Quantitative Methods for Finance
Third Edition

A Pearson Custom Publication

Quantitative Methods for Finance

Third Edition

Compiled from:

Mathematics for Economics and Business
Sixth Edition
by Ian Jacques

Basic Business Statistics: Concepts and Applications
Eleventh Edition
by Mark L. Berenson, David M. Levine
and Timothy C. Krehbiel

PEARSON
Custom Publishing

Pearson Education Limited
Edinburgh Gate
Harlow
Essex CM20 2JE

And associated companies throughout the world

Visit us on the World Wide Web at:
www.pearsoned.co.uk

First published 2007
This Custom Book Edition © 2010 Published by Pearson Education Limited

Compiled from:

Mathematics for Economics and Business
Sixth Edition
Ian Jacques
ISBN 978 0 273 72216 8

Copyright © Addison-Wesley Publishers Ltd, 1991, 1994
Copyright © Pearson Education Limited 1999, 2009

Basic Business Statistics: Concepts and Applications
Eleventh Edition
Mark L. Berenson, David M. Levine and Timothy C. Krehbiel
ISBN 978 0 13 603260 1

Copyright © 2009, 2006, 2004, 2002, 1999 by Pearson Education, Inc.,
Upper Saddle River, New Jersey, 07458.

ISBN 978 1 84959 182 9

Printed and bound in Great Britain by Henry Ling Limited at the Dorset Press,
Dorchester, DT1 1HD.

Contents

PREFACE

Quantitative Methods for Finance is a compulsory module within three degrees at Durham University: Business Finance, Business and Accounting & Finance. The module aims to introduce students to the essential mathematical and statistical techniques necessary in those degrees, to support other year 1 modules and to provide a foundation for further study in later years.

The material is concerned with mathematics and statistics as languages and how they can facilitate the study of business and finance. This module is certainly *not* about mathematics for its own sake. The first Term is devoted to some basic mathematical methods and applications, including elementary algebra and the use of graphs, analysis of linear and non-linear relationships, the technique of differential calculus and its use in problems of optimisation. The second and third terms are devoted to introductory probability and statistical analysis with an applied focus on business and financial data. By the end of the module students should have acquired an array of mathematical and statistical skills widely used in business and finance.

There are excellent textbooks available which cover the analytical mathematics of this module, and there are equally excellent textbooks available which cover the probability and statistical material of this module. However, there is no one textbook which satisfactorily covers the entire syllabus.

Traditionally we have recommended that students purchase two books:

Jacques, Ian (2006), *Mathematics for Economics and Business*. 5th Edition, Pearson Education. ISBN: 0-273-70195-9.

and

Berenson, Mark L., Levine, David M. and Krehbiel, Timothy C., (2005), *Basic Business Statistics: Concepts and Applications*. 10th Edition, Pearson Education. ISBN: 0-13-153686-9.

However, the syllabus of this module focuses on specific material of each book, and does not draw on either of them in their entirety. To address this we have worked with the Publisher and have created a 'customised textbook' which brings together those specific chapters of each book which form the module.

As a customised text, we have sought to incorporate only those chapters on which the syllabus of your module is based, and have omitted all those which are, in this regard, superfluous. This has substantially reduced your financial outlay on texts for the module, as you, the hard-pressed student, now need only purchase one text for the whole syllabus, rather than two separate texts. The new text has its own pagination, but has also retained the original versions' pagination in order that your use of the Indexes (available on the Web at www.coursecompass.com) is fully operational.

The primary driving motivations in this customised text are three-fold:

1. you now have access, in one text, to all the material of the syllabus;
2. by eliminating the material from each original text which is not part of the syllabus, you only need buy what is absolutely essential;
3. by focussing on the module syllabus, each original text becomes abridged which generates a very significant cost-saving.

There is, as far as we can perceive, only one slight downside. The originals have been scanned to create the new text and in so doing one aspect only of the original has been lost, namely the colour of the source printing. This is a very small potential loss and affects very few diagrams. If this is important to you then you are, of course, free to purchase the original texts (copies of which are, of course, available in the Library). It is our opinion that this is a very small price to pay for the compact nature of the single text now available.

The original Jacques text has an associated website and this is, of course, fully available to all purchasers of the customised text. Similarly, the software available with the original Berenson *et al.* text and the associated website are both fully available to those who choose this customised text. All students are encouraged to engage with the module and manage their own learning through proper and effective use of these websites and, for example, to test their own understanding through the various multiple-choice questions.

We hope that you, like us, are delighted with this innovation.

Professor Adrian C Darnell, Module Leader, June 2006.

Section A

Mathematical Analysis

CHAPTER 1
Linear Equations

The main aim of this chapter is to introduce the mathematics of linear equations. This is an obvious first choice in an introductory text, since it is an easy topic which has many applications. There are seven sections, which are intended to be read in the order that they appear.

Sections 1.1, 1.2, 1.3, 1.4 and 1.6 are devoted to mathematical methods. They serve to revise the rules of arithmetic and algebra, which you probably met at school but may have forgotten. In particular, the properties of negative numbers and fractions are considered. A reminder is given on how to multiply out brackets and how to manipulate mathematical expressions. You are also shown how to solve simultaneous linear equations. Systems of two equations in two unknowns can be solved using graphs, which are described in Section 1.3. However, the preferred method uses elimination, which is considered in Section 1.4. This algebraic approach has the advantage that it always gives an exact solution and it extends readily to larger systems of equations.

The remaining two sections are reserved for applications in microeconomics and macroeconomics. You may be pleasantly surprised by how much economic theory you can analyse using just the basic mathematical tools considered here. Section 1.5 introduces the fundamental concept of an economic function and describes how to calculate equilibrium prices and quantities in supply and demand theory. Section 1.7 deals with national income determination in simple macroeconomic models.

The first six sections underpin the rest of the book and are essential reading. The final section is not quite as important and can be omitted at this stage.

SECTION 1.1
Introduction to algebra

Objectives

At the end of this section you should be able to:

- Add, subtract, multiply and divide negative numbers.
- Understand what is meant by an algebraic expression.
- Evaluate algebraic expressions numerically.
- Simplify algebraic expressions by collecting like terms.
- Multiply out brackets.
- Factorize algebraic expressions.

ALGEBRA IS BORING

There is no getting away from the fact that algebra *is* boring. Doubtless there are a few enthusiasts who get a kick out of algebraic manipulation, but economics and business students are rarely to be found in this category. Indeed, the mere mention of the word 'algebra' is enough to strike fear into the heart of many a first-year student. Unfortunately, you cannot get very far with mathematics unless you have completely mastered this topic. An apposite analogy is the game of chess. Before you can begin to play a game of chess it is necessary to go through the tedium of learning the moves of individual pieces. In the same way it is essential that you learn the rules of algebra before you can enjoy the 'game' of mathematics. Of course, just because you know the rules does not mean that you are going to excel at the game and no one is expecting you to become a grandmaster of mathematics. However, you should at least be able to follow the mathematics presented in economics books and journals, as well as being able to solve simple problems for yourself.

Advice

If you have studied mathematics recently then you will find the material in the first few sections of the book fairly straightforward. You may prefer just to try the questions in the starred exercise at the end of each section to get yourself back up to speed. However, if it has been some time since you have studied this subject our advice is very different. Please work through the material thoroughly even if it is vaguely familiar. Make sure that you do the problems as they arise, checking your answers with those on the website. The material has been broken down into three subsections:

- negative numbers
- expressions
- brackets.

You might like to work through these subsections on separate occasions to enable the ideas to sink in. To rush this topic now is likely to give you only a half-baked understanding which will result in hours of frustration when you study the later chapters of this book.

1.1.1 Negative numbers

In mathematics numbers are classified into one of three types: positive, negative or zero. At school you were probably introduced to the idea of a negative number via the temperature on a thermometer scale measured in degrees centigrade. A number such as −5 would then be interpreted as a temperature of 5 degrees below freezing. In personal finance a negative bank balance would indicate that an account is in 'in the red' or 'in debit'. Similarly, a firm's profit of −500 000 signifies a loss of half a million.

The rules for the multiplication of negative numbers are

$$\boxed{\text{negative}} \times \boxed{\text{negative}} = \boxed{\text{positive}}$$
$$\boxed{\text{negative}} \times \boxed{\text{positive}} = \boxed{\text{negative}}$$

It does not matter in which order two numbers are multiplied, so

$$\boxed{\text{positive}} \times \boxed{\text{negative}} = \boxed{\text{negative}}$$

These rules produce

$$(-2) \times (-3) = 6$$
$$(-4) \times 5 = -20$$
$$7 \times (-5) = -35$$

respectively. Also, because division is the same sort of operation as multiplication (it just undoes the result of multiplication and takes you back to where you started), exactly the same rules apply when one number is divided by another. For example,

$$(-15) \div (-3) = 5$$
$$(-16) \div 2 = -8$$
$$2 \div (-4) = -1/2$$

In general, to multiply or divide lots of numbers it is probably simplest to ignore the signs to begin with and just to work the answer out. The final result is negative if the total number of minus signs is odd and positive if the total number is even.

Example

Evaluate

(a) $(-2) \times (-4) \times (-1) \times 2 \times (-1) \times (-3)$ **(b)** $\dfrac{5 \times (-4) \times (-1) \times (-3)}{(-6) \times 2}$

Solution

(a) Ignoring the signs gives

$$2 \times 4 \times 1 \times 2 \times 1 \times 3 = 48$$

There are an odd number of minus signs (in fact, five) so the answer is −48.

(b) Ignoring the signs gives

$$\frac{5 \times 4 \times 1 \times 3}{6 \times 2} = \frac{60}{12} = 5$$

There are an even number of minus signs (in fact, four) so the answer is 5.

Advice

Attempt the following problem yourself both with and without a calculator. On most machines a negative number such as –6 is entered by pressing the button labelled $\boxed{(-)}$ followed by 6.

Practice Problem

1. **(1)** Without using a calculator evaluate

    (a) $5 \times (-6)$ **(b)** $(-1) \times (-2)$ **(c)** $(-50) \div 10$

    (d) $(-5) \div (-1)$ **(e)** $2 \times (-1) \times (-3) \times 6$ **(f)** $\dfrac{2 \times (-1) \times (-3) \times 6}{(-2) \times 3 \times 6}$

    (2) Confirm your answer to part (1) using a calculator.

To add or subtract negative numbers it helps to think in terms of a number line:

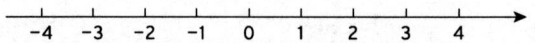

If b is a positive number then

$$a - b$$

can be thought of as an instruction to start at a and to move b units to the left. For example,

$$1 - 3 = -2$$

because if you start at 1 and move 3 units to the left, you end up at –2:

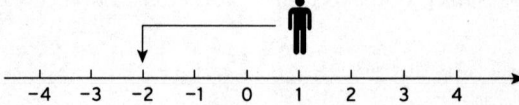

Similarly,

$$-2 - 1 = -3$$

because 1 unit to the left of –2 is –3.

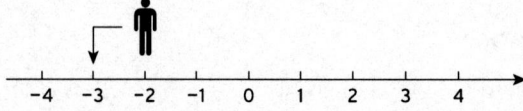

On the other hand,

$$a - (-b)$$

is taken to be $a + b$. This follows from the rule for multiplying two negative numbers, since

$$-(-b) = (-1) \times (-b) = b$$

Consequently, to evaluate

$$a - (-b)$$

you start at a and move b units to the right (that is, in the positive direction). For example,

$$-2 - (-5) = -2 + 5 = 3$$

because if you start at -2 and move 5 units to the right you end up at 3.

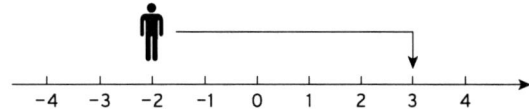

Example

Evaluate

(a) $-32 - 4$

(b) $-68 - (-62)$

Solution

(a) $-32 - 4 = -36$ because 4 units to the left of -32 is -36.

(b) $-68 - (-62) = -68 + 62 = -6$ because 62 units to the right of -68 is -6.

Practice Problem

2. (1) Without using a calculator evaluate

    (a) $1 - 2$ **(b)** $-3 - 4$ **(c)** $1 - (-4)$

    (d) $-1 - (-1)$ **(e)** $-72 - 19$ **(f)** $-53 - (-48)$

(2) Confirm your answer to part (1) using a calculator.

1.1.2 Expressions

In algebra letters are used to represent numbers. In pure mathematics the most common letters used are x and y. However, in applications it is helpful to choose letters that are more meaningful, so we might use Q for quantity and I for investment. An algebraic expression is then simply a combination of these letters, brackets and other mathematical symbols such as $+$ or $-$. For example, the expression

$$P\left(1 + \frac{r}{100}\right)^n$$

can be used to work out how money in a savings account grows over a period of time. The letters P, r and n represent the original sum invested (called the principal – hence the use of the letter P), the rate of interest and the number of years, respectively. To work it all out, you not only need to replace these letters by actual numbers, but you also need to understand the various conventions that go with algebraic expressions such as this.

In algebra when we multiply two numbers represented by letters we usually suppress the multiplication sign between them. The product of a and b would simply be written as ab without bothering to put the multiplication sign between the symbols. Likewise when a number represented by the letter Y is doubled we write $2Y$. In this case we not only suppress the multiplication sign but adopt the convention of writing the number in front of the letter. Here are some further examples:

$P \times Q$ is written as PQ

$d \times 8$ is written as $8d$

$n \times 6 \times t$ is written as $6nt$

$z \times z$ is written as z^2 (using the index 2 to indicate squaring a number)

$1 \times t$ is written as t (since multiplying by 1 does not change a number)

In order to evaluate these expressions it is necessary to be given the numerical value of each letter. Once this has been done you can work out the final value by performing the operations in the following order:

Brackets first   (B)

Indices second   (I)

Division and Multiplication third   (DM)

Addition and Subtraction fourth   (AS)

This is sometimes remembered using the acronym BIDMAS and it is essential that this ordering is used for working out all mathematical calculations. For example, suppose you wish to evaluate each of the following expressions when $n = 3$:

$2n^2$ and $(2n)^2$

Substituting $n = 3$ into the first expression gives

$2n^2 = 2 \times 3^2$ (the multiplication sign is revealed when we switch from algebra to numbers)

$ = 2 \times 9$ (according to BIDMAS indices are worked out before multiplication)

$ = 18$

whereas in the second expression we get

$(2n)^2 = (2 \times 3)^2$ (again the multiplication sign is revealed)

$ = 6^2$ (according to BIDMAS we evaluate the inside of the brackets first)

$ = 36$

The two answers are not the same so the order indicated by BIDMAS really does matter. Looking at the previous list notice that there is a tie between multiplication and division for third place, and another tie between addition and subtraction for fourth place. These pairs of operations have equal priority and under these circumstances you work from left to right when evaluating expressions. For example, substituting $x = 5$ and $y = 4$ in the expression, $x - y + 2$, gives

$x - y + 2 = 5 - 4 + 2$

$ = 1 + 2$ (reading from left to right, subtraction comes first)

$ = 3$

Example

(a) Find the value of $2x - 3y$ when $x = 9$ and $y = 4$.

(b) Find the value of $2Q^2 - 4Q + 150$ when $Q = 10$.

(c) Find the value of $5a - 2b + c$ when $a = 4$, $b = 6$ and $c = 1$.

(d) Find the value of $(12 - t) - (t - 1)$ when $t = 4$.

Solution

(a) $2x - 3y = 2 \times 9 - 3 \times 4$ (substituting numbers)

$\qquad = 18 - 12$ (multiplication has priority over subtraction)

$\qquad = 6$

(b) $2Q^2 + 4Q + 150 = 2 \times 10^2 + 4 \times 10 + 150$ (substituting numbers)

$\qquad = 2 \times 100 + 4 \times 10 + 150$ (indices have priority over multiplication and addition)

$\qquad = 200 + 40 + 150$ (multiplication has priority over addition)

$\qquad = 390$

(c) $5a - 2b + c = 5 \times 4 - 2 \times 6 + 1$ (substituting numbers)

$\qquad = 20 - 12 + 1$ (multiplication has priority over addition and subtraction)

$\qquad = 8 + 1$ (addition and subtraction have equal priority so work from left to right)

$\qquad = 9$

(d) $(12 - t) - (t - 1) = (12 - 4) - (4 - 1)$ (substituting numbers)

$\qquad = 8 - 3$ (brackets first)

$\qquad = 5$

Practice Problem

3. Evaluate each of the following by replacing the letters by the given numbers:

(a) $2Q + 5$ when $Q = 7$.

(b) $5x^2y$ when $x = 10$ and $y = 3$.

(c) $4d - 3f + 2g$ when $d = 7$, $f = 2$ and $g = 5$.

(d) $a(b + 2c)$ when $a = 5$, $b = 1$ and $c = 3$.

Like terms are multiples of the same letter (or letters). For example, $2P$, $-34P$ and $0.3P$ are all multiples of P and so are like terms. In the same way, xy, $4xy$ and $69xy$ are all multiples of xy so are like terms. If an algebraic expression contains like terms which are added or subtracted together then it can be simplified to produce an equivalent shorter expression.

Example

Simplify each of the following expressions (where possible):

(a) $2a + 5a - 3a$

(b) $4P - 2Q$

(c) $3w + 9w^2 + 2w$

(d) $3xy + 2y^2 + 9x + 4xy - 8x$

Solution

(a) All three are like terms since they are all multiples of a so the expression can be simplified:

$$2a + 5a - 3a = 4a$$

(b) The terms $4P$ and $2Q$ are unlike because one is a multiple of P and the other is a multiple of Q so the expression cannot be simplified.

(c) The first and last are like terms since they are both multiples of w so we can collect these together and write

$$3w + 9w^2 + 2w = 5w + 9w^2$$

This cannot be simpified any further because $5w$ and $9w^2$ are unlike terms.

(d) The terms $3xy$ and $4xy$ are like terms, and $9x$ and $8x$ are also like terms. These pairs can therefore be collected together to give

$$3xy + 2y^2 + 9x + 4xy - 8x = 7xy + 2y^2 + x$$

Notice that we write just x instead of $1x$ and also that no further simplication is possible since the final answer involves three unlike terms.

Practice Problem

4. Simplify each of the following expressions, where possible:

(a) $2x + 6y - x + 3y$ (b) $5x + 2y - 5x + 4z$ (c) $4Y^2 + 3Y - 43$

(d) $8r^2 + 4s - 6rs - 3s - 3s^2 + 7rs$ (e) $2e^2 + 5f - 2e^2 - 9f$ (f) $3w + 6W$

(g) $ab - ba$

1.1.3 Brackets

It is useful to be able to take an expression containing brackets and rewrite it as an equivalent expression without brackets and vice versa. The process of removing brackets is called 'expanding brackets' or 'multiplying out brackets'. This is based on the **distributive law**, which states that for any three numbers a, b and c

$$a(b + c) = ab + ac$$

It is easy to verify this law in simple cases. For example, if $a = 2$, $b = 3$ and $c = 4$ then the left-hand side is

$$2(3 + 4) = 2 \times 7 = 14$$

However,

$$ab = 2 \times 3 = 6 \text{ and } ac = 2 \times 4 = 8$$

and so the right-hand side is $6 + 8$, which is also 14.

This law can be used when there are any number of terms inside the brackets. We have

$$a(b + c + d) = ab + ac + ad$$
$$a(b + c + d + e) = ab + ac + ad + ae$$

and so on.

It does not matter in which order two numbers are multiplied, so we also have

$$(b + c)a = ba + ca$$
$$(b + c + d)a = ba + ca + da$$
$$(b + c + d + e)a = ba + ca + da + ea$$

Example

Multiply out the brackets in

(a) $x(x - 2)$

(b) $2(x + y - z) + 3(z + y)$

(c) $x + 3y - (2y + x)$

Solution

(a) The use of the distributive law to multiply out $x(x - 2)$ is straightforward. The x outside the bracket multiplies the x inside to give x^2. The x outside the bracket also multiplies the -2 inside to give $-2x$. Hence

$$x(x - 2) = x^2 - 2x$$

(b) To expand

$$2(x + y - z) + 3(z + y)$$

we need to apply the distributive law twice. We have

$$2(x + y - z) = 2x + 2y - 2z$$
$$3(z + y) = 3z + 3y$$

Adding together gives

$$2(x + y - z) + 3(z + y) = 2x + 2y - 2z + 3z + 3y$$
$$= 2x + 5y + z \quad \text{(collecting like terms)}$$

(c) It may not be immediately apparent how to expand

$$x + 3y - (2y + x)$$

However, note that

$$-(2y + x)$$

is the same as

$$(-1)(2y + x)$$

which expands to give

$$(-1)(2y) + (-1)x = -2y - x$$

Hence

$$x + 3y - (2y + x) = x + 3y - 2y - x = y$$

after collecting like terms.

Advice

In this example the solutions are written out in painstaking detail. This is done to show you precisely how the distributive law is applied. The solutions to all three parts could have been written down in only one or two steps of working. You are, of course, at liberty to compress the working in your own solutions, but please do not be tempted to overdo this. You might want to check your answers at a later date and may find it difficult if you have tried to be too clever.

Practice Problem

5. Multiply out the brackets, simplifying your answer as far as possible.

(a) $(5 - 2z)z$ (b) $6(x - y) + 3(y - 2x)$ (c) $x - y + z - (x^2 + x - y)$

Before we leave this topic a word of warning is in order. Be careful when removing brackets from very simple expressions such as those considered in part (c) in the above worked example and practice problem. A common mistake is to write

$$(a + b) - (c + d) = a + b - c + d \quad \textbf{This is NOT true}$$

The distributive law tells us that the -1 multiplying the second bracket applies to the d as well as the c so the correct answer has to be

$$(a + b) - (c + d) = a + b - c - d$$

In algebra, it is sometimes useful to reverse the procedure and put the brackets back in. This is called **factorization**. Consider the expression $12a + 8b$. There are many numbers which divide into both 8 and 12. However, we always choose the biggest number, which is 4 in this case, so we attempt to take the factor of 4 outside the brackets:

$$12a + 8b = 4(? + ?)$$

where the ? indicate some mystery terms inside the brackets. We would like 4 multiplied by the first term in the brackets to be $12a$ so we are missing $3a$. Likewise if we are to generate an $8b$ the second term in the brackets will have to be $2b$.

Hence

$$12a + 8b = 4(3a + 2b)$$

As a check, notice that when you expand the brackets on the right-hand side you really do get the expression on the left-hand side.

Example

Factorize

(a) $6x - 3x^2$

(b) $5a - 10b + 20c$

Solution

(a) Both terms have a common factor of 3. Also, because $x^2 = x \times x$, both $6x$ and $-3x^2$ have a factor of x. Hence we can take out a common factor of $3x$ altogether.

$$6x - 3x^2 = 3x(2) - 3x(x) = 3x(2 - x)$$

(b) All three terms have a common factor of 5 so we write

$$5a - 10b + 20c = 5(a) - 5(2b) + 5(4c) = 5(a - 2b + 4c)$$

Practice Problem

6. Factorize

    (a) $7d + 21$ **(b)** $16w - 20q$ **(c)** $6x - 3y + 9z$ **(d)** $5Q - 10Q^2$

We conclude our discussion of brackets by describing how to multiply two brackets together. In the expression $(a + b)(c + d)$ the two terms a and b must each multiply the single bracket $(c + d)$ so

$$(a + b)(c + d) = a(c + d) + b(c + d)$$

The first term $a(c + d)$ can itself be expanded as $ac + ad$. Likewise, $b(c + d) = bc + bd$. Hence

$$(a + b)(c + d) = ac + ad + bc + bd$$

This procedure then extends to brackets with more than two terms:

$$(a + b)(c + d + e) = a(c + d + e) + b(c + d + e) = ac + ad + ae + bc + bd + be$$

Example

Multiply out the brackets

(a) $(x + 1)(x + 2)$ **(b)** $(x + 5)(x - 5)$ **(c)** $(2x - y)(x + y - 6)$

simplifying your answer as far as possible.

Solution

(a)
$$\begin{aligned}(x + 1)(x + 2) &= x(x + 2) + (1)(x + 2) \\ &= x^2 + 2x + x + 2 \\ &= x^2 + 3x + 2\end{aligned}$$

(b)
$$\begin{aligned}(x + 5)(x - 5) &= x(x - 5) + 5(x - 5) \\ &= x^2 - 5x + 5x - 25 \\ &= x^2 - 25\end{aligned}$$

the x's cancel

(c)
$$\begin{aligned}(2x - y)(x + y - 6) &= 2x(x + y - 6) - y(x + y - 6) \\ &= 2x^2 + 2xy - 12x - yx - y^2 + 6y \\ &= 2x^2 + xy - 12x - y^2 + 6y\end{aligned}$$

Practice Problem

7. Multiply out the brackets.

   (a) $(x + 3)(x - 2)$
   (b) $(x + y)(x - y)$
   (c) $(x + y)(x + y)$
   (d) $(5x + 2y)(x - y + 1)$

Looking back at part (b) of the previous worked example, notice that

$$(x + 5)(x - 5) = x^2 - 25 = x^2 - 5^2$$

Quite generally

$$\begin{aligned}(a + b)(a - b) &= a(a - b) + b(a - b) \\ &= a^2 - ab + ba - b^2 \\ &= a^2 - b^2\end{aligned}$$

The result

$$\boxed{a^2 - b^2 = (a + b)(a - b)}$$

is called the **difference of two squares** formula. It provides a quick way of factorizing certain expressions.

Example

Factorize the following expressions:

(a) $x^2 - 16$ **(b)** $9x^2 - 100$

Solution

(a) Noting that

$$x^2 - 16 = x^2 - 4^2$$

we can use the difference of two squares formula to deduce that

$$x^2 - 16 = (x + 4)(x - 4)$$

(b) Noting that

$$9x^2 - 100 = (3x)^2 - (10)^2$$

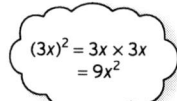

$(3x)^2 = 3x \times 3x$
$= 9x^2$

we can use the difference of two squares formula to deduce that

$$9x^2 - 100 = (3x + 10)(3x - 10)$$

Practice Problem

8. Factorise the following expressions:

   (a) $x^2 - 64$ **(b)** $4x^2 - 81$

Advice

This completes your first piece of mathematics. We hope that you have not found it quite as bad as you first thought. There now follow a few extra problems to give you more practice. Not only will they help to strengthen your mathematical skills, but also they should improve your overall confidence. There are two alternative exercises available. Exercise 1.1 is suitable for students whose mathematics may be rusty and who need to consolidate their understanding. Exercise 1.1* contains more challenging problems and so is more suitable for those students who have found this section very easy.

Key Terms

Distributive law   The law of arithmetic which states that $a(b + c) = ab + ac$ for any numbers, a, b, c.

Factorization   The process of writing an expression as a product of simpler expressions using brackets.

Like terms   Multiples of the same algebraic symbol.

Exercise 1.1

1. Without using a calculator evaluate

(a) $10 \times (-2)$ **(b)** $(-1) \times (-3)$ **(c)** $(-8) \div 2$ **(d)** $(-5) \div (-5)$

(e) $24 \div (-2)$ **(f)** $(-10) \times (-5)$ **(g)** $\dfrac{20}{-4}$ **(h)** $\dfrac{-27}{-9}$

(i) $(-6) \times 5 \times (-1)$ **(j)** $\dfrac{2 \times (-6) \times 3}{(-9)}$

2. Without using a calculator evaluate

(a) $5 - 6$ **(b)** $-1 - 2$ **(c)** $6 - 17$ **(d)** $-7 + 23$

(e) $-7 - (-6)$ **(f)** $-4 - 9$ **(g)** $7 - (-4)$ **(h)** $-9 - (-9)$

(i) $12 - 43$ **(j)** $2 + 6 - 10$

3. Without using a calculator evaluate

(a) $5 \times 2 - 13$ **(b)** $\dfrac{-30 - 6}{-18}$ **(c)** $\dfrac{(-3) \times (-6) \times (-1)}{2 - 3}$ **(d)** $5 \times (1 - 4)$

(e) $1 - 6 \times 7$ **(f)** $-5 + 6 \div 3$ **(g)** $2 \times (-3)^2$ **(h)** $-10 + 2^2$

(i) $(2)^2 - 5 \times 6 + 1$ **(j)** $\dfrac{(-4)^2 \times (-3) \times (-1)}{(-2)^3}$

4. Simplify each of the following algebraic expressions:

(a) $2 \times P \times Q$ **(b)** $I \times 8$ **(c)** $3 \times x \times y$

(d) $4 \times q \times w \times z$ **(e)** $b \times b$ **(f)** $k \times 3 \times k$

5. Simplify the following algebraic expressions by collecting like terms:

(a) $6w - 3w + 12w + 4w$ **(b)** $6x + 5y - 2x - 12y$

(c) $3a - 2b + 6a - c + 4b - c$ **(d)** $2x^2 + 4x - x^2 - 2x$

(e) $2cd + 4c - 5dc$ **(f)** $5st + s^2 - 3ts + t^2 + 9$

6. Without using a calculator find the value of the following:

(a) $2x - y$ when $x = 7$ and $y = 4$.

(b) $x^2 - 5x + 12$ when $x = 6$.

(c) $2m^3$ when $m = 10$.

(d) $5fg^2 + 2g$ when $f = 2$ and $g = 3$.

(e) $2v + 4w - (4v - 7w)$ when $v = 20$ and $w = 10$.

7. If $x = 2$ and $y = -3$ evaluate

(a) $2x + y$ **(b)** $x - y$ **(c)** $3x + 4y$

(d) xy **(e)** $5xy$ **(f)** $4x - 6xy$

8. (a) Without using a calculator, work out the value of $(-4)^2$.

   (b) Press the following key sequence on your calculator:

   $\boxed{(-)}$ $\boxed{4}$ $\boxed{x^2}$

   Explain carefully why this does not give the same result as part (a) and give an alternative key sequence that *does* give the correct answer.

9. Without using a calculator work out

   (a) $(5 - 2)^2$ **(b)** $5^2 - 2^2$

   Is it true in general that $(a - b)^2 = a^2 - b^2$?

10. Use your calculator to work out the following. Round your answer, if necessary, to 2 decimal places.

   (a) $5.31 \times 8.47 - 1.01^2$ **(b)** $(8.34 + 2.27)/9.41$

   (c) $9.53 - 3.21 + 4.02$ **(d)** $2.41 \times 0.09 - 1.67 \times 0.03$

   (e) $45.76 - (2.55 + 15.83)$ **(f)** $(3.45 - 5.38)^2$

   (g) $4.56(9.02 + 4.73)$ **(h)** $6.85/(2.59 + 0.28)$

11. Multiply out the brackets:

   (a) $7(x - y)$ **(b)** $3(5x - 2y)$ **(c)** $4(x + 3)$ **(d)** $7(3x - 1)$

   (e) $3(x + y + z)$ **(f)** $x(3x - 4)$ **(g)** $y + 2z - 2(x + 3y - z)$

12. Factorize

   (a) $25c + 30$ **(b)** $9x - 18$ **(c)** $x^2 + 2x$

   (d) $16x - 12y$ **(e)** $4x^2 - 6xy$ **(f)** $10d - 15e + 50$

13. Multiply out the brackets:

   (a) $(x + 2)(x + 5)$ **(b)** $(a + 4)(a - 1)$ **(c)** $(d + 3)(d - 8)$ **(d)** $(2s + 3)(3s + 7)$

   (e) $(2y + 3)(y + 1)$ **(f)** $(5t + 2)(2t - 7)$ **(g)** $(3n + 2)(3n - 2)$ **(h)** $(a - b)(a - b)$

14. Simplify the following expressions by collecting together like terms:

   (a) $2x + 3y + 4x - y$ **(b)** $2x^2 - 5x + 9x^2 + 2x - 3$

   (c) $5xy + 2x + 9yx$ **(d)** $7xyz + 3yx - 2zyx + yzx - xy$

   (e) $2(5a + b) - 4b$ **(f)** $5(x - 4y) + 6(2x + 7y)$

   (g) $5 - 3(p - 2)$ **(h)** $x(x - y + 7) + xy + 3x$

15. Use the formula for the difference of two squares to factorize

   (a) $x^2 - 4$ **(b)** $Q^2 - 49$ **(c)** $x^2 - y^2$ **(d)** $9x^2 - 100y^2$

16. Simplify the following algebraic expressions:

   (a) $3x - 4x^2 - 2 + 5x + 8x^2$ **(b)** $x(3x + 2) - 3x(x + 5)$

Exercise 1.1*

1. Without using a calculator evaluate

(a) $(12 - 8) - (6 - 5)$ (b) $12 - (8 - 6) - 5$ (c) $12 - 8 - 6 - 5$

2. Put a pair of brackets in the left-hand side of each of the following to give correct statements:

(a) $2 - 7 - 9 + 3 = -17$

(b) $8 - 2 + 3 - 4 = -1$

(c) $7 - 2 - 6 + 10 = 1$

3. Without using a calculator work out the value of each of the following expressions in the case when $a = 3$, $b = -4$ and $c = -2$:

(a) $a(b - c)$ (b) $3c(a + b)$ (c) $a^2 + 2b + 3c$ (d) $2abc^2$

(e) $\dfrac{c + b}{2a}$ (f) $\sqrt{2(b^2 - c)}$ (g) $\dfrac{b}{2c} - \dfrac{a}{3b}$ (h) $5a - b^3 - 4c^2$

4. Without using a calculator evaluate each of the following expressions in the case when $x = -1$, $y = -2$ and $z = 3$:

(a) $x^3 + y^2 + z$ (b) $\sqrt{\left(\dfrac{x^2 + y^2 + z}{x^2 + 2xy - z} \right)}$ (c) $\dfrac{xyz(x + z)(z - y)}{(x + y)(x - z)}$

5. Multiply out the brackets and simplify

$(x - y)(x + y) - (x + 2)(x - y + 3)$

6. Simplify

(a) $x - y - (y - x)$ (b) $(x - ((y - x) - y))$ (c) $x + y - (x - y) - (x - (y - x))$

7. Multiply out the brackets:

(a) $(x + 4)(x - 6)$ (b) $(2x - 5)(3x - 7)$ (c) $2x(3x + y - 2)$

(d) $(3 + g)(4 - 2g + h)$ (e) $(2x + y)(1 - x - y)$ (f) $(a + b + c)(a - b - c)$

8. Factorize

(a) $9x - 12y$ (b) $x^2 - 6x$ (c) $10xy + 15x^2$

(d) $3xy^2 - 6x^2y + 12xy$ (e) $x^3 - 2x^2$ (f) $60x^4y^6 - 15x^2y^4 + 20xy^3$

9. Use the formula for the difference of two squares to factorize

(a) $p^2 - 25$ (b) $9c^2 - 64$ (c) $32v^2 - 50d^2$ (d) $16x^4 - y^4$

10. Evaluate the following without using a calculator:

(a) $50\,563^2 - 49\,437^2$ (b) $90^2 - 89.99^2$

(c) $759^2 - 541^2$ (d) $123\,456\,789^2 - 123\,456\,788^2$

SECTION 1.2
Further algebra

Objectives

At the end of this section you should be able to:

- Simplify fractions by cancelling common factors.
- Add, subtract, multiply and divide fractions.
- Solve equations by doing the same thing to both sides.
- Recognize the symbols $<$, $>$, $\leq$ and $\geq$.
- Solve linear inequalities.

This section is broken down into three manageable subsections:

- fractions
- equations
- inequalities.

The advice offered in Section 1.1 applies equally well here. Please try to study these topics on separate occasions and be prepared to put the book down and work through the practice problems as they arise in the text.

1.2.1 Fractions

For a numerical fraction such as

$$\frac{7}{8}$$

the number 7, on the top, is called the **numerator** and the number 8, on the bottom, is called the **denominator**. In this book we are also interested in the case when the numerator and denominator involve letters as well as numbers. These are referred to as **algebraic fractions**. For example,

$$\frac{1}{x^2 - 2} \quad \text{and} \quad \frac{2x^2 - 1}{y + z}$$

are both algebraic fractions. The letters x, y and z are used to represent numbers, so the rules for the manipulation of algebraic fractions are the same as those for ordinary numerical fractions. It is therefore essential that you are happy manipulating numerical fractions without a calculator so that you can extend this skill to fractions with letters.

Two fractions are said to be **equivalent** if they represent the same numerical value. We know that $\frac{3}{4}$ is equivalent to $\frac{6}{8}$ since they are both equal to the decimal number 0.75. It is also intuitively obvious. Imagine breaking a bar of chocolate into four equal pieces and eating three of them. You eat the same amount of chocolate as someone who breaks the bar into eight equal pieces and eats six of them. Each piece is only half the size so you need to compensate by eating twice as many. Formally we say that when the numerator and denominator are both multiplied by the same number the value of the fraction remains unchanged. In this example we have

$$\frac{3}{4} = \frac{3 \times 2}{4 \times 2} = \frac{6}{8}$$

This process can be reversed so equivalent fractions are produced when the numerator and denominator are both divided by the same number. For example,

$$\frac{16}{24} = \frac{16/8}{24/8} = \frac{2}{3}$$

so the fractions $\frac{16}{24}$ and $\frac{2}{3}$ are equivalent. A fraction is said to be in its simplest form or reduced to its lowest terms when there are no factors common to both the numerator and denominator. To express any given fraction in its simplest form you need to find the highest common factor of the numerator and denominator and then divide top and bottom of the fraction by this.

Example

Reduce each of the following fractions to its lowest terms:

(a) $\dfrac{14}{21}$ (b) $\dfrac{48}{60}$ (c) $\dfrac{2x}{3xy}$ (d) $\dfrac{3a}{6a + 3b}$ (e) $\dfrac{x - 2}{(x - 2)(x + 1)}$

Solution

(a) The largest number which divides into both 14 and 21 is 7 so we choose to divide top and bottom by 7:

$$\frac{14}{21} = \frac{14/7}{21/7} = \frac{2}{3}$$

An alternative way of writing this (which will be helpful when we tackle algebraic fractions) is:

$$\frac{14}{21} = \frac{2 \times \cancel{7}}{3 \times \cancel{7}} = \frac{2}{3}$$

(b) The highest common factor of 48 and 60 is 12 so we write:

$$\frac{48}{60} = \frac{4 \times \cancel{12}}{5 \times \cancel{12}} = \frac{4}{5}$$

(c) The factor x is common to both $2x$ and $3xy$ so we need to divide top and bottom by x, that is, we cancel the x's:

$$\frac{2x}{3xy} = \frac{2 \times \cancel{x}}{3 \times \cancel{x} \times y} = \frac{2}{3y}$$

(d) Factorizing the denominator gives

$$6a + 3b = 3(2a + b)$$

which shows that there is a common factor of 3 in the top and bottom which can be cancelled:

$$\frac{3a}{6a+3b}=\frac{\cancel{3}a}{\cancel{3}(2a+b)}=\frac{a}{2a+b}$$

(e) We see immediately that there is a common factor of $(x-2)$ in the top and bottom so this can be cancelled:

$$\frac{\cancel{x-2}}{\cancel{(x-2)}(x+1)}=\frac{1}{x+1}$$

Before we leave this topic a word of warning is in order. Notice that you can only cancel by dividing by a **factor** of the numerator or denominator. In part (d) of the above example you must not get carried away and attempt to cancel the a's, and write something daft like:

$$\frac{a}{2a+b}=\frac{1}{2+b}\qquad\textbf{This is NOT true}$$

To see that this is totally wrong let us try substituting numbers, $a=3$, $b=4$, say, into both sides. The left-hand side gives $\dfrac{a}{2a+b}=\dfrac{3}{2\times3+4}=\dfrac{3}{10}$ whereas the right-hand side gives $\dfrac{1}{2+b}=\dfrac{1}{2+4}=\dfrac{1}{6}$, which is not the same value.

Practice Problem

1. Reduce each of the following fractions to its lowest terms:

(a) $\dfrac{9}{15}$ (b) $\dfrac{24}{30}$ (c) $\dfrac{x}{2xy}$ (d) $\dfrac{3x}{6x+9x^2}$ (e) $\dfrac{x(x+1)}{x(x-4)(x+1)}$

The rules for multiplication and division are as follows:

to multiply fractions you multiply their corresponding numerators and denominators

In symbols,

$$\frac{a}{b}\times\frac{c}{d}=\frac{a\times c}{b\times d}=\frac{ac}{bd}$$

to divide by a fraction you turn it upside down and multiply

In symbols,

$$\frac{a}{b}\div\frac{c}{d}=\frac{a}{b}\times\frac{d}{c}\qquad\text{turn the divisor upside down}$$

$$=\frac{ad}{bc}\qquad\text{rule for multiplying fractions}$$

Example

Calculate

(a) $\dfrac{2}{3} \times \dfrac{5}{4}$ **(b)** $2 \times \dfrac{6}{13}$ **(c)** $\dfrac{6}{7} \div \dfrac{4}{21}$ **(d)** $\dfrac{1}{2} \div 3$

Solution

(a) The multiplication rule gives

$$\frac{2}{3} \times \frac{5}{4} = \frac{2 \times 5}{3 \times 4} = \frac{10}{12}$$

We could leave the answer like this, although it can be simplified by dividing top and bottom by 2 to get $^5/_6$. It is also valid to 'cancel' by 2 at the very beginning: that is,

$$\frac{{}^1\cancel{2}}{3} \times \frac{5}{\cancel{4}_2} = \frac{1 \times 5}{3 \times 2} = \frac{5}{6}$$

(b) The whole number 2 is equivalent to the fraction $^2/_1$, so

$$2 \times \frac{6}{13} = \frac{2}{1} \times \frac{6}{13} = \frac{2 \times 6}{1 \times 13} = \frac{12}{13}$$

(c) To calculate

$$\frac{6}{7} \div \frac{4}{21}$$

the divisor is turned upside down to get $^{21}/_4$ and then multiplied to get

$$\frac{6}{7} \div \frac{4}{21} = \frac{{}^3\cancel{6}}{\cancel{7}_1} \times \frac{\cancel{21}^3}{\cancel{4}_2} = \frac{3 \times 3}{1 \times 2} = \frac{9}{2}$$

(d) We write 3 as $^3/_1$, so

$$\frac{1}{2} \div 3 = \frac{1}{2} \div \frac{3}{1} = \frac{1}{2} \times \frac{1}{3} = \frac{1}{6}$$

Practice Problem

2. (1) Without using a calculator evaluate

(a) $\dfrac{1}{2} \times \dfrac{3}{4}$ **(b)** $7 \times \dfrac{1}{14}$ **(c)** $\dfrac{2}{3} \div \dfrac{8}{9}$ **(d)** $\dfrac{8}{9} \div 16$

(2) Confirm your answer to part (1) using a calculator.

The rules for addition and subtraction are as follows:

> to add (or subtract) two fractions you write them as equivalent fractions
> with a common denominator and add (or subtract) their numerators

Example

Calculate

(a) $\dfrac{1}{5} + \dfrac{2}{5}$ (b) $\dfrac{1}{4} + \dfrac{2}{3}$ (c) $\dfrac{7}{12} - \dfrac{5}{8}$

Solution

(a) The fractions $^1/_5$ and $^2/_5$ already have the same denominator, so to add them we just add their numerators to get

$$\frac{1}{5} + \frac{2}{5} = \frac{1+2}{5} = \frac{3}{5}$$

(b) The fractions $^1/_4$ and $^2/_5$ have denominators 4 and 3. One number that is divisible by both 3 and 4 is 12, so we choose this as the common denominator. Now 4 goes into 12 exactly 3 times, so

$$\frac{1}{4} = \frac{1 \times 3}{4 \times 3} = \frac{3}{12}$$

> multiply top and bottom by 3

and 3 goes into 12 exactly 4 times, so

$$\frac{2}{3} = \frac{2 \times 4}{3 \times 4} = \frac{8}{12}$$

> multiply top and bottom by 4

Hence

$$\frac{1}{4} + \frac{2}{3} = \frac{3}{12} + \frac{8}{12} = \frac{3+8}{12} = \frac{11}{12}$$

(c) The fractions $^7/_{12}$ and $^5/_8$ have denominators 12 and 8. One number that is divisible by both 12 and 8 is 24, so we choose this as the common denominator. Now 12 goes into 24 exactly twice, so

$$\frac{7}{12} = \frac{7 \times 2}{24} = \frac{14}{24}$$

and 8 goes into 24 exactly 3 times, so

$$\frac{5}{8} = \frac{5 \times 3}{24} = \frac{15}{24}$$

Hence

$$\frac{7}{12} - \frac{5}{8} = \frac{14}{24} - \frac{15}{24} = -\frac{1}{24}$$

It is not essential that the lowest common denominator is used. Any number will do provided that it is divisible by the two original denominators. If you are stuck then you could always multiply the original two denominators together. In part (c) the denominators multiply to give 96, so this can be used instead. Now

$$\frac{7}{12} = \frac{7 \times 8}{96} = \frac{56}{96}$$

and

$$\frac{5}{8} = \frac{5 \times 12}{96} = \frac{60}{96}$$

so

$$\frac{7}{12} - \frac{5}{8} = \frac{56}{96} - \frac{60}{96} = \frac{56 - 60}{96} = \frac{-1}{24} = -\frac{1}{24}$$

as before.

Notice how the final answer to part (c) of this example has been written. We have simply used the fact that when a negative number is divided by a positive number the answer is negative. It is standard practice to write negative fractions like this so we would write $-\frac{3}{4}$ in preference to either $\frac{3}{-4}$ or $\frac{-3}{4}$ and, of course, $\frac{-3}{-4}$ is written as $\frac{3}{4}$.

Before we leave this topic a word of warning is in order. Notice that you can only add or subtract fractions after you have gone to the trouble of finding a common denominator. In particular, the following short-cut does not give the correct answer:

$$\frac{a}{b} + \frac{c}{d} = \frac{a+c}{b+d} \qquad \textbf{This is NOT true}$$

As usual you can check for yourself that it is complete rubbish by using actual numbers of your own choosing.

Practice Problem

3. (1) Without using a calculator evaluate

$$\textbf{(a)}\ \frac{3}{7} - \frac{1}{7} \qquad \textbf{(b)}\ \frac{1}{3} + \frac{2}{5} \qquad \textbf{(c)}\ \frac{7}{18} - \frac{1}{4}$$

(2) Confirm your answer to part (1) using a calculator.

Provided that you can manipulate ordinary fractions, there is no reason why you should not be able to manipulate algebraic fractions just as easily, since the rules are the same.

Example

Find expressions for each of the following:

$$\textbf{(a)}\ \frac{x}{x-1} \times \frac{2}{x(x+4)} \qquad \textbf{(b)}\ \frac{2}{x-1} \div \frac{x}{x-1} \qquad \textbf{(c)}\ \frac{x+1}{x^2+2} + \frac{x-6}{x^2+2} \qquad \textbf{(d)}\ \frac{x}{x+2} - \frac{1}{x+1}$$

Solution

(a) To multiply two fractions we multiply their corresponding numerators and denominators, so

$$\frac{x}{x-1} \times \frac{2}{x(x+4)} = \frac{2x}{(x-1)x(x+4)} = \frac{2}{(x-1)(x+4)}$$

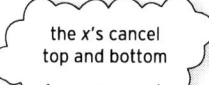

the *x*'s cancel top and bottom

(b) To divide by

$$\frac{x}{x-1}$$

we turn it upside down and multiply, so

$$\frac{2}{x-1} \div \frac{x}{x-1} = \frac{2}{x-1} \times \frac{x-1}{x} = \frac{2}{x}$$

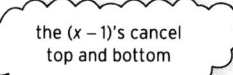

the (*x* − 1)'s cancel top and bottom

(c) The fractions

$$\frac{x+1}{x^2+2} \text{ and } \frac{x-6}{x^2+2}$$

already have the same denominator, so to add them we just add their numerators to get

$$\frac{x+1}{x^2+2} + \frac{x-6}{x^2+2} = \frac{x+1+x-6}{x^2+2} = \frac{2x-5}{x^2+2}$$

(d) The fractions

$$\frac{x}{x+2} \text{ and } \frac{1}{x+1}$$

have denominators $x+2$ and $x+1$. An obvious common denominator is given by their product, $(x+2)(x+1)$. Now $x+2$ goes into $(x+2)(x+1)$ exactly $x+1$ times, so

$$\frac{x}{x+2} = \frac{x(x+1)}{(x+2)(x+1)}$$

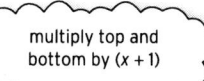

multiply top and bottom by (*x* + 1)

Also $x+1$ goes into $(x+2)(x+1)$ exactly $x+2$ times, so

$$\frac{1}{x+1} = \frac{(x+2)}{(x+2)(x+1)}$$

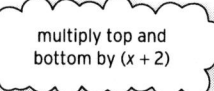

multiply top and bottom by (*x* + 2)

Hence

$$\frac{x}{x+2} - \frac{1}{x+1} = \frac{(x+1)}{(x+2)(x+1)} - \frac{(x+2)}{(x+2)(x+1)} = \frac{x(x+1)-(x+2)}{(x+2)(x+1)}$$

It is worth multiplying out the brackets on the top to simplify: that is,

$$\frac{x^2+x-x-2}{(x+2)(x+1)} = \frac{x^2-2}{(x+2)(x+1)}$$

Practice Problem

4. Find expressions for the following algebraic fractions, simplifying your answers as far as possible.

(a) $\dfrac{5}{x-1} \times \dfrac{x-1}{x+2}$ (b) $\dfrac{x^2}{x+10} \div \dfrac{x}{x+1}$ (c) $\dfrac{4}{x+1} + \dfrac{1}{x+1}$ (d) $\dfrac{2}{x+1} - \dfrac{1}{x+2}$

1.2.2 Equations

In Section 1.1.2 and again in Section 1.2.1 we have seen how to re-write an algebraic expression in a simpler but equivalent form. For example, when we write things like

$$x^2 + 3x + 3x^2 - 10x = 4x^2 - 7x \qquad \text{(collecting like terms)}$$

or

$$\frac{x}{x+2} - \frac{1}{x+1} = \frac{x^2-2}{(x+2)(x+1)} \qquad \text{(part (d) of the previous worked example)}$$

we have at the back of our minds the knowledge that the left- and right-hand sides are identical so that each statement is true for all possible values of x. For this reason the above relations are called **identities**. Compare these with statements such as:

$$7x - 1 = 13$$

or

$$x^2 - 5x = 1$$

These relations are called **equations** and are only true for particular values of x which need to be found. It turns out that the first equation above has just one solution whereas the second has two solutions. The latter is called a quadratic equation and will be considered in the next chapter.

One naïve approach to the solution of equations such as $7x - 1 = 13$ might be to use trial and error: that is, we could just keep guessing values of x until we find the one that works. Can you see what x is in this case? However, a more reliable and systematic approach is to actually solve this equation using the rules of mathematics. In fact, the only rule that we need is:

> you can apply whatever mathematical operation you like to an equation,
> *provided that you do the same thing to both sides*

There is only one exception to this rule: you must never divide both sides by zero. This should be obvious because a number such as 11/0 does not exist. (If you do not believe this, try dividing 11 by 0 on your calculator.)

The first obstacle that prevents us from writing down the value of x immediately from the equation $7x - 1 = 13$ is the presence of the −1 on the left-hand side. This can be removed by adding 1. For this to be legal we must also add 1 to the right-hand side to get

$$7x - 1 + 1 = 13 + 1$$
$$7x = 14$$

The second obstacle is the number 7 which is multiplying the *x*. This can be removed by dividing the left-hand side by 7. Of course, we must also do the same thing to the right-hand side to get

$$\frac{7x}{7} = \frac{14}{7}$$

$$x = 2$$

This is no doubt the solution that you spotted earlier by simple trial and error and you may be wondering why you need to bother with the formal method. The reason is simple: guesswork will not help to solve more complicated equations in which the solution is non-obvious or even simple equations in which the solution is a fraction. In these circumstances we need to follow the approach of 'balancing the equation' described above.

Example

Solve

(a) $6x + 1 = 10x - 9$ **(b)** $3(x - 1) + 2(2x + 1) = 4$

(c) $\dfrac{20}{3x - 1} = 7$ **(d)** $\dfrac{9}{x + 2} = \dfrac{7}{2x + 1}$ **(e)** $\sqrt{\dfrac{2x}{x - 6}} = 2$

Solution

(a) To solve

$$6x + 1 = 10x - 9$$

the strategy is to collect terms involving *x* on one side of the equation, and to collect all of the number terms on to the other side. It does not matter which way round this is done. In this particular case, there are more *x*'s on the right-hand side than there are on the left-hand side. Consequently, to avoid negative numbers, you may prefer to stack the *x* terms on the right-hand side. The details are as follows:

$$1 = 4x - 9 \quad \text{(subtract } 6x \text{ from both sides)}$$

$$10 = 4x \quad \text{(add 9 to both sides)}$$

$$\frac{10}{4} = x \quad \text{(divide both sides by 4)}$$

Hence $x = {}^5\!/_2 = 2{}^1\!/_2$.

(b) The novel feature of the equation

$$3(x - 1) + 2(2x + 1) = 4$$

is the presence of brackets. To solve it, we first remove the brackets by multiplying out, and then collect like terms:

$$3x - 3 + 4x + 2 = 4 \quad \text{(multiply out the brackets)}$$

$$7x - 1 = 4 \quad \text{(collect like terms)}$$

Note that this equation is now of the form that we know how to solve:

$$7x = 5 \quad \text{(add 1 to both sides)}$$

$$x = \frac{5}{7} \quad \text{(divide both sides by 7)}$$

(c) The novel feature of the equation

$$\frac{20}{3x - 1} = 7$$

is the fact that it involves an algebraic fraction. This can easily be removed by multiplying both sides by the bottom of the fraction:

$$\frac{20}{3x - 1} \times (3x - 1) = 7(3x - 1)$$

which cancels down to give

$$20 = 7(3x - 1)$$

The remaining steps are similar to those in part (b):

$20 = 21x - 7$ (multiply out the brackets)

$27 = 21x$ (add 7 to both sides)

$\dfrac{27}{21} = x$ (divide both sides by 21)

Hence $x = {}^9/_7 = 1{}^2/_7$.

(d) The next equation,

$$\frac{9}{x + 2} = \frac{7}{2x + 1}$$

looks particularly daunting since there are fractions on both sides. However, these are easily removed by multiplying both sides by the denominators, in turn:

$$9 = \frac{7(x + 2)}{2x + 1}$$ (multiply both sides by $x + 2$)

$9(2x + 1) = 7(x + 2)$ (multiply both sides by $2x + 1$)

With practice you can do these two steps simultaneously and write this as the first line of working. The procedure of going straight from

$$\frac{9}{x + 2} = \frac{7}{2x + 1}$$

to

$$9(2x + 1) = 7(x + 2)$$

is called 'cross-multiplication'. In general, if

$$\frac{a}{b} = \frac{c}{d}$$

then

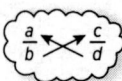

$$ad = bc$$

The remaining steps are similar to those used in the earlier parts of this example:

$$18x + 9 = 7x + 14 \quad \text{(multiply out the brackets)}$$
$$11x + 9 = 14 \quad \text{(subtract } 7x \text{ from both sides)}$$
$$11x = 5 \quad \text{(subtract 9 from both sides)}$$
$$x = \frac{5}{11} \quad \text{(divide both sides by 11)}$$

(e) The left-hand side of the final equation

$$\sqrt{\frac{2x}{x-6}} = 2$$

is surrounded by a square root, which can easily be removed by squaring both sides to get

$$\frac{2x}{x-6} = 4$$

The remaining steps are 'standard':

$$2x = 4(x-6) \quad \text{(multiply both sides by } x - 6)$$
$$2x = 4x - 24 \quad \text{(multiply out the brackets)}$$
$$-2x = -24 \quad \text{(subtract } 4x \text{ from both sides)}$$
$$x = 12 \quad \text{(divide both sides by } -2)$$

Looking back over each part of the previous example, notice that there is a common strategy. In each case, the aim is to convert the given equation into one of the form

$$ax + b = c$$

which is the sort of equation that we can easily solve. If the original equation contains brackets then remove them by multiplying out. If the equation involves fractions then remove them by cross-multiplying.

Advice

If you have the time, it is always worth checking your answer by substituting your solution back into the original equation. For the last part of the above example, putting $x = 12$ into $\sqrt{\dfrac{2x}{x-6}}$ gives

$$\sqrt{\frac{2 \times 12}{12 - 6}} = \sqrt{\frac{24}{6}} = \sqrt{4} = 2 \quad \checkmark$$

Practice Problem

5. Solve each of the following equations. Leave your answer as a fraction, if necessary.

(a) $4x + 1 = 25$ (b) $4x + 5 = 5x - 7$ (c) $3(3 - 2x) + 2(x - 1) = 10$

(d) $\dfrac{4}{x-1} = 5$ (e) $\dfrac{3}{4} = \dfrac{5}{x-1}$

1.2.3 Inequalities

In Section 1.1.1 we made use of a **number line:**

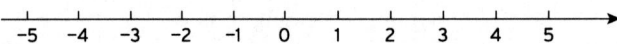

Now, although only whole numbers are marked on this diagram, it is implicitly assumed that it can also be used to indicate fractions and decimal numbers as well. To each point on the line there corresponds a particular number. Conversely, every number can be represented by a particular point on the line. For example, $-2\frac{1}{2}$ lies exactly halfway between -3 and -2. Similarly, $4\frac{7}{8}$ lies $\frac{7}{8}$ths of the way between 4 and 5. In theory, we can even find a point on the line corresponding to a number such as $\sqrt{2}$, although it may be difficult to sketch such a point accurately in practice. My calculator gives the value of $\sqrt{2}$ to be 1.414 213 56 to eight decimal places. This number therefore lies just less than halfway between 1 and 2.

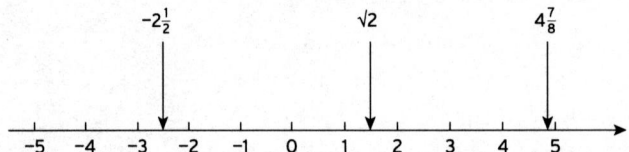

A number line can be used to decide whether or not one number is greater or less than another number. We say that a number a is greater than a number b if a lies to the right of b on the line and write this as

$a > b$

Likewise, we say that a is less than b if a lies to the left of b and write this as

$a < b$

From the diagram we see that

$-2 > -4$

because -2 lies to the right of 4. This is equivalent to the statement

$-4 < -2$

Similarly,

$0 > -1$ (or equivalently $-1 < 0$)
$2 > -2\frac{1}{2}$ (or equivalently $-2\frac{1}{2} < 2$)
$4\frac{7}{8} > \sqrt{2}$ (or equivalently $\sqrt{2} < 4\frac{7}{8}$)

There are occasions when we would like the letters a and b to stand for mathematical expressions rather than actual numbers. In this situation we sometimes use the symbols $\geq$ and $\leq$ to mean 'greater than or equal to' and 'less than or equal to' respectively.

We have already seen that we can manipulate equations in any way we like, provided that we do the same thing to both sides. An obvious question to ask is whether this rule extends to inequalities. To investigate this, consider the following example.

Example

Starting with the true statement

$1 < 3$

decide which of the following are valid operations when performed on both sides:

(a) add 4   **(b)** add −5   **(c)** multiply by 2   **(d)** multiply by −6

Solution

(a) If we add 4 to both sides of the inequality

$1 < 3$ (1)

then we obtain

$5 < 7$

which is a true statement.

(b) If we add −5 to both sides of inequality (1) then we obtain

$-4 < -2$

which is also true.

(c) If we multiply both sides of inequality (1) by 2 then we obtain

$2 < 6$

which is again true.

(d) So far so good, but if we now multiply both sides of inequality (1) by −6 then we obtain

$-6 < -18$

which is false. In fact, quite the reverse is true, since −6 lies to the right of −18 on the number line and so −6 is actually greater than −18. This indicates that the rule needs modifying before we can extend it to inequalities and that we need to be careful when manipulating such things.

Practice Problem

6. Starting with the true statement

$6 > 3$

decide which of the following are valid operations when performed on both sides:

(a) add 6   **(b)** multiply by 2   **(c)** subtract 3

(d) add −3   **(e)** divide by 3   **(f)** multiply by −4

(g) multiply by −1 **(h)** divide by −3   **(i)** add −10

These examples show that the usual rule does apply to inequalities with the important proviso that

> **if both sides are multiplied or divided by a negative number then the sense of the inequality is reversed**

By this we mean that '>' changes to '<', '≤' changes to '≥' and so on.

Example

Simplify the inequality

$$2x + 3 < 4x + 7$$

Solution

The first problem is to decide what is meant by the word 'simplify'. At the moment there are x's on both sides of the inequality sign and it would obviously look neater if these were collected together. We do this by subtracting $4x$ from both sides to get

$$-2x + 3 < 7$$

We can also put all of the constant terms on to the right-hand side by subtracting 3 from both sides to get

$$-2x < 4$$

This is certainly an improvement, but we can go further to make the inequality even more meaningful. We may divide both sides by -2 to get

$$x > -2$$

Notice that the sense has been reversed at this stage because we have divided by a negative number. We have therefore shown that any number x satisfies the original inequality provided that it lies to the right of the number -2 on the number line.

Advice

You should check your answer using a couple of test values. Substituting $x = 1$ (which lies to the right of -2, so should work) into both sides of the original inequality $2x + 3 < 4x + 7$ gives $5 < 11$, which is true. On the other hand, substituting $x = -3$ (which lies to the left of -2, so should fail) gives $-3 < -5$, which is false.

Of course, just checking a couple of numbers like this does not prove that the final inequality is correct, but it should protect you against gross blunders.

Practice Problem

7. Simplify the inequalities

    (a) $2x < 3x + 7$ **(b)** $21x - 19 \geq 4x + 15$

Key Terms

Algebraic fraction   Ratio of two expressions; $p(x)/q(x)$ where $p(x)$ and $q(x)$ are algebraic expressions such as $ax^2 + bx + c$ or $dx + e$.

Denominator   The number (or expression) on the bottom of a fraction.

Equation   Equality of two algebraic expressions which is only true for certain values of the variable.

Equivalent fractions   Fractions which may appear different but which have the same numerical value.

Identity   Equality of two algebraic expressions which is true for all values of the variable.

Number line   An infinite line on which the points represent real numbers by their (signed) distance from the origin.

Numerator   The number (or expression) on the top of a fraction.

Exercise 1.2

1. Reduce each of the following numerical fractions to their lowest terms:

    (a) $\dfrac{13}{26}$ (b) $\dfrac{9}{12}$ (c) $\dfrac{18}{30}$ (d) $\dfrac{24}{72}$ (e) $\dfrac{36}{27}$

2. Reduce each of the following algebraic fractions to their lowest terms:

    (a) $\dfrac{6x}{9}$ (b) $\dfrac{x}{2x^2}$ (c) $\dfrac{b}{abc}$ (d) $\dfrac{4x}{6x^2y}$ (e) $\dfrac{15a^2b}{20ab^2}$

3. By factorizing the numerators and/or denominators of each of the following fractions reduce each to its lowest terms:

    (a) $\dfrac{2p}{4q + 6r}$ (b) $\dfrac{x}{x^2 - 4x}$ (c) $\dfrac{3ab}{6a^2 + 3a}$ (d) $\dfrac{14d}{21d - 7de}$ (e) $\dfrac{x + 2}{x^2 - 4}$

4. Which one of the following algebraic fractions can be simplified? Explain why the other two fractions cannot be simplified.

    $$\dfrac{x - 1}{2x - 2}, \dfrac{x - 2}{x + 2}, \dfrac{5t}{10t - s}$$

5. (1) Without using a calculator work out the following giving your answer in its lowest terms:

    (a) $\dfrac{1}{7} + \dfrac{2}{7}$ (b) $\dfrac{2}{9} - \dfrac{5}{9}$ (c) $\dfrac{1}{2} + \dfrac{1}{3}$ (d) $\dfrac{3}{4} - \dfrac{2}{5}$ (e) $\dfrac{1}{6} + \dfrac{2}{9}$ (f) $\dfrac{1}{6} + \dfrac{2}{3}$

    (g) $\dfrac{5}{6} \times \dfrac{3}{4}$ (h) $\dfrac{4}{15} \div \dfrac{2}{3}$ (i) $\dfrac{7}{8} \times \dfrac{2}{3}$ (j) $\dfrac{2}{75} \div \dfrac{4}{5}$ (k) $\dfrac{2}{9} \div 3$ (l) $3 \div \dfrac{2}{7}$

    (2) Use your calculator to check your answers to part (1).

6. Work out each of the following, simplifying your answer as far as possible:

(a) $\dfrac{2}{3x}+\dfrac{1}{3x}$ (b) $\dfrac{2}{x}\times\dfrac{x}{5}$ (c) $\dfrac{3}{x}-\dfrac{2}{x^2}$ (d) $\dfrac{7}{x}+\dfrac{2}{y}$ (e) $\dfrac{a}{2}\div\dfrac{a}{6}$

(f) $\dfrac{5c}{12}+\dfrac{5d}{18}$ (g) $\dfrac{x+2}{y-5}\times\dfrac{y-5}{x+3}$ (h) $\dfrac{4gh}{7}\div\dfrac{2g}{9h}$ (i) $\dfrac{t}{4}\div 5$ (j) $\dfrac{P}{Q}\times\dfrac{Q}{P}$

7. Solve each of the following equations. If necessary give your answer as a mixed fraction reduced to its lowest terms.

(a) $x+2=7$ (b) $3x=18$ (c) $\dfrac{x}{9}=2$ (d) $x-4=-2$

(e) $2x-3=17$ (f) $3x+4=1$ (g) $\dfrac{x}{6}-7=3$ (h) $3(x-1)=2$

(i) $4-x=9$ (j) $6x+2=5x-1$ (k) $5(3x+8)=10$ (l) $2(x-3)=5(x+1)$

(m) $\dfrac{4x-7}{3}=2$ (n) $\dfrac{4}{x+1}=1$ (o) $5-\dfrac{1}{x}=1$

8. Which of the following inequalities are true?

(a) $-2<1$ (b) $-6>-4$ (c) $3<3$

(d) $3\le 3$ (e) $-21\ge -22$ (f) $4<\sqrt{25}$

9. Simplify the following inequalities:

(a) $2x>x+1$ (b) $7x+3\le 9+5x$ (c) $x-5>4x+4$ (d) $x-1<2x-3$

10. Simplify the following algebraic expression:

$$\dfrac{4}{x^2y}\div\dfrac{2x}{y}$$

11. (a) Solve the equation

$$6(2+x)=5(1-4x)$$

(b) Solve the inequality

$$3x+6\ge 5x-14$$

Exercise 1.2*

1. Simplify each of the following algebraic fractions:

(a) $\dfrac{2x-6}{4}$ (b) $\dfrac{9x}{6x^2-3x}$ (c) $\dfrac{4x+16}{x+4}$ (d) $\dfrac{x-1}{1-x}$

(e) $\dfrac{x+6}{x^2-36}$ (f) $\dfrac{(x+3)(2x-5)}{(2x-5)(x+4)}$ (g) $\dfrac{3x}{6x^3-15x^2+9x}$ (h) $\dfrac{4x^2-25y^2}{6x-15y}$

2. (1) Without using your calculator evaluate

(a) $\dfrac{4}{5} \times \dfrac{25}{28}$

(b) $\dfrac{2}{7} \times \dfrac{14}{25} \times \dfrac{5}{8}$

(c) $\dfrac{9}{16} \div \dfrac{3}{8}$

(d) $\dfrac{2}{5} \times \dfrac{1}{12} \div \dfrac{8}{25}$

(e) $\dfrac{10}{13} - \dfrac{12}{13}$

(f) $\dfrac{5}{9} + \dfrac{2}{3}$

(g) $2\dfrac{3}{5} + 1\dfrac{3}{7}$

(h) $5\dfrac{9}{10} - \dfrac{1}{2} + 1\dfrac{2}{5}$

(i) $3\dfrac{3}{4} \times 1\dfrac{3}{5}$

(j) $\dfrac{3}{5} \times \left(2\dfrac{1}{3} + \dfrac{1}{2}\right)$

(k) $\dfrac{5}{6} \times \left(2\dfrac{1}{3} - 1\dfrac{2}{5}\right)$

(l) $\left(3\dfrac{1}{3} \div 2\dfrac{1}{6}\right) \div \dfrac{5}{13}$

(2) Confirm your answer to part (1) using a calculator.

3. Find expressions for the following fractions:

(a) $\dfrac{x^2 + 6x}{x - 2} \times \dfrac{x - 2}{x}$

(b) $\dfrac{1}{x} \div \dfrac{1}{x + 1}$

(c) $\dfrac{2}{xy} + \dfrac{3}{xy}$

(d) $\dfrac{x}{2} + \dfrac{x + 1}{3}$

(e) $\dfrac{3}{x} + \dfrac{4}{x + 1}$

(f) $\dfrac{3}{x} + \dfrac{5}{x^2}$

(g) $x - \dfrac{2}{x + 1}$

(h) $\dfrac{5}{x(x + 1)} - \dfrac{2}{x} + \dfrac{3}{x + 1}$

4. Solve the following equations:

(a) $5(2x + 1) = 3(x - 2)$

(b) $5(x + 2) + 4(2x - 3) = 11$

(c) $5(1 - x) = 4(10 + x)$

(d) $3(3 - 2x) - 7(1 - x) = 10$

(e) $9 - 5(2x - 1) = 6$

(f) $\dfrac{3}{2x + 1} = 2$

(g) $\dfrac{2}{x - 1} = \dfrac{3}{5x + 4}$

(h) $\dfrac{x}{2} + 3 = 7$

(i) $5 - \dfrac{x}{3} = 2$

(j) $\dfrac{5(x - 3)}{2} = \dfrac{2(x - 1)}{5}$

(k) $\sqrt{(2x - 5)} = 3$

(l) $(x + 3)(x - 1) = (x + 4)(x - 3)$

(m) $(x + 2)^2 + (2x - 1)^2 = 5x(x + 1)$

(n) $\dfrac{2x + 7}{3} = \dfrac{x - 4}{6} + \dfrac{1}{2}$

(o) $\sqrt{\dfrac{45}{2x - 1}} = 3$

(p) $\dfrac{4}{x} - \dfrac{3}{4} = \dfrac{1}{4x}$

5. Two-thirds of Ariadne's money together with five-sevenths of Brian's money is equal to three-fifths of Catriona's money. If Ariadne has \$2.40 and Catriona has \$11.25, write down an equation that you could use to work out how much Brian has. Solve this equation.

6. An amount \$$P$ is placed in a savings account. The interest rate is r% compounded annually so that after n years the savings, S, will be

$$S = P\left(1 + \dfrac{r}{100}\right)^n$$

(a) Find S when $P = 2000$, $n = 5$ and $r = 10$.

(b) Find P when $S = 65\ 563.62$, $n = 3$ and $r = 3$.

(c) Find r when $S = 7320.50$, $P = 5000$, and $n = 4$.

7. Solve the following inequalities:

(a) $2x - 19 > 7x + 24$ (b) $2(x - 1) < 5(3x + 2)$ (c) $\dfrac{2x - 1}{5} \geq \dfrac{x - 3}{2}$

(d) $3 + \dfrac{x}{3} < 2(x + 4)$ (e) $x < 2x + 1 \leq 7$

8. List all the whole numbers that satisfy both of the following inequalities simultaneously:

$-7 \leq 2x < 6$ and $4x + 1 \leq x + 2$

9. (a) Simplify

$$\frac{31x - 8}{(2x - 1)(x + 2)} - \frac{14}{x + 2}$$

(b) Solve the equation

$$\frac{x + 1}{8} = \frac{x + 3}{4} - \frac{1}{2}$$

(c) Simplify the inequality

$$(2x + 1)(x - 5) \leq 2(x + 2)(x - 4)$$

10. Simplify

$$\frac{x^2}{x + 1} \div \frac{2x}{x^2 - 1}$$

SECTION 1.3
Graphs of linear equations

Objectives

At the end of this section you should be able to:

* Plot points on graph paper given their coordinates.
* Sketch a line by finding the coordinates of two points on the line.
* Solve simultaneous linear equations graphically.
* Sketch a line by using its slope and intercept.

Consider the two straight lines shown in Figure 1.1. The horizontal line is referred to as the **x axis** and the vertical line is referred to as the **y axis**. The point where these lines intersect is known as the **origin** and is denoted by the letter O. These lines enable us to identify uniquely any point, P, in terms of its **coordinates** (x, y). The first number, x, denotes the horizontal distance along the x axis and the second number, y, denotes the vertical distance along the y axis. The arrows on the axes indicate the positive direction in each case.

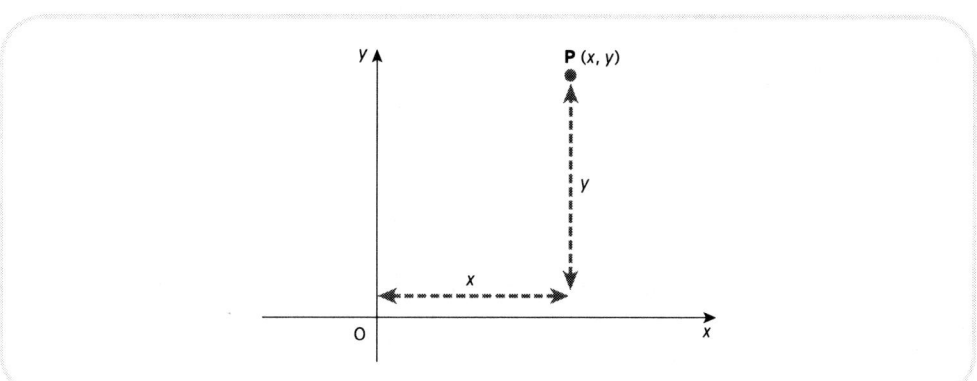

Figure 1.1

Example

Plot the points A(2, 3), B(−1, 4), C(−3, −1), D(3, −2) and E(5, 0).

Solution

The point A with coordinates (2, 3) is obtained by starting at the origin, moving 2 units to the right and then moving 3 units vertically upwards. Similarly, the point B with coordinates (−1, 4) is located 1 unit to the left of O (because the x coordinate is negative) and 4 units up. These points, together with C(−3, −1), D(3, −2) and E(5, 0) are plotted in Figure 1.2.

Note that the point C lies in the bottom left-hand quadrant since its x and y coordinates are both negative. It is also worth noticing that E actually lies on the x axis since its y coordinate is zero. Likewise, a point with coordinates of the form $(0, y)$ for some number y would lie somewhere on the y axis. Of course, the point with coordinates $(0, 0)$ is the origin, O.

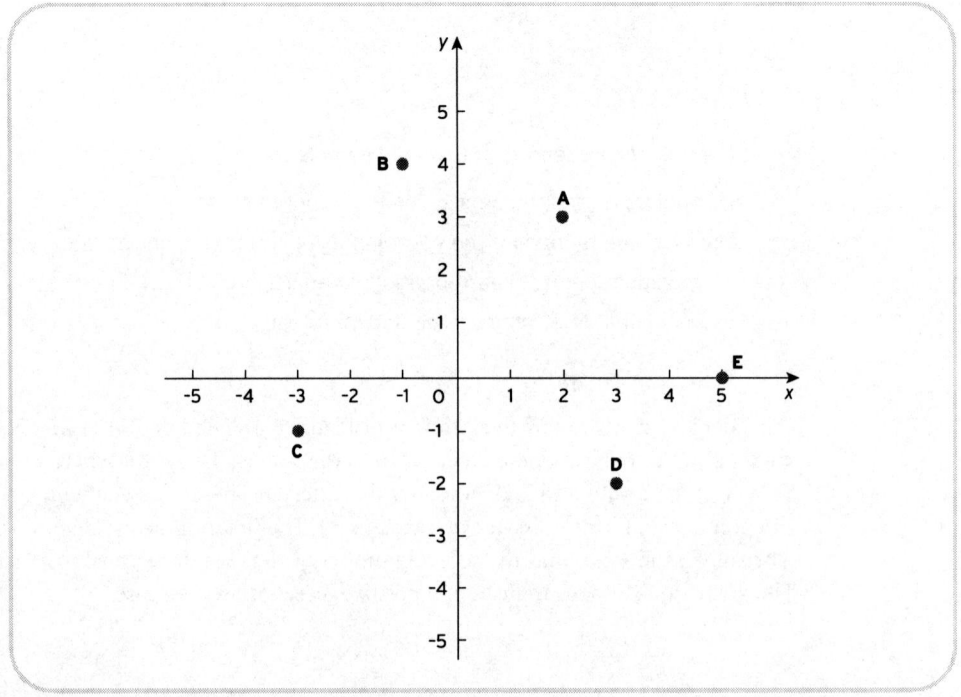

Figure 1.2

Practice Problem

1. Plot the following points on graph paper. What do you observe?

$(2, 5), (1, 3), (0, 1), (-2, -3), (-3, -5)$

In economics we need to do rather more than just plot individual points on graph paper. We would like to be able to sketch curves represented by equations and to deduce information from such a picture. We restrict our attention in this section to those equations whose graphs are straight lines, deferring consideration of more general curve sketching until Chapter 2.

In Practice Problem 1 you will have noticed that the five points $(2, 5), (1, 3), (0, 1), (-2, -3)$ and $(-3, -5)$ all lie on a straight line. In fact, the equation of this line is

$$-2x + y = 1$$

Any point lies on this line if its x and y coordinates satisfy this equation. For example, $(2, 5)$ lies on the line because when the values $x = 2$ and $y = 5$ are substituted into the left-hand side of the equation we obtain

$$-2(2) + 5 = -4 + 5 = 1$$

which is the right-hand side of the equation. The other points can be checked similarly (Table 1.1).

Table 1.1

Point	Check	
(1, 3)	$-2(1) + 3 = -2 + 3 = 1$	✓
(0, 1)	$-2(0) + 1 = 0 + 1 = 1$	✓
(−2, −3)	$-2(-2) - 3 = 4 - 3 = 1$	✓
(−3, −5)	$-2(-3) - 5 = 6 - 5 = 1$	✓

The general equation of a straight line takes the form

$$\boxed{\text{a multiple of } x} + \boxed{\text{a multiple of } y} = \boxed{\text{a number}}$$

that is,

$$dx + ey = f$$

for some given numbers d, e and f. Consequently, such an equation is called a **linear equation**. The numbers d and e are referred to as the **coefficients**. The coefficients of the linear equation,

$$-2x + y = 1$$

are -2 and 1 (the coefficient of y is 1 because y can be thought of as $1 \times y$).

Example

Decide which of the following points lie on the line $5x - 2y = 6$:

A(0, −3), B(2, 2), C(−10, −28) and D(4, 8)

Solution

$$5(0) - 2(-3) = 0 - (-6) = 0 + 6 = 6$$
$$5(2) - 2(2) = 10 - 4 = 6$$
$$5(-10) - 2(-28) = -50 - (-56) = -50 + 56 = 6$$
$$5(4) - 2(8) = 20 - 16 = 4 \neq 6$$

Hence points A, B and C lie on the line, but D does not.

Practice Problem

2. Check that the points

(−1, 2), (−4, 4), (5, −2), (2, 0)

all lie on the line

$$2x + 3y = 4$$

and hence sketch this line on graph paper. Does the point (3, −1) lie on this line?

In general, to sketch a line from its mathematical equation, it is sufficient to calculate the coordinates of any two distinct points lying on it. These two points can be plotted on graph paper and a ruler used to draw the line passing through them. One way of finding the coordinates of a point on a line is simply to choose a numerical value for x and to substitute it into the equation.

The equation can then be used to deduce the corresponding value of *y*. The whole process can be repeated to find the coordinates of the second point by choosing another value for *x*.

Example

Sketch the line

$$4x + 3y = 11$$

Solution

For the first point, let us choose $x = 5$. Substitution of this number into the equation gives

$$4(5) + 3y = 11$$
$$20 + 3y = 11$$

The problem now is to solve this equation for *y*:

$3y = -9$ (subtract 20 from both sides)

$y = -3$ (divide both sides by 3)

Consequently, the coordinates of one point on the line are $(5, -3)$.

For the second point, let us choose $x = -1$. Substitution of this number into the equation gives

$$4(-1) + 3y = 11$$
$$-4 + 3y = 11$$

This can be solved for *y* as follows:

$3y = 15$ (add 4 to both sides)

$y = 5$ (divide both sides by 3)

Hence $(-1, 5)$ lies on the line, which can now be sketched on graph paper as shown in Figure 1.3.

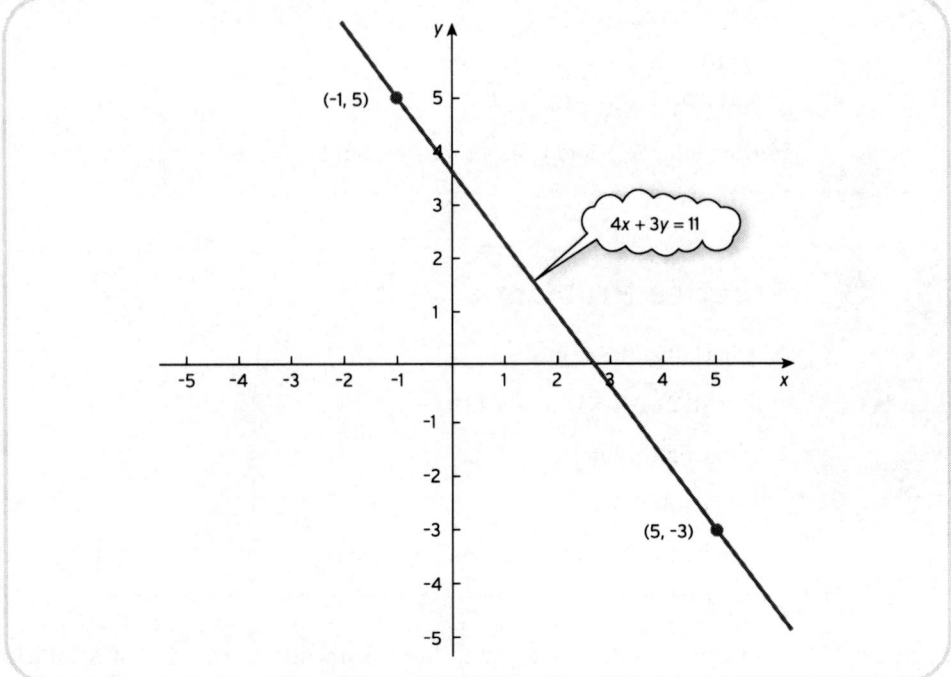

Figure 1.3

Practice Problem

3. Find the coordinates of two points on the line

$$3x - 2y = 4$$

by taking $x = 2$ for the first point and $x = -2$ for the second point. Hence sketch its graph.

In this example we arbitrarily picked two values of x and used the linear equation to work out the corresponding values of y. There is nothing particularly special about the variable x. We could equally well have chosen values for y and solved the resulting equations for x. In fact, the easiest thing to do (in terms of the amount of arithmetic involved) is to put $x = 0$ and find y and then to put $y = 0$ and find x.

Example

Sketch the line

$$2x + y = 5$$

Solution

Setting $x = 0$ gives

$$2(0) + y = 5$$
$$0 + y = 5$$
$$y = 5$$

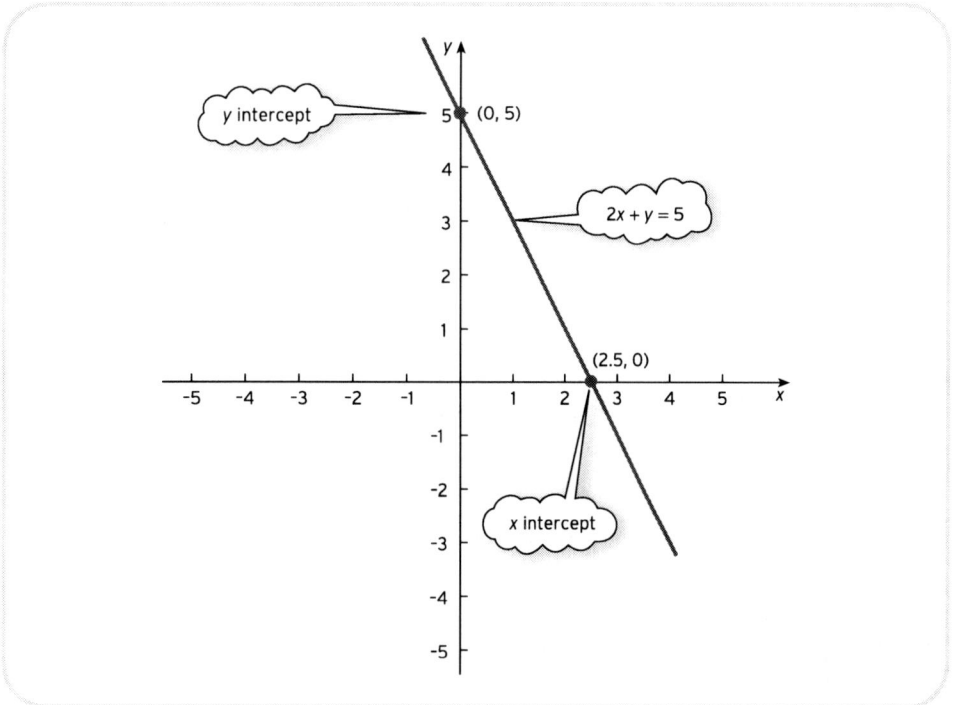

Figure 1.4

Hence (0, 5) lies on the line.
Setting $y = 0$ gives

$$2x + 0 = 5$$
$$2x = 5$$
$$x = 5/2 \quad \text{(divide both sides by 2)}$$

Hence (5/2, 0) lies on the line.

The line $2x + y = 5$ is sketched in Figure 1.4. Notice how easy the algebra is using this approach. The two points themselves are also slightly more meaningful. They are the points where the line intersects the coordinate axes.

Practice Problem

4. Find the coordinates of the points where the line

$$x - 2y = 2$$

intersects the axes. Hence sketch its graph.

In economics it is sometimes necessary to handle more than one equation at the same time. For example, in supply and demand analysis we are interested in two equations, the supply equation and the demand equation. Both involve the same variables Q and P, so it makes sense to sketch them on the same diagram. This enables the market equilibrium quantity and price to be determined by finding the point of intersection of the two lines. We shall return to the analysis of supply and demand in Section 1.5. There are many other occasions in economics and business studies when it is necessary to determine the coordinates of points of intersection. The following is a straightforward example which illustrates the general principle.

Example

Find the point of intersection of the two lines

$$4x + 3y = 11$$
$$2x + y = 5$$

Solution

We have already seen how to sketch these lines in the previous two examples. We discovered that

$$4x + 3y = 11$$

passes through (5, −3) and (−1, 5), and that

$$2x + y = 5$$

passes through (0, 5) and (5/2, 0).

These two lines are sketched on the same diagram in Figure 1.5, from which the point of intersection is seen to be (2, 1).

It is easy to verify that we have not made any mistakes by checking that (2, 1) lies on both lines. It lies on

$4x + 3y = 11$ because $4(2) + 3(1) = 8 + 3 = 11$ ✓

and lies on $2x + y = 5$ because $2(2) + 1 = 4 + 1 = 5$ ✓

For this reason, we say that $x = 2$, $y = 1$, is the solution of the **simultaneous linear equations**

$$4x + 3y = 11$$
$$2x + y = 5$$

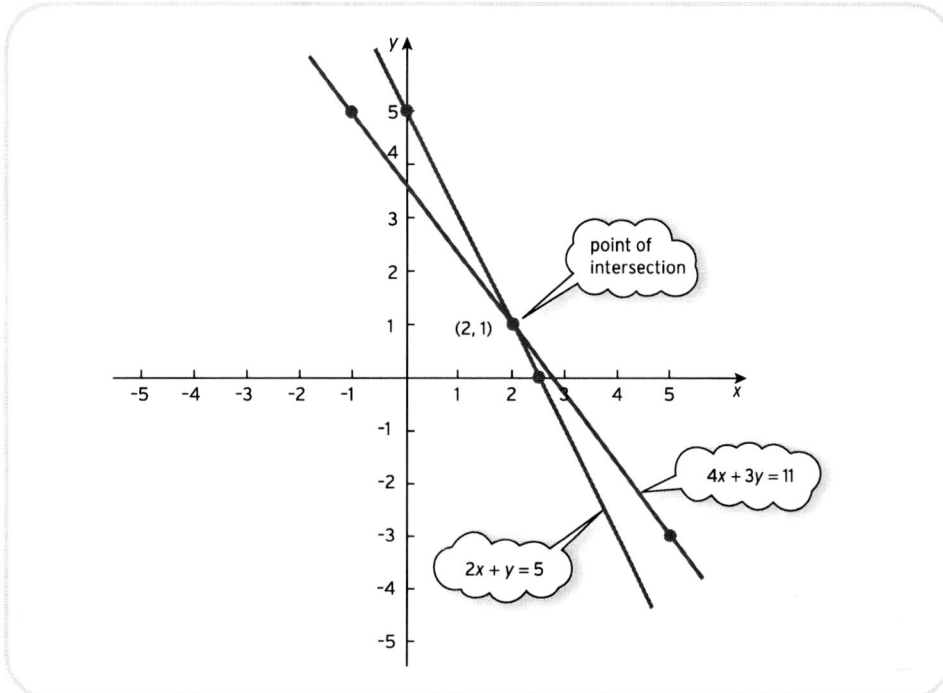

Figure 1.5

Practice Problem

5. Find the point of intersection of

$$3x - 2y = 4$$
$$x - 2y = 2$$

[Hint: you might find your answers to Problems 3 and 4 useful.]

Quite often it is not necessary to produce an accurate plot of an equation. All that may be required is an indication of the general shape together with a few key points or features. It can be shown that, provided e is non-zero, any equation given by

$$dx + ey = f$$

can be rearranged into the special form

$$y = ax + b$$

An example showing you how to perform such a rearrangement will be considered in a moment. The coefficients a and b have particular significance, which we now examine. To be specific, consider

$$y = 2x - 3$$

in which $a = 2$ and $b = -3$.

When x is taken to be zero, the value of y is

$$y = 2(0) - 3 = -3$$

The line passes through $(0, -3)$, so the y intercept is -3. This is just the value of b. In other words, the constant term, b, represents the **intercept** on the y axis.

In the same way it is easy to see that a, the coefficient of x, determines the **slope** of the line. The slope of a straight line is simply the change in the value of y brought about by a 1 unit increase in the value of x. For the equation

$$y = 2x - 3$$

let us choose $x = 5$ and increase this by a single unit to get $x = 6$. The corresponding values of y are then

$$y = 2(5) - 3 = 10 - 3 = 7$$
$$y = 2(6) - 3 = 12 - 3 = 9$$

respectively. The value of y increases by 2 units when x rises by 1 unit. The slope of the line is therefore 2, which is the value of a. The slope of a line is fixed throughout its length, so it is immaterial which two points are taken. The particular choice of $x = 5$ and $x = 6$ was entirely arbitrary. You might like to convince yourself of this by choosing two other points, such as $x = 20$ and $x = 21$, and repeating the previous calculations.

A graph of the line

$$y = 2x - 3$$

is sketched in Figure 1.6. This is sketched using the information that the intercept is -3 and that for every 1 unit along we go 2 units up. In this example the coefficient of x is positive. This does not have to be the case. If a is negative then for every increase in x there is a corresponding decrease in y, indicating that the line is downhill. If a is zero then the equation is just

$$y = b$$

indicating that y is fixed at b and the line is horizontal. The three cases are illustrated in Figure 1.7.

It is important to appreciate that in order to use the slope–intercept approach it is necessary for the equation to be written as

$$y = ax + b$$

If a linear equation does not have this form, it is usually possible to perform a preliminary rearrangement to isolate the variable y on the left-hand side, as the following example demonstrates.

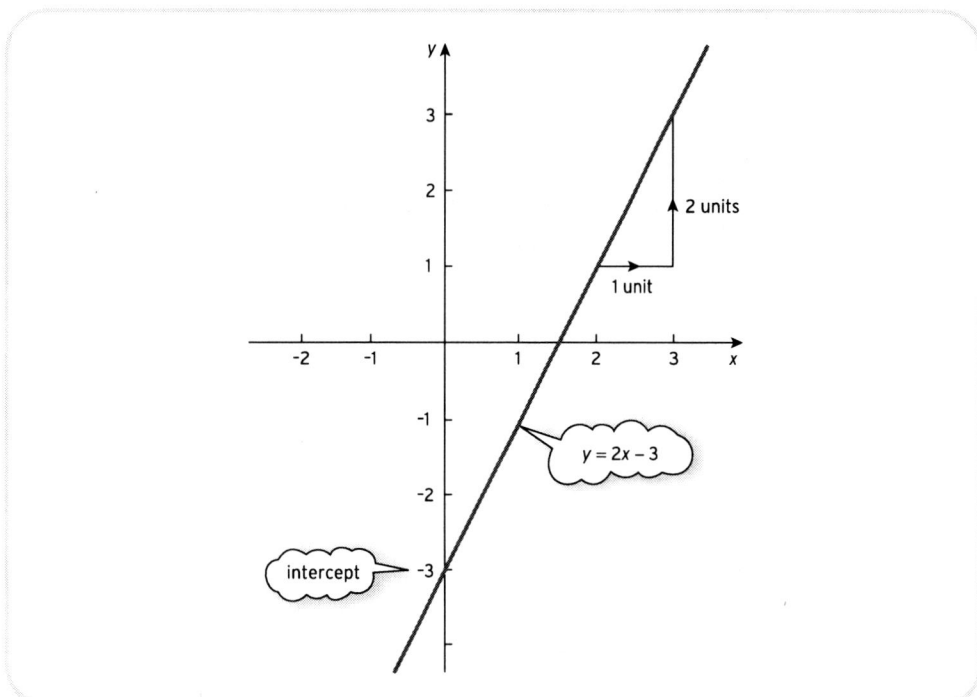

Figure 1.6

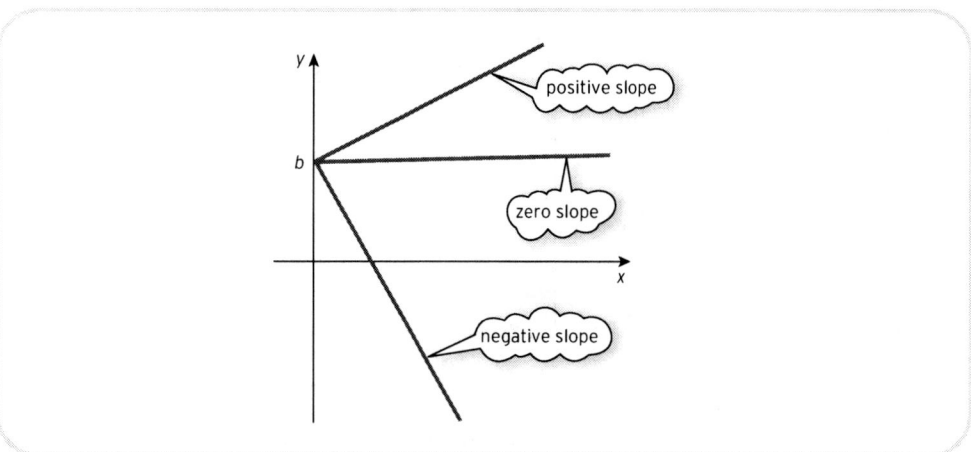

Figure 1.7

Example

Use the slope–intercept approach to sketch the line

$$2x + 3y = 12$$

Solution

We can remove the x term on the left-hand side of

$$2x + 3y = 12$$

by subtracting $2x$. As usual, to balance the equation we must also subtract $2x$ from the right-hand side to get

$$3y = 12 - 2x$$

We now just divide through by 3 to get

$$y = 4 - \tfrac{2}{3}x$$

This is now in the required form with $a = -2/3$ and $b = 4$. The line is sketched in Figure 1.8. A slope of $-2/3$ means that, for every 1 unit along, we go $2/3$ units down (or, equivalently, for every 3 units along, we go 2 units down). An intercept of 4 means that it passes through $(0, 4)$.

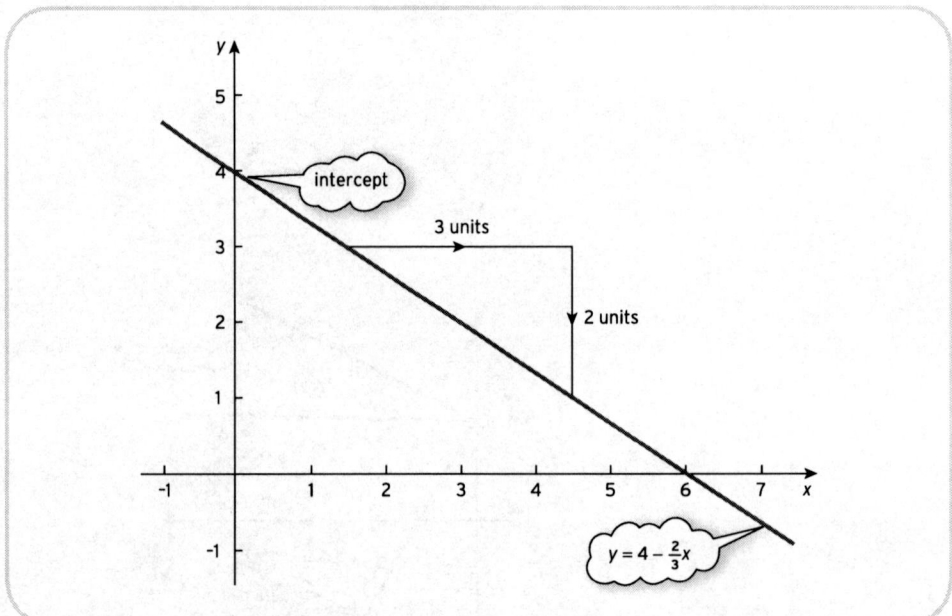

Figure 1.8

Practice Problem

6. Use the slope–intercept approach to sketch the lines

   (a) $y = x + 2$

   (b) $4x + 2y = 1$

Example   EXCEL

(a) Use Excel to draw the graphs of

$$y = 3x + 2$$
$$y = -2x + 2$$
$$y = \tfrac{1}{2}x + 2$$

on the same set of axes, taking values of x between -3 and 3.

(b) On another set of axes, use Excel to draw the graphs of

$$y = 2x$$
$$y = 2x - 3$$
$$y = 2x + 1$$

for $-3 \le x \le 3$.

(c) What do you notice about the two sets of graphs?

Solution

(a) To draw graphs with Excel, we first have to set up a table of values. By giving a title to each column, we will be able to label the graphs at a later stage, so we type the headings x, $y = 3x + 2$, $y = -2x + 2$ and $y = x/2 + 2$ in cells A1, B1, C1 and D1 respectively.

The x values are now typed into the first column, as shown in the diagram below. In the next three columns, we generate the corresponding values for y by entering formulae for each of the three lines.

The formula for the first graph goes in cell B2. As the x value is in cell A2, we type

`=3*A2+2`

	A	B	C	D
1	x	y = 3x + 2	y = -2x + 2	y = x/2 + 2
2		-3	=3*A2+2	
3		-2		
4		-1		
5		0		
6		1		
7		2		
8		3		
9				
10				

By clicking and dragging this formula down the second column (up to, and including, cell B8), the values of y are calculated.

Similarly, the formula for calculating the y coordinates for the second line is entered into cell C2 as

`=-2*A2+2`

and the formula for the third line is entered into cell D2 as

`=A2/2+2`

To plot these points on a graph, we highlight all the cells in the table, including the column titles, and click on the Chart Wizard button on the toolbar. The Chart Wizard box will appear:

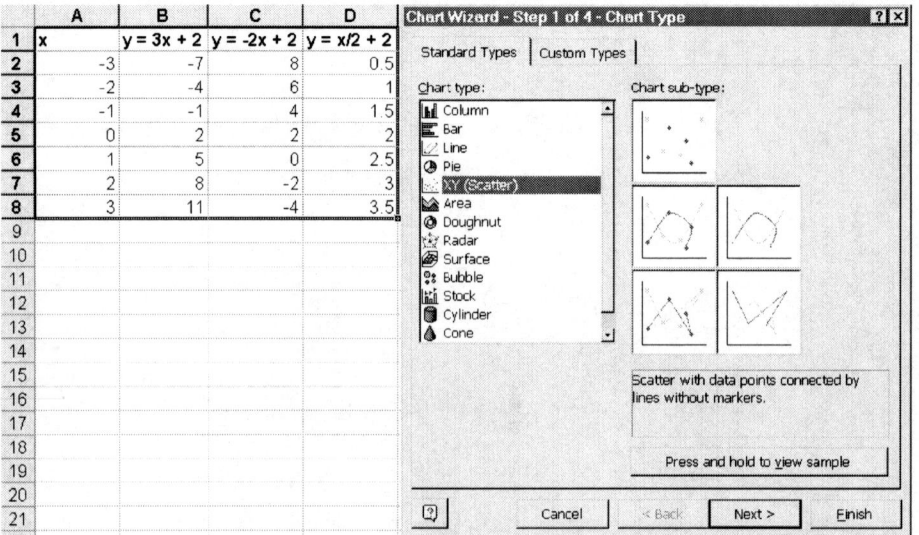

From the list of chart types, we choose **XY (Scatter)**, and then choose an appropriate sub-type. As we are plotting straight lines, we have selected **Scatter with data points connected by lines without markers**.

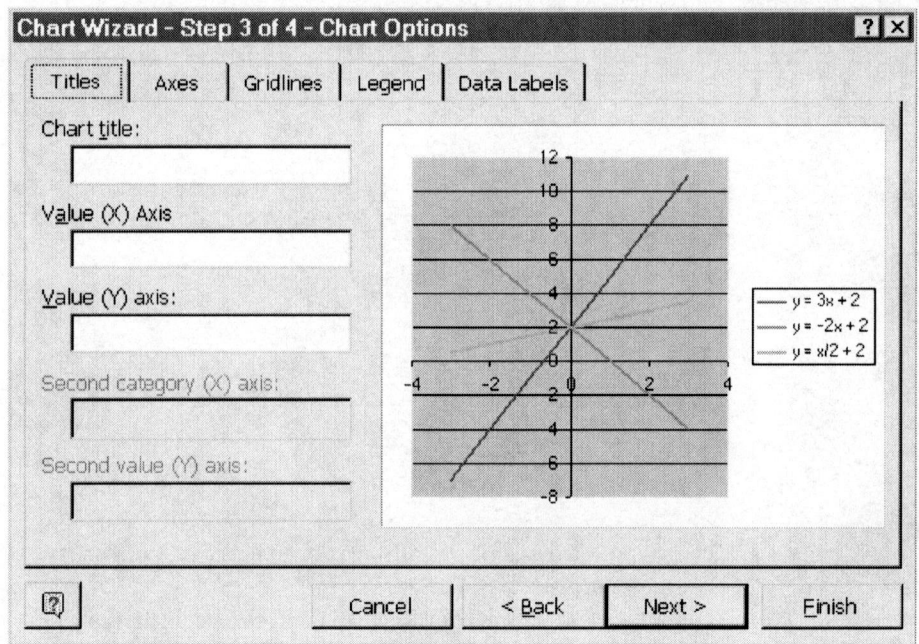

Click Next to see a preview of the graph, with the option to change the range of the cells that have been plotted. If the graph looks wrong, it is usually because the wrong cells have been highlighted before going into Chart Wizard, so go back and check this, rather than altering the range.

The third screen allows you to label your graph, and alter its gridlines. You should always label your axes, but you could, for example, delete the Legend if you feel it is inappropriate. Adding gridlines can make it easier to read values off the graph.

Finally, we click Next and Finish, to transfer the graph on to the spreadsheet, as shown in Figure 1.9. Notice that Excel provides a key showing which line is which.

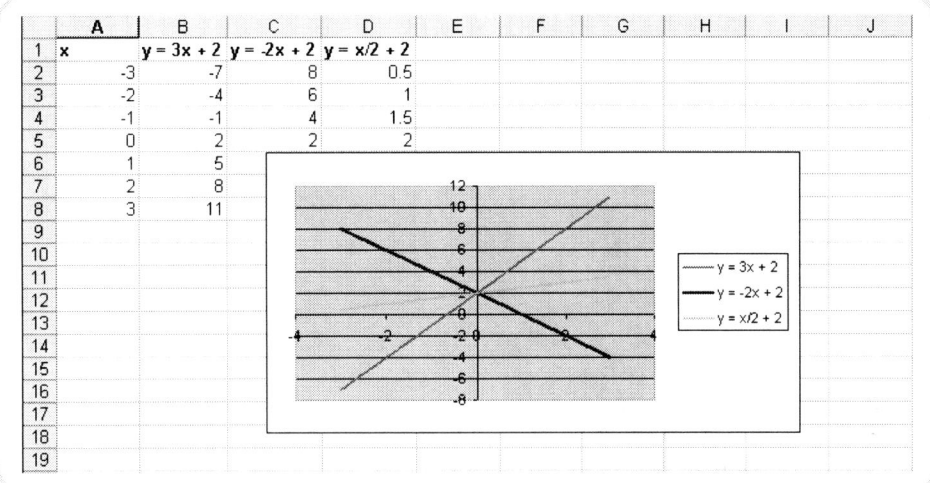

Figure 1.9

(b) Following the same procedure for the three lines

$$y = 2x$$

$$y = 2x - 3$$

$$y = 2x + 1$$

produces a graph as shown in Figure 1.10.

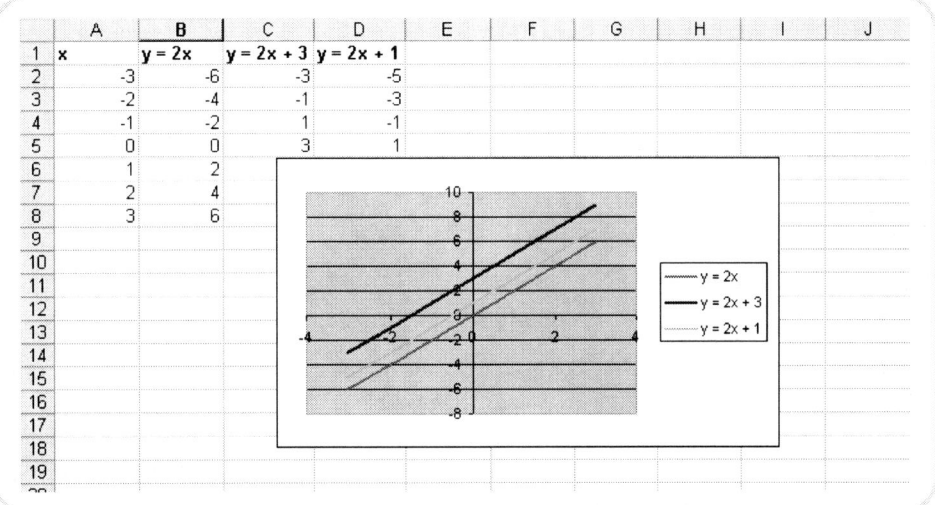

Figure 1.10

(c) Notice that in part (a), all of the graphs cut the y axis at the point (0, 2). In part (b), the graphs are parallel, which means that they have the same gradient.

This illustrates the fact that every straight line has an equation of the form

$$y = ax + b$$

where a is the gradient, and b is the intercept on the y axis.

In (a), the value of b in each equation is equal to 2, so all of the lines cut the y axis at this point.

In (b), the value of a in each equation is equal to 2, so all of the lines have the same gradient and are parallel.

It is very useful to be able to recognize these properties from the equations, as it means we have a fairly good idea of what our graph should look like even before we draw it.

Key Terms

Coefficient   A numerical multiplier of the variables in an algebraic term, such as the numbers 4 and 7 in the expression $4x + 7yz^2$.

Coordinates   A set of numbers that determine the position of a point relative to a set of axes.

Intercept   The point(s) where a graph crosses one of the coordinate axes.

Linear equation   An equation of the form $y = ax + b$.

Origin   The point where the coordinate axes intersect.

Simultaneous linear equations   A set of linear equations in which there are (usually) the same number of equations and unknowns. The solution consists of values of the unknowns which satisfy all of the equations at the same time.

Slope of a line   Also known as the gradient, it is the change in the value of y when x increases by 1 unit.

x axis   The horizontal coordinate axis pointing from left to right.

y axis   The vertical coordinate axis pointing upwards.

Exercise 1.3

1. On graph paper draw axes with values of x and y between −3 and 10, and plot the following points:

   P (4, 0), Q (−2, 9), R (5, 8), S (−1, −2)

   Hence find the coordinates of the point of intersection of the line passing through P and Q, and the line passing through R and S.

2. By substituting values into the equation, decide which of the following points lie on the line, $x + 4y = 12$:

   A(12, 0), B(2, 2), C(4, 2), D(−8, 5), E(0, 3)

3. For the line $3x - 5y = 8$,

(a) Find the value of x when $y = 2$.

(b) Find the value of y when $x = 1$.

Hence write down the coordinates of two points which lie on this line.

4. If $4x + 3y = 24$, complete the following table and hence sketch this line.

x	y
0	
	0
3	

5. Solve the following pairs of simultaneous linear equations graphically:

(a) $-2x + y = 2$
$2x + y = -6$

(b) $3x + 4y = 12$
$x + 4y = 8$

(c) $2x + y = 4$
$4x - 3y = 3$

(d) $x + y = 1$
$6x + 5y = 15$

6. State the value of the slope and y-intercept for each of the following lines:

(a) $y = 5x + 9$

(b) $y = 3x - 1$

(c) $y = 13 - x$

(d) $-x + y = 4$

(e) $4x + 2y = 5$

(f) $5x - y = 6$

7. Use the slope–intercept approach to produce a rough sketch of the following lines:

(a) $y = -x$

(b) $x - 2y = 6$

Exercise 1.3*

1. Which of the following points lie on the line $3x - 5y = 25$?

(5, −2), (10, 1), (−5, 0), (5, 10), (−5, 10), (0, −5)

2. Solve the following pairs of simultaneous equations graphically:

(a) $y = 3x - 1$
$y = 2x + 1$

(b) $2x + y = 6$
$x - y = -3$

(c) $2x + 3y = 5$
$5x - 2y = -16$

(d) $3x + 4y = -12$
$-2x + 3y = 25$

3. State the value of the slope and y intercept for each of the following lines:

(a) $y = 7x - 34$

(b) $y = 1 - x$

(c) $3x - 2y = 6$

(d) $-4x + 2y = 5$

(e) $x - 5y = 0$

(f) $y = 2$

(g) $x = 4$

4. Identify the two lines in the following list which are parallel:

   (a) $3x + 5y = 2$ **(b)** $5x - 3y = 1$ **(c)** $5x + 3y = 13$
   (d) $10x - 6y = 9$ **(e)** $y = 0.6x + 2$

5. **(a)** The Wonderful Mobile Phone Company charges $70 per month, and calls cost $0.50 per minute. If I use my phone for x minutes in a month, write down an expression for the total cost in terms of x.

   (b) Repeat part (a) for the Fantastic Mobile Phone Company, which charges $20 per month and $1 per minute.

   (c) Plot both graphs on the same axes and hence find the call time per month which gives the same total cost for these two companies.

6. **(1)** Show that the lines $ax + by = c$ and $dx + ey = f$ are parallel whenever $ae - bd = 0$.

   (2) Use the result of part (1) to comment on the solution of the following simultaneous equations:

   $$2x - 4y = 1$$
   $$-3x + 6y = 7$$

7. Write down the coordinates of the points where the line $ax + by = c$ intercepts the axes.

SECTION 1.4
Algebraic solution of simultaneous linear equations

Objectives

At the end of this section you should be able to:

* Solve a system of two simultaneous linear equations in two unknowns using elimination.
* Detect when a system of equations does not have a solution.
* Detect when a system of equations has infinitely many solutions.
* Solve a system of three simultaneous linear equations in three unknowns using elimination.

In Section 1.3 a graphical method was described for the solution of simultaneous linear equations. Both lines are sketched on the same piece of graph paper and the coordinates of the point of intersection are then simply read off from the diagram. Unfortunately this approach has several drawbacks. It is not always easy to decide on a suitable scale for the axes. Even if the scale allows all four points (two from each line) to fit on the diagram, there is no guarantee that the point of intersection itself also lies on it. When this happens you have no alternative but to throw away your graph paper and to start again, choosing a smaller scale in the hope that the solution will now fit. The second drawback concerns the accuracy of the graphical solution. All of the problems in Section 1.3 were deliberately chosen so that the answers had nice numbers in them; whole numbers such as -1, 2 and 5 or at worst simple fractions such as $\frac{1}{2}$, $2\frac{1}{2}$ and $-\frac{1}{4}$. In practice, the coefficients of the equations may well involve decimals and we might expect a decimal solution. Indeed, even if the coefficients are whole numbers the solution itself could involve nasty fractions such as 7/8 or perhaps something like 231/571. A moment's thought should convince you that in these circumstances it is virtually impossible to obtain the solution graphically, even if we use a really large scale and our sharpest HB pencil in the process. The final drawback concerns the nature of the problem itself. Quite frequently in economics we need to solve three equations in three unknowns or maybe four equations in four unknowns. Unfortunately, the graphical method of solution does not extend to these cases.

In this section an alternative method of solution is described which relies on algebra. It is called the **elimination method**, since each stage of the process eliminates one (or more) of the unknowns. This method always produces the exact solution and can be applied to systems of equations larger than just two equations in two unknowns. In order to illustrate the method, we return to the simple example considered in the previous section:

$$4x + 3y = 11 \tag{1}$$

$$2x + \ y = 5 \tag{2}$$

The coefficient of x in equation (1) is 4 and the coefficient of x in equation (2) is 2. If these numbers had turned out to be exactly the same then we could have eliminated the variable x by subtracting one equation from the other. However, we can arrange for this to be the case by multiplying the left-hand side of the second equation by 2. Of course, we must also remember to multiply the right-hand side of the second equation by 2 in order for this operation to be valid. The second equation then becomes

$$4x + 2y = 10 \qquad\qquad (3)$$

We may now subtract equation (3) from (1) to get

$$y = 1$$

You may like to think of this in terms of the usual layout for the subtraction of two ordinary numbers: that is,

$$
\begin{aligned}
4x + 3y &= 11 \\
4x + 2y &= 10 - \\
\hline
y &= 1
\end{aligned}
$$

the x's cancel when you subtract

This number can now be substituted into one of the original equations to deduce x. From equation (1)

$$
\begin{aligned}
4x + 3(1) &= 11 \quad \text{(substitute } y = 1) \\
4x + 3 &= 1 \\
4x &= 8 \quad \text{(subtract 3 from both sides)} \\
x &= 2 \quad \text{(divide both sides by 4)}
\end{aligned}
$$

Hence the solution is $x = 2$, $y = 1$. As a check, substitution of these values into the other original equation (2) gives

$$2(2) + 1 = 5 \quad \checkmark$$

The method of elimination can be summarized as follows.

Step 1

Add/subtract a multiple of one equation to/from a multiple of the other to eliminate x.

Step 2

Solve the resulting equation for y.

Step 3

Substitute the value of y into one of the original equations to deduce x.

Step 4

Check that no mistakes have been made by substituting both x and y into the other original equation.

Example

Solve the system of equations

$$3x + 2y = 1 \qquad (1)$$
$$-2x + \ y = 2 \qquad (2)$$

Solution

Step 1

The coefficients of x in equations (1) and (2) are 3 and -2 respectively. We can arrange for these to be the same size (but of opposite sign) by multiplying equation (1) by 2 and multiplying (2) by 3. The new equations will then have x coefficients of 6 and -6, so we can eliminate x this time by adding the equations together. The details are as follows.

Doubling the first equation produces

$$6x + 4y = 2 \qquad (3)$$

Tripling the second equation produces

$$-6x + 3y = 6 \qquad (4)$$

If equation (4) is added to equation (3) then

$$
\begin{array}{r}
6x + 4y = 2 \\
-6x + 3y = 6 \ + \\
\hline
7y = 8
\end{array}
\qquad (5)
$$

> the x's cancel when you add

Step 2

Equation (5) can be solved by dividing both sides by 7 to get

$$y = 8/7$$

Step 3

If 8/7 is substituted for y in equation (1) then

$$3x + 2\left(\frac{8}{7}\right) = 1$$

$$3x + \frac{16}{7} = 1$$

$$3x = 1 - \frac{16}{7} \qquad \text{(subtract 16/7 from both sides)}$$

$$3x = \frac{7 - 16}{7} \qquad \text{(put over a common denominator)}$$

$$3x = -\frac{9}{7}$$

$$x = \frac{1}{3} \times \left(-\frac{9}{7}\right) \qquad \text{(divide both sides by 3)}$$

$$x = -\frac{3}{7}$$

The solution is therefore $x = -3/7$, $y = 8/7$.

Step 4

As a check, equation (2) gives

$$-2\left(-\frac{3}{7}\right) + \frac{8}{7} = \frac{6}{7} + \frac{8}{7} = \frac{6 + 8}{7} = \frac{14}{7} = 2 \quad ✓$$

Advice

In the general description of the method, we suggested that the variable x is eliminated in step 1. There is nothing special about x. We could equally well eliminate y at this stage and then solve the resulting equation in step 2 for x.

You might like to solve the above example using this alternative strategy. You need to double equation (2) and then subtract from (1).

Practice Problem

1. **(a)** Solve the equations

$$3x - 2y = 4$$
$$x - 2y = 2$$

by eliminating one of the variables.

(b) Solve the equations

$$3x + 5y = 19$$
$$-5x + 2y = -11$$

by eliminating one of the variables.

The following examples provide further practice in using the method and illustrate some special cases which may occur.

Example

Solve the system of equations

$$x - 2y = 1$$
$$2x - 4y = -3$$

Solution

Step 1

The variable x can be eliminated by doubling the first equation and subtracting the second:

both the x's and the y's cancel!

$$
\begin{array}{r}
2x - 4y = 2 \\
2x - 4y = -3 \ - \\
\hline
0 = 5
\end{array}
$$

The statement '0 = 5' is clearly nonsense and something has gone seriously wrong. To understand what is going on here, let us try and solve this problem graphically.

The line $x - 2y = 1$ passes through the points $(0, -1/2)$ and $(1, 0)$ (check this). The line $2x - 4y = -3$ passes through the points $(0, 3/4)$ and $(-3/2, 0)$ (check this). Figure 1.11 shows that these lines are parallel and so they do not intersect. It is therefore not surprising that we were unable to find a solution using algebra, because this system of equations does not have one. We could have deduced this before when subtracting the equations. The equation that only involves y in step 2 can be written as

$$0y = 5$$

and the problem is to find a value of y for which this equation is true. No such value exists, since

$$\boxed{\text{zero}} \times \boxed{\text{any number}} = \boxed{\text{zero}}$$

and so the original system of equations does not have a solution.

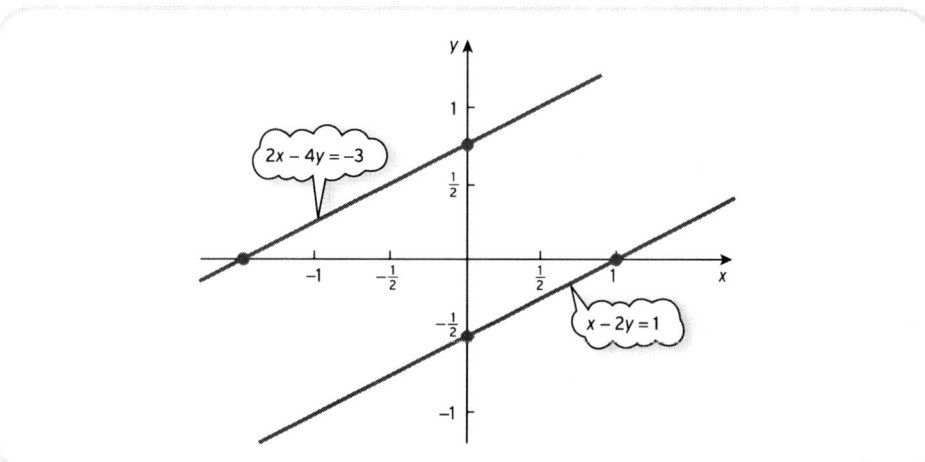

Figure 1.11

Example

Solve the equations

$$2x - 4y = 1$$
$$5x - 10y = 5/2$$

Solution

Step 1
The variable x can be eliminated by multiplying the first equation by 5, multiplying the second equation by 2 and subtracting

$$10x - 20y = 5$$
$$\underline{10x - 20y = 5 -}$$
$$0 = 0$$

everything cancels including the right-hand side!

Again, it is easy to explain this using graphs. The line $2x - 4y = 1$ passes through $(0, -1/4)$ and $(1/2, 0)$. The line $5x - 10y = 5/2$ passes through $(0, -1/4)$ and $(1/2, 0)$. Consequently, both equations represent the same line. From Figure 1.12 the lines intersect along the whole of their length and any point on this line is a solution. This particular system of equations has infinitely many solutions. This can also be deduced algebraically. The equation involving y in step 2 is

$$0y = 0$$

which is true for any value of y.

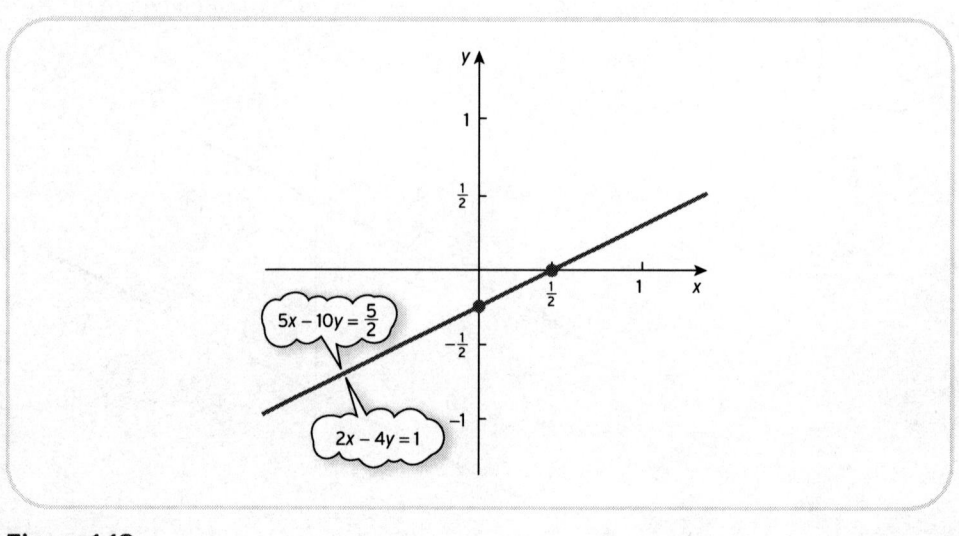

Figure 1.12

These examples show that a system of equations can possess a unique solution, no solution or infinitely many solutions. Algebraically, this can be detected in step 2. If the equation resulting from the elimination of x looks like

$$\boxed{\text{any non-zero number}} \times \boxed{y} = \boxed{\text{any number}}$$

then the equations have a unique solution, or if it looks like

$$\boxed{\text{zero}} \times \boxed{y} = \boxed{\text{any non-zero number}}$$

then the equations have no solution, or if it looks like

$$\boxed{\text{zero}} \times \boxed{y} = \boxed{\text{zero}}$$

then the equations have infinitely many solutions.

It is interesting to notice how the graphical approach 'saved the day' in the previous two examples. They show how useful pictures are as an aid to understanding in mathematics.

Practice Problem

2. Attempt to solve the following systems of equations:

(a) $3x - 6y = -2$ **(b)** $-5x + y = 4$

      $-4x + 8y = -1$ $10x - 2y = -8$

Comment on the nature of the solution in each case.

We now show how the algebraic method can be used to solve three equations in three unknowns. As you might expect, the details are more complicated than for just two equations, but the principle is the same. We begin with a simple example to illustrate the general method. Consider the system

$$x + 3y - z = 4 \tag{1}$$
$$2x + y + 2z = 10 \tag{2}$$
$$3x - y + z = 4 \tag{3}$$

The objective is to find three numbers x, y and z which satisfy these equations simultaneously. Our previous work suggests that we should begin by eliminating x from all but one of the equations.

The variable x can be eliminated from the second equation by multiplying equation (1) by 2 and subtracting equation (2):

$$\begin{array}{r} 2x + 6y - 2z = 8 \\ 2x + y + 2z = 10\ - \\ \hline 5y - 4z = -2 \end{array} \tag{4}$$

Similarly, we can eliminate x from the third equation by multiplying equation (1) by 3 and subtracting equation (3):

$$\begin{array}{r} 3x + 9y - 3z = 12 \\ 3x - y + z = 4\ - \\ \hline 10y - 4z = 8 \end{array} \tag{5}$$

At this stage the first equation is unaltered but the second and third equations of the system have changed to equations (4) and (5) respectively, so the current equations are

$$x + 3y - z = 4 \tag{1}$$
$$5y - 4z = -2 \tag{4}$$
$$10y - 4z = 8 \tag{5}$$

Notice that the last two equations constitute a system of just two equations in two unknowns, y and z. This, of course, is precisely the type of problem that we already know how to solve. Once y and z have been calculated, the values can be substituted into equation (1) to deduce x.

We can eliminate y in the last equation by multiplying equation (4) by 2 and subtracting equation (5):

$$\begin{array}{r} 10y - 8z = -4 \\ 10y - 4z = 8\ - \\ \hline -4z = -12 \end{array} \tag{6}$$

Collecting together the current equations gives

$$x + 3y - z = 4 \tag{1}$$
$$5y - 4z = -2 \tag{4}$$
$$-4z = -12 \tag{6}$$

From the last equation,

$$z = \frac{-12}{-4} = 3 \quad \text{(divide both sides by } -4\text{)}$$

If this is substituted into equation (4) then

$$5y - 4(3) = -2$$
$$5y - 12 = -2$$
$$5y = 10 \quad \text{(add 12 to both sides)}$$
$$y = 2 \quad \text{(divide both sides by 5)}$$

Finally, substituting $y = 2$ and $z = 3$ into equation (1) produces

$$x + 3(2) - 3 = 4$$
$$x + 3 = 4$$
$$x = 1 \quad \text{(subtract 3 from sides)}$$

Hence the solution is $x = 1$, $y = 2$, $z = 3$.

As usual, it is possible to check the answer by putting these numbers back into the original equations (1), (2) and (3):

$$1 + 3(2) - 3 = 4 \quad \checkmark$$
$$2(1) + 2 + 2(3) = 10 \quad \checkmark$$
$$3(1) - 2 + 3 = 4 \quad \checkmark$$

The general strategy may be summarized as follows. Consider the system

$$?x + ?y + ?z = ?$$
$$?x + ?y + ?z = ?$$
$$?x + ?y + ?z = ?$$

where ? denotes some numerical coefficient.

Step 1

Add/subtract multiples of the first equation to/from multiples of the second and third equations to eliminate x. This produces a new system of the form

$$?x + ?y + ?z = ?$$
$$?y + ?z = ?$$
$$?y + ?z = ?$$

Step 2

Add/subtract a multiple of the second equation to/from a multiple of the third to eliminate y. This produces a new system of the form

$$?x + ?y + ?z = ?$$
$$?y + ?z = ?$$
$$?z = ?$$

Step 3

Solve the last equation for z. Substitute the value of z into the second equation to deduce y. Finally, substitute the values of both y and z into the first equation to deduce x.

Step 4

Check that no mistakes have been made by substituting the values of x, y and z into the original equations.

It is possible to adopt different strategies from that suggested above. For example, it may be more convenient to eliminate z from the last equation in step 2 rather than y. However, it is important to notice that we use the second equation to do this, not the first. Any attempt to use the first equation in step 2 would reintroduce the variable x into the equations, which is the last thing we want to do at this stage.

Example

Solve the equations

$$4x + y + 3z = 8 \qquad (1)$$
$$-2x + 5y + z = 4 \qquad (2)$$
$$3x + 2y + 4z = 9 \qquad (3)$$

Solution

Step 1

To eliminate x from the second equation we multiply it by 2 and add to equation (1):

$$
\begin{aligned}
4x + y + 3z &= 8 \\
-4x + 10y + 2z &= 8\ + \\
\hline
11y + 5z &= 16
\end{aligned}
\qquad (4)
$$

To eliminate x from the third equation we multiply equation (1) by 3, multiply equation (3) by 4 and subtract:

$$
\begin{aligned}
12x + 3y + 9z &= 24 \\
12x + 8y + 16z &= 36\ - \\
\hline
-5y - 7z &= -12
\end{aligned}
\qquad (5)
$$

This produces a new system:

$$4x + y + 3z = 8 \qquad (1)$$
$$11y + 5z = 16 \qquad (4)$$
$$-5y - 7z = -12 \qquad (5)$$

Step 2

To eliminate y from the new third equation (that is, equation (5)) we multiply equation (4) by 5, multiply equation (5) by 11 and add:

$$
\begin{aligned}
55y + 25z &= 80 \\
-55y - 77z &= -132\ + \\
\hline
-52z &= -52
\end{aligned}
\qquad (6)
$$

This produces a new system

$$4x + y + 3z = 8 \qquad (1)$$
$$11y + 5z = 16 \qquad (4)$$
$$-52z = -52 \qquad (6)$$

Step 3
The last equation gives

$$z = \frac{-52}{-52} = 1 \quad \text{(divide both sides by } -52)$$

If this is substituted into equation (4) then

$$11y + 5(1) = 16$$
$$11y + 5 = 16$$
$$11y = 11 \quad \text{(subtract 5 from both sides)}$$
$$y = 1 \quad \text{(divide both sides by 11)}$$

Finally, substituting $y = 1$ and $z = 1$ into equation (1) produces

$$4x + 1 + 3(1) = 8$$
$$4x + 4 = 8$$
$$4x = 4 \quad \text{(subtract 5 from both sides)}$$
$$x = 1 \quad \text{(divide both sides by 4)}$$

Hence the solution is $x = 1$, $y = 1$, $z = 1$.

Step 4
As a check the original equations (1), (2) and (3) give

$$4(1) + 1 + 3(1) = 8 \quad \checkmark$$
$$-2(1) + 5(1) + 1 = 4 \quad \checkmark$$
$$3(1) + 2(1) + 4(1) = 9 \quad \checkmark$$

respectively.

Practice Problem

3. Solve the following system of equations:

$$2x + 2y - 5z = -5 \qquad (1)$$
$$x - y + z = 3 \qquad (2)$$
$$-3x + y + 2z = -2 \qquad (3)$$

As you might expect, it is possible for three simultaneous linear equations to have either no solution or infinitely many solutions. An illustration of this is given in Question 4 of Exercise 1.4*. The method described in this section has an obvious extension to larger systems of equations. However, the calculations are extremely tedious to perform by hand. Fortunately there are many computer packages available which are capable of solving large systems accurately and efficiently (a matter of a few seconds to solve 10 000 equations in 10 000 unknowns).

Key Terms

Elimination method   The method in which variables are removed from a system of simultaneous equations by adding (or subtracting) a multiple of one equation to (or from) a multiple of another.

Exercise 1.4

1. Use the elimination method to solve the following pairs of simultaneous linear equations:

   (a) $-2x + y = 2$ **(b)** $3x + 4y = 12$ **(c)** $2x + y = 4$ **(d)** $x + y = 1$
   $\ 2x + y = -6$ $\ x + 4y = 8$ $\ 4x - 3y = 3$ $\ 6x + 5y = 15$

2. Sketch the following lines on the same diagram:

   $$2x - 3y = 6, \quad 4x - 6y = 18, \quad x - \frac{3}{2}y = 3$$

   Hence comment on the nature of the solutions of the following systems of equations:

   (a) $2x - 3y = 6$ **(b)** $4x - 6y = 18$
   $\ x - \dfrac{3}{2}y = 3$ $\ x - \dfrac{3}{2}y = 3$

3. Use the elimination method to attempt to solve the following systems of equations. Comment on the nature of the solution in each case.

   (a) $-3x + 5y = 4$ **(b)** $6x - 2y = 3$
   $\ 9x - 15y = -12$ $\ 15x - 5y = 4$

4. If the following system of linear equations has infinitely many solutions, find the value of k.

   $$6x - 4y = 2$$
   $$-3x + 2y = k$$

Exercise 1.4*

1. Solve the following pairs of simultaneous equations:

   (a) $y = 3x - 1$ **(b)** $2x + y = 6$ **(c)** $2x + 3y = 5$ **(d)** $3x + 4y = -12$

      $y = 2x + 1$ $x - y = -3$ $5x - 2y = -16$ $-2x + 3y = 25$

2. Write down a possible set of values of the numbers a and b for which the simultaneous equations:

   (a) $2x + 3y = 4$ have infinitely many solutions

      $ax + 6y = b$

   (b) $4x - 6y = 1$ have no solutions

      $2x + ay = b$

3. Solve the following systems of equations:

   (a) $x - 3y + 4z = 5$ (1)   **(b)** $3x + 2y - 2z = -5$ (1)

      $2x + y + z = 3$ (2) $4x + 3y + 3z = 17$ (2)

      $4x + 3y + 5z = 1$ (3) $2x - y + z = -1$ (3)

4. Attempt to solve the following systems of equations. Comment on the nature of the solution in each case.

   (a) $x - 2y + z = -2$ (1)   **(b)** $2x + 3y - z = 13$ (1)

      $x + y - 2z = 4$ (2) $x - 2y + 2z = -3$ (2)

      $-2x + y + z = 12$ (3) $3x + y + z = 10$ (3)

5. If the following system of equations has infinitely many solutions, find the value of the constant, k.

   $x + 2y - 5z = 1$

   $2x - y + 3z = 4$

   $4x + 3y - 7z = k$

   What can you say about the nature of the solution for other values of k?

SECTION 1.5
Supply and demand analysis

Objectives

At the end of this section you should be able to:

- Use the function notation, $y = f(x)$.
- Identify the endogenous and exogenous variables in an economic model.
- Identify and sketch a linear demand function.
- Identify and sketch a linear supply function.
- Determine the equilibrium price and quantity for a single-commodity market both graphically and algebraically.
- Determine the equilibrium price and quantity for a multicommodity market by solving simultaneous linear equations.

Microeconomics is concerned with the analysis of the economic theory and policy of individual firms and markets. In this section we focus on one particular aspect known as market equilibrium, in which the supply and demand balance. We describe how the mathematics introduced in the previous two sections can be used to calculate the equilibrium price and quantity. However, before we do this it is useful to explain the concept of a function. This idea is central to nearly all applications of mathematics in economics.

A **function**, f, is a rule which assigns to each incoming number, x, a uniquely defined outgoing number, y. A function may be thought of as a 'black box' that performs a dedicated arithmetic calculation. As an example, consider the rule 'double and add 3'. The effect of this rule on two specific incoming numbers, 5 and -17, is illustrated in Figure 1.13.

Unfortunately, such a representation is rather cumbersome. There are, however, two alternative ways of expressing this rule which are more concise. We can write either

$$y = 2x + 3 \quad \text{or} \quad f(x) = 2x + 3$$

The first of these is familiar to you from our previous work; corresponding to any incoming number, x, the right-hand side tells you what to do with x to generate the outgoing number, y.

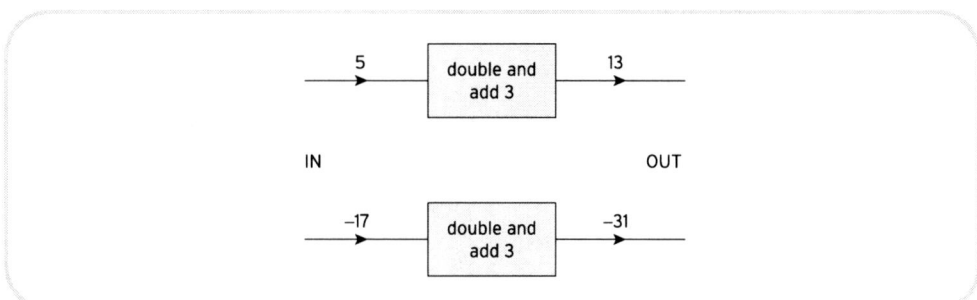

Figure 1.13

The second notation is also useful. It has the advantage that it involves the label f, which is used to name the rule. If, in a piece of economic theory, there are two or more functions, we can use different labels to refer to each one. For example, a second function might be

$$g(x) = -3x + 10$$

and we subsequently identify the respective functions simply by referring to them by name: that is, as either f or g.

The new notation also enables the information conveyed in Figure 1.13 to be written

$f(5) = 13$ read 'f of 5 equals 13'

$f(-17) = -31$ read 'f of -17 equals -31'

The number inside the brackets is the incoming value, x, and the right-hand side is the corresponding outgoing value, y.

Example

(a) If $f(x) = 2x^2 - 3x$ find the value of $f(5)$.

(b) If $g(Q) = \dfrac{3}{5 + 2Q}$ find the value of $g(2)$.

Solution

(a) Substituting $x = 5$ into $2x^2 - 3x$ gives

$$f(5) = 2 \times 5^2 - 3 \times 5$$
$$= 2 \times 25 - 3 \times 5 \quad \text{BIDMAS}$$
$$= 50 - 15 = 35$$

(b) Although the letter Q is used instead of x, the procedure is the same:

$$g(2) = \frac{3}{5 + 2 \times 2} = \frac{3}{9} = \frac{1}{3}$$

Practice Problem ❓

1. Evaluate

   (a) $f(25)$ **(b)** $f(1)$ **(c)** $f(17)$ **(d)** $g(0)$ **(e)** $g(48)$ **(f)** $g(16)$

   for the two functions

   $$f(x) = -2x + 50$$
   $$g(x) = -\tfrac{1}{2}x + 25$$

   Do you notice any connection between f and g?

The incoming and outgoing variables are referred to as the **independent** and **dependent** variables respectively. The value of y clearly 'depends' on the actual value of x that is fed into the function. For example, in microeconomics the quantity demanded, Q, of a good depends on the market price, P. We might express this as

$Q = f(P)$

Such a function is called a **demand** function. Given any particular formula for $f(P)$ it is then a simple matter to produce a picture of the corresponding demand curve on graph paper. There is, however, a difference of opinion between mathematicians and economists on how this should be done. If your quantitative methods lecturer is a mathematician then he or she is likely to plot Q on the vertical axis and P on the horizontal axis. Economists, on the other hand, normally plot them the other way round with Q on the horizontal axis. In doing so, we are merely noting that since Q is related to P then, conversely, P must be related to Q, and so there is a function of the form

$P = g(Q)$

The two functions, f and g, are said to be **inverse** functions: that is, f is the inverse of g and, equivalently, g is the inverse of f. We adopt the economists' approach in this book. In subsequent chapters we shall investigate other microeconomic functions such as total revenue, average cost, and profit. It is conventional to plot each of these against Q (that is, with Q on the horizontal axis), so it makes sense to be consistent and to do the same here.

Written in the form $P = g(Q)$, the demand function tells us that P is a function of Q but it gives us no information about the precise relationship between these two variables. To find this we need to know the form of the function which can be obtained either from economic theory or from empirical evidence. For the moment we hypothesize that the function is linear so that

$P = aQ + b$

for some appropriate constants (called **parameters**), a and b. Of course, in reality, the relationship between price and quantity is likely to be much more complicated than this. However, the use of linear functions makes the mathematics nice and easy, and the result of any analysis at least provides a first approximation to the truth. The process of identifying the key features of the real world and making appropriate simplifications and assumptions is known as **modelling**. Models are based on economic laws and help to explain and predict the behaviour of real-world situations. Inevitably there is a conflict between mathematical ease and the model's accuracy. The closer the model comes to reality, the more complicated the mathematics is likely to be.

A graph of a typical linear demand function is shown in Figure 1.14 (overleaf). Elementary theory shows that demand usually falls as the price of a good rises and so the slope of the line is negative. Mathematically, P is then said to be a **decreasing** function of Q.

In symbols we write

$a < 0$  read 'a is less than zero'

It is also apparent from the graph that the intercept, b, is positive: that is,

$b > 0$  read 'b is greater than zero'

In fact, it is possible in theory for the demand curve to be horizontal with $a = 0$. This corresponds to perfect competition and we shall return to this special case in Chapter 4.

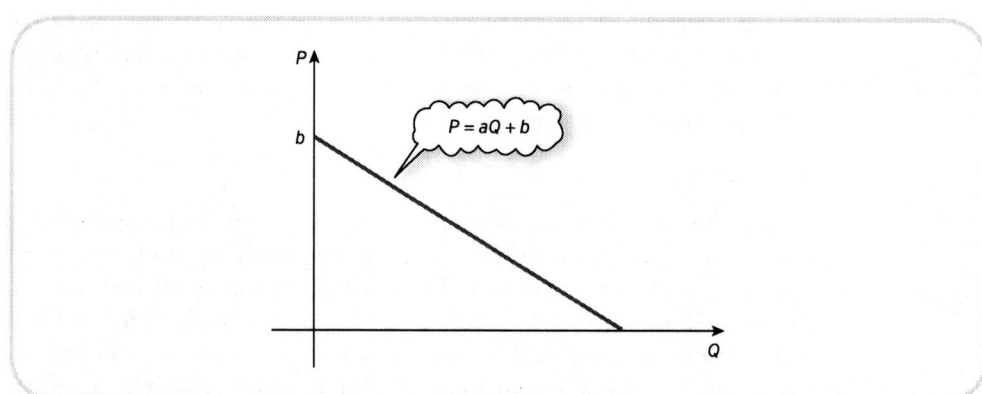

Figure 1.14

Example

Sketch a graph of the demand function

$$P = -2Q + 50$$

Hence, or otherwise, determine the value of

(a) P when $Q = 9$
(b) Q when $P = 10$

Solution

For the demand function

$$P = -2Q + 50$$

$a = -2$, $b = 50$, so the line has a slope of -2 and an intercept of 50. For every 1 unit along, the line goes down by 2 units, so it must cross the horizontal axis when $Q = 25$. (Alternatively, note that when $P = 0$ the equation reads $0 = -2Q + 50$, with solution $Q = 25$.) The graph is sketched in Figure 1.15.

(a) Given any quantity, Q, it is straightforward to use the graph to find the corresponding price, P. A line is drawn vertically upwards until it intersects the demand curve and the value of P is read off from the vertical axis. From Figure 1.15, when $Q = 9$ we see that $P = 32$. This can also be found by substituting $Q = 9$ directly into the demand function to get

$$P = -2(9) + 50 = 32$$

(b) Reversing this process enables us to calculate Q from a given value of P. A line is drawn horizontally until it intersects the demand curve and the value of Q is read off from the horizontal axis. Figure 1.15 indicates that $Q = 20$ when $P = 10$. Again this can be found by calculation. If $P = 10$ then the equation reads

$$10 = -2Q + 50$$
$$-40 = -2Q \quad \text{(subtract 50 from both sides)}$$
$$20 = Q \quad \text{(divide both sides by } -2)$$

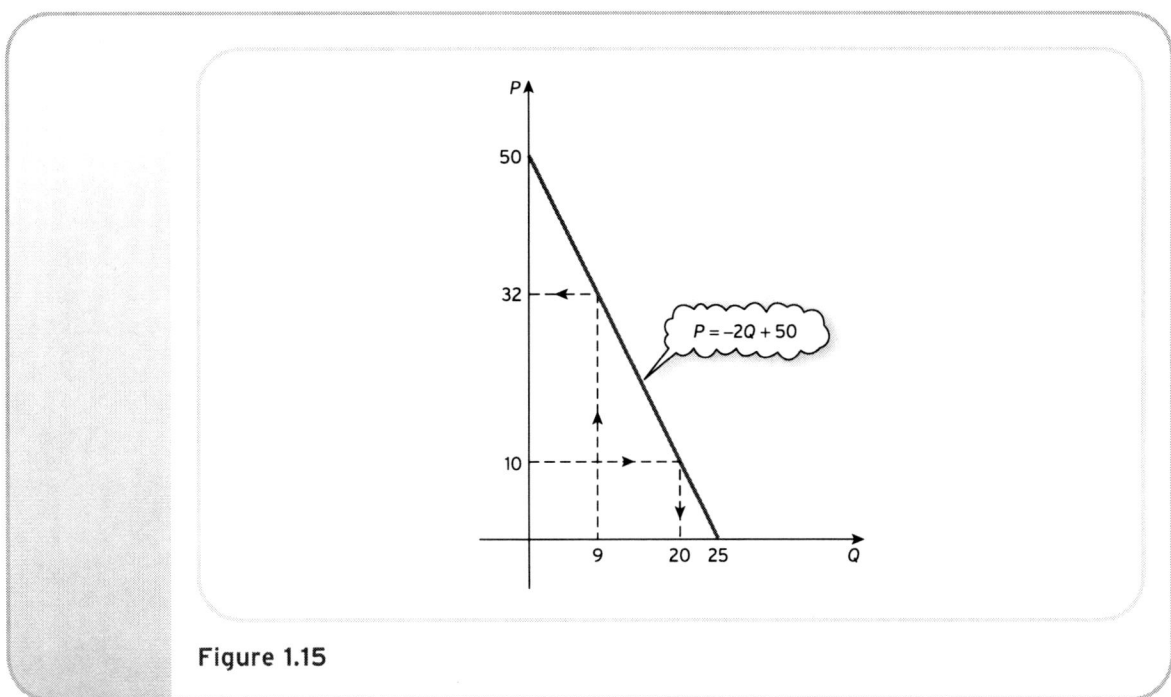

Figure 1.15

Practice Problem

2. Sketch a graph of the demand function

$$P = -3Q + 75$$

Hence, or otherwise, determine the value of

(a) P when $Q = 23$

(b) Q when $P = 18$

The model of consumer demand given so far is fairly crude in that it assumes that quantity depends solely on the price, P, of the good being considered. In practice, Q depends on other factors as well. These include the incomes of consumers, Y, the price of substitutable goods, P_S, the price of complementary goods, P_C, advertising expenditure, A, and consumers' tastes, T. A **substitutable** good is one that could be consumed instead of the good under consideration. For example, in the transport industry, buses and taxis could obviously be substituted for each other in urban areas. A **complementary** good is one that is used in conjunction with other goods. For example, music CDs and hi-fi systems are consumed together. Mathematically, we say that Q is a function of P, Y, P_S, P_C, A and T. This is written

$$Q = f(P, Y, P_S, P_C, A, T)$$

where the variables inside the brackets are separated by commas. In terms of a 'black box' diagram, this is represented with six incoming lines and one outgoing line as shown in Figure 1.16 (overleaf). In our previous discussion it was implicitly assumed that the variables Y, P_S, P_C, A and T are held fixed. We describe this situation by calling Q and P **endogenous** variables, since they are allowed to vary and are determined within the model. The remaining variables are called **exogenous**, since they are constant and are determined outside the model.

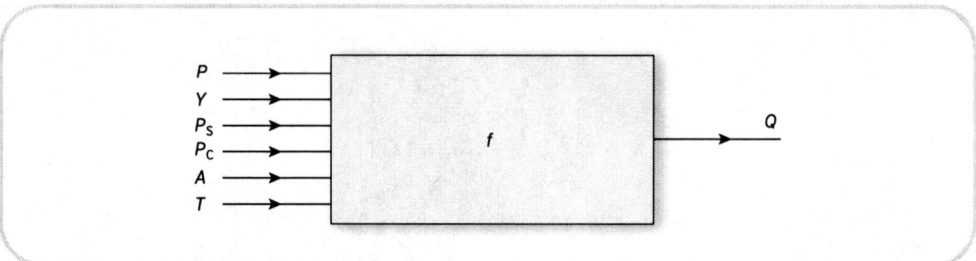

Figure 1.16

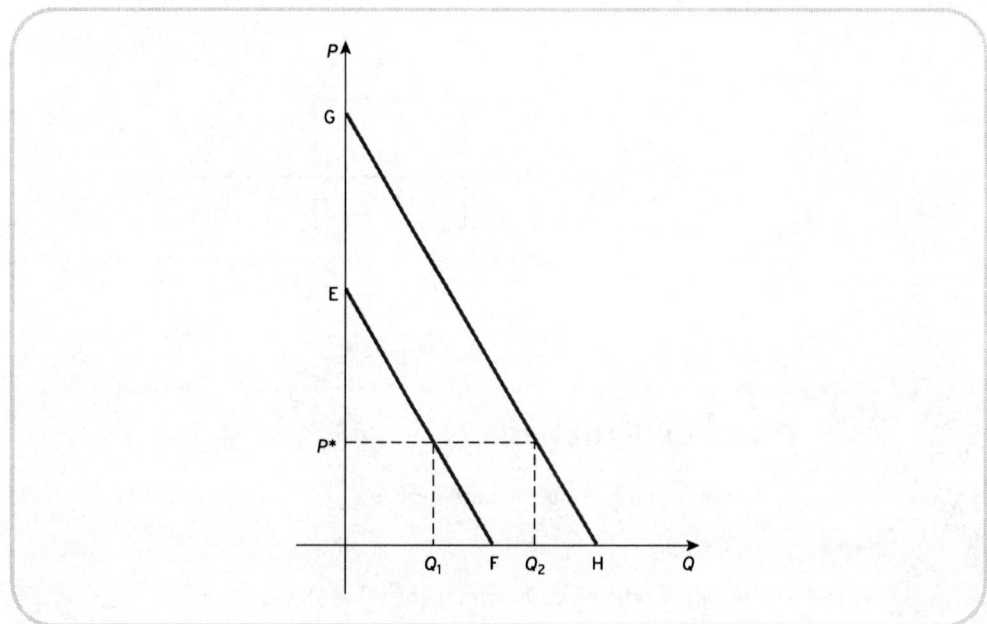

Figure 1.17

Let us return now to the standard demand curve shown in Figure 1.17 as the line EF. This is constructed on the assumption that Y, P_S, P_C, A and T are all constant. Notice that when the price is P^* the quantity demanded is Q_1. Now suppose that income, Y, increases. We would normally expect the demand to rise because the extra income buys more goods at price P^*. The effect is to shift the demand curve to the right because at price P^* consumers can afford the larger number of goods, Q_2. From Figure 1.17 we deduce that if the demand curve is

$$P = aQ + b$$

then a rise in income causes the intercept, b, to increase.

We conclude that if one of the exogenous variables changes then the whole demand curve moves, whereas if one of the endogenous variables changes, we simply move along the fixed curve.

Incidentally, it is possible that, for some goods, an increase in income actually causes the demand curve to shift to the left. In the 1960s and 1970s, most western economies saw a decline in the domestic consumption of coal as a result of an increase in income. In this case, higher wealth meant that more people were able to install central heating systems which use alternative forms of energy. Under these circumstances the good is referred to as an **inferior good**. On the other hand, a **superior good** is one whose demand rises as income rises. Cars and electrical goods are obvious examples of superior goods. Currently, concern about global warming is also reducing demand for coal. This factor can be incorporated as part of taste, although it is difficult to handle mathematically since it is virtually impossible to quantify taste and so to define T numerically.

The **supply** function is the relation between the quantity, Q, of a good that producers plan to bring to the market and the price, P, of the good. A typical linear supply curve is indicated in Figure 1.18. Economic theory indicates that, as the price rises, so does the supply. Mathematically, P is then said to be an **increasing** function of Q. A price increase encourages existing producers to raise output and entices new firms to enter the market. The line shown in Figure 1.18 has equation

$$P = aQ + b$$

with slope $a > 0$ and intercept $b > 0$. Note that when the market price is equal to b the supply is zero. It is only when the price exceeds this threshold level that producers decide that it is worth supplying any good whatsoever.

Again this is a simplification of what happens in the real world. The supply function does not have to be linear and the quantity supplied, Q, is influenced by things other than price. These exogenous variables include the prices of factors of production (that is, land, capital, labour and enterprise), the profits obtainable on alternative goods, and technology.

In microeconomics we are concerned with the interaction of supply and demand. Figure 1.19 shows typical supply and demand curves sketched on the same diagram. Of particular significance is the point of intersection. At this point the market is in **equilibrium** because the quantity supplied exactly matches the quantity demanded. The corresponding price, P_0, and quantity, Q_0, are called the equilibrium price and quantity.

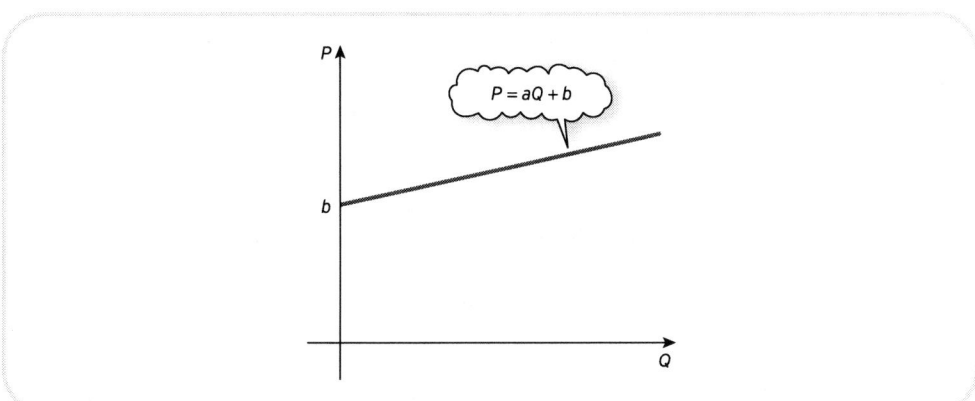

Figure 1.18

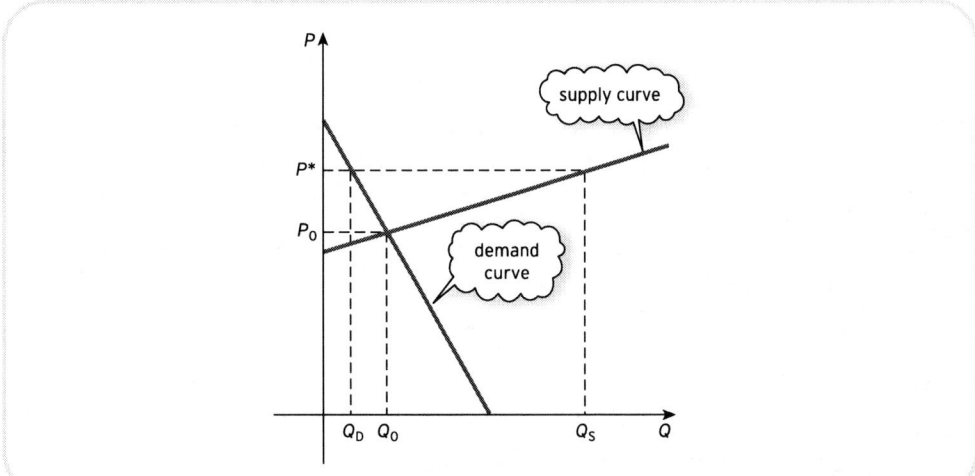

Figure 1.19

In practice, it is often the deviation of the market price away from the equilibrium price that is of most interest. Suppose that the market price, P^*, exceeds the equilibrium price, P_0. From Figure 1.19 the quantity supplied, Q_S, is greater than the quantity demanded, Q_D, so there is excess supply. There are stocks of unsold goods, which tend to depress prices and cause firms to cut back production. The effect is for 'market forces' to shift the market back down towards equilibrium. Likewise, if the market price falls below equilibrium price then demand exceeds supply. This shortage pushes prices up and encourages firms to produce more goods, so the market drifts back up towards equilibrium.

Example

The demand and supply functions of a good are given by

$$P = 2Q_D + 50$$
$$P = \tfrac{1}{2}Q_S + 25$$

where P, Q_D and Q_S denote the price, quantity demanded and quantity supplied respectively.

(a) Determine the equilibrium price and quantity.

(b) Determine the effect on the market equilibrium if the government decides to impose a fixed tax of \$5 on each good.

Solution

(a) The demand curve has already been sketched in Figure 1.15. For the supply function

$$P = \tfrac{1}{2}Q_S + 25$$

we have $a = \tfrac{1}{2}$, $b = 25$, so the line has a slope of $\tfrac{1}{2}$ and an intercept of 25. It therefore passes through $(0, 25)$. For a second point, let us choose $Q_S = 20$, say. The corresponding value of P is

$$P = \tfrac{1}{2}(20) + 25 = 35$$

so the line also passes through $(20, 35)$. The points $(0, 25)$ and $(20, 35)$ can now be plotted and the supply curve sketched. Figure 1.20 shows both the demand and supply curves sketched on the same diagram. The point of intersection has coordinates $(10, 30)$, so the equilibrium quantity is 10 and the equilibrium price is 30.

It is possible to calculate these values using algebra. In equilibrium, $Q_D = Q_S$. If this common value is denoted by Q then the demand and supply equations become

$$P = 2Q + 50 \quad \text{and} \quad P = \tfrac{1}{2}Q + 25$$

This represents a pair of simultaneous equations for the two unknowns P and Q, and so could be solved using the elimination method described in the previous section. However, this is not strictly necessary because it follows immediately from the above equations that

$$-2Q + 50 = \tfrac{1}{2}Q + 25$$

since both sides are equal to P. This can be rearranged to calculate Q:

$$-2\tfrac{1}{2}Q + 50 = 25 \quad \text{(subtract } \tfrac{1}{2}Q \text{ from both sides)}$$
$$-2\tfrac{1}{2}Q = -25 \quad \text{(subtract 50 from both sides)}$$
$$Q = 10 \quad \text{(divide both sides by } -2\tfrac{1}{2})$$

Finally, P can be found by substituting this value into either of the original equations.

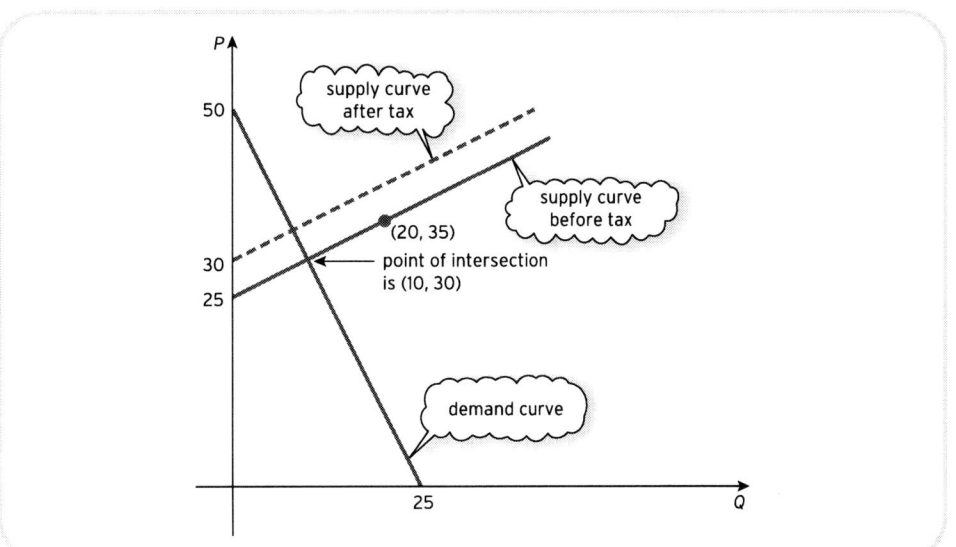

Figure 1.20

The demand equation gives

$$P = -2(10) + 50 = 30$$

As a check, the supply equation gives

$$P = \tfrac{1}{2}(10) + 25 = 30 \quad ✓$$

(b) If the government imposes a fixed tax of $5 per good then the money that the firm actually receives from the sale of each good is the amount, P, that the consumer pays, less the tax, 5: that is, $P - 5$. Mathematically, this problem can be solved by replacing P by $P - 5$ in the supply equation to get the new supply equation

$$P - 5 = \tfrac{1}{2}Q_S + 25$$

that is,

$$P = \tfrac{1}{2}Q_S + 30$$

The remaining calculations proceed as before. In equilibrium, $Q_D = Q_S$. Again setting this common value to be Q gives

$$P = -2Q + 50$$
$$P = \tfrac{1}{2}Q + 30$$

Hence

$$-2Q + 50 = \tfrac{1}{2}Q + 30$$

which can be solved as before to give $Q = 8$. Substitution into either of the above equations gives $P = 34$. (Check the details.)

Graphically, the introduction of tax shifts the supply curve upwards by 5 units. Obviously the demand curve is unaltered. The dashed line in Figure 1.20 shows the new supply curve, from which the new equilibrium quantity is 8 and equilibrium price is 34. Note the effect that government taxation has on the market equilibrium price. This has risen to $34 and so not all of the tax is passed on to the consumer. The consumer pays an additional $4 per good. The remaining $1 of tax must, therefore, be paid by the firm.

Practice Problem

3. The demand and supply functions of a good are given by

$$P = -4Q_D + 120$$
$$P = \tfrac{1}{3}Q_S + 29$$

where P, Q_D and Q_S denote the price, quantity demanded and quantity supplied respectively.

(a) Calculate the equilibrium price and quantity.

(b) Calculate the new equilibrium price and quantity after the imposition of a fixed tax of $13 per good. Who pays the tax?

Example   EXCEL

The demand and supply functions of a good are given by

$$P = -\tfrac{1}{2}Q_D + 20$$
$$P = \tfrac{1}{3}(Q_S + 10)$$

The government imposes a fixed tax, $\$\alpha$, on each good. Determine the equilibrium price and quantity in the case when

(a) $\alpha = 0$

(b) $\alpha = 5$

(c) $\alpha = 10$

(d) $\alpha = 2.50$

In each case, calculate the tax paid by the consumer and comment on these values.

Solution

(a) In the case when $\alpha = 0$, there is no tax and the demand and supply functions are as given above. In equilibrium, $Q_D = Q_S$, so by writing this value as Q, we can find the equilibrium position by solving the simultaneous equations

$$P = -\tfrac{1}{2}Q + 20$$
$$P = \tfrac{1}{3}(Q + 10)$$

In Excel, we first set up a table of values for Q. In Figure 1.21, the label Q has been put in cell A1, and values from 0 to 40 (going up in steps of 10) occupy cells A2 to A6. At this stage, we need to enter a formula for calculating the corresponding values of P using each of the equations in turn. As the first value of Q is in cell A2, we type

```
=-A2/2+20
```

in cell B2 for the demand function, and

```
=1/3*(A2+10)
```

in cell C2 for the supply function. By clicking and dragging down the columns, Excel will generate corresponding values for demand and supply.

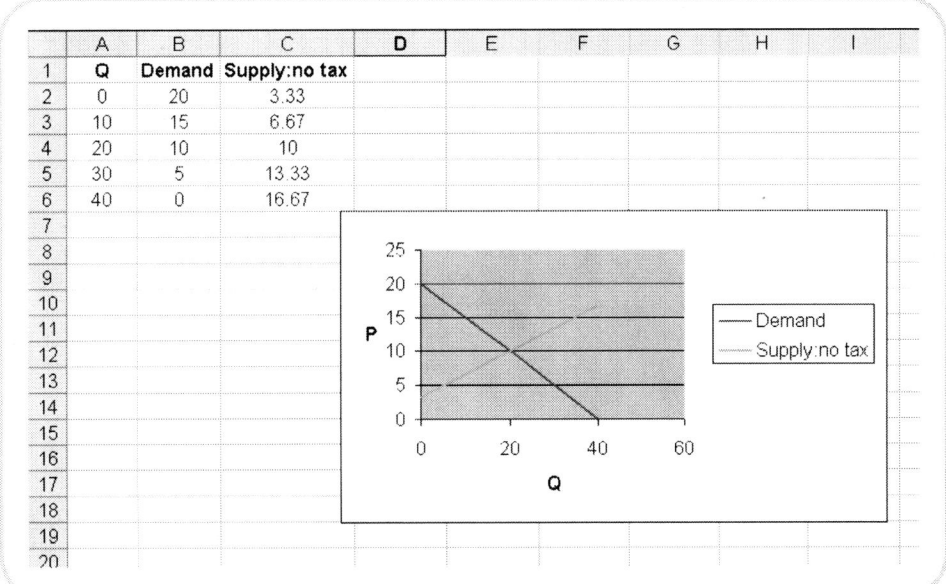

Figure 1.21

You will find that the values in the third column look very unfriendly to start with, as they have lots of figures after the decimal point. However, these can be removed by highlighting these numbers, and clicking on the Decrease Decimal icon, which can be found on the toolbar:

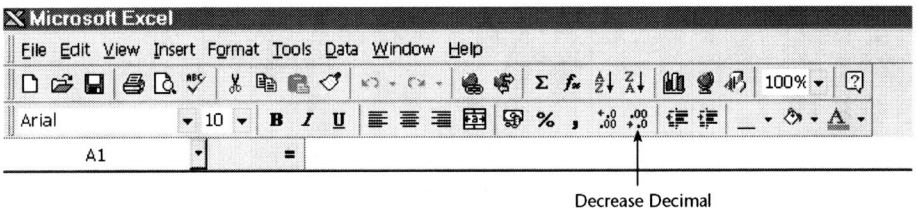

This has the effect of reducing the number of decimal places by rounding. Each time you click the icon, another decimal place is removed. As we are dealing with money, we round to 2 decimal places.

Finally, we highlight the contents of the first three columns and use Chart Wizard to create a diagram showing the demand and supply functions, as shown in Figure 1.21.

From the graph, it can be seen that the lines cross when $Q = 20$ and $P = 10$, which gives us the equilibrium position. This can also be seen by looking at the fourth row of the table.

(b) If the government imposes a tax of \$5 per item, the company producing the goods now receives \$5 less per item sold. The supply equation now becomes

$$P - 5 = \frac{1}{3}(Q_S + 10)$$

so that

$$P = \frac{1}{3}(Q_S + 10) + 5 \text{ (add 5 to both sides)}$$

The demand function remains unchanged. We can extend our spreadsheet from part (a) to include an extra column for this amended supply function, and we can then plot this extra line on the same graph. This can be done by typing

```
=1/3*(A2+10)+5
```

in cell D2, and dragging down to D6.

It is possible to alter the type of line drawn by the Chart Wizard by clicking on the line you wish to change. This should highlight the points that were plotted. Select **Format** from the menu bar, and then click on **Data Series**, **Patterns** and finally scroll through the styles of lines available and select the one required. Figure 1.22 shows the new spreadsheet.

Notice that the effect of the tax is to move the supply line up by 5, and the position of equilibrium has moved to (14, 13). This means that the price has increased from \$10 to \$13, with the consumer paying an additional \$3 in tax. The remaining \$2 is therefore paid by the company.

(c) The calculations in (b) can obviously be repeated by editing the formula for the supply equation in cell D2 to

```
=1/3*(A2+10)+10
```

The equilibrium quantity and price are now

$$Q = 8 \quad \text{and} \quad P = 16$$

so the consumer pays \$6 of this tax.

(d) Changing D2 to

```
=1/3*(A2+10)+2.5
```

Figure 1.22

gives equilibrium values

$$Q = 17 \quad \text{and} \quad P = 11.5$$

so the consumer pays \$1.50 of the tax.

Notice that, as expected, the consumer pays increasing amounts of tax as the value of α increases. More significantly, notice that the *fraction* of the tax paid by the consumer is the same in each case. For example, in part (c), the consumer pays \$6 of the \$10 tax, which is $^3/_5$ of the tax. You might like to check that in cases (b) and (d) the tax is also split in the ratio of 3:2. We shall investigate this further in Question 8 in Exercise 1.5* at the end of this section.

We conclude this section by considering a more realistic model of supply and demand, taking into account substitutable and complementary goods. Let us suppose that there are two goods in related markets, which we call good 1 and good 2. The demand for either good depends on the prices of both good 1 and good 2. If the corresponding demand functions are linear then

$$Q_{D_1} = a_1 + b_1 P_1 + c_1 P_2$$
$$Q_{D_2} = a_2 + b_2 P_1 + c_2 P_2$$

where P_i and Q_{D_i} denote the price and demand for the ith good and a_i, b_i, c_i are parameters. For the first equation, $a_1 > 0$ because there is a positive demand when the prices of both goods are zero. Also, $b_1 < 0$ because the demand of a good falls as its price rises. The sign of c_1 depends on the nature of the goods. If the goods are substitutable then an increase in the price of good 2 would mean that consumers would switch from good 2 to good 1, causing Q_{D_1} to increase. Substitutable goods are therefore characterized by a positive value of c_1. On the other hand, if the goods are complementary then a rise in the price of either good would see the demand fall, so c_1 is negative. Similar results apply to the signs of a_2, b_2 and c_2. The calculation of the equilibrium price and quantity in a two-commodity market model is demonstrated in the following example.

Example

The demand and supply functions for two interdependent commodities are given by

$$Q_{D_1} = 10 - 2P_1 + P_2$$
$$Q_{D_2} = 5 + 2P_1 - 2P_2$$
$$Q_{S_1} = -3 + 2P_1$$
$$Q_{S_2} = -2 + 3P_2$$

where Q_D, Q_S and P_i denote the quantity demanded, quantity supplied and price of good i respectively. Determine the equilibrium price and quantity for this two-commodity model.

Solution

In equilibrium, we know that the quantity supplied is equal to the quantity demanded for each good, so that

$$Q_{D_1} = Q_{S_1} \quad \text{and} \quad Q_{D_2} = Q_{S_2}$$

Let us write these respective common values as Q_1 and Q_2. The demand and supply equations for good 1 then become

$$Q_1 = 10 - 2P_1 + P_2$$
$$Q_1 = -3 + 2P_1$$

Hence

$$10 - 2P_1 + P_2 = -3 + 2P_1$$

since both sides are equal to Q_1. It makes sense to tidy this equation up a bit by collecting all of the unknowns on the left-hand side and putting the constant terms on to the right-hand side:

$$10 - 4P_1 + P_2 = -3 \quad \text{(subtract } 2P_1 \text{ from both sides)}$$
$$-4P_1 + P_2 = -13 \quad \text{(subtract 10 from both sides)}$$

We can perform a similar process for good 2. The demand and supply equations become

$$Q_2 = 5 + 2P_1 - 2P_2$$
$$Q_2 = -2 + 3P_2$$

because $Q_{D_2} = Q_{S_2} = Q_2$ in equilibrium. Hence

$$5 + 2P_1 - 2P_2 = -2 + 3P_2$$
$$5 + 2P_1 - 5P_2 = -2 \quad \text{(subtract } 3P_2 \text{ from both sides)}$$
$$2P_1 - 5P_2 = -7 \quad \text{(subtract 5 from both sides)}$$

We have therefore shown that the equilibrium prices, P_1 and P_2, satisfy the simultaneous linear equations

$$-4P_1 + P_2 = -13 \tag{1}$$
$$2P_1 - 5P_2 = -7 \tag{2}$$

which can be solved by elimination. Following the steps described in Section 1.2 we proceed as follows.

Step 1
Double equation (2) and add to equation (1) to get

$$\begin{array}{r} -4P_1 + P_2 = -13 \\ 4P_1 - 10P_2 = -14\ + \\ \hline -9P_2 = -27 \end{array} \tag{3}$$

Step 2
Divide both sides of equation (3) by -9 to get $P_2 = 3$.

Step 3
If this is substituted into equation (1) then

$$-4P_1 + 3 = -13$$
$$-4P_1 \quad = -16 \quad \text{(subtract 3 from both sides)}$$
$$P_1 \quad = 4 \quad \text{(divide both sides by } -4)$$

Step 4

As a check, equation (2) gives

$$2(4) - 5(3) = -7 \quad ✓$$

Hence $P_1 = 4$ and $P_2 = 3$.

Finally, the equilibrium quantities can be deduced by substituting these values back into the original supply equations. For good 1,

$$Q_1 = -3 + 2P_1 = -3 + 2(4) = 5$$

For good 2,

$$Q_2 = -2 + 3P_2 = -2 + 3(3) = 7$$

As a check, the demand equations also give

$$Q_1 = 10 - 2P_1 + P_2 = 10 - 2(4) + 3 = 5 \quad ✓$$
$$Q_2 = 5 + 2P_1 - 2P_2 = 5 + 2(4) - 2(3) = 7 \quad ✓$$

Practice Problem

4. The demand and supply functions for two interdependent commodities are given by

$$Q_{D_1} = 40 - 5P_1 - P_2$$
$$Q_{D_2} = 50 - 2P_1 - 4P_2$$
$$Q_{S_1} = -3 + 4P_1$$
$$Q_{S_2} = -7 + 3P_2$$

where Q_D, Q_S and P_i denote the quantity demanded, quantity supplied and price of good i respectively. Determine the equilibrium price and quantity for this two-commodity model. Are these goods substitutable or complementary?

For a two-commodity market the equilibrium prices and quantities can be found by solving a system of two simultaneous equations. Exactly the same procedure can be applied to a three-commodity market, which requires the solution of a system of three simultaneous equations.

Advice

An example of a three-commodity model can be found in Question 6 of Exercise 1.5*. Alternative methods and further examples are described in Chapter 7. In general, with n goods it is necessary to solve n equations in n unknowns and, as pointed out in Section 1.4, this is best done using a computer package whenever n is large.

Key Terms

Complementary goods   A pair of goods consumed together. As the price of either goes up, the demand for both goods goes down.

Decreasing function   A function, $y = f(x)$, in which y decreases as x increases.

Demand function   A relationship between the quantity demanded and various factors that affect demand, including price.

Dependent variable   A variable whose value is determined by that taken by the independent variables; in $y = f(x)$, the dependent variable is y.

Endogenous variable   A variable whose value is determined within a model.

Equilibrium (market)   This state occurs when quantity supplied and quantity demanded are equal.

Exogenous variable   A variable whose value is determined outside a model.

Function   A rule that assigns to each incoming number, x, a uniquely defined outgoing number, y.

Increasing function   A function, $y = f(x)$, in which y increases as x increases.

Independent variable   A variable whose value determines that of the dependent variable; in $y = f(x)$, the independent variable is x.

Inferior good   A good whose demand decreases as income increases.

Inverse function   A function, written f^{-1}, which reverses the effect of a given function, f, so that $x = f^{-1}(y)$ when $y = f(x)$.

Modelling   The creation of piece of mathematical theory which represents (a simplification of) some aspect of practical economics.

Parameter   A constant whose value affects the specific values but not the general form of a mathematical expression such as the constants a, b and c in $ax^2 + bx + c$.

Substitutable goods   A pair of goods that are alternatives to each other. As the price of one of them goes up, the demand for the other rises.

Superior good   A good whose demand increases as income increases.

Supply function   A relationship between the quantity supplied and various factors that affect supply, including price.

Exercise 1.5

1. If $f(x) = 3x + 15$ and $g(x) = \frac{1}{3}x - 5$, evaluate

    (a) $f(2)$ **(b)** $f(10)$ **(c)** $f(0)$ **(d)** $g(21)$ **(e)** $g(45)$ **(f)** $g(15)$

    What word describes the relationship between f and g?

2. Sketch a graph of the supply function

    $$P = \frac{1}{3}Q + 7$$

    Hence, or otherwise, determine the value of

    (a) P when $Q = 12$

    (b) Q when $P = 10$

    (c) Q when $P = 4$

3. The demand function of a good is

$$Q = 100 - P + 2Y + \tfrac{1}{2}A$$

where Q, P, Y and A denote quantity demanded, price, income and advertising expenditure respectively.

(a) Calculate the demand when $P = 10$, $Y = 40$ and $A = 6$. Assuming that price and income are fixed, calculate the additional advertising expenditure needed to raise demand to 179 units.

(b) Is this good inferior or superior?

4. The demand, Q, for a certain good depends on its own price, P, and the price of an alternative good, P_A, according to

$$Q = 30 - 3P + P_A$$

(a) Find Q if $P = 4$ and $P_A = 5$.

(b) Is the alternative good substitutable or complementary? Give a reason for your answer.

(c) Determine the value of P if $Q = 23$ and $P_A = 11$.

5. (a) Copy and complete the following table of values for the supply function ❓

$$P = \tfrac{1}{2}Q + 20$$

Q	0		50
P		25	

Hence, or otherwise, draw an accurate sketch of this function using axes with values of Q and P between 0 and 50.

(b) On the same axes draw the graph of the demand function

$$P = 50 - Q$$

and hence find the equilibrium quantity and price.

(c) The good under consideration is superior. Describe the effect on the equilibrium quantity and price when income rises.

6. The demand and supply functions of a good are given by

$$P = -3Q_D + 48$$
$$P = \tfrac{1}{2}Q_S + 23$$

Find the equilibrium quantity if the government imposes a fixed tax of $4 on each good.

7. The demand and supply functions for two interdependent commodities are given by

$$Q_{D_1} = 100 - 2P_1 + P_2$$
$$Q_{D_2} = 5 + 2P_1 - 3P_2$$
$$Q_{S_1} = -10 + P_1$$
$$Q_{S_2} = -5 + 6P_2$$

where Q_D, Q_S and P_i denote the quantity demanded, quantity supplied and price of good i respectively. Determine the equilibrium price and quantity for this two-commodity model.

8. A demand equation of a certain good is given by

$$Q = -20P + 0.04Y + 4T + 3P_r$$

where Q and P denote the quantity and price of the good, Y is income, T is taste, and P_r is the price of a related good.

(a) Calculate Q when $P = 8$, $Y = 1000$, $T = 15$ and $P_r = 30$.

(b) Is the related good, substitutable or complementary? Give a reason for your answer.

(c) Find the value of P when $Q = 235$, $Y = 8000$, $T = 30$ and $P_r = 25$.

(d) The exogenous variables are now fixed at $Y = 2000$, $T = 10$ and $P_r = 5$. State the values of the slope and vertical intercept when the demand equation is sketched with

    (i) P on the horizontal axis and Q on the vertical axis
    (ii) Q on the horizontal axis and P on the vertical axis.

9. (**Excel**) The demand function of a good is given by

$$Q = 100 - 2P + Y - 3P_A$$

where Q, P, Y and P_A denote quantity, price, income and price of an alternative good, respectively. For each of the following cases, tabulate values of Q, when P is 0, 20, 40, 60. Hence sketch all three demand curves on the same diagram.

(a) $Y = 20$, $P_A = 10$

(b) $Y = 50$, $P_A = 10$

(c) $Y = 20$, $P_A = 16$

Is the good inferior or superior?
Is the alternative good substitutable or complementary?
Give reasons for your answers.

Exercise 1.5*

1. Describe the effect on the demand curve due to an increase in

    (a) the price of substitutable goods
    (b) the price of complementary goods
    (c) advertising expenditure.

2. If the line, $P = -\frac{2}{3}Q + 6$, is sketched with P on the horizontal axis, and Q on the vertical axis, find the gradient, m, and the vertical intercept, c.

3. If the demand function of a good is

$$2P + 3Q_D = 60$$

where P and Q_D denote price and quantity demanded respectively, find the largest and smallest values of P for which this function is economically meaningful.

4. The demand and supply functions of a good are given by

$$P = -5Q_D + 80$$
$$P = 2Q_S + 10$$

where P, Q_D and Q_S denote price, quantity demanded and quantity supplied respectively.

(1) Find the equilibrium price and quantity

  (a) graphically   **(b)** algebraically

(2) If the government deducts, as tax, 15% of the market price of each good, determine the new equilibrium price and quantity.

5. The supply and demand equations of a good are given by

$$P = Q_S + 8$$
$$P = -3Q_D + 80$$

where P, Q_S and Q_D denote price, quantity supplied and quantity demanded respectively.

(a) Find the equilibrium price and quantity if the government imposes a fixed tax of $36 on each good.

(b) Find the corresponding value of the government's tax revenue.

6. The demand and supply functions for three interdependent commodities are

$$Q_{D_1} = 15 - P_1 + 2P_2 + P_3$$
$$Q_{D_2} = 9 + P_1 - P_2 - P_3$$
$$Q_{D_3} = 8 + 2P_1 - P_2 - 4P_3$$
$$Q_{S_1} = -7 + P_1$$
$$Q_{S_2} = -4 + 4P_2$$
$$Q_{S_3} = -5 + 2P_3$$

where Q_{D_i}, Q_{S_i} and P_i denote the quantity demanded, quantity supplied and price of good i respectively. Determine the equilibrium price and quantity for this three-commodity model.

7. The demand and supply functions of a good are given by

$$P = -3Q_D + 60$$
$$P = 2Q_S + 40$$

respectively. If the government decides to impose a tax of t per good, show that the equilibrium quantity is given by

$$Q = 4 - \tfrac{1}{5}t$$

and write down a similar expression for the equilibrium price.

(a) If it is known that the equilibrium quantity is 3, work out the value of t.

  How much of this tax is paid by the firm?

(b) If, instead of imposing a tax, the government provides a subsidy of $5 per good, find the new equilibrium price and quantity.

---

8. (**Excel**) The supply and demand functions of a good are given by

$$P = -Q_D + 240$$
$$P = 60 + 2Q_S$$

where P, Q_D and Q_S denote price, quantity demanded and quantity supplied respectively. Sketch graphs of both functions on the same diagram, on the range $0 \leq Q \leq 80$, and hence find the equilibrium price. The government now imposes a fixed tax, \$60, on each good. Draw the new supply equation on the same diagram and hence find the new equilibrium price. What fraction of the \$60 tax is paid by the consumer?

Consider replacing the demand function by the more general equation

$$P = -kQ_D + 240$$

By repeating the calculations above, find the fraction of the tax paid by the consumer for the case when k is

(a) 2   (b) 3   (c) 4

State the connection between this fraction and the value of k. Use this connection to predict how much tax is paid by the consumer when $k = 6$.

SECTION 1.6
Transposition of formulae

Objectives

At the end of this section you should be able to:

* Manipulate formulae.
* Draw a flow chart representing a formula.
* Use a reverse flow chart to transpose a formula.
* Change the subject of a formula involving several letters.

Mathematical modelling involves the use of formulae to represent the relationship between economic variables. In microeconomics we have already seen how useful supply and demand formulae are. These provide a precise relationship between price and quantity. For example, the connection between price, P, and quantity, Q, might be modelled by

$$P = -4Q + 100$$

Given any value of Q it is trivial to deduce the corresponding value of P by merely replacing the symbol Q by a number. A value of $Q = 2$, say, gives

$$P = -4 \times 2 + 100$$
$$= -8 + 100$$
$$= 92$$

On the other hand, given P, it is necessary to solve an equation to deduce Q. For example, when $P = 40$, the equation is

$$-4Q + 100 = 40$$

which can be solved as follows:

$$-4Q = -60 \quad \text{(subtract 100 from both sides)}$$
$$Q = 15 \quad \text{(divide both sides by } -4\text{)}$$

This approach is reasonable when only one or two values of P are given. However, if we are given many values of P, it is clearly tedious and inefficient for us to solve the equation each time to find Q. The preferred approach is to **transpose** the formula for P. In other words, we rearrange the formula

$$P = \text{an expression involving } Q$$

into

$$Q = \text{an expression involving } P$$

Written this way round, the formula enables us to find Q by replacing P by a number. For the specific formula

$$-4Q + 100 = P$$

the steps are

$$-4Q = P - 100 \quad \text{(subtract 100 from both sides)}$$

$$Q = \frac{P - 100}{-4} \quad \text{(divide both sides by } -4\text{)}$$

Notice that

$$\frac{P - 100}{-4} = \frac{P}{-4} - \frac{100}{-4}$$

$$= -\tfrac{1}{4}P + 25$$

so the rearranged formula simplifies to

$$Q = -\tfrac{1}{4}P + 25$$

If we now wish to find Q when $P = 40$, we immediately get

$$Q = -\tfrac{1}{4} \times 40 + 25$$

$$= -10 + 25$$

$$= 15$$

The important thing to notice about the algebra is that the individual steps are identical to those used previously for solving the equation

$$-4Q + 100 = 40$$

i.e. the operations are again

'subtract 100 from both sides'

followed by

'divide both sides by -4'

Example

Make x the subject of the formula

$$\tfrac{1}{7}x - 2 = y$$

Solution

If you needed to solve an equation such as $\tfrac{1}{7}x - 2 = 4$, say, you would first add 2 to both sides and then multiply both sides by 7. Performing the same operations to the general equation

$$\tfrac{1}{7}x - 2 = y$$

gives

$$\tfrac{1}{7}x = y + 2 \quad \text{(add 2 to both sides)}$$

$$x = 7(y + 2) \quad \text{(multiply both sides by 7)}$$

If desired, you can multiply out the brackets to give the alternative version:

$$x = 7y + 14$$

Practice Problem

1. (a) Solve the equation

$$\tfrac{1}{2}Q + 13 = 17$$

State clearly exactly what operation you have performed to both sides at each stage of your solution.

(b) By performing the same operations as part (a), rearrange the formula

$$\tfrac{1}{2}Q + 13 = P$$

into the form

$$Q = \text{an expression involving } P$$

(c) By substituting $P = 17$ into the formula derived in part (b), check that this agrees with your answer to part (a).

In general, there are two issues concerning formula transposition. Firstly, we need to decide what to do to both sides of the given formula and the order in which they should be performed. Secondly, we need to carry out these steps accurately. The first of these is often the more difficult. However, there is a logical strategy that can be used to help. To illustrate this, consider the task of making Q the subject of

$$P = \tfrac{1}{3}Q + 5$$

that is, of rearranging this formula into the form

$$Q = \text{an expression involving } P$$

Imagine starting with a value of Q and using a calculator to work out P from

$$P = \tfrac{1}{3}Q + 5$$

The diagram below shows that two operations are required and indicates the order in which they must be done. This diagram is called a **flow chart**.

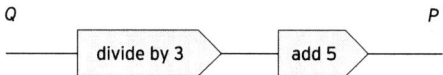

To go backwards from P to Q we need to undo these operations. Now the reverse of 'divide by 3' is 'multiply by 3' and the reverse of 'add 5' is 'subtract 5', so the operations needed to transpose the formula are as follows:

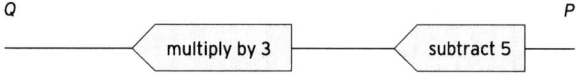

This diagram is called a **reverse flow chart**. The process is similar to that of unwrapping a parcel (or peeling an onion); you start by unwrapping the outer layer first and work inwards. If we now actually perform these steps in the order specified by the reverse flow chart, we get

$$\tfrac{1}{3}Q + 5 = P$$
$$\tfrac{1}{3}Q \quad\ = P - 5 \qquad \text{(subtract 5 from both sides)}$$
$$Q \quad\ = 3(P - 5) \quad \text{(multiply both sides by 3)}$$

The rearranged formula can be simplified by multiplying out the brackets to give

$Q = 3P - 15$

Incidentally, if you prefer, you can actually use the reverse flow chart itself to perform the algebra for you. All you have to do is to pass the letter P through the reverse flow chart. Working from right to left gives

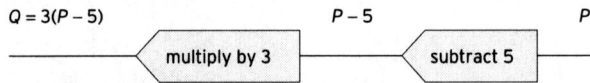

Notice that by taking P as the input to the box 'subtract 5' gives the output $P - 5$, and if the whole of this is taken as the input to the box 'multiply by 3', the final output is the answer, $3(P - 5)$. Hence

$Q = 3(P - 5)$

Example

Make x the subject of

(a) $y = \sqrt{\dfrac{x}{5}}$ (b) $y = \dfrac{4}{2x + 1}$

Solution

(a) To go from x to y the operations are

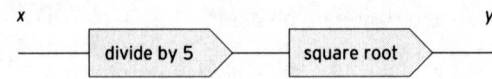

so the steps needed to transpose the formula are

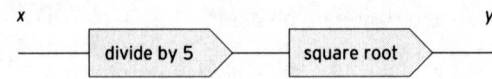

The algebraic details are as follows:

$$\sqrt{\dfrac{x}{5}} = y$$

$$\dfrac{x}{5} = y^2 \quad \text{(square both sides)}$$

$$x = 5y^2 \quad \text{(multiply both sides by 5)}$$

Hence the transposed formula is

$x = 5y^2$

Alternatively, if you prefer, the reverse flow chart can be used directly to obtain

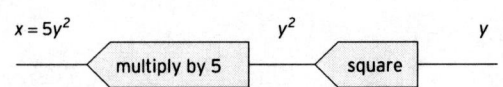

Hence

$$x = 5y^2$$

(b) The forwards flow chart is

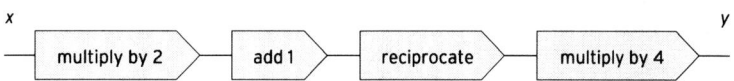

so the reverse flow chart is

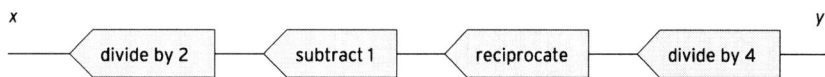

The algebraic details are as follows:

$$\frac{4}{2x + 1} = y$$

$$\frac{1}{2x + 1} = \frac{y}{4} \qquad \text{(divide both sides by 4)}$$

$$2x + 1 = \frac{4}{y} \qquad \text{(reciprocate both sides)}$$

$$2x = \frac{4}{y} - 1 \qquad \text{(subtract 1 from both sides)}$$

$$= \frac{1}{2}\left(\frac{4}{y} - 1\right) \qquad \text{(divide both sides by 2)}$$

which can be simplified, by multiplying out the brackets, to give

$$x = \frac{2}{y} - \frac{1}{2}$$

Again, the reverse flow chart can be used directly to obtain

$$x = \frac{1}{2}\left(\frac{4}{y} - 1\right) \qquad \frac{4}{y} - 1 \qquad \frac{4}{y} \qquad \frac{y}{4} \qquad y$$

$$\longleftarrow \boxed{\text{divide by 2}} \longleftarrow \boxed{\text{subtract 1}} \longleftarrow \boxed{\text{reciprocate}} \longleftarrow \boxed{\text{divide by 4}} \longleftarrow$$

Practice Problem

2. Use flow charts to make x the subject of the following formulae:

(a) $y = 6x^2$ **(b)** $y = \dfrac{1}{7x - 1}$

The following example contains two difficult instances of transposition. In both cases the letter x appears more than once on the right-hand side. If this happens, the technique based on flow charts cannot be used. However, it may still be possible to perform the manipulation even if some of the steps may not be immediately obvious.

Example

Transpose the following equations to express x in terms of y:

(a) $ax = bx + cy + d$ **(b)** $y = \dfrac{x+1}{x-2}$

Solution

(a) In the equation

$$ax = bx + cy + d$$

there are terms involving x on both sides and since we are hoping to rearrange this into the form

$$x = \text{an expression involving } y$$

it makes sense to collect the x's on the left-hand side. To do this we subtract bx from both sides to get

$$ax - bx = cy + d$$

Notice that x is a common factor of the left-hand side, so the distributive law can be applied 'in reverse' to take the x outside the brackets: that is,

$$(a - b)x = cy + d$$

Finally, both sides are divided by $a - b$ to get

$$x = \frac{cy + d}{a - b}$$

which is of the desired form.

(b) It is difficult to see where to begin with the equation

$$y = \frac{x+1}{x-2}$$

because there is an x in both the numerator and the denominator. Indeed, the thing that is preventing us getting started is precisely the fact that the expression is a fraction. We can, however, remove the fraction simply by multiplying both sides by the denominator to get

$$(x - 2)y = x + 1$$

and if we multiply out the brackets then

$$xy - 2y = x + 1$$

We want to rearrange this into the form

$$x = \text{an expression involving } y$$

so we collect the x's on the left-hand side and put everything else on to the right-hand side. To do this we first add $2y$ to both sides to get

$$xy = x + 1 + 2y$$

and then subtract x from both sides to get

$$xy - x = 1 + 2y$$

The distributive law can now be applied 'in reverse' to take out the common factor of x: that is,

$$(y - 1)x = 1 + 2y$$

Finally, dividing through by $y - 1$ gives

$$x = \frac{1 + 2y}{y - 1}$$

Advice

This example contains some of the hardest algebraic manipulation seen so far in this book. I hope that you managed to follow the individual steps. However, it all might appear as if we have 'pulled rabbits out of hats'. You may feel that, if left on your own, you are never going to be able to decide what to do at each stage. Unfortunately there is no watertight strategy that always works, although the following five-point plan is worth considering if you get stuck.

To transpose a given equation of the form

y = an expression involving x

into an equation of the form

x = an expression involving y

you proceed as follows:

Step 1   Remove fractions.
Step 2   Multiply out the brackets.
Step 3   Collect all of the x's on to the left-hand side.
Step 4   Take out a factor of x.
Step 5   Divide by the coefficient of x.

You might find it helpful to look back at the previous example in the light of this strategy. In part (b) it is easy to identify each of the five steps. Part (a) also used this strategy, starting with the third step.

Example

Make x the subject of

$$y = \sqrt{\frac{ax + b}{cx + d}}$$

Solution

In this formula there is a square root symbol surrounding the right-hand side. This can be removed by squaring both sides to get

$$y^2 = \frac{ax + b}{cx + d}$$

We now apply the five-step strategy:

Step 1 $(cx + d)y^2 = ax + b$

Step 2 $cxy^2 + dy^2 = ax + b$

Step 3 $cxy^2 - ax = b - dy^2$

Step 4 $(cy^2 - a)x = b - dy^2$

Step 5 $x = \dfrac{b - dy^2}{cy^2 - a}$

Practice Problem

3. Transpose the following formulae to express x in terms of y:

(a) $x - ay = cx + y$

(b) $y = \dfrac{x - 2}{x + 4}$

Key Terms

Flow chart A diagram consisting of boxes of instructions indicating a sequence of operations and their order.

Reverse flow chart A flow chart indicating the inverse of the original sequence of operations in reverse order.

Transpose a formula The rearrangement of a formula to make one of the other letters the subject.

Exercise 1.6

1. Make Q the subject of

$P = 2Q + 8$

Hence find the value of Q when $P = 52$.

2. Write down the formula representing each of the following flow charts

x y

(a) ──── ⟩ double ⟩ ── ⟩ add 5 ⟩ ────

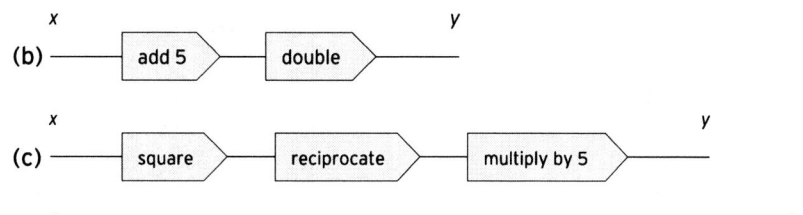

3. Draw flow charts for each of the following formulae:

(a) $y = 5x + 3$ **(b)** $y = 5(x + 3)$ **(c)** $y = 6x - 9$ **(d)** $y = 4x^2 - 6$

(e) $y = \dfrac{x}{2} + 7$ **(f)** $y = \dfrac{2}{x}$ **(g)** $y = \dfrac{2}{x + 3}$

4. Make x the subject of each of the following formulae:

(a) $y = 9x - 6$ **(b)** $y = (x + 4)/3$ **(c)** $y = \dfrac{x}{2}$

(d) $y = \dfrac{x}{5} + 8$ **(e)** $y = \dfrac{1}{x + 2}$ **(f)** $y = \dfrac{4}{3x - 7}$

5. Transpose the formulae:

     (a) $Q = aP + b$ to express P in terms of Q

     (b) $Y = aY + b + I$ to express Y in terms of I

     (c) $Q = \dfrac{1}{aP + b}$ to express P in terms of Q

6. Make x the subject of the formula

$$y = \frac{3}{x} - 2$$

Exercise 1.6*

1. (1) Draw flow charts for each of the following formulae:

     (a) $y = 9x + 1$ **(b)** $y = 3 - x$ **(c)** $y = 5x^2 - 8$

     (d) $y = \sqrt{(3x + 5)}$ **(e)** $y = \dfrac{4}{x^2 + 8}$

(2) Hence, or otherwise, express x in terms of y in each case.

2. Make x the subject of the following formulae: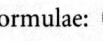

(a) $\dfrac{a}{x} + b = \dfrac{c}{x}$ (b) $a - x = \dfrac{b + x}{a}$ (c) $e + \sqrt{x + f} = g$

(d) $a\sqrt{\left(\dfrac{x - n}{m}\right)} = \dfrac{a^2}{b}$ (e) $\dfrac{\sqrt{x - m}}{n} = \dfrac{1}{m}$ (f) $\dfrac{\sqrt{x} + a}{\sqrt{x} - b} = \dfrac{b}{a}$

3. Transpose the formula

$$V = \frac{5t + 1}{t - 1}$$

to express t in terms of V.

Hence, or otherwise, find the value of t when $V = 5.6$.

4. Make r the subject of the formula

$$S = P\left(1 + \frac{r}{100}\right)^n$$

5. Rearrange the formula

$$Y = \frac{-aT + b + I + G}{1 - a + at}$$

to make each of the following letters the subject:

(a) G (b) T (c) t (d) a

SECTION 1.7
National income determination

Objectives

At the end of this section you should be able to:

- Identify and sketch linear consumption functions.
- Identify and sketch linear savings functions.
- Set up simple macroeconomic models.
- Calculate equilibrium national income.
- Analyse IS and LM schedules.

Macroeconomics is concerned with the analysis of economic theory and policy at a national level. In this section we focus on one particular aspect known as national income determination. We describe how to set up simple models of the national economy which enable equilibrium levels of income to be calculated. Initially we assume that the economy is divided into two sectors, households and firms. Firms use resources such as land, capital, labour and raw materials to produce goods and services. These resources are known as **factors of production** and are taken to belong to households. **National income** represents the flow of income from firms to households given as payment for these factors. Households can then spend this money in one of two ways. Income can be used for the consumption of goods produced by firms or it can be put into savings. Consumption, C, and savings, S, are therefore functions of income, Y: that is,

$$C = f(Y)$$
$$S = g(Y)$$

for some appropriate consumption function, f, and savings function, g. Moreover, C and S are normally expected to increase as income rises, so f and g are both increasing functions.

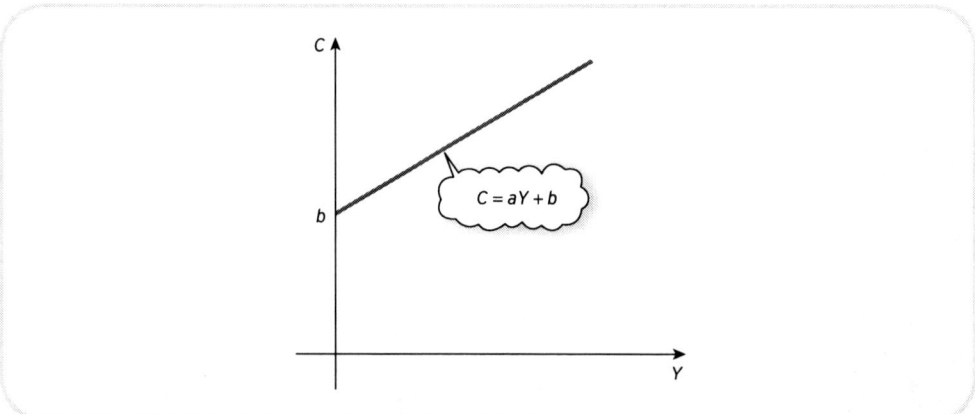

Figure 1.23

We begin by analysing the **consumption function**. As usual we need to quantify the precise relationship between C and Y. If this relationship is linear then a graph of a typical consumption function is shown in Figure 1.23. It is clear from this graph that if

$$C = aY + b$$

then $a > 0$ and $b > 0$. The intercept b is the level of consumption when there is no income (that is, when $Y = 0$) and is known as **autonomous consumption**. The slope, a, is the change in C brought about by a 1 unit increase in Y and is known as the **marginal propensity to consume** (MPC). As previously noted, income is used up in consumption and savings so that

$$Y = C + S$$

It follows that only a proportion of the 1 unit increase in income is consumed; the rest goes into savings. Hence the slope, a, is generally smaller than 1: that is, $a < 1$. It is standard practice in mathematics to collapse the two separate inequalities $a > 0$ and $a < 1$ into the single inequality

$$0 < a < 1$$

The relation

$$Y = C + S$$

enables the precise form of the savings function to be determined from any given consumption function. This is illustrated in the following example.

Example

Sketch a graph of the consumption function

$$C = 0.6Y + 10$$

Determine the corresponding savings function and sketch its graph.

Solution

The graph of the consumption function

$$C = 0.6Y + 10$$

has intercept 10 and slope 0.6. It passes through $(0, 10)$. For a second point, let us choose $Y = 40$, which gives $C = 34$. Hence the line also passes through $(40, 34)$. The consumption function is sketched in Figure 1.24.

To find the savings function we use the relation

$$Y = C + S$$

which gives

$$
\begin{aligned}
S &= Y - C && \text{(subtract } C \text{ from both sides)} \\
&= Y - (0.6Y + 10) && \text{(substitute } C) \\
&= Y - 0.6Y - 10 && \text{(multiply out the brackets)} \\
&= 0.4Y - 10 && \text{(collect terms)}
\end{aligned}
$$

The savings function is also linear. Its graph has intercept -10 and slope 0.4. This is sketched in Figure 1.25 using the fact that it passes through $(0, -10)$ and $(25, 0)$.

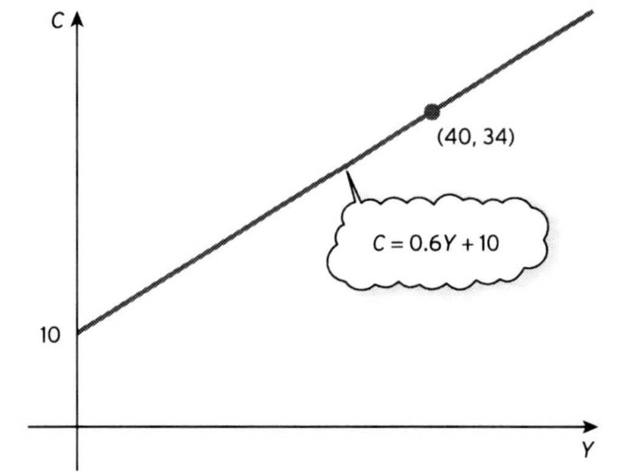

Figure 1.24

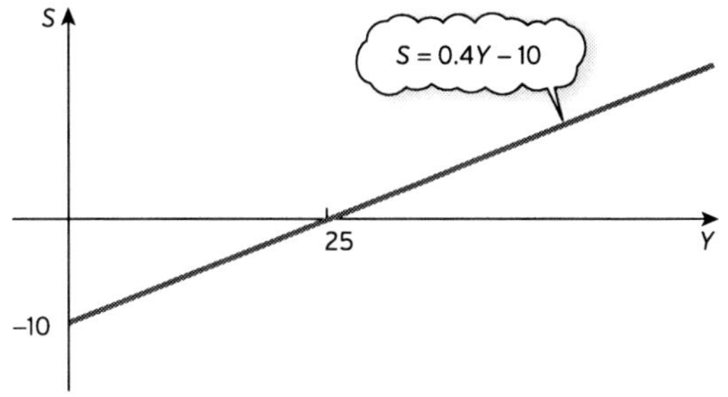

Figure 1.24

Figure 1.25

Figure 1.25

Practice Problem

1. Determine the savings function that corresponds to the consumption function

$$C = 0.8Y + 25$$

For the general consumption function

$$C = aY + b$$

we have

$$S = Y - C$$
$$= Y - (aY + b) \quad \text{(substitute } C\text{)}$$
$$= Y - aY - b \quad \text{(multiply out the brackets)}$$
$$= (1 - a)Y - b \quad \text{(take out a common factor of } Y\text{)}$$

The slope of the savings function is called the **marginal propensity to save** (MPS) and is given by $1 - a$: that is,

$$\text{MPS} = 1 - a = 1 - \text{MPC}$$

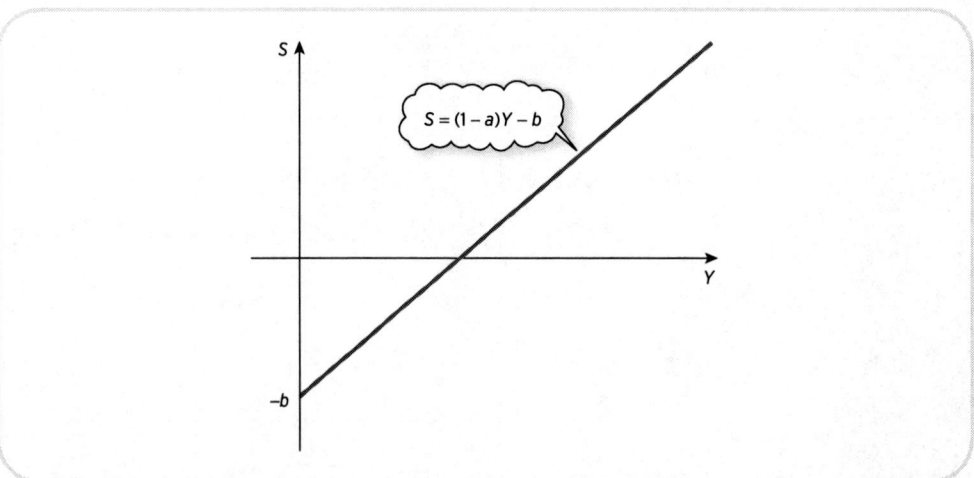

Figure 1.26

Moreover, since $a < 1$ we see that the slope, $1 - a$, is positive. Figure 1.26 shows the graph of this savings function. One interesting feature, which contrasts with other economic functions considered so far, is that it is allowed to take negative values. In particular, note that **autonomous savings** (that is, the value of S when $Y = 0$) are equal to $-b$, which is negative because $b > 0$. This is to be expected because whenever consumption exceeds income, households must finance the excess expenditure by withdrawing savings.

> ## Advice
>
> The result, MPC + MPS = 1, is always true, even if the consumption function is non-linear. A proof of this generalization can be found on page 295.

The simplest model of the national economy is illustrated in Figure 1.27, which shows the circular flow of income and expenditure. This is fairly crude, since it fails to take into account government activity or foreign trade. In this diagram **investment**, I, is an injection into the circular flow in the form of spending on capital goods.

Let us examine this more closely and represent the diagrammatic information in symbols. Consider first the box labelled 'Households'. The flow of money entering this box is Y and the flow leaving it is $C + S$. Hence we have the familiar relation

$$Y = C + S$$

For the box labelled 'Firms' the flow entering it is $C + I$ and the flow leaving it is Y, so

$$Y = C + I$$

Suppose that the level of investment that firms plan to inject into the economy is known to be some fixed value, I^*. If the economy is in equilibrium, the flow of income and expenditure balance so that

$$Y = C + I^*$$

From the assumption that the consumption function is

$$C = aY + b$$

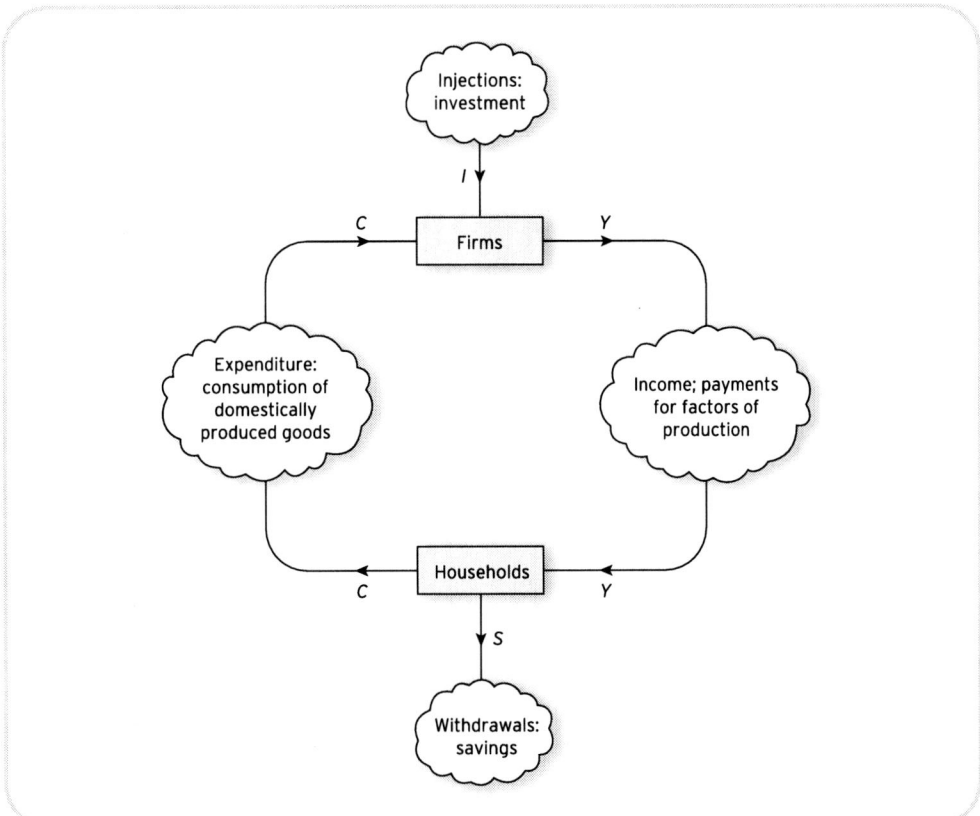

Figure 1.27

for given values of a and b these two equations represent a pair of simultaneous equations for the two unknowns Y and C. In these circumstances C and Y can be regarded as endogenous variables, since their precise values are determined within the model, whereas I^* is fixed outside the model and is exogenous.

Example

Find the equilibrium level of income and consumption if the consumption function is

$$C = 0.6Y + 10$$

and planned investment $I = 12$.

Solution

We know that

$$Y = C + I \qquad \text{(from theory)}$$
$$C = 0.6Y + 10 \quad \text{(given in problem)}$$
$$I = 12 \qquad \text{(given in problem)}$$

If the value of I is substituted into the first equation then

$$Y = C + 12$$

The expression for C can also be substituted to give

$$Y = 0.6Y + 10 + 12$$

$$Y = 0.6Y + 22$$

$$0.4Y = 22 \qquad \text{(subtract } 0.6Y \text{ from both sides)}$$

$$Y = 55 \qquad \text{(divide both sides by 0.4)}$$

The corresponding value of C can be deduced by putting this level of income into the consumption function to get

$$C = 0.6(55) + 10 = 43$$

The equilibrium income can also be found graphically by plotting expenditure against income. In this example the aggregate expenditure, $C + I$, is given by $0.6Y + 22$. This is sketched in Figure 1.28 using the fact that it passes through $(0, 22)$ and $(80, 70)$. Also sketched is the '45° line', so called because it makes an angle of 45° with the horizontal. This line passes through the points $(0, 0)$, $(1, 1)$, ..., $(50, 50)$ and so on. In other words, at any point on this line expenditure and income are in balance. The equilibrium income can therefore be found by inspecting the point of intersection of this line and the aggregate expenditure line, $C + I$. From Figure 1.28 this occurs when $Y = 55$, which is in agreement with the calculated value.

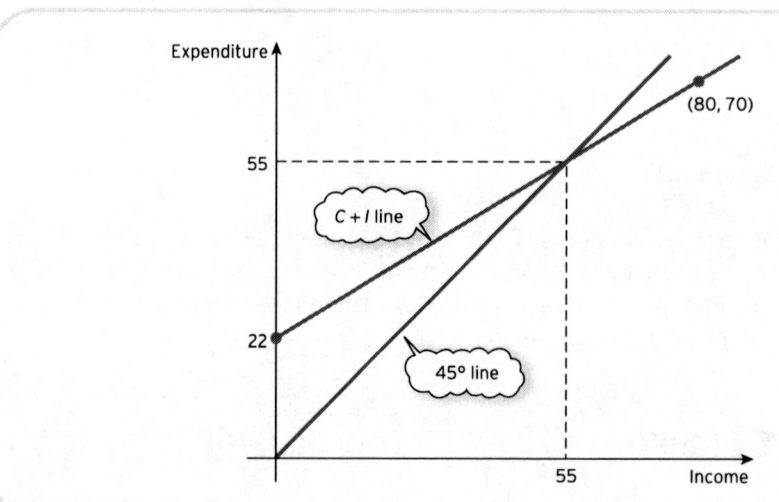

Figure 1.28

Practice Problem

2. Find the equilibrium level of income if the consumption function is

$$C = 0.8Y + 25$$

and planned investment $I = 17$. Calculate the new equilibrium income if planned investment rises by 1 unit.

To make the model more realistic let us now include **government expenditure**, G, and **taxation**, T, in the model. The injections box in Figure 1.27 now includes government expenditure in addition to investment, so

$$Y = C + I + G$$

We assume that planned government expenditure and planned investment are autonomous with fixed values G^* and I^* respectively, so that in equilibrium

$$Y = C + I^* + G^*$$

The withdrawals box in Figure 1.27 now includes taxation. This means that the income that households have to spend on consumer goods is no longer Y but rather $Y - T$ (income less tax), which is called **disposable income**, Y_d. Hence

$$C = aY_d + b$$

with

$$Y_d = Y - T$$

In practice, the tax will either be autonomous ($T = T^*$ for some lump sum T^*) or be a proportion of national income ($T = tY$ for some proportion t), or a combination of both ($T = tY + T^*$).

Example

Given that

$$G = 20$$
$$I = 35$$
$$C = 0.9Y_d + 70$$
$$T = 0.2Y + 25$$

calculate the equilibrium level of national income.

Solution

At first sight this problem looks rather forbidding, particularly since there are so many variables. However, all we have to do is to write down the relevant equations and to substitute systematically one equation into another until only Y is left.

We know that

$Y = C + I + G$	(from theory)	(1)
$G = 20$	(given in problem)	(2)
$I = 35$	(given in problem)	(3)
$C = 0.9Y_d + 70$	(given in problem)	(4)
$T = 0.2Y + 25$	(given in problem)	(5)
$Y_d = Y - T$	(from theory)	(6)

This represents a system of six equations in six unknowns. The obvious thing to do is to put the fixed values of G and I into equation (1) to get

$$Y = C + 35 + 20 = C + 55 \tag{7}$$

This has at least removed G and I, so there are only three more variables (C, Y_d and T) left to eliminate. We can remove T by substituting equation (5) into (6) to get

$$Y_d = Y - (0.2Y + 25)$$
$$= Y - 0.2Y - 25$$
$$= 0.8Y - 25 \tag{8}$$

and then remove Y_d by substituting equation (8) into (4) to get

$$C = 0.9(0.8Y - 25) + 70$$
$$= 0.72Y - 22.5 + 70$$
$$= 0.72Y + 47.5 \tag{9}$$

We can eliminate C by substituting equation (9) into (7) to get

$$Y = C + 55$$
$$= 0.72Y + 47.5 + 55$$
$$= 0.72Y + 102.5$$

Finally, solving for Y gives

$$0.28Y = 102.5 \quad \text{(subtract } 0.72Y \text{ from both sides)}$$
$$Y = 366 \quad \text{(divide both sides by 0.28)}$$

Practice Problem ❓

3. Given that

$$G = 40$$
$$I = 55$$
$$C = 0.8Y_d + 25$$
$$T = 0.1Y + 10$$

calculate the equilibrium level of national income.

To conclude this section we return to the simple two-sector model:

$$Y = C + I$$
$$C = aY + b$$

Previously, the investment, I, was taken to be constant. It is more realistic to assume that planned investment depends on the rate of interest, r. As the interest rate rises, so investment falls and we have a relationship

$$I = cr + d$$

where $c < 0$ and $d > 0$. Unfortunately, this model consists of three equations in the four unknowns Y, C, I and r, so we cannot expect it to determine national income uniquely. The best we can do is to eliminate C and I, say, and to set up an equation relating Y and r. This is most easily understood by an example. Suppose that

$$C = 0.8Y + 100$$
$$I = -20r + 1000$$

We know that the commodity market is in equilibrium when

$$Y = C + I$$

Substitution of the given expressions for C and I into this equation gives

$$Y = (0.8Y + 100) + (-20r + 1000)$$
$$= 0.8Y - 20r + 1100$$

which rearranges as

$$0.2Y + 20r = 1100$$

This equation, relating national income, Y, and interest rate, r, is called the **IS schedule**.

We obviously need some additional information before we can pin down the values of Y and r. This can be done by investigating the equilibrium of the money market. The money market is said to be in equilibrium when the supply of money, M_S, matches the demand for money, M_D: that is, when

$$M_S = M_D$$

There are many ways of measuring the **money supply**. In simple terms it can be thought of as consisting of the notes and coins in circulation, together with money held in bank deposits. The level of M_S is assumed to be controlled by the central bank and is taken to be autonomous, so that

$$M_S = M_S^*$$

for some fixed value M_S^*.

The demand for money comes from three sources: transactions, precautions and speculations. The **transactions demand** is used for the daily exchange of goods and services, whereas the **precautionary demand** is used to fund any emergencies requiring unforeseen expenditure. Both are assumed to be proportional to national income. Consequently, we lump these together and write

$$L_1 = k_1 Y$$

where L_1 denotes the aggregate transaction–precautionary demand and k_1 is a positive constant. The **speculative demand** for money is used as a reserve fund in case individuals or firms decide to invest in alternative assets such as government bonds. In Chapter 3 we show that, as interest rates rise, speculative demand falls. We model this by writing

$$L_2 = k_2 r + k_3$$

where L_2 denotes speculative demand, k_2 is a negative constant and k_3 is a positive constant. The total demand, M_D, is the sum of the transaction–precautionary demand and speculative demand: that is,

$$M_D = L_1 + L_2$$
$$= k_1 Y + k_2 r + k_3$$

If the money market is in equilibrium then

$$M_S = M_D$$

that is,

$$M_S^* = k_1 Y + k_2 r + k_3$$

This equation, relating national income, Y, and interest rate, r, is called the **LM schedule**. If we assume that equilibrium exists in both the commodity and money markets then the IS and LM schedules provide a system of two equations in two unknowns, Y and r. These can easily be solved either by elimination or by graphical methods.

Example

Determine the equilibrium income and interest rate given the following information about the commodity market:

$$C = 0.8Y + 100$$
$$I = -20r + 1000$$

and the money market:

$$M_S = 2375$$
$$L_1 = 0.1Y$$
$$L_2 = -25r + 2000$$

What effect would a decrease in the money supply have on the equilibrium levels of Y and r?

Solution

The IS schedule for these particular consumption and investment functions has already been obtained in the preceding text. It was shown that the commodity market is in equilibrium when

$$0.2Y + 20r = 1100 \tag{1}$$

For the money market we see that the money supply is

$$M_S = 2375$$

and that the total demand for money (that is, the sum of the transaction–precautionary demand, L_1, and the speculative demand, L_2) is

$$M_D = L_1 + L_2 = 0.1Y - 25r + 2000$$

The money market is in equilibrium when

$$M_S = M_D$$

that is,

$$2375 = 0.1Y - 25r + 2000$$

The LM schedule is therefore given by

$$0.1Y - 25r = 375 \tag{2}$$

Equations (1) and (2) constitute a system of two equations for the two unknowns Y and r. The steps described in Section 1.2 can be used to solve this system:

Step 1
Double equation (2) and subtract from equation (1) to get

$$0.2Y + 20r = 1100$$
$$\underline{0.2Y - 50r = 750 \ -}$$
$$70r = 350 \qquad\qquad (3)$$

Step 2
Divide both sides of equation (3) by 70 to get

$$r = 5$$

Step 3
Substitute $r = 5$ into equation (1) to get

$$0.2Y + 100 = 1100$$
$$0.2Y = 1000 \quad \text{(subtract 100 from both sides)}$$
$$Y = 5000 \quad \text{(divide both sides by 0.2)}$$

Step 4
As a check, equation (2) gives

$$0.1(5000) - 25(5) = 375 \quad \checkmark$$

The equilibrium levels of Y and r are therefore 5000 and 5 respectively.

To investigate what happens to Y and r as the money supply falls, we could just take a smaller value of M_S such as 2300 and repeat the calculations. However, it is more instructive to perform the investigation graphically. Figure 1.29 shows the IS and LM curves plotted on the same diagram with r on the horizontal axis and Y on the vertical axis. These lines intersect at (5, 5000), confirming the equilibrium levels of interest rate and income obtained by calculation. Any change in the money supply will obviously have no effect on the IS curve. On the other hand, a change in the money supply does affect the LM curve. To see this, let us return to the general LM schedule

$$k_1Y + k_2r + k_3 = M_S^*$$

and transpose it to express Y in terms of r:

$$k_1Y = -k_2r - k_3 + M_S^* \qquad \text{(subtract } k_2r + k_3 \text{ from both sides)}$$
$$Y = \left(\frac{-k_2}{k_1}\right)r + \frac{-k_3 + M_S^*}{k_1} \quad \text{(divide both sides by } k_1)$$

Expressed in this form, we see that the LM schedule has slope $-k_2/k_1$ and intercept $(-k_3 + M_S^*)/k_1$.

Any decrease in M_S^* therefore decreases the intercept (but not the slope) and the LM curve shifts downwards. This is indicated by the dashed line in Figure 1.29. The point of intersection shifts both downwards and to the right. We deduce that, as the money supply falls, interest rates rise and national income decreases (assuming that both the commodity and money markets remain in equilibrium).

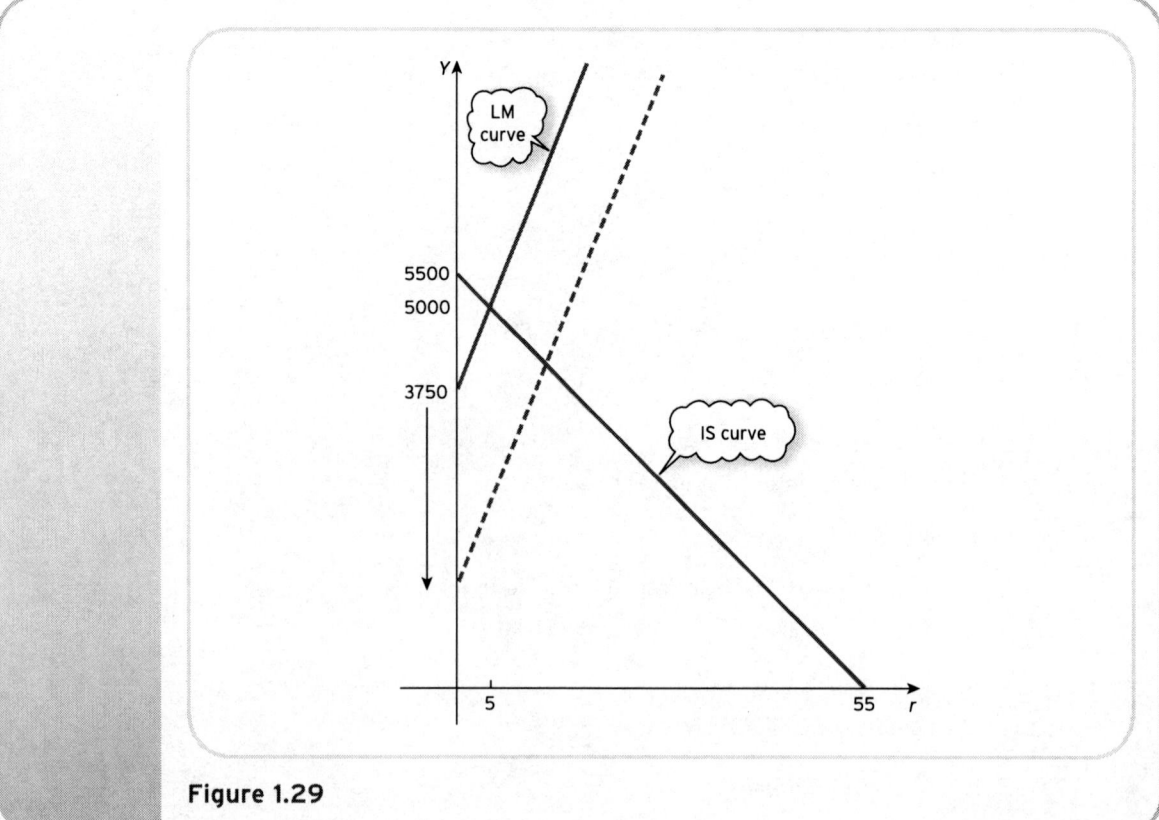

Figure 1.29

Advice

It is possible to produce general formulae for the equilibrium level of income in terms of various parameters used to specify the model. As you might expect, the algebra is a little harder but it does allow for a more general investigation into the effects of varying these parameters. We will return to this in Section 5.3.

Practice Problem

4. Determine the equilibrium income, Y, and interest rate, r, given the following information about the commodity market

$$C = 0.7Y + 85$$

$$I = -50r + 1200$$

and the money market

$$M_S = 500$$

$$L_1 = 0.2Y$$

$$L_2 = -40r + 230$$

Sketch the IS and LM curves on the same diagram. What effect would an increase in the value of autonomous investment have on the equilibrium values of Y and r?

Example   EXCEL

(a) Given the consumption function

$$C = 800 + 0.9Y$$

and the investment function

$$I = 8000 - 800r$$

find an equation for the IS schedule.

(b) Given the money supply

$$M_S = 28\ 500$$

and the demand for money

$$M_D = 0.75Y - 1500r$$

find an equation for the LM schedule.

(c) By plotting the IS–LM diagram, find the equilibrium values of national income, Y, and interest rate, r. If the autonomous investment increases by 1000, what effect will this have on the equilibrium position?

Solution

(a) The IS schedule is given by an equation relating national income, Y, and interest rate, r. In equilibrium, $Y = C + I$. By substituting the equations given in (a) into this equilibrium equation, we eliminate C and I, giving

$$Y = 800 + 0.9Y + 8000 - 800r$$

$$0.1Y = 8800 - 800r \qquad \text{(subtract } 0.9Y \text{ from both sides)}$$

$$Y = 88\ 000 - 8000r \quad \text{(divide both sides by 0.1)}$$

(b) The LM schedule is also given by an equation relating Y and r, but this time it is derived from the equilibrium of the money markets: that is, when $M_S = M_D$. Substituting the equations given in (b) into this equilibrium equation gives

$$0.75Y - 1500r = 28\ 500$$

$$0.75Y = 28\ 500 + 1500r \quad \text{(add } 1500r \text{ to both sides)}$$

$$Y = 38\ 000 + 2000r \quad \text{(divide both sides by 0.75)}$$

(c) To find the equilibrium position, we plot these two lines on a graph using Excel in the usual way. We need to choose values for r and then work out corresponding values for Y. It is most likely that r will lie somewhere between 0 and 10, so values of r are tabulated between 0 and 10, going up in steps of 2. We type the formula

```
=88000-8000*A2
```

in cell B2 and type

```
=38000+2000*A2
```

in cell C2. The values of Y are then generated by clicking and dragging down the columns. Figure 1.30 shows the completed Excel screen.

Placing the cursor at the point of intersection tells us that the lines cross when

$$r = 5\% \quad \text{and} \quad Y = 48\ 000$$

If the autonomous investment increases by 1000, the equation for the IS schedule will change, as the equation for investment now becomes

$$I = 9000 - 800r$$

giving

$$Y = 98\,000 - 8000r$$

The new IS schedule can be plotted on the same graph by adding a column of figures into the spreadsheet, as shown in Figure 1.31.

Notice that the point of intersection has shifted both upwards and to the right. The equilibrium position has now changed, resulting in a rise in interest rates to 6% and an increase in income to 50 000.

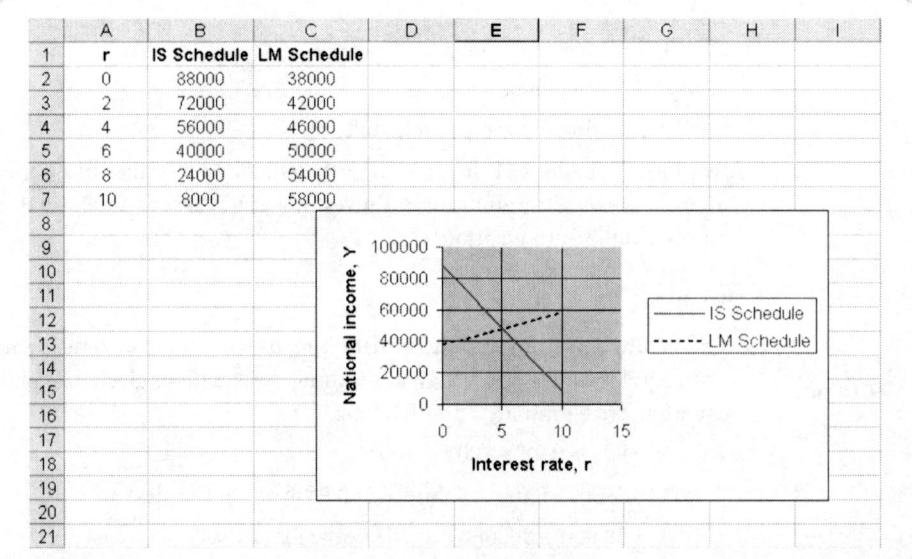

Figure 1.30

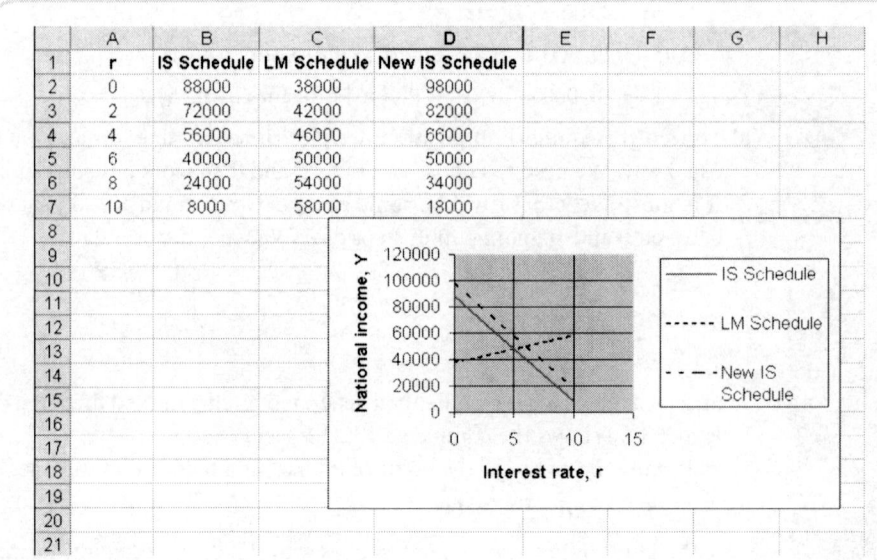

Figure 1.31

Key Terms

Autonomous consumption   The level of consumption when there is no income.

Autonomous savings   The withdrawals from savings when there is no income.

Consumption function   The relationship between national income and consumption.

Disposable income   Household income after the deduction of taxes and the addition of benefits.

Factors of production   The inputs to the production of goods and services: land, capital, labour and raw materials.

Government expenditure   The total amount of money spent by government on defence, education, health, police, etc.

Investment   The creation of output not for immediate consumption.

IS schedule   The equation relating national income and interest rate based on the assumption of equilibrium in the goods market.

LM schedule   The equation relating national income and interest rate based on the assumption of equilibrium in the money market.

Marginal propensity to consume   The fraction of a rise in national income which goes on consumption. It is the slope of the consumption function.

Marginal propensity to save   The fraction of a rise in national income which goes into savings. It is the slope of the savings function.

Money supply   The notes and coins in circulation together with money held in bank deposits.

National income   The flow of money from firms to households.

Precautionary demand for money   Money held in reserve by individuals or firms to fund unforeseen future expenditure.

Speculative demand for money   Money held back by firms or individuals for the purpose of investing in alternative assets, such as government bonds, at some future date.

Taxation   Money paid to government based on an individual's income and wealth (direct taxation) together with money paid by suppliers of goods or services based on expenditure (indirect taxation).

Transactions demand for money   Money used for everyday transactions of goods and services.

Exercise 1.7

1. If the consumption function is given by

    $$C = 0.7Y + 40$$

    state the values of

    (a) autonomous consumption

    (b) marginal propensity to consume.

    Transpose this formula to express Y in terms of C and hence find the value of Y when $C = 110$.

2. Write down expressions for the savings function given that the consumption function is

    (a) $C = 0.9Y + 72$ **(b)** $C = 0.8Y + 100$

3. For a closed economy with no government intervention the consumption function is

$$C = 0.6Y + 30$$

and planned investment is

$$I = 100$$

Calculate the equilibrium level of

(a) national income
(b) consumption
(c) savings.

4. A consumption function is given by $C = aY + b$.
It is known that when $Y = 10$, the value of C is 28, and that when $Y = 30$, the value of C is 44.
By solving a pair of simultaneous equations, find the values of a and b, and deduce that the corresponding savings function is given by

$$S = 0.2Y - 20$$

Determine the equilibrium level of income when planned investment $I = 13$.

5. Given that

$$G = 50$$
$$I = 40$$
$$C = 0.75Y_d + 45$$
$$T = 0.2Y + 80$$

calculate the equilibrium level of national income.

Exercise 1.7*

1. Write down an expression for the savings function, simplified as far as possible, given that the consumption function is

(a) $C = 0.7Y + 30$ **(b)** $C = \dfrac{Y^2 + 500}{Y + 10}$

2. If

$$C = aY + b$$
$$Y = C + I$$
$$I = I*$$

show that

$$Y = \frac{b + I*}{1 - a}$$

and obtain a similar expression for C in terms of a, b and $I*$.

3. Transpose the formula

$$Y = \frac{b + I^*}{1 - a}$$

to express a in terms of Y, b and I.

4. An open economy is in equilibrium when

$$Y = C + I + G + X - M$$

where

Y = national income

C = consumption

I = investment

G = government expenditure

X = exports

M = imports

Determine the equilibrium level of income given that

$C = 0.8Y + 80$

$I = 70$

$G = 130$

$X = 100$

$M = 0.2Y + 50$

5. Given that

consumption,	$C = 0.8Y + 60$
investment,	$I = -30r + 740$
money supply,	$M_S = 4000$
transaction–precautionary demand for money,	$M_S = 0.15Y$
speculative demand for money,	$L_2 = -20r + 3825$

determine the values of national income, Y, and interest rate, r, on the assumption that both the commodity and the money markets are in equilibrium.

6. Consider the national income model

$Y = C + I$

$C = aY_d + 50$

$I = 24$

$Y_d = Y - T$

$T = 20$

Show that the equilibrium level of national income is given by

$$Y = \frac{74 - 20a}{1 - a}$$

Transpose this equation to express a in terms of Y.

Hence, or otherwise, find the value of a for which $Y = 155$ and find the value of C.

7. (**Excel**) Consider the consumption function

$$C = 120 + 0.8Y_d$$

where Y_d is disposable income.

Write down expressions for C, in terms of national income, Y, when there is

(**a**) no tax

(**b**) a lump sum tax of $100

(**c**) a proportional tax in which the proportion is 0.25.

Sketch all three functions on the same diagram, over the range $0 \leq Y \leq 800$, and briefly describe any differences or similarities between them.

Sketch the 45 degree line, $C = Y$, on the same diagram, and hence estimate equilibrium levels of national income in each case.

8. (**Excel**) If the consumption function is

$$C = 0.9Y + 20$$

and planned investment $I = 10$, write down an expression for the aggregate expenditure, $C + I$, in terms of Y.

Draw graphs of aggregate expenditure, and the 45 degree line, on the same diagram, over the range $0 \leq Y \leq 500$. Deduce the equilibrium level of national income.

Describe what happens to the aggregate expenditure line in the case when

(**a**) the marginal propensity to consume falls to 0.8

(**b**) planned investment rises to 15

and find the new equilibrium income in each case.

CHAPTER 2
Non-linear Equations

The main aim of this chapter is to describe the mathematics of non-linear equations. The approach is similar to that of Chapter 1. There are four sections. Section 2.1 should be read before Section 2.2, and Section 2.3 should be read before Section 2.4.

The first section investigates the simplest non-linear equation, known as a quadratic. A quadratic equation can easily be solved either by factorizing it as the product of two linear factors or by using a special formula. You are also shown how to sketch the graphs of quadratic functions. The techniques are illustrated by finding the equilibrium price and quantity for quadratic supply and demand functions.

Section 2.2 introduces additional functions in microeconomics, including revenue and profit. There is very little new material in this section. It mainly consists of applying the ideas of Section 2.1 to sketch graphs of quadratic revenue and profit functions and to find their maximum values.

Finally, the topic of algebra, which we started in Chapter 1, is completed by investigating the rules of indices and logarithms. The basic concepts are covered in Section 2.3. The notation and rules of indices are extremely important and are used frequently in subsequent chapters. Section 2.4 focuses on two specific functions, namely the exponential and natural logarithm functions. If you run into difficulty, or are short of time, then this section could be omitted, particularly if you do not intend to study the next chapter on the mathematics of finance.

SECTION 2.1
Quadratic functions

Objectives

At the end of this section you should be able to:

- Solve a quadratic equation using 'the formula'.
- Solve a quadratic equation given its factorization.
- Sketch the graph of a quadratic function using a table of function values.
- Sketch the graph of a quadratic function by finding the coordinates of the intercepts.
- Solve quadratic inequalities.
- Determine equilibrium price and quantity given a pair of quadratic demand and supply functions.

The first chapter considered the topic of linear mathematics. In particular, we described how to sketch the graph of a linear function and how to solve a linear equation (or system of simultaneous linear equations). It was also pointed out that not all economic functions are of this simple form. In assuming that the demand and supply graphs are straight lines, we are certainly making the mathematical analysis easy, but we may well be sacrificing realism. It may be that the demand and supply graphs are curved and, in these circumstances, it is essential to model them using more complicated functions. The simplest non-linear function is known as a **quadratic** and takes the form

$$f(x) = ax^2 + bx + c$$

for some parameters a, b and c. (In fact, even if the demand function is linear, functions derived from it, such as total revenue and profit, turn out to be quadratic. We investigate these functions in the next section.) For the moment we concentrate on the mathematics of quadratics and show how to sketch graphs of quadratic functions and how to solve quadratic equations.

Consider the elementary equation

$$x^2 - 9 = 0$$

> x^2 is an abbreviation for $x \times x$

It is easy to see that the expression on the left-hand side is a special case of the above with $a = 1$, $b = 0$ and $c = -9$. To solve this equation we add 9 to both sides to get

$$x^2 = 9$$

so we need to find a number, x, which when multiplied by itself produces the value 9. A moment's thought should convince you that there are exactly two numbers that work, namely 3 and −3 because

$$3 \times 3 = 9 \quad \text{and} \quad (-3) \times (-3) = 9$$

These two solutions are called the **square roots** of 9. The symbol $\sqrt{\ }$ is reserved for the positive square root, so in this notation the solutions are $\sqrt{9}$ and $-\sqrt{9}$. These are usually combined and written $\pm\sqrt{9}$. The equation

$$x^2 - 9 = 0$$

is trivial to solve because the number 9 has obvious square roots. In general, it is necessary to use a calculator to evaluate square roots. For example, the equation

$$x^2 - 2 = 0$$

can be written as

$$x^2 = 2$$

and so has solutions $x = \pm\sqrt{2}$. My calculator gives 1.414 213 56 (correct to 8 decimal places) for the square root of 2, so the above equation has solutions

1.414 213 56   and   −1.414 213 56

Example

Solve the following quadratic equations:

(a) $5x^2 - 80 = 0$ **(b)** $x^2 + 64 = 0$ **(c)** $(x + 4)^2 = 81$

Solution

(a) $5x^2 - 80 = 0$

$\quad\quad 5x^2 = 80$ (add 80 to both sides)

$\quad\quad\quad x^2 = 16$ (divide both sides by 5)

$\quad\quad\quad\ x = \pm 4$ (square root both sides)

(b) $x^2 + 64 = 0$

$\quad\quad x^2 = -64$ (subtract 64 from both sides)

This equation does not have a solution because you cannot square a real number and get a negative answer.

(c) $(x + 4)^2 = 81$

$\quad x + 4 = \pm 9$ (square root both sides)

The two solutions are obtained by taking the + and − signs separately. Taking the + sign,

$\quad x + 4 = 9$ so $x = 9 - 4 = 5$

Taking the − sign,

$\quad x + 4 = -9$ so $x = -9 - 4 = -13$

The two solutions are 5 and −13.

Practice Problem

1. Solve the following quadratic equations. (Round your solutions to 2 decimal places if necessary.)

   (a) $x^2 - 100 = 0$ **(b)** $2x^2 - 8 = 0$ **(c)** $x^2 - 3 = 0$ **(d)** $x^2 - 5.72 = 0$

   (e) $x^2 + 1 = 0$ **(f)** $3x^2 + 6.21 = 0$ **(g)** $x^2 = 0$

All of the equations considered in Practice Problem 1 are of the special form

$$ax^2 + c = 0$$

in which the coefficient of x is zero. To solve more general quadratic equations we use a formula that enables the solutions to be calculated in a few lines of working. It can be shown that

$$ax^2 + bx + c = 0$$

has solutions

$$x = \frac{-b \pm \sqrt{(b^2 - 4ac)}}{2a}$$

The following example describes how to use this formula. It also illustrates the fact (which you have already discovered in Practice Problem 1) that a quadratic equation can have two solutions, one solution or no solutions.

Example

Solve the quadratic equations

(a) $2x^2 + 9x + 5 = 0$ **(b)** $x^2 - 4x + 4 = 0$ **(c)** $3x^2 - 5x + 6 = 0$

Solution

(a) For the equation

$$2x^2 + 9x + 5 = 0$$

we have $a = 2$, $b = 9$ and $c = 5$. Substituting these values into the formula

$$x = \frac{-b \pm \sqrt{(b^2 - 4ac)}}{2a}$$

gives

$$x = \frac{-9 \pm \sqrt{(9^2 - 4(2)(5))}}{2(2)}$$

$$= \frac{-9 \pm \sqrt{(81 - 40)}}{4}$$

$$= \frac{-9 \pm \sqrt{41}}{4}$$

The two solutions are obtained by taking the + and − signs separately: that is,

$$\frac{-9+\sqrt{41}}{4} = -0.649 \quad \text{(correct to 3 decimal places)}$$

$$\frac{-9-\sqrt{41}}{4} = -3.851 \quad \text{(correct to 3 decimal places)}$$

It is easy to check that these are solutions by substituting them into the original equation. For example, putting $x = -0.649$ into

$$2x^2 + 9x + 5$$

gives

$$2(-0.649)^2 + 9(-0.649) + 5 = 0.001\ 402$$

which is close to zero, as required. We cannot expect to produce an exact value of zero because we rounded $\sqrt{41}$ to 3 decimal places. You might like to check for yourself that −3.851 is also a solution.

(b) For the equation

$$x^2 - 4x + 4 = 0$$

we have $a = 1$, $b = -4$ and $c = 4$. Substituting these values into the formula

$$x = \frac{-b \pm \sqrt{(b^2 - 4ac)}}{2a}$$

gives

$$x = \frac{-(-4) \pm \sqrt{((-4^2) - 4(1)(4))}}{2(1)}$$

$$= \frac{4 \pm \sqrt{(16 - 16)}}{2}$$

$$= \frac{4 \pm \sqrt{0}}{2}$$

$$= \frac{4 \pm 0}{2}$$

Clearly we get the same answer irrespective of whether we take the + or the − sign here. In other words, this equation has only one solution, $x = 2$. As a check, substitution of $x = 2$ into the original equation gives

$$(2)^2 - 4(2) + 4 = 0$$

(c) For the equation

$$3x^2 - 5x + 6 = 0$$

we have $a = 3$, $b = -5$ and $c = 6$. Substituting these values into the formula

$$x = \frac{-b \pm \sqrt{(b^2 - 4ac)}}{2a}$$

gives

$$x = \frac{-(-5) \pm \sqrt{((-5^2) - 4(3)(6))}}{2(3)}$$

$$= \frac{5 \pm \sqrt{(25 - 72)}}{6}$$

$$= \frac{5 \pm \sqrt{(-47)}}{6}$$

The number under the square root sign is negative and, as you discovered in Practice Problem 1, it is impossible to find the square root of a negative number. We conclude that the quadratic equation

$$3x^2 - 5x + 6 = 0$$

has no solutions.

This example demonstrates the three cases that can occur when solving quadratic equations. The precise number of solutions that an equation can have depends on whether the number under the square root sign is positive, zero or negative. The number $b^2 - 4ac$ is called the **discriminant** because the sign of this number discriminates between the three cases that can occur.

- If $b^2 - 4ac > 0$ then there are two solutions

$$x = \frac{-b + \sqrt{(b^2 - 4ac)}}{2a} \quad \text{and} \quad x = \frac{-b - \sqrt{(b^2 - 4ac)}}{2a}$$

- If $b^2 - 4ac = 0$ then there is one solution

$$x = \frac{-b \pm \sqrt{0}}{2a} = \frac{-b}{2a}$$

- If $b^2 - 4ac < 0$ then there are no solutions because $\sqrt{(b^2 - 4ac)}$ does not exist.

Practice Problem

2. Solve the following quadratic equations (where possible):

(a) $2x^2 - 19x - 10 = 0$ (b) $4x^2 + 12x + 9 = 0$

(c) $x^2 + x + 1 = 0$ (d) $x^2 - 3x + 10 = 2x + 4$

You may be familiar with another method for solving quadratic equations. This is based on the factorization of a quadratic into the product of two linear factors. Section 1.1 described how to multiply out two brackets. One of the examples in that section showed that

$$(x + 1)(x + 2) = x^2 + 3x + 2$$

Consequently, the solutions of the equation

$$x^2 + 3x + 2 = 0$$

are the same as those of

$$(x + 1)(x + 2) = 0$$

Now the only way that two numbers can be multiplied together to produce a value of zero is when (at least) one of the numbers is zero.

if *ab* = 0 then either *a* = 0 or *b* = 0 (or both)

It follows that either

$x + 1 = 0$ with solution $x = -1$

or

$x + 2 = 0$ with solution $x = -2$

The quadratic equation

$$x^2 + 3x + 2 = 0$$

therefore has two solutions, $x = -1$ and $x = -2$.

The difficulty with this approach is that it is impossible, except in very simple cases, to work out the factorization from any given quadratic, so the preferred method is to use the formula. However, if you are lucky enough to be given the factorization, or perhaps clever enough to spot the factorization for yourself, then it does provide a viable alternative.

Example

Write down the solutions to the following quadratic equations:

(a) $x(3x - 4) = 0$ **(b)** $(x - 7)^2 = 0$

Solution

(a) If $x(3x - 4) = 0$ then either $x = 0$ or $3x - 4 = 0$

The first gives the solution $x = 0$ and the second gives $x = {}^4/_3$.

(b) If $(x - 7)(x - 7) = 0$ then either $x - 7 = 0$ or $x - 7 = 0$

Both options lead to the same solution, $x = 7$.

Practice Problem

3. Write down the solutions to the following quadratic equations. (There is no need to multiply out the brackets.)

(a) $(x - 4)(x + 3) = 0$

(b) $x(10 - 2x) = 0$

(c) $(2x - 6)^2 = 0$

One important feature of linear functions is that their graphs are always straight lines. Obviously the intercept and slope vary from function to function, but the shape is always the same. It turns out that a similar property holds for quadratic functions. Now, whenever you are asked to produce a graph of an unfamiliar function, it is often a good idea to tabulate the function, to plot these points on graph paper and to join them up with a smooth curve. The precise number of points to be taken depends on the function but, as a general rule, between 5 and 10 points usually produce a good picture.

Example

Sketch a graph of the square function, $f(x) = x^2$.

Solution

A table of values for the simple square function

$$f(x) = x^2$$

is given by

x	−3	−2	−1	0	1	2	3
$f(x)$	9	4	1	0	1	4	9

The first row of the table gives a selection of 'incoming' numbers, x, while the second row shows the corresponding 'outgoing' numbers, y. Points with coordinates (x, y) are then plotted on graph paper to produce the curve shown in Figure 2.1. For convenience, different scales are used on the x and y axes.

Mathematicians call this curve a **parabola**, whereas economists refer to it as **U-shaped**. Notice that the graph is symmetric about the y axis with a minimum point at the origin; if a mirror is placed along the y axis then the left-hand part is the image of the right-hand part.

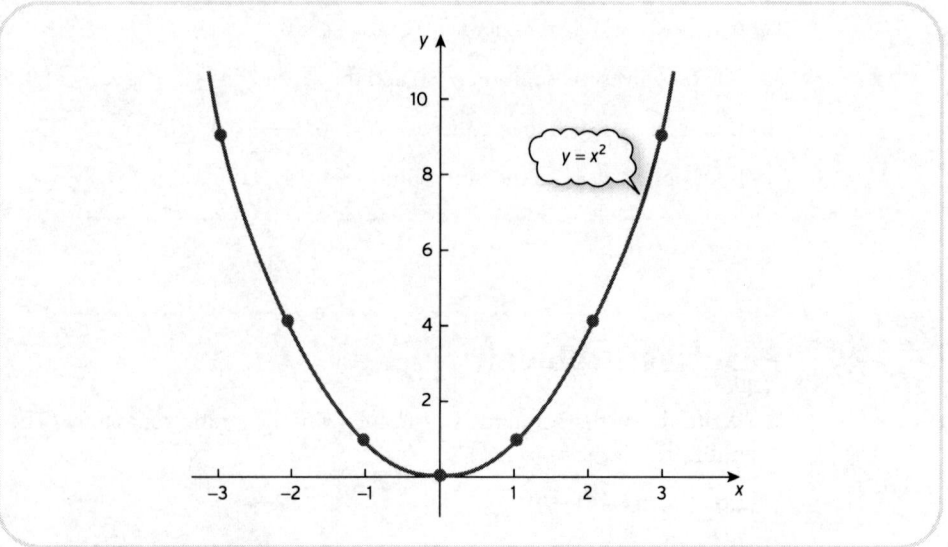

Figure 2.1

Advice

The following problem is designed to give you an opportunity to tabulate and sketch graphs of more general quadratic functions. Please remember that when you substitute numbers into a formula you must use BIDMAS to decide the order of the operations. For example, in part (a) you need to substitute $x = -1$ into $4x^2 - 12x + 5$. You get

$$4(-1)^2 - 12(-1) + 5$$
$$= 4 + 12 + 5$$
$$= 21$$

Note also that when using a calculator you must use brackets when squaring negative numbers. In this case a possible sequence of key presses might be

Practice Problem

4. Complete the following tables of function values and hence sketch a graph of each quadratic function.

(a) $f(x) = 4x^2 - 12x + 5$

x	−1	0	1	2	3	4
$f(x)$						

(b) $f(x) = -x^2 + 6x - 9$

x	0	1	2	3	4	5	6
$f(x)$							

(c) $f(x) = -2x^2 + 4x - 6$

x	−2	−1	0	1	2	3	4
$f(x)$							

The results of Practice Problem 4 suggest that the graph of a quadratic is always parabolic. Furthermore, whenever the coefficient of x^2 is positive, the graph bends upwards and is a 'happy' parabola (U shape). A selection of U-shaped curves is shown in Figure 2.2 (overleaf). Similarly, when the coefficient of x^2 is negative, the graph bends downwards and is a 'sad' parabola (inverted U shape). A selection of inverted U-shaped curves is shown in Figure 2.3 (overleaf).

The task of sketching graphs from a table of function values is extremely tedious, particularly if only a rough sketch is required. It is usually more convenient just to determine a few key points on the curve. The obvious points to find are the intercepts with the coordinate axes, since these enable us to 'tether' the parabola down in the various positions shown in Figures 2.2 and 2.3. The curve crosses the y axis when $x = 0$. Evaluating the function

$$f(x) = ax^2 + bx + c$$

at $x = 0$ gives

$$f(0) = a(0)^2 + b(0) + c = c$$

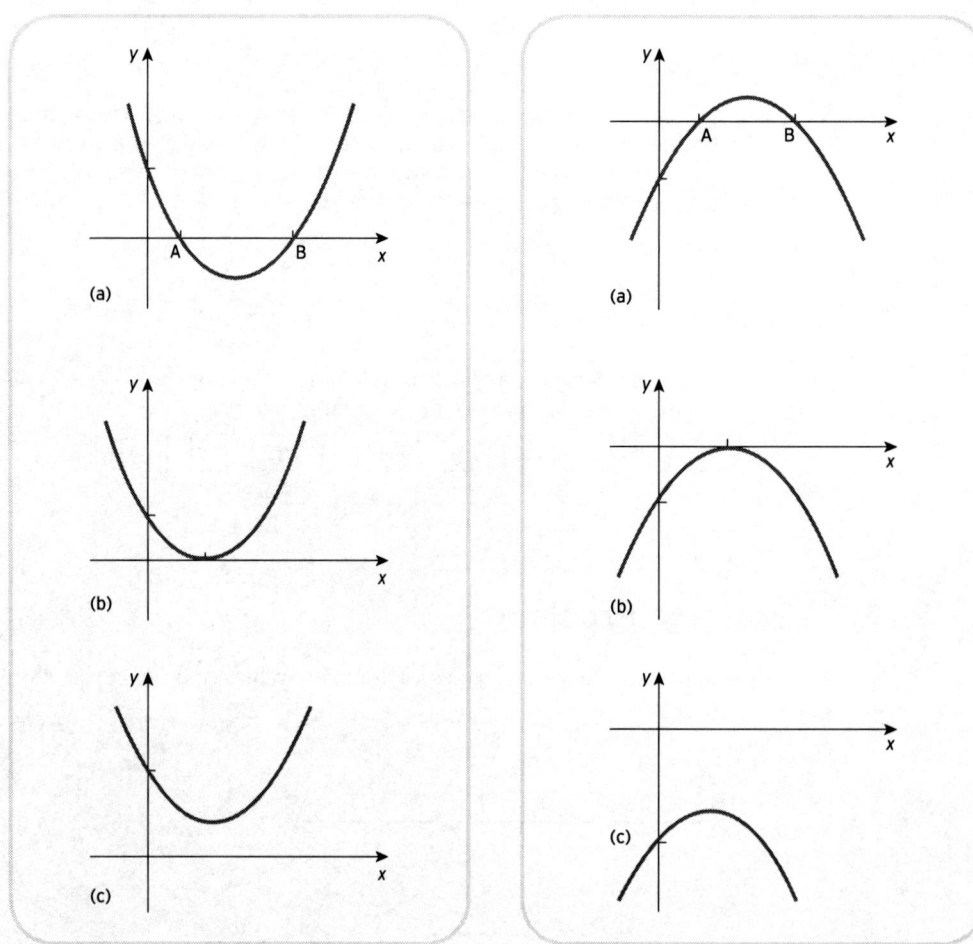

Figure 2.2   **Figure 2.3**

so the constant term determines where the curve cuts the vertical axis (as it did for linear functions). The curve crosses the x axis when $y = 0$ or, equivalently, when $f(x) = 0$, so we need to solve the quadratic equation

$$ax^2 + bx + c = 0$$

This can be done using 'the formula' and the solutions are the points where the graph cuts the horizontal axis. In general, a quadratic equation can have two, one or no solutions and these possibilities are illustrated in cases (a), (b) and (c) respectively in Figures 2.2 and 2.3. In case (a) the curve crosses the x axis at A, turns round and crosses it again at B, so there are two solutions. In case (b) the curve turns round just as it touches the x axis, so there is only one solution. Finally, in case (c) the curve turns round before it has a chance to cross the x axis, so there are no solutions.

The strategy for sketching the graph of a quadratic function

$$f(x) = ax^2 + bx + c$$

may now be stated.

Step 1

Determine the basic shape. The graph has a U shape if $a > 0$, and an inverted U shape if $a < 0$.

Step 2

Determine the y intercept. This is obtained by substituting $x = 0$ into the function, which gives $y = c$.

Step 3

Determine the x intercepts (if any). These are obtained by solving the quadratic equation

$$ax^2 + bx + c = 0$$

This three-step strategy is illustrated in the following example.

Example

Give a rough sketch of the graph of the following quadratic function:

$$f(x) = -x^2 + 8x - 12$$

Solution

For the function

$$f(x) = -x^2 + 8x - 12$$

the strategy is as follows.

Step 1

The coefficient of x^2 is -1, which is negative, so the graph is a 'sad' parabola with an inverted U shape.

Step 2

The constant term is -12, so the graph crosses the vertical axis at $y = -12$.

Step 3

For the quadratic equation

$$-x^2 + 8x - 12 = 0$$

the formula gives

$$x = \frac{-8 \pm \sqrt{(8^2 - 4(-1)(-12))}}{2(-1)} = \frac{-8 \pm \sqrt{(64 - 48)}}{-2}$$

$$= \frac{-8 \pm \sqrt{16}}{-2} = \frac{-8 \pm 4}{-2}$$

so the graph crosses the horizontal axis at

$$x = \frac{-8 + 4}{-2} = 2$$

and

$$x = \frac{-8 - 4}{-2} = 6$$

The information obtained in steps 1–3 is sufficient to produce the sketch shown in Figure 2.4 (overleaf).

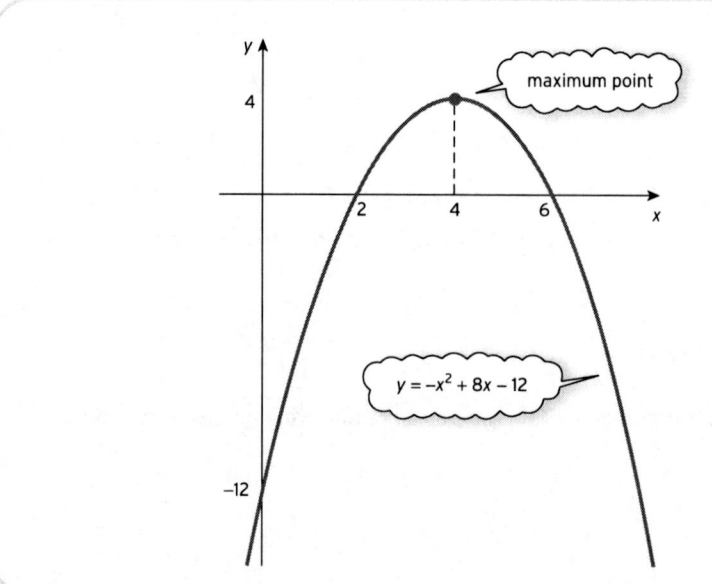

Figure 2.4

In fact, we can go even further in this case and locate the coordinates of the turning point – that is, the maximum point – on the curve. By symmetry, the x coordinate of this point occurs exactly halfway between $x = 2$ and $x = 6$: that is, at

$$x = \tfrac{1}{2}(2 + 6) = 4$$

The corresponding y coordinate is found by substituting $x = 4$ into the function to get

$$f(4) = -(4)^2 + 8(4) - 12 = 4$$

The maximum point on the curve therefore has coordinates $(4, 4)$.

Practice Problem

5. Use the three-step strategy to produce rough graphs of the following quadratic functions:

   (a) $f(x) = 2x^2 - 11x - 6$ **(b)** $f(x) = x^2 - 6x + 9$

One useful by-product of our work on sketching graphs is that it enables us to solve quadratic inequalities with no extra effort.

Example

Solve the following quadratic inequalities

   (a) $-x^2 + 8x - 12 > 0$ **(b)** $-x^2 + 8x - 12 \leq 0$

Solution

The graph of the function $f(x) = -x^2 + 8x - 12$ has already been sketched in Figure 2.4.

The parabola lies above the x axis (that is, the line $y = 0$) between 2 and 6 and is below the x axis outside these values.

(a) The quadratic function takes positive values when the graph is above the x axis so the inequality has solution, $2 < x < 6$. The values of 2 and 6 must be excluded from the solution since we require the quadratic to be strictly greater than zero.

(b) The graph is on or below the x axis at or to the left of 2, and at or to the right of 6, so the complete solution is $x \le 2$ and $x \ge 6$.

Practice Problem

6. Use your answers to Practice Problem 5 to write down the solution to each of the following quadratic inequalities:

(a) $2x^2 - 11x - 6 \le 0$ **(b)** $x^2 - 6x + 9 > 0$

We conclude this section by seeing how to solve a particular problem in microeconomics. In Section 1.5 the concept of market equilibrium was introduced and in each of the problems the supply and demand functions were always given to be linear. The following example shows this to be an unnecessary restriction and indicates that it is almost as easy to manipulate quadratic supply and demand functions.

Example

Given the supply and demand functions

$$P = Q_S^2 + 14Q_S + 22$$
$$P = -Q_D^2 - 10Q_D + 150$$

calculate the equilibrium price and quantity.

Solution

In equilibrium, $Q_S = Q_D$, so if we denote this equilibrium quantity by Q, the supply and demand functions become

$$P = Q^2 + 14Q + 22$$
$$P = -Q^2 - 10Q + 150$$

Hence

$$Q^2 + 14Q + 22 = -Q^2 - 10Q + 150$$

since both sides are equal to P. Collecting like terms gives

$$2Q^2 + 24Q - 128 = 0$$

which is just a quadratic equation in the variable Q. Before using the formula to solve this it is a good idea to divide both sides by 2 to avoid large numbers. This gives

$$Q^2 + 12Q - 64 = 0$$

and so

$$Q = \frac{-12 \pm \sqrt{((12^2) - 4(1)(-64))}}{2(1)}$$

$$= \frac{-12 \pm \sqrt{(400)}}{2}$$

$$= \frac{-12 \pm 20}{2}$$

The quadratic equation has solutions $Q = -16$ and $Q = 4$. Now the solution $Q = -16$ can obviously be ignored because a negative quantity does not make sense. The equilibrium quantity is therefore 4. The equilibrium price can be calculated by substituting this value into either the original supply or demand equation.

From the supply equation,

$$P = 4^2 + 14(4) + 22 = 94$$

As a check, the demand equation gives

$$P = -(4)^2 - 10(4) + 150 = 94 \quad ✓$$

You might be puzzled by the fact that we actually obtain two possible solutions, one of which does not make economic sense. The supply and demand curves are sketched in Figure 2.5. This shows that there are indeed two points of intersection confirming the mathematical solution. However, in economics the quantity and price are both positive, so the functions are only defined in the top right-hand (that is, positive) quadrant. In this region there is just one point of intersection, at (4, 94).

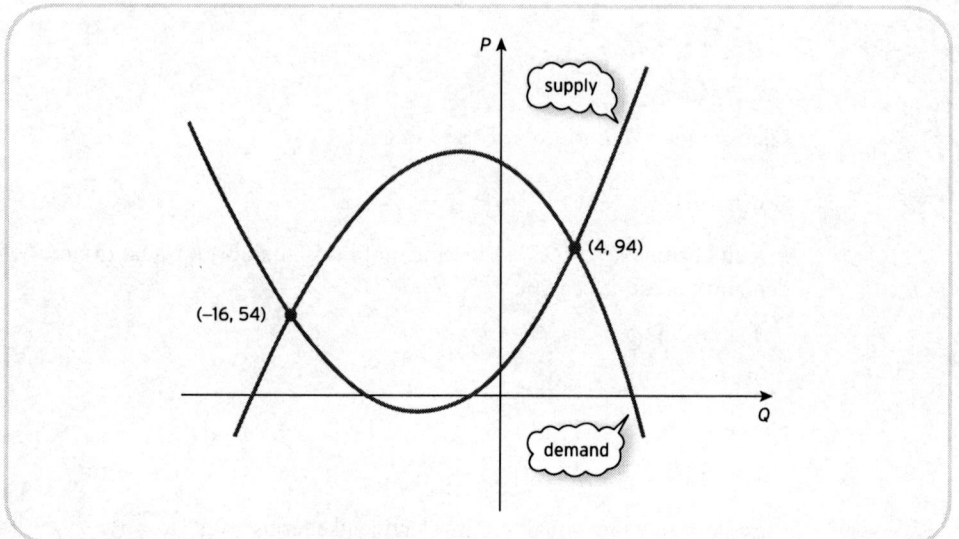

Figure 2.5

Practice Problem

7. Given the supply and demand functions

$$P = 2Q_S^2 + 10Q_S + 10$$
$$P = -Q_D^2 - 5Q_D + 52$$

calculate the equilibrium price and quantity.

Key Terms

Discriminant The number $b^2 - 4ac$, which is used to indicate the number of solutions of the quadratic equation $ax^2 + bx + c = 0$.

Parabola The shape of the graph of a quadratic function.

Quadratic function A function of the form $f(x) = ax^2 + bx + c$ where $a \neq 0$.

Square root A number that when multiplied by itself equals a given number; the solutions of the equation $x^2 = c$ which are written $\pm\sqrt{c}$.

U-shaped curve A term used by economists to describe a curve, such as a parabola, which bends upwards, like the letter U.

Exercise 2.1

1. Solve the following quadratic equations:

   (a) $x^2 = 81$ **(b)** $x^2 = 36$ **(c)** $2x^2 = 8$

   (d) $(x - 1)^2 = 9$ **(e)** $(x + 5)^2 = 16$

2. Write down the solutions of the following equations:

   (a) $(x - 1)(x + 3) = 0$ **(b)** $(2x - 1)(x + 10) = 0$ **(c)** $x(x + 5) = 0$

   (d) $(3x + 5)(4x - 9) = 0$ **(e)** $(5 - 4x)(x - 5) = 0$

3. Use 'the formula' to solve the following quadratic equations. (Round your answers to 2 decimal places.)

   (a) $x^2 - 5x + 2 = 0$ **(b)** $2x^2 + 5x + 1 = 0$ **(c)** $-3x^2 + 7x + 2 = 0$

   (d) $x^2 - 3x - 1 = 0$ **(e)** $2x^2 + 8x + 8 = 0$ **(f)** $x^2 - 6x + 10 = 0$

4. Solve the equation $f(x) = 0$ for each of the following quadratic functions:

   (a) $f(x) = x^2 - 16$ **(b)** $f(x) = x(100 - x)$ **(c)** $f(x) = -x^2 + 22x - 85$

   (d) $f(x) = x^2 - 18x + 81$ **(e)** $f(x) = 2x^2 + 4x + 3$

5. Sketch the graphs of the quadratic functions given in Question 4.

6. Use the results of Question 5 to solve each of the following inequalities:

(a) $x^2 - 16 \geq 0$ (b) $x(100 - x) > 0$ (c) $-x^2 + 22x - 85 \geq 0$

(d) $x^2 - 18x + 81 \leq 0$ (e) $2x^2 + 4x + 3 > 0$

7. Given the quadratic supply and demand functions

$$P = Q_S^2 + 2Q_S + 12$$
$$P = -Q_D^2 - 4Q_D + 68$$

determine the equilibrium price and quantity.

8. Given the supply and demand functions

$$P = Q_S^2 + 2Q_S + 7$$
$$P = -Q_D + 25$$

determine the equilibrium price and quantity.

Exercise 2.1*

1. Solve the following quadratic equations:

(a) $x^2 = 169$ (b) $(x - 5)^2 = 64$ (c) $(2x - 7)^2 = 121$

2. Find the solutions (in terms of d) of the quadratic equation

$$x^2 + 6dx - 7d^2 = 0$$

3. Write down the solutions of the following equations:

(a) $(x - 3)(x + 8) = 0$ (b) $(3x - 2)(2x + 9) = 0$ (c) $x(4x - 3) = 0$

(d) $(6x - 1)^2 = 0$ (e) $(x - 2)(x + 1)(4 - x) = 0$

4. Solve the following quadratic equations, rounding your answers to 2 decimal places, if necessary:

(a) $x^2 - 15x + 56 = 0$ (b) $2x^2 - 5x + 1 = 0$ (c) $4x^2 - 36 = 0$

(d) $x^2 - 14x + 49 = 0$ (e) $3x^2 + 4x + 7 = 0$ (f) $x^2 - 13x + 200 = 16x + 10$

5. Solve the following inequalities:

(a) $x^2 \geq 64$ (b) $x^2 - 10x + 9 \leq 0$ (c) $2x^2 + 15x + 7 < 0$

(d) $-3x^2 + 2x + 5 \geq 0$ (e) $x^2 + 2x + 1 \leq 0$

6. One solution of the quadratic equation

$$x^2 - 8x + c = 0$$

is known to be $x = 2$. Find the second solution.

7. Find the value of k so that the equation

$x^2 - 10x + 2k = 8x - k$

has exactly one root.

8. Given the supply and demand functions

$P = Q_S^2 + 10Q_S + 30$

$P = -Q_D^2 - 8Q_D + 200$

calculate the equilibrium price, correct to 2 decimal places.

9. A pottery can make B bowls and P plates in a week according to the relation

$2B^2 + 5B + 25P = 525$

(a) If it makes 5 bowls, how many plates can it make in a week?

(b) What is the maximum number of bowls that it can produce in a week?

10. Given the supply and demand functions

$Q_S = (P + 8)\sqrt{P + 20}$

$Q_D = \dfrac{460 - 12P - 3P^2}{\sqrt{P + 20}}$

calculate the equilibrium price and quantity.

SECTION 2.2

Revenue, cost and profit

Objectives

At the end of this section you should be able to:

● Sketch the graphs of the total revenue, total cost, average cost and profit functions.

● Find the level of output that maximizes total revenue.

● Find the level of output that maximizes profit.

● Find the break-even levels of output.

The main aim of this section is to investigate one particular function in economics, namely profit. By making reasonable simplifying assumptions, the profit function is shown to be quadratic and so the methods developed in Section 2.1 can be used to analyse its properties. We describe how to find the levels of output required for a firm to break even and to maximize profit. The **profit** function is denoted by the Greek letter π (pi, pronounced 'pie') and is defined to be the difference between total revenue, TR, and total cost, TC: that is,

$$\pi = \text{TR} - \text{TC}$$

This definition is entirely sensible because TR is the amount of money received by the firm from the sale of its goods and TC is the amount of money that the firm has to spend to produce these goods. We begin by considering the total revenue and total cost functions in turn.

The **total revenue** received from the sale of Q goods at price P is given by

$$\text{TR} = PQ$$

For example, if the price of each good is $70 and the firm sells 300 then the revenue is

$$\$70 \times 300 = \$21\ 000$$

Given any particular demand function, expressing P in terms of Q, it is a simple matter to obtain a formula for TR solely in terms of Q. A graph of TR against Q can then be sketched.

Example

Given the demand function

$$P = 100 - 2Q$$

express TR as a function of Q and hence sketch its graph.

(a) For what values of Q is TR zero?

(b) What is the maximum value of TR?

Solution

Total revenue is defined by

$$\text{TR} = PQ$$

and, since $P = 100 - 2Q$, we have

$$\text{TR} = (100 - 2Q)Q = 100Q - 2Q^2$$

This function is quadratic and so its graph can be sketched using the strategy described in Section 2.1.

Step 1
The coefficient of Q^2 is negative, so the graph has an inverted U shape.

Step 2
The constant term is zero, so the graph crosses the TR axis at the origin.

Step 3
To find where the curve crosses the horizontal axis, we could use 'the formula'. However, this is not necessary, since it follows immediately from the factorization

$$\text{TR} = (100 - 2Q)Q$$

that TR = 0 when either $100 - 2Q = 0$ or $Q = 0$. In other words, the quadratic equation has two solutions, $Q = 0$ and $Q = 50$.

The total revenue curve is shown in Figure 2.6.

- From Figure 2.6 the total revenue is zero when $Q = 0$ and $Q = 50$.

- By symmetry, the parabola reaches its maximum halfway between 0 and 50, that is at $Q = 25$. The corresponding total revenue is given by

$$\text{TR} = 100(25) - 2(25)^2 = 1250$$

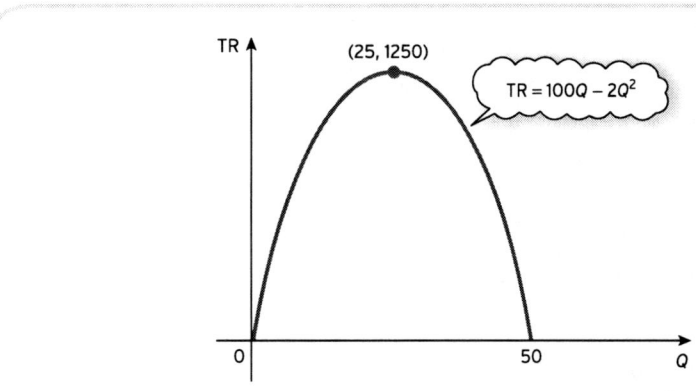

Figure 2.6

Practice Problem

1. Given the demand function

$$P = 1000 - Q$$

express TR as a function of Q and hence sketch a graph of TR against Q. What value of Q maximizes total revenue and what is the corresponding price?

In general, given the linear demand function

$$P = aQ + b \quad (a < 0, b > 0)$$

the total revenue function is

$$\begin{aligned} TR = PQ &= (aQ + b)Q \\ &= aQ^2 + bQ \end{aligned}$$

This function is quadratic in Q and, since $a < 0$, the TR curve has an inverted U shape. Moreover, since the constant term is zero, the curve always intersects the vertical axis at the origin. This fact should come as no surprise to you; if no goods are sold, the revenue must be zero.

We now turn our attention to the **total cost** function, TC, which relates the production costs to the level of output, Q. As the quantity produced rises, the corresponding cost also rises, so the TC function is increasing. However, in the short run, some of these costs are fixed. **Fixed costs**, FC, include the cost of land, equipment, rent and possibly skilled labour. Obviously, in the long run all costs are variable, but these particular costs take time to vary, so can be thought of as fixed in the short run. **Variable costs**, on the other hand, vary with output and include the cost of raw materials, components, energy and unskilled labour. If VC denotes the variable cost per unit of output then the total variable cost, TVC, in producing Q goods is given by

$$TVC = (VC)Q$$

The total cost is the sum of the contributions from the fixed and variable costs, so is given by

$$TC = FC + (VC)Q$$

Now although this is an important economic function, it does not always convey the information necessary to compare individual firms. For example, suppose that an international car company operates two plants, one in the USA and one in Europe, and suppose that the total annual costs are known to be $200 million and $45 million respectively. Which of these two plants is regarded as the more efficient? Unfortunately, unless we also know the total number of cars produced it is impossible to make any judgement. The significant function here is not the total cost, but rather the average cost per car. If the plants in the USA and Europe manufacture 80 000 and 15 000 cars, respectively, their corresponding average costs are

$$\frac{200\ 000\ 000}{80\ 000} = 2500$$

and

$$\frac{45\ 000\ 000}{15\ 000} = 3000$$

On the basis of these figures, the plant in the USA appears to be the more efficient. In practice, other factors would need to be taken into account before deciding to increase or decrease the scale of operation in either country.

In general, the **average cost** function, AC, is obtained by dividing the total cost by output, so that

$$\begin{aligned} AC = \frac{TC}{Q} &= \frac{FC + (VC)Q}{Q} \\ &= \frac{FC}{Q} + \frac{(VC)Q}{Q} \\ &= \frac{FC}{Q} + VC \end{aligned}$$

Example

Given that fixed costs are 1000 and that variable costs are 4 per unit, express TC and AC as functions of Q. Hence sketch their graphs.

Solution

We are given that FC = 1000 and VC = 4, so

$$TC = 1000 + 4Q$$

and

$$AC = \frac{TC}{Q} = \frac{1000 + 4Q}{Q}$$

$$= \frac{1000}{Q} + 4$$

The graph of the total cost function is easily sketched. It is a straight line with intercept 1000 and slope 4. It is sketched in Figure 2.7. The average cost function is of a form that we have not met before, so we have no prior knowledge about its basic shape. Under these circumstances it is useful to tabulate the function. The tabulated values are then plotted on graph paper and a smooth curve obtained by joining the points together. One particular table of function values is

Q	100	250	500	1000	2000
AC	14	8	6	5	4.5

These values are readily checked. For instance, when $Q = 100$

$$AC = \frac{1000}{100} + 4 = 10 + 4 = 14$$

A graph of the average cost function, based on this table, is sketched in Figure 2.8 (overleaf). This curve is known as a **rectangular hyperbola** and is sometimes referred to by economists as being **L-shaped**.

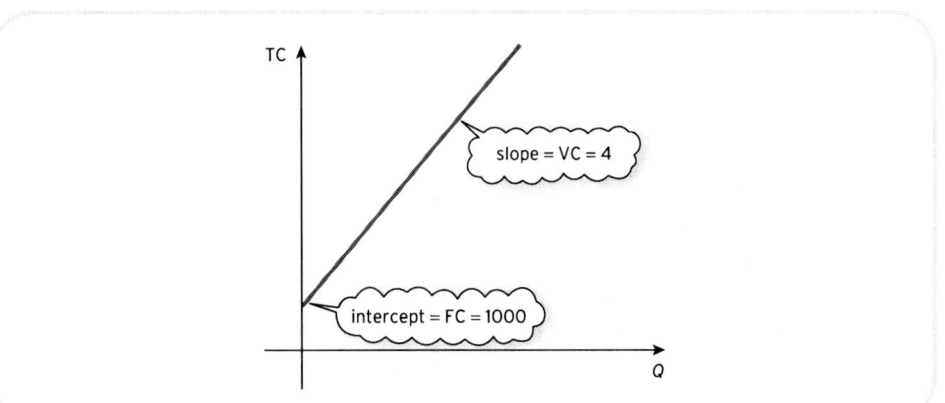

Figure 2.7

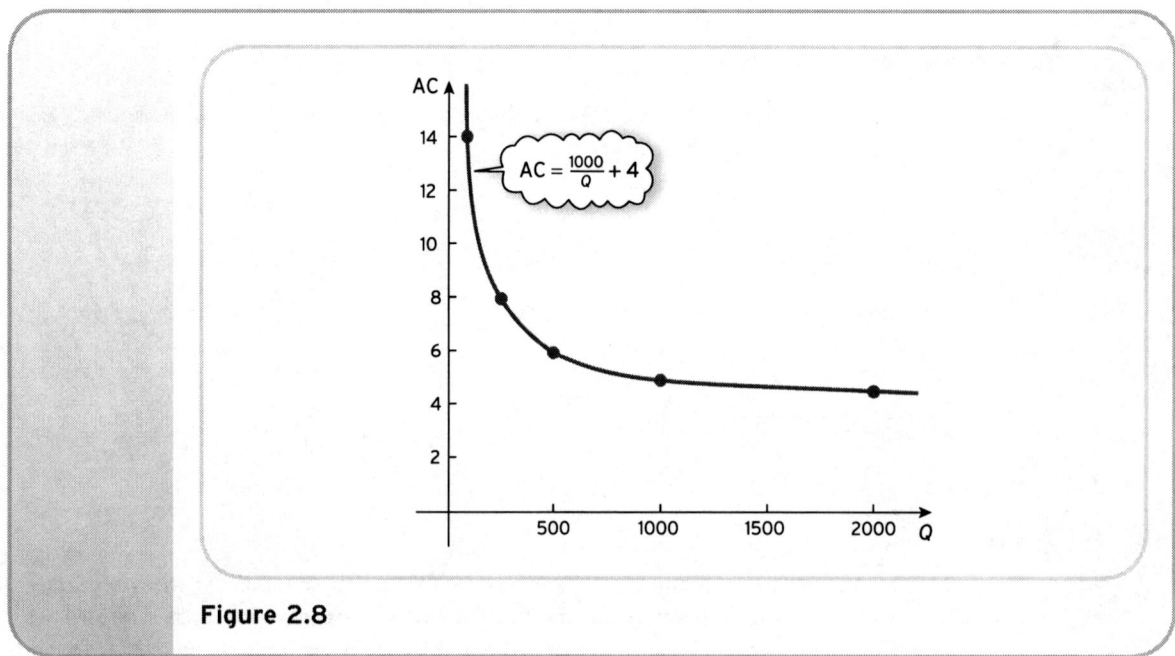

Figure 2.8

Practice Problem

2. Given that fixed costs are 100 and that variable costs are 2 per unit, express TC and AC as functions of Q. Hence sketch their graphs.

In general, whenever the variable cost, VC, is a constant the total cost function,

$$TC = FC + (VC)Q$$

is linear. The intercept is FC and the slope is VC. For the average cost function

$$AC = \frac{FC}{Q} + VC$$

note that if Q is small, then FC/Q is large, so the graph bends sharply upwards as Q approaches zero. As Q increases, FC/Q decreases and eventually tails off to zero for large values of Q. The AC curve therefore flattens off and approaches VC as Q gets larger and larger. This phenomenon is hardly surprising, since the fixed costs are shared between more and more goods, so have little effect on AC for large Q. The graph of AC therefore has the basic L shape shown in Figure 2.9. This discussion assumes that VC is a constant. In practice, this may not be the case and VC might depend on Q. The TC graph is then no longer linear and the AC graph becomes U-shaped rather than L-shaped. An example of this can be found in Question 5 in Exercise 2.2 at the end of this section.

Figure 2.10 shows typical TR and TC graphs sketched on the same diagram. These are drawn on the assumption that the demand function is linear (which leads to a quadratic total revenue function) and that the variable costs are constant (which leads to a linear total cost function). The horizontal axis represents quantity, Q. Strictly speaking the label Q means different things for the two functions. For the revenue function, Q denotes the quantity of goods actually sold, whereas for the cost function it denotes the quantity produced. In sketching both graphs on

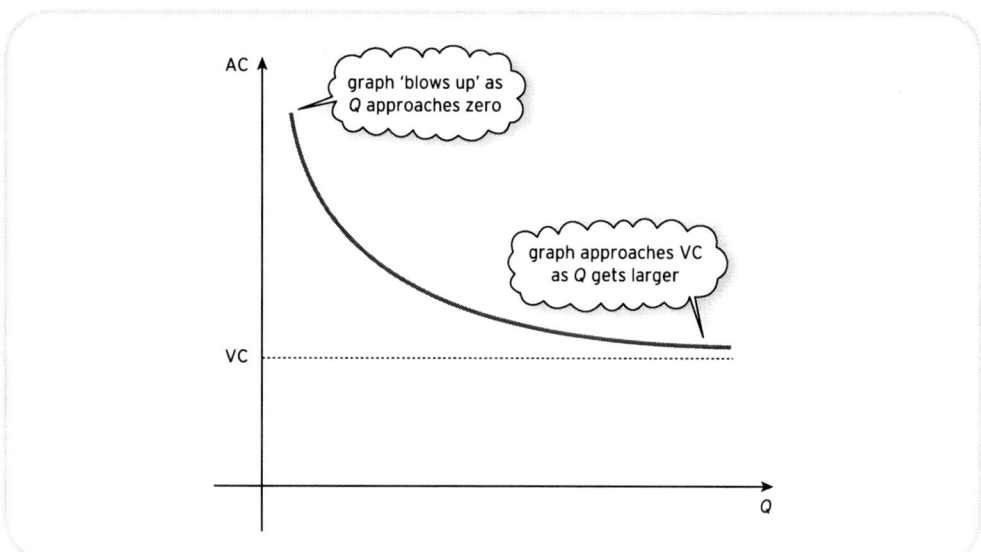

Figure 2.9

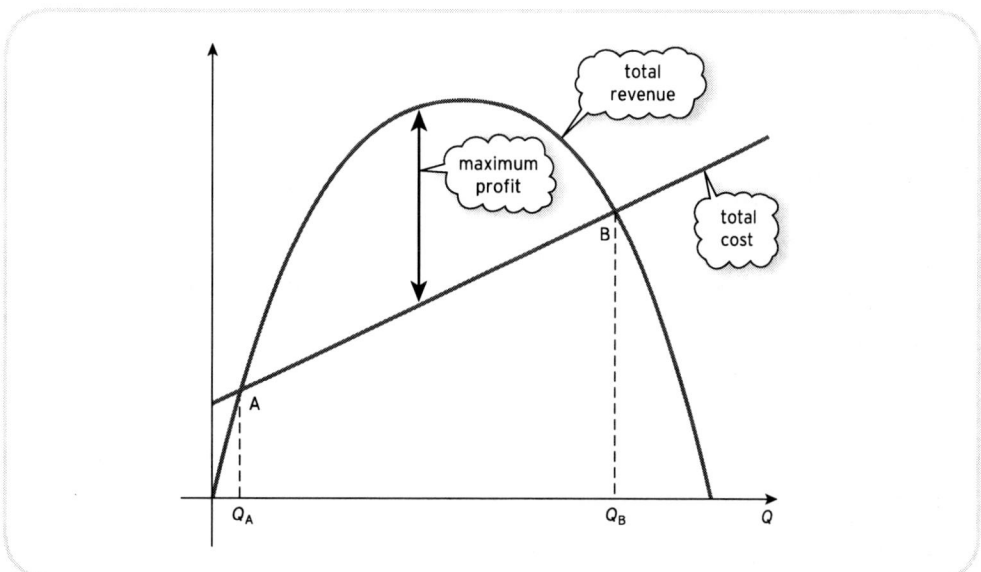

Figure 2.10

the same diagram we are implicitly assuming that these two values are the same and that the firm sells all of the goods that it produces.

The two curves intersect at precisely two points, A and B, corresponding to output levels Q_A and Q_B. At these points the cost and revenue are equal and the firm breaks even. If $Q < Q_A$ or $Q > Q_B$ then the TC curve lies above that of TR, so cost exceeds revenue. For these levels of output the firm makes a loss. If $Q_A < Q < Q_B$ then revenue exceeds cost and the firm makes a profit that is equal to the vertical distance between the revenue and cost curves. The maximum profit occurs where the gap between them is largest. The easiest way of calculating maximum profit is to obtain a formula for profit directly in terms of Q using the defining equation

$$\pi = TR - TC$$

Example

If fixed costs are 4, variable costs per unit are 1 and the demand function is

$$P = 10 - 2Q$$

obtain an expression for π in terms of Q and hence sketch a graph of π against Q.

(a) For what values of Q does the firm break even?

(b) What is the maximum profit?

Solution

We begin by obtaining expressions for the total cost and total revenue. For this problem, $FC = 4$ and $VC = 1$, so

$$TC = FC + (VC)Q = 4 + Q$$

The given demand function is $P = 10 - 2Q$
so $TR = PQ = (10 - 2Q)Q = 10Q - 2Q^2$
Hence the profit is given by

$$\pi = TR - TC$$
$$= (10 - 2Q^2) - (4 + Q)$$
$$= 10Q - 2Q^2 - 4 - Q$$
$$= -2Q^2 + 9Q - 4$$

To sketch a graph of the profit function we follow the strategy described in Section 2.1.

Step 1
The coefficient of Q^2 is negative, so the graph has an inverted U shape.

Step 2
The constant term is -4, so the graph crosses the vertical axis when $\pi = -4$.

Step 3
The graph crosses the horizontal axis when $\pi = 0$, so we need to solve the quadratic equation

$$-2Q^2 + 9Q - 4 = 0$$

This can be done using 'the formula' to get

$$Q = \frac{-9 \pm \sqrt{81 - 32}}{2(-2)} = \frac{-9 \pm 7}{-4}$$

so $Q = 0.5$ and $Q = 4$.
   The profit curve is sketched in Figure 2.11.

(a) From Figure 2.11 we see that profit is zero when $Q = 0.5$ and $Q = 4$.

(b) By symmetry, the parabola reaches its maximum halfway between 0.5 and 4: that is, at

$$Q = \tfrac{1}{2}(0.5 + 4) = 2.25$$

The corresponding profit is given by

$$\pi = -2(2.25)^2 + 9(2.25) - 4 = 6.125$$

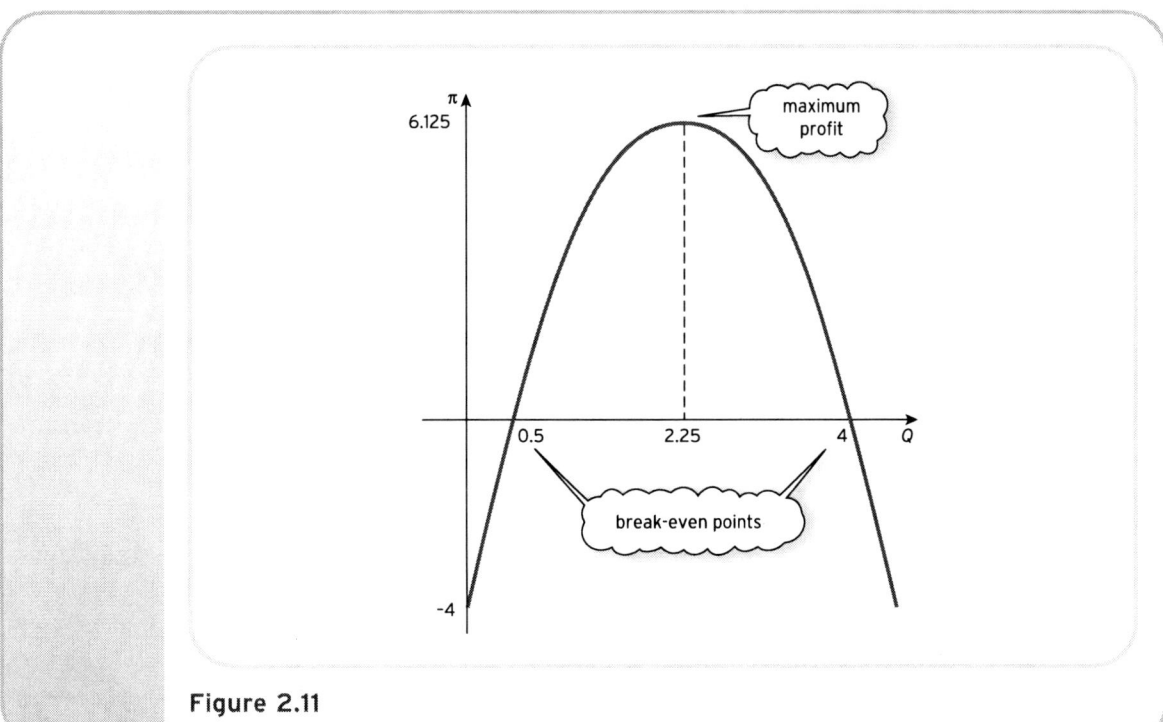

Figure 2.11

Advice

It is important to notice the use of brackets in the previous derivation of π. A common student mistake is to forget to include the brackets and just to write down

$$\pi = \text{TR} - \text{TC}$$
$$= 10Q - 2Q^2 - 4 + Q$$
$$= -2Q^2 + 11Q - 4$$

This cannot be right, since the whole of the total cost needs to be subtracted from the total revenue, not just the fixed costs. You might be surprised to learn that many economics students make this sort of blunder, particularly under examination conditions. I hope that if you have carefully worked through Section 1.1 on basic algebra then you will not fall into this category.

Practice Problem ❷

3. If fixed costs are 25, variable costs per unit are 2 and the demand function is

$$P = 20 - Q$$

obtain an expression for π in terms of Q and hence sketch its graph.

(a) Find the levels of output which give a profit of 31.

(b) Find the maximum profit and the value of Q at which it is achieved.

Example   EXCEL

A firm's profit function is given by

$$\pi = -Q^3 + 21Q - 18$$

Draw a graph of π against Q, over the range $0 \leq Q \leq 5$, and hence estimate

(a) the interval in which $\pi \geq 0$

(b) the maximum profit

Solution

Figure 2.12 shows the tabulated values of Q which have been entered in cells A4 to A8. In the second column, cell B4 contains the formula to work out the corresponding values of π:

    =-(A4)^3+21*A4-18

This has been replicated down the profit column by clicking and dragging in the usual way.

It can be seen that the maximum profit occurs somewhere between 2 and 4, so it makes sense to add a few extra entries in here so that the graph can be plotted more accurately in this region.

Initially, inserting extra rows for $Q = 2.5$ and 3.5 shows that the maximum occurs between 2.5 and 3. Inserting a few more rows enables us to pinpoint the maximum profit value more accurately, as shown in Figure 2.13. At this stage, we can be confident that the maximum profit occurs between $Q = 2.6$ and $Q = 2.7$. The graph of the firm's profit function based on this table of values can now be drawn using the Chart Wizard, as shown in Figure 2.13.

This diagram shows that

(a) the firm makes a profit for values of Q between 0.9 and 4.1

(b) the maximum profit is about 19.

	A	B
1	**Profit function**	
2		
3	**Q**	**Profit**
4	0	-18
5	1	2
6	2	16
7	3	18
8	4	2
9	5	-38
10		

Figure 2.12

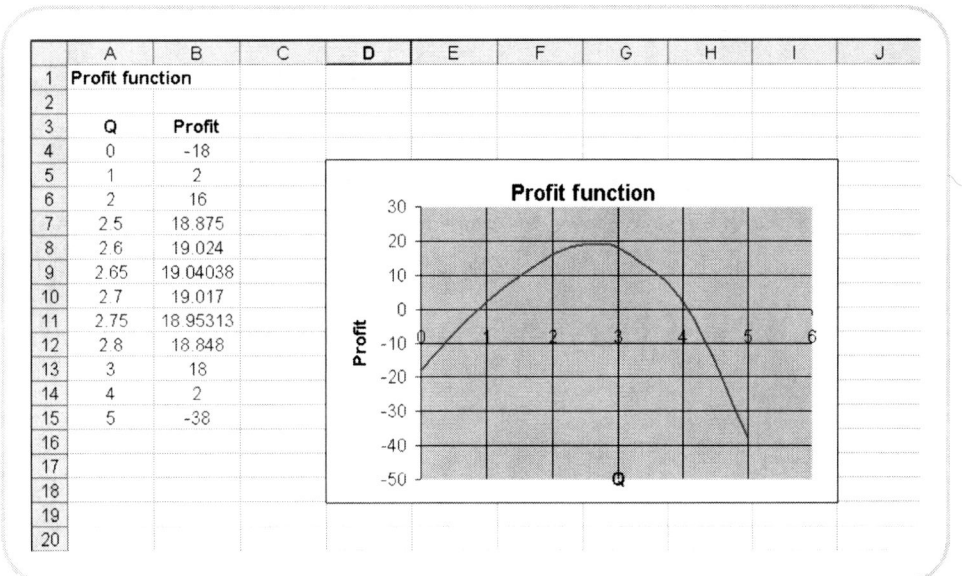

Figure 2.13

Key Terms

Average cost   Total cost per unit of output: AC = TC/Q.

Fixed costs   Total costs that are independent of output.

L-shaped curve   A term used by economists to describe the graph of a function, such as $f(x) = a + \dfrac{b}{x}$, which bends roughly like the letter L.

Profit   Total revenue minus total cost: $\pi = TR - TC$

Rectangular hyperbola   A term used by mathematicians to describe the graph of a function, such as $f(x) = a + \dfrac{b}{x}$, which is a hyperbola with horizontal and vertical asymptotes.

Total cost   The sum of the total variable and fixed costs: TC = TVC + FC.

Total revenue   A firm's total earnings from the sales of a good: TR = PQ.

Variable costs   Total costs that change according to the amount of output produced.

Exercise 2.2

1. **(a)** If the demand function of a good is given by

   $$P = 80 - 3Q$$

   find the price when $Q = 10$, and deduce the total revenue.

   (b) If fixed costs are 100 and variable costs are 5 per unit find the total cost when $Q = 10$.

   (c) Use your answers to parts (a) and (b) to work out the corresponding profit.

2. Given the following demand functions, express TR as a function of Q and hence sketch the graphs of TR against Q:

   (a) $P = 4$ **(b)** $P = 7/Q$ **(c)** $P = 10 - 4Q$

3. Given the following total revenue functions, find the corresponding demand functions:

   (a) $TR = 50Q - 4Q^2$ **(b)** $TR = 10$

4. Given that fixed costs are 500 and that variable costs are 10 per unit, express TC and AC as functions of Q. Hence sketch their graphs.

5. Given that fixed costs are 1 and that variable costs are $Q + 1$ per unit, express TC and AC as functions of Q. Hence sketch their graphs.

6. Find an expression for the profit function given the demand function

   $$2Q + P = 25$$

   and the average cost function

   $$AC = \frac{32}{Q} + 5$$

   Find the values of Q for which the firm

   (a) breaks even

   (b) makes a loss of 432 units

   (c) maximizes profit.

7. Sketch, on the same diagram, graphs of the total revenue and total cost functions,

   $$TR = -2Q^2 + 14Q$$
   $$TC = 2Q + 10$$

   (1) Use your graphs to estimate the values of Q for which the firm

   (a) breaks even

   (b) maximizes profit.

   (2) Confirm your answer to part (1) using algebra.

8. The demand function for a firm's product is given by $P = 60 - Q$.
Fixed costs are 100, and the variable costs per good are $Q + 6$.

(a) Write down an expression for total revenue, TR, in terms of Q and sketch a graph of TR against Q, indicating clearly the intercepts with the coordinate axes.

(b) Write down an expression for total costs, TC, in terms of Q and deduce that the average cost function is given by

$$AC = Q + 6 + \frac{100}{Q}$$

Copy and complete the following table of function values:

Q	2	5	10	15	20
AC	58				

Draw an accurate graph of AC against Q and state the value of Q that minimizes average cost.

(c) Show that the profit function is given by

$$\pi = 2(2 - Q)(Q - 25)$$

State the values of Q for which the firm breaks even and determine the maximum profit.

EXERCISE 2.2*

1. If fixed costs are 30, variable costs per unit are $Q + 3$, and the demand function is

$$P + 2Q = 50$$

show that the associated profit function is

$$\pi = -3Q^2 + 47Q - 30.$$

Find the break-even values of Q and deduce the maximum profit.

2. The profit function of a firm is of the form

$$\pi = aQ^2 + bQ + c$$

If it is known that $\pi = 9$, 34 and 19 when $Q = 1$, 2 and 3 respectively, write down a set of three simultaneous equations for the three unknowns, a, b and c. Solve this system to find a, b and c. Hence find the profit when $Q = 4$.

3. A firm's average cost function is given by

$$AC = \frac{800}{Q} + 2Q + 18$$

(a) Find, to the nearest whole number, the value of Q at the lowest point on the graph of AC plotted against Q, in the interval, $0 \le Q \le 30$.

(b) State the value of the fixed costs.

4. If the demand equation is $aP + bQ = c$, fixed costs are d, and variable costs are e per unit, find expressions, in terms of Q, for each of the following economic functions:

(a) total revenue   **(b)** total cost   **(c)** average cost   **(d)** profit

5. The Ennerdale Bank charges its customers for every withdrawal: $0.50 per cheque and $0.25 for each cash machine withdrawal. The North Borsetshire Bank charges customers a fixed annual charge of $15 and each debit (cheque or machine) costs a further $0.30. You may assume that there are no other withdrawals, that the account never goes overdrawn and that any interest due is negligible.

(a) The proportion of withdrawals that are through cheques is a and the total number of withdrawals made during the year is N. If the cost of operating the two accounts is the same, show that

$$a = \frac{1}{5} + \frac{60}{N}$$

Sketch the graph of this relationship.

(b) What advice can you offer new customers if at least 60% of the customer's annual withdrawals are from cash machines?

6. (Excel) Tabulate values of the total cost function

$$TC = 0.01Q^3 + 0.5Q^2 + Q + 1000$$

when Q is $0, 2, 4, \ldots, 30$ and hence plot a graph of this function on the range $0 \le Q \le 30$. Use this graph to estimate the value of Q for which $TC = 1400$.

7. (Excel) A firm's total revenue and total cost functions are given by

$$TR = -0.5Q^2 + 24Q$$
$$TC = Q\sqrt{Q} + 100$$

Sketch these graphs on the same diagram on the range $0 \le Q \le 48$. Hence estimate the values of Q for which the firm

(a) breaks even   **(b)** maximizes profit.

SECTION 2.3
Indices and logarithms

Objectives

At the end of this section you should be able to:

○ Evaluate b^n in the case when n is positive, negative, a whole number or a fraction.

○ Simplify algebraic expressions using the rules of indices.

○ Investigate the returns to scale of a production function.

○ Evaluate logarithms in simple cases.

○ Use the rules of logarithms to solve equations in which the unknown occurs as a power.

Advice

This section is quite long with some important ideas. If you are comfortable using the rules of indices and already know what a logarithm is, you should be able to read through the material in one sitting, concentrating on the applications. However, if your current understanding is hazy (or non-existent), you should consider studying this topic on separate occasions. To help with this, the material in this section has been split into the following convenient sub-sections:

● index notation
● rules of indices
● logarithms
● summary.

2.3.1 Index notation

We have already used b^2 as an abbreviation for $b \times b$. In this section we extend the notation to b^n for any value of n, positive, negative, whole number or fraction. In general, if

$$M = b^n$$

we say that b^n is the **exponential form of M to base b**. The number n is then referred to as the **index**, **power** or **exponent**. An obvious way of extending

$$b^2 = b \times b$$

to other positive whole-number powers, n, is to define

$$b^3 = b \times b \times b$$
$$b^4 = b \times b \times b \times b$$

and, in general,

$$\boxed{b^n = b \times b \times b \times b \times \ldots b}$$

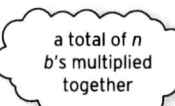
a total of n b's multiplied together

To include the case of negative powers, consider the following table of values of 2^n:

2^{-3}	2^{-2}	2^{-1}	2^0	2^1	2^2	2^3	2^4
?	?	?	?	2	4	8	16

To work from left to right along the completed part of the table, all you have to do is to multiply each number by 2. Equivalently, if you work from right to left, you simply divide by 2. It makes sense to continue this pattern beyond $2^1 = 2$. Dividing this by 2 gives

$$2^0 = 2 \div 2 = 1$$

and dividing again by 2 gives

$$2^{-1} = 1 \div 2 = \frac{1}{2}$$

and so on. The completed table is then

2^{-3}	2^{-2}	2^{-1}	2^0	2^1	2^2	2^3	2^4
$\frac{1}{8}$	$\frac{1}{4}$	$\frac{1}{2}$	1	2	4	8	16

Notice that

$$2^{-1} = \frac{1}{2} = \frac{1}{2^1}$$

$$2^{-2} = \frac{1}{4} = \frac{1}{2^2}$$

$$2^{-3} = \frac{1}{8} = \frac{1}{2^3}$$

In other words, negative powers are evaluated by taking the reciprocal of the corresponding positive power. Motivated by this particular example, we define

$$\boxed{b^0 = 1}$$

and

$$\boxed{b^{-n} = \frac{1}{b^n}}$$

where n is any positive whole number.

Example

Evaluate

(a) 3^2 (b) 4^3 (c) 7^0 (d) 5^1 (e) 5^{-1}
(f) $(-2)^6$ (g) 3^{-4} (h) $(-2)^3$ (i) $(1.723)^0$

Solution

Using the definitions

$$b^n = b \times b \times b \times \ldots \times b$$
$$b^0 = 1$$
$$b^{-n} = \frac{1}{b^n}$$

we obtain

(a) $3^2 = 3 \times 3 = 9$

(b) $4^3 = 4 \times 4 \times 4 = 64$

(c) $7^0 = 1$

because any number raised to the power of zero equals 1.

(d) $5^1 = 5$

(e) $5^{-1} = \dfrac{1}{5^{-1}} = \dfrac{1}{5}$

(f) $(-2)^6 = (-2) \times (-2) \times (-2) \times (-2) \times (-2) \times (-2) = 64$

where the answer is positive because there are an even number of minus signs.

(g) $3^{-4} = \dfrac{1}{3^4} = \dfrac{1}{3 \times 3 \times 3 \times 3} = \dfrac{1}{81}$

(h) $(-2)^{-3} = \dfrac{1}{(-2)^3} = \dfrac{1}{(-2) \times (-2) \times (-2)} = -\dfrac{1}{8}$

where the answer is negative because there are an odd number of minus signs.

(i) $(1.723)^0 = 1$

Practice Problem

1. **(1)** Without using a calculator evaluate

    (a) 10^2 **(b)** 10^1 **(c)** 10^0 **(d)** 10^{-1} **(e)** 10^{-2} **(f)** $(-1)^{100}$

    (g) $(-1)^{99}$ **(h)** 7^{-3} **(i)** $(-9)^2$ **(j)** $(72\ 101)^1$ **(k)** $(2.718)^0$

    (2) Confirm your answer to part (1) using a calculator.

We handle fractional powers in two stages. We begin by defining b^m where m is a reciprocal such as $^1/_2$ or $^1/_8$ and then consider more general fractions such as $^3/_4$ or $^3/_8$ later. Assuming that n is a positive whole number, we define

$$\boxed{b^{1/n} = n\text{th root of } b}$$

By this we mean that $b^{1/n}$ is a number which, when raised to the power n, produces b. In symbols, if $c = b^{1/n}$ then $c^n = b$. Using this definition,

$$9^{1/2} = \text{square root of } 9 \quad = 3 \quad (\text{because } 3^2 = 9)$$
$$8^{1/3} = \text{cube root of } 8 \quad = 2 \quad (\text{because } 2^3 = 8)$$
$$625^{1/4} = \text{fourth root of } 625 \quad = 5 \quad (\text{because } 5^4 = 625)$$

Of course, the nth root of a number may not exist. There is no number c satisfying $c^2 = -4$, for example, and so $(-4)^{1/2}$ is not defined. It is also possible for some numbers to have more than one nth root. For example, there are two values of c which satisfy $c^4 = 16$, namely $c = 2$ and $c = -2$. In these circumstances it is standard practice to take the positive root, so $16^{1/4} = 2$.

We now turn our attention to the case of b^m, where m is a general fraction of the form p/q for some whole numbers p and q. What interpretation are we going to put on a number such as $16^{3/4}$? To be consistent with our previous definitions, the numerator, 3, can be thought of as an instruction for us to raise 16 to the power of 3, and the denominator tells us to take the fourth root. In fact, it is immaterial in which order these two operations are carried out. If we begin by cubing 16 we get

$$16^3 = 16 \times 16 \times 16 = 4096$$

and taking the fourth root of this gives

$$16^{3/4} = (4096)^{1/4} = 8 \quad \text{(because } 8^4 = 4096\text{)}$$

On the other hand, taking the fourth root first gives

$$16^{1/4} = 2 \quad \text{(because } 2^4 = 16\text{)}$$

and cubing this gives

$$16^{3/4} = 2^3 = 8$$

which is the same answer as before. We therefore see that

$$(16^3)^{1/4} = (16^{1/4})^3$$

This result holds for any base b and fraction p/q (provided that q is positive), so we define

$$\boxed{b^{p/q} = (b^p)^{1/q} = (b^{1/q})^p}$$

Example

Evaluate

(a) $8^{4/3}$ **(b)** $25^{-3/2}$

Solution

(a) To evaluate $8^{4/3}$ we need both to raise the number to the power of 4 and to find a cube root. Choosing to find the cube root first,

$$8^{4/3} = (8^{1/3})^4 = 2^4 = 16$$

(b) Again it is easy to find the square root of 25 first before raising the number to the power of -3, so

$$25^{-3/2} = (25^{1/2})^{-3} = 5^{-3} = \frac{1}{5^3} = \frac{1}{125}$$

For this particular exponential form we have actually carried out three distinct operations. The minus sign tells us to reciprocate, the fraction $^1/_2$ tells us to take the square root and the 3 tells us to cube. You might like to check for yourself that you get the same answer irrespective of the order in which these three operations are performed.

Advice

Given that we are allowed to perform these operations in any order, it is usually easier to find the qth root first to avoid having to spot roots of large numbers.

Practice Problem

2. (1) Without using your calculator, evaluate

(a) $16^{1/2}$ (b) $27^{1/3}$ (c) $4^{5/2}$ (d) $8^{-2/3}$ (e) $1^{-17/25}$

(2) Confirm your answer to part (1) using a calculator.

2.3.2 Rules of indices

There are two reasons why the exponential form is useful. Firstly, it is a convenient shorthand for what otherwise might be a very lengthy number. The exponential form

$$9^8$$

is much easier to write down than either of the equivalent forms

$$9 \times 9 \times 9 \times 9 \times 9 \times 9 \times 9 \times 9$$

or

$$43\ 046\ 721$$

Secondly, there are four basic rules of indices which facilitate the manipulation of such numbers. The four rules may be stated as follows:

> *Rule 1* $b^m \times b^n = b^{m+n}$
>
> *Rule 2* $b^m \div b^n = b^{m-n}$
>
> *Rule 3* $(b^m)^n = b^{mn}$
>
> *Rule 4* $(ab)^n = a^n b^n$

It is certainly not our intention to provide mathematical proofs in this book. However, it might help you to remember these rules if we give you a justification based on some simple examples. We consider each rule in turn.

Rule 1

Suppose we want to multiply together 2^2 and 2^5. Now $2^2 = 2 \times 2$ and $2^5 = 2 \times 2 \times 2 \times 2 \times 2$, so

$$2^2 \times 2^5 = (2 \times 2) \times (2 \times 2 \times 2 \times 2 \times 2)$$

Notice that we are multiplying together a total of seven 2s and so by definition this is just 2^7: that is,

$$2^2 \times 2^5 = 2^7 = 2^{2+5}$$

This confirms rule 1, which tells you that if you multiply two numbers, all you have to do is to add the indices.

Rule 2

Suppose we want to divide 2^2 by 2^5. This gives

$$\frac{\cancel{2} \times \cancel{2}}{2 \times 2 \times 2 \times \cancel{2} \times \cancel{2}} = \frac{1}{2 \times 2 \times 2} = \frac{1}{2^3}$$

Now, by definition, reciprocals are denoted by negative indices, so this is just 2^{-3}: that is,

$$2^2 \div 2^5 = 2^{-3} = 2^{2-5}$$

This confirms rule 2, which tells you that if you divide two numbers, all you have to do is to subtract the indices.

Rule 3

Suppose we want to raise 10^2 to the power 3. By definition, for any number b,

$$b^3 = b \times b \times b$$

so replacing b by 10^2 we have

$$(10^2)^3 = 10^2 \times 10^2 \times 10^2 = (10 \times 10) \times (10 \times 10) \times (10 \times 10) = 10^6$$

because there are six 10s multiplied together: that is,

$$(10^2)^3 = 10^6 = 10^{2 \times 3}$$

This confirms rule 3, which tells you that if you take a 'power of a power', all you have to do is to multiply the indices.

Rule 4

Suppose we want to raise 2×3 to the power 4. By definition,

$$b^4 = b \times b \times b \times b$$

so replacing b by 2×3 gives

$$(2 \times 3)^4 = (2 \times 3) \times (2 \times 3) \times (2 \times 3) \times (2 \times 3)$$

and, because it does not matter in which order numbers are multiplied, this can be written as

$$(2 \times 2 \times 2 \times 2) \times (3 \times 3 \times 3 \times 3)$$

that is,

$$(2 \times 3)^4 = 2^4 \times 3^4$$

This confirms rule 4, which tells you that if you take the power of a product of two numbers, all you have to do is to take the power of each number separately and multiply.

A word of warning is in order regarding these laws. Notice that in rules 1 and 2 the bases of the numbers involved are the same. These rules do not apply if the bases are different. For example, rule 1 gives no information about

$$2^4 \times 3^5$$

Similarly, please notice that in rule 4 the numbers a and b are multiplied together. For some strange reason, some business and economics students seem to think that rule 4 also applies to addition, so that

$$(a + b)^n = a^n + b^n \qquad \text{This statement is \textbf{NOT TRUE}}$$

It would make algebraic manipulation a whole lot easier if it were true, but I am afraid to say that it is definitely false! If you need convincing of this, note, for example, that

$$(1 + 2)^3 = 3^3 = 27$$

which is not the same as

$$1^3 + 2^3 = 1 + 8 = 9$$

One variation of rule 4 which is true is

$$\left(\frac{a}{b}\right)^n = \frac{a^n}{b^n} \quad (b \neq 0)$$

This is all right because division (unlike addition or subtraction) is the same sort of operation as multiplication. In fact,

$$\left(\frac{a}{b}\right)^n$$

can be thought of as

$$\left(a \times \frac{1}{b}\right)^n$$

so applying rule 4 to this product gives

$$a^n\left(\frac{1}{b}\right)^n = \frac{a^n}{b^n}$$

as required.

Advice

There might be occasions (such as in examinations!) when you only half remember a rule or perhaps think that you have discovered a brand new rule for yourself. If you are ever worried about whether some rule is legal or not, you should always check it out by trying numbers, just as we did for $(a + b)^n$. Obviously, one numerical example which actually works does not prove that the rule will always work. However, one example which fails is good enough to tell you that your supposed rule is rubbish.

The following example demonstrates how rules 1–4 are used to simplify algebraic expressions.

Example

Simplify

(a) $x^{1/4} \times x^{3/4}$ **(b)** $\dfrac{x^2 y^3}{x^4 y}$ **(c)** $(x^2 y^{-1/3})^3$

Solution

(a) The expression

$$x^{1/4} \times x^{3/4}$$

represents the product of two numbers in exponential form with the same base. From rule 1 we may add the indices to get

$$x^{1/4} \times x^{3/4} = x^{1/4+3/4} = x^1$$

which is just x.

(b) The expression

$$\frac{x^2 y^3}{x^4 y}$$

is more complicated than that in part (a) since it involves numbers in exponential form with two different bases, x and y. From rule 2,

$$\frac{x^2}{x^4}$$

may be simplified by subtracting indices to get

$$x^2 \div x^4 = x^{2-4} = x^{-2}$$

Similarly,

$$\frac{y^3}{y} = y^3 \div y^1 = y^{3-1} = y^2$$

Hence

$$\frac{x^2 y^3}{x^4 y} = x^{-2} y^2$$

It is not possible to simplify this any further, because x^{-2} and y^2 have different bases. However, if you prefer, this can be written as

$$\frac{y^2}{x^2}$$

because negative powers denote reciprocals.

(c) An obvious first step in the simplification of

$$(x^2 y^{-1/3})^3$$

is to apply rule 4, treating x^2 as the value of a and $y^{-1/3}$ as b to get

$$(x^2 y^{-1/3})^3 = (x^2)^3 (y^{-1/3})^3$$

Rule 3 then allows us to write

$$(x^2)^3 = x^{2 \times 3} = x^6$$
$$(y^{-1/3})^3 = y^{(-1/3) \times 3} = y^{-1}$$

Hence

$$(x^2 y^{-1/3})^3 = x^6 y^{-1}$$

As in part (b), if you think it looks neater, you can write this as

$$\frac{x^6}{y}$$

because negative powers denote reciprocals.

Practice Problem

3. Simplify

(a) $(x^{3/4})^8$ **(b)** $\dfrac{x^2}{x^{3/2}}$ **(c)** $(x^2 y^4)^3$ **(d)** $\sqrt{x}(x^{5/2} + y^3)$

[Hint: in part (d) note that $\sqrt{x} = x^{1/2}$ and multiply out the brackets.]

There are occasions throughout this book when we use the rules of indices and definitions of b^n. For the moment, we concentrate on one specific application where we see these ideas in action. The output, Q, of any production process depends on a variety of inputs, known as **factors of production**. These comprise land, capital, labour and enterprise. For simplicity we restrict our attention to capital and labour. **Capital**, K, denotes all man-made aids to production such as buildings, tools and plant machinery. **Labour**, L, denotes all paid work in the production process. The dependence of Q on K and L may be written

$$Q = f(K, L)$$

which is called a **production function**. Once this relationship is made explicit, in the form of a formula, it is straightforward to calculate the level of production from any given combination of inputs. For example, if

$$Q = 100K^{1/3}L^{1/2}$$

then the inputs $K = 27$ and $L = 100$ lead to an output

$$Q = 100(27)^{1/3}(100)^{1/2}$$
$$= 100(3)(10)$$
$$= 3000$$

Of particular interest is the effect on output when inputs are scaled in some way. If capital and labour both double, does the production level also double, does it go up by more than double or does it go up by less than double? For the particular production function,

$$Q = 100K^{1/3}L^{1/2}$$

we see that, when K and L are replaced by $2K$ and $2L$, respectively,

$$Q = 100(2K)^{1/3}(2L)^{1/2}$$

Now, by rule 4,

$$(2K)^{1/3} = 2^{1/3}K^{1/3} \text{ and } (2L)^{1/2} = 2^{1/2}L^{1/2}$$

so

$$Q = 100(2^{1/3}K^{1/3})(2^{1/2}L^{1/2})$$
$$= (2^{1/3}2^{1/2})(100K^{1/3}L^{1/2})$$

The second term, $100K^{1/3}L^{1/2}$, is just the original value of Q, so we see that the output is multiplied by

$$2^{1/3}2^{1/2}$$

Using rule 1, this number may be simplified by adding the indices to get

$$2^{1/3}2^{1/2} = 2^{5/6}$$

Moreover, because 5/6 is less than 1, the scale factor is smaller than 2. In fact, my calculator gives

$$2^{5/6} = 1.78 \text{ (to 2 decimal places)}$$

so output goes up by just less than double.

It is important to notice that the above argument does not depend on the particular value, 2, that is taken as the scale factor. Exactly the same procedure can be applied if the inputs, K and L, are scaled by a general number λ (where λ is a Greek letter pronounced 'lambda'). Replacing K and L by λK and λL respectively in the formula

$$Q = 100K^{1/3}L^{1/2}$$

gives

$$Q = 100(\lambda K)^{1/3}(\lambda L)^{1/2}$$
$$= 100\lambda^{1/3}K^{1/3}\lambda^{1/2}L^{1/2} \qquad \text{(rule 4)}$$
$$= (\lambda^{1/3}\lambda^{1/2})(100K^{1/3}L^{1/2})$$
$$= \lambda^{5/6}(100K^{1/3}L^{1/2}) \qquad \text{(rule 1)}$$

We see that the output gets scaled by $\lambda^{5/6}$, which is smaller than λ since the power, 5/6, is less than 1. We describe this by saying that the production function exhibits decreasing returns to scale.

In general, a function

$$Q = f(K, L)$$

is said to be **homogeneous** if

$$f(\lambda K, \lambda L) = \lambda^n f(K, L)$$

for some number, n. This means that when both variables K and L are multiplied by λ we can pull out all of the λs as a common factor, λ^n. The power, n, is called the **degree of homogeneity**. In the previous example we showed that

$$f(\lambda K, \lambda L) = \lambda^{5/6}f(K, L)$$

and so it is homogeneous of degree 5/6. In general, if the degree of homogeneity, n, satisfies:

- $n < 1$, the function is said to display **decreasing returns to scale**
- $n = 1$, the function is said to display **constant returns to scale**
- $n > 1$, the function is said to display **increasing returns to scale**.

Example

Show that the following production function is homogeneous and find its degree of homogeneity:

$$Q = 2K^{1/2}L^{3/2}$$

Does this function exhibit decreasing returns to scale, constant returns to scale or increasing returns to scale?

Solution

We are given that

$$f(K, L) = 2K^{1/2}L^{3/2}$$

so replacing K by λK and L by λL gives

$$f(\lambda K, \lambda L) = 2(\lambda K)^{1/2}(\lambda L)^{3/2}$$

We can pull out all of the λs by using rule 4 to get

$$2\lambda^{1/2}K^{1/2}\lambda^{3/2}L^{3/2}$$

and then using rule 1 to get

$$\lambda^2(2K^{1/2}L^{3/2})$$

$$\lambda^{1/2}\lambda^{3/2} = \lambda^{1/2+3/2} = \lambda^2$$

We have therefore shown that

$$f(\lambda K, \lambda L) = \lambda^2 f(K, L)$$

and so the function is homogeneous of degree 2. Moreover, since 2 > 1 we deduce that it has increasing returns to scale.

Practice Problem ❷

4. Show that the following production functions are homogeneous and comment on their returns to scale:

(a) $Q = 7KL^2$ **(b)** $Q = 50K^{1/4}L^{3/4}$

You may well have noticed that all of the production functions considered so far are of the form

$$Q = AK^{\alpha}L^{\beta}$$

for some positive constants, A, α and β. (The Greek letters α and β are pronounced 'alpha' and 'beta' respectively.) Such functions are called **Cobb–Douglas** production functions. It is easy to see that they are homogeneous of degree $\alpha + \beta$ because if

$$f(K, L) = AK^{\alpha}L^{\beta}$$

then

$$\begin{aligned} f(\lambda K, \lambda L) &= A(\lambda K)^{\alpha}(\lambda L)^{\beta} \\ &= A\lambda^{\alpha}K^{\alpha}\lambda^{\beta}L^{\beta} \quad \text{(rule 4)} \\ &= \lambda^{\alpha+\beta}(AK^{\alpha}L^{\beta}) \quad \text{(rule 1)} \\ &= \lambda^{\alpha+\beta}f(K, L) \end{aligned}$$

Consequently, Cobb–Douglas production functions exhibit

- decreasing returns to scale, if $\alpha + \beta < 1$
- constant returns to scale, if $\alpha + \beta = 1$
- increasing returns to scale, if $\alpha + \beta > 1$.

By the way, not all production functions are of this type. Indeed, it is not even necessary for a production function to be homogeneous. Some examples illustrating these cases are given in Question 5 in Exercise 2.3 and Question 5 in Exercise 2.3* at the end of this section. We shall return to the topic of production functions in Chapter 5.

2.3.3 Logarithms

At the beginning of this section we stated that if a number, M, is expressed as

$$M = b^n$$

then b^n is called the exponential form of M to base b. The approach taken so far has simply been to evaluate M from any given values of b and n. In practice, it may be necessary to reverse this process and to find n from known values of M and b. To solve the equation

$$32 = 2^n$$

we need to express 32 as a power of 2. In this case it is easy to work out n by inspection. Simple trial and error easily gives $n = 5$ because

$$2^5 = 32$$

We describe this expression by saying that the logarithm of 32 to base 2 is 5. In symbols we write

$$\log_2 32 = 5$$

Quite generally,

> **if $M = b^n$ then $\log_b M = n$**

where n is called the logarithm of M to base b.

Advice

Students have been known to regard logarithms as something rather abstract and difficult to understand. There is, however, no need to worry about logarithms, since they simply provide an alternative way of thinking about numbers such as b^n. Read through the following example and then try Practice Problem 5 for yourself. You might discover that they are easier than you expect.

Example

Evaluate

(a) $\log_3 9$ **(b)** $\log_4 2$ **(c)** $\log_7 \frac{1}{7}$

Solution

(a) To find the value of $\log_3 9$ we convert the problem into one involving powers. From the definition of a logarithm to base 3 we see that the statement

$$\log_3 9 = n$$

is equivalent to

$$9 = 3^n$$

The problem of finding the logarithm of 9 to base 3 is exactly the same as that of writing 9 as a power of 3. The solution of this equation is clearly $n = 2$ since

$$9 = 3^2$$

Hence $\log_3 9 = 2$.

(b) Again to evaluate $\log_4 2$ we merely rewrite

$$\log_4 2 = n$$

in exponential form as

$$2 = 4^n$$

The problem of finding the logarithm of 2 to base 4 is exactly the same as that of writing 2 as a power of 4. The value of 2 is obtained from 4 by taking the square root, which involves raising 4 to the power of $^1/_2$, so

$$2 = 4^{1/2}$$

Hence $\log_2 4 = ^1/_2$.

(c) If

$$\log_7 {}^1/_7 = n$$

then

$$^1/_7 = 7^n$$

The value of $^1/_7$ is found by taking the reciprocal of 7, which involves raising 7 to the power of -1: that is,

$$^1/_7 = 7^{-1}$$

Hence $\log_7 {}^1/_7 = -1$.

Practice Problem

5. **(1)** Write down the values of n which satisfy

    (a) $1000 = 10^n$ **(b)** $100 = 10^n$ **(c)** $10 = 10^n$

    (d) $1 = 10^n$ **(e)** $\dfrac{1}{10} = 10^n$ **(f)** $\dfrac{1}{100} = 10^n$

(2) Use your answer to part (1) to write down the values of

    (a) $\log_{10} 1000$ **(b)** $\log_{10} 100$ **(c)** $\log_{10} 10$

    (d) $\log_{10} 1$ **(e)** $\log_{10} {}^1/_{10}$ **(f)** $\log_{10} {}^1/_{100}$

(3) Confirm your answer to part (2) using a calculator.

Given the intimate relationship between exponentials and logarithms, you should not be too surprised to learn that logarithms satisfy three rules that are comparable with those for indices. The rules of logarithms are as follows:

Rule 1 $\log_b(x \times y) = \log_b x + \log_b y$

Rule 2 $\log_b(x \div y) = \log_b x - \log_b y$

Rule 3 $\log_b x^m = m\log_b x$

A long time ago, before the pocket calculator was invented, people used tables of logarithms to perform complicated arithmetic calculations. It was generally assumed that everyone could add or subtract numbers using pen and paper, but that people found it hard to multiply and divide. The first two rules gave a means of converting calculations involving multiplication and division into easier calculations involving addition and subtraction. For example, to work out

$$1.765\ 12 \times 25.329\ 71$$

we would first look up the logarithms of 1.765 12 and 25.329 71 using tables and then add these logarithms together on paper. According to rule 1, the value obtained is just the logarithm of the answer. Finally, using tables of antilogarithms (which in effect raised the base to an appropriate power), the result of the calculation was obtained. Fortunately for us, this is all history and we can now perform arithmetic calculations in a fraction of the time it took our predecessors to multiply or divide two numbers. This might suggest that logarithms are redundant. However, the idea of a logarithm remains an important one. The logarithm function itself – that is,

$$f(x) = \log_b(x)$$

is of value and we shall investigate its properties later in the book. For the time being we first show how to use the laws of logarithms in algebra and then demonstrate how logarithms can be used to solve algebraic equations in which the unknown appears as a power. This technique will be of particular use in the next chapter when we solve compound interest problems.

Example

Use the rules of logarithms to express each of the following as a single logarithm:

(a) $\log_b x + \log_b y - \log_b z$ **(b)** $2\log_b x - 3\log_b y$

Solution

(a) The first rule of logs shows that the *sum* of two logs can be written as the log of a *product*, so

$$\log_b x + \log_b y - \log_b z = \log_b(xy) - \log_b z$$

Also, according to rule 2, the *difference* of two logs is the log of a *quotient*, so we can simplify further to get

$$\log_b\left(\frac{xy}{z}\right)$$

(b) Given any combination of logs such as

$$2\log_b x - 3\log_b y$$

the trick is to use the third rule to 'get rid' of the coefficients. Since

$$2\log_b x = \log_b x^2 \quad \text{and} \quad 3\log_b y = \log_b y^3$$

we see that

$$2\log_b x - 3\log_b y = \log_b x^2 - \log_b y^3$$

Only now can we use the second rule of logs, which allows us to write the expression as the single logarithm

$$\log_b\left(\frac{x^2}{y^3}\right)$$

Practice Problem

6. Use the rules of logs to express each of the following as a single logarithm:

(a) $\log_b x - \log_b y + \log_b z$ (b) $4\log_b x + 2\log_b y$

Before we leave this topic a word of warning is in order. Be careful to learn the rules of logs correctly. A common mistake is to misread rule 1 as

$\log_b(x + y) = \log_b x + \log_b y$ **This is NOT true**

Remember that logs are just a posh way of thinking about indices and it is when you *multiply* numbers together you end up adding the indices, so the correct version has to be

$\log_b(xy) = \log_b x + \log_b y$

Example

Find the value of x which satisfies

(a) $200(1.1)^x = 20\,000$ (b) $5^x = 2(3)^x$

Solution

(a) An obvious first step in the solution of

$$200(1.1)^x = 20\,000$$

is to divide both sides by 200 to get

$$(1.1)^x = 100$$

In Chapter 1 it was pointed out that we can do whatever we like to an equation, provided that we do the same thing to both sides. In particular, we may take logarithms of both sides to get

$$\log(1.1)^x = \log(100)$$

Now by rule 3 we have

$$\log(1.1)^x = x\log(1.1)$$

so the equation becomes

$$x\log(1.1) = \log(100)$$

Notice the effect that rule 3 has on the equation. It brings the unknown down to the same level as the rest of the expression. This is the whole point of taking logarithms, since it converts an equation in which the unknown appears as a power into one which can be solved using familiar algebraic methods. Dividing both sides of the equation

$$x\log(1.1) = \log(100)$$

by $\log(1.1)$ gives

$$x = \frac{\log(100)}{\log(1.1)}$$

So far no mention has been made of the base of the logarithm. The above equation for x is true no matter what base is used. It makes sense to use logarithms to base 10 because all scientific calculators have this facility as one of their function keys. Using base 10, my calculator gives

$$x = \frac{\log(100)}{\log(1.1)} = \frac{2}{0.041\,392\,685} = 48.32$$

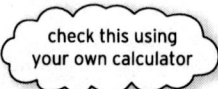 check this using your own calculator

to 2 decimal places.

As a check, if this number is substituted back into the original equation, then

$$200(1.1)^x = 200(1.1)^{48.32} = 20\,004 \quad ✓$$

We cannot expect to obtain the exact answer, because we rounded x to only two decimal places.

(b) To solve

$$5^x = 2(3)^x$$

we take logarithms of both sides to get

$$\log(5^x) = \log(2 \times 3^x)$$

The right-hand side is the logarithm of a product and, according to rule 1, can be written as the sum of the logarithms, so the equation becomes

$$\log(5^x) = \log(2) + \log(3^x)$$

As in part (a) the key step is to use rule 3 to 'bring down the powers'. If rule 3 is applied to both $\log(5^x)$ and $\log(3^x)$ then the equation becomes

$$x\log(5) = \log(2) + x\log(3)$$

This is now the type of equation that we know how to solve. We collect x's on the left-hand side to get

$$x\log(5) - x\log(3) = \log(2)$$

and then pull out a common factor of x to get

$$x[\log(5) - \log(3)] = \log(2)$$

Now, by rule 2, the difference of two logarithms is the same as the logarithm of their quotient, so

$$\log(5) - \log(3) = \log(5 \div 3)$$

Hence the equation becomes

$$x\log\left(\frac{5}{3}\right) = \log(2)$$

so

$$x = \frac{\log(2)}{\log(5/3)}$$

Finally, taking logarithms to base 10 using a calculator gives

$$x = \frac{0.301\ 029\ 996}{0.221\ 848\ 750} = 1.36$$

to 2 decimal places.

As a check, the original equation

$$5^x = 2(3)^x$$

becomes

$$5^{1.36} = 2(3)^{1.36}$$

that is,

$$8.92 = 8.91 \quad \checkmark$$

Again the slight discrepancy is due to rounding errors in the value of x.

Practice Problem

7. Solve the following equations for x:

(a) $3^x = 7$ (b) $5(2)^x = 10^x$

Advice

In this section we have met a large number of definitions and rules concerning indices and logarithms. For convenience, we have collected these together in the form of a summary. The facts relating to indices are particularly important and you should make every effort to memorize these before proceeding with the rest of this book.

2.3.4 Summary

Indices

If n is a positive whole number then

$$b^n = b \times b \times \ldots \times b$$
$$b^0 = 1$$
$$b^{-n} = 1/b^n$$
$$b^{1/n} = n\text{th root of } b$$

Also, if p and q are whole numbers with $q > 0$ then

$$b^{p/q} = (b^p)^{1/q} = (b^{1/q})^p$$

The four rules of indices are:

Rule 1 $b^m \times b^n = b^{m+n}$

Rule 2 $b^m \div b^n = b^{m-n}$

Rule 3 $(b^m)^n = b^{mn}$

Rule 4 $(ab)^n = a^n b^n$

Logarithms

If $M = b^n$ then $n = \log_b M$. The three rules of logarithms are:

Rule 1 $\log_b(x \times y) = \log_b x + \log_b y$

Rule 2 $\log_b(x \div y) = \log_b x - \log_b y$

Rule 3 $\log_b x^m = m\log_b x$

Key Terms

Capital   Man-made assets used in the production of goods and services.

Cobb–Douglas production function   A production function of the form: $Q = AK^\alpha L^\beta$.

Constant returns to scale   Exhibited by a production function when a given percentage increase in input leads to the same percentage increase in output: $f(\lambda K, \lambda L) = \lambda f(K, L)$.

Decreasing returns to scale   Exhibited by a production function when a given percentage increase in input leads to a smaller percentage increase in output: $f(\lambda K, \lambda L) = \lambda^n f(K, L)$ where $0 < n < 1$.

Degree of homogeneity   The number n in the relation $f(\lambda K, \lambda L) = \lambda^n f(K, L)$.

Exponent   A superscript attached to a variable; the number 5 is the exponent in the expression, $2x^5$.

Exponential form   A representation of a number which is written using powers. For example, 2^5 is the exponential form of the number 32.

Factors of production   The inputs into the production of goods and services: labour, land, capital and raw materials.

Homogeneous function   A function with the property that when all of the inputs are multiplied by a constant, λ, the output is multiplied by λ^n where n is the degree of homogeneity.

Increasing returns to scale   Exhibited by a production function when a given percentage increase in input leads to a larger percentage increase in output: $f(\lambda K, \lambda L) = \lambda^n f(K, L)$ where $n > 1$.

Index   Another word for exponent.

Labour   All forms of human input to the production process.

Logarithm   The power to which a base must be raised to yield a particular number.

Power   Another word for exponent. If this is a positive integer then it gives the number of times a number is multiplied by itself.

Production function   The relationship between the output of a good and the inputs used to produce it.

Exercise 2.3

1. **(1)** Without using your calculator evaluate

   (a) 8^2 **(b)** 2^1 **(c)** 3^{-1} **(d)** 17^0 **(e)** $1^{1/5}$ **(f)** $36^{1/2}$ **(g)** $8^{2/3}$ **(h)** $49^{-3/2}$

   (2) Confirm your answer to part (1) using a calculator.

2. Use the rules of indices to simplify

   (a) $a^3 \times a^8$ **(b)** $\dfrac{b^7}{b^2}$ **(c)** $(c^2)^3$ **(d)** $\dfrac{x^4 y^5}{x^2 y^3}$ **(e)** $(xy^2)^3$

   (f) $y^3 \div y^7$ **(g)** $(x^{1/2})^8$ **(h)** $f^2 \times f^4 \times f$ **(i)** $\sqrt{(y^6)}$ **(j)** $\dfrac{x^3}{x^{-2}}$

3. Write the following expressions using index notation ❓

   (a) $\sqrt{x}$ **(b)** $\dfrac{1}{x^2}$ **(c)** $\sqrt[3]{x}$ **(d)** $\dfrac{1}{x}$ **(e)** $\dfrac{1}{\sqrt{x}}$ **(f)** $x\sqrt{x}$

4. For the production function, $Q = 200K^{1/4}L^{2/3}$ find the output when

   (a) $K = 16, L = 27$ **(b)** $K = 10\,000, L = 1000$

5. Which of the following production functions are homogeneous? For those functions which are homogeneous write down their degrees of homogeneity and comment on their returns to scale.

   (a) $Q = 500K^{1/3}L^{1/4}$

   (b) $Q = 3LK + L^2$

   (c) $Q = L + 5L^2K^3$

6. Write down the values of x which satisfy each of the following equations:

   (a) $5^x = 25$ **(b)** $3^x = \dfrac{1}{3}$ **(c)** $2^x = \dfrac{1}{8}$

   (d) $2^x = 64$ **(e)** $100^x = 10$ **(f)** $8^x = 1$

7. Write down the value of

   (a) $\log_b b^2$ **(b)** $\log_b b$ **(c)** $\log_b 1$ **(d)** $\log_b \sqrt{b}$ **(e)** $\log_b (1/b)$

8. Use the rules of logs to express each of the following as a single log:

   (a) $\log_b x + \log_b z$

   (b) $3\log_b x - 2\log_b y$

   (c) $\log_b y - 3\log_b z$

9. Express the following in terms of $\log_b x$ and $\log_b y$:

   (a) $\log_b x^2 y$

   (b) $\log_b \left(\dfrac{x}{y^2} \right)$

   (c) $\log_b x^2 y^7$

10. Solve the following equations for x. Give your answers to 2 decimal places.

(a) $5^x = 8$ (b) $10^x = 50$ (c) $1.2^x = 3$ (d) $1000 \times 1.05^x = 1500$

11. (1) State the values of

(a) $\log_2 32$ (b) $\log_9\left(\dfrac{1}{3}\right)$

(2) Use the rules of logs to express

$2\log_b x - 4\log_b y$

as a single logarithm.

(3) Use logs to solve the equation

$10(1.05)^x = 300$

Give your answer correct to 1 decimal place.

12. (1) State the values of x that satisfy the following equations:

(a) $81 = 3^x$ (b) $\dfrac{1}{25} = 5^x$ (c) $16^{1/2} = 2^x$

(2) Use the rules of indices to simplify:

(a) $\dfrac{x^6 y^9}{x^3 y^8}$ (b) $(x^3 y)^5$ (c) $\sqrt{\dfrac{x^9 y^4}{x^5}}$

Exercise 2.3*

1. (1) Evaluate the following without using a calculator

(a) $32^{3/5}$ (b) $64^{-5/6}$ (c) $\left(\dfrac{1}{125}\right)^{-4/3}$ (d) $\left(3\dfrac{3}{8}\right)^{2/3}$ (e) $\left(2\dfrac{1}{4}\right)^{-1/2}$

(2) Confirm your answer to part (1) using a calculator.

2. Use the rules of indices to simplify

(a) $y^{3/2} \times y^{1/2}$ (b) $\dfrac{x^2 y}{xy^{-1}}$ (c) $(xy^{1/2})^4$

(d) $(p^2)^{1/3} \div (p^{1/3})^2$ (e) $(24q)^{1/3} \div (3q)^{1/3}$ (f) $(25p^2 q^4)^{1/2}$

3. Write the following expressions using index notation

(a) $\dfrac{1}{x^7}$ (b) $\sqrt[4]{x}$ (c) $\dfrac{1}{x\sqrt{x}}$ (d) $2x^5\sqrt{x}$ (e) $\dfrac{8}{x(\sqrt[3]{x})}$

4. If $a = \dfrac{2\sqrt{x}}{y^3}$ and $b = 3x^4 y$, simplify $\dfrac{4b}{a^2}$

5. Show that the production function

$Q = A[bK^\alpha + (1-b)L^\alpha]^{1/\alpha}$

is homogeneous and displays constant returns to scale.

6. Solve the following equations:

(a) $2^{3x} = 4$ 　　　　　　(b) $4 \times 2^x = 32$ 　　　　　　(c) $8^x = 2 \times \left(\dfrac{1}{2}\right)^x$

7. Use the rules of logs to express each of the following as a single log:

(a) $\log_b(xy) - \log_b x - \log_b y$

(b) $3\log_b x - 2\log_b y$

(c) $\log_b y + 5\log_b x - 2\log_b z$

(d) $2 + 3\log_b x$

8. Express the following in terms of $\log_b x$, $\log_b y$ and $\log_b z$:

(a) $\log_b(x^2 y^3 z^4)$

(b) $\log_b\left(\dfrac{x^4}{y^2 z^5}\right)$

(c) $\log_b\left(\dfrac{x}{\sqrt{yz}}\right)$

9. If $\log_b 2 = p$, $\log_b 3 = q$ and $\log_b 10 = r$, express the following in terms of p, q and r:

(a) $\log_b\left(\dfrac{1}{3}\right)$ 　　(b) $\log_b 12$ 　　　　(c) $\log_b 0.000\,3$ 　　　(d) $\log_b 600$

10. Solve the following equations. Round your answers to 2 decimal places.

(a) $10(1.07)^x = 2000$ 　(b) $10^{x-1} = 3$ 　　　　(c) $5^{x-2} = 5$ 　　　　(d) $2(7)^{-x} = 3^x$

11. Solve the inequalities giving the bounds to 3 decimal places:

(a) $3^{2x+1} \le 7$ 　　　　(b) $0.8^x < 0.04$

12. Solve the equation

$$\log_{10}(x + 2) + \log_{10} x - 1 = \log_{10}\left(\dfrac{3}{2}\right)$$

13. (1) Define the term *homogeneous* when used to describe a production function $f(K, L)$.

(2) If the production function

$$f(K, L) = 4K^m L^{1/3} + 3K$$

is homogeneous, state the value of m.

Does the function display decreasing, constant or increasing returns to scale?

14. (1) State the values of x that satisfy the following equations:

(a) $4 = 8^x$ 　　　(b) $5 = \left(\dfrac{1}{25}\right)^x$

(2) Express y in terms of x:

$$2\log_a x = \log_a 7 + \log_a y$$

15. Show that $2\log_{10} x - \dfrac{1}{2}\log_{10} y - \dfrac{1}{3}\log_{10} 1000$ can be simplified to

$$\log_{10}\left(\sqrt{\dfrac{x^4}{y}}\right) - 1$$

SECTION 2.4

The exponential and natural logarithm functions

Objectives

At the end of this section you should be able to:

- Sketch graphs of general exponential functions.
- Understand how the number e is defined.
- Use the exponential function to model growth and decay.
- Use log graphs to find unknown parameters in simple models.
- Use the natural logarithm function to solve equations.

In the previous section we described how to define numbers of the form b^x, and discussed the idea of a logarithm, $\log_b x$. It turns out that there is one base (the number $e = 2.718\ 281\dots$) that is particularly important in mathematics. The purpose of this present section is to introduce you to this strange number and to consider a few simple applications.

Example

Sketch the graphs of the functions

(a) $f(x) = 2^x$ **(b)** $g(x) = 2^{-x}$

Comment on the relationship between these graphs.

Solution

(a) As we pointed out in Section 2.3, a number such as 2^x is said to be in exponential form. The number 2 is called the base and x is called the exponent. Values of this function are easily found either by pressing the power key $\boxed{x^y}$ on a calculator or by using the definition of b^n given in Section 2.3. A selection of these is given in the following table:

x	−3	−2	−1	0	1	2	3	4	5
2^x	0.125	0.25	0.5	1	2	4	8	16	32

A graph of $f(x)$ based on this table is sketched in Figure 2.14. Notice that the graph approaches the x axis for large negative values of x and it rises rapidly as x increases.

(b) The negative exponential

$$g(x) = 2^{-x}$$

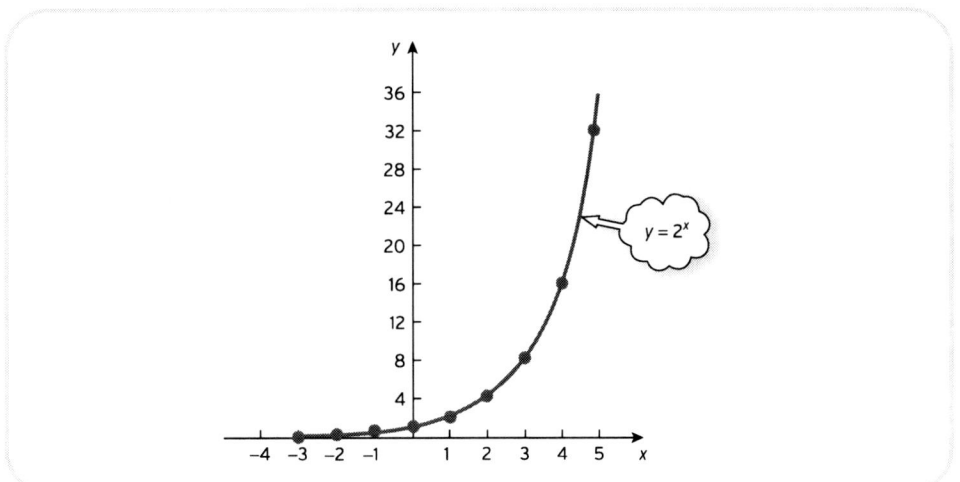

Figure 2.14

has values

x	-5	-4	-3	-2	-1	0	1	2	3
2^{-x}	32	16	8	4	2	1	0.5	0.25	0.125

This function is sketched in Figure 2.15. It is worth noticing that the numbers appearing in the table of 2^{-x} are the same as those of 2^{x} but arranged in reverse order. Hence the graph of 2^{-x} is obtained by reflecting the graph of 2^{x} in the y axis.

Figure 2.14 displays the graph of a particular exponential function, 2^{x}. Quite generally, the graph of any exponential function

$$f(x) = b^x$$

has the same basic shape provided $b > 1$. The only difference is that larger values of b produce steeper curves. A similar comment applies to the negative exponential, b^{-x}.

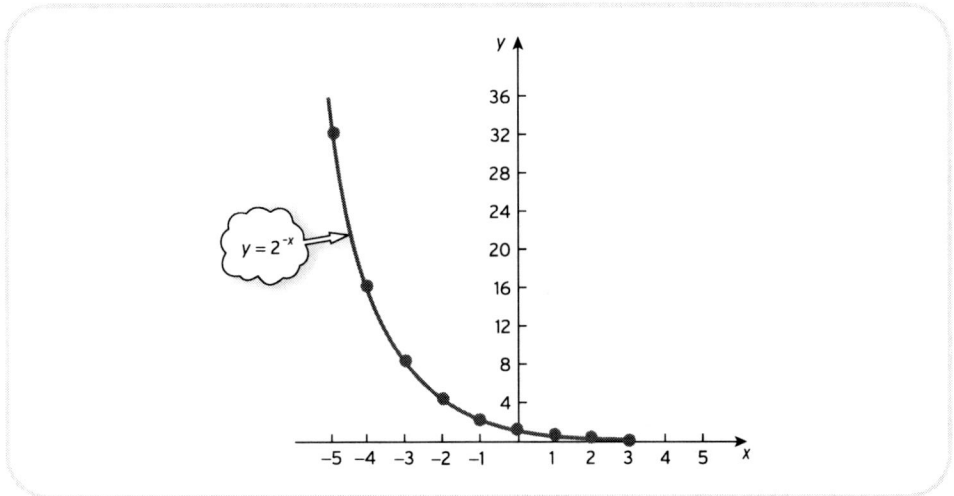

Figure 2.15

Practice Problem

1. Complete the following table of function values of 3^x and 3^{-x} and hence sketch their graphs.

x	-3	-2	-1	0	1	2	3
3^x							
3^{-x}							

Obviously there is a whole class of functions, each corresponding to a different base, b. Of particular interest is the case when b takes the value

2.718 281 828 459 . . .

This number is written as e and the function

$$f(x) = e^x$$

is referred to as *the* **exponential function**. In fact, it is not necessary for you to understand where this number comes from. All scientific calculators have an e^x button and you may simply wish to accept the results of using it. However, it might help your confidence if you have some appreciation of how it is defined. To this end consider the following example and subsequent problem.

Example

Evaluate the expression

$$\left(1 + \frac{1}{m}\right)^m$$

where $m = 1, 10, 100$ and 1000, and comment briefly on the behaviour of this sequence.

Solution

Substituting the values $m = 1, 10, 100$ and 1000 into

$$\left(1 + \frac{1}{m}\right)^m$$

gives

$$\left(1 + \frac{1}{1}\right)^1 = 2^1 = 2$$

$$\left(1 + \frac{1}{10}\right)^{10} = (1.1)^{10} = 2.593\ 742\ 460$$

$$\left(1 + \frac{1}{100}\right)^{100} = (1.01)^{100} = 2.704\ 813\ 829$$

$$\left(1 + \frac{1}{1000}\right)^{1000} = (1.001)^{1000} = 2.716\ 923\ 932$$

The numbers are clearly getting bigger as m increases. However, the rate of increase appears to be slowing down, suggesting that numbers are converging to some fixed value.

The following problem gives you an opportunity to continue the sequence and to discover for yourself the limiting value.

Practice Problem

2. (a) Use the power key x^y on your calculator to evaluate

$$\left(1 + \frac{1}{m}\right)^m$$

where $m = 10\,000$, $100\,000$ and $1\,000\,000$.

(b) Use your calculator to evaluate e^1 and compare with your answer to part (a).

Hopefully, the results of Practice Problem 2 should convince you that as m gets larger, the value of

$$\left(1 + \frac{1}{m}\right)^m$$

approaches a limiting value of $2.718\,281\,828\ldots$, which we choose to denote by the letter e. In symbols we write

$$e = \lim_{m \to \infty}\left(1 + \frac{1}{m}\right)^m$$

The significance of this number can only be fully appreciated in the context of calculus, which we study in Chapter 4. However, it is useful at this stage to consider some preliminary examples. These will give you practice in using the e^x button on your calculator and will give you some idea how this function can be used in modelling.

Advice

The number e has a similar status in mathematics as the number π and is just as useful. It arises in the mathematics of finance, which we discuss in the next chapter. You might like to glance through Section 3.2 now if you need convincing of the usefulness of e.

Example

The percentage, y, of households possessing refrigerators, t years after they have been introduced in a developed country, is modelled by

$$y = 100 - 95e^{-0.15t}$$

(1) Find the percentage of households that have refrigerators

    (a) at their launch

    (b) after 1 year

    (c) after 10 years

    (d) after 20 years.

(2) What is the market saturation level?

(3) Sketch a graph of y against t and hence give a qualitative description of the growth of refrigerator ownership over time.

Solution

(1) To calculate the percentage of households possessing refrigerators now and in 1, 10 and 20 years' time, we substitute $t = 0, 1, 10$ and 20 into the formula

$$y = 100 - 95e^{-0.15t}$$

to get

    (a) $y(0) = 100 - 95e^0 = 5\%$

    (b) $y(1) = 100 - 95e^{-0.15} = 18\%$

    (c) $y(10) = 100 - 95e^{-1.5} = 79\%$

    (d) $y(20) = 100 - 95e^{-3.0} = 95\%$

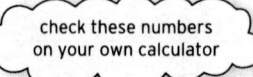

check these numbers on your own calculator

(2) To find the saturation level we need to investigate what happens to y as t gets ever larger. We know that the graph of a negative exponential function has the basic shape shown in Figure 2.15. Consequently, the value of $e^{-0.15t}$ will eventually approach zero as t increases. The market saturation level is therefore given by

$$y = 100 - 95(0) = 100\%$$

(3) A graph of y against t, based on the information obtained in parts (1) and (2), is sketched in Figure 2.16.

    This shows that y grows rapidly to begin with, but slows down as the market approaches saturation level. An economic variable which increases over time but approaches a fixed value like this is said to display **limited growth**. A saturation level of 100% indicates that eventually all households are expected to possess refrigerators, which is not surprising given the nature of the product.

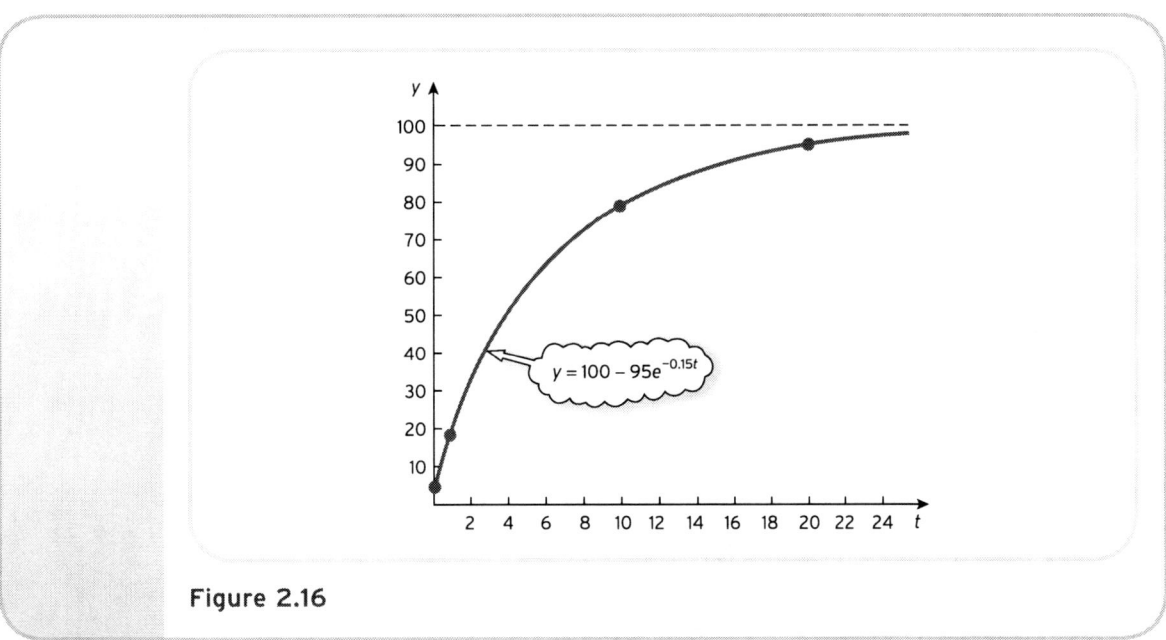

Figure 2.16

Practice Problem

3. The percentage, y, of households possessing camcorders t years after they have been launched is modelled by

$$y = \frac{55}{1 + 800e^{-0.3t}}$$

(1) Find the percentage of households that have camcorders

   (a) at their launch

   (b) after 10 years

   (c) after 20 years

   (d) after 30 years.

(2) What is the market saturation level?

(3) Sketch a graph of y against t and hence give a qualitative description of the growth of camcorder ownership over time.

In Section 2.3 we noted that if a number M can be expressed as b^n then n is called the logarithm of M to base b. In particular, for base e,

   if $M = e^n$ then $n = \log_e M$

We call logarithms to base e **natural logarithms**. These occur sufficiently frequently to warrant their own notation. Rather than writing $\log_e M$ we simply put $\ln M$ instead. The three rules of logs can then be stated as

> *Rule 1* $\ln(x \times y) = \ln x + \ln y$
>
> *Rule 2* $\ln(x \div y) = \ln x - \ln y$
>
> *Rule 3* $\ln x^m = m \ln x$

Example

Use the rules of logs to express

(a) $\ln\left(\dfrac{x}{\sqrt{y}}\right)$ in terms of $\ln x$ and $\ln y$

(b) $3 \ln p + \ln q - 2 \ln r$ as a single logarithm.

Solution

(a) In this part we need to 'expand', so we read the rules of logs from left to right:

$$\ln\left(\frac{x}{\sqrt{y}}\right) = \ln x - \ln\sqrt{y} \quad \text{(rule 2)}$$

$$= \ln x - \ln y^{1/2} \quad \text{(fractional powers denote roots)}$$

$$= \ln x - \frac{1}{2}\ln y \quad \text{(rule 3)}$$

(b) In this part we need to reverse this process and so read the rules from right to left:

$$3 \ln p + \ln q - 2 \ln r = \ln p^3 + \ln q - \ln r^2 \quad \text{(rule 3)}$$

$$= \ln(p^3 q) - \ln r^2 \quad \text{(rule 1)}$$

$$= \ln\left(\frac{p^3 q}{r^2}\right) \quad \text{(rule 2)}$$

Practice Problem

4. Use the rules of logs to express

  (a) $\ln(a^2 b^3)$ in terms of $\ln a$ and $\ln b$

  (b) $\frac{1}{2} \ln x - 3 \ln y$ as a single logarithm.

As we pointed out in Section 2.3, logs are particularly useful for solving equations in which the unknown occurs as a power. If the base is the number e then the equation can be solved by using natural logarithms.

Example

An economy is forecast to grow continuously so that the gross national product (GNP), measured in billions of dollars, after t years is given by

$$\text{GNP} = 80e^{0.02t}$$

After how many years is GNP forecast to be \$88 billion? What does the model predict about the value of GNP in the long run?

Solution

We need to solve

$$88 = 80e^{0.02t}$$

for t. Dividing through by 80 gives

$$1.1 = e^{0.02t}$$

Using the definition of natural logarithms we know that

$$\text{if } M = e^n \text{ then } n = \ln M$$

If we apply this definition to the equation

$$1.1 = e^{0.02t}$$

we deduce that

$$0.02t = \ln 1.1 = 0.095\ 31 \ldots \quad \text{(check this using your own calculator)}$$

so

$$t = \frac{0.095\ 31}{0.02} = 4.77$$

We therefore deduce that GNP reaches a level of \$88 billion after 4.77 years.

A graph of GNP plotted against time would be similar in shape to the graph in Figure 2.14. This shows that GNP just keeps on rising over time (in fact at an increasing rate). Such a model is said to display **unlimited growth**.

Practice Problem ❷

5. During a recession a firm's revenue declines continuously so that the revenue, TR (measured in millions of dollars), in t years' time is modelled by

$$\text{TR} = 5e^{-0.15t}$$

(a) Calculate the current revenue and also the revenue in 2 years' time.

(b) After how many years will the revenue decline to \$2.7 million?

One important (but rather difficult) problem in modelling is to extract a mathematical formula from a table of numbers. If this relationship is of the form of an exponential then it is possible to estimate values for some of the parameters involved.

Advice

The following example shows how to find such a formula from data points. This is an important skill. However, it is not crucial to your understanding of subsequent material in this book. You may wish to miss this out on first reading and move straight on to the Exercises at the end of this chapter.

Example

The values of GNP, g, measured in billions of dollars, over a period of t years was observed to be

t (years)	2	5	10	20
g (billions of dollars)	12	16	27	74

Model the growth of GNP using a formula of the form

$$g = Be^{At}$$

for appropriate values of A and B. Hence estimate the value of GNP after 15 years.

Solution

Figure 2.17 shows the four points plotted with g on the vertical axis and t on the horizontal axis. The basic shape of the curve joining these points certainly suggests that an exponential function is likely to provide a reasonable model, but it gives no information about what values to use for the parameters A and B. However, since one of the unknown parameters, A, occurs as a power in the relation

$$g = Be^{At}$$

it is a good idea to take natural logs of both sides to get

$$\ln g = \ln(Be^{At})$$

The rules of logs enable us to expand the right-hand side to get

$$\ln(Be^{At}) = \ln B + \ln(e^{At}) \quad \text{(rule 1)}$$
$$= \ln B + At \quad \text{(definition of a log to base e)}$$

Hence

$$\ln g = At + \ln B$$

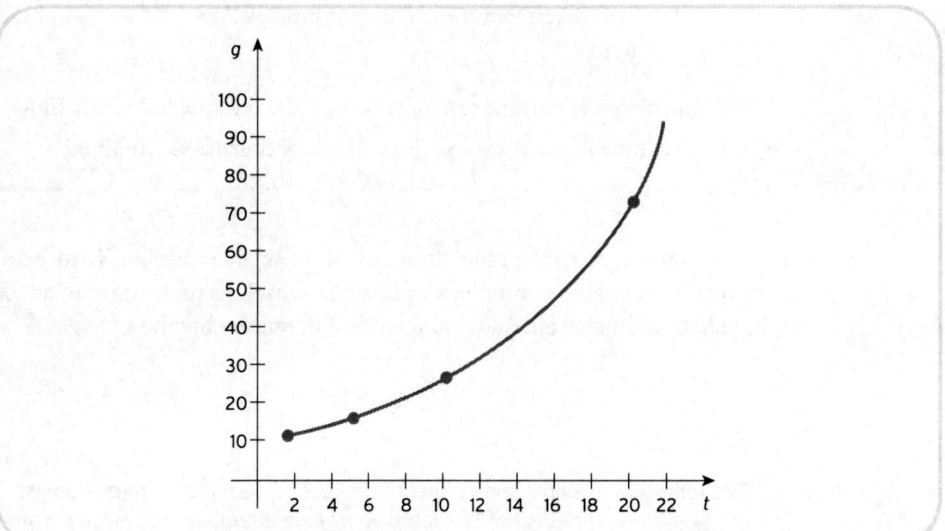

Figure 2.17

Although this does not look like it at first sight, this relation is actually the equation of a straight line! To see this recall that the usual equation of a line is $y = ax + b$. The log equation is indeed of this form if we put

$$y = \ln g \quad \text{and} \quad x = t$$

The equation then becomes

$$y = Ax + \ln B$$

so a graph of $\ln g$ plotted on the vertical axis with t plotted on the horizontal axis should produce a straight line with slope A and with an intercept on the vertical axis of $\ln B$.

Figure 2.18 shows this graph based on the table of values

$x = t$	2	5	10	20
$y = \ln g$	2.48	2.77	3.30	4.30

As one might expect, the points do not exactly lie on a straight line, since the formula is only a model. However, the line sketched in Figure 2.18 is a remarkably good fit. The slope can be calculated as

$$A = \frac{4 - 3}{18.6 - 7.6} = 0.09$$

and the vertical intercept can be read off the graph as 2.25. This is $\ln B$ and so

$$B = e^{2.25} = 9.49$$

Hence the formula for the approximate relation between g and t is

$$g = 9.49e^{0.09t}$$

An estimate of the GNP after 15 years can be obtained by substituting $t = 15$ into this formula to get

$$g = 36.6 \quad \text{(billion dollars)}$$

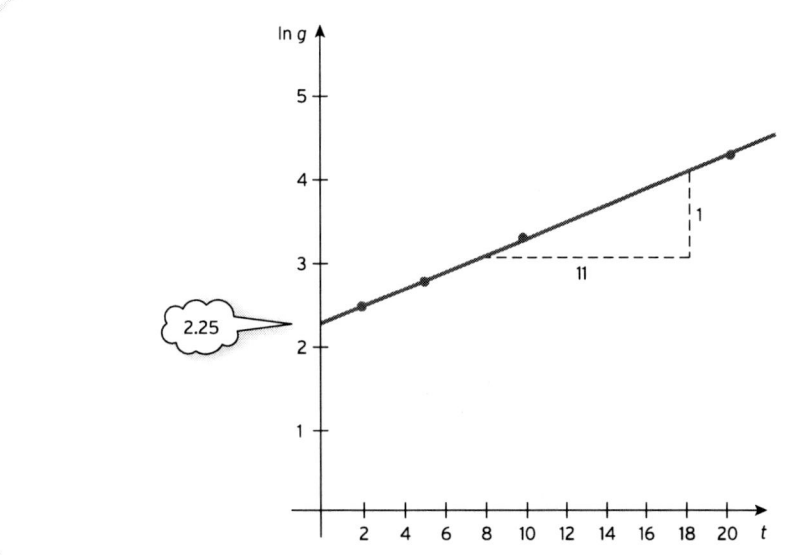

Figure 2.18

Practice Problem

6. Immediately after the launch of a new product, the monthly sales figures (in thousands) are as follows:

t (months)	1	3	6	12
s (sales)	1.8	2.7	5.0	16.5

(1) Complete the following table of values of ln s:

t	1	3	6	12
ln s	0.59		1.61	

(2) Plot these points on graph paper with the values of ln s on the vertical axis and t on the horizontal axis. Draw a straight line passing close to these points. Write down the value of the vertical intercept and calculate the slope.

(3) Use your answers to part (2) to estimate the values of A and B in the relation $s = Be^{At}$.

(4) Use the exponential model derived in part (3) to estimate the sales when

(a) $t = 9$ (b) $t = 60$

Which of these estimates would you expect to be the more reliable? Give a reason for your answer.

Key Terms

Exponential function   The function, $f(x) = e^x$; an exponential function in which the base is the number e = 2.718 281. . . .

Limited growth   Used to describe an economic variable which increases over time but which tends to a fixed quantity.

Natural logarithm   A logarithm to base, e; if $M = e^n$ then n is the natural logarithm of M and we write, $n = \ln M$.

Unlimited growth   Used to describe an economic variable which increases without bound.

Exercise 2.4

1. The number of items, N, produced each day by an assembly-line worker, t days after an initial training period, is modelled by

$$N = 100 - 100e^{-0.4t}$$

(1) Calculate the number of items produced daily

(a) 1 day after the training period

(b) 2 days after the training period

(c) 10 days after the training period.

(2) What is the worker's daily production in the long run?

(3) Sketch a graph of N against t and explain why the general shape might have been expected.

2. Use the rules of logs to expand each of the following:

(a) $\ln xy$

(b) $\ln xy^4$

(c) $\ln(xy)^2$

(d) $\ln \dfrac{x^5}{y^7}$

(e) $\ln \sqrt{\dfrac{x}{y}}$

(f) $\ln \sqrt{\dfrac{xy^3}{z}}$

3. Use the rules of logs to express each of the following as a single logarithm:

(a) $\ln x + 2 \ln x$

(b) $4 \ln x - 3 \ln y + 5 \ln z$

4. Solve each of the following equations. (Round your answer to 2 decimal places.)

(a) $e^x = 5.9$

(b) $e^x = 0.45$

(c) $e^x = -2$

(d) $e^{3x} = 13.68$

(e) $e^{-5x} = 0.34$

(f) $4e^{2x} = 7.98$

5. The value of a second-hand car reduces exponentially with age, so that its value $\$y$ after t years can be modelled by the formula

$$y = Ae^{-at}$$

If the car was \$50 000 when new and was worth \$38 000 after 2 years, find the values of A and a, correct to 3 decimal places.

Use this model to predict the value of the car

(a) when the car is 5 years old

(b) in the long run.

6. **(Excel)** Tabulate values of the following functions for $x = 0, 0.2, 0.4, \ldots, 2$. Hence sketch graphs of these functions, on the same diagram, over the range $0 \le x \le 2$. Discuss, in qualitative terms, any differences or similarities between these functions:

(a) $y = x$ **(b)** $y = x^2$ **(c)** $y = x^3$ **(d)** $y = \sqrt{x}$ **(e)** $y = e^x$

[In Excel, e^x is typed EXP(x).]

Exercise 2.4*

1. The value (in cents) of shares, t years after their flotation on the stock market, is modelled by

$$V = 6e^{0.8t}$$

Find the increase in the value of these shares, 4 years and 2 months later. Give your answer to the nearest cent.

2. Solve each of the following equations, correct to 2 decimal places:

(a) $6e^{-2x} = 0.62$ **(b)** $5 \ln(4x) = 9.84$ **(c)** $3 \ln(5x) - 2 \ln(x) = 7$

3. A team of financial advisers guiding the launch of a national newspaper has modelled the future circulation of the newspaper by the equation

$$N = c(1 - e^{-kt})$$

where N is the daily circulation after t days of publication, and c and k are positive constants. Transpose this formula to show that

$$t = \frac{1}{k} \ln\left(\frac{c}{c - N}\right)$$

When the paper is launched, audits show that

$$c = 700\,000 \quad \text{and} \quad k = \frac{1}{30} \ln 2$$

(a) Calculate the daily circulation after 30 days of publication.

(b) After how many days will the daily circulation first reach 525 000?

(c) What advice can you give the newspaper proprietor if it is known that the paper will break even only if the daily circulation exceeds 750 000?

4. A Cobb–Douglas production function is given by

$$Q = 3L^{1/2}K^{1/3}$$

Find an expression for $\ln Q$ in terms of $\ln L$ and $\ln K$.

If a graph were to be sketched of $\ln Q$ against $\ln K$ (for varying values of Q and K but with L fixed), explain briefly why the graph will be a straight line and state its slope and vertical intercept.

5. The following table gives data relating a firm's output, Q and labour, L:

L	1	2	3	4	5
Q	0.50	0.63	0.72	0.80	0.85

The firm's short-run production function is believed to be of the form

$$Q = AL^n$$

(a) Show that

$$\ln Q = n \ln L + \ln A$$

(b) Using the data supplied, copy and complete the following table:

$\ln L$		0.69		1.39	
$\ln Q$	−0.69		−0.33		−0.16

Plot these points with $\ln L$ on the horizontal axis and $\ln Q$ on the vertical axis. Draw a straight line passing as close as possible to all five points.

(c) By finding the slope and vertical intercept of the line sketched in part (b), estimate the values of the parameters n and A.

6. (a) Multiply out the brackets

$$(3y - 2)(y + 5)$$

(b) Solve the equation

$$3e^{2x} + 13e^{x} = 10$$

Give your answer correct to 3 decimal places.

7. (a) Make y the subject of the equation

$$x = ae^{by}$$

(b) Make x the subject of the equation

$$y = \ln(3 + e^{2x})$$

8. (Excel) Tabulate values of the functions $\ln x$, $\log_{10}x$ and $\log_{6}x$ for $x = 0.2, 0.4, 0.6, 0.8, 1.0,$ 2, 3, 4, . . . , 8. Hence sketch graphs of these functions on the same diagram, over the range $0.2 \le x \le 8$.

Briefly comment on any similarities and differences between them.

[In Excel, natural logs and logs to base 10 are typed as $LN(x)$ and $LOG(x)$ respectively. In general, to find the logarithm of a number x to base n, type $LOG(x, n)$.]

9. (Excel) The demand function of a good can be modelled approximately by

$$P = 100 - \frac{2}{3}Q^{n}$$

(a) Show that if this relation is exact then a graph of $\ln(150 - 1.5P)$ against $\ln Q$ will be a straight line passing through the origin with slope n.

(b) For the data given below, tabulate the values of $\ln(150 - 1.5P)$ and $\ln Q$. Find the line of best fit and hence estimate the value of n correct to 1 decimal place.

Q	10	50	60	100	200	400
P	95	85	80	70	50	20

CHAPTER 4
Differentiation

This chapter provides a simple introduction to the general topic of calculus. In fact, 'calculus' is a Latin word and a literal translation of it is 'stone'. Unfortunately, all too many students interpret this as meaning a heavy millstone that they have to carry around with them! However, as we shall see, the techniques of calculus actually provide us with a quick way of performing calculations. (The process of counting was originally performed using stones a long time ago.)

There are eight sections, which should be read in the order that they appear. It should be possible to omit Sections 4.5 and 4.7 at a first reading and Section 4.6 can be read any time after Section 4.3.

Section 4.1 provides a leisurely introduction to the basic idea of differentiation. The material is explained using pictures, which will help you to understand the connection between the underlying mathematics and the economic applications in later sections.

There are six rules of differentiation, which are evenly split between Sections 4.2 and 4.4. Section 4.2 considers the easy rules that all students will need to know. However, if you are on a business studies or accountancy course, or are on a low-level economics route, then the more advanced rules in Section 4.4 may not be of relevance and could be ignored. As far as possible, examples given in later sections and chapters are based on the easy rules only so that such students are not disadvantaged. However, the more advanced rules are essential to any proper study of mathematical economics and their use in deriving general results is unavoidable.

Sections 4.3 and 4.5 describe standard economic applications. Marginal functions associated with revenue, cost, production, consumption and savings functions are all discussed in Section 4.3. The important topic of elasticity is described in Section 4.5. The distinction is made between price elasticity along an arc and price elasticity at a point. Familiar results involving general linear demand functions and the relationship between price elasticity of demand and revenue are derived.

Sections 4.6 and 4.7 are devoted to the topic of optimization, which is used to find the maximum and minimum values of economic functions. In the first half of Section 4.6 we concentrate on the mathematical technique. The second half contains four examination-type problems, all taken from economics, which are solved in detail. In Section 4.7, mathematics is used to derive general results relating to the optimization of profit and production functions.

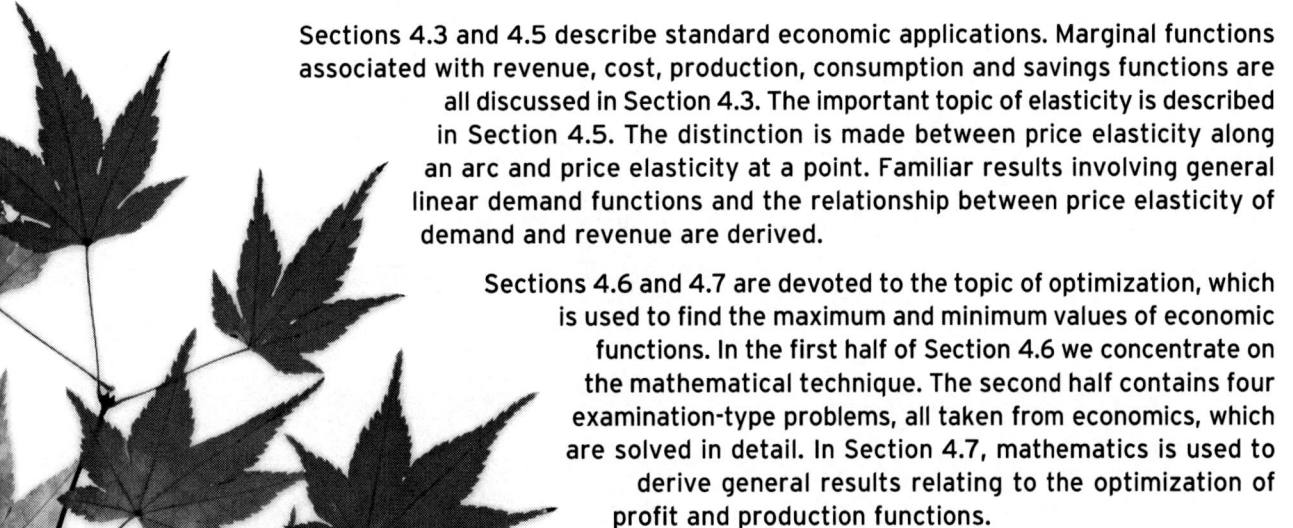

The final section revises two important mathematical functions, namely the exponential and natural logarithm functions. We describe how to differentiate these functions and illustrate their use in economics.

Differentiation is probably the most important topic in the whole book, and one that we shall continue in Chapters 5 and 6, since it provides the necessary background theory for much of mathematical economics. You are therefore advised to make every effort to attempt the problems given in each section. The prerequisites include an understanding of the concept of a function together with the ability to manipulate algebraic expressions. These are covered in Chapters 1 and 2, and if you have worked successfully through this material, you should find that you are in good shape to begin calculus.

SECTION 4.1
The derivative of a function

Objectives

At the end of this section you should be able to:

- Find the slope of a straight line given any two points on the line.
- Detect whether a line is uphill, downhill or horizontal using the sign of the slope.
- Recognize the notation $f'(x)$ and dy/dx for the derivative of a function.
- Estimate the derivative of a function by measuring the slope of a tangent.
- Differentiate power functions.

This introductory section is designed to get you started with differential calculus in a fairly painless way. There are really only three things that we are going to do. We discuss the basic idea of something called a derived function, give you two equivalent pieces of notation to describe it and finally show you how to write down a formula for the derived function in simple cases.

In Chapter 1 the slope of a straight line was defined to be the change in the value of y brought about by a 1 unit increase in x. In fact, it is not necessary to restrict the change in x to a 1 unit increase. More generally, the **slope**, or **gradient**, of a line is taken to be the change in y divided by the corresponding change in x as you move between any two points on the line. It is customary to denote the change in y by Δy, where Δ is the Greek letter 'delta'.

Likewise, the change in x is written Δx. In this notation we have

$$\boxed{\text{slope} = \frac{\Delta y}{\Delta x}}$$

Example

Find the slope of the straight line passing through

(a) A $(1, 2)$ and B $(3, 4)$ **(b)** A $(1, 2)$ and C $(4, 1)$ **(c)** A $(1, 2)$ and D $(5, 2)$

Solution

(a) Points A and B are sketched in Figure 4.1. As we move from A to B, the y coordinate changes from 2 to 4, which is an increase of 2 units, and the x coordinate changes from 1 to 3, which is also an increase of 2 units. Hence

$$\text{slope} = \frac{\Delta y}{\Delta x} = \frac{4 - 2}{3 - 1} = \frac{2}{2} = 1$$

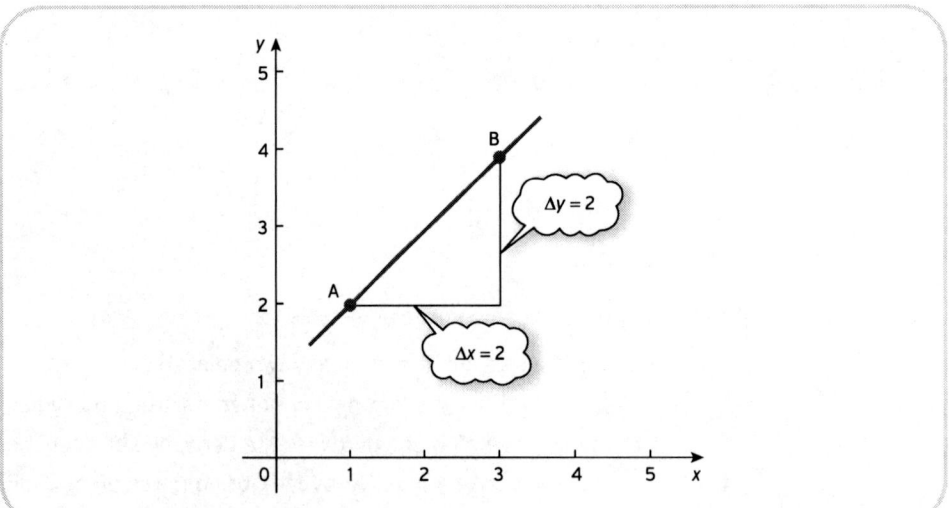

Figure 4.1

(b) Points A and C are sketched in Figure 4.2. As we move from A to C, the y coordinate changes from 2 to 1, which is a decrease of 1 unit, and the x coordinate changes from 1 to 4, which is an increase of 3 units. Hence

$$\text{slope} = \frac{\Delta y}{\Delta x} = \frac{1-2}{4-1} = \frac{-1}{3}$$

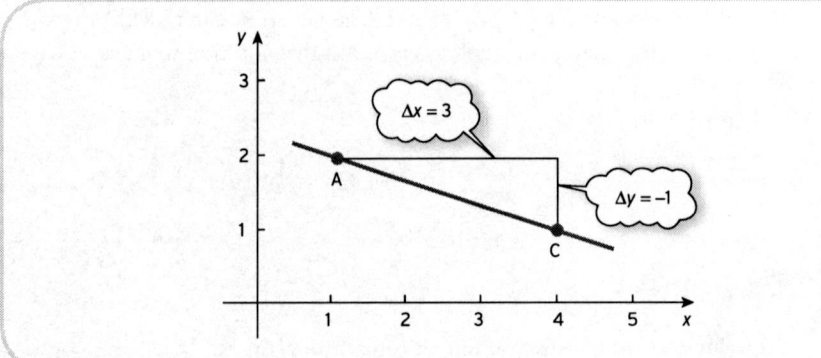

Figure 4.2

(c) Points A and D are sketched in Figure 4.3. As we move from A to D, the y coordinate remains fixed at 2, and the x coordinate changes from 1 to 5, which is an increase of 4 units. Hence

$$\text{slope} = \frac{\Delta y}{\Delta x} = \frac{2-2}{5-1} = \frac{0}{4} = 0$$

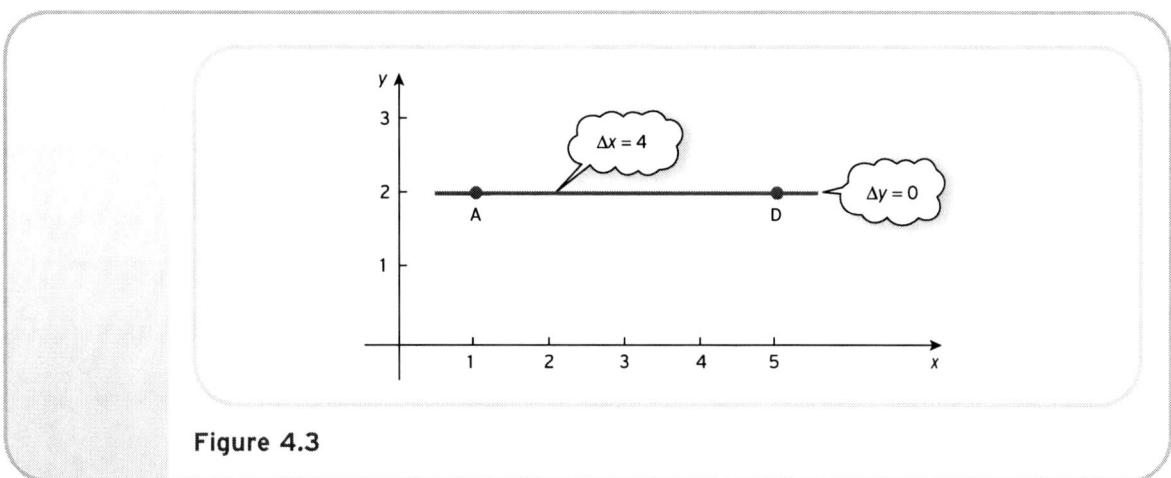

Figure 4.3

Practice Problem

1. Find the slope of the straight line passing through

    (a) E (−1, 3) and F (3, 11)   **(b)** E (−1, 3) and G (4, −2)   **(c)** E (−1, 3) and H (49, 3)

From these examples we see that the gradient is positive if the line is uphill, negative if the line is downhill and zero if the line is horizontal.

Unfortunately, not all functions in economics are linear, so it is necessary to extend the definition of slope to include more general curves. To do this we need the idea of a tangent, which is illustrated in Figure 4.4.

A straight line which passes through a point on a curve and which just touches the curve at this point is called a **tangent**. The slope, or gradient, of a curve at $x = a$ is then defined to be that of the tangent at $x = a$. Since we have already seen how to find the slope of a straight line, this gives us a precise way of measuring the slope of a curve. A simple curve together with a selection of tangents at various points is shown in Figure 4.5 (overleaf). Notice how each tangent passes through exactly one point on the curve and strikes a glancing blow. In this case, the slopes of the tangents increase as we move from left to right along the curve. This reflects the fact that the curve is flat at $x = 0$ but becomes progressively steeper further away.

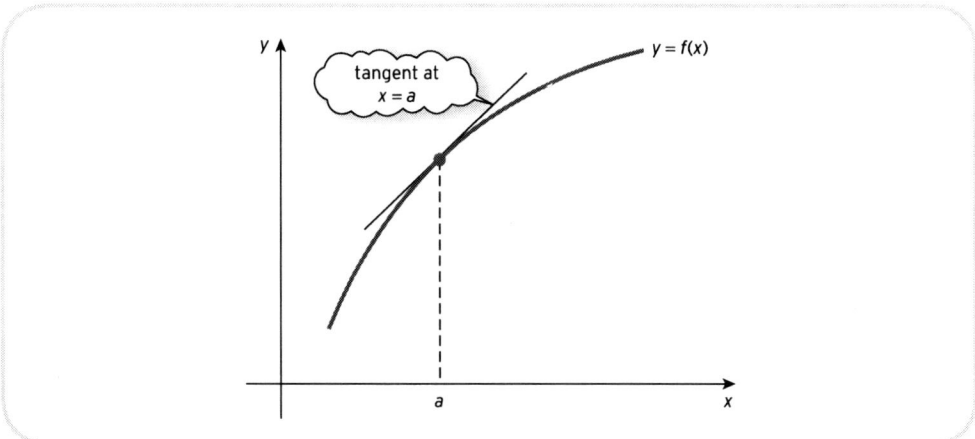

Figure 4.4

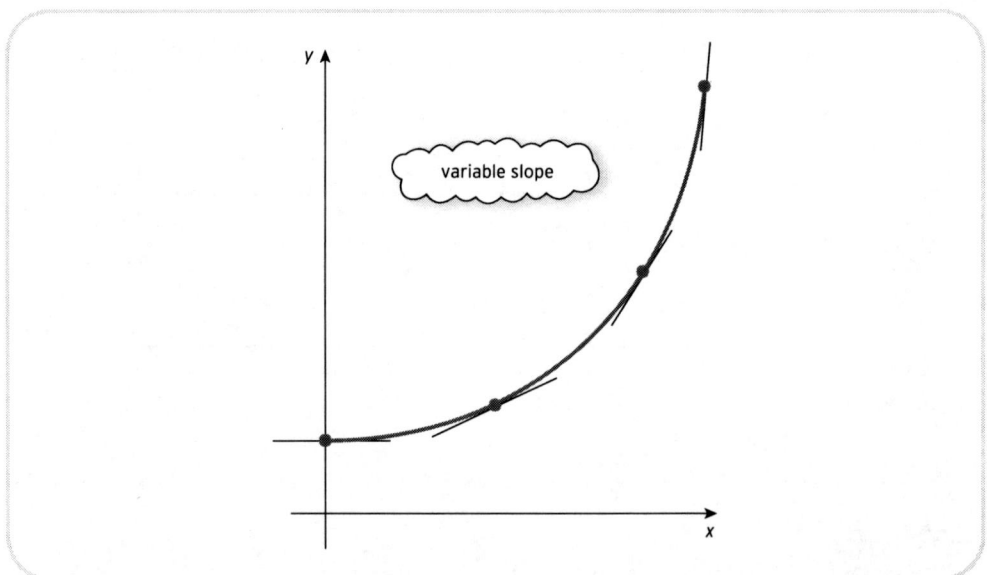

Figure 4.5

This highlights an important difference between the slope of a straight line and the slope of a curve. In the case of a straight line, the gradient is fixed throughout its length and it is immaterial which two points on a line are used to find it. For example, in Figure 4.6 all of the ratios $\Delta y/\Delta x$ have the value $^1/_2$. However, as we have just seen, the slope of a curve varies as we move along it. In mathematics we use the symbol

$$f'(a) \qquad \text{read 'f dashed of a'}$$

to represent the slope of the graph of a function f at $x = a$. This notation conveys the maximum amount of information with the minimum of fuss. As usual, we need the label f to denote which function we are considering. We certainly need the a to tell us at which point on the curve the gradient is being measured. Finally, the 'prime' symbol $'$ is used to distinguish the gradient from the function value. The notation $f(a)$ gives the height of the curve above the x axis at $x = a$, whereas $f'(a)$ gives the gradient of the curve at this point.

The slope of the graph of a function is called the **derivative** of the function. It is interesting to notice that corresponding to each value of x there is a uniquely defined derivative $f'(x)$. In other

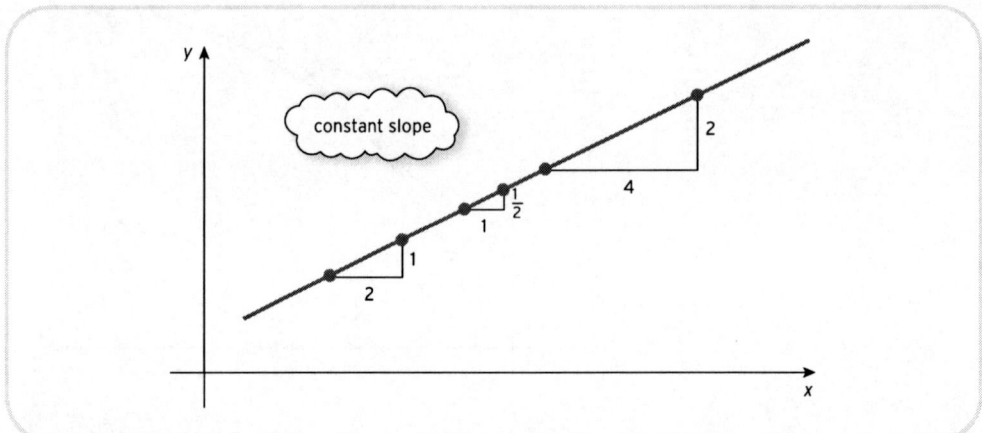

Figure 4.6

words, the rule 'find the slope of the graph of f at x' defines a function. This slope function is usually referred to as the **derived function**. An alternative notation for the derived function is

$$\frac{dy}{dx}$$ (read 'dee y by dee x')

Historically, this symbol arose from the corresponding notation $\Delta y / \Delta x$ for the gradient of a straight line; the letter 'd' is the English equivalent of the Greek letter Δ. However, it is important to realize that

$$\frac{dy}{dx}$$

does not mean 'dy divided by dx'. It should be thought of as a single symbol representing the derivative of y with respect to x. It is immaterial which notation is used, although the context may well suggest which is more appropriate. For example, if we use

$$y = x^2$$

to identify the square function then it is natural to use

$$\frac{dy}{dx}$$

for the derived function. On the other hand, if we use

$$f(x) = x^2$$

then $f'(x)$ seems more appropriate.

Example

Complete the following table of function values and hence sketch an accurate graph of $f(x) = x^2$.

x	−2.0	−1.5	−1.0	−0.5	0.0	0.5	1.0	1.5	2.0
$f(x)$									

Draw the tangents to the graph at $x = -1.5, -0.5, 0, 0.5$ and 1.5. Hence estimate the values of $f'(-1.5), f'(-0.5), f'(0), f'(0.5)$ and $f'(1.5)$.

Solution

Using a calculator we obtain

x	−2.0	−1.5	−1.0	−0.5	0.0	0.5	1.0	1.5	2.0
$f(x)$	4	2.25	1	0.25	0	0.25	1	2.25	4

The corresponding graph of the square function is sketched in Figure 4.7. From the graph we see that the slopes of the tangents are

$$f'(-1.5) = \frac{-1.5}{0.5} = -3$$

$$f'(-0.5) = \frac{-1.5}{0.5} = -1$$

$$f'(0) = 0$$

$$f'(0.5) = \frac{0.5}{0.5} = 1$$

$$f'(1.5) = \frac{1.5}{0.5} = 3$$

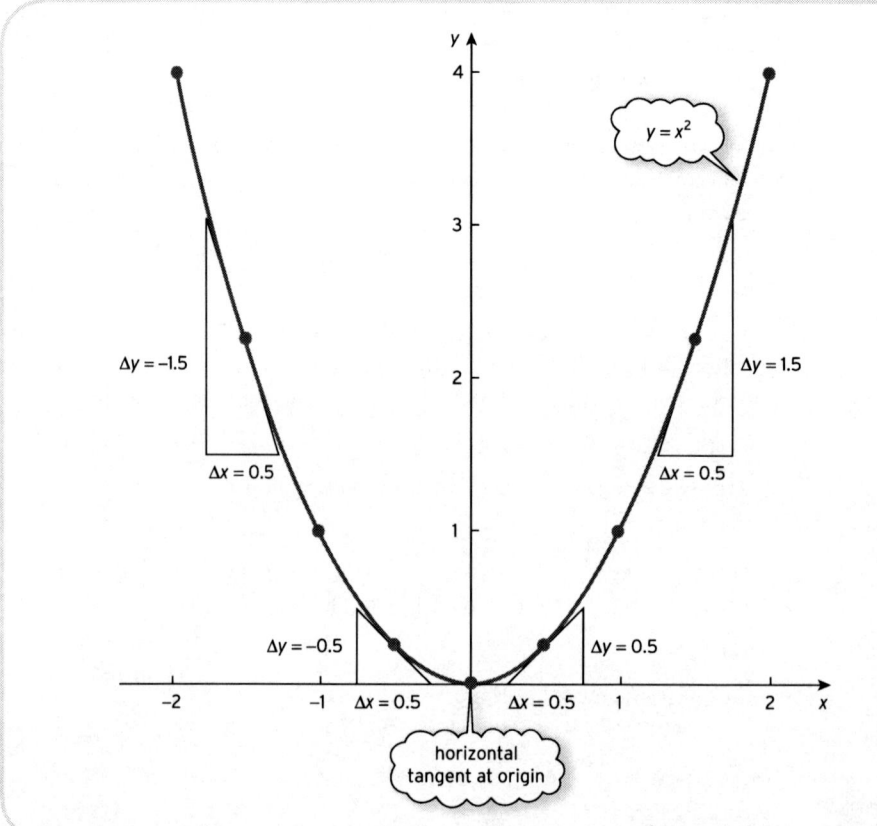

Figure 4.7

The value of $f'(0)$ is zero because the tangent is horizontal at $x = 0$. Notice that

$$f'(-1.5) = -f'(1.5) \quad \text{and} \quad f'(-0.5) = -f'(0.5)$$

This is to be expected because the graph is symmetric about the y axis. The slopes of the tangents to the left of the y axis have the same size as those of the corresponding tangents to the right. However, they have opposite signs since the curve slopes downhill on one side and uphill on the other.

Practice Problem

2. Complete the following table of function values and hence sketch an accurate graph of $f(x) = x^3$.

x	−1.50	−1.25	−1.00	−0.75	−0.50	−0.25	0.00
$f(x)$		−1.95			−0.13		

x	0.25	0.50	0.75	1.00	1.25	1.50
$f(x)$		0.13			1.95	

Draw the tangents to the graph at $x = -1$, 0 and 1. Hence estimate the values of $f'(-1)$, $f'(0)$ and $f'(1)$.

Practice Problem 2 should convince you how hard it is in practice to calculate $f'(a)$ exactly using graphs. It is impossible to sketch a perfectly smooth curve using graph paper and pencil, and it is equally difficult to judge, by eye, precisely where the tangent should be. There is also the problem of measuring the vertical and horizontal distances required for the slope of the tangent. These inherent errors may compound to produce quite inaccurate values for $f'(a)$. Fortunately, there is a really simple formula that can be used to find $f'(a)$ when f is a power function. It can be proved that

$$\text{if } f(x) = x^n \text{ then } f'(x) = nx^{n-1}$$

or, equivalently,

$$\text{if } y = x^n \text{ then } \frac{dy}{dx} = nx^{n-1}$$

The process of finding the derived function symbolically (rather than using graphs) is known as **differentiation**. In order to differentiate x^n all that needs to be done is to bring the power down to the front and then to subtract 1 from the power:

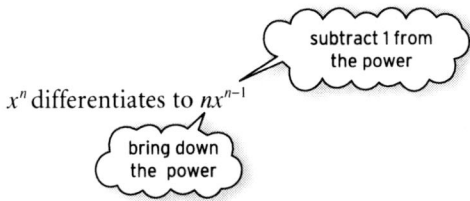

x^n differentiates to nx^{n-1}

To differentiate the square function we set $n = 2$ in this formula to deduce that

$$f(x) = x^2 \text{ differentiates to } f'(x) = 2x^{2-1}$$

that is,

$$f'(x) = 2x^1 = 2x$$

Using this result we see that

$$f'(-1.5) = 2 \times (-1.5) = -3$$
$$f'(-0.5) = 2 \times (-0.5) = -1$$
$$f'(0) = 2 \times (0) = 0$$
$$f'(0.5) = 2 \times (0.5) = 1$$
$$f'(1.5) = 2 \times (1.5) = 3$$

which are in agreement with the results obtained graphically in the preceding example.

Practice Problem

3. If $f(x) = x^3$ write down a formula for $f'(x)$. Calculate $f'(-1), f'(0)$ and $f'(1)$. Confirm that these are in agreement with your rough estimates obtained in Practice Problem 2.

Example

Differentiate

(a) $y = x^4$ **(b)** $y = x^{10}$ **(c)** $y = x$ **(d)** $y = 1$ **(e)** $y = 1/x^4$ **(f)** $y = \sqrt{x}$

Solution

(a) To differentiate $y = x^4$ we bring down the power (that is, 4) to the front and then subtract 1 from the power (that is, $4 - 1 = 3$) to deduce that

$$\frac{dy}{dx} = 4x^3$$

(b) Similarly,

$$\text{if } y = x^{10} \text{ then } \frac{dy}{dx} = 10x^9$$

(c) To use the general formula to differentiate x we first need to express $y = x$ in the form $y = x^n$ for some number n. In this case $n = 1$ because $x^1 = x$, so

$$\frac{dy}{dx} = 1x^0 = 1 \text{ since } x^0 = 1$$

This result is also obvious from the graph of $y = x$ sketched in Figure 4.8.

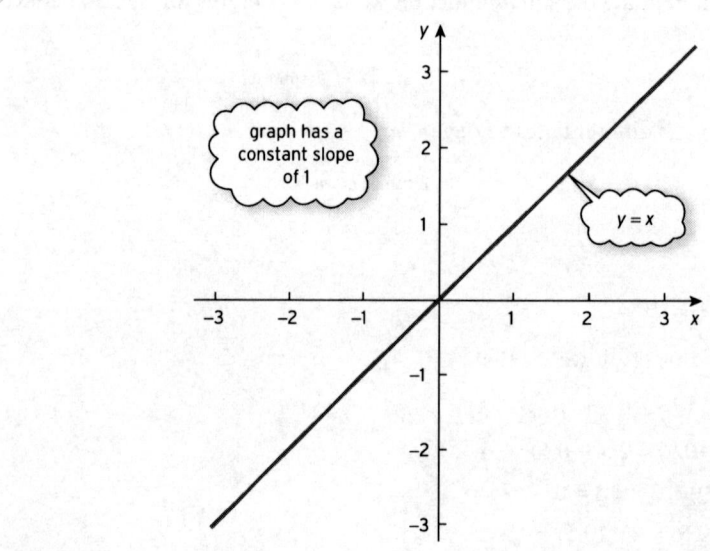

Figure 4.8

(d) Again, to differentiate 1 we need to express $y = 1$ in the form $y = x^n$. In this case $n = 0$ because $x^0 = 1$, so

$$\frac{dy}{dx} = 0x^{-1} = 0$$

This result is also obvious from the graph of $y = 1$ sketched in Figure 4.9.

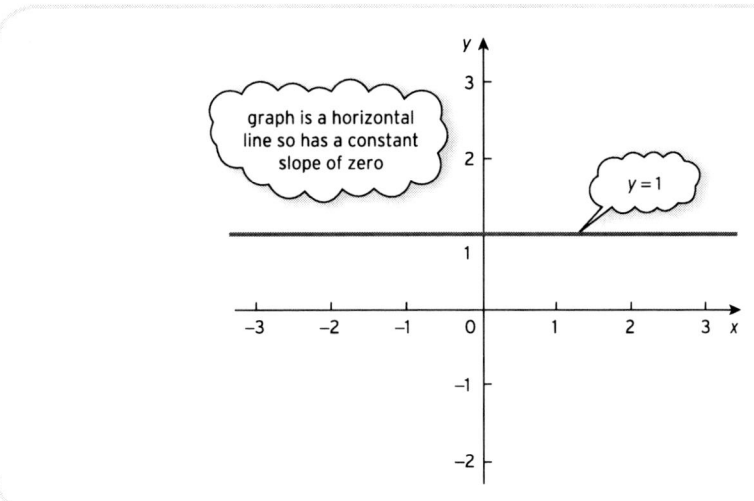

Figure 4.9

(e) Noting that $1/x^4 = x^{-4}$ it follows that

$$\text{if } y = \frac{1}{x^4} \text{ then } \frac{dy}{dx} = -4x^{-5} = -\frac{4}{x^5}$$

The power has decreased to -5 because $-4 - 1 = -5$.

(f) Noting that $\sqrt{x} = x^{1/2}$ it follows that if

$$y = \sqrt{x} \text{ then } \frac{dy}{dx} = \frac{1}{2}x^{-1/2}$$

$$= \frac{1}{2x^{1/2}} \quad \text{negative powers denote reciprocals}$$

$$= \frac{1}{2\sqrt{x}} \quad \text{fractional powers denote roots}$$

The power has decreased to $-\frac{1}{2}$ because $\frac{1}{2} - 1 = -\frac{1}{2}$.

Practice Problem

4. Differentiate

(a) $y = x^5$ **(b)** $y = x^6$ **(c)** $y = x^{100}$ **(d)** $y = 1/x$ **(e)** $y = 1/x^2$

[Hint: in parts (d) and (e) note that $1/x = x^{-1}$ and $1/x^2 = x^{-2}$]

In more advanced books on mathematics the derivative is defined via the concept of a limit and is usually written in symbols as

$$\frac{dy}{dx} = \lim_{\Delta x \to 0} \frac{\Delta y}{\Delta x}$$

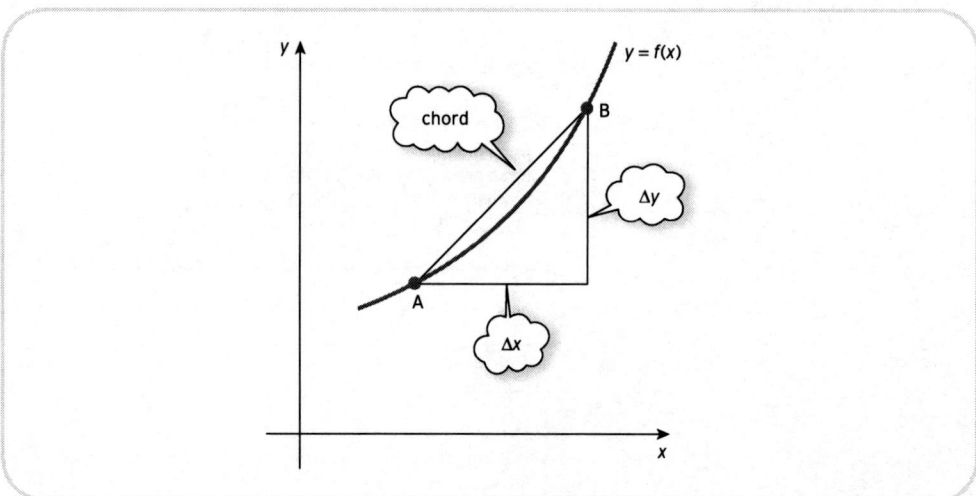

Figure 4.10

We have deliberately not introduced the derivative to you in this way because the notation can appear frightening to non-mathematics specialists. Look at Figure 4.10. Points A and B both lie on the curve $y = f(x)$ and their x and y coordinates differ by Δx and Δy respectively. A line AB which joins two points on the curve is known as a **chord** and it has slope $\Delta y / \Delta x$.

Now look at Figure 4.11, which shows a variety of chords, AB_1, AB_2, AB_3, . . . , corresponding to smaller and smaller 'widths' Δx. As the right-hand end points, B_1, B_2, B_3, . . . , get closer to A, the 'width', Δx, tends to zero. More significantly, the slope of the chord gets closer to that of the tangent at A. We describe this by saying that in the limit, as Δx tends to zero, the slope of the chord, $\Delta y / \Delta x$, is equal to that of the tangent. This limit is written

$$\lim_{\Delta x \to 0} \frac{\Delta y}{\Delta x}$$

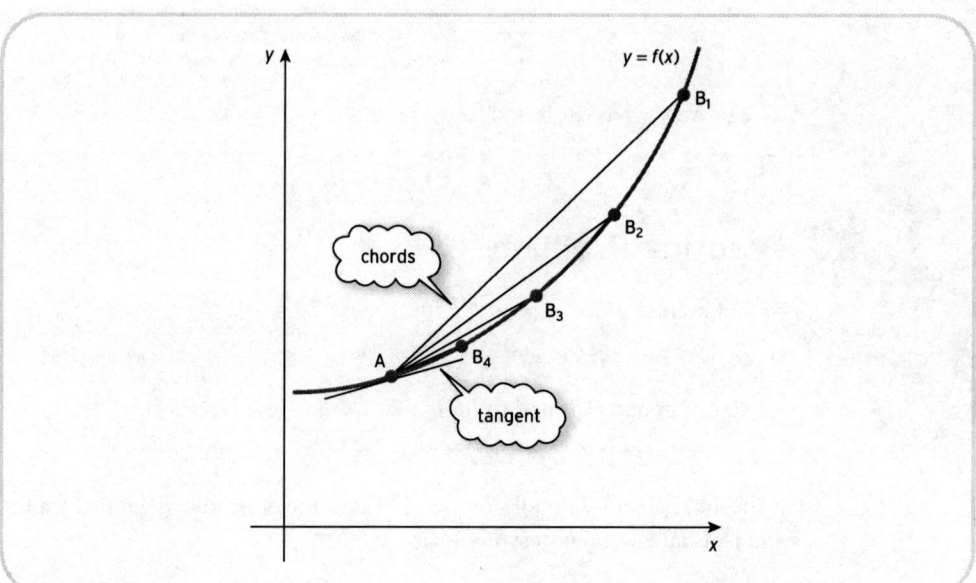

Figure 4.11

We deduce that the formal definition

$$\frac{dy}{dx} = \lim_{\Delta x \to 0} \frac{\Delta y}{\Delta x}$$

coincides with the idea that dy/dx represents the slope of the tangent, which is the approach adopted in this book.

Advice

If you have met differentiation before, you might be interested in using this definition to prove results. You are advised to consult Appendix 1 on the website.

Key Terms

Chord   A line joining two points on a curve.

Derivative   The gradient of the tangent to a curve at a point. The derivative at $x = a$ is written $f'(a)$.

Derived function   The rule, f', which gives the gradient of a function, f, at a general point.

Differentiation   The process or operation of determining the first derivative of a function.

Gradient   The gradient of a line measures steepness and is the vertical change divided by the horizontal change between any two points on the line. The gradient of a curve at a point is that of the tangent at that point.

Slope   An alternative word for gradient.

Tangent   A line that just touches a curve at a point.

Exercise 4.1

1. Find the slope of the straight line passing through
   (a) $(2, 5)$ and $(4, 9)$ **(b)** $(3, -1)$ and $(7, -5)$ **(c)** $(7, 19)$ and $(4, 19)$

2. Verify that the points $(0, 2)$ and $(3, 0)$ lie on the line
   $$2x + 3y = 6$$
   Hence find the slope of this line. Is the line uphill, downhill or horizontal?

3. Sketch the graph of the function
   $$f(x) = 5$$
   Explain why it follows from this that
   $$f'(x) = 0$$

4. Differentiate the function
   $$f(x) = x^7$$

Hence calculate the slope of the graph of

$$y = x^7$$

at the point $x = 2$.

5. Differentiate

(a) $y = x^8$ (b) $y = x^{50}$ (c) $y = x^{19}$ (d) $y = x^{999}$

6. Differentiate the following functions, giving your answer in a similar form, without negative or fractional indices:

(a) $f(x) = \dfrac{1}{x^3}$ (b) $f(x) = \sqrt{x}$ (c) $f(x) = \dfrac{1}{\sqrt{x}}$ (d) $y = x\sqrt{x}$

7. Complete the following table of function values for the function, $f(x) = x^2 - 2x$:

x	-1	-0.5	0	0.5	1	1.5	2	2.5
$x^2 - 2x$								

Sketch the graph of this function and, by measuring the slope of the tangents, estimate

(a) $f'(-0.5)$ (b) $f'(1)$ (c) $f'(1.5)$

Exercise 4.1*

1. Verify that the points $(0, b)$ and $(1, a + b)$ lie on the line

$$y = ax + b$$

Hence show that this line has slope a.

2. Differentiate each of the following functions expressing your answer in a similar form:

(a) $y = x^{15}$ (b) $x^4\sqrt{x}$ (c) $y = \sqrt[3]{x}$ (d) $\dfrac{1}{\sqrt[4]{x}}$ (e) $\dfrac{\sqrt{x}}{x^7}$

3. For each of the graphs

(a) $y = \sqrt{x}$ (b) $y = x\sqrt{x}$ (c) $y = \dfrac{1}{\sqrt{x}}$

A is the point where $x = 4$, and B is the point where $x = 4.1$. In each case find

(i) the y coordinates of A and B

(ii) the gradient of the chord AB

(iii) the value of $\dfrac{dy}{dx}$ at A.

Compare your answers to parts (ii) and (iii).

4. Find the coordinates of the point(s) at which the curve has the specified gradient.

(a) $y = x^{2/3}$, gradient $= \dfrac{1}{3}$ (b) $y = x^5$, gradient $= 405$

(c) $y = \dfrac{1}{x^2}$, gradient $= 16$ (d) $y = \dfrac{1}{x\sqrt{x}}$, gradient $= -\dfrac{3}{64}$

SECTION 4.2
Rules of differentiation

Objectives

At the end of this section you should be able to:

- Use the constant rule to differentiate a function of the form $cf(x)$.
- Use the sum rule to differentiate a function of the form $f(x) + g(x)$.
- Use the difference rule to differentiate a function of the form $f(x) - g(x)$.
- Evaluate and interpret second-order derivatives.

Advice

In this section we consider three elementary rules of differentiation. Subsequent sections of this chapter describe various applications to economics. However, before you can tackle these successfully, you must have a thorough grasp of the basic techniques involved. The problems in this section are repetitive in nature. This is deliberate. Although the rules themselves are straightforward, it is necessary for you to practise them over and over again before you can become proficient in using them. In fact, you will not be able to get much further with the rest of this book until you have mastered the rules of this section.

Rule 1 The constant rule

If $h(x) = cf(x)$ then $h'(x) = cf'(x)$

for any constant c.

This rule tells you how to find the derivative of a constant multiple of a function:

differentiate the function and multiply by the constant

Example

Differentiate

(a) $y = 2x^4$ **(b)** $y = 10x$

Solution

(a) To differentiate $2x^4$ we first differentiate x^4 to get $4x^3$ and then multiply by 2. Hence

If $y = 2x^4$ then $\dfrac{dy}{dx} = 2(4x^3) = 8x^3$

(b) To differentiate $10x$ we first differentiate x to get 1 and then multiply by 10. Hence

If $y = 10x$ then $\dfrac{dy}{dx} = 10(1) = 10$

Practice Problem

1. Differentiate

   (a) $y = 4x^3$ **(b)** $y = 2/x$

The constant rule can be used to show that

> **constants differentiate to zero**

To see this, note that the equation

$$y = c$$

is the same as

$$y = cx^0$$

because $x^0 = 1$. By the constant rule we first differentiate x^0 to get $0x^{-1}$ and then multiply by c. Hence

$$\text{if } y = c \quad \text{then} \quad \frac{dy}{dx} = c(0x^{-1}) = 0$$

This result is also apparent from the graph of $y = c$, sketched in Figure 4.12, which is a horizontal line c units away from the x axis. It is an important result and explains why lone constants lurking in mathematical expressions disappear when differentiated.

Rule 2 The sum rule

$$\text{If } h(x) = f(x) + g(x) \quad \text{then} \quad h'(x) = f'(x) + g'(x)$$

This rule tells you how to find the derivative of the sum of two functions:

> **differentiate each function separately and add**

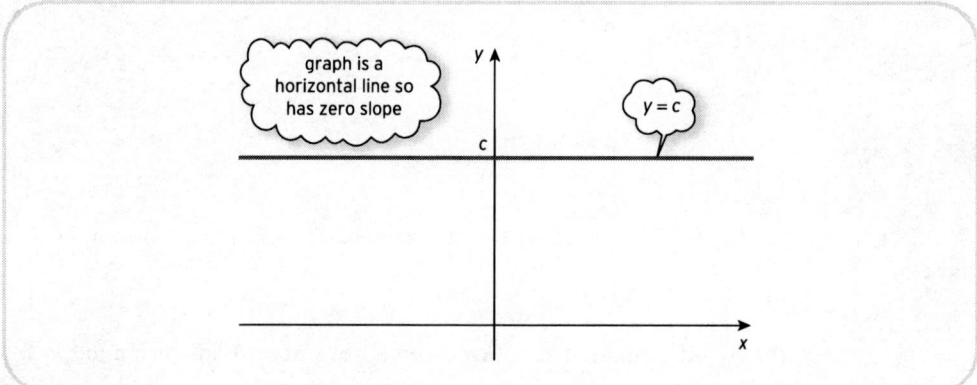

Figure 4.12

Example

Differentiate

(a) $y = x^2 + x^{50}$ (b) $y = x^3 + 3$

Solution

(a) To differentiate $x^2 + x^{50}$ we need to differentiate x^2 and x^{50} separately and add. Now

$\quad x^2$ differentiates to $2x$

and

$\quad x^{50}$ differentiates to $50x^{49}$

so

$\quad$ if $y = x^2 + x^{50}$ then $\dfrac{dy}{dx} = 2x + 50x^{49}$

(b) To differentiate $x^3 + 3$ we need to differentiate x^3 and 3 separately and add. Now

$\quad x^3$ differentiates to $3x^2$

and

$\quad 3$ differentiates to 0

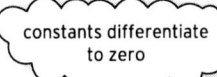

constants differentiate to zero

so

$\quad$ if $y = x^3 + 3$ then $\dfrac{dy}{dx} = 3x^2 + 0 = 3x^2$

Practice Problem

2. Differentiate

$\quad$ (a) $y = x^5 + x$ (b) $y = x^2 + 5$

Rule 3 The difference rule

$\quad$ If $h(x) = f(x) - g(x)$ then $h'(x) = f'(x) - g'(x)$

This rule tells you how to find the derivative of the difference of two functions:

differentiate each function separately and subtract

Example

Differentiate

(a) $y = x^5 - x^2$ **(b)** $y = x - \dfrac{1}{x^2}$

Solution

(a) To differentiate $x^5 - x^2$ we need to differentiate x^5 and x^2 separately and subtract. Now

x^5 differentiates to $5x^4$

and

x^2 differentiates to $2x$

so

if $y = x^5 - x^2$ then $\dfrac{dy}{dx} = 5x^4 - 2x$

(b) To differentiate $x - \dfrac{1}{x^2}$ we need to differentiate x and $\dfrac{1}{x^2}$ separately and subtract. Now

x differentiates to 1

and

$\dfrac{1}{x^2}$ differentiates to $-\dfrac{2}{x^3}$

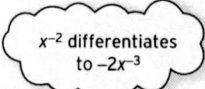

x^{-2} differentiates to $-2x^{-3}$

so

if $y = x - \dfrac{1}{x^2}$ then $\dfrac{dy}{dx} = 1 - \left(-\dfrac{2}{x^3}\right) = 1 + \dfrac{2}{x^3}$

Practice Problem

3. Differentiate

(a) $y = x^2 - x^3$ **(b)** $y = 50 - \dfrac{1}{x^3}$

It is possible to combine these three rules and so to find the derivative of more involved functions, as the following example demonstrates.

Example

Differentiate

(a) $y = 3x^5 + 2x^3$ **(b)** $y = x^3 + 7x^2 - 2x + 10$ **(c)** $y = 2\sqrt{x} + \dfrac{3}{x}$

Solution

(a) The sum rule shows that to differentiate $3x^5 + 2x^3$ we need to differentiate $3x^5$ and $2x^3$ separately and add. By the constant rule

$3x^5$ differentiates to $3(5x^4) = 15x^4$

and

$2x^3$ differentiates to $2(3x^2) = 6x^2$

so

if $y = 3x^5 + 2x^3$ then $\dfrac{dy}{dx} = 15x^4 + 6x^2$

With practice you will soon find that you can just write the derivative down in a single line of working by differentiating term by term. For the function

$y = 3x^5 + 2x^3$

we could just write

$\dfrac{dy}{dx} = 3(5x^4) + 2(3x^2) = 15x^4 + 6x^2$

(b) So far we have only considered expressions comprising at most two terms. However, the sum and difference rules still apply to lengthier expressions, so we can differentiate term by term as before. For the function

$y = x^3 + 7x^2 - 2x + 10$

we get

$\dfrac{dy}{dx} = 3x^2 + 7(2x) - 2(1) + 0 = 3x^2 + 14x - 2$

(c) To differentiate

$y = 2\sqrt{x} + \dfrac{3}{x}$

we first rewrite it using the notation of indices as

$y = 2x^{1/2} + 3x^{-1}$

Differentiating term by term then gives

$\dfrac{dy}{dx} = 2\left(\dfrac{1}{2}\right)x^{-1/2} + 3(-1)x^{-2} = x^{-1/2} - 3x^{-2}$

which can be written in the more familiar form

$= \dfrac{1}{\sqrt{x}} - \dfrac{3}{x^2}$

Practice Problem

4. Differentiate

(a) $y = 9x^5 + 2x^2$ **(b)** $y = 5x^8 - \dfrac{3}{x}$

(c) $y = x^2 + 6x + 3$ **(d)** $y = 2x^4 + 12x^3 - 4x^2 + 7x - 400$

Whenever a function is differentiated, the thing that you end up with is itself a function. This suggests the possibility of differentiating a second time to get the 'slope of the slope function'. This is written as

$f''(x)$  read 'f double dashed of x'

or

$\dfrac{d^2y}{dx^2}$ read 'dee two y by dee x squared'

For example, if

$f(x) = 5x^2 - 7x + 12$

then differentiating once gives

$f'(x) = 10x - 7$

and if we now differentiate $f'(x)$ we get

$f''(x) = 10$

The function $f'(x)$ is called the **first-order derivative** and $f''(x)$ is called the **second-order derivative**.

Example

Evaluate $f''(1)$ where

$f(x) = x^7 + \dfrac{1}{x}$

Solution

To find $f''(1)$ we need to differentiate

$f(x) = x^7 + x^{-1}$

twice and put $x = 1$ into the end result. Differentiating once gives

$f'(x) = 7x^6 + (-1)x^{-2} = 7x^6 - x^{-2}$

and differentiating a second time gives

$f''(x) = 7(6x^5) - (-2)x^{-3} = 42x^5 + 2x^{-3}$

Finally, substituting $x = 1$ into

$f''(x) = 42x^5 + \dfrac{2}{x^3}$

gives

$f''(1) = 42 + 2 = 44$

Practice Problem

5. Evaluate $f''(6)$ where

$$f(x) = 4x^3 - 5x^2$$

It is possible to give a graphical interpretation of the sign of the second-order derivative. Remember that the first-order derivative, $f'(x)$, measures the gradient of a curve. If the derivative of $f'(x)$ is positive (that is, if $f''(x) > 0$) then $f'(x)$ is increasing. This means that the graph gets steeper as you move from left to right and so the curve bends upwards. On the other hand, if $f''(x) < 0$, the gradient, $f'(x)$ must be decreasing, so the curve bends downwards. These two cases are illustrated in Figure 4.13. For this function, $f''(x) < 0$ to the left of $x = a$, and $f''(x) > 0$ to the right of $x = a$. At $x = a$ itself, the curve changes from bending downwards to bending upwards and at this point, $f''(a) = 0$.

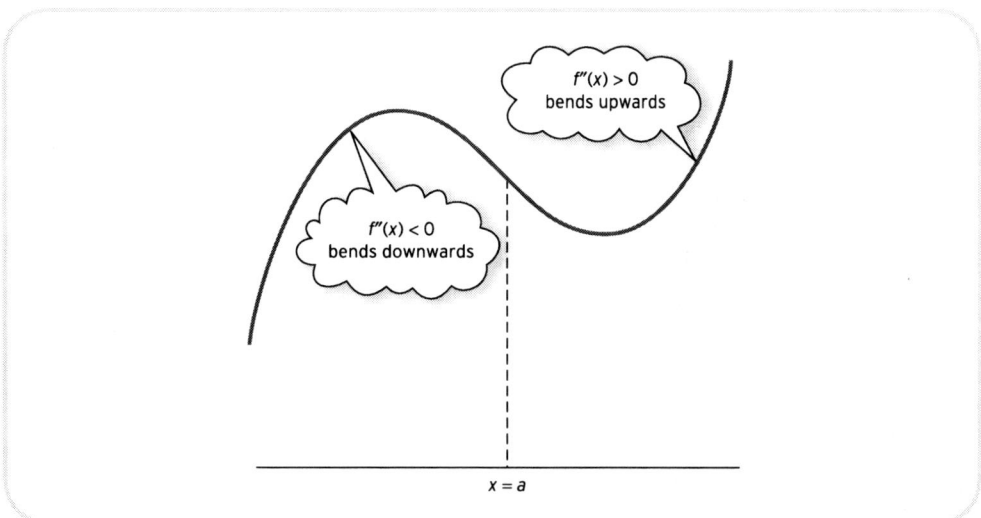

Figure 4.13

Example

Use the second-order derivative to show that the graph of the quadratic

$$y = ax^2 + bx + c$$

bends upwards when $a > 0$ and bends downwards when $a < 0$.

Solution

If $y = ax^2 + bx + c$ then $\dfrac{dy}{dx} = 2ax + b$ and $\dfrac{d^2y}{dx^2} = 2a$

If $a > 0$ then $\dfrac{d^2y}{dx^2} = 2a > 0$ so the parabola bends upwards

If $a < 0$ then $\dfrac{d^2y}{dx^2} = 2a < 0$ so the parabola bends downwards

Of course, if $a = 0$, the equation reduces to $y = bx + c$, which is the equation of a straight line, so the graph bends neither upwards nor downwards.

Throughout this section the functions have all been of the form $y = f(x)$, where the letters x and y denote the variables involved. In economic functions, different symbols are used. It should be obvious, however, that we can still differentiate such functions by applying the rules of this section. For example, if a supply function is given by

$$Q = P^2 + 3P + 1$$

and we need to find the derivative of Q with respect to P then we can apply the sum and difference rules to obtain

$$\frac{dQ}{dP} = 2P + 3$$

Key Terms

First-order derivative   The rate of change of a function with respect to its independent variable. It is the same as the 'derivative' of a function, $y = f(x)$, and is written as $f'(x)$ or dy/dx.

Second-order derivative   The derivative of the first-order derivative. The expression obtained when the original function, $y = f(x)$, is differentiated twice in succession and is written as $f''(x)$ or d^2y/dx^2.

Exercise 4.2

1. Differentiate ❓

    (a) $y = 5x^2$

    (b) $y = \dfrac{3}{x}$

    (c) $y = 2x + 3$

    (d) $y = x^2 + x + 1$

    (e) $y = x^2 - 3x + 2$

    (f) $y = 3x - \dfrac{7}{x}$

    (g) $y = 2x^3 - 6x^2 + 49x - 54$

    (h) $y = ax + b$

    (i) $y = ax^2 + bx + c$

    (j) $y = 4\sqrt{x} - \dfrac{3}{x} + \dfrac{7}{x^2}$

2. Evaluate $f'(x)$ for each of the following functions at the given point:

    (a) $f(x) = 3x^9$ at $x = 1$

    (b) $f(x) = x^2 - 2x$ at $x = 3$

    (c) $f(x) = x^3 - 4x^2 + 2x - 8$ at $x = 0$

    (d) $f(x) = 5x^4 - \dfrac{4}{x^4}$ at $x = -1$

    (e) $f(x) = \sqrt{x} - \dfrac{2}{x}$ at $x = 4$

3. By writing $x^2\left(x^2 + 2x - \dfrac{5}{x^2}\right) = x^4 + 2x^3 - 5$ differentiate $x^2\left(x^2 + 2x - \dfrac{5}{x^2}\right)$.

Use a similar approach to differentiate

(a) $x^2(3x - 4)$

(b) $x(3x^3 - 2x^2 + 6x - 7)$

(c) $(x + 1)(x - 6)$

(d) $\dfrac{x^2 - 3}{x}$

(e) $\dfrac{x - 4x^2}{x^3}$

(f) $\dfrac{x^2 - 3x + 5}{x^2}$

4. Find expressions for d^2y/dx^2 in the case when

(a) $y = 7x^2 - x$

(b) $y = \dfrac{1}{x^2}$

(c) $y = ax + b$

5. Evaluate $f''(2)$ for the function

$$f(x) = x^3 - 4x^2 + 10x - 7$$

6. If $f(x) = x^2 - 6x + 8$, evaluate $f'(3)$. What information does this provide about the graph of $y = f(x)$ at $x = 3$?

7. By writing $\sqrt{4x} = \sqrt{4} \times \sqrt{x} = 2\sqrt{x}$, differentiate $\sqrt{4x}$.
Use a similar approach to differentiate

(a) $\sqrt{25x}$ **(b)** $\sqrt[3]{27x}$ **(c)** $\sqrt[4]{16x^3}$ **(d)** $\sqrt{\dfrac{25}{x}}$

8. Find expressions for ❷

(a) $\dfrac{dQ}{dP}$ for the supply function $Q = P^2 + P + 1$

(b) $\dfrac{d(TR)}{dQ}$ for the total revenue function $TR = 50Q - 3Q^2$

(c) $\dfrac{d(AC)}{dQ}$ for the average cost function $AC = \dfrac{30}{Q} + 10$

(d) $\dfrac{dC}{dY}$ for the consumption function $C = 3Y + 7$

(e) $\dfrac{dQ}{dL}$ for the production function $Q = 10\sqrt{L}$

(f) $\dfrac{d\pi}{dQ}$ for the profit function $\pi = -2Q^3 + 15Q^2 - 24Q - 3$

Exercise 4.2*

1. Find the value of the first-order derivative of the function

$$y = 3\sqrt{x} - \frac{81}{x} + 13$$

when $x = 9$.

2. Find expressions for

(a) $\dfrac{dQ}{dP}$ for the supply function $Q = 2P^2 + P + 1$

(b) $\dfrac{d(TR)}{dQ}$ for the total revenue function $TR = 40Q - 3Q\sqrt{Q}$

(c) $\dfrac{d(AC)}{dQ}$ for the average cost function $AC = \dfrac{20}{Q} + 7Q + 25$

(d) $\dfrac{dC}{dY}$ for the consumption function $C = Y(2Y + 3) + 10$

(e) $\dfrac{dQ}{dL}$ for the production function $Q = 200L + 4\sqrt[4]{L}$

(f) $\dfrac{d\pi}{dQ}$ for the profit function $\pi = -Q^3 + 20Q^2 - 7Q - 1$

3. Find the value of the second-order derivative of the following function at the point $x = 4$:

$$f(x) = -2x^3 + 4x^2 + x - 3$$

What information does this provide about the shape of the graph of $f(x)$ at this point?

4. Consider the graph of the function

$$f(x) = 2x^5 - 3x^4 + 2x^2 - 17x + 31$$

at $x = -1$.
   Giving reasons for your answers,

(a) state whether the tangent slopes uphill, downhill or is horizontal

(b) state whether the graph bends downwards or upwards.

5. Use the second-order derivative to show that the graph of the cubic,

$$f(x) = ax^3 + bx^2 + cx + d \ (a > 0)$$

bends upwards when $x > -b/3a$ and bends downwards when $x = -b/3a$.

6. Find the equation of the tangent to the curve

$$y = 4x^3 - 5x^2 + x - 3$$

at the point where it crosses the y axis.

SECTION 4.3
Marginal functions

Objectives

At the end of this section you should be able to:

- Calculate marginal revenue and marginal cost.
- Derive the relationship between marginal and average revenue for both a monopoly and perfect competition.
- Calculate marginal product of labour.
- State the law of diminishing marginal productivity using the notation of calculus.
- Calculate marginal propensity to consume and marginal propensity to save.

At this stage you may be wondering what on earth differentiation has got to do with economics. In fact, we cannot get very far with economic theory without making use of calculus. In this section we concentrate on three main areas that illustrate its applicability:

- revenue and cost
- production
- consumption and savings.

We consider each of these in turn.

4.3.1 Revenue and cost

In Chapter 2 we investigated the basic properties of the revenue function, TR. It is defined to be PQ, where P denotes the price of a good and Q denotes the quantity demanded. In practice, we usually know the demand equation, which provides a relationship between P and Q. This enables a formula for TR to be written down solely in terms of Q. For example, if

$$P = 100 - 2Q$$

then

$$TR = PQ = (100 - 2Q)Q = 100Q - 2Q^2$$

The formula can be used to calculate the value of TR corresponding to any value of Q. Not content with this, we are also interested in the effect on TR of a change in the value of Q from some existing level. To do this we introduce the concept of marginal revenue. The **marginal revenue**, MR, of a good is defined by

$$MR = \frac{d(TR)}{dQ}$$

marginal revenue is the derivative of total revenue with respect to demand

For example, the marginal revenue function corresponding to

$$TR = 100Q - 2Q^2$$

is given by

$$\frac{d(TR)}{dQ} = 100 - 4Q$$

If the current demand is 15, say, then

$$MR = 100 - 4(15) = 40$$

You may be familiar with an alternative definition often quoted in elementary economics textbooks. Marginal revenue is sometimes taken to be the change in TR brought about by a 1 unit increase in Q. It is easy to check that this gives an acceptable approximation to MR, although it is not quite the same as the exact value obtained by differentiation. For example, substituting $Q = 15$ into the total revenue function considered previously gives

$$TR = 100(15) - 2(15)^2 = 1050$$

An increase of 1 unit in the value of Q produces a total revenue

$$TR = 100(16) - 2(16)^2 = 1088$$

This is an increase of 38, which, according to the non-calculus definition, is the value of MR when Q is 15. This compares with the exact value of 40 obtained by differentiation.

It is instructive to give a graphical interpretation of these two approaches. In Figure 4.14 the point A lies on the TR curve corresponding to a quantity Q_0. The exact value of MR at this point is equal to the derivative

$$\frac{d(TR)}{dQ}$$

and so is given by the slope of the tangent at A. The point B also lies on the curve but corresponds to a 1 unit increase in Q. The vertical distance from A to B therefore equals the change in TR when Q increases by 1 unit. The slope of the chord joining A and B is

$$\frac{\Delta(TR)}{\Delta Q} = \frac{\Delta(TR)}{1} = \Delta(TR)$$

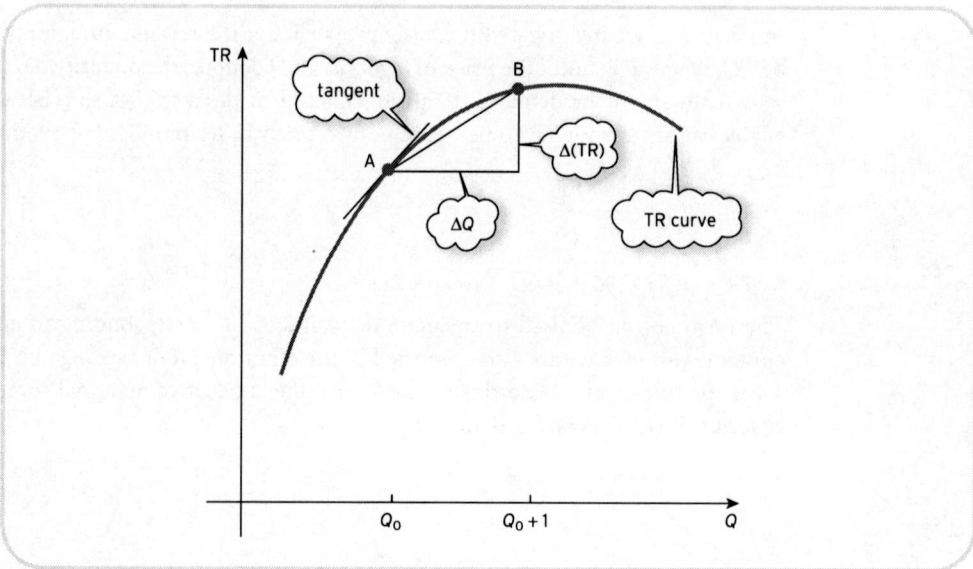

Figure 4.14

In other words, the slope of the chord is equal to the value of MR obtained from the non-calculus definition. Inspection of the diagram reveals that the slope of the tangent is approximately the same as that of the chord joining A and B. In this case the slope of the tangent is slightly the larger of the two, but there is not much in it. We therefore see that the 1 unit increase approach produces a reasonable approximation to the exact value of MR given by

$$\frac{d(TR)}{dQ}$$

Example

If the demand function is

$$P = 120 - 3Q$$

find an expression for TR in terms of Q.
   Find the value of MR at $Q = 10$ using

(a) differentiation

(b) the 1 unit increase approach

Solution

$$TR = PQ = (120 - 3Q)Q = 120Q - 3Q^2$$

(a) The general expression for MR is given by

$$\frac{d(TR)}{dQ} = 120 - 6Q$$

so at $Q = 10$,

$$MR = 120 - 6 \times 10 = 60$$

(b) From the non-calculus definition we need to find the change in TR as Q increases from 10 to 11.

Putting $Q = 10$ gives $TR = 120 \times 10 - 3 \times 10^2 = 900$
Putting $Q = 11$ gives $TR = 120 \times 11 - 3 \times 11^2 = 957$
and so $MR \simeq 57$

Practice Problem

1. If the demand function is

    $$P = 60 - Q$$

    find an expression for TR in terms of Q.

    (1) Differentiate TR with respect to Q to find a general expression for MR in terms of Q. Hence write down the exact value of MR at $Q = 50$.

    (2) Calculate the value of TR when

    (a) $Q = 50$ **(b)** $Q = 51$

    and hence confirm that the 1 unit increase approach gives a reasonable approximation to the exact value of MR obtained in part (1).

The approximation indicated by Figure 4.14 holds for any value of ΔQ. The slope of the tangent at A is the marginal revenue, MR. The slope of the chord joining A and B is $\Delta(TR)/\Delta Q$. It follows that

$$MR \simeq \frac{\Delta(TR)}{\Delta Q}$$

This equation can be transposed to give

$$\Delta(TR) \simeq MR \times \Delta Q \qquad \text{multiply both sides by } \Delta Q$$

that is,

$$\boxed{\text{change in total revenue}} \simeq \boxed{\text{marginal revenue}} \times \boxed{\text{change in demand}}$$

Moreover, Figure 4.14 shows that the smaller the value of ΔQ, the better the approximation becomes. This, of course, is similar to the argument used at the end of Section 4.1 when we discussed the formal definition of a derivative as a limit.

Example

If the total revenue function of a good is given by

$$100Q - Q^2$$

write down an expression for the marginal revenue function. If the current demand is 60, estimate the change in the value of TR due to a 2 unit increase in Q.

Solution

If

$$TR = 100Q - Q^2$$

then

$$MR = \frac{d(TR)}{dQ}$$

$$= 100 - 2Q$$

When $Q = 60$

$$MR = 100 - 2(60) = -20$$

If Q increases by 2 units, $\Delta Q = 2$ and the formula

$$\Delta(TR) \simeq MR \times \Delta Q$$

shows that the change in total revenue is approximately

$$(-20) \times 2 = -40$$

A 2 unit increase in Q therefore leads to a decrease in TR of about 40.

Practice Problem ❷

2. If the total revenue function of a good is given by

$$1000Q - 4Q^2$$

write down an expression for the marginal revenue function. If the current demand is 30, find the approximate change in the value of TR due to a

(a) 3 unit increase in Q

(b) 2 unit decrease in Q.

The simple model of demand, originally introduced in Section 1.5, assumed that price, P, and quantity, Q, are linearly related according to an equation

$$P = aQ + b$$

where the slope, a, is negative and the intercept, b, is positive. A downward-sloping demand curve such as this corresponds to the case of a **monopolist**. A single firm, or possibly a group of firms forming a cartel, is assumed to be the only supplier of a particular product and so has control over the market price. As the firm raises the price, so demand falls. The associated total revenue function is given by

$$\begin{aligned} \text{TR} &= PQ \\ &= (aQ + b)Q \\ &= aQ^2 + bQ \end{aligned}$$

An expression for marginal revenue is obtained by differentiating TR with respect to Q to get

$$\text{MR} = 2aQ + b$$

It is interesting to notice that, on the assumption of a linear demand equation, the marginal revenue is also linear with the same intercept, b, but with slope $2a$. The marginal revenue curve slopes downhill exactly twice as fast as the demand curve. This is illustrated in Figure 4.15(a).

The **average revenue**, AR, is defined by

$$\text{AR} = \frac{\text{TR}}{Q}$$

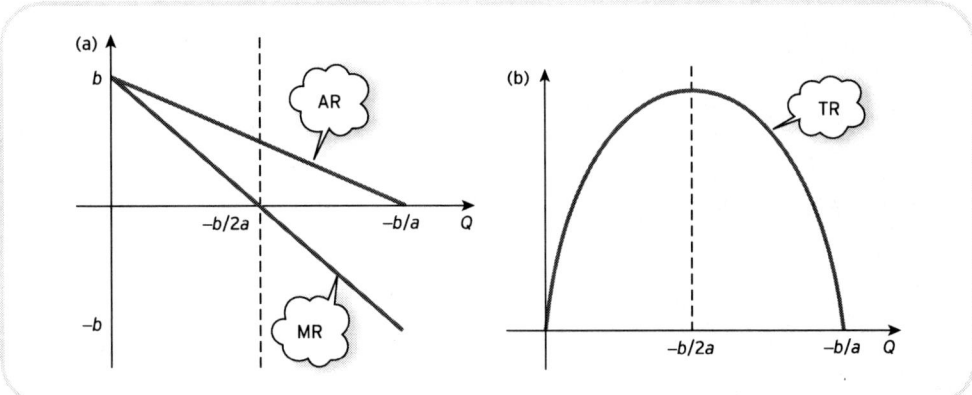

Figure 4.15

and, since TR = PQ, we have

$$AR = \frac{PQ}{Q} = P$$

For this reason the demand curve is labelled average revenue in Figure 4.15(a). The above derivation of the result AR = P is independent of the particular demand function. Consequently, the terms 'average revenue curve' and 'demand curve' are synonymous.

Figure 4.15(a) shows that the marginal revenue takes both positive and negative values. This is to be expected. The total revenue function is a quadratic and its graph has the familiar parabolic shape indicated in Figure 4.15(b). To the left of $-b/2a$ the graph is uphill, corresponding to a positive value of marginal revenue, whereas to the right of this point it is downhill, giving a negative value of marginal revenue. More significantly, at the maximum point of the TR curve, the tangent is horizontal with zero slope and so MR is zero.

At the other extreme from a monopolist is the case of **perfect competition**. For this model we assume that there are a large number of firms all selling an identical product and that there are no barriers to entry into the industry. Since any individual firm produces a tiny proportion of the total output, it has no control over price. The firm can sell only at the prevailing market price and, because the firm is relatively small, it can sell any number of goods at this price. If the fixed price is denoted by b then the demand function is

$P = b$

and the associated total revenue function is

TR = $PQ = bQ$

An expression for marginal revenue is obtained by differentiating TR with respect to Q and, since b is just a constant, we see that

MR = b

In the case of perfect competition, the average and marginal revenue curves are the same. They are horizontal straight lines, b units above the Q axis as shown in Figure 4.16.

So far we have concentrated on the total revenue function. Exactly the same principle can be used for other economic functions. For instance, we define the **marginal cost**, MC, by

$$MC = \frac{d(TC)}{dQ}$$

marginal cost is the derivative of total cost with respect to output

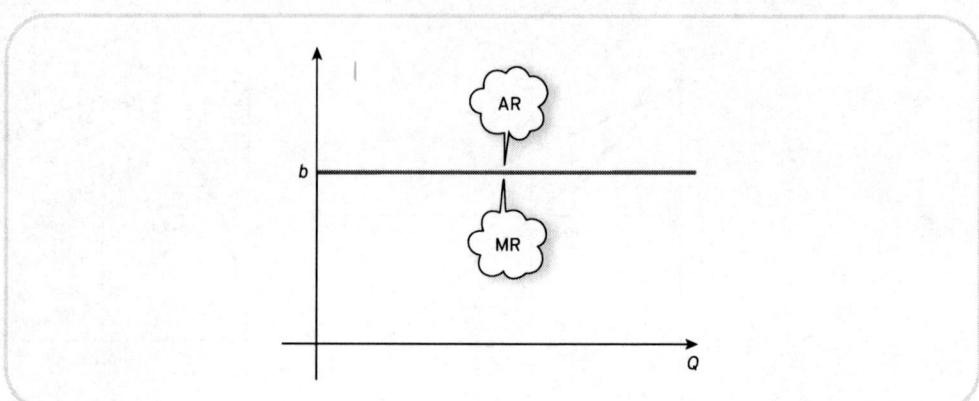

Figure 4.16

Again, using a simple geometrical argument, it is easy to see that if Q changes by a small amount ΔQ then the corresponding change in TC is given by

$$\Delta(TC) \simeq MC \times \Delta Q$$

$$\boxed{\text{change in total cost}} \simeq \boxed{\text{marginal cost}} \times \boxed{\text{change in output}}$$

In particular, putting $\Delta Q = 1$ gives

$$\Delta(TC) \simeq MC$$

so that MC gives the approximate change in TC when Q increases by 1 unit.

Example

If the average cost function of a good is

$$AC = 2Q + 6 + \frac{13}{Q}$$

find an expression for MC. If the current output is 15, estimate the effect on TC of a 3 unit decrease in Q.

Solution

We first need to find an expression for TC using the given formula for AC. Now we know that the average cost is just the total cost divided by Q: that is,

$$AC = \frac{TC}{Q}$$

Hence

$$TC = (AC)Q$$

$$= \left(2Q + 6 + \frac{13}{Q}\right)Q$$

and, after multiplying out the brackets, we get

$$TC = 2Q^2 + 6Q + 13$$

In this formula the last term, 13, is independent of Q so must denote the fixed costs. The remaining part, $2Q^2 + 6Q$, depends on Q so represents the total variable costs. Differentiating gives

$$MC = \frac{d(TC)}{dQ}$$

$$= 4Q + 6$$

Notice that because the fixed costs are constant they differentiate to zero and so have no effect on the marginal cost. When $Q = 15$,

$$MC = 4(15) + 6 = 66$$

Also, if Q decreases by 3 units then $\Delta Q = -3$. Hence the change in TC is given by

$$\Delta(TC) \simeq MC \times \Delta Q = 66 \times (-3) = -198$$

so TC decreases by 198 units approximately.

Practice Problem ❓

3. Find the marginal cost given the average cost function

$$AC = \frac{100}{Q} + 2$$

Deduce that a 1 unit increase in Q will always result in a 2 unit increase in TC, irrespective of the current level of output.

4.3.2 Production

Production functions were introduced in Section 2.3. In the simplest case output, Q, is assumed to be a function of labour, L, and capital, K. Moreover, in the short run the input K can be assumed to be fixed, so Q is then only a function of one input L. (This is not a valid assumption in the long run and in general Q must be regarded as a function of at least two inputs. Methods for handling this situation are considered in the next chapter.) The variable L is usually measured in terms of the number of workers or possibly in terms of the number of worker hours. Motivated by our previous work, we define the **marginal product of labour**, MP_L, by

$$MP_L = \frac{dQ}{dL}$$

> **marginal product of labour is the derivative of output with respect to labour**

As before, this gives the approximate change in Q that results from using 1 more unit of L.

Example

If the production function is

$$Q = 300\sqrt{L} - 4L$$

where Q denotes output and L denotes the size of the workforce, calculate the value of MP_L when

(a) $L = 1$
(b) $L = 9$
(c) $L = 100$
(d) $L = 2500$

and discuss the implications of these results.

Solution

If

$$Q = 300\sqrt{L} - 4L = 300L^{1/2} - 4L$$

then

$$\text{MP}_L = \frac{dQ}{dL}$$

$$= 300(\tfrac{1}{2}L^{-1/2}) - 4$$

$$= 150L^{-1/2} - 4$$

$$= \frac{150}{\sqrt{L}} - 4$$

(a) When $L = 1$

$$\text{MP}_L = \frac{150}{\sqrt{1}} - 4$$

(b) When $L = 9$

$$\text{MP}_L = \frac{150}{\sqrt{9}} - 4 = 46$$

(c) When $L = 100$

$$\text{MP}_L = \frac{150}{\sqrt{100}} - 4 = 11$$

(d) When $L = 2500$

$$\text{MP}_L = \frac{150}{\sqrt{2500}} - 4 = -1$$

Notice that the values of MP_L decline with increasing L. Part (a) shows that if the workforce consists of only one person then to employ two people would increase output by approximately 146. In part (b) we see that to increase the number of workers from 9 to 10 would result in about 46 additional units of output. In part (c) we see that a 1 unit increase in labour from a level of 100 increases output by only 11. In part (d) the situation is even worse. This indicates that to increase staff actually reduces output! The latter is a rather surprising result, but it is borne out by what occurs in real production processes. This may be due to problems of overcrowding on the shopfloor or to the need to create an elaborate administration to organize the larger workforce.

This example illustrates the **law of diminishing marginal productivity** (sometimes called the **law of diminishing returns**). It states that the increase in output due to a 1 unit increase in labour will eventually decline. In other words, once the size of the workforce has reached a certain threshold level, the marginal product of labour will get smaller. In the previous example, the value of MP_L continually goes down with rising L. This is not always so. It is possible for the marginal product of labour to remain constant or to go up to begin with for small values of L. However, if it is to satisfy the law of diminishing marginal productivity then there must be some value of L above which MP_L decreases.

A typical product curve is sketched in Figure 4.17, which has slope

$$\frac{dQ}{dL} = \text{MP}_L$$

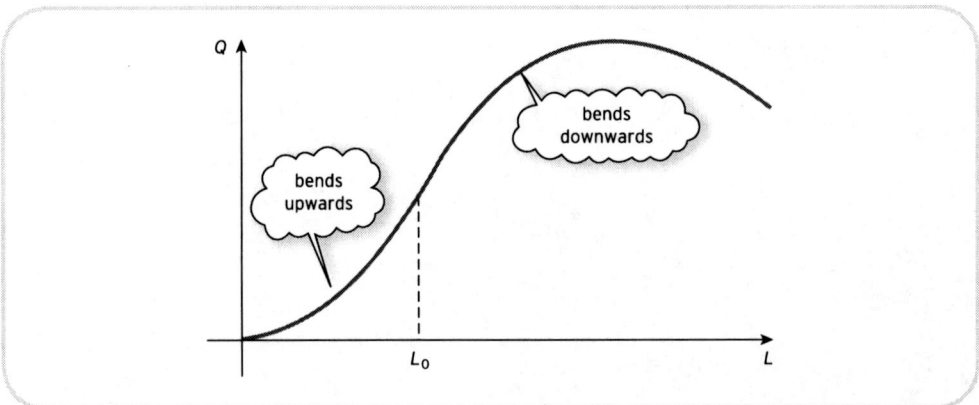

Figure 4.17

Between 0 and L_0 the curve bends upwards, becoming progressively steeper, and so the slope function, MP_L, increases. Mathematically, this means that the slope of MP_L is positive: that is,

$$\frac{d(MP_L)}{dQ} > 0$$

Now MP_L is itself the derivative of Q with respect to L, so we can use the notation for the second derivative and write this as

$$\frac{d^2Q}{dL^2} > 0$$

Similarly, if L exceeds the threshold value of L_0, then Figure 4.17 shows that the product curve bends downwards and the slope decreases. In this region, the slope of the slope function is negative, so that

$$\frac{d^2Q}{dL^2} < 0$$

The law of diminishing returns states that this must happen eventually: that is,

$$\frac{d^2Q}{dL^2} < 0$$

for sufficiently large L.

Practice Problem ❷

4. A Cobb–Douglas production function is given by

$$Q = 5L^{1/2}K^{1/2}$$

Assuming that capital, K, is fixed at 100, write down a formula for Q in terms of L only. Calculate the marginal product of labour when

(a) $L = 1$ **(b)** $L = 9$ **(c)** $L = 10\,000$

Verify that the law of diminishing marginal productivity holds in this case.

4.3.3 Consumption and savings

In Chapter 1 the relationship between consumption, C, savings, S, and national income, Y, was investigated. If we assume that national income is only used up in consumption and savings then

$$Y = C + S$$

Of particular interest is the effect on C and S due to variations in Y. Expressed simply, if national income rises by a certain amount, are people more likely to go out and spend their extra income on consumer goods or will they save it? To analyse this behaviour we use the concepts **marginal propensity to consume**, MPC, and **marginal propensity to save**, MPS, which are defined by

$$\text{MPC} = \frac{dC}{dY} \quad \text{and} \quad \text{MPS} = \frac{dS}{dY}$$

---

marginal propensity to consume is the derivative of consumption with respect to income

marginal propensity to save is the derivative of savings with respect to income

---

These definitions are consistent with those given in Section 1.7, where MPC and MPS were taken to be the slopes of the linear consumption and savings curves, respectively. At first sight it appears that, in general, we need to work out two derivatives in order to evaluate MPC and MPS. However, this is not strictly necessary. Recall that we can do whatever we like to an equation provided we do the same thing to both sides. Consequently, we can differentiate both sides of the equation

$$Y = C + S$$

with respect to Y to deduce that

$$\frac{dY}{dY} = \frac{dC}{dY} + \frac{dS}{dY} = \text{MPC} + \text{MPS}$$

Now we are already familiar with the result that when we differentiate x with respect to x the answer is 1. In this case Y plays the role of x, so

$$\frac{dY}{dY} = 1$$

Hence

$$1 = \text{MPC} + \text{MPS}$$

This formula is identical to the result given in Section 1.7 for simple linear functions. In practice, it means that we need only work out one of the derivatives. The remaining derivative can then be calculated directly from this equation.

Example

If the consumption function is

$$C = 0.01Y^2 + 0.2Y + 50$$

calculate MPC and MPS when $Y = 30$.

Solution

In this example the consumption function is given, so we begin by finding MPC. To do this we differentiate C with respect to Y. If

$$C = 0.01Y^2 + 0.2Y + 50$$

then

$$\frac{dC}{dY} = 0.02Y + 0.2$$

so, when $Y = 30$,

$$MPC = 0.02(30) + 0.2 = 0.8$$

To find the corresponding value of MPS we use the formula

$$MPC + MPS = 1$$

which gives

$$MPS = 1 - MPC = 1 - 0.8 = 0.2$$

This indicates that when national income increases by 1 unit (from its current level of 30) consumption rises by approximately 0.8 units, whereas savings rise by only about 0.2 units. At this level of income the nation has a greater propensity to consume than it has to save.

Practice Problem

5. If the savings function is given by

$$S = 0.02Y^2 - Y + 100$$

calculate the values of MPS and MPC when $Y = 40$. Give a brief interpretation of these results.

Key Terms

Average revenue   Total revenue per unit of output: $AR = TR/Q = P$.

Law of diminishing marginal productivity (law of diminishing returns)   Once the size of the workforce exceeds a particular value, the increase in output due to a 1 unit increase in labour will decline: $d^2Q/dL^2 < 0$ for sufficiently large L.

Marginal cost   The cost of producing 1 more unit of output: $MC = d(TC)/dQ$.

Marginal product of labour   The extra output produced by 1 more unit of labour: $MP_L = dQ/dL$.

Marginal propensity to consume   The fraction of a rise in national income which goes on consumption: $MPC = dC/dY$.

Marginal propensity to save   The fraction of a rise in national income which goes into savings: $MPS = dS/dY$.

Marginal revenue   The extra revenue gained by selling 1 more unit of a good: $MR = d(TR)/dQ$.

Monopolist   The only firm in the industry.

Perfect competition   A situation in which there are no barriers to entry in an industry where there are many firms selling an identical product at the market price.

Exercise 4.3

1. If the demand function is

   $$P = 100 - 4Q$$

   find expressions for TR and MR in terms of Q. Hence estimate the change in TR brought about by a 0.3 unit increase in output from a current level of 12 units.

2. If the demand function is

   $$P = 80 - 3Q$$

   show that

   $$MR = 2P - 80$$

3. A monopolist's demand function is given by

   $$P + Q = 100$$

   Write down expressions for TR and MR in terms of Q and sketch their graphs. Find the value of Q which gives a marginal revenue of zero and comment on the significance of this value.

4. If the average cost function of a good is

   $$AC = \frac{15}{Q} + 2Q + 9$$

   find an expression for TC. What are the fixed costs in this case? Write down an expression for the marginal cost function.

5. A firm's production function is

   $$Q = 50L - 0.01L^2$$

   where L denotes the size of the workforce. Find the value of MP_L in the case when

   (a) $L = 1$ **(b)** $L = 10$ **(c)** $L = 100$ **(d)** $L = 1000$

   Does the law of diminishing marginal productivity apply to this particular function?

6. If the consumption function is

   $$C = 50 + 2\sqrt{Y}$$

   calculate MPC and MPS when $Y = 36$ and give an interpretation of these results.

7. If the consumption function is

   $$C = 0.02Y^2 + 0.1Y + 25$$

   find the value of Y when MPS = 0.38.

Exercise 4.3*

1. A firm's demand function is given by

$$P = 100 - 4\sqrt{Q} - 3Q$$

(a) Write down an expression for total revenue, TR, in terms of Q.

(b) Find an expression for the marginal revenue, MR, and find the value of MR when $Q = 9$.

(c) Use the result of part (b) to *estimate* the change in TR when Q increases by 0.25 units from its current level of 9 units and compare this with the exact change in TR.

2. The consumption function is

$$C = 0.01Y^2 + 0.8Y + 100$$

(a) Calculate the values of MPC and MPS when $Y = 8$.

(b) Use the fact that $C + S = Y$ to obtain a formula for S in terms of Y. By differentiating this expression find the value of MPS at $Y = 8$ and verify that this agrees with your answer to part (a).

3. The fixed costs of producing a good are 100 and the variable costs are $2 + Q/10$ per unit.

(a) Find expressions for TC and MC.

(b) Evaluate MC at $Q = 30$ and hence estimate the change in TC brought about by a 2 unit increase in output from a current level of 30 units.

(c) At what level of output does MC = 22?

4. Show that the law of diminishing marginal productivity holds for the production function

$$Q = 6L^2 - 0.2L^3$$

5. A firm's production function is given by

$$Q = 5\sqrt{L} - 0.1L$$

(a) Find an expression for the marginal product of labour, MP_L.

(b) Solve the equation $MP_L = 0$ and briefly explain the significance of this value of L.

(c) Show that the law of diminishing marginal productivity holds for this function.

6. A firm's average cost function takes the form

$$AC = 4Q + a + \frac{6}{Q}$$

and it is known that MC = 35 when $Q = 3$. Find the value of AC when $Q = 6$.

SECTION 4.4

Further rules of differentiation

Objectives

At the end of this section you should be able to:

- Use the chain rule to differentiate a function of a function.
- Use the product rule to differentiate the product of two functions.
- Use the quotient rule to differentiate the quotient of two functions.
- Differentiate complicated functions using a combination of rules.

Section 4.2 introduced you to the basic rules of differentiation. Unfortunately, not all functions can be differentiated using these rules alone. For example, we are unable to differentiate the functions

$$x\sqrt{(2x-3)} \quad \text{and} \quad \frac{x}{x^2+1}$$

using just the constant, sum or difference rules. The aim of the present section is to describe three further rules which allow you to find the derivative of more complicated expressions. Indeed, the totality of all six rules will enable you to differentiate any mathematical function. Although you may find that the rules described in this section take you slightly longer to grasp than before, they are vital to any understanding of economic theory.

The first rule that we investigate is called the chain rule and it can be used to differentiate functions such as

$$y = (2x+3)^{10} \quad \text{and} \quad y = \sqrt{(1+x^2)}$$

The distinguishing feature of these expressions is that they represent a 'function of a function'. To understand what we mean by this, consider how you might evaluate

$$y = (2x+3)^{10}$$

on a calculator. You would first work out an intermediate number u, say, given by

$$u = 2x + 3$$

and then raise it to the power of 10 to get

$$y = u^{10}$$

This process is illustrated using the flow chart in Figure 4.18 (overleaf). Note how the incoming number x is first processed by the inner function, 'double and add 3'. The output u from this is then passed on to the outer function, 'raise to the power of 10', to produce the final outgoing number y.

The function

$$y = \sqrt{(1+x^2)}$$

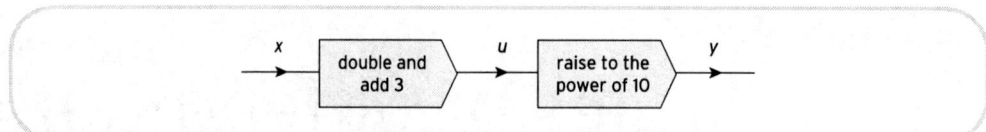

Figure 4.18

can be viewed in the same way. To calculate y you perform the inner function, 'square and add 1', followed by the outer function, 'take square roots'.

The chain rule for differentiating a function of a function may now be stated.

Rule 4 The chain rule

If y is a function of u, which is itself a function of x, then

$$\frac{dy}{dx} = \frac{dy}{du} \times \frac{du}{dx}$$

> **differentiate the outer function and multiply by the derivative of the inner function**

To illustrate this rule, let us return to the function

$$y = (2x + 3)^{10}$$

in which

$$y = u^{10} \quad \text{and} \quad u = 2x + 3$$

Now

$$\frac{dy}{du} = 10u^9 = 10(2x + 3)^9$$

$$\frac{du}{dx} = 2$$

The chain rule then gives

$$\frac{dy}{dx} = \frac{dy}{du} \times \frac{du}{dx} = 10(2x + 3)^9(2) = 20(2x + 3)^9$$

With practice it is possible to perform the differentiation without explicitly introducing the variable u. To differentiate

$$y = (2x + 3)^{10}$$

we first differentiate the outer power function to get

$$10(2x + 3)^9$$

and then multiply by the derivative of the inner function, $2x + 3$, which is 2, so

$$\frac{dy}{dx} = 20(2x + 3)^9$$

Example

Differentiate

(a) $y = (3x^2 - 5x + 2)^4$

(b) $y = \dfrac{1}{3x + 7}$

(c) $y = \sqrt{(1 + x^2)}$

Solution

(a) The chain rule shows that to differentiate $(3x^2 - 5x + 2)^4$ we first differentiate the outer power function to get

$$4(3x^2 - 5x + 2)^3$$

and then multiply by the derivative of the inner function, $3x^2 - 5x + 2$, which is $6x - 5$. Hence if

$$y = (3x^2 - 5x + 2)^4 \quad \text{then} \quad \frac{dy}{dx} = 4(3x^2 - 5x + 2)^3(6x - 5)$$

(b) To use the chain rule to differentiate

$$y = \frac{1}{3x + 7}$$

recall that reciprocals are denoted by negative powers, so that

$$y = (3x + 7)^{-1}$$

The outer power function differentiates to get

$$-(3x + 7)^{-2}$$

and the inner function, $3x + 7$, differentiates to get 3. By the chain rule we just multiply these together to deduce that

$$\text{if} \quad y = \frac{1}{3x + 7} \quad \text{then} \quad \frac{dy}{dx} = -(3x + 7)^{-2}(3) = \frac{-3}{(3x + 7)^2}$$

(c) To use the chain rule to differentiate

$$y = \sqrt{(1 + x^2)}$$

recall that roots are denoted by fractional powers, so that

$$y = (1 + x^2)^{1/2}$$

The outer power function differentiates to get

$$\frac{1}{2}(1 + x^2)^{-1/2}$$

and the inner function, $1 + x^2$, differentiates to get $2x$. By the chain rule we just multiply these together to deduce that

$$\text{if} \quad y = \sqrt{(1 + x^2)} \quad \text{then} \quad \frac{dy}{dx} = \frac{1}{2}(1 + x^2)^{-1/2}(2x) = \frac{x}{\sqrt{(1 + x^2)}}$$

Practice Problem

1. Differentiate

   (a) $y = (3x - 4)^5$ **(b)** $y = (x^2 + 3x + 5)^3$ **(c)** $y = \dfrac{1}{2x - 3}$ **(d)** $y = \sqrt{(4x - 3)}$

The next rule is used to differentiate the product of two functions, $f(x)g(x)$. In order to give a clear statement of this rule, we write

$$u = f(x) \quad \text{and} \quad v = g(x)$$

Rule 5 The product rule

$$\text{If} \quad y = uv \quad \text{then} \quad \frac{dy}{dx} = u\frac{dv}{dx} + v\frac{du}{dx}$$

This rule tells you how to differentiate the product of two functions:

multiply each function by the derivative of the other and add

Example

Differentiate

(a) $y = x^2(2x + 1)^3$ **(b)** $x\sqrt{(6x + 1)}$ **(c)** $y = \dfrac{x}{1 + x}$

Solution

(a) The function $x^2(2x + 1)^3$ involves the product of two simpler functions, namely x^2 and $(2x + 1)^3$, which we denote by u and v respectively. (It does not matter which function we label u and which we label v. The same answer is obtained if u is $(2x + 1)^3$ and v is x^2. You might like to check this for yourself later.) Now if

$$u = x^2 \quad \text{and} \quad v = (2x +1)^3$$

then

$$\frac{du}{dx} = 2x \quad \text{and} \quad \frac{dv}{dx} = 6(2x +1)^2$$

where we have used the chain rule to find dv/dx. By the product rule,

$$\frac{dy}{dx} = u\frac{dv}{dx} + v\frac{du}{dx}$$

$$= x^2[6(2x + 1)^2] + (2x + 1)^3(2x)$$

The first term is obtained by leaving u alone and multiplying it by the derivative of v. Similarly, the second term is obtained by leaving v alone and multiplying it by the derivative of u.

If desired, the final answer may be simplified by taking out a common factor of $2x(2x + 1)^2$. This factor goes into the first term $3x$ times and into the second $2x + 1$ times. Hence

$$\frac{dy}{dx} = 2x(2x + 1)^2[3x + (2x + 1)] = 2x(2x + 1)^2(5x + 1)$$

(b) The function $x\sqrt{(6x + 1)}$ involves the product of the simpler functions

$$u = x \quad \text{and} \quad v = \sqrt{(6x + 1)} = (6x + 1)^{1/2}$$

for which

$$\frac{du}{dx} = 1 \quad \text{and} \quad \frac{dv}{dx} = \frac{1}{2}(6x + 1)^{-1/2} \times 6 = 3(6x + 1)^{-1/2}$$

where we have used the chain rule to find dv/dx. By the product rule,

$$\frac{dy}{dx} = u\frac{dv}{dx} + v\frac{du}{dx}$$

$$= x[3(6x + 1)^{-1/2}] + (6x + 1)^{1/2}(1)$$

$$= \frac{3x}{\sqrt{(6x + 1)}} + \sqrt{(6x + 1)}$$

If desired, this can be simplified by putting the second term over a common denominator $\sqrt{(6x + 1)}$

To do this we multiply the top and bottom of the second term by $\sqrt{(6x + 1)}$ to get

$$\frac{6x + 1}{\sqrt{(6x + 1)}} \qquad \boxed{\sqrt{(6x+1)} \times \sqrt{(6x+1)} = 6x+1}$$

Hence

$$\frac{dy}{dx} = \frac{3x + (6x + 1)}{\sqrt{(6x + 1)}} = \frac{9x + 1}{\sqrt{(6x + 1)}}$$

(c) At first sight it is hard to see how we can use the product rule to differentiate

$$\frac{x}{1 + x}$$

since it appears to be the quotient and not the product of two functions. However, if we recall that reciprocals are equivalent to negative powers, we may rewrite it as

$$x(1 + x)^{-1}$$

It follows that we can put

$$u = x \quad \text{and} \quad v = (1 + x)^{-1}$$

which gives

$$\frac{du}{dx} = 1 \quad \text{and} \quad \frac{dv}{dx} = -(1 + x)^{-2}$$

where we have used the chain rule to find dv/dx. By the product rule

$$\frac{dy}{dx} = u\frac{dv}{dx} + v\frac{du}{dx}$$

$$\frac{dy}{dx} = x[-(1+x)^{-2}] + (1+x)^{-1}(1)$$

$$= \frac{-x}{(1+x)^2} + \frac{1}{1+x}$$

If desired, this can be simplified by putting the second term over a common denominator

$$(1+x)^2$$

To do this we multiply the top and bottom of the second term by $1 + x$ to get

$$\frac{1+x}{(1+x)^2}$$

Hence

$$\frac{dy}{dx} = \frac{-x}{(1+x)^2} + \frac{1+x}{(1+x)^2} = \frac{-x + (1+x)}{(1+x)^2} = \frac{1}{(1+x)^2}$$

Practice Problem

2. Differentiate

(a) $y = x(3x-1)^6$ **(b)** $y = x^3\sqrt{(2x+3)}$ **(c)** $y = \dfrac{x}{x-2}$

Advice

You may have found the product rule the hardest of the rules so far. This may have been due to the algebraic manipulation that is required to simplify the final expression. If this is the case, do not worry about it at this stage. The important thing is that you can use the product rule to obtain some sort of an answer even if you cannot tidy it up at the end. This is not to say that the simplification of an expression is pointless. If the result of differentiation is to be used in a subsequent piece of theory, it may well save time in the long run if it is simplified first.

One of the most difficult parts of Practice Problem 2 is part (c), since this involves algebraic fractions. For this function, it is necessary to manipulate negative indices and to put two individual fractions over a common denominator. You may feel that you are unable to do either of these processes with confidence. For this reason we conclude this section with a rule that is specifically designed to differentiate this type of function. The rule itself is quite complicated. However, as will become apparent, it does the algebra for you, so you may prefer to use it rather than the product rule when differentiating algebraic fractions.

Rule 6 The quotient rule

If $y = \dfrac{u}{v}$ then $\dfrac{dy}{dx} = \dfrac{v\,du/dx - u\,dv/dx}{v^2}$

This rule tells you how to differentiate the quotient of two functions:

> **bottom times derivative of top, minus top times derivative of bottom,
> all over bottom squared**

Example

Differentiate

(a) $y = \dfrac{x}{1 + x}$ **(b)** $y = \dfrac{x^2}{2 - x^3}$

Solution

(a) In the quotient rule, u is used as the label for the numerator and v is used for the denominator, so to differentiate

$$\frac{x}{1 + x}$$

we must take

$$u = x \quad \text{and} \quad v = 1 + x$$

for which

$$\frac{du}{dx} = 1 \quad \text{and} \quad \frac{dv}{dx} = 1$$

By the quotient rule

$$\frac{dy}{dx} = \frac{v\,du/dx - u\,dv/dx}{v^2}$$

$$= \frac{(1 + x)(1) - x(1)}{(1 + x^2)}$$

$$= \frac{1 + x - x}{(1 + x)^2}$$

$$= \frac{1}{(1 + x)^2}$$

Notice how the quotient rule automatically puts the final expression over a common denominator. Compare this with the algebra required to obtain the same answer using the product rule in part (c) of the previous example.

(b) The numerator of the algebraic fraction

$$\frac{1 + x^2}{2 - x^3}$$

is $1 + x^2$ and the denominator is $2 - x^3$, so we take

$$u = 1 + x^2 \quad \text{and} \quad v = 2 - x^3$$

for which

$$\frac{\mathrm{d}u}{\mathrm{d}x} = 2x \quad \text{and} \quad \frac{\mathrm{d}v}{\mathrm{d}x} = -3x^2$$

By the quotient rule

$$\frac{\mathrm{d}y}{\mathrm{d}x} = \frac{v\,\mathrm{d}u/\mathrm{d}x - u\,\mathrm{d}v/\mathrm{d}x}{v^2}$$

$$= \frac{(2 - x^3)(2x) - (1 + x^2)(-3x^2)}{(2 - x^3)^2}$$

$$= \frac{4x - 2x^4 + 3x^2 + 3x^4}{(2 - x^3)^2}$$

$$= \frac{x^4 + 3x^2 + 4x}{(2 - x^3)^2}$$

Practice Problem

3. Differentiate

(a) $y = \dfrac{x}{x - 2}$ **(b)** $y = \dfrac{x - 1}{x + 1}$

[You might like to check that your answer to part (a) is the same as that obtained in Practice Problem 2(c).]

Advice

The product and quotient rules give alternative methods for the differentiation of algebraic fractions. It does not matter which rule you go for; use whichever rule is easiest for you.

Exercise 4.4

1. Use the chain rule to differentiate

(a) $y = (5x + 1)^3$ (b) $y = (2x - 7)^8$ (c) $y = (x + 9)^5$

(d) $y = (4x^2 - 7)^3$ (e) $y = (x^2 + 4x - 3)^4$ (f) $y = \sqrt{(2x + 1)}$

(g) $y = \dfrac{1}{3x + 1}$ (h) $y = \dfrac{1}{(4x - 3)^2}$ (i) $y = \dfrac{1}{\sqrt{(2x + 5)}}$

2. Use the product rule to differentiate

(a) $x(3x + 4)^2$ (b) $x^2(x - 2)^3$ (c) $x\sqrt{(x + 2)}$

(d) $(x - 1)(x + 6)^3$ (e) $(2x + 1)(x + 5)^3$ (f) $x^3(2x - 5)^4$

3. Use the quotient rule to differentiate

(a) $y = \dfrac{x}{x - 5}$ (b) $y = \dfrac{x}{(x + 7)}$ (c) $y = \dfrac{x + 3}{x - 2}$

(d) $y = \dfrac{2x + 9}{3x + 1}$ (e) $\dfrac{x}{(5x + 6)}$ (f) $y = \dfrac{x + 4}{3x - 7}$

4. Differentiate

$$y = (5x + 7)^2$$

(a) by using the chain rule

(b) by first multiplying out the brackets and then differentiating term by term.

5. Differentiate

$$y = x^5(x + 2)^2$$

(a) by using the product rule

(b) by first multiplying out the brackets and then differentiating term by term.

6. Find expressions for marginal revenue in the case when the demand equation is given by

(a) $P = (100 - Q)^3$ (b) $\dfrac{1000}{Q + 4}$

7. If the consumption function is

$$C = \dfrac{300 + 2Y^2}{1 + Y}$$

calculate MPC and MPS when $Y = 36$ and give an interpretation of these results.

Exercise 4.4*

1. Use the chain rule to differentiate

    (a) $y = (2x + 1)^{10}$ **(b)** $y = (x^2 + 3x - 5)^3$ **(c)** $y = \dfrac{1}{7x - 3}$

    (d) $y = \dfrac{1}{x^2 + 1}$ **(e)** $y = \sqrt{(8x - 1)}$ **(f)** $y = \dfrac{1}{\sqrt[3]{(6x - 5)}}$

2. Use the product rule to differentiate

    (a) $y = x^2(x + 5)^3$ **(b)** $y = x^5(4x + 5)^2$ **(c)** $y = x^4\sqrt{(x + 1)}$

3. Use the quotient rule to differentiate

    (a) $y = \dfrac{x^2}{x + 4}$ **(b)** $y = \dfrac{2x - 1}{x + 1}$ **(c)** $y = \dfrac{x^3}{\sqrt{(x - 1)}}$

4. Differentiate

    (a) $y = x(x - 3)^4$ **(b)** $y = x\sqrt{(2x - 3)}$ **(c)** $y = \dfrac{x^3}{(3x + 5)^2}$ **(d)** $y = \dfrac{x}{x^2 + 1}$

    (e) $y = \dfrac{ax + b}{cx + d}$ **(f)** $y = (ax + b)^m(cx + d)^n$ **(g)** $y = x(x + 2)^2(x + 3)^3$

5. Find an expression, simplified as far as possible, for the second-order derivative of the function, $y = \dfrac{x}{2x + 1}$.

6. Find expressions for marginal revenue in the case when the demand equation is given by

    (a) $P = \sqrt{(100 - 2Q)}$ **(b)** $P = \dfrac{1000}{\sqrt{2 + Q}}$

7. Determine the marginal propensity to consume for the consumption function

    $$C = \dfrac{650 + 2Y^2}{9 + Y}$$

    when $Y = 21$, correct to 3 decimal places.

    Deduce the corresponding value of the marginal propensity to save and comment on the implications of these results.

SECTION 4.5
Elasticity

> ## Objectives
>
> At the end of this section you should be able to:
>
> * Calculate price elasticity averaged along an arc.
> * Calculate price elasticity evaluated at a point.
> * Decide whether supply and demand are inelastic, unit elastic or elastic.
> * Understand the relationship between price elasticity of demand and revenue.
> * Determine the price elasticity for general linear demand functions.

One important problem in business is to determine the effect on revenue of a change in the price of a good. Let us suppose that a firm's demand curve is downward-sloping. If the firm lowers the price then it will receive less for each item, but the number of items sold increases. The formula for total revenue, TR, is

$$TR = PQ$$

and it is not immediately obvious what the net effect on TR will be as P decreases and Q increases. The crucial factor here is not the absolute changes in P and Q but rather the proportional or percentage changes. Intuitively, we expect that if the percentage rise in Q is greater than the percentage fall in P then the firm experiences an increase in revenue. Under these circumstances we say that demand is **elastic**, since the demand is relatively sensitive to changes in price. Similarly, demand is said to be **inelastic** if demand is relatively insensitive to price changes. In this case, the percentage change in quantity is less than the percentage change in price. A firm can then increase revenue by raising the price of the good. Although demand falls as a result, the increase in price more than compensates for the reduced volume of sales and revenue rises. Of course, it could happen that the percentage changes in price and quantity are equal, leaving revenue unchanged. We use the term **unit elastic** to describe this situation.

We quantify the responsiveness of demand to price change by defining the **price elasticity of demand** to be

$$E = \frac{\text{percentage change in demand}}{\text{percentage change in price}}$$

Notice that because the demand curve slopes downwards, a positive change in price leads to a negative change in quantity and vice versa. Consequently, the value of E is always negative. It is conventional to avoid this by deliberately changing the sign and taking

$$E = -\frac{\text{percentage change in demand}}{\text{percentage change in price}}$$

which makes E positive. The previous classification of demand functions can now be restated more succinctly in terms of E:

Demand is said to be

- inelastic if $E < 1$
- unit elastic if $E = 1$
- elastic if $E > 1$.

Advice

You should note that not all economists adopt the convention of ignoring the sign to make E positive. If the negative sign is left in, the demand will be inelastic if $E = -1$, unit elastic if $E > -1$ and elastic if $E < -1$. You should check with your lecturer the particular convention that you need to adopt.

As usual, we denote the changes in P and Q by ΔP and ΔQ respectively, and seek a formula for E in terms of these symbols. To motivate this, suppose that the price of a good is \$12 and that it rises to \$18. A moment's thought should convince you that the percentage change in price is then 50%. You can probably work this out in your head without thinking too hard. However, it is worthwhile identifying the mathematical process involved. To obtain this figure we first express the change

$$18 - 12 = 6$$

as a fraction of the original to get

$$\frac{6}{12} = 0.5$$

and then multiply by 100 to express it as a percentage. This simple example gives us a clue as to how we might find a formula for E. In general, the percentage change in price is

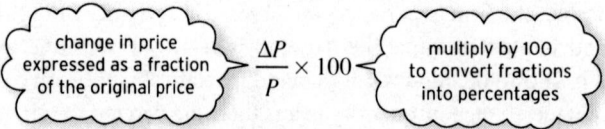

Similarly, the percentage change in quantity is

$$\frac{\Delta Q}{Q} \times 100$$

Hence

$$E = -\left(\frac{\Delta Q}{Q} \times 100 \right) \div \left(\frac{\Delta P}{P} \times 100 \right)$$

Now, when we divide two fractions we turn the denominator upside down and multiply, so

$$E = -\left(\frac{\Delta Q}{Q} \times \cancel{100} \right) \times \left(\frac{P}{\cancel{100} \times \Delta P} \right)$$

$$= -\frac{P}{Q} \times \frac{\Delta Q}{\Delta P}$$

A typical demand curve is illustrated in Figure 4.19, in which a price fall from P_1 to P_2 causes an increase in demand from Q_1 to Q_2.

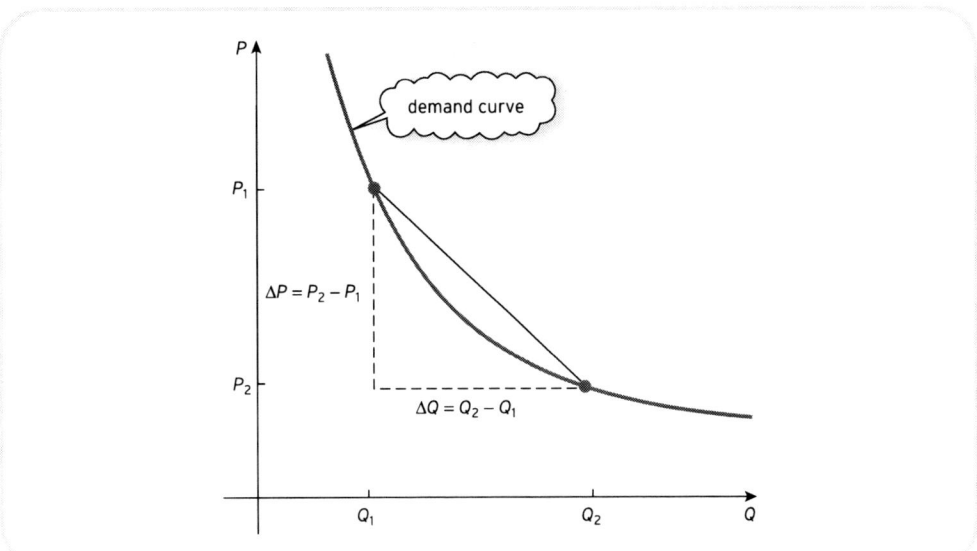

Figure 4.19

Example

Determine the elasticity of demand when the price falls from 136 to 119, given the demand function

$$P = 200 - Q^2$$

Solution

In the notation of Figure 4.19 we are given that

$$P_1 = 136 \text{ and } P_2 = 119$$

The corresponding values of Q_1 and Q_2 are obtained from the demand equation

$$P = 200 - Q^2$$

by substituting $P = 136$ and 119 respectively and solving for Q. For example, if $P = 136$ then

$$136 = 200 - Q^2$$

which rearranges to give

$$Q^2 = 200 - 136 = 64$$

This has solution $Q = \pm 8$ and, since we can obviously ignore the negative quantity, we have $Q_1 = 8$. Similarly, setting $P = 119$ gives $Q_2 = 9$. The elasticity formula is

$$E = -\frac{P}{Q} \times \frac{\Delta Q}{\Delta P}$$

and the values of ΔP and ΔQ are easily worked out to be

$$\Delta P = 119 - 136 = -17$$

$$\Delta Q = 9 - 8 = 1$$

However, it is not at all clear what to take for P and Q. Do we take P to be 136 or 119? Clearly we are going to get two different answers depending on our choice. A sensible compromise is to use their average and take

$$P = \tfrac{1}{2}(136 + 119) = 127.5$$

Similarly, averaging the Q values gives

$$Q = \tfrac{1}{2}(8 + 9) = 8.5$$

Hence

$$E = -\frac{127.5}{8.5} \times \left(\frac{1}{-17}\right) = 0.88$$

The particular application of the general formula considered in the previous example provides an estimate of elasticity averaged over a section of the demand curve between (Q_1, P_1) and (Q_2, P_2). For this reason it is called **arc elasticity** and is obtained by replacing P by $\tfrac{1}{2}(P_1 + P_2)$ and Q by $\tfrac{1}{2}(Q_1 + Q_2)$ in the general formula.

Practice Problem

1. Given the demand function

    $$P = 1000 - 2Q$$

    calculate the arc elasticity as P falls from 210 to 200.

A disappointing feature of the previous example is the need to compromise and calculate the elasticity averaged along an arc rather than calculate the exact value at a point. A formula for the latter can easily be deduced from

$$E = -\frac{P}{Q} \times \frac{\Delta Q}{\Delta P}$$

by considering the limit as ΔQ and ΔP tend to zero in Figure 4.19. All that happens is that the arc shrinks to a point and the ratio $\Delta Q/\Delta P$ tends to dQ/dP. The price elasticity at a point (**point elasticity**) may therefore be found from

$$E = -\frac{P}{Q} \times \frac{dQ}{dP}$$

Example

Given the demand function

$$P = 50 - 2Q$$

find the elasticity when the price is 30. Is demand inelastic, unit elastic or elastic at this price?

Solution

To find dQ/dP we need to differentiate Q with respect to P. However, we are actually given a formula for P in terms of Q, so we need to transpose

$$P = 50 - 2Q$$

for Q. Adding $2Q$ to both sides gives

$$P + 2Q = 50$$

and if we subtract P then

$$2Q = 50 - P$$

Finally, dividing through by 2 gives

$$Q = 25 - \tfrac{1}{2}P$$

Hence

$$\frac{\mathrm{d}Q}{\mathrm{d}P} = -\tfrac{1}{2}$$

We are given that $P = 30$ so, at this price, demand is

$$Q = 25 - \tfrac{1}{2}(30) = 10$$

These values can now be substituted into

$$E = -\frac{P}{Q} \times \frac{\mathrm{d}Q}{\mathrm{d}P}$$

to get

$$E = -\frac{30}{10} \times \left(-\frac{1}{2}\right) = 1.5$$

Moreover, since $1.5 > 1$, demand is elastic at this price.

Practice Problem

2. Given the demand function

$$P = 100 - Q$$

calculate the price elasticity of demand when the price is

(a) 10   **(b)** 50   **(c)** 90

Is the demand inelastic, unit elastic or elastic at these prices?

It is quite common in economics to be given the demand function in the form

$$P = f(Q)$$

where P is a function of Q. In order to evaluate elasticity it is necessary to find

$$\frac{dQ}{dP}$$

which assumes that Q is actually given as a function of P. Consequently, we may have to transpose the demand equation and find an expression for Q in terms of P before we perform the differentiation. This was the approach taken in the previous example. Unfortunately, if $f(Q)$ is a complicated expression, it may be difficult, if not impossible, to carry out the initial rearrangement to extract Q. An alternative approach is based on the fact that

$$\frac{dQ}{dP} = \frac{1}{dP/dQ}$$

A proof of this can be obtained via the chain rule, although we omit the details. This result shows that we can find dQ/dP by just differentiating the original demand function to get dP/dQ and reciprocating.

Example

Given the demand function

$$P = -Q^2 - 4Q + 96$$

find the price elasticity of demand when $P = 51$. If this price rises by 2%, calculate the corresponding percentage change in demand.

Solution

We are given that $P = 51$, so to find the corresponding demand we need to solve the quadratic equation

$$-Q^2 - 4Q + 96 = 51$$

that is,

$$-Q^2 - 4Q + 45 = 0$$

To do this we use the standard formula

$$\frac{-b \pm \sqrt{(b^2 - 4ac)}}{2a}$$

discussed in Section 2.1, which gives

$$Q = \frac{-(-4) \pm \sqrt{((-4)^2 - 4(-1)(45))}}{2(-1)}$$

$$= \frac{4 \pm \sqrt{196}}{-2}$$

$$= \frac{4 \pm 14}{-2}$$

The two solutions are -9 and 5. As usual, the negative value can be ignored, since it does not make sense to have a negative quantity, so $Q = 5$.

To find the value of E we also need to calculate

$$\frac{dQ}{dP}$$

from the demand equation, $P = -Q^2 - 4Q + 96$. It is not at all easy to transpose this for Q. Indeed, we would have to use the formula for solving a quadratic, as before, replacing the number 51 with the letter P. Unfortunately this expression involves square roots and the subsequent differentiation is quite messy. (You might like to have a go at this yourself!) However, it is easy to differentiate the given expression with respect to Q to get

$$\frac{dP}{dQ} = -2Q - 4$$

and so

$$\frac{dQ}{dP} = \frac{1}{dP/dQ} = \frac{1}{-2Q - 4}$$

Finally, putting $Q = 5$ gives

$$\frac{dQ}{dP} = -\frac{1}{14}$$

The price elasticity of demand is given by

$$E = -\frac{P}{Q} \times \frac{dQ}{dP}$$

and if we substitute $P = 51$, $Q = 5$ and $dQ/dP = -1/14$ we get

$$E - \frac{51}{5} \times \left(-\frac{1}{14}\right) = 0.73$$

To discover the effect on Q due to a 2% rise in P we return to the original definition

$$E = -\frac{\text{percentage change in demand}}{\text{percentage change in price}}$$

We know that $E = 0.73$ and that the percentage change in price is 2, so

$$0.73 = -\frac{\text{percentage change in price}}{2}$$

which shows that demand changes by

$$-0.73 \times 2 = -1.46\%$$

A 2% rise in price therefore leads to a fall in demand of 1.46%.

Practice Problem

3. Given the demand equation

$$P = -Q^2 - 10Q + 150$$

find the price elasticity of demand when $Q = 4$. Estimate the percentage change in price needed to increase demand by 10%.

The **price elasticity of supply** is defined in an analogous way to that of demand. We define

$$E = \frac{\text{percentage change in supply}}{\text{percentage change in price}}$$

This time, however, there is no need to fiddle the sign. An increase in price leads to an increase in supply, so E is automatically positive. In symbols,

$$E = \frac{P}{Q} \times \frac{\Delta Q}{\Delta P}$$

If (Q_1, P_1) and (Q_2, P_2) denote two points on the supply curve then arc elasticity is obtained, as before, by setting

$$\Delta P = P_2 - P_1$$
$$\Delta Q = Q_2 - Q_1$$
$$P = 1/2(P_1 + P_2)$$
$$Q = 1/2(Q_1 + Q_2)$$

The corresponding formula for point elasticity is

$$E = \frac{P}{Q} \times \frac{dQ}{dP}$$

Example

Given the supply function

$$P = 10 + \sqrt{Q}$$

find the price elasticity of supply

(a) averaged along an arc between $Q = 100$ and $Q = 105$

(b) at the point $Q = 100$.

Solution

(a) We are given that

$$Q_1 = 100, Q_2 = 105$$

so that

$$P_1 = 10 + \sqrt{100} = 20 \text{ and } P_2 = 10 + \sqrt{105} = 20.247$$

Hence

$$\Delta P = 20.247 - 20 = 0.247, \qquad \Delta Q = 105 - 100 = 5$$

$$P = \frac{1}{2}(20 + 20.247) = 20.123, \qquad Q = \frac{1}{2}(100 + 105) = 102.5$$

The formula for arc elasticity gives

$$E = \frac{P}{Q} \times \frac{\Delta Q}{\Delta P} = \frac{20.123}{102.5} \times \frac{5}{0.247} = 3.97$$

(b) To evaluate the elasticity at the point $Q = 100$, we need to find the derivative, $\dfrac{dQ}{dP}$. The supply equation

$$P = 10 + Q^{1/2}$$

differentiates to give

$$\frac{dP}{dQ} = \frac{1}{2}Q^{-1/2} = \frac{1}{2\sqrt{Q}}$$

so that

$$\frac{dQ}{dP} = 2\sqrt{Q}$$

At the point $Q = 100$, we get

$$\frac{dQ}{dP} = 2\sqrt{100} = 20$$

The formula for point elasticity gives

$$E = \frac{P}{Q} \times \frac{dQ}{dP} = \frac{20}{100} \times 20 = 4$$

Notice that, as expected, the answers to parts (a) and (b) are nearly the same.

Practice Problem

4. If the supply equation is

$$Q = 150 + 5P + 0.1P^2$$

calculate the price elasticity of supply

(a) averaged along an arc between $P = 9$ and $P = 11$

(b) at the point $P = 10$.

Advice

The concept of elasticity can be applied to more general functions and we consider some of these in the next chapter. For the moment we investigate the theoretical properties of demand elasticity. The following material is more difficult to understand than the foregoing, so you may prefer just to concentrate on the conclusions and skip the intermediate derivations.

We begin by analysing the relationship between elasticity and marginal revenue. Marginal revenue, MR, is given by

$$MR = \frac{d(TR)}{dQ}$$

Now TR is equal to the product PQ, so we can apply the product rule to differentiate it. If

$u = P$ and $v = Q$

then

$$\frac{du}{dQ} = \frac{dP}{dQ} \text{ and } \frac{dv}{dQ} = \frac{dQ}{dQ} = 1$$

By the product rule

$$MR = u\frac{dv}{dQ} + v\frac{du}{dQ}$$

$$= P + Q \times \frac{dP}{dQ}$$

$$= P\left(1 + \frac{Q}{P} \times \frac{dP}{dQ}\right)$$

check this by multiplying out the brackets

Now

$$-\frac{P}{Q} \times \frac{dQ}{dP} = E$$

so

$$\frac{Q}{P} \times \frac{dP}{dQ} = -\frac{1}{E}$$

turn both sides upside down and multiply by –1

This can be substituted into the expression for MR to get

$$MR = P\left(1 - \frac{1}{E}\right)$$

The connection between marginal revenue and demand elasticity is now complete, and this formula can be used to justify the intuitive argument that we gave at the beginning of this section concerning revenue and elasticity. Observe that if $E < 1$ then $1/E > 1$, so MR is negative for any value of P. It follows that the revenue function is decreasing in regions where demand is inelastic, because MR determines the slope of the revenue curve. Similarly, if $E > 1$ then $1/E < 1$, so MR is positive for any price, P, and the revenue curve is upwards. In other words, the revenue function is increasing in regions where demand is elastic. Finally, if $E = 1$ then MR is 0, and so the slope of the revenue curve is horizontal at points where demand is unit elastic.

Throughout this section we have taken specific functions and evaluated the elasticity at particular points. It is more instructive to consider general functions and to deduce general expressions for elasticity. Consider the standard linear downward-sloping demand function

$P = aQ + b$

when $a < 0$ and $b > 0$. As noted in Section 4.3, this typifies the demand function faced by a monopolist. To transpose this equation for Q, we subtract b from both sides to get

$aQ = P - b$

and then divide through by a to get

$$Q = \frac{1}{a}(P - b)$$

Hence

$$\frac{dQ}{dP} = \frac{1}{a}$$

The formula for elasticity of demand is

$$E = -\frac{P}{Q} \times \frac{dQ}{dP}$$

so replacing Q by $(1/a)(P - b)$ and dQ/dP by $1/a$ gives

$$E = \frac{-P}{(1/a)(P - b)} \times \frac{1}{a}$$

$$= \frac{-P}{P - b}$$

$$= \frac{P}{b - P}$$

> multiply top and bottom by −1

Notice that this formula involves P and b but not a. Elasticity is therefore independent of the slope of linear demand curves. In particular, this shows that, corresponding to any price P, the elasticities of the two demand functions sketched in Figure 4.20 are identical. This is perhaps a rather surprising result. We might have expected demand to be more elastic at point A than at point B, since A is on the steeper curve. However, the mathematics shows that this is not the case. (Can you explain, in economic terms, why this is so?)

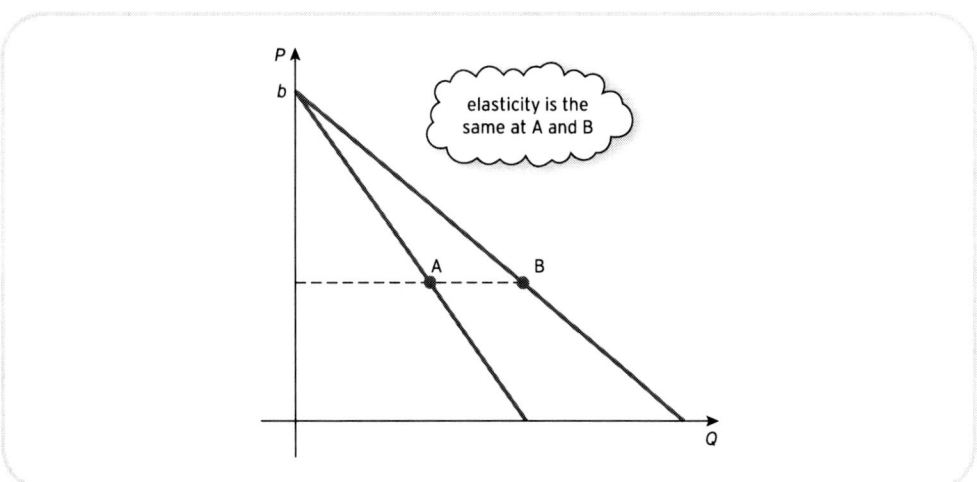

Figure 4.20

Another interesting feature of the result

$$E = \frac{P}{b - P}$$

is the fact that b occurs in the denominator of this fraction, so that corresponding to any price, P, the larger the value of the intercept, b, the smaller the elasticity. In Figure 4.21 (overleaf), elasticity at C is smaller than that at D because C lies on the curve with the larger intercept.

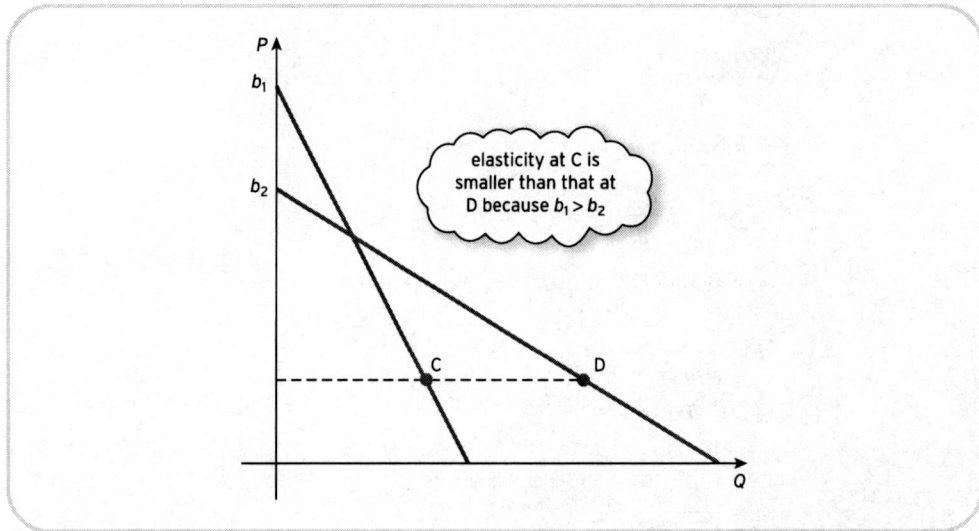

Figure 4.21

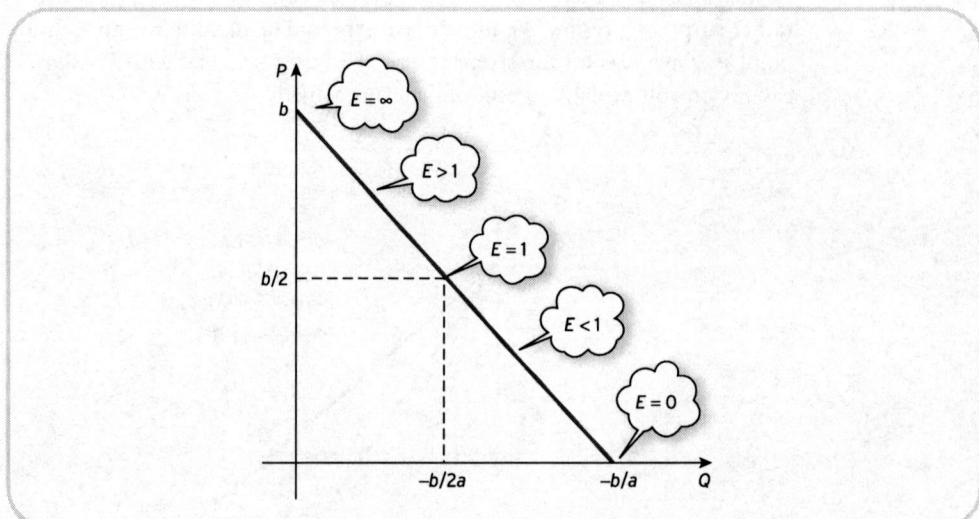

Figure 4.22

The dependence of E on P is also worthy of note. It shows that elasticity varies along a linear demand curve. This is illustrated in Figure 4.22. At the left-hand end, $P = b$, so

$$E = \frac{b}{b-b} = \frac{b}{0} = \infty$$ (read 'infinity')

At the right-hand end, $P = 0$, so

$$E = \frac{0}{b-0} = \frac{0}{b} = 0$$

As you move down the demand curve, the elasticity decreases from ∞ to 0, taking all possible values. Demand is unit elastic when $E = 1$ and the price at which this occurs can be found by solving

$$\frac{P}{b-P} = 1 \text{ for } P$$

$$P = b - P \qquad \text{(multiply both sides by } b - P)$$
$$2P = b \qquad \text{(add } P \text{ to both sides)}$$
$$P = \frac{b}{2} \qquad \text{(divide both sides by 2)}$$

The corresponding quantity can be found by substituting $P = b/2$ into the transposed demand equation to get

$$Q = \frac{1}{a}\left(\frac{b}{2} - b\right) = -\frac{b}{2a}$$

Demand is unit elastic exactly halfway along the demand curve. To the left of this point $E > 1$ and demand is elastic, whereas to the right $E < 1$ and demand is inelastic.

In our discussion of general demand functions, we have concentrated on those which are represented by straight lines since these are commonly used in simple economic models. There are other possibilities and Question 4 in Exercise 4.5* investigates a class of functions that have constant elasticity.

Key Terms

Arc elasticity   Elasticity measured between two points on a curve.

Elastic demand   Where the percentage change in demand is more than the corresponding percentage change in price: $E > 1$.

Inelastic demand   Where the percentage change in demand is less than the corresponding percentage change in price: $E < 1$.

Point elasticity   Elasticity measured at a particular point on a curve, e.g. for a supply curve, $E = \frac{P}{Q} \times \frac{dQ}{dP}$.

Price elasticity of demand   A measure of the responsiveness of the change in demand due to a change in price: −(percentage change in demand) ÷ (percentage change in price).

Price elasticity of supply   A measure of the responsiveness of the change in supply due to a change in price: (percentage change in supply) ÷ (percentage change in price).

Unit elasticity demand   Where the percentage change in demand is the same as the percentage change in price: $E = 1$.

Exercise 4.5

1. Given the demand function

   $$P = 500 - 4Q^2$$

   calculate the price elasticity of demand averaged along an arc joining $Q = 8$ and $Q = 10$.

2. Find the price elasticity of demand at the point $Q = 9$ for the demand function

   $$P = 500 - 4Q^2$$

   and compare your answer with that of Question 1.

3. Find the price elasticity of demand at $P = 6$ for each of the following demand functions:
   (a) $P = 30 - 2Q$
   (b) $P = 30 - 12Q$
   (c) $P = \sqrt{(100 - 2Q)}$

4. Consider the supply equation

   $$Q = 4 + 0.1P^2$$

   (a) Write down an expression for dQ/dP.
   (b) Show that the supply equation can be rearranged as

   $$P = \sqrt{(10Q - 40)}$$

   Differentiate this to find an expression for dP/dQ.
   (c) Use your answers to parts (a) and (b) to verify that

   $$\frac{dQ}{dP} = \frac{1}{dP/dQ}$$

   (d) Calculate the elasticity of supply at the point $Q = 14$.

5. If the supply equation is

   $$Q = 7 + 0.1P + 0.004P^2$$

   find the price elasticity of supply if the current price is 80.
   (a) Is supply elastic, inelastic or unit elastic at this price?
   (b) Estimate the percentage change in supply if the price rises by 5%.

Exercise 4.5*

1. Find the elasticity for the demand function

   $$Q = 80 - 2P - 0.5P^2$$

   averaged along an arc joining $Q = 32$ to $Q = 50$. Give your answer to two decimal places.

2. Consider the supply equation

   $$P = 7 + 2Q^2$$

   By evaluating the price elasticity of supply at the point $P = 105$, estimate the percentage increase in supply when the price rises by 7%.

3. If the demand equation is

$$Q + 4P = 60$$

find a general expression for the price elasticity of demand in terms of P. For what value of P is demand unit elastic?

4. Show that the price elasticity of demand is constant for the demand functions

$$P = \frac{A}{Q^n}$$

where A and n are positive constants.

5. Find a general expression for the point elasticity of supply for the function,

$$Q = aP + b \quad (a > 0)$$

Deduce that the supply function is

(a) unit elastic when $b = 0$

(b) inelastic when $b > 0$.

Give a brief geometrical interpretation of these results.

6. A supply function is given by

$$Q = 40 + 0.1P^2$$

(1) Find the price elasticity of supply averaged along an arc between $P = 11$ and $P = 13$. Give your answer correct to 3 decimal places.

(2) Find an expression for price elasticity of supply at a general point, P.

Hence:

(a) Estimate the percentage change in supply when the price increases by 5% from its current level of 17. Give your answer correct to 1 decimal place.

(b) Find the price at which supply is unit elastic.

7. (a) Show that the elasticity of the supply function

$$P = aQ + b$$

is given by

$$E = \frac{P}{P - b}$$

(b) Consider the two supply functions

$$P = 2Q + 5 \text{ and } P = aQ + b$$

The quantity supplied is the same for both functions when $P = 10$, and at this point, the price elasticity of supply for the second function is five times larger than that for the first function. Find the values of a and b.

SECTION 4.6

Optimization of economic functions

Objectives

At the end of this section you should be able to:

- Use the first-order derivative to find the stationary points of a function.
- Use the second-order derivative to classify the stationary points of a function.
- Find the maximum and minimum points of an economic function.
- Use stationary points to sketch graphs of economic functions.

In Section 2.1 a simple three-step strategy was described for sketching graphs of quadratic functions of the form

$$f(x) = ax^2 + bx + c$$

The basic idea is to solve the corresponding equation

$$ax^2 + bx + c = 0$$

to find where the graph crosses the x axis. Provided that the quadratic equation has at least one solution, it is then possible to deduce the coordinates of the maximum or minimum point of the parabola. For example, if there are two solutions, then by symmetry the graph turns round at the point exactly halfway between these solutions. Unfortunately, if the quadratic equation has no solution then only a limited sketch can be obtained using this approach.

In this section we show how the techniques of calculus can be used to find the coordinates of the turning point of a parabola. The beauty of this approach is that it can be used to locate the maximum and minimum points of any economic function, not just those represented by quadratics. Look at the graph in Figure 4.23. Points B, C, D, E, F and G are referred to as the **stationary points** (sometimes called **critical points**, **turning points** or **extrema**) of the function. At a stationary point the tangent to the graph is horizontal and so has zero slope.

Consequently, at a stationary point of a function $f(x)$,

$$f'(x) = 0$$

The reason for using the word 'stationary' is historical. Calculus was originally used by astronomers to predict planetary motion. If a graph of the distance travelled by an object is sketched against time then the speed of the object is given by the slope, since this represents the rate of change of distance with respect to time. It follows that if the graph is horizontal at some point then the speed is zero and the object is instantaneously at rest: that is, stationary.

Stationary points are classified into one of three types: local maxima, local minima and stationary points of inflection.

At a **local maximum** (sometimes called a relative maximum) the graph falls away on both sides. Points B and E are the local maxima for the function sketched in Figure 4.23. The word

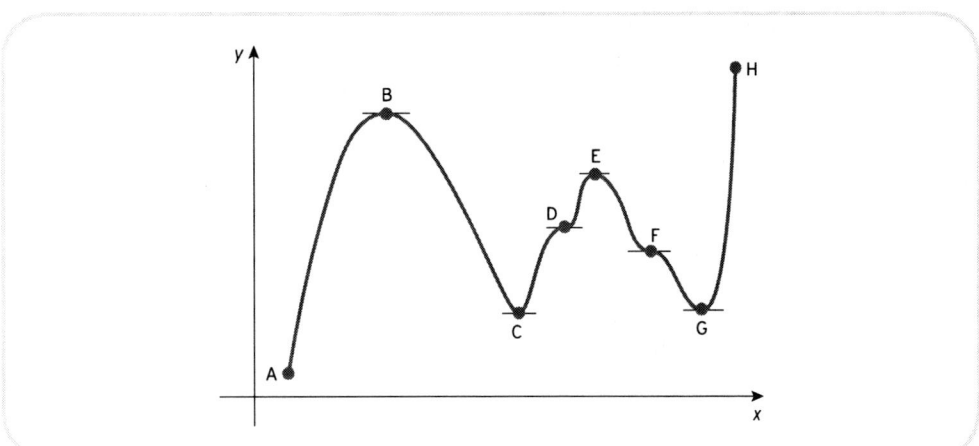

Figure 4.23

'local' is used to highlight the fact that, although these are the maximum points relative to their locality or neighbourhood, they may not be the overall or global maximum. In Figure 4.23 the highest point on the graph actually occurs at the right-hand end, H, which is not a stationary point, since the slope is not zero at H.

At a **local minimum** (sometimes called a relative minimum) the graph rises on both sides. Points C and G are the local minima in Figure 4.23. Again, it is not necessary for the global minimum to be one of the local minima. In Figure 4.23 the lowest point on the graph occurs at the left-hand end, A, which is not a stationary point.

At a **stationary point of inflection** the graph rises on one side and falls on the other. The stationary points of inflection in Figure 4.23 are labelled D and F. These points are of little value in economics, although they do sometimes assist in sketching graphs of economic functions. Maxima and minima, on the other hand, are important. The calculation of the maximum points of the revenue and profit functions is clearly worthwhile. Likewise, it is useful to be able to find the minimum points of average cost functions.

For most examples in economics, the local maximum and minimum points coincide with the global maximum and minimum. For this reason we shall drop the word 'local' when describing stationary points. However, it should always be borne in mind that the global maximum and minimum could actually be attained at an end point and this possibility may need to be checked. This can be done by comparing the function values at the end points with those of the stationary points and then deciding which of them gives rise to the largest or smallest values.

Two obvious questions remain. How do we find the stationary points of any given function and how do we classify them? The first question is easily answered. As we mentioned earlier, stationary points satisfy the equation

$$f'(x) = 0$$

so all we need do is to differentiate the function, to equate to zero and to solve the resulting algebraic equation. The classification is equally straightforward. It can be shown that if a function has a stationary point at $x = a$ then

- if $f''(a) > 0$ then $f(x)$ has a minimum at $x = a$
- if $f''(a) < 0$ then $f(x)$ has a maximum at $x = a$.

Therefore, all we need do is to differentiate the function a second time and to evaluate this second-order derivative at each point. A point is a minimum if this value is positive and a maximum if this value is negative. These facts are consistent with our interpretation of the second-order derivative in Section 4.2. If $f''(a) > 0$ the graph bends upwards at $x = a$ (points C and G in Figure 4.23). If $f''(a) < 0$ the graph bends downwards at $x = a$ (points B and E in Figure 4.23). There is, of course, a third possibility, namely $f''(a) = 0$. Sadly, when this happens it provides no information whatsoever about the stationary point. The point $x = a$ could be a maximum, minimum or inflection. This situation is illustrated in Question 2 in Exercise 4.6* at the end of this section.

> ### Advice
>
> If you are unlucky enough to encounter this case, you can always classify the point by tabulating the function values in the vicinity and use these to produce a local sketch.

To summarize, the method for finding and classifying stationary points of a function, $f(x)$, is as follows:

Step 1

Solve the equation $f'(x) = 0$ to find the stationary points, $x = a$.

Step 2

If

- $f''(a) > 0$ then the function has a minimum at $x = a$
- $f''(a) < 0$ then the function has a maximum at $x = a$
- $f''(a) = 0$ then the point cannot be classified using the available information.

Example

Find and classify the stationary points of the following functions. Hence sketch their graphs.

(a) $f(x) = x^2 - 4x + 5$ **(b)** $f(x) = 2x^3 + 3x^2 - 12x + 4$

Solution

(a) In order to use steps 1 and 2 we need to find the first- and second-order derivatives of the function

$$f'(x) = x^2 - 4x + 5$$

Differentiating once gives

$$f'(x) = 2x - 4$$

and differentiating a second time gives

$$f''(x) = 2$$

Step 1

The stationary points are the solutions of the equation

$$f'(x) = 0$$

so we need to solve

$$2x - 4 = 0$$

This is a linear equation so has just one solution. Adding 4 to both sides gives

$$2x = 4$$

and dividing through by 2 shows that the stationary point occurs at

$$x = 2$$

Step 2

To classify this point we need to evaluate

$$f''(2)$$

In this case

$$f''(x) = 2$$

for all values of x, so in particular

$$f''(2) = 2$$

This number is positive, so the function has a minimum at $x = 2$.

We have shown that the minimum point occurs at $x = 2$. The corresponding value of y is easily found by substituting this number into the function to get

$$y = (2)^2 - 4(2) + 5 = 1$$

so the minimum point has coordinates $(2, 1)$. A graph of $f(x)$ is shown in Figure 4.24.

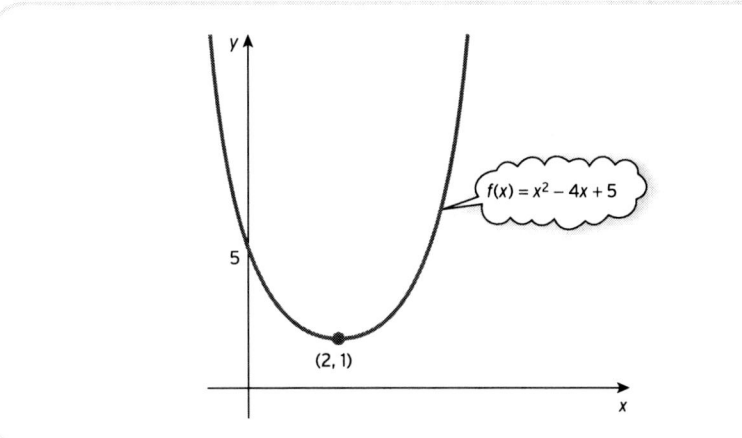

Figure 4.24

(b) In order to use steps 1 and 2 we need to find the first- and second-order derivatives of the function

$$f(x) = 2x^3 + 3x^2 - 12x + 4$$

Differentiating once gives

$$f'(x) = 6x^2 + 6x - 12$$

and differentiating a second time gives

$$f''(x) = 12x + 6$$

Step 1

The stationary points are the solutions of the equation

$$f'(x) = 0$$

so we need to solve

$$6x^2 + 6x - 12 = 0$$

This is a quadratic equation and so can be solved using 'the formula'. However, before doing so, it is a good idea to divide both sides by 6 to avoid large numbers. The resulting equation

$$x^2 + x - 2 = 0$$

has solution

$$x = \frac{-1 \pm \sqrt{(1^2 - 4(1)(-2))}}{2(1)} = \frac{-1 \pm \sqrt{9}}{2} = \frac{-1 \pm 3}{2} = -2, 1$$

In general, whenever $f(x)$ is a cubic function the stationary points are the solutions of a quadratic equation, $f'(x) = 0$. Moreover, we know from Section 2.1 that such an equation can have two, one or no solutions. It follows that a cubic equation can have two, one or no stationary points. In this particular example we have seen that there are two stationary points, at $x = -2$ and $x = 1$.

Step 2

To classify these points we need to evaluate $f''(-2)$ and $f''(1)$. Now

$$f''(-2) = 12(-2) + 6 = -18$$

This is negative, so there is a maximum at $x = -2$. When $x = -2$,

$$y = 2(-2)^3 + 3(-2)^2 - 12(-2) + 4 = 24$$

so the maximum point has coordinates $(-2, 24)$. Now

$$f''(1) = 12(1) + 6 = 18$$

This is positive, so there is a minimum at $x = 1$. When $x = 1$,

$$y = 2(1)^3 + 3(1)^2 - 12(1) + 4 = -3$$

so the minimum point has coordinates $(1, -3)$.

This information enables a partial sketch to be drawn as shown in Figure 4.25. Before we can be confident about the complete picture it is useful to plot a few more points such as those below:

x	−10	0	10
y	−1816	4	2184

This table indicates that when x is positive the graph falls steeply downwards from a great height. Similarly, when x is negative the graph quickly disappears off the bottom of the page. The curve cannot wiggle and turn round except at the two stationary points already plotted (otherwise it would have more stationary points, which we know is not the case). We now have enough information to join up the pieces and so sketch a complete picture as shown in Figure 4.26.

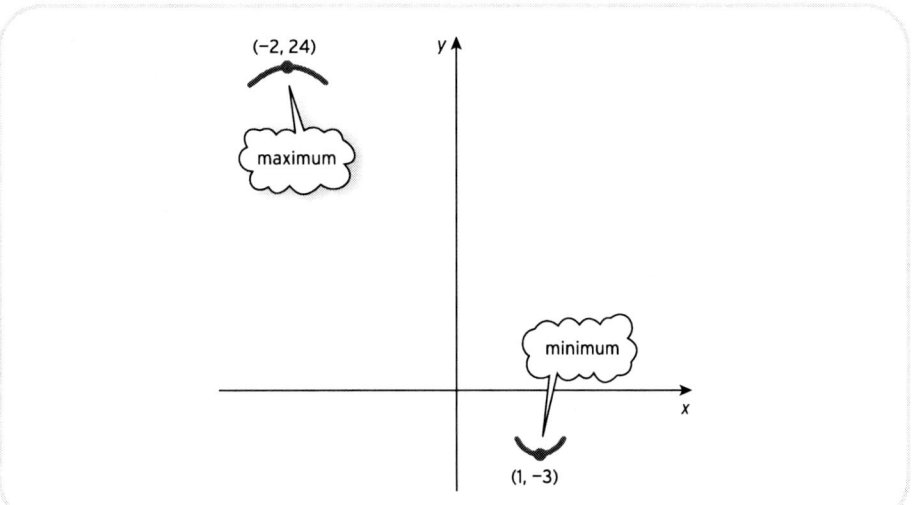

Figure 4.25

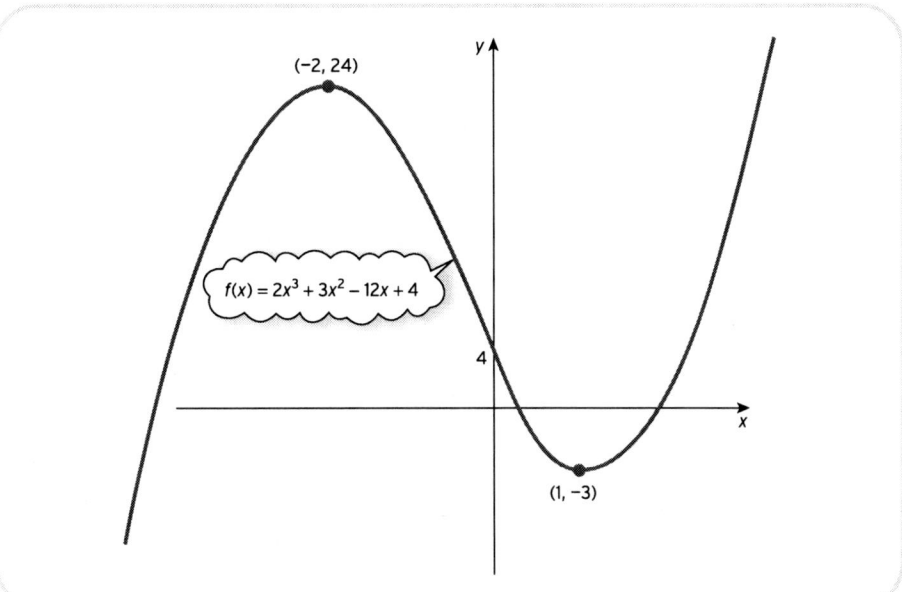

Figure 4.26

In an ideal world it would be nice to calculate the three points at which the graph crosses the *x* axis. These are the solutions of

$$2x^3 + 3x^2 - 12x + 4 = 0$$

There is a formula for solving cubic equations, just as there is for quadratic equations, but it is extremely complicated and is beyond the scope of this book.

Practice Problem

1. Find and classify the stationary points of the following functions. Hence sketch their graphs.

(a) $y = 3x^2 + 12x - 35$ **(b)** $y = -2x^3 + 15x^2 - 36x + 27$

The task of finding the maximum and minimum values of a function is referred to as **optimization**. This is an important topic in mathematical economics. It provides a rich source of examination questions and we devote the remaining part of this section and the whole of the next to applications of it. In this section we demonstrate the use of stationary points by working through four 'examination-type' problems in detail. These problems involve the optimization of specific revenue, cost, profit and production functions. They are not intended to exhaust all possibilities, although they are fairly typical. The next section describes how the mathematics of optimization can be used to derive general theoretical results.

Example

A firm's short-run production function is given by

$$Q = 6L^2 - 0.2L^3$$

where L denotes the number of workers.

(a) Find the size of the workforce that maximizes output and hence sketch a graph of this production function.

(b) Find the size of the workforce that maximizes the average product of labour. Calculate MP_L and AP_L at this value of L. What do you observe?

Solution

(a) In the first part of this example we want to find the value of L which maximizes

$$Q = 6L^2 - 0.2L^3$$

Step 1
At a stationary point

$$\frac{dQ}{dL} = 12L - 0.6L^2 = 0$$

This is a quadratic equation and so we could use 'the formula' to find L. However, this is not really necessary in this case because both terms have a common factor of L and the equation may be written as

$$L(12 - 0.6L) = 0$$

It follows that either

$$L = 0 \text{ or } 12 - 0.6L = 0$$

that is, the equation has solutions

$$L = 0 \text{ and } L = 12/0.6 = 20$$

Step 2

It is obvious on economic grounds that $L = 0$ is a minimum and presumably $L = 20$ is the maximum. We can, of course, check this by differentiating a second time to get

$$\frac{d^2Q}{dL^2} = 12 - 1.2L$$

When $L = 0$,

$$\frac{d^2Q}{dL^2} = 12 > 0$$

which confirms that $L = 0$ is a minimum. The corresponding output is given by

$$Q = 6(0)^2 - 0.2(0)^3 = 0$$

as expected. When $L = 20$,

$$\frac{d^2Q}{dL^2} = -12 < 0$$

which confirms that $L = 20$ is a maximum.

The firm should therefore employ 20 workers to achieve a maximum output

$$Q = 6(20)^2 - 0.2(20)^3 = 800$$

We have shown that the minimum point on the graph has coordinates $(0, 0)$ and the maximum point has coordinates $(20, 800)$. There are no further turning points, so the graph of the production function has the shape sketched in Figure 4.27.

It is possible to find the precise values of L at which the graph crosses the horizontal axis. The production function is given by

$$Q = 6L^2 - 0.2L^3$$

so we need to solve

$$6L^2 - 0.2L^3 = 0$$

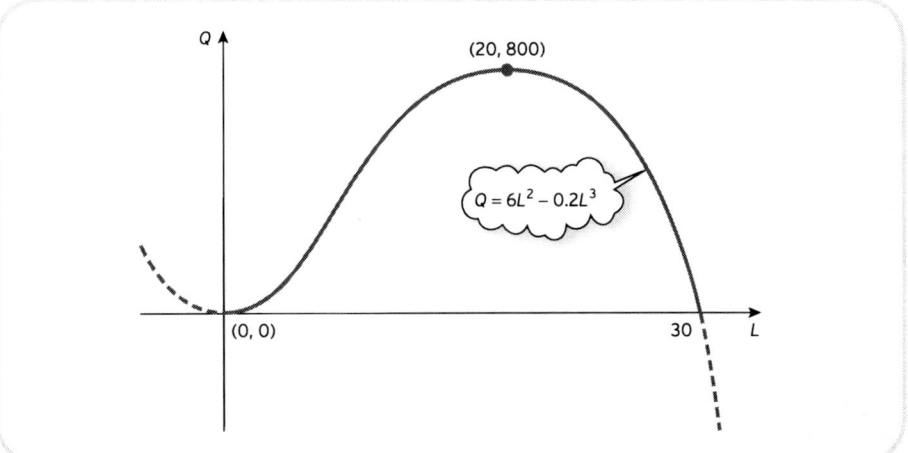

Figure 4.27

We can take out a factor of L^2 to get

$$L^2(6 - 0.2L) = 0$$

Hence, either

$$L^2 = 0 \text{ or } 6 - 0.2L = 0$$

The first of these merely confirms the fact that the curve passes through the origin, whereas the second shows that the curve intersects the L axis at $L = 6/0.2 = 30$.

(b) In the second part of this example we want to find the value of L which maximizes the average product of labour. This is a concept that we have not met before in this book, although it is not difficult to guess how it might be defined.

The **average product of labour**, AP_L, is taken to be total output divided by labour, so that in symbols

$$AP_L = \frac{Q}{L}$$

This is sometimes called **labour productivity**, since it measures the average output per worker.

In this example,

$$AP_L = \frac{6L^2 - 0.2L^3}{L} = 6L - 0.2L^2$$

Step 1

At a stationary point

$$\frac{d(AP_L)}{dL} = 0$$

so

$$6 - 0.4L = 0$$

which has solution $L = 6/0.4 = 15$.

Step 2

To classify this stationary point we differentiate a second time to get

$$\frac{d^2(AP_L)}{dL^2} = -0.4 < 0$$

which shows that it is a maximum.

The labour productivity is therefore greatest when the firm employs 15 workers. In fact, the corresponding labour productivity, AP_L, is

$$6(15) - 0.2(15)^2 = 45$$

In other words, the largest number of goods produced per worker is 45.

Finally, we are invited to calculate the value of MP_L at this point. To find an expression for MP_L we need to differentiate Q with respect to L to get

$$MP_L = 12L - 0.6L^2$$

When $L = 15$,

$$MP_L = 12(15) - 0.6(15)^2 = 45$$

We observe that at $L = 15$ the values of MP_L and AP_L are equal.

In this particular example we discovered that at the point of maximum average product of labour

| marginal product of labour | = | average product of labour |

There is nothing special about this example and in the next section we show that this result holds for any production function.

Practice Problem

2. A firm's short-run production function is given by

$$Q = 300L^2 - L^4$$

where L denotes the number of workers. Find the size of the workforce that maximizes the average product of labour and verify that at this value of L

$$MP_L = AP_L$$

Example

The demand equation of a good is

$$P + Q = 30$$

and the total cost function is

$$TC = \frac{1}{2}Q^2 + 6Q + 7$$

(a) Find the level of output that maximizes total revenue.

(b) Find the level of output that maximizes profit. Calculate MR and MC at this value of Q. What do you observe?

Solution

(a) In the first part of this example we want to find the value of Q which maximizes total revenue. To do this we use the given demand equation to find an expression for TR and then apply the theory of stationary points in the usual way.

The total revenue is defined by

$$TR = PQ$$

We seek the value of Q which maximizes TR, so we express TR in terms of the variable Q only. The demand equation

$$P + Q = 30$$

can be rearranged to get

$$P = 30 - Q$$

Hence

$$TR = (30 - Q)Q$$
$$= 30Q - Q^2$$

Step 1

At a stationary point

$$\frac{d(TR)}{dQ} = 0$$

so

$$30 - 2Q = 0$$

which has solution $Q = 30/2 = 15$.

Step 2

To classify this point we differentiate a second time to get

$$\frac{d^2(TR)}{dQ^2} = -2$$

This is negative, so TR has a maximum at $Q = 15$.

(b) In the second part of this example we want to find the value of Q which maximizes profit. To do this we begin by determining an expression for profit in terms of Q. Once this has been done, it is then a simple matter to work out the first- and second-order derivatives and so to find and classify the stationary points of the profit function.

The profit function is defined by

$$\pi = TR - TC$$

From part (a)

$$TR = 30Q - Q^2$$

We are given the total cost function

$$TC = \tfrac{1}{2}Q^2 + 6Q + 7$$

Hence

$$\pi = (30Q - Q^2) - (\tfrac{1}{2}Q^2 + 6Q + 7)$$
$$= 30Q - Q^2 - \tfrac{1}{2}Q^2 - 6Q - 7$$
$$= -\tfrac{3}{2}Q^2 + 24Q - 7$$

Step 1

At a stationary point

$$\frac{d\pi}{dQ} = 0$$

so

$$-3Q + 24 = 0$$

which has solution $Q = 24/3 = 8$.

Step 2

To classify this point we differentiate a second time to get

$$\frac{d^2\pi}{dQ^2} = -3$$

This is negative, so π has a maximum at $Q = 8$. In fact, the corresponding maximum profit is

$$\pi = -\tfrac{3}{2}(8)^2 + 24(8) - 7 = 89$$

Finally, we are invited to calculate the marginal revenue and marginal cost at this particular value of Q. To find expressions for MR and MC we need only differentiate TR and TC, respectively. If

$$\text{TR} = 30Q - Q^2$$

then

$$\text{MR} = \frac{d(\text{TR})}{dQ}$$
$$= 30 - 2Q$$

so when $Q = 8$

$$\text{MR} = 30 - 2(8) = 14$$

If

$$\text{TC} = \tfrac{1}{2}Q^2 + 6Q + 7$$

then

$$\text{MC} = \frac{d(\text{TC})}{dQ}$$
$$= Q + 6$$

so when $Q = 8$

$$\text{MC} = 8 + 6 = 14$$

We observe that at $Q = 8$, the values of MR and MC are equal.

In this particular example we discovered that at the point of maximum profit,

$$\boxed{\text{marginal revenue}} = \boxed{\text{marginal cost}}$$

There is nothing special about this example and in the next section we show that this result holds for any profit function.

Practice Problem

3. The demand equation of a good is given by

$$P + 2Q = 20$$

and the total cost function is

$$Q^3 - 8Q^2 + 20Q + 2$$

(a) Find the level of output that maximizes total revenue.

(b) Find the maximum profit and the value of Q at which it is achieved. Verify that, at this value of Q, MR = MC.

Example

The cost of building an office block, x floors high, is made up of three components:

(1) $10 million for the land

(2) $¼ million per floor

(3) specialized costs of $10 000$x$ per floor.

How many floors should the block contain if the average cost per floor is to be minimized?

Solution

The $10 million for the land is a fixed cost because it is independent of the number of floors. Each floor costs $¼ million, so if the building has x floors altogether then the cost will be 250 000x.

In addition there are specialized costs of 10 000x per floor, so if there are x floors this will be

$$(10\ 000x)x = 10\ 000x^2$$

Notice the square term here, which means that the specialized costs rise dramatically with increasing x. This is to be expected, since a tall building requires a more complicated design. It may also be necessary to use more expensive materials.

The total cost, TC, is the sum of the three components: that is,

$$TC = 10\ 000\ 000 + 250\ 000x + 10\ 000x^2$$

The average cost per floor, AC, is found by dividing the total cost by the number of floors: that is,

$$AC = \frac{TC}{x} = \frac{10\ 000\ 000 + 250\ 000 + 10\ 000x^2}{x}$$

$$= \frac{10\ 000\ 000}{x} + 250\ 000 + 10\ 000x$$

$$= 10\ 000\ 000x^{-1} + 250\ 000 + 10\ 000x$$

Step 1

At a stationary point

$$\frac{d(AC)}{dx} = 0$$

In this case

$$\frac{d(AC)}{dx} = -10\ 000\ 000x^{-2} + 10\ 000 = \frac{-10\ 000\ 000}{x^2} + 10\ 000$$

so we need to solve

$$10\ 000 = \frac{10\ 000\ 000}{x^2} \quad \text{or equivalently} \quad 10\ 000x^2 = 10\ 000\ 000$$

Hence

$$x^2 = \frac{10\ 000\ 000}{10\ 000} = 1000$$

This has solution

$$x = \pm\sqrt{1000} = \pm 31.6$$

We can obviously ignore the negative value because it does not make sense to build an office block with a negative number of floors, so we can deduce that $x = 31.6$.

Step 2

To confirm that this is a minimum we need to differentiate a second time. Now

$$\frac{d(AC)}{dx} = -10\,000\,000x^{-2} + 10\,000$$

so

$$\frac{d^2(AC)}{dx^2} = -2(-10\,000\,000)x^{-3} = \frac{20\,000\,000}{x^3}$$

When $x = 31.6$ we see that

$$\frac{d^2(AC)}{dx^2} = \frac{20\,000\,000}{(31.6)^3} = 633.8$$

It follows that $x = 31.6$ is indeed a minimum because the second-order derivative is a positive number.

At this stage it is tempting to state that the answer is 31.6. This is mathematically correct but is a physical impossibility since x must be a whole number. To decide whether to take x to be 31 or 32 we simply evaluate AC for these two values of x and choose the one that produces the lower average cost.

When $x = 31$,

$$AC = \frac{10\,000\,000}{31} + 250\,000 + 10\,000(31) = \$882\,581$$

When $x = 32$,

$$AC = \frac{10\,000\,000}{32} + 250\,000 + 10\,000(32) = \$882\,500$$

Therefore an office block 32 floors high produces the lowest average cost per floor.

Practice Problem

4. The total cost function of a good is given by

$$TC = Q^2 + 3Q + 36$$

Calculate the level of output that minimizes average cost. Find AC and MC at this value of Q. What do you observe?

Example

The supply and demand equations of a good are given by

$$P = Q_S + 8$$

and

$$P = -3Q_D + 80$$

respectively.

The government decides to impose a tax, t, per unit. Find the value of t which maximizes the government's total tax revenue on the assumption that equilibrium conditions prevail in the market.

Solution

The idea of taxation was first introduced in Chapter 1. In Section 1.5 the equilibrium price and quantity were calculated from a given value of t. In this example t is unknown but the analysis is exactly the same. All we need to do is to carry the letter t through the usual calculations and then to choose t at the end so as to maximize the total tax revenue.

To take account of the tax we replace P by $P - t$ in the supply equation. This is because the price that the supplier actually receives is the price, P, that the consumer pays less the tax, t, deducted by the government. The new supply equation is then

$$P - t = Q_S + 8$$

so that

$$P = Q_S + 8 + t$$

In equilibrium

$$Q_S = Q_D$$

If this common value is denoted by Q then the supply and demand equations become

$$P = Q + 8 + t$$
$$P = -3Q + 80$$

Hence

$$Q + 8 + t = -3Q + 80$$

since both sides are equal to P. This can be rearranged to give

$$Q = -3Q + 72 - t \quad \text{(subtract } 8 + t \text{ from both sides)}$$
$$4Q = 72 - t \quad \text{(add } 3Q \text{ to both sides)}$$
$$Q = 18 - \tfrac{1}{4}t \quad \text{(divide both sides by 4)}$$

Now, if the number of goods sold is Q and the government raises t per good then the total tax revenue, T, is given by

$$T = tQ$$
$$= t(18 - \tfrac{1}{4}t)$$
$$= 18t - \tfrac{1}{4}t^2$$

This then is the expression that we wish to maximize.

Step 1
At a stationary point

$$\frac{dT}{dt} = 0$$

so

$$18 - \tfrac{1}{2}t = 0$$

which has solution

$$t = 36$$

Step 2
To classify this point we differentiate a second time to get

$$\frac{d^2T}{dt^2} = \tfrac{1}{2} < 0$$

which confirms that it is a maximum.

Hence the government should impose a tax of \$36 on each good.

Practice Problem

5. The supply and demand equations of a good are given by

$$P = \tfrac{1}{2}Q_S + 25$$

and

$$P = -2Q_D + 50$$

respectively.

The government decides to impose a tax, t, per unit. Find the value of t which maximizes the government's total tax revenue on the assumption that equilibrium conditions prevail in the market.

We conclude this section by describing the use of a computer package to solve optimization problems. Although a spreadsheet could be used to do this, by tabulating the values of a function, it cannot handle the associated mathematics. A symbolic computation system such as Maple, Matlab, Mathcad or Derive can not only sketch the graphs of functions, but also differentiate and solve algebraic equations. Consequently, it is possible to obtain the exact solution using one of these packages. In this book we have chosen to use Maple.

Advice

A simple introduction to this package is described in the Getting Started section at the very beginning of this book. If you have not used Maple before, go back and read through this section now.

The following example makes use of three basic Maple instructions: `plot`, `diff` and `solve`. As the name suggests, `plot` produces a graph of a function by joining together points which are accurately plotted over a specified range of values. The instruction `diff`, not surprisingly, differentiates a given expression with respect to any stated variable, and `solve` finds the exact solution of an equation.

Example   MAPLE

The price, P, of a good varies over time, t, during a 15-year period according to

$$P = 0.064t^3 - 1.44t^2 + 9.6t + 10 \ (0 \le t \le 15)$$

(a) Sketch a graph of this function and use it to estimate the local maximum and minimum points.

(b) Find the exact coordinates of these points using calculus.

Solution

It is convenient to give the cubic expression the name price, and to do this in Maple, we type

```
>price:=0.064*t^3-1.44*t^2+9.6*t+10;
```

(a) To plot a graph of this function for values of t between 0 and 15 we type

```
>plot(price,t=0..15);
```

Maple responds by producing a graph of price over the specified range (see Figure 4.28). The graph shows that there is one local maximum and one local minimum. (It also shows very clearly that the overall, or global, minimum and maximum occur at the ends, 0 and 15 respectively.) If you now move the cursor to some point on the plot (not on the graph itself) and click, you will discover that two things happen. You will first notice

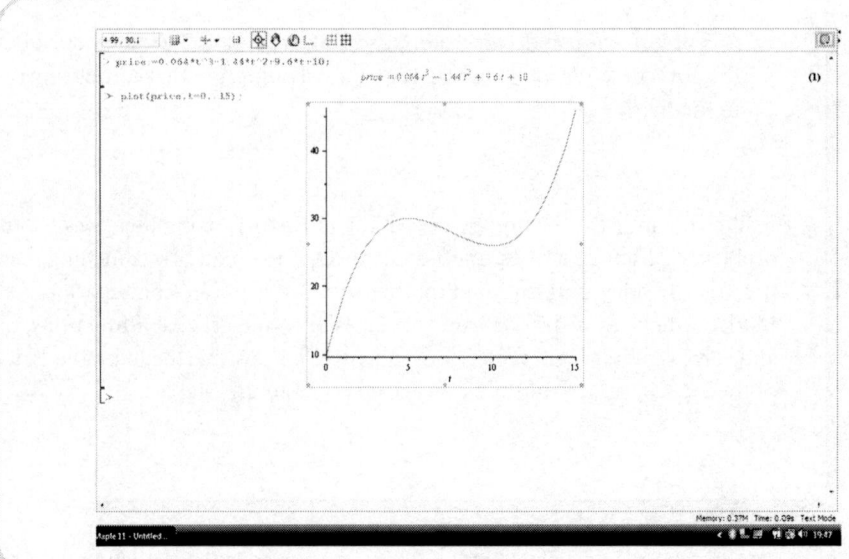

Figure 4.28

that the graph is now surrounded by a box. More significantly, if you look carefully at the top of the screen, you will see that a graphics toolbar has appeared. In the left-hand corner of this is a small window containing the coordinates of the position of the cursor. To estimate the local maximum and minimum all you need do is to move the cursor over the relevant points, and read off the answer from the screen. Looking carefully at Figure 4.28, in which the cursor is positioned over the local maximum, we see that the coordinates of this point are approximately (4.99, 30.1). A similar estimate could be found for the local minimum point. It is worth spending a few minutes having some fun by pressing the other buttons on the graphics toolbar to discover many useful features provided by Maple.

(b) To find the exact coordinates we need to use calculus. The simple instruction

```
>diff(price,t);
```

will produce the first derivative of price with respect to t. However, since we want to equate this to zero and solve the associated equation, it makes sense to give this a name. You can use whatever combination of symbols you like for a name in Maple, provided it does not begin with a number and it has not already been reserved by Maple. So, you are not allowed to use 1deriv, say (because it starts with the digit 1), or subs (which Maple recognizes as one of its own in-house instructions for substituting numbers for letters in an expression). If we choose to call it deriv1 we type:

```
>deriv1:=diff(price,t);
```

and Maple responds with

```
deriv1:=.192t²-2.88t+9.6
```

To find the stationary points, we need to equate this to zero and solve for t. This is achieved in Maple by typing:

```
>solve(deriv1=0,t);
```

and Maple responds with:

```
10.,5.
```

These are the values of t at the stationary points. It is clear from the graph in Figure 4.28 that $t = 5$ is a local maximum and $t = 10$ is a local minimum. To find the price at the maximum we substitute $t = 5$ into the expression for price, so we type:

```
>subs(t=5,price);
```

and Maple responds with

```
30.000
```

To find the price at the local minimum we edit the instruction to create

```
>subs(t=10,price);
```

and Maple responds with

```
26.000
```

The local maximum and minimum have coordinates (5, 30) and (10, 26) respectively.

Key Terms

Average product of labour (labour productivity)   Output per worker: $AP_L = Q/L$.

Maximum (local) point   A point on a curve which has the highest function value in comparison with other values in its neighbourhood; at such a point the first-order derivative is zero and the second-order derivative is either zero or negative.

Minimum (local) point   A point on a curve which has the lowest function value in comparison with other values in its neighbourhood; at such a point the first-order derivative is zero and the second-order derivative is either zero or positive.

Optimization   The determination of the optimal (usually stationary) points of a function.

Stationary point of inflection   A stationary point that is neither a maximum nor a minimum; at such a point both the first- and second-order derivatives are zero.

Stationary points (critical points, turning points, extrema)   Points on a graph at which the tangent is horizontal; at a stationary point the first-order derivative is zero.

Exercise 4.6

1. Find and classify the stationary points of the following functions. Hence give a rough sketch of their graphs. ❓

   (a) $y = -x^2 + x + 1$ **(b)** $y = x^2 - 4x + 4$ **(c)** $y = x^2 - 20x + 105$ **(d)** $y = -x^3 + 3x$

2. If the demand equation of a good is ❓

   $$P = 40 - 2Q$$

   find the level of output that maximizes total revenue.

3. A firm's short-run production function is given by ❓

   $$Q = 30L^2 - 0.5L^3$$

   Find the value of L which maximizes AP_L and verify that $MP_L = AP_L$ at this point.

4. If the fixed costs are 13 and the variable costs are $Q + 2$ per unit, show that the average cost function is

   $$AC = \frac{13}{Q} + Q + 2$$

   (a) Calculate the values of AC when $Q = 1, 2, 3, \ldots, 6$. Plot these points on graph paper and hence produce an accurate graph of AC against Q.

   (b) Use your graph to estimate the minimum average cost.

   (c) Use differentiation to confirm your estimate obtained in part (b).

5. The demand and total cost functions of a good are

   $$4P + Q - 16 = 0$$

   and

   $$TC = 4 + 2Q - \frac{3Q^2}{10} + \frac{Q^3}{20}$$

   respectively.

(a) Find expressions for TR, π, MR and MC in terms of Q.

(b) Solve the equation

$$\frac{d\pi}{dQ} = 0$$

and hence determine the value of Q which maximizes profit.

(c) Verify that, at the point of maximum profit, MR = MC.

6. The supply and demand equations of a good are given by

$$3P - Q_S = 3$$

and

$$2P + Q_D = 14$$

respectively.

The government decides to impose a tax, t, per unit. Find the value of t (in dollars) which maximizes the government's total tax revenue on the assumption that equilibrium conditions prevail in the market.

7. A manufacturer has fixed costs of \$200 each week, and the variable costs per unit can be expressed by the function, VC = $2Q - 36$

(a) Find an expression for the total cost function and deduce that the average cost function is given by

$$AC = \frac{200}{Q} + 2Q - 36$$

(b) Find the stationary point of this function and show that this is a minimum.

(c) Verify that, at this stationary point, average cost is the same as marginal cost.

8. (Maple) Plot a graph of each of the following functions over the specified range of values and use these graphs to estimate the coordinates of all of the stationary points. Use calculus to find the exact coordinates of these points.

(a) $y = 3x^4 - 28x^3 + 84x^2 - 96x + 30$ $(0 \le x \le 5)$

(b) $y = x^4 - 8x^3 + 18x^2 - 10$ $(-1 \le x \le 4)$

(c) $y = \dfrac{x}{x^2 + 1}$ $(-4 \le x \le 4)$

9. (Maple) The total cost, TC, and total revenue, TR, functions of a good are given by

$$TC = 80Q - \frac{15}{2}Q^2 + \frac{1}{3}Q^3 \text{ and } TR = 50Q - Q^2$$

Obtain Maple expressions for π, MC and MR, naming them profit, MC and MR respectively. Plot all three functions on the same diagram using the instruction:

```
plot({profit,MC,MR},Q=0..14);
```

Use this diagram to show that

(a) when the profit is a minimum, MR = MC and the MC curve cuts the MR curve from above

(b) when the profit is a maximum, MR = MC and the MC curve cuts the MR curve from below.

Exercise 4.6*

1. A firm's demand function is

   $$P = 60 - 0.5Q$$

   If fixed costs are 10 and variable costs are $Q + 3$ per unit, find the maximum profit.

2. Show that all of the following functions have a stationary point at $x = 0$. Verify in each case that $f''(0) = 0$. Classify these points by producing a rough sketch of each function.

   (b) $f(x) = x^3$ **(b)** $f(x) = x^4$ **(c)** $f(x) = -x^6$

3. If fixed costs are 15 and the variable costs are $2Q$ per unit, write down expressions for TC, AC and MC. Find the value of Q which minimizes AC and verify that AC = MC at this point. ❓

4. An electronic components firm launches a new product on 1 January. During the following year a rough estimate of the number of orders, S, received t days after the launch is given by ❓

   $$S = t^2 - 0.002t^3$$

   (a) What is the maximum number of orders received on any one day of the year?

   (b) After how many days does the firm experience the greatest increase in orders?

5. If the demand equation of a good is

   $$P = \sqrt{(1000 - 4Q)}$$

   find the value of Q which maximizes total revenue.

6. A firm's total cost and demand functions are given by

   $$TC = Q^2 + 50Q + 10 \text{ and } P = 200 - 4Q$$

   respectively.

   (a) Find the level of output needed to maximize the firm's profit.

   (b) The government imposes a tax of $\$t$ per good. If the firm adds this tax to its costs and continues to maximize profit, show that the price of the good increases by two-fifths of the tax, irrespective of the value of t.

7. Given that the cubic function, $f(x) = x^3 + ax^2 + bx + c$ has a stationary point at $(2, 5)$, and that it passes through $(1, 3)$, find the values of a, b and c.

8. (Maple)

   (a) Attempt to use Maple to plot a graph of the function $y = 1/x$ over the range $-4 \le x \le 4$. What difficulty do you encounter? Explain briefly why this has occurred for this particular function.

   (b) One way of avoiding the difficulty in part (a) is to restrict the range of the y values. Produce a plot by typing

   ```
   plot(1/x,x=-4..4,y=-3..3);
   ```

(c) Use the approach suggested in part (b) to plot a graph of the curve

$$y = \frac{x - 3}{(x + 1)(x - 2)}$$

on the interval $-2 \leq x \leq 6$. Use calculus to find all of the stationary points.

9. (**Maple**) A firm's short-run production function is given by

$$Q = 300L^{0.8}(240 - 5L)^{0.5} \quad (0 \leq L \leq 48)$$

where L is the size of the workforce. Plot a graph of this function and hence estimate the level of employment needed to maximize output. Confirm this by using differentiation.

SECTION 4.7
Further optimization of economic functions

Objectives

At the end of this section you should be able to:

- Show that, at the point of maximum profit, marginal revenue equals marginal cost.
- Show that, at the point of maximum profit, the slope of the marginal revenue curve is less than that of marginal cost.
- Maximize profits of a firm with and without price discrimination in different markets.
- Show that, at the point of maximum average product of labour, average product of labour equals marginal product of labour.

The previous section demonstrated how mathematics can be used to optimize particular economic functions. Those examples suggested two important results:

1. If a firm maximizes profit then MR = MC.
2. If a firm maximizes average product of labour then $AP_L = MP_L$.

Although these results were found to hold for all of the examples considered in Section 4.6, it does not necessarily follow that the results are always true. The aim of this section is to prove these assertions without reference to specific functions and hence to demonstrate their generality.

Advice

You may prefer to skip these proofs at a first reading and just concentrate on the worked example (and Practice Problem 1 and Question 3 in Exercise 4.7*) on price discrimination.

Justification of the first result turns out to be really quite easy. Profit, π, is defined to be the difference between total revenue, TR, and total cost, TC: that is,

$$\pi = TR - TC$$

To find the stationary points of π we differentiate with respect to Q and equate to zero: that is,

$$\frac{d\pi}{dQ} = \frac{d(TR)}{dQ} - \frac{d(TC)}{dQ} = 0$$

where we have used the difference rule to differentiate the right-hand side. In Section 4.3 we defined

$$MR = \frac{d(TR)}{dQ} \text{ and } MC = \frac{d(TC)}{dQ}$$

so the previous equation is equivalent to

$$MR - MC = 0$$

and so MR = MC as required.

The stationary points of the profit function can therefore be found by sketching the MR and MC curves on the same diagram and inspecting the points of intersection. Figure 4.29 shows typical marginal revenue and marginal cost curves. The result

$$MR = MC$$

holds for any stationary point. Consequently, if this equation has more than one solution then we need some further information before we can decide on the profit-maximizing level of output. In Figure 4.29 there are two points of intersection, Q_1 and Q_2, and it turns out (as you discovered in Practice Problem 3 and Question 5 of Exercise 4.6 in the previous section) that one of these is a maximum while the other is a minimum. Obviously, in any actual example, we can classify these points by evaluating second-order derivatives. However, it would be nice to make this decision just by inspecting the graphs of marginal revenue and marginal cost. To see how this can be done let us return to the equation

$$\frac{d\pi}{dQ} = MR - MC$$

and differentiate again with respect to Q to get

$$\frac{d^2\pi}{dQ^2} = \frac{d(MR)}{dQ} - \frac{d(MC)}{dQ}$$

Now if $d^2\pi/dQ^2 < 0$ then the profit is a maximum. This will be so when

$$\frac{d(MR)}{dQ} < \frac{d(MC)}{dQ}$$

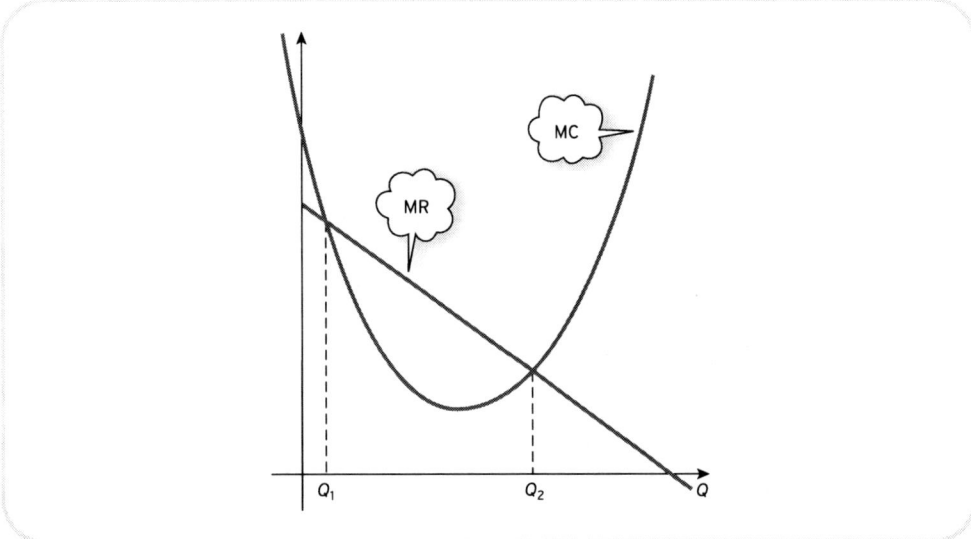

Figure 4.29

that is, when the slope of the marginal revenue curve is less than the slope of the marginal cost curve.

Looking at Figure 4.29, we deduce that this criterion is true at Q_2, so this must be the desired level of output needed to maximize profit. Note also from Figure 4.29 that the statement 'the slope of the marginal revenue curve is less than the slope of the marginal cost curve' is equivalent to saying that 'the marginal cost curve cuts the marginal revenue curve from below'. It is this latter form that is often quoted in economics textbooks. A similar argument shows that, at a minimum point, the marginal cost curve cuts the marginal revenue curve from above and so we can deduce that profit is a minimum at Q_1 in Figure 4.29. In practice, the task of sketching the graphs of MR and MC and reading off the coordinates of the points of intersection is not an attractive one, particularly if MR and MC are complicated functions. However, it might turn out that MR and MC are both linear, in which case a graphical approach is feasible.

Practice Problem ❓

1. A monopolist's demand function is

$$P = 25 - 0.5Q$$

The fixed costs of production are 7 and the variable costs are $Q + 1$ per unit.

(a) Show that

$$\text{TR} = 25Q - 0.5Q^2 \text{ and } \text{TC} = Q^2 + Q + 7$$

and deduce the corresponding expressions for MR and MC.

(b) Sketch the graphs of MR and MC on the same diagram and hence find the value of Q which maximizes profit.

Quite often a firm identifies more than one market in which it wishes to sell its goods. For example, a firm might decide to export goods to several countries and demand conditions are likely to be different in each one. The firm may be able to take advantage of this and increase overall profit by charging different prices in each country. The theoretical result 'marginal revenue equals marginal cost' can be applied in each market separately to find the optimal pricing policy.

Example

A firm is allowed to charge different prices for its domestic and industrial customers. If P_1 and Q_1 denote the price and demand for the domestic market then the demand equation is

$$P_1 + Q_1 = 500$$

If P_2 and Q_2 denote the price and demand for the industrial market then the demand equation is

$$2P_2 + 3Q_2 = 720$$

The total cost function is

$$\text{TC} = 50\,000 + 20Q$$

where $Q = Q_1 + Q_2$. Determine the prices (in dollars) that the firm should charge to maximize profits:

(a) with price discrimination

(b) without price discrimination.

Compare the profits obtained in parts (a) and (b).

Solution

(a) The important thing to notice is that the total cost function is independent of the market and so marginal costs are the same in each case. In fact, since

$$\text{TC} = 50\,000 + 20Q$$

we have MC = 20. All we have to do to maximize profits is to find an expression for the marginal revenue for each market and to equate this to the constant value of marginal cost.

Domestic market

The demand equation

$$P_1 + Q_1 = 500$$

rearranges to give

$$P_1 = 500 - Q_1$$

so the total revenue function for this market is

$$\text{TR}_1 = (500 - Q_1)Q_1 = 500Q_1 - Q_1^2$$

Hence

$$\text{MR}_1 = \frac{d(\text{TR}_1)}{dQ_1} = 500 - 2Q_1$$

For maximum profit

$$\text{MR}_1 = \text{MC}$$

so

$$500 - 2Q_1 = 20$$

which has solution $Q_1 = 240$. The corresponding price is found by substituting this value into the demand equation to get

$$P_1 = 500 - 240 = \$260$$

To maximize profit the firm should charge its domestic customers \$260 per good.

Industrial market

The demand equation

$$2P_2 + 3Q_2 = 720$$

rearranges to give

$$P_2 = 360 - \tfrac{3}{2}Q_2$$

so the total revenue function for this market is

$$\text{TR}_2 = (360 - \tfrac{3}{2}Q_2)Q_2 = 360Q_2 - \tfrac{3}{2}Q_2^2$$

Hence

$$MR_2 = \frac{d(TR_2)}{dQ_2} = 360 - 3Q_2$$

For maximum profit

$$MR_2 = MC$$

so

$$360 - 3Q_2 = 20$$

which has solution $Q_2 = 340/3$. The corresponding price is obtained by substituting this value into the demand equation to get

$$P_2 = 360 - \frac{3}{2}\left(\frac{340}{3}\right) = \$190$$

To maximize profits the firm should charge its industrial customers \$190 per good, which is lower than the price charged to its domestic customers.

(b) If there is no price discrimination then $P_1 = P_2 = P$, say, and the demand functions for the domestic and industrial markets become

$$P + Q_1 = 500$$

and

$$2P + 3Q_2 = 720$$

respectively. We can use these to deduce a single demand equation for the combined market. We need to relate the price, P, of each good to the total demand, $Q = Q_1 + Q_2$.

This can be done by rearranging the given demand equations for Q_1 and Q_2 and then adding. For the domestic market

$$Q_1 = 500 - P$$

and for the industrial market

$$Q_2 = 240 - \tfrac{2}{3}P$$

Hence

$$Q = Q_1 + Q_2 = 740 - \tfrac{5}{3}P$$

The demand equation for the combined market is therefore

$$Q + \tfrac{5}{3}P = 740$$

The usual procedure for profit maximization can now be applied. This demand equation rearranges to give

$$P = 444 - \tfrac{3}{5}Q$$

enabling the total revenue function to be written down as

$$TR = \left(444 - \frac{5}{3}Q\right)Q = 444Q - \frac{3Q^2}{5}$$

Hence

$$MR = \frac{d(TR)}{dQ} = 444 - \frac{6}{5}Q$$

For maximum profit

$$MR = MC$$

so

$$444 - \frac{6}{5}Q_2 = 20$$

which has solution $Q = 1060/3$. The corresponding price is found by substituting this value into the demand equation to get

$$P = 444 - \frac{3}{5}\left(\frac{1060}{3}\right) = \$232$$

To maximize profit without discrimination the firm needs to charge a uniform price of \$232 for each good. Notice that this price lies between the prices charged to its domestic and industrial customers with discrimination.

To evaluate the profit under each policy we need to work out the total revenue and subtract the total cost. In part (a) the firm sells 240 goods at \$260 each in the domestic market and sells 340/3 goods at \$190 each in the industrial market, so the total revenue received is

$$240 \times 260 + \frac{340}{3} \times 190 = \$83\ 933.33$$

The total number of goods produced is

$$240 + \frac{340}{3} = \frac{1060}{3}$$

so the total cost is

$$50\ 000 + 20 \times \frac{1060}{3} = \$57\ 066.67$$

Therefore the profit with price discrimination is

$$83\ 933.33 - 57\ 066.67 = \$26\ 866.67$$

In part (b) the firm sells 1060/3 goods at \$232 each, so total revenue is

$$\frac{1060}{3} \times 232 = \$81\ 973.33$$

Now the total number of goods produced under both pricing policies is the same: that is, 1060/3. Consequently, the total cost of production in part (b) must be the same as part (a): that is,

$$TC = \$57\ 066.67$$

The profit without price discrimination is

$$81\ 973.33 - 57\ 066.67 = \$24\ 906.66$$

As expected, the profits are higher with discrimination than without.

Practice Problem

2. A firm has the possibility of charging different prices in its domestic and foreign markets. The corresponding demand equations are given by

$$Q_1 = 300 - P_1$$
$$Q_2 = 400 - 2P_2$$

The total cost function is

$$TC = 5000 + 100Q$$

where $Q = Q_1 + Q_2$.

Determine the prices (in dollars) that the firm should charge to maximize profits

(a) with price discrimination

(b) without price discrimination.

Compare the profits obtained in parts (a) and (b).

In the previous example and in Practice Problem 2 we assumed that the marginal costs were the same in each market. The level of output that maximizes profit with price discrimination was found by equating marginal revenue to this common value of marginal cost. It follows that the marginal revenue must be the same in each market. In symbols

$$MR_1 = MC \text{ and } MR_2 = MC$$

so

$$MR_1 = MR_2$$

This fact is obvious on economic grounds. If it were not true then the firm's policy would be to increase sales in the market where marginal revenue is higher and to decrease sales by the same amount in the market where the marginal revenue is lower. The effect would be to increase revenue while keeping costs fixed, thereby raising profit. This property leads to an interesting result connecting price, P, with elasticity of demand, E. In Section 4.5 we derived the formula

$$MR = P\left(1 - \frac{1}{E}\right)$$

If we let the price elasticity of demand in two markets be denoted by E_1 and E_2 corresponding to prices P_1 and P_2 then the equation

$$MR_1 = MR_2$$

becomes

$$P_1\left(1 - \frac{1}{E_1}\right) = P_2\left(1 - \frac{1}{E_2}\right)$$

This equation holds whenever a firm chooses its prices P_1 and P_2 to maximize profits in each market. Note that if $E_1 < E_2$ then this equation can only be true if $P_1 > P_2$. In other words, the firm charges the higher price in the market with the lower elasticity of demand.

Practice Problem

3. Calculate the price elasticity of demand at the point of maximum profit for each of the demand functions given in Practice Problem 2 with price discrimination. Verify that the firm charges the higher price in the market with the lower elasticity of demand.

The previous discussion concentrated on profit. We now turn our attention to average product of labour and prove result (2) stated at the beginning of this section. This concept is defined by

$$AP_L = \frac{Q}{L}$$

where Q is output and L is labour. The maximization of AP_L is a little more complicated than before, since it is necessary to use the quotient rule to differentiate this function. In the notation of Section 4.4 we write

$$u = Q \quad \text{and} \quad v = L$$

so

$$\frac{du}{dL} = \frac{dQ}{dL} = MP_L \quad \text{and} \quad \frac{dv}{dL} = \frac{dL}{dL} = 1$$

where we have used the fact that the derivative of output with respect to labour is the marginal product of labour.

The quotient rule gives

$$\frac{d(AP_L)}{dL} = \frac{v\,du/dL - u\,dv/dL}{v^2}$$

$$= \frac{L(MP_L) - Q(1)}{L^2}$$

$$= \frac{MP_L - Q/L}{L} \qquad \text{divide top and bottom by } L$$

$$= \frac{MP_L - AP_L}{L} \qquad \text{by definition, } AP_L = \frac{Q}{L}$$

At a stationary point

$$\frac{d(AP_L)}{dL} = 0$$

so

$$\frac{MP_L - AP_L}{L} = 0$$

Hence

$$MP_L = AP_L$$

as required.

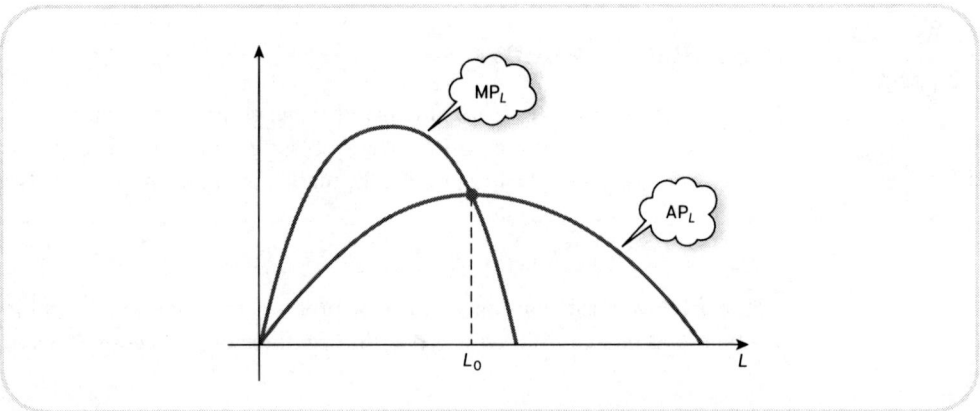

Figure 4.30

This analysis shows that, at a stationary point of the average product of labour function, the marginal product of labour equals the average product of labour. The above argument provides a formal proof that this result is true for any average product of labour function. Figure 4.30 shows typical average and marginal product functions. Note that the two curves intersect at the peak of the AP_L curve. To the left of this point the AP_L function is increasing, so that

$$\frac{d(AP_L)}{dL} > 0$$

Now we have just seen that

$$\frac{d(AP_L)}{dL} = \frac{MP_L - AP_L}{L}$$

so we deduce that, to the left of the maximum, $MP_L > AP_L$. In other words, in this region the graph of marginal product of labour lies above that of average product of labour. Similarly, to the right of the maximum, AP_L is decreasing, so that

$$\frac{d(AP_L)}{dL} < 0$$

and hence $MP_L < AP_L$. The graph of marginal product of labour therefore lies below that of average product of labour in this region.

We deduce that if the stationary point is a maximum then the MP_L curve cuts the AP_L curve from above. A similar argument can be used for any average function. The particular case of the average cost function is investigated in Question 6 in Exercise 4.7*.

Exercise 4.7*

1. A firm's demand function is

    $P = aQ + b \ (a < 0, b > 0)$

    Fixed costs are c and variable costs per unit are d.

    (a) Write down general expressions for TR and TC.

    (b) By differentiating the expressions in part (a), deduce MR and MC.

    (c) Use your answers to (b) to show that profit, π, is maximized when

    $$Q = \frac{d - b}{2a}$$

2. **(a)** In Section 4.5 the following relationship between marginal revenue, MR, and price elasticity of demand, E, was derived:

    $$MR = P \left(1 - \frac{1}{E} \right)$$

    Use this result to show that at the point of maximum total revenue, $E = 1$.

    (b) Verify the result of part (a) for the demand function

    $2P + 3Q = 60$

3. The demand functions for a firm's domestic and foreign markets are

    $P_1 = 50 - 5Q_1$

    $P_2 = 30 - 4Q_2$

    and the total cost function is

    $TC = 10 + 10Q$

    where $Q = Q_1 + Q_2$. Determine the prices needed to maximize profit

    (a) with price discrimination

    (b) without price discrimination.

    Compare the profits obtained in parts (a) and (b).

4. Show that if the marginal cost curve cuts the marginal revenue curve from above then profit is a minimum.

5. The economic order quantity, EOQ, is used in cost accounting to minimize the total cost, TC, to order and carry a firm's stock over the period of a year.

    The annual cost of placing orders, ACO, is given by

    $$ACO = \frac{(ARU)(CO)}{EOQ}$$

    where

    ARU = annual required units

    CO = cost per order

The annual carrying cost, ACC, is given by

$$\text{ACC} = (\text{CU})(\text{CC})\frac{(\text{EOQ})}{2}$$

where

CU = cost per unit

CC = carrying cost

and (EOQ)/2 provides an estimate of the average number of units in stock at any given time of the year. Assuming that ARU, CO, CU and CC are all constant, show that the total cost

$$\text{TC} = \text{ACO} + \text{ACC}$$

is minimized when

$$\text{EOQ} = \sqrt{\frac{2(\text{ARU})(\text{CO})}{(\text{CU})(\text{CC})}}$$

6. (a) Show that, at a stationary point of an average cost function, average cost equals marginal cost.

(b) Show that if the marginal cost curve cuts the average cost curve from below then average cost is a minimum.

7. In a competitive market the equilibrium price, P, and quantity, Q, are found by setting $Q_S = Q_D = Q$ in the supply and demand equations ❓

$$P = aQ_S + b \ (a > 0, b > 0)$$
$$P = cQ_D + d \ (c > 0, d > 0)$$

If the government levies an excise tax, t, per unit, show that

$$Q = \frac{d - b - t}{a + c}$$

Deduce that the government's tax revenue, $T = tQ$, is maximized by taking

$$t = \frac{d - b}{2}$$

SECTION 4.8

The derivative of the exponential and natural logarithm functions

Objectives

At the end of this section you should be able to:

● Differentiate the exponential function.

● Differentiate the natural logarithm function.

● Use the chain, product and quotient rules to differentiate combinations of these functions.

● Appreciate the use of the exponential function in economic modelling.

In this section we investigate the derived functions associated with the exponential and natural logarithm functions, e^x and $\ln x$. The approach that we adopt is similar to that used in Section 4.1. The derivative of a function determines the slope of the graph of a function. Consequently, to discover how to differentiate an unfamiliar function we first produce an accurate sketch and then measure the slopes of the tangents at selected points.

Advice

The functions, e^x and $\ln x$ were first introduced in Section 2.4. You might find it useful to remind yourself how these functions are defined before working through the rest of the current section.

Example

Complete the following table of function values and hence sketch a graph of $f(x) = e^x$:

x	−2.0	−1.5	−1.0	0.0	0.5	1.0	1.5
$f(x)$							

Draw tangents to the graph at $x = -1, 0$ and 1. Hence estimate the values of $f'(-1), f'(0)$ and $f'(1)$. Suggest a general formula for the derived function $f'(x)$.

Solution

Using a calculator we obtain

x	−2.0	−1.5	−1.0	−0.5	0.0	0.5	1.0	1.5
$f(x)$	0.14	0.22	0.37	0.61	1.00	1.65	2.72	4.48

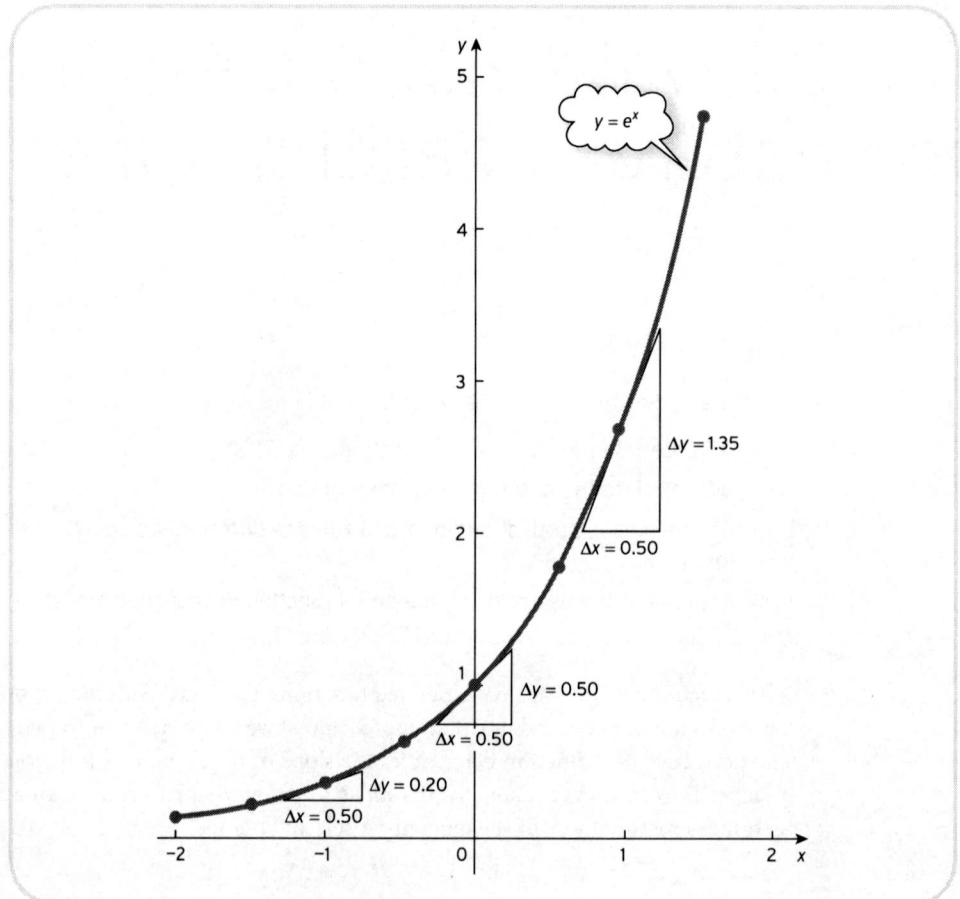

Figure 4.31

The corresponding graph of the exponential function is sketched in Figure 4.31. From the graph we see that the slopes of the tangents are

$$f'(-1) = \frac{0.20}{0.50} = 0.4$$

$$f'(0) = \frac{0.50}{0.50} = 1.0$$

$$f'(1) = \frac{1.35}{0.50} = 2.7$$

These results are obtained by measurement and so are quoted to only 1 decimal place. We cannot really expect to achieve any greater accuracy using this approach.

The values of x, $f(x)$ and $f'(x)$ are summarized in the following table. The values of $f(x)$ are rounded to 1 decimal place in order to compare with the graphical estimates of $f'(x)$.

x	−1	0	1
$f(x)$	0.4	1.0	2.7
$f'(x)$	0.4	1.0	2.7

Notice that the values of $f(x)$ and $f'(x)$ are identical to within the accuracy quoted.

These results suggest that the slope of the graph at each point is the same as the function value at that point: that is, e^x differentiates to itself. Symbolically,

if $f(x) = e^x$ then $f'(x) = e^x$

or, equivalently,

if $y = e^x$ then $\dfrac{dy}{dx} = e^x$

Practice Problem

1. Use your calculator to complete the following table of function values and hence sketch an accurate graph of $f(x) = \ln x$:

x	0.50	1.00	1.50	2.00	2.50	3.00	3.50	4.00
$f(x)$			0.41				1.25	

Draw the tangents to the graph at $x = 1, 2$ and 3. Hence estimate the values of $f'(1), f'(2)$ and $f'(3)$. Suggest a general formula for the derived function $f'(x)$.
[Hint: for the last part you may find it helpful to rewrite your estimates of $f'(x)$ as simple fractions.]

In fact, it is possible to prove that, for any value of the constant m,

$$\boxed{\;\text{if}\quad y = e^{mx}\quad \text{then}\quad \dfrac{dy}{dx} = me^{mx}\;}$$

and

$$\boxed{\;\text{if}\quad y = \ln mx\quad \text{then}\quad \dfrac{dy}{dx} = \dfrac{1}{x}\;}$$

In particular, we see by setting $m = 1$ that

e^x differentiates to e^x

and that

$\ln x$ differentiates to $\dfrac{1}{x}$

which agree with our practical investigations.

Example

Differentiate

(a) $y = e^{2x}$

(b) $y = e^{-7x}$

(c) $y = \ln 5x$ $(x > 0)$

(d) $y = \ln 559x$ $(x > 0)$

Solution

(a) Setting $m = 2$ in the general formula shows that

$$\text{if} \quad y = e^{2x} \quad \text{then} \quad \frac{dy}{dx} = 2e^{2x}$$

Notice that when exponential functions are differentiated the power itself does not change. All that happens is that the coefficient of x comes down to the front.

(b) Setting $m = -7$ in the general formula shows that

$$\text{if} \quad y = e^{-7x} \quad \text{then} \quad \frac{dy}{dx} = -7e^{-7x}$$

(c) Setting $m = 5$ in the general formula shows that

$$\text{if} \quad y = \ln 5x \quad \text{then} \quad \frac{dy}{dx} = \frac{1}{x}$$

Notice the restriction $x > 0$ stated in the question. This is needed to ensure that we do not attempt to take the logarithm of a negative number, which is impossible.

(d) Setting $m = 559$ in the general formula shows that

$$\text{if} \quad y = \ln 559x \quad \text{then} \quad \frac{dy}{dx} = \frac{1}{x}$$

Notice that we get the same answer as part (c). The derivative of the natural logarithm function does not depend on the coefficient of x. This fact may seem rather strange but it is easily accounted for. The third rule of logarithms shows that $\ln 559x$ is the same as

$$\ln 559 + \ln x$$

The first term is merely a constant, so differentiates to zero, and the second term differentiates to $1/x$.

Practice Problem

2. Differentiate

    (a) $y = e^{3x}$ **(b)** $y = e^{-x}$ **(c)** $y = \ln 3x \ (x > 0)$ **(d)** $y = \ln 51\ 234x \ (x > 0)$

The chain rule can be used to explain what happens to the m when differentiating e^{mx}. The outer function is the exponential, which differentiates to itself, and the inner function is mx, which differentiates to m. Hence, by the chain rule,

$$\text{if} \quad y = e^{mx} \quad \text{then} \quad \frac{dy}{dx} = e^{mx} \times m = me^{mx}$$

Similarly, noting that the natural logarithm function differentiates to the reciprocal function,

$$\text{if} \quad y = \ln mx \quad \text{then} \quad \frac{dy}{dx} = \frac{1}{mx} \times m = \frac{1}{x}$$

The chain, product and quotient rules can be used to differentiate more complicated functions involving e^x and $\ln x$.

Example

Differentiate

(a) $y = x^3 e^{2x}$ **(b)** $y = \ln(x^2 + 2x + 1)$ **(c)** $y = \dfrac{e^{3x}}{x^2 + 2}$

Solution

(a) The function $x^3 e^{2x}$ involves the product of two simpler functions, x^3 and e^{2x}, so we need to use the product rule to differentiate it. Putting

$$u = x^3 \quad \text{and} \quad v = e^{2x}$$

gives

$$\frac{du}{dx} = 3x^2 \quad \text{and} \quad \frac{dv}{dx} = 2e^{2x}$$

By the product rule

$$\frac{dy}{dx} = u\frac{dv}{dx} + v\frac{du}{dx} = x^3[2e^{2x}] + e^{2x}[3x^2] = 2x^3 e^{2x} + 3x^2 e^{2x}$$

There is a common factor of $x^2 e^{2x}$, which goes into the first term $2x$ times and into the second term three times. Hence

$$\frac{dy}{dx} = x^2 e^{2x}(2x + 3)$$

(b) The expression $\ln(x^2 + 2x + 1)$ can be regarded as a function of a function, so we can use the chain rule to differentiate it. We first differentiate the outer log function to get

$$\frac{1}{x^2 + 2x + 1}$$

and then multiply by the derivative of the inner function, $x^2 + 2x + 1$, which is $2x + 2$. Hence

$$\frac{dy}{dx} = \frac{2x + 2}{x^2 + 2x + 1}$$

(c) The function

$$\frac{e^{3x}}{x^2 + 2}$$

is the quotient of the simpler functions

$$u = e^{3x} \quad \text{and} \quad v = x^2 + 2$$

for which

$$\frac{du}{dx} = 3e^{3x} \quad \text{and} \quad \frac{dv}{dx} = 2x$$

By the quotient rule

$$\frac{dy}{dx} = \frac{v\dfrac{du}{dx} - u\dfrac{dv}{dx}}{v^2} = \frac{(x^2 + 2)(3e^{3x}) - e^{3x}(2x)}{(x^2 + 2)^2} = \frac{e^{3x}[3(x^2 + 2) - 2x]}{(x^2 + 2)^2} = \frac{e^{3x}(3x^2 - 2x + 6)}{(x^2 + 2)^2}$$

Practice Problem

3. Differentiate

(a) $y = x^4 \ln x$

(b) $y = e^{v^2}$

(c) $y = \dfrac{\ln x}{x + 2}$

Advice

If you ever need to differentiate a function of the form:

ln(an inner function involving products, quotients or powers of x)

then it is usually quicker to use the rules of logs to expand the expression before you begin. The three rules are

Rule 1 $\ln(x \times y) = \ln x + \ln y$
Rule 2 $\ln(x \div y) = \ln x - \ln y$
Rule 3 $\ln x^m = m\ln x$

The following example shows how to apply this 'trick' in practice.

Example

Differentiate

(a) $y = \ln(x(x + 1)^4)$ (b) $y = \ln\left(\dfrac{x}{\sqrt{(x + 5)}}\right)$

Solution

(a) From rule 1

$$\ln(x(x + 1)^4) = \ln x + \ln(x + 1)^4$$

which can be simplified further using rule 3 to give

$$y = \ln x + 4 \ln(x + 1)$$

Differentiation of this new expression is simple. We see immediately that

$$\frac{dy}{dx} = \frac{1}{x} + \frac{4}{x + 1}$$

If desired the final answer can be put over a common denominator

$$\frac{1}{x} + \frac{4}{x + 1} = \frac{(x + 1) + 4x}{x(x + 1)} = \frac{5x + 1}{x(x + 1)}$$

(b) The quickest way to differentiate

$$y = \ln\left(\frac{x}{\sqrt{(x + 5)}}\right)$$

is to expand first to get

$$y = \ln x - \ln(x + 5)^{1/2} \quad \text{(rule 2)}$$
$$= \ln x - \tfrac{1}{2}\ln(x + 5) \quad \text{(rule 3)}$$

Again this expression is easy to differentiate:

$$\frac{dy}{dx} = \frac{1}{x} - \frac{1}{2(x + 5)}$$

If desired, this can be written as a single fraction:

$$\frac{1}{x} - \frac{1}{2(x + 5)} = \frac{2(x + 5) - x}{2x(x + 5)} = \frac{x + 10}{2x(x + 5)}$$

Practice Problem

4. Differentiate the following functions by first expanding each expression using the rules of logs:

(a) $y = \ln(x^3(x + 2)^4)$ **(b)** $y = \ln\left(\dfrac{x^2}{2x + 3}\right)$

Exponential and natural logarithm functions provide good mathematical models in many areas of economics and we conclude this chapter with some illustrative examples.

Example

A firm's short-run production function is given by

$$Q = L^2 e^{-0.01L}$$

Find the value of L that maximizes the average product of labour.

Solution

The average product of labour is given by

$$\text{AP}_L = \frac{Q}{L} = \frac{L^2 e^{-0.01L}}{L} = L e^{-0.01L}$$

To maximize this function we adopt the strategy described in Section 4.6.

Step 1
At a stationary point

$$\frac{d(\text{AP}_L)}{dL} = 0$$

To differentiate $L e^{-0.01L}$, we use the product rule. If

$$u = L \quad \text{and} \quad v = e^{-0.01L}$$

then

$$\frac{du}{dL} = 1 \quad \text{and} \quad \frac{dv}{dL} = -0.01e^{-0.01L}$$

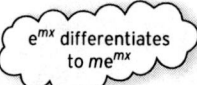

e^{mx} differentiates to me^{mx}

By the product rule

$$\frac{d(AP_L)}{dL} = u\frac{dv}{dL} + v\frac{du}{dL} = L(-0.01e^{-0.01L}) + e^{-0.01L} = (1 - 0.01L)e^{-0.01L}$$

We know that a negative exponential is never equal to zero. (Although $e^{-0.01L}$ gets ever closer to zero as L increases, it never actually reaches it for finite values of L.) Hence the only way that

$$(1 - 0.01L)e^{-0.01L}$$

can equal zero is when

$$1 - 0.01L = 0$$

which has solution $L = 100$.

Step 2
To show that this is a maximum we need to differentiate a second time. To do this we apply the product rule to

$$(1 - 0.01L)e^{-0.01L}$$

taking

$$u = 1 - 0.01L \quad \text{and} \quad v = e^{-0.01L}$$

for which

$$\frac{du}{dL} = -0.01 \quad \text{and} \quad \frac{dv}{dL} = -0.01e^{-0.01L}$$

Hence

$$\frac{d^2(AP_L)}{dL^2} = u\frac{dv}{dL} + v\frac{du}{dL} = (1 - 0.01L)(-0.01e^{-0.01L}) + e^{-0.01L}(-0.01) = (-0.02 + 0.0001L)e^{-0.01L}$$

Finally, putting $L = 100$ into this gives

$$\frac{d^2(AP_L)}{dL^2} = -0.0037$$

The fact that this is negative shows that the stationary point, $L = 100$, is indeed a maximum.

Practice Problem

5. The demand function of a good is given by

$$Q = 1000e^{-0.2P}$$

If fixed costs are 100 and the variable costs are 2 per unit, show that the profit function is given by

$$\pi = 1000Pe^{-0.2P} - 2000e^{-0.2P} - 100$$

Find the price needed to maximize profit.

Example

A firm estimates that the total revenue received from the sale of Q goods is given by

$$TR = \ln(1 + 1000Q^2)$$

Calculate the marginal revenue when $Q = 10$.

Solution

The marginal revenue function is obtained by differentiating the total revenue function. To differentiate $\ln(1 + 1000Q^2)$ we use the chain rule. We first differentiate the outer log function to get

$$\frac{1}{1 + 1000Q^2}$$

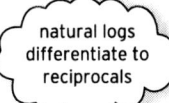
natural logs differentiate to reciprocals

and then multiply by the derivative of the inner function, $1 + 1000Q^2$, to get $2000Q$. Hence

$$MR = \frac{d(TR)}{dQ} = \frac{2000Q}{1 + 1000Q^2}$$

At $Q = 10$,

$$MR = \frac{2000(10)}{1 + 1000(10)^2} = 0.2$$

Practice Problem

6. If the demand equation is

$$P = 200 - 40 \ln(Q + 1)$$

calculate the price elasticity of demand when $Q = 20$.

Exercise 4.8

1. Write down the derivative of

(a) $y = e^{6x}$ (b) $y = e^{-342x}$ (c) $y = 2e^{-x} + 4e^x$ (d) $y = 10e^{4x} - 2x^2 + 7$

2. If \$4000 is saved in an account offering a return of 4% compounded continuously the future value, S, after t years is given by

$$S = 4000e^{0.04t}$$

(1) Calculate the value of S when

(a) $t = 5$ (b) $t = 5.01$

and hence estimate the rate of growth at $t = 5$. Round your answers to 2 decimal places.

(2) Write down an expression for $\dfrac{dS}{dt}$ and hence find the exact value of the rate of growth after 5 years.

3. Write down the derivative of

   (a) $y = \ln(3x)$ $(x > 0)$ **(b)** $y = \ln(-13x)$ $(x < 0)$

4. Use the chain rule to differentiate

   (a) $y = e^{x^3}$ **(b)** $y = \ln(x^4 + 3x^2)$

5. Use the product rule to differentiate

   (a) $y = x^4 e^{2x}$ **(b)** $y = x \ln x$

6. Use the quotient rule to differentiate

   (a) $y = \dfrac{e^{4x}}{x^2 + 2}$ **(b)** $y = \dfrac{e^x}{\ln x}$

7. Find and classify the stationary points of

   (a) $y = xe^{-x}$ **(b)** $y = \ln x - x$

   Hence sketch their graphs.

8. Find the output needed to maximize profit given that the total cost and total revenue functions are

   $$\text{TC} = 2Q \quad \text{and} \quad \text{TR} = 100 \ln(Q + 1)$$

   respectively.

9. If a firm's production function is given by

   $$Q = 700Le^{-0.02L}$$

   find the value of L that maximizes output.

10. The demand function of a good is given by

   $$P = 100e^{-0.1Q}$$

   Show that demand is unit elastic when $Q = 10$.

Exercise 4.8*

1. Differentiate:

   (a) $y = e^{2x} - 3e^{-4x}$ **(b)** xe^{4x} **(c)** $\dfrac{e^{-x}}{x^2}$ **(d)** $x^m \ln x$ **(e)** $x(\ln x - 1)$

   (f) $\dfrac{x^n}{\ln x}$ **(g)** $\dfrac{e^{mx}}{(ax + b)^n}$ **(h)** $\dfrac{e^{ax}}{(\ln bx)^n}$ **(i)** $\dfrac{e^x - 1}{e^x + 1}$

2. Use the rules of logarithms to expand each of the following functions. Hence write their derivatives.

   (a) $y = \ln\left(\dfrac{x}{x+1}\right)$ **(b)** $y = \ln(x\sqrt{(3x - 1)})$ **(c)** $y = \ln\sqrt{\dfrac{x+1}{x-1}}$

3. The growth rate of an economic variable, y, is defined to be $\dfrac{dy}{dt} \div y$.

Use this definition to find the growth rate of the variable, $y = Ae^{kt}$.

4. Differentiate the following functions with respect to x, simplifying your answers as far as possible:

(a) $y = x^4 e^{-2x^2}$ (b) $y = \ln\left(\dfrac{3x}{(x+1)^2}\right)$

5. Find and classify the stationary points of

(a) $y = xe^{ax}$ (b) $y = \ln(ax^2 + bx)$

where $a < 0$.

6. (a) Use the quotient rule to show that the derivative of the function

$$y = \frac{2x + 1}{\sqrt{4x + 3}}$$

is given by

$$\frac{4(x + 1)}{(4x + 3)\sqrt{4x + 3}}$$

(b) Use the chain rule to differentiate the function

$$y = \ln\left(\frac{2x + 1}{\sqrt{4x + 3}}\right)$$

(c) Confirm that your answer to part (b) is correct by first expanding

$$\ln\left(\frac{2x + 1}{\sqrt{4x + 3}}\right)$$

using the rules of logs and then differentiating.

7. A firm's short-run production function is given by

$$Q = L^3 e^{-0.02L}$$

Find the value of L that maximises the average product of labour.

8. Find an expression for the price elasticity of demand for each of the demand curves:

(a) $P = 100e^{-Q}$ (b) $P = 500 - 75\ln(2Q + 1)$

9. Find an expression for the marginal revenue for each of the following demand curves:

(a) $P = \dfrac{e^{Q^2}}{Q^2}$ (b) $P = \ln\left(\dfrac{2Q}{3Q + 1}\right)$

CHAPTER 5
Partial Differentiation

This chapter continues the topic of calculus by describing how to differentiate functions of more than one variable. In many ways this chapter can be regarded as the climax of the whole book. It is the summit of the mathematical mountain that we have been merrily climbing. Not only are the associated mathematical ideas and techniques quite sophisticated, but also partial differentiation provides a rich source of applications. In one sense there is no new material presented here. If you know how to differentiate a function of one variable then you also know how to partially differentiate a function of several variables because the rules are the same. Similarly, if you can optimize a function of one variable then you need have no fear of unconstrained and constrained optimization. Of course, if you cannot use the elementary rules of differentiation or cannot find the maximum and minimum values of a function as described in Chapter 4 then you really are fighting a lost cause. Under these circumstances you are best advised to omit this chapter entirely. There is no harm in doing this, because it does not form the prerequisite for any of the later topics. However, you will miss out on one of the most elegant and useful branches of mathematics.

There are six sections to this chapter. It is important that Sections 5.1 and 5.2 are read first, but the remaining sections can be studied in any order. Sections 5.1 and 5.2 follow the familiar pattern. We begin by looking at the mathematical techniques and then use them to determine marginal functions and elasticities. Section 5.3 describes the multiplier concept and completes the topic of statics which you studied in Chapter 1.

The final three sections are devoted to optimization. For functions of several variables, optimization problems are split into two groups, unconstrained and constrained. Unconstrained problems, tackled in Section 5.4, involve the maximization and minimization of functions in which the variables are free to take any values whatsoever. In a constrained problem only certain combinations of the variables are examined. For example, a firm might wish to minimize costs but is constrained by the need to satisfy production quotas, or an individual might want to maximize utility but is subject to a budgetary constraint, and so on. There are two ways of solving constrained problems: the method of substitution and the method of Lagrange multipliers, described in Sections 5.5 and 5.6 respectively.

SECTION 5.1

Functions of several variables

Objectives

At the end of this section you should be able to:

- Use the function notation, $z = f(x, y)$.
- Determine the first-order partial derivatives, f_x and f_y.
- Determine the second-order partial derivatives, f_{xx}, f_{xy}, f_{yx} and f_{yy}.
- Appreciate that, for most functions, $f_{xy} = f_{yx}$.
- Use the small increments formula.
- Perform implicit differentiation.

Most relationships in economics involve more than two variables. The demand for a good depends not only on its own price but also on the price of substitutable and complementary goods, incomes of consumers, advertising expenditure and so on. Likewise, the output from a production process depends on a variety of inputs, including land, capital and labour. To analyse general economic behaviour we must extend the concept of a function, and particularly the differential calculus, to functions of several variables.

A **function, f, of two variables** is a rule that assigns to each incoming pair of numbers, (x, y), a uniquely defined outgoing number, z. This is illustrated in Figure 5.1. The 'black box' f performs some arithmetic operation on x and y to produce z. For example, the rule might be 'multiply the two numbers together and add twice the second number'. In symbols we write this either as

$$f(x, y) = xy + 2y$$

or as

$$z = xy + 2y$$

In order to be able to evaluate the function we have to specify the numerical values of both x and y.

Figure 5.1

Example

If $f(x, y) = xy + 2y$ evaluate

(a) $f(3, 4)$ **(b)** $f(4, 3)$

Solution

(a) Substituting $x = 3$ and $y = 4$ gives

$$f(3, 4) = 3(4) + 2(4) = 20$$

(b) Substituting $x = 4$ and $y = 3$ gives

$$f(4, 3) = 4(3) + 2(3) = 18$$

Note that, for this function, $f(3, 4)$ is not the same as $f(4, 3)$, so in general we must be careful to write down the correct ordering of the variables.

We have used the labels x and y for the two incoming numbers (called the **independent** variables) and z for the outgoing number (called the **dependent** variable). We could equally well have written the above function as

$$y = x_1 x_2 + 2x_2$$

say, using x_1 and x_2 to denote the independent variables and using y this time to denote the dependent variable. The use of subscripts may seem rather cumbersome, but it does provide an obvious extension to functions of more than two variables. In general, a function of n variables can be written

$$y = f(x_1, x_2, \ldots, x_n)$$

Practice Problem

1. If

$$f(x, y) = 5x + xy^2 - 10$$

and

$$g(x_1, x_2, x_3) = x_1 + x_2 + x_3$$

evaluate

(a) $f(0, 0)$ **(b)** $f(1, 2)$ **(c)** $f(2, 1)$ **(d)** $g(5, 6, 10)$ **(e)** $g(0, 0, 0)$ **(f)** $g(10, 5, 6)$

A function of one variable can be given a pictorial description using graphs, which help to give an intuitive feel for its behaviour. Figure 5.2 shows the graph of a typical function

$$y = f(x)$$

in which the horizontal axis determines the incoming number, x, and the vertical axis determines the corresponding outgoing number, y. The height of the curve directly above any point on the x axis represents the value of the function at this point.

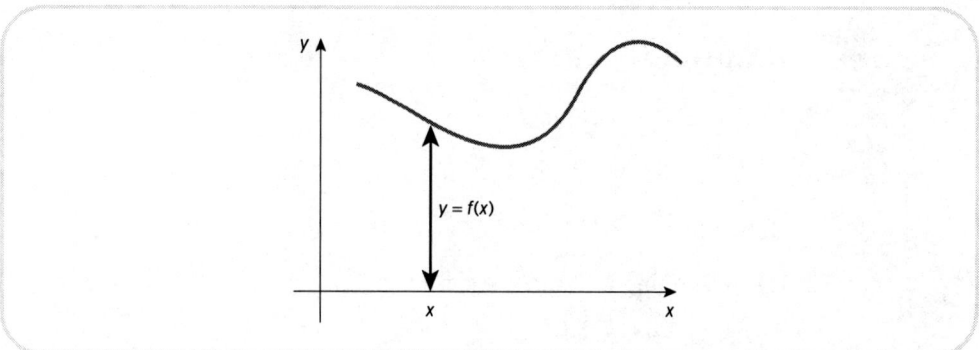

Figure 5.2

An obvious question to ask is whether there is a pictorial representation of functions of several variables. The answer is yes in the case of functions of two variables, although it is not particularly easy to construct. A function

$$z = f(x, y)$$

can be thought of as a surface, rather like a mountain range, in three-dimensional space as shown in Figure 5.3. If you visualize the incoming point with coordinates (x, y) as lying in a horizontal plane then the height of the surface, z, directly above it represents the value of the function at this point. As you can probably imagine, it is not an easy task to sketch the surface by hand from an equation such as

$$f(x, y) = xy^3 + 4x$$

although three-dimensional graphics packages are available for most computers which can produce such a plot.

Advice

There is an example which describes how to use Maple to produce a three-dimensional plot at the end of the next section. If you are interested, you might like to read the example now and see if you can produce graphs of some of the functions considered here.

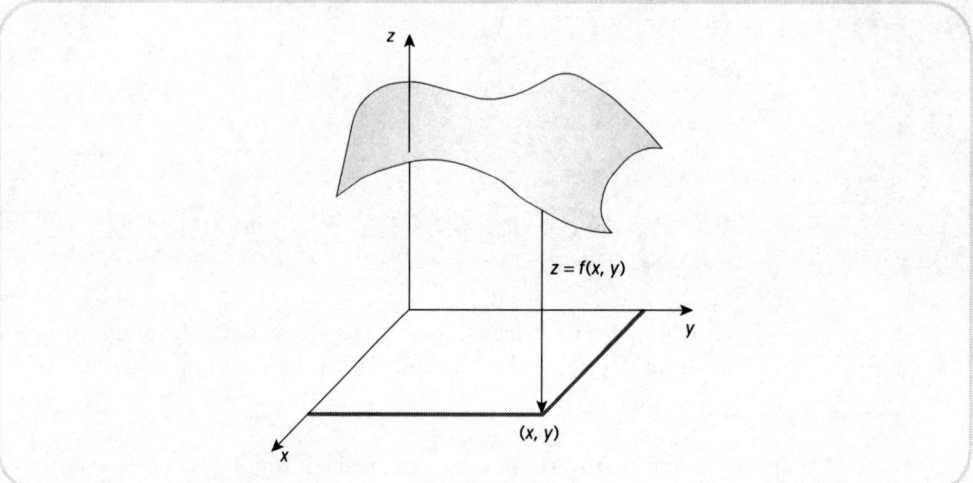

Figure 5.3

It is impossible to provide any sort of graphical interpretation for functions of more than two variables. For example, a function of, say, four variables would require five dimensions, one for each of the incoming variables and a further one for the outgoing variable! In spite of this setback we can still perform the task of differentiating functions of several variables and, as we shall see in the remaining sections of this chapter, such derivatives play a vital role in analysing economic behaviour.

Given a function of two variables,

$$z = f(x, y)$$

we can determine two first-order derivatives. The **partial derivative of f with respect to x** is written as

$$\frac{\partial z}{\partial x} \quad \text{or} \quad \frac{\partial f}{\partial x} \quad \text{or} \quad f_x$$

and is found by differentiating f with respect to x, with y held constant. Similarly, the **partial derivative of f with respect to y** is written as

$$\frac{\partial z}{\partial y} \quad \text{or} \quad \frac{\partial f}{\partial y} \quad \text{or} \quad f_y$$

and is found by differentiating f with respect to y, with x held constant. We use curly d's in the notation

$$\frac{\partial f}{\partial x}$$

read 'partial dee f by dee x'

to distinguish partial differentiation of functions of several variables from ordinary differentiation of functions of one variable. The alternative notation, f_x, is analogous to the f' notation for ordinary differentiation.

Example

Find the first-order partial derivatives of the functions

(a) $f(x, y) = x^2 + y^3$ **(b)** $f(x, y) = x^2 y$

Solution

(a) To differentiate the function

$$f(x, y) = x^2 + y^3$$

with respect to x we work as follows. By the sum rule we know that we can differentiate each part separately and add. Now, when we differentiate x^2 with respect to x we get $2x$. However, when we differentiate y^3 with respect to x we get 0. To see this, note from the definition of partial differentiation with respect to x that the variable y is held constant. Of course, if y is a constant then so is y^3 and, as we discovered in Chapter 4, constants differentiate to zero. Hence

$$\frac{\partial f}{\partial x} = 2x + 0 = 2x$$

In the same way

$$\frac{\partial f}{\partial y} = 0 + 3y^2 = 3y^2$$

This time x is held constant, so x^2 goes to zero, and when we differentiate y^3 with respect to y we get $3y^2$.

(b) To differentiate the function

$$f(x, y) = x^2 y$$

with respect to x, we differentiate in the normal way, taking x as the variable while pretending that y is a constant. Now, when we differentiate a constant multiple of x^2 we differentiate x^2 to get $2x$ and then multiply by the constant. For example,

$$7x^2 \quad \text{differentiates to} \quad 7(2x) = 14x$$
$$-100x^2 \quad \text{differentiates to} \quad -100(2x) = -200x$$

and

$$cx^2 \quad \text{differentiates to} \quad c(2x) = 2cx$$

for any constant c. In our case, y, plays the role of a constant, so

$$x^2 y \quad \text{differentiates to} \quad (2x)y = 2xy$$

Hence

$$f_x = 2xy$$

Similarly, to find f_y we treat y as the variable and x as a constant in the expression

$$f(x, y) = x^2 y$$

Now, when we differentiate a constant multiple of y we just get the constant, so cy differentiates to c. In our case, x^2 plays the role of c, so $x^2 y$ differentiates to x^2. Hence

$$f_y = x^2$$

Practice Problem

2. Find expressions for the first-order partial derivatives for the functions

(a) $f(x, y) = 5x^4 - y^2$ **(b)** $f(x, y) = x^2 y^3 - 10x$

In general, when we differentiate a function of two variables, the thing we end up with is itself a function of two variables. This suggests the possibility of differentiating a second time. In fact there are four **second-order partial derivatives**. We write

$$\frac{\partial^2 z}{\partial x^2} \quad \text{or} \quad \frac{\partial^2 f}{\partial x^2} \quad \text{or} \quad f_{xx}$$

for the function obtained by differentiating twice with respect to x,

$$\frac{\partial^2 z}{\partial y^2} \quad \text{or} \quad \frac{\partial^2 f}{\partial y^2} \quad \text{or} \quad f_{yy}$$

for the function obtained by differentiating twice with respect to y,

$$\frac{\partial^2 z}{\partial y \partial x} \quad \text{or} \quad \frac{\partial^2 f}{\partial y \partial x} \quad \text{or} \quad f_{yx}$$

for the function obtained by differentiating first with respect to x and then with respect to y, and

$$\frac{\partial^2 z}{\partial x \partial y} \quad \text{or} \quad \frac{\partial^2 f}{\partial x \partial y} \quad \text{or} \quad f_{xy}$$

for the function obtained by differentiating first with respect to y and then with respect to x.

Example

Find expressions for the second-order partial derivatives f_{xx}, f_{yy}, f_{yx} and f_{xy} for the functions

(a) $f(x, y) = x^2 + y^3$ **(b)** $f(x, y) = x^2 y$

Solution

(a) The first-order partial derivatives of the function

$$f(x, y) = x^2 + y^3$$

have already been found and are given by

$$f_x = 2x, \quad f_y = 3y^2$$

To find f_{xx} we differentiate f_x with respect to x to get

$$f_{xx} = 2$$

To find f_{yy} we differentiate f_y with respect to y to get

$$f_{yy} = 6y$$

To find f_{yx} we differentiate f_x with respect to y to get

$$f_{yx} = 0$$

Note how f_{yx} is obtained. Starting with the original function

$$f(x, y) = x^2 + y^3$$

we first differentiate with respect to x to get $2x$ and when we differentiate this with respect to y we keep x constant, so it goes to zero. Finally, to find f_{xy} we differentiate f_y with respect to x to get

$$f_{xy} = 0$$

Note how f_{xy} is obtained. Starting with the original function

$$f(x, y) = x^2 + y^3$$

we first differentiate with respect to y to get $3y^2$ and when we differentiate this with respect to x we keep y constant, so it goes to zero.

(b) The first-order partial derivatives of the function

$$f(x, y) = x^2 y$$

have already been found and are given by

$$f_x = 2xy, \quad f_y = x^2$$

Hence

$$f_{xx} = 2y, \quad f_{yy} = 0, \quad f_{yx} = 2x, \quad f_{xy} = 2x$$

Practice Problem

3. Find expressions for the second-order partial derivatives of the functions

(a) $f(x, y) = 5x^4 - y^2$ **(b)** $f(x, y) = x^2 y^3 - 10x$

[Hint: you might find your answer to Practice Problem 2 useful.]

Looking back at the expressions obtained in the previous example and Practice Problem 3, notice that in all cases

$$\frac{\partial^2 f}{\partial y \partial x} = \frac{\partial^2 f}{\partial x \partial y}$$

$f_{yx} = f_{xy}$

It can be shown that this result holds for all functions that arise in economics. It is immaterial in which order the partial differentiation is performed. Differentiating with respect to x then y gives the same expression as differentiating with respect to y then x. (In fact, there are some weird mathematical functions for which this result is not true, although they need not concern us.)

Although we have concentrated exclusively on functions of two variables, it should be obvious how to work out partial derivatives of functions of more than two variables. For the general function

$$y = f(x_1, x_2, \ldots, x_n)$$

there are n first-order partial derivatives, written as

$$\frac{\partial f}{\partial x_i} \quad \text{or} \quad f_i \quad (i = 1, 2, \ldots, n)$$

which are found by differentiating with respect to one variable at a time, keeping the remaining $n - 1$ variables fixed. The second-order partial derivatives are determined in an analogous way.

Example

Find the derivative, f_{31}, for the function

$$f(x_1, x_2, x_3) = x_1^3 + x_1 x_3^2 + 5x_2^4$$

Solution

We need to find

$$f_{31} = \frac{\partial^2 f}{\partial x_3 \partial x_1}$$

which denotes the function obtained by differentiating first with respect to x_1 and then with respect to x_3. Differentiating with respect to x_1 gives

$$f_1 = \frac{\partial f}{\partial x_1} = 3x_1^2 + x_3^2$$

and if we further differentiate this with respect to x_3 we get

$$f_{31} = \frac{\partial^2 f}{\partial x_3 \partial x_1} = 2x_3$$

In fact, as we have just noted for functions of two variables, we get the same answer if we differentiate in reverse order. You might like to check this for yourself.

Practice Problem

4. Find expressions for the partial derivatives f_1, f_{11} and f_{21} in the case when

$$f(x_1, x_2, x_3) = x_1 x_2 + x_1^5 - x_2^2 x_3$$

We have seen how to work out partial derivatives but have yet to give any meaning to them. To provide an interpretation of a partial derivative, let us take one step back for a moment and recall the corresponding situation for functions of one variable of the form

$$y = f(x)$$

The derivative, dy/dx, gives the rate of change of y with respect to x. In other words, if x changes by a small amount Δx then the corresponding change in y satisfies

$$\Delta y \simeq \frac{dy}{dx} \Delta x$$

Moreover, the accuracy of the approximation improves as Δx becomes smaller and smaller.

Advice

You might like to remind yourself of the reasoning behind this approximation, which was explained graphically in Section 4.3.1.

Given the way in which a partial derivative is found, we can deduce that for a function of two variables

$$z = f(x, y)$$

if x changes by a small amount Δx and y is held fixed then the corresponding change in z satisfies

$$\Delta z \simeq \frac{\partial z}{\partial x}\Delta x$$

Similarly, if y changes by Δy and x is fixed then z changes by

$$\Delta z \simeq \frac{\partial z}{\partial y}\Delta y$$

In practice, of course, x and y may both change simultaneously. If this is the case then the net change in z will be the sum of the individual changes brought about by changes in x and y separately, so that

$$\boxed{\Delta z \simeq \frac{\partial z}{\partial x}\Delta x + \frac{\partial z}{\partial y}\Delta y}$$

This is referred to as the **small increments formula**. Although this is only an approximation, it can be shown that for most functions the corresponding error tends to zero as Δx and Δy both tend to zero. For this reason the formula is sometimes quoted with an equality sign and written as

$$dz = \frac{\partial z}{\partial x}dx + \frac{\partial z}{\partial y}dy$$

where the symbols dx, dy and dz are called **differentials** and represent limiting values of Δx, Δy and Δz, respectively.

Example

If

$$z = x^3 y - y^3 x$$

evaluate

$$\frac{\partial z}{\partial x} \quad \text{and} \quad \frac{\partial z}{\partial y}$$

at the point $(1, 3)$. Hence estimate the change in z when x increases from 1 to 1.1 and y decreases from 3 to 2.8 simultaneously.

Solution

If

$$z = x^3 y - y^3 x$$

then

$$\partial z/\partial x = 3x^2 y - y^3 \quad \text{and} \quad \partial z/\partial y = x^3 - 3y^2 x$$

so at the point $(1, 3)$

$$\frac{\partial z}{\partial x} = 3(1)^2 (3) - 3^3 = -18$$

$$\frac{\partial z}{\partial y} = 1^3 - 3(3)^2 (1) = -26$$

Now, since x increases from 1 to 1.1, the change in x is

$$\Delta x = 0.1$$

> positive numbers denote increases

and, since y decreases from 3 to 2.8, the change in y is

$$\Delta y = -0.2$$

> negative numbers denote decreases

The small increments formula states that

$$\Delta z \simeq \frac{\partial z}{\partial x} \Delta x + \frac{\partial z}{\partial y} \Delta y$$

The change in z is therefore

$$\Delta z \simeq (-18)(0.1) + (-26)(-0.2) = 3.4$$

so z increases by approximately 3.4.

Practice Problem ❷

5. If

$$z = xy - 5x + 2y$$

evaluate

$$\frac{\partial z}{\partial x} \quad \text{and} \quad \frac{\partial z}{\partial y}$$

at the point $(2, 6)$.

(a) Use the small increments formula to estimate the change in z as x decreases from 2 to 1.9 and y increases from 6 to 6.1.

(b) Confirm your estimate of part (a) by evaluating z at $(2, 6)$ and $(1.9, 6.1)$.

One important application of the small increments formula is to implicit differentiation. We hope by now that you are entirely happy differentiating functions of one variable such as

$$y = x^3 + 2x^2 + 5$$

> $\frac{dy}{dx} = 3x^2 + 4x$

Suppose, however, that you are asked to find dy/dx given the equation

$$y^3 + 2xy^2 - x = 5$$

This is much more difficult. The reason for the difference is that in the first case y is given explicitly in terms of x whereas in the second case the functional dependence of y on x is only given implicitly. You would need to somehow rearrange this equation and to write y in terms of x before you could differentiate it. Unfortunately, this is an impossible task because of the presence of the y^3 term. The trick here is to regard the expression on the left-hand side of the equation as a function of the two variables x and y, so that

$$f(x, y) = y^3 + 2xy^2 - x$$

or, equivalently,

$$z = y^3 + 2xy^2 - x$$

The equation

$$y^3 + 2xy^2 - x = 5$$

then reads

$$z = 5$$

In general, the differential form of the small increments formula states that

$$dz = \frac{\partial z}{\partial x}dx + \frac{\partial z}{\partial y}dy$$

In our particular case, z takes the constant value of 5, so does not change. Hence $dz = 0$ and the formula reduces to

$$0 = \frac{\partial z}{\partial x}dx + \frac{\partial z}{\partial y}dy$$

which rearranges as

$$\frac{\partial z}{\partial y}dy = -\frac{\partial z}{\partial x}dx$$

that is,

$$\frac{dy}{dx} = -\frac{\partial z/\partial x}{\partial z/\partial y}$$

This formula can be used to find dy/dx given any implicit function

$$f(x, y) = \text{constant}$$

that is,

$$\boxed{\text{if} \quad f(x, y) = \text{constant} \quad \text{then} \quad \frac{dy}{dx} = -\frac{f_x}{f_y}}$$

The technique of finding dy/dx from $-f_x/f_y$ is called **implicit differentiation** and can be used whenever it is difficult or impossible to obtain an explicit representation for y in terms of x.

Example

Use implicit differentiation to find an expression for dy/dx given that

$$y^3 + 2xy^2 - x = 5$$

Solution
For the function

$$f(x, y) = y^3 + 2xy^2 - x$$

we have

$$f_x = 2y^2 - 1 \text{ and } f_y = 3y^2 + 4xy$$

so that

$$\frac{dy}{dx} = -\frac{f_x}{f_y} = -\left(\frac{2y^2 - 1}{3y^2 + 4xy}\right) = \frac{-2y^2 + 1}{3y^2 + 4xy}$$

Advice

There is an alternative way of thinking about implicit differentiation which is based on the chain rule and does not depend on partial differentiation at all. This is described in Appendix 2 on the website. You might find it easier to use than the method described above.

Practice Problem

6. Use implicit differentiation to find expressions for dy/dx given that

  (a) $xy - y^3 + y = 0$ **(b)** $y^5 - xy^2 = 10$

Key Terms

Dependent variable A variable whose value is determined by that taken by the independent variables; in $z = f(x, y)$, the dependent variable is z.

Differentials Limiting values of incremental changes. In the limit, the approximation $\Delta z \approx \frac{\partial z}{\partial x} \times \Delta x$ becomes $dz = \frac{\partial z}{\partial x} \times dx$ where dz and dx are the differentials.

Function of two variables A rule that assigns to each pair of incoming numbers, x and y, a uniquely defined outgoing number, z.

Implicit differentiation The process of obtaining dy/dx where the function is not given explicitly as an expression for y in terms of x.

Independent variable Variables whose values determine that of the dependent variable; in $z = f(x, y)$, the independent variables are x and y.

Partial derivative The derivative of a function of two or more variables with respect to one of these variables, the others being regarded as constant.

Second-order partial derivative The partial derivative of a first-order partial derivative. For example, f_{xy} is the second-order partial derivative when f is differentiated first with respect to y and then with respect to x.

Small increments formula The result $\Delta z \simeq \dfrac{\partial z}{\partial x}\Delta x + \dfrac{\partial z}{\partial y}\Delta y$

Exercise 5.1

1. If

$$f(x, y) = 3x^2 y^3$$

evaluate $f(2, 3)$, $f(5, 1)$ and $f(0, 7)$.

2. Write down expressions for the first-order partial derivatives, $\dfrac{\partial z}{\partial x}$ and $\dfrac{\partial z}{\partial y}$ for

(a) $z = x^2 + 4y^5$ **(b)** $z = 3x^3 - 2e^y$ **(c)** $z = xy + 6y$ **(d)** $z = x^6 y^2 + 5y^3$

3. If

$$f(x, y) = x^4 y^5 - x^2 + y^2$$

write down expressions for the first-order partial derivatives, f_x and f_y. Hence evaluate $f_x(1, 0)$ and $f_y(1, 1)$.

4. Use the small increments formula to estimate the change in

$$z = x^2 y^4 - x^6 + 4y$$

when

(a) x increases from 1 to 1.1 and y remains fixed at 0

(b) x remains fixed at 1 and y decreases from 0 to -0.5

(c) x increases from 1 to 1.1 and y decreases from 0 to -0.5.

5. **(a)** If

$$f(x, y) = y - x^3 + 2x$$

write down expressions for f_x and f_y. Hence use implicit differentiation to find dy/dx given that

$$y - x^3 + 2x = 1$$

(b) Confirm your answer to part (a) by rearranging the equation

$$y - x^3 + 2x = 1$$

to give y explicitly in terms of x and using ordinary differentiation.

Exercise 5.1*

1. If

$$f(x, y) = 2xy + 3x$$

verify that $f(5, 7) \neq f(7, 5)$. Find all pairs of numbers, (x, y) for which $f(x, y) = f(y, x)$.

2. Find expressions for all first- and second-order partial derivatives of the following functions. In each case verify that

$$\frac{\partial^2 z}{\partial y \partial x} = \frac{\partial^2 z}{\partial x \partial y}$$

  (a) $z = xy$ **(b)** $z = e^x y$ **(c)** $z = x^2 + 2x + y$ **(d)** $z = 16x^{1/4}y^{3/4}$ **(e)** $z = \dfrac{y}{x^2} + \dfrac{x}{y}$

3. If
$$z = x^2 y^3 - 10xy + y^2$$

evaluate z_x and z_y at the point $(2, 3)$. Hence estimate the change in z as x increases by 0.2 and y decreases by 0.1.

4. Verify that $x = 1$, $y = -1$ satisfy the equation $x^2 - 2y^3 = 3$. Use implicit differentiation to find the value of dy/dx at this point.

5. A function of three variables is given by

$$f(x_1, x_2, x_3) = \frac{x_1 x_3^2}{x_2} + \ln(x_2 x_3)$$

Find all of the first- and second-order derivatives of this function and verify that

$$f_{12} = f_{21}, \quad f_{13} = f_{31} \quad \text{and} \quad f_{23} = f_{32}$$

6. Write down an expression for a function, $f(x, y)$, with first-order partial derivatives,

$$\frac{\partial f}{\partial x} = 3xy(xy + 2) \qquad \frac{\partial f}{\partial y} = x^2(2xy + 3)$$

7. Evaluate the second-order partial derivative, f_{23}, of the function

$$f(x_1, x_2, x_3) = \frac{x_3 x_2^3}{x_1} + x_2 e^{x_3}$$

at the point, $(3, 2, 0)$.

8. Find the value of $\dfrac{dy}{dx}$ at the point $(-2, 1)$ for the function which is defined implicitly by

$$x^2 y - \frac{x}{y} = 6$$

SECTION 5.2
Partial elasticity and marginal functions

Objectives

At the end of this section you should be able to:

- Calculate partial elasticities.
- Calculate marginal utilities.
- Calculate the marginal rate of commodity substitution along an indifference curve.
- Calculate marginal products.
- Calculate the marginal rate of technical substitution along an isoquant.
- State Euler's theorem for homogeneous production functions.

The first section of this chapter described the technique of partial differentiation. Hopefully, you have discovered that partial differentiation is no more difficult than ordinary differentiation. The only difference is that for functions of several variables you have to be clear at the outset which letter in a mathematical expression is to be the variable, and to bear in mind that all remaining letters are then just constants in disguise! Once you have done this, the actual differentiation itself obeys the usual rules. In Sections 4.3 and 4.5 we considered various microeconomic applications. Given the intimate relationship between ordinary and partial differentiation, you should not be too surprised to learn that we can extend these applications to functions of several variables. We concentrate on three main areas:

- elasticity of demand
- utility
- production.

We consider each of these in turn.

5.2.1 Elasticity of demand

Suppose that the demand, Q, for a certain good depends on its price, P, the price of an alternative good, P_A, and the income of consumers, Y, so that

$$Q = f(P, P_A, Y)$$

for some demand function, f.

Of particular interest is the responsiveness of demand to changes in any one of these three variables. This can be measured quantitatively using elasticity. The **(own) price elasticity of demand** is defined to be

$$E_P = -\frac{\text{percentage change in } Q}{\text{percentage change in } P}$$

with P_A and Y held constant. This definition is identical to the one given in Section 4.5, so following the same mathematical argument presented there we deduce that

$$E_P = -\frac{P}{Q} \times \frac{\partial Q}{\partial P}$$

The partial derivative notation is used here because Q is now a function of several variables, and P_A and Y are held constant.

Advice

You may recall that the introduction of the minus sign is an artificial device designed to make E_P positive. This policy is not universal and you are advised to check which convention your own tutor uses.

In an analogous way we can measure the responsiveness of demand to changes in the price of the alternative good. The **cross-price elasticity of demand** is defined to be

$$E_{P_A} = \frac{\text{percentage change in } Q}{\text{percentage change in } P_A}$$

with P and Y held constant. Again, the usual mathematical argument shows that

$$E_{P_A} = \frac{P_A}{Q} \times \frac{\partial Q}{\partial P_A}$$

The sign of E_{P_A} could turn out to be positive or negative depending on the nature of the alternative good. If the alternative good is substitutable then Q increases as P_A rises, because consumers buy more of the given good as it becomes relatively less expensive. Consequently,

$$\frac{\partial Q}{\partial P_A} > 0$$

and so $E_{P_A} > 0$. If the alternative good is complementary then Q decreases as P_A rises, because the bundle of goods as a whole becomes more expensive. Consequently,

$$\frac{\partial Q}{\partial P_A} < 0$$

and so $E_{P_A} < 0$.

Finally, the **income elasticity of demand** is defined to be

$$E_Y = \frac{\text{percentage change in } Q}{\text{percentage change in } Y}$$

and can be found from

$$E_Y = \frac{Y}{Q} \times \frac{\partial Q}{\partial Y}$$

Again, E_Y can be positive or negative. If the good is superior then demand rises as income rises and E_Y is positive. However, if the good is inferior then demand falls as income rises and E_Y is negative.

Example

Given the demand function

$$Q = 100 - 2P + P_A + 0.1Y$$

where $P = 10$, $P_A = 12$ and $Y = 1000$, find the

(a) price elasticity of demand

(b) cross-price elasticity of demand

(c) income elasticity of demand.

Is the alternative good substitutable or complementary?

Solution

We begin by calculating the value of Q when $P = 10$, $P_A = 12$ and $Y = 1000$. The demand equation gives

$$Q = 100 - 2(10) + 12 + 0.1(1000) = 192$$

(a) To find the price elasticity of demand we partially differentiate

$$Q = 100 - 2P + P_A + 0.1Y$$

with respect to P to get

$$\frac{\partial Q}{\partial Y} = -2$$

Hence

$$E_P = -\frac{P}{Q} \times \frac{\partial Q}{\partial P} = -\frac{10}{192} \times (-2) = 0.10$$

(b) To find the cross-price elasticity of demand we partially differentiate

$$Q = 100 - 2P + P_A + 0.1Y$$

with respect to P_A to get

$$\frac{\partial Q}{\partial P_A} = 1$$

Hence

$$E_{P_A} = \frac{P_A}{Q} \times \frac{\partial Q}{\partial P_A} = \frac{12}{192} \times 1 = 0.06$$

The fact that this is positive shows that the two goods are substitutable.

(c) To find the income elasticity of demand we partially differentiate

$$Q = 100 - 2P + P_A + 0.1Y$$

with respect to Y to get

$$\frac{\partial Q}{\partial Y} = 0.1$$

Hence

$$E_Y = \frac{Y}{Q} \times \frac{\partial Q}{\partial Y} = \frac{1000}{192} \times 0.1 = 0.52$$

Practice Problem ❓

1. Given the demand function

    $$Q = 500 - 3P - 2P_A + 0.01Y$$

    where $P = 20$, $P_A = 30$ and $Y = 5000$, find

    (a) the price elasticity of demand

    (b) the cross-price elasticity of demand

    (c) the income elasticity of demand.

    If income rises by 5%, calculate the corresponding percentage change in demand. Is the good inferior or superior?

5.2.2 Utility

So far in this book we have concentrated almost exclusively on the behaviour of producers. In this case it is straightforward to identify the primary objective, which is to maximize profit. We now turn our attention to consumers. Unfortunately, it is not so easy to identify the motivation for their behaviour. One tentative suggestion is that consumers try to maximize earned income. However, if this were the case then individuals would try to work 24 hours a day for 7 days a week, which is not so. In practice, people like to allocate a reasonable proportion of time to leisure activities.

Consumers are faced with a choice of how many hours each week to spend working and how many to devote to leisure. In the same way, a consumer needs to decide how many items of various goods to buy and has a preference between the options available. To analyse the behaviour of consumers quantitatively we associate with each set of options a number, U, called **utility**, which indicates the level of satisfaction. Suppose that there are two goods, G1 and G2, and that the consumer buys x_1 items of G1 and x_2 items of G2. The variable U is then a function of x_1 and x_2, which we write as

$$U = U(x_1, x_2)$$

If

$$U(3, 7) = 20 \quad \text{and} \quad U(4, 5) = 25$$

for example, then the consumer derives greater satisfaction from buying four items of G1 and five items of G2 than from buying three items of G1 and seven items of G2.

Utility is a function of two variables, so we can work out two first-order partial derivatives,

$$\frac{\partial U}{\partial x_1} \quad \text{and} \quad \frac{\partial U}{\partial x_2}$$

The derivative

$$\frac{\partial U}{\partial x_1}$$

gives the rate of change of U with respect to x_i and is called the **marginal utility of** x_i. If x_i changes by a small amount Δx_i and the other variable is held fixed then the change in U satisfies

$$\Delta U \simeq \frac{\partial U}{\partial x_i} \Delta x_i$$

If x_1 and x_2 both change then the net change in U can be found from the small increments formula

$$\Delta U \simeq \frac{\partial U}{\partial x_1}\Delta x_1 + \frac{\partial U}{\partial x_2}\Delta x_2$$

Example

Given the utility function

$$U = x_1^{1/4}x_2^{3/4}$$

determine the value of the marginal utilities

$$\frac{\partial U}{\partial x_1} \quad \text{and} \quad \frac{\partial U}{\partial x_2}$$

when $x_1 = 100$ and $x_2 = 200$. Hence estimate the change in utility when x_1 decreases from 100 to 99 and x_2 increases from 200 to 201.

Solution

If

$$U = x_1^{1/4}x_2^{3/4}$$

then

$$\frac{\partial U}{\partial x_1} = {}^1\!/_4 x_1^{-3/4}x_2^{3/4} \quad \text{and} \quad \frac{\partial U}{\partial x_2} = {}^3\!/_4 x_1^{1/4}x_2^{-1/4}$$

so when $x_1 = 100$ and $x_2 = 200$

$$\frac{\partial U}{\partial x_1} = {}^1\!/_4(100)^{-3/4}(200)^{3/4} = 0.42$$

$$\frac{\partial U}{\partial x_2} = {}^3\!/_4(100)^{1/4}(200)^{-1/4} = 0.63$$

Now x_1 decreases by 1 unit, so

$$\Delta x_1 = -1$$

and x_2 increases by 1 unit, so

$$\Delta x_2 = 1$$

The small increments formula states that

$$\Delta U \simeq \frac{\partial U}{\partial x_1}\Delta x_1 + \frac{\partial U}{\partial x_2}\Delta x_2$$

The change in utility is therefore

$$\Delta U \simeq (0.42)(-1) + (0.63)(1) = 0.21$$

Note that for the particular utility function

$$U = x_1^{1/4} x_2^{3/4}$$

given in the above example, the second-order derivatives

$$\frac{\partial^2 U}{\partial x_1^2} = \frac{-3}{16} x_1^{-7/4} x_2^{3/4} \quad \text{and} \quad \frac{\partial^2 U}{\partial x_2^2} = \frac{-3}{16} x_1^{1/4} x_2^{-5/4}$$

are both negative. Now $\partial^2 U / \partial x_1^2$ is the partial derivative of marginal utility $\partial U / \partial x_1$ with respect to x_1. The fact that this is negative means that marginal utility of x_1 decreases as x_1 rises. In other words, as the consumption of good G1 increases, each additional item of G1 bought confers less utility than the previous item. A similar property holds for G2. This is known as the **law of diminishing marginal utility**.

Advice

You might like to compare this with the law of diminishing marginal productivity discussed in Section 4.3.2.

Practice Problem

2. An individual's utility function is given by

$$U = 1000x_1 + 450x_2 + 5x_1x_2 - 2x_1^2 - x_2^2$$

where x_1 is the amount of leisure measured in hours per week and x_2 is earned income measured in dollars per week.

Determine the value of the marginal utilities

$$\frac{\partial U}{\partial x_1} \quad \text{and} \quad \frac{\partial U}{\partial x_2}$$

when $x_1 = 138$ and $x_2 = 500$.

Hence estimate the change in U if the individual works for an extra hour, which increases earned income by \$15 per week.

Does the law of diminishing marginal utility hold for this function?

It was pointed out in Section 5.1 that functions of two variables could be represented by surfaces in three dimensions. This is all very well in theory, but in practice the task of sketching such a surface by hand is virtually impossible. This difficulty has been faced by geographers for years and the way they circumvent the problem is to produce a two-dimensional contour map. A contour is a curve joining all points at the same height above sea level. Exactly the same device can be used for utility functions. Rather than attempt to sketch the surface, we draw an **indifference map**. This consists of **indifference curves** joining points (x_1, x_2) which give the same value of utility. Mathematically, an indifference curve is defined by an equation

$$U(x_1, x_2) = U_0$$

for some fixed value of U_0. A typical indifference map is sketched in Figure 5.4 (overleaf).

Points A and B both lie on the lower indifference curve, $U_0 = 20$. Point A corresponds to the case when the consumer buys a_1 units of G1 and a_2 units of G2. Likewise, point B corresponds

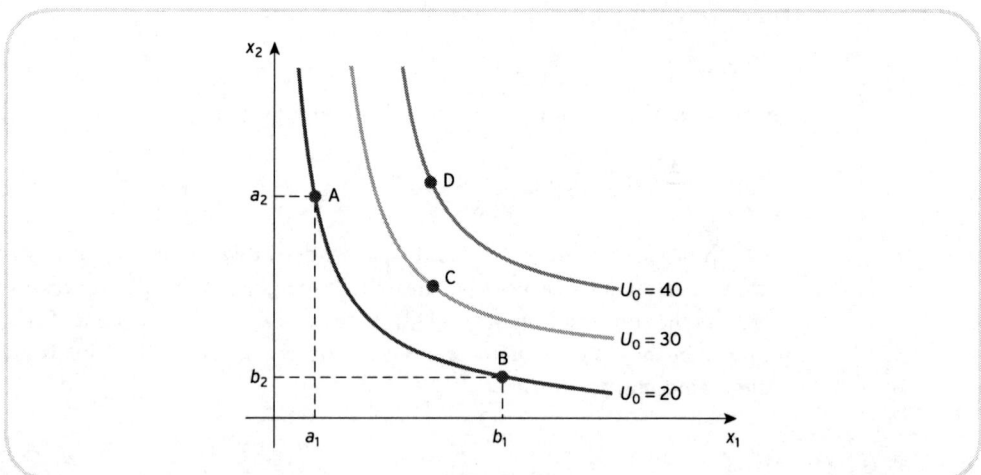

Figure 5.4

to the case when the consumer buys b_1 units of G1 and b_2 units of G2. Both of these combinations yield the same level of satisfaction and the consumer is indifferent to choosing between them. In symbols we have

$$U(a_1, a_2) = 20 \quad \text{and} \quad U(b_1, b_2) = 20$$

Points C and D lie on indifference curves that are further away from the origin. The combinations of goods that these points represent yield higher levels of utility and so are ranked above those of A and B.

Indifference curves are usually downward-sloping. If fewer purchases are made of G1 then the consumer has to compensate for this by buying more of type G2 to maintain the same level of satisfaction. Note also from Figure 5.4 that the slope of an indifference curve varies along its length, taking large negative values close to the vertical axis and becoming almost zero as the curve approaches the horizontal axis. Again this is to be expected for any function that obeys the law of diminishing marginal utility. A consumer who currently owns a large number of items of G2 and relatively few of G1 is likely to value G1 more highly. Consequently, he or she might be satisfied in sacrificing a large number of items of G2 to gain just one or two extra items of G1. In this region the marginal utility of x_1 is much greater than that of x_2, which accounts for the steepness of the curve close to the vertical axis. Similarly, as the curve approaches the horizontal axis, the situation is reversed and the curve flattens off. We quantify this exchange of goods by introducing the **marginal rate of commodity substitution**, MRCS. This is defined to be the increase in x_2 necessary to maintain a constant value of utility when x_1 decreases by 1 unit. This is illustrated in Figure 5.5.

Starting at point E, we move 1 unit to the left. The value of MRCS is then the vertical distance that we need to travel if we are to remain on the indifference curve passing through E. Now this sort of '1 unit change' definition is precisely the approach that we took in Section 4.3 when discussing marginal functions. In that section we actually defined the marginal function to be the derived function and we showed that the '1 unit change' definition gave a good approximation to it. If we do the same here then we can define

$$\text{MRCS} = -\frac{dx_2}{dx_1}$$

The derivative, dx_2/dx_1, determines the slope of an indifference curve when x_1 is plotted on the horizontal axis and x_2 is plotted on the vertical axis. This is negative, so we deliberately put a

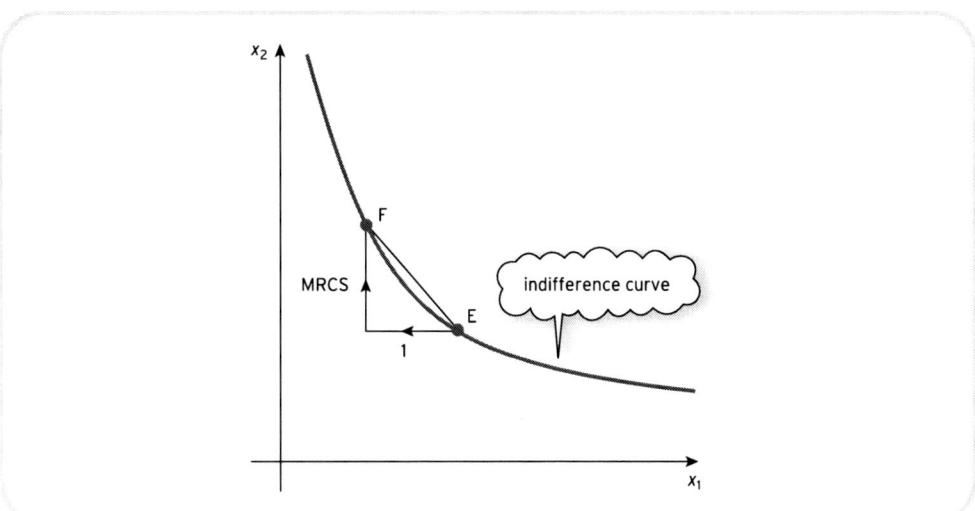

Figure 5.5

minus sign in front to make MRCS positive. This definition is useful only if we can find the equation of an indifference curve with x_2 given explicitly in terms of x_1. However, we may only know the utility function

$$U(x_1, x_2)$$

so that the indifference curve is determined implicitly from an equation

$$U(x_1, x_2) = U_0$$

This is precisely the situation that we discussed at the end of Section 5.1. The formula for implicit differentiation gives

$$\frac{\mathrm{d}x_2}{\mathrm{d}x_1} = -\frac{\partial U/\partial x_1}{\partial U/\partial x_2}$$

Hence

$$\text{MRCS} = -\frac{\mathrm{d}x_2}{\mathrm{d}x_1} = \frac{\partial U/\partial x_1}{\partial U/\partial x_2}$$

> **marginal rate of commodity substitution is the marginal
> utility of x_1 divided by the marginal utility of x_2**

Example

Given the utility function

$$U = x_1^{1/2} x_2^{1/2}$$

find a general expression for MRCS in terms of x_1 and x_2.

Calculate the particular value of MRCS for the indifference curve that passes through (300, 500). Hence estimate the increase in x_2 required to maintain the current level of utility when x_1 decreases by 3 units.

Solution

If

$$U = x_1^{1/2} x_2^{1/2}$$

then

$$\frac{\partial U}{\partial x_1} = \frac{1}{2} x_1^{-1/2} x_2^{1/2} \quad \text{and} \quad \frac{\partial U}{\partial x_2} = \frac{1}{2} x_1^{1/2} x_2^{-1/2}$$

Using the result

$$\text{MRCS} = \frac{\partial U / \partial x_1}{\partial U / \partial x_2}$$

we see that

$$\text{MRCS} = \frac{\frac{1}{2} x_1^{-1/2} x_2^{1/2}}{\frac{1}{2} x_1^{1/2} x_2^{-1/2}}$$

> rule 2 of indices;
> $b^m \div b^n = b^{m-n}$

$$= x_1^{-1} x_2^1$$

$$= \frac{x_2}{x_1}$$

> $b^1 = b,$
> $b^{-1} = \dfrac{1}{b}$

At the point (300, 500)

$$\text{MRCS} = \frac{500}{300} = \frac{5}{3}$$

Now MRCS approximates the increase in x_2 required to maintain a constant level of utility when x_1 decreases by 1 unit. In this example x_1 decreases by 3 units, so we multiply MRCS by 3. The approximate increase in x_2 is

$$\frac{5}{3} \times 3 = 5$$

We can check the accuracy of this approximation by evaluating U at the old point (300, 500) and the new point (297, 505). We get

$$U(300, 500) = (300)^{1/2}(500)^{1/2} = 387.30$$

$$U(297, 505) = (297)^{1/2}(505)^{1/2} = 387.28$$

This shows that, to all intents and purposes, the two points do indeed lie on the same indifference curve.

Practice Problem

3. Calculate the value of MRCS for the utility function given in Practice Problem 2 at the point (138, 500). Hence estimate the increase in earned income required to maintain the current level of utility if leisure time falls by 2 hours per week.

5.2.3 Production

Production functions were first introduced in Section 2.3. We assume that output, Q, depends on capital, K, and labour, L, so we can write

$$Q = f(K, L)$$

Such functions can be analysed in a similar way to utility functions. The partial derivative

$$\frac{\partial Q}{\partial K}$$

gives the rate of change of output with respect to capital and is called the **marginal product of capital**, MP_K. If capital changes by a small amount ΔK, with labour held constant, then the corresponding change in Q is given by

$$\Delta Q \simeq \frac{\partial Q}{\partial K} \Delta K$$

Similarly,

$$\frac{\partial Q}{\partial L}$$

gives the rate of change of output with respect to labour and is called the **marginal product of labour**, MP_L. If labour changes by a small amount ΔL, with capital held constant, then the corresponding change in Q is given by

$$\Delta Q \simeq \frac{\partial Q}{\partial L} \Delta L$$

If K and L both change simultaneously, then the net change in Q can be found from the small increments formula

$$\Delta Q \simeq \frac{\partial Q}{\partial K} \Delta K + \frac{\partial Q}{\partial L} \Delta L$$

The contours of a production function are called **isoquants**. In Greek 'iso' means 'equal', so the word 'isoquant' literally translates as 'equal quantity'. Points on an isoquant represent all possible combinations of inputs (K, L) which produce a constant level of output, Q_0. A typical isoquant map is sketched in Figure 5.6 (overleaf). Notice that we have adopted the standard convention of plotting labour on the horizontal axis and capital on the vertical axis.

The lower curve determines the input pairs needed to output 100 units. Higher levels of output correspond to isoquants further away from the origin. Again, the general shape of the curves is to be expected. For example, as capital is reduced it is necessary to increase labour to compensate and so maintain production levels. Moreover, if capital continues to decrease, the rate of substitution of labour for capital goes up. We quantify this exchange of inputs by defining the **marginal rate of technical substitution**, MRTS, to be

$$-\frac{dK}{dL}$$

so that MRTS is the positive value of the slope of an isoquant. As in the case of a utility function, the formula for implicit differentiation shows that

$$\text{MRTS} = \frac{\partial Q/\partial L}{\partial Q/\partial K} = \frac{MP_L}{MP_K}$$

marginal rate of technical substitution is the marginal product of labour divided by the marginal product of capital

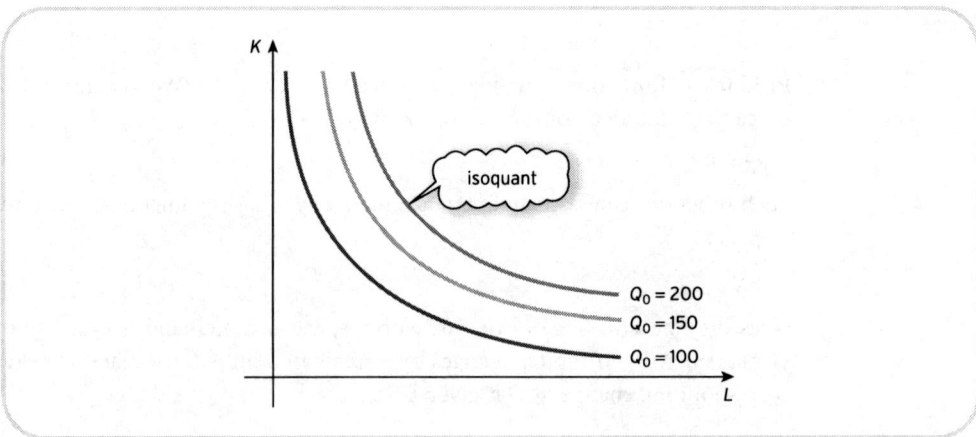

Figure 5.6

Example

Find an expression for MRTS for the general Cobb–Douglas production function

$$Q = AK^{\alpha}L^{\beta}$$

where A, α and β are positive constants.

Solution

We begin by finding the marginal products. Partial differentiation of

$$Q = AK^{\alpha}L^{\beta}$$

with respect to K and L gives

$$MP_K = \alpha AK^{\alpha-1}L^{\beta} \quad \text{and} \quad MP_L = \beta AK^{\alpha}L^{\beta-1}$$

Hence

$$MRTS = \frac{MP_L}{MP_K} = \frac{\beta AK^{\alpha}L^{\beta-1}}{\alpha AK^{\alpha-1}L^{\beta}} = \frac{\beta K}{\alpha L}$$

Practice Problem

4. Given the production function

$$Q = K^2 + 2L^2$$

write down expressions for the marginal products

$$\frac{\partial Q}{\partial K} \quad \text{and} \quad \frac{\partial Q}{\partial L}$$

Hence show that

(a) $MRTS = \dfrac{2L}{K}$

(b) $K\dfrac{\partial Q}{\partial K} + L\dfrac{\partial Q}{\partial L} = 2Q$

Recall that a production function is described as being homogeneous of degree n if, for any number λ,

$$f(\lambda K, \lambda L) = \lambda^n f(K, L)$$

A production function is then said to display decreasing returns to scale, constant returns to scale or increasing returns to scale, depending on whether $n < 1$, $n = 1$ or $n > 1$, respectively. One useful result concerning homogeneous functions is known as **Euler's theorem**, which states that

$$\boxed{K\frac{\partial f}{\partial K} + L\frac{\partial f}{\partial L} = nf(K, L)}$$

In fact, you have already verified this in Practice Problem 4(b) for the particular production function

$$Q = K^2 + 2L^2$$

which is easily shown to be homogeneous of degree 2. We have no intention of proving this theorem, although you are invited to confirm its validity for general Cobb–Douglas production functions in Question 4 in Exercise 5.2* at the end of this section.

The special case $n = 1$ is worthy of note because the right-hand side is then simply $f(K, L)$, which is equal to the output, Q. Euler's theorem for homogeneous production functions of degree 1 states that

$$\boxed{\text{Capital times marginal product of capital}} + \boxed{\text{labour times marginal product of labour}} = \boxed{\text{total output}}$$

If each input factor is paid an amount equal to its marginal product then each term on the left-hand side gives the total bill for that factor. For example, if each unit of labour is paid MP_L then the cost of L units of labour is $L(MP_L)$. Provided that the production function displays constant returns to scale, Euler's theorem shows that the sum of the factor payments is equal to the total output.

We conclude this section with an example that shows how the computer package Maple can be used to handle functions of two variables.

Example   MAPLE

Consider the production function

$$Q = 2K^{0.2}L^{0.8} \quad (0 \le K \le 1000, 0 \le L \le 1000)$$

(a) Draw a three-dimensional plot of this function together with its isoquant map.

(b) Use the instruction `diff` to find an expression for MRTS.

Solution

(a) Let us name this function `prod`. To do this, we type

```
>prod:=2*K^0.2*L^0.8;
```

The instruction for a three-dimensional plot is `plot3d`. This is used in the same way as ordinary plot. The only difference is that we must specify the range of both K and L, so we type

```
>plot3d(prod,K=0..1000,L=0..1000);
```

If you do this, you get a most uninspiring picture of the surface. Most of the surface is 'coming straight towards you', so you cannot see it properly. Maple does, however, allow you to rotate the surface to get a better perspective. To do this, click on the surface to make the graphics toolbar appear. This is shown in Figure 5.7.

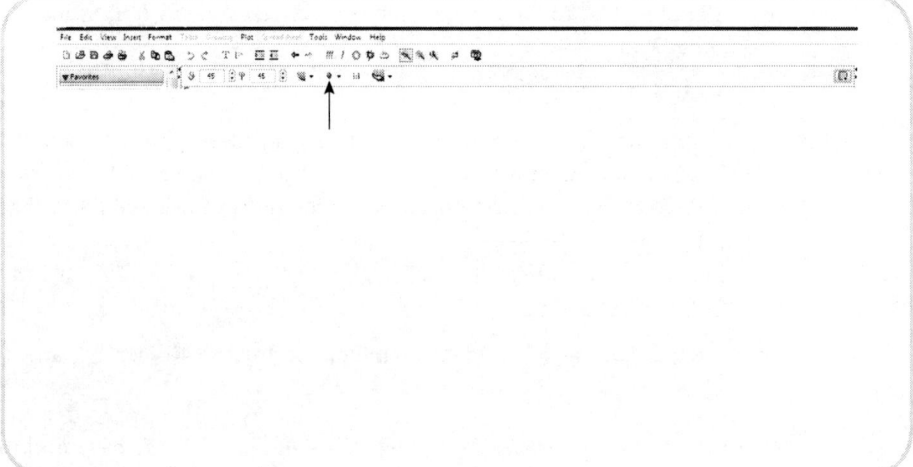

Figure 5.7

Advice

It is well worth playing around with some of the buttons on the toolbar to investigate some of the useful features of the package. For example, click on the first indicated button and choose the first option (which looks like a red ball and choose the first option). This creates a cuboid on the screen. To rotate the axes, simply hold the mouse button down and drag the cursor around. Figure 5.8 shows one such perspective with the origin at the front. It shows clearly how the output rises with increasing capital and labour and that this effect is more pronounced with increasing values of L than K.

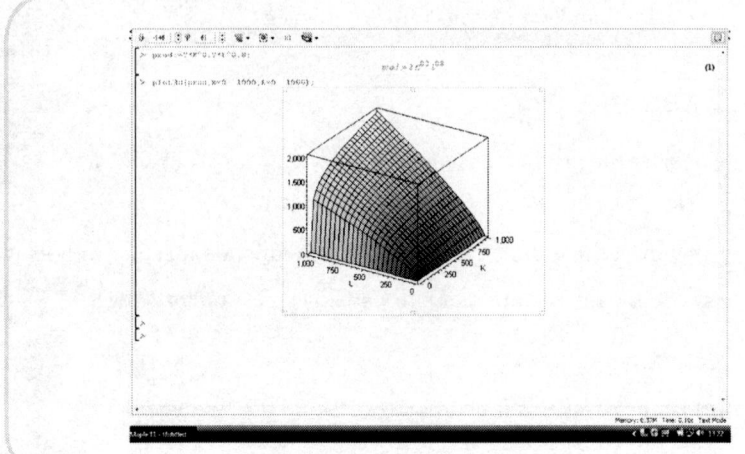

Figure 5.8

To obtain an isoquant map we need to call up the more sophisticated plotting routines, from which we select the one called `contourplot`. You type

```
>with(plots):
```

> you can end this command with a colon ':'

followed by

```
>contourplot(prod,K=0..1000,L=0..1000);
```

The response from Maple is the isoquant map shown in Figure 5.9.

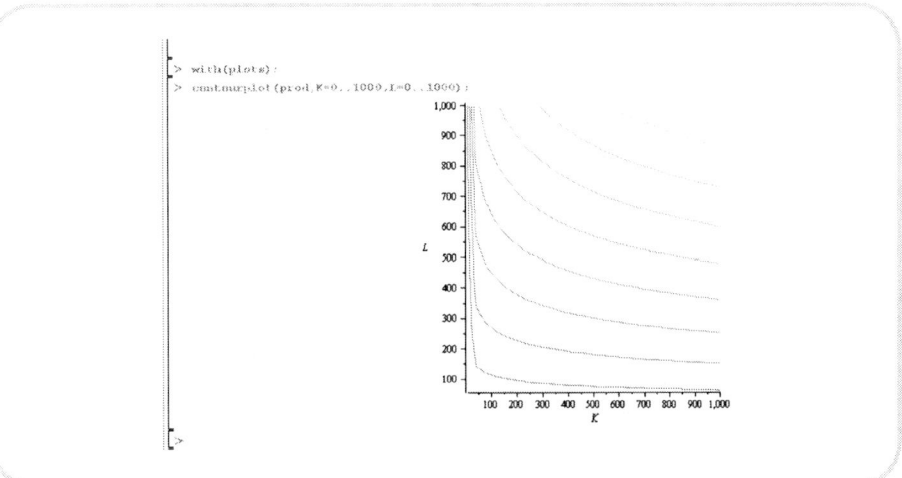

Figure 5.9

(b) Partial differentiation is performed, as usual, via the instruction `diff`.
Typing

```
>diff(prod,K);
```

performs the differentiation with respect to K and shows that MP_K is given by

$$\frac{0.4L^{0.8}}{K^{0.8}}$$

Typing

```
>diff(prod,L);
```

performs the differentiation with respect to L and shows that MP_L is given by

$$\frac{1.6K^{0.2}}{L^{0.2}}$$

The MRTS is found by dividing one by the other. In fact, this can be done in a single line:

```
>MRTS:=diff(prod,L)/diff(prod,K);
```

which gives

$$MRTS = \frac{4K}{L}$$

Key Terms

Cross-price elasticity of demand   The responsiveness of demand for one good to a change in the price of another: (percentage change in quantity) ÷ (percentage change in the price of the alternative good).

Euler's theorem   If each input is paid the value of its marginal product, the total costs of these inputs is equal to total output, provided there are constant returns to scale.

Income elasticity of demand   The responsiveness of demand for one good to a change in income: (percentage change in quantity) ÷ (percentage change in income).

Indifference curve   A curve indicating all combinations of two goods which give the same level of utility.

Indifference map   A diagram showing the graphs of a set of indifference curves. The further the curve is from the origin, the greater the level of utility.

Isoquant   A curve indicating all combinations of two factors which give the same level of output.

Law of diminishing marginal utility   The law which states that the increase in utility due to the consumption of an additional good will eventually decline: $\partial^2 U / \partial x_i^2 < 0$ for sufficiently large x_i.

Marginal product of capital   The additional output produced by a 1 unit increase in capital: $MP_K = \partial Q / \partial K$

Marginal product of labour   The additional output produced by a 1 unit increase in labour: $MP_L = \partial Q / \partial L$.

Marginal rate of commodity substitution (MRCS)   The amount by which one input needs to increase to maintain a constant value of utility when the other input decreases by 1 unit: $MRTS = \partial U / \partial x_1 \div \partial U / \partial x_2$.

Marginal rate of technical substitution (MRTS)   The amount by which capital needs to rise to maintain a constant level of output when labour decreases by 1 unit: $MRTS = MP_L / MP_K$.

Marginal utility   The extra satisfaction gained by consuming 1 extra unit of a good: $\partial U / \partial x_1$.

Price elasticity of demand   The responsiveness of demand for one good to a change in its own price: $-$(percentage change in quantity) ÷ (percentage change in the price).

Utility   The satisfaction gained from the consumption of a good.

Exercise 5.2

1. Given the demand function

    $$Q = 1000 - 5P - P_A^2 + 0.005Y^3$$

    where $P = 15$, $P_A = 20$ and $Y = 100$, find the income elasticity of demand.

    Give your answer correct to 2 decimal places.

2. Given the demand function

    $$Q = 200 - 2P - P_A + 0.1Y^2$$

    where $P = 10$, $P_A = 15$ and $Y = 100$, find

    (a) the price elasticity of demand

    (b) the cross-price elasticity of demand

    (c) the income elasticity of demand.

    Estimate the percentage change in demand if P_A rises by 3%. Is the alternative good substitutable or complementary?

3. Given the demand function

$$Q = \frac{P_A Y^2}{P}$$

where $P_A = 10$, $Y = 2$ and $P = 4$, find the income elasticity of demand. If P_A and P are fixed, estimate the percentage change in Y needed to raise Q by 2%.

4. Given the utility function

$$U = x_1^{1/2} x_2^{1/3}$$

determine the value of the marginal utilities

$$\frac{\partial U}{\partial x_1} \quad \text{and} \quad \frac{\partial U}{\partial x_2}$$

at the point $(25, 8)$. Hence

(a) estimate the change in utility when x_1 and x_2 both increase by 1 unit

(b) find the marginal rate of commodity substitution at this point.

5. Evaluate MP_K and MP_L for the production function

$$Q = 2LK + \sqrt{L}$$

given that the current levels of K and L are 7 and 4, respectively. Hence

(a) write down the value of MRTS

(b) estimate the increase in capital needed to maintain the current level of output given a 1 unit decrease in labour.

6. If $Q = 2K^3 + 3L^2K$ show that $K(MP_K) + L(MP_L) = 3Q$.

7. (**Maple**) Consider the production function

$$Q = L(5\sqrt{K} + \sqrt{L}) \quad (0 \leq K \leq 3, 0 \leq L \leq 5)$$

(a) Draw a three-dimensional plot of this function. Rotate the axes to give a clear view of the surface. Draw the corresponding isoquant map.

(b) Find an expression for MRTS.

(c) Given that $L = 4$, find the value of K for which MRTS $= 2$.

Exercise 5.2*

1. The demand function of a good is given by

$$Q = 500 - 4P + 0.02Y$$

Price and income are known to be $P = 20$ and $Y = 14\,000$, respectively.

(a) Find the income elasticity of demand.

(b) Estimate the percentage change in demand when income rises by 8%, and comment on the growth potential of this good in an expanding economy.

2. Find the value of the marginal rate of technical substitution for the production function,

$$Q = 300K^{2/3}L^{1/2}$$

when, $K = 40$, $L = 60$.

3. A utility function is given by

$$U = x_1^{2/3}x_2^{1/2}$$

Find the value of x_2 if the points, $(64, 256)$ and $(512, x_2)$ lie on the same indifference curve.

4. Verify Euler's theorem for the Cobb–Douglas production function

$$Q = AK^{\alpha}K^{\beta}$$

[Hint: this function was shown to be homogeneous of degree $\alpha + \beta$ in Section 2.3.]

5. If a firm's production function is given by

$$Q = 5L + 7K$$

sketch the isoquant corresponding an output level, $Q = 700$. Use your graph to find the value of MRTS and confirm this using partial differentiation.

6. A firm's production function is given by

$$Q = 10\sqrt{(KL)} + 3L$$

with $K = 90$ and $L = 40$.

(a) Find the values of the marginal products, MP_K and MP_L.

(b) Use the results of part (a) to estimate the overall effect on Q when K increases by three units and L decreases by two units.

(c) State the value of the marginal rate of technical substitution and give an interpretation of this value.

7. A firm's production function is

$$Q = A[bK^{\alpha} + (1 - b)L^{\alpha}]^{1/\alpha}$$

(a) Show that the marginal rate of technical substitution is given by

$$\text{MRTS} = \frac{1 - b}{b}\left(\frac{K}{L}\right)^{1-\alpha}$$

(b) Show that the marginal products satisfy the relation

$$K\frac{\partial Q}{\partial K} + L\frac{\partial Q}{\partial L} = Q$$

8. The demand function of a good is given by

$$Q = a - bP - cP_A + dY$$

where P is the price of the good, P_A is the price of an alternative good, Y is income, and the coefficients, a, b, c and d are all positive. It is known that $P = 50$, $P_A = 30$, $Y = 1000$ and $Q = 5000$.

(a) Is the alternative good substitutable or complementary? Give a reason for your answer.

(b) Find expressions, in terms of b, c and d for the

   (i)   price elasticity of demand

   (ii) cross-price elasticity of demand

   (iii) income elasticity of demand.

(c) The cross-price elasticity is -0.012. The income elasticity is four times the price elasticity. When income increases by 10%, the demand increases by 2%. Determine the values of a, b, c and d.

9. (**Maple**) Consider the production function

$$Q = (0.3K^{-3} + 0.7L^{-3})^{-1/3} \quad (1 \le K \le 10, \ 1 \le L \le 10)$$

(a) Draw a three-dimensional plot of this function. Rotate the axes to give a clear view of the surface.

(b) Draw the corresponding isoquant map. Deduce that the marginal rate of technical substitution diminishes with increasing L.

(c) Find an expression for MRTS.

(d) Find the slope of the isoquant $Q = 4$ at the point $L = 8$.

SECTION 5.3

Comparative statics

The simplest macroeconomic model, discussed in Section 1.7, assumes that there are two sectors, households and firms, and that household consumption, C, is modelled by a linear relationship of the form

$$C = aY + b \tag{1}$$

In this equation Y denotes national income and a and b are parameters. The parameter a is the marginal propensity to consume and lies in the range $0 < a < 1$. The parameter b is the autonomous consumption and satisfies $b > 0$. In equilibrium

$$Y = C + I \tag{2}$$

where I denotes investment, which is assumed to be given by

$$I = I^* \tag{3}$$

for some constant I^*. Equations (1), (2) and (3) describe the structure of the model and as such are called **structural equations.** Substituting equations (1) and (3) into equation (2) gives

$$Y = aY + b + I^*$$

$$Y - aY = b + I^* \qquad \text{(subtract } aY \text{ from both sides)}$$

$$(1 - a)Y = b + I^* \qquad \text{(take out a common factor of } Y\text{)}$$

$$Y = \frac{b + I^*}{1 - a} \qquad \text{(divide both sides by } 1 - a\text{)}$$

This is known as the **reduced form** because it compresses the model into a single equation in which the endogenous variable, Y, is expressed in terms of the exogenous variable, I^*, and parameters, a and b. The process of analysing the equilibrium level of income in this way is referred to as **statics** because it assumes that the equilibrium state is attained instantaneously. The branch of mathematical economics which investigates time dependence is known as **dynamics** and is considered in Additional Topic 2 on the website.

We should like to do rather more than just to calculate the equilibrium values here. In particular, we are interested in the effect on the endogenous variables in a model brought about by changes in the exogenous variables and parameters. This is known as **comparative statics**, since we seek to compare the effects obtained by varying each variable and parameter in turn. The actual mechanism for change will be ignored and it will be assumed that the system returns to equilibrium instantaneously. The equation

$$Y = \frac{b + I^*}{1 - a}$$

shows that Y is a function of three variables, a, b and I^*, so we can write down three partial derivatives

$$\frac{\partial Y}{\partial a}, \frac{\partial Y}{\partial b}, \frac{\partial Y}{\partial I^*}$$

The only hard one to work out is the first, and this is found using the chain rule by writing

$$Y = (b + I^*)(1 - a)^{-1}$$

which gives

$$\frac{\partial Y}{\partial a} = (b + I^*)(-1)(1 - a)^{-2}(-1) = \frac{b + I^*}{(1 - a)^2}$$

To interpret this derivative let us suppose that the marginal propensity to consume, a, changes by Δa with b and I^* held constant. The corresponding change in Y is given by

$$\Delta Y = \frac{\partial Y}{\partial a}\Delta a$$

Strictly speaking, the '=' sign should really be '≈'. However, as we have seen in the previous two sections, provided that Δa is small the approximation is reasonably accurate. In any case we could argue that the model itself is only a first approximation to what is really happening in the economy and so any further small inaccuracies that are introduced are unlikely to have any significant effect on our conclusions. The above equation shows that the change in national income is found by multiplying the change in the marginal propensity to consume by the partial derivative $\partial Y/\partial a$. For this reason the partial derivative is called the **marginal propensity to consume multiplier** for Y. In the same way, $\partial Y/\partial b$ and $\partial Y/\partial I^*$ are called the **autonomous consumption multiplier** and the **investment multiplier**, respectively.

Multipliers enable us to explain the behaviour of the model both qualitatively and quantitatively. The qualitative behaviour can be described simply by inspecting the multipliers as they stand, before any numerical values are assigned to the variables and parameters. It is usually possible to state whether the multipliers are positive or negative and hence whether an increase in an exogenous variable or parameter leads to an increase or decrease in the corresponding endogenous variable. In the present model it is apparent that the marginal propensity to consume multiplier for Y is positive because it is known that b and I^* are both positive, and the denominator $(1 - a)^2$ is clearly positive. Therefore, national income rises whenever a rises.

Once the exogenous variables and parameters have been assigned specific numerical values, the behaviour of the model can be explained quantitatively. For example, if $b = 10$, $I^* = 30$ and $a = 0.5$ then the marginal propensity to consume multiplier is

$$\frac{b + I^*}{(1 - a)^2} = \frac{10 + 30}{(1 - 0.5)^2} = 160$$

This means that when the marginal propensity to consume rises by, say, 0.02 units the change in national income is

$$160 \times 0.02 = 3.2$$

Of course, if a, b and I^* change by amounts Δa, Δb and ΔI^* simultaneously then the small increments formula shows that the change in Y can be found from

$$\Delta Y = \frac{\partial Y}{\partial a} \Delta a + \frac{\partial Y}{\partial b} \Delta b + \frac{\partial Y}{\partial I^*} \Delta I^*$$

Example

Use the equation

$$Y = \frac{b + I^*}{1 - a}$$

to find the investment multiplier.

Deduce that an increase in investment always leads to an increase in national income.

Calculate the change in national income when investment rises by 4 units and the marginal propensity to consume is 0.6.

Solution

Writing

$$Y = \frac{b}{1 - a} + \frac{I^*}{1 - a}$$

we see that

$$\frac{\partial Y}{\partial I^*} = \frac{1}{1 - a}$$

which is positive because $a < 1$. Therefore national income rises whenever I^* rises.

When $a = 0.6$ the investment multiplier is

$$\frac{1}{1 - a} = \frac{1}{1 - 0.6} = \frac{1}{0.4} = 2.5$$

so that when investment rises by 4 units the change in national income is

$$2.5 \times 4 = 10$$

Practice Problem

1. By substituting

$$Y = \frac{b + I^*}{1 - a}$$

into

$$C = aY + b$$

write down the reduced equation for C in terms of a, b and I^*. Hence show that the investment multiplier for C is

$$\frac{a}{1 - a}$$

Deduce that an increase in investment always leads to an increase in consumption. Calculate the change in consumption when investment rises by 2 units if the marginal propensity to consume is $1/2$.

The following example is more difficult because it involves three sectors: households, firms and government. However, the basic strategy for analysing the model is the same. We first obtain the reduced form, which is differentiated to determine the relevant multipliers. These can then be used to discuss the behaviour of national income both qualitatively and quantitatively.

Example

Consider the three-sector model

$$Y = C + I + G \tag{1}$$
$$C = aY_d + b \qquad (0 < a < 1, b > 0) \tag{2}$$
$$Y_d = Y - T \tag{3}$$
$$T = tY + T^* \qquad (0 < t < 1, T^* > 0) \tag{4}$$
$$I = I^* \qquad (I^* > 0) \tag{5}$$
$$G = G^* \qquad (G^* > 0) \tag{6}$$

where G denotes government expenditure and T denotes taxation.

(a) Show that

$$Y = \frac{-aT^* + b + I^* + G^*}{1 - a + at}$$

(b) Write down the government expenditure multiplier and autonomous taxation multiplier. Deduce the direction of change in Y due to increases in G^* and T^*.

(c) If it is government policy to finance any increase in expenditure, ΔG^*, by an increase in autonomous taxation, ΔT^*, so that

$$\Delta G^* = \Delta T^*$$

show that national income rises by an amount that is less than the rise in expenditure.

(d) If $a = 0.7$, $b = 50$, $T^* = 200$, $t = 0.2$, $I^* = 100$ and $G^* = 300$, calculate the equilibrium level of national income, Y, and the change in Y due to a 10 unit increase in government expenditure.

Solution

(a) We need to 'solve' equations (1)–(6) for Y. An obvious first move is to substitute equations (2), (5) and (6) into equation (1) to get

$$Y = aY_d + b + I^* + G^* \tag{7}$$

Now from equations (3) and (4)

$$
\begin{aligned}
Y_d &= Y - T \\
&= Y - (tY + T^*) \\
&= Y - tY - T^*
\end{aligned}
$$

so this can be put into equation (7) to get

$$
\begin{aligned}
Y &= a(Y - tY - T^*) + b + I^* + G^* \\
&= aY - atY - aT^* + b + I^* + G^*
\end{aligned}
$$

Collecting terms in Y on the left-hand side gives

$$(1 - a + at)Y = -aT^* + b + I^* + G^*$$

which produces the desired equation

$$Y = \frac{-aT^* + b + I^* + G^*}{1 - a + at}$$

(b) The government expenditure multiplier is

$$\frac{\partial Y}{\partial G^*} = \frac{1}{1 - a + at}$$

and the autonomous taxation multiplier is

$$\frac{\partial Y}{\partial T^*} = \frac{-a}{1 - a + at}$$

We are given that $a < 1$, so $1 - a > 0$. Also, we know that a and t are both positive, so their product, at, must be positive. The expression $(1 - a) + at$ is therefore positive, being the sum of two positive terms. The government expenditure multiplier is therefore positive, which shows that any increase in G^* leads to an increase in Y. The autonomous taxation multiplier is negative because its numerator is negative and its denominator is positive. This shows that any increase in T^* leads to a decrease in Y.

(c) Government policy is to finance a rise in expenditure out of autonomous taxation, so that

$$\Delta G^* = \Delta T^*$$

From the small increments formula

$$\Delta Y = \frac{\partial Y}{\partial G^*} \Delta G^* + \frac{\partial Y}{\partial T^*} \Delta T^*$$

we deduce that

$$\Delta Y = \left(\frac{\partial Y}{\partial G^*} + \frac{\partial Y}{\partial T^*} \right) \Delta G^* = \left(\frac{1}{1-a+at} + \frac{-a}{1-a+at} \right) \Delta G^* = \left(\frac{1-a}{1-a+at} \right) \Delta G^*$$

The multiplier

$$\frac{1-a}{1-a+at}$$

is called the **balanced budget multiplier** and is positive because the numerator and denominator are both positive. An increase in government expenditure leads to an increase in national income. However, the denominator is greater than the numerator by an amount at, so that

$$\frac{1-a}{1-a+at} < 1$$

and $\Delta Y < \Delta G^*$, showing that the rise in national income is less than the rise in expenditure.

(d) To solve this part of the problem we simply substitute the numerical values $a = 0.7$, $b = 50$, $T^* = 200$, $t = 0.2$, $I^* = 100$ and $G^* = 300$ into the results of parts (a) and (b). From part (a)

$$Y = \frac{-aT^* + b + I^* + G^*}{1-a+at} = \frac{-0.7(200) + 50 + 100 + 300}{1 - 0.7 + 0.7(0.2)} = 704.5$$

From part (b) the government expenditure multiplier is

$$\frac{1}{1-a+at} = \frac{1}{0.44} = 2.27$$

and we are given that $\Delta G^* = 10$, so the change in national income is

$$2.27 \times 10 = 22.7$$

Practice Problem

2. Consider the four-sector model

$$Y = C + I + G + X - M$$

$$C = aY + b \qquad\qquad (0 < a < 1, b > 0)$$

$$I = I^* \qquad\qquad (I^* > 0)$$

$$G = G^* \qquad\qquad (G^* > 0)$$

$$X = X^* \qquad\qquad (X^* > 0)$$

$$M = mY + M^* \qquad\qquad (0 < m < 1, M^* > 0)$$

where X and M denote exports and imports respectively and m is the marginal propensity to import.

(a) Show that

$$Y = \frac{b + I^* + G^* + X^* - M^*}{1 - a + m}$$

(b) Write down the autonomous export multiplier

$$\frac{\partial Y}{\partial X*}$$

and the marginal propensity to import multiplier

$$\frac{\partial Y}{\partial m}$$

Deduce the direction of change in Y due to increases in $X*$ and m.

(c) If $a = 0.8$, $b = 120$, $I* = 100$, $G* = 300$, $X* = 150$, $m = 0.1$ and $M* = 40$, calculate the equilibrium level of national income, Y, and the change in Y due to a 10 unit increase in autonomous exports.

So far, all of the examples of comparative statics that we have considered have been taken from macroeconomics. The same approach can be used in microeconomics. For example, let us analyse the equilibrium price and quantity in supply and demand theory.

Figure 5.10 illustrates the simple linear one-commodity market model described in Section 1.5. The equilibrium values of price and quantity are determined from the point of intersection of the supply and demand curves. The supply curve is a straight line with a positive slope and intercept, so its equation may be written as

$$P = aQ_S + b \qquad (a > 0, b > 0)$$

The demand equation is also linear but has a negative slope and a positive intercept, so its equation may be written as

$$P = -cQ_D + d \qquad (c > 0, d > 0)$$

It is apparent from Figure 5.10 that in order for these two lines to intersect in the positive quadrant, it is necessary for the intercept on the demand curve to lie above that on the supply curve, so we require

$$d > b$$

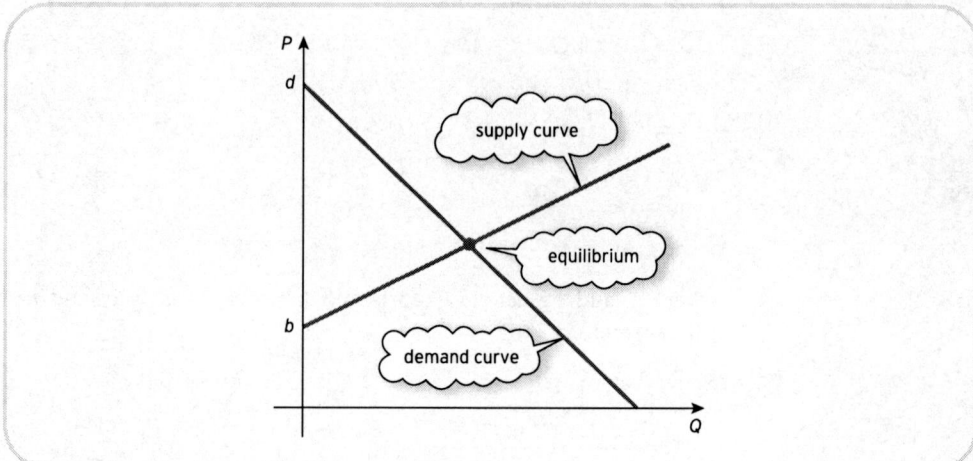

Figure 5.10

or equivalently

$$d - d > 0$$

In equilibrium Q_S and Q_D are equal. If we let their common value be denoted by Q then the supply and demand equations become

$$P = aQ + b$$
$$P = -cQ + d$$

and so

$$aQ + b = -cQ + b$$

since both sides are equal to P.

To solve for Q we first collect like terms together, which gives

$$(a + c)Q = d - b$$

and then divide by the coefficient of Q to get

$$Q = \frac{d - b}{a + c}$$

(Incidentally, this confirms the restriction $d - b > 0$. If this were not true then Q would be either zero or negative, which does not make economic sense.)

Equilibrium quantity is a function of the four parameters a, b, c and d, so there are four multipliers

$$\frac{\partial Q}{\partial a} = -\frac{d - b}{(a + c)^2}$$

$$\frac{\partial Q}{\partial b} = -\frac{1}{a + c}$$

$$\frac{\partial Q}{\partial c} = -\frac{d - b}{(a + c)^2}$$

$$\frac{\partial Q}{\partial d} = \frac{1}{a + c}$$

where the chain rule is used to find $\partial Q/\partial a$ and $\partial Q/\partial c$.

We noted previously that all of the parameters are positive and that $d - b > 0$, so

$$\frac{\partial Q}{\partial a} < 0, \frac{\partial Q}{\partial b} < 0, \frac{\partial Q}{\partial c} < 0 \quad \text{and} \quad \frac{\partial Q}{\partial d} > 0$$

This shows that an increase in a, b or c causes a decrease in Q, whereas an increase in d causes an increase in Q.

Example

Give a graphical confirmation of the sign of the multiplier

$$\frac{\partial Q}{\partial a}$$

Solution

From the supply equation

$$P = aQ_S + b$$

we see that a small increase in the value of the parameter a causes the supply curve to become slightly steeper, as indicated by the dashed line in Figure 5.11. The effect is to shift the point of intersection to the left and so the equilibrium quantity decreases from Q_1 to Q_2 which is consistent with a negative value of the multiplier, $\partial Q/\partial a$.

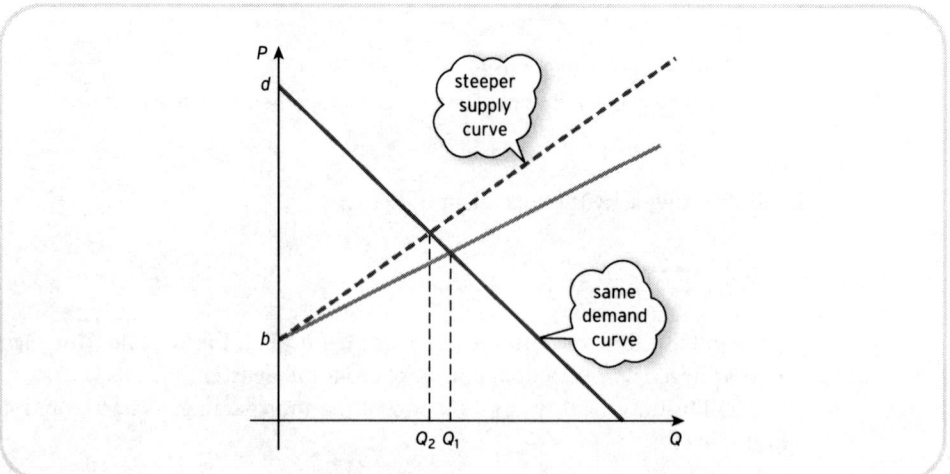

Figure 5.11

Given any pair of supply and demand equations, we can easily calculate the effect on the equilibrium quantity. For example, consider the equations

$$P = Q_S + 1$$
$$P = -2Q_D + 5$$

and let us suppose that we need to calculate the change in equilibrium quantity when the coefficient of Q_S increases from 1 to 1.1. In this case we have

$$a = 1, b = 1, c = 2, d = 5$$

To find ΔQ we first evaluate the multiplier

$$\frac{\partial Q}{\partial a} = -\frac{d-b}{(a+c)^2} = -\frac{5-1}{(1+2)^2} = -0.44$$

and then multiply by 0.1 to get

$$\Delta Q = (-0.44) \times 0.1 = -0.044$$

An increase of 0.1 in the slope of the supply curve therefore produces a decrease of 0.044 in the equilibrium quantity.

Practice Problem

3. Give a graphical confirmation of the sign of the multiplier

$$\frac{\partial Q}{\partial d}$$

for the linear one-commodity market model

$$P = aQ_S + b \qquad (a > 0, b > 0)$$
$$P = -cQ_D + d \qquad (c > 0, d > 0)$$

Throughout this section all of the relations in each model have been assumed to be linear. It is possible to analyse non-linear relations in a similar way, although this is beyond the scope of this book.

Advice

We shall return to this topic again in Chapter 7 when we use Cramer's rule to solve the structural equations of a linear model.

Key Terms

Autonomous consumption multiplier The number by which you multiply the change in autonomous consumption to deduce the corresponding change in, say, national income: $\partial Y/\partial b$.

Balanced budget multiplier The number by which you multiply the change in government expenditure to deduce the corresponding change in, say, national income: $\partial Y/\partial G^*$, assuming that this change is financed entirely by a change in taxation.

Comparative statics Examination of the effect on equilibrium values due to changes in the parameters of an economic model.

Dynamics Analysis of how equilibrium values vary over time.

Investment multiplier The number by which you multiply the change in investment to deduce the corresponding change in, say, national income: $\partial Y/\partial I^*$.

Marginal propensity to consume multiplier The number by which you multiply the change in MPC to deduce the corresponding change in, say, national income: $\partial Y/\partial a$.

Reduced form The final equation obtained when exogenous variables are eliminated in the course of solving a set of structural equations in a macroeconomic model.

Statics The determination of the equilibrium values of variables in an economic model which do not change over time.

Structural equations A collection of equations that describe the equilibrium conditions of a macroeconomic model.

Exercise 5.3*

1. Consider the three-sector model

    $$Y = C + I + G \tag{1}$$
    $$C = aY_d + b \qquad (0 < a < 1, b > 0) \tag{2}$$
    $$Y_d = Y - T \tag{3}$$
    $$T = T^* \qquad (T^* > 0) \tag{4}$$
    $$I = I^* \qquad (I^* > 0) \tag{5}$$
    $$G = G^* \qquad (G^* > 0) \tag{6}$$

    (a) Show that

    $$C = \frac{aI^* + aG^* - aT^* + b}{1 - a}$$

    (b) Write down the investment multiplier for C. Decide the direction of change in C due to an increase in I^*.

    (c) If $a = 0.9$, $b = 80$, $I^* = 60$, $G^* = 40$, $T^* = 20$, calculate the equilibrium level of consumption, C, and also the change in C due to a 2 unit change in investment.

2. The reduced form of a macroeconomic model is

    $$Y = \frac{b + I^* + G^* - aT^*}{1 - a - at}$$

    where t is the marginal rate of taxation.

    Find an expression for the marginal rate of taxation multiplier.

3. Consider the four-sector macroeconomic model

    $$Y = C + I + G + X - M$$
    $$C = aY_d + b \qquad (0 < a < 1, b > 0)$$
    $$Y_d = Y - T$$
    $$T = tY + T^* \qquad (0 < t < 1, T^* > 0)$$
    $$I = I^* \qquad (I^* > 0)$$
    $$G = G^* \qquad (G^* > 0)$$
    $$X = X^* \qquad (X^* > 0)$$
    $$M = mY_d + M^* \qquad (0 < m < 1, M^* > 0)$$

    (1) Show that

    $$Y = \frac{b + (m - a)T^* + I^* + G^* + X^* - M^*}{1 - a + at + m - mt}$$

    (2) (a) Write down the autonomous taxation multiplier. Deduce that an increase in T^* causes a decrease in Y on the assumption that a country's marginal propensity to import, m, is less than its marginal propensity to consume, a.

    (b) Write down the government expenditure multiplier. Deduce that an increase in G^* causes an increase in Y.

(3) Let $a = 0.7, b = 150, t = 0.25, m = 0.1, T^* = 100, I^* = 100, G^* = 500, M^* = 300$ and $X^* = 160$.

(a) Calculate the equilibrium level of national income.

(b) Calculate the change in Y due to an 11 unit increase in G^*.

(c) Find the increase in autonomous taxation required to restore Y to its level calculated in part (a).

4. Show that the equilibrium price for a linear one-commodity market model

$$P = aQ_S + b \qquad (a > 0, b > 0)$$
$$P = -cQ_D + d \qquad (c > 0, d > 0)$$

where $d - b > 0$, is given by

$$P = \frac{ad + bc}{a + c}$$

Find expressions for the multipliers

$$\frac{\partial P}{\partial a}, \frac{\partial P}{\partial b}, \frac{\partial P}{\partial c}, \frac{\partial P}{\partial d}$$

and deduce the direction of change in P due to an increase in a, b, c or d.

5. Consider the three-sector macroeconomic model

$$Y = C + I + G$$
$$C = aY_d + b \qquad (0 < a < 1, b > 0)$$
$$Y_d = Y - T$$
$$T = T^* \qquad (T^* > 0)$$
$$I = I^* \qquad (I^* > 0)$$
$$G = G^* \qquad (G^* > 0)$$

(a) Show that

$$Y = \frac{1}{1 - a}(b - aT^* + I^* + G^*)$$

(b) Write down expressions for the government expenditure multiplier, $\dfrac{\partial Y}{\partial G^*}$, and the taxation multiplier, $\dfrac{\partial Y}{\partial T^*}$, and deduce that if both government expenditure and taxation increase by one unit then the equilibrium value of income also rises by one unit, irrespective of the value of a.

State the value of the balanced budget multiplier.

6. (1) For the commodity market

$$Y = C + I$$
$$C = aY + b \qquad (0 < a < 1, b > 0)$$
$$I = cr + d \qquad (c < 0, d > 0)$$

where r is the interest rate.

Show that, when the commodity market is in equilibrium,

$$(1 - a)Y - cr = b + d$$

(2) For the money market

(money supply) $\qquad M_S = M_S^*$ $\qquad (M_S^* > 0)$

(total demand for money) $\quad M_D = k_1 Y + k_2 r + k_3$ $\quad (k_1 > 0, k_2 < 0, k_3 > 0)$

(equilibrium) $\qquad M_D = M_S$

Show that when the money market is in equilibrium

$$k_1 Y + k_2 r = M_S^* - k_3$$

(3) (a) By solving the simultaneous equations derived in parts (1) and (2) show that when the commodity and money markets are both in equilibrium

$$Y = \frac{k_2(b + d) + c(M_S^* - k_3)}{(1 - a)k_2 + ck_1}$$

(b) Write down the money supply multiplier, $\partial Y / \partial M_S^*$ and deduce that an increase in M_S^* causes an increase in Y.

7 Consider the three-sector model

$$Y = C + I$$
$$C = aY_d + b \quad (0 < a < 1, b > 0)$$
$$Y_d = Y - T$$
$$T = tY + T^* \quad (0 < t < 1, T^* > 0)$$
$$I = cr + d \quad (c < 0, d > 0)$$

(a) Show that

$$Y = \frac{b + d - aT^* + cr}{1 - a(1 - t)}$$

(b) Find expressions for the multipliers, $\dfrac{\partial Y}{\partial c}$ and $\dfrac{\partial Y}{\partial a}$.

(c) State whether the value of Y increases or decreases as a result of an increase in the value of c. Give a reason for your answer.

(d) If $a = 0.8$, $b = 100$, $t = 0.25$, $T^* = 250$, $c = -60$, $d = 1700$ and $r = 8$, calculate the equilibrium level of income, Y, and use the multiplier obtained in part (b) to estimate the change in Y due to a 0.01 increase in the marginal propensity to consume.

SECTION 5.4
Unconstrained optimization

Objectives

At the end of this section you should be able to:

● Use the first-order partial derivatives to find the stationary points of a function of two variables.

● Use the second-order partial derivatives to classify the stationary points of a function of two variables.

● Find the maximum profit of a firm that produces two goods.

● Find the maximum profit of a firm that sells a single good in different markets with price discrimination.

As you might expect, methods for finding the maximum and minimum points of a function of two variables are similar to those used for functions of one variable. However, the nature of economic functions of several variables forces us to subdivide optimization problems into two types, unconstrained and constrained. To understand the distinction, consider the utility function

$$U(x_1, x_2) = x_1^{1/4}x_2^{3/4}$$

The value of U measures the satisfaction gained from buying x_1 items of a good G1 and x_2 items of a good G2. The natural thing to do here is to try to pick x_1 and x_2 to make U as large as possible, thereby maximizing utility. However, a moment's thought should convince you that, as it stands, this problem does not have a finite solution. The factor $x_1^{1/4}$ can be made as large as we please by taking ever-increasing values of x_1 and likewise for the factor $x_2^{3/4}$. In other words, utility increases without bound as more and more items of goods G1 and G2 are bought. In practice, of course, this does not occur, since there is a limit to the amount of money that an individual has to spend on these goods. For example, suppose that the cost of each item of G1 and G2 is $2 and $3, respectively, and that we allocate $100 for the purchase of these goods. The total cost of buying x_1 items of G1 and x_2 items of G2 is

$$2x_1 + 3x_2$$

so we require

$$2x_1 + 3x_2 = 100$$

The problem now is to maximize the utility function

$$U = x_1^{1/4}x_2^{3/4}$$

subject to the budgetary constraint

$$2x_1 + 3x_2 = 100$$

The constraint prevents us from taking ever-increasing values of x_1 and x_2 and leads to a finite solution.

We describe how to solve constrained optimization problems in the following two sections. For the moment we concentrate on the simple case of optimizing functions

$$z = f(x, y)$$

without any constraints. This is typified by the problem of profit maximization, which usually has a finite solution without the need to impose constraints. In a sense the constraints are built into the profit function, which is defined by

$$\pi = \text{TR} - \text{TC}$$

because there is a conflict between trying to make total revenue, TR, as large as possible while trying to make total cost, TC, as small as possible.

Let us begin by recalling how to find and classify stationary points of functions of one variable

$$y = f(x)$$

In Section 4.6 we used the following strategy:

Step 1

Solve the equation

$$f'(x) = 0$$

to find the stationary points, $x = a$.

Step 2

If

- $f''(a) > 0$ then the function has a minimum at $x = a$
- $f''(a) < 0$ then the function has a maximum at $x = a$
- $f''(a) = 0$ then the point cannot be classified using the available information.

For functions of two variables

$$z = f(x, y)$$

the stationary points are found by solving the simultaneous equations

$$\frac{\partial z}{\partial x} = 0$$

$$\frac{\partial z}{\partial y} = 0$$

that is,

$$f_x(x, y) = 0$$

$$f_y(x, y) = 0$$

This is a natural extension of the one-variable case. We first write down expressions for the first-order partial derivatives and then equate to zero. This represents a system of two equations for the two unknowns x and y, which we hope can be solved. Stationary points obtained in this way can be classified into one of three types: **minimum**, **maximum** and **saddle point**.

Figure 5.12(a) shows the shape of a surface in the neighbourhood of a minimum. It can be thought of as the bottom of a bowl-shaped valley. If you stand at the minimum point and walk in any direction then you are certain to start moving upwards. Mathematically, we can classify a stationary point (a, b) as a minimum provided that all three of the following conditions hold:

$$\frac{\partial^2 z}{\partial x^2} > 0, \ \frac{\partial^2 z}{\partial y^2} > 0, \ \left(\frac{\partial^2 z}{\partial x^2}\right)\left(\frac{\partial^2 z}{\partial y^2}\right) - \left(\frac{\partial^2 z}{\partial x \partial y}\right)^2 > 0$$

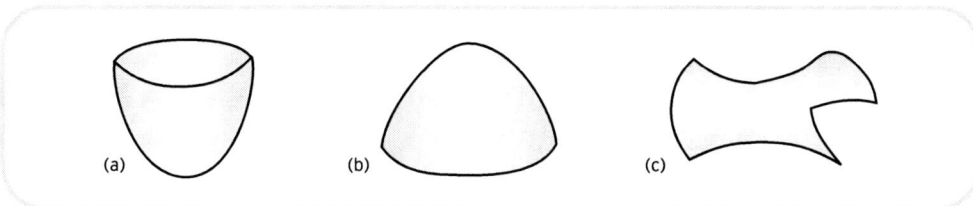

Figure 5.12

when $x = a$ and $y = b$: that is,

$$f_{xx}(a, b) > 0, \qquad f_{yy}(a, b) > 0, \qquad f_{xx}(a, b)f_{yy}(a, b) - [f_{xy}(a, b)]^2 > 0$$

This triple requirement is obviously more complicated than the single condition needed in the case of a function of one variable. However, once the second-order partial derivatives have been evaluated at the stationary point, the three conditions are easily checked.

Figure 5.12(b) shows the shape of a surface in the neighbourhood of a maximum. It can be thought of as the summit of a mountain. If you stand at the maximum point and walk in any direction then you are certain to start moving downwards. Mathematically, we can classify a stationary point (a, b) as a maximum provided that all three of the following conditions hold:

$$\frac{\partial^2 z}{\partial x^2} < 0, \frac{\partial^2 z}{\partial y^2} < 0, \quad \left(\frac{\partial^2 z}{\partial x^2}\right)\left(\frac{\partial^2 z}{\partial y^2}\right) - \left(\frac{\partial^2 z}{\partial x \partial y}\right)^2 > 0$$

when $x = a$ and $y = b$: that is,

$$f_{xx}(a, b) < 0, \qquad f_{yy}(a, b) < 0, \qquad f_{xx}(a, b)f_{yy}(a, b) - [f_{xy}(a, b)]^2 > 0$$

Of course, any particular mountain range may well have lots of valleys and summits. Likewise, a function of two variables can have more than one minimum or maximum.

Figure 5.12(c) shows the shape of a surface in the neighbourhood of a saddle point. As its name suggests, it can be thought of as the middle of a horse's saddle. If you sit at this point and edge towards the head or tail then you start moving upwards. On the other hand, if you edge sideways then you start moving downwards (and will probably fall off!). Mathematically, we can classify a stationary point (a, b) as a saddle point provided that the following single condition holds:

$$\left(\frac{\partial^2 z}{\partial x^2}\right)\left(\frac{\partial^2 z}{\partial y^2}\right) - \left(\frac{\partial^2 z}{\partial x \partial y}\right)^2 < 0$$

when $x = a$ and $y = b$: that is,

$$f_{xx}(a, b)f_{yy}(a, b) - [f_{xy}(a, b)]^2 < 0$$

To summarize, the method for finding and classifying stationary points of a function $f(x, y)$ is as follows:

Step 1

Solve the simultaneous equations

$$f_x(x, y) = 0$$
$$f_y(x, y) = 0$$

to find the stationary points, (a, b).

Step 2

If

- $f_{xx} > 0, f_{yy} > 0$ and $f_{xx}f_{yy} - f_{xy}^2 > 0$ at (a, b) then the function has a minimum at (a, b)
- $f_{xx} < 0, f_{yy} < 0$ and $f_{xx}f_{yy} - f_{xy}^2 > 0$ at (a, b) then the function has a maximum at (a, b)
- $f_{xx}f_{yy} - f_{xy}^2 < 0$ at (a, b) then the function has a saddle point at (a, b).

Advice

The second-order conditions needed to classify a stationary point can be expressed more succinctly using Hessians. Details are given in Appendix 3 on the website, although you will need to be familiar with determinants of 2×2 matrices, which are covered later in Section 7.2.

Example

Find and classify the stationary points of the function

$$f(x, y) = x^3 - 3x + xy^2$$

Solution

In order to use steps 1 and 2 we need to find all first- and second-order partial derivatives of the function

$$f(x, y) = x^3 - 3x + xy^2$$

These are easily worked out as

$$f_x = 3x^2 - 3 + y^2$$
$$f_y = 2xy$$
$$f_{xx} = 6x$$
$$f_{xy} = 2y$$
$$f_{yy} = 2x$$

Step 1

The stationary points are the solutions of the simultaneous equations

$$f_x(x, y) = 0$$
$$f_y(x, y) = 0$$

so we need to solve

$$3x^2 - 3 + y^2 = 0$$
$$2xy = 0$$

There have been many occasions throughout this book when we have solved simultaneous equations. So far these have been linear. This time, however, we need to solve a pair of non-linear equations. Unfortunately, there is no standard method for solving such systems. We have to rely on our wits in any particular instance. The trick here is to begin with the second equation

$$2xy = 0$$

The only way that the product of three numbers can be equal to zero is when one or more of the individual numbers forming the product are zero. We know that $2 \neq 0$, so either $x = 0$ or $y = 0$. We investigate these two possibilities separately:

- Case 1: $x = 0$. Substituting $x = 0$ into the first equation

$$3x^2 - 3 + y^2 = 0$$

gives

$$-3 + y^2 = 0$$

that is,

$$y^2 = 3$$

There are therefore two possibilities for y to go with $x = 0$, namely $y = \sqrt{3}$ and $y = \sqrt{3}$. Hence $(0, -\sqrt{3})$ and $(0, \sqrt{3})$ are stationary points.

- Case 2: $y = 0$. Substituting $y = 0$ into the first equation

$$3x^2 - 3 + y^2 = 0$$

gives

$$3x^2 - 3 = 0$$

that is,

$$x^2 = 1$$

There are therefore two possibilities for x to go with $y = 0$, namely $x = -1$ and $x = 1$. Hence $(-1, 0)$ and $(1, 0)$ are stationary points.

These two cases indicate that there are precisely four stationary points, $(0, -\sqrt{3})$, $(0, \sqrt{3})$, $(-1, 0)$, $(1, 0)$.

Step 2

To classify these points we need to evaluate the second-order partial derivatives

$$f_{xx} = 6x, \qquad f_{yy} = 2x, \qquad f_{xy} = 2y$$

at each point and check the signs of

$$f_{xx}, f_{yy}, \qquad f_{xx}f_{yy} - f_{xy}^2$$

- Point $(0, -\sqrt{3})$

$$f_{xx} = 6(0) = 0, \qquad f_{yy} = 2(0) = 0, \qquad f_{xy} = -2\sqrt{3}$$

Hence

$$f_{xx}f_{yy} - f_{xy}^2 = 0(0) - (2\sqrt{3})^2 = -12 < 0$$

and so $(0, -\sqrt{3})$ is a saddle point.

- Point $(0, \sqrt{3})$

$$f_{xx} = 6(0) = 0, \qquad f_{yy} = 2(0) = 0, \qquad f_{xy} = 2\sqrt{3}$$

Hence

$$f_x f_{yy} - f_{xy}^2 = 0(0) - (2\sqrt{3})^2 = -12 < 0$$

and so $(0, \sqrt{3})$ is a saddle point.

- Point $(-1, 0)$

$$f_{xx} = 6(-1) = -6, \qquad f_{yy} = 2(-1) = -2, \quad f_{xy} = 2(0) = 0$$

Hence

$$f_{xx}f_{yy} - f_{xy}^2 = (-6)(-2) - 0^2 = 12 > 0$$

and so $(-1, 0)$ is not a saddle point. Moreover, since

$$f_{xx} < 0 \quad \text{and} \quad f_{yy} < 0$$

we deduce that $(-1, 0)$ is a maximum.

- Point $(1, 0)$

$$f_{xx} = 6(1) = 6, \qquad f_{yy} = 2(1) = 2, \qquad f_{xy} = 2(0) = 0$$

Hence

$$f_{xx}f_{yy} - f_{xy}^2 = 6(2) - 0^2 = 12 > 0$$

and so $(1, 0)$ is not a saddle point. Moreover, since

$$f_{xx} > 0 \qquad \text{and} \qquad f_{yy} > 0$$

we deduce that $(1, 0)$ is a minimum.

Practice Problem

1. Find and classify the stationary points of the function

$$f(x, y) = x^2 + 6y - 3y^2 + 10$$

We now consider two examples from economics, both involving the maximization of profit. The first considers the case of a firm producing two different goods, whereas the second involves a single good sold in two different markets.

Example

A firm is a perfectly competitive producer and sells two goods G1 and G2 at $1000 and $800, respectively, each. The total cost of producing these goods is given by

$$TC = 2Q_1^2 + 2Q_1Q_2 + Q_2^2$$

where Q_1 and Q_2 denote the output levels of G1 and G2, respectively. Find the maximum profit and the values of Q_1 and Q_2 at which this is achieved.

Solution

The fact that the firm is perfectly competitive tells us that the price of each good is fixed by the market and does not depend on Q_1 and Q_2. The actual prices are stated in the question as $1000 and $800. If the firm sells Q_1 items of G1 priced at $1000 then the revenue is

$$TR_1 = 1000Q_1$$

Similarly, if the firm sells Q_2 items of G2 priced at \$800 then the revenue is

$$TR_2 = 800Q_2$$

The total revenue from the sale of both goods is then

$$TR = TR_1 + TR_2 = 1000Q_1 + 800Q_2$$

We are given that the total cost is

$$TC = 2Q_1^2 + 2Q_1Q_2 + Q_2^2$$

so the profit function is

$$\pi = TR - TC$$
$$= (1000Q_1 + 800Q_2) - (2Q_1^2 + 2Q_1Q_2 + Q_2^2)$$
$$= 1000Q_1 + 800Q_2 - 2Q_1^2 - 2Q_1Q_2 - Q_2^2$$

This is a function of the two variables, Q_1 and Q_2, that we wish to optimize. The first- and second-order partial derivatives are

$$\frac{\partial \pi}{\partial Q_1} = 1000 - 4Q_1 - 2Q_2$$

$$\frac{\partial \pi}{\partial Q_2} = 800 - 2Q_1 - 2Q_2$$

$$\frac{\partial^2 \pi}{\partial Q_1^2} = -4$$

$$\frac{\partial^2 \pi}{\partial Q_1 \partial Q_2} = -2$$

$$\frac{\partial^2 \pi}{\partial Q_2^2} = -2$$

The two-step strategy then gives the following:

Step 1
At a stationary point

$$\frac{\partial \pi}{\partial Q_1} = 0$$

$$\frac{\partial \pi}{\partial Q_2} = 0$$

so we need to solve the simultaneous equations

$$1000 - 4Q_1 - 2Q_2 = 0$$
$$800 - 2Q_1 - 2Q_2 = 0$$

that is,

$$4Q_1 + 2Q_2 = 1000 \tag{1}$$
$$2Q_1 + 2Q_2 = 800 \tag{2}$$

The variable Q_2 can be eliminated by subtracting equation (2) from (1) to get

$$2Q_1 = 200$$

and so $Q_1 = 100$. Substituting this into either equation (1) or (2) gives $Q_2 = 300$. The profit function therefore has one stationary point at $(100, 300)$.

Step 2

To show that the point really is a maximum we need to check that

$$\frac{\partial^2 \pi}{\partial Q_1^2} < 0, \ \frac{\partial^2 \pi}{\partial Q_2^2} < 0, \ \left(\frac{\partial^2 \pi}{\partial Q_1^2}\right)\left(\frac{\partial^2 \pi}{\partial Q_2^2}\right) - \left(\frac{\partial^2 \pi}{\partial Q_1 \partial Q_2}\right)^2 > 0$$

at this point. In this example the second-order partial derivatives are all constant. We have

$$\frac{\partial^2 \pi}{\partial Q_1^2} = -4 < 0 \quad \checkmark$$

$$\frac{\partial^2 \pi}{\partial Q_2^2} = -2 < 0 \quad \checkmark$$

$$\left(\frac{\partial^2 \pi}{\partial Q_1^2}\right)\left(\frac{\partial^2 \pi}{\partial Q_2^2}\right) - \left(\frac{\partial^2 \pi}{\partial Q_1 \partial Q_2}\right)^2 = (-4)(-2) - (-2)^2 = 4 > 0 \quad \checkmark$$

confirming that the firm's profit is maximized by producing 100 items of G1 and 300 items of G2.

The actual value of this profit is obtained by substituting $Q_1 = 100$ and $Q_2 = 300$ into the expression

$$\pi = 1000Q_1 + 800Q_2 - 2Q_1^2 - 2Q_1Q_2 - Q_2^2$$

to get

$$\pi = 1000(100) + 800(300) - 2(100)^2 - 2(100)(300) - (300)^2 = \$170\,000$$

Practice Problem

2. A firm is a monopolistic producer of two goods G1 and G2. The prices are related to quantities Q_1 and Q_2 according to the demand equations

$$P_1 = 50 - Q_1$$
$$P_2 = 95 - 3Q_2$$

If the total cost function is

$$TC = Q_1^2 + 3Q_1Q_2 + Q_2^2$$

show that the firm's profit function is

$$\pi = 50Q_1 - 2Q_1^2 - 95Q_2 - 4Q_2^2 - 3Q_1Q_2$$

Hence find the values of Q_1 and Q_2 which maximize π and deduce the corresponding prices.

Example

A firm is allowed to charge different prices for its domestic and industrial customers. If P_1 and Q_1 denote the price and demand for the domestic market then the demand equation is

$$P_1 + Q_1 = 500$$

If P_2 and Q_2 denote the price and demand for the industrial market then the demand equation is

$$2P_2 + 3Q_2 = 720$$

The total cost function is

$$TC = 50\,000 + 20Q$$

where $Q = Q_1 + Q_2$. Determine the firm's pricing policy that maximizes profit with price discrimination and calculate the value of the maximum profit.

Solution

The topic of price discrimination has already been discussed in Section 4.7. This particular problem is identical to the worked example solved in that section using ordinary differentiation. You might like to compare the details of the two approaches.

Our current aim is to find an expression for profit in terms of Q_1 and Q_2 which can then be optimized using partial differentiation. For the domestic market the demand equation is

$$P_1 + Q_1 = 500$$

which rearranges as

$$P_1 = 500 - Q_1$$

The total revenue function for this market is then

$$TR_1 = P_1Q_1 = (500 - Q_1)Q_1 = 500Q_1 - Q_1^2$$

For the industrial market the demand equation is

$$2P_2 + 3Q_2 = 720$$

which rearranges as

$$P_2 = 360 - {}^3\!/_2Q_2$$

The total revenue function for this market is then

$$TR_2 = P_2Q_2 = (360 - {}^3\!/_2Q_2)Q_2 = 360Q_2 - {}^3\!/_2Q_2^2$$

The total revenue received from sales in both markets is

$$TR = TR_1 + TR_2 = 500Q_1 - Q_1^2 + 360Q_2 - {}^3\!/_2Q_2^2$$

The total cost of producing these goods is given by

$$TC = 50\,000 + 20Q$$

and, since $Q = Q_1 + Q_2$, we can write this as

$$TC = 50\,000 + 20(Q_1 + Q_2)$$
$$= 50\,000 + 20Q_1 + 20Q_2$$

The firm's profit function is therefore

$$\pi = \text{TR} - \text{TC}$$
$$= (500Q_1 - Q_1^2 + 360Q_2 - \tfrac{3}{2}Q_2^2) - (50\,000 + 20Q_1 + 20Q_2)$$
$$480Q_1 - Q_1^2 + 340Q_2 - \tfrac{3}{2}Q_2^2 - 50\,000$$

This is a function of the two variables, Q_1 and Q_2, that we wish to optimize. The first- and second-order partial derivatives are

$$\frac{\partial \pi}{\partial Q_1} = 480 - 2Q_1$$

$$\frac{\partial \pi}{\partial Q_2} = 340 - 3Q_2$$

$$\frac{\partial^2 \pi}{\partial Q_1^2} = -2$$

$$\frac{\partial^2 \pi}{\partial Q_1 \partial Q_2} = 0$$

$$\frac{\partial^2 \pi}{\partial Q_2^2} = -3$$

The two-step strategy gives the following:

Step 1

At a stationary point

$$\frac{\partial \pi}{\partial Q_1} = 0$$

$$\frac{\partial \pi}{\partial Q_2} = 0$$

so we need to solve the simultaneous equations

$$480 - 2Q_1 = 0$$
$$340 - 3Q_2 = 0$$

These are easily solved because they are 'uncoupled'. The first equation immediately gives

$$Q_1 = \frac{480}{2} = 240$$

while the second gives

$$Q_2 = \frac{240}{3}$$

Step 2

It is easy to check that the conditions for a maximum are satisfied:

$$\frac{\partial^2 \pi}{\partial Q_1^2} = -2 < 0$$

$$\frac{\partial^2 \pi}{\partial Q_2^2} = -3 < 0$$

$$\left(\frac{\partial^2 \pi}{\partial Q_1^2}\right)\left(\frac{\partial^2 \pi}{\partial Q_2^2}\right) - \left(\frac{\partial^2 \pi}{\partial Q_1 \partial Q_2}\right)^2 = (-2)(-3) - 0^2 = 6 > 0$$

The question actually asks for the optimum prices rather than the quantities. These are found by substituting

$$Q_1 = 240 \quad \text{and} \quad Q_2 = \frac{340}{3}$$

into the corresponding demand equations. For the domestic market

$$P_1 = 500 - Q_1 = 500 - 240 = \$260$$

For the industrial market

$$P_2 = 360 - \frac{3}{2}Q_1 = 360 - \frac{3}{2}\left(\frac{340}{3}\right) = \$190$$

Finally, we substitute the values of Q_1 and Q_2 into the profit function

$$\pi = 480Q_1 - Q_1^2 + 340Q_2 - \tfrac{3}{2}Q_2^2 - 50\,000$$

to deduce that the maximum profit is \$26 866.67.

Practice Problem

3. A firm has the possibility of charging different prices in its domestic and foreign markets. The corresponding demand equations are given by

$$Q_1 = 300 - P_1$$
$$Q_2 = 400 - 2P_2$$

The total cost function is

$$TC = 5000 + 100Q$$

where $Q = Q_1 + Q_2$. Determine the prices that the firm should charge to maximize profit with price discrimination and calculate the value of this profit.

[You have already solved this particular example in Practice Problem 2(a) of Section 4.7.]

Example   MAPLE

A utility function is given by

$$U = 4x_1 + 2x_2 - x_1^2 - x_1^2 + x_1x_2 \quad (0 \le x_1 \le 5, 0 \le x_2 \le 5)$$

where x_1 and x_2 denote the number of units of goods 1 and 2 that are consumed.

(a) Draw a three-dimensional plot of this function and hence estimate the values of x_1 and x_2 at the stationary point. Is this a maximum, minimum or saddle point?

(b) Find the exact values of x_1 and x_2 at the stationary point using calculus.

Solution

(a) We can name this function `utility` by typing

```
>utility:=4*x1+2*x2-x1^2-x2^2+x1*x2;
```

and then plot the surface by typing

```
>plot3d(utility,x1=0..5,x2=0..5);
```

This surface, rotated so that the origin is to the front of the picture, is drawn in Figure 5.13, which shows that there is just one stationary point. This is clearly a maximum with approximate coordinates (3, 3).

(b) The partial derivatives are worked out by typing

```
>derivx1:=diff(utility,x1);
```

which gives

$$derivx1:=4-2x1+x2$$

and then typing

```
>derivx2:=diff(utility,x2);
```

which gives

$$derivx1:=2-2x2+x1$$

The stationary point is then found by setting each of these derivatives to zero and solving the resulting simultaneous equations. This is achieved by typing

```
>solve({derivx1=0,derivx2=0},{x1,x2});
```

which generates the response

$$\left\{ x_2 = \frac{8}{3}, x_1 = \frac{10}{3} \right\}$$

so we conclude that the utility function has a maximum point when

$$x_1 = \frac{10}{3} \text{ and } x_2 = \frac{8}{3}$$

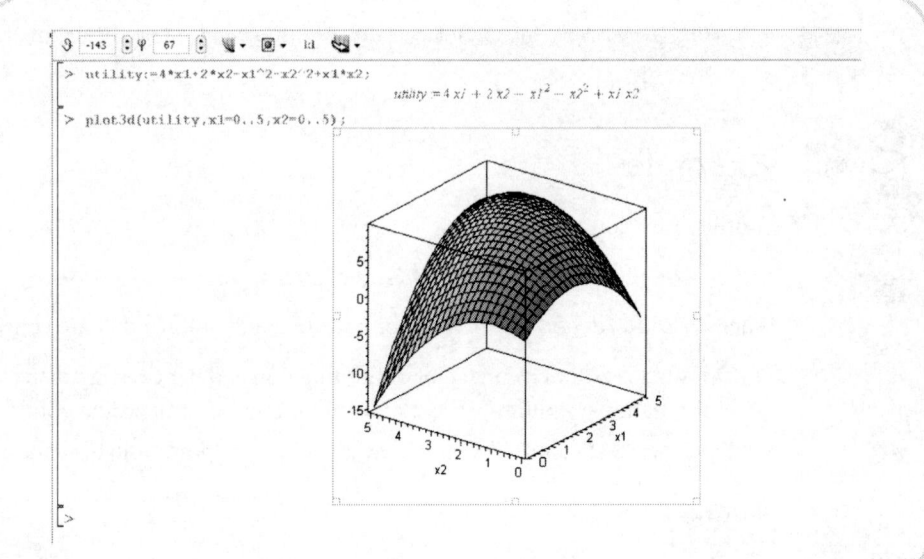

Figure 5.13

Key Terms

Maximum point A point on a surface which has the highest function value in comparison with other values in its neighbourhood; at such a point the surface looks like the top of a mountain.

Minimum point A point on a surface which has the lowest function value in comparison with other values in its neighbourhood; at such a point the surface looks like the bottom of a valley or bowl.

Saddle point A stationary point which is neither a maximum or minimum and at which the surface looks like the middle of a horse's saddle.

Exercise 5.4

1. Find and classify the stationary points of the following functions:

    (a) $f(x, y) = x^3 + y^3 - 3x - 3y$ **(b)** $f(x, y) = x^3 + 3xy^2 - 3x^2 - 3y^2 + 10$

2. A firm's profit function for the production of two goods is given by

    $$\pi = 24Q_1 - Q_1^2 - Q_1Q_2 - 2Q_2^2 + 33Q_2 - 43$$

    Find the output levels needed to maximize profit. Use second-order derivatives to confirm that the stationary point is a maximum.

3. A firm is a perfectly competitive producer and sells two goods G1 and G2 at \$70 and \$50, respectively, each. The total cost of producing these goods is given by

    $$TC = Q_1^2 + Q_1Q_2 + Q_2^2$$

    where Q_1 and Q_2 denote the output levels of G1 and G2. Find the maximum profit and the values of Q_1 and Q_2 at which this is achieved.

4. An individual's utility function is given by

    $$U = 260x_1 + 310x_2 + 5x_1x_2 - 10x_1^2 - x_2^2$$

    where x_1 is the amount of leisure measured in hours per week and x_2 is earned income measured in dollars per week. Find the values of x_1 and x_2 which maximize U. What is the corresponding hourly rate of pay?

5. A monopolist produces the same product at two factories. The cost functions for each factory are as follows: ❷

    $$TC_1 = 8Q_1 \quad \text{and} \quad TC_2 = Q_2^2$$

    The demand function for the good is

    $$P = 100 - 2Q$$

    where $Q = Q_1 + Q_2$. Find the values of Q_1 and Q_2 which maximize profit.

6. (**Maple**) Draw the surface representing each of the following functions. By rotating the surface, estimate the x and y values of the stationary points and state whether they are maxima, minima or saddle points. Use calculus to find the exact location of these points.

    (a) $z = x^2 + y^2 - 2x - 4y + 15$ $(0 \le x \le 4, 0 \le y \le 4)$

    (b) $z = 39 - x^2 - y^2 - 2y$ $(-2 \le x \le 2, -2 \le y \le 2)$

    (c) $z = x^2 - y^2 - 4x + 4y$ $(0 \le x \le 4, 0 \le y \le 4)$

Exercise 5.4*

1. Find and classify the stationary points of the function

   $$f(x, y) = x^3 + x^2 - xy + y^2 + 10$$

2. A firm's production function is given by

   $$Q = 2L^{1/2} + 3K^{1/2}$$

   where Q, L and K denote the number of units of output, labour and capital. Labour costs are \$2 per unit, capital costs are \$1 per unit and output sells at \$8 per unit. Show that the profit function is

   $$\pi = 16L^{1/2} + 24K^{1/2} - 2L - K$$

   and hence find the maximum profit and the values of L and K at which it is achieved.

3. An additional cost of \$50 per unit is incurred by a firm when selling to its non-EU customers compared to its EU customers. The demand function is the same in both markets and is given by

   $$20P + Q = 5000$$

   and the total cost function is given by

   $$TC = 40Q + 2000$$

   where Q is total demand.

   Find the maximum profit with price discrimination.

4. The demand functions for a firm's domestic and foreign markets are

   $$P_1 = 50 - 5Q_1$$
   $$P_2 = 30 - 4Q_2$$

   and the total cost function is

   $$TC = 10 + 10Q$$

   where $Q = Q_1 + Q_2$. Determine the prices needed to maximize profit with price discrimination and calculate the value of the maximum profit.

   [You have already solved this particular example in Question 3(a) in Exercise 4.7*.]

5. A firm is able to sell its product in two different markets. The corresponding demand functions are

   $$P_1 + 2Q_1 = 100$$
   $$2P_2 + Q_2 = 2a$$

   and the total cost function is

   $$TC = 500 + 10Q$$

   where $Q = Q_1 + Q_2$ and a is a positive constant.

Determine, in terms of a, the prices needed to maximize profit

(a) with price discrimination

(b) without price discrimination.

Show that the profit with price discrimination is always greater than the profit without discrimination, irrespective of the value of a.

6. **(Maple)** A monopolistic producer charges different prices at home and abroad. The demand functions of the domestic and foreign markets are given by

$$P_1 + Q_1 = 100 \quad \text{and} \quad P_2 + 2Q_2 = 80$$

respectively. The firm's total cost function is

$$\text{TC} = (Q_1 + Q_2)^2$$

(a) Show that the firm's profit function is given by

$$\pi = 100Q_1 + 80Q_2 - 2Q_1^2 - 3Q_2^2 - 2Q_1Q_2$$

Use calculus to show that profit is maximized when $Q_1 = 22$ and $Q_2 = 6$, and find the corresponding prices.

(b) The foreign country believes that the firm is guilty of dumping because the good sells at a higher price in the home market, so decides to restrict the sales to a maximum of 2, so that $Q_2 \leq 2$. By plotting π in the region $0 \leq Q_1 \leq 30$, $0 \leq Q_2 \leq 2$, explain why the profit is maximized when $Q_2 = 2$. Use calculus to find value of Q_1, and compare the corresponding profit with that of the free market in part (a).

SECTION 5.5
Constrained optimization

Objectives

At the end of this section you should be able to:

● Give a graphical interpretation of constrained optimization.

● Show that when a firm maximizes output subject to a cost constraint, the ratio of marginal product to price is the same for all inputs.

● Show that when a consumer maximizes utility subject to a budgetary constraint, the ratio of marginal utility to price is the same for all goods.

● Use the method of substitution to solve constrained optimization problems in economics.

Advice

In this section we begin by proving some theoretical results before describing the method of substitution. You might prefer to skip the theory at a first reading, and begin with the two worked examples.

In Section 5.4 we described how to find the optimum (that is, maximum or minimum) of a function of two variables

$$z = f(x, y)$$

where the variables x and y are free to take any values. As we pointed out at the beginning of that section, this assumption is unrealistic in many economic situations. An individual wishing to maximize utility is subject to an income constraint and a firm wishing to maximize output is subject to a cost constraint.

In general, we want to optimize a function,

$$z = f(x, y)$$

called the **objective** function subject to a constraint

$$\varphi(x, y) = M$$

Here φ, the Greek letter phi, is a known function of two variables and M is a known constant. The problem is to pick the pair of numbers (x, y) which maximizes or minimizes $f(x, y)$ as before. This time, however, we limit the choice of pairs to those which satisfy

$$\varphi(x, y) = M$$

A graphical interpretation should make this clear. To be specific, let us suppose that a firm wants to maximize output and that the production function is of the form

$$Q = f(K, L)$$

Let the costs of each unit of capital and labour be P_K and P_L respectively. The cost to the firm of using as input K units of capital and L units of labour is

$$P_K K + P_L L$$

so if the firm has a fixed amount, M, to spend on these inputs then

$$P_K K + P_L L = M$$

The problem is one of trying to maximize the objective function

$$Q = f(K, L)$$

subject to the cost constraint

$$P_K K + P_L L = M$$

Sketched in Figure 5.14 is a typical isoquant map. As usual, points on any one isoquant yield the same level of output and as output rises the isoquants themselves move further away from the origin. Also sketched in Figure 5.14 is the cost constraint. This is called an **isocost curve** because it gives all combinations of K and L which can be bought for a fixed cost, M.

The fact that

$$P_K K + P_L L = M$$

is represented by a straight line should come as no surprise to you by now. We can even rewrite it in the more familiar '$y = ax + b$' form and so identify its slope and intercept. In Figure 5.14, L is plotted on the horizontal axis and K is plotted on the vertical axis, so we need to rearrange

$$P_K K + P_L L = M$$

to express K in terms of L. Subtracting $P_L L$ from both sides and dividing through by P_K gives

$$K = \left(-\frac{P_L}{P_K} \right) L + \frac{M}{P_K}$$

The isocost curve is therefore a straight line with slope $-P_L/P_K$ and intercept M/P_L. Graphically, our constrained problem is to choose that point on the isocost line which maximizes output. This is given by the point labelled A in Figure 5.14. Point A certainly lies on the isocost line and it maximizes output because it also lies on the highest isoquant. Other points, such as B and C,

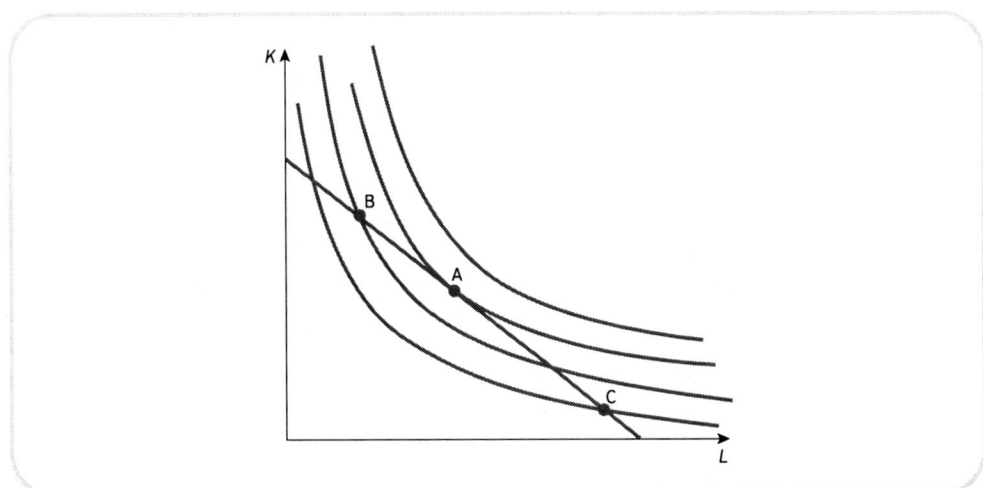

Figure 5.14

also satisfy the constraint but they lie on lower isoquants and so yield smaller levels of output than A. Point A is characterized by the fact that the isocost line is tangential to an isoquant. In other words, the slope of the isocost line is the same as that of the isoquant at A.

Now we have already shown that the isocost line has slope $-P_L/P_K$. In Section 5.2 we defined the marginal rate of technical substitution, MRTS, to be minus the slope of an isoquant, so at point A we must have

$$\frac{P_L}{P_K} = \text{MRTS}$$

We also showed that

$$\text{MRTS} = \frac{\text{MP}_L}{\text{MP}_K}$$

so

$$\frac{P_L}{P_K} = \frac{\text{MP}_L}{\text{MP}_K}$$

> **the ratio of the input prices is equal to the ratio of their marginal products**

This relationship can be rearranged as

$$\frac{\text{MP}_L}{P_L} = \frac{\text{MP}_K}{P_K}$$

so when output is maximized subject to a cost constraint

> **the ratio of marginal product to price is the same for all inputs**

The marginal product determines the change in output due to a 1 unit increase in input. This optimization condition therefore states that the last dollar spent on labour yields the same addition to output as the last dollar spent on capital.

The above discussion has concentrated on production functions. An analogous situation arises when we maximize utility functions

$$U = U(x_1, x_2)$$

where x_1, x_2 denote the number of items of goods G1, G2 that an individual buys. If the prices of these goods are denoted by P_1 and P_2 and the individual has a fixed budget, M, to spend on these goods then the corresponding constraint is

$$P_1 x_1 + P_2 x_2 = M$$

This budgetary constraint plays the role of the cost constraint, and indifference curves are analogous to isoquants. Consequently, we analyze the problem by superimposing the budget line on an indifference map. The corresponding diagram is virtually indistinguishable from that of Figure 5.14. The only change is that the axes would be labelled x_1 and x_2 rather than L and K. Once again, the maximum point of the constrained problem occurs at the point of tangency, so that at this point the slope of the budget line is that of an indifference curve. Hence

$$\frac{P_1}{P_2} = \text{MRCS}$$

In Section 5.2 we derived the result

$$\text{MRCS} = \frac{\partial U/\partial x_1}{\partial U/\partial x_2}$$

Writing the partial derivatives $\partial U/\partial x_i$ more concisely as U_i we can deduce that

$$\frac{P_1}{P_2} = \frac{U_1}{U_2}$$

that is,

the ratio of the prices of the goods is equal to the ratio of their marginal utilities

Again, this relationship can be rearranged into the more familiar form

$$\frac{U_1}{P_1} = \frac{U_2}{P_2}$$

so when utility is maximized subject to a budgetary constraint,

the ratio of marginal utility to price is the same for all goods consumed

If individuals allocate their budgets between goods in this way then utility is maximized when the last dollar spent on each good yields the same addition to total utility. Under these circumstances, the consumer has achieved maximum satisfaction within the constraint of a fixed budget, so there is no tendency to reallocate income between these goods. Obviously, the consumer's equilibrium will be affected if there is a change in external conditions such as income or the price of any good. For example, suppose that P_1 suddenly increases, while P_2 and M remain fixed. If this happens then the equation

$$\frac{U_1}{P_1} = \frac{U_2}{P_2}$$

turns into an inequality

$$\frac{U_1}{P_1} < \frac{U_2}{P_2}$$

so equilibrium no longer holds. Given that P_1 has increased, consumers find that the last dollar spent no longer buys as many items of G1, so utility can be increased by purchasing more of G2 and less of G1. By the law of diminishing marginal utility, the effect is to increase U_1 and to decrease U_2. The process of reallocation continues until the ratio of marginal utilities to prices is again equal and equilibrium is again established.

The graphical approach provides a useful interpretation of constrained optimization. It has also enabled us to justify some familiar results in microeconomics. However, it does not give us a practical way of actually solving such problems. It is very difficult to produce an accurate isoquant or indifference map from any given production or utility function. We now describe an alternative approach, known as the **method of substitution**. To illustrate the method we begin with an easy example.

Example

Find the minimum value of the objective function

$$z = -2x^2 + y^2$$

subject to the constraint $y = 2x - 1$.

Solution

In this example we need to optimize the function

$$z = -2x^2 + y^2$$

given that x and y are related by

$$y = 2x - 1$$

The obvious thing to do is to substitute the expression for y given by the constraint directly into the function that we are trying to optimize to get

$$z = -2x^2 + (2x - 1)^2$$
$$= -2x^2 + 4x^2 - 4x + 1$$
$$= 2x^2 - 4x + 1$$

Note the wonderful effect that this has on z. Instead of z being a function of two variables, x and y, it is now just a function of the one variable, x. Consequently, the minimum value of z can be found using the theory of stationary points discussed in Chapter 4.

At a stationary point

$$\frac{dz}{dx} = 0$$

that is,

$$4x - 4 = 0$$

which has solution $x = 1$. Differentiating a second time we see that

$$\frac{d^2z}{dx^2} = 4 > 0$$

confirming that the stationary point is a minimum. The value of z can be found by substituting $x = 1$ into

$$z = 2x^2 - 4x + 1$$

to get

$$z = 2(1)^2 - 4(1) + 1 = -1$$

It is also possible to find the value of y at the minimum. To do this we substitute $x = 1$ into the constraint

$$y = 2x - 1$$

to get

$$y = 2(1) - 1 = 1$$

The constrained function therefore has a minimum value of -1 at the point $(1, 1)$.

The method of substitution for optimizing

$$z = f(x, y)$$

subject to

$$\varphi(x, y) = M$$

may be summarized as follows:

Step 1

Use the constraint

$$\varphi(x, y) = M$$

to express y in terms of x.

Step 2

Substitute this expression for y into the objective function

$$z = f(x, y)$$

to write z as a function of x only.

Step 3

Use the theory of stationary points of functions of one variable to optimize z.

Practice Problem ❷

1. Find the maximum value of the objective function

   $$z = 2x^2 - 3xy + 2y + 10$$

   subject to the constraint $y = x$.

Advice

The most difficult part of the three-step strategy is step 1, where we rearrange the given constraint to write y in terms of x. In the previous example and in Practice Problem 1 this step was exceptionally easy because the constraint was linear. In both cases the constraint was even presented in the appropriate form to begin with, so no extra work was required. In general, if the constraint is non-linear, it may be difficult or impossible to perform the initial rearrangement. If this happens then you could try working the other way round and expressing x in terms of y, although there is no guarantee that this will be possible either. However, when step 1 can be tackled successfully, the method does provide a really quick way of solving constrained optimization problems.

To illustrate this we now use the method of substitution to solve two economic problems that both involve production functions. In the first example output is maximized subject to cost constraint and in the second example cost is minimized subject to an output constraint.

Example

A firm's unit capital and labour costs are $1 and $2 respectively. If the production function is given by

$$Q = 4LK + L^2$$

find the maximum output and the levels of K and L at which it is achieved when the total input costs are fixed at $105. Verify that the ratio of marginal product to price is the same for both inputs at the optimum.

Solution

We are told that 1 unit of capital costs $1 and that 1 unit of labour costs $2. If the firm uses K units of capital and L units of labour then the total input costs are

$$K + 2L$$

This is fixed at $105, so

$$K + 2L = 105$$

The mathematical problem is to maximize the objective function

$$Q = 4LK + L^2$$

subject to the constraint

$$K + 2L = 105$$

The three-step strategy is as follows:

Step 1

Rearranging the constraint to express K in terms of L gives

$$K = 105 - 2L$$

Step 2

Substituting this into the objective function

$$Q = 4LK + L^2$$

gives

$$Q = 4L(105 - 2L) + L^2 = 420L - 7L^2$$

and so output is now a function of the one variable, L.

Step 3

At a stationary point

$$\frac{dQ}{dL} = 0$$

that is,

$$420 - 14L = 0$$

which has solution $L = 30$. Differentiating a second time gives

$$\frac{d^2Q}{dL^2} = -14 < 0$$

confirming that the stationary point is a maximum.

The maximum output is found by substituting $L = 30$ into the objective function

$$Q = 420L - 7L^2$$

to get

$$Q = 420(30) - 7(30)^2 = 6300$$

The corresponding level of capital is found by substituting $L = 30$ into the constraint

$$K = 105 - 2L$$

to get

$$K = 105 - 2(30) = 45$$

The firm should therefore use 30 units of labour and 45 units of capital to produce a maximum output of 6300.

Finally, we are asked to check that the ratio of marginal product to price is the same for both inputs. From the formula

$$Q = 4LK + L^2$$

we see that the marginal products are given by

$$\text{MP}_L = \frac{\partial Q}{\partial L} = 4K + 2L \quad \text{and} \quad \text{MP}_K = \frac{\partial Q}{\partial K} = 4L$$

so at the optimum

$$\text{MP}_L = 4(45) + 2(30) = 240$$

and

$$\text{MP}_K = 4(30) = 120$$

The ratios of marginal products to prices are then

$$\frac{\text{MP}_L}{P_L} = \frac{240}{2} = 120$$

and

$$\frac{\text{MP}_K}{P_K} = \frac{120}{1} = 120$$

which are seen to be the same.

Practice Problem

2. An individual's utility function is given by

$$U = x_1 x_2$$

where x_1 and x_2 denote the number of items of two goods, G1 and G2. The prices of the goods are $2 and $10, respectively. Assuming that the individual has $400 available to spend on these goods, find the utility-maximizing values of x_1 and x_2. Verify that the ratio of marginal utility to price is the same for both goods at the optimum.

Example

A firm's production function is given by

$$Q = 2K^{1/2}L^{1/2}$$

Unit capital and labour costs are \$4 and \$3 respectively. Find the values of K and L which minimize total input costs if the firm is contracted to provide 160 units of output.

Solution

Given that capital and labour costs are \$4 and \$3 per unit, the total cost of using K units of capital and L units of labour is

$$TC = 4K + 3L$$

The firm's production quota is 160, so

$$2K^{1/2}L^{1/2} = 160$$

The mathematical problem is to minimize the objective function

$$TC = 4K + 3L$$

subject to the constraint

$$2K^{1/2}L^{1/2} = 160$$

Step 1

Rearranging the constraint to express L in terms of K gives

$$L^{1/2} = \frac{80}{K^{1/2}} \qquad \text{(divide both sides by } 2K^{1/2}\text{)}$$

$$L = \frac{6400}{K} \qquad \text{(square both sides)}$$

Step 2

Substituting this into the objective function

$$TC = 4K + 3L$$

gives

$$TC = 4K + \frac{19\,200}{K}$$

and so total cost is now a function of the one variable, K.

Step 3

At a stationary point

$$\frac{d(TC)}{dK} = 0$$

that is,

$$4 - \frac{19\,200}{K^2} = 0$$

This can be written as

$$4 = \frac{19\,200}{K^2}$$

so that

$$K^2 = \frac{19\,200}{4} = 4800$$

Hence

$$K = \sqrt{4800} = 69.28$$

Differentiating a second time gives

$$\frac{d^2(TC)}{dK^2} = \frac{38\,400}{K^3} > 0 \quad \text{because} \quad K > 0$$

confirming that the stationary point is a minimum.

Finally, the value of L can be found by substituting $K = 69.28$ into the constraint

$$L = \frac{6400}{K}$$

to get

$$L = \frac{6400}{69.28} = 92.38$$

We are not asked for the minimum cost, although this could easily be found by substituting the values of K and L into the objective function.

Practice Problem

3. A firm's total cost function is given by

$$TC = 3x_1^2 + 2x_1 x_2 + 7x_2^2$$

where x_1 and x_2 denote the number of items of goods G1 and G2, respectively, that are produced. Find the values of x_1 and x_2 which minimize costs if the firm is committed to providing 40 goods of either type in total.

Key Terms

Isocost curve   A line showing all combinations of two factors which can be bought for a fixed cost.

Method of substitution   The method of solving constrained optimization problems whereby the constraint is used to eliminate one of the variables in the objective function.

Objective function   A function that one seeks to optimize (usually) subject to constraints.

Exercise 5.5

1. **(a)** Make y the subject of the formula $9x + 3y = 2$.

    (b) The function,

    $$z = 3xy$$

    is subject to the constraint

    $$9x + 3y = 2$$

    Use your answer to part (a) to show that

    $$z = 2x - 9x^2$$

    Hence find the maximum value of z and the corresponding values of x and y.

2. Find the maximum value of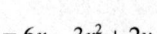

    $$z = 6x - 3x^2 + 2y$$

    subject to the constraint

    $$y - x^2 = 2$$

3. Find the maximum value of

    $$z = 80x - 0.1x^2 + 100y - 0.2y^2$$

    subject to the constraint

    $$x + y = 500$$

4. A firm's production function is given by

    $$Q = 50KL$$

    Unit capital and labour costs are \$2 and \$3 respectively. Find the values of K and L which minimize total input costs if the production quota is 1200.

5. The total cost of producing x items of product A and y items of product B is

    $$TC = 22x^2 + 8y^2 - 5xy$$

    If the firm is committed to producing 20 items in total, write down the constraint connecting x and y. Hence find the number of each type that should be produced to minimize costs.

6. Find the maximum value of the utility function, $U = x_1x_2$, subject to the budgetary constraint, $x_1 + 4x_2 = 360$.

Exercise 5.5*

1. **(a)** Find the minimum value of the objective function

   $$z = 9x^2 + 2y^2 - 3xy$$

   subject to the constraint,

   $$x + y = 40.$$

   (b) Find the maximum value of the objective function

   $$-16x^2 - 2y^2 + 4x + 9y + 2xy$$

   subject to the constraint,

   $$y = 4x$$

2. A firm's production function is given by

   $$Q = 10K^{1/2}L^{1/4}$$

   Unit capital and labour costs are \$4 and \$5 respectively and the firm spends a total of \$60 on these inputs. Find the values of K and L which maximize output.

3. A firm's production function is given by

   $$Q = 2L^{1/2} + 3K^{1/2}$$

   where Q, L and K denote the number of units of output, labour and capital respectively. Labour costs are \$2 per unit, capital costs are \$1 per unit and output sells at \$8 per unit. If the firm is prepared to spend \$99 on input costs, find the maximum profit and the values of K and L at which it is achieved.

   [You might like to compare your answer with the corresponding unconstrained problem that you solved in Question 2 of Exercise 5.4*.]

4. A consumer's utility function is

   $$U = \ln x_1 + 2 \ln x_2$$

   Find the values of x_1 and x_2 which maximize U subject to the budgetary constraint

   $$2x_1 + 3x_2 = 18$$

SECTION 5.6

Lagrange multipliers

Objectives

At the end of this section you should be able to:

- Use the method of Lagrange multipliers to solve constrained optimization problems.
- Give an economic interpretation of Lagrange multipliers.
- Use Lagrange multipliers to maximize a Cobb-Douglas production function subject to a cost constraint.
- Use Lagrange multipliers to show that when a firm maximizes output subject to a cost constraint, the ratio of marginal product to price is the same for all inputs.

We now describe the method of Lagrange multipliers for solving constrained optimization problems. This is the preferred method, since it handles non-linear constraints and problems involving more than two variables with ease. It also provides some additional information that is useful when solving economic problems.

To optimize an objective function

$$f(x, y)$$

subject to a constraint

$$\varphi(x, y) = M$$

we work as follows.

Step 1

Define a new function

$$g(x, y, \lambda) = f(x, y) + \lambda[M - \varphi(x, y)]$$

Step 2

Solve the simultaneous equations

$$\frac{\partial g}{\partial x} = 0$$

$$\frac{\partial g}{\partial y} = 0$$

$$\frac{\partial g}{\partial \lambda} = 0$$

for the three unknowns, x, y and λ.

The basic steps of the method are straightforward. In step 1 we combine the objective function and constraint into a single function. To do this we first rearrange the constraint as

$$M - \varphi(x, y)$$

and multiply by the scalar (i.e. number) λ (the Greek letter 'lambda'). This scalar is called the **Lagrange multiplier**. Finally, we add on the objective function to produce the new function

$$g(x, y, \lambda) = f(x, y) + \lambda[M - \varphi(x, y)]$$

This is called the **Lagrangian** function. The right-hand side involves the three letters x, y and λ, so g is a function of three variables.

In step 2 we work out the three first-order partial derivatives

$$\frac{\partial g}{\partial x}, \frac{\partial g}{\partial y}, \frac{\partial g}{\partial \lambda}$$

and equate these to zero to produce a system of three simultaneous equations for the three unknowns x, y and λ. The point (x, y) is then the optimal solution of the constrained problem. The number λ can also be given a meaning and we consider this later. For the moment we consider a simple example to get us started.

Example

Use Lagrange multipliers to find the optimal value of

$$x^2 - 3xy + 12x$$

subject to the constraint

$$2x + 3y = 6$$

Solution

Step 1
In this example

$$f(x, y) = x^2 - 3xy + 12x$$
$$\varphi(x, y) = 2x + 3y$$
$$M = 6$$

so the Lagrangian function is given by

$$g(x, y, \lambda) = x^2 - 3xy + 12x + \lambda(6 - 2x - 3y)$$

Step 2
Working out the three partial derivatives of g gives

$$\frac{\partial g}{\partial x} = 2x - 3y + 12 - 2\lambda$$

$$\frac{\partial g}{\partial y} = -3x - 3\lambda$$

$$\frac{\partial g}{\partial \lambda} = -6 - 2x - 3y$$

so we need to solve the simultaneous equations

$$2x - 3y + 12 - 2\lambda = 0$$
$$-3x - 3\lambda = 0$$
$$6 - 2x - 3y = 0$$

that is,

$$2x - 3y - 2\lambda = -12 \tag{1}$$

$$-3x - 3\lambda = 0 \tag{2}$$

$$2x + 3y = 6 \tag{3}$$

We can eliminate x from equation (2) by multiplying equation (1) by 3, multiplying equation (2) by 2 and adding. Similarly, x can be eliminated from equation (3) by subtracting equation (3) from (1). These operations give

$$-9y - 12\lambda = -36 \tag{4}$$

$$-6y - 2\lambda = -18 \tag{5}$$

The variable y can be eliminated by multiplying equation (4) by 6 and equation (5) by 9, and subtracting to get

$$-54\lambda = -54 \tag{6}$$

so $\lambda = 1$. Substituting this into equations (5) and (2) gives $y = 8/3$ and $x = -1$ respectively.

The optimal solution is therefore $(1, 8/3)$ and the corresponding value of the objective function

$$x^2 - 3xy + 12x$$

is

$$(-1)^2 - 3(1)(^8/_3) + 12(-1) = -3$$

Practice Problem

1. Use Lagrange multipliers to optimize

$$2x^2 - xy$$

subject to

$$x + y = 12$$

Looking back at the worked example and your own solution to Practice Problem 1, notice that the third equation in step 2 is just a restatement of the original constraint. It is easy to see that this is always the case because if

$$g(x, y, \lambda) = f(x, y) + \lambda[M - \varphi(x, y)]$$

then

$$\frac{\partial g}{\partial \lambda} = M - \varphi(x, y)$$

The equation

$$\frac{\partial g}{\partial \lambda} = 0$$

then implies the constraint

$$\varphi(x, y) = M$$

It is possible to make use of second-order partial derivatives to classify the optimal point. Unfortunately, these conditions are quite complicated and are considered in Appendix 3 on the website. In all problems that we consider there is only a single optimum and it is usually obvious on economic grounds whether it is a maximum or a minimum.

Example

A monopolistic producer of two goods, G1 and G2, has a joint total cost function

$$TC = 10Q_1 + Q_1Q_2 + 10Q_2$$

where Q_1 and Q_2 denote the quantities of G1 and G2 respectively. If P_1 and P_2 denote the corresponding prices then the demand equations are

$$P_1 = 50 - Q_1 + Q_2$$
$$P_2 = 30 + 2Q_1 - Q_2$$

Find the maximum profit if the firm is contracted to produce a total of 15 goods of either type. Estimate the new optimal profit if the production quota rises by 1 unit.

Solution

The first thing that we need to do is to write down expressions for the objective function and constraint. The objective function is profit and is given by

$$\pi = TR - TC$$

The total cost function is given to be

$$TC = 10Q_1 + Q_1Q_2 + 10Q_2$$

However, we need to use the demand equations to obtain an expression for TR. Total revenue from the sale of G1 is

$$TR_1 = P_1Q_1 = (50 - Q_1 + Q_2)Q_1 + 50Q_1 - Q_1^2 + Q_2Q_1$$

and total revenue from the sale of G2 is

$$TR_2 = P_2Q_2 = (30 + 2Q_1 - Q_2)Q_2 = 30Q_2 + 2Q_1Q_2 - Q_2^2$$

so

$$TR = TR_1 + TR_2$$
$$= 50Q_1 - Q_1^2 + Q_2Q_1 + 30Q_2 + 2Q_1Q_2 - Q_2^2$$
$$= 50Q_1 - Q_1^2 + 3Q_1Q_2 + 30Q_2 - Q_2^2$$

Hence

$$\pi = TR - TC$$
$$= (50Q_1 - Q_1^2 + 3Q_1Q_2 + 30Q_2 - Q_2^2) - (10Q_1 + Q_1Q_2 + 10Q_2)$$
$$= 40Q_1 + Q_1^2 + 2Q_1Q_2 + 20Q_2 - Q_2^2$$

The constraint is more easily determined. We are told that the firm produces 15 goods in total, so

$$Q_1 + Q_2 = 15$$

The mathematical problem is to maximize the objective function

$$\pi = 40Q_1 - Q_1^2 + 2Q_1Q_2 + 20Q_2 - Q_2^2$$

subject to the constraint

$$Q_1 + Q_2 = 15$$

Step 1
The Lagrangian function is

$$g(Q_1, Q_2, \lambda) = 40Q_1 - Q_1^2 + 2Q_1Q_2 + 20Q_2 - Q_2^2 + \lambda(15 - Q_1 - Q_2)$$

Step 2
The simultaneous equations

$$\frac{\partial g}{\partial Q_1} = 0, \frac{\partial g}{\partial Q_2} = 0, \frac{\partial g}{\partial \lambda} = 0$$

are

$$40 - 2Q_1 + 2Q_2 - \lambda = 0$$
$$2Q_1 + 20 - 2Q_2 - \lambda = 0$$
$$15 - Q_1 - Q_2 = 0$$

that is,

$$-2Q_1 + 2Q_2 - \lambda = -40 \tag{1}$$
$$2Q_1 - 2Q_2 - \lambda = -20 \tag{2}$$
$$Q_1 + Q_2 = 15 \tag{3}$$

The obvious way of solving this system is to add equations (1) and (2) to get

$$-2\lambda = -60$$

so $\lambda = 30$. Putting this into equation (1) gives

$$-2Q_1 + 2Q_2 = -10 \tag{4}$$

Equations (3) and (4) constitute a system of two equations for the two unknowns Q_1 and Q_2. We can eliminate Q_1 by multiplying equation (3) by 2 and adding equation (4) to get

$$4Q_2 = 20$$

so $Q_2 = 5$. Substituting this into equation (3) gives

$$Q_1 = 15 - 5 = 10$$

The maximum profit is found by substituting $Q_1 = 10$ and $Q_2 = 5$ into the formula for π to get

$$\pi = 40(10) - (10)^2 + 2(10)(5) + 20(5) - 5^2 = 475$$

The final part of this example wants us to find the new optimal profit when the production quota rises by 1 unit. One way of doing this is just to repeat the calculations replacing the previous quota of 15 by 16, although this is extremely tedious and not strictly necessary. There is a convenient shortcut based on the value of the Lagrange multiplier λ. To understand this, let us replace the production quota, 15, by the variable M, so that the Lagrangian function is

$$g(Q_1, Q_2, \lambda, M) = 40Q_1 - Q_1^2 + 2Q_1Q_2 + 20Q_2 - Q_2^2 + \lambda(M - Q_1 - Q_2)$$

The expression on the right-hand side involves Q_1, Q_2, λ and M, so g is now a function of four variables. If we partially differentiate with respect to M then

$$\frac{\partial g}{\partial M} = \lambda$$

We see that λ is a multiplier not only in the mathematical but also in the economic sense. It represents the (approximate) change in g due to a 1 unit increase in M. Moreover, if the constraint is satisfied, then

$$Q_1 + Q_2 = M$$

and the expression for g reduces to

$$40Q_1 - Q_1^2 + 2Q_1Q_2 + 20Q_2 - Q_2^2$$

which is equal to the profit. The value of the Lagrange multiplier represents the change in optimal profit brought about by a 1 unit increase in the production quota. In this case, $\lambda = 30$, so the profit rises by 30 to become 505.

The interpretation placed on the value of λ in this example applies quite generally. Given an objective function

$$f(x, y)$$

and constraint

$$\varphi(x, y) = M$$

the value of λ gives the approximate change in the optimal value of f due to a 1 unit increase in M.

Practice Problem

2. A consumer's utility function is given by

$$U(x_1, x_2) = 2x_1x_2 + 3x_1$$

where x_1 and x_2 denote the number of items of two goods G1 and G2 that are bought. Each item costs \$1 for G1 and \$2 for G2. Use Lagrange multipliers to find the maximum value of U if the consumer's income is \$83. Estimate the new optimal utility if the consumer's income rises by \$1.

Example

Use Lagrange multipliers to find expressions for K and L which maximize output given by a Cobb–Douglas production function

$$Q = AK^\alpha L^\beta \quad (A, \alpha \text{ and } \beta \text{ are positive constants})$$

subject to a cost constraint

$$P_K K + P_L L = M$$

Solution

This example appears very hard at first sight because it does not involve specific numbers. However, it is easy to handle such generalized problems provided that we do not panic.

Step 1
The Lagrangian function is

$$g(K, L, \lambda) = AK^{\alpha}L^{\beta} + \lambda(M - P_K K - P_L L)$$

Step 2
The simultaneous equations

$$\frac{\partial g}{\partial K} = 0, \quad \frac{\partial g}{\partial L} = 0, \quad \frac{\partial g}{\partial \lambda} = 0$$

are

$$A\alpha K^{\alpha-1}L^{\beta} - \lambda P_K = 0 \tag{1}$$
$$A\beta K^{\alpha-1}L^{\beta-1} - \lambda P_L = 0 \tag{2}$$
$$M - P_K K - P_L L = 0 \tag{3}$$

These equations look rather forbidding. Before we begin to solve them it pays to simplify equations (1) and (2) slightly by introducing $Q = AK^{\alpha}L^{\beta}$. Notice that

$$A\alpha K^{\alpha-1}L^{\beta} = \frac{\alpha(AK^{\alpha}L^{\beta})}{K} = \frac{\alpha Q}{K}$$

$$A\beta K^{\alpha}L^{\beta-1} = \frac{\beta(AK^{\alpha}L^{\beta})}{L} = \frac{\beta Q}{L}$$

so equations (1), (2) and (3) can be written

$$\frac{\alpha Q}{K} - \lambda P_K = 0 \tag{4}$$

$$\frac{\beta Q}{L} - \lambda P_L = 0 \tag{5}$$

$$P_K K + P_L L = M \tag{6}$$

Equations (4) and (5) can be rearranged to give

$$\lambda = \frac{\alpha Q}{P_K K} \quad \text{and} \quad \lambda = \frac{\beta Q}{P_L L}$$

so that

$$\frac{\alpha Q}{P_K K} = \frac{\beta Q}{P_L L}$$

and hence

$$\frac{P_K K}{\alpha} = \frac{P_L L}{\beta} \quad \text{(divide both sides by } Q \text{ and turn both sides upside down)}$$

that is,

$$P_K K = \frac{\alpha}{\beta} P_L L \quad \text{(multiply through by } \alpha\text{)} \tag{7}$$

Substituting this into equation (6) gives

$$\frac{\alpha}{\beta}P_L L + P_L L = M$$

$$\alpha L + \beta L = \frac{\beta M}{P_L} \qquad \text{(multiply through by } \beta/P_L)$$

$$(\alpha + \beta)L = \frac{\beta M}{P_L} \qquad \text{(factorize)}$$

$$L = \frac{\beta M}{(\alpha + \beta)P_L} \qquad \text{(divide through by } \alpha + \beta)$$

Finally, we can put this into equation (7) to get

$$P_K K = \frac{\alpha M}{\alpha + \beta}$$

so

$$K = \frac{\alpha M}{(\alpha + \beta)P_K}$$

The values of K and L which optimize Q are therefore

$$\frac{\alpha M}{(\alpha + \beta)P_K} \quad \text{and} \quad \frac{\beta M}{(\alpha + \beta)P_L}$$

Practice Problem

3. Use Lagrange multipliers to find expressions for x_1 and x_2 which maximize the utility function

$$U = x_1^{1/2} + x_2^{1/2}$$

subject to the general budgetary constraint

$$P_1 x_1 + P_2 x_2 = M$$

The previous example illustrates the power of mathematics when solving economics problems. The main advantage of using algebra and calculus rather than just graphs and tables of numbers is their generality. In future, if we need to maximize any particular Cobb–Douglas production function subject to any particular cost constraint, then all we have to do is to quote the result of the previous example. By substituting specific values of M, α, β, P_K and P_L into the general formulas for K and L, we can write down the solution in a matter of seconds. In fact, we can use mathematics to generalize still further. Rather than work with production functions of a prescribed form such as

$$Q = AK^\alpha L^\beta$$

we can obtain results pertaining to any production function

$$Q = f(K, L)$$

For instance, we can use Lagrange multipliers to justify a result that we derived graphically in Section 5.5. At the beginning of that section we showed that when output is maximized subject to a cost constraint, the ratio of marginal product to price is the same for all inputs. To obtain this result using Lagrange multipliers we simply write down the Lagrangian function

$$g(K, L, \lambda) = f(K, L) + \lambda(M - P_K K - P_L L)$$

which corresponds to a production function

$$f(K, L)$$

and cost constraint

$$P_K K + P_L L = M$$

The simultaneous equations

$$\frac{\partial g}{\partial K} = 0, \quad \frac{\partial g}{\partial L} = 0, \quad \frac{\partial g}{\partial \lambda} = 0$$

are

$$\text{MP}_K - \lambda P_K = 0 \tag{1}$$
$$\text{MP}_L - \lambda P_L = 0 \tag{2}$$
$$M - P_K K - P_L L = 0 \tag{3}$$

because

$$\frac{\partial f}{\partial K} = \text{MP}_K \quad \text{and} \quad \frac{\partial f}{\partial K} = \text{MP}_L$$

Equations (1) and (2) can be rearranged to give

$$\lambda = \frac{\text{MP}_K}{P_K} \quad \text{and} \quad \lambda = \frac{\text{MP}_L}{P_L}$$

so

$$\frac{\text{MP}_K}{P_K} = \frac{\text{MP}_L}{P_L}$$

as required.

Key Terms

Lagrange multiplier   The number λ which is used in the Lagrangian function. In economics this gives the change in the value of the objective function when the value of the constraint is increased by 1 unit.

Lagrangian   The function $f(x, y) + \lambda[M - \varphi(x, y)]$, where $f(x, y)$ is the objective function and $\phi(x, y) = M$ is the constraint. The stationary point of this function is the solution of the associated constrained optimization problem.

Advice

There now follow some additional problems for you to try. If you feel that you need even more practice then you are advised to rework the questions in Section 5.5 using Lagrange multipliers.

Exercise 5.6

1. Use Lagrange multipliers to find the maximum value of

   $z = x + 2xy$

   subject to the constraint

   $x + 2y = 5$

2. **(a)** Use Lagrange multipliers to find the maximum value of

   $z = 4xy$

   subject to the constraint

   $x + 2y = 40$

   State the associated values of x, y and λ.

   (b) Repeat part (a) when the constraint is changed to

   $x + 2y = 41$

   (c) Verify that the value of the Lagrange multiplier in part (a) is approximately the same as the change in the optimal value of z when the right-hand side of the constraint is increased by one unit.

3. A firm's production function is given by

   $Q = KL$

   Unit capital and labour costs are \$2 and \$1 respectively. Find the maximum level of output if the total cost of capital and labour is \$6.

4. A monopolistic producer of two goods, G1 and G2, has a total cost function

   $TC = 5Q_1 + 10Q_2$

   where Q_1 and Q_2 denote the quantities of G1 and G2 respectively. If P_1 and P_2 denote the corresponding prices then the demand equations are

   $P_1 = 50 - Q_1 - Q_2$
   $P_2 = 100 - Q_1 - 4Q_2$

   Find the maximum profit if the firm's total costs are fixed at \$100. Estimate the new optimal profit if total costs rise to \$101.

Exercise 5.6*

1. A firm that manufactures speciality bicycles has a profit function

    $$\pi = 5x^2 - 10xy + 3y^2 + 240x$$

    where x denotes the number of frames and y denotes the number of wheels. Find the maximum profit assuming that the firm does not want any spare frames or wheels left over at the end of the production run.

2. Find the maximum value of

    $$Q = 10\sqrt{(KL)}$$

    subject to the cost constraint

    $$K + 4L = 16$$

    Estimate the change in the optimal value of Q if the cost constraint is changed to

    $$K + 4L = 17$$

3. A consumer's utility function is given by

    $$U = \alpha \ln x_1 + \beta \ln x_2$$

    Find the values of x_1 and x_2 which maximize U subject to the budgetary constraint

    $$P_1 x_1 + P_2 x_2 = M$$

4. An advertising agency spends $\$x$ on a newspaper campaign and a further $\$y$ promoting its client's products on local radio. It receives 15% commission on all sales that the client receives. The agency has $\$10\,000$ to spend in total, and the client earns $\$M$ from its sales, where

    $$M = \frac{100\,000x}{50 + x} + \frac{40\,000y}{30 + y}$$

    Use the method of Lagrange multipliers to determine how much should be spent on advertising in newspapers and on radio to maximize the agency's net income. Give your answers correct to 2 decimal places.

5. A firm produces three goods, A, B and C. The number of items of each are x, y and z, respectively. The firm is committed to producing a total number of 30 items of types A and B. The firm's associated profit function is

    $$\pi = 8x + 12y + 4z - 0.5x^2 - 0.5y^2 - z^2$$

    How many goods of each type must be produced to maximize profit subject to the constraint?

6. A firm decides to invest x units of capital in project A and y units in project B. The expected return for one unit of investment is \$400 in project A and \$800 in project B. However, in order to meet the expectations of the firm's ethical and environmental policy the values of x and y must satisfy the constraint

$$x^2 + y^2 - 4x - 6y = 195$$

How many units of each type should the firm buy in order to maximize total return?

Section B

Probability and Statistics

CHAPTER ONE

INTRODUCTION AND DATA COLLECTION

LEARNING OBJECTIVES

This chapter will help you learn:

- How statistics is used in business
- The sources of data used in business
- The types of data used in business
- The basics of Microsoft Excel
- The basics of Minitab

1.1 WHY LEARN STATISTICS

People use numbers every day to describe or analyze the world we live in. For example, consider these recent headlines:

- "Why Experts Are Concerned about the Growing Tendency of Employees to Work on Vacation" (K. Stech, *Newsday*, September 4, 2006, p. F4)—Twenty-one percent of employees work sometimes, often, or very often on vacation, and 43% return feeling overwhelmed by all they have to do.
- "Americans Gulping More Bottled Water" (*USA Today*, February 28, 2007, p. 1D)—The annual per capita consumption of bottled water has increased from 18.8 gallons in 2001 to 28.3 gallons in 2006.
- "Paying More with Plastic" (*USA Today*, March 6, 2007, p. 1D)—Consumer payment with credit cards increased from 18% in 1995 to 25% in 2005, while payment in cash decreased to 14% from 21%.
- "The Real Most Valuable Players" (R. Adams, *The Wall Street Journal*, April 14, 2007, pp. P1, P4)—Economists have developed models to predict the real value of player performance and have related it to player salary.

You will make better sense of the numbers in the stories behind these headlines if you understand statistics. **Statistics** is the branch of mathematics that transforms numbers into useful information for decision makers. Statistics provides a way of understanding and then reducing—but not eliminating—the variation that is part of any decision-making process, and also can tell you the known risks associated with making a decision.

Statistics does this by providing a set of methods for analyzing the numbers. These methods help you to find patterns in "the numbers" and enable you to determine whether differences in "the numbers" are just due to chance. As you learn these methods, you will also learn the appropriate conditions for using those methods. And because so many statistical methods must be computerized in order to be of practical benefit, as you learn statistics you also need to learn about the programs that help apply statistics in the business world.

1.2 STATISTICS IN THE BUSINESS WORLD

In the business world, statistics has four important applications:

- To summarize business data
- To draw conclusions from that data
- To make reliable forecasts about business activities
- To improve business processes

The field of statistics consists of two branches, descriptive statistics and inferential statistics.

Descriptive statistics focuses on collecting, summarizing, presenting and analyzing a set of data. You are probably familiar with presentations such as tables and charts, and statistics such as the mean and median from your previous school experience.

Inferential statistics uses data that have been collected from a small group to draw conclusions about a larger group. These methods are used to make decisions about which investment might lead to a higher return and what marketing strategy might lead to increased sales.

Looking at the first bulleted point above, descriptive statistics allows you to create different tables and charts to summarize your data. It also provides statistical measures such as the mean, median, and standard deviation to describe different characteristics of your data.

Drawing conclusions from your data is the heart of inferential statistics. Using these methods enables you to make decisions based on data rather than just on intuition.

Making reliable forecasts involves developing statistical models for prediction. These models enable you to develop more accurate predictions of future activities.

Improving business processes involves using managerial approaches that focus on quality improvement such as Six Sigma. These approaches are data-driven and use statistical methods as an integral part of the quality improvement approach.

To help you develop the necessary skills for making better decisions, every chapter of *Basic Business Statistics* has a Using Statistics scenario. Although the scenarios are fictional, they represent realistic situations in which you will be asked to make decisions while using Microsoft Excel or Minitab to transform data into statistical information. For example, in one chapter, you will be asked to decide the location in a supermarket that best enhances sales of a cola drink, and in another chapter, you will be asked to forecast sales for a clothing store.

USING STATISTICS @ Good Tunes

Good Tunes, a growing four-store home entertainment systems retailer, seeks to double their number of stores within the next three years. The managers have decided to approach local area banks for the funding needed to underwrite this expansion. They need to prepare an electronic slide show and a formal prospectus that will argue that Good Tunes is a thriving business and a good candidate for expansion.

You have been asked to assist in the process of preparing the slide show and prospectus. What data should you include that will convince bankers to extend the credit that Good Tunes needs? How should you present that data?

In this scenario, you must identify the most relevant data for the bankers. Because Good Tunes is an ongoing business, you can start by reviewing the company's records, which show both its current and past status. Because Good Tunes is a retailer, presenting data about the company's sales seems a reasonable thing to do. You could include the details of every sales transaction that has occurred for the past few years as a way of demonstrating that Good Tunes is a thriving business.

However, presenting the bankers with the thousands of transactions would overwhelm them and not be very useful. As mentioned in Section 1.1, you need to transform the transactions data into information by summarizing the details of each transaction in some useful way that would allow the bankers to (perhaps) uncover a favorable pattern about the sales over time.

One piece of information that the bankers would presumably want to see is the yearly dollar sales totals. Tallying and totaling sales is a common process of transforming data into information. When you tally sales—or any other relevant data about Good Tunes you choose to use—you follow normal business practice and tally by a business period such as by month, quarter, or year. When you do so, you end up with multiple values: sales for this year, sales for last year, sales for the year before that, and so on. How to determine the best way to refer to these multiple values requires learning the basic vocabulary of statistics.

1.3 BASIC VOCABULARY OF STATISTICS

Variables are characteristics of items or individuals and are what you analyze when you use a statistical method. For the Good Tunes scenario, sales, expenses by year, and net profit by year are variables that the bankers would want to analyze.

VARIABLE

A **variable** is a characteristic of an item or individual.

When used in everyday speech, *variable* suggests that something changes or varies, and you would expect the sales, expenses, and net profit to have different values from year to year. These different values are the **data** associated with a variable, and more simply, the "data" to be analyzed.

Variables can differ for reasons other than time. For example, if you conducted an analysis of the composition of a large lecture class, you would probably want to include the variables class standing, gender, and major field of study. These variables would vary, too, because each student in the class is different. One student might be a sophomore, male, economics major, while another may be a junior, female, finance major.

You also need to remember that values are meaningless unless their variables have **operational definitions**. These definitions are universally accepted meanings that are clear to all associated with an analysis. Even though the operational definition for sales per year might seem clear, miscommunication could occur if one person was referring to sales per year for the entire chain of stores and another to sales per year per store. Even individual values for variables sometimes need definition—for the class standing variable, for example, what *exactly* is meant by the words *sophomore* and *junior?* (Perhaps the most famous example of vague definitions was the definition of a valid vote in the state of Florida during the 2000 U.S. presidential election. Vagueness about the operational definitions there ultimately required a U.S. Supreme Court ruling.)

Four other basic vocabulary terms are population, sample, parameter, and statistic.

POPULATION

A **population** consists of all the items or individuals about which you want to draw a conclusion.

SAMPLE

A **sample** is the portion of a population selected for analysis.

PARAMETER

A **parameter** is a numerical measure that describes a characteristic of a population.

STATISTIC

A **statistic** is a numerical measure that describes a characteristic of a sample.

All the Good Tunes sales transactions for a specific year, all the customers who shopped at Good Tunes this weekend, all the full-time students enrolled in a college, and all the registered voters in Ohio are examples of populations. Examples of samples from these four populations would be 200 Good Tunes sales transactions randomly selected by an auditor for study, 30 Good Tunes customers asked to complete a customer satisfaction survey, 50 full-time students selected for a marketing study, and 500 registered voters in Ohio contacted via telephone for a political poll. In each sample, the transactions or people in the sample represent a portion of the items or individuals that make up the population.

The mean amount spent by all customers who shopped at Good Tunes this weekend is an example of a parameter because the amount spent in the entire population is needed. In contrast, the mean amount spent by the 30 customers completing the customer satisfaction survey is an example of a statistic because the amount spent by only the sample of 30 people is required.

Coming Attractions

From the Authors' Desktop

If you are someone who likes to skim quickly through a book to learn a book's organization, you should know that we have organized the chapters of this book according to the four business tasks first listed in Section 1.2. We use those tasks—summarizing business data, drawing conclusions from that data, making reliable forecasts about business activities, and improving business processes—as a way of organizing our chapters.

Chapters 1 through 3 discuss methods of presenting and describing information. Chapters 4 through 12 and Chapter 17 discuss drawing conclusions about populations using sample information. Chapters 13 through 16 provide ways of making reliable forecasts and Chapter 18 introduces you to how you can apply statistical methods to improve business processes.

Don't worry if your instructor does not cover all of these chapters—introductory business statistics courses vary in their scope, length, and number of college credits. Tradi-tionally, instructors start with descriptive statistics because some of these methods may already be familiar to you from everyday activities and that's the main reason we've put them in the first three chapters. Chapter 4 discusses probability concepts that are needed in Chapters 5 through 7. Chapters 8 through 12 cover inferential statistics. Chapter 8 introduces the confidence interval approach, while Chapter 9 develops the fundamental hypothesis testing concepts that are expanded on in Chapters 10 through 12. Understanding these concepts will allow you to fully answer questions such as "How can you make decisions about the many based on a few?"—a question business people uneducated in statistics often ask when they challenge the use of statistics. Chapters 13 through 16 cover regression and time-series models that are used to make reliable forecasts. Chapter 13 develops the simple regression model, while Chapters 14 through 16 expand the simple model to more complex situations. Chapter 18 provides some background into the total quality management and Six Sigma quality improvement approaches and introduces statistical methods used in quality improvement.

Remember that the goal of this book is *not* for you to become a statistician. The goal is to help you understand and apply appropriately the statistical methods commonly used in the area of business in which you are most interested—be it accounting, economics, finance, information systems, marketing, or management.

By the way, if you are the type of person who likes to read the last page of a book first, please don't. Introductory business statistics is somewhat cumulative and if you jump to the back of the book, you may find things a bit puzzling if you are only just beginning to learn statistics. So if you have happened to notice things such as strange-looking tables, don't fret—by the time you get to the point in this book where you need to use such tables, you will know how to use them effectively.

1.4 DATA COLLECTION

The managers at Good Tunes believe that they will have a stronger argument for expansion if they can show the bankers that the customers of Good Tunes are highly satisfied with the service they received. How could the managers demonstrate that good service was the typical customer experience at Good Tunes?

In the Good Tunes scenario on page 3, sales per year was automatically collected as part of normal business activities. The managers now face the twin challenges to first identify relevant variables for a customer satisfaction study and then devise a method for **data collection**, that is, collecting the values for those variables.

Many different types of circumstances, such as the following, require data collection:

- A marketing research analyst needs to assess the effectiveness of a new television advertisement.
- A pharmaceutical manufacturer needs to determine whether a new drug is more effective than those currently in use.
- An operations manager wants to improve a manufacturing process.
- An auditor wants to review the financial transactions of a company in order to determine whether the company is in compliance with generally accepted accounting principles.

In each of these examples, and for the Good Tunes managers as well, collecting data from every item or individual in the population would be too difficult or too time-consuming. Because this is the typical case, data collection almost always involves collecting data from a sample. (Chapter 7 discusses methods of sample selection.)

Data sources are classified as being either **primary sources** or **secondary sources**. When the data collector is the one using the data for analysis, the source is primary. When the person performing the statistical analysis is not the data collector, the source is secondary. Organizations and individuals that collect and publish data typically use that data as a primary source and then let others use it as a secondary source. For example, the United States federal government collects and distributes data in this way for both public and private purposes. The Bureau of Labor Statistics collects data on employment and also distributes the monthly consumer price index. The Census Bureau oversees a variety of ongoing surveys regarding population, housing, and manufacturing and undertakes special studies on topics such as crime, travel, and health care.

Sources of data fall into one of four categories:

- Data distributed by an organization or an individual
- A designed experiment
- A survey
- An observational study

Market research firms and trade associations distribute data pertaining to specific industries or markets. Investment services such as Mergent (see **www.mergent.com**) provide financial data on a company-by-company basis. Syndicated services such as AC Nielsen provide clients with data that enables the comparison of client products with those of their competitors. Daily newspapers are filled with numerical information regarding stock prices, weather conditions, and sports statistics.

Outcomes of a designed experiment are another data source. These outcomes are the result of an experiment, such as a test of several laundry detergents to compare how well each detergent removes a certain type of stain. Developing proper experimental designs is a subject mostly beyond the scope of this book because such designs often involve sophisticated statistical procedures. However, some of the fundamental experimental design concepts are discussed in Chapters 10 through 12.

Conducting a survey is a third type of data source. People being surveyed are asked questions about their beliefs, attitudes, behaviors, and other characteristics. For example, people could be asked their opinion about which laundry detergent best removes a certain type of stain. (This could lead to a result different from a designed experiment seeking the same answer.)

Conducting an observational study is the fourth important data source. A researcher collects data by directly observing a behavior, usually in a natural or neutral setting. Observational studies are a common tool for data collection in business. For example, market researchers use

FIGURE 1.1

Questions about the Good Tunes customer experience

1. How many days did it take from the time you ordered your merchandise to the time you received it?_____

2. Did you buy any merchandise that was featured in the Good Tunes Sunday newspaper sales flyer for the week of your purchase? Yes _____ No_____

3. Was this your first purchase at Good Tunes? Yes _____ No_____

4. Are you likely to buy additional merchandise from Good Tunes in the next 12 months? Yes _____ No_____

5. How much money (in U.S. dollars) do you expect to spend on stereo and consumer electronics equipment in the next 12 months?_____

6. How do you rate the overall service provided by Good Tunes with respect to your recent purchase?

Excellent ☐   Very good ☐   Fair ☐   Poor ☐

7. How do you rate the selection of products offered by Good Tunes with respect to other retailers of home entertainment systems?

Excellent ☐   Very good ☐   Fair ☐   Poor ☐

8. How do you rate the quality of the items you recently purchased from Good Tunes?

Excellent ☐   Very good ☐   Fair ☐   Poor ☐

focus groups to elicit unstructured responses to open-ended questions posed by a moderator to a target audience. Observational study techniques are also used to enhance teamwork or improve the quality of products and services.

Identifying the most appropriate source is a critical task because if biases, ambiguities, or other types of errors flaw the data being collected, even the most sophisticated statistical methods will not produce useful information. For the Good Tunes example, variables relevant to the customer experience could take the form of survey questions related to various aspects of the customer experience, examples of which are shown in Figure 1.1. The survey might also ask questions that seek to classify customers into groups for later analysis.

One good way for Good Tunes to avoid data-collection flaws would be to distribute the questionnaire to a random sample of customers (Chapter 7 explains how to collect a random sample). A poor way would be to rely on a business-rating Web site that allows online visitors to rate a merchant. Such Web sites cannot provide assurance that those who do the ratings are representative of the population of customers, or that they even *are* customers.

The Buzz about Web Surveys

From the Authors' Desktop

Many marketers have become interested in using Web-based surveys and ratings sites to promote their products and services. Although many Internet users visit these sites, they give little thought to the use and misuse of such sites.

Not knowing how the data have been collected makes all of the information on such sites suspect. *The New York Times* has reported that Internet travel sites now closely monitor submitted reviews to avoid fraudulent claims (C. Elliott, "Hotel Reviews Online: In Bed with Hope, Half-Truths and Hype," *The New York Times*, February 7, 2006, pp. C1, C8). However, it's hard to imagine how such sites can offset the influence of offers such as one made by a Key West (Florida) hotel that offered guests a 10% discount if they posted a rave review on a particular travel Web site! Other articles, including one by the travel writer Arthur Frommer, have noted how unscrupulous marketers have manipulated the "buzz" on the Internet to either promote or undermine the reputation of specific travel companies (A. Frommer, "Be Careful about Public Web Site Comments," *Palm Beach Post*, February 25, 2007, p. E3).

Even when shielded from unscrupulous marketers, Web-based surveys can produce suspect results, if the survey is conducted inappropriately. In redesigning Microsoft Office 2007, Microsoft personnel explained that they had been influenced by the anonymous data that an ongoing "customer experience improvement program" had collected. Noting that experienced users usually decline the opportunity to participate in that program, at least one commentator suggested that the data collected were somehow *biased*, unrepresentative of the population of all Microsoft Office users.

Have you ever received a request asking you to rate a business or post an online opinion? Are you more or less likely to do so if asked directly? And would receiving an incentive, as the Key West hotel offered, affect your actions? When writing an early draft of this section, one of the authors received a message from Marriott International that urged all to rate the Marriott travel loyalty program a perfect "10" in the voting for the Freddie Awards sponsored by *InsideFlyer* magazine. Even though he had never heard of the awards or the magazine, he went online and voted. Only later did he learn that the magazine and its awards were targeted to businesspeople who frequently travel. He wondered how his "infrequent flyer" opinion would color the results. (In the end, Marriott International was happy—it won numerous "Freddies" and even sent a note to its customers thanking them for helping in the voting.)

If you do use a rating Web site, be sure to check out the "fine print" on your next visit. How does the Web site collect its ratings? What business relationships does the Web site have with the businesses that are rated on the site? Most Web sites explain their online privacy policy. Perhaps they should also explain their online "data collection policy."

1.5 TYPES OF VARIABLES

Statisticians classify variables as either being categorical or numerical and further classify numerical variables as having either discrete or continuous values. Figure 1.2 shows the relationships and provides examples of each type of variable.

FIGURE 1.2

Types of variables

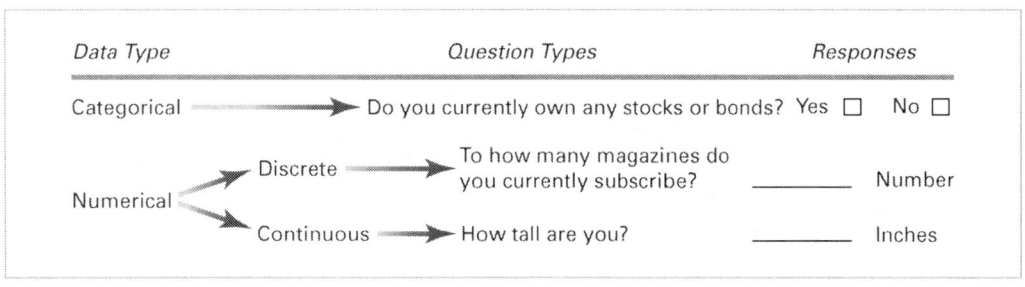

Data Type	Question Types	Responses
Categorical	Do you currently own any stocks or bonds?	Yes ☐ No ☐
Numerical — Discrete	To how many magazines do you currently subscribe?	_____ Number
Numerical — Continuous	How tall are you?	_____ Inches

Categorical variables (also known as **qualitative variables**) have values that can only be placed into categories, such as yes and no. "Do you currently own stocks and bonds?" and Questions 2 through 4 in Figure 1.1 are examples of categorical variables, all of which have yes or no as their values. Categorical variables can also have more than two possible responses. For example, you could ask customers to indicate the day of the week on which they made their purchases. In Figure 1.1, there are four possible responses to Questions 6 through 8.

Numerical variables (also known as **quantitative variables**) have values that represent quantities. For example, Questions 1 and 5 in Figure 1.1 are numerical variables. Numerical variables are further subdivided as discrete or continuous variables.

Discrete variables have numerical values that arise from a counting process. "The number of magazines subscribed to" is an example of a discrete numerical variable because the response is one of a finite number of integers. You subscribe to zero, one, two, and so on magazines. The number of items that a customer purchases is also a discrete numerical variable because you are counting the number of items purchased.

Continuous variables produce numerical responses that arise from a measuring process. The time you wait for teller service at a bank is an example of a continuous numerical variable because the response takes on any value within a *continuum*, or interval, depending on the precision of the measuring instrument. For example, your waiting time could be 1 minute, 1.1 minutes, 1.11 minutes, or 1.113 minutes, depending on the precision of the measuring device you use.

Theoretically, with sufficient precision of measurement, no two continuous values are identical. As a practical matter, however, most measuring devices are not precise enough to detect small differences, and tied values for a continuous variable (i.e., two or more items or individuals with the same value) are often found in experimental or survey data.

Levels of Measurement and Measurement Scales

Using levels of measurement is another way of classifying data. There are four widely recognized levels of measurement: nominal, ordinal, interval, and ratio scales.

Nominal and Ordinal Scales

Data from a categorical variable are measured on a nominal scale or on an ordinal scale. A **nominal scale** (see Figure 1.3) classifies data into distinct categories in which no ranking is implied. In the Good Tunes customer satisfaction survey, the answer to the question "Are you likely to buy additional merchandise from Good Tunes in the next 12 months?" is an example of a nominal scaled variable, as are your favorite soft drink, your political party affiliation, and your gender. Nominal scaling is the weakest form of measurement because you cannot specify any ranking across the various categories.

FIGURE 1.3

Examples of nominal scales

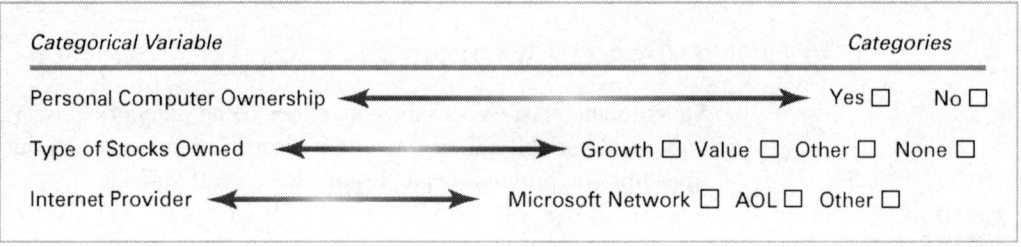

An **ordinal scale** classifies data into distinct categories in which ranking is implied. In the Good Tunes survey, the answers to the question "How do you rate the overall service provided by Good Tunes with respect to your recent purchase?" represent an ordinal scaled variable because the responses "excellent, very good, fair, and poor" are ranked in order of satisfaction level. Figure 1.4 lists other examples of ordinal scaled variables.

FIGURE 1.4

Examples of ordinal scales

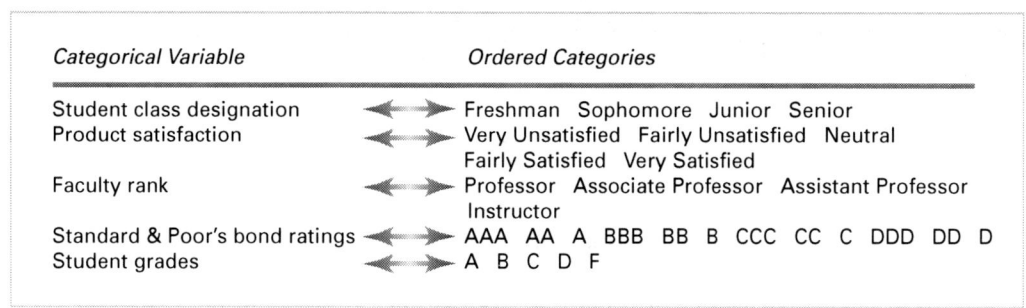

Ordinal scaling is a stronger form of measurement than nominal scaling because an observed value classified into one category possesses more of a property than does an observed value classified into another category. However, ordinal scaling is still a relatively weak form of measurement because the scale does not account for the amount of the differences *between* the categories. The ordering implies only *which* category is "greater," "better," or "more preferred"—not by *how much*.

Interval and Ratio Scales   Data from a numerical variable are measured on an interval or a ratio scale. An **interval scale** (see Figure 1.5) is an ordered scale in which the difference between measurements is a meaningful quantity but does not involve a true zero point. For example, a noontime temperature reading of 67 degrees Fahrenheit is 2 degrees warmer than a noontime reading of 65 degrees. In addition, the 2 degrees Fahrenheit difference in the noontime temperature readings is the same as if the two noontime temperature readings were 74 and 76 degrees Fahrenheit because the difference has the same meaning anywhere on the scale.

FIGURE 1.5

Examples of interval and ratio scales

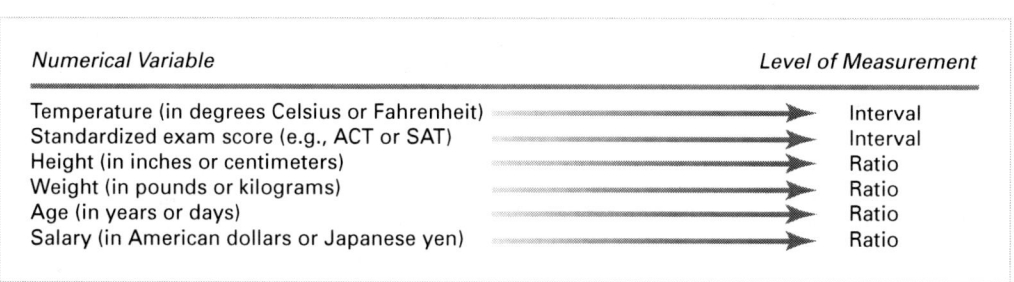

A **ratio scale** is an ordered scale in which the difference between the measurements involves a true zero point, as in height, weight, age, or salary measurements. In the Good Tunes customer satisfaction survey, the amount of money (in U.S. dollars) you expect to spend on stereo equipment in the next 12 months is an example of a ratio scaled variable. As another example, a person who weighs 240 pounds is twice as heavy as someone who weighs 120 pounds. Temperature is a trickier case: Fahrenheit and Celsius (centigrade) scales are interval but not ratio scales; the "zero" value is arbitrary, not real. You cannot say that a noontime temperature reading of 4 degrees Fahrenheit is twice as hot as 2 degrees Fahrenheit. But a Kelvin temperature reading, in which zero degrees means no molecular motion, is ratio scaled. In contrast, the Fahrenheit and Celsius scales use arbitrarily selected zero-degree beginning points.

Data measured on an interval scale or on a ratio scale constitute the highest levels of measurement. They are stronger forms of measurement than an ordinal scale because you can determine not only which observed value is the largest but also by how much.

PROBLEMS FOR SECTION 1.5

Learning the Basics

1.1 Three different beverages are sold at a fast-food restaurant—soft drinks, tea, and coffee.
a. Explain why the type of beverage sold is an example of a categorical variable.
b. Explain why the type of beverage sold is an example of a nominal scaled variable.

1.2 Soft drinks are sold in three sizes at a fast-food restaurant—small, medium, and large. Explain why the size of the soft drink is an example of an ordinal scaled variable.

1.3 Suppose that you measure the time it takes to download an MP3 file from the Internet.
a. Explain why the download time is a continuous numerical variable.
b. Explain why the download time is a ratio scaled variable.

Applying the Concepts

SELF Test **1.4** For each of the following variables, determine whether the variable is categorical or numerical. If the variable is numerical, determine whether the variable is discrete or continuous. In addition, determine the level of measurement for each of the following.
a. Number of telephones per household
b. Length of the longest long-distance call made per month
c. Whether someone in the household owns a cell phone
d. Whether there is a high-speed Internet connection in the household

1.5 The following information is collected from students upon exiting the campus bookstore during the first week of classes:
a. Amount of time spent shopping in the bookstore
b. Number of textbooks purchased
c. Academic major
d. Gender
Classify each of these variables as categorical or numerical. If the variable is numerical, determine whether the variable is discrete or continuous. In addition, determine the level of measurement for these variables.

1.6 For each of the following variables, determine whether the variable is categorical or numerical. If the variable is numerical, determine whether the variable is discrete or continuous. In addition, determine the level of measurement for each of the following.
a. Name of Internet provider
b. Amount of time spent surfing the Internet per week

c. Number of e-mails received in a week
d. Number of online purchases made in a month

1.7 For each of the following variables, determine whether the variable is categorical or numerical. If the variable is numerical, determine whether the variable is discrete or continuous. In addition, determine the level of measurement for each of the following.
a. Amount of money spent on clothing in the past month
b. Favorite department store
c. Most likely time period during which shopping for clothing takes place (weekday, weeknight, or weekend)
d. Number of pairs of shoes owned

1.8 Suppose the following information is collected from Robert Keeler on his application for a home mortgage loan at the Metro County Savings and Loan Association:
a. Monthly payments: $1,427
b. Number of jobs in past 10 years: 1
c. Annual family income: $86,000
d. Marital status: Married
Classify each of the responses by type of data and level of measurement.

1.9 One of the variables most often included in surveys is income. Sometimes the question is phrased "What is your income (in thousands of dollars)?" In other surveys, the respondent is asked to "Place an X in the circle corresponding to your income level" and given a number of income ranges from which to choose.
a. In the first format, explain why income might be considered either discrete or continuous.
b. Which of these two formats would you prefer to use if you were conducting a survey? Why?
c. Which of these two formats would likely bring you a greater rate of response? Why?

1.10 If two students score a 90 on the same examination, what arguments could be used to show that the underlying variable—test score—is continuous?

1.11 The director of market research at a large department store chain wanted to conduct a survey throughout a metropolitan area to determine the amount of time working women spend shopping for clothing in a typical month.
a. Describe both the population and the sample of interest, and indicate the type of data the director might want to collect.
b. Develop a first draft of the questionnaire needed in (a) by writing a series of three categorical questions and three numerical questions that you feel are appropriate for this survey.

1.6 BUSINESS STATISTICS AND COMPUTERS

During the past 30 years, computerization has made practical the application of new statistical methods that require complex calculations and the collection and analysis of very large sets of data. As the cost of computer processing has dropped over time, the use of these new methods has migrated from those few who were fortunate to have access to specialized "statistical" calculators or large mainframe computers to all those using a typical desktop PC. Statistical functionality is so commonplace today that many simple statistical tasks, once done exclusively with pencil and paper or simple hand calculators, are now done electronically with the assistance of an appropriate computer program.

Minitab and Microsoft Excel are examples of desktop PC programs that people use for statistics. Minitab is an example of a **statistical package**, a program engineered from the ground up to perform statistical analysis as accurately as possible. Microsoft Excel is a general purpose data analysis program found in Microsoft Office that evolved from electronic spreadsheets used in accounting and financial applications. Today Excel is a multifunction data analysis tool. Typical of a general purpose tool, Excel can perform many functions, but none as well as other programs that are more singularly focused (see References 1, 2, and 5). Minitab and Excel are two very different programs and their differences have led to an ongoing debate in business schools about which program is more appropriate for teaching introductory statistics. Adherents of each program point to their program's strengths: Minitab as a complete statistical solution; Excel as a common desktop tool found in many business functional areas (and in many different business school courses).

Although you are probably more familiar with Microsoft Excel than with Minitab, you may be surprised to learn that that both programs share many similarities. This is no coincidence as Minitab was inspired by Omnitab, a mainframe computer program from the 1960s that can be considered an ancestor to all electronic spreadsheet programs. Both Minitab and Excel use **worksheets** (their name for spreadsheets) to store the data you have collected for analysis. Worksheets are tabular arrangements of data, in which the intersections of rows and columns form **cells**, boxes into which you make entries. In Minitab, the data for each variable are placed in individual columns, and this also is the standard practice when using Excel. (The Excel instructions in this book assume this standard practice.) Both Excel and Minitab allow you to save worksheets, programming information, and results in one file, called **workbooks** in Excel and **projects** in Minitab.

Among their differences, Excel uses worksheets to store certain programming information as well as to present results of a statistical analysis whereas Minitab generally displays these things in separate windows. Minitab allows you to save individual worksheets in separate Minitab worksheet (.mtw) files. (The Student CD-ROM packaged with this book contains the data for problems and chapter examples as both Excel workbook files and Minitab worksheet files.)

Because the details of using Microsoft Excel and Minitab differ, you will find at the end of every chapter separate appendices for Microsoft Excel, PHStat2 (the Excel add-in that simplifies your use of Excel as explained in Section P1.1 on page 22), and Minitab. These appendices will help you to re-create the in-chapter examples and help solve the problems listed in the chapter. Should you be new to computing, you can review Appendix C that discusses the minimal computing skills you need to operate Excel (with or without PHStat2) or Minitab effectively. Appendix C also reviews the conventions used to describe computer operations.

If you use the Microsoft Excel appendices, you will occasionally find paired sections—one that gives instructions for Excel 97, 2000, 2002, or 2003; and the other that gives instructions for Excel 2007—that reflect changes Microsoft has made to Office 2007.

Regardless of which program you end up using, be aware that using computer programs to assist in statistical decision making is a necessary and commonplace occurrence in business today.

Learning to Use Programs *Properly*

From the Authors' Desktop

When you learn something, you usually get feedback that you use constructively to improve your productivity. Providing feedback is one reason instructors give tests. When you get the results of a test, you can reflect on how well you have properly learned the subject matter. Unfortunately, when learning to use programs such as Microsoft Excel or Minitab while studying business statistics, feedback opportunities can be rare. You either get a usable result (good) or fail to do so (bad). This good–bad, pass–fail type of feedback cannot help you to acquire the skills and good habits you need to use programs effectively. We hope the following checklist will.

You are using programs *properly* if you can:

1. Understand how to operate the program. You will not get far if you have not mastered the mechanical tasks of working with a program. These tasks include how to start the program, load or enter data, and select commands or otherwise instruct the program what you want it to do for you.

The end-of-chapter Sections E1, P1, and M1 introduce you to the tasks you need for using either Microsoft Excel or Minitab. Begin with these tasks and don't waste your time teaching yourself every command or trying to memorize every program function. Learn about additional features in a just-in-time fashion, that is, only when you need to use them. In addition, if you own or manage the computer that you use, know how to use the Internet to retrieve and apply program updates and to get technical assistance.

2. Understand the underlying statistical concepts. Make sure you understand what a program is doing as it creates its information. As a minimum, be informed about what each menu selection you make does or calculates. Be knowledgeable enough to be able to justify your choice of using a particular statistical method. Don't rely on memorizing keystroke or mouse clicks alone.

3. Understand how to organize and present information. Plan how you are going to store and use your data for analysis. Think about how to best arrange and label your data. If using Microsoft Excel, place results on their own worksheets, apart from the worksheet used to store the data to be analyzed. Also think about using worksheet and chart formatting features (see Section E1.1 on page 16 and Section E1.2 on page 17) to enhance the visual presentation and to correct formatting errors that Excel makes. If using Minitab, think about the organization and visual layout of your saved project files.

4. Know how to review results for errors. Never assume that any results you create in a program are free of errors. Always review results for obvious errors such as "impossible" results (a mean smaller than any data value). If you have entered formulas into a worksheet, examine them individually, looking for errors.

5. Make secure and clearly named backups of your work. Make backup copies of your work on a regular basis. Physically separate the backup copies by writing to a separate disk; two copies of a file on the same disk is not an example of a true backup. Do not name files or backups "file1" or "my file" or other names that do not clearly identify your work.

SUMMARY

In this chapter, you have been introduced to the role of statistics in turning data into information and the importance of using computer programs such as Microsoft Excel and Minitab. In addition, you have studied data collection and the various types of data used in business. In conjunction with the Using Statistics scenario, you were asked to review the customer survey used by the Good Tunes company (see page 6). The first and fifth questions of the survey shown will produce numerical data. Questions 2 through 4 will produce nominal categorical data. Questions 6 through 8 will produce ordinal categorical data. The responses to the first question (number of days) are discrete, and the responses to the fifth question (amount of money spent) are continuous. In the next two chapters, tables and charts and a variety of descriptive numerical measures that are useful for data analysis are developed.

KEY TERMS

categorical variables
cell
continuous variable
data
data collection
descriptive statistics
discrete variables
inferential statistics
interval scale
nominal scale

numerical variables
operational definition
ordinal scale
parameter
population
primary source
projects
qualitative variables
quantitative variables
ratio scale

sample
secondary source
statistic
statistical package
statistics
variable
workbooks
worksheets

CHAPTER REVIEW PROBLEMS

Checking Your Understanding

1.12 What is the difference between a sample and a population?

1.13 What is the difference between a statistic and a parameter?

1.14 What is the difference between descriptive and inferential statistics?

1.15 What is the difference between a categorical variable and a numerical variable?

1.16 What is the difference between a discrete variable and a continuous variable?

1.17 What is an operational definition and why is it so important?

1.18 What are the four levels of measurement scales?

Applying the Concepts

1.19 The Data and Story Library, **lib.stat.cmu.edu/DASL**, is an online library of data files and stories that illustrate the use of basic statistical methods. The stories are classified by method and by topic. Go to this site and click on **List all topics**. Pick a story and summarize how statistics were used in the story.

1.20 Go to the official Microsoft Excel Web site, **www.microsoft.com/office/excel**, or the official Minitab Web site, **www.minitab.com**. Explain how you think Microsoft Excel or Minitab could be useful in the field of statistics.

1.21 The Gallup organization releases the results of recent polls at its Web site, **www.galluppoll.com**. Go to this site and read today's top story.
a. Describe the population of interest.
b. Describe the sample that was collected.
c. Describe a parameter of interest.
d. Describe the statistic used to describe the parameter in (c).

1.22 According to its homepage, "Swivel is a place where curious people explore data—all kinds of data." Go to **www.swivel.com** and explore a data set of interest to you.
a. Which of the four sources of data best describes the source of the data set you selected?
b. Describe a variable in the data set you selected.
c. Is the variable categorical or numerical?
d. If the variable in (c) is numerical, is it discrete or continuous?

1.23 At the U.S. Census Bureau site, **www.census.gov**, click **Survey of Business Owners** in the "Business & Industry" section and read about The Survey of Business Owners. Click on **Sample SBO-1 Form** to view a survey form.
a. Give an example of a categorical variable found in this survey.
b. Give an example of a numerical variable found in this survey.
c. Is the variable you selected in (b) discrete or continuous?

1.24 An online survey of almost 53,000 people (N. Hellmich, "Americans Go for the Quick Fix for Dinner," *USA Today*, February 14, 2005, p. B1) indicated that 37% decide what to make for dinner at home at the last minute and that the amount of time to prepare dinner averages 12 minutes, while the amount of time to cook dinner averages 28 minutes.
a. Which of the four categories of data sources listed in Section 1.4 on page 6 do you think were used in this study?
b. Name a categorical variable discussed in this article.
c. Name a numerical variable discussed in this article.

1.25 Three professors at Northern Kentucky University compared two different approaches to teaching courses in the school of business (M. W. Ford, D. W. Kent, and S. Devoto, "Learning from the Pros: Influence of Web-Based Expert Commentary on Vicarious Learning about Financial Markets," *Decision Sciences Journal of Innovative Education*, January 2007, 5(1), 43–63). At the time of the study, there were 2,100 students in the business school and 96 students were involved in the study. Demographic data collected on these 96 students included class (freshman, sophomore, junior, senior), age, gender, and major.
a. Describe the population of interest.
b. Describe the sample that was collected.
c. For each of the four demographic variables mentioned above, indicate if they are categorical or numerical.
d. For each of the four demographic variables, indicate their level of measurement.

1.26 A manufacturer of cat food was planning to survey households in the United States to determine purchasing habits of cat owners. Among the questions to be included are those that relate to
1. where cat food is primarily purchased.
2. whether dry or moist cat food is purchased.
3. the number of cats living in the household.
4. whether the cat is pedigreed.
a. Describe the population.
b. For each of the four items listed, indicate whether the variable is categorical or numerical. If it is numerical, is it discrete or continuous?

c. Develop five categorical questions for the survey.
d. Develop five numerical questions for the survey.

Student Survey Data Base

1.27 A sample of 50 undergraduate students answered the following survey.

1. What is your gender? Female _____ Male _____
2. What is your age (*as of last birthday*)? _____
3. What is your height (*in inches*)? _____
4. What is your current registered class designation?
    Freshman _____ Sophomore _____
    Junior _____ Senior _____
5. What is your major area of study?
    Accounting _____ Economics/Finance _____
    Information Systems _____
    International Business _____ Management _____
    Marketing/Retailing _____ Other _____
    Undecided _____
6. At the present time, do you plan to attend graduate school? Yes _____ No _____ Not sure _____
7. What is your current cumulative grade point average?
    _____
8. What would you expect your starting annual salary (*in $000*) to be if you were to seek employment immediately after obtaining your bachelor's degree?
    _____
9. What do you anticipate your salary to be (*in $000*) after five years of full-time work experience? _____
10. What is your current employment status?
    Full-time _____ Part-time _____
    Unemployed _____
11. How many clubs, groups, organizations, or teams are you currently affiliated with on campus?
12. How satisfied are you with the student advisement services on campus? _____
    Extremely 1 2 3 4 5 6 7 Extremely
    unsatisfied   Neutral   satisfied
13. About how much money did you spend this semester for textbooks and supplies? _____

The results of the survey are in the file `Undergradsurvey`.
a. Which variables in the survey are categorical?
b. Which variables in the survey are numerical?
c. Which variables are discrete numerical variables?

1.28 A sample of 40 MBA students answered the following survey:

1. What is your gender? Female _____ Male _____
2. What is your age (*as of last birthday*)? _____
3. What is your height (*in inches*)? _____
4. What is your current major area of study?
    Accounting _____ Economics/Finance _____
    Information Systems _____
    International Business _____ Management _____
    Marketing/Retailing _____ Other _____
    Undecided _____
5. What is your graduate cumulative grade point average? _____
6. What was your undergraduate area of specialization?
    Biological Sciences _____ Business
    Administration _____ Computers or Math _____
    Education _____ Engineering _____
    Humanities _____ Performing Arts _____
    Physical Sciences _____ Social Sciences _____
    Other _____
7. What was your undergraduate cumulative grade point average? _____
8. What was your GMAT score? _____
9. What is your current employment status? _____
    Full-time _____ Part-time _____
    Unemployed _____
10. How many different full-time jobs have you held in the past 10 years? _____
11. What do you expect your annual salary (*in $000*) to be immediately after completion of the MBA program? _____
12. What do you anticipate your salary to be (*in $000*) after five years of full-time work experience following the completion of the MBA program? _____
13. How satisfied are you with the student advisement services on campus?
    Extremely 1 2 3 4 5 6 7 Extremely
    unsatisfied   Neutral   satisfied
14. About how much money did you spend this semester for textbooks and supplies? _____

The results of the survey are in the file `Gradsurvey`.
a. Which variables in the survey are categorical?
b. Which variables in the survey are numerical?
c. Which variables are discrete numerical variables?

END-OF-CHAPTER CASES

At the end of most chapters, you will find a continuing case study that allows you to apply statistics to problems faced by the management of the *Springville Herald*, a daily newspaper. Complementing this case are a series of Web Cases that extend many of the Using Statistics scenarios that begin each chapter.

LEARNING WITH THE WEB CASES

People use statistical techniques to help communicate and present important information to others both inside and outside their businesses. Every day, as in these examples, people misuse these techniques:

- A sales manager working with an "easy-to-use" charting program chooses an inappropriate chart that obscures data relationships.
- The editor of an annual report presents a chart of revenues with an abridged *Y*-axis that creates the false impression of greatly rising revenues.
- An analyst generates meaningless statistics about a set of categorical data, using analyses designed for numerical data.

Identifying and preventing misuses of statistics, whether intentional or not, is an important responsibility for all managers. The Web Cases help you develop the skills necessary for this important task.

Web Cases send you to Web sites that are related to the Using Statistics scenarios that begin each chapter. You review internal documents as well as publicly stated claims, seeking to identify and correct the misuses of statistics. Unlike a traditional case study, but much like real-world situations, not all of the information you encounter will be relevant to your task, and you may occasionally discover conflicting information that you need to resolve before continuing with the case.

To assist your learning, the Web Case for each chapter begins with the learning objective and a summary of the problem or issue at hand. Each case directs you to one or more Web pages where you can discover information to answer case questions that help guide your exploration. If you prefer, you can view these pages by opening corresponding HTML files that can be found in the **Web Case** folder on the Student CD-ROM. You can find an index of all files/pages by opening the `SpringvilleCC.htm` file in the **Web Case** folder or by visiting the Springville Chamber of Commerce page, at **www.prenhall.com/Springville/SpringvilleCC.htm**.

Web Case Example

To illustrate how to learn from a Web Case, open a Web browser and link to **www.prenhall.com/Springville/Good_Tunes.htm**, or open the `Good_Tunes.htm` file in the Student CD-ROM **Web Case** folder. This Web page represents the home page of Good Tunes, the online retailer mentioned in the Using Statistics scenario in this chapter. Recall that the privately held Good Tunes is seeking financing to expand its business by opening retail locations. Because it is in management's interest to show that Good Tunes is a thriving business, it is not too surprising to discover the "our best sales year ever" claim in the "Good Times at Good Tunes" entry at the top of their home page.

The claim also serves as a hyperlink, so click on **our best sales year ever** to display the page that supports the claim. How would you support such a claim? with a table of numbers? a chart? remarks attributed to a knowledgeable source? Good Tunes has used a chart to present "two years ago" and "latest twelve months" sales data by category. Are there any problems with the choices made on this Web page? *Absolutely!*

First, note that there are no scales for the symbols used, so it is impossible to know what the actual sales volumes are. In fact, as you will learn in Section 2.6, charts that incorporate symbols in this way are considered examples of *chartjunk* and would never be used by people seeking to properly use graphs.

This important point aside, another question that arises is whether the sales data represent the number of units sold or something else. The use of the symbols creates the impression that unit sales data are being presented. If the data are unit sales, does such data best support the claim being made, or would something else, such as dollar volumes, be a better indicator of sales at Good Tunes?

Then there are those curious chart labels. "Latest twelve months" is ambiguous; it could include months from the current year as well as months from one year ago and therefore may not be an equivalent time period to "two years ago." But the business was established in 1997, and the claim being made is "best sales year ever," so why hasn't management included sales figures for *every* year?

Is Good Tunes management hiding something, or are they just unaware of the proper use of statistics? Either way, they have failed to properly communicate a vital aspect of their story.

In subsequent Web Cases, you will be asked to provide this type of analysis, using the open-ended questions of the case as your guide. Not all the cases are as straightforward as this sample, and some cases include perfectly appropriate applications of statistics.

REFERENCES

1. McCullough, B. D., and B. Wilson, "On the Accuracy of Statistical Procedures in Microsoft Excel 97," *Computational Statistics and Data Analysis*, 31 (1999), 27–37.

2. McCullough, B. D., and B. Wilson, "On the Accuracy of Statistical Procedures in Microsoft Excel 2003," *Computational Statistics and Data Analysis*, 49 (2005), 1244–52.

3. *Microsoft Excel 2007* (Redmond, WA: Microsoft Corporation, 2007).
4. *Minitab Release 15* (State College, PA: Minitab, Inc., 2006).
5. Nash, J. C., "Spreadsheets in Statistical Practice—Another Look," *The American Statistician*, 60 (2006), 287–89.

Appendix E1
Introduction to Microsoft Excel

E1.1 OPENING AND SAVING WORKBOOKS

As discussed in Section 1.6, Microsoft Excel uses worksheets that are stored in workbooks. You open and save workbooks by selecting the storage folder to use and then specifying the file name of the workbook. You begin the process by selecting **File** from the Excel menu bar in Excel 97–2003 or by clicking the **Office Button** in Excel 2007. You then select either **Open** or **Save As**. These selections display nearly identical Open and Save As dialog boxes that vary only slightly owing to the different Excel versions (Figure E1.1 shows the Excel 2007 Save As dialog box).

Inside these dialog boxes, you select the storage folder using the drop-down list at the top of these dialog boxes. You enter, or select from the list box, a file name for the workbook in the **File name** box. You click **Open** or **Save** to complete the task. Sometimes when saving files, you will want to change the file type before you click **Save**. If you use Excel 2007 and want to save your workbook in the format used by earlier Excel versions, select **Excel 97–2003 Workbook (*.xls)** from the **Save as type** drop-down list before you click **Save** (shown in Figure E1.1). If you use any version of Excel and want to save data in a form that can be opened by programs that cannot open Excel workbooks, you might select either **Text (Tab delimited) (*.txt)** or **CSV (Comma delimited) (*.csv)** as the save type.

When you go to open a file and cannot find its name in the list box, verify that the current **Look in** folder is the correct one. If that fails to help, change the file type to **All Files (*.*)** to see all files in the current folder. (This technique will help you discover inadvertent misspellings or missing file extensions that otherwise prevents the file from being displayed.)

Although all versions of Microsoft Excel include a **Save** command, you should avoid this choice until you gain experience. Using Save makes it too easy for you to inad-

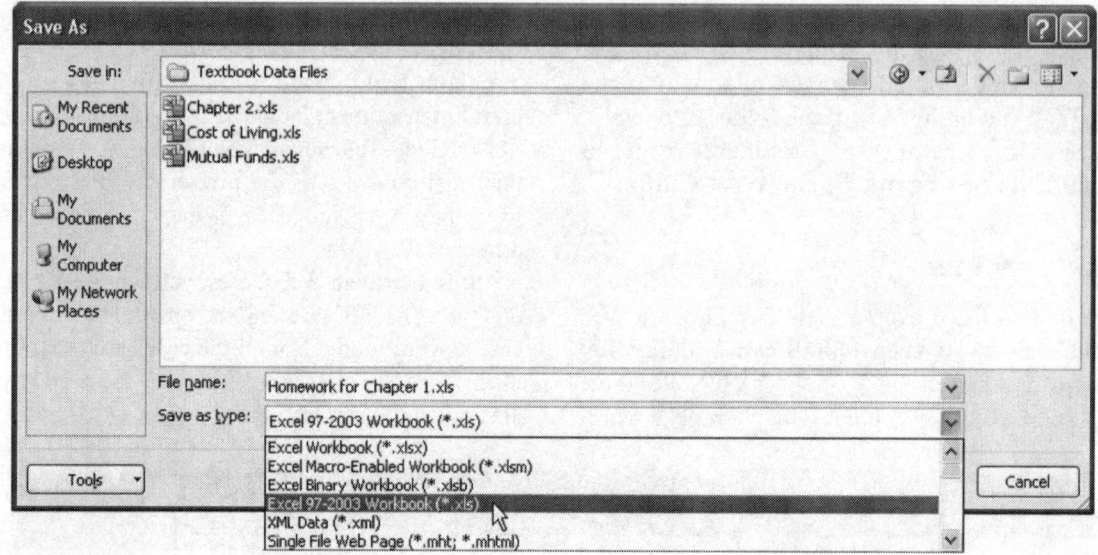

FIGURE E1.1

Save As dialog box (Excel 2007 version)

vertently overwrite your work, and in Excel 2007, it saves your workbook in the new **.xlsx** workbook format that cannot be used by earlier Excel versions. If you open a workbook from a nonmodifiable source, such as the Student CD-ROM, Excel will mark the workbook "read-only," so you must use Save As to save any changes you make to the workbook. (Excel will prevent you from using Save in such situations.)

E1.2 CREATING NEW WORKBOOKS

You create a new workbook through a straightforward process that varies depending on the version of Excel you are using. In Excel 97 or 2000, you select **File ➜ New**. In Excel 2002 (also known as Excel XP) or 2003, you select **File ➜ New** and then click **Blank workbook** in the New Workbook task pane. In Excel 2007, you click **Office Button ➜ New** and in the New Workbook dialog box, you first click **Blank workbook** and then **Create**.

New workbooks are created with a fixed number of worksheets. You can delete extra worksheets or insert more sheets by right-clicking a sheet tab and clicking either **Delete** or **Insert**.

E1.3 PRINTING WORKSHEETS

When you want to print the contents of a workbook, you should print one sheet at a time to get the best results. You print sheets by first previewing their printed form onscreen and then making any adjustments to the worksheet and/or to the print setup settings.

To print a specific worksheet, you first click on the sheet tab of that worksheet to make the worksheet the currently active one. Then you display the Print Preview window. If you use a version of Excel other than 2007, select **File ➜ Print Preview**. If you use Excel 2007, click **Office Button**, move the mouse pointer over **Print** (do not click) and select **Print Preview** from the Preview and Print gallery.

The Print Preview windows for all Excel versions are similar to one another. Figure E1.2 shows a partial window for Excel 2003 (top) and Excel 2007 (bottom). If the preview contains errors or displays the worksheet in an undesirable manner, click **Close** (or **Close Print Preview** in Excel 2007), make the changes necessary, and reselect the preview command. You can customize your printout by clicking **Setup** (or **Page Setup**) and making the appropriate entries in the Page Setup dialog box, which is similar

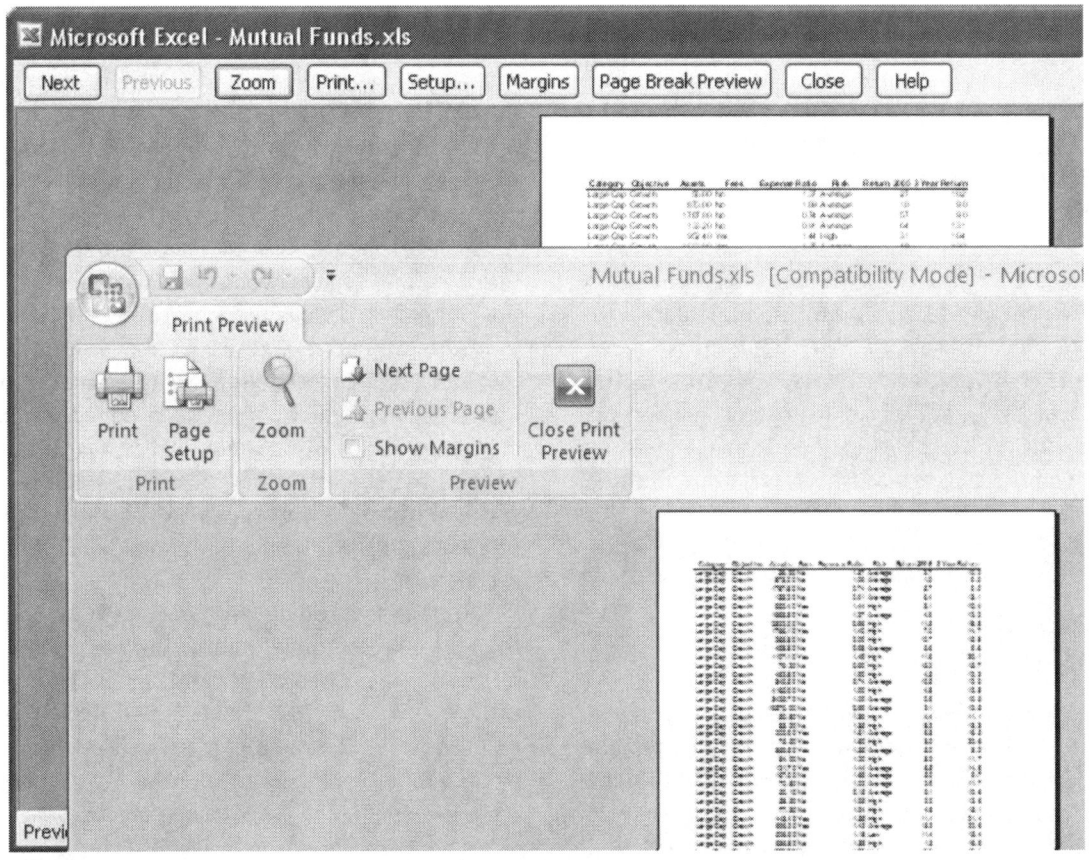

FIGURE E1.2

Partial Print Preview windows (Excel 2003 and 2007 versions)

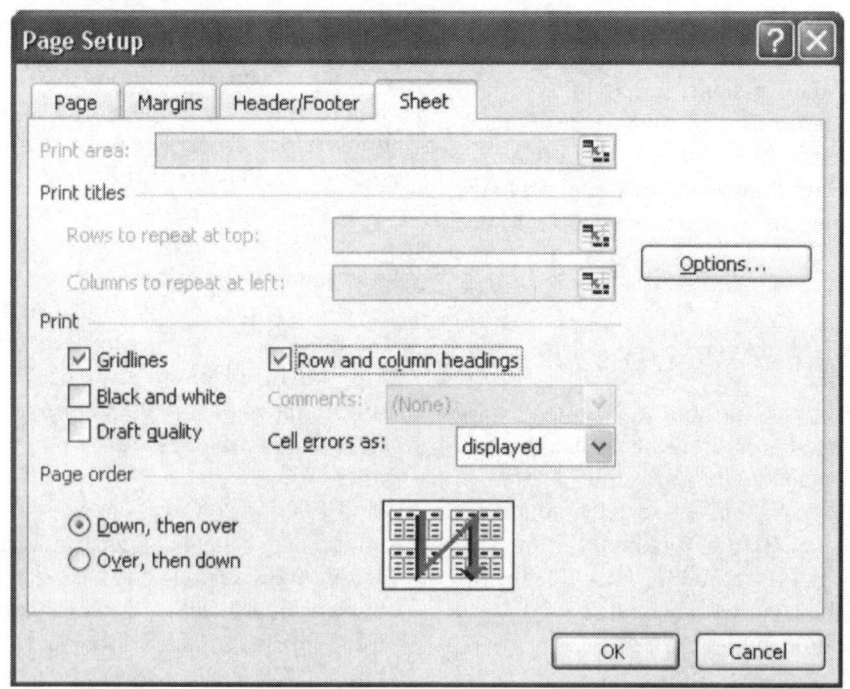

FIGURE E1.3

Sheet tab of the Page Setup dialog box (Excel 2003 version)

for all Excel versions. For example, to print your worksheet with grid lines and numbered row and lettered column headings (similar to the appearance of the worksheet onscreen), you click the **Sheet** tab in the Page Setup dialog box and then click **Gridlines** and **Row and column headings** and click **OK** (see Figure E1.3). (You can find more information about using Page Setup in Section F4 of Appendix F.)

When you are ready to print, you can click **Print** in the Print Preview window, but to gain maximum control over your printout, click **Close** (or **Close Print Preview**) and then select **File → Print** (Excel 97–2003) or **Office Button → Print** (Excel 2007). In the Print dialog box that appears, you can select the printer to use, make sure you are printing only the currently active worksheet, or print multiple copies at once.

E1.4 WORKSHEET ENTRIES AND REFERENCES

As first discussed in Section 1.6, worksheets are tabular arrangements of data in which standard practice dictates that you enter the data for each variable in individual columns. You use the cursor keys or your pointing device to move a **cell pointer** through a worksheet and to select a cell for entry. As you type an entry, it appears in the formula bar, and you place that entry into the cell by either pressing

the **Tab** or **Enter** keys or clicking the checkmark button in the formula bar.

As you enter the data for a variable in a column, follow the standard practice of using the row 1 cell to store a name or label for the variable. Should you be entering two or more sets of data, consider placing each set of data in a separate worksheet.

In worksheets that you use for intermediate calculations or final results, you might enter **formulas**, instructions to perform a calculation or some other task, in addition to the numeric and text entries you otherwise make into cells. Proper formulas use values found in one or more other cells to produce a new displayed result. The displayed results automatically change; that is, the formula is recalculated, when the values in other cells change. (Such **recalculation** was the original novel feature of spreadsheet programs and led to such programs being widely used in accounting.)

To refer to a cell in a formula, you use a **cell address** in the form **SheetName!ColumnRow**. For example, **Data!A2** refers to the cell in the Data worksheet that is in column A and row 2. You can also use just the *ColumnRow* portion of a full address, for example, **A2**, if you are referring to a cell on the same worksheet as the one into which you are entering a formula. If the sheet name contains spaces or special characters, for example, **City Data** or **Figure-1.2**, you must enclose the sheet name in a pair of single quotes, as in **'City Data'!A2** or **'Figure-1.2'!A2**.

When you want to refer to a group of cells, for example, to the cells of a column that store the data for a particular variable, you use a **cell range**. A cell range names the upper leftmost cell and the lower rightmost cell of the group using the form ***SheetName!UpperLeftCell:LowerRightCell***. For example, the cell range **Data!B1:B51** identifies the cells in the UndergradSurvey.xls workbook that store the data for the gender variable (with cell B1 storing the variable label "Gender" as explained earlier). Cell ranges can extend over multiple columns; the cell range **Data!B1:E51** in the same workbook would refer to the data for the gender, age, height, and class variables.

As with a single cell reference, you can skip the *SheetName!* part of the reference if you are referring to a cell range on the current worksheet, and, must use a pair of single quotes if a sheet name contains spaces or special characters. However, in many cases in the Excel instructions in this book, including the sheet name will be necessary in a cell reference in order to get the proper results. Because sheet names are used so frequently, you should change the names that Excel assigns to worksheets (names in the form **Sheet1**, **Sheet2**, and so on) to more meaningful words or phrases. To do so, double-click a sheet tab, type the new name, and press **Enter**.

(Although not a form used in this book, cell references can include a workbook name in the form **'[*Workbook Name*]*SheetName*'!*ColumnRow*** or **'[*WorkbookName*]*SheetName*'!*UpperLeftCell:LowerRightCell***. You may discover such references if you inadvertently copy certain types of worksheets or chart sheets from one workbook to another.)

E1.5 ENTERING FORMULAS INTO WORKSHEETS

You enter formulas by typing the equal sign symbol (=) and then a combination of mathematical or other data-processing operations. For simple formulas, you use the symbols +, −, *, /, and ∧ for the operations addition, subtraction, multiplication, division, and exponentiation (a number raised to a power), respectively. For example, the formula **=Data!B2 + Data!B3 + Data!B4** adds the contents of the cells B2, B3, and B4 of the Data worksheet and displays the sum as the value in the cell containing the formula. You can also use **worksheet functions** in formulas to simplify formulas.

To use a worksheet function in a formula, either type the function as shown in the instructions in this book or use the Excel Function Wizard feature to insert the function. To use this feature, select **Insert ➔ Function** (Excel 97–2003) or **Formulas ➔ Function Wizard** (Excel 2007) and then make entries and selections in one or more dialog boxes.

E1.6 VERIFYING FORMULAS AND WORKSHEETS

If you use formulas in your worksheets, you should review and verify formulas before you use their results. To view the formulas in a worksheet, press **Ctrl+`** (grave accent key). To restore the original view, the results of the formulas, press **Ctrl+`** a second time.

As you create and use more complicated worksheets, you may want to visually examine the relationships among a formula and the cells it uses (called the precedents) and the cells that use the results of the formula (the dependents). To display arrows that visually show these relationships, use the formula auditing feature of Excel. Select **Tools ➔ Auditing** (Excel 97 or 2000), or **Tools ➔ Formula Auditing** (Excel 2002 or 2003), or **Formulas** (Excel 2007). Then select one of the choices from the **auditing** submenu (Excel 97–2003) or from the **Formula Auditing** group (Excel 2007). When you are finished, selecting **Remove All Arrows** restores your display by removing all auditing arrows.

E1.7 ENHANCING WORKBOOK PRESENTATION

By formatting the display of individual cells and by rearranging the contents of your workbook, you can enhance the presentation of your workbook.

You can find the most common cell-formatting operations on the Formatting toolbar (Excel 97–2003) or in the Home tab (Excel 2007). Most worksheets shown as illustrations in this book use the **Boldface**, **Fill Color**, **Merge-and-Center**, and **Borders** features to highlight particular cells or cell ranges. Experiment with these features to develop your own style that maximizes the effectiveness of your presentations.

You may also want to rearrange the content of your workbooks. Use the copy-and-paste combination keystroke shortcuts, **Crtl+C** and **Ctrl+V**, to copy content from one cell to another on the same worksheet. Copying cells that contain formulas is not necessarily as straightforward as you might expect. If your formula uses references in the format discussed in Section E1.4, Excel will change to reflect the difference, or offset, between the original (source) cell and the cell into which you are pasting the formula (the target cell). For example, when you copy the formula =A2 + B2 in cell C2 down to cell C3, an offset of one row, Excel pastes the formula =A3 + B3 in C3 to reflect that one-row offset. Cell ranges also get changed, so if you copy the formula =SUM(A1:A4) from cell A5 to cell B5, the formula is changed to =SUM(B1:B4).

You can stop Excel from making such changes by inserting a U.S. dollar symbol ($) before either the column letter or

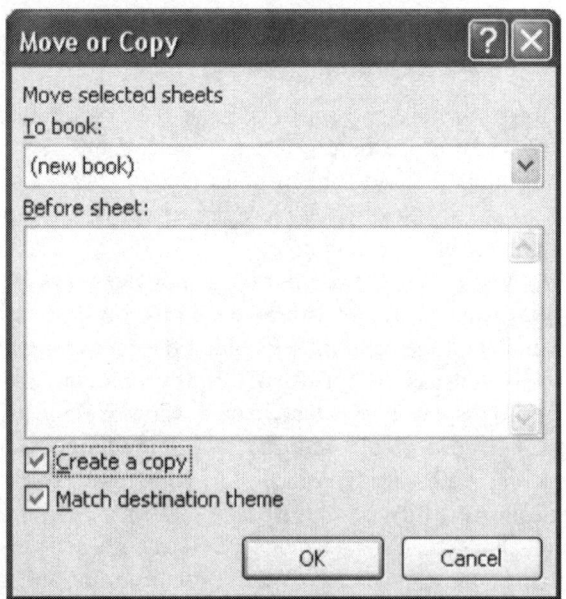

FIGURE E1.4
Move or Copy dialog box (Excel 2007 version)

row number (or both) of a cell reference to form an **absolute reference**, for example, $A\$2. Do not confuse the use of the U.S. dollar symbol with the format operation that displays numbers as U.S. currency values. To format cell values for U.S. currency display, you use the **Currency ($)** format button, available on the Formatting toolbar (Excel 97–2003) and in the Number group of **Home** tab (Excel 2007).

Finally, you can also copy entire worksheets for convenience or clarity. To copy a worksheet to a new workbook, you first select the worksheet by clicking its sheet tab. Then you right-click the tab and select **Move or Copy** from the shortcut menu that appears. In the **To book** drop-down list of the Move or Copy dialog box (see Figure E1.4), first select **(new book)** or the name of the preexisting target workbook, and then click **Create a copy** and then click **OK**.

E1.8 USING ADD-INS

Add-ins can simplify the task of creating something to add to a workbook. Add-ins are programming components not included in the main Excel program and may need to be **installed**, or added, to your computer system separately. Add-ins are not always available for you to use because they can be disabled by other users or system security settings. However, the little extra effort you need to ensure that the right add-ins are installed and enabled is well worth the features that add-ins bring to Excel.

As you use Microsoft Excel with this book, you will use the Excel **Analysis ToolPak** add-in for some statistical

tasks. The Analysis ToolPak add-in (which the book simply calls the "ToolPak" from this point forward) adds statistical procedures to Excel, but creates worksheets that do not contain formulas. Should you later change your data, you must repeat the ToolPak procedure to get updated results. Some Excel versions come with the ToolPak preinstalled; others require that you separately install this component from your Microsoft Office or Excel program setup disk. (See Appendix F for additional information about installing the ToolPak.)

As you use Microsoft Excel, you may choose to use **PHStat2**, the Prentice Hall statistics add-in that is included on the Student CD-ROM. If you plan to use PHStat2, you first need to run its setup program, using the instructions found in Appendix F and in the Student CD-ROM PHStat2 readme file. PHStat2 adds a PHStat menu of procedures to the Excel menu bar in Excel 97–2003 and the Add-ins tab in Excel 2007. Unlike the ToolPak, PHStat2 usually creates worksheets that contain formulas and that will produce new results as the underlying data changes. Sometimes, though, PHStat2 asks the ToolPak to create sheets on its behalf, and the resulting sheets are similar to the no-formulas sheets that the ToolPak creates. In many such cases, PHStat2 enhances the sheets it asks the ToolPak to create, correcting errors the ToolPak makes or adding new formula-based calculations. (If you plan to use PHStat2, be sure to read Appendix P1, which immediately follows this appendix.)

In all Excel versions other than Excel 97, all add-ins that you open will be screened by Microsoft Office security components. If you use Excel 2000, 2002, or 2003, you can

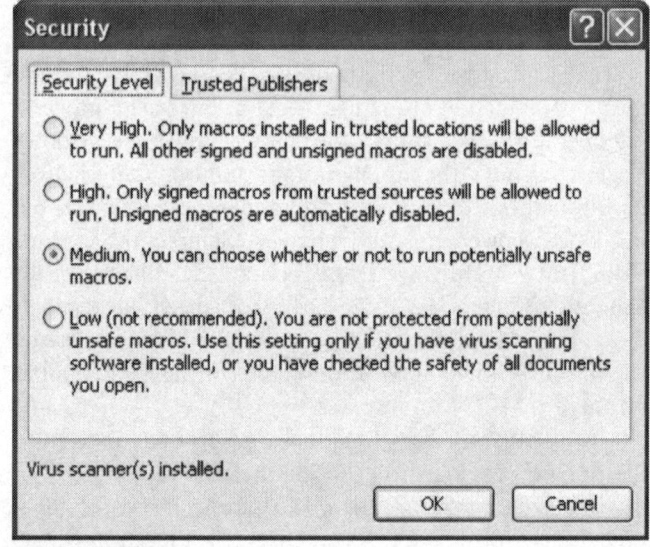

FIGURE E1.5
Security dialog box (Excel 2003 version)

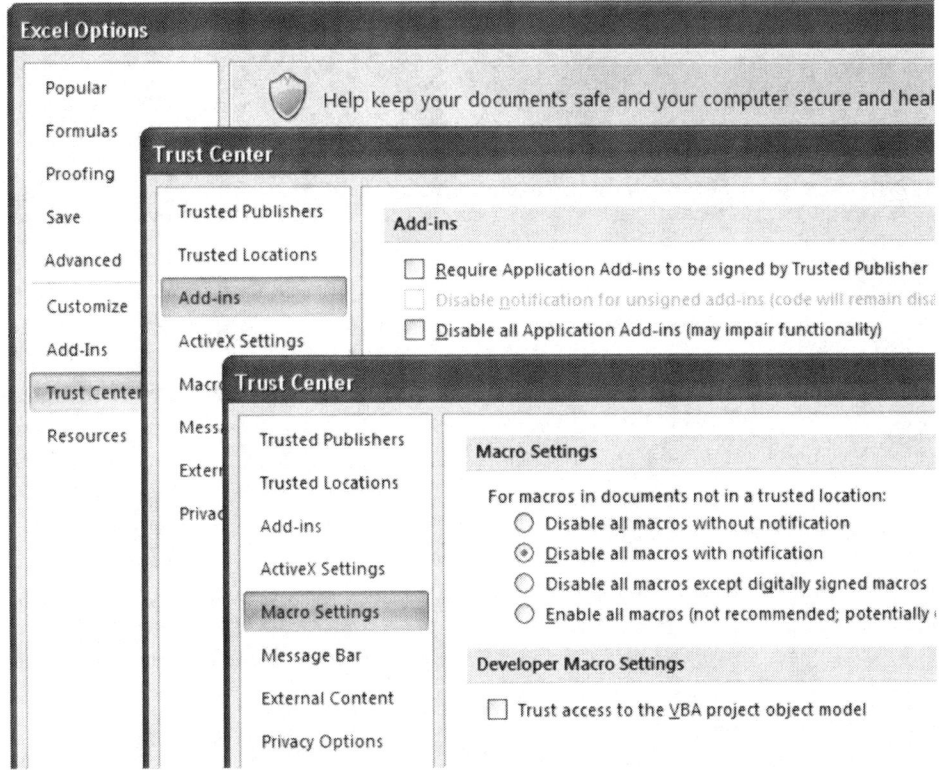

FIGURE E1.6

Excel Options and Trust Center panes (Excel 2007)

review and change the security settings by selecting **Tools** → **Macro** → **Security** to display a Security dialog box (similar to the one shown in Figure E1.5 for Excel 2003). To use an add-in such as PHStat2 that is "not signed," you would click **Medium** and then click **OK**.

If you use Excel 2007, click the **Office Button**, and then click **Excel Options** in the Office menu. In the Excel Options dialog box (see Figure E1.6) click **Trust Center** in the left pane to display information about security issues. Then click **Trust Center Settings** (obscured in Figure E1.6) to display the Trust Center dialog box. To use an add-in such as PHStat2 that is not signed, click **Add-Ins** in the left pane, and then clear all checkboxes in the right pane (see Figure E1.6). Then click **Macro Settings** in the left pane and click **Disable all macros with notification** in the right pane (see Figure E1.6). On some systems, you may also have to click **Trusted Locations** in the left pane and add the file location of the add-in.

With the Security screen set to an appropriate level, you will see a macro virus warning dialog box when you open an add-in such as PHStat2. Figure E1.7 shows the Excel 2003 and Excel 2007 warning boxes. You click the **Enable Macros** button to allow virus-free add-ins, such as PHStat2, to be opened and used.

FIGURE E1.7

Macro warning dialog boxes (Excel 2003 and 2007)

Appendix P1
Introduction to PHStat2

P1.1 OVERVIEW

PHStat2 is software that makes using Microsoft Excel as distraction-free as possible. As a student studying statistics, you can use PHStat2 to maximize your focus on mastering statistics and minimize your worries about learning every little detail about Excel. When combined with the ToolPak add-in, you can use a beginner's knowledge of Microsoft Excel to illustrate nearly all of the statistical methods presented in this book.

PHStat2 was not designed to be used commercially and you should not see it as a replacement for or an equivalent to statistical programs such as Minitab, SPSS, JMP, and SAS. Because PHStat2 emphasizes learning, PHStat2 tries to use the methods of calculation that an introductory statistics student can easily follow, including manual calculation methods presented in this book. In other cases, PHStat2 uses preexisting Microsoft Excel methods to produce results that are too complex to manually calculate or present to the learner. These design choices occasionally produce results that are not as precise or accurate as those produced by commercial programs, which use methods of calculation that are fine-tuned for precision and accuracy. Even though these differences will not be significant for most sets of data and are *not* significant for all data used in chapter examples and problems, they could be if you used PHStat2 with data that happen to have unusual properties.

P1.2 HOW PHSTAT2 PRESENTS ITS RESULTS

PHStat2 creates new worksheets and chart sheets inserted into the currently active workbook. Cells containing important values and results are highlighted by a light yellow tint and boldface text. These cells and the cells that hold intermediate calculations are usually only minimally numerically formatted. For some procedures, the values in these cells will have an excessive number of seemingly significant digits and you may want to change the numeric formatting for such cells for presentation purposes.

Worksheets that contain cells tinted in light turquoise are designed to be interactive and you can change the numeric values of those cells to produce different results without reselecting the PHStat2 procedure.

P1.3 USING PHSTAT2

When properly loaded, PHStat2 adds the PHStat menu entry to the Excel 97–2003 menu bar or the Add-Ins tab of Excel 2007. Selecting **PHStat** for either of these displays the PHStat menu (see Figure P1.1). You make selections from this menu, as discussed in the PHStat2 appendices of later chapters, to select and run a PHStat2 procedure.

In addition to selecting procedures, you can select **About PHStat** to view information about the PHStat2 version that you are using, or select **Help for PHStat** to display the PHStat2 help system inside Microsoft Excel (this feature is not available for Windows Vista users).

To use PHStat2, make sure you have read Section E1.8 "Using Add-Ins," the Student CD-ROM **PHStat2 readme file** and the appropriate sections of Appendix F. If you are inexperienced in the task of installing programs on your computer system, you may additionally want to seek assistance from a friend or campus help center if you plan to install PHStat2 on your system. General assistance is also available through the PHStat2 Website, **www.prenhall.com/phstat**.

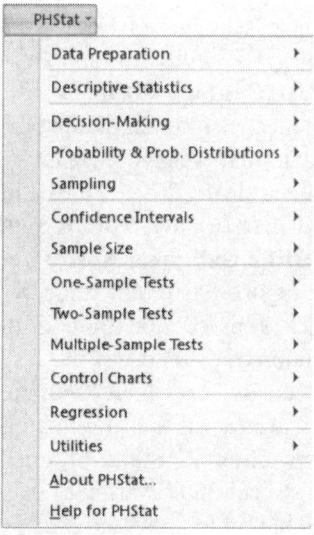

FIGURE P1.1

PHStat Menu

Appendix M1
Introduction to Minitab

M1.1 OVERVIEW

Minitab is a statistical program that initially evolved from efforts at the Pennsylvania State University to improve the teaching of statistics. Over the years, Minitab's accuracy and its availability for many different types of computer systems have attracted such corporate customers as the Ford Motor Company, 3M, and General Electric. This combination of having large-scale commercial acceptance and the legacy of being designed for statistics education makes Minitab an attractive program to use in business statistics courses.

As first discussed in Section 1.6, you create Minitab **projects** to store all of your data and results. A project includes several components: a **session area** that contains all your statistical tables; a **Project Manager** that summarizes the project contents; Minitab worksheets that store your data; and graphs of your data. Project components appear as separate windows *inside* the Minitab window. When you start Minitab, you typically see a new project that contains only the session area and one worksheet window. (You can view other components by selecting them in the Minitab **Windows** menu.) You can open and save an entire project or, as is done in this book, open and save individual worksheets.

M1.2 USING MINITAB WORKSHEETS

You enter data for each variable in individual columns of a Minitab worksheet. Minitab worksheets are organized as numbered rows and columns numbered in the form Cn in which C1 is the first column, C2 is the second column, and so forth. You enter variable labels in a special unnumbered row that precedes row 1. You refer to individual variables either using their column number, such as **C1**, or through their variable labels, such as **Risk**. If a variable label is a phrase such as **Return 2006**, you enter the label with a pair of single quotation marks, for example, as **'Return 2006'**. (In this book, variable labels are generally used to refer to variables, a practice that can minimize errors.)

By default, Minitab names open worksheets serially in the form of Worksheet1, Worksheet2, and so on. Better names are ones that reflect the content of the worksheets, such as Mutual Funds for a worksheet that contains mutual funds data. To give a sheet a descriptive name, open the Project Manager window, right-click the icon for the worksheet, and select **Rename** from the shortcut menu and type in the new name.

M1.3 OPENING AND SAVING WORKSHEETS AND OTHER COMPONENTS

You open worksheets to use data that have been created by you or others at an earlier time. To open a Minitab worksheet:

1. Select **File → Open Worksheet**.
2. In the Open Worksheet dialog box that appears (see Figure M1.1 on page 24), select the file to be opened and then click **Open**.

If you cannot find your file, you may need to do one or more of the following:

- Use the scroll bars or the slider, if present, to scroll through the entire list of files.
- Select the correct folder from the **Look in** drop-down list at the top of the dialog box.
- Change the **Files of type** value from the drop-down list at the bottom of the dialog box. You should select **Text (*.txt)** from the list to see text files, **Excel (*.xls, *.xlsx)** to see Microsoft Excel files, and so forth. To list every file in the folder, select **All Files(*.*)**.

To save a Minitab worksheet:

1. Select **File → Save Current Worksheet As**.
2. In the Save Worksheet As dialog box that appears (similar to the Open Worksheet dialog box), enter the name for your worksheet in the **File name** box and then click **Save**.

If applicable, you can also do the following:

- Change to another folder by selecting that folder from the **Save in** drop-down list.
- Change the **Save as type** value to something other than the default choice, **Minitab**. "**Minitab Portable**" or an earlier version of **Minitab**, such as "**Minitab 13**", are commonly chosen alternatives.

After saving your work, you should consider saving your file a second time, using a different name, in order to create a backup copy of your work. Files opened from non-writable disks, such as the Student CD-ROM, cannot be saved to their original files.

To open an entire Minitab Project, select **File → Open Project**. To save a Minitab Project, select **File → Save Project As**. When you use these commands, the dialog box

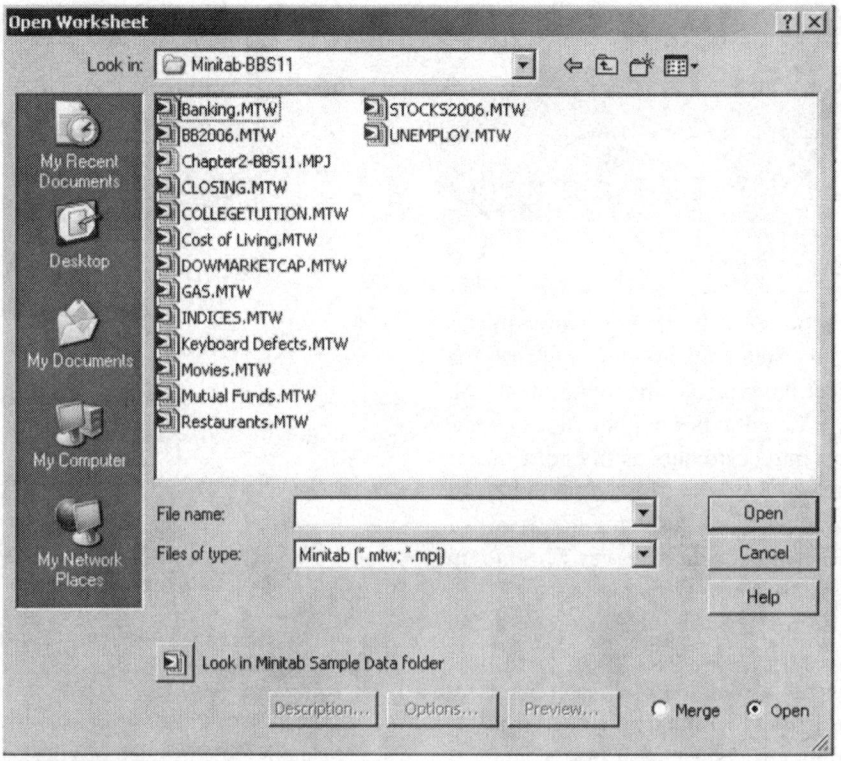

FIGURE M1.1

Open Worksheet dialog box

that appears will contain an **Options** button that you can click to selectively open (or save) parts of your project.

Individual graphs and the session window can also be saved separately by first selecting their windows and then selecting **File → Save Graph As** or **File → Save Session Window As**, as appropriate. Minitab graphs can be saved in either a Minitab graph format or any one of several common graphics formats, and session files can be saved as simple or formatted text files.

M1.4 PRINTING WORKSHEETS, GRAPHS, AND SESSIONS

To print a specific worksheet, graph, or session:

1. Select the window that contains the worksheet, graph, or session to be printed.
2. Select **File → Print** *object*, where *object* is either **Worksheet**, **Graph**, or **Session Window**, depending on what you seek to print.

If you are printing a graph or a session window, you will then see the Print dialog box. If you are printing a worksheet, you will first see a Data Window Print Options dialog box (Figure M1.2) that allows you to select formatting options for your printout (the default selections should be fine for most of your printouts). Click **OK** in that dialog box to proceed to the Print dialog box.

The Print dialog box contains settings to select the printer to be used, what pages to print, and the number of copies to produce (1 is the default). If you need to change these settings, change them before clicking **OK** to create your printout.

After printing, you should verify the contents of your printout. Most printing failures will trigger the display of onscreen information that you can use to determine the source of the failure. You can change the paper size or paper orientation of your printout by selecting **File → Print Setup** and then making the appropriate entries in the dialog box that appears. (Click **OK** when you are finished making entries.)

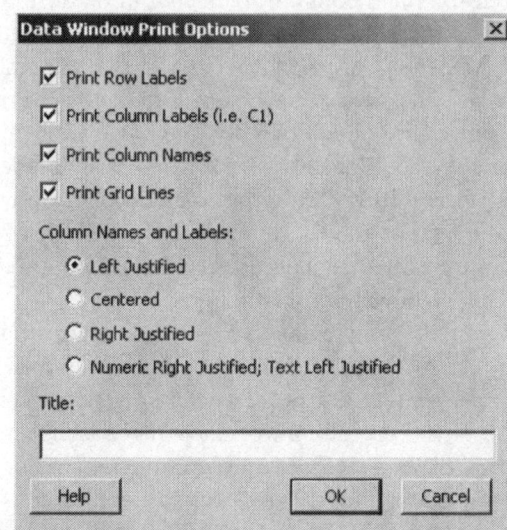

FIGURE M1.2

Data Window Print Options dialog box

CHAPTER TWO

PRESENTING DATA IN TABLES AND CHARTS

USING STATISTICS @ Choice Is Yours, Part I

LEARNING OBJECTIVES

In this chapter, you learn:

- To develop tables and charts for categorical data
- To develop tables and charts for numerical data
- The principles of properly presenting graphs

USING STATISTICS @ Choice Is Yours, Part I

Choice Is Yours is a service that helps customers make wise investment choices. You've been hired to assist investors interested in mutual funds, a market basket of securities. According to **investopedia.com**, "A mutual fund is nothing more than a collection of stocks and/or bonds. You can think of a mutual fund as a company that brings together a group of people and invests their money in stocks, bonds, and other securities. Each investor owns shares, which represent a portion of the holdings of the fund." (You can learn more about mutual funds at **www.investopedia.com/university/mutualfunds/**.)

The Choice Is Yours company previously selected a sample of 868 mutual funds that it believes might be of interest to its customers. You have been asked to present data about these funds in a way that will help customers make good investment choices. What facts about each mutual fund would you collect to help customers compare and contrast the many funds?

A good starting point would be to collect data that would help customers classify mutual funds into various categories. You could research such things as the amount of risk involved in a fund's investment strategy and whether the fund focuses on growth securities, those companies that are expected to grow quickly in the next year, or on value securities, those companies whose stock prices are currently considered undervalued. You might also investigate whether a mutual fund specializes in a certain size company and whether the fund charges management fees that would reduce the percentage return earned by an investor.

Of course, you would want to know how well the fund performed in the past. You would also want to supply the customer with several measures of each fund's past performance. Even though past performance is no assurance of future performance, past data could give customers insight into how well each mutual fund has been managed.

As you further think about your task, you realize that all these data for all 868 mutual funds would be a lot for anyone to review. How could you "get your hands around" such data and explore it in a comprehensible manner?

To *get* your hands around the data described in this chapter's Using Statistics scenario, you need to use methods of descriptive statistics, defined in Chapter 1 as the branch of statistics that collects, summarizes, presents and analyzes data. In this scenario, you need to use descriptive techniques for both categorical variables (to help investors classify the mutual funds) and numerical variables (to help show the return each fund has achieved). Reading this chapter will help you prepare tables and charts that are appropriate for both types of variables. You'll also learn techniques to help answer questions that require two variables, such as "Do growth-oriented mutual funds have lower returns than value mutual funds?" and "Do growth funds tend to be riskier investments than value funds?"

Many examples in this chapter use a sample of 868 mutual funds, the data for which you can find in the Data worksheet of the Mutual Funds.xls *workbook or in the Minitab worksheet* Mutual Funds.mtw *on the Student CD-ROM.*

2.1 TABLES AND CHARTS FOR CATEGORICAL DATA

When you have categorical data, you tally responses into categories and then present the frequency or percentage in each category in tables and charts.

The Summary Table

A **summary table** indicates the frequency, amount, or percentage of items in a set of categories so that you can see differences between categories. A summary table lists the categories in one column and the frequency, amount, or percentage in a different column or columns. Table 2.1 illustrates a summary table based on a recent survey (see the `Banking` file) that asked people where they prefer to do their banking (K. Chu, "Online Banks Launch Checking Accounts," *USA Today*, January 18, 2007, p. 1B). In Table 2.1, the most common choices are in person at branch and on the Internet, followed by drive-through service at branch and ATM. Very few respondents mentioned automated or live telephone.

TABLE 2.1

Banking Preference

Banking Preference	Percentage (%)
ATM	16
Automated or live telephone	2
Drive-through service at branch	17
In person at branch	41
Internet	24

EXAMPLE 2.1

SUMMARY TABLE OF LEVELS OF RISK OF MUTUAL FUNDS

The 868 mutual funds that are part of the Using Statistics scenario (see page 26) are classified according to their risk level, categorized as low, average, and high. Construct a summary table of the mutual funds, categorized by risk.

SOLUTION From Table 2.2, you can see that fewer than 25% of the funds are low-risk funds. There are more high-risk funds (355, or 40.90%) than low-risk (202, or 23.27%) or average-risk funds (311, or 35.83%). More than 75% of the funds are average risk or high risk.

TABLE 2.2

Frequency and Percentage Summary Table Pertaining to Risk Level for 868 Mutual Funds

Fund Risk Level	Number of Funds	Percentage of Funds (%)
Low	202	23.27
Average	311	35.83
High	355	40.90
Total	868	100.00

The Bar Chart

In a **bar chart**, a bar shows each category. The length of the bar represents the amount, frequency, or percentage of values falling into a category. Figure 2.1 on page 28 displays the bar chart for where people prefer to do their banking presented in Table 2.1.

Bar charts allow you to compare percentages in different categories. In Figure 2.1, respondents are most likely to bank in person at a branch and on the Internet, followed by drive-through service at a branch and ATM. Very few respondents mentioned automated or live telephone.

FIGURE 2.1

Microsoft Excel bar chart for where people prefer to do their banking.

See Sections E2.4 or P2.3 to create this. (Minitab users, see Section M2.2 to create an equivalent chart.)

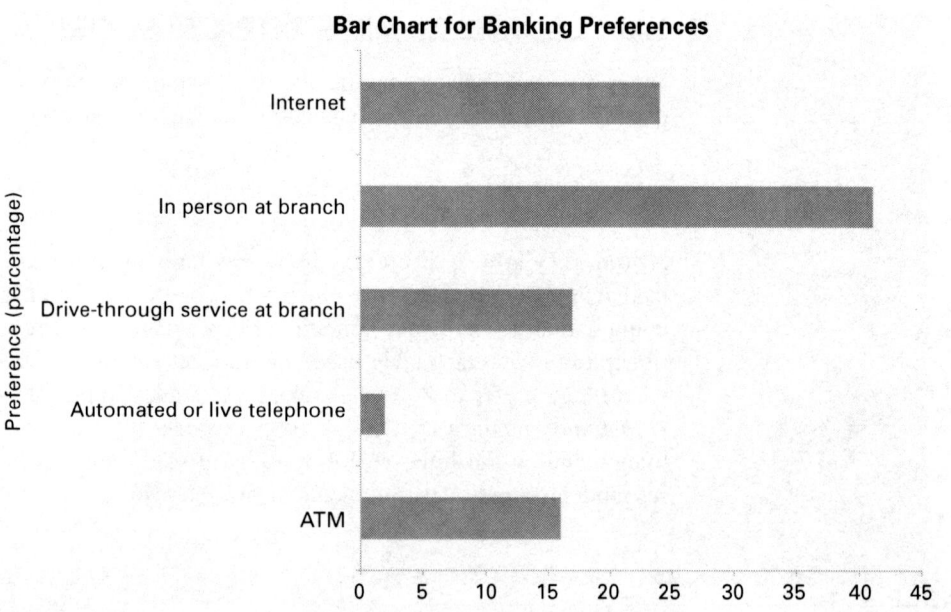

Bar Chart for Banking Preferences

EXAMPLE 2.2

BAR CHART OF LEVELS OF RISK OF MUTUAL FUNDS

Construct a bar chart for the levels of risk of mutual funds (based on the information in Table 2.2 on page 27) and interpret the results.

SOLUTION From Figure 2.2, you can see that approximately 200 of the funds are low risk, whereas more than 650 of the 868 funds are either average risk or high risk. There are more high-risk funds than average-risk or low-risk funds.

FIGURE 2.2

Microsoft Excel bar chart of the levels of risk of mutual funds

See Sections E2.4 or P2.3 to create this. (Minitab users, see Section M2.2 to create an equivalent chart.)

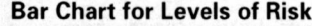

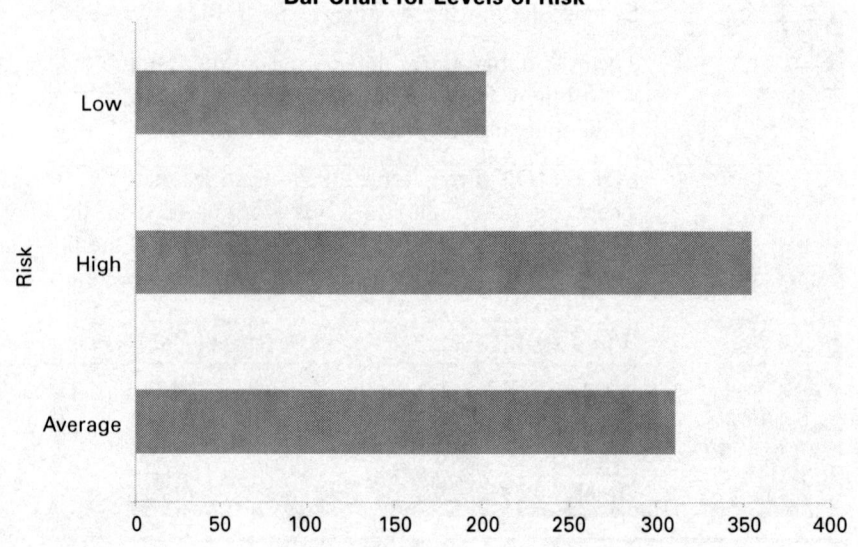

Bar Chart for Levels of Risk

The Pie Chart

The **pie chart** is a circle broken up into slices that represent categories. The size of each slice of the pie varies according to the percentage in each category. In Table 2.1 on page 27, for example, 41% of the respondents stated that they prefer to bank in person at the branch. Thus, in constructing the pie chart, the 360 degrees that makes up a circle is multiplied by 0.41, resulting in a slice of the pie that takes up 147.6 degrees of the 360 degrees of the circle. From Figure 2.3, you can see that the pie chart lets you visualize the portion of the entire pie that is in each category. In this figure, bank in person at the branch takes 41% of the pie and automated or live telephone takes only 2%.

FIGURE 2.3

Microsoft Excel pie chart for where people prefer to do their banking

See Sections E2.4 or P2.3 to create this. (Minitab users, see Section M2.3 to create an equivalent chart.)

Pie Chart for Banking Preferences

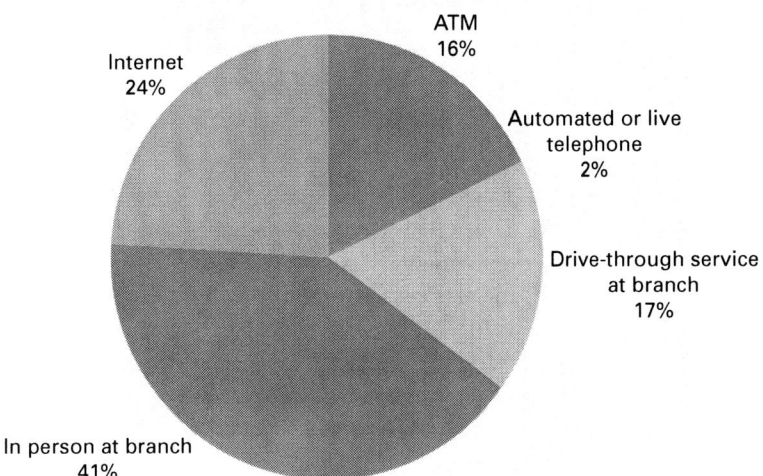

Which chart should you use—a bar chart or a pie chart? The selection of a particular chart often depends on your intention. If a comparison of categories is most important, you should use a bar chart. If observing the portion of the whole that is in a particular category is most important, you should use a pie chart.

EXAMPLE 2.3

PIE CHART OF LEVELS OF RISK OF MUTUAL FUNDS

Construct a pie chart for the levels of risk of mutual funds (see Table 2.2 on page 27) and interpret the results.

SOLUTION From Figure 2.4, you can see that 41% of the funds are high risk, 36% are average risk, and only 23% are low risk.

FIGURE 2.4

Microsoft Excel pie chart of the levels of risk of mutual funds

See Sections E2.4 or P2.3 to create this. (Minitab users, see Section M2.3 to create an equivalent chart.)

Pie Chart for Levels of Risk

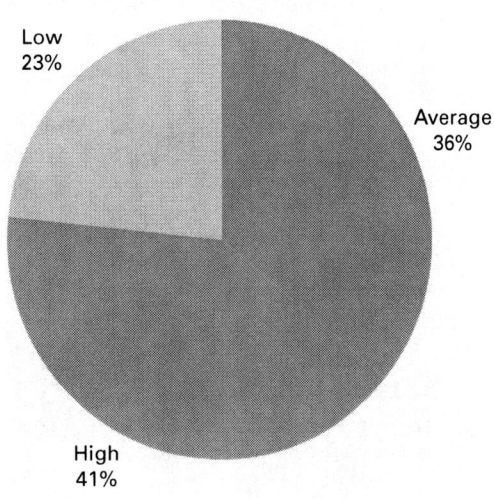

The Pareto Chart

In a **Pareto chart**, the responses in the categories are plotted in descending order, according to their frequencies, and are combined with a cumulative percentage line on the same chart. The Pareto chart can identify situations in which the Pareto principle occurs.

PARETO PRINCIPLE

The **Pareto principle** exists when the majority of items in a set of data occur in a small number of categories and the few remaining items are spread out over a large number of categories. These two groups are often referred to as the "vital few" and the "trivial many."

The Pareto chart has the ability to separate the "vital few" from the "trivial many," enabling you to focus on the important categories. In situations in which the data involved consist of defective or nonconforming items, the Pareto chart is a powerful tool for prioritizing improvement efforts.

Table 2.3 presents data for a large injection-molding company that manufactures plastic components used in computer keyboards, washing machines, automobiles, and television sets (see the **Keyboard defects** file). The data presented in Table 2.3 consist of all computer keyboards with defects produced during a three-month period.

TABLE 2.3

Summary Table of Causes of Defects in Computer Keyboards in a Three-Month Period

Cause	Frequency	Percentage
Black spot	413	6.53
Damage	1,039	16.43
Jetting	258	4.08
Pin mark	834	13.19
Scratches	442	6.99
Shot mold	275	4.35
Silver streak	413	6.53
Sink mark	371	5.87
Spray mark	292	4.62
Warpage	1,987	31.42
Total	6,324	100.01*

*Result differs slightly from 100.00 due to rounding.
Source: *Extracted from U. H. Acharya and C. Mahesh, "Winning Back the Customer's Confidence: A Case Study on the Application of Design of Experiments to an Injection-Molding Process,"* Quality Engineering, 11, 1999, pp. 357–363.

Table 2.4 presents a summary table for the computer keyboard data in which the categories are ordered based on the frequency of defects present (rather than arranged alphabetically). The percentages and cumulative percentages for the ordered categories are also included as part of the table.

TABLE 2.4

Ordered Summary Table of Causes of Defects in Computer Keyboards in a Three-Month Period

Cause	Frequency	Percentage	Cumulative Percentage
Warpage	1,987	31.42	31.42
Damage	1,039	16.43	47.85
Pin mark	834	13.19	61.04
Scratches	442	6.99	68.03
Black spot	413	6.53	74.56
Silver streak	413	6.53	81.09
Sink mark	371	5.87	86.96
Spray mark	292	4.62	91.58
Shot mold	275	4.35	95.93
Jetting	258	4.08	100.01*
Total	6,324	100.01*	

*Result differs slightly from 100.00 due to rounding.

In Table 2.4, the first category listed is warpage (with 31.42% of the defects), followed by damage (with 16.43%), followed by pin mark (with 13.19%). The two most frequently occurring categories, warpage and damage, account for 47.85% of the defects; the three most frequently occurring categories—warpage, damage, and pin mark—account for 61.04% of the defects, and so on. Figure 2.5 is a Pareto chart based on the results displayed in Table 2.4.

FIGURE 2.5

Microsoft Excel Pareto
chart for the keyboard
defects data

*See Sections E2.5 or P2.4 to
create this. (Minitab users,
see Section M2.4 to create
an equivalent chart.)*

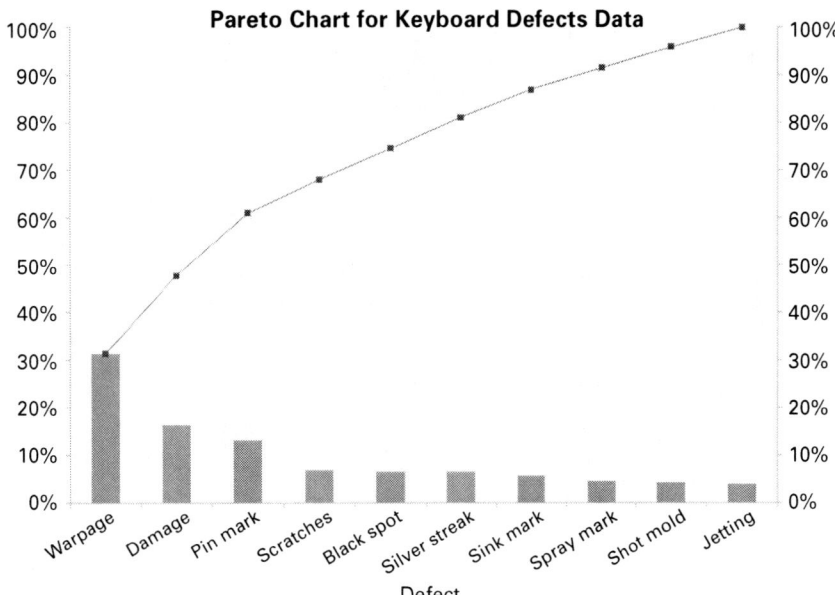

Figure 2.5 presents the bars vertically, along with a cumulative percentage line. The cumulative line is plotted at the midpoint of each category, at a height equal to the cumulative percentage. If you follow the line, you see that these first three categories account for about 60% of the defects. Because the categories in the Pareto chart are ordered by the frequency of occurrences, decision makers can see where to concentrate efforts to improve the process. Attempts to reduce defects due to warpage, damage, and pin marks should produce the greatest payoff. Then, efforts can be made to reduce scratches, black spots, and silver streaks.

In order for a Pareto chart to include all categories, even those with few defects, in some situations you need to include a category labeled *Other* or *Miscellaneous*. In these situations, the bar representing these categories should be placed to the right of the other bars.

EXAMPLE 2.4

PARETO CHART OF BANKING PREFERENCE

Construct a Pareto chart of banking preference (see Table 2.1 on page 27).

SOLUTION In Figure 2.6, in person at branch and on the Internet account for 65% of the banking preferences; 98% of the respondents would prefer in person at branch, on the Internet, drive-through at branch, and ATM.

FIGURE 2.6

Microsoft Excel Pareto
chart for banking
preference

*See Sections E2.5 or P2.4 to
create this. (Minitab users,
see Section M2.4 to create
an equivalent chart.)*

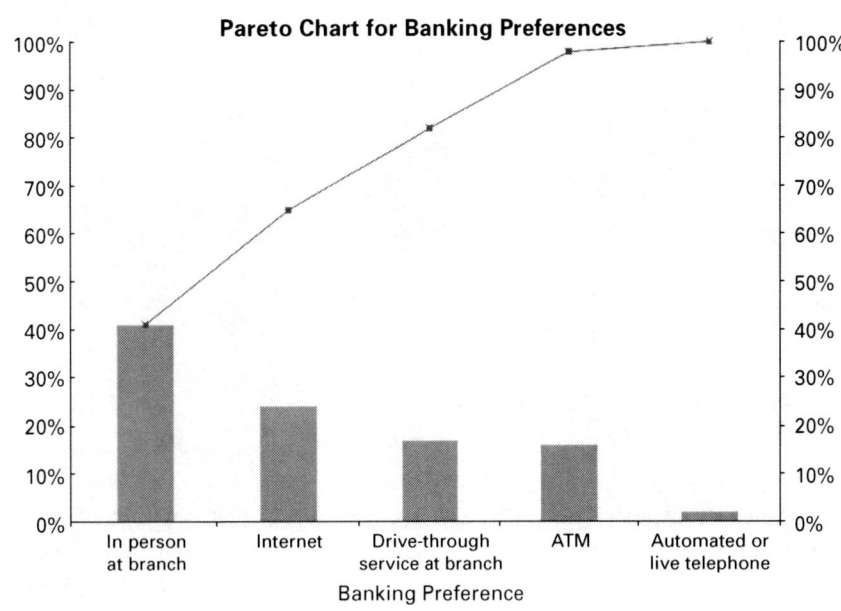

PROBLEMS FOR SECTION 2.1

Learning the Basics

2.1 A categorical variable has three categories with the following frequencies of occurrence:

Category	Frequency
A	13
B	28
C	9

a. Compute the percentage of values in each category.
b. Construct a bar chart.
c. Construct a pie chart.
d. Construct a Pareto chart.

2.2 A categorical variable has four categories with the following percentages of occurrence:

Category	Percentage	Category	Percentage
A	12	C	35
B	29	D	24

a. Construct a bar chart.
b. Construct a pie chart.
c. Construct a Pareto chart.

Applying the Concepts

2.3 A survey of 705 workers asked how much they used the Internet at work. The results (*USA Today, Snapshots*, March 21, 2006, p. 1B) were as follows:

Use of the Internet at Work	%
Too much	5
More than I should	4
Within limits	60
Very little	5
Do not use	26

a. Construct a bar chart, a pie chart, and a Pareto chart.
b. Which graphical method do you think is best to portray these data?
c. Based on this survey, what conclusions can you reach about the use of the Internet at work?

2.4 A survey of 1,264 women asked who was their most trusted shopping advisers. The results (*USA Today, Snapshots*, October 19, 2006, p. 1B) were as follows:

Shopping Advisers	%
Advertising	7
Friends/family	45
Manufacturer Web sites	5
News media	11
Online user reviews	13
Retail Web sites	4
Salespeople	1
Other	14

a. Construct a bar chart, a pie chart, and a Pareto chart.
b. Which graphical method do you think is best to portray these data?
c. What conclusions can you reach concerning women's most trusted shopping advisers?

2.5 What changes in their compensation package do workers in the United States want most? A survey by Hudson-Index.com indicated the following:

Perks	%
More money	42
Better health care	20
Better retirement	12
Work/family balance	10
Other	16

Source: *Adapted from Anne R. Carey and Chad Palmer, "What Workers Want,"* **www.usatoday.com***, April 9, 2007.*

a. Construct a bar chart, a pie chart, and a Pareto chart.
b. Which graphical method do you think is best to portray these data?
c. What conclusions can you reach concerning which perks workers want most?

2.6 The following table represents the U.S. sources of electric energy in a recent year:

Source	%
Coal	50
Hydropower	7
Natural gas	18
Nuclear	20
Oil	3
Renewables	2

Source: *International Energy Agency.*

a. Construct a Pareto chart.
b. What percentage of electricity is derived from coal, nuclear energy, or natural gas?

c. Construct a pie chart.

d. For these data, do you prefer the Pareto chart or the pie chart? Why?

2.7 An article (K. Delaney, "How Search Engine Rules Cause Sites to Go Missing," *The Wall Street Journal*, March 13, 2007, pp. B1, B4) discussed the amount of Internet search results that Web surfers typically scan before selecting one. The following table represents the results for a sample of 2,369 people:

Amount of Internet Search Results Scanned	Percentage (%)
A few search results	23
First page of search results	39
First two pages	19
First three pages	9
More than first three pages	10

a. Construct a bar chart and a pie chart.

b. Which graphical method do you think is best to portray these data?

c. What conclusions can you reach concerning how people scan Internet search results?

2.8 U.S. companies spent more than $250 billion in advertising in 2005 (K. Delaney, "In Latest Deal, Google Steps Further into World of Old Media," *The Wall Street Journal*, January 18, 2006, pp. A1, A6). The spending was as follows:

Media	Amount ($billions)	Percentage (%)
Cinema	0.4	0.16
Direct mail	44.5	17.35
Internet	10.0	3.90
Magazines	23.9	9.32
Newspapers	50.2	19.57
Outdoor	5.7	2.22
Radio	20.6	8.03
TV	55.4	21.60
Other	45.8	17.86

a. Construct a bar chart and a pie chart.

b. Which graphical method do you think is best to portray these data?

c. What conclusions can you reach concerning how U.S. companies spend their advertising dollars?

2.9 Medication errors are a serious problem in hospitals. The following data represent the root causes of pharmacy errors at a hospital during a recent time period:

Reason for Failure	Frequency
Additional instructions	16
Dose	23
Drug	14
Duplicate order entry	22
Frequency	47
Omission	21
Order not discontinued when received	12
Order not received	52
Patient	5
Route	4
Other	8

a. Construct a Pareto chart.

b. Discuss the "vital few" and "trivial many" reasons for the root causes of pharmacy errors.

2.10 The following data represent complaints about hotel rooms:

Reason	Number
Room dirty	32
Room not stocked	17
Room not ready	12
Room too noisy	10
Room needs maintenance	17
Room has too few beds	9
Room doesn't have promised features	7
No special accommodations	2

a. Construct a Pareto chart.

b. What reasons for complaints do you think the hotel should focus on if it wants to reduce the number of complaints? Explain.

2.2 ORGANIZING NUMERICAL DATA

When the number of data values is large, you can organize numerical data into an ordered array or a stem-and-leaf display to help understand the information you have. Suppose you decide to undertake a study that compares the cost of a restaurant meal in an urban area to the cost of a similar meal in the suburbs outside the city. The data file Restaurants contains the data for 50 urban restaurants and 50 suburban restaurants, as shown in Table 2.5. The data are not arranged in order from lowest to highest. This arrangement makes it difficult to arrive at conclusions concerning the price of meals in the two geographical areas.

TABLE 2.5

Price per Person at 50 Urban Restaurants and 50 Suburban Restaurants

Urban

65	48	32	27	47	45	36	55	48	33
45	46	39	44	45	63	54	20	55	73
51	34	28	65	44	43	50	29	33	41
41	52	48	48	38	52	33	40	36	51
39	38	22	35	35	16	74	57	52	68

Suburban

47	43	44	41	44	48	50	48	38	36
28	25	44	55	20	36	30	44	24	32
29	42	53	27	68	34	30	24	61	34
47	29	26	42	54	51	34	39	39	40
42	40	61	27	37	37	40	39	43	36

The Ordered Array

An **ordered array** is a sequence of data, in rank order, from the smallest value to the largest value. Table 2.6 contains ordered arrays for the cost of meals at urban restaurants and suburban restaurants. From Table 2.6 you can see that the cost of a meal at the urban restaurants is between $16 and $74 and the cost of a meal at the suburban restaurants is between $20 and $68.

TABLE 2.6

Ordered Array of Cost per Person at 50 Urban Restaurants and 50 Suburban Restaurants

Urban

16	20	22	27	28	29	32	33	33	33
34	35	35	36	36	38	38	39	39	40
41	41	43	44	44	45	45	45	46	47
48	48	48	48	50	51	51	52	52	52
54	55	55	57	63	65	65	68	73	74

Suburban

20	24	24	25	26	27	27	28	29	29
30	30	32	34	34	34	36	36	36	37
37	38	39	39	39	40	40	40	41	42
42	42	43	43	44	44	44	44	47	47
48	48	50	51	53	54	55	61	61	68

The Stem-and-Leaf Display

A **stem-and-leaf display** organizes data into groups (called stems) so that the values within each group (the leaves) branch out to the right on each row. The resulting display allows you to see how the data are distributed and where concentrations of data exist. To see how to construct a stem-and-leaf display, suppose that 15 students from your class eat lunch at a fast-food restaurant. The following data are the amounts ($) spent for lunch:

5.40 4.30 4.80 5.50 7.30 8.50 6.10 4.80 4.90 4.90 5.50 3.50 5.90 6.30 6.60

To form the stem-and-leaf display, you use the units as the stems and round the decimals (the leaves) to one decimal place. For example, the first value is 5.40. Its stem (row) is 5, and its leaf is 4. The second value is 4.30. Its stem (row) is 4, and its leaf is 3. You continue with the remainder of the 15 values and then reorder the leaves within each stem as follows:

```
3 | 5
4 | 38899
5 | 4559
6 | 136
7 | 3
8 | 5
```

EXAMPLE 2.5 STEM-AND-LEAF DISPLAY OF THE 2006 RETURN OF THE LOW-RISK MUTUAL FUNDS

In this chapter's Using Statistics scenario, you are interested in studying the past performance of low-risk mutual funds. One measure of past performance is the return in 2006. Construct a stem-and-leaf display of the return in 2006 for the low-risk funds.

SOLUTION From Figure 2.7, you can conclude that:

• The lowest return in 2006 was 1.
• The highest return in 2006 was 28.
• The returns in 2006 were concentrated between 14 and 23.
• Only one mutual fund had a 2006 return below 5, and only two low-risk mutual funds had a 2006 return above 25.

Notice that due to the large number of values, Minitab subdivides each stem into five sub-stems containing leaves with 0 and 1, 2 and 3, 4 and 5, 6 and 7, and 8 and 9.

FIGURE 2.7

Minitab Stem-and-Leaf Display of the Returns of Low-Risk Mutual Funds in 2006

See Section M2.5 to create this. (PHStat2 users, see Section P2.5 to create an equivalent display.)

```
Stem-and-leaf of Return 2006-Low Risk  N = 202
Leaf Unit = 1.0

    1    0  1
    1    0
    2    0  5
    6    0  6667
   13    0  8888899
   26    1  0000001111111
   33    1  2223333
   66    1  444444444444444455555555555555555555
  (40)   1  6666666666666666666666666677777777777777
   96    1  888888888888888888888888888999999999999999999999999999999999
   38    2  0000000000000001111111111
   13    2  2222223333
    3    2  4
    2    2  6
    1    2  8
```

PROBLEMS FOR SECTION 2.2

Learning the Basics

2.11 Form an ordered array, given the following data from a sample of $n = 7$ midterm exam scores in accounting:

68 94 63 75 71 88 64

2.12 Form a stem-and-leaf display, given the following data from a sample of $n = 7$ midterm exam scores in finance:

80 54 69 98 93 53 74

2.13 Form an ordered array, given the following data from a sample of $n = 7$ midterm exam scores in marketing:

88 78 78 73 91 78 85

2.14 Form an ordered array, given the following stem-and-leaf display from a sample of $n = 7$ midterm exam scores in information systems:

```
5 | 0
6 |
7 | 446
8 | 19
9 | 2
```

Applying the Concepts

2.15 The following is a stem-and-leaf display representing the amount of gasoline purchased, in gallons (with leaves in tenths of gallons), for a sample of 25 cars that use a particular service station on the New Jersey Turnpike:

```
 9 | 147
10 | 02238
11 | 12556677
12 | 223489
13 | 02
```

a. Place the data into an ordered array.
b. Which of these two displays seems to provide more information? Discuss.
c. What amount of gasoline (in gallons) is most likely to be purchased?
d. Is there a concentration of the purchase amounts in the center of the distribution?

2.16 As player salaries have increased, the cost of attending baseball games has increased dramatically. The following data in the file **BB2006** (extracted from K. Belson, "Oh Yeah, There's a Ballgame Too," *The New York Times*, October 22, 2006, Business, pp. 1, 7–8) represent the cost of four tickets, two beers, four soft drinks, four hot dogs, two game programs, two baseball caps, and the parking fee for one car for each of the 30 major league baseball teams.

Team	Cost($)	Team	Cost($)
Baltimore	159	Chicago Cubs	219
Boston	288	Cincinnati	157
Chicago White Sox	191	Colorado	141
Cleveland	158	Florida	154
Detroit	163	Houston	192
Kansas City	120	Los Angeles	175
Los Angeles Angels	134	Dodgers	
Minnesota	149	Milwaukee	132
New York Yankees	209	New York Mets	207
Oakland	170	Philadelphia	194
Seattle	186	Pittsburgh	139
Tampa Bay	130	St. Louis	209
Texas	134	San Diego	180
Toronto	183	San Francisco	202
Arizona	148	Washington	170
Atlanta	146		

a. Place the data into an ordered array.
b. Construct a stem-and-leaf display for these data.

c. Which of these two displays seems to provide more information? Discuss.
d. Around what value, if any, are the costs of attending a baseball game concentrated? Explain.

2.17 The file **MoviePrices** contains data on the price for two tickets, with online service charges, large popcorn, and two medium soft drinks at a sample of six theater chains:

$36.15 $31.00 $35.05 $40.25 $33.75 $43.00

Source: *Extracted from K. Kelly, "The Multiplex Under Siege," The Wall Street Journal, December 24–25, 2005, pp. P1, P5.*

a. Place the data into an ordered array.
b. Construct a stem-and-leaf display for these data.
c. Which of these two displays seems to provide more information? Discuss.
d. Around what value, if any, are the movie prices concentrated? Explain.

✓ **SELF Test** **2.18** The file **Chicken** contains data on the total fat, in grams per serving, for a sample of 20 chicken sandwiches from fast-food chains. The data are as follows:

7 8 4 5 16 20 20 24 19 30 23 30 25 19 29 29 30 30 40 56

Source: *Extracted from "Fast Food: Adding Health to the Menu," Consumer Reports, September 2004, pp. 28–31.*

a. Place the data into an ordered array.
b. Construct a stem-and-leaf display.
c. Does the ordered array or the stem-and-leaf display provide more information? Discuss.
d. Around what value, if any, are the total fat amounts concentrated? Explain.

2.19 The data in the file **Batterylife** represent the battery life, in shots, for a sample of 12 three pixel digital cameras:

300 180 85 170 380 460 260 35 380 120 110 240

Source: *Extracted from "Cameras: More Features in the Mix," Consumer Reports, July 2005, pp. 14–18.*

a. Place the data into an ordered array.
b. Construct a stem-and-leaf display.
c. Does the ordered array or the stem-and-leaf display provide more information? Discuss.
d. Around what value, if any, is the battery life concentrated? Explain.

2.3 TABLES AND CHARTS FOR NUMERICAL DATA

When you have a data set that contains a large number of values, reaching conclusions from an ordered array or a stem-and-leaf display can be difficult. In such circumstances, you need to present data in tables and charts such as the frequency and percentage distributions, histogram, polygon, and cumulative percentage polygon (ogive).

The Frequency Distribution

The **frequency distribution** is a summary table in which the data are arranged into numerically ordered **classes**. In constructing a frequency distribution, you must give attention to selecting the appropriate *number* of classes for the table, determining a suitable *width* of a class, and establishing the *boundaries* of each **class grouping** to avoid overlapping.

The number of classes you use depends on the number of values in the data. Larger numbers of values allow for a larger number of classes. In general, the frequency distribution should have at least 5 classes but no more than 15. Having too few or too many classes provides little new information.

When developing a frequency distribution, you define each class by class intervals of equal width. To determine the **width of a class interval**, you divide the **range** (highest value − lowest value) of the data by the number of classes desired.

Determining the Width of a Class Interval

$$\text{Width of interval} = \frac{\text{Range}}{\text{number of classes}} \qquad (2.1)$$

Because the urban restaurant data consist of a sample of 50 restaurants, 10 classes are acceptable. From the ordered array in Table 2.6 on page 34, the range of the data is $74 − $16 = $58. Using Equation (2.1), you approximate the width of the class interval as follows:

$$\text{Width of interval} = \frac{58}{10} = 5.8$$

You should choose an interval width that simplifies reading and interpretation. Therefore, instead of using an interval width of $5.80, you should select an interval width of $5.00.

To construct the frequency distribution table, you should establish clearly defined **class boundaries** for each class so that the values can be properly tallied into the classes. You place each value in one and only one class. You must avoid overlapping of classes.

Because you have set the width of each class interval for the restaurant data at $5, you need to establish the boundaries of the various classes so as to include the entire range of values. Whenever possible, you should choose these boundaries to simplify reading and interpretation. Thus, for the urban restaurants, because the cost ranges from $16 to $74, the first class interval ranges from $15 to less than $20, the second from $20 to less than $25, and so on, until they have been tallied into 12 classes. Each class has an interval width of $5, without overlapping. The center of each class, the **class midpoint**, is halfway between the lower boundary of the class and the upper boundary of the class. Thus, the class midpoint for the class from $15 to under $20 is $17.50, the class midpoint for the class from $20 to under $25 is $22.50, and so on. Table 2.7 is a frequency distribution of the cost per meal for the 50 urban restaurants and the 50 suburban restaurants.

TABLE 2.7

Frequency Distribution of the Cost per Meal for 50 Urban Restaurants and 50 Suburban Restaurants

Cost per Meal ($)	Urban Frequency	Suburban Frequency
15 but less than 20	1	0
20 but less than 25	2	3
25 but less than 30	3	7
30 but less than 35	5	6
35 but less than 40	8	9
40 but less than 45	6	13
45 but less than 50	9	4
50 but less than 55	7	4
55 but less than 60	3	1
60 but less than 65	1	2
65 but less than 70	3	1
70 but less than 75	2	0
Total	50	50

The frequency distribution allows you to draw conclusions about the major characteristics of the data. For example, Table 2.7 shows that the cost of meals at urban restaurants is concentrated between $30 and $55, and the cost of meals at suburban restaurants is clustered between $25 and $45.

If the data set does not contain many values, one set of class boundaries may provide a different picture than another set. For example, for the restaurant data, using a class-interval width of 6.0 instead of 5.0 (as was used in Table 2.7) may cause shifts in the way the values distribute among the classes.

You can also get shifts in data concentration when you choose different lower and upper class boundaries. Fortunately, as the sample size increases, alterations in the selection of class boundaries affect the concentration of data less and less.

EXAMPLE 2.6

FREQUENCY DISTRIBUTION OF THE 2006 RETURN FOR GROWTH AND VALUE MUTUAL FUNDS

In the Using Statistics scenario, you are interested in comparing the 2006 return of growth and value mutual funds. Construct frequency distributions for the growth funds and the value funds.

SOLUTION The 2006 returns of the growth funds are highly concentrated between 0 and 15, whereas the 2006 returns of the value funds are highly concentrated between 10 and 25 (see Table 2.8). You should not directly compare the frequencies of the growth funds and the value funds because there are 464 growth funds and 404 value funds in the sample. Proportions or relative frequencies and percentages are introduced below.

TABLE 2.8

Frequency Distribution of the 2006 Return for Growth and Value Mutual Funds

2006 Return	Growth Frequency	Value Frequency
−10 but less than −5	6	0
−5 but less than 0	21	0
0 but less than 5	75	1
5 but less than 10	189	14
10 but less than 15	121	102
15 but less than 20	39	208
20 but less than 25	12	71
25 but less than 30	1	7
30 but less than 35	0	0
35 but less than 40	0	1
Total	464	404

The Relative Frequency Distribution and the Percentage Distribution

Because you usually want to know the proportion or the percentage of the total that is in each group, the relative frequency distribution or the percentage distribution is preferred to the frequency distribution.

The **proportion** in each group is equal to the number of frequencies in each class divided by the total number of values. The **relative frequency** is another word for the proportion. You then compute the percentage in each group by multiplying the proportion by 100%.

Computing the Proportion or Relative Frequency

The proportion or relative frequency is the number of frequencies in each class divided by the total number of values.

$$\text{Proportion} = \text{Relative Frequency} = \frac{\text{frequency in each class}}{\text{total number of values}} \qquad \textbf{(2.2)}$$

Thus, if there are 80 values and the frequency in a certain class is 20, the proportion of frequencies in that class is

$$\frac{20}{80} = 0.25$$

and the percentage is

$$0.25 \times 100\% = 25\%$$

When you are comparing two or more groups that have different sample sizes, you must use either a relative frequency distribution or a percentage distribution. You form the **relative frequency distribution** by first determining the frequency (the number of values) in each class and then dividing by the total number of values. See Equation (2.2). For example, in Table 2.7 on page 37, there are 50 urban restaurants and the cost per meal at 3 of these restaurants is between 25 and 30. Therefore, as shown in Table 2.9, the proportion (or relative frequency) of meals that cost between $25 and $30 at urban restaurants is

$$\frac{6}{50} = 0.12$$

You form the **percentage distribution** by multiplying each proportion (or relative frequency) by 100%. Thus, the proportion of meals at urban restaurants that cost between $50 and $55 is 7 divided by 50, or 0.14, and the percentage is 14%. Table 2.9 presents the relative frequency distribution and percentage distribution of the cost of meals at urban and suburban restaurants.

TABLE 2.9

Relative Frequency Distribution and Percentage Distribution of the Cost of Meals at Urban and Suburban Restaurants

Cost per Meal ($)	Urban Relative Frequency	Urban Percentage	Suburban Relative Frequency	Suburban Percentage
15 but less than 20	0.02	2.0	0.00	0.0
20 but less than 25	0.04	4.0	0.06	6.0
25 but less than 30	0.06	6.0	0.14	14.0
30 but less than 35	0.10	10.0	0.12	12.0
35 but less than 40	0.16	16.0	0.18	18.0
40 but less than 45	0.12	12.0	0.26	26.0
45 but less than 50	0.18	18.0	0.08	8.0
50 but less than 55	0.14	14.0	0.08	8.0
55 but less than 60	0.06	6.0	0.02	2.0
60 but less than 65	0.02	2.0	0.04	4.0
65 but less than 70	0.06	6.0	0.02	2.0
70 but less than 75	0.04	4.0	0.00	0.0
Total	1.00	100.0	1.00	100.0

From Table 2.9, you conclude that meals cost more at urban restaurants than at suburban restaurants. Also 18% of the meals cost between $45 and $50 at urban restaurants as compared to 8% of the meals at suburban restaurants; and only 6% of the meals cost between $25 and $30 at urban restaurants as compared to 14% of the meals at suburban restaurants.

EXAMPLE 2.7

RELATIVE FREQUENCY DISTRIBUTION AND PERCENTAGE DISTRIBUTION OF THE 2006 RETURN FOR GROWTH AND VALUE MUTUAL FUNDS

In the Using Statistics scenario, you are interested in comparing the 2006 return for growth and value mutual funds. Construct relative frequency distributions and percentage distributions for the growth funds and the value funds.

SOLUTION You conclude (see Table 2.10) that the 2006 return for the growth funds is much lower than for the value funds. 5.82% of growth funds have negative returns, while none of the value funds have negative returns. Of the growth funds, 16.16% have returns between 0 and 5 as compared to only 0.25% of the value funds. Also, more of the value funds have higher returns. For example, 51.49% of the value funds have a return between 15 and 20, whereas only 8.41% of the growth funds have a return between 15 and 20.

TABLE 2.10

Relative Frequency Distribution and Percentage Distribution of the 2006 Return for Growth and Value Mutual Funds

2006 Return	Growth Proportion	Growth Percentage	Value Proportion	Value Percentage
−10 but less than −5	0.0129	1.29	0.0000	0.00
−5 but less than 0	0.0453	4.53	0.0000	0.00
0 but less than 5	0.1616	16.16	0.0025	0.25
5 but less than 10	0.4073	40.73	0.0347	3.47
10 but less than 15	0.2608	26.08	0.2525	25.25
15 but less than 20	0.0841	8.41	0.5149	51.49
20 but less than 25	0.0259	2.59	0.1757	17.57
25 but less than 30	0.0022	0.22	0.0173	1.73
30 but less than 35	0.0000	0.00	0.0000	0.00
35 but less than 40	0.0000	0.00	0.0025	0.25
Total*	1.0001	100.01	1.0001	100.01

*Error due to rounding

The Cumulative Distribution

The **cumulative percentage distribution** provides a way of presenting information about the percentage of items that are less than a certain value. For example, you might want to know what percentage of the urban restaurant meals cost less than $20, less than $30, less than $50, and so on. The percentage distribution is used to form the cumulative percentage distribution. Table 2.11 illustrates how to develop the cumulative percentage distribution for the cost of meals at urban restaurants. This table shows that 0.00% of the meals cost less than $15, 2% cost

TABLE 2.11

Developing the Cumulative Percentage Distribution for the Cost of Meals at Urban Restaurants

Cost per Meal ($)	Percentage	Percentage of Meals Less Than Lower Boundary of Class Interval
15 but less than 20	2	0
20 but less than 25	4	2
25 but less than 30	6	6 = 2 + 4
30 but less than 35	10	12 = 2 + 4 + 6
35 but less than 40	16	22 = 2 + 4 + 6 + 10
40 but less than 45	12	38 = 2 + 4 + 6 + 10 + 16
45 but less than 50	18	50 = 2 + 4 + 6 + 10 + 16 + 12
50 but less than 55	14	68 = 2 + 4 + 6 + 10 + 16 + 12 + 18
55 but less than 60	6	82 = 2 + 4 + 6 + 10 + 16 + 12 + 18 + 14
60 but less than 65	2	88 = 2 + 4 + 6 + 10 + 16 + 12 + 18 + 14 + 6
65 but less than 70	6	90 = 2 + 4 + 6 + 10 + 16 + 12 + 18 + 14 + 6 + 2
70 but less than 75	4	96 = 2 + 4 + 6 + 10 + 16 + 12 + 18 + 14 + 6 + 2 + 6
75 but less than 80	0	100 = 2 + 4 + 6 + 10 + 16 + 12 + 18 + 14 + 6 + 2 + 6 + 4

less than $20, 6% cost less than $25 (because 4% of the meals cost between $20 and $25), and so on, until all 100% of the meals cost less than $75.

Table 2.12 summarizes the cumulative percentages of the cost of urban and suburban restaurant meals. The cumulative distribution clearly shows that the cost of meals is lower in suburban restaurants than in urban restaurants. Table 2.12 shows that 20% of the meals at suburban restaurants cost less than $30 as compared to only 12% of the meals at urban restaurants; 32% of the meals at suburban restaurants cost less than $35 as compared to only 22% of the meals at urban restaurants; and 76% of the meals at suburban restaurants cost less than $45 as compared to only 50% of the meals at urban restaurants.

TABLE 2.12

Cumulative Percentage Distributions of the Cost of Urban and Suburban Restaurant Meals

Cost ($)	Urban Percentage of Restaurants with Meals Less Than Indicated Value	Suburban Percentage of Restaurants with Meals Less Than Indicated Value
15	0	0
20	2	0
25	6	6
30	12	20
35	22	32
40	38	50
45	50	76
50	68	84
55	82	92
60	88	94
65	90	98
70	96	100
75	100	100

EXAMPLE 2.8

CUMULATIVE PERCENTAGE DISTRIBUTION OF THE 2006 RETURN FOR GROWTH AND VALUE MUTUAL FUNDS

In the Using Statistics scenario, you are interested in comparing the 2006 return of growth and value mutual funds. Construct cumulative percentage distributions for the growth funds and the value funds.

SOLUTION The cumulative distribution in Table 2.13 indicates that more of the growth funds have lower returns than the value funds. The table shows that 5.82% of the growth funds have negative returns as compared to none of the value funds; 21.98% of the growth funds have returns below 5 as compared to 0.25% of the value funds; and 62.71% of the growth funds have returns below 10 as compared to 3.72% of the value funds.

TABLE 2.13

Cumulative Percentage Distributions of the 2006 Return for Growth and Value Funds

2006 Return	Growth Fund Percentage Less Than Indicated Value	Value Fund Percentage Less Than Indicated Value
−10	0.00	0.00
−5	1.29	0.00
0	5.82	0.00
5	21.98	0.25
10	62.71	3.72
15	88.79	28.97
20	97.20	80.46
25	99.79	98.03
30	100.00	99.76
35	100.00	99.76
40	100.01*	100.01*

*Error due to rounding.

The Histogram

A **histogram** is a bar chart for grouped numerical data in which the frequencies or percentages of each group of numerical data are represented as individual vertical bars. In a histogram, there are no gaps between adjacent bars as there is in a bar chart of categorical data. You display the variable of interest along the horizontal (X) axis. The vertical (Y) axis represents either the frequency or the percentage of values per class interval.

Figure 2.8 displays a Microsoft Excel frequency histogram for the cost of meals at urban restaurants and suburban restaurants. The histogram for urban restaurants indicates that the cost of meals is concentrated between approximately $30 and $55. Very few meals at urban restaurants cost less than $20 or more than $60. The histogram for suburban restaurants shows that the cost of meals is concentrated between $25 and $45. Very few meals at suburban restaurants cost less than $20 or more than $55.

FIGURE 2.8

Microsoft Excel histograms for the cost of restaurant meals— Panel A Urban Restaurants and Panel B Suburban Restaurants

See Sections E2.9 or P2.6 to create this. (Minitab users, see Section M2.6 to create an equivalent chart.)

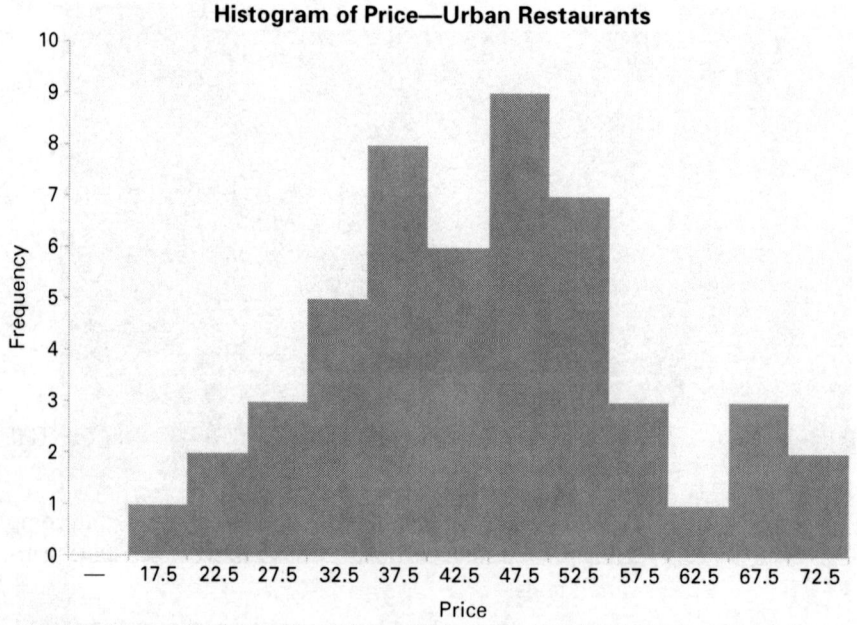

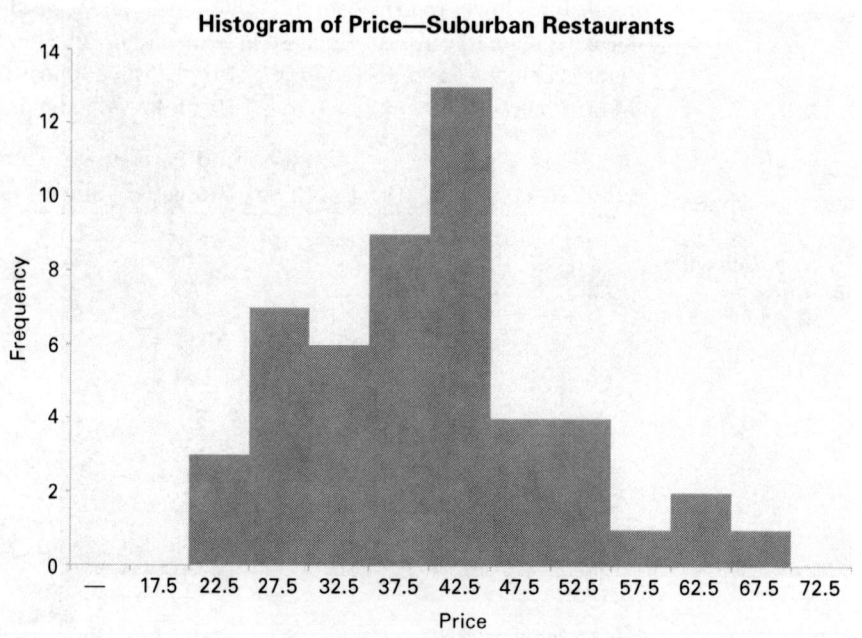

EXAMPLE 2.9

HISTOGRAM OF THE 2006 RETURN FOR GROWTH AND VALUE MUTUAL FUNDS

In the Using Statistics scenario, you are interested in comparing the 2006 return of growth and value mutual funds. Construct histograms for the growth funds and the value funds.

SOLUTION Figure 2.9 shows that the distribution of the growth funds has more low returns as compared to the value funds, which have more high returns. The return for growth funds is concentrated between 0 and 15, whereas the return for value funds is concentrated between 10 and 25.

FIGURE 2.9

Microsoft Excel Histograms of the 2006 return for growth and value funds

See Sections E2.9 or P2.6 to create this. (Minitab users, see Section M2.6 to create an equivalent chart.)

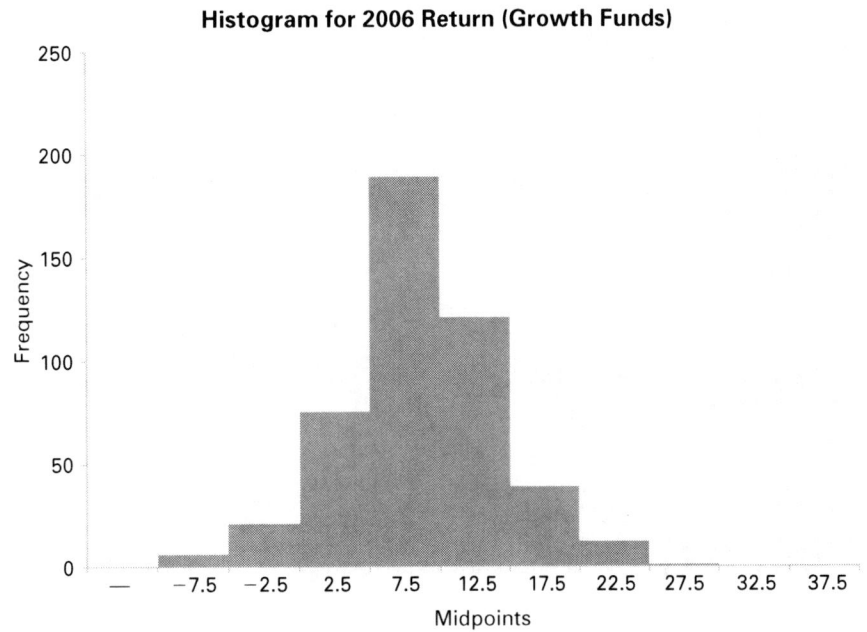

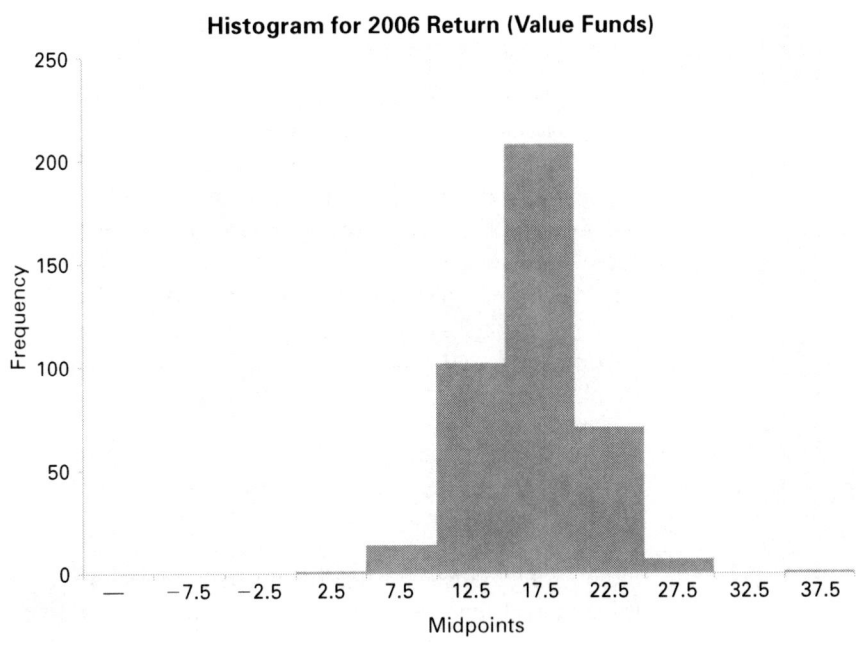

The Polygon

Constructing multiple histograms on the same graph when comparing two or more sets of data is confusing. Superimposing the vertical bars of one histogram on another histogram makes interpretation difficult. When there are two or more groups, you should use a percentage polygon.

> PERCENTAGE POLYGON
>
> A **percentage polygon** is formed by having the midpoint of each class represent the data in that class and then connecting the sequence of midpoints at their respective class percentages.

Figure 2.10 displays percentage polygons for the cost of meals at urban and suburban restaurants. The polygon for the cost of meals at suburban restaurants is concentrated to the left of (corresponding to lower cost) the polygon for the cost of meals at urban restaurants. The highest percentage of meals at the suburban restaurants are for a class midpoint of $42.50, whereas the highest percentage of meals at the urban restaurants are for a class midpoint of $47.50.

FIGURE 2.10

Microsoft Excel percentage polygons of the cost of restaurant meals for urban and suburban restaurants

See Section P2.7 to create this.

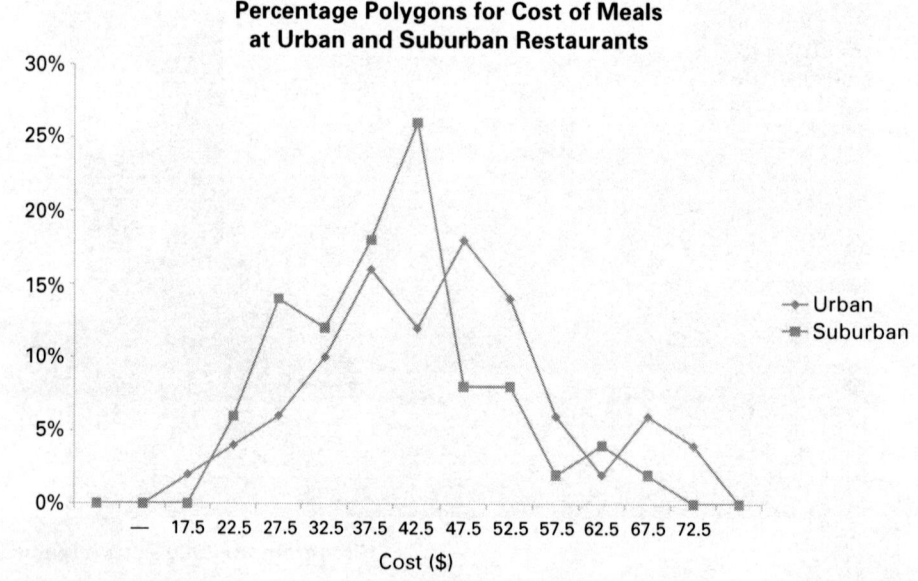

The polygons in Figure 2.10 have points whose values on the X axis represent the midpoint of the class interval. For example, look at the points plotted on the Y axis at 42.5 ($42.50). The point for the cost of meals at suburban restaurants (the higher one) represents the fact that 26% of the meals at these restaurants cost between $40 and $45. The point for the cost of meals at urban restaurants (the lower one) represents the fact that 12% of meals at these restaurants cost between $40 and $45.

When you construct polygons or histograms, the vertical (Y) axis should show the true zero, or "origin," so as not to distort the character of the data. The horizontal (X) axis does not need to show the zero point for the variable of interest, although the range of the variable should include the major portion of the axis.

EXAMPLE 2.10

PERCENTAGE POLYGONS OF THE 2006 RETURN FOR GROWTH AND VALUE MUTUAL FUNDS

In the Using Statistics scenario, you are interested in comparing the 2006 return of growth and value mutual funds. Construct percentage polygons for the 2006 return for growth funds and value funds.

SOLUTION Figure 2.11 shows that the distribution of the 2006 return of growth funds is lower than the value funds, which has more high returns. The highest percentage of 2006 returns for the growth funds is at 7.5, whereas the highest percentage of 2006 returns for the value funds is at 17.5.

FIGURE 2.11

Microsoft Excel percentage polygons of the 2006 return

See Section P2.7 to create this.

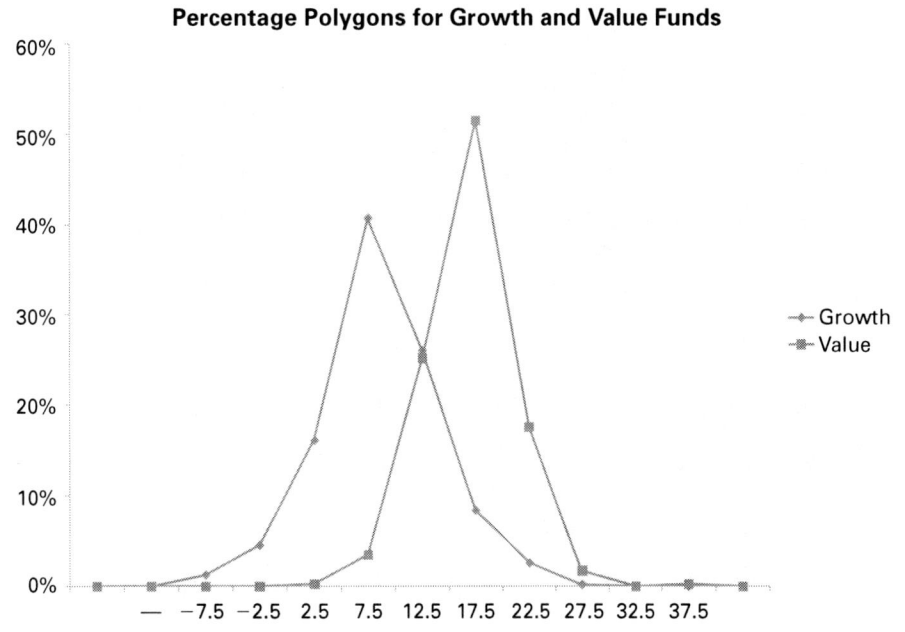

The Cumulative Percentage Polygon (Ogive)

The **cumulative percentage polygon**, or **ogive**, displays the variable of interest along the X axis and the cumulative percentages along the Y axis.

Figure 2.12 illustrates the Microsoft Excel cumulative percentage polygons of the cost of meals at urban and suburban restaurants. Most of the curve of the cost of meals at the urban restaurants is located to the right of the curve for the suburban restaurants. This indicates that the urban restaurants have fewer meals that cost below a particular value. For example, 38% of the meals at urban restaurants cost less than $40 as compared to 50% of the meals at suburban restaurants.

FIGURE 2.12

Microsoft Excel cumulative percentage polygons of the cost of restaurant meals at urban and suburban restaurants

See Section P2.7 to create this.

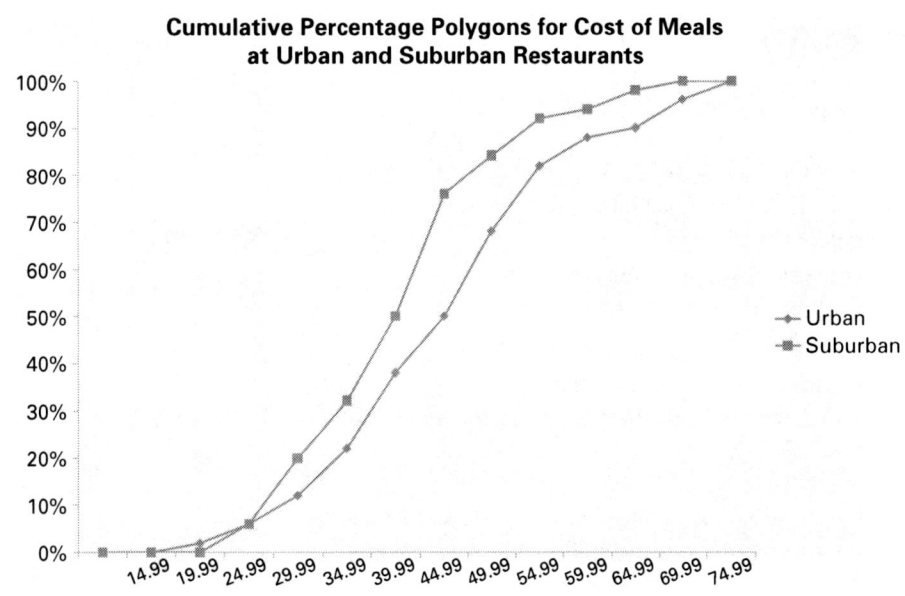

EXAMPLE 2.11   CUMULATIVE PERCENTAGE POLYGONS OF THE 2006 RETURN FOR GROWTH AND VALUE MUTUAL FUNDS

In the Using Statistics scenario, you are interested in comparing the 2006 return of growth and value mutual funds. Construct cumulative percentage polygons of the 2006 return for the growth funds and the value funds.

SOLUTION   Figure 2.13 illustrates the Microsoft Excel cumulative percentage polygons of the 2006 return for growth and value funds. The curve for the 2006 return of value funds is located to the right of the curve for the growth funds. This indicates that the value funds have fewer 2006 returns below a particular value. For example, 88.79% of the growth funds have 2006 returns less than 15 as compared to 28.97% of the value funds. You can conclude that, in general, the value funds outperformed the growth funds in 2006.

FIGURE 2.13

Microsoft Excel cumulative percentage polygons of the 2006 return of growth funds and value funds

See Section P2.7 to create this.

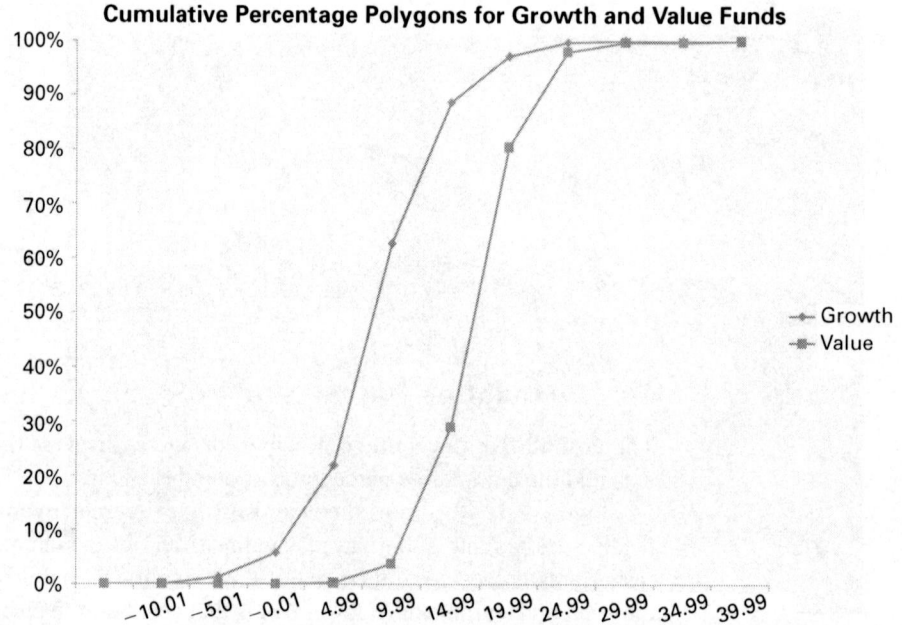

PROBLEMS FOR SECTION 2.3

Learning the Basics

2.20   The values for a set of data vary from 11.6 to 97.8.
a. If these values are grouped into nine classes, indicate the class boundaries.
b. What class-interval width did you choose?
c. What are the nine class midpoints?

2.21   The GMAT scores from a sample of 50 applicants to an MBA program indicate that none of the applicants scored below 450. A frequency distribution was formed by choosing class intervals 450 to 499, 500 to 549, and so on, with the last class having an interval from 700 to 749. Two applicants scored in the interval 450 to 499, and 16 applicants scored in the interval 500 to 549.
a. What percentage of applicants scored below 500?

b. What percentage of applicants scored between 500 and 549?
c. What percentage of applicants scored below 550?
d. What percentage of applicants scored below 750?

Applying the Concepts

2.22   The following data (contained in the file **Utility**) represent the cost of electricity during July 2007 for a random sample of 50 one-bedroom apartments in a large city:

Raw Data on Utility Charges ($)

96	171	202	178	147	102	153	197	127	82
157	185	90	116	172	111	148	213	130	165
141	149	206	175	123	128	144	168	109	167
95	163	150	154	130	143	187	166	139	149
108	119	183	151	114	135	191	137	129	158

a. Form a frequency distribution and a percentage distribution that have class intervals with the upper class boundaries $99, $119, and so on.
b. Construct a histogram and a percentage polygon.
c. Form a cumulative percentage distribution and plot a cumulative percentage polygon.
d. Around what amount does the monthly electricity cost seem to be concentrated?

2.23 As player salaries have increased, the cost of attending baseball games has increased dramatically. The data in the file BB2006 (extracted from K. Belson, "Oh Yeah, There's a Ballgame Too," *The New York Times*, October 22, 2006, pp. B1, B7–8) represent the cost of four tickets, two beers, four soft drinks, four hot dogs, two game programs, two baseball caps, and the parking fee for one car for each of the 30 major league teams. The following is a histogram created for these data.

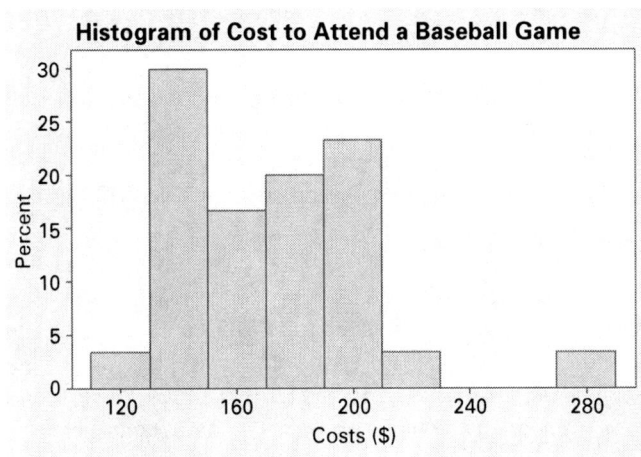

Histogram of Cost to Attend a Baseball Game

What conclusions can you reach concerning the cost of attending a baseball game at different ballparks?

2.24 The data in the file PropertyTaxes contains the property taxes per capita for the fifty states and the District of Columbia. The following is a histogram and cumulative percentage polygon created for these data.

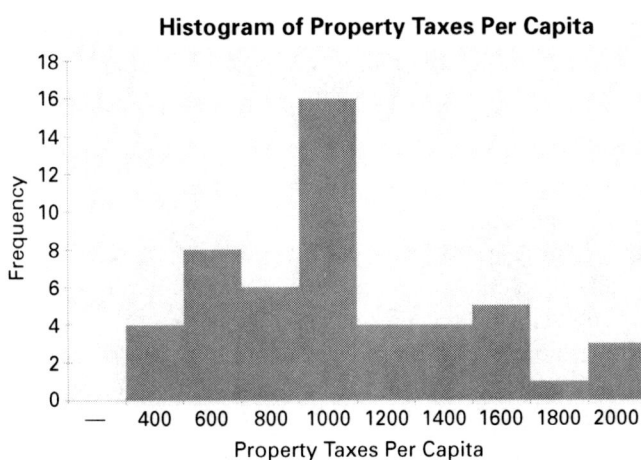

Histogram of Property Taxes Per Capita

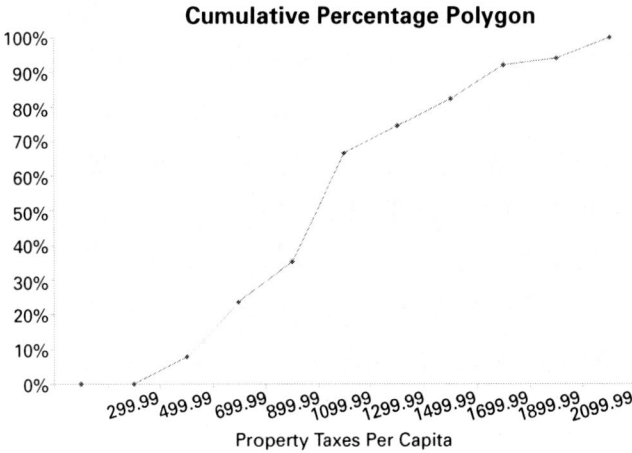

Cumulative Percentage Polygon

What conclusions can you reach concerning the property taxes per capita?

2.25 One operation of a mill is to cut pieces of steel into parts that will later be used as the frame for front seats in an automobile. The steel is cut with a diamond saw and requires the resulting parts to be within ±0.005 inch of the length specified by the automobile company. The following data (contained in the file Steel) comes from a sample of 100 steel parts. The measurement reported is the difference in inches between the actual length of the steel part, as measured by a laser measurement device, and the specified length of the steel part. For example, the first value, −0.002, represents a steel part that is 0.002 inch shorter than the specified length.

−0.002	0.002	0.0005	−0.0015	−0.001
0.0005	0.001	0.001	−0.0005	−0.001
0.0025	0.001	0.0005	−0.0015	0.0005
0.001	0.001	0.001	−0.0005	−0.0025
0.002	−0.002	0.0025	−0.0005	0.0025
0.001	−0.003	0.001	−0.001	0.002
0.005	−0.0015	0.000	−0.0015	0.0025
−0.002	−0.0005	−0.0025	0.0025	−0.002
0.000	0.000	−0.001	0.001	0.000
0.001	−0.0025	0.0035	0.0005	−0.0005
−0.0025	−0.003	0.000	0.000	−0.001
−0.003	−0.001	−0.003	0.002	0.000
0.001	0.002	−0.002	−0.0005	−0.002
−0.0005	−0.001	−0.001	0.0005	0.000
0.000	0.000	−0.0015	0.0005	0.000
−0.003	0.003	−0.0015	0.000	0.0020
−0.001	0.0015	−0.002	−0.0005	−0.003
0.0005	0.000	0.001	0.002	−0.0005
0.0025	0.000	−0.0025	0.001	−0.002
−0.0025	−0.0025	−0.0005	−0.0015	−0.002

a. Construct a percentage histogram.

b. Is the steel mill doing a good job in meeting the requirements set by the automobile company? Explain.

✓ SELF
✓ Test **2.26** A manufacturing company produces steel housings for electrical equipment. The main component part of the housing is a steel trough that is made out of a 14-gauge steel coil. It is produced using a 250-ton progressive punch press with a wipe-down operation that puts two 90-degree forms in the flat steel to make the trough. The distance from one side of the form to the other is critical because of weatherproofing in outdoor applications. The company requires that the width of the trough be between 8.31 inches and 8.61 inches. The following (contained in the file **Trough**) are the widths of the troughs, in inches, for a sample of 49 troughs.

8.312 8.343 8.317 8.383 8.348 8.410 8.351 8.373

8.481 8.422 8.476 8.382 8.484 8.403 8.414 8.419

8.385 8.465 8.498 8.447 8.436 8.413 8.489 8.414

8.481 8.415 8.479 8.429 8.458 8.462 8.460 8.444

8.429 8.460 8.412 8.420 8.410 8.405 8.323 8.420

8.396 8.447 8.405 8.439 8.411 8.427 8.420 8.498

8.409

a. Construct a frequency distribution and a percentage distribution.

b. Construct a percentage histogram and a percentage polygon.

c. Plot a cumulative percentage polygon.

d. What can you conclude about the number of troughs that will meet the company's requirements of troughs being between 8.31 and 8.61 inches wide?

2.27 The manufacturing company in Problem 2.26 also produces electric insulators. If the insulators break when in use, a short circuit is likely to occur. To test the strength of the insulators, destructive testing in high-powered labs is carried out to determine how much *force* is required to break the insulators. Force is measured by observing how many pounds must be applied to the insulator before it breaks. The strengths of 30 insulators (contained in the file **Force**) are as follows:

1,870 1,728 1,656 1,610 1,634 1,784 1,522 1,696

1,592 1,662 1,866 1,764 1,734 1,662 1,734 1,774

1,550 1,756 1,762 1,866 1,820 1,744 1,788 1,688

1,810 1,752 1,680 1,810 1,652 1,736

a. Construct a frequency distribution and a percentage distribution.

b. Construct a percentage histogram and a percentage polygon.

c. Plot a cumulative percentage polygon.

d. What can you conclude about the strength of the insulators if the company requires a force measurement of at least 1,500 pounds before breaking?

2.28 The ordered arrays in the accompanying table (and contained in the file **Bulbs**) deal with the life (in hours) of a sample of forty 100-watt lightbulbs produced by Manufacturer A and a sample of forty 100-watt lightbulbs produced by Manufacturer B.

Manufacturer A					Manufacturer B				
684	697	720	773	821	819	836	888	897	903
831	835	848	852	852	907	912	918	942	943
859	860	868	870	876	952	959	962	986	992
893	899	905	909	911	994	1,004	1,005	1,007	1,015
922	924	926	926	938	1,016	1,018	1,020	1,022	1,034
939	943	946	954	971	1,038	1,072	1,077	1,077	1,082
972	977	984	1,005	1,014	1,096	1,100	1,113	1,113	1,116
1,016	1,041	1,052	1,080	1,093	1,153	1,154	1,174	1,188	1,230

a. Form a frequency distribution and a percentage distribution for each manufacturer, using the following class-interval widths for each distribution:
1. Manufacturer A: 650 but less than 750, 750 but less than 850, and so on.
2. Manufacturer B: 750 but less than 850, 850 but less than 950, and so on.

b. Construct percentage histograms on separate graphs and plot the percentage polygons on one graph.

c. Form cumulative percentage distributions and plot cumulative percentage polygons on one graph.

d. Which manufacturer has bulbs with a longer life—Manufacturer A or Manufacturer B? Explain.

2.29 The following data (contained in the file **Drink**) represent the amount of soft drink in a sample of fifty 2-liter bottles:

2.109 2.086 2.066 2.075 2.065 2.057 2.052 2.044 2.036 2.038

2.031 2.029 2.025 2.029 2.023 2.020 2.015 2.014 2.013 2.014

2.012 2.012 2.012 2.010 2.005 2.003 1.999 1.996 1.997 1.992

1.994 1.986 1.984 1.981 1.973 1.975 1.971 1.969 1.966 1.967

1.963 1.957 1.951 1.951 1.947 1.941 1.941 1.938 1.908 1.894

a. Construct a frequency distribution and a percentage distribution.

b. Construct a histogram and a percentage polygon.

c. Form a cumulative percentage distribution and plot a cumulative percentage polygon.

d. On the basis of the results of (a) through (c), does the amount of soft drink filled in the bottles concentrate around specific values?

2.4 CROSS TABULATIONS

The study of patterns that may exist between two or more categorical variables is common in business. Often, by cross-tabulating the data, these patterns can be explained. You can present **cross tabulations** in tabular form (contingency tables) or graphical form (side-by-side charts).

The Contingency Table

A **contingency table** presents the results of two categorical variables. The joint responses are classified so that the categories of one variable are located in the rows and the categories of the other variable are located in the columns. The values located at the intersections of the rows and columns are called **cells**. Depending on the type of contingency table constructed, the cells for each row-column combination contain the frequency, the percentage of the overall total, the percentage of the row total, or the percentage of the column total.

Suppose that in the Using Statistics scenario, you want to examine whether there is any pattern or relationship between the level of risk and the objective of the mutual fund (growth versus value). Table 2.14 summarizes this information for all 868 mutual funds.

TABLE 2.14

Contingency Table Displaying Fund Objective and Fund Risk

See Sections E2.11, P2.8, or M2.7 to create this.

	RISK LEVEL			
OBJECTIVE	**High**	**Average**	**Low**	**Total**
Growth	302	140	22	464
Value	53	171	180	404
Total	355	311	202	868

You construct this contingency table by tallying the joint responses for each of the 868 mutual funds with respect to objective and risk into one of the six possible cells in the table. The first fund listed in the Mutual Funds file is classified as a growth fund with a low risk. Thus, you tally this joint response into the cell that is the intersection of the first row and third column. The remaining 867 joint responses are recorded in a similar manner. Each cell contains the frequency for the row-column combination.

In order to further explore any possible pattern or relationship between objective and fund risk, you can construct contingency tables based on percentages. You first convert these results into percentages based on the following three totals:

1. The overall total (i.e., the 868 mutual funds)
2. The row totals (i.e., 464 growth funds and 404 value funds)
3. The column totals (i.e., 355 high, 311 average, and 202 low)

Tables 2.15, 2.16, and 2.17 summarize these percentages.

TABLE 2.15

Contingency Table Displaying Fund Objective and Fund Risk, Based on Percentage of Overall Total

	RISK LEVEL			
OBJECTIVE	**High**	**Average**	**Low**	**Total**
Growth	34.79	16.13	2.53	53.46
Value	6.11	19.70	20.74	46.54
Total	40.90	35.83	23.27	100.00

TABLE 2.16

Contingency Table Displaying Fund Objective and Fund Risk, Based on Percentage of Row Total

	RISK LEVEL			
OBJECTIVE	**High**	**Average**	**Low**	**Total**
Growth	65.09	30.17	4.74	100.00
Value	13.12	42.33	44.55	100.00
Total	40.90	35.83	23.27	100.00

TABLE 2.17

Contingency Table Displaying Fund Objective and Fund Risk, Based on Percentage of Column Total

	RISK LEVEL			
OBJECTIVE	High	Average	Low	Total
Growth	85.07	45.02	10.89	53.46
Value	14.93	54.98	89.11	46.54
Total	100.00	100.00	100.00	100.00

Table 2.15 shows that 40.9% of the mutual funds sampled are high risk, 53.46% are growth funds, and 34.79% are high-risk funds that are growth funds. Table 2.16 shows that 65.09% of the growth funds are high risk and 4.74% are low risk. Table 2.17 shows that 85.07% of the high-risk funds and only 10.89% of the low-risk funds are growth funds. The tables reveal that growth funds are more likely to be high risk, whereas value funds are more likely to be low risk.

The Side-by-Side Bar Chart

A useful way to visually display the results of cross-classification data is by constructing a **side-by-side bar chart**. Figure 2.14, which uses the data from Table 2.14 on page 49, is a Microsoft Excel side-by-side bar chart that compares the three fund risk levels, based on their objectives. An examination of Figure 2.14 reveals results consistent with those of Tables 2.15, 2.16, and 2.17: Growth funds are more likely to be high risk, whereas value funds are more likely to be low risk.

FIGURE 2.14

Microsoft Excel side-by-side bar chart for fund objective and risk

See Sections E2.12 or P2.8 to create this. (Minitab users, see Section M2.8 to create an equivalent chart.)

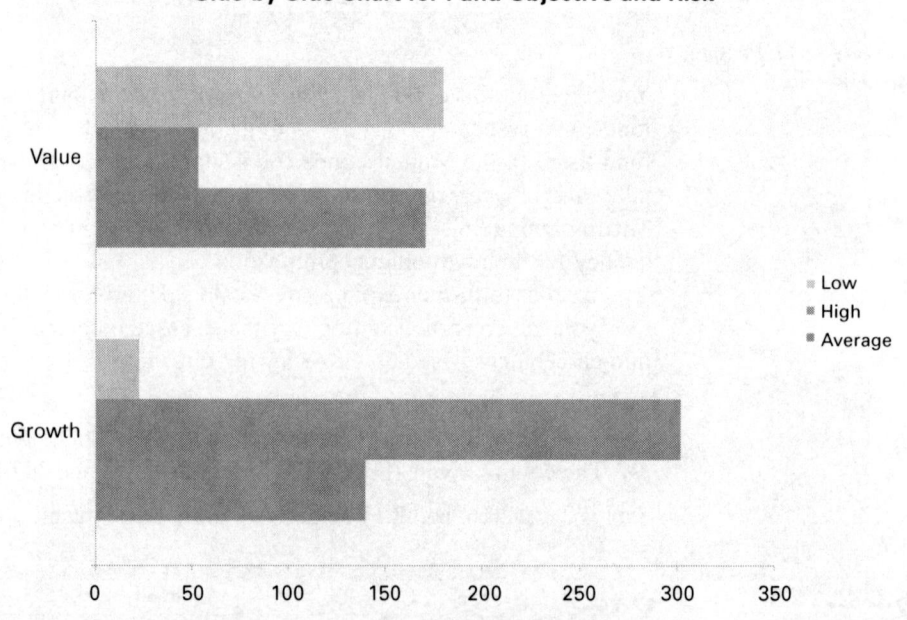

Side-by-Side Chart for Fund Objective and Risk

PROBLEMS FOR SECTION 2.4

Learning the Basics

2.30 The following data represent the responses to two questions asked in a survey of 40 college students majoring in business—What is your gender? (male = M; female = F) and What is your major? (accounting = A; computer information systems = C; marketing = M):

Gender:	M	M	M	F	M	F	F	M	F	M	F	M	M	M	M	F	F	M	F	F
Major:	A	C	C	M	A	C	A	A	C	C	A	A	A	M	C	M	A	A	A	C
Gender:	M	M	M	M	F	M	F	F	M	M	F	M	M	M	M	F	M	F	M	M
Major:	C	C	A	A	M	M	C	A	A	A	C	C	A	A	A	A	C	C	A	C

a. Tally the data into a contingency table where the two rows represent the gender categories and the three columns represent the academic-major categories.

b. Form contingency tables based on percentages of all 40 student responses, based on row percentages and based on column percentages.

c. Using the results from (a), construct a side-by-side bar chart of gender based on student major.

2.31 Given the following contingency table, construct a side-by-side bar chart comparing A and B for each of the three-column categories:

	1	2	3	Total
A	20	40	40	100
B	80	80	40	200

Applying the Concepts

2.32 The results of a study made as part of a yield improvement effort at a semiconductor manufacturing facility provided defect data for a sample of 450 wafers. The following table presents a summary of the responses to two questions: Was a particle found on the die that produced the wafer? and Is the wafer good or bad?

QUALITY OF WAFER	CONDITION OF DIE		
	No Particles	Particles	Totals
Good	320	14	334
Bad	80	36	116
Totals	400	50	450

Source: *Extracted from S. W. Hall, "Analysis of Defectivity of Semiconductor Wafers by Contingency Table,"* Proceedings Institute of Environmental Sciences, Vol. 1 *(1994), pp. 177–183.*

a. Construct contingency tables based on total percentages, row percentages, and column percentages.

b. Construct a side-by-side bar chart of quality of wafers based on condition of die.

c. What conclusions do you draw from these analyses?

2.33 Each day at a large hospital, several hundred laboratory tests are performed. The rate at which these tests are done improperly (and therefore need to be redone) seems steady, at about 4%. In an effort to get to the root cause of these nonconformances (i.e., tests that need to be redone), the director of the lab decided to keep records over a period of one week. The laboratory tests were subdivided by the shift of workers who performed the lab tests. The results are as follows:

LAB TESTS PERFORMED	SHIFT		
	Day	Evening	Total
Nonconforming	16	24	40
Conforming	654	306	960
Total	670	330	1,000

a. Construct contingency tables based on total percentages, row percentages, and column percentages.

b. Which type of percentage—row, column, or total—do you think is most informative for these data? Explain.

c. What conclusions concerning the pattern of nonconforming laboratory tests can the laboratory director reach?

SELF Test **2.34** A sample of 500 shoppers was selected in a large metropolitan area to determine various information concerning consumer behavior. Among the questions asked was "Do you enjoy shopping for clothing?" The results are summarized in the following cross-classification table:

ENJOY SHOPPING FOR CLOTHING	GENDER		
	Male	Female	Total
Yes	136	224	360
No	104	36	140
Total	240	260	500

a. Construct contingency tables based on total percentages, row percentages, and column percentages.

b. Construct a side-by-side bar chart of enjoying shopping for clothing based on gender.

c. What conclusions do you draw from these analyses?

2.35 As more Americans use cell phones, they question where it is okay to talk on cell phones. The following is a table of results, in percentages, for 2000 and 2006 (extracted from W. Koch, "Businesses Put a Lid on Chatterboxes," *USA Today*, February 7, 2006, p. 3A):

OK TO TALK ON A CELL PHONE IN A RESTAURANT	YEAR	
	2000	2006
Yes	31	21
No	69	79
Total	100	100

a. Construct a side-by-side bar chart.

b. Discuss the changes in attitude concerning the use of cell phones in restaurants between 2000 and 2006.

2.36 An experiment was conducted by James Choi, David Laibson, and Brigitte Madrian to study the choices made in fund selection. When presented with four S&P 500 index funds that were identical except for their fees, undergraduate and MBA students chose the funds as follows (in percentages). Note that because the funds are identical, the best choice is the fund with the lowest fee.

Fund	Student Group	
	Undergraduate	**MBA**
Lowest fee	19	19
Second-lowest fee	37	40
Third-lowest fee	17	23
Highest fee	27	18

Source: *Extracted from J. Choi, D. Laibson, and B. Madrian, "Why Does the Law of One Practice Fail? An Experiment on Mutual Funds,"* **www.som.yale.edu/faculty/jjc83/fees.pdf**.

a. Construct a side-by-side bar chart for the two student groups.
b. What do these results tell you about the differences between undergraduate and MBA students in their ability to choose S&P 500 index funds?

2.37 Where people turn to for news is different for various age groups. A study indicated where different age groups primarily get their news.

Media	Age Group		
	Under 36	**36–50**	**50+**
Local TV	107	119	133
National TV	73	102	127
Radio	75	97	109
Local newspaper	52	79	107
Internet	95	83	76

a. Construct a side-by-side bar chart for the three age groups.
b. What differences are there in the age groups?

2.5   SCATTER PLOTS AND TIME-SERIES PLOTS

When analyzing a single numerical variable such as the cost of a restaurant meal or the 2006 return, the appropriate charts to use include histograms, polygons, and cumulative percentage polygons, developed in Section 2.3. This section discusses scatter plots and time-series plots, which are used when you have two numerical variables.

The Scatter Plot

You use a **scatter plot** to examine possible relationships between two numerical variables. For each observation, you plot one variable on the horizontal X axis and the other variable on the vertical Y axis. For example, a marketing analyst could study the effectiveness of advertising by comparing weekly sales volumes and weekly advertising expenditures. Or a human resources director interested in the salary structure of the company could compare the employees' years of experience with their current salaries.

To demonstrate a scatter plot, you can examine the relationship between the cost of different items in various cities (extracted from K. Spors, "Keeping Up with . . . Yourself," *The Wall Street Journal*, April 11, 2005, p. R4). Table 2.18 provides the cost of a fast-food hamburger meal and the cost of two movie tickets in 10 cities around the world. The `Cost of Living` file contains the complete data set.

TABLE 2.18

Cost of a Fast-Food Hamburger Meal and Cost of Two Movie Tickets in 10 Cities

City	Hamburger	Movie Tickets
Tokyo	5.99	32.66
London	7.62	28.41
New York	5.75	20.00
Sydney	4.45	20.71
Chicago	4.99	18.00
San Francisco	5.29	19.50
Boston	4.39	18.00
Atlanta	3.70	16.00
Toronto	4.62	18.05
Rio de Janeiro	2.99	9.90

For each city, you plot the cost of a fast-food hamburger meal on the X axis, and the cost of two movie tickets on the Y axis. Figure 2.15 presents a Microsoft Excel scatter plot for these two variables.

FIGURE 2.15

Microsoft Excel scatter plot of the cost of a fast-food hamburger meal and the cost of two movie tickets

See Sections E2.13 or P2.9 to create this. (Minitab users, see Section M2.9 to create an equivalent chart.)

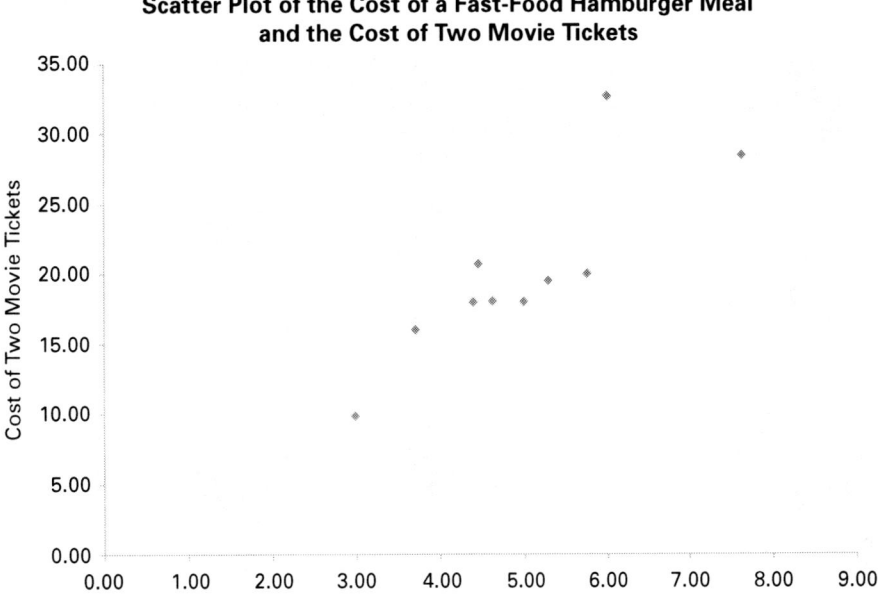

Although there is some variation, there appears to be a clearly increasing (positive) relationship between the cost of a fast-food hamburger meal and the cost of two movie tickets. In other words, cities in which the cost of a fast-food hamburger meal is low seem to also have a low cost of two movie tickets. Other pairs of variables may have a decreasing (negative) relationship in which one variable decreases as the other increases. The scatter plot will be studied again in Chapter 3, when the coefficient of correlation and the covariance are presented, and in Chapter 13, when regression analysis is developed.

The Time-Series Plot

A **time-series plot** is used to study patterns in the values of a numerical variable over time. Each value is plotted as a point in two dimensions with the time period on the horizontal X axis and the variable of interest on the Y axis.

To demonstrate a time-series plot, you can examine the yearly movie attendance, in billions, from 1999 to 2006 (extracted from C. Passy, "Good Night and Good Luck," *Palm Beach Post*, February 5, 2006, p. 1J and S. Bowles, "Box Office Breaks Its Downward Cycle," *USA Today*, March 7, 2007, p. 1D). Table 2.19 presents the data for the yearly movie attendance (see

TABLE 2.19

Movie Attendance, in Billions, from 1999 to 2006

Year	Attendance
1999	1.47
2000	1.42
2001	1.49
2002	1.63
2003	1.57
2004	1.53
2005	1.41
2006	1.45

the file **Movies**). Figure 2.16 is a time-series plot of the movie attendance (in billions) from 1999 to 2006. You can see that although movie attendance increased from 1999 to 2002, it declined from 2003 to 2005, before increasing slightly in 2006. Attendance in 2005 and 2006 was below attendance in 1999.

FIGURE 2.16

Microsoft Excel time-series plot of movie attendance from 1999 to 2006

See Section E2.14 to create this. (Minitab users, see Section M2.9 to create an equivalent chart.)

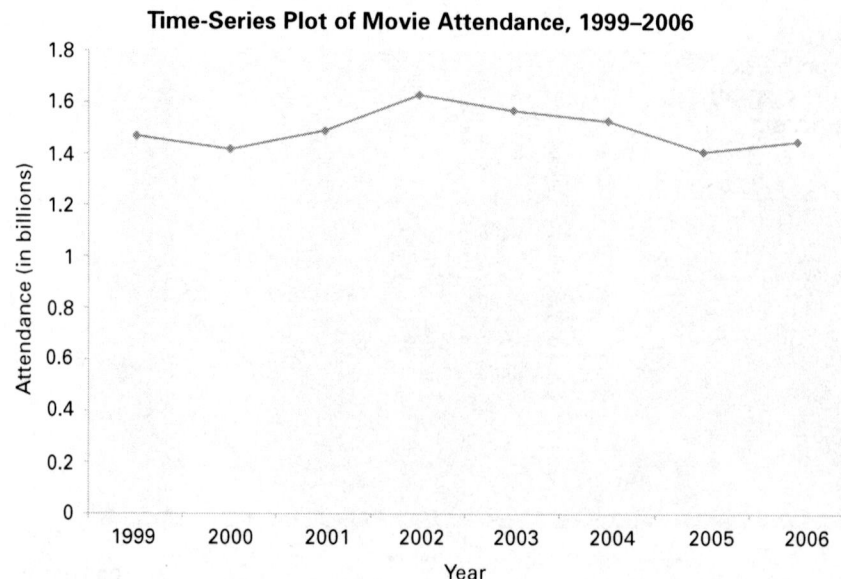

PROBLEMS FOR SECTION 2.5

Learning the Basics

2.38 The following is a set of data from a sample of $n = 11$ items:

$$X \quad 7 \quad 5 \quad 8 \quad 3 \quad 6 \quad 10 \quad 12 \quad 4 \quad 9 \quad 15 \quad 18$$
$$Y \quad 21 \quad 15 \quad 24 \quad 9 \quad 18 \quad 30 \quad 36 \quad 12 \quad 27 \quad 45 \quad 54$$

a. Construct a scatter plot.
b. Is there a relationship between X and Y? Explain.

2.39 The following is a series of annual sales (in millions of dollars) over an 11-year period (1996 to 2006):

Year 1996 1997 1998 1999 2000 2001 2002 2003 2004 2005 2006

Sales 13.0 17.0 19.0 20.0 20.5 20.5 20.5 20.0 19.0 17.0 13.0

a. Construct a time-series plot.
b. Does there appear to be any change in real annual sales over time? Explain.

Applying the Concepts

2.40 There are several methods for calculating fuel economy. The following table (contained in the file **Mileage**) indicates the mileage as calculated by owners and by current government standards for nine car models:

Car	Owner	Government
2005 Ford F-150	14.3	16.8
2005 Chevrolet Silverado	15.0	17.8
2002 Honda Accord LX	27.8	26.2
2002 Honda Civic	27.9	34.2
2004 Honda Civic Hybrid	48.8	47.6
2002 Ford Explorer	16.8	18.3
2005 Toyota Camry	23.7	28.5
2003 Toyota Corolla	32.8	33.1
2005 Toyota Prius	37.3	56.0

Source: Extracted from J. Healey, "Fuel Economy Calculations to be Altered," USA Today, January 11, 2006, p. 1B.

a. Construct a scatter plot with owner mileage on the X axis and current government standards mileage on the Y axis.
b. Does there appear to be a relationship between owner and current government standards mileage? If so, is the relationship positive or negative?

2.41 The file **Chicken** contains data on the calories and total fat (in grams per serving) for a sample of 20 chicken sandwiches from fast-food chains:

Sandwich	Calories	Fat
Wendy's Ultimate Chicken Grill	360	7
Baja Fresh Original Baja Taco with Charbroiled Chicken	370	8
Burger King Smoky BBQ Fire-Grilled Chicken Baguette	380	4
Quiznos Sub Honey Bourbon Chicken on Wheat Bread	400	5
McDonald's Chicken McGrill	400	16
Blimpie Grilled Chicken Hot Sub	470	20
Subway Oven-Roasted Chicken Breast	470	20
Blimpie Buffalo Chicken Hot Sub	500	24
Wendy's Spicy Chicken Fillet	510	19
Taco Bell Ranchero Chicken Soft Taco (two tacos)	540	30
KFC Oven-Roasted Chicken Tender Wrap	550	23
Subway Buffalo Chicken Sub	550	30
Burger King Chicken Whopper	570	25
Au Bon Pain Arizona Chicken	580	19
Boston Market Rotisserie Chicken Carver	640	29
Chipolte Soft Tacos with Chicken (three tacos)	660	29
Cosi Grilled Chicken with Tomato, Basil, and Mozzarella	720	30
Atlanta Bread Company Chargrilled Chicken Pesto Panini	740	30
Corner Bakery Café Chicken Pomodori Panini	910	40
Panera Bread Tuscan Chicken on Rosemary & Onion Focaccia	950	56

Source: *Extracted from "Fast food: Adding Health to the Menu,"* Consumer Reports, *September 2004, pp. 28–31.*

a. Construct a scatter plot with calories on the X axis and total fat on the Y axis.

b. What conclusions can you reach about the relationship between the calories and total fat in chicken sandwiches?

2.42 College basketball is big business, with coaches' salaries, revenues, and expenses in millions of dollars. The file Colleges-Basketball contains the coaches' salary and revenue for college basketball at selected schools in a recent year (extracted from R. Adams, "Pay for Playoffs," *The Wall Street Journal*, March 11–12, 2006, pp. P1, P8).

a. Do you think schools with higher revenues also have higher coaches' salaries?

b. Construct a scatter plot with revenue on the X axis and coaches' salaries on the Y axis.

c. Does the scatter plot confirm or contradict your answer to (a)?

2.43 College football players trying out for the NFL are given the Wonderlic standardized intelligence test. The file Wonderlic contains the average Wonderlic scores of football players trying out for the NFL and the graduation rate for football players at selected schools (extracted from S. Walker, "The NFL's Smartest Team," *The Wall Street Journal*, September 30, 2005, pp. W1, W10).

a. Construct a scatter plot with average Wonderlic score on the X axis and graduation rate on the Y axis.

b. What conclusions can you reach about the relationship between the average Wonderlic score and graduation rate?

2.44 The U.S. Bureau of Labor Statistics compiles data on a wide variety of workforce issues. The following table (contained in the file Unemploy) gives the monthly seasonally adjusted civilian unemployment rate for the United States from 2000 to 2006:

Month	2000	2001	2002	2003	2004	2005	2006
January	4.0	4.2	5.7	5.8	5.7	5.2	4.7
February	4.1	4.2	5.7	5.9	5.6	5.4	4.8
March	4.0	4.3	5.7	5.9	5.7	5.1	4.7
April	3.8	4.4	5.9	6.0	5.5	5.1	4.7
May	4.0	4.3	5.8	6.1	5.6	5.1	4.6
June	4.0	4.5	5.8	6.3	5.6	5.0	4.6
July	4.0	4.6	5.8	6.2	5.5	5.0	4.8
August	4.1	4.9	5.7	6.1	5.4	4.9	4.7
September	3.9	5.0	5.7	6.1	5.4	5.1	4.6
October	3.9	5.3	5.7	6.0	5.4	4.9	4.4
November	3.9	5.5	5.9	5.9	5.4	5.0	4.5
December	3.9	5.7	6.0	5.7	5.4	4.9	4.5

Source: *"U.S. Bureau of Labor Statistics,"* **www.bls.gov**, *March 30, 2007.*

a. Construct a time-series plot of the U.S. unemployment rate.

b. Does there appear to be any pattern?

2.45 In 2005, five million people in the United States subscribed to online dating services. The subscribers spent, on average, $99 for the services provided, thus generating nearly $500 million for the online dating companies. The following table (contained in the file Dating) gives the number of subscribers (in millions) to U.S. dating Web sites from 2000 to 2005:

Year	Number of Subscribers (millions)
2000	0.7
2001	1.6
2002	2.8
2003	4.3
2004	4.7
2005	5.0

Source: *Extracted from "Making an E-Match,"* National Geographic, *February, 2006, p. 128.*

a. Construct a time-series plot.

b. Do you think the number of subscribers is increasing or decreasing? Do you think the *rate* of growth is increasing or decreasing? Explain.

2.46 The following table contained in the file `Tvchannels` (extracted from "At Home With More TV Channels," *USA Today*, April 10, 2007, p. A1) shows the average number of TV channels that the U.S. home received from 1985 to 2005:

Year	Number of TV Channels Received
1985	18.8
1990	33.2
1995	41.1
2000	61.4
2005	96.4

a. Construct a time-series plot for the average number of TV channels that the U.S. home received from 1985 to 2005.

b. What pattern, if any, is present in the data?

c. If you had to make a prediction of the average number of TV channels that the U.S. home will receive in 2010, what would you predict?

2.47 The following data, contained in the file `Deals`, provide the number of mergers and acquisitions made during January 1 through January 11 of each year from 1995 to 2006 (extracted from "Back of the Envelope," *The New York Times*, January 13, 2006, p. C7):

Year	Deals
1995	715
1996	865
1997	708
1998	861
1999	931
2000	939
2001	1,031
2002	893
2003	735
2004	759
2005	1,013
2006	622

a. Construct a time-series plot.

b. What pattern, if any, is present in the data?

c. If you had to make a prediction of the mergers and acquisitions made during January 1 through January 11, 2007, what would you predict?

2.6 MISUSING GRAPHS AND ETHICAL ISSUES

Good graphical displays clearly and unambiguously reveal what the data convey. Unfortunately, many graphs presented in the media (broadcast, print, and online) are incorrect, misleading, or so unnecessarily complicated that they should never be used. To illustrate the misuse of graphs, the chart presented in Figure 2.17 is similar to one that was printed in *Time* magazine as part of an article on increasing exports of wine from Australia to the United States.

In Figure 2.17, the wineglass icon representing the 6.77 million gallons for 1997 does not appear to be almost twice the size of the wineglass icon representing the 3.67 million gallons for 1995, nor does the wineglass icon representing the 2.25 million gallons for 1992 appear to be twice the size of the wineglass icon representing the 1.04 million gallons for 1989. Part of the reason for this is that the three-dimensional wineglass icon is used to represent the two dimensions of exports and time. Although the wineglass presentation may catch the eye, the data should instead be presented in a summary table or a time-series plot.

FIGURE 2.17

"Improper" display of Australian wine exports to the United States, in millions of gallons

Source: *Adapted from S. Watterson, "Liquid Gold— Australians Are Changing the World of Wine. Even the French Seem Grateful,"* Time, November 22, 1999, p. 68.

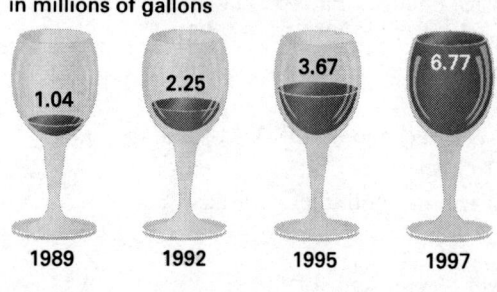

We're drinking more . . .
Australian wine exports to the U.S.
in millions of gallons

1.04 — 1989
2.25 — 1992
3.67 — 1995
6.77 — 1997

In addition to the type of distortion created by the wineglass icons in the *Time* magazine graph displayed in Figure 2.17, improper use of the vertical and horizontal axes leads to distortions. Figure 2.18 presents another graph used in the same *Time* magazine article.

FIGURE 2.18

"Improper" display of amount of land planted with grapes for the wine industry

Source: *Adapted from S. Watterson, "Liquid Gold—Australians Are Changing the World of Wine. Even the French Seem Grateful,"* Time, November 22, 1999, pp. 68–69.

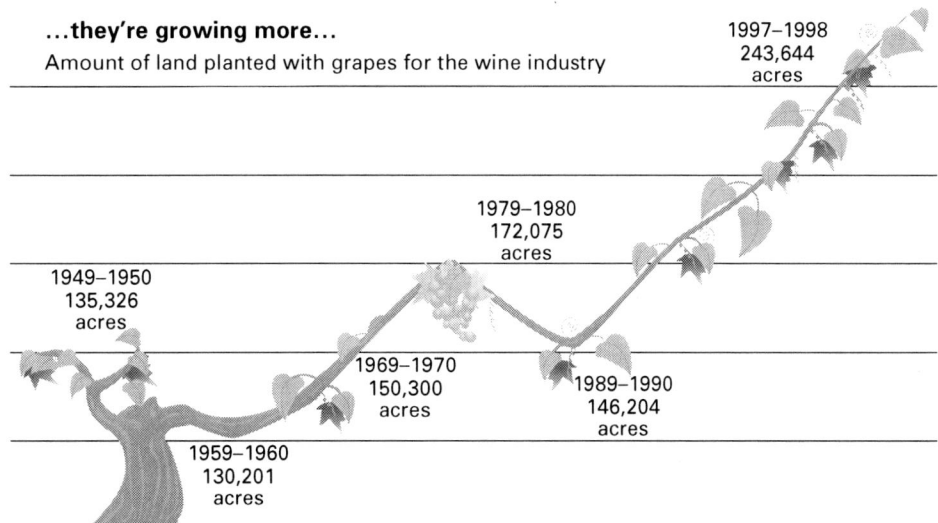

...they're growing more...
Amount of land planted with grapes for the wine industry

1997–1998 243,644 acres
1979–1980 172,075 acres
1949–1950 135,326 acres
1969–1970 150,300 acres
1989–1990 146,204 acres
1959–1960 130,201 acres

There are several problems in this graph. First, there is no zero point on the vertical axis. Second, the acreage of 135,326 for 1949–1950 is plotted above the acreage of 150,300 for 1969–1970. Third, it is not obvious that the difference between 1979–1980 and 1997–1998 (71,569 acres) is approximately 3.5 times the difference between 1979–1980 and 1969–1970 (21,775 acres). Fourth, there are no scale values on the horizontal axis. Years are plotted next to the acreage totals, not on the horizontal axis. Fifth, the values for the time dimension are not properly spaced along the horizontal axis. The value for 1979–1980 is much closer to 1989–1990 than it is to 1969–1970.

Other types of eye-catching displays that you typically see in magazines and newspapers often include information that is not necessary and just adds excessive clutter. Figure 2.19 represents one such display. The graph in Figure 2.19 shows those products with the largest market share for soft drinks in 1999. The graph suffers from too much clutter, although it is designed to show the differences in market share among the soft drinks. The display of the fizz for each soft drink takes up too much of the graph relative to the data. The same information could have been conveyed with a bar chart or pie chart.

FIGURE 2.19

"Improper" plot of market share of soft drinks in 1999

Source: *Adapted from Anne B. Carey and Sam Ward, "Coke Still Has Most Fizz,"* USA Today, May 10, 2000, p. 1B.

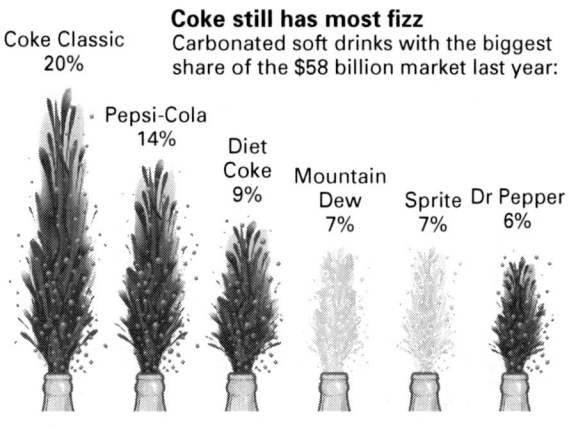

Coke still has most fizz
Carbonated soft drinks with the biggest share of the $58 billion market last year:

Coke Classic 20%
Pepsi-Cola 14%
Diet Coke 9%
Mountain Dew 7%
Sprite 7%
Dr Pepper 6%

Some guidelines for developing good graphs are as follows:

- The graph should not distort the data.
- The graph should not contain **chartjunk**, unnecessary adornments that convey no useful information.
- Any two-dimensional graph should contain a scale for each axis.
- The scale on the vertical axis should begin at zero.
- All axes should be properly labeled.
- The graph should contain a title.
- The simplest possible graph should be used for a given set of data.

Often these guidelines are unknowingly violated by individuals unaware of how to construct appropriate graphs.

Ethical Concerns

Inappropriate graphs raise ethical concerns. Such graphs can obscure unfavorable information or create false impressions of data, even if the inappropriate chart was developed naively. Consider the following sets of sales trend charts as shown in Figure 2.20. A casual viewer of these charts might think model B had the best sales trend and that models A and D had similar trends. A more careful examination of these line graphs shows that model B has the weakest sales trend and that model C and D actually have the *same* sales trend. A casual viewer gets misled because of the inconsistent scaling of the *Y* axis.

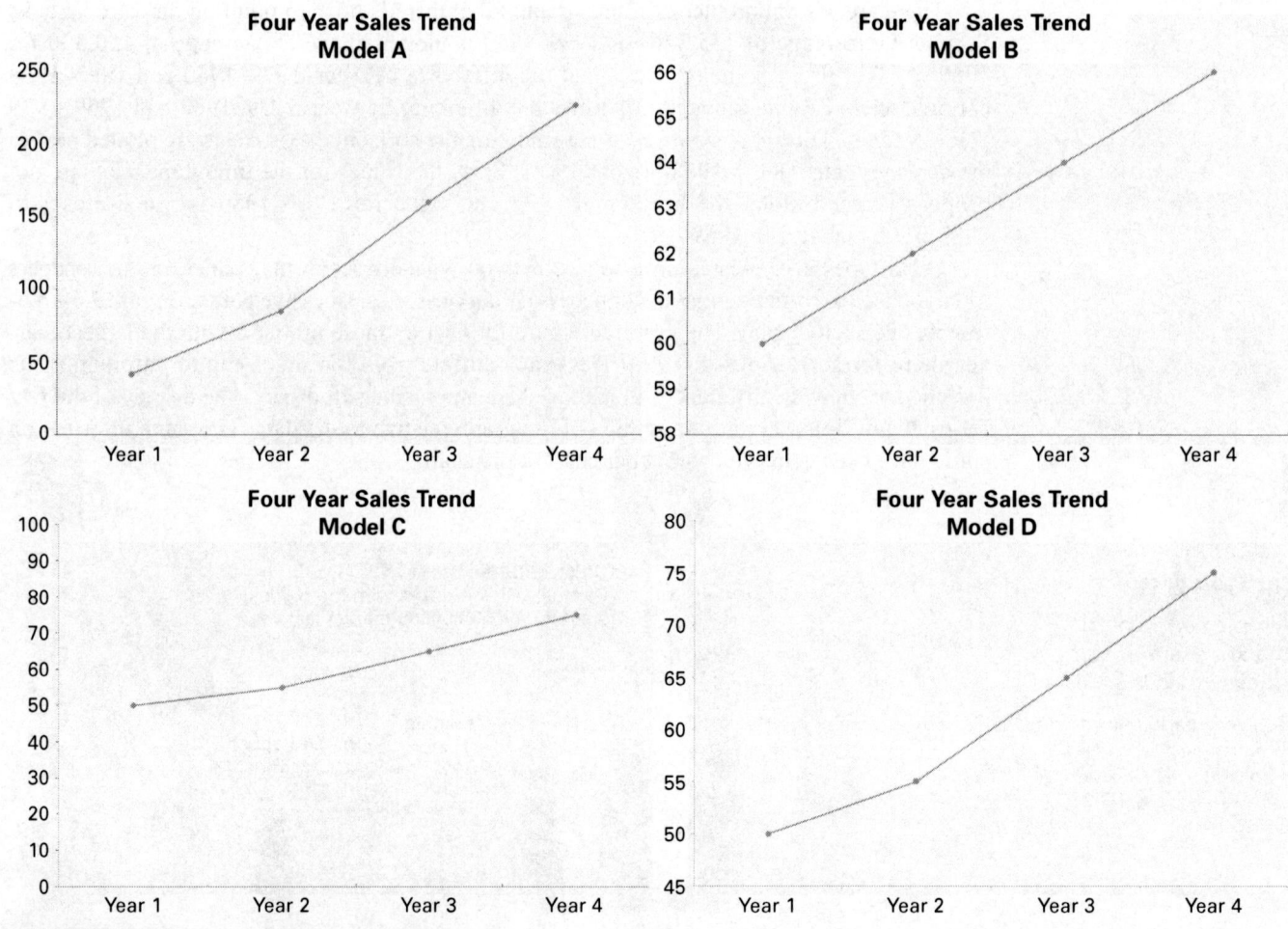

FIGURE 2.20 Four sales trend charts

Pretty, But Not Witty or Wise

In the Leonard Bernstein and Stephen Sondheim musical, *West Side Story*, the character Maria sings of being "pretty and witty and wise." In the business world, pretty charts are not necessarily smart or witty or wise.

You may get tempted to create pretty charts if you use programs such as Microsoft Excel. Excel allows you to easily create fancy charts that may appear pretty, but are unwise choices. Taking a simple pie chart and making it prettier by adding exploded 3D slices is unwise as this can complicate a viewer's interpretation of the data. Uncommon chart choices such as doughnut, radar, surface, bubble, cone, and pyramid charts may look visually striking, but obscure the data in most cases.

To be smart and wise and effective, try to make sure that the tables and charts you create are simple and clear, so that the information presented can be easily interpreted.

PROBLEMS FOR SECTION 2.6

Applying the Concepts

2.48 (Student Project) Bring to class a chart from a Web site, newspaper, or magazine that you believe to be a poorly drawn representation of a numerical variable. Be prepared to submit the chart to the instructor with comments as to why you believe it is inappropriate. Do you believe that the intent of the chart is to purposely mislead the reader? Also, be prepared to present and comment on this in class.

2.49 (Student Project) Bring to class a chart from a Web site, newspaper, or magazine that you believe to be a poorly drawn representation of a categorical variable. Be prepared to submit the chart to the instructor with comments as to why you consider it inappropriate. Do you believe that the intent of the chart is to purposely mislead the reader? Also, be prepared to present and comment on this in class.

2.50 (Student Project) According to its home page, Swivel is "a place where curious people explore data—all kinds of data." Go to **www.swivel.com** and explore the various graphical displays.
a. Select a graphical display that you think does a good job revealing what the data convey. Discuss why you think it is a good graphical display.
b. Select a graphical display that you think needs a lot of improvement. Discuss why you think that it is a poorly constructed graphical display.

2.51 The following visual display contains an overembellished chart similar to one that appeared in *USA Today*, dealing with the average consumer's Valentine's Day spending ("USA Today Snapshots: The Price of Romance," *USA Today*, February 14, 2007, p. 1B).

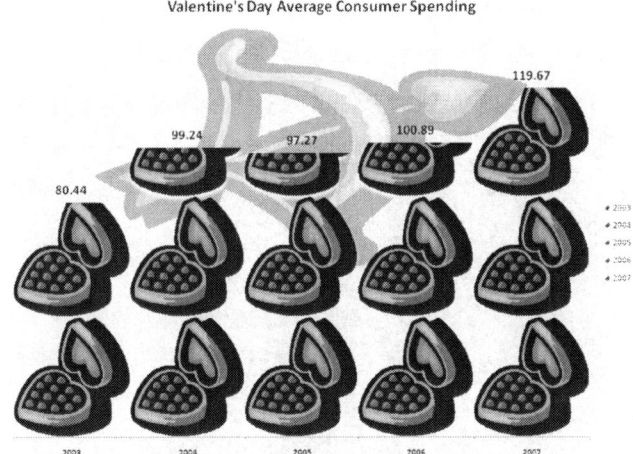

Valentine's Day Average Consumer Spending

a. Describe at least one good feature of this visual display.
b. Describe at least one bad feature of this visual display.
c. Redraw the graph, using the guidelines given on page 58.

2.52 The following visual display contains an overembellished chart similar to one that appeared in *USA Today*, dealing with the estimated number of hours the typical American will spend using various media ("USA Today Snapshots: Minding Their Media," *USA Today*, March 2, 2007, p. 1B).

Media Usage
Estimated number of hours the typical American will spend using various media this year.

Listening to music — 175
Reading newspapers — 175
Using Internet —
Listening to Radio — 974
Watching TV — 1555

a. Describe at least one good feature of this visual display.
b. Describe at least one bad feature of this visual display.
c. Redraw the graph, using the guidelines given on page 58.

2.53 The following visual display contains an overembellished chart similar to one that appeared in *USA Today*, dealing with which card is safer to use ("USA Today Snapshots: Credit Card vs. Debit Card," *USA Today*, March 14, 2007, p. 1B).

Credit Card vs. Debit Card: Which one is safer to use?

Don't Mind 49%
Credit Card 32%
Debit Card 19%
1234
123 45 6789 1234

a. Describe at least one good feature of this visual display.
b. Describe at least one bad feature of this visual display.
c. Redraw the graph, using the guidelines given on page 58.

2.54 An article in *The New York Times* (D. Rosato, "Worried About the Numbers? How About the Charts?" *The New York Times*, September 15, 2002, p. B7) reported on research done on annual reports of corporations by Professor Deanna Oxender Burgess of Florida Gulf Coast University. Professor Burgess found that even slight distortions in a chart changed readers' perception of the information. The article displayed sales information from the annual report of Zale Corporation and showed how results were exaggerated.

Using Internet or library sources, study the most recent annual report of a selected corporation. Find at least one chart in the report that you think needs improvement and develop an improved version of the chart. Explain why you believe the improved chart is better than the one included in the annual report.

2.55 Figures 2.1, 2.3, and 2.6 consist of a bar chart, a pie chart, and a Pareto chart for where people prefer to do their banking.
a. Use the chart features of Microsoft Excel to construct an exploded pie chart, doughnut chart, a cone chart, and a pyramid chart for where people prefer to do their banking.
b. Which graphs do you prefer—the bar chart, pie chart, and Pareto chart or the exploded pie chart, doughnut chart, cone chart, and pyramid chart? Explain.

2.56 Figures 2.2 and 2.4 consist of a bar chart and a pie chart for the risk level for the mutual fund data.
a. Use the chart features of Microsoft Excel to develop an exploded pie chart, a doughnut chart, a cone chart, and a pyramid chart for the risk level of the mutual funds.
b. Do you prefer the bar chart and pie chart, or the exploded pie chart, doughnut chart, cone chart, and pyramid chart? Explain.

SUMMARY

As you can see in Table 2.20, this chapter discusses data presentation. You have used various tables and charts to draw conclusions about where people prefer to bank, about the cost of restaurant meals in an urban area and its suburbs, and about the set of mutual funds that were first introduced in the Using Statistics scenario at the beginning of the chapter. Now that you have studied tables and charts, in Chapter 3 you will learn about a variety of numerical descriptive measures useful for data analysis and interpretation.

TABLE 2.20

Roadmap for Selecting Tables and Charts

	Type of Data	
Type of Analysis	**Numerical**	**Categorical**
Tabulating, organizing, and graphically presenting the values of a variable	Ordered array, stem-and-leaf display, frequency distribution, relative frequency distribution, percentage distribution, cumulative percentage distribution, histogram, polygon, cumulative percentage polygon **(Sections 2.2 and 2.3)**	Summary table, bar chart, pie chart, Pareto chart **(Section 2.1)**
Graphically presenting the relationship between two variables	Scatter plot, time-series plot **(Section 2.5)**	Contingency table, side-by-side bar chart **(Section 2.4)**

KEY EQUATIONS

Width of Interval

$$\text{Width of interval} = \frac{\text{Range}}{\text{number of classes}} \qquad (2.1)$$

Proportion

$$\text{Proportion} = \text{Relative Frequency} = \frac{\text{Frequency in each class}}{\text{total number of values}} \qquad (2.2)$$

KEY TERMS

bar chart
cells
chartjunk
class boundaries
class grouping
class midpoint
classes
contingency table
cross tabulations
cumulative percentage distribution

cumulative percentage polygon (ogive)
frequency distribution
histogram
ogive (cumulative percentage polygon)
ordered array
Pareto chart
Pareto principle
percentage distribution
percentage polygon

pie chart
proportion
range
relative frequency
relative frequency distribution
scatter plot
side-by-side bar chart
stem-and-leaf display
summary table
time-series plot
width of a class interval

CHAPTER REVIEW PROBLEMS

Checking Your Understanding

2.57 How do histograms and polygons differ in terms of construction and use?

2.58 Why would you construct a summary table?

2.59 What are the advantages and/or disadvantages of using a bar chart, a pie chart, or a Pareto chart?

2.60 Compare and contrast the bar chart for categorical data with the histogram for numerical data.

2.61 What is the difference between a time-series plot and a scatter plot?

2.62 Why is it said that the main feature of the Pareto chart is its ability to separate the "vital few" from the "trivial many"? Discuss.

2.63 What are the three different ways to break down the percentages in a contingency table?

Applying the Concepts

2.64 The following data represent the breakdown of the price of a new college textbook:

Revenue Categories	Percentage	
Publisher	64.8	
Manufacturing costs		32.3
Marketing and promotion		15.4
Administrative costs and taxes		10.0
After-tax profit		7.1
Bookstore	22.4	
Employee salaries and benefits		11.3
Operations		6.6
Pretax profit		4.5
Author	11.6	
Freight	1.2	

Source: *Extracted from T. Lewin, "When Books Break the Bank,"* The New York Times, *September 16, 2003, pp. B1, B4.*

a. Using the four categories publisher, bookstore, author, and freight, construct a bar chart, a pie chart, and a Pareto chart.
b. Using the four subcategories of publisher and three subcategories of bookstore along with the author and freight categories, construct a Pareto chart.
c. Based on the results of (a) and (b), what conclusions can you reach concerning who gets the revenue from the sales of new college textbooks? Do any of these results surprise you? Explain.

2.65 The following data represent the global market share for plasma TVs and LCD TVs in the fourth quarter of 2005:

Company	Plasma TVs (%)	Company	LCD TVs (%)
Hitachi	7.3	LGE	6.5
LGE	15.4	Phillips/Magnavox	14.2
Panasonic	26.0	Samsung	11.6
Phillips	13.3	Sharp	13.6
Samsung	14.4	Sony	14.6
Others	23.6	Others	39.5

Source: *Extracted from Y. Kkageyama, "Flat-Panel TVs Proving Savior of Japanese Electronics Makers," The Palm Beach Post, April 23, 2006, p. F3.*

a. For plasma TVs and LCD TVs, separately construct a bar chart, a pie chart, and a Pareto chart.
b. Based on the results of (a), explain how the market share of plasma TVs differs from the market share of LCD TVs.

2.66 The following data represent energy consumption and renewable energy consumption in the United States in 2005:

Energy Source	%*	Renewable Energy Source	%*
Coal	23.0	Ethanol	10.1
Hydroelectric power	2.7	Geothermal	10.8
Natural gas	22.2	Solar	1.9
Nuclear electric power	8.1	Waste	17.1
Petroleum	40.5	Wind	4.5
Renewable fuels	3.3	Wood	55.5

*Percentages do not add to 100% due to rounding.
Source: *Energy Information Administration, 2006.*

*Percentages do not add to 100% due to rounding.
Source: *Energy Information Administration, 2006.*

a. For energy consumption and renewable energy consumption, separately construct a bar chart, a pie chart, and a Pareto chart.
b. Based on the results of (a), what conclusions can you reach about energy consumption and renewable energy consumption in the United States in 2005?

2.67 The following data represent proven conventional oil reserves, in billions of barrels, subdivided by region and country:

Region and Country	Proven Conventional Reserves (Billions of Barrels)	
North America	54.8	
Mexico		28.3
United States		21.8
Canada		4.7
Central and South America	95.2	
Venezuela		76.9
Brazil		8.1
Other Central and South America		10.2
Western Europe	17.2	
Norway		9.5
Britain		5.0
Other Western Europe		2.7
Africa	74.9	
Libya		29.5
Nigeria		22.5
Algeria		9.2
Angola		5.4
Other Africa		8.3
Middle East	683.6	
Saudi Arabia		259.2
Iraq		112.5
United Arab Emirates		97.8
Kuwait		94.0
Iran		89.7
Qatar		13.2
Oman		5.5
Other Middle East		11.7
Far East and Oceania	44.0	
China		24.0
Indonesia		5.0
India		4.7
Other Far East and Oceania		10.3
Eastern Europe and Former USSR	59.0	
Russia		48.6
Kazakhstan		5.4
Other Eastern Europe and Former USSR		5.0

Source: *U.S. Department of Energy.*

a. Using the set of countries, construct a bar chart, a pie chart, and a Pareto chart.

b. Using the set of regions, construct a bar chart, a pie chart, and a Pareto chart.

c. Which graphical method do you think is best to portray these data?

d. Based on the results of (a) and (b), what conclusions can you make concerning the proven conventional oil reserves for the different countries and regions?

2.68 People conduct hundreds of millions of search queries every day. In response, businesses are estimated to spend almost $20 billion annually on online ad spending (K. J. Delaney, "The New Benefits of Web-Search Queries," *The Wall Street Journal*, February 6, 2007, p. B3). The following represents the categories of online ad spending and the results of a Yahoo! keyword tool for searches related to sneakers.

Estimated 2007 U.S. Online Ad Spending

Type	Spending ($billions)
Classified	3.32
Display ads	3.90
Paid search	8.29
Rich media/video	2.15
Other	1.85
Total	19.51

Results of a Yahoo! Keyword Tool for Searches Related to "Sneakers"

Search result	Number of Occurrences
Jordan sneaker	13,240
Nike sneaker	8,139
Puma sneaker	6,768
Sneaker	58,995
Sneaker pimps*	15,357

*Sneaker pimps is a British electropop band.

a. For type of online ad spending, construct a bar chart, a pie chart, and a Pareto chart.

b. Which graphical method do you think is best to portray these data?

c. For the results of "sneakers" searches, construct a bar chart, a pie chart, and a Pareto chart.

d. Which graphical method do you think is best to portray these data?

e. What conclusions can you reach concerning online ad spending and the results of "sneakers" searches?

2.69 The owner of a restaurant serving Continental-style entrées is interested in studying patterns of patron demand for the Friday-to-Sunday weekend time period. Records are maintained that indicate the type of entrée ordered. The data are as follows:

Type of Entrée	Number Served
Beef	187
Chicken	103
Duck	25
Fish	122
Pasta	63
Shellfish	74
Veal	26

a. Construct a percentage summary table for the types of entrées ordered.

b. Construct a bar chart, a pie chart, and a Pareto chart for the types of entrées ordered.

c. Do you prefer a Pareto chart or a pie chart for these data? Why?

d. What conclusions can the restaurant owner reach concerning demand for different types of entrées?

2.70 Suppose that the owner of the restaurant in Problem 2.69 is also interested in studying the demand for dessert during the same time period. She decided that two other variables, along with whether a dessert was ordered, are to be studied: the gender of the individual and whether a beef entrée is ordered. The results are as follows:

	GENDER		
DESSERT ORDERED	Male	Female	Total
Yes	96	40	136
No	224	240	464
Total	320	280	600

	BEEF ENTRÉE		
DESSERT ORDERED	Yes	No	Total
Yes	71	65	136
No	116	348	464
Total	187	413	600

a. For each of the two contingency tables, construct a contingency table of row percentages, column percentages, and total percentages.

b. Which type of percentage (row, column, or total) do you think is most informative for each gender? for beef entrée? Explain.

c. What conclusions concerning the pattern of dessert ordering can the owner of the restaurant reach?

2.71 The following data (extracted from R. Wolf, "Paper-Trail Voting Gets Organized Opposition," *USA Today*, April 24, 2007, p. 2A) represent the method for recording votes in the November 2006 election, broken down by percentage of counties in the United States using each method and the number of counties using each method in 2000 and 2006.

Method	Percentage of Counties Using Method
Electronic	36.6
Hand-counted paper ballots	1.8
Lever	2.0
Mixed	3.0
Optically scanned paper ballots	56.2
Punch card	0.4

	Number of Counties	
Method	2000	2006
Electronic	309	1,142
Hand-counted paper ballots	370	57
Lever	434	62
Mixed	149	92
Optically scanned paper ballots	1,279	1,752
Punch card	572	13

a. Construct a pie chart and a Pareto chart for the percentage of counties using the various methods.

b. Construct side-by-side bar charts, by year, for the number of counties using the various methods.

c. Which type of graphical display is more helpful in depicting the data? Explain.

d. What conclusions can you reach concerning the type of voting method used in November 2006?

e. What differences are there in the methods used in 2000 and 2006?

2.72 In summer 2000, a growing number of warranty claims on Firestone tires sold on Ford SUVs prompted Firestone and Ford to issue a major recall. An analysis of warranty-claims data helped identify which models to recall. A breakdown of 2,504 warranty claims based on tire size is given in the following table:

Tire Size	Warranty Claims
23575R15	2,030
311050R15	137
30950R15	82
23570R16	81
331250R15	58
25570R16	54
Others	62

Source: *Extracted from Robert L. Simison, "Ford Steps Up Recall Without Firestone," The Wall Street Journal, August 14, 2000, p. A3.*

The 2,030 warranty claims for the 23575R15 tires can be categorized into ATX models and Wilderness models. The type of incident leading to a warranty claim, by model type, is summarized in the following table:

Incident	ATX Model Warranty Claims	Wilderness Warranty Claims
Tread separation	1,365	59
Blowout	77	41
Other/unknown	422	66
Total	1,864	166

Source: *Extracted from Robert L. Simison, "Ford Steps Up Recall Without Firestone," The Wall Street Journal, August 14, 2000, p. A3.*

a. Construct a Pareto chart for the number of warranty claims by tire size. What tire size accounts for most of the claims?

b. Construct a pie chart to display the percentage of the total number of warranty claims for the 23575R15 tires that come from the ATX model and Wilderness model. Interpret the chart.

c. Construct a Pareto chart for the type of incident causing the warranty claim for the ATX model. Does a certain type of incident account for most of the claims?

d. Construct a Pareto chart for the type of incident causing the warranty claim for the Wilderness model. Does a certain type of incident account for most of the claims?

2.73 One of the major measures of the quality of service provided by any organization is the speed with which the organization responds to customer complaints. A large family-held department store selling furniture and flooring, including carpet, had undergone a major expansion in the past several years. In particular, the flooring department had expanded from 2 installation crews to an installation supervisor, a measurer, and 15 installation crews. During a recent year, the company got 50 complaints concerning carpet installation. The following data (contained in the file Furniture) represent the number of days between the receipt of the complaint and the resolution of the complaint:

54   5   35 137   31 27 152   2 123 81 74 27

11 19 126 110 110 29   61 35   94 31 26   5

12   4 165   32   29 28   29 26   25   1 14 13

13 10   5   27   4 52   30 22   36 26 20 23

33 68

a. Construct a frequency distribution and a percentage distribution.

b. Construct a histogram and a percentage polygon.

c. Form a cumulative percentage distribution and plot a cumulative percentage polygon (ogive).

d. On the basis of the results of (a) through (c), if you had to tell the president of the company how long a customer should expect to wait to have a complaint resolved, what would you say? Explain.

2.74 Data concerning 71 of the best-selling domestic beers in the United States are located in the file Domesticbeer . The values for three variables are included: percentage alcohol, number of calories per 12 ounces, and number of carbohydrates (in grams) per 12 ounces.

Source: *Extracted from* **www.Beer100.com**, *May 4, 2007.*

a. Construct a percentage histogram for each of the three variables.

b. Construct three scatter plots: percentage alcohol versus calories, percentage alcohol versus carbohydrates, and calories versus carbohydrates.

c. Discuss the information you learned from studying the graphs in (a) and (b).

2.75 The data in the file Spending are the federal *per capita* spending, in thousands of dollars, for each state in 2004.

a. Develop an ordered array.

b. Plot a percentage histogram.

c. What conclusions can you reach about the differences in federal per-capita spending between the states?

2.76 The data in the file Savings are the yields for a money market account, a one-year certificate of deposit (CD), and a five-year CD for 37 banks in south Florida, as of March 9, 2007 (extracted from **www.Bankrate.com**, March 9, 2007).

a. Construct a percentage histogram for each of the three variables.

b. Construct three scatter plots: money market account versus one-year CD, money market account versus five-year CD, and one-year CD versus five-year CD.

c. Discuss the information you learned from studying the graphs in (a) and (b).

2.77 The data in the file Ceo represent the total compensation (in $millions) of CEOs of the 150 large public companies that filed proxies by March 31, 2007, by revenue (extracted from "C.E.O. Pay: The New Rules," *The New York Times*, April 8, 2007, pp. 10B, 11B).

a. Construct a frequency distribution and a percentage distribution.

b. Construct a histogram and a percentage polygon.

c. Construct a cumulative percentage distribution and plot a cumulative percentage polygon (ogive).

d. Based on (a) through (c), what conclusions can you reach concerning CEO compensation in 2006?

e. Are there any companies whose CEO has a total compensation below $500,000? If so, go to the company's Web site and see if you can find out a reason why the CEO has a total compensation below $500,000.

2.78 Studies conducted by a manufacturer of "Boston" and "Vermont" asphalt shingles have shown product weight to be a major factor in customers' perception of quality. Moreover, the weight represents the amount of raw materials being used and is therefore very important to the company from a cost standpoint. The last stage of the assembly line packages the shingles before the packages are placed on wooden pallets. When a pallet is full (a pallet for most brands holds 16 squares of shingles), it is weighed, and the measurement is recorded. The company expects pallets of its "Boston" brand-name shingles to weigh at least 3,050 pounds but less than 3,260 pounds. For the company's "Vermont" brand-name shingles, pallets should weigh at least 3,600 pounds but less than 3,800. The file Pallet contains the weights (in pounds) from a sample of 368 pallets of "Boston" shingles and 330 pallets of "Vermont" shingles.

a. For the "Boston" shingles, construct a frequency distribution and a percentage distribution having eight class intervals, using 3,015, 3,050, 3,085, 3,120, 3,155, 3,190, 3,225, 3,260, and 3,295 as the class boundaries.

b. For the "Vermont" shingles, construct a frequency distribution and a percentage distribution having seven class intervals, using 3,550, 3,600, 3,650, 3,700, 3,750, 3,800, 3,850, and 3,900 as the class boundaries.

c. Construct percentage histograms for the "Boston" shingles and for the "Vermont" shingles.

d. Comment on the distribution of pallet weights for the "Boston" and "Vermont" shingles. Be sure to identify the percentage of pallets that are underweight and overweight.

2.79 The data in the file States represent the results of the American Community Survey, a sampling of households taken in all states during the 2000 U.S. Census. For each of the variables average travel-to-work time in minutes, percentage of homes with eight or more rooms, median household income, and percentage of mortgage-paying homeowners whose housing costs exceed 30% of income:

a. Construct a frequency distribution and a percentage distribution.

b. Construct a histogram and a percentage polygon.

c. Construct a cumulative percentage distribution and plot a cumulative percentage polygon.

d. What conclusions about these four variables can you make based on the results of (a) through (c)?

2.80 The data in the file Protein indicate calorie and cholesterol information concerning popular protein foods (fresh red meats, poultry, and fish).

Source: *U.S. Department of Agriculture.*

a. Construct a percentage histogram for the amount of calories.

b. Construct a percentage histogram for the amount of cholesterol.

c. What conclusions can you reach from your analyses in (a) and (b)?

2.81 In Figure 2.15 on page 53, a scatter plot of the relationship between the cost of a fast-food hamburger meal and the cost of movie tickets in 10 different cities was constructed. The file Cost of Living also includes the overall cost index, the monthly rent for a two-bedroom apartment, the cost of a cup of coffee with service, the cost of dry-cleaning a men's blazer, and the cost of toothpaste.

a. Construct six separate scatter plots. For each, use the overall cost index as the Y axis. Use the monthly rent for a two-bedroom apartment, the costs of a cup of coffee with service, a fast-food hamburger meal, dry-cleaning a men's blazer, toothpaste, and movie tickets as the X axis.

b. What conclusions can you reach about the relationship of the overall cost index to these six variables?

2.82 In Problem 2.41 on page 54, using the data in the file Chicken, you constructed a scatter plot of calories with the total fat content of chicken sandwiches.

a. Construct a scatter plot of calories on the Y axis and carbohydrates on the X axis.

b. Construct a scatter plot of calories on the Y axis and sodium on the X axis.

c. Which variable (total fat, carbohydrates, or sodium) seems to be most closely related to calories? Explain.

2.83 The file Gas contains the weekly average price of gasoline in the United States from January 3, 2005, to April 2, 2007. Prices are in dollars per gallon.

Source: *"U.S. Department of Energy,"* **www.eia.doe.gov**, *April 3, 2007.*

a. Construct a time-series plot.

b. What pattern, if any, is present in the data?

2.84 The data contained in the file Drink represent the amount of soft drink filled in a sample of 50 consecutive 2-liter bottles. The results are listed horizontally in the order of being filled:

2.109 2.086 2.066 2.075 2.065 2.057 2.052 2.044 2.036 2.038

2.031 2.029 2.025 2.029 2.023 2.020 2.015 2.014 2.013 2.014

2.012 2.012 2.012 2.010 2.005 2.003 1.999 1.996 1.997 1.992

1.994 1.986 1.984 1.981 1.973 1.975 1.971 1.969 1.966 1.967

1.963 1.957 1.951 1.951 1.947 1.941 1.941 1.938 1.908 1.894

a. Construct a time-series plot for the amount of soft drink on the Y axis and the bottle number (going consecutively from 1 to 50) on the X axis.

b. What pattern, if any, is present in these data?

c. If you had to make a prediction of the amount of soft drink filled in the next bottle, what would you predict?

d. Based on the results of (a) through (c), explain why it is important to construct a time-series plot and not just a histogram, as was done in Problem 2.29 on page 48.

2.85 The S&P 500 Index tracks the overall movement of the stock market by considering the stock prices of 500 large corporations. The data file Stocks2006 contains weekly data for this index as well as the weekly closing stock price for three companies during 2006. The variables included are:

WEEK—Week ending on date given
S&P—Weekly closing value for the S&P 500 Index
GE—Weekly closing stock price for General Electric
TARGET—Weekly closing stock price for Target
SARA LEE—Weekly closing stock price for Sara Lee

Source: *Extracted from* **finance.yahoo.com**, *April 3, 2007.*

a. Construct a time-series plot for the weekly closing values of the S&P 500 Index, General Electric, Target, and Sara Lee.

b. Explain any patterns present in the plots.

c. Write a short summary of your findings.

2.86 (Class Project) Let each student in the class respond to the question "Which carbonated soft drink do you most prefer?" so that the teacher can tally the results into a summary table.

a. Convert the data to percentages and construct a Pareto chart.

b. Analyze the findings.

2.87 (Class Project) Let each student in the class be cross-classified on the basis of gender (male, female) and current employment status (yes, no) so that the teacher can tally the results.

a. Construct a table with either row or column percentages, depending on which you think is more informative.

b. What would you conclude from this study?

c. What other variables would you want to know regarding employment in order to enhance your findings?

Report Writing Exercises

2.88 Referring to the results from Problem 2.78 on page 65 concerning the weight of "Boston" and "Vermont" shingles, write a report that evaluates whether the weight of the pallets of the two types of shingles are what the company expects. Be sure to incorporate tables and charts into the report.

2.89 Referring to the results from Problem 2.72 on page 64 concerning the warranty claims on Firestone tires, write a report that evaluates warranty claims on Firestone tires sold on Ford SUVs. Be sure to incorporate tables and charts into the report.

Team Project

The data file **Mutual Funds** contains information regarding nine variables from a sample of 868 mutual funds. The variables are:

Category—Type of stocks comprising the mutual fund (small cap, mid cap, large cap)

Objective—Objective of stocks comprising the mutual fund (growth or value)

Assets—In millions of dollars

Fees—Sales charges (no or yes)

Expense ratio—Ratio of expenses to net assets in percentage

2006 return—Twelve-month return in 2006

Three-year return—Annualized return, 2004–2006

Five-year return—Annualized return, 2002–2006

Risk—Risk-of-loss factor of the mutual fund (low, average, or high)

2.90 For the expense ratio:

a. Construct a percentage histogram.

b. Plot percentage polygons of the expense ratio for mutual funds that have fees and mutual funds that do not have fees on the same graph.

c. What conclusions about the expense ratio can you reach based on the results of (a) and (b)?

2.91 For the three-year annualized return from 2004 to 2006:

a. Construct a percentage histogram.

b. Plot percentage polygons of the three-year annualized return from 2004 to 2006 for growth mutual funds and value mutual funds on the same graph.

c. What conclusions about the three-year annualized return from 2004 to 2006 can you reach based on the results of (a) and (b)?

2.92 For the five-year annualized return from 2002 to 2006:

a. Construct a percentage histogram.

b. Plot percentage polygons of the five-year annualized return from 2004 to 2006 for growth mutual funds and value mutual funds on the same graph.

c. What conclusions about the five-year annualized return from 2004 to 2006 can you reach based on the results of (a) and (b)?

Student Survey Database

2.93 Problem 1.27 on page 14 describes a survey of 50 undergraduate students (see the file **Undergradsurvey**). For these data, construct all the appropriate tables and charts and write a report summarizing your conclusions.

2.94 Problem 1.27 on page 14 describes a survey of 50 undergraduate students (see the file **Undergradsurvey**).

a. Select a sample of 50 undergraduate students at your school and conduct a similar survey for those students.

b. For the data collected in (a), construct all the appropriate tables and charts and write a report summarizing your conclusions.

c. Compare the results of (b) to those of Problem 2.93.

2.95 Problem 1.28 on page 14 describes a survey of 40 MBA students (see the file **Gradsurvey**). For these data, construct all appropriate tables and charts and write a report summarizing your conclusions.

2.96 Problem 1.28 on page 14 describes a survey of 40 MBA students (see the file **Gradsurvey**).

a. Select a sample of 40 MBA students in your MBA program and conduct a similar survey for those students.

b. For the data collected in (a), construct all the appropriate tables and charts and write a report summarizing your conclusions.

c. Compare the results of (b) to those of Problem 2.95.

MANAGING THE *SPRINGVILLE HERALD*

Advertising fees are an important source of revenue for any newspaper. In an attempt to boost these revenues and to minimize costly errors, the management of the *Herald* has established a task force charged with improving customer service in the advertising department. Open a Web browser and link to **www.prenhall.com/HeraldCase/Ad_Errors.htm** (or open the `Ad_Errors.htm` file in the Student CD-ROM's Herald Case folder) to review the task force's data collec-

tion. Identify the data that are important in describing the customer service problems. For each set of data you identify, construct the graphical presentation you think is most appropriate for the data and explain your choice. Also, suggest what other information concerning the different types of errors would be useful to examine. Offer possible courses of action for either the task force or management to take that would support the goal of improving customer service.

WEB CASE

In the Using Statistics scenario, you were asked to gather information to help make wise investment choices. Sources for such information include brokerage firms and investment counselors. Apply your knowledge about the proper use of tables and charts in this Web Case about the claims of foresight and excellence by a Springville financial services firm.

Visit the EndRun Financial Services Web site at **www.prenhall.com/Springville/EndRun.htm** (or open the `EndRun.htm` file in the Student CD-ROM's Web Case folder). Review the company's investment claims and supporting data and then answer the following.

1. How does the presentation of the general information about EndRun on its home page affect your perception of the business?

2. Is EndRun's claim about having more winners than losers a fair and accurate reflection of the quality of its investment service? If you do not think that the claim is a fair and accurate one, provide an alternate presentation that you think is fair and accurate.

3. EndRun's "Big Eight" mutual funds are part of the sample found in the `Mutual Funds` worksheet. Is there any other relevant data from that file that could have been included in the Big Eight table? How would that new data alter your perception of EndRun's claims?

4. EndRun is proud that all Big Eight funds have gained in value over the past five years. Do you agree that EndRun should be proud of its selections? Why or why not?

REFERENCES

1. Huff, D., *How to Lie with Statistics* (New York: Norton, 1954).
2. *Microsoft Excel 2007* (Redmond, WA: Microsoft Corporation, 2007).
3. *Minitab for Windows Version 15* (State College, PA: Minitab, Inc., 2006).
4. Tufte, E. R., *Beautiful Evidence* (Cheshire, CT: Graphics Press, 2006).
5. Tufte, E. R., *Envisioning Information* (Cheshire, CT: Graphics Press, 1990).
6. Tufte, E. R., *The Visual Display of Quantitative Information*, 2nd ed. (Cheshire, CT: Graphics Press, 2002).
7. Tufte, E. R., *Visual Explanations* (Cheshire, CT: Graphics Press, 1997).
8. Wainer, H., *Visual Revelations: Graphical Tales of Fate and Deception from Napoleon Bonaparte to Ross Perot* (New York: Copernicus/Springer-Verlag, 1997).

Appendix E2
Using Microsoft Excel for Tables and Charts

E2.1 INTRODUCTION

This appendix describes how to use Microsoft Excel to create tables and charts. If you plan to use PHStat2 with Microsoft Excel, read Appendix P2 "Using PHStat2 for Tables and Charts." Because Excel 2007 changes many table and chart features, some appendix sections contain paired sets of instructions, such as Sections E2.2A and E2.2B, one for use with Excel 97–2003, the other for use with Excel 2007. Use only the set of instructions that applies to the Excel version that you have.

Before continuing, you should review the material in Appendix E1 and Appendix C if you have not done so already.

Occasionally PHStat2 will be the only reasonable way to accomplish a task using Microsoft Excel. In such cases, an Excel appendix section will refer you to the appropriate PHStat2 appendix section.

E2.2 CREATING SUMMARY TABLES

To create a summary table from unsummarized data, you create a PivotTable. To create a summary table from data already summarized in table form, enter the contents of the table into a blank worksheet, using row 1 cells for column headings.

You create a PivotTable by dragging the variable names of the unsummarized data into a form or template. Because the process differs between Excel 97–2003 and Excel 2007, use the instructions of either Sections E2.2A or E2.2B to complete this task.

E2.2A CREATING PIVOTTABLES (EXCEL 97–2003)

To create a PivotTable in Excel 97–2003, open to the worksheet that contains your unsummarized data and select **Data → PivotTable Report** (Excel 97) or **Data → PivotTable and PivotChart Report** (Excel 2000–2003). When you make these selections you start the PivotTable Wizard, a sequence of three dialog boxes (four in Excel 97) that step you through the process of creating a PivotTable. Figure E2.1 shows the dialog boxes for Excel 2003. (Other

versions have similar dialog boxes; Excel 97 uses four dialog boxes, breaking the third box into two.)

You step through these dialog boxes by clicking **Next** to advance to the next dialog box or **Back** to move back to a previous one. At any point, you can click **Cancel** to stop creating a PivotTable or click **Finish** to end the wizard and create a PivotTable. To create a summary table, make the following entries in the Wizard Step dialog boxes:

Wizard Step 1 Click **Microsoft Excel list or database** as the source data and **PivotTable** as the report type. (You do not select a report type in Microsoft Excel 97; PivotTable is assumed.)

Wizard Step 2 Enter the cell range of the data to be summarized in the PivotTable. This cell range must contain variable labels (column headings) in the first row of the range because the wizard, in Step 3, will use the cells in the first row as the names for your variables.

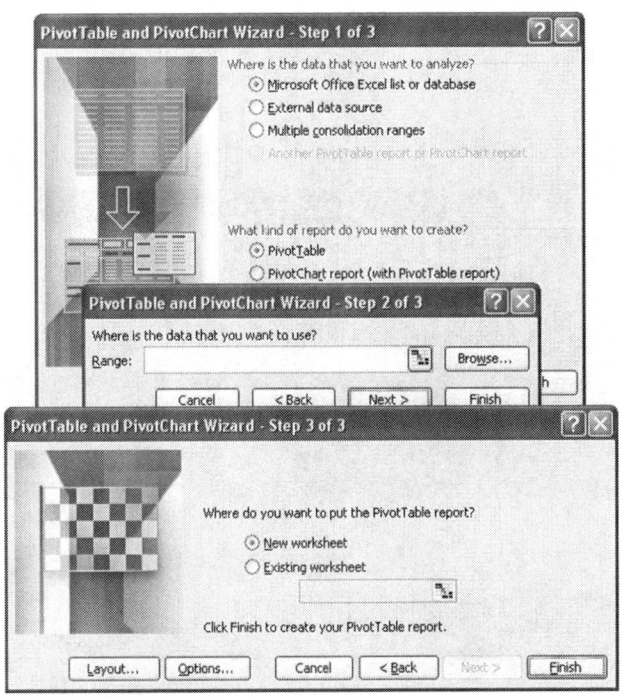

FIGURE E2.1 PivotTable Wizard steps (Excel 2003)

Wizard Step 3 First, click the **New worksheet** option as the location for your PivotTable. Then click **Layout** to display the Layout dialog box (see Figure E2.2). Design your table using the instructions in the next paragraph and then click **OK** to return to the Step 3 box. Then, click **Options** to display the PivotTable Options dialog box (see Figure E2.2). Enter **0** as the **For empty cells, show** value and click **OK** to return to the Wizard Step 3 dialog box. Then, click **Finish** to create the PivotTable.

(If you use Excel 97, the Layout dialog box appears as the Step 3 dialog box. When you click **Next** in this box, you then see a Step 4 dialog box that contains location options. There is no Options button in either the Step 3 or Step 4 dialog boxes in Excel 97.)

In the Layout dialog box of Step 3, drag the label of the variable to be summarized and drop it in the ROW area. Drag a second copy of this same label and drop it in the DATA area. This second label changes to **Count of variable** name to indicate that a count, or tally, of the occurrences of each category will be shown in the DATA area.

After Excel creates the PivotTable, close any floating PivotTable toolbar windows. Enter a title in cell A1 of the new worksheet that contains your PivotTable. Also, rename the new worksheet, using a descriptive name. In cell C4, enter **Percentage** and in cell C5, enter the formula in the form **=B5/B$n**, in which *n* is the row that contains the Grand Total. (If you do not understand the significance of the $ symbol, you can review Section E1.7.) For example, if the Grand Total row is row 8, enter **=B5/B$8**. Copy this formula down through all the category rows and format the cell range that contains these formulas for percentage display. Further adjust the table display as is necessary, using

Section E1.7 as your guide. (You may also need to adjust the width of columns by dragging the column rules at the top of the worksheet.)

E2.2B CREATING PIVOTTABLES (EXCEL 2007)

To create a PivotTable in Excel 2007, open to the worksheet that contains your unsummarized data and select **Insert → PivotTable**. In the Create PivotTable dialog box (see Figure E2.3), leave the **Select a table or range** option selected and change, if necessary, the **Table/Range** cell range. (In Figure E2.3, the cell range is for the mutual funds data found in the Data worksheet of **Mutual Funds.xls**.) Select the **New Worksheet** option and click **OK**.

In the PivotTable Field List task pane, drag the label of the variable to be summarized and drop it in the **Row Labels** box. Drag a second copy of this same label and drop it in the Σ **Values** box. This second label changes to **Count of variable name** to indicate that a count, or tally, of the occurrences of each category will be shown in the DATA area.

Right-click the PivotTable and click **Table Options** in the shortcut menu that appears. In the PivotTable Options dialog box (a reorganized version of the older one shown in Figure E2.2), click the **Layout & Format** tab, check **For empty cells show**, enter **0** as its value, and then click **OK**. Close the PivotTable Field List task pane. Enter a title in cell A1 of the new worksheet that contains your PivotTable. Also, rename the new worksheet, using a descriptive name.

In cell C4, enter **Percentage** and in cell C5, enter the formula in the form **=B5/B$n**, in which *n* is the row that

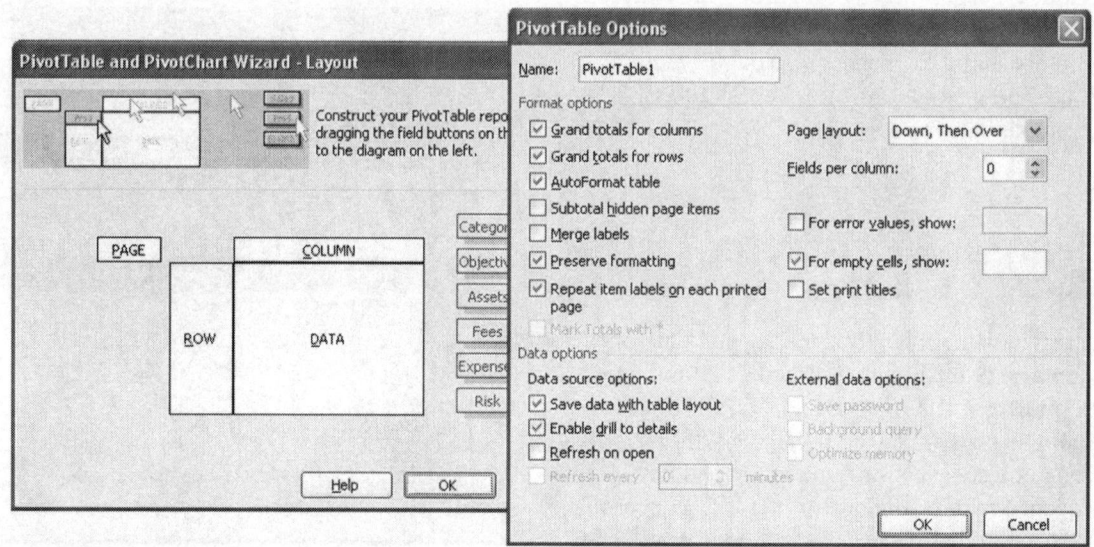

FIGURE E2.2 PivotTable Layout and Options dialog boxes (Excel 2000–2003)

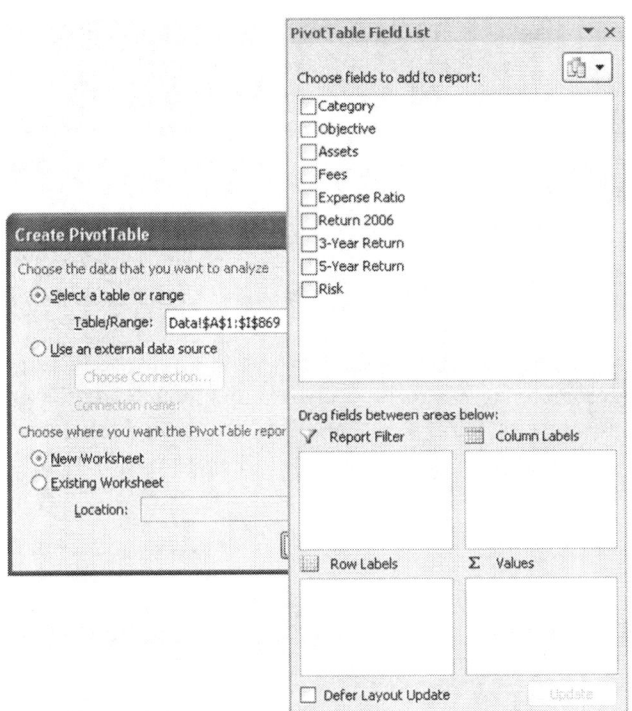

FIGURE E2.3 Create PivotTable dialog box and PivotTable Field List task pane (Excel 2007)

contains the Grand Total. (If you do not understand the significance of the $ symbol, you can review Section E1.7.) For example, if the Grand Total row is row 8, enter =B5/B$8. Copy this formula down through all the category rows and format the cell range that contains these formulas for percentage display. Further adjust the table display as is necessary, using Section E1.7 as your guide. (You may also need to adjust the width of columns by dragging the column rules at the top of the worksheet.)

E2.3 CREATING CHARTS: OVERVIEW

Although Microsoft Excel contains many features that create tables and charts, you can easily get improper results or otherwise get frustrated if you do not properly organize your worksheet data first. In Excel, charts are linked to sets of worksheet data, and the arrangement of that data influences the chart Excel creates. For example, when creating a scatter plot, Excel will always consider the first column of data as the *X* variable data. If you wanted to create the scatter plot of the cost of a fast-food hamburger meal and the cost of two movie tickets (Figure 2.15 on page 53), you would want to place the meal costs in a column to the left of the column containing the ticket costs.

The best way to avoid arrangement errors is to place your data on a separate worksheet using consecutive columns starting with column A. (Data worksheets in the Student CD-ROM Excel workbook files have this arrangement.) If you are using Microsoft Excel 2007, you should also select your data by dragging the mouse over your data, as explained in Appendix C, to prevent Excel 2007 from making a "bad" guess as to the table or chart you seek.

With these simple steps you will eliminate the most common errors that occur when using Excel charting features. However, creating a chart using Excel charting features does not necessarily end your task. Many charts will need minor reformatting to pass the strictest presentation standards. Illustrations in this book reflect such formatting and appendix sections throughout the book include reformatting instructions when appropriate.

Some charts, especially those created in Excel 97–2003, contain colored backgrounds (typically gray) that can interfere with clear printing or displaying of the chart. To remove the background in an Excel 97–2003 chart, right-click the background and click **Format Plot Area** in the shortcut menu. In the dialog box that appears, click the **None** option of the **Area** group and click **OK**. (This was done for all the charts shown in this book.) To remove a background in Excel 2007, right-click the chart background and select **Layout → Plot Area** and select **None** in the Plot Area gallery.

Occasionally, you may open to a chart sheet and see only part of a (too-large) chart or see a (too-small) chart surrounded by a too-large frame mat. To display an optimally sized chart in Excel 97–2003, open to the chart sheet and press **Esc**. Select **View → Zoom** and then, in the Zoom dialog box, select the **Fit selection** option and click **OK**. To display an optimally sized chart in Excel 2007, use the Zoom slider on the lower right of the Excel window frame or click the chart and then select **Format** and use the items in the Size group. Finally, if the symbols, captions, and/or legends and titles prove too big or too small for you, you can usually change these elements by right-clicking over them and clicking the shortcut menu choice that contains the word **Format**.

If you use PHStat2, the charts created by PHStat2 will generally include these minor reformatting and enhancements discussed above.

E2.3A CREATING CHARTS (EXCEL 97–2003)

To create a chart in Excel 97–2003, open to the worksheet containing your unsummarized data and select **Insert → Chart** to begin the Chart Wizard, a sequence of four dialog boxes that step you through the process of creating a chart. (Figure E2.4 shows these dialog boxes for Excel 2003. Excel 97, 2000, and 2002 have similar sets of dialog boxes.) To create a chart, make the following entries in the Wizard Step dialog boxes:

Wizard Step 1   Choose the chart type from either the **Standard Types** or **Custom Types** tab. Most of the charts you create in this text are chart types found in the Standard Types tab.

Wizard Step 2   Enter the cell range of the data to be charted in the **Data Range** tab. For some types of charts, you also enter the cell range or ranges that contain chart labeling information in the **Series** tab. Cell ranges in the Series tab must always be entered with their worksheet names as a formula, in the form =*SheetName*!*CellRange*.

Wizard Step 3   Enter titles and select formatting options for your chart in the various tabs of this dialog box. Unless told otherwise in later instructions, make the following entries and selections:

In the **Titles** tab, enter a title and enter axis labels if appropriate. In the **Axes** tab, click both the (X) axis and (Y) axis check boxes and click **Automatic** under the (X) axis check box. In the **Gridlines** tab, clear all the check boxes. In the **Legend** tab, clear the **Show legend** check box. In the **Data Labels** tab, click the **None** option under the **Data labels** heading. In the **Data Table** tab, clear the **Show data table** check box. (Not all tabs are displayed for all chart types. If a tab is not displayed, skip the instructions for the tab.)

Wizard Step 4   Click the **As new sheet** option to place the chart on its own chart sheet. Then click **Finish** to create the chart.

*Because the Wizard Step 4 dialog box instructions never vary, they are not explicitly listed in later instructions. You should always click **As new sheet** and **Finish** in this dialog box when you create a chart.*

If you discover a mistake in your chart after your chart is created, right-click the chart and select **Chart Type, Source Data, Chart Options**, or **Location** to return to versions of the Wizard Step 1, Step 2, Step 3, or Step 4 dialog boxes, respectively.

E2.3B CREATING CHARTS (EXCEL 2007)

To create a chart in Excel 2007, open to the worksheet that contains your unsummarized data. Select the cell range of the data to be charted. If your cell range contains two non-

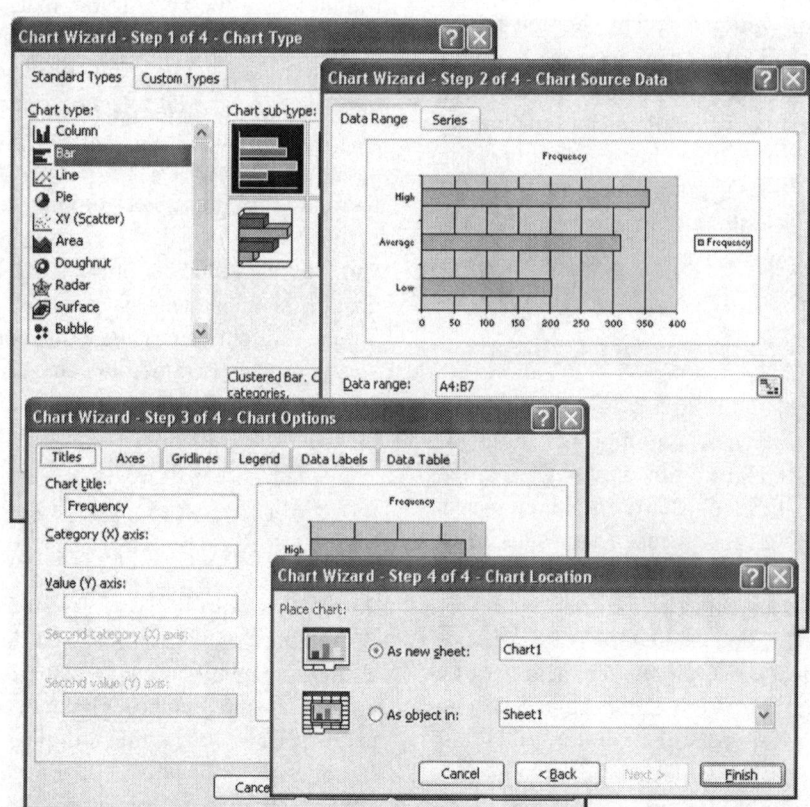

FIGURE E2.4 Chart Wizard dialog boxes (Excel 2003)

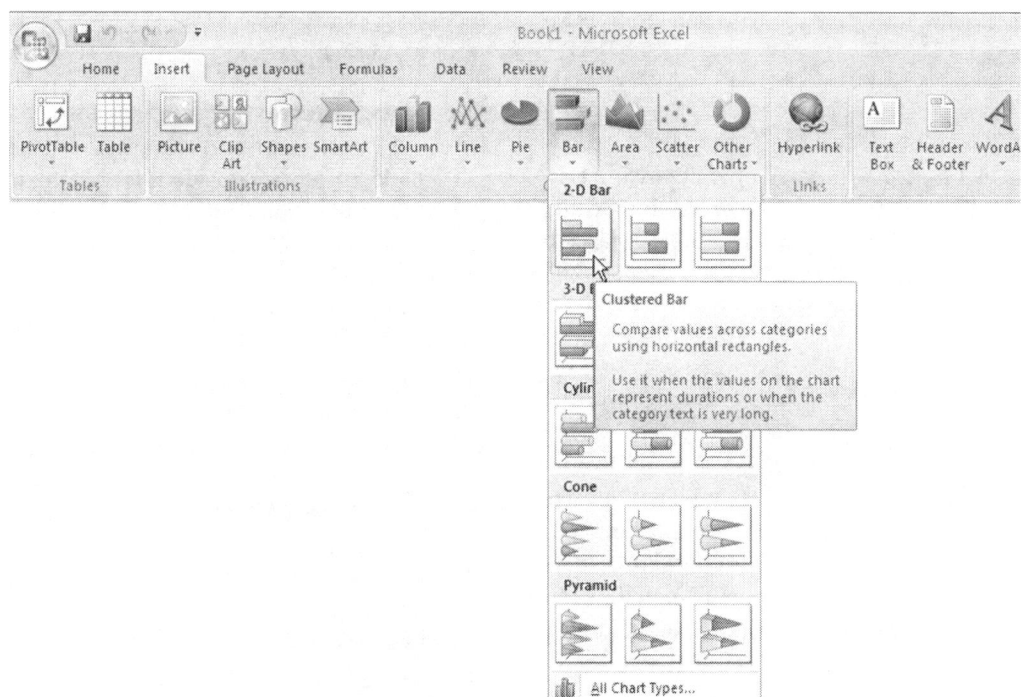

FIGURE E2.5 Selecting a chart sub-type (Excel 2007)

adjacent areas, hold down the **Ctrl** key as you drag and select each area. Select **Insert** and in the **Charts** group, click the chart type. From the drop-down gallery that appears, click the chart sub-type you want. To help distinguish sub-types, move the mouse pointer over a sub-type and wait for a description to be displayed. In Figure E2.5, the description for the bar chart "clustered bar" sub-type is displayed.

Customize your chart by clicking the chart and selecting the **Layout** tab of the Chart Tools ribbon group (or PivotChart Tools, if the chart is based on a PivotTable). Review the settings for the members of the **Labels** and **Axes** groups in this tab. Unless told otherwise in later instructions, make the following entries and selections (for a given chart type, some of these items may be disabled and not available):

Click **Chart Title** and choose either **Centered Overlay Title** or **Above Chart**. Click **Axes Titles** ➔ **Primary Horizontal Axis Title** ➔ **Title Below Axis**. Click **Axes Titles** ➔ **Primary Vertical Axis Title** ➔ **Rotated Title**. (For charts with secondary axes, select **Title Below Axis** as the **Secondary Horizontal Axis Title** and **None** as the **Secondary Vertical Axis Title**.) Click **Data Labels** ➔ **None** and click **Data Table** ➔ **None**.

Click **Axes** ➔ **Primary Horizontal Title** ➔ **Show Left to Right Axis**. Click **Axes** ➔ **Primary Vertical Title** ➔ **Show Default Axis**. Some charts have secondary axes; for such charts, select **None** as the **Secondary Horizontal**

Axis Title and **Show Default Axis** as the **Secondary Vertical Axis Title**. Click **Gridlines**. Select **None** for both the **Primary Horizontal Gridlines** and **Primary Vertical Gridlines**. Also select **None** for secondary gridlines, if the chart contains those as well.

Excel 2007 creates charts on worksheets. To move a chart to its own chart sheet (recommended), right-click the chart frame and click **Move Chart** in the shortcut menu that appears. In the Move Chart dialog box that appears, select the **New sheet** option and click **OK**.

E2.4 CREATING BAR AND PIE CHARTS: OVERVIEW

You create bar and pie charts from summary tables such as PivotTables using Excel charting features. You cannot create bar and pie charts directly from unsummarized data using Excel unless you use PHStat2.

E2.4A CREATING BAR AND PIE CHARTS (EXCEL 97–2003)

Open to the worksheet that contains your summary table. If your summary table is a PivotTable, click a cell that is outside your PivotTable. Select **Insert** ➔ **Chart** to begin the

Chart Wizard and make the following entries in the Wizard Step dialog boxes:

Wizard Step 1 Click the **Standard Types** tab. For a bar chart, click **Bar** as the **Chart type** and then click the first **Chart sub-type** choice, labeled **Clustered Bar** when selected. For a pie chart, click **Pie** as the **Chart type** and then click the first **Chart sub-type** choice, labeled **Pie** when selected.

Wizard Step 2 Click the **Data Range** tab and enter the cell range of the category labels and the frequency counts as the **Data range**. If you used the instructions in Section E2.2 to create your summary table, this range will always start with cell A4 and end with a cell in column B. (You do not include the column C cells that contain the percentages.) Click the **Columns** option if it is visible. In some Excel versions the model chart shown in the dialog box contains additional boxed labels that you can ignore for now.

Wizard Step 3 Click the **Titles** tab. Enter a title as the **Chart title** and, if you are creating a bar chart, enter appropriate values for the **Category (X) axis** and **Value (Y) axis** titles. For a bar chart, click, in turn, the **Axes**, **Gridlines**, **Legend**, **Data Labels**, and **Data Table** tabs and adjust the settings, as discussed in Section E2.3A on page 72. For a pie chart, click the **Legend** tab and clear **Show legend** and then click the **Data Labels** tab. If you are using Excel 97 or Excel 2000, click the **Show label and percent** option; otherwise, click **Category name** and **Percentage**.

If the chart created contains the additional boxed labels, such as "Drop Page Fields Here," that you ignored in the Step 2 dialog box, right-click the category drop-down list on the chart sheet and click **Hide PivotChart Field Buttons**. This eliminates the clutter and makes your chart look more like the ones throughout Chapter 2.

E2.4B CREATING BAR AND PIE CHARTS (EXCEL 2007)

Open to the worksheet that contains your summary table. Click a cell inside your table and then select **Insert**. For a bar chart, click **Column** in the Charts group, and then click **Clustered Column** in the chart gallery. For a pie chart, click **Pie** in the Charts group, and then click **Pie** in the chart gallery. Adjust chart settings as discussed in Section E2.3B on page 73.

E2.5 CREATING PARETO CHARTS: OVERVIEW

You create a Pareto chart from a modified summary table by using Excel charting features. You modify your summary table by adding a column for cumulative percentage. If you have used the Section E2.2 instructions to create a PivotTable, enter the heading **Cumulative Pctage** in cell D4 and enter the formula =C5 in cell D5. In cell D6, enter the formula =C6+D5 and copy this formula down through all the category rows of the summary table. Format the column D cell range that contains formulas for percentage display. Adjust the number of decimals displayed and the width of column D as necessary.

If you use Excel 2007, click cell B5 (the first frequency) and select **Home → Sort & Filter** (in the Editing group) → **Sort Largest to Smallest**. If you use Excel 97–2003, right-click cell A4 and click **Field Settings** in the shortcut menu (**Field**, if using Microsoft Excel 97). In the PivotTable Field dialog box that appears (see Figure E2.6), click **Advanced**. In the PivotTable Field Advanced Options dialog box that appears (also see Figure E2.4), select the **Descending** option and **Count of** *variable* from the **Using field** drop-down list. Click **OK** to return to the PivotTable Field dialog box and then click **OK** in that dialog box to return to the worksheet. (These last steps reorder the category rows in the table in descending order.)

With these changes, you can proceed to creating the actual Pareto chart using the instructions appropriate for the Excel version you use.

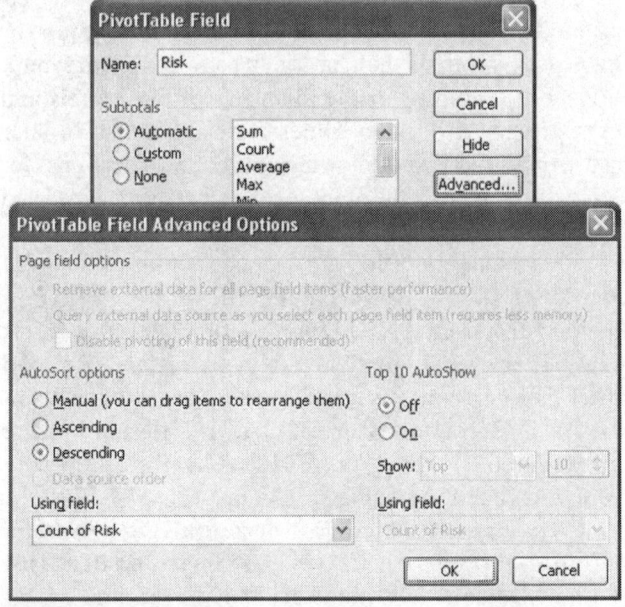

FIGURE E2.6 PivotTable Field and PivotTable Field Advanced Options dialog boxes (Excel 97–2003)

E2.5A CREATING A PARETO CHART (EXCEL 97–2003)

With your workbook opened to the worksheet that contains the modified summary table, click a cell that is outside the summary table. Select **Insert → Chart** to begin the Chart Wizard and make the following entries in the Wizard Step dialog boxes:

Wizard Step 1 Click the **Custom Types** tab. Click **Built-in** and then click **Line - Column on 2 Axes** as the **Chart type**.

Wizard Step 2 Click the **Data Range** tab. Enter the cell range of the percentage and cumulative percentage frequencies, without their column headings, in the **Data range** edit box. This range will always start with cell C4 and end with a cell in column D. Click the **Columns** option in the **Series in** group and then click the **Series** tab. Enter as a **formula** the column A cell range that contains the category labels as the **Category (X) axis labels**. Leave the **Second category (X) axis labels** box blank, if it appears.

Wizard Step 3 Click the **Titles** tab. Enter a title as the **Chart title**, the name of the variable in the **Category (X) axis** edit box, and **Percentage** in the **Value (Y) axis** edit box. Leave the other two boxes blank. Click, in turn, the **Gridlines**, **Legend**, **Data Labels**, and **Data Table** tabs and use the settings discussed in Section E2.3A.

The Pareto chart that the wizard creates contains a secondary (right) *Y*-axis scale that improperly extends past 100%. To correct this error, right-click that axis (you will see the popup message **Secondary Value Axis** when your mouse is properly positioned) and click **Format Axis** in the shortcut menu. In the **Scale** tab of the Format Axis dialog box, change the **Maximum** value to **1** and click **OK**. Right-click the primary (left) axis and repeat these instructions if the left axis needs rescaling too (you will see the popup message **Value Axis** when your mouse is properly positioned).

E2.5B CREATING A PARETO CHART (EXCEL 2007)

Select the cell range of the data to be charted. (This range will begin with cell C4, if you used the Section E2.2B instructions to create a PivotTable.) Select **Insert → Column** (in the Charts group) and select the first sub-type, identified as **Clustered Column** when you move the mouse pointer over that sub-type and pause. Select **Format**

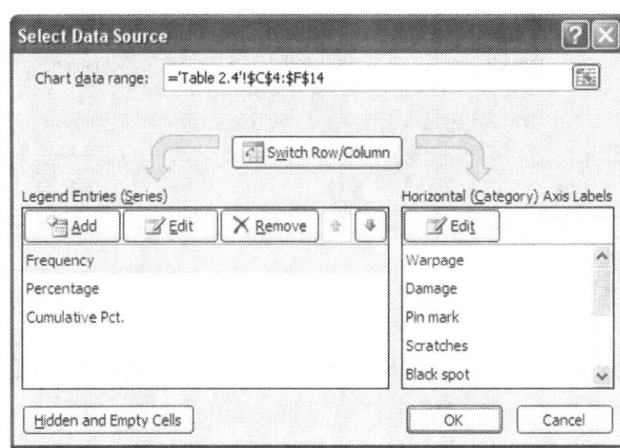

FIGURE E2.7 The Select Data Source dialog box (Excel 2007)

and select the cumulative percentage series from the drop-down list in the Current Selection group. Then select **Format Selection** (from the same group) and in the Format Data Series dialog box select the **Secondary Axis** in the **Series Options** panel and click **Close**. With the cumulative percentage series still selected in the Current Selection group, select **Design → Change Chart Type**, and in the **Change Chart Type** gallery, select the line chart identified as **Line with Markers** and click **OK**.

If your chart contains extraneous plots—for example, a plot of percentage frequencies—delete such plots one series at a time by doing the following: Select **Format** and then select an extraneous series from the drop-down list in the Current Selection group. Select **Design → Select Data**. In the Select Data Source dialog box (see Figure E2.7), select the extraneous **Legend Entries** series (**Percentage** in Figure E2.7) and click **Remove** and then **OK**.

Relocate your chart to a chart sheet and customize your chart, using the instructions in Section E.2.3B. If the secondary (right) *Y*-axis scale improperly extends past 100%, right-click the axis and click **Format Axis** in the shortcut menu. In the **Scale** tab of the Format Axis dialog box, change the value in the **Maximum** edit box to **1** and click **Close**. Right-click the primary (left) axis and repeat these instructions if the left axis needs rescaling too.

E2.6 CREATING ORDERED ARRAYS

To create an ordered array, first organize your worksheet so that each variable appears in its own column, enter a variable column heading in row 1, and enter the values for the variable starting in row 2. Select the data to be sorted. If you use Excel 97–2003, select **Data ➔ Sort**. In the Sort dialog box, select the variable to be sorted from the Sort by drop-down list. Click the **Ascending** option button, click **Header row**, and click **OK**. If you use Excel 2007, select **Home ➔ Sort & Filter** (in the Editing group) ➔ **Sort Smallest to Largest**.

E2.7 CREATING STEM-AND-LEAF DISPLAYS

No Microsoft Excel features directly create stem-and-leaf displays. Use PHStat2 Section P2.5 to create a stem-and-leaf display in Excel.

E2.8 CREATING BINS FOR FREQUENCY DISTRIBUTIONS

To create frequency distributions using Excel features, you must first translate your class groupings into what Excel calls **bins**.

Bins are numbers in an ordered list that define ranges for each row of a frequency distribution or each bar of a histogram. Unlike class groupings, which have well-defined lower and upper boundary values, the boundary values of each bin are implied. For a particular bin number, the range defined is all values that are less than or equal to the bin number and that are greater than the previous bin number, which must be a lesser value.

In Chapter 2, Tables 2.7– 2.11 use class groupings in the form *valueA but less than valueB*. You can translate class groupings in this form into nearly equivalent bins by creating a list of bin numbers that are slightly less than each *valueB* that appears in the class groupings. For example, the Table 2.7 class groupings on page 37 could be translated into nearly equivalent bins by using this list of bin numbers: 14.99 ("slightly less" than 15.0), 19.99, 24.99, 29.99, 34.99, 39.99, 44.99, 49.99, 54.99, 59.99, 64.99, 69.99, and 74.99).

If you have class groupings in the form "all values from *valueA* to *valueB*," such as the set 0.0 through 4.9, 5.0 through 9.9, 10.0 through 14.9, and 15.0 through 19.9, you can approximate each class grouping by choosing a bin number slightly more than each *valueB*, as in this list of bin numbers: 4.99 (slightly more than 4.9), 9.99, 14.99, and 19.99.

Because the first bin number always represents a range with no explicit lower boundary (other than negative infinity), a first bin can never have a midpoint. (You may have noticed in this chapter that in the charts in which midpoints are used as labels, the first bin is labeled with – and not with a midpoint.) To enter a list of bin numbers, use a blank column in the worksheet that contains your unsummarized data, entering the column heading "Bins" in the row 1 cell.

Unlike the frequency distributions shown in Tables 2.8, 2.10, and 2.13, you typically include frequency, percentage frequency, and cumulative percentage frequencies as columns of one table and not as separate tables. Also, unlike what is done in Chapter 2, in Excel, you create frequency distributions for individual categories, one at a time (e.g., growth funds or value funds) and not frequency distributions that contain two categories (e.g., growth and value funds). To create multiple category tables, such as Tables 2.8, 2.10, and 2.13, you must combine columns from the individual tables using copy-and-paste operations.

E2.9 CREATING FREQUENCY DISTRIBUTIONS AND HISTOGRAMS

To create frequency distributions and histograms from unsummarized data, use the ToolPak **Histogram** procedure. This procedure requires that you first translate your class groupings into bins, as explained in the previous section.

Open to the worksheet that contains the unsummarized data and verify that bin values have been placed in their own column. Begin the ToolPak add-in and select **Histogram** from the **Analysis Tools** list and then click **OK**. In the Histogram dialog box (see Figure E2.8), enter the cell range of the data to be summarized as the **Input Range**. Enter the cell range of the list of bin numbers (including the column heading "Bins") as the **Bin Range**. (If you leave Bin Range blank, the procedure creates a set of bins for you, but such bins are often not as well chosen as the ones you can specify yourself.) Click **Labels** to indicate that the first cells of the Input Range and Bin Range contain a label. Click **New Worksheet Ply** and **Cumulative Percentage**, and then click **Chart Output** (if you want to create a histogram). Click **OK** to create the frequency distribution (and histogram) on a new worksheet.

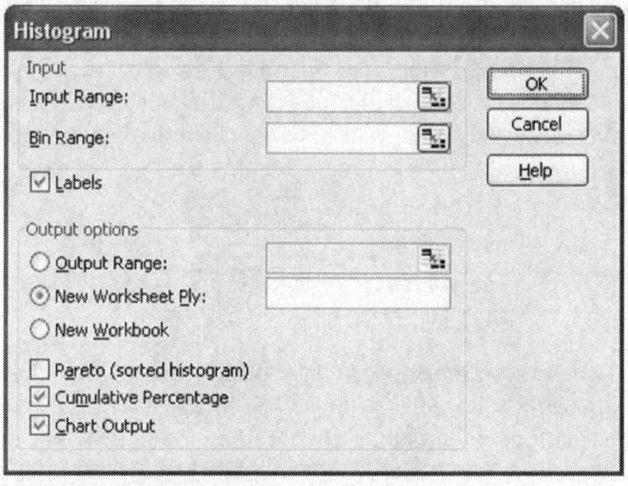

FIGURE E2.8 The Data Analysis Histogram dialog box

The frequency distribution that the ToolPak creates improperly contains an open-ended bin labeled **More**. To eliminate the More class, first manually add the frequency count of the More row to the count of the preceding bin and set the cumulative percentage of the preceding bin to 100%. Then, select the entire row containing the More row. Next, select **Edit → Delete** in Excel 97–2003 or right-click the selected row in Excel 2007. In the Delete dialog box, click **Shift cells up** and then click **OK**.

As you correct your frequency distribution, your histogram also changes, and the bar representing the incorrect More group disappears. However, the histogram will still contain these errors: There are gaps between the bars, the bins are labeled with their maximum bin values and not with their midpoint values, and the secondary *Y*-axis scale exceeds 100%.

To eliminate the gaps between bars, right-click inside one of the histogram bars. (You will see a popup message that begins with **Series 'Frequency'** when your mouse is properly positioned.) Click **Format Data Series** in the shortcut menu to display the Format Data Series dialog box. If you use Excel 97–2003, click the **Options** tab, change the value of **Gap width** to 0, and click **OK**. If you use Excel 2007, move the **Gap Width** slider to **No Gap** in the **Series Options** panel of this dialog box.

To change the bin labels, enter the list of midpoint values in column D of the worksheet. Cell D2 should contain the heading **Midpoints** and cell D3 should contain --- (which you should enter as '– to avoid an error). Right-click the tinted background of the chart. (You will see the ToolTip **Plot Area** when your mouse is properly positioned.) Click **Source Data** (Excel 97–2003) or **Select Data** (Excel 2007) in the shortcut menu. If you use Excel 97–2003, select the **Series** tab in the Source Data dialog box and enter the cell range of the midpoints as a formula, in the form =*SheetName*!*CellRange*, in the **Category (X) axis labels** box. Then delete the entry for the **Second category(X) axis labels** and click **OK**. If you use Excel 2007, click the **Edit** button under the **Horizontal (Categories) Axis Labels** heading in the Select Data Source dialog box. In the Axis Labels dialog box, enter the cell range of the midpoints as a formula, in the form =*SheetName*!*CellRange*, and click **OK**. (This range should start with the first midpoint value and not with the midpoint column heading.) Click **OK** a second time (in the original dialog box) to complete the task.

To rescale the secondary *Y*-axis, right-click on the secondary (right) *Y*-axis. (You will see a popup message that includes the words **Secondary** and **Axis** when your mouse is properly positioned.) Click **Format Axis** in the shortcut menu. If you use Excel 97–2003, change the **Maximum** in the **Scale** tab of the Format Axis dialog box to **1** and click **OK**. If you use Excel 2007, select the **Fixed** option for **Maximum** and enter **1** as the maximum value in the **Axis Options** panel of the Format Axis dialog box, and then click **OK**.

If you want to add a percentage frequency column to the frequency distribution, select column C and then select **Insert → Columns**. In the new column C, enter the heading **Percentage** in cell C2. Enter the formula **=B3/SUM(B:B)** in cell C3 and copy the formula down the column through the rest of the frequency distribution. Format column C for percentage display to complete the column.

E2.10 CREATING PERCENTAGE AND CUMULATIVE PERCENTAGE POLYGONS

No Microsoft Excel features directly create percentage or cumulative percentage polygons. Use PHStat2 Section P2.7 to create a polygon in Excel.

E2.11 CREATING CONTINGENCY TABLES: OVERVIEW

You create a contingency table from unsummarized data by creating a PivotTable using instructions adapted from Section E2.2. To create a contingency table from data already summarized in table form, enter the contents of the table into a blank worksheet, using the column A and row 1 cells for row and column headings.

E2.11A CREATING CONTINGENCY TABLES (EXCEL 97–2003)

Adapt the instructions of Section E2.2A, "Creating PivotTables (Excel 97–2003)." When you get to the Step 3 instructions, modify them as follows. In the Layout dialog box in Step 3, first drag the label of the first variable to be summarized and drop it in the ROW area. Drag a second copy of this same label and drop it in the DATA area. (The label changes to **Count of variable name**.) Then drag the label of the second variable and drop it in the COLUMN area. In the PivotTable Options dialog box, also in Step 3, verify that both **Grand total for columns** and **Grand totals for rows** are checked (they should be) and that you have entered **0** as the **For empty cells, show** value. (Excel 97 does not contain this options dialog box.)

E2.11B CREATING CONTINGENCY TABLES (EXCEL 2007)

Adapt the instructions of Section E2.2B, "Creating PivotTables (Excel 2007)." When you get to the instructions for using the PivotTable Field List task pane, modify them as follows. In the PivotTable Field List task pane, drag the label of the variable to be summarized and drop it in the **Row Labels** box. Drag a second copy of this same label and drop it in the **Σ Values** box. (This second label changes to **Count of variable name**.) Then drag the label of the second variable and drop it in the **Column Labels** area. When you later right-click the PivotTable, click **Pivot Table Options** in the shortcut menu. In the **Total & Filters** tab of the PivotTable Options dialog box, verify that both **Show grand totals for columns** and **Show grand totals for rows** are checked. Also, as stated in Section E2.2B, click the **Layout & Format** tab, check **For empty cells show**, and enter **0** as its value, and then click **OK**.

E2.12 CREATING SIDE-BY-SIDE CHARTS

You use Excel charting features to create a side-by-side chart from a contingency table of two categorical variables.

E2.12A CREATING SIDE-BY-SIDE CHARTS (EXCEL 97–2003)

To create a side-by-side chart, open to the worksheet containing the contingency table. First, click a cell that is outside the contingency table. Then, select **Insert → Chart** to begin the Chart Wizard and make the following entries in the Wizard Step dialog boxes:

Wizard Step 1 Click **Bar** from the **Standard Types Chart type** box and leave the first **Chart sub-type** selected.

Wizard Step 2 If you are using a PivotTable, click the PivotTable when the **Data range** box is selected to have Excel fill in the proper cell range. If you are using a manually entered contingency table, enter the rectangular range that excludes the total row and the total column but that includes the row and column headings.

Wizard Step 3 Click the **Titles** tab. Enter a title as the **Chart title** and appropriate values for the **Category (X) axis** and **Value (Y) axis** titles. (Unlike other charts, Excel considers the horizontal axis to be the *Value (Y) axis* and the vertical axis of this chart to be the *Category (X) axis*, which is different from what you might otherwise expect.) Click the **Legend** tab and click **Show legend**. Use the formatting settings for **Axes**, **Gridlines**, **Data Labels**, and **Data Table** tabs that are given in Section E2.3A on page 72.

If field buttons appear on the chart, right-click any button and click **Hide PivotChart Field Buttons** in the shortcut menu.

E2.12B CREATING SIDE-BY-SIDE CHARTS (EXCEL 2007)

To create a side-by-side chart, open to the worksheet that contains the contingency table. If your contingency table is also a PivotTable, click a cell inside the PivotTable; otherwise, select the cell range of the contingency table, including row and column headings, but excluding the total row and total column.

Select **Insert → Bar** and click the **Clustered Bar** gallery choice. If your chart contains reversed row and column variables and is not based on a PivotTable, right-click the chart and click **Select Data** in the shortcut menu. In the Select Data Source dialog box, click **Switch Row/Column** and then click **OK**. If your chart has reversed variables and is based on a PivotTable, you have to reorder your variables in the PivotTable in order to get the correct chart. Finish by relocating your chart to a chart sheet and customizing your chart, using the instructions in Section E.2.3B on page 73, with this exception: When you click **Legend**, select **Show Legend at Right**.

E2.13 CREATING SCATTER PLOTS: OVERVIEW

You use Excel charting features to create scatter plots. To create a scatter plot, the variable columns to be plotted must be arranged *X* variable column first, then *Y* variable column, reading left-to-right. (If your data are arranged *Y* then *X*, first cut and paste the *Y* variable column so it appears to the right of the *X* variable column before continuing.)

E2.13A CREATING SCATTER PLOTS (EXCEL 97–2003)

Open to the worksheet containing the properly arranged columns. Select **Insert → Chart** (to begin the Chart Wizard) and make the following entries in the Wizard Step dialog boxes:

Wizard Step 1 Click **XY (Scatter)** from the Standard Types Chart type box and click the first Chart sub-type.

Wizard Step 2 Enter the cell range of the two variables in the **Data range** box and select the **Columns** option. If the two variables are in nonadjacent columns, first type or point to the cell range of the first variable, then type a comma, then type or point to the cell range of the second variable, and then press **Enter**. Do not make any entries in the **Series** tab of this dialog box.

Wizard Step 3 Click the **Titles** tab. Enter a title as the **Chart title** and enter appropriate values for the **Value (X) axis** and **Value (Y) axis** titles. Click, in turn, the **Axes**, **Gridlines**, **Legend**, and **Data Labels** tabs and use the formatting settings given in Section E2.3A on page 72.

E2.13B CREATING SCATTER PLOTS (EXCEL 2007)

Open to the worksheet containing the properly arranged columns. Select **Insert → Scatter** and click the **Scatter with only Markers** gallery choice. Finish by relocating your chart to a chart sheet and customizing your chart using the instructions in Section E.2.3B on page 73.

E2.14 CREATING TIME-SERIES PLOTS

You create time-series plots by using Excel charting features with a time-series worksheet in which the time periods have been entered into columns. If your data are arranged with the numerical variable before the time variable, first cut and paste the numerical variable column so it appears to the right of the time variable column before continuing.

E2.14A CREATING A TIME-SERIES PLOT (EXCEL 97–2003)

Open to the worksheet containing the properly arranged columns. Select **Insert → Chart** to begin the Chart Wizard and make the following entries in the Wizard Step dialog boxes:

Wizard Step 1 Click **Line** from the Standard Types Chart type box and select the first Chart sub-type in the second row, identified as **Line with markers displayed at each data value**.

Wizard Step 2 Enter the cell range of the two variables in the **Data range** box and select the **Columns** option. If the variables are in nonadjacent columns, first type or point to the cell range of the first variable, then type a comma, then type or point to the cell range of the second variable, and then press **Enter**. Do not make any entries in the **Series** tab of this dialog box.

Wizard Step 3 Click the **Titles** tab. Enter a title as the **Chart title** and enter appropriate values for the **Value (X) axis** and **Value (Y) axis** titles. Click, in turn, the **Axes**, **Gridlines**, **Legend**, **Data Labels**, and **Data Table** tabs and use the formatting settings that are given in Section E2.3A on page 72.

E2.14B CREATING A TIME-SERIES PLOT (EXCEL 2007)

Open to the worksheet containing the properly arranged columns. In the Select Data Source dialog box, select **Insert → XY (Scatter) → Scatter with Straight Lines and Markers**. Finish by relocating your chart to a chart sheet and customizing your chart using the instructions in Section E.2.3B on page 73.

Appendix P2
Using PHStat2 for Tables and Charts

P2.1 INTRODUCTION

Before continuing, you should review the material in Appendix P1 that presents a general introduction to using PHStat2. You should also review Appendix F and the PHStat2 readme file on the Student CD-ROM if you plan to install PHStat2 on your computer system. Note that for some tasks that are straightforward to do in Excel, there is no equivalent PHStat2 procedure (use the appropriate Excel appendix section for such tasks).

P2.2 CREATING SUMMARY TABLES

To create summary charts, use **PHStat → Descriptive Statistics → One-Way Tables & Charts**. This procedure accepts either unsummarized data (**Raw Categorical Data**) or data in the form of categories that have already been tallied (**Table of Frequencies**). In both cases, the procedure uses the Excel PivotTable feature to create a summary table.

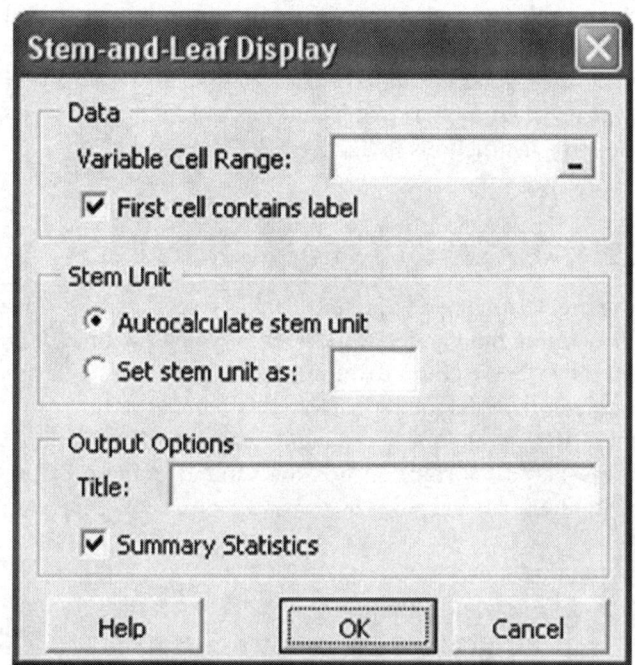

P2.3 CREATING CHARTS

To create summary charts, use various Output Options of the **PHStat → Descriptive Statistics → One-Way Tables & Charts** procedure discussed in the previous section. The options use Excel charting features to create a percentage column, bar, pie, or Pareto chart. (The charts are created with the custom formatting discussed in Sections E2.3 and E2.5.)

P2.4 CREATING PARETO CHARTS

To create summary charts, use the **Pareto Chart** Output Options of the **PHStat → Descriptive Statistics → One-Way Tables & Charts** procedure discussed in Section P2.2.

P2.5 CREATING STEM-AND-LEAF DISPLAYS

To create a stem-and-leaf display, use **PHStat → Descriptive Statistics → Stem-and-Leaf Display**. This procedure creates a stem-and-leaf display from the unsummarized data in the **Variable Cell Range**. The stem-and-leaf display

appears as a series of formatted worksheet labels in a new worksheet. If you click **Summary Statistics**, a table of summary statistics is included on that new worksheet.

The **Set stem unit as** option should be used sparingly and, if you use this option, the stem unit you specify must be a power of ten. Only use this option if **Autocalculate stem unit** creates a display that has too few or too many stems.

P2.6 CREATING FREQUENCY DISTRIBUTIONS AND HISTOGRAMS

To create a frequency distribution and histogram from unsummarized data, use **PHStat → Descriptive Statistics → Histogram & Polygons**. This procedure accepts data either for a single group or multiple groups as either unstacked data (column by column) or stacked data (one column). If you use the **Multiple Groups – Stacked** option, you will also need to enter the **Grouping Variable Cell Range**.

This procedure silently uses the ToolPak Histogram procedure but corrects several errors made by the ToolPak procedure. Because the ToolPak is used silently, you must specify a cell range for bins (and not class groupings). Because the first bin will always be open-ended towards negative infinity, this bin will never have a true midpoint. Therefore, the command expects that your **Midpoints Cell Range** will be one cell smaller than your **Bins Cell Range** and will assign the first midpoint to the second class. (Review Section E2.8 "Creating Bins for Frequency Distributions" on page 76 if you are not familiar with the Excel bins concept.)

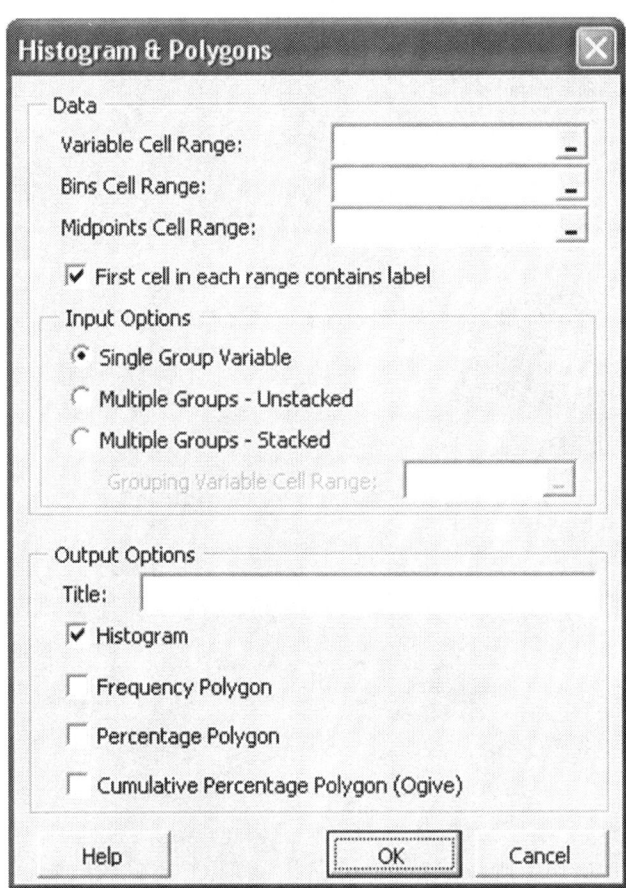

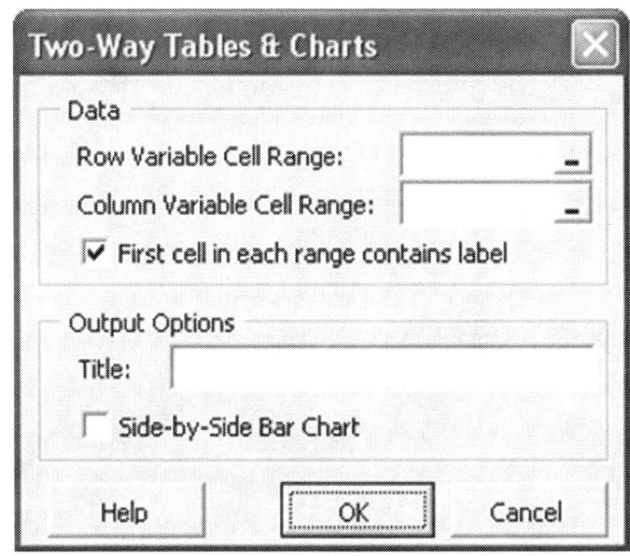

P2.8 CREATING CONTINGENCY TABLES AND SIDE-BY-SIDE CHARTS

To create a contingency table and, optionally, a side-by-side chart from unsummarized data, use **PHStat → Descriptive Statistics → Two-Way Tables & Charts**. This procedure uses the Excel PivotTable feature to create a contingency table. Click **Side-by-Side Bar Chart** to optionally create the side-by-side chart.

P2.7 CREATING PERCENTAGE AND CUMULATIVE PERCENTAGE POLYGONS

To create percentage and cumulative percentage polygons, use the Output Options of the **PHStat → Descriptive Statistics → Histogram & Polygons** procedure discussed in the previous section. The options use Excel charting features to create a percentage polygon and/or cumulative percentage polygon, as well as a frequency polygon.

P2.9 CREATING SCATTER PLOTS

To create a scatter plot, use the **Scatter Diagram** Output Option of the **PHStat → Regression → Simple Linear Regression** procedure. For full information about using this procedure, see Section P13.2 on page 632.

Appendix M2
Using Minitab for Tables and Charts

You can use Minitab to create many of the tables and charts discussed in this chapter. If you are new to Minitab, make sure to review Appendix M1, "Introduction to Minitab," that starts on page 23, before continuing.

M2.1 UNSTACKING DATA

Data are usually arranged so that all of the values of a variable are stacked vertically down a column. In many cases, you need to separately analyze different subgroups in terms of a numerical variable of interest. For example, in the mutual fund data, you may want to analyze the 2006 percentage return for the growth funds separately from the 2006 percentage return for the value funds. This can be accomplished by unstacking the 2006 percentage return variable so that the 2006 percentage returns for the growth funds are located in one column and the 2006 percentage returns for the value funds are located in a different column.

To unstack the growth and value funds data:

1. Open the `Mutual Funds.mtw` worksheet.
2. Select **Data → Unstack Columns**.

In the Unstack Columns dialog box (see Figure M2.1):

3. Enter **'Return 2006'** in the **Unstack the data in** box and **Objective** in the **Using subscripts in** box.
4. Click the **After last column in use** option and **Name the columns containing the unstacked data**.
5. Click **OK**.

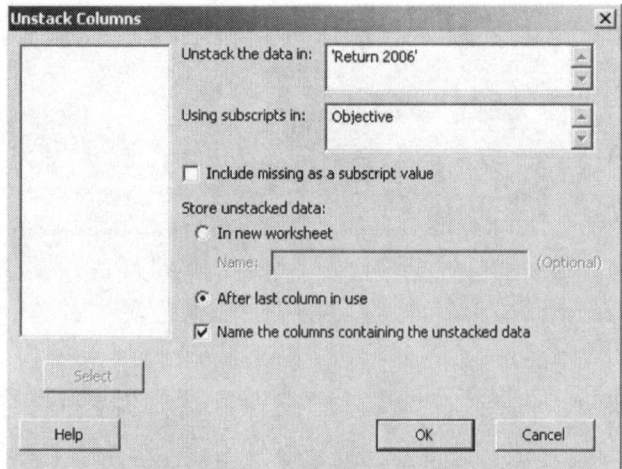

FIGURE M2.1 Minitab Unstack Columns dialog box

The new variables Return2006_Growth and Return2006_Value appear in columns C10 and C11. (You can change these variable names by editing their values in the cell at the top of these columns.)

M2.2 CREATING BAR CHARTS

To create the bar chart in Figure 2.1 on page 28:

1. Open the `Banking.mtw` worksheet.
2. Select **Graph → Bar Chart**.

In the Bar Charts dialog box (see Figure M2.2):

3. Select **Values from a table** from the **Bars represent** drop-down list. (Make this selection because the fre-

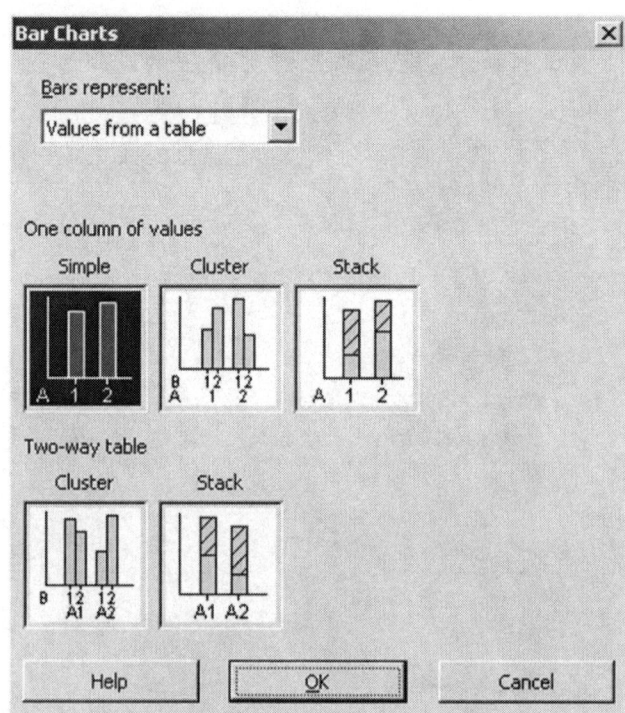

FIGURE M2.2 Minitab Bar Charts dialog box

quencies in each category are provided. If you are using raw data such as is found in the `Mutual Funds.mtw` worksheet, select **Counts of unique values** instead.)

4. In the gallery of choices, click **Simple**.
5. Click **OK**.

In the Bar Chart - Values from a table, One column of values, Simple dialog box (see Figure M2.3):

6. Enter **'Percentage (%)'** in the **Graph variables** box.
7. Enter **'Banking Preference'** in the **Categorical variable** box.
8. Click **OK** (to create the chart).

To modify the bar chart by changing the colors for the bars and borders in the bar chart:

1. Right-click one of the bars of the bar chart.
2. Select **Edit Bars** from the shortcut menu.

In the **Attributes** tab of the Edit Bars dialog box:

3. Click **Custom** under the **Fill Pattern** heading and make selections from the **Type** and **Background color** drop-down lists.
4. Click **Custom** under the **Border and Fill Lines** heading and make selections from the **Type**, **Color**, and **Size** drop-down lists.
5. At the bottom of the dialog box, click **OK**.

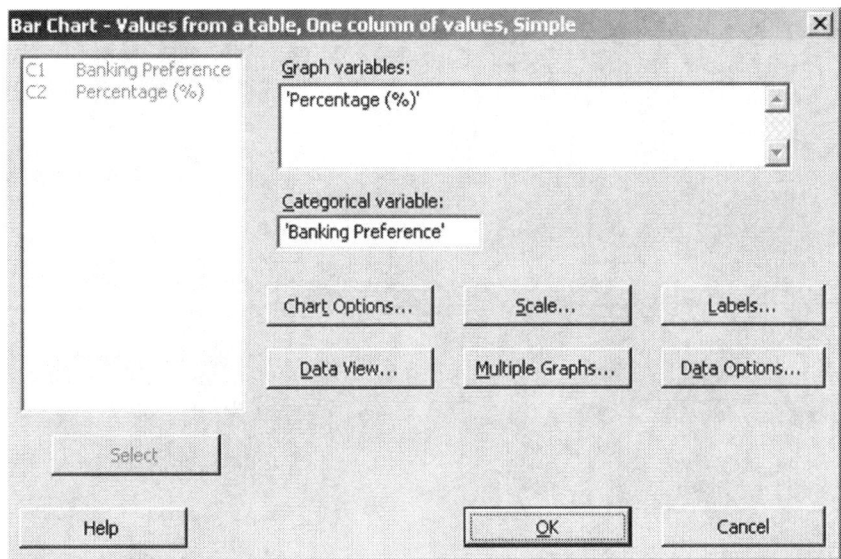

FIGURE M2.3 Minitab Bar Chart - Values from a table, One column of values, Simple dialog box

M2.3 CREATING PIE CHARTS

To create a pie chart similar to Figure 2.4 on page 29:

1. Open the **Mutual Funds.mtw** worksheet.
2. Select **Graph ➜ Pie Chart**.

In the Pie Chart dialog box (see Figure M2.4):

3. Click **Chart counts of unique values.**

(If you used a worksheet such as **Banking.mtw** that contained the frequencies in each category, you would click

Chart values from a table and not **Chart counts of unique values**.)

4. Enter **Risk** in the **Categorical variables** box.
5. Click **Labels**.

In the Pie Chart - Labels dialog box (see Figure M2.5):

6. Click the **Slice Labels** tab.
7. Click **Category name** and **Percent**.
8. Click **OK** (to return to the original Pie Chart dialog box).
9. Back in the original Pie Chart dialog box, click **OK**.

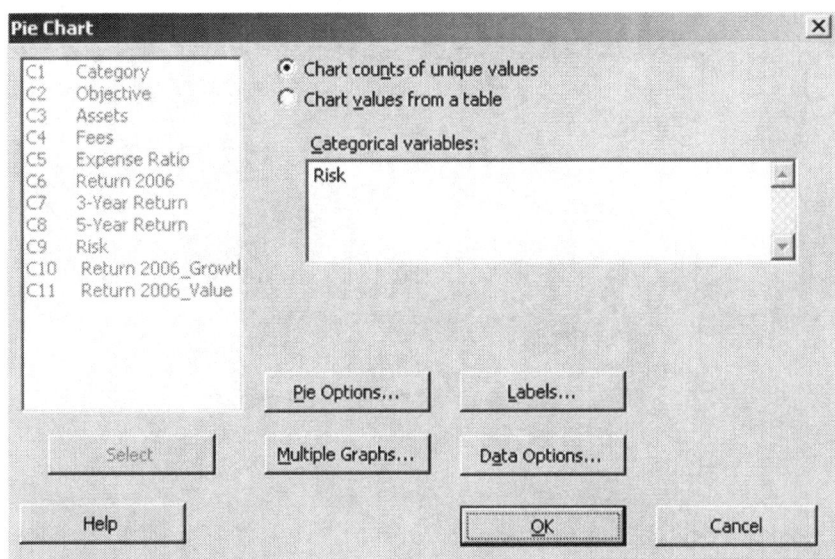

FIGURE M2.4 Minitab Pie Chart dialog box

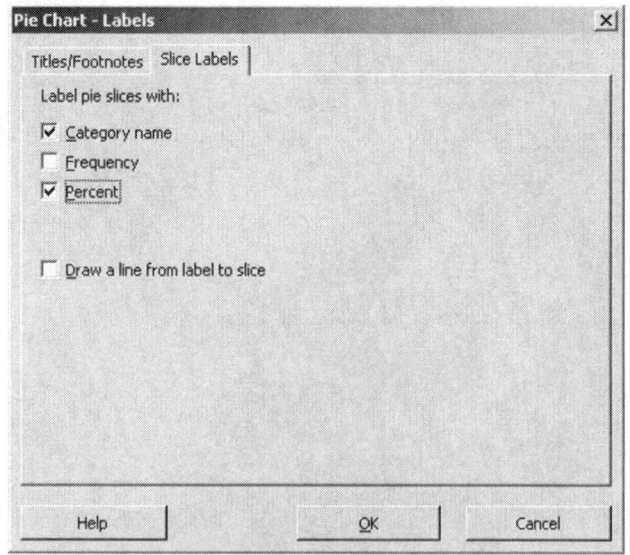

FIGURE M2.5 Minitab Pie Charts - Labels dialog box

M2.4 CREATING PARETO CHARTS

To create the Pareto chart of Figure 2.5 on page 31:

1. Open the **Keyboard Defects.mtw** worksheet. (This worksheet contains the causes of the defects in column C1 and the frequency of defects in column C2.)
2. Select **Stat → Quality Tools → Pareto Chart**.

In the Pareto Chart dialog box (see Figure M2.6):

3. Click **Chart defects table**.
4. Enter **Defect** in the **Labels in** box.
5. Enter **Frequency** in the **Frequencies in** box.
6. Click **Do not combine**.
7. Click **OK**.

If the variable of interest was located in a single column and is in raw form with each row indicating a type of error,

you would click **Charts defects data in** and enter the appropriate column number or variable name in the **Chart defects data in** box before doing steps 6 and 7.

M2.5 CREATING STEM-AND-LEAF DISPLAYS

To create the stem-and-leaf display of the 2006 returns for all the mutual funds:

1. Open the **Mutual Funds.mtw** worksheet.
2. Select **Graph → Stem-and-Leaf**.

In the Stem-and-Leaf dialog box (see Figure M2.7):

3. Enter **'Return 2006'** in the **Graph variables** box.
4. Click **OK**.

M2.6 CREATING HISTOGRAMS

To create the histogram of the 2006 returns for all the mutual funds:

1. Open the **Mutual Funds.mtw** worksheet.
2. Select **Graph → Histogram**.
3. In the gallery of the Histograms dialog box (see Figure M2.8), click **Simple** and then click **OK**.
4. In the Histogram-Simple dialog box (see Figure M2.9), enter **'Return 2006'** in the **Graph variables** box and then click **OK** (to create the chart).

To modify the histogram by changing the colors for the bars and borders in the histogram:

1. Right-click one of the bars of the histogram.
2. Select **Edit Bars** from the shortcut menu.

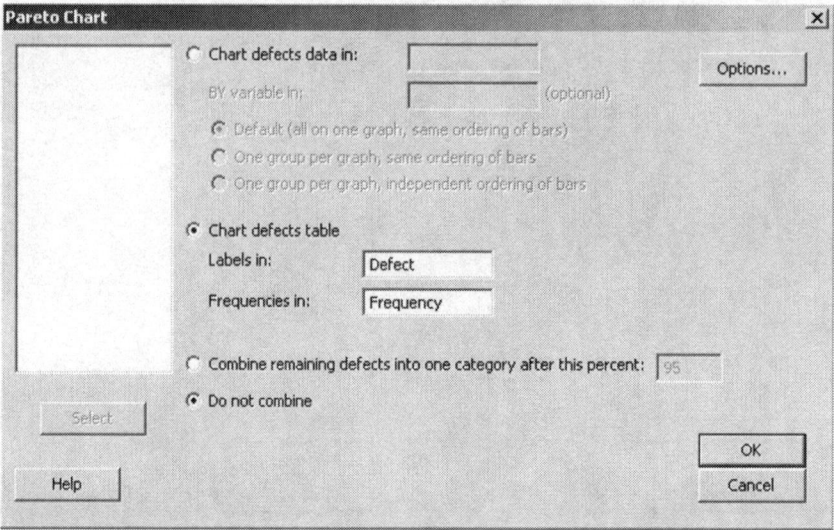

FIGURE M2.6 Minitab Pareto Chart dialog box

FIGURE M2.7
Minitab Stem-and-Leaf
dialog box

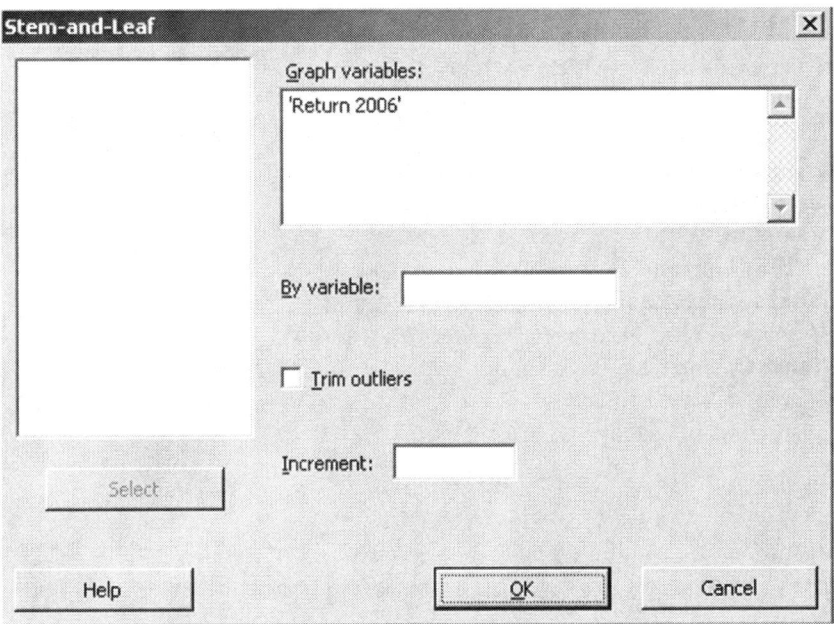

FIGURE M2.8
Minitab Histograms
dialog box

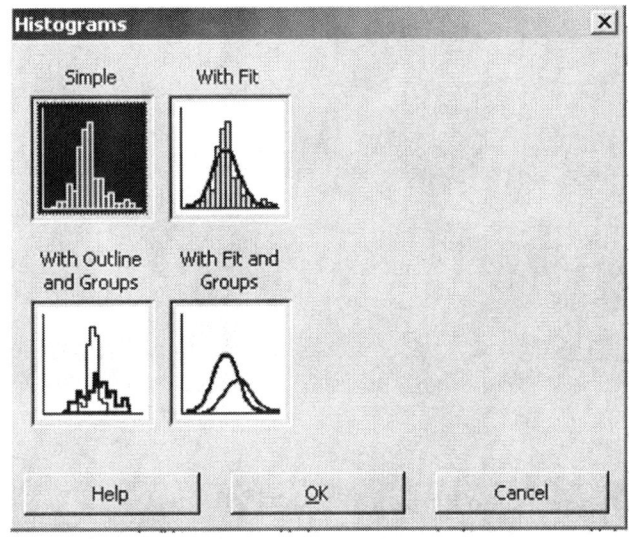

FIGURE M2.9
Minitab Histogram-
Simple dialog box

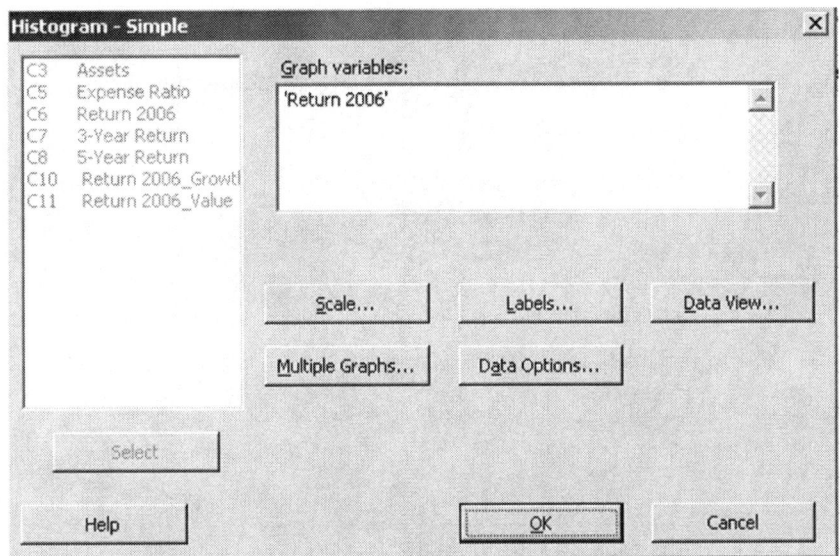

In the **Attributes** tab of the Edit Bars dialog box:

3. Click **Custom** under the **Fill Pattern** heading and make selections from the **Type** and **Background color** drop-down lists.
4. Click **Custom** under the **Border and Fill Lines** heading and make selections from the **Type**, **Color**, and **Size** drop-down lists.
5. In the **Binning** tab of the same dialog box, click **Midpoint** to specify midpoints or click **Cutpoint** to specify class limits. Then click **Midpoint/Cutpoint positions** and enter the set of midpoint or cutpoints values in the box.
6. Click **OK** (to complete the modifications).

If you wish to create separate histograms for the growth and value funds similar to Figure 2.9 on page 43, do the following:

7. Enter **'Return2006_Growth'** and **'Return2006_Value'** in the **Graph variables** box.
8. Select **Multiple Graphs**.
9. In the By Variables tab, select the **On separate graphs** button and then click **OK**.
10. Click **OK** again to construct the graphs.

M2.7 CREATING CROSS-TABULATION TABLES

To create cross-tabulation tables similar to Tables 2.14 through 2.17 on pages 49–50:

1. Open the Mutual Funds.mtw worksheet.
2. Select **Stat** → **Tables** → **Cross Tabulation and Chi-Square**.

In the Cross Tabulation and Chi-Square dialog box (see Figure M2.10):

3. Enter **Objective** in the **For rows** box.
4. Enter **Risk** in the **For columns** box.
5. Click **Counts**, **Row percents**, **Column percents**, and **Total percents**.
6. Click **OK**.

M2.8 CREATING SIDE-BY-SIDE BAR CHARTS

To create a side-by-side bar chart similar to Figure 2.14 on page 50:

1. Open the Mutual Funds.mtw worksheet.
2. Select **Graph** → **Bar Chart**

In the Bar Charts dialog box (similar to Figure M2.2 on page 82):

3. Select **Counts of unique values** from the **Bars represent** drop-down list (because you are using raw data).
4. In the gallery of choices, click **Cluster**.
5. Click **OK**.

In the Bar Chart-Counts of unique values, Cluster dialog box (see Figure M2.11):

6. Enter **Objective** and **Risk** in the **Categorical variables (2–4, outermost first)** box.
7. Click **OK**.

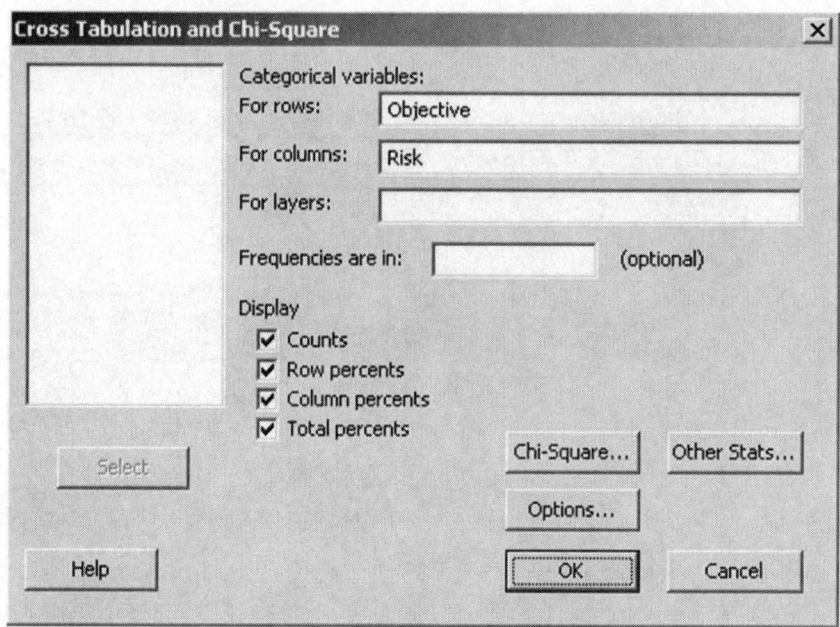

FIGURE M2.10 Minitab Cross Tabulation and Chi-Square dialog box

FIGURE M2.11
Minitab Bar Chart -
Counts of unique
values, Cluster dialog
box

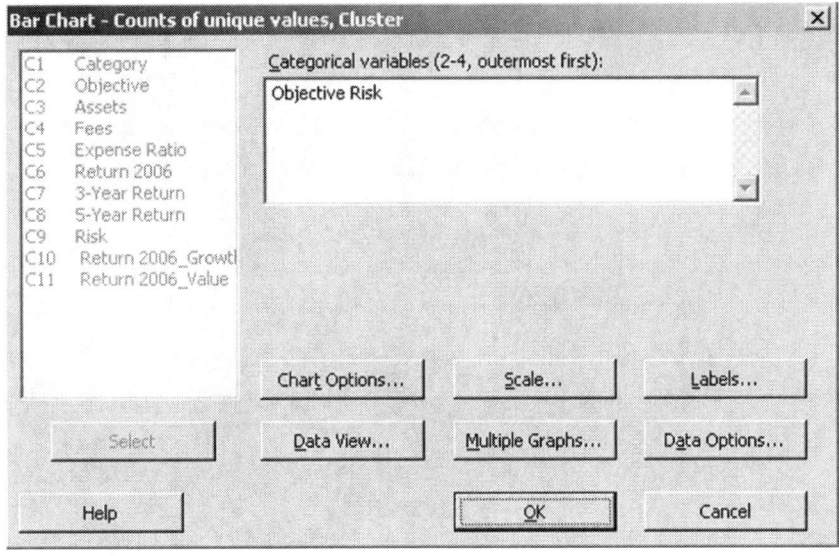

M2.9 CREATING SCATTER PLOT AND TIME-SERIES PLOTS

To create the scatter plot of the cost of a hamburger and the cost of movie tickets (see Figure 2.15 on page 53):

1. Open the `Cost of Living.mtw` worksheet.
2. Select **Graph ➜ Scatterplot**.

In the Scatterplots dialog box (see Figure M2.12):

3. In the gallery, click **Simple**.
4. Click **OK**.

In the Scatterplot - Simple dialog box (see Figure M2.13 on page 88):

5. Enter **'Movie Tickets'** in the row 1 **Y variables** cell.
6. Enter **Hamburger** in the row 1 **X variables** cell.
7. Click **OK (** to create the chart).

To create a time-series plot, use the same eight-step process, entering the variable of interest in step 5 and the time period variable in step 6.

FIGURE M2.12
Minitab Scatterplots
dialog box

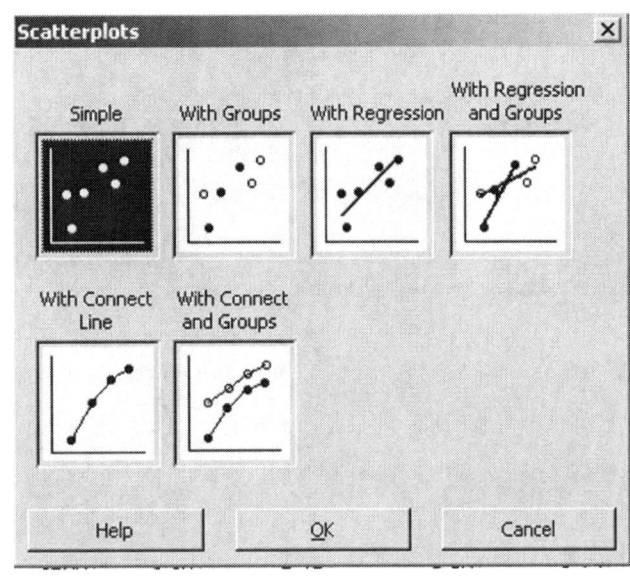

FIGURE M2.13
Minitab Scatterplot -
Simple dialog box

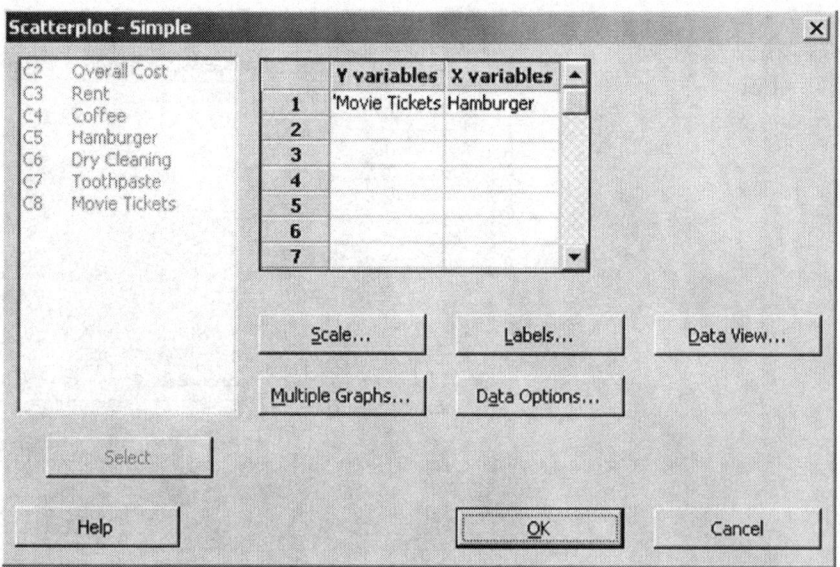

CHAPTER THREE

NUMERICAL DESCRIPTIVE MEASURES

LEARNING OBJECTIVES

In this chapter, you learn:

- To describe the properties of central tendency, variation, and shape in numerical data
- To calculate descriptive summary measures for a population
- To calculate descriptive summary measures from frequency distribution
- To construct and interpret a boxplot
- To describe the covariance and the coefficient of correlation

USING STATISTICS @ Choice Is Yours, Part II

The tables and charts you prepared for the sample of 868 mutual funds has proved useful to the customers of the Choice Is Yours service. However, customers have become frustrated trying to evaluate mutual fund performance. Although they know how the 2006 returns are distributed, they have no idea what a typical 2006 rate of return would be for a particular category of mutual funds, such as low-risk funds, nor do they know how that typical value compares to the typical values of other categories. They also have no idea of the extent of the variability in the 2006 rate of return. Are all the values relatively similar, or do they include very small and very large values? Are there a lot of small values and a few large ones, or vice versa, or are there a similar number of small and large values?

How could you help the customers get answers to these questions so that they could better evaluate the mutual funds?

The customers in the Using Statistics scenario are asking questions about numerical variables. When summarizing and describing numerical variables, you need to do more than just prepare the tables and charts discussed in Chapter 2. You need to consider the central tendency, variation, and shape of each numerical variable.

> **CENTRAL TENDENCY**
>
> The **central tendency** is the extent to which all the data values group around a typical or central value.
>
> **VARIATION**
>
> The **variation** is the amount of dispersion, or scattering, of values away from a central value.
>
> **SHAPE**
>
> The **shape** is the pattern of the distribution of values from the lowest value to the highest value.

This chapter discusses ways you can measure the central tendency, variation, and shape of a variable. You will also learn about the covariance and the coefficient of correlation, which help measure the strength of the association between two numerical variables. Using these measures would give the customers of the Choice Is Yours service the answers they seek.

3.1 MEASURES OF CENTRAL TENDENCY

Most sets of data show a distinct tendency to group around a central point. When people talk about an "average value" or the "middle value" or the "most frequent value," they are talking informally about the mean, median, and mode—three measures of central tendency.

The Mean

The **arithmetic mean** (typically referred to as the **mean**) is the most common measure of central tendency. The mean is the only common measure in which all the values play an equal role. The mean serves as a "balance point" in a set of data (like the fulcrum on a seesaw). You calculate the mean by adding together all the values in a data set and then dividing that sum by the number of values in the data set.

The symbol $\bar{X}$, called *X-bar*, is used to represent the mean of a sample. For a sample containing n values, the equation for the mean of a sample is written as

$$\bar{X} = \frac{\text{sum of the values}}{\text{number of values}}$$

Using the series $X_1, X_2, \ldots, X_n$ to represent the set of n values and n to represent the number of values in the sample, the equation becomes:

$$\bar{X} = \frac{X_1 + X_2 + \cdots + X_n}{n}$$

By using summation notation (discussed fully in Appendix B), you replace the numerator $X_1 + X_2 + \cdots + X_n$ by the term $\sum_{i=1}^{n} X_i$, which means sum all the X_i values from the first X value, X_1, to the last X value, X_n, to form Equation (3.1), a formal definition of the sample mean.

Sample Mean

The **sample mean** is the sum of the values divided by the number of values.

$$\bar{X} = \frac{\sum_{i=1}^{n} X_i}{n} \tag{3.1}$$

where

$\bar{X}$ = sample mean

n = number of values or sample size

X_i = ith value of the variable X

$\sum_{i=1}^{n} X_i$ = summation of all X_i values in the sample

Because all the values play an equal role, a mean is greatly affected by any value that is greatly different from the others in the data set. When you have such extreme values, you should avoid using the mean as a measure of central tendency.

The mean can suggest a typical or central value for a data set. For example, if you knew the typical time it takes you to get ready in the morning, you might be able to better plan your morning and minimize any excessive lateness (or earliness) going to your destination. Suppose you define the time to get ready as the time (rounded to the nearest minute) from when you get out of bed to when you leave your home. You collect the times shown below for 10 consecutive workdays (stored in the data file Times):

Day:	1	2	3	4	5	6	7	8	9	10
Time (minutes):	39	29	43	52	39	44	40	31	44	35

The mean time is 39.6 minutes, computed as follows:

$$\bar{X} = \frac{\text{sum of the values}}{\text{number of values}}$$

$$\bar{X} = \frac{\sum_{i=1}^{n} X_i}{n}$$

$$\bar{X} = \frac{39 + 29 + 43 + 52 + 39 + 44 + 40 + 31 + 44 + 35}{10}$$

$$= \frac{396}{10} = 39.6$$

Even though no one day in the sample actually had the value 39.6 minutes, allotting about 40 minutes to get ready would be a good rule for planning your mornings. The mean is a good measure of central tendency in this case because the data set does not contain any exceptionally small or large values.

Consider a case in which the value on Day 4 is 102 minutes instead of 52 minutes. This extreme value causes the mean to rise to 44.6 minutes, as follows:

$$\bar{X} = \frac{\text{sum of the values}}{\text{number of values}}$$

$$\bar{X} = \frac{\sum_{i=1}^{n} X_i}{n}$$

$$\bar{X} = \frac{446}{10} = 44.6$$

The one extreme value has increased the mean by more than 10%, from 39.6 to 44.6 minutes. In contrast to the original mean that was in the "middle" (i.e., greater than 5 of the getting-ready times and less than the 5 other times), the new mean is greater than 9 of the 10 getting-ready times. Because of the extreme value, now the mean is not a good measure of central tendency.

EXAMPLE 3.1   THE MEAN CALORIES FOR COFFEE DRINKS

The data in the file **CoffeeDrink** represent the calories of 16-ounce iced coffee drinks at Dunkin' Donuts and Starbucks:

Product	Calories
Dunkin' Donuts Iced Mocha Swirl latte (whole milk)	240
Starbucks Coffee Frappuccino blended coffee	260
Dunkin' Donuts Coffee Coolatta (cream)	350
Starbucks Iced Coffee Mocha Expresso (whole milk and whipped cream)	350
Starbucks Mocha Frappuccino blended coffee (whipped cream)	420
Starbucks Chocolate Brownie Frappuccino blended coffee (whipped cream)	510
Starbucks Chocolate Frappuccino Blended Crème (whipped cream)	530

Source: *Extracted from "Coffee as Candy at Dunkin' Donuts and Starbucks,"* Consumer Reports, *June 2004, p. 9.*

Compute the mean number of calories for the iced coffee drinks.

SOLUTION The mean number of calories is 380, calculated as follows:

$$\bar{X} = \frac{\text{sum of the values}}{\text{number of values}}$$

$$\bar{X} = \frac{\sum_{i=1}^{n} X_i}{n}$$

$$= \frac{2660}{7} = 380$$

The Median

The **median** is the middle value in a set of data that has been ranked from smallest to largest. Half the values are smaller than or equal to the median, and half the values are larger than or equal to the median. The median is not affected by extreme values, so you can use the median when extreme values are present.

To calculate the median for a set of data, you first rank the values from smallest to largest and then use Equation (3.2) to compute the rank of the value that is the median.

Median

$$\text{Median} = \frac{n+1}{2} \text{ ranked value} \tag{3.2}$$

You compute the median value by following one of two rules:

- **Rule 1** If there are an *odd* number of values in the data set, the median is the middle-ranked value.
- **Rule 2** If there are an *even* number of values in the data set, then the median is the *average* of the two middle-ranked values.

To compute the median for the sample of 10 times to get ready in the morning, you rank the daily times as follows:

Ranked values:

29   31   35   39   39   40   43   44   44   52

Ranks:

1   2   3   4   5   6   7   8   9   10

↑

Median = 39.5

Because the result of dividing $n + 1$ by 2 is $(10 + 1)/2 = 5.5$ for this sample of 10, you must use Rule 2 and average the fifth and sixth ranked values, 39 and 40. Therefore, the median is 39.5. The median of 39.5 means that for half the days, the time to get ready is less than or equal to 39.5 minutes, and for half the days, the time to get ready is greater than or equal to 39.5 minutes. In this case, the median time to get ready of 39.5 minutes is very close to the mean time to get ready of 39.6 minutes.

EXAMPLE 3.2   COMPUTING THE MEDIAN FROM AN ODD-SIZED SAMPLE

The data in the file **CoffeeDrink** (see Example 3.1 on page 92) represent the calories of 16-ounce iced coffee drinks at Dunkin' Donuts and Starbucks. Compute the median number of calories for the iced coffee drinks at Dunkin' Donuts and Starbucks.

SOLUTION Because the result of dividing $n + 1$ by 2 is $(7 + 1)/2 = 4$ for this sample of seven, using Rule 1, the median is the fourth ranked value. The number of calories of 16-ounce iced coffee drinks at Dunkin' Donuts and Starbucks are ranked from the smallest to the largest:

Ranked values:

240   260   350   350   420   510   530

Ranks:

1   2   3   4   5   6   7

↑

Median = 350

The median number of calories is 350. Half the drinks had equal to or less than 350 calories, and half the drinks had equal to or more than 350 calories.

The Mode

The **mode** is the value in a set of data that appears most frequently. Like the median and unlike the mean, extreme values do not affect the mode. Often, there is no mode or there are several modes in a set of data. For example, consider the time-to-get-ready data shown below:

29   31   35   39   39   40   43   44   44   52

There are two modes, 39 minutes and 44 minutes, because each of these values occurs twice.

EXAMPLE 3.3   DETERMINING THE MODE

A systems manager in charge of a company's network keeps track of the number of server failures that occur in a day. Determine the mode for the following data, which represents the number of server failures in a day for the past two weeks:

1   3   0   3   26   2   7   4   0   2   3   3   6   3

SOLUTION The ordered array for these data is

0   0   1   2   2   3   3   3   3   3   4   6   7   26

Because 3 appears five times, more times than any other value, the mode is 3. Thus, the systems manager can say that the most common occurrence is having three server failures in a day. For this data set, the median is also equal to 3, and the mean is equal to 4.5. The extreme value 26 is an outlier. For these data, the median and the mode better measure central tendency than the mean.

A set of data has no mode if none of the values is "most typical." Example 3.4 presents a data set with no mode.

EXAMPLE 3.4   DATA WITH NO MODE

The bounced check fees ($) for a sample of 10 banks was

$$26 \quad 28 \quad 20 \quad 21 \quad 22 \quad 25 \quad 18 \quad 23 \quad 15 \quad 30$$

Compute the mode.

SOLUTION These data have no mode. None of the values is most typical because each value appears once.

The Geometric Mean

The **geometric mean** measures the rate of change of a variable over time. Equation (3.3) defines the geometric mean.

> **Geometric Mean**
>
> The geometric mean is the nth root of the product of n values.
>
> $$\bar{X}_G = (X_1 \times X_2 \times \cdots \times X_n)^{1/n} \qquad \textbf{(3.3)}$$

The **geometric mean rate of return** measures the average percentage return of an investment over time. Equation (3.4) defines the geometric mean rate of return.

> **Geometric Mean Rate of Return**
>
> $$\bar{R}_G = [(1+R_1) \times (1+R_2) \times \cdots \times (1+R_n)]^{1/n} - 1 \qquad \textbf{(3.4)}$$
>
> where R_i is the rate of return in time period i

To illustrate these measures, consider an investment of $100,000 that declined to a value of $50,000 at the end of Year 1 and then rebounded back to its original $100,000 value at the end of Year 2. The rate of return for this investment for the two-year period is 0 because the starting and ending value of the investment is unchanged. However, the arithmetic mean of the yearly rates of return of this investment is

$$\bar{X} = \frac{(-0.50) + (1.00)}{2} = 0.25 \text{ or } 25\%$$

because the rate of return for Year 1 is

$$R_1 = \left(\frac{50,000 - 100,000}{100,000} \right) = -0.50 \text{ or } -50\%$$

and the rate of return for Year 2 is

$$R_2 = \left(\frac{100,000 - 50,000}{50,000}\right) = 1.00 \text{ or } 100\%$$

Using Equation (3.4), the geometric mean rate of return for the two years is

$$\begin{aligned}
\bar{R}_G &= [(1+R_1) \times (1+R_2)]^{1/n} - 1 \\
&= [(1+(-0.50)) \times (1+(1.0))]^{1/2} - 1 \\
&= [(0.50) \times (2.0)]^{1/2} - 1 \\
&= [1.0]^{1/2} - 1 \\
&= 1 - 1 = 0
\end{aligned}$$

Thus, the geometric mean rate of return more accurately reflects the (zero) change in the value of the investment for the two-year period than does the arithmetic mean.

EXAMPLE 3.5 COMPUTING THE GEOMETRIC MEAN RATE OF RETURN

The percentage change in the Russell 2000 Index of the stock prices of 2,000 small companies was +4.55% in 2005 and +17.00% in 2006. Compute the geometric rate of return.

SOLUTION Using Equation (3.4), the geometric mean rate of return in the Russell 2000 Index for the two years is

$$\begin{aligned}
\bar{R}_G &= [(1+R_1) \times (1+R_2)]^{1/n} - 1 \\
&= [(1+(0.0455)) \times (1+(0.1700))]^{1/2} - 1 \\
&= [(1.0455) \times (1.1700)]^{1/2} - 1 \\
&= [1.223235]^{1/2} - 1 \\
&= 1.106 - 1 = 0.106
\end{aligned}$$

The geometric mean rate of return in the Russell 2000 Index for the two years is 10.6%.

3.2 VARIATION AND SHAPE

In addition to central tendency, every data set can be characterized by its variation and shape. Variation measures the **spread**, or **dispersion**, of values in a data set. One simple measure of variation is the range, the difference between the largest and smallest values. More commonly used in statistics are the standard deviation and variance, two measures explained later in this section. The shape of a data set represents a pattern of all the values, from the lowest to highest value. As you will learn later in this section, many data sets have a pattern that looks approximately like a bell, with a peak of values somewhere in the middle.

The Range

The **range** is the simplest numerical descriptive measure of variation in a set of data.

> **Range**
> The range is equal to the largest value minus the smallest value.
>
> $$\text{Range} = X_{\text{largest}} - X_{\text{smallest}} \qquad (3.5)$$

To determine the range of the times to get ready in the morning, you rank the data from smallest to largest:

$$29 \quad 31 \quad 35 \quad 39 \quad 39 \quad 40 \quad 43 \quad 44 \quad 44 \quad 52$$

Using Equation (3.5), the range is 52 − 29 = 23 minutes. The range of 23 minutes indicates that the largest difference between any two days in the time to get ready in the morning is 23 minutes.

EXAMPLE 3.6   COMPUTING THE RANGE IN THE CALORIES IN ICED COFFEE DRINKS

The data in the file **CoffeeDrink** (see Example 3.1 on page 92) represent the calories of 16-ounce iced coffee drinks at Dunkin' Donuts and Starbucks. Compute the range in the number of calories for the iced coffee drinks at Dunkin' Donuts and Starbucks.

SOLUTION Ranked from smallest to largest, the number of calories for the seven iced coffee drinks are

$$240 \quad 260 \quad 350 \quad 350 \quad 420 \quad 510 \quad 530$$

Therefore, using Equation (3.5), the range = 530 − 240 = 290. The largest difference in the number of calories between any two iced coffee drinks is 290.

The range measures the *total spread* in the set of data. Although the range is a simple measure of the total variation in the data, it does not take into account *how* the data are distributed between the smallest and largest values. In other words, the range does not indicate whether the values are evenly distributed throughout the data set, clustered near the middle, or clustered near one or both extremes. Thus, using the range as a measure of variation when at least one value is an extreme value is misleading.

The Variance and the Standard Deviation

Although the range is a simple measure of variation, it does not take into consideration how the values distribute or cluster between the extremes. Two commonly used measures of variation that take into account how all the values in the data are distributed are the **variance** and the **standard deviation**. These statistics measure the "average" scatter around the mean—how larger values fluctuate above it and how smaller values distribute below it.

A simple measure of variation around the mean might take the difference between each value and the mean and then sum these differences. However, if you did that, you would find that because the mean is the balance point in a set of data, for *every* set of data, these differences would sum to zero. One measure of variation that differs from data set to data set *squares* the difference between each value and the mean and then sums these squared differences. In statistics, this quantity is called a **sum of squares** (or **SS**). This sum is then divided by the number of values minus 1 (for sample data) to get the sample variance (S^2). The square root of the sample variance is the sample standard deviation (S).

Because the sum of squares is a sum of squared differences that by the rules of arithmetic will always be nonnegative, *neither the variance nor the standard deviation can ever be negative*. For virtually all sets of data, the variance and standard deviation will be a positive value, although both of these statistics will be zero if there is no variation at all in a set of data and each value in the sample is the same.

For a sample containing n values, $X_1, X_2, X_3, \ldots, X_n$, the sample variance (given by the symbol S^2) is

$$S^2 = \frac{(X_1 - \bar{X})^2 + (X_2 - \bar{X})^2 + \cdots + (X_n - \bar{X})^2}{n-1}$$

Equation (3.6) expresses the sample variance using summation notation, and Equation (3.7) expresses the sample standard deviation.

Sample Variance

The **sample variance** is the sum of the squared differences around the mean divided by the sample size minus one.

$$S^2 = \frac{\displaystyle\sum_{i=1}^{n} (X_i - \bar{X})^2}{n-1} \tag{3.6}$$

where

$$\bar{X} = \text{mean}$$

$$n = \text{sample size}$$

$$X_i = i\text{th value of the variable } X$$

$$\sum_{i=1}^{n} (X_i - \bar{X})^2 = \text{summation of all the squared differences between the } X_i \text{ values and } \bar{X}$$

Sample Standard Deviation

The **sample standard deviation** is the square root of the sum of the squared differences around the mean divided by the sample size minus one.

$$S = \sqrt{S^2} = \sqrt{\frac{\displaystyle\sum_{i=1}^{n} (X_i - \bar{X})^2}{n-1}} \tag{3.7}$$

If the denominator were n instead of $n-1$, Equation (3.6) [and the inner term in Equation (3.7)] would calculate the average of the squared differences around the mean. However, $n-1$ is used because of certain desirable mathematical properties possessed by the statistic S^2 that make it appropriate for statistical inference (which is discussed in Chapter 7). As the sample size increases, the difference between dividing by n and by $n-1$ becomes smaller and smaller.

You will most likely use the sample standard deviation as your measure of variation [defined in Equation (3.7)]. Unlike the sample variance, which is a squared quantity, the standard deviation is always a number that is in the same units as the original sample data. The standard deviation helps you to know how a set of data clusters or distributes around its mean. For almost all sets of data, the majority of the observed values lie within an interval of plus and minus one standard deviation above and below the mean. Therefore, knowledge of the mean and the standard deviation usually helps define where at least the majority of the data values are clustering.

To hand-calculate the sample variance, S^2, and the sample standard deviation, S, do the following:

1. Compute the difference between each value and the mean.
2. Square each difference.
3. Add the squared differences.
4. Divide this total by $n - 1$ to get the sample variance.
5. Take the square root of the sample variance to get the sample standard deviation.

Table 3.1 shows the first four steps for calculating the variance and standard deviation for the getting-ready-times data with a mean ($\bar{X}$) equal to 39.6. (See page 92 for the calculation of the mean.) The second column of Table 3.1 shows step 1. The third column of Table 3.1 shows step 2. The sum of the squared differences (step 3) is shown at the bottom of Table 3.1. This total is then divided by $10 - 1 = 9$ to compute the variance (step 4).

TABLE 3.1

Computing the Variance of the Getting-Ready Times

$\bar{X} = 39.6$		
Time (X)	Step 1: $(X_i - \bar{X})$	Step 2: $(X_i - \bar{X})^2$
39	−0.60	0.36
29	−10.60	112.36
43	3.40	11.56
52	12.40	153.76
39	−0.60	0.36
44	4.40	19.36
40	0.40	0.16
31	−8.60	73.96
44	4.40	19.36
35	−4.60	21.16
	Step 3: Sum:	Step 4: Divide by ($n - 1$):
	412.40	45.82

You can also calculate the variance by substituting values for the terms in Equation (3.6):

$$S^2 = \frac{\sum_{i=1}^{n}(X_i - \bar{X})^2}{n-1}$$

$$= \frac{(39 - 39.6)^2 + (29 - 39.6)^2 + \cdots + (35 - 39.6)^2}{10 - 1}$$

$$= \frac{412.4}{9}$$

$$= 45.82$$

Because the variance is in squared units (in squared minutes, for these data), to compute the standard deviation, you take the square root of the variance. Using Equation (3.7) on page 98, the sample standard deviation, S, is

$$S = \sqrt{S^2} = \sqrt{\frac{\sum_{i=1}^{n}(X_i - \bar{X})^2}{n-1}} = \sqrt{45.82} = 6.77$$

This indicates that the getting-ready times in this sample are clustering within 6.77 minutes around the mean of 39.6 minutes (i.e., clustering between $\bar{X} - 1S = 32.83$ and $\bar{X} + 1S = 46.37$). In fact, 7 out of 10 getting-ready times lie within this interval.

Using the second column of Table 3.1, you can also calculate the sum of the differences between each value and the mean to be zero. For any set of data, this sum will always be zero:

$$\sum_{i=1}^{n}(X_i - \bar{X}) = 0 \text{ for all sets of data}$$

This property is one of the reasons that the mean is used as the most common measure of central tendency.

EXAMPLE 3.7

COMPUTING THE VARIANCE AND STANDARD DEVIATION OF THE NUMBER OF CALORIES IN ICED COFFEE DRINKS

The data in the file CoffeeDrink (see Example 3.1 on page 92) represent the calories of 16-ounce iced coffee drinks at Dunkin' Donuts and Starbucks. Compute the variance and standard deviation of the calories in 16-ounce iced coffee drinks.

SOLUTION Table 3.2 illustrates the computation of the variance and standard deviation for the calories in 16-ounce iced coffee drinks.

TABLE 3.2

Computing the Variance of the Calories in 16-ounce Iced Coffee Drinks

$\bar{X} = 380$

Calories	Step 1: $(X_i - \bar{X})$	Step 2: $(X_i - \bar{X})^2$
240	−140	19,600
260	−120	14,400
350	−30	900
350	−30	900
420	40	1600
510	130	16,900
530	150	22,500
	Step 3: Sum:	Step 4: Divide by $(n-1)$:
	76,800	12,800

Using Equation (3.6) on page 98:

$$S^2 = \frac{\sum_{i=1}^{n}(X_i - \bar{X})^2}{n-1}$$

$$= \frac{(240-380)^2 + (260-380)^2 + \cdots + (530-380)^2}{7-1}$$

$$= \frac{76,800}{6}$$

$$= 12,800$$

Using Equation (3.7) on page 98, the sample standard deviation, S, is

$$S = \sqrt{S^2} = \sqrt{\frac{\sum_{i=1}^{n}(X_i - \bar{X})^2}{n-1}} = \sqrt{12,800} = 113.1371$$

The standard deviation of 113.1371 indicates that the calories in the iced coffee drinks are clustering within 113.1371 around the mean of 380 (i.e., clustering between $\bar{X} - 1S = 266.8629$ and $\bar{X} + 1S = 493.1371$). In fact, 42.9% (3 out of 7) of the calories lie within this interval.

The following summarizes the characteristics of the range, variance, and standard deviation:

- The more the data are spread out or dispersed, the larger the range, variance, and standard deviation.
- The more the data are concentrated or homogeneous, the smaller the range, variance, and standard deviation.
- If the values are all the same (so that there is no variation in the data), the range, variance, and standard deviation will all equal zero.
- None of the measures of variation (the range, standard deviation, and variance) can *ever* be negative.

The Coefficient of Variation

Unlike the previous measures of variation presented, the **coefficient of variation** is a *relative measure* of variation that is always expressed as a percentage rather than in terms of the units of the particular data. The coefficient of variation, denoted by the symbol CV, measures the scatter in the data relative to the mean.

Coefficient of Variation

The coefficient of variation is equal to the standard deviation divided by the mean, multiplied by 100%.

$$CV = \left(\frac{S}{\bar{X}}\right)100\% \tag{3.8}$$

where

$$S = \text{sample standard deviation}$$
$$\bar{X} = \text{sample mean}$$

For the sample of 10 getting-ready times, because $\bar{X} = 39.6$ and $S = 6.77$, the coefficient of variation is

$$CV = \left(\frac{S}{\bar{X}}\right)100\% = \left(\frac{6.77}{39.6}\right)100\% = 17.10\%$$

For the getting-ready times, the standard deviation is 17.1% of the size of the mean.

The coefficient of variation is very useful when comparing two or more sets of data that are measured in different units, as Example 3.8 illustrates.

EXAMPLE 3.8   COMPARING TWO COEFFICIENTS OF VARIATION WHEN TWO VARIABLES HAVE DIFFERENT UNITS OF MEASUREMENT

The operations manager of a package delivery service is deciding whether to purchase a new fleet of trucks. When packages are stored in the trucks in preparation for delivery, you need to consider two major constraints—the weight (in pounds) and the volume (in cubic feet) for each item.

The operations manager samples 200 packages and finds that the mean weight is 26.0 pounds, with a standard deviation of 3.9 pounds, and the mean volume is 8.8 cubic feet, with a standard deviation of 2.2 cubic feet. How can the operations manager compare the variation of the weight and the volume?

SOLUTION Because the measurement units differ for the weight and volume constraints, the operations manager should compare the relative variability in the two types of measurements. For weight, the coefficient of variation is

$$CV_W = \left(\frac{3.9}{26.0}\right)100\% = 15\%$$

For volume, the coefficient of variation is

$$CV_V = \left(\frac{2.2}{8.8}\right)100\% = 25\%$$

Thus, relative to the mean, the package volume is much more variable than the package weight.

Z Scores

An **extreme value** or **outlier** is a value located far away from the mean. Z scores are useful in identifying outliers. The larger the Z score, the greater the distance from the value to the mean. The **Z score** is the difference between the value and the mean, divided by the standard deviation.

Z Scores

$$Z = \frac{X - \bar{X}}{S} \tag{3.9}$$

For the time-to-get-ready data, the mean is 39.6 minutes, and the standard deviation is 6.77 minutes. The time to get ready on the first day is 39.0 minutes. You compute the Z score for Day 1 by using Equation (3.9):

$$Z = \frac{X - \bar{X}}{S}$$

$$= \frac{39.0 - 39.6}{6.77}$$

$$= -0.09$$

Table 3.3 shows the Z scores for all 10 days. The largest Z score is 1.83 for Day 4, on which the time to get ready was 52 minutes. The lowest Z score was -1.57 for Day 2, on which the time to get ready was 29 minutes. As a general rule, a Z score is considered an outlier if it is less than -3.0 or greater than $+3.0$. None of the times met that criterion to be considered outliers.

TABLE 3.3

Z Scores for the 10 Getting-Ready Times

	Time (X)	Z Score
	39	-0.09
	29	-1.57
	43	0.50
	52	1.83
	39	-0.09
	44	0.65
	40	0.06
	31	-1.27
	44	0.65
	35	-0.68
Mean	39.6	
Standard deviation	6.77	

EXAMPLE 3.9

COMPUTING THE Z SCORES OF THE NUMBER OF CALORIES IN ICED COFFEE DRINKS

The data in the file `CoffeeDrink` (see Example 3.1 on page 92) represent the calories of 16-ounce iced coffee drinks at Dunkin' Donuts and Starbucks. Compute the Z scores of the calories of 16-ounce iced coffee drinks.

SOLUTION Table 3.4 illustrates the Z scores of the calories of 16-ounce iced coffee drinks. The largest Z score is 1.33, for an iced coffee drink with 530 calories. The lowest Z score is -1.24, for an iced coffee drink with 240 calories. There are no apparent outliers in these data because none of the Z scores are less than -3 or greater than $+3$.

TABLE 3.4

Z Scores of the Number of Calories in Iced Coffee Drinks

	Calories	Z Scores
	240	-1.24
	260	-1.06
	350	-0.27
	350	-0.27
	420	0.35
	510	1.15
	530	1.33
Mean	380	
Standard Deviation	113.1371	

Shape

Shape is the pattern of the distribution of data values throughout the entire range of all the values. A distribution is either symmetrical or skewed. In a **symmetrical** distribution, the values below the mean are distributed exactly as the values above the mean. In this case, the low and high values balance each other out. In a **skewed** distribution, the values are not symmetrical around the mean. This skewness results in an imbalance of low values or high values.

Shape influences the relationship of the mean to the median in the following ways:

- Mean < median: negative, or left-skewed
- Mean = median: symmetric, or zero skewness
- Mean > median: positive, or right-skewed

Figure 3.1 depicts three data sets, each with a different shape.

FIGURE 3.1

A comparison of three data sets differing in shape

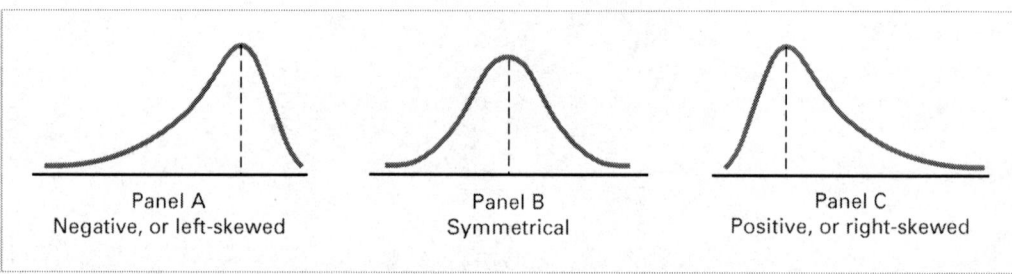

Panel A
Negative, or left-skewed

Panel B
Symmetrical

Panel C
Positive, or right-skewed

The data in Panel A are negative, or **left-skewed**. In this panel, most of the values are in the upper portion of the distribution. A long tail and distortion to the left is caused by some extremely small values. These extremely small values pull the mean downward so that the mean is less than the median.

The data in Panel B are symmetrical. Each half of the curve is a mirror image of the other half of the curve. The low and high values on the scale balance, and the mean equals the median.

The data in Panel C are positive, or **right-skewed**. In this panel, most of the values are in the lower portion of the distribution. A long tail on the right is caused by some extremely large values. These extremely large values pull the mean upward so that the mean is greater than the median.

Microsoft Excel ToolPak Descriptive Statistics Results

The Microsoft Excel ToolPak Descriptive Statistics procedure (see Appendix E3.1) computes the mean, median, mode, standard deviation, variance, range, minimum, maximum, and count (sample size) and displays these statistics on a new worksheet. In addition, the procedure calculates and displays the standard error, the kurtosis, and skewness, three statistics not discussed previously in this section. The standard error, discussed in Chapter 7, is the standard deviation divided by the square root of the sample size. Skewness measures the lack of symmetry in the data. A skewness value of zero indicates a symmetrical distribution. A positive value indicates right-skewness whereas a negative value indicates left-skewness. Kurtosis measures the relative concentration of values in the center of the distribution, as compared with the tails. A kurtosis value of zero indicates a bell-shaped distribution. A negative value indicates a distribution that is flatter than a bell-shaped distribution. A positive value indicates a distribution with a sharper peak than a bell-shaped distribution.

Figure 3.2 shows the results of using the Descriptive Statistics procedure to calculate separate descriptive summary measures for growth and value mutual funds. (The procedure was used twice, and the results that appeared on two separate worksheets were consolidated on one sheet.)

FIGURE 3.2

ToolPak descriptive
statistics for growth and
value funds 2006 return

*See Section E3.1 to create
this.*

	A	B	C
1	*Descriptive Statistics for Return 2006*		
2		Growth	Value
3	Mean	8.7103	16.8829
4	Standard Error	0.2515	0.1968
5	Median	8.6000	16.8500
6	Mode	7.5000	16.6000
7	Standard Deviation	5.4178	3.9553
8	Sample Variance	29.3524	15.6446
9	Kurtosis	0.7390	1.4329
10	Skewness	-0.0118	0.0371
11	Range	37.5	32.2
12	Minimum	-9.0	2.8
13	Maximum	28.5	35.0
14	Sum	4041.6	6820.7
15	Count	464	404

In examining the results, there are large differences in the 2006 return for the growth and value funds. The value funds had a mean 2006 return of 16.8829 and a median return of 16.85. This compares to a mean of 8.7103 and a median of 8.6 for the growth funds. This means that half of the value funds had returns of 16.85 or better, and half the growth funds had returns of only 8.6 or better. The growth funds had a larger standard deviation than the value funds. Neither the growth nor the value funds showed any skewness because their measures of skewness were very close to 0. Both the growth and value funds exhibited positive kurtosis, meaning that the distribution of the returns had a sharper peak than a bell-shaped distribution.

Minitab Descriptive Statistics Results

As shown in Figure 3.3, for descriptive statistics, Minitab computes the sample size (labeled as N), the mean, the standard deviation (labeled as StDev), the coefficient of variation (labeled as CoefVar), first and third quartiles (see Section 3.5), median, maximum, range, and the interquartile range (labeled as IQR—see Section 3.5). In addition, Minitab computes skewness and kurtosis statistics. A skewness value of zero indicates a symmetrical distribution. A positive value indicates right-skewness whereas a negative value indicates left-skewness. Kurtosis measures the relative concentration of values in the center of the distribution, as compared with the tails. A kurtosis value of zero indicates a bell-shaped distribution. A negative value indicates a distribution that is flatter than a bell-shaped distribution. A positive value indicates a distribution with a sharper peak than a bell-shaped distribution.

FIGURE 3.3

Minitab descriptive
statistics of the 2006
returns for growth and
value funds

*See Section M3.1 to create
this.*

Descriptive Statistics: Return 2006

Variable	Objective	N	Mean	StDev	CoefVar	Minimum	Q1	Median
Return 2006	Growth	464	8.710	5.418	62.20	-9.000	5.325	8.600
	Value	404	16.883	3.955	23.43	2.800	14.500	16.850

Variable	Objective	Q3	Maximum	Range	IQR	Skewness	Kurtosis
Return 2006	Growth	12.400	28.500	37.500	7.075	-0.01	0.74
	Value	19.500	35.000	32.200	5.000	0.04	1.43

In examining the results, there are large differences in the 2006 return for the growth and value funds. The value funds had a mean 2006 return of 16.883 and a median return of 16.85. This compares to a mean of 8.7103 and a median of 8.60 for the growth funds. This means that half of the value funds had returns of 16.85 or better, and half the growth funds had returns of only 8.60 or better. The growth funds had a larger standard deviation than the value funds. Neither the growth nor the value funds showed any skewness because their skewness statistics were very close to 0. Both the growth and value funds exhibited positive kurtosis, meaning that the distribution of the returns had a sharper peak than a bell-shaped distribution.

VISUAL EXPLORATIONS: Exploring Descriptive Statistics

You can use the Visual Explorations Descriptive Statistics procedure to see the effect of changing data values on measures of central tendency, variation, and shape. Open the visual explorations.xla add-in workbook (see Appendix D) and select **VisualExplorations → Descriptive Statistics** (Excel 97–2003) or **Add-ins → VisualExplorations → Descriptive Statistics** (Excel 2007) from the Microsoft Excel menu bar. Read the instructions in the pop-up box (see illustration below) and click **OK** to examine a dot-scale diagram for the sample of 10 getting-ready times used throughout this chapter. (Review Section E1.8 on page 20 for more information on using add-ins, if necessary.)

Experiment by entering an extreme value such as 10 minutes into one of the tinted cells of column A. Which measures are affected by this change? Which ones are not? You can flip between the "before" and "after" diagrams by repeatedly pressing **Ctrl + Z** (undo) followed by **Ctrl + Y** (redo) to help see the changes the extreme value caused in the diagram.

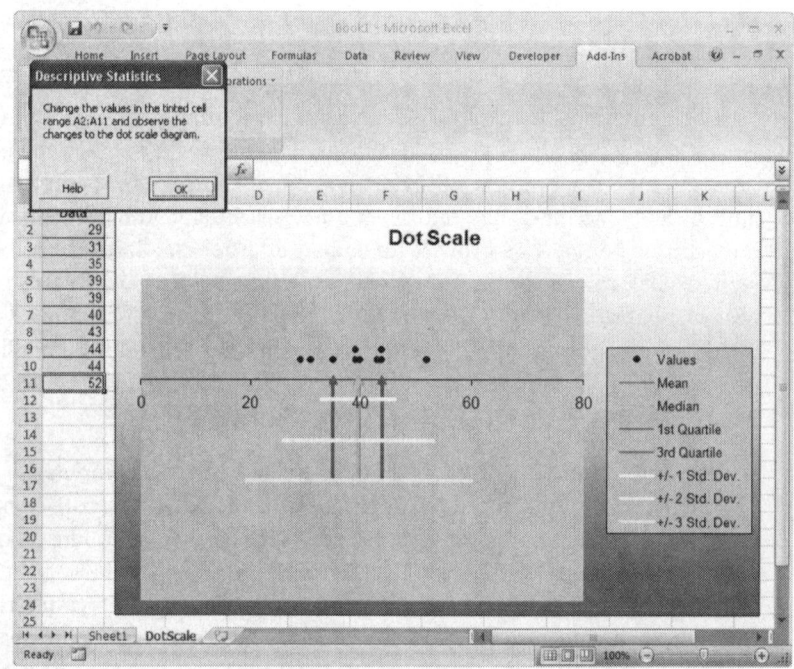

PROBLEMS FOR SECTIONS 3.1 AND 3.2

Learning the Basics

3.1 The following is a set of data from a sample of $n = 5$:

$$7 \quad 4 \quad 9 \quad 8 \quad 2$$

a. Compute the mean, median, and mode.
b. Compute the range, variance, standard deviation, and coefficient of variation.
c. Compute the Z scores. Are there any outliers?
d. Describe the shape of the data set.

3.2 The following is a set of data from a sample of $n = 6$:

$$7 \quad 4 \quad 9 \quad 7 \quad 3 \quad 12$$

a. Compute the mean, median, and mode.
b. Compute the range, variance, standard deviation, and coefficient of variation.
c. Compute the Z scores. Are there any outliers?
d. Describe the shape of the data set.

3.3 The following set of data is from a sample of $n = 7$:

$$12 \quad 7 \quad 4 \quad 9 \quad 0 \quad 7 \quad 3$$

a. Compute the mean, median, and mode.
b. Compute the range, variance, standard deviation, and coefficient of variation.
c. Compute the Z scores. Are there any outliers?
d. Describe the shape of the data set.

3.4 The following is a set of data from a sample of $n = 5$:

$$7 \quad -5 \quad -8 \quad 7 \quad 9$$

a. Compute the mean, median, and mode.
b. Compute the range, variance, standard deviation, and coefficient of variation.
c. Compute the Z scores. Are there any outliers?
d. Describe the shape of the data set.

3.5 Suppose the rate of return for a particular stock during the past two years was 10% and 30%. Compute the geometric mean rate of return. (*Note:* A rate of return of 10% is recorded as 0.10, and a rate of return of 30% is recorded as 0.30.)

Applying the Concepts

3.6 The operations manager of a plant that manufactures tires wants to compare the actual inner diameters of two grades of tires, each of which is expected to be 575 millimeters. A sample of five tires of each grade was selected, and the results representing the inner diameters of the tires, ranked from smallest to largest, are as follows:

Grade X	Grade Y
568 570 575 578 584	573 574 575 577 578

a. For each of the two grades of tires, compute the mean, median, and standard deviation.
b. Which grade of tire is providing better quality? Explain.
c. What would be the effect on your answers in (a) and (b) if the last value for grade Y were 588 instead of 578? Explain.

3.7 According to the U.S. Census Bureau, in February 2007 the median sales price of new houses was $250,000 and the mean sales price was $331,000 (U.S. Census Bureau News, **www.census.gov**, March 26, 2007).
a. Interpret the median sales price.
b. Interpret the mean sales price.
c. Discuss the shape of the price of new houses.

SELF Test **3.8** The data in the file Movieprices contain the price for two tickets with online service charges, large popcorn, and two medium soft drinks at a sample of six theater chains:

$36.15 $31.00 $35.05 $40.25 $33.75 $43.00

Source: *Extracted from K. Kelly, "The Multiplex Under Siege," The Wall Street Journal, December 24–25, 2005, pp. P1, P5.*

a. Compute the mean and median.
b. Compute the variance, standard deviation, range, and coefficient of variation.
c. Are the data skewed? If so, how?
d. Based on the results of (a) through (c), what conclusions can you reach concerning the cost of going to the movies?

3.9 The data in the file Sedans represent the overall miles per gallon (MPG) of 2007 family sedans (4 cylinder).

Model	MPG	Model	MPG
Volkswagen Passat	24	Mazda	23
Nissan Altima	25	Ford Fusion	23
Toyota Camry Hybrid	34	Mercury Milan	23
Honda Accord	24	Toyota Prius	44
Kia Optima	23	Chevrolet Malibu	24
Toyota Camry LE	24	Mitsubishi Galant	23
Subaru Legacy	18	Pontiac G6	22
Hyundai Sonata	23	Chrysler Sebring	23

Source: *Extracted from "Vehicle Ratings," Consumer Reports, April 2007, pp. 36–37.*

a. Compute the mean, median, and mode.
b. Compute the variance, standard deviation, range, coefficient of variation, and Z scores.
c. Are the data skewed? If so, how?
d. Compare the results of (a) through (c) to those of Problem 3.10 (a) through (c) that refer to the miles per gallon of small SUVs.

3.10 The data in the file SUV represent the overall miles per gallon (MPG) of 2007 small SUVs.

Model	MPG	Model	MPG
Toyota RAV4 6-cyl	22	Mercury Mariner	18
Hyundai Santa Fe	18	Luxury	
Toyota RAV4 4-cyl	23	Mazda Tribute	18
Subaru Forester	20	Nissan Xterra	17
Sports 2.5 XT		Honda Element	21
Honda CR-V	21	Suzuki Grand Vitara	18
Subaru Forester	22	Chevrolet Equinox	18
Sports 2.5 X		Pontiac Torrent	18
Mitsubishi Outlander	19	Jeep Compass	22
Hyundai Tucson	18	Saturn Vue	19
Kia Sportage	18	Saturn Vue Hybrid	24
Ford Escape Hybrid	26	Kia Sorento	15
Mercury Mariner	26	Jeep Liberty	15
Hybrid		Toyota FJ Cruiser	17
Suzuki XL-7	17	Dodge Nitro	16
Ford Escape	18	Jeep Wrangler	15

Source: *Extracted from "Vehicle Ratings," Consumer Reports, April 2007, pp.42–43.*

a. Compute the mean, median, and mode.

b. Compute the variance, standard deviation, range, coefficient of variation, and Z scores.

c. Are the data skewed? If so, how?

d. Compare the results of (a) through (c) to those of Problem 3.9 (a) through (c) that refer to the miles per gallon of 4-cylinder family sedans.

3.11 The data in the file Chicken contain the total fat, in grams per serving, for a sample of 20 chicken sandwiches from fast-food chains. The data are as follows:

7 8 4 5 16 20 20 24 19 30 23 30 25 19 29 29 30 30 40 56

Source: *Extracted from "Fast Food: Adding Health to the Menu," Consumer Reports, September 2004, pp. 28–31.*

a. Compute the mean, median, and mode.

b. Compute the variance, standard deviation, range, coefficient of variation, and Z scores. Are there any outliers? Explain.

c. Are the data skewed? If so, how?

d. Based on the results of (a) through (c), what conclusions can you reach concerning the total fat of chicken sandwiches?

3.12 The data in the file Batterylife represent the battery life (in shots) for a sample of 12 three-pixel digital cameras:

300 180 85 170 380 460 260 35 380 120 110 240

Source: *Extracted from "Cameras: More Features in the Mix," Consumer Reports, July 2005, pp. 14–18.*

a. Compute the mean, median, and mode.

b. Compute the variance, standard deviation, range, coefficient of variation, and Z scores. Are there any outliers? Explain.

c. Are the data skewed? If so, how?

d. Based on the results of (a) through (c), what conclusions can you reach concerning the battery life (in shots) for three-pixel digital cameras?

3.13 Is there a difference in the variation of the yields of different types of investments between banks? The data in the file Bankyield represent the nationwide highest yields for money market accounts and five-year CDs as of March 12, 2007:

Money Market	Five-Year CD
5.35	5.95
5.31	5.89
5.30	5.83
5.30	5.83
5.25	5.79

Source: *Extracted from www.Bankrate.com, March 12, 2007.*

a. For money market accounts and five-year CDs, separately compute the variance, standard deviation, range, and coefficient of variation.

b. Based on the results of (a), do money market accounts or five-year CDs have more variation in the highest yields offered? Explain.

3.14 The data in the file Themeparks contain the starting admission price (in $) for one-day tickets to 10 theme parks in the United States:

58 63 41 42 29 50 62 43 40 40

Source: *Extracted from C. Jackson and E. Gamerman, "Rethinking the Thrill Factor," The Wall Street Journal, April 15–16, 2006, pp. P1, P4.*

a. Compute the mean, median, and mode.

b. Compute the range, variance, and standard deviation.

c. Based on the results of (a) and (b), what conclusions can you reach concerning the starting admission price for one-day tickets.

d. Suppose that the first value was 98 instead of 58. Repeat (a) through (c), using this value. Comment on the difference in the results.

3.15 A bank branch located in a commercial district of a city has developed an improved process for serving customers during the noon-to-1:00 p.m. lunch period. The waiting time, in minutes (defined as the time the customer enters the line to when he or she reaches the teller window), of a sample of 15 customers during this hour is recorded over a period of one week. The results are contained in the data file Bank1 and are listed below:

4.21 5.55 3.02 5.13 4.77 2.34 3.54 3.20 4.50
6.10 0.38 5.12 6.46 6.19 3.79

a. Compute the mean and median.

b. Compute the variance, standard deviation, range, coefficient of variation, and Z scores. Are there any outliers? Explain.

c. Are the data skewed? If so, how?

d. As a customer walks into the branch office during the lunch hour, she asks the branch manager how long she can expect to wait. The branch manager replies, "Almost certainly less than five minutes." On the basis of the results of (a) through (c), evaluate the accuracy of this statement.

3.16 Suppose that another branch, located in a residential area, is also concerned with the noon-to-1 p.m. lunch hour. The waiting time, in minutes (defined as the time the customer enters the line to when he or she reaches the teller window), of a sample of 15 customers during this hour is recorded over a period of one week. The results are contained in the data file Bank2 and are listed below:

9.66 5.90 8.02 5.79 8.73 3.82 8.01 8.35 10.49
6.68 5.64 4.08 6.17 9.91 5.47

a. Compute the mean and median.

b. Compute the variance, standard deviation, range, coefficient of variation and Z scores. Are there any outliers? Explain.

c. Are the data skewed? If so, how?

d. As a customer walks into the branch office during the lunch hour, he asks the branch manager how long he can expect to wait. The branch manager replies, "Almost certainly less than five minutes." On the basis of the results of (a) through (c), evaluate the accuracy of this statement.

3.17 General Electric (GE) is one of the world's largest companies; it develops, manufactures, and markets a wide range of products, including medical diagnostic imaging devices, jet engines, lighting products, and chemicals. Through its affiliate, NBC Universal, GE produces and delivers network television and motion pictures. In 2004, GE's stock price rose 20.6%, but in 2005, the price dropped 1.4%.
Source: *Extracted from* **www.finance.yahoo.com**, *April 17, 2006.*

a. Compute the geometric mean rate of increase for the two-year period 2004–2005. (*Hint:* Denote an increase of 20.6% as $R_1 = 0.206$.)

b. If you purchased $1,000 of GE stock at the start of 2004, what was its value at the end of 2005?

c. Compare the result of (b) to that of Problem 3.18(b).

d. In 2006, GE's stock price increased by 6.2%. Compute the geometric mean rate of increase for the three-year period 2004–2006.

3.18 TASER International, Inc., develops, manufactures, and sells nonlethal self-defense devices known as tasers. Marketing primarily to law enforcement, corrections institutions, and the military, TASER's popularity has enjoyed a roller-coaster ride. The stock price in 2004 increased 361.4%, but in 2005, it decreased 78.0%.
Source: *Extracted from* **finance.yahoo.com**, *April 17, 2006.*

a. Compute the geometric mean rate of increase for the two-year period 2004–2005. (*Hint:* Denote an increase of 361.4% as $R_1 = 3.614$.)

b. If you purchased $1,000 of TASER stock at the start of 2004, what was its value at the end of 2005?

c. Compare the result of (b) to that of Problem 3.17(b).

d. In 2006, TASER's stock price increased by 9.3%. Compute the geometric mean rate of increase for the three-year period 2004–2006.

3.19 In 2002, all the major stock market indexes decreased dramatically as the attacks on 9/11 drove stock prices spiraling downward. Stocks soon rebounded, but what type of mean return did investors experience over the five-year period from 2002 to 2006? The data in the following table (contained in the data file **Indices**) represent the total rate of return (in percentage) for the Dow Jones Industrial Average (DJIA), the Standard & Poor's 500 (S&P 500), and the technology-heavy NASDAQ Composite (Nasdaq).

Year	DJIA	S&P 500	Nasdaq
2006	16.3	13.6	9.5
2005	−0.6	2.9	1.4
2004	3.4	9.1	8.6
2003	30.0	26.4	50.0
2002	−16.8	−24.2	−31.5

Source: *Extracted from* **finance.yahoo.com**, *April 26, 2007.*

a. Calculate the geometric mean rate of return for the DJIA, S&P 500, and Nasdaq.

b. What conclusions can you reach concerning the geometric rates of return of the three market indexes?

c. Compare the results of (b) to those of Problem 3.20(b).

3.20 In 2002–2006, precious metals changed rapidly in value. The data in the following table (contained in the data file **Metals**) represent the total rate of return (in percentage) for platinum, gold, and silver:

Year	Platinum	Gold	Silver
2006	15.9	23.2	46.1
2005	12.3	17.8	29.5
2004	5.7	4.6	14.2
2003	36.0	19.9	27.8
2002	24.6	25.6	3.3

Source: *Extracted from* **kitco.com**, *April 26, 2007.*

a. Calculate the geometric mean rate of return for platinum, gold, and silver.

b. What conclusions can you reach concerning the geometric rates of return of the three precious metals?

c. Compare the results of (b) to those of Problem 3.19(b).

3.3 NUMERICAL DESCRIPTIVE MEASURES FOR A POPULATION

Sections 3.1 and 3.2 present various statistics that described the properties of central tendency and variation for a sample. If your data set represents numerical measurements for an entire population, you need to calculate and interpret parameters, summary measures for a population. In this section, you will learn about three descriptive population parameters: the population mean, population variance, and population standard deviation.

To help illustrate these parameters, first review Table 3.5, which contains the one-year return for the five largest bond funds (in terms of total assets) as of March 29, 2007. (The data are contained in the file **Largest bonds**.)

TABLE 3.5

One-Year Return for the
Population Consisting
of the Five Largest
Bond Funds

Bond Fund	One-Year Return
Pimco: Total Rtn; Inst	6.1
Vanguard Tot Bd; Inv	6.2
American Funds Bond; A	7.2
Franklin CA TF Inc; A	5.9
Vanguard GNMA; Inv	5.5

Source: *Extracted from* The Wall Street Journal, *March 29, 2007, p. C4.*

The Population Mean

The **population mean** is represented by the symbol μ, the Greek lowercase letter mu. Equation (3.10) defines the population mean.

Population Mean

The population mean is the sum of the values in the population divided by the population size N.

$$\mu = \frac{\sum\limits_{i=1}^{N} X_i}{N} \tag{3.10}$$

where

$$\mu = \text{population mean}$$

$$X_i = i\text{th value of the variable } X$$

$$\sum_{i=1}^{N} X_i = \text{summation of all } X_i \text{ values in the population}$$

To compute the mean one-year return for the population of bond funds given in Table 3.5, use Equation (3.10):

$$\mu = \frac{\sum\limits_{i=1}^{N} X_i}{N} = \frac{6.1 + 6.2 + 7.2 + 5.9 + 5.5}{5} = \frac{30.9}{5} = 6.18$$

Thus, the mean percentage return for these bond funds is 6.18.

The Population Variance and Standard Deviation

The **population variance** and the **population standard deviation** measure variation in a population. Like the related sample statistics, the population standard deviation is the square root of the population variance. The symbol σ^2, the Greek lowercase letter sigma squared, represents the population variance, and the symbol σ, the Greek lowercase letter sigma, represents the population standard deviation. Equations (3.11) and (3.12) define these parameters. The denominators for the right-side terms in these equations use N and not the $(n-1)$ term that is used in the equations for the sample variance and standard deviation [see Equations (3.6) and (3.7) on page 98].

Population Variance

The population variance is the sum of the squared differences around the population mean divided by the population size N.

$$\sigma^2 = \frac{\sum_{i=1}^{N}(X_i - \mu)^2}{N}$$

(3.11)

where

μ = population mean

X_i = ith value of the variable X

$\sum_{i=1}^{N}(X_i - \mu)^2$ = summation of all the squared differences between the X_i values and μ

Population Standard Deviation

$$\sigma = \sqrt{\frac{\sum_{i=1}^{N}(X_i - \mu)^2}{N}}$$

(3.12)

To compute the population variance for the data of Table 3.5, you use Equation (3.11):

$$\sigma^2 = \frac{\sum_{i=1}^{N}(X_i - \mu)^2}{N}$$

$$= \frac{(6.1 - 6.18)^2 + (6.2 - 6.18)^2 + (7.2 - 6.18)^2 + (5.9 - 6.18)^2 + (5.5 - 6.18)^2}{5}$$

$$= \frac{0.0064 + 0.0004 + 1.0444 + 0.0784 + 0.4624}{5}$$

$$= \frac{1.588}{5} = 0.3176$$

Thus, the variance of the one-year returns is 0.3176 squared percentage return. The squared units make the variance hard to interpret. You should use the standard deviation that is expressed in the original units of the data (percentage return). From Equation (3.12),

$$\sigma = \sqrt{\sigma^2} = \sqrt{\frac{\sum_{i=1}^{N}(X_i - \mu)^2}{N}} = \sqrt{0.3176} = 0.5636$$

Therefore, the typical percentage return differs from the mean of 6.18 by approximately 0.56. This small amount of variation suggests that these large bond funds produce results that do not differ greatly.

The Empirical Rule

In most data sets, a large portion of the values tend to cluster somewhere near the median. In right-skewed data sets, this clustering occurs to the left of the mean—that is, at a value less than the mean. In left-skewed data sets, the values tend to cluster to the right of the mean—that is, greater than the mean. In symmetrical data sets, where the median and mean are the same, the values often tend to cluster around the median and mean, producing a bell-shaped distribution. You can use the **empirical rule** to examine the variability in bell-shaped distributions:

- Approximately 68% of the values are within a distance of ±1 standard deviation from the mean.
- Approximately 95% of the values are within a distance of ±2 standard deviations from the mean.
- Approximately 99.7% of the values are within a distance of ±3 standard deviations from the mean.

The empirical rule helps you measure how the values distribute above and below the mean and can help you identify outliers. The empirical rule implies that for bell-shaped distributions, only about 1 out of 20 values will be beyond two standard deviations from the mean in either direction. As a general rule, you can consider values not found in the interval $\mu \pm 2\sigma$ as potential outliers. The rule also implies that only about 3 in 1,000 will be beyond three standard deviations from the mean. Therefore, values not found in the interval $\mu \pm 3\sigma$ are almost always considered outliers.

EXAMPLE 3.10   USING THE EMPIRICAL RULE

A population of 12-ounce cans of cola is known to have a mean fill-weight of 12.06 ounces and a standard deviation of 0.02. The population is known to be bell-shaped. Describe the distribution of fill-weights. Is it very likely that a can will contain less than 12 ounces of cola?

SOLUTION

$$\mu \pm \sigma = 12.06 \pm 0.02 = (12.04,\ 12.08)$$

$$\mu \pm 2\sigma = 12.06 \pm 2(0.02) = (12.02,\ 12.10)$$

$$\mu \pm 3\sigma = 12.06 \pm 3(0.02) = (12.00,\ 12.12)$$

Using the empirical rule, approximately 68% of the cans will contain between 12.04 and 12.08 ounces, approximately 95% will contain between 12.02 and 12.10 ounces, and approximately 99.7% will contain between 12.00 and 12.12 ounces. Therefore, it is highly unlikely that a can will contain less than 12 ounces.

For heavily skewed data sets, or those not appearing bell-shaped for any other reason, the Chebyshev rule discussed next should be applied instead of the empirical rule.

The Chebyshev Rule

The **Chebyshev rule** (reference 1) states that for any data set, regardless of shape, the percentage of values that are found within distances of k standard deviations from the mean must be at least

$$(1 - 1/k^2) \times 100\%$$

You can use this rule for any value of k greater than 1. Consider $k = 2$. The Chebyshev rule states that at least $[1 - (1/2)^2] \times 100\% = 75\%$ of the values must be found within ±2 standard deviations of the mean.

The Chebyshev rule is very general and applies to any type of distribution. The rule indicates *at least* what percentage of the values fall within a given distance from the mean. However, if the data set is approximately bell-shaped, the empirical rule will more accurately reflect the greater concentration of data close to the mean. Table 3.6 compares the Chebyshev and empirical rules.

TABLE 3.6		% of Values Found in Intervals Around the Mean	
How Data Vary Around the Mean	Interval	Chebyshev (any distribution)	Empirical Rule (bell-shaped distribution)
	$(\mu - \sigma, \mu + \sigma)$	At least 0%	Approximately 68%
	$(\mu - 2\sigma, \mu + 2\sigma)$	At least 75%	Approximately 95%
	$(\mu - 3\sigma, \mu + 3\sigma)$	At least 88.89%	Approximately 99.7%

EXAMPLE 3.11

USING THE CHEBYSHEV RULE

As in Example 3.10, a population of 12-ounce cans of cola is known to have a mean fill-weight of 12.06 ounces and a standard deviation of 0.02. However, the shape of the population is unknown, and you cannot assume that it is bell-shaped. Describe the distribution of fill-weights. Is it very likely that a can will contain less than 12 ounces of cola?

SOLUTION

$$\mu \pm \sigma = 12.06 \pm 0.02 = (12.04, 12.08)$$

$$\mu \pm 2\sigma = 12.06 \pm 2(0.02) = (12.02, 12.10)$$

$$\mu \pm 3\sigma = 12.06 \pm 3(0.02) = (12.00, 12.12)$$

Because the distribution may be skewed, you cannot use the empirical rule. Using the Chebyshev rule, you cannot say anything about the percentage of cans containing between 12.04 and 12.08 ounces. You can state that at least 75% of the cans will contain between 12.02 and 12.10 ounces and at least 88.89% will contain between 12.00 and 12.12 ounces. Therefore, between 0 and 11.11% of the cans will contain less than 12 ounces.

You can use these two rules for understanding how data are distributed around the mean when you have sample data. In each case, you use the value you calculated for $\bar{X}$ in place of μ and the value you calculated for S in place of σ. The results you compute using the sample statistics are *approximations* because you used sample statistics $(\bar{X}, S)$ and not population parameters (μ, σ).

PROBLEMS FOR SECTION 3.3

Learning the Basics

3.21 The following is a set of data for a population with $N = 10$:

    7   5   11   8   3   6   2   1   9   8

a. Compute the population mean.
b. Compute the population standard deviation.

3.22 The following is a set of data for a population with $N = 10$:

    7   5   6   6   6   4   8   6   9   3

a. Compute the population mean.
b. Compute the population standard deviation.

Applying the Concepts

3.23 The data in the file **Tax** represent the quarterly sales tax receipts (in thousands of dollars) submitted to the

comptroller of the Village of Fair Lake for the period ending March 2007 by all 50 business establishments in that locale:

10.3	11.1	9.6	9.0	14.5
13.0	6.7	11.0	8.4	10.3
13.0	11.2	7.3	5.3	12.5
8.0	11.8	8.7	10.6	9.5
11.1	10.2	11.1	9.9	9.8
11.6	15.1	12.5	6.5	7.5
10.0	12.9	9.2	10.0	12.8
12.5	9.3	10.4	12.7	10.5
9.3	11.5	10.7	11.6	7.8
10.5	7.6	10.1	8.9	8.6

a. Compute the mean, variance, and standard deviation for this population.

b. What percentage of these businesses have quarterly sales tax receipts within ±1, ±2, or ±3 standard deviations of the mean?

c. Compare and contrast your findings with what would be expected on the basis of the empirical rule. Are you surprised at the results in (b)?

3.24 Consider a population of 1,024 mutual funds that primarily invest in large companies. You have determined that μ, the mean one-year total percentage return achieved by all the funds, is 8.20 and that σ, the standard deviation, is 2.75. According to the empirical rule, what percentage of these funds is expected to be

a. within ±1 standard deviation of the mean?

b. within ±2 standard deviations of the mean?

c. According to the Chebyshev rule, what percentage of these funds are expected to be within ±1, ±2, or ±3 standard deviations of the mean?

d. According to the Chebyshev rule, at least 93.75% of these funds are expected to have one-year total returns between what two amounts?

3.25 The file **Collegetuition** contains the tuition and fees for public four-year colleges in each of the 50 states for the 2006–2007 school year. The amounts do not include room and board. The file also contains the percentage increase in tuition and fees from 2005–2006 to 2006–2007 (extracted from Sandra Block, "Rising Costs Make Climb to Higher Education Steeper," **usatoday.com**, January 12, 2007).

a. Compute the population mean and population standard deviation for tuition and fees.

b. Interpret the parameters in (a).

c. Compute the population mean and population standard deviation for the percentage increase from 2005–2006 to 2006–2007.

d. Interpret the parameters in (c).

3.26 The data in the file **Energy** contains the per-capita energy consumption, in kilowatt hours, for each of the 50 states and the District of Columbia during a recent year.

a. Compute the mean, variance, and standard deviation for the population.

b. What proportion of these states has average per-capita energy consumption within ±1 standard deviation of the mean, within ±2 standard deviations of the mean, and within ±3 standard deviations of the mean?

c. Compare and contrast your findings versus what would be expected based on the empirical rule. Are you surprised at the results in (b)?

d. Repeat (a) through (c) with the District of Columbia removed. How have the results changed?

3.27 Thirty companies comprise the DJIA. Just how big are these companies? One common method to measure the size of a company is to use its market capitalization, which is computed by taking the number of stock shares multiplied by the price of a share of stock. On April 25, 2007, the market capitalization of these companies ranged from General Motors's $17.4 billion to Exxon-Mobil's $453.9 billion. The entire population of market capitalization values is recorded in the file **Dowmarketcap**.

Source: *Extracted from* **money.cnn.com**, *April 25, 2007.*

a. Calculate the mean and standard deviation of the market capitalization for this population of 30 companies.

b. Interpret the parameters calculated in (a).

3.4 COMPUTING NUMERICAL DESCRIPTIVE MEASURES FROM A FREQUENCY DISTRIBUTION

Sometimes you have only a frequency distribution, not the raw data. When this occurs, you can compute approximations to the mean and the standard deviation.

When you have data from a sample that has been summarized into a frequency distribution, you can compute an approximation of the mean by assuming that all values within each class interval are located at the midpoint of the class.

Approximating the Mean from a Frequency Distribution

$$\bar{X} = \frac{\sum_{j=1}^{c} m_j f_j}{n} \qquad \qquad (3.13)$$

where

$$\bar{X} = \text{sample mean}$$

$$n = \text{number of values or sample size}$$

$$c = \text{number of classes in the frequency distribution}$$

$$m_j = \text{midpoint of the } j\text{th class}$$

$$f_j = \text{number of values in the } j\text{th class}$$

To calculate the standard deviation from a frequency distribution, you assume that all values within each class interval are located at the midpoint of the class.

Approximating the Standard Deviation From a Frequency Distribution

$$S = \sqrt{\frac{\sum_{j=1}^{c}(m_j - \bar{X})^2 f_j}{n-1}} \qquad (3.14)$$

Example 3.12 illustrates the computation of the mean and the standard deviation from a frequency distribution.

EXAMPLE 3.12   APPROXIMATING THE MEAN AND STANDARD DEVIATION FROM A FREQUENCY DISTRIBUTION

Consider the frequency distribution of the 2006 return of value funds (Table 3.7). Compute the mean and standard deviation.

TABLE 3.7

Frequency Distribution of the 2006 Return for Value Mutual Funds

2006 Return	Frequency
0 to under 5	1
5 to under 10	14
10 to under 15	102
15 to under 20	208
20 to under 25	71
25 to under 30	7
30 to under 35	0
35 to under 40	1
Total	404

SOLUTION The computations that you need to calculate the approximations of the mean and standard deviation of the 2006 return for value mutual funds are summarized in Table 3.8 on page 116. Using Equation (3.13) on page 114,

$$\bar{X} = \sqrt{\frac{\sum_{j=1}^{c} m_j f_j}{n}}$$

$$\bar{X} = \frac{6,850.0}{404} = 16.9554$$

TABLE 3.8

Computations Needed for Approximating the Mean and Standard Deviation of the 2006 return for Value Mutual Funds

Percentage Return	Frequency (f_j)	Midpoint (m_j)	$m_j f_j$	$(m_j - \bar{X})$	$(m_j - \bar{X})^2$	$(m_j - \bar{X})^2 f_j$
0 to under 5	1	2.5	2.5	−14.45545	208.9599	208.9599
5 to under 10	14	7.5	105.0	−9.45545	89.4055	1,251.6763
10 to under 15	102	12.5	1,275.0	−4.45545	19.8510	2,024.8015
15 to under 20	208	17.5	3,640.0	0.54455	0.2965	61.6802
20 to under 25	71	22.5	1,597.5	5.54455	30.7421	2,182.6880
25 to under 30	7	27.5	192.5	10.54455	111.1876	778.3134
30 to under 35	0	32.5	0.0	15.54455	241.6332	0.0000
35 to under 40	1	37.5	37.5	20.54455	422.0787	422.0787
	404		6,850.0			6,930.1980

and using Equation (3.14) on page 115

$$S = \sqrt{\frac{\sum_{i=1}^{c} (m_j - \bar{X})^2 f_j}{n-1}}$$

$$S = \sqrt{\frac{6930.198}{404 - 1}}$$

$$= \sqrt{17.196521}$$

$$= 4.1469$$

PROBLEMS FOR SECTION 3.4

Learning the Basics

3.28 Given the following frequency distribution for $n = 100$:

Class Intervals	Frequency
0—Under 10	10
10—Under 20	20
20—Under 30	40
30—Under 40	20
40—Under 50	10
	100

Approximate
a. the mean.
b. the standard deviation.

3.29 Given the following frequency distribution for $n = 100$:

Class Intervals	Frequency
0—Under 10	40
10—Under 20	25
20—Under 30	15
30—Under 40	15
40—Under 50	5
	100

Approximate
a. the mean.
b. the standard deviation.

Applying the Concepts

3.30 A wholesale appliance distributing firm wished to study its accounts receivable for two successive months. Two independent samples of 50 accounts were selected for each of the two months. The results are summarized in the following table:

Amount	March Frequency	April Frequency
$0 to under $2,000	6	10
$2,000 to under $4,000	13	14
$4,000 to under $6,000	17	13
$6,000 to under $8,000	10	10
$8,000 to under $10,000	4	0
$10,000 to under $12,000	0	3
Total	50	50

For each month, approximate the
a. mean.
b. standard deviation.
c. On the basis of (a) and (b), do you think the mean and the standard deviation of the accounts receivable have changed substantially from March to April? Explain.

3.31 The following table contains the cumulative frequency distributions and cumulative percentage distributions of braking distance (in feet) at 80 miles per hour for a sample of 25 U.S.-manufactured automobile models and for a sample of 72 foreign-made automobile models in a recent year:

Braking Distance (in Ft)	U.S.-Made Automobile Models "Less Than" Indicated Values		Foreign-Made Automobile Models "Less Than" Indicated Values	
	Number	Percentage	Number	Percentage
210	0	0.0	0	0.0
220	1	4.0	1	1.4
230	2	8.0	4	5.6
240	3	12.0	19	26.4
250	4	16.0	32	44.4
260	8	32.0	54	75.0
270	11	44.0	61	84.7

(continued)

Braking Distance (in Ft)	U.S.-Made Automobile Models "Less Than" Indicated Values		Foreign-Made Automobile Models "Less Than" Indicated Values	
	Number	Percentage	Number	Percentage
280	17	68.0	68	94.4
290	21	84.0	68	94.4
300	23	92.0	70	97.2
310	25	100.0	71	98.6
320	25	100.0	72	100.0

For U.S.- and foreign-made automobiles:
a. Construct a frequency distribution for each group.
b. On the basis of the results of (a), approximate the mean of the braking distance.
c. On the basis of the results of (a), approximate the standard deviation of the braking distance.
d. On the basis of the results of (b) and (c), do U.S.- and foreign-made automobiles seem to differ in their braking distance? Explain.

3.32 The following data represent the distribution of the ages of employees within two different divisions of a publishing company.

Age of Employees (Years)	A Frequency	B Frequency
20—Under 30	8	15
30—Under 40	17	32
40—Under 50	11	20
50—Under 60	8	4
60—Under 70	2	0

For each of the two divisions (*A* and *B*), approximate the
a. mean.
b. standard deviation.
c. On the basis of the results of (a) and (b), do you think there are differences in the age distribution between the two divisions? Explain.

3.5 QUARTILES AND THE BOXPLOT

Sections 3.1 through 3.3 discuss measures of central tendency, variation, and shape. Another way of describing numerical data is through an exploratory data analysis that includes the quartiles, the five-number summary, and the boxplot (references 4 and 5).

Quartiles

Quartiles split a set of data into four equal parts—the **first quartile, Q_1,** divides the smallest 25.0% of the values from the other 75.0% that are larger. The **second quartile, Q_2,** is the median—50.0% of the values are smaller than the median and 50.0% are larger. The **third**

quartile, Q_3, divides the smallest 75.0% of the values from the largest 25.0%. Equations (3.15) and (3.16) define the first and third quartiles.[1]

First Quartile, Q_1

25.0% of the values are smaller than or equal to Q_1, the first quartile, and 75.0% are larger than or equal to the first quartile, Q_1.

$$Q_1 = \frac{n+1}{4} \text{ ranked value} \qquad (3.15)$$

Third Quartile, Q_3

75.0% of the values are smaller than or equal to the third quartile, Q_3, and 25.0% are larger than or equal to the third quartile, Q_3.

$$Q_3 = \frac{3(n+1)}{4} \text{ ranked value} \qquad (3.16)$$

Use the following rules to calculate the quartiles from a set of ranked values:

- **Rule 1** If the ranked value is a whole number, then the quartile is equal to that ranked value. For example, if the sample size $n = 7$, the first quartile, Q_1, is equal to the $(7 + 1)/4 =$ second ranked value.
- **Rule 2** If the ranked value is a fractional half (2.5, 4.5, etc.), then the quartile is equal to the average of the corresponding ranked values. For example, if the sample size $n = 9$, the first quartile, Q_1, is equal to the $(9 + 1)/4 = 2.5$ ranked value, halfway between the second ranked value and the third ranked value.
- **Rule 3** If the ranked value is neither a whole number nor a fractional half, you round the result to the nearest integer and select that ranked value. For example, if the sample size $n = 10$, the first quartile, Q_1, is equal to the $(10 + 1)/4 = 2.75$ ranked value. Round 2.75 to 3 and use the third ranked value.

To illustrate the computation of the quartiles for the time-to-get-ready data, rank the following data from smallest to largest:

Ranked values:

29 31 35 39 39 40 43 44 44 52

Ranks:

1 2 3 4 5 6 7 8 9 10

The first quartile is the $(n + 1)/4 = (10 + 1)/4 = 2.75$ ranked value. Using Rule 3, you round up to the third ranked value. The third ranked value for the time-to-get-ready data is 35 minutes. You interpret the first quartile of 35 to mean that on 25% of the days, the time to get ready is less than or equal to 35 minutes, and on 75% of the days, the time to get ready is greater than or equal to 35 minutes.

The third quartile is the $3(n + 1)/4 = 3(10 + 1)/4 = 8.25$ ranked value. Using Rule 3 for quartiles, you round this down to the eighth ranked value. The eighth ranked value is 44 minutes. Thus, on 75% of the days, the time to get ready is less than or equal to 44 minutes, and on 25% of the days, the time to get ready is greater than or equal to 44 minutes.

EXAMPLE 3.13   COMPUTING THE QUARTILES

The data in the file CoffeeDrink (see Example 3.1 on page 92) represent the calories of 16-ounce iced coffee drinks at Dunkin' Donuts and Starbucks. Compute the first quartile (Q_1) and third quartile (Q_3) number of calories for the iced coffee drinks at Dunkin' Donuts and Starbucks.

SOLUTION Ranked from smallest to largest, the number of calories for the seven iced coffee drinks are:

Ranked values:

$$240 \quad 260 \quad 350 \quad 350 \quad 420 \quad 510 \quad 530$$

Ranks:

$$1 \quad\quad 2 \quad\quad 3 \quad\quad 4 \quad\quad 5 \quad\quad 6 \quad\quad 7$$

For these data

$$Q_1 = \frac{(n+1)}{4} \text{ ranked value}$$

$$= \frac{7+1}{4} \text{ ranked value} = 2\text{nd ranked value}$$

Therefore, using Rule 1, Q_1 is the second ranked value. Because the second ranked value is 260, the first quartile, Q_1, is 260.

To find the third quartile, Q_3:

$$Q_3 = \frac{3(n+1)}{4} \text{ ranked value}$$

$$= \frac{3(7+1)}{4} \text{ ranked value} = 6\text{th ranked value}$$

Therefore, using Rule 1, Q_3 is the sixth ranked value. Because the sixth ranked value is 510, Q_3 is 510.

The first quartile of 260 indicates that 25% of the iced coffee drinks have calories that are below or equal to 260 and 75% are greater than or equal to 260. The third quartile of 510 indicates that 75% of the iced coffee drinks have calories that are below or equal to 510 and 25% are greater than or equal to 510.

The Interquartile Range

The **interquartile range** (also called **midspread**) is the difference between the third and first quartiles in a set of data.

Interquartile Range

The interquartile range is the difference between the third quartile and the first quartile.

$$\text{Interquartile range} = Q_3 - Q_1 \qquad\qquad \textbf{(3.17)}$$

The interquartile range measures the spread in the middle 50% of the data. Therefore, it is not influenced by extreme values. To determine the interquartile range of the times to get ready

$$29 \quad 31 \quad 35 \quad 39 \quad\quad 39 \quad 40 \quad 43 \quad 44 \quad 44 \quad 52$$

you use Equation (3.17) and the earlier results on page 118, $Q_1 = 35$ and $Q_3 = 44$:

$$\text{Interquartile range} = 44 - 35 = 9 \text{ minutes}$$

Therefore, the interquartile range in the time to get ready is 9 minutes. The interval 35 to 44 is often referred to as the *middle fifty*.

EXAMPLE 3.14

COMPUTING THE INTERQUARTILE RANGE FOR THE NUMBER OF CALORIES IN ICED COFFEE DRINKS

The data in the file **CoffeeDrink** (see Example 3.1 on page 92) represent the calories of 16-ounce iced coffee drinks at Dunkin' Donuts and Starbucks. Compute the interquartile range of the number of calories of 16-ounce iced coffee drinks.

SOLUTION Ranked from smallest to largest, the number of calories for the seven iced coffee drinks are:

$$240 \quad 260 \quad 350 \quad 350 \quad 420 \quad 510 \quad 530$$

Using Equation (3.17) and the earlier results on page 119, $Q_1 = 260$ and $Q_3 = 510$:

$$\text{Interquartile range} = 510 - 260 = 250$$

Therefore, the interquartile range of the number of calories of 16-ounce iced coffee drinks is 250 calories.

Because the interquartile range does not consider any value smaller than Q_1 or larger than Q_3, it cannot be affected by extreme values. Summary measures such as the median, Q_1, Q_3, and the interquartile range, which cannot be influenced by extreme values, are called **resistant measures**.

The Five-Number Summary

A **five-number summary** that consists of

$$X_{\text{smallest}} \quad Q_1 \quad \text{Median} \quad Q_3 \quad X_{\text{largest}}$$

provides a way to determine the shape of a distribution. Table 3.9 explains how the relationships among the "five numbers" allows you to recognize the shape of a data set.

For the sample of 10 getting-ready times, the smallest value is 29 minutes and the largest value is 52 minutes (see page 91). Calculations done on pages 93 and 119 show that the median = 39.5, $Q_1 = 35$, and $Q_3 = 44$. Therefore, the five-number summary is

$$29 \quad 35 \quad 39.5 \quad 44 \quad 52$$

The distance from X_{smallest} to the median ($39.5 - 29 = 10.5$) is slightly less than the distance from the median to X_{largest} ($52 - 39.5 = 12.5$). The distance from X_{smallest} to Q_1 ($35 - 29 = 6$) is slightly less than the distance from Q_3 to X_{largest} ($52 - 44 = 8$). Therefore, the getting-ready times are slightly right-skewed.

TABLE 3.9

Relationships Among the Five-Number Summary and the Type of Distribution

| | Type of Distribution | | |
Comparison	Left-Skewed	Symmetric	Right-Skewed
The distance from $X_{smallest}$ to the median versus the distance from the median to $X_{largest}$.	The distance from $X_{smallest}$ to the median is greater than the distance from the median to $X_{largest}$.	Both distances are the same.	The distance from $X_{smallest}$ to the median is less than the distance from the median to $X_{largest}$.
The distance from $X_{smallest}$ to Q_1 versus the distance from Q_3 to $X_{largest}$.	The distance from $X_{smallest}$ to Q_1 is greater than the distance from Q_3 to $X_{largest}$.	Both distances are the same.	The distance from $X_{smallest}$ to Q_1 is less than the distance from Q_3 to $X_{largest}$.
The distance from Q_1 to the median versus the distance from the median to Q_3.	The distance from Q_1 to the median is greater than the distance from the median to Q_3.	Both distances are the same.	The distance from Q_1 to the median is less than the distance from the median to Q_3.

EXAMPLE 3.15   COMPUTING THE FIVE-NUMBER SUMMARY OF THE NUMBER OF CALORIES IN ICED COFFEE DRINKS

The data in the file CoffeeDrink (see Example 3.1 on page 92) represent the calories of 16-ounce iced coffee drinks at Dunkin' Donuts and Starbucks. Compute the five-number summary of the number of calories of 16-ounce iced coffee drinks.

SOLUTION From previous computations for the calories of 16-ounce iced coffee drinks (see pages 94 and 119), the median = 350, $Q_1 = 260$, and $Q_3 = 510$. In addition, the smallest value in the data set is 240, and the largest value is 530. Therefore, the five-number summary is

$$240 \quad 260 \quad 350 \quad 510 \quad 530$$

The three comparisons listed in Table 3.9 are used to evaluate skewness. The distance from $X_{smallest}$ to the median ($350 - 240 = 110$) is less than the distance ($530 - 350 = 180$) from the median to $X_{largest}$. The distance from $X_{smallest}$ to Q_1 ($260 - 240 = 20$) is the same as the distance from Q_3 to $X_{largest}$ ($530 - 510 = 20$). The distance from Q_1 to the median ($350 - 260 = 90$) is less than the distance from the median to Q_3 ($510 - 350 = 160$). Two comparisons indicate a right-skewed distribution whereas the other indicates a symmetric distribution. Therefore, you can conclude that the number of calories in iced coffee drinks is right-skewed.

The Boxplot

A **boxplot** provides a graphical representation of the data based on the five-number summary. Figure 3.4 on page 122 illustrates the boxplot for the getting-ready times. The vertical line drawn within the box represents the median. The vertical line at the left side of the box represents the location of Q_1, and the vertical line at the right side of the box represents the location of Q_3. Thus, the box contains the middle 50% of the values. The lower 25% of the data are represented by a line connecting the left side of the box to the location of the smallest value, $X_{smallest}$. Similarly, the upper 25% of the data are represented by a line connecting the right side of the box to $X_{largest}$.

FIGURE 3.4

Boxplot for the getting ready times

See Appendix E3.3 or P3.1 to create this. (Use Section M3.2 to create the Minitab equivalent.)

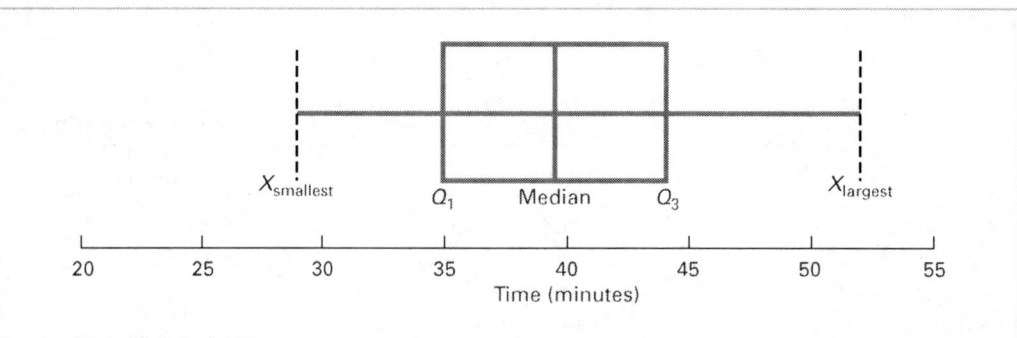

The boxplot of the getting-ready times in Figure 3.4 indicates very slight right-skewness because the distance between the median and the highest value is slightly greater than the distance between the lowest value and the median. Also, the right tail is slightly longer than the left tail.

EXAMPLE 3.16   THE BOXPLOTS OF THE 2006 RETURNS OF GROWTH AND VALUE MUTUAL FUNDS

The 868 mutual funds (Mutual Funds) that are part of the Using Statistics scenario (see page 90) are classified according to whether the mutual funds are growth or value funds. Construct the boxplot of the 2006 returns for growth and value mutual funds.

SOLUTION Figure 3.5 shows the PHStat2 boxplot of the 2006 return for the growth and value mutual funds and Figure 3.6 is a Minitab boxplot. The median return, the quartiles, and the minimum and maximum return are much higher for the value funds than for the growth funds. Both the growth and value funds appear to be fairly symmetrical between the quartiles, but the value funds seem to have more extremely high returns.

FIGURE 3.5

PHStat2 boxplots of the 2006 return for growth and value mutual funds

See Appendix E3.3 or P3.1 to create this.

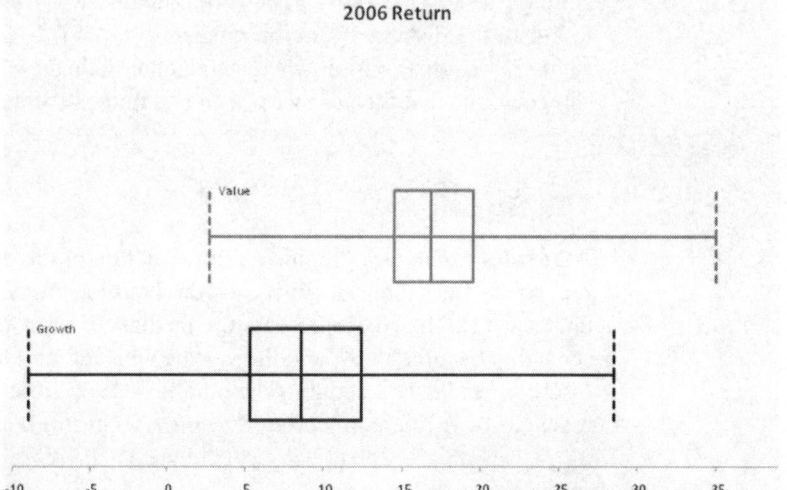

FIGURE 3.6

Minitab boxplots of the 2006 return for growth and value mutual funds

See Appendix M3.2 to create this.

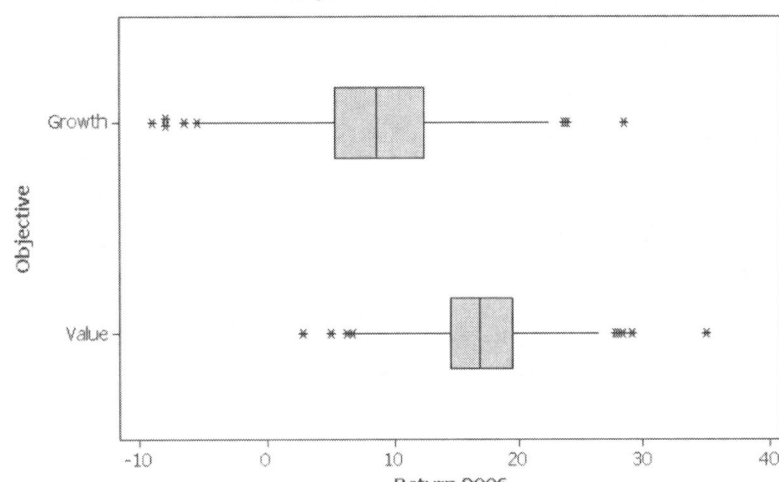

Boxplot of Return 2006

Notice that in Figure 3.6, several * appear in the boxplots. This indicates outliers that are more than 1.5 times the interquartile range beyond the quartiles.

Figure 3.7 demonstrates the relationship between the boxplot and the polygon for four different types of distributions. (*Note:* The area under each polygon is split into quartiles corresponding to the five-number summary for the boxplot.)

FIGURE 3.7

Boxplots and corresponding polygons for four distributions

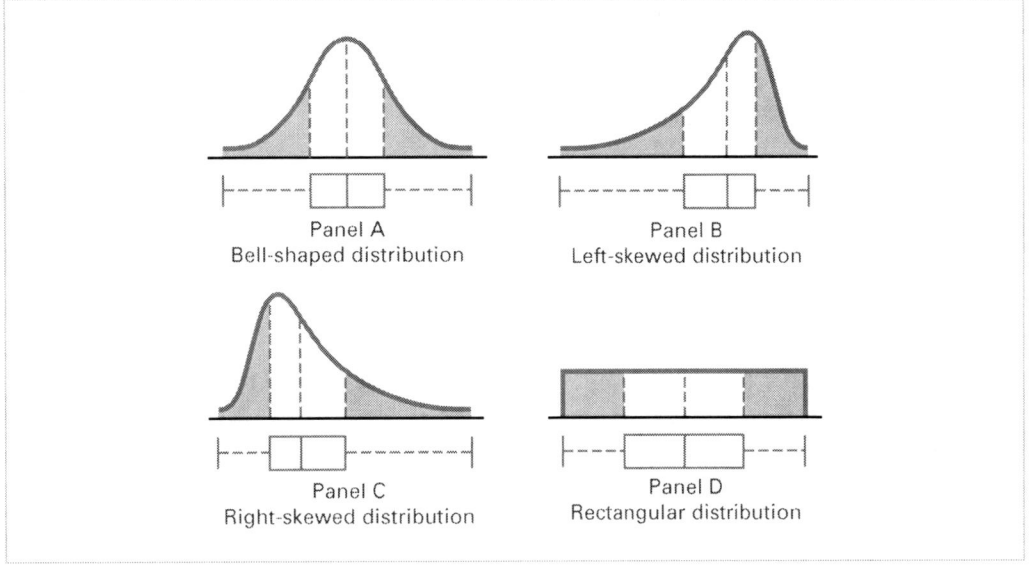

Panel A
Bell-shaped distribution

Panel B
Left-skewed distribution

Panel C
Right-skewed distribution

Panel D
Rectangular distribution

Panels A and D of Figure 3.7 are symmetrical. In these distributions, the mean and median are equal. In addition, the length of the left tail is equal to the length of the right tail, and the median line divides the box in half.

Panel B of Figure 3.7 is left-skewed. The few small values distort the mean toward the left tail. For this left-skewed distribution, there is a heavy clustering of values at the high end of the scale (i.e., the right side); 75% of all values are found between the left edge of the box (Q_1) and the end of the right tail ($X_{largest}$). There is a long left tail that contains the smallest 25% of the values, demonstrating the lack of symmetry in this data set.

Panel C of Figure 3.7 is right-skewed. The concentration of values is on the low end of the scale (i.e., the left side of the boxplot). Here, 75% of all data values are found between the beginning of the left tail ($X_{smallest}$) and the right edge of the box (Q_3). There is a long right tail that contains the largest 25% of the values, demonstrating the lack of symmetry in this data set.

PROBLEMS FOR SECTION 3.5

Learning the Basics

3.33 The following is a set of data from a sample of $n = 5$:

7   4   9   8   2

a. Compute the first quartile (Q_1), the third quartile (Q_3), and the interquartile range.
b. List the five-number summary.
c. Construct a boxplot and describe the shape.
d. Compare your answer in (c) with that from Problem 3.1(d) on page 106. Discuss.

3.34 The following is a set of data from a sample of $n = 6$:

7   4   9   7   3   12

a. Compute the first quartile (Q_1), the third quartile (Q_3), and the interquartile range.
b. List the five-number summary.
c. Construct a boxplot and describe the shape.
d. Compare your answer in (c) with that from Problem 3.2(d) on page 106. Discuss.

3.35 The following is a set of data from a sample of $n = 7$:

12   7   4   9   0   7   3

a. Compute the first quartile (Q_1), the third quartile (Q_3), and the interquartile range.
b. List the five-number summary.
c. Construct a boxplot and describe the shape.
d. Compare your answer in (c) with that from Problem 3.3(d) on page 107. Discuss.

3.36 The following is a set of data from a sample of $n = 5$:

7   −5   −8   7   9

a. Compute the first quartile (Q_1), the third quartile (Q_3), and the interquartile range.
b. List the five-number summary.
c. Construct a boxplot and describe the shape.
d. Compare your answer in (c) with that from Problem 3.4(d) on page 107. Discuss.

Applying the Concepts

3.37 The data file Chicken contains the total fat, in grams per serving, for a sample of 20 chicken sandwiches from fast-food chains. The data are as follows:

7   8   4   5   16   20   20   24   19   30
23   30   25   19   29   29   30   30   40   56

Source: *Extracted from "Fast Food: Adding Health to the Menu,"* Consumer Reports, *September 2004, pp. 28–31.*

a. Compute the first quartile (Q_1), the third quartile (Q_3), and the interquartile range.

b. List the five-number summary.
c. Construct a boxplot and describe the shape.

3.38 The data in the file Batterylife represent the battery life (in shots) for a sample of three-pixel digital cameras:

300 180 85 170 380 460 260 35 380 120 110 240

Source: *Extracted from "Cameras: More Features in the Mix,"* Consumer Reports, *July 2005, pp. 14–18.*

a. Compute the first quartile (Q_1), the third quartile (Q_3), and the interquartile range.
b. List the five-number summary.
c. Construct a boxplot and describe the shape.

3.39 The data file Themeparks contains data on the starting admission price (in $) for one-day tickets to 10 theme parks in the United States:

58   63   41   42   29   50   62   43   40   40

Source: *Extracted from C. Jackson and E. Gamerman, "Rethinking the Thrill Factor,"* The Wall Street Journal, *April 15–16, 2006, pp. P1, P4.*

a. Compute the first quartile (Q_1), the third quartile (Q_3), and the interquartile range.
b. List the five-number summary.
c. Construct a boxplot and describe the shape.

SELF Test **3.40** The data in the file SUV represent the overall miles per gallon (MPG) of 2007 small SUVs.

Model	MPG	Model	MPG
Toyota RAV4 6-cyl	22	Mazda Tribute	18
Hyundai Santa Fe	18	Mercury Mariner	18
Toyota RAV4 4-cyl	23	Luxury	
Subaru Forester Sports 2.5 XT	20	Nissan Xterra	17
		Honda Element	21
Honda CR-V	21	Suzuki Grand Vitara	18
Subaru Forester Sports 2.5 X	22	Chevrolet Equinox	18
		Pontiac Torrent	18
Mitsubishi Outlander	19	Jeep Compass	22
Hyundai Tucson	18	Saturn Vue	19
Kia Sportage	18	Saturn Vue Hybrid	24
Ford Escape Hybrid	26	Kia Sorento	15
Mercury Mariner Hybrid	26	Jeep Liberty	15
		Toyota FJ Cruiser	17
Suzuki XL-7	17	Dodge Nitro	16
Ford Escape	18	Jeep Wrangler	15

Source: *Extracted from "Vehicle Ratings,"* Consumer Reports, *April 2007, pp. 42–43.*

a. Compute the first quartile (Q_1), the third quartile (Q_3), and the interquartile range.
b. List the five-number summary.
c. Construct a boxplot and describe the shape.

3.41 The data in the file **Savings** are the yields for a money market account, a one-year certificate of deposit (CD), and a five-year CD for 37 banks in South Florida as of March 9, 2007 (extracted from **Bankrate.com**, March 9, 2007).
a. List the five-number summary for the yield of the money market account, one-year CD, and a five-year CD.
b. Construct a boxplot for the yield of the money market account, one-year CD, and a five-year CD.
c. What similarities and differences are there in the distributions for the yield of the money market account, one-year CD, and a five-year CD?

3.42 A bank branch located in a commercial district of a city has developed an improved process for serving customers during the noon-to-1:00 p.m. lunch period. The waiting time, in minutes (defined as the time the customer enters the line to when he or she reaches the teller window), of a sample of 15 customers during this hour is recorded over a period of one week. The results are contained in the data file **Bank1** and are listed below:

4.21 5.55 3.02 5.13 4.77 2.34 3.54 3.20
4.50 6.10 0.38 5.12 6.46 6.19 3.79

Another branch, located in a residential area, is also concerned with the noon-to-1 p.m. lunch hour. The waiting time, in minutes (defined as the time the customer enters the line to when he or she reaches the teller window), of a sample of 15 customers during this hour is recorded over a period of one week. The results are contained in the data file **Bank2** and are listed below:

9.66 5.90 8.02 5.79 8.73 3.82 8.01 8.35
10.49 6.68 5.64 4.08 6.17 9.91 5.47

a. List the five-number summaries of the waiting times at the two bank branches.
b. Construct boxplots and describe the shape of the distribution for the two bank branches.
c. What similarities and differences are there in the distributions of the waiting time at the two bank branches?

3.6 THE COVARIANCE AND THE COEFFICIENT OF CORRELATION

In Section 2.5, you used scatter plots to visually examine the relationship between two numerical variables. This section presents two numerical measures of the relationship between two numerical variables: the covariance and the coefficient of correlation.

The Covariance

The **covariance** measures the strength of the linear relationship between two numerical variables (X and Y). Equation (3.18) defines the **sample covariance**, and Example 3.17 illustrates its use.

The Sample Covariance

$$\text{cov}(X,Y) = \frac{\sum_{i=1}^{n}(X_i - \bar{X})(Y_i - \bar{Y})}{n-1} \qquad (3.18)$$

EXAMPLE 3.17   COMPUTING THE SAMPLE COVARIANCE

In Figure 2.15 on page 53, you examined the relationship between the cost of a fast-food hamburger meal and the cost of two movie tickets in 10 cities around the world (extracted from K. Spors, "Keeping Up with . . . Yourself," *The Wall Street Journal*, April 11, 2005, p. R4). The data file **Cost of living** contains the complete data set. Compute the sample covariance.

SOLUTION Table 3.10 provides the cost of a fast-food hamburger meal and the cost of two movie tickets in 10 cities around the world.

TABLE 3.10

Cost of a Fast-Food
Hamburger Meal and
Cost of Two Movie
Tickets in 10 Cities

City	Hamburger	Movie Tickets
Tokyo	5.99	32.66
London	7.62	28.41
New York	5.75	20.00
Sydney	4.45	20.71
Chicago	4.99	18.00
San Francisco	5.29	19.50
Boston	4.39	18.00
Atlanta	3.70	16.00
Toronto	4.62	18.05
Rio de Janeiro	2.99	9.90

Figure 3.8 contains a Microsoft Excel worksheet that calculates the covariance for these data. The Calculations area of Figure 3.8 breaks down Equation (3.18) into a set of smaller calculations. From cell C20, or by using Equation (3.18) directly, you find that the covariance is 6.8378:

$$cov(X,Y) = \frac{61.5399}{10-1}$$

$$= 6.8378$$

FIGURE 3.8

Microsoft Excel
worksheet for the
covariance between the
cost of a fast-food
hamburger meal and
the cost of two movie
tickets in 10 cities

*See Appendix E3.4 to
create this.*

	A	B	C	
1	Covariance Analysis			
2				
3	Hamburger Meal	Movie Ticket	(X-XBar)(Y-YBar)	
4	5.99	32.66	12.6749	=(A4 - C16) * (B4 - C17)
5	7.62	28.41	21.8860	=(A5 - C16) * (B5 - C17)
6	5.75	20.00	-0.0948	=(A6 - C16) * (B6 - C17)
7	4.45	20.71	-0.3105	=(A7 - C16) * (B7 - C17)
8	4.99	18.00	-0.0234	=(A8 - C16) * (B8 - C17)
9	5.29	19.50	-0.1938	=(A9 - C16) * (B9 - C17)
10	4.39	18.00	1.2504	=(A10 - C16) * (B10 - C17)
11	3.70	16.00	5.2733	=(A11 - C16) * (B11 - C17)
12	4.62	18.05	0.7442	=(A12 - C16) * (B12 - C17)
13	2.99	9.90	20.3335	=(A13 - C16) * (B13 - C17)
14				
15		Calculations		
16		XBar	4.9790	=AVERAGE(A4:A13)
17		YBar	20.1230	=AVERAGE(B4:B13)
18		n-1	9	=COUNT(A4:A13) - 1
19		Sum	61.5399	=SUM(C4:C13)
20		Covariance	6.8378	=C19 / C18

The covariance has a major flaw as a measure of the linear relationship between two numerical variables. Because the covariance can have any value, you are unable to determine the relative strength of the relationship. In other words, you cannot tell whether the value 6.8378 is an indication of a strong relationship or a weak relationship. To better determine the relative strength of the relationship, you need to compute the coefficient of correlation.

The Coefficient of Correlation

The **coefficient of correlation** measures the relative strength of a linear relationship between two numerical variables. The values of the coefficient of correlation range from −1 for a perfect negative correlation to +1 for a perfect positive correlation. Perfect means that if the points were plotted in a scatter plot, all the points could be connected with a straight line. When dealing with population data for two numerical variables, the Greek letter ρ is used as the symbol for the coefficient of correlation. Figure 3.9 illustrates three different types of association between two variables.

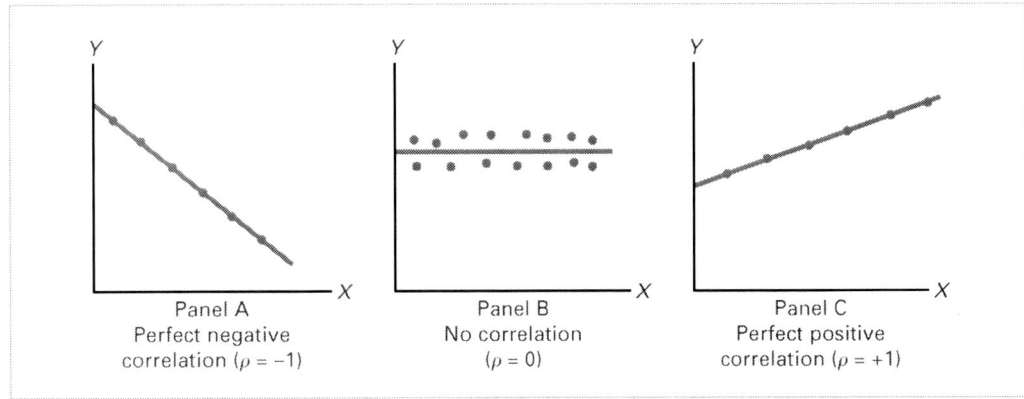

Panel A
Perfect negative
correlation ($\rho = -1$)

Panel B
No correlation
($\rho = 0$)

Panel C
Perfect positive
correlation ($\rho = +1$)

In Panel A of Figure 3.9, there is a perfect negative linear relationship between X and Y. Thus, the coefficient of correlation, ρ, equals -1, and when X increases, Y decreases in a perfectly predictable manner. Panel B shows a situation in which there is no relationship between X and Y. In this case, the coefficient of correlation, ρ, equals 0, and as X increases, there is no tendency for Y to increase or decrease. Panel C illustrates a perfect positive relationship where ρ equals $+1$. In this case, Y increases in a perfectly predictable manner when X increases.

Correlation alone cannot prove that there is a causation effect—that is, that the change in the value of one variable caused the change in the other variable. A strong correlation can be produced simply by chance, by the effect of a third variable not considered in the calculation of the correlation, or by a cause-and-effect relationship. You would need to perform additional analysis to determine which of these three situations actually produced the correlation. Therefore, you can say that causation implies correlation, but correlation alone does not imply causation.

Equation (3.19) defines the **sample coefficient of correlation**, r.

The Sample Coefficient of Correlation

$$r = \frac{\text{cov}(X,Y)}{S_X S_Y} \qquad (3.19)$$

where

$$\text{cov}(X, Y) = \frac{\displaystyle\sum_{i=1}^{n}(X_i - \bar{X})(Y_i - \bar{Y})}{n-1}$$

$$S_X = \sqrt{\frac{\displaystyle\sum_{i=1}^{n}(X_i - \bar{X})^2}{n-1}}$$

$$S_Y = \sqrt{\frac{\displaystyle\sum_{i=1}^{n}(Y_i - \bar{Y})^2}{n-1}}$$

When you have sample data, you calculate the sample coefficient of correlation, r. When using sample data, you are unlikely to have a sample coefficient of exactly $+1$, 0, or -1. Figure 3.10 presents scatter plots along with their respective sample coefficients of correlation, r, for six data sets, each of which contains 100 values of X and Y.

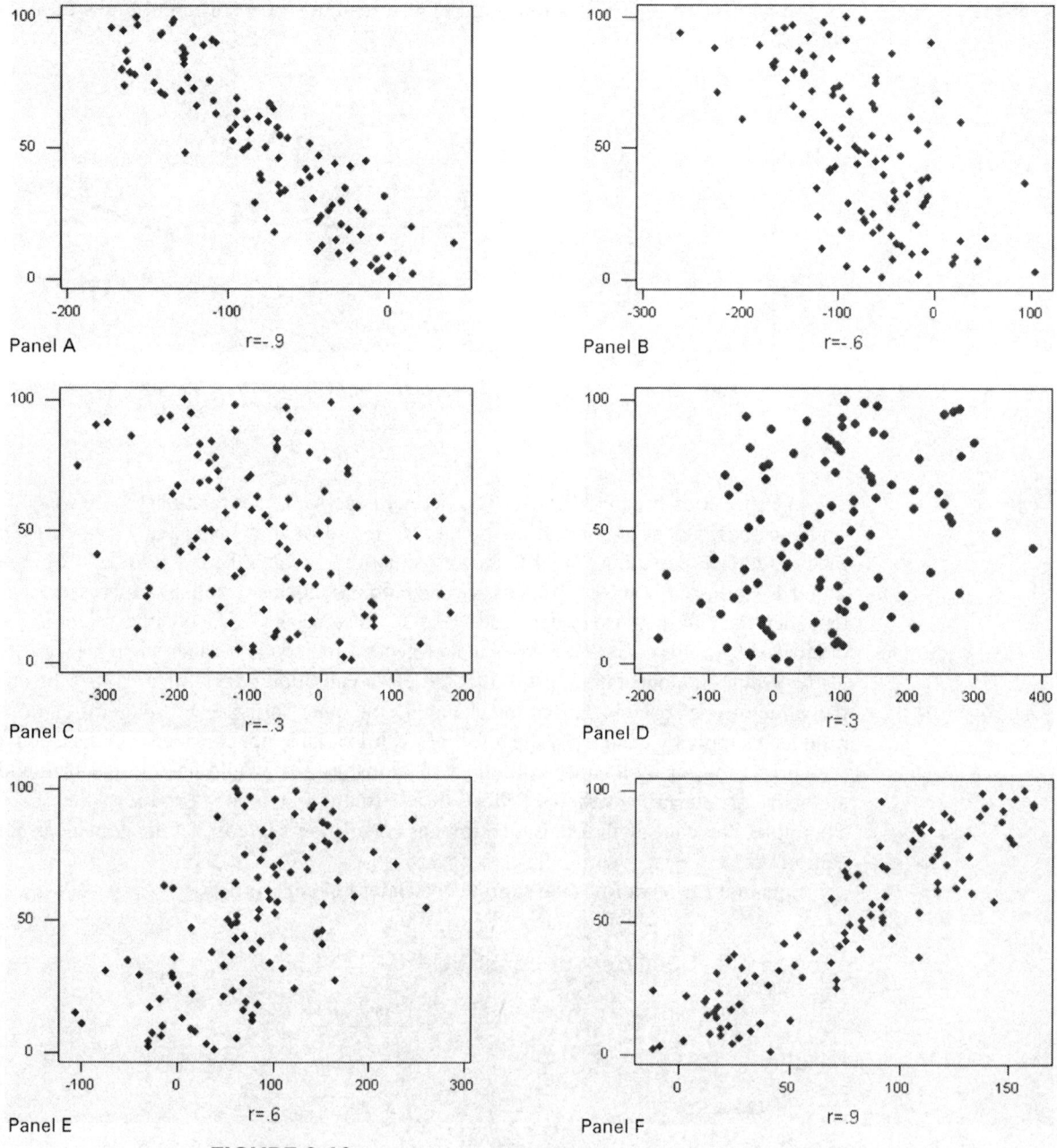

FIGURE 3.10

Six Minitab scatter plots and their sample coefficients of correlation, *r*

In Panel A, the coefficient of correlation, *r*, is −0.9. You can see that for small values of *X*, there is a very strong tendency for *Y* to be large. Likewise, the large values of *X* tend to be paired with small values of *Y*. The data do not all fall on a straight line, so the association between *X* and *Y* cannot be described as perfect. The data in Panel B have a coefficient of correlation equal to −0.6, and the small values of *X* tend to be paired with large values of *Y*. The linear relationship between *X* and *Y* in Panel B is not as strong as that in Panel A. Thus, the coefficient of correlation in Panel B is not as negative as that in Panel A. In Panel C, the linear relationship between *X* and *Y* is very weak, *r* = −0.3, and there is only a slight tendency for the small values of *X* to be paired with the larger values of *Y*. Panels D through F depict data sets that have positive coefficients of correlation because small values of *X* tend to be paired with small values of *Y*, and the large values of *X* tend to be associated with large values of *Y*.

EXAMPLE 3.18

COMPUTING THE SAMPLE COEFFICIENT OF CORRELATION

Consider the cost of a fast-food hamburger meal and the cost of two movie tickets in 10 cities around the world (see Table 3.10 on page 126). From Figure 3.11 and Equation (3.19), compute the sample coefficient of correlation.

SOLUTION
$$r = \frac{\text{cov}(X,Y)}{S_X S_Y}$$

$$= \frac{6.8378}{(1.2925)(6.337)}$$

$$= 0.8348$$

FIGURE 3.11

Microsoft Excel worksheet for the sample coefficient of correlation, r, between the cost of a fast-food hamburger meal and two movie tickets

See Appendix E3.5 to create this. (Use Section M3.3 to create the Minitab equivalent.)

	A	B	C	D	E
1	Hamburger Meal	Movie Ticket	(X-XBar)²	(Y-YBar)²	(X-XBar)(Y-YBar)
2	5.99	32.66	1.0221	157.1764	12.6749
3	7.62	28.41	6.9749	68.6744	21.8860
4	5.75	20.00	0.5944	0.0151	-0.0948
5	4.45	20.71	0.2798	0.3446	-0.3105
6	4.99	18.00	0.0001	4.5071	-0.0234
7	5.29	19.50	0.0967	0.3881	-0.1938
8	4.39	18.00	0.3469	4.5071	1.2504
9	3.70	16.00	1.6358	16.9991	5.2733
10	4.62	18.05	0.1289	4.2973	0.7442
11	2.99	9.90	3.9561	104.5097	20.3335
12		Sums:	15.03589	361.41901	61.5399
13					
14				Calculations	
15				XBar	4.979	=AVERAGE(A2:A11)
16				YBar	20.123	=AVERAGE(B2:B11)
17				n-1	9	=COUNT(A2:A11)-1
18				Covariance	6.83777	=E12 / E17
19				Sₓ	1.2925	=SQRT(C12 / E17)
20				Sᵧ	6.3370	=SQRT(D12 / E17)
21				r	0.8348	=CORREL(A2:A11, B2:B11)

The cost of a fast-food hamburger meal and the cost of two movie tickets are positively correlated. Those cities with the lowest cost of a fast-food hamburger meal tend to be associated with the lowest cost of two movie tickets. Those cities with the highest cost of a fast-food hamburger meal tend to be associated with the highest cost of two movie tickets. This relationship is strong, as indicated by a coefficient of correlation, $r = 0.8348$.

You cannot assume that having a low cost of a fast-food hamburger meal caused the low cost of two movie tickets. You can only say that this is what tended to happen in the sample.

In summary, the coefficient of correlation indicates the linear relationship, or association, between two numerical variables. When the coefficient of correlation gets closer to $+1$ or -1, the linear relationship between the two variables is stronger. When the coefficient of correlation is near 0, little or no linear relationship exists. The sign of the coefficient of correlation indicates whether the data are positively correlated (i.e., the larger values of X are typically paired with the larger values of Y) or negatively correlated (i.e., the larger values of X are typically paired with the smaller values of Y). The existence of a strong correlation does not imply a causation effect. It only indicates the tendencies present in the data.

PROBLEMS FOR SECTION 3.6

Learning the Basics

3.43 The following is a set of data from a sample of $n = 11$ items:

$$X \quad 7 \quad 5 \quad 8 \quad 3 \quad 6 \quad 10 \quad 12 \quad 4 \quad 9 \quad 15 \quad 18$$

$$Y \quad 21 \quad 15 \quad 24 \quad 9 \quad 18 \quad 30 \quad 36 \quad 12 \quad 27 \quad 45 \quad 54$$

a. Compute the covariance.
b. Compute the coefficient of correlation.
c. How strong is the relationship between X and Y? Explain.

Applying the Concepts

3.44 An article (P. Lim, "An Around-the-World Ticket for Your Portfolio," *The New York Times*, June 3, 2007, p. B5) that discussed investment in foreign stocks (over the last five years) stated that the coefficient of correlation between the return on investment of U.S. stocks (as expressed by the S & P 500) and the German stock market was 0.89, U.S. stocks (as expressed by the S & P 500) and Brazilian stock market was 0.68, and U.S. stocks (as expressed by the S & P 500) and the Japanese stock market was 0.29. What conclusions can you make about the strength of the relationship between the return on investment of U.S. stocks and each of these three other types of investments?

3.45 According to the Mortgage Bankers Association, home mortgage applications were rising as lower loan rates fostered home purchases and refinancings ("Mortgage Applications Creep Up as Rates Fall," **www.usatoday.com**, April 25, 2007).

a. Is the article implying that the number of home mortgages and loan rates are positively correlated, negatively correlated, or independent?
b. If you believe that the article is implying that the number of home mortgages and loan rates are correlated, do you believe that there is a cause-and-effect relationship? Discuss.

✓ SELF Test **3.46** The data in the file CoffeeDrink represent the calories and fat, in grams, of 16-ounce iced coffee drinks at Dunkin' Donuts and Starbucks:

Product	Calories	Fat
Dunkin' Donuts Iced Mocha Swirl latte (whole milk)	240	8.0
Starbucks Coffee Frappuccino blended coffee	260	3.5
Dunkin' Donuts Coffee Coolatta (cream)	350	22.0

Product	Calories	Fat
Starbucks Iced Coffee Mocha Expresso (whole milk and whipped cream)	350	20.0
Starbucks Mocha Frappuccino blended coffee (whipped cream)	420	16.0
Starbucks Chocolate Brownie Frappuccino blended coffee (whipped cream)	510	22.0
Starbucks Chocolate Frappuccino Blended Crème (whipped cream)	530	19.0

Source: *Extracted from "Coffee as Candy at Dunkin' Donuts and Starbucks,"* Consumer Reports, *June 2004, p. 9.*

a. Compute the covariance.
b. Compute the coefficient of correlation.
c. Which do you think is more valuable in expressing the relationship between calories and fat—the covariance or the coefficient of correlation? Explain.
d. What conclusions can you reach about the relationship between calories and fat?

3.47 There are several methods for calculating fuel economy. The following table (contained in the file Mileage) indicates the mileage, as calculated by owners and by current government standards:

Car	Owner	Government
2005 Ford F-150	14.3	16.8
2005 Chevrolet Silverado	15.0	17.8
2002 Honda Accord LX	27.8	26.2
2002 Honda Civic	27.9	34.2
2004 Honda Civic Hybrid	48.8	47.6
2002 Ford Explorer	16.8	18.3
2005 Toyota Camry	23.7	28.5
2003 Toyota Corolla	32.8	33.1
2005 Toyota Prius	37.3	56.0

Source: *Extracted from J. Healey, "Fuel Economy Calculations to Be Altered,"* USA Today, *January 11, 2006, p. 1B.*

a. Compute the covariance.
b. Compute the coefficient of correlation.
c. Which do you think is more valuable in expressing the relationship between owner and current government standards mileage—the covariance or the coefficient of correlation? Explain.
d. What conclusions can you reach about the relationship between owner and current government standards mileage?

3.48 College basketball is big business, with coaches' salaries, revenues, and expenses in millions of dollars. The data file Colleges-basketball contains the coaches' salaries and revenue for college basketball at selected schools in a recent year (extracted from R. Adams, "Pay for Playoffs," *The Wall Street Journal*, March 11–12, 2006, pp. P1, P8).

a. Compute the covariance.

b. Compute the coefficient of correlation.

c. What conclusions can you reach about the relationship between a coach's salary and revenue?

3.49 College football players trying out for the NFL are given the Wonderlic standardized intelligence test. The data in the file Wonderlic contains the average Wonderlic score of football players trying out for the NFL and the graduation rate for football players at selected schools (extracted from S. Walker, "The NFL's Smartest Team," *The Wall Street Journal*, September 30, 2005, pp. W1, W10).

a. Compute the covariance.

b. Compute the coefficient of correlation.

c. What conclusions can you reach about the relationship between the average Wonderlic score and graduation rate?

Presenting Descriptive Statistics: Pitfalls and Ethical Issues

From the Authors' Desktop

This chapter describes how a set of numerical data can be characterized by the statistics that measure the properties of central tendency, variation, and shape. In business, descriptive statistics such as the ones you have learned about are frequently included in summary reports that are prepared periodically.

The volume of information available on the Internet, in newspapers, and in magazines has produced much skepticism about the objectivity of data. When you are reading information that contains descriptive statistics, you should keep in mind the quip often attributed to the famous nineteenth-century British statesman Benjamin Disraeli: "There are three kinds of lies: lies, damned lies, and statistics."

For example, in examining statistics that are provided, you need to compare the mean and the median. Are they similar or are they very different? Or, is only the mean provided? The answers to these questions will enable you to know whether the data are skewed or symmetrical and whether the median might be a better measure of central tendency than the mean. In addition, you should look to see whether the standard deviation has been included in the statistics provided. Without the standard deviation, it is difficult to determine the amount of variation that exists in the data.

Ethical considerations arise when you are deciding what results to include in a report. You should document both good and bad results. In addition, when making oral presentations and presenting written reports, you need to give results in a fair, objective, and neutral manner. Unethical behavior occurs when you selectively fail to report pertinent findings that are detrimental to the support of a particular position.

SUMMARY

In this and the previous chapter, you studied descriptive statistics—how data are presented in tables and charts, and then summarized, described, analyzed, and interpreted. When dealing with the mutual fund data, you were able to present useful information through the use of pie charts, histograms, and other graphical methods. You explored characteristics of past performance, such as central tendency, variability, and shape, using numerical descriptive measures, such as the mean, median, quartiles, range, standard deviation, and coefficient of correlation. Table 3.11 provides a list of the numerical descriptive measures covered in this chapter.

In the next chapter, the basic principles of probability are presented in order to bridge the gap between the subject of descriptive statistics and the subject of inferential statistics.

TABLE 3.11

Summary of Numerical Descriptive Measures

Type of Analysis	Numerical Data
Describing central tendency, variation, and shape of a numerical variable	Mean, median, mode, quartiles, geometric mean, range, interquartile range, variance, standard deviation, coefficient of variation, Z scores, boxplot (**Sections 3.1, 3.2, 3.5**)
Describing the relationship between two numerical variables	Covariance, coefficient of correlation (**Section 3.6**)

KEY EQUATIONS

Sample Mean

$$\bar{X} = \frac{\sum_{i=1}^{n} X_i}{n} \tag{3.1}$$

Median

$$\text{Median} = \frac{n+1}{2} \text{ ranked value} \tag{3.2}$$

Geometric Mean

$$\bar{X}_G = (X_1 \times X_2 \times \cdots \times X_n)^{1/n} \tag{3.3}$$

Geometric Mean Rate of Return

$$\bar{R}_G = [(1+R_1) \times (1+R_2) \times \cdots \times (1+R_n)]^{1/n} - 1 \tag{3.4}$$

Range

$$\text{Range} = X_{\text{largest}} - X_{\text{smallest}} \tag{3.5}$$

Sample Variance

$$S^2 = \frac{\sum_{i=1}^{n} (X_i - \bar{X})^2}{n-1} \tag{3.6}$$

Sample Standard Deviation

$$S = \sqrt{S^2} = \sqrt{\frac{\sum_{i=1}^{n} (X_i - \bar{X})^2}{n-1}} \tag{3.7}$$

Coefficient of Variation

$$CV = \left(\frac{S}{\bar{X}}\right) 100\% \tag{3.8}$$

Z Scores

$$Z = \frac{X - \bar{X}}{S} \tag{3.9}$$

Population Mean

$$\mu = \frac{\sum_{i=1}^{N} X_i}{N} \tag{3.10}$$

Population Variance

$$\sigma^2 = \frac{\sum_{i=1}^{N} (X_i - \mu)^2}{N} \tag{3.11}$$

Population Standard Deviation

$$\sigma = \sqrt{\frac{\sum_{i=1}^{N} (X_i - \mu)^2}{N}} \tag{3.12}$$

Mean of a Frequency Distribution

$$\bar{X} = \frac{\sum_{j=1}^{c} m_j f_j}{n} \tag{3.13}$$

Standard Deviation of a Frequency Distribution

$$S = \sqrt{\frac{\sum_{j=1}^{c} (m_j - \bar{X})^2 f_j}{n-1}} \tag{3.14}$$

First Quartile Q_1

$$Q_1 = \frac{n+1}{4} \text{ ranked value} \tag{3.15}$$

Third Quartile Q_3

$$Q_3 = \frac{3(n+1)}{4} \text{ ranked value} \tag{3.16}$$

Interquartile Range

$$\text{Interquartile range} = Q_3 - Q_1 \tag{3.17}$$

Sample Covariance

$$\text{cov}(X,Y) = \frac{\sum_{i=1}^{n}(X_i - \bar{X})(Y_i - \bar{Y})}{n-1} \qquad (3.18)$$

Sample Coefficient of Correlation

$$r = \frac{\text{cov}(X,Y)}{S_X S_Y} \qquad (3.19)$$

KEY TERMS

arithmetic mean   90
boxplot   121
central tendency   90
Chebyshev rule   112
coefficient of correlation   126
coefficient of variation   101
covariance   125
dispersion   96
empirical rule   112
extreme value   102
five-number summary   120
geometric mean   95
geometric mean rate of return   95
interquartile range   119
left-skewed   104

mean   90
median   93
midspread   119
mode   94
outlier   102
population mean   110
population standard deviation   110
population variance   110
Q_1: first quartile   117
Q_2: second quartile   117
Q_3: third quartile   117
quartiles   117
range   97
resistant measure   120
right-skewed   104

sample coefficient of correlation   127
sample covariance   125
sample mean   91
sample standard deviation   98
sample variance   98
shape   90
skewed   104
spread   96
standard deviation   97
sum of squares (*SS*)   98
symmetrical   104
variance   97
variation   90
Z score   102

CHAPTER REVIEW PROBLEMS

Checking Your Understanding

3.50 What are the properties of a set of numerical data?

3.51 What is meant by the property of central tendency?

3.52 What are the differences among the mean, median, and mode, and what are the advantages and disadvantages of each?

3.53 How do you interpret the first quartile, median, and third quartile?

3.54 What is meant by the property of variation?

3.55 What does the *Z* score measure?

3.56 What are the differences among the various measures of variation, such as the range, interquartile range, variance, standard deviation, and coefficient of variation, and what are the advantages and disadvantages of each?

3.57 How does the empirical rule help explain the ways in which the values in a set of numerical data cluster and distribute?

3.58 How do the empirical rule and the Chebyshev rule differ?

3.59 What is meant by the property of shape?

3.60 How do the covariance and the coefficient of correlation differ?

Applying the Concepts

3.61 The American Society for Quality (ASQ) conducted a salary survey of all its members. ASQ members work in all areas of manufacturing and service-related institutions, with a common theme of an interest in quality. For the U.S. survey, e-mails were sent to 70,645 members, and 10,848 valid responses were received. The two most common job titles were manager and quality engineer. Another title is Master Black Belt, who is a person who takes a leadership role as the keeper of the Six Sigma process (see Section 18.8). Descriptive statistics concerning salaries for these three titles are given on page 134 (extracted from M. Edmund, "Elevation Almost Everywhere," *Quality Progress*, December 2006, pp. 21–48). Compare the salaries of managers, quality engineers, and Master Black Belts.

Title	Sample Size	Minimum	Maximum	Standard Deviation	Mean	Median
Manager	2,615	25,000	178,000	22,266	80,837	80,000
Quality Engineer	1,617	25,000	160,000	17,316	68,028	66,000
Master Black Belt	155	46,000	200,000	25,010	106,617	105,000

3.62 In New York State, savings banks are permitted to sell a form of life insurance called savings bank life insurance (SBLI). The approval process consists of underwriting, which includes a review of the application, a medical information bureau check, possible requests for additional medical information and medical exams, and a policy compilation stage during which the policy pages are generated and sent to the bank for delivery. The ability to deliver approved policies to customers in a timely manner is critical to the profitability of this service to the bank. During a period of one month, a random sample of 27 approved policies was selected, and the following total processing times in days were recorded; the data are contained in the file Insurance:

73 19 16 64 28 28 31 90 60 56 31 56 22 18

45 48 17 17 17 91 92 63 50 51 69 16 17

a. Compute the mean, median, first quartile, and third quartile.
b. Compute the range, interquartile range, variance, standard deviation, and coefficient of variation.
c. Construct a boxplot. Are the data skewed? If so, how?
d. What would you tell a customer who enters the bank to purchase this type of insurance policy and asks how long the approval process takes?

3.63 One of the major measures of the quality of service provided by any organization is the speed with which it responds to customer complaints. A large family-held department store selling furniture and flooring, including carpet, had undergone a major expansion in the past several years. In particular, the flooring department had expanded from 2 installation crews to an installation supervisor, a measurer, and 15 installation crews. A sample of 50 complaints concerning carpet installation was selected during a recent year. The data in the file Furniture represent the number of days between the receipt of a complaint and the resolution of the complaint:

54   5   35 137 31 27 152   2 123 81 74 27 11

19 126 110 110 29 61   35 94   31 26   5 12   4

165 32 29 28 29 26 25   1 14 13 13 10   5

27   4 52 30 22 36 26 20 23 33 68

a. Compute the mean, median, first quartile, and third quartile.

b. Compute the range, interquartile range, variance, standard deviation, and coefficient of variation.
c. Construct a boxplot. Are the data skewed? If so, how?
d. On the basis of the results of (a) through (c), if you had to tell the president of the company how long a customer should expect to wait to have a complaint resolved, what would you say? Explain.

3.64 A manufacturing company produces steel housings for electrical equipment. The main component part of the housing is a steel trough that is made out of a 14-gauge steel coil. It is produced using a 250-ton progressive punch press with a wipe-down operation, putting two 90-degree forms in the flat steel to make the trough. The distance from one side of the form to the other is critical because of weatherproofing in outdoor applications. The company requires that the width of the trough be between 8.31 inches and 8.61 inches. The data file Trough contains the widths of the troughs, in inches, for a sample of $n = 49$:

8.312 8.343 8.317 8.383 8.348 8.410 8.351 8.373 8.481 8.422

8.476 8.382 8.484 8.403 8.414 8.419 8.385 8.465 8.498 8.447

8.436 8.413 8.489 8.414 8.481 8.415 8.479 8.429 8.458 8.462

8.460 8.444 8.429 8.460 8.412 8.420 8.410 8.405 8.323 8.420

8.396 8.447 8.405 8.439 8.411 8.427 8.420 8.498 8.409

a. Calculate the mean, median, range, and standard deviation for the width. Interpret these measures of central tendency and variability.
b. List the five-number summary.
c. Construct a boxplot and describe its shape.
d. What can you conclude about the number of troughs that will meet the company's requirement of troughs being between 8.31 and 8.61 inches wide?

3.65 The manufacturing company in Problem 3.64 also produces electric insulators. If the insulators break when in use, a short circuit is likely to occur. To test the strength of the insulators, destructive testing is carried out to determine how much force is required to break the insulators. Force is measured by observing how many pounds must be applied to the insulator before it breaks. The data from 30 insulators from this experiment are contained in the file Force:

1,870 1,728 1,656 1,610 1,634 1,784 1,522 1,696 1,592 1,662

1,866 1,764 1,734 1,662 1,734 1,774 1,550 1,756 1,762 1,866

1,820 1,744 1,788 1,688 1,810 1,752 1,680 1,810 1,652 1,736

a. Calculate the mean, median, range, and standard deviation for the force needed to break the insulator.
b. Interpret the measures of central tendency and variability in (a).
c. Construct a boxplot and describe its shape.

d. What can you conclude about the strength of the insulators if the company requires a force measurement of at least 1,500 pounds before breakage?

3.66 The data contained in the file Tuition2006 consist of the in-state tuition and fees and the out-of-state tuition and fees for four-year colleges with the highest percentage of students graduating within six years.

Source: *U.S. Department of Education, 2006.*

For each variable:
a. Compute the mean, median, first quartile, and third quartile.
b. Compute the range, interquartile range, variance, standard deviation, and coefficient of variation.
c. Construct a boxplot. Are the data skewed? If so, how?
d. Compute the coefficient of correlation between the in-state tuition and fees and the out-of-state tuition and fees.
e. What conclusions can you reach concerning the in-state tuition and fees and the out-of-state tuition and fees?

3.67 A quality characteristic of interest for a tea-bag-filling process is the weight of the tea in the individual bags. If the bags are underfilled, two problems arise. First, customers may not be able to brew the tea to be as strong as they wish. Second, the company may be in violation of the truth-in-labeling laws. For this product, the label weight on the package indicates that, on average, there are 5.5 grams of tea in a bag. If the mean amount of tea in a bag exceeds the label weight, the company is giving away product. Getting an exact amount of tea in a bag is problematic because of variation in the temperature and humidity inside the factory, differences in the density of the tea, and the extremely fast filling operation of the machine (approximately 170 bags per minute). The data in the file Teabags shown below provide the weight, in grams, of a sample of 50 tea bags produced in one hour by a single machine:

5.65 5.44 5.42 5.40 5.53 5.34 5.54 5.45 5.52 5.41

5.57 5.40 5.53 5.54 5.55 5.62 5.56 5.46 5.44 5.51

5.47 5.40 5.47 5.61 5.53 5.32 5.67 5.29 5.49 5.55

5.77 5.57 5.42 5.58 5.58 5.50 5.32 5.50 5.53 5.58

5.61 5.45 5.44 5.25 5.56 5.63 5.50 5.57 5.67 5.36

a. Compute the mean, median, first quartile, and third quartile.
b. Compute the range, interquartile range, variance, standard deviation, and coefficient of variation.
c. Interpret the measures of central tendency and variation within the context of this problem. Why should the company producing the tea bags be concerned about the central tendency and variation?
d. Construct a boxplot. Are the data skewed? If so, how?

e. Is the company meeting the requirement set forth on the label that, on average, there are 5.5 grams of tea in a bag? If you were in charge of this process, what changes, if any, would you try to make concerning the distribution of weights in the individual bags?

3.68 The manufacturer of Boston and Vermont asphalt shingles provides its customers with a 20-year warranty on most of its products. To determine whether a shingle will last as long as the warranty period, accelerated-life testing is conducted at the manufacturing plant. Accelerated-life testing exposes the shingle to the stresses it would be subject to in a lifetime of normal use via an experiment in a laboratory setting that takes only a few minutes to conduct. In this test, a shingle is repeatedly scraped with a brush for a short period of time, and the shingle granules removed by the brushing are weighed (in grams). Shingles that experience low amounts of granule loss are expected to last longer in normal use than shingles that experience high amounts of granule loss. In this situation, a shingle should experience no more than 0.8 gram of granule loss if it is expected to last the length of the warranty period. The data file Granule contains a sample of 170 measurements made on the company's Boston shingles and 140 measurements made on Vermont shingles.
a. List the five-number summary for the Boston shingles and for the Vermont shingles.
b. Construct side-by-side boxplots for the two brands of shingles and describe the shapes of the distributions.
c. Comment on the shingles' ability to achieve a granule loss of 0.8 gram or less.

3.69 A study conducted by Zagat Survey concluded that many first-rate restaurants are located in hotels across the United States. Travelers can find quality food, service, and décor without leaving their hotels. The top-rated hotel restaurant is The French Room, located in The Adolphus Hotel in Dallas, Texas. The estimated price for dinner, including one drink and tip, at The French Room is $80. The highest price reported is $179 at Alain Ducasse, located in the Jumeirah Essex House in New York City (extracted from Gary Stoller, "Top Restaurants Check into Luxury Hotels," *USA Today*, April 11, 2006, p. 5B). The file Bestrest contains the top 100 hotel restaurants in the United States and the variables state, city, restaurant, hotel, cost (estimated price of dinner including one drink and tip), and rating (1 to 100, with 1 the top-rated restaurant).
a. Construct the five-number summary of dinner price.
b. Construct a boxplot of dinner price and interpret the distribution of dinner prices.
c. Calculate and interpret the correlation coefficient of the rating and dinner price.

3.70 The data in the file Chicken contains the characteristics for a sample of 20 chicken sandwiches from fast-food chains.

a. Compute the correlation coefficient between calories and carbohydrates.

b. Compute the correlation coefficient between calories and sodium.

c. Compute the correlation coefficient between calories and total fat.

d. Which variable (total fat, carbohydrates, or sodium) seems to be most closely related to calories? Explain.

3.71 In Example 3.18 on page 129, the correlation coefficient between the cost of a fast-food hamburger meal and the cost of movie tickets in 10 different cities was computed. The data file `Cost of living` also includes the overall cost index, the monthly rent for a two-bedroom apartment, and the costs of a cup of coffee with service, dry cleaning for a men's blazer, and toothpaste.

a. Compute the correlation coefficient between the overall cost index and the monthly rent for a two-bedroom apartment, the cost of a cup of coffee with service, the cost of a fast-food hamburger meal, the cost of dry-cleaning a men's blazer, the cost of toothpaste, and the cost of movie tickets. (There will be six separate correlation coefficients.)

b. What conclusions can you reach about the relationship of the overall cost index to each of these six variables?

3.72 The data in the file `Spending` is the per-capita spending, in thousands of dollars, for each state in 2004.

a. Compute the mean, median, first quartile, and third quartile.

b. Compute the range, interquartile range, variance, standard deviation, and coefficient of variation.

c. Construct a boxplot. Are the data skewed? If so, how?

d. What conclusions can you reach concerning per-capita spending, in thousands of dollars, for each state in 2004?

3.73 The data in the file `CEO` represent the total compensation (in $millions) of CEOs of the 100 largest companies, by revenue (extracted from "Special Report: Executive Compensation," *USA Today*, April 10, 2006, pp. 3B, 4B).

a. Compute the mean, median, first quartile, and third quartile.

b. Compute the range, interquartile range, variance, standard deviation, and coefficient of variation.

c. Construct a boxplot. Are the data skewed? If so, how?

d. What conclusions can you draw concerning the total compensation (in $millions) of CEOs?

3.74 You are planning to study for your statistics examination with a group of classmates, one of whom you particularly want to impress. This individual has volunteered to use Microsoft Excel or Minitab to get the needed summary information, tables, and charts for a data set containing several numerical and categorical variables assigned by the instructor for study purposes. This person comes over to you with the printout and exclaims, "I've got it all–the means, the medians, the standard deviations, the boxplots, the pie charts—for all our variables. The problem is, some of the output looks weird—like the boxplots for gender and for major and the pie charts for grade point index and for height. Also, I can't understand why Professor Krehbiel said we can't get the descriptive stats for some of the variables—I got them for everything! See, the mean for height is 68.23, the mean for grade point index is 2.76, the mean for gender is 1.50, the mean for major is 4.33." What is your reply?

Report Writing Exercises

3.75 Data concerning 71 of the best-selling domestic beers in the United States are located in the file `Domesticbeer`. The values for three variables are included: percentage alcohol, number of calories per 12 ounces, and number of carbohydrates (in grams) per 12 ounces.

Source: *Extracted from* **www.Beer100.com**, *May 4, 2007.*

Your task is to write a report based on a complete descriptive evaluation of each of the numerical variables—percentage alcohol, number of calories per 12 ounces, and number of carbohydrates (in grams) per 12 ounces. Appended to your report should be all appropriate tables, charts, and numerical descriptive measures.

Team Projects

The data file `Mutual Funds` contains information regarding nine variables from a sample of 868 mutual funds:

Category—Type of stocks comprising the mutual fund (small cap, mid cap, large cap)

Objective—Objective of stocks comprising the mutual fund (growth or value)

Assets—In millions of dollars

Fees—Sales charges (no or yes)

Expense ratio—Ratio of expenses to net assets in percentage

Risk—Risk-of-loss factor of the mutual fund (low, average, high)

2006 return—Twelve-month return in 2006

Three-year return—Annualized return, 2004–2006

Five-year return—Annualized return, 2002–2006

3.76 For expense ratio in percentage, three-year return, and five-year return,

a. Compute the mean, median, first quartile, and third quartile.

b. Compute the range, interquartile range, variance, standard deviation, and coefficient of variation.

c. Construct a boxplot. Are the data skewed? If so, how?

d. What conclusions can you reach concerning these variables?

3.77 You wish to compare mutual funds that have fees to those that do not have fees. For each of these two groups, for the variables expense ratio in percentage, 2006 return, three-year return, and five-year return,
a. Compute the mean, median, first quartile, and third quartile.
b. Compute the range, interquartile range, variance, standard deviation, and coefficient of variation.
c. Construct a boxplot. Are the data skewed? If so, how?
d. What conclusions can you reach about differences between mutual funds that have fees and those that do not have fees?

3.78 You wish to compare mutual funds that have a growth objective to those that have a value objective. For each of these two groups, for the variables expense ratio in percentage, three-year return, and five-year return,
a. Compute the mean, median, first quartile, and third quartile.
b. Compute the range, interquartile range, variance, standard deviation, and coefficient of variation.
c. Construct a boxplot. Are the data skewed? If so, how?
d. What conclusions can you reach about differences between mutual funds that have a growth objective and those that have a value objective?

3.79 You wish to compare small cap, mid cap, and large cap mutual funds. For each of these three groups, for the variables expense ratio in percentage, 2006 return, three-year return, and five-year return,
a. Compute the mean, median, first quartile, and third quartile.
b. Compute the range, interquartile range, variance, standard deviation, and coefficient of variation.
c. Construct a boxplot. Are the data skewed? If so, how?
d. What conclusions can you reach about differences between small cap, mid cap, and large cap mutual funds?

Student Survey Data Base

3.80 Problem 1.27 on page 14 describes a survey of 50 undergraduate students (see the file Undergradsurvey). For these data, for each numerical variable,
a. Compute the mean, median, first quartile, and third quartile.
b. Compute the range, interquartile range, variance, standard deviation, and coefficient of variation.
c. Construct a boxplot. Are the data skewed? If so, how?
d. Write a report summarizing your conclusions.

3.81 Problem 1.27 on page 14 describes a survey of 50 undergraduate students (see the file Undergradsurvey).
a. Select a sample of 50 undergraduate students at your school and conduct a similar survey for those students.
b. For the data collected in (a), repeat (a) through (d) of Problem 3.80.
c. Compare the results of (b) to those of Problem 3.80.

3.82 Problem 1.28 on page 14 describes a survey of 40 MBA students (see the file Gradsurvey). For these data, for each numerical variable,
a. Compute the mean, median, first quartile, and third quartile.
b. Compute the range, interquartile range, variance, standard deviation, and coefficient of variation.
c. Construct a boxplot. Are the data skewed? If so, how?
d. Write a report summarizing your conclusions.

3.83 Problem 1.28 on page 14 describes a survey of 40 MBA students (see the file Gradsurvey).
a. Select a sample of 40 graduate students from your MBA program and conduct a similar survey for those students.
b. For the data collected in (a), repeat (a) through (d) of Problem 3.82.
c. Compare the results of (b) to those of Problem 3.82.

MANAGING THE *SPRINGVILLE HERALD*

For what variable in the Chapter 2 "Managing the *Springville Herald*" case (see page 68) are numerical descriptive measures needed? For the variable you identify:

1. Compute the appropriate numerical descriptive measures, and construct a boxplot.

2. Identify another graphical display that might be useful and construct it. What conclusions can you form from that plot that cannot be made from the boxplot?

3. Summarize your findings in a report that can be included with the task force's study.

WEB CASE

Apply your knowledge about the proper use of numerical descriptive measures in this continuing Web Case from Chapter 2.

Visit EndRun Financial Services, at **www.prenhall.com/ Springville/EndRun.htm** (or open the `EndRun.htm` file in the Student CD-ROM Web Case folder) a second time and reexamine their supporting data and then answer the following:

1. Can descriptive measures be computed for any variables? How would such summary statistics support EndRun's claims? How would those summary statistics affect your perception of EndRun's record?

2. Evaluate the methods EndRun used to summarize the results of its customer survey (see **www.prenhall.com/ Springville/ER_Survey.htm** or the `ER_Survey.htm` file on the Student CD-ROM Web Case folder). Is there anything you would do differently to summarize these results?

3. Note that the last question of the survey has fewer responses than the other questions. What factors may have limited the number of responses to that question?

REFERENCES

1. Kendall, M. G., A. Stuart, and J. K. Ord, *Kendall's Advanced Theory of Statistics, Volume 1: Distribution Theory*, 6th ed. (New York: Oxford University Press, 1994).
2. *Microsoft Excel 2007* (Redmond, WA: Microsoft Corporation, 2007).
3. *Minitab for Windows Version 15* (State College, PA: Minitab, Inc., 2006).
4. Tukey, J., *Exploratory Data Analysis* (Reading, MA: Addison-Wesley, 1977).
5. Velleman, P. F., and D. C. Hoaglin, *Applications, Basics, and Computing of Exploratory Data Analysis* (Boston: Duxbury Press, 1981).

Appendix E3
Using Microsoft Excel for Descriptive Statistics

E3.1 Computing Measures of Central Tendency, Variation, and Shape

You compute measures of central tendency, variation, and shape by either using the ToolPak Descriptive Statistics procedure or by using worksheet functions. Use the ToolPak procedure when you want to create a list of summary statistics similar to the one shown in Figure 3.2 on page 105. Use worksheet functions when you want to add one or a few descriptive measures to a worksheet (as is done in Figure 3.8 on page 126).

Using ToolPak Descriptive Statistics

Open to the worksheet containing your data to be summarized. Select **Tools → Data Analysis** (Excel 97–2003) or **Data → Data Analysis** (Excel 2007). In the Data Analysis dialog box, select **Descriptive Statistics** from the **Analysis Tools** list and then click **OK**. In the Descriptive Statistics dialog box (shown in Figure E3.1), enter the cell range of the data as the **Input Range**. Click the **Columns** option and **Labels in first row**. Finish by clicking **New Worksheet Ply**, **Summary statistics**, **Kth Largest**, and **Kth Smallest**, and then **OK**.

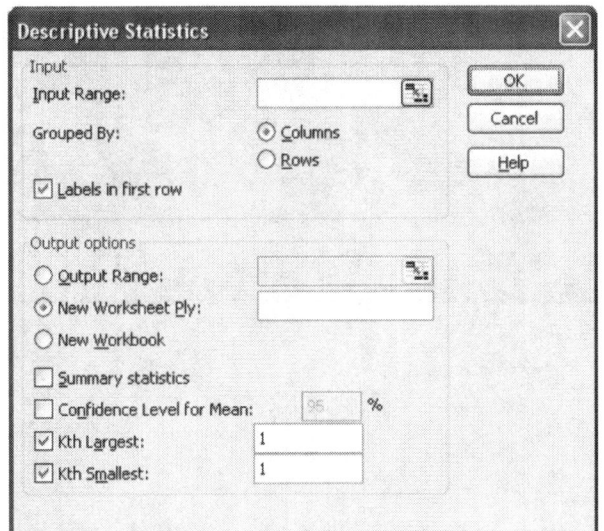

FIGURE E3.1

ToolPak Descriptive Statistics dialog box

To compute descriptive statistics for a variable by sub-groups, as was done in Figure 3.2 on page 105 for the growth and value subgroups, first sort your data by the categorical variable to which the subgroups belong. Next, repeat the instructions given on page 138 for each subgroup using the cell range of the subgroup and the New Worksheet Ply option each time. Then copy and paste the results found in the second and subsequent worksheets to this first sheet to create a multiple column table similar to the one shown in Figure 3.2.

Using Worksheet Functions

You use the worksheet functions SUM, COUNT, AVERAGE (for mean), MEDIAN, MODE, QUARTILE, or GEOMEAN to compute measures of central tendency or STDEV, VAR, MIN, MAX, LARGE, or SMALL to compute measures of shape and variation. For all but QUARTILE, enter a formula in the form *=WorksheetFunction(cell range of data to be summarized)*. For QUARTILE enter the formula in the form *= WorksheetFunction(cell range of data to be summarized, quartile number)*. Use 1 as the *quartile number* to compute the first quartile, 2 to compute the second quartile (the median), or 3 to compute the third quartile. In Excel versions earlier than Excel 2003, you may encounter some minor errors in results when using the QUARTILE function.

E3.2 Computing Measures for a Population

To compute the population variance and standard deviation use the worksheet functions VARP and STDEVP. To use either function, enter a formula into a blank cell in the form *=WorksheetFunction(cell range of data to be summarized)*.

E3.3 Creating Boxplots

You create boxplots by entering a five-number summary into the tinted cell range B2:B6 of the **Plot** worksheet of the Boxplot.xls workbook. The workbook uses the contents of this range to create a boxplot on the Plot worksheet.

E3.4 Computing the Covariance

You compute the covariance by making entries in the **Covariance** worksheet of the Covariance.xls workbook, shown in Figure 3.8 on page 126. If you want to use this worksheet with other pairs of variables, follow the instructions in the worksheet for modifying the table area. The worksheet gains its flexibility by the cell C18 formula that uses the COUNT function to determine the sample size n. This allows the worksheet to always use the proper value of $n - 1$ for the covariance calculation when you change the size of the table area.

E3.5 Computing the Coefficient of Correlation

You compute the correlation coefficient by making entries in the **Correlation** worksheet of the Correlation.xls workbook, shown in Figure 3.11 on page 129. If you want to use this worksheet with other pairs of variables, follow the instructions in the worksheet for modifying the table area. This worksheet shares some of the design of the covariance worksheet discussed in the previous section.

This worksheet uses the CORREL function in the formula $=CORREL(A2:A11, B2:B11)$ in cell E21 to compute the correlation coefficient. Because the covariance, S_X, and S_Y are computed elsewhere in this worksheet, the formula $=E18/(E19 * E20)$ could also be used to compute the correlation coefficient statistic.

Appendix P3
Using PHStat2 for Descriptive Statistics

P3.1 Creating Boxplots

To create boxplots, use **PHStat → Descriptive Statistics → Boxplot**. This procedure accepts data for a single group or multiple groups as either unstacked data (column by column) or stacked data (one column). If you use the **Multiple Groups-Stacked** option, you will also need to enter the **Grouping Variable Cell Range**.

The procedure creates a custom worksheet and then uses Excel charting features to create a boxplot from the data of that worksheet. If you click **Five-Number Summary**, a five-number summary appears on a separate worksheet.

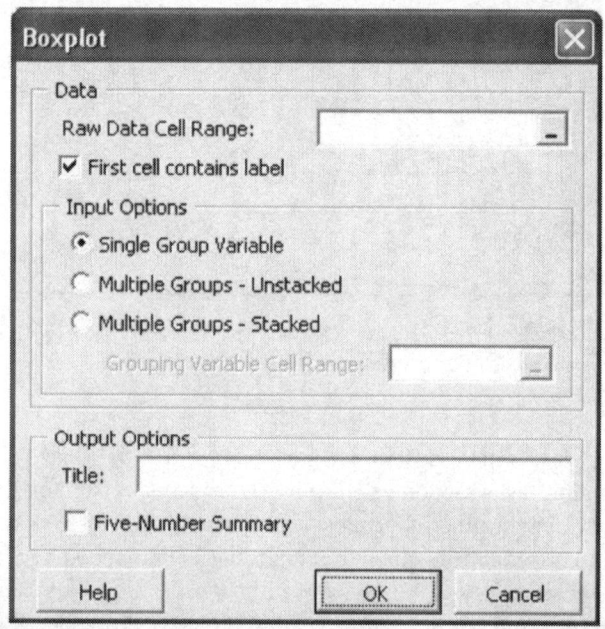

Appendix M3
Using Minitab for Descriptive Statistics

M3.1 Computing Descriptive Statistics

To create descriptive statistics for the 2006 return for different objectives shown in Figure 3.3 on page 106:

1. Open the **Mutual Funds.mtw** worksheet.
2. Select **Stat → Basic Statistics → Display Descriptive Statistics**.

In the Display Descriptive Statistics dialog box (see Figure M3.1):

3. Enter **'Return 2006'** in the **Variables** box.
4. Enter **Objective** in the **By variables (optional)** box.
5. Click **Statistics**.
6. In the Display Descriptive Statistics - Statistics dialog box (see Figure M3.2), select **Mean**, **Standard deviation**, **Coefficient of variation**, **First quartile**, **Median**, **Third quartile**, **Interquartile range**, **Minimum**, **Maximum**, **Range**, **Skewness**, **Kurtosis**,

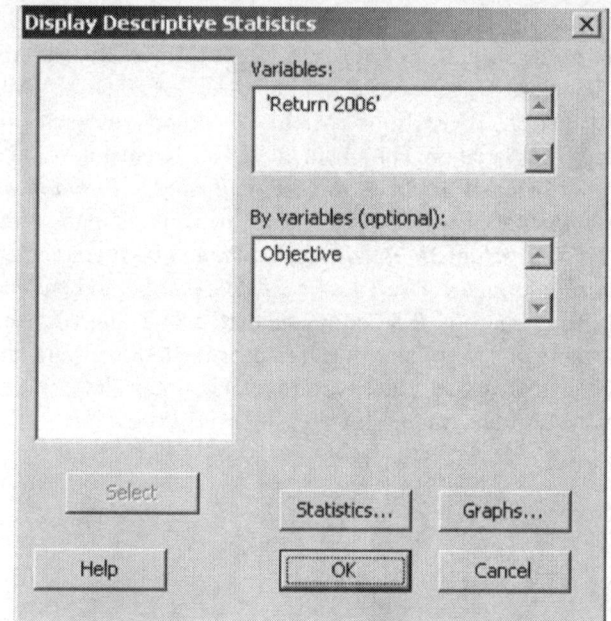

FIGURE M3.1

Minitab Display Descriptive Statistics dialog box

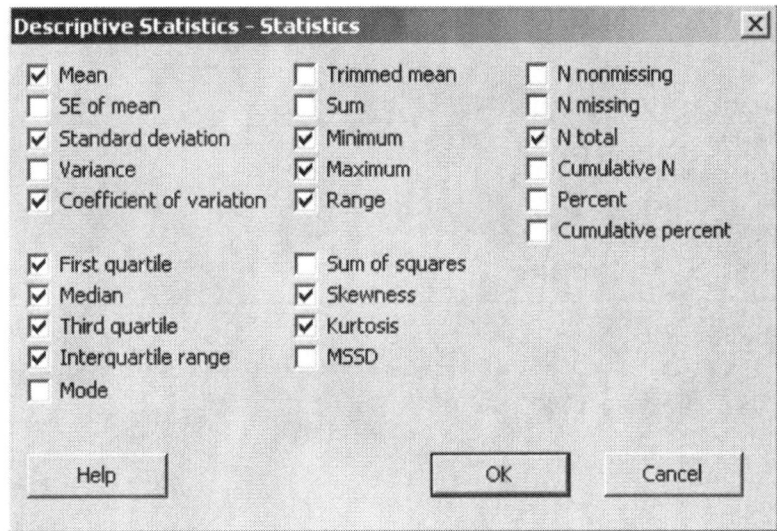

FIGURE M3.2
Minitab Display Descriptive Statistics - Statistics dialog box

and **N total** and then click **OK** to return to the Display Descriptive Statistics dialog box.

7. Back in the Display Descriptive Statistics dialog box, click **OK**.

M3.2 Creating Boxplots

To create a boxplot for the 2006 return for different objectives shown in Figure 3.6 on page 123:

1. Open the **Mutual Funds.mtw** worksheet.
2. Select **Graph → Boxplot**.

In the Boxplots dialog box (see Figure M3.3):

3. Click **With Groups** in the **One Y** gallery. (You would click **Simple** in the **One Y** gallery if you were creating a boxplot for one group.)
4. Click **OK**.

In the Boxplot - One Y, With Groups dialog box (see Figure M3.4):

5. Enter **'Return 2006'** in the **Graph variables** box.
6. Enter **Objective** in the **Categorical variables** box.
7. Click the **Scale** button.
8. Select the **Transpose value and category scales** box.
9. Click **OK**.
10. Click **OK** (to create the boxplot).

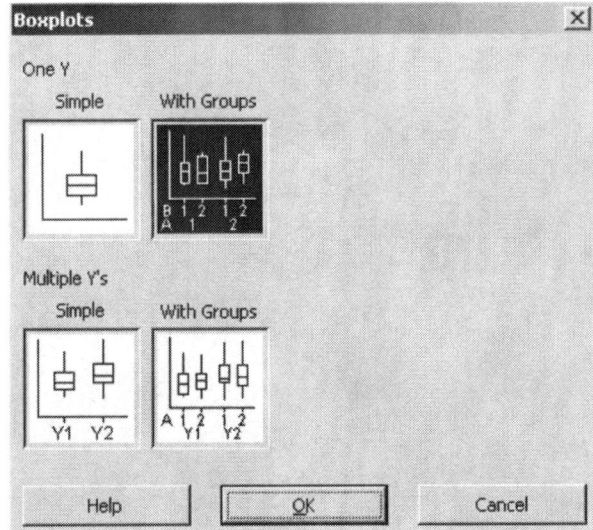

FIGURE M3.3
Minitab Boxplots dialog box

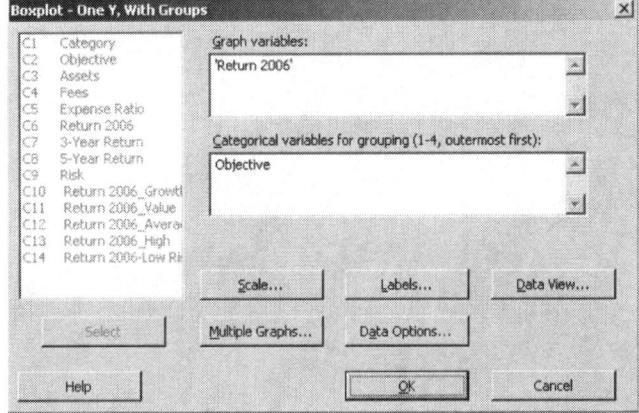

FIGURE M3.4
Minitab Boxplots - One Y, With Groups dialog box

M3.3 Computing the Coefficient of Correlation

To compute the coefficient of correlation for the cost of a fast-food hamburger meal and the cost of two movie tickets in ten cities (see Table 3.10 on page 126):

1. Open the `Cost of Living.mtw` worksheet.
2. Select **Stat → Basic Statistics → Correlation**.

In the Correlation dialog box (see Figure M3.5):

3. Enter **Hamburger** and **'Movie Tickets'** in the **Variables** box.
4. Click **OK**.

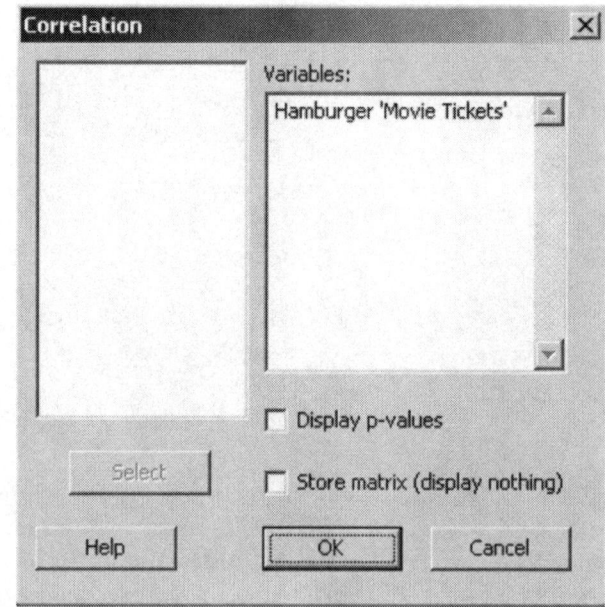

FIGURE M3.5
Minitab Correlation dialog box

CHAPTER
FOUR

BASIC PROBABILITY

USING STATISTICS @ M&R Electronics World

LEARNING OBJECTIVES

In this chapter, you learn:

- Basic probability concepts
- Conditional probability
- To use Bayes' theorem to revise probabilities
- Various counting rules

USING STATISTICS @ M&R Electronics World

As the marketing manager for M&R Electronics World, you are analyzing the survey results of an intent-to-purchase study. This study asked the heads of 1,000 households about their intentions to purchase a big-screen television (defined as 36 inches or larger) sometime during the next 12 months. Investigations of this type are known as *intent-to-purchase studies*. As a follow-up, you plan to survey the same people 12 months later to see whether such a television was purchased. In addition, for households purchasing big-screen televisions, you would like to know whether the television they purchased was a plasma screen, whether they also purchased a digital video recorder (DVR) in the past 12 months, and whether they were satisfied with their purchase of the big-screen television.

You are expected to use the results of this survey to plan a new marketing strategy that will enhance sales and better target those households likely to purchase multiple or more expensive products. What questions can you ask in this survey? How can you express the relationships among the various intent-to-purchase responses of individual households?

In previous chapters, you learned descriptive methods to summarize categorical and numerical variables. In this chapter, you will learn about probability to answer questions such as the following:

- What is the probability that a household is planning to purchase a big-screen television in the next year?
- What is the probability that a household will actually purchase a big-screen television?
- What is the probability that a household is planning to purchase a big-screen television and actually purchases the television?
- Given that the household is planning to purchase a big-screen television, what is the probability that the purchase is made?
- Does knowledge of whether a household *plans* to purchase the television change the likelihood of predicting whether the household *will* purchase the television?
- What is the probability that a household that purchases a big-screen television will purchase a plasma-screen television?
- What is the probability that a household that purchases a big-screen television with a plasma screen will also purchase a DVR?
- What is the probability that a household that purchases a big-screen television will be satisfied with the purchase?

With answers to questions such as these, you can begin to make decisions about your marketing strategy. Should your strategy for selling more big-screen televisions target those households that have indicated an intent to purchase? Should you concentrate on selling plasma screens? Is it likely that households that purchase big-screen televisions with plasma screens can be easily persuaded to also purchase DVRs?

The principles of probability help bridge the worlds of descriptive statistics and inferential statistics. Reading this chapter will help you learn about different types of probabilities, how to compute probabilities, and how to revise probabilities in light of new information. Probability principles are the foundation for the probability distribution, the concept of mathematical expectation, and the binomial, hypergeometric, and Poisson distributions, topics that are discussed in Chapter 5.

4.1 BASIC PROBABILITY CONCEPTS

What is meant by the word *probability*? A **probability** is the numeric value representing the chance, likelihood, or possibility a particular event will occur, such as the price of a stock increasing, a rainy day, a defective product, or the outcome five in a single toss of a die. In all these instances, the probability involved is a proportion or fraction whose value ranges between 0 and 1, inclusive. An event that has no chance of occurring (i.e., the **impossible event**) has a probability of 0. An event that is sure to occur (i.e., the **certain event**) has a probability of 1.

There are three types of probability:

- *A priori*
- Empirical
- Subjective

In *a priori* **probability**, the probability of success is based on prior knowledge of the process involved. In the simplest case, where each outcome is equally likely, the chance of occurrence of the event is defined in Equation (4.1).

Probability of Occurrence

$$\text{Probability of occurrence} = \frac{X}{T} \qquad (4.1)$$

where

X = number of ways in which the event occurs

T = total number of possible outcomes

Consider a standard deck of cards that has 26 red cards and 26 black cards. The probability of selecting a black card is $26/52 = 0.50$ because there are $X = 26$ black cards and $T = 52$ total cards. What does this probability mean? If each card is replaced after it is selected, does it mean that 1 out of the next 2 cards selected will be black? No, because you cannot say for certain what will happen on the next several selections. However, you can say that in the long run, if this selection process is continually repeated, the proportion of black cards selected will approach 0.50.

EXAMPLE 4.1

FINDING *A PRIORI* PROBABILITIES

A standard six-sided die has six faces. Each face of the die contains either one, two, three, four, five, or six dots. If you roll a die, what is the probability that you will get a face with five dots?

SOLUTION Each face is equally likely to occur. Because there are six faces, the probability of getting a face with five dots is $\frac{1}{6}$.

The preceding examples use the *a priori* probability approach because the number of ways the event occurs and the total number of possible outcomes are known from the composition of the deck of cards or the faces of the die.

In the **empirical probability** approach, the outcomes are based on observed data, not on prior knowledge of a process. Surveys are often used to generate empirical probabilities. Examples of this type of probability are the proportion of individuals in the Using Statistics scenario who actually purchase a big-screen television, the proportion of registered voters who prefer a certain political candidate, and the proportion of students who have part-time jobs. For example, if you take a survey of students, and 60% state that they have part-time jobs, then there is a 0.60 probability that an individual student has a part-time job.

The third approach to probability, **subjective probability**, differs from the other two approaches because subjective probability differs from person to person. For example, the development team for a new product may assign a probability of 0.6 to the chance of success for the product, even though the president of the company may be less optimistic and assign a probability of 0.3. The assignment of subjective probabilities to various outcomes is usually based on a combination of an individual's past experience, personal opinion, and analysis of a particular situation. Subjective probability is especially useful in making decisions in situations in which you cannot use *a priori* probability or empirical probability.

Events and Sample Spaces

The basic elements of probability theory are the individual outcomes of a variable under study. You need the following definitions to understand probabilities.

EVENT
Each possible outcome of a variable is referred to as an **event**.
A **simple event** is described by a single characteristic.

For example, when you toss a coin, the two possible outcomes are heads and tails. Each of these represents a simple event. When you roll a standard six-sided die in which the six faces of the die contain either one, two, three, four, five, or six dots, there are six possible simple events. An event can be any one of these simple events, a set of them, or a subset of all of them. For example, the event of an *even number of dots* consists of three simple events (i.e., two, four, or six dots).

JOINT EVENT
A **joint event** is an event that has two or more characteristics.

Getting two heads on the toss of two coins is an example of a joint event because it consists of heads on the toss of the first coin and heads on the toss of the second coin.

COMPLEMENT
The **complement** of event A (represented by the symbol A') includes all events that are not part of A.

The complement of a head is a tail because that is the only event that is not a head. The complement of face five is not getting face five. Not getting face five consists of getting face one, two, three, four, or six.

SAMPLE SPACE
The collection of all the possible events is called the **sample space**.

The sample space for tossing a coin consists of heads and tails. The sample space when rolling a die consists of one, two, three, four, five, and six dots. Example 4.2 demonstrates events and sample spaces.

EXAMPLE 4.2

EVENTS AND SAMPLE SPACES

The Using Statistics scenario on page 144 concerns M&R Electronics World. Table 4.1 presents the results of the sample of 1,000 households in terms of purchase behavior for big-screen televisions.

TABLE 4.1

Purchase Behavior for Big-Screen Televisions

PLANNED TO PURCHASE	ACTUALLY PURCHASED		
	Yes	No	Total
Yes	200	50	250
No	100	650	750
Total	300	700	1,000

What is the sample space? Give examples of simple events and joint events.

SOLUTION The sample space consists of the 1,000 respondents. Simple events are "planned to purchase," "did not plan to purchase," "purchased," and "did not purchase." The complement of the event "planned to purchase" is "did not plan to purchase." The event "planned to purchase and actually purchased" is a joint event because the respondent must plan to purchase the television *and* actually purchase it.

Contingency Tables and Venn Diagrams

There are several ways in which you can view a particular sample space. One way involves assigning the appropriate events to a **contingency table** (see Section 2.4) such as the one displayed in Table 4.1. You get the values in the cells of the table by subdividing the sample space of 1,000 households according to whether someone planned to purchase and actually purchased the big-screen television set. For example, 200 of the respondents planned to purchase a big-screen television set and subsequently did purchase the big-screen television set.

A second way to present the sample space is by using a **Venn diagram**. This diagram graphically represents the various events as "unions" and "intersections" of circles. Figure 4.1 on page 148 presents a typical Venn diagram for a two-variable situation, with each variable having only two events (A and A', B and B'). The circle on the left (the red one) represents all events that are part of A. The circle on the right (the yellow one) represents all events that are part of B. The area contained within circle A and circle B (center area) is the intersection of A and B (written as $A \cap B$), because it is part of A and also part of B. The total area of the two circles is the union of A and B (written as $A \cup B$) and contains all outcomes that are just part of event A, just part of event B, or part of both A and B. The area in the diagram outside of $A \cup B$ contains outcomes that are neither part of A nor part of B.

You must define A and B in order to develop a Venn diagram. You can define either event as A or B, as long as you are consistent in evaluating the various events. For the large-screen television example, you can define the events as follows:

A = planned to purchase B = actually purchased

A' = did not plan to purchase B' = did not actually purchase

In drawing the Venn diagram (see Figure 4.2 on page 148), you must determine the value of the intersection of A and B so that the sample space can be divided into its parts. $A \cap B$ consists of all 200 households who planned to purchase and actually purchased a big-screen television set. The remainder of event A (planned to purchase) consists of the 50 households who planned to purchase a big-screen television set but did not actually purchase one. The remainder of event

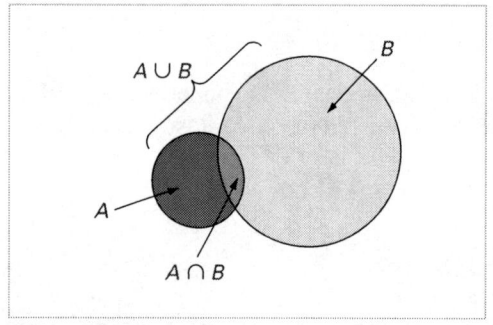

FIGURE 4.1

Venn diagram for events A and B

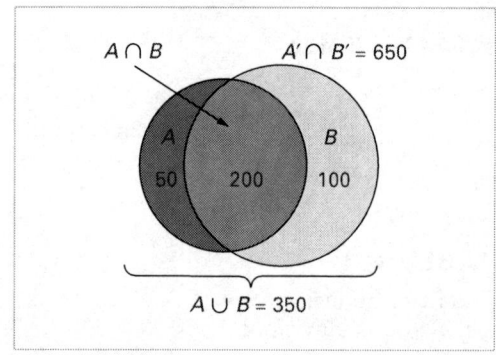

FIGURE 4.2

Venn diagram for the M&R Electronics World example

B (actually purchased) consists of the 100 households who did not plan to purchase a big-screen television set but actually purchased one. The remaining 650 households represent those who neither planned to purchase nor actually purchased a big-screen television set.

Simple Probability

Now you can answer some of the questions posed in the Using Statistics scenario. Because the results are based on data collected in a survey (refer to Table 4.1), you can use the empirical probability approach.

As stated previously, the most fundamental rule for probabilities is that they range in value from 0 to 1. An impossible event has a probability of 0, and an event that is certain to occur has a probability of 1.

Simple probability refers to the probability of occurrence of a simple event, $P(A)$. A simple probability in the Using Statistics scenario is the probability of planning to purchase a big-screen television. How can you determine the probability of selecting a household that planned to purchase a big-screen television? Using Equation (4.1) on page 145:

$$\text{Probability of occurrence} = \frac{X}{T}$$

$$P(\text{Planned to purchase}) = \frac{\text{Number who planned to purchase}}{\text{Total number of households}}$$

$$= \frac{250}{1,000} = 0.25$$

Thus, there is a 0.25 (or 25%) chance that a household planned to purchase a big-screen television. Example 4.3 illustrates another application of simple probability.

EXAMPLE 4.3

COMPUTING THE PROBABILITY THAT THE BIG-SCREEN TELEVISION PURCHASED IS A PLASMA SCREEN

In the Using Statistics follow-up survey, additional questions were asked of the 300 households that actually purchased big-screen televisions. Table 4.2 indicates the consumers' responses to whether the television purchased was a plasma screen and whether they also purchased a DVR in the past 12 months.

Find the probability that if a household that purchased a big-screen television is randomly selected, the television purchased is a plasma screen.

TABLE 4.2

Purchase Behavior Regarding Plasma-Screen Televisions and DVR

PURCHASED PLASMA SCREEN	PURCHASED DVR		
	Yes	**No**	**Total**
Plasma screen	38	42	80
Not plasma screen	70	150	220
Total	108	192	300

SOLUTION Using the following definitions:

A = purchased a plasma screen $\qquad B$ = purchased a DVR

A' = did not purchase a plasma screen $\quad B'$ = did not purchase a DVR

$$P(\text{Plasma screen}) = \frac{\text{Number of plasma-screen televisions}}{\text{Total number of televisions}}$$

$$= \frac{80}{300} = 0.267$$

There is a 26.7% chance that a randomly selected big-screen television purchase is a purchase of a plasma-screen television.

Joint Probability

Whereas simple or marginal probability refers to the probability of occurrence of simple events, **joint probability** refers to the probability of an occurrence involving two or more events. An example of joint probability is the probability that you will get heads on the first toss of a coin and heads on the second toss of a coin.

Referring to Table 4.1 on page 147, those individuals who planned to purchase and actually purchased a big-screen television consist only of the outcomes in the single cell "yes—planned to purchase *and* yes—actually purchased." Because this group consists of 200 households, the probability of picking a household that planned to purchase *and* actually purchased a big-screen television is

$$P(\text{Planned to purchase } and \text{ actually purchased}) = \frac{\text{Planned to purchase } and \text{ actually purchased}}{\text{Total number of respondents}}$$

$$= \frac{200}{1,000} = 0.20$$

Example 4.4 also demonstrates how to determine joint probability.

EXAMPLE 4.4

DETERMINING THE JOINT PROBABILITY THAT A BIG-SCREEN TELEVISION CUSTOMER PURCHASED A PLASMA-SCREEN TELEVISION AND A DVR

In Table 4.2, the purchases are cross-classified as plasma screen or not plasma screen and whether or not the household purchased a DVR. Find the probability that a randomly selected household that purchased a big-screen television also purchased a plasma-screen television and a DVR.

SOLUTION Using Equation (4.1) on page 145,

$$P(\text{Plasma screen } and \text{ DVR}) = \frac{\text{Number that purchased a plasma screen } and \text{ a DVR}}{\text{Total number of big-screen television purchasers}}$$

$$= \frac{38}{300} = 0.127$$

Therefore, there is a 12.7% chance that a randomly selected household that purchased a big-screen television purchased a plasma-screen television and a DVR.

Marginal Probability

The **marginal probability** of an event consists of a set of joint probabilities. You can determine the marginal probability of a particular event by using the concept of joint probability just discussed. For example, if B consists of two events, B_1 and B_2, then $P(A)$, the probability of event A, consists of the joint probability of event A occurring with event B_1 and the joint probability of event A occurring with event B_2. You use Equation (4.2) to compute marginal probabilities.

Marginal Probability

$$P(A) = P(A \text{ and } B_1) + P(A \text{ and } B_2) + \cdots + P(A \text{ and } B_k) \qquad \textbf{(4.2)}$$

where $B_1, B_2, \ldots, B_k$ are k mutually exclusive and collectively exhaustive events, defined as follows:

Two events are **mutually exclusive** if both the events cannot occur simultaneously.
A set of events is **collectively exhaustive** if one of the events must occur.

Heads and tails in a coin toss are mutually exclusive events. The result of a coin toss cannot simultaneously be a head and a tail. Heads and tails in a coin toss are also collectively exhaustive events. One of them must occur. If heads does not occur, tails must occur. If tails does not occur, heads must occur. Being male and being female are mutually exclusive and collectively exhaustive events. No one is both (the two are mutually exclusive), and everyone is one or the other (the two are collectively exhaustive).

You can use Equation (4.2) to compute the marginal probability of "planned to purchase" a big-screen television:

$$P(\text{Planned to purchase}) = P(\text{Planned to purchase } and \text{ purchased})$$
$$+ P(\text{Planned to purchase } and \text{ did not purchase})$$

$$= \frac{200}{1,000} + \frac{50}{1,000}$$

$$= \frac{250}{1,000} = 0.25$$

You get the same result if you add the number of outcomes that make up the simple event "planned to purchase."

General Addition Rule

How do you find the probability of event "A or B"? You need to consider the occurrence of either event A or event B or both A and B. For example, how can you determine the probability that a household planned to purchase *or* actually purchased a big-screen television? The event "planned to purchase *or* actually purchased" includes all households that planned to purchase and all households that actually purchased the big-screen television. You examine each cell of the contingency table (Table 4.1 on page 147) to determine whether it is part of this event. From Table 4.1, the cell "planned to purchase *and* did not actually purchase" is part of the event because it includes respondents who planned to purchase. The cell "did not plan to purchase *and* actually purchased" is included because it contains respondents who actually purchased. Finally, the cell "planned to purchase *and* actually purchased" has both characteristics of interest. Therefore, one way to calculate the probability of "planned to purchase *or* actually purchased" is:

$$P(\text{Planned to purchase } or \text{ actually purchased}) = P(\text{Planned to purchase } and \text{ did not actually purchase}) + P(\text{Did not plan to purchase } and \text{ actually purchased}) + P(\text{Planned to purchase } and \text{ actually purchased})$$

$$= \frac{50}{1,000} + \frac{100}{1,000} + \frac{200}{1,000} = \frac{350}{1,000} = 0.35$$

Often, it is easier to determine $P(A \text{ or } B)$, the probability of the event $A \text{ or } B$, by using the **general addition rule**, defined in Equation (4.3).

> **General Addition Rule**
>
> The probability of $A \text{ or } B$ is equal to the probability of A plus the probability of B minus the probability of $A \text{ and } B$.
>
> $$P(A \text{ or } B) = P(A) + P(B) - P(A \text{ and } B) \qquad (4.3)$$

Applying Equation (4.3) to the previous example produces the following result:

$$P(\text{Planned to purchase } or \text{ actually purchased}) = P(\text{Planned to purchase}) + P(\text{Actually purchased}) - P(\text{Planned to purchase } and \text{ actually purchased})$$

$$= \frac{250}{1,000} + \frac{300}{1,000} - \frac{200}{1,000}$$

$$= \frac{350}{1,000} = 0.35$$

The general addition rule consists of taking the probability of A and adding it to the probability of B and then subtracting the probability of the joint event $A \text{ and } B$ from this total because the joint event has already been included in computing both the probability of A and the probability of B. Referring to Table 4.1 on page 147, if the outcomes of the event "planned to purchase" are added to those of the event "actually purchased," the joint event "planned to purchase *and* actually purchased" has been included in each of these simple events. Therefore, because this joint event has been double-counted, you must subtract it to provide the correct result. Example 4.5 illustrates another application of the general addition rule.

EXAMPLE 4.5   USING THE GENERAL ADDITION RULE FOR THE HOUSEHOLDS THAT PURCHASED BIG-SCREEN TELEVISIONS

In Example 4.3 on page 148, the purchases were cross-classified in Table 4.2 on page 149 as a plasma screen or not a plasma screen and whether or not the household purchased a DVR. Find the probability that among households that purchased a big-screen television, they purchased a plasma-screen television or a DVR.

SOLUTION Using Equation (4.3),

$$P(\text{Plasma screen } or \text{ DVR}) = P(\text{Plasma screen}) + P(\text{DVR}) - P(\text{Plasma screen } and \text{ DVR})$$

$$= \frac{80}{300} + \frac{108}{300} - \frac{38}{300}$$

$$= \frac{150}{300} = 0.50$$

Therefore, there is a 50.0% chance that a randomly selected household that purchased a big-screen television purchased a plasma-screen television or a DVR.

PROBLEMS FOR SECTION 4.1

Learning the Basics

4.1 Two coins are tossed.
a. Give an example of a simple event.
b. Give an example of a joint event.
c. What is the complement of a head on the first toss?

4.2 An urn contains 12 red balls and 8 white balls. One ball is to be selected from the urn.
a. Give an example of a simple event.
b. What is the complement of a red ball?

4.3 Given the following contingency table:

	B	*B'*
A	10	20
A'	20	40

What is the probability of
a. event *A*?
b. event *A'*?
c. event *A and B*?
d. event *A or B*?

4.4 Given the following contingency table:

	B	*B'*
A	10	30
A'	25	35

What is the probability of
a. event *A'*?
b. event *A and B*?
c. event *A' and B'*?
d. event *A' or B'*?

Applying the Concepts

4.5 For each of the following, indicate whether the type of probability involved is an example of *a priori* probability, empirical probability, or subjective probability.
a. The next toss of a fair coin will land on heads.
b. Italy will win soccer's World Cup the next time the competition is held.
c. The sum of the faces of two dice will be seven.
d. The train taking a commuter to work will be more than 10 minutes late.

4.6 For each of the following, state whether the events created are mutually exclusive and collectively exhaustive. If they are not mutually exclusive and collectively exhaustive, either reword the categories to make them mutually exclusive and collectively exhaustive or explain why that would not be useful.
a. Registered voters in the United States were asked whether they registered as Republicans or Democrats.
b. Each respondent was classified by the type of car he or she drives: American, European, Japanese, or none.
c. People were asked, "Do you currently live in (i) an apartment or (ii) a house?"
d. A product was classified as defective or not defective.

4.7 Which of the following events occur with a probability of zero? For each, state why or why not.
a. A voter in the United States who is registered as a Republican and a Democrat
b. A voter in the United States who is female and registered as a Republican
c. An automobile that is a Ford and a Toyota
d. An automobile that is a Toyota and was manufactured in the United States

4.8 According to an Ipsos poll, the perception of unfairness in the U.S. tax code is spread fairly evenly across income groups, age groups, and education levels. In an April 2006 survey of 1,005 adults, Ipsos reported that almost 60% of all people said the code is unfair, whereas slightly more than 60% of those making more than $50,000 viewed the code as unfair ("People Cry Unfairness," *The Cincinnati Enquirer*, April 16, 2006, p. A8). Suppose that the following contingency table represents the specific breakdown of responses:

U.S. TAX CODE	INCOME LEVEL		
	Less Than $50,000	**More Than $50,000**	**Total**
Fair	225	180	405
Unfair	280	320	600
Total	505	500	1,005

a. Give an example of a simple event.
b. Give an example of a joint event.
c. What is the complement of "tax code is fair"?
d. Why is "tax code is fair *and* makes less than $50,000" a joint event?

4.9 Referring to the contingency table in Problem 4.8, if a respondent is selected at random, what is the probability that he or she
a. thinks the tax code is unfair?
b. thinks the tax code is unfair *and* makes less than $50,000?
c. thinks the tax code is unfair *or* makes less than $50,000?
d. Explain the difference in the results in (b) and (c).

SELF Test **4.10** A yield improvement study at a semiconductor manufacturing facility provided defect data for a sample of 450 wafers. The following table presents a summary of the responses to two questions: "Was a particle found on the die that produced the wafer?" and "Is the wafer good or bad?"

QUALITY OF WAFER	CONDITION OF DIE		
	No Particles	**Particles**	**Totals**
Good	320	14	334
Bad	80	36	116
Totals	400	50	450

Source: *Extracted from S. W. Hall, "Analysis of Defectivity of Semiconductor Wafers by Contingency Table,"* Proceedings Institute of Environmental Sciences, Vol. 1, *1994, pp. 177–183.*

a. Give an example of a simple event.
b. Give an example of a joint event.
c. What is the complement of a good wafer?
d. Why is a "good wafer" and a die "with particles" a joint event?

4.11 Referring to the contingency table in Problem 4.10, if a wafer is selected at random, what is the probability that

a. it was produced from a die with no particles?
b. it is a bad wafer *and* was produced from a die with no particles?
c. it is a bad wafer *or* was produced from a die with no particles?
d. Explain the difference in the results in (b) and (c).

4.12 An experiment was conducted to study the choices made in mutual fund selection. Undergraduate and MBA students were presented with different S&P 500 Index funds that were identical except for fees. Suppose 100 undergraduate students and 100 MBA students were selected. Partial results are shown in the following table:

FUND	STUDENT GROUP	
	Undergraduate	**MBA**
Highest-cost fund	27	18
Not highest-cost fund	73	82

Source: *Extracted from J. J. Choi, D. Laibson, and B. C. Madrian, Why Does the Law of One Price Fail?* **www.som.yale.edu/faculty/jjc83/fees.pdf**.

If a student is selected at random, what is the probability that he or she
a. selected the highest-cost fund?
b. selected the highest-cost fund *and* is an undergraduate?
c. selected the highest-cost fund *or* is an undergraduate?
d. Explain the difference in the results in (b) and (c).

4.13 Where people turn to for news is different for various age groups. Suppose that a study conducted on this issue (extracted from P. Johnson, "Young People Turn to the Web for News," *USA Today*, March 23, 2006, p. 9D) was based on 200 respondents who were between the ages of 36 and 50, and 200 respondents who were over age 50. Of the 200 respondents who were between the ages of 36 and 50, 82 got their news primarily from newspapers. Of the 200 respondents who were over age 50, 104 got their news primarily from newspapers. Construct a contingency table or a Venn diagram to evaluate the probabilities. If a respondent is selected at random, what is the probability that he or she
a. got news primarily from newspapers?
b. got news primarily from newspapers and is over 50 years old?
c. got news primarily from newspapers or is over 50 years old?
d. Explain the difference in the results in (b) and (c).

4.14 A sample of 500 respondents was selected in a large metropolitan area to study consumer behavior. Among the questions asked was "Do you enjoy shopping for clothing?" Of 240 males, 136 answered yes. Of 260 females, 224 answered yes. Construct a contingency table or a Venn diagram to evaluate the probabilities. What is the probability that a respondent chosen at random

a. enjoys shopping for clothing?
b. is a female *and* enjoys shopping for clothing?
c. is a female *or* enjoys shopping for clothing?
d. is a male *or* a female?

4.15 Each year, ratings are compiled concerning the performance of new cars during the first 90 days of use. Suppose that the cars have been categorized according to whether the car needs warranty-related repair (yes or no) and the country in which the company manufacturing the car is based (United States or not United States). Based on the data collected, the probability that the new car needs warranty repair is 0.04, the probability that the car was manufactured by a U.S.-based company is 0.60, and the probability that the new car needs a warranty repair *and* was manufactured by a U.S.-based company is 0.025. Construct a contingency table or a Venn diagram to evaluate the probabilities of a warranty-related repair. What is the probability that a new car selected at random

a. needs a warranty repair?
b. needs a warranty repair *and* was manufactured by a U.S.-based company?
c. needs a warranty repair *or* was manufactured by a U.S.-based company?
d. needs a warranty repair *or* was not manufactured by a U.S.-based company?

4.2 CONDITIONAL PROBABILITY

Each example in Section 4.1 involves finding the probability of an event when sampling from the entire sample space. How do you determine the probability of an event if certain information about the events involved is already known?

Computing Conditional Probabilities

Conditional probability refers to the probability of event *A*, given information about the occurrence of another event *B*.

Conditional Probability

The probability of *A* given *B* is equal to the probability of *A and B* divided by the probability of *B*.

$$P(A \mid B) = \frac{P(A \text{ and } B)}{P(B)} \tag{4.4a}$$

The probability of *B* given *A* is equal to the probability of *A and B* divided by the probability of *A*.

$$P(B \mid A) = \frac{P(A \text{ and } B)}{P(A)} \tag{4.4b}$$

where

$$P(A \text{ and } B) = \text{joint probability of } A \text{ and } B$$

$$P(A) = \text{marginal probability of } A$$

$$P(B) = \text{marginal probability of } B$$

Referring to the Using Statistics scenario involving the purchase of big-screen televisions, suppose you were told that a household planned to purchase a big-screen television. Now, what is the probability that the household actually purchased the television? In this example, the objective is to find *P*(Actually purchased | Planned to purchase). Here you are given the information that the household planned to purchase the big-screen television. Therefore, the sample space does not consist of all 1,000 households in the survey. It consists of only those households that planned to purchase the big-screen television. Of 250 such households, 200 actually purchased the big-screen television. Therefore, based on Table 4.1 on page 147, the probability that a household actually purchased the big-screen television given that he or she planned to purchase is

$$P(\text{Actually purchased} \mid \text{Planned to purchase}) = \frac{\text{Planned to purchase } and \text{ actually purchased}}{\text{Planned to purchase}}$$

$$= \frac{200}{250} = 0.80$$

You can also use Equation (4.4b) to compute this result:

$$P(B \mid A) = \frac{P(A \text{ and } B)}{P(A)}$$

where

$$A = \text{planned to purchase}$$

$$B = \text{actually purchased}$$

then

$$P(\text{Actually purchased} \mid \text{Planned to purchase}) = \frac{200/1,000}{250/1,000}$$

$$= \frac{200}{250} = 0.80$$

Example 4.6 further illustrates conditional probability.

EXAMPLE 4.6   FINDING A CONDITIONAL PROBABILITY OF PURCHASING A DVR

Table 4.2 on page 149 is a contingency table for whether the household purchased a plasma-screen television and whether the household purchased a DVR. If a household purchased a plasma-screen television, what is the probability that it also purchased a DVR?

SOLUTION Because you know that the household purchased a plasma-screen television, the sample space is reduced to 80 households. Of these 80 households, 38 also purchased a DVR. Therefore, the probability that a household purchased a DVR, given that the household purchased a plasma-screen television, is:

$$P(\text{Purchased DVR} \mid \text{Purchased plasma screen}) = \frac{\text{Number purchasing plasma screen } and \text{ DVR}}{\text{Number purchasing plasma screen}}$$

$$= \frac{38}{80} = 0.475$$

If you use Equation (4.4b) on page 154:

$$A = \text{Purchased plasma-screen television} \quad B = \text{Purchased DVR}$$

then

$$P(B \mid A) = \frac{P(A \text{ and } B)}{P(A)} = \frac{38/300}{80/300} = 0.475$$

Therefore, given that the household purchased a plasma-screen television, there is a 47.5% chance that the household also purchased a DVR. You can compare this conditional probability to the marginal probability of purchasing a DVR, which is 108/300 = 0.36, or 36%. These results tell you that households that purchased plasma-screen televisions are more likely to purchase DVRs than are households that purchased big-screen televisions that are not plasma-screen televisions.

Decision Trees

In Table 4.1 on page 147, households are classified according to whether they planned to purchase and whether they actually purchased big-screen televisions. A **decision tree** is an alternative to the contingency table. Figure 4.3 represents the decision tree for this example.

FIGURE 4.3

Decision tree for M&R Electronics World example

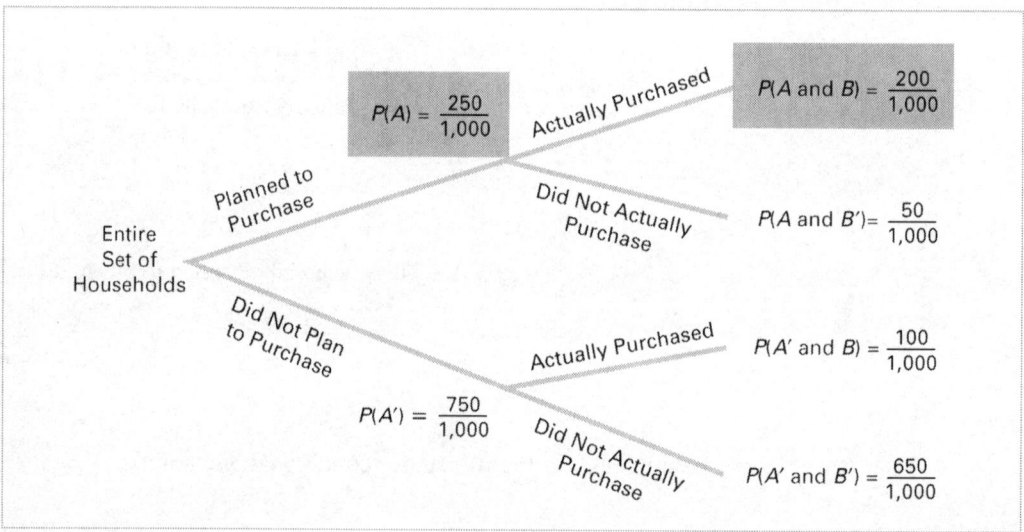

In Figure 4.3, beginning at the left with the entire set of households, there are two "branches" for whether or not the household planned to purchase a big-screen television. Each of these branches has two subbranches, corresponding to whether the household actually purchased or did not actually purchase the big-screen television. The probabilities at the end of the initial branches represent the marginal probabilities of A and A'. The probabilities at the end of each of the four subbranches represent the joint probability for each combination of events A and B. You compute the conditional probability by dividing the joint probability by the appropriate marginal probability.

For example, to compute the probability that the household actually purchased, given that the household planned to purchase the big-screen television, you take P(Planned to purchase *and* actually purchased) and divide by P(Planned to purchase). From Figure 4.3:

$$P(\text{Actually purchased} \mid \text{Planned to purchase}) = \frac{200/1{,}000}{250/1{,}000}$$

$$= \frac{200}{250} = 0.80$$

Example 4.7 illustrates how to construct a decision tree.

EXAMPLE 4.7   FORMING THE DECISION TREE FOR THE HOUSEHOLDS THAT PURCHASED BIG-SCREEN TELEVISIONS

Using the cross-classified data in Table 4.2 on page 149, construct the decision tree. Use the decision tree to find the probability that a household purchased a DVR, given that the household purchased a plasma-screen television.

SOLUTION The decision tree for purchased a DVR and a plasma-screen television is displayed in Figure 4.4. Using Equation (4.4b) on page 154 and the following definitions,

$$A = \text{Purchased plasma-screen television}$$

$$B = \text{Purchased DVR}$$

$$P(B \mid A) = \frac{P(A \text{ and } B)}{P(A)} = \frac{38/300}{80/300} = 0.475$$

FIGURE 4.4

Decision tree for purchased a DVR and a plasma-screen television

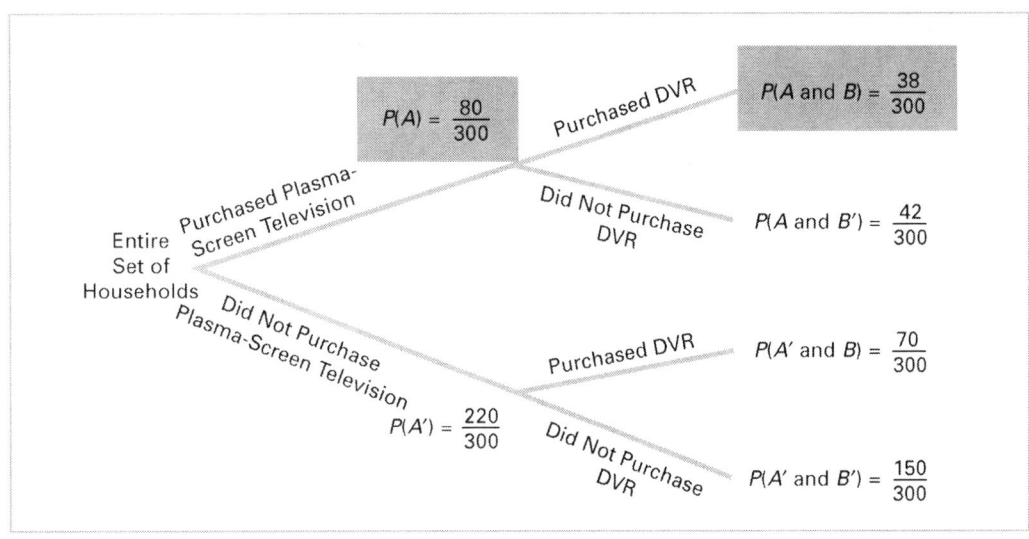

Independence

In the example concerning the purchase of big-screen televisions, the conditional probability is $200/250 = 0.80$ that the selected household actually purchased the big-screen television, given that the household planned to purchase. The simple probability of selecting a household that actually purchased is $300/1,000 = 0.30$. This result shows that the prior knowledge that the household planned to purchase affected the probability that the household actually purchased the television. In other words, the outcome of one event is *dependent* on the outcome of a second event.

When the outcome of one event does *not* affect the probability of occurrence of another event, the events are said to be independent. **Independence** can be determined by using Equation (4.5).

Independence

Two events, A and B, are independent if and only if

$$P(A \mid B) = P(A) \qquad\qquad (4.5)$$

where

$$P(A \mid B) = \text{conditional probability of } A \text{ given } B$$

$$P(A) = \text{marginal probability of } A$$

Example 4.8 demonstrates the use of Equation (4.5).

EXAMPLE 4.8   DETERMINING INDEPENDENCE

In the follow-up survey of the 300 households that actually purchased big-screen televisions, the households were asked if they were satisfied with their purchases. Table 4.3 cross-classifies the responses to the satisfaction question with the responses to whether the television was a plasma-screen television.

TABLE 4.3

Satisfaction with Purchase of Big-Screen Televisions

	SATISFIED WITH PURCHASE?		
TYPE OF TELEVISION	Yes	No	Total
Plasma screen	64	16	80
Not plasma screen	176	44	220
Total	240	60	300

Determine whether being satisfied with the purchase and type of television purchased are independent.

SOLUTION For these data,

$$P(\text{Satisfied} \mid \text{Plasma screen}) = \frac{64/300}{80/300} = \frac{64}{80} = 0.80$$

which is equal to

$$P(\text{Satisfied}) = \frac{240}{300} = 0.80$$

Thus, being satisfied with the purchase and type of television purchased are independent. Knowledge of one event does not affect the probability of the other event.

Multiplication Rules

By manipulating the formula for conditional probability, you can determine the joint probability $P(A \text{ and } B)$ from the conditional probability of an event. The **general multiplication rule** is derived using Equation (4.4a) on page 154:

$$P(A \mid B) = \frac{P(A \text{ and } B)}{P(B)}$$

and solving for the joint probability $P(A \text{ and } B)$.

General Multiplication Rule

The probability of A and B is equal to the probability of A given B times the probability of B.

$$P(A \text{ and } B) = P(A \mid B)P(B) \tag{4.6}$$

Example 4.9 demonstrates the use of the general multiplication rule.

EXAMPLE 4.9   USING THE MULTIPLICATION RULE

Consider the 80 households that purchased plasma-screen televisions. In Table 4.3 on page 158 you see that 64 households are satisfied with their purchase and 16 households are dissatisfied. Suppose two households are randomly selected from the 80 customers. Find the probability that both households are satisfied with their purchase.

SOLUTION Here you can use the multiplication rule in the following way. If:

$$A = \text{second household selected is satisfied}$$
$$B = \text{first household selected is satisfied}$$

then, using Equation (4.6),

$$P(A \text{ and } B) = P(A \mid B)P(B)$$

The probability that the first household is satisfied with the purchase is 64/80. However, the probability that the second household is also satisfied with the purchase depends on the result of the first selection. If the first household is not returned to the sample after the satisfaction level is determined (i.e., sampling without replacement), the number of households remaining is 79. If the first household is satisfied, the probability that the second is also satisfied is 63/79 because 63 satisfied households remain in the sample. Therefore,

$$P(A \text{ and } B) = \left(\frac{63}{79}\right)\left(\frac{64}{80}\right) = 0.6380$$

There is a 63.80% chance that both of the households sampled will be satisfied with their purchase.

The **multiplication rule for independent events** is derived by substituting $P(A)$ for $P(A \mid B)$ in Equation (4.6).

Multiplication Rule for Independent Events

If A and B are independent, the probability of A and B is equal to the probability of A times the probability of B.

$$P(A \text{ and } B) = P(A)P(B) \qquad (4.7)$$

If this rule holds for two events, A and B, then A and B are independent. Therefore, there are two ways to determine independence:

1. Events A and B are independent if, and only if, $P(A \mid B) = P(A)$.
2. Events A and B are independent if, and only if, $P(A \text{ and } B) = P(A)P(B)$.

Marginal Probability Using the General Multiplication Rule

In Section 4.1, marginal probability was defined using Equation (4.2) on page 150. You can state the equation for marginal probability by using the general multiplication rule. If

$$P(A) = P(A \text{ and } B_1) + P(A \text{ and } B_2) + \cdots + P(A \text{ and } B_k)$$

then, using the general multiplication rule, Equation (4.8) defines the marginal probability.

> **Marginal Probability Using the General Multiplication Rule**
> $$P(A) = P(A \mid B_1)P(B_1) + P(A \mid B_2)P(B_2) + \cdots + P(A \mid B_k)P(B_k) \quad \textbf{(4.8)}$$
>
> where $B_1, B_2, \ldots, B_k$ are k mutually exclusive and collectively exhaustive events.

To illustrate this equation, refer to Table 4.1 on page 147. Let

$$P(A) = \text{probability of "planned to purchase"}$$
$$P(B_1) = \text{probability of "actually purchased"}$$
$$P(B_2) = \text{probability of "did not actually purchase"}$$

Then, using Equation (4.8), the probability of planned to purchase is:

$$P(A) = P(A \mid B_1)P(B_1) + P(A \mid B_2)P(B_2)$$
$$= \left(\frac{200}{300}\right)\left(\frac{300}{1,000}\right) + \left(\frac{50}{700}\right)\left(\frac{700}{1,000}\right)$$
$$= \frac{200}{1,000} + \frac{50}{1,000} = \frac{250}{1,000} = 0.25$$

PROBLEMS FOR SECTION 4.2

Learning the Basics

4.16 Given the following contingency table:

	B	B'
A	10	20
A'	20	40

What is the probability of
a. $A \mid B$?
b. $A \mid B'$?
c. $A' \mid B'$?
d. Are events A and B independent?

4.17 Given the following contingency table:

	B	B'
A	10	30
A'	25	35

What is the probability of
a. $A \mid B$?
b. $A' \mid B'$?
c. $A \mid B'$?
d. Are events A and B independent?

4.18 If $P(A \text{ and } B) = 0.4$ and $P(B) = 0.8$, find $P(A \mid B)$.

4.19 If $P(A) = 0.7$, $P(B) = 0.6$, and A and B are independent, find $P(A \text{ and } B)$.

4.20 If $P(A) = 0.3$, $P(B) = 0.4$, and $P(A \text{ and } B) = 0.2$, are A and B independent?

Applying the Concepts

4.21 Where people turn to for news is different for various age groups. Suppose that a study conducted on this issue (extracted from P. Johnson, "Young People Turn to the Web for News," *USA Today*, March 23, 2006, p. 9D) was based on 200 respondents who were between the ages of 36 and 50 and 200 respondents who were over age 50. Of the 200 respondents who were between the ages of 36 and 50, 82 got their news primarily from newspapers. Of the 200 respondents who were over age 50, 104 got their news primarily from newspapers.
a. Given that a respondent is over age 50, what then is the probability that he or she gets news primarily from newspapers?
b. Given that a respondent gets news primarily from newspapers, what is the probability that he or she is over age 50?
c. Explain the difference in the results in (a) and (b).
d. Are the two events, whether the respondent is over age 50 and whether he or she gets news primarily from newspapers, independent?

4.22 A yield improvement study at a semicon- ductor manufacturing facility provided defect data for a sample of 450 wafers. The following table pre- sents a summary of the responses to two questions: "Were particles found on the die that produced the wafer?" and "Is the wafer good or bad?"

QUALITY OF WAFER	CONDITION OF DIE		
	No Particles	**Particles**	**Totals**
Good	320	14	334
Bad	80	36	116
Totals	400	50	450

Source: *Extracted from S. W. Hall, "Analysis of Defectivity of Semiconductor Wafers by Contingency Table,"* Proceedings Institute of Environmental Sciences, Vol. 1, *1994, pp. 177–183.*

a. Suppose you know that a wafer is bad. What is the probability that it was produced from a die that had particles?
b. Suppose you know that a wafer is good. What is the prob- ability that it was produced from a die that had particles?
c. Are the two events, a good wafer and a die with no par- ticles, independent? Explain.

4.23 According to an Ipsos poll, the perception of unfair- ness in the U.S. tax code is spread fairly evenly across income groups, age groups, and education levels. In an April 2006 survey of 1,005 adults, Ipsos reported that almost 60% of all people said the code is unfair, whereas slightly more than 60% of those making more than $50,000 viewed the code as unfair ("People Cry Unfairness," *The Cincinnati Enquirer*, April 16, 2006, p. A8). Suppose that the following contingency table represents the specific breakdown of responses:

	INCOME LEVEL		
	Less Than $50,000	**More Than $50,000**	**Total**
Fair	225	180	405
Unfair	280	320	600
Total	505	500	1,005

a. Given that a respondent earns less than $50,000, what is the probability that he or she said that the tax code is fair?
b. Given that a respondent earns more than $50,000, what is the probability that he or she said that the tax code is fair?
c. Is income level independent of attitude about whether the tax code is fair? Explain.

4.24 An experiment was conducted to study the choices made in mutual fund selection. Undergraduate and MBA students were presented with different S&P 500 Index funds that were identical except for fees. Suppose 100 undergraduate students and 100 MBA students were selected. Partial results are shown in the following table:

FUND	STUDENT GROUP	
	Undergraduate	**MBA**
Highest-cost fund	27	18
Not highest-cost fund	73	82

Source: *Extracted from J. J. Choi, D. Laibson, and B. C. Madrian,* Why Does the Law of One Price Fail? ***www.som.yale.edu/faculty/ jjc83/fees.pdf.***

a. Given that a student is an undergraduate, what is the probability that he or she selected the highest-cost fund?
b. Given that a student selected the highest-cost fund, what is the probability that he or she is an undergraduate?
c. Explain the difference in the results in (a) and (b).
d. Are the two events "student group" and "fund selected" independent? Explain.

4.25 A sample of 500 respondents was selected in a large metropolitan area to study consumer behavior, with the fol- lowing results:

ENJOYS SHOPPING FOR CLOTHING	GENDER		
	Male	**Female**	**Total**
Yes	136	224	360
No	104	36	140
Total	240	260	500

a. Suppose the respondent chosen is a female. What is the probability that she does not enjoy shopping for clothing?
b. Suppose the respondent chosen enjoys shopping for cloth- ing. What is the probability that the individual is a male?
c. Are enjoying shopping for clothing and the gender of the individual independent? Explain.

4.26 Each year, ratings are compiled concerning the per- formance of new cars during the first 90 days of use. Suppose that the cars have been categorized according to whether the car needs warranty-related repair (yes or no) and the country in which the company manufacturing the car is based (United States or not United States). Based on the data collected, the probability that the new car needs a warranty repair is 0.04, the probability that the car is man- ufactured by a U.S.-based company is 0.60, and the proba- bility that the new car needs a warranty repair *and* was manufactured by a U.S.-based company is 0.025.
a. Suppose you know that a company based in the United States manufactured a particular car. What is the proba- bility that the car needs warranty repair?
b. Suppose you know that a company based in the United States did not manufacture a particular car. What is the probability that the car needs warranty repair?
c. Are need for warranty repair and location of the com- pany manufacturing the car independent?

4.27 In 36 of the 57 years from 1950 through 2006, the S&P 500 finished higher after the first 5 days of trading. In 31 of those 36 years, the S&P 500 finished higher for the year. Is a good first week a good omen for the upcoming year? The following table gives the first-week and annual performance over this 57-year period:

S&P 500'S ANNUAL PERFORMANCE

FIRST WEEK	Higher	Lower
Higher	31	5
Lower	11	10

a. If a year is selected at random, what is the probability that the S&P 500 finished higher for the year?
b. Given that the S&P 500 finished higher after the first five days of trading, what is the probability that it finished higher for the year?
c. Are the two events "first-week performance" and "annual performance" independent? Explain.
d. Look up the performance after the first five days of 2007 and the 2007 annual performance of the S&P 500 at **finance.yahoo.com**. Comment on the results.

4.28 A standard deck of cards is being used to play a game. There are four suits (hearts, diamonds, clubs, and spades), each having 13 faces (ace, 2, 3, 4, 5, 6, 7, 8, 9, 10, jack, queen, and king), making a total of 52 cards. This complete deck is thoroughly mixed, and you will receive the first 2 cards from the deck without replacement.
a. What is the probability that both cards are queens?
b. What is the probability that the first card is a 10 and the second card is a 5 or 6?
c. If you were sampling with replacement, what would be the answer in (a)?
d. In the game of blackjack, the picture cards (jack, queen, king) count as 10 points, and the ace counts as either 1 or 11 points. All other cards are counted at their face value. Blackjack is achieved if 2 cards total 21 points. What is the probability of getting blackjack in this problem?

4.29 A box of nine gloves contains two left-handed gloves and seven right-handed gloves.
a. If two gloves are randomly selected from the box without replacement, what is the probability that both gloves selected will be right-handed?
b. If two gloves are randomly selected from the box without replacement, what is the probability there will be one right-handed glove and one left-handed glove selected?
c. If three gloves are selected with replacement, what is the probability that all three will be left-handed?
d. If you were sampling with replacement, what would be the answers to (a) and (b)?

4.3 BAYES' THEOREM

Bayes' theorem is used to revise previously calculated probabilities based on new information. Developed by Thomas Bayes in the eighteenth century (see references 1, 2, and 5), Bayes' theorem is an extension of what you previously learned about conditional probability.

You can apply Bayes' theorem to the situation in which M&R Electronics World is considering marketing a new model of television. In the past, 40% of the televisions introduced by the company have been successful, and 60% have been unsuccessful. Before introducing the television to the marketplace, the marketing research department conducts an extensive study and releases a report, either favorable or unfavorable. In the past, 80% of the successful televisions had received favorable market research reports, and 30% of the unsuccessful televisions had received favorable reports. For the new model of television under consideration, the marketing research department has issued a favorable report. What is the probability that the television will be successful?

Bayes' theorem is developed from the definition of conditional probability. To find the conditional probability of B given A, consider Equation (4.4b) [originally presented on page 154 and shown below]:

$$P(B \mid A) = \frac{P(A \text{ and } B)}{P(A)} = \frac{P(A \mid B)P(B)}{P(A)}$$

Bayes' theorem is derived by substituting Equation (4.8) on page 160 for $P(A)$ in the denominator of Equation (4.4b).

Bayes' Theorem

$$P(B_i \mid A) = \frac{P(A \mid B_i)P(B_i)}{P(A \mid B_1)P(B_1) + P(A \mid B_2)P(B_2) + \cdots + P(A \mid B_k)P(B_k)} \quad \text{(4.9)}$$

where B_i is the ith event out of k mutually exclusive and collectively exhaustive events.

To use Equation (4.9) for the television-marketing example, let

$$\text{event } S = \text{successful television} \qquad \text{event } F = \text{favorable report}$$
$$\text{event } S' = \text{unsuccessful television} \qquad \text{event } F' = \text{unfavorable report}$$

and

$$P(S) = 0.40 \qquad P(F \mid S) = 0.80$$
$$P(S') = 0.60 \qquad P(F \mid S') = 0.30$$

Then, using Equation (4.9),

$$P(S \mid F) = \frac{P(F \mid S)P(S)}{P(F \mid S)P(S) + P(F \mid S')P(S')}$$
$$= \frac{(0.80)(0.40)}{(0.80)(0.40) + (0.30)(0.60)}$$
$$= \frac{0.32}{0.32 + 0.18} = \frac{0.32}{0.50}$$
$$= 0.64$$

The probability of a successful television, given that a favorable report was received, is 0.64. Thus, the probability of an unsuccessful television, given that a favorable report was received, is $1 - 0.64 = 0.36$. Table 4.4 summarizes the computation of the probabilities, and Figure 4.5 presents the decision tree.

TABLE 4.4

Bayes' Theorem Calculations for the Television-Marketing Example

Event S_i	Prior Probability $P(S_i)$	Conditional Probability $P(F \mid S_i)$	Joint Probability $P(F \mid S_i)P(S_i)$	Revised Probability $P(S_i \mid F)$
S = successful television	0.40	0.80	0.32	$P(S \mid F) = 0.32/0.50$ $= 0.64$
S' = unsuccessful television	0.60	0.30	0.18 0.50	$P(S' \mid F) = 0.18/0.50$ $= 0.36$

FIGURE 4.5

Decision tree for marketing a new television

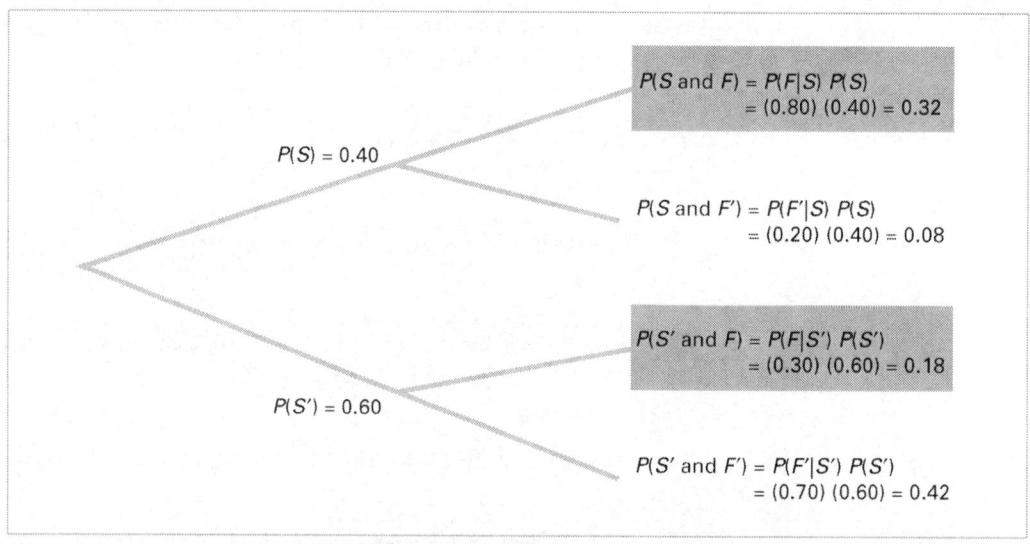

Example 4.10 applies Bayes' theorem to a medical diagnosis problem.

EXAMPLE 4.10

USING BAYES' THEOREM IN A MEDICAL DIAGNOSIS PROBLEM

The probability that a person has a certain disease is 0.03. Medical diagnostic tests are available to determine whether the person actually has the disease. If the disease is actually present, the probability that the medical diagnostic test will give a positive result (indicating that the disease is present) is 0.90. If the disease is not actually present, the probability of a positive test result (indicating that the disease is present) is 0.02. Suppose that the medical diagnostic test has given a positive result (indicating that the disease is present). What is the probability that the disease is actually present? What is the probability of a positive test result?

SOLUTION Let

$$\text{event } D = \text{has disease} \qquad \text{event } T = \text{test is positive}$$
$$\text{event } D' = \text{does not have disease} \qquad \text{event } T' = \text{test is negative}$$

and

$$P(D) = 0.03 \qquad P(T \mid D) = 0.90$$
$$P(D') = 0.97 \qquad P(T \mid D') = 0.02$$

Using Equation (4.9) on page 163,

$$P(D \mid T) = \frac{P(T \mid D)P(D)}{P(T \mid D)P(D) + P(T \mid D')P(D')}$$

$$= \frac{(0.90)(0.03)}{(0.90)(0.03) + (0.02)(0.97)}$$

$$= \frac{0.0270}{0.0270 + 0.0194} = \frac{0.0270}{0.0464}$$

$$= 0.582$$

The probability that the disease is actually present, given that a positive result has occurred (indicating that the disease is present), is 0.582. Table 4.5 summarizes the computation of the probabilities, and Figure 4.6 presents the decision tree.

TABLE 4.5

Bayes' Theorem
Calculations for the
Medical Diagnosis
Problem

Event D_i	Prior Probability $P(D_i)$	Conditional Probability $P(T \mid D_i)$	Joint Probability $P(T \mid D_i)P(D_i)$	Revised Probability $P(D_i \mid T)$
D = has disease	0.03	0.90	0.0270	$P(D \mid T) = 0.0270/0.0464$ $= 0.582$
D' = does not have disease	0.97	0.02	0.0194	$P(D' \mid T) = 0.0194/0.0464$ $= 0.418$
			0.0464	

FIGURE 4.6

Decision tree for the
medical diagnosis
problem

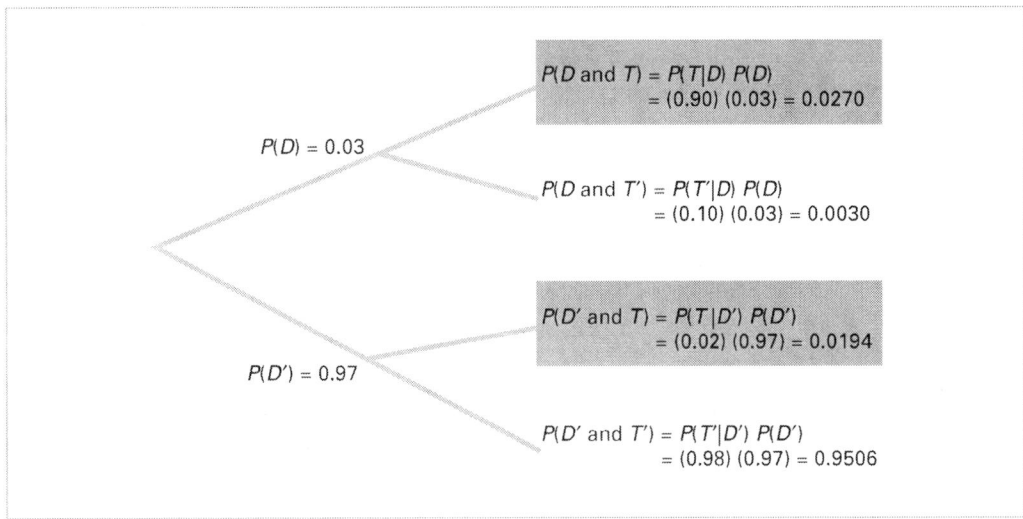

$P(D) = 0.03$

$P(D \text{ and } T) = P(T|D)\ P(D)$
$= (0.90)\ (0.03) = 0.0270$

$P(D \text{ and } T') = P(T'|D)\ P(D)$
$= (0.10)\ (0.03) = 0.0030$

$P(D') = 0.97$

$P(D' \text{ and } T) = P(T|D')\ P(D')$
$= (0.02)\ (0.97) = 0.0194$

$P(D' \text{ and } T') = P(T'|D')\ P(D')$
$= (0.98)\ (0.97) = 0.9506$

The denominator in Bayes' theorem represents $P(T)$, the probability of a positive test result, which in this case is 0.0464, or 4.64%.

Divine Providence and Spam

From The Authors' Desktop

Would you guess that the author of *Divine Benevolence: Or, An Attempt to Prove That the Principal End of the Divine Providence and Government Is the Happiness of His Creatures* also wrote *An Essay Towards Solving a Problem in the Doctrine of Chances*? Probably not, but, in fact, both essays were written by Thomas Bayes, who was a minister and theologian by training. Don't feel bad if you made a wrong guess—later in this passage you will see how your wrong guess illustrates a modern-day application of Bayesian statistics—spam, or junk mail, filters.

An Essay Towards Solving . . . introduced Bayes' theorem, discussed in Section 4.3. After writing the essay, Bayes put it aside, and we only know about the paper because a friend published it after Bayes' death in 1763. His friend thought the essay proved the existence of God; Bayes, himself, was more modest about the essay, noting "so far as mathe-

matics do not tend to make men more sober and rational thinkers . . . they are only to be considered as an amusement, which ought not to take us off from serious business." *(Please do not use this as an excuse for not doing your statistics homework.)*

In spite of his friend's enthusiasm, Bayes' theorem was soon dismissed by the majority of mathematicians, who felt, among other reasons, that establishing the prior probabilities needed by the theorem would ultimately be nothing more than an example of setting subjective probabilities. Others, who had a more accepting view, noted that the prior probabilities would need to be constantly updated and therefore were concerned about the impossibility of keeping track of all the results that would be needed in order to constantly update those probabilities (to better reflect current experience).

Although always championed by a minority of statisticians, and notably, a number of nonstatisticians, Bayes' theorem remained at

the fringes of respectable statistics for more than 150 years. The theorem began its long return from statistical exile when *An Essay Towards . . .* was republished in 1940, with commentary by W. Edwards Deming. (Ironically, like Bayes' theorem, many of Deming's own ideas would also be ignored, only to be widely accepted later on, as Chapter 18 explains.) But it took the data-processing power of modern computer systems to bring Bayesian statistics into the mainstream of research.

Today, applications of Bayesian statistics are allowing computer programs to "mine" large databases in order to discover hidden patterns. Your favorite Internet search engine may use some Bayesian techniques, as well, to deliver Internet links most likely to be relevant to your search. But of all the Bayesian applications in use, the one you've most likely experienced involves spam, the unwanted junk mail that clogs your e-mail inbox.

Return to the question that opens this *From The Authors' Desktop.* Implicit in this question is the expectation that word frequencies vary by subject matter. A statistics book would very likely contain the word *statistics* as well as words such as *chance*, *problem*, and *solving*. An eighteenth-century book about theology and religion would be more likely to contain the uppercase forms of *Divine* and *Providence*. Likewise, there are words very unlikely to appear in either book, such as the words *sedimentary*, *igneous*, and *metamorphic* (types of rocks), and there are words that are likely to appear in both such as the common words *a*, *an*, and *the*.

That the words are either likely or unlikely suggests an application of probability theory. Of course, likely and unlikely are fuzzy concepts, and we could never be completely sure if we had classified a book correctly. After all, a book about the underground film director John Waters (of *Hairspray* fame) might talk about him traveling with the late star of many of his movies, *Divine*, to see *Providence* (as in Rhode Island). Still, we would probably not mistake such a book for an eighteenth-century book on theology if we considered other words, such as *film* and *movie*, which are unlikely to be found in an eighteenth-century publication.

Classifying books into one of several categories creates complications too difficult to explain here, but what if we looked at the simpler problem of trying to classify a newly arrived e-mail message as either spam or a legitimate message (sometimes called "ham" in this context)? More specifically, what if we focused on all the e-mails sent to one address? And what if we added something to that person's e-mail program that would track word frequencies associated with spam and ham messages in order to constantly update the prior probabilities that Bayes' theorem needs? When researchers realized all this was possible, Bayesian spam filters got their start.

These filters ask, "What is the probability that an e-mail is spam, given the presence of a certain word?" Using Bayes' theorem, the filters can calculate this probability by multiplying the probability of finding the word in a spam e-mail, $P(A|B)$ in Equation (4.9), by the

probability that the e-mail is spam, $P(B)$, and dividing by the probability of finding the word in an e-mail, the denominator in Equation (4.9).

Bayesian spam filters quickly proved superior to simple keyword filters in both identifying spam and avoiding labeling a ham message as spam. Most Bayesian spam filters ignore common words found in both ham and spam e-mails. These filters also take shortcuts by focusing on a small set of words that have a high probability of being found in a spam e-mail and on words that have a low probability of being found in a spam e-mail.

As spammers (people who sent junk e-mail) learned of these new filters, they tried to outfox them. Having learned that Bayesian filters might be assigning a high $P(A|B)$ value to words like Viagra, commonly found in early spam messages, spammers thought they could fool the filter by misspelling the word as Vi@gr@ or V1agra. What they failed to realize was that the misspelled variants were even more likely to be found in a spam message than the original word. Thus, the misspelled variants made the job even easier for the Bayesian filters. Of course, through all the e-mails, the filters are constantly being retrained—that is, updating probabilities and noting when the user indicates a particular e-mail marked as ham is really spam. So, the initial Vi@gr@ e-mails were mismarked as ham, but the filter quickly learns to treat such messages as spam. (Don't worry about filters marking a ham message as spam; most filters are set up with a bias in their probabilities that minimizes such occurrences.)

Other spammers, reading a little bit about filters, decided to add "good" words, words that would have a very low $P(A|B)$ value, or "rare" words, words not frequently encountered in e-mails. This, they thought, should change the result as the filter evaluated the text of an e-mail and led the filter to enable their spam messages to be viewed as ham messages. But these spammers overlooked the fact that the conditional probabilities are constantly updated and that words once considered "good" would be discarded

by the filter as their $P(A|B)$ value increased. They also failed to realize that, as "rare" words started to show up in spam messages (and yet still rarely in ham messages), those words acted like the misspelled variants they had tried earlier.

After these attacks were beaten back by Bayesian filters, spammers apparently started learning more about Bayesian statistics. Some figured that they could "break" Bayesian filters by inserting random words in their messages. Those random words would affect the filter by causing it to see many words whose $P(A|B)$ value would be low. The Bayesian filter would begin to label many spam messages as ham and end up being of no practical use. Because the Internet still contains some Web pages and posts that triumph this approach, we will leave it to you to figure out why this method of attack cannot succeed in the long run and why this method is not as initially successful as some would claim.

Today, spammers are still trying to outwit Bayesian filters. Some spammers have decided to eliminate all or most of the words in their messages and replace them with graphics so that Bayesian filters will have very few words with which to work. But this approach will fail too, as Bayesian filters are rewritten to consider things other than words in a message. After all, Bayes' theorem is all about events, and "graphics present with no text" is as valid an event as "*some word* present in e-mail."

In truth, for a variety of reasons, including expediency, most e-mail filters today use a combination of techniques that includes applying Bayesian statistics. And although the war against Bayesian filters will escalate over time, it's a war that statistics dooms spammers to lose in the long run.

Bayesian spam filters illustrate how applications of statistics can show up in your life in very unexpected ways and how a knowledge of statistics is an important component of being a well-educated person. You will discover more unexpected examples as you read through the rest of this book.

PROBLEMS FOR SECTION 4.3

Learning the Basics

4.30 If $P(B) = 0.05$, $P(A \mid B) = 0.80$, $P(B') = 0.95$, and $P(A \mid B') = 0.40$, find $P(B \mid A)$.

4.31 If $P(B) = 0.30$, $P(A \mid B) = 0.60$, $P(B') = 0.70$, and $P(A \mid B') = 0.50$, find $P(B \mid A)$.

Applying the Concepts

4.32 In Example 4.10 on page 164, suppose that the probability that a medical diagnostic test will give a positive result if the disease is not present is reduced from 0.02 to 0.01. Given this information,

a. if the medical diagnostic test has given a positive result (indicating that the disease is present), what is the probability that the disease is actually present?

b. if the medical diagnostic test has given a negative result (indicating that the disease is not present), what is the probability that the disease is not present?

4.33 An advertising executive is studying television viewing habits of married men and women during prime-time hours. Based on past viewing records, the executive has determined that during prime time, husbands are watching television 60% of the time. When the husband is watching television, 40% of the time the wife is also watching. When the husband is not watching television, 30% of the time the wife is watching television. Find the probability that

a. if the wife is watching television, the husband is also watching television.

b. the wife is watching television in prime time.

 4.34 Olive Construction Company is determining whether it should submit a bid for a new shopping center. In the past, Olive's main competitor, Base Construction Company, has submitted bids 70% of the time. If Base Construction Company does not bid on a job, the probability that Olive Construction Company will get the job is 0.50. If Base Construction Company bids on a job, the probability that Olive Construction Company will get the job is 0.25.

a. If Olive Construction Company gets the job, what is the probability that Base Construction Company did not bid?

b. What is the probability that Olive Construction Company will get the job?

4.35 Laid-off workers who become entrepreneurs because they cannot find meaningful employment with another company are known as *entrepreneurs by necessity*. *The Wall Street Journal* reports that these entrepreneurs by necessity are less likely to grow into large businesses than are *entrepreneurs by choice* (J. Bailey, "Desire—More Than Need—Builds a Business," *The Wall Street Journal*, May 21, 2001, p. B4). This article states that 89% of the entrepreneurs in the United States are entrepreneurs by choice and 11% are entrepreneurs by necessity. Only 2% of entrepreneurs by necessity expect their new business to employ 20 or more people within five years, whereas 14% of entrepreneurs by choice expect to employ at least 20 people within five years.

a. If an entrepreneur is selected at random, and that individual expects that his or her new business will employ 20 or more people within five years, what is the probability that this individual is an entrepreneur by choice?

b. Discuss several possible reasons why entrepreneurs by choice are more likely to believe that they will grow their businesses.

4.36 The editor of a textbook publishing company is trying to decide whether to publish a proposed business statistics textbook. Information on previous textbooks published indicates that 10% are huge successes, 20% are modest successes, 40% break even, and 30% are losers. However, before a publishing decision is made, the book will be reviewed. In the past, 99% of the huge successes received favorable reviews, 70% of the moderate successes received favorable reviews, 40% of the break-even books received favorable reviews, and 20% of the losers received favorable reviews.

a. If the proposed textbook receives a favorable review, how should the editor revise the probabilities of the various outcomes to take this information into account?

b. What proportion of textbooks receives favorable reviews?

4.37 A municipal bond service has three rating categories (*A, B,* and *C*). Suppose that in the past year, of the municipal bonds issued throughout the United States, 70% were rated *A*, 20% were rated *B*, and 10% were rated *C*. Of the municipal bonds rated *A*, 50% were issued by cities, 40% by suburbs, and 10% by rural areas. Of the municipal bonds rated *B*, 60% were issued by cities, 20% by suburbs, and 20% by rural areas. Of the municipal bonds rated *C*, 90% were issued by cities, 5% by suburbs, and 5% by rural areas.

a. If a new municipal bond is to be issued by a city, what is the probability that it will receive an *A* rating?

b. What proportion of municipal bonds are issued by cities?

c. What proportion of municipal bonds are issued by suburbs?

4.4   COUNTING RULES

In Equation (4.1) on page 145, the probability of occurrence of an outcome was defined as the number of ways the outcome occurs, divided by the total number of possible outcomes. In many instances, there are a large number of possible outcomes and determining the exact number can be difficult. In these circumstances, rules for counting the number of possible outcomes have been developed. This section presents five different counting rules.

> ### Counting Rule 1
>
> If any one of k different mutually exclusive and collectively exhaustive events can occur on each of n trials, the number of possible outcomes is equal to
>
> $$k^n \qquad (4.10)$$

EXAMPLE 4.11   COUNTING RULE 1

Suppose you toss a coin five times. What is the number of different possible outcomes (the sequences of heads and tails)?

SOLUTION If you toss a coin (having two sides) five times, using Equation (4.10), the number of outcomes is $2^5 = 2 \times 2 \times 2 \times 2 \times 2 = 32$.

EXAMPLE 4.12   ROLLING A DIE TWICE

Suppose you roll a die twice. How many different possible outcomes can occur?

SOLUTION If a die (having six sides) is rolled twice, using Equation (4.10), the number of different outcomes is $6^2 = 36$.

The second counting rule is a more general version of the first and allows for the number of possible events to differ from trial to trial.

> ### Counting Rule 2
>
> If there are k_1 events on the first trial, k_2 events on the second trial, . . . , and k_n events on the nth trial, then the number of possible outcomes is
>
> $$(k_1)(k_2) \cdots (k_n) \qquad (4.11)$$

EXAMPLE 4.13   COUNTING RULE 2

A state motor vehicle department would like to know how many license plate numbers are available if the license plates consist of three letters followed by three numbers (0 through 9).

SOLUTION Using Equation (4.11), if a license plate consists of three letters followed by three numbers, the total number of possible outcomes is $(26)(26)(26)(10)(10)(10) = 17,576,000$.

EXAMPLE 4.14   DETERMINING THE NUMBER OF DIFFERENT DINNERS

A restaurant menu has a price-fixed complete dinner that consists of an appetizer, entrée, beverage, and dessert. You have a choice of five appetizers, ten entrées, three beverages, and six desserts. Determine the total number of possible dinners.

SOLUTION Using Equation (4.11), the total number of possible dinners is $(5)(10)(3)(6) = 900$.

The third counting rule involves computing the number of ways that a set of items can be arranged in order.

> **Counting Rule 3**
>
> The number of ways that all n items can be arranged in order is
>
> $$n! = (n)(n-1)\cdots(1) \tag{4.12}$$
>
> where $n!$ is called n *factorial* and $0!$ is defined as 1.

EXAMPLE 4.15

COUNTING RULE 3

If a set of six books is to be placed on a shelf, in how many ways can the six books be arranged?

SOLUTION To begin, you must realize that any of the six books could occupy the first position on the shelf. Once the first position is filled, there are five books to choose from in filling the second position. You continue this assignment procedure until all the positions are occupied. The number of ways that you can arrange six books is

$$n! = 6! = (6)(5)(4)(3)(2)(1) = 720$$

In many instances you need to know the number of ways in which a subset of the entire group of items can be arranged in *order*. Each possible arrangement is called a **permutation**.

> **Counting Rule 4**
>
> *Permutations:* The number of ways of arranging X objects selected from n objects in order is
>
> $$_nP_X = \frac{n!}{(n-X)!} \tag{4.13}$$
>
> where
>
> n = the total number of objects
>
> X = the number of objects to be arranged
>
> $n!$ = n factorial = $n(n-1)\cdots(1)$
>
> P is the symbol for permutations.[1]

[1]On many scientific calculators, there is a button labeled nPr that allows you to compute permutations. The symbol r is used instead of X.

EXAMPLE 4.16

COUNTING RULE 4

Modifying Example 4.15, if you have six books, but there is room for only four books on the shelf, in how many ways can you arrange these books on the shelf?

SOLUTION Using Equation (4.13), the number of ordered arrangements of four books selected from six books is equal to

$$_nP_X = \frac{n!}{(n-X)!} = \frac{6!}{(6-4)!} = \frac{(6)(5)(4)(3)(2)(1)}{(2)(1)} = 360$$

In many situations you are not interested in the *order* of the outcomes, but only in the number of ways that X items can be selected from n items, *irrespective of order*. Each possible selection is called a **combination**.

Counting Rule 5

Combinations: The number of ways of selecting X objects from n objects, irrespective of order, is equal to

$$_nC_X = \frac{n!}{X!(n-X)!} \qquad (4.14)$$

where

$$n = \text{the total number of objects}$$
$$X = \text{the number of objects to be arranged}$$
$$n! = n \text{ factorial} = n(n-1)\ldots(1)$$
$$C \text{ is the symbol for combinations.}[2]$$

---

[2]*On many scientific calculators, there is a button labeled nCr that allows you to compute combinations. The symbol r is used instead of X.*

Comparing this rule to the previous one, you see that it differs only in the inclusion of a term $X!$ in the denominator. When permutations were used, all of the arrangements of the X objects are distinguishable. With combinations, the $X!$ possible arrangements of objects are irrelevant.

EXAMPLE 4.17

COUNTING RULE 5

Modifying Example 4.16, if the order of the books on the shelf is irrelevant, in how many ways can you arrange these books on the shelf?

SOLUTION Using Equation (4.14), the number of combinations of four books selected from six books is equal to

$$_nC_X = \frac{n!}{X!(n-X)!} = \frac{6!}{4!(6-4)!} = \frac{(6)(5)(4)(3)(2)(1)}{(4)(3)(2)(1)(2)(1)} = 15$$

PROBLEMS FOR SECTION 4.4

Applying the Concepts

4.38 If there are ten multiple-choice questions on an exam, each having three possible answers, how many different sequences of answers are there?

4.39 A lock on a bank vault consists of three dials, each with 30 positions. In order for the vault to open, each of the three dials must be in the correct position.
a. How many different possible "dial combinations" are there for this lock?

b. What is the probability that if you randomly select a position on each dial, you will be able to open the bank vault?

c. Explain why "dial combinations" are not mathematical combinations expressed by Equation (4.14).

4.40 a. If a coin is tossed seven times, how many different outcomes are possible?

b. If a die is tossed seven times, how many different outcomes are possible?

c. Discuss the differences in your answers to (a) and (b).

4.41 A particular brand of women's jeans is available in seven different sizes, three different colors, and three different styles. How many different jeans does the store manager need to order to have one pair of each type?

SELF Test **4.42** You would like to make a salad that consists of lettuce, tomato, cucumber, and peppers. You go to the supermarket intending to purchase one variety of each of these ingredients. You discover that there are eight varieties of lettuce, four varieties of tomatoes, three varieties of cucumbers, and three varieties of peppers for sale at the supermarket. How many different salads can you make?

4.43 If each letter is used once, how many different four-letter "words" can be made from the letters E, L, O, and V?

SELF Test **4.44** In Major League Baseball, there are five teams in the Eastern Division of the National League: Atlanta, Florida, New York, Philadelphia, and Washington. How many different orders of finish are there for these five teams? (Assume that there are no ties in the standings.) Do you believe that all these orders are equally likely? Discuss.

4.45 Referring to Problem 4.44, how many different orders of finish are possible for the first four positions?

4.46 A gardener has six rows available in his vegetable garden to place tomatoes, eggplant, peppers, cucumbers, beans, and lettuce. Each vegetable will be allowed one and only one row. How many ways are there to position these vegetables in his garden?

4.47 The Trifecta at the local racetrack consists of picking the correct order of finish of the first three horses in the ninth race. If there are 12 horses entered in today's ninth race, how many Trifecta outcomes are there?

SELF Test **4.48** The Quinella at the local racetrack consists of picking the horses that will place first and second in a race *irrespective* of order. If eight horses are entered in a race, how many Quinella combinations are there?

4.49 A student has seven books that she would like to place in her backpack. However, there is only room for four books. Regardless of the arrangement, how many ways are there of placing four books into her backpack?

4.50 A daily lottery is conducted in which two winning numbers are selected out of 100 numbers. How many different combinations of winning numbers are possible?

4.51 A reading list for a course contains 20 articles. How many ways are there to choose three articles from this list?

4.5 ETHICAL ISSUES AND PROBABILITY

Ethical issues can arise when any statements related to probability are presented to the public, particularly when these statements are part of an advertising campaign for a product or service. Unfortunately, many people are not comfortable with numerical concepts (see reference 4) and tend to misinterpret the meaning of the probability. In some instances, the misinterpretation is not intentional, but in other cases, advertisements may unethically try to mislead potential customers.

One example of a potentially unethical application of probability relates to advertisements for state lotteries. When purchasing a lottery ticket, the customer selects a set of numbers (such as 6) from a larger list of numbers (such as 54). Although virtually all participants know that they are unlikely to win the lottery, they also have very little idea of how unlikely it is for them to select all 6 winning numbers from the list of 54 numbers. They have even less idea of the probability of winning a consolation prize by selecting either 4 or 5 winning numbers.

Given this background, you might consider a recent commercial for a state lottery that stated, "We won't stop until we have made everyone a millionaire" to be deceptive and possibly unethical. Do you think the state has any intention of ever stopping the lottery, given the fact that the state relies on it to bring millions of dollars into the treasury? Is it possible that the lottery can make everyone a millionaire? Is it ethical to suggest that the purpose of the lottery is to make everyone a millionaire?

Another example of a potentially unethical application of probability relates to an investment newsletter promising a 90% probability of a 20% annual return on investment. To make the claim in the newsletter an ethical one, the investment service needs to (a) explain the basis on which this probability estimate rests, (b) provide the probability statement in another format, such as 9 chances in 10, and (c) explain what happens to the investment in the 10% of the cases in which a 20% return is not achieved (e.g., is the entire investment lost?).

PROBLEMS FOR SECTION 4.5

Applying the Concepts

4.52 Write an advertisement for the state lottery that ethically describes the probability of winning a certain prize.

4.53 Write an advertisement for the investment newsletter that ethically states the probability of a 20% return on an investment.

SUMMARY

This chapter develops concepts concerning basic probability, conditional probability, and Bayes' theorem. In the next chapter, important discrete probability distributions such as the binomial, hypergeometric, and Poisson distributions are developed.

KEY EQUATIONS

Probability of Occurrence

$$\text{Probability of occurrence} = \frac{X}{T} \quad \text{(4.1)}$$

Marginal Probability

$$P(A) = P(A \text{ and } B_1) + P(A \text{ and } B_2) + \cdots + P(A \text{ and } B_k) \quad \text{(4.2)}$$

General Addition Rule

$$P(A \text{ or } B) = P(A) + P(B) - P(A \text{ and } B) \quad \text{(4.3)}$$

Conditional Probability

$$P(A \mid B) = \frac{P(A \text{ and } B)}{P(B)} \quad \text{(4.4a)}$$

$$P(B \mid A) = \frac{P(A \text{ and } B)}{P(A)} \quad \text{(4.4b)}$$

Independence

$$P(A \mid B) = P(A) \quad \text{(4.5)}$$

General Multiplication Rule

$$P(A \text{ and } B) = P(A \mid B)P(B) \quad \text{(4.6)}$$

Multiplication Rule for Independent Events

$$P(A \text{ and } B) = P(A)P(B) \quad \text{(4.7)}$$

Marginal Probability Using the General Multiplication Rule

$$P(A) = P(A \mid B_1)P(B_1) + P(A \mid B_2)P(B_2) + \cdots + P(A \mid B_k)P(B_k) \quad \text{(4.8)}$$

Bayes' Theorem

$$P(B_i \mid A) = \frac{P(A \mid B_i)P(B_i)}{P(A \mid B_1)P(B_1) + P(A \mid B_2)P(B_2) + \cdots + P(A \mid B_k)P(B_k)} \quad \text{(4.9)}$$

Counting Rule 1

$$k^n \quad \text{(4.10)}$$

Counting Rule 2

$$(k_1)(k_2) \cdots (k_n) \quad \text{(4.11)}$$

Counting Rule 3

$$n! = (n)(n-1) \cdots (1) \quad \text{(4.12)}$$

Permutations

$$_nP_X = \frac{n!}{(n-X)!} \quad \text{(4.13)}$$

Combinations

$$_nC_X = \frac{n!}{X!(n-X)!} \quad \text{(4.14)}$$

KEY TERMS

CHAPTER REVIEW PROBLEMS

Checking Your Understanding

4.54 What are the differences between *a priori* probability, empirical probability, and subjective probability?

4.55 What is the difference between a simple event and a joint event?

4.56 How can you use the general addition rule to find the probability of occurrence of event *A* or *B*?

4.57 What is the difference between mutually exclusive events and collectively exhaustive events?

4.58 How does conditional probability relate to the concept of independence?

4.59 How does the multiplication rule differ for events that are and are not independent?

4.60 How can you use Bayes' theorem to revise probabilities in light of new information?

4.61 In Bayes' theorem, how does the prior probability differ from the revised probability?

Applying the Concepts

4.62 From April 2 to April 5, 2007, Gallup poll conducted a nationwide telephone survey with randomly selected adults. Each respondent was asked, "In politics, as of today, do you consider yourself a Republican, a Democrat, or an Independent?" Of the 1008 responses received, 36% considered themselves Independents, 34% Democrats, and 30% Republicans ("Party Affiliation," **www.galluppoll.com**, April 17, 2007). Suppose that at this time you randomly selected three adults in the United States.

a. What is the probability that all three consider themselves Republican?

b. What is the probability that all three consider themselves Democrats?

c. What is the probability that all three consider themselves Independents?

d. What is the probability that you select one Republican, one Democrat, and one Independent?

e. Is the approach you used in (a) through (d) an example of *a priori*, empirical, or subjective probability?

4.63 A survey of 500 men and 500 women, designed to study financial tensions between couples, asked how likely each was to hide purchases, cash, or investments from his or her partner. The following table summarizes the results.

TYPE	LIKELY TO HIDE	
	Men	**Women**
Auto-related	66	36
Cash	126	133
Clothes	62	116
Electronics	79	56
Entertainment	96	76
Food	74	94
Investments	76	52
Travel	53	39

Source: *Extracted from L. Wei, "Your Money Manager as Financial Therapist,"* The Wall Street Journal, *November 5–6, 2005, p. B4.*

For each type of purchase, construct a contingency table or a Venn diagram of likely to hide (yes or no) with gender. If a respondent is chosen at random, what is the probability that

a. he or she is likely to hide a clothing purchase?

b. he or she is likely to hide investments?

c. the person is a male and is likely to hide auto-related purchases?

d. the person is a female and is likely to hide clothing purchases?

e. Given that the person hides investments, what is the probability that the person is a male?

f. Are any of the types of things that couples hide independent of the gender of the respondent? Explain.

4.64 A survey by the Pew Research Center ("Snapshots: Goals of 'Gen next' vs. 'Gen X'," *USA Today*, March 27, 2007, p. 1A) indicated that 81% of 18- to 25-year-olds had getting rich as a goal as compared to 62% of 26- to 40-year-olds. Suppose that the survey was based on 500 respondents from each of the two groups.

a. Form a contingency table or a Venn diagram.
b. Give an example of a simple event and a joint event.
c. What is the probability that a randomly selected respondent has a goal of getting rich?
d. What is the probability that a randomly selected respondent has a goal of getting rich and is in the 26- to 40-year-old group?
e. Are the events "age group" and "has getting rich as a goal" independent? Explain.

4.65 The owner of a restaurant serving Continental-style entrées was interested in studying ordering patterns of patrons for the Friday-to-Sunday weekend time period. Records were maintained that indicated the demand for dessert during the same time period. The owner decided to study two other variables, along with whether a dessert was ordered: the gender of the individual and whether a beef entrée was ordered. The results are as follows:

	GENDER		
DESSERT ORDERED	**Male**	**Female**	**Total**
Yes	96	40	136
No	224	240	464
Total	320	280	600

	BEEF ENTRÉE		
DESSERT ORDERED	**Yes**	**No**	**Total**
Yes	71	65	136
No	116	348	464
Total	187	413	600

A waiter approaches a table to take an order. What is the probability that the first customer to order at the table

a. orders a dessert?
b. orders a dessert *or* a beef entrée?
c. is a female *and* does not order a dessert?
d. is a female *or* does not order a dessert?
e. Suppose the first person that the waiter takes the dessert order from is a female. What is the probability that she does not order dessert?
f. Are gender and ordering dessert independent?
g. Is ordering a beef entrée independent of whether the person orders dessert?

4.66 Unsolicited commercial e-mail messages containing product advertisements, commonly referred to as spam, are routinely deleted before being read by more than 80% of all e-mail users. Furthermore, a small percentage of those reading the spam actually follow through and purchase items. Yet many companies use these unsolicited e-mail advertisements because of the extremely low cost involved. Movies Unlimited, a mail-order video and DVD business in Philadelphia, is one of the more successful companies in terms of generating sales through this form of e-marketing. Ed Weiss, general manager of Movies Unlimited, estimates that somewhere from 15% to 20% of the company's e-mail recipients read the advertisements. Moreover, approximately 15% of those who read the advertisements place orders (S. Forster, "E-Marketers Look to Polish Spam's Rusty Image," *The Wall Street Journal*, May 20, 2002, p. D2).

a. Using Mr. Weiss's lower estimate that the probability a recipient will read the advertisement is 0.15, what is the probability that a recipient will read the advertisement and place an order?
b. Movies Unlimited uses a 175,000-customer database to send e-mail advertisements. If an e-mail advertisement is sent to everyone in its customer database, how many customers do you expect will read the advertisement and place an order?
c. If the probability a recipient will read the advertisement is 0.20, what is the probability that a recipient will read the advertisement and place an order?
d. What is your answer to (b) if the probability that a recipient will read the advertisement is 0.20?

4.67 An experiment was conducted by James Choi, David Laibson, and Brigitte Madrian to study the choices made in fund selection. Suppose 100 undergraduate students and 100 MBA students were selected. When presented with four S&P 500 Index funds that were identical except for their fees, undergraduate and MBA students chose the funds as follows:

	STUDENT GROUP	
FUND	**Undergraduate**	**MBA**
Lowest-cost fund	19	19
Second-lowest-cost fund	37	40
Third-lowest-cost fund	17	23
Highest-cost fund	27	18

Source: *Extracted from J. J. Choi, D. Laibson, and B. C. Madrian, Why Does the Law of One Price Fail?* **www.som.yale.edu/faculty/jjc83/fees.pdf**.

If a student is selected at random, what is the probability that he or she

a. selected the lowest- or second-lowest cost fund?
b. selected the lowest-cost fund and is an undergraduate?
c. selected the lowest-cost fund or is an undergraduate?
d. Given that the student is an undergraduate, what is the probability that he or she selected the highest-cost fund?
e. Do you think undergraduate students and graduate students differ in their fund selection? Explain.

4.68 Sport utility vehicles (SUVs), vans, and pickups are generally considered to be more prone to roll over than cars. In 1997, 24.0% of all highway fatalities involved rollovers; 15.8% of all fatalities in 1997 involved SUVs, vans, and pickups, given that the fatality involved a rollover. Given that a rollover was not involved, 5.6% of all fatalities involved SUVs, vans, and pickups (A. Wilde Mathews, "Ford Ranger, Chevy Tracker Tilt in Test," *The Wall Street Journal*, July 14, 1999, p. A2). Consider the following definitions:

   A = fatality involved an SUV, van, or pickup

   B = fatality involved a rollover

a. Use Bayes' theorem to find the probability that a fatality involved a rollover, given that the fatality involved an SUV, a van, or a pickup.
b. Compare the result in (a) to the probability that a fatality involved a rollover and comment on whether SUVs, vans, and pickups are generally more prone to rollover accidents than other vehicles.

4.69 Enzyme-linked immunosorbent assay (ELISA) is the most common type of screening test for detecting the HIV virus. A positive result from an ELISA indicates that the HIV virus is present. For most populations, ELISA has a high degree of sensitivity (to detect infection) and specificity (to detect noninfection). (See HIVInsite, at **HIVInsite.ucsf.edu**.) Suppose that the probability a person is infected with the HIV virus for a certain population is 0.015. If the HIV virus is actually present, the probability that the ELISA test will give a positive result is 0.995. If the HIV virus is not actually present, the probability of a positive result from an ELISA is 0.01. If the ELISA has given a positive result, use Bayes' theorem to find the probability that the HIV virus is actually present.

Team Project

The data file **Mutual Funds** contains information regarding four categorical variables from a sample of 868 mutual funds. The variables are:
   Category—Type of stocks comprising the mutual fund (small cap, mid cap, large cap)
   Objective—Objective of stocks comprising the mutual fund (growth or value)
   Fees—Sales charges (no or yes)
   Risk—Risk-of-loss factor of the mutual fund (low, average, high)

4.70 Construct contingency tables of category and objective, category and fees, category and risk, objective and fees, and fees and risk.
a. For each of these contingency tables, compute all the conditional and marginal probabilities.

b. Based on (a), what conclusions can you reach about whether these variables are independent?

Student Survey Data Base

4.71 Problem 1.27 on page 14 describes a survey of 50 undergraduate students (see the file **Undergradsurvey**). For these data, construct contingency tables of gender and major, gender and graduate school intention, gender and employment status, class and graduate school intention, class and employment status, major and graduate school intention, and major and employment status.
a. For each of these contingency tables, compute all the conditional and marginal probabilities.
b. Based on (a), what conclusions can you reach about whether these variables are independent?

4.72 Problem 1.27 on page 14 describes a survey of 50 undergraduate students (see the file **Undergradsurvey**).
a. Select a sample of 50 undergraduate students at your school and conduct a similar survey for those students.
b. For these data, construct contingency tables of gender and major, gender and graduate school intention, gender and employment status, class and graduate school intention, class and employment status, major and graduate school intention, and major and employment status. For each of these contingency tables, compute all the conditional and marginal probabilities.
c. Based on (b), what conclusions can you reach about whether these variables are independent?
d. Compare the results of (c) to those of Problem 4.71(b).

4.73 Problem 1.28 on page 14 describes a survey of 40 MBA students (see the file **Gradsurvey**). For these data, construct contingency tables of gender and graduate major, gender and undergraduate major, gender and employment status, graduate major and undergraduate major, and graduate major and employment status.
a. For each of these contingency tables, compute all the conditional and marginal probabilities.
b. Based on (b), what conclusions can you reach about whether these variables are independent?

4.74 Problem 1.28 on page 14 describes a survey of 40 MBA students (see the file **Gradsurvey**).
a. Select a sample of 40 MBA students from your MBA program and conduct a similar survey for those students.
b. For these data, construct contingency tables of gender and graduate major, gender and undergraduate major, gender and employment status, graduate major and undergraduate major, and graduate major and employment status. For each of these contingency tables, compute all the conditional and marginal probabilities.
c. Based on (b), what conclusions can you reach about whether these variables are independent?
d. Compare the results of (c) to those of Problem 4.73(b).

WEB CASE

Apply your knowledge about contingency tables and the proper application of simple and joint probabilities in this continuing Web Case from Chapter 3.

Visit the EndRun Guaranteed Investment Package (GIP) Web page, at **www.prenhall.com/Springville/ER_Guaranteed.htm** or open this Web page file from the Student CD-ROM Web Case folder. Read the claims and examine the supporting data. Then answer the following:

1. How accurate is the claim of the probability of success for EndRun's GIP? In what ways is the claim misleading? How would you calculate and state the probability of having an annual rate of return not less than 15%?
2. What mistake was made in reporting the 7% probability claim? Using the table found on the "Winning Probabilities" Web page, **ER_Guaranteed3.htm**, compute the proper probabilities for the group of investors.
3. Are there any probability calculations that would be appropriate for rating an investment service? Why or why not?

REFERENCES

1. Bellhouse, D. R., "The Reverend Thomas Bayes, FRS: A Biography to Celebrate the Tercentenary of His Birth," *Statistical Science* 19 (2004), 3–43.
2. Lowd, D., and C. Meek, "Good Word Attacks on Statistical Spam Filters," presented at the Second Conference on Email and Anti-Spam, CEAS 2005.
3. *Microsoft Excel 2007* (Redmond, WA: Microsoft Corp., 2007).
4. Paulos, J. A., *Innumeracy* (New York: Hill and Wang, 1988).
5. Silberman, S., "The Quest for Meaning," *Wired 8.02*, February 2000.
6. T. Zeller, "The Fight Against V1@gra (and Other Spam)," *The New York Times*, May 21, 2006, pp. B1, B6.

Appendix E4

Using Microsoft Excel for Basic Probability

E4.1 Computing Basic Probabilities (all Excel versions)

To compute basic probabilities, open to the **Probabilities** worksheet of the **Probabilities.xls** workbook. Enter event labels and counts in the tinted cells in rows 3 through 6. Figure E4.1 shows a completed worksheet for the "Purchase Behavior for Big-Screen Television" data of Table 4.1 on page 147. Also shown offset in Figure E4.1 are the formulas this worksheet uses to compute the various probabilities.

The worksheet also "computes" the *labels* for the probabilities table with formulas that use the ampersand (**&**) operator to combine parts of a label. For example, the cell A10 formula **="P(" & B5 & ")"** asks Excel to combine the contents of B5 (**Yes**) to the label **"P("** to get **"P(Yes"** and then to "add" **")"** to get **"P(Yes)"** and form the formula **="P(Yes)"**—a novel, but acceptable, way of entering the label value **P(Yes)** in a cell.

	A	B	C	D	E
1	**Probabilities for Purchase Behavior for Big-Screen Televisions**				
2					
3	**Sample Space**		**Actually Purchased**		
4			**Yes**	**No**	Totals
5	**Planned to Purchase**	**Yes**	200	50	250
6		**No**	100	650	750
7		Totals	300	700	1000
8					
9	**Simple Probabilities**				
10	P(Yes)	0.25			
11	P(No)	0.75			
12	P(Yes)	0.30			
13	P(No)	0.70			
14					
15	**Joint Probabilities**				
16	P(Yes and Yes)	0.20			
17	P(Yes and No)	0.05			
18	P(No and Yes)	0.10			
19	P(No and No)	0.65			
20					
21	**Addition Rule**				
22	P(Yes or Yes)	0.35			
23	P(Yes or No)	0.90			
24	P(No or Yes)	0.95			
25	P(No or No)	0.80			

Simple Probabilities	
="P(" & B5 & ")"	=E5 / E7
="P(" & B6 & ")"	=E6 / E7
="P(" & C4 & ")"	=C7 / E7
="P(" & D4 & ")"	=D7 / E7
Joint Probabilities	
="P(" & B5 & " and " & C4 & ")"	=C5 / E7
="P(" & B5 & " and " & D4 & ")"	=D5 / E7
="P(" & B6 & " and " & C4 & ")"	=C6 / E7
="P(" & B6 & " and " & D4 & ")"	=D6 / E7
Addition Rule	
="P(" & B5 & " or " & C4 & ")"	=B10 + B12 - B16
="P(" & B5 & " or " & D4 & ")"	=B10 + B13 - B17
="P(" & B6 & " or " & C4 & ")"	=B11 + B12 - B18
="P(" & B6 & " or " & D4 & ")"	=B11 + B13 - B19

FIGURE E4.1

Probabilities worksheet

E4.2 Using Bayes' Theorem (all Excel versions)

You calculate probabilities using Bayes' theorem by making entries in the cell range B5:C6 of the **Bayes** worksheet of the Bayes.xls workbook. Figure E4.2 shows a completed worksheet for the television-marketing example shown in Table 4.4 on page 163.

	A	B	C	D	E
1	Bayes Theorem Calculations				
2					
3			Probabilities		
4	Event	Prior	Conditional	Joint	Revised
5	S	0.4	0.8	0.32	0.64
6	S'	0.6	0.3	0.18	0.36
7			Total:	0.5	

Joint	Revised
=B5 * C5	=D5 / D7
=B6 * C6	=D6 / D7
=D5 + D6	

FIGURE E4.2
Bayes' theorem worksheet

Appendix P4
Using PHStat2 for Basic Probability

P4.1 Computing Basic Probabilities

To compute basic probabilities, use **PHStat → Probability & Prob. Distributions → Simple & Joint Probabilities**.

This procedure inserts a **Basic Probabilities** worksheet similar to Figure E4.1 on page 176 into the current workbook. To use the worksheet, fill in the Sample Space area with your data. (Unlike most PHStat2 procedures, this procedure does *not* display a dialog box.)

CHAPTER
FIVE

SOME IMPORTANT DISCRETE PROBABILITY DISTRIBUTIONS

USING STATISTICS @ Saxon Home Improvement

5.1 THE PROBABILITY DISTRIBUTION FOR A DISCRETE RANDOM VARIABLE
Expected Value of a Discrete Random Variable
Variance and Standard Deviation of a Discrete Random Variable

5.2 COVARIANCE AND ITS APPLICATION IN FINANCE
Covariance
Expected Value, Variance, and Standard Deviation of the Sum of Two Random Variables
Portfolio Expected Return and Portfolio Risk

5.3 BINOMIAL DISTRIBUTION

5.4 POISSON DISTRIBUTION

5.5 HYPERGEOMETRIC DISTRIBUTION

5.6 (CD-ROM TOPIC) USING THE POISSON DISTRIBUTION TO APPROXIMATE THE BINOMIAL DISTRIBUTION

From the Authors' Desktop: Probability Distributions— More Likely Than You Think

E5 USING MICROSOFT EXCEL FOR DISCRETE PROBABILITY DISTRIBUTIONS

P5 USING PHSTAT2 FOR DISCRETE PROBABILITY DISTRIBUTIONS

M5 USING MINITAB FOR DISCRETE PROBABILITY DISTRIBUTIONS

LEARNING OBJECTIVES

In this chapter, you learn:

- The properties of a probability distribution
- To compute the expected value and variance of a probability distribution
- To calculate the covariance and understand its use in finance
- To compute probabilities from binomial, Poisson, and hypergeometric distributions
- How to use the binomial, Poisson, and hypergeometric distributions to solve business problems

USING STATISTICS @ Saxon Home Improvement

Accounting information systems collect, process, store, transform, and distribute financial information to decision makers both internal and external to a business organization (see reference 7). These systems continuously audit accounting information, looking for errors or incomplete or improbable information. For example, when customers of the Saxon Home Improvement Company submit online orders, the company's accounting information system reviews the order forms for possible mistakes. Any questionable invoices are *tagged* and included in a daily *exceptions report*. Recent data collected by the company show that the likelihood is 0.10 that an order form will be tagged. Saxon would like to determine the likelihood of finding a certain number of tagged forms in a sample of a specific size. For example, what would be the likelihood that none of the order forms are tagged in a sample of four forms? That one of the order forms is tagged?

How could the Saxon Home Improvement Company determine the solution to this type of probability problem? One way is to use a model, or small-scale representation, that approximates the process. By using such an approximation, Saxon managers could make inferences about the actual order process. Model building is a difficult task for some endeavors, and, in this case, the Saxon managers can use *probability distributions*, mathematical models suited for solving the type of probability problems the managers are facing. Reading this chapter will help you learn about characteristics of a probability distribution and how to specifically apply the binomial, Poisson, and hypergeometric distributions to business problems.

5.1 THE PROBABILITY DISTRIBUTION FOR A DISCRETE RANDOM VARIABLE

In Section 1.5, a *numerical variable* was defined as a variable that yielded numerical responses, such as the number of magazines you subscribe to or your height. Numerical variables are classified as *discrete* or *continuous*. Continuous numerical variables produce outcomes that come from a measuring process (e.g., your height). Discrete numerical variables produce outcomes that come from a counting process (e.g., the number of magazines you subscribe to). This chapter deals with probability distributions that represent discrete numerical variables.

PROBABILITY DISTRIBUTION FOR A DISCRETE RANDOM VARIABLE

A **probability distribution for a discrete random variable** is a mutually exclusive listing of all the possible numerical outcomes along with the probability of occurrence of each outcome.

For example, Table 5.1 gives the distribution of the number of mortgages approved per week at the local branch office of a bank. The listing in Table 5.1 is collectively exhaustive because all possible outcomes are included. Thus, the probabilities sum to 1. Figure 5.1 is a graphical representation of Table 5.1.

TABLE 5.1

Probability Distribution of the Number of Home Mortgages Approved per Week

Home Mortgages Approved per Week	Probability
0	0.10
1	0.10
2	0.20
3	0.30
4	0.15
5	0.10
6	0.05

FIGURE 5.1

Probability distribution of the number of home mortgages approved per week

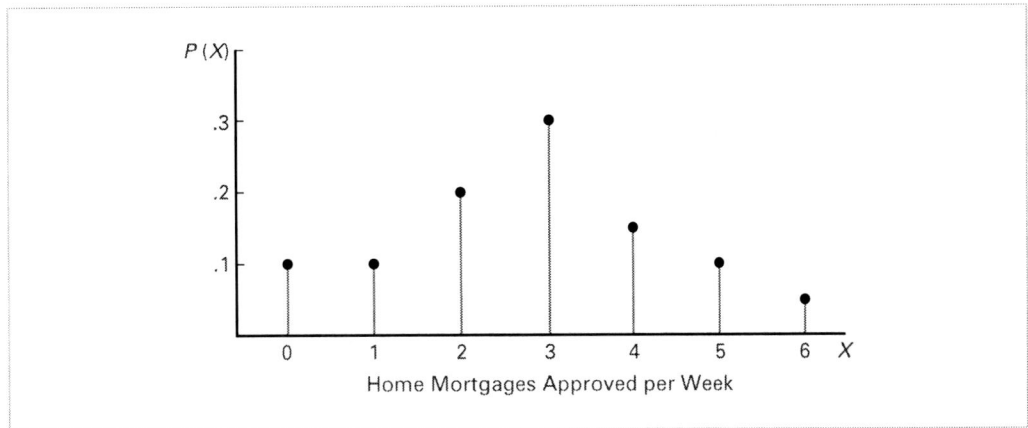

Expected Value of a Discrete Random Variable

The mean, μ, of a probability distribution is the **expected value** of its random variable. To calculate the expected value, you multiply each possible outcome, X, by its corresponding probability, $P(X)$, and then sum these products.

Expected Value, μ, of a Discrete Random Variable

$$\mu = E(X) = \sum_{i=1}^{N} X_i P(X_i) \qquad (5.1)$$

where

X_i = the ith outcome of the discrete random variable X

$P(X_i)$ = probability of occurrence of the ith outcome of X

For the probability distribution of the number of home mortgages approved per week (Table 5.1), the expected value is computed below using Equation (5.1) and is also shown in Table 5.2.

$$\mu = E(X) = \sum_{i=1}^{N} X_i P(X_i)$$

$$= (0)(0.1) + (1)(0.1) + (2)(0.2) + (3)(0.3) + (4)(0.15) + (5)(0.1) + (6)(0.05)$$

$$= 0 + 0.1 + 0.4 + 0.9 + 0.6 + 0.5 + 0.3$$

$$= 2.8$$

TABLE 5.2

Computing the Expected Value of the Number of Home Mortgages Approved per Week

Home Mortgages Approved per Week (X_i)	$P(X_i)$	$X_i P(X_i)$
0	0.10	$(0)(0.10) = 0.0$
1	0.10	$(1)(0.10) = 0.1$
2	0.20	$(2)(0.20) = 0.4$
3	0.30	$(3)(0.30) = 0.9$
4	0.15	$(4)(0.15) = 0.6$
5	0.10	$(5)(0.10) = 0.5$
6	0.05	$(6)(0.05) = 0.3$
	1.00	$\mu = E(X) = 2.8$

The expected value is 2.8. The expected value of 2.8 for the number of mortgages approved is not a possible outcome because the actual number of mortgages approved in a given week must be an integer value. The expected value represents the *mean* number of mortgages approved per week.

Variance and Standard Deviation of a Discrete Random Variable

You compute the variance of a probability distribution by multiplying each possible squared difference $[X_i - E(X)]^2$ by its corresponding probability, $P(X_i)$, and then summing the resulting products. Equation (5.2) defines the **variance of a discrete random variable**.

Variance of a Discrete Random Variable

$$\sigma^2 = \sum_{i=1}^{N} [X_i - E(X)]^2 P(X_i) \tag{5.2}$$

where

$$X_i = \text{the } i\text{th outcome of the discrete random variable } X$$

$$P(X_i) = \text{probability of occurrence of the } i\text{th outcome of } X$$

Equation (5.3) defines the **standard deviation of a discrete random variable**.

Standard Deviation of a Discrete Random Variable

$$\sigma = \sqrt{\sigma^2} = \sqrt{\sum_{i=1}^{N} [X_i - E(X)]^2 P(X_i)} \tag{5.3}$$

The variance and the standard deviation of the number of home mortgages approved per week are computed below and in Table 5.3, using Equations (5.2) and (5.3):

$$\sigma^2 = \sum_{i=1}^{N} [X_i - E(X)]^2 P(X_i)$$

$$= (0-2.8)^2(0.10) + (1-2.8)^2(0.10) + (2-2.8)^2(0.20) + (3-2.8)^2(0.30)$$

$$\quad + (4-2.8)^2(0.15) + (5-2.8)^2(0.10) + (6-2.8)^2(0.05)$$

$$= 0.784 + 0.324 + 0.128 + 0.012 + 0.216 + 0.484 + 0.512$$

$$= 2.46$$

TABLE 5.3	**Home Mortgages Approved per Week (X_i)**	**$P(X_i)$**	**$X_i P(X_i)$**	**$[X_i - E(X)]^2 P(X_i)$**
Computing the Variance and Standard Deviation of the Number of Home Mortgages Approved per Week	0	0.10	(0)(0.10) = 0.0	$(0 - 2.8)^2(0.10) = 0.784$
	1	0.10	(1)(0.10) = 0.1	$(1 - 2.8)^2(0.10) = 0.324$
	2	0.20	(2)(0.20) = 0.4	$(2 - 2.8)^2(0.20) = 0.128$
	3	0.30	(3)(0.30) = 0.9	$(3 - 2.8)^2(0.30) = 0.012$
	4	0.15	(4)(0.15) = 0.6	$(4 - 2.8)^2(0.15) = 0.216$
	5	0.10	(5)(0.10) = 0.5	$(5 - 2.8)^2(0.10) = 0.484$
	6	0.05	(6)(0.05) = 0.3	$(6 - 2.8)^2(0.05) = 0.512$
		1.00	$\mu = E(X) = 2.8$	$\sigma^2 = 2.46$

and

$$\sigma = \sqrt{\sigma^2} = \sqrt{2.46} = 1.57$$

Thus, the mean number of mortgages approved per week is 2.8, the variance is 2.46, and the standard deviation is 1.57.

PROBLEMS FOR SECTION 5.1

Learning the Basics

5.1 Given the following probability distributions:

Distribution A		**Distribution B**	
X	$P(X)$	X	$P(X)$
0	0.50	0	0.05
1	0.20	1	0.10
2	0.15	2	0.15
3	0.10	3	0.20
4	0.05	4	0.50

a. Compute the expected value for each distribution.
b. Compute the standard deviation for each distribution.
c. Compare the results of distributions A and B.

5.2 Given the following probability distributions:

Distribution C		**Distribution D**	
X	$P(X)$	X	$P(X)$
0	0.20	0	0.10
1	0.20	1	0.20
2	0.20	2	0.40
3	0.20	3	0.20
4	0.20	4	0.10

a. Compute the expected value for each distribution.
b. Compute the standard deviation for each distribution.
c. Compare the results of distributions C and D.

Applying the Concepts

5.3 How many credit cards do you have in your wallet? According to a survey by Ipsos, a large survey research company, 26% of adults in the United States reported having no credit cards; 38% reported having one or two; 20% three or four; 15% five or more; and 1% reported "not sure" ("Snapshots," **www.usatoday.com**, April 18, 2006). Suppose that the following table contains the complete probability distribution for the number of credit cards owned by adults in the United States:

Number of Credit Cards (X)	**$P(X)$**
0	0.26
1	0.22
2	0.16
3	0.12
4	0.08
5	0.06
6	0.04
7	0.03
8	0.02
9	0.01

a. Compute the mean number of credit cards owned by a U.S. adult.
b. Compute the standard deviation.

SELF Test **5.4** The following table contains the probability distribution for the number of traffic accidents daily in a small city:

Number of Accidents Daily (X)	P(X)
0	0.10
1	0.20
2	0.45
3	0.15
4	0.05
5	0.05

a. Compute the mean number of accidents per day.
b. Compute the standard deviation.

5.5 The manager of a large computer network has developed the following probability distribution of the number of interruptions per day:

Interruptions (X)	P(X)
0	0.32
1	0.35
2	0.18
3	0.08
4	0.04
5	0.02
6	0.01

a. Compute the expected number of interruptions per day.
b. Compute the standard deviation.

5.6 In the carnival game Under-or-Over-Seven, a pair of fair dice is rolled once, and the resulting sum determines whether the player wins or loses his or her bet. For example, the player can bet $1 that the sum will be under 7—that is, 2, 3, 4, 5, or 6. For this bet, the player wins $1 if the result is under 7 and loses $1 if the outcome equals or is greater than 7. Similarly, the player can bet $1 that the sum will be over 7—that is, 8, 9, 10, 11, or 12. Here, the player wins $1 if the result is over 7 but loses $1 if the result is 7 or under. A third method of play is to bet $1 on the outcome 7. For this bet, the player wins $4 if the result of the roll is 7 and loses $1 otherwise.
a. Construct the probability distribution representing the different outcomes that are possible for a $1 bet on under 7.

b. Construct the probability distribution representing the different outcomes that are possible for a $1 bet on over 7.
c. Construct the probability distribution representing the different outcomes that are possible for a $1 bet on 7.
d. Show that the expected long-run profit (or loss) to the player is the same, no matter which method of play is used.

5.7 The number of arrivals per minute at a bank located in the central business district of a large city was recorded over a period of 200 minutes with the following results:

Arrivals	Frequency
0	14
1	31
2	47
3	41
4	29
5	21
6	10
7	5
8	2

a. Compute the expected number of arrivals per day.
b. Compute the standard deviation.

5.8 The manager of a commercial mortgage department of a large bank has collected data during the past two years concerning the number of commercial mortgages approved per week. The results from these two years (104 weeks) indicated the following:

Number of Commercial Mortgages Approved	Frequency
0	13
1	25
2	32
3	17
4	9
5	6
6	1
7	1

a. Compute the expected number of mortgages approved per week.
b. Compute the standard deviation.

5.2   COVARIANCE AND ITS APPLICATION IN FINANCE

In Section 5.1, the expected value, variance, and standard deviation of a discrete random variable of a probability distribution were discussed. In this section, the covariance between two variables is introduced and applied to portfolio management, a topic of great interest to financial analysts.

Covariance

The **covariance**, σ_{XY}, measures the strength of the relationship between two numerical random variables, X and Y. A positive covariance indicates a positive relationship. A negative covariance indicates a negative relationship. A covariance of 0 indicates that the two variables are independent. Equation (5.4) defines the covariance.

Covariance

$$\sigma_{XY} = \sum_{i=1}^{N}[X_i - E(X)][Y_i - E(Y)]P(X_iY_i) \qquad (5.4)$$

where

X = discrete random variable X

X_i = ith outcome of X

Y = discrete random variable Y

Y_i = ith outcome of Y

$P(X_iY_i)$ = probability of occurrence of the ith outcome of X and the ith outcome of Y

$i = 1, 2, \ldots, N$

To illustrate the covariance, suppose that you are deciding between two alternative investments for the coming year. The first investment is a mutual fund that consists of the stocks that comprise the Dow Jones Industrial Average. The second investment is a mutual fund that is expected to perform best when economic conditions are weak. Table 5.4 summarizes your estimate of the returns (per $1,000 investment) under three economic conditions, each with a given probability of occurrence.

TABLE 5.4

Estimated Returns for Each Investment Under Three Economic Conditions

		Investment	
$P(X_iY_i)$	**Economic Condition**	**Dow Jones Fund**	**Weak-Economy Fund**
0.2	Recession	−$100	+$200
0.5	Stable economy	+100	+50
0.3	Expanding economy	+250	−100

The expected value and standard deviation for each investment and the covariance of the two investments are computed as follows:

Let X = Dow Jones fund, and Y = weak-economy fund

$E(X) = \mu_X = (-100)(0.2) + (100)(0.5) + (250)(0.3) = \$105$

$E(Y) = \mu_Y = (+200)(0.2) + (50)(0.5) + (-100)(0.3) = \$35$

$Var(X) = \sigma_X^2 = (-100 - 105)^2(0.2) + (100 - 105)^2(0.5) + (250 - 105)^2(0.3)$

$\qquad = 14,725$

$\sigma_X = \$121.35$

$$Var(Y) = \sigma_Y^2 = (200-35)^2(0.2)+(50-35)^2(0.5)+(-100-35)^2(0.3)$$

$$= 11,025$$

$$\sigma_Y = \$105.00$$

$$\sigma_{XY} = (-100-105)(200-35)(0.2)+(100-105)(50-35)(0.5)$$

$$+(250-105)(-100-35)(0.3)$$

$$= -6,765-37.5-5,872.5$$

$$= -12,675$$

Thus, the Dow Jones fund has a higher expected value (i.e., larger expected return) than the weak-economy fund but also has a higher standard deviation (i.e., more risk). The covariance of $-12,675$ between the two investments indicates a negative relationship in which the two investments are varying in the *opposite* direction. Therefore, when the return on one investment is high, typically, the return on the other is low.

Expected Value, Variance, and Standard Deviation of the Sum of Two Random Variables

Equations (5.1) through (5.3) defined the expected value, variance, and standard deviation of a probability distribution and Equation (5.4) defined the covariance between two variables, X and Y. The **expected value of the sum of two random variables** is equal to the sum of the expected values. The **variance of the sum of two random variables** is equal to the sum of the variances plus twice the covariance. The **standard deviation of the sum of two random variables** is the square root of the variance of the sum of two random variables.

Expected Value of the Sum of Two Random Variables

$$E(X+Y) = E(X) + E(Y) \tag{5.5}$$

Variance of the Sum of Two Random Variables

$$Var(X+Y) = \sigma_{X+Y}^2 = \sigma_X^2 + \sigma_Y^2 + 2\sigma_{XY} \tag{5.6}$$

Standard Deviation of the Sum of Two Random Variables

$$\sigma_{X+Y} = \sqrt{\sigma_{X+Y}^2} \tag{5.7}$$

To illustrate the expected value, variance, and standard deviation of the sum of two random variables, consider the two investments previously discussed. If X = Dow Jones fund and Y = weak-economy fund, using Equations (5.5), (5.6), and (5.7),

$$E(X+Y) = E(X)+E(Y) = 105+35 = \$140$$

$$\sigma_{X+Y}^2 = \sigma_X^2 + \sigma_Y^2 + 2\sigma_{XY}$$

$$= 14,725+11,025+(2)(-12,675)$$

$$= 400$$

$$\sigma_{X+Y} = \$20$$

The expected value of the sum of the Dow Jones fund and the weak-economy fund is $140, with a standard deviation of $20. The standard deviation of the sum of the two investments is much less than the standard deviation of either single investment because there is a large negative covariance between the investments.

Portfolio Expected Return and Portfolio Risk

Now that the covariance and the expected value and standard deviation of the sum of two random variables have been defined, these concepts can be applied to the study of a group of assets referred to as a **portfolio**. Investors combine assets into portfolios to reduce their risk (see references 1 and 2). Often, the objective is to maximize the return while minimizing the risk. For such portfolios, rather than studying the sum of two random variables, each investment is weighted by the proportion of assets assigned to that investment. Equations (5.8) and (5.9) define the **portfolio expected return** and **portfolio risk**.

Portfolio Expected Return

The portfolio expected return for a two-asset investment is equal to the weight assigned to asset X multiplied by the expected return of asset X plus the weight assigned to asset Y multiplied by the expected return of asset Y.

$$E(P) = wE(X) + (1 - w)E(Y) \qquad (5.8)$$

where

$E(P)$ = portfolio expected return

w = proportion of the portfolio value assigned to asset X

$(1 - w)$ = proportion of the portfolio value assigned to asset Y

$E(X)$ = expected return of asset X

$E(Y)$ = expected return of asset Y

Portfolio Risk

$$\sigma_p = \sqrt{w^2 \sigma_X^2 + (1-w)^2 \sigma_Y^2 + 2w(1-w)\sigma_{XY}} \qquad (5.9)$$

In the previous example, you evaluated the expected return and risk of two different investments, a Dow Jones fund and a weak-economy fund. You also computed the covariance of the two investments. Now, suppose that you wish to form a portfolio of these two investments that consists of an equal investment in each of these two funds. To compute the portfolio expected return and the portfolio risk, using Equations (5.8) and (5.9), with $w = 0.50$, $E(X) = \$105$, $E(Y) = \$35$, $\sigma_X^2 = 14{,}725$, $\sigma_Y^2 = 11{,}025$, and $\sigma_{XY} = -12{,}675$,

$$E(P) = (0.5)(105) + (1 - 0.5)(35) = \$70$$

$$\sigma_p = \sqrt{(0.5)^2(14{,}725) + (1 - 0.5)^2(11{,}025) + 2(0.5)(1 - 0.5)(-12{,}675)}$$

$$= \sqrt{100} = \$10$$

Thus, the portfolio has an expected return of $70 for each $1,000 invested (a return of 7%) and has a portfolio risk of $10. The portfolio risk here is small because there is a large negative covariance between the two investments. The fact that each investment performs best under different circumstances reduces the overall risk of the portfolio.

PROBLEMS FOR SECTION 5.2

Learning the Basics

5.9 Given the following probability distributions for variables X and Y:

$P(X_iY_i)$	X	Y
0.4	100	200
0.6	200	100

Compute
a. $E(X)$ and $E(Y)$.
b. σ_X and σ_Y.
c. σ_{XY}.
d. $E(X + Y)$.

5.10 Given the following probability distributions for variables X and Y:

$P(X_iY_i)$	X	Y
0.2	−100	50
0.4	50	30
0.3	200	20
0.1	300	20

Compute
a. $E(X)$ and $E(Y)$.
b. σ_X and σ_Y.
c. σ_{XY}.
d. $E(X + Y)$.

5.11 Two investments, X and Y, have the following characteristics:

$$E(X) = \$50, \ E(Y) = \$100, \ \sigma_X^2 = 9,000,$$

$$\sigma_Y^2 = 15,000, \text{ and } \sigma_{XY} = 7,500.$$

If the weight of portfolio assets assigned to investment X is 0.4, compute the
a. portfolio expected return.
b. portfolio risk.

Applying the Concepts

5.12 The process of being served at a bank consists of two independent parts—the time waiting in line and the time it

takes to be served by the teller. Suppose that the time waiting in line has an expected value of 4 minutes, with a standard deviation of 1.2 minutes, and the time it takes to be served by the teller has an expected value of 5.5 minutes, with a standard deviation of 1.5 minutes. Compute the
a. expected value of the total time it takes to be served at the bank.
b. standard deviation of the total time it takes to be served at the bank.

5.13 In the portfolio example in this section (see page 187), half the portfolio assets are invested in the Dow Jones fund and half in a weak-economy fund. Recalculate the portfolio expected return and the portfolio risk if
a. 30% of the portfolio assets are invested in the Dow Jones fund and 70% in a weak-economy fund.
b. 70% of the portfolio assets are invested in the Dow Jones fund and 30% in a weak-economy fund.
c. Which of the three investment strategies (30%, 50%, or 70% in the Dow Jones fund) would you recommend? Why?

✓ SELF Test **5.14** You are trying to develop a strategy for investing in two different stocks. The anticipated annual return for a $1,000 investment in each stock under four different economic conditions has the following probability distribution:

		Returns	
Probability	Economic Condition	Stock X	Stock Y
0.1	Recession	−100	50
0.3	Slow growth	0	150
0.3	Moderate growth	80	−20
0.3	Fast growth	150	−100

Compute the
a. expected return for stock X and for stock Y.
b. standard deviation for stock X and for stock Y.
c. covariance of stock X and stock Y.
d. Would you invest in stock X or stock Y? Explain.

5.15 Suppose that in Problem 5.14 you wanted to create a portfolio that consists of stock X and stock Y. Compute the portfolio expected return and portfolio risk for each of the following percentages invested in stock X:

a. 30%
b. 50%
c. 70%
d. On the basis of the results of (a) through (c), which portfolio would you recommend? Explain.

5.16 You are trying to develop a strategy for investing in two different stocks. The anticipated annual return for a $1,000 investment in each stock under four different economic conditions has the following probability distribution:

		Returns	
Probability	Economic Condition	Stock X	Stock Y
0.1	Recession	−50	−100
0.3	Slow growth	20	50
0.4	Moderate growth	100	130
0.2	Fast growth	150	200

Compute the
a. expected return for stock X and for stock Y.
b. standard deviation for stock X and for stock Y.
c. covariance of stock X and stock Y.
d. Would you invest in stock X or stock Y? Explain.

5.17 Suppose that in Problem 5.16 you wanted to create a portfolio that consists of stock X and stock Y. Compute the portfolio expected return and portfolio risk for each of the following percentages invested in stock X:
a. 30%
b. 50%
c. 70%
d. On the basis of the results of (a) through (c), which portfolio would you recommend? Explain.

5.18 You plan to invest $1,000 in a corporate bond fund or in a common stock fund. The following information about

the annual return (per $1,000) of each of these investments under different economic conditions is available, along with the probability that each of these economic conditions will occur:

Probability	Economic Condition	Corporate Bond Fund	Common Stock Fund
0.10	Recession	−30	−150
0.15	Stagnation	50	−20
0.35	Slow growth	90	120
0.30	Moderate growth	100	160
0.10	High growth	110	250

Compute the
a. expected return for the corporate bond fund and for the common stock fund.
b. standard deviation for the corporate bond fund and for the common stock fund.
c. covariance of the corporate bond fund and the common stock fund.
d. Would you invest in the corporate bond fund or the common stock fund? Explain.

5.19 Suppose that in Problem 5.18 you wanted to create a portfolio that consists of the corporate bond fund and the common stock fund. Compute the portfolio expected return and portfolio risk for each of the following situations:
a. $300 in the corporate bond fund and $700 in the common stock fund.
b. $500 in each fund.
c. $700 in the corporate bond fund and $300 in the common stock fund.
d. On the basis of the results of (a) through (c), which portfolio would you recommend? Explain.

5.3 BINOMIAL DISTRIBUTION

This section and the three that follow use mathematical models to solve business problems.

> **MATHEMATICAL MODEL**
> A **mathematical model** is a mathematical expression that represents a variable of interest.

When a mathematical expression is available, you can compute the exact probability of occurrence of any particular outcome of the variable.

The **binomial distribution** is one of the most useful mathematical models. You use the binomial distribution when the discrete random variable is the number of events of interest in a sample of n observations. The binomial distribution has four basic properties:

- The sample consists of a fixed number of observations, n.
- Each observation is classified into one of two mutually exclusive and collectively exhaustive categories.

- The probability of an observation being classified as the event of interest, π, is constant from observation to observation. Thus, the probability of an observation being classified as not being the event of interest, $1 - \pi$, is constant over all observations.
- The outcome of any observation is independent of the outcome of any other observation. To ensure independence, the observations can be randomly selected either from an *infinite population without replacement* or from a *finite population with replacement*.

Returning to the Using Statistics scenario presented on page 180 concerning the accounting information system, suppose the event of interest is defined as a tagged order form. You are interested in the number of tagged order forms in a given sample of orders.

What results can occur? If the sample contains four orders, there could be none, one, two, three, or four tagged order forms. The binomial random variable, the number of tagged order forms, cannot take on any other value because the number of tagged order forms cannot be more than the sample size, n, and cannot be less than zero. Therefore, the binomial random variable has a range from 0 to n.

Suppose that you observe the following result in a sample of four orders:

First Order	Second Order	Third Order	Fourth Order
Tagged	Tagged	Not tagged	Tagged

What is the probability of having three tagged order forms in a sample of four orders in this particular sequence? Because the historical probability of a tagged order is 0.10, the probability that each order occurs in the sequence is

First Order	Second Order	Third Order	Fourth Order
$\pi = 0.10$	$\pi = 0.10$	$1 - \pi = 0.90$	$\pi = 0.10$

Each outcome is independent of the others because the order forms were selected from an extremely large or practically infinite population without replacement. Therefore, the probability of having this particular sequence is

$$\pi\pi(1 - \pi)\pi = \pi^3(1 - \pi)^1$$

$$= (0.10)(0.10)(0.10)(0.90)$$

$$= (0.10)^3(0.90)^1$$

$$= 0.0009$$

This result indicates only the probability of three tagged order forms (events of interest) from a sample of four order forms in a *specific sequence*. To find the number of ways of selecting X objects from n objects, *irrespective of sequence*, you use the **rule of combinations** given in Equation (5.10) below and previously defined in Equation (4.14) on page 170.

Combinations

The number of combinations[1] of selecting X objects out of n objects is given by

$$_nC_X = \frac{n!}{X!(n - X)!} \tag{5.10}$$

where

$n! = (n)(n - 1) \cdots (1)$ is called n factorial. By definition, $0! = 1$.

[1] On many scientific calculators, there is a button labeled $_nC_r$ that allows you to compute the number of combinations. The symbol r is used instead of X.

With $n = 4$ and $X = 3$, there are

$$_nC_X = \frac{n!}{X!(n-X)!} = \frac{4!}{3!(4-3)!} = \frac{4\times3\times2\times1}{(3\times2\times1)(1)} = 4$$

such sequences. The four possible sequences are:

Sequence 1 = *tagged, tagged, tagged, not tagged*, with probability
$$\pi\pi\pi(1-\pi) = \pi^3(1-\pi)^1 = 0.0009$$

Sequence 2 = *tagged, tagged, not tagged, tagged*, with probability
$$\pi\pi(1-\pi)\pi = \pi^3(1-\pi)^1 = 0.0009$$

Sequence 3 = *tagged, not tagged, tagged, tagged*, with probability
$$\pi(1-\pi)\pi\pi = \pi^3(1-\pi)^1 = 0.0009$$

Sequence 4 = *not tagged, tagged, tagged, tagged*, with probability
$$(1-\pi)\pi\pi\pi = \pi^3(1-\pi)^1 = 0.0009$$

Therefore, the probability of three tagged order forms is equal to

(Number of possible sequences) $\times$ (Probability of a particular sequence)
$$= (4) \times (0.0009) = 0.0036$$

You can make a similar, intuitive derivation for the other possible outcomes of the random variable—zero, one, two, and four tagged order forms. However, as n, the sample size, gets large, the computations involved in using this intuitive approach become time-consuming. Equation (5.11) is the mathematical model that provides a general formula for computing any binomial probability from the binomial distribution with the number of events of interest, X, given the values of n and π.

Binomial Distribution

$$P(X) = \frac{n!}{X!(n-X)!}\pi^X(1-\pi)^{n-X} \qquad (5.11)$$

where

$P(X)$ = probability of X events of interest, given n and π

n = number of observations

π = probability of an event of interest

$1-\pi$ = probability of not having an event of interest

X = number of events of interest in the sample ($X = 0, 1, 2, \ldots, n$)

Equation (5.11) restates what you had intuitively derived. The binomial variable X can have any integer value X from 0 through n. In Equation (5.11), the product

$$\pi^X(1-\pi)^{n-X}$$

represents the probability of exactly X events of interest from n observations in a *particular sequence*.

The term

$$\frac{n!}{X!(n-X)!}$$

represents the number of *combinations* of the X events of interest from the n observations that are possible. Hence, given the number of observations, n, and the probability of an event of interest, π, the probability of X events of interest is:

$$P(X) = (\text{Number of possible sequences}) \times (\text{Probability of a particular sequence})$$

$$= \frac{n!}{X!(n-X)!} \pi^X (1-\pi)^{n-X}$$

Example 5.1 illustrates the use of Equation (5.11).

EXAMPLE 5.1   DETERMINING $P(X = 3)$, GIVEN $n = 4$ AND $\pi = 0.1$

If the likelihood of a tagged order form is 0.1, what is the probability that there are three tagged order forms in the sample of four?

SOLUTION Using Equation (5.11) on page 191, the probability of three tagged orders from a sample of four is

$$P(X = 3) = \frac{4!}{3!(4-3)!}(0.1)^3(1-0.1)^{4-3}$$

$$= \frac{4!}{3!(4-3)!}(0.1)^3(0.9)^1$$

$$= 4(0.1)(0.1)(0.1)(0.9) = 0.0036$$

Examples 5.2 and 5.3 show the computations for other values of X.

EXAMPLE 5.2   DETERMINING $P(X \geq 3)$, GIVEN $n = 4$ AND $\pi = 0.1$

If the likelihood of a tagged order form is 0.1, what is the probability that there are three or more (i.e., at least three) tagged order forms in the sample of four?

SOLUTION In Example 5.1, you found that the probability of *exactly* three tagged order forms from a sample of four is 0.0036. To compute the probability of *at least* three tagged order forms, you need to add the probability of three tagged order forms to the probability of four tagged order forms. The probability of four tagged order forms is

$$P(X = 4) = \frac{4!}{4!(4-4)!}(0.1)^4(1-0.1)^{4-4}$$

$$= \frac{4!}{4!(0)!}(0.1)^4(0.9)^0$$

$$= 1(0.1)(0.1)(0.1)(0.1) = 0.0001$$

Thus, the probability of at least three tagged order forms is

$$P(X \geq 3) = P(X = 3) + P(X = 4)$$

$$= 0.0036 + 0.0001$$

$$= 0.0037$$

There is a 0.37% chance that there will be at least three tagged order forms in a sample of four.

EXAMPLE 5.3   DETERMINING $P(X < 3)$, GIVEN $n = 4$ AND $\pi = 0.1$

If the likelihood of a tagged order form is 0.1, what is the probability that there are less than three tagged order forms in the sample of four?

SOLUTION The probability that there are less than three tagged order forms is

$$P(X < 3) = P(X = 0) + P(X = 1) + P(X = 2)$$

Using Equation (5.11) on page 191, these probabilities are

$$P(X = 0) = \frac{4!}{0!(4-0)!}(0.1)^0(1-0.1)^{4-0} = 0.6561$$

$$P(X = 1) = \frac{4!}{1!(4-1)!}(0.1)^1(1-0.1)^{4-1} = 0.2916$$

$$P(X = 2) = \frac{4!}{2!(4-2)!}(0.1)^2(1-0.1)^{4-2} = 0.0486$$

Therefore, $P(X < 3) = 0.6561 + 0.2916 + 0.0486 = 0.9963$. $P(X < 3)$ could also be calculated from its complement, $P(X \geq 3)$, as follows:

$$P(X < 3) = 1 - P(X \geq 3)$$
$$= 1 - 0.0037 = 0.9963$$

Computations such as those in Example 5.3 can become tedious, especially as n gets large. To avoid computational drudgery, you can find many binomial probabilities directly from Table E.6 (in Appendix E), a portion of which is reproduced in Table 5.5. Table E.6 provides binomial probabilities for $X = 0, 1, 2, \ldots, n$ for various selected combinations of n and π. For example, to find the probability of exactly two events of interest in a sample of four when the probability of an event is 0.1, you first find $n = 4$ and then look in the row $X = 2$ and column $\pi = 0.10$. The result is 0.0486.

TABLE 5.5

Finding a Binomial Probability for $n = 4$, $X = 2$, and $\pi = 0.1$

| | | | | π | |
n	X	0.01	0.02	....	0.10
4	0	0.9606	0.9224	....	0.6561
	1	0.0388	0.0753	....	0.2916
	2	0.0006	0.0023	....	0.0486
	3	0.0000	0.0000	....	0.0036
	4	0.0000	0.0000	....	0.0001

Source: *Table E.6.*

You can also compute the binomial probabilities given in Table E.6 by using Microsoft Excel or Minitab as shown in Figures 5.2 and 5.3 (note that Minitab uses the letter p instead of π to denote the probability of an event of interest).

FIGURE 5.2

Microsoft Excel
worksheet for
computing binomial
probabilities

*See Section E5.3 or P5.2 to
create this.*

	A	B	
1	Tagged Orders		
2			
3	Data		
4	Sample size	4	
5	Probability of an event of interest	0.1	
6			
7	Statistics		
8	Mean	0.4	=B4 * B5
9	Variance	0.36	=B8 * (1 - B5)
10	Standard deviation	0.6	=SQRT(B9)
11			
12	Binomial Probabilities Table		
13	X	P(X)	
14	0	0.6561	=BINOMDIST(A14, B4, B5, FALSE)
15	1	0.2916	=BINOMDIST(A15, B4, B5, FALSE)
16	2	0.0486	=BINOMDIST(A16, B4, B5, FALSE)
17	3	0.0036	=BINOMDIST(A17, B4, B5, FALSE)
18	4	0.0001	=BINOMDIST(A18, B4, B5, FALSE)

FIGURE 5.3

Minitab results for
computing binomial
probabilities

*See Section M5.1 to create
this.*

```
          Binomial with n = 4 and p = 0.1

          x    P( X = x )
          0      0.6561
          1      0.2916
          2      0.0486
          3      0.0036
          4      0.0001
```

The shape of a binomial probability distribution depends on the values of n and π. Whenever $\pi = 0.5$, the binomial distribution is symmetrical, regardless of how large or small the value of n. When $\pi \neq 0.5$, the distribution is skewed. The closer π is to 0.5 and the larger the number of observations, n, the less skewed the distribution becomes. For example, the distribution of the number of tagged order forms is highly skewed to the right because $\pi = 0.1$ and $n = 4$ (see Figure 5.4).

FIGURE 5.4

Microsoft Excel
histogram of the
binomial probability
distribution with $n = 4$
and $\pi = 0.1$

*See Section E5.3 and E2.9
or P5.2 to create this.*

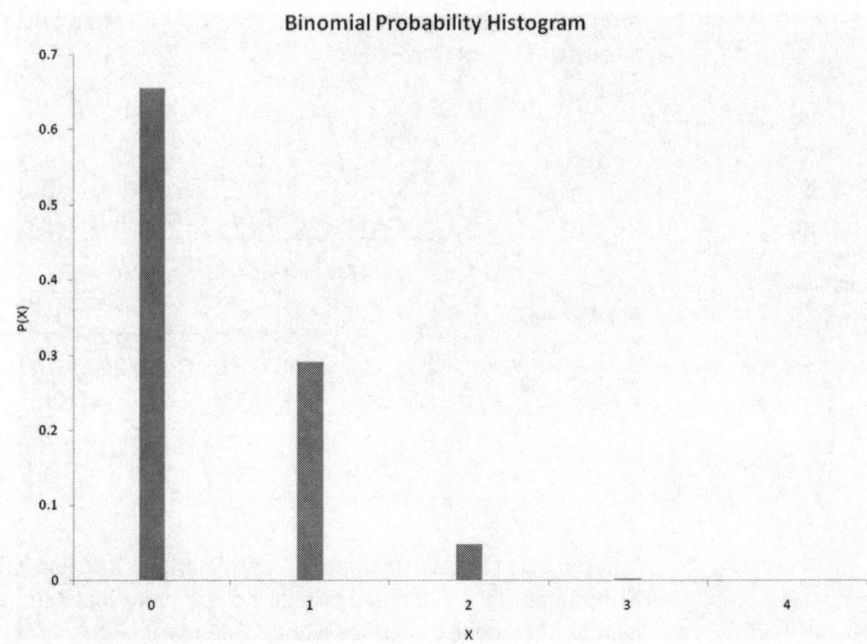

Binomial Probability Histogram

The mean (or expected value) of the binomial distribution is equal to the product of n and π. Instead of using Equation (5.1) on page 181 to compute the mean of the probability distribution, you use Equation (5.12) to compute the mean for variables that follow the binomial distribution.

Mean of the Binomial Distribution

The mean, μ, of the binomial distribution is equal to the sample size, n, multiplied by the probability of an event of interest, π.

$$\mu = E(X) = n\pi \tag{5.12}$$

On the average, over the long run, you theoretically expect $\mu = E(X) = n\pi = (4)(0.1) = 0.4$ tagged order form in a sample of four orders.

The standard deviation of the binomial distribution is calculated using Equation (5.13).

Standard Deviation of the Binomial Distribution

$$\sigma = \sqrt{\sigma^2} = \sqrt{Var(X)} = \sqrt{n\pi(1-\pi)} \tag{5.13}$$

The standard deviation of the number of tagged order forms is

$$\sigma = \sqrt{4(0.1)(0.9)} = 0.60$$

You get the same result if you use Equation (5.3) on page 182.

Example 5.4 applies the binomial distribution to service at a fast-food restaurant.

EXAMPLE 5.4   COMPUTING BINOMIAL PROBABILITIES

Accuracy in taking orders at a drive-through window is important for fast-food chains. Each month, *QSR Magazine*, **www.qsrmagazine.com**, publishes the results of its surveys. Accuracy is measured as the percentage of orders that are filled correctly. In a recent month, the percentage of orders filled correctly at McDonald's was approximately 91%. If a sample of three orders is taken, what are the mean and standard deviation of the binomial distribution for the number of orders filled correctly? Suppose that you go to the drive-through window at McDonald's and place an order. Two friends of yours independently place orders at the drive-through window at the same McDonald's. What are the probabilities that all three, that none of the three, and that at least two of the three orders will be filled correctly?

SOLUTION   Because there are three orders and the probability of a correct order is 0.91, $n = 3$ and $\pi = 0.91$. Using Equations (5.12) and (5.13),

$$\mu = E(X) = n\pi = 3(0.91) = 2.73$$

$$\sigma = \sqrt{\sigma^2} = \sqrt{Var(X)} = \sqrt{n\pi(1-\pi)}$$

$$= \sqrt{3(0.91)(0.09)}$$

$$= \sqrt{0.2457} = 0.4957$$

Using Equation (5.11) on page 191,

$$P(X = 3) = \frac{3!}{3!(3-3)!}(0.91)^3(1-0.91)^{3-3}$$

$$= \frac{3!}{3!(3-3)!}(0.91)^3(0.09)^0$$

$$= 1(0.91)(0.91)(0.91)(1) = 0.7536$$

$$P(X = 0) = \frac{3!}{0!(3-0)!}(0.91)^0(1-0.91)^{3-0}$$

$$= \frac{3!}{0!(3-0)!}(0.91)^0(0.09)^3$$

$$= 1(1)(0.09)(0.09)(0.09) = 0.0007$$

$$P(X = 2) = \frac{3!}{2!(3-2)!}(0.91)^2(1-0.91)^{3-2}$$

$$= \frac{3!}{2!(3-2)!}(0.91)^2(0.09)^1$$

$$= 3(0.91)(0.91)(0.09) = 0.2236$$

$$P(X \geq 2) = P(X = 2) + P(X = 3)$$

$$= 0.2236 + 0.7536$$

$$= 0.9772$$

The mean number of orders filled correctly in a sample of three orders is 2.73, and the standard deviation is 0.4957. The probability that all three orders are filled correctly is 0.7536, or 75.36%. The probability that none of the orders are filled correctly is 0.0007, or 0.07%. The probability that at least two orders are filled correctly is 0.9772, or 97.72%.

In this section, you have been introduced to the binomial distribution. The binomial distribution is an important mathematical model in many business situations.

PROBLEMS FOR SECTION 5.3

Learning the Basics

5.20 Determine the following:
a. For $n = 4$ and $\pi = 0.12$, what is $P(X = 0)$?
b. For $n = 10$ and $\pi = 0.40$, what is $P(X = 9)$?
c. For $n = 10$ and $\pi = 0.50$, what is $P(X = 8)$?
d. For $n = 6$ and $\pi = 0.83$, what is $P(X = 5)$?

5.21 If $n = 5$ and $\pi = 0.40$, what is the probability that
a. $X = 4$?
b. $X \leq 3$?
c. $X < 2$?
d. $X > 1$?

5.22 Determine the mean and standard deviation of the random variable X in each of the following binomial distributions:
a. $n = 4$ and $\pi = 0.10$
b. $n = 4$ and $\pi = 0.40$
c. $n = 5$ and $\pi = 0.80$
d. $n = 3$ and $\pi = 0.50$

Applying the Concepts

5.23 The increase or decrease in the price of a stock between the beginning and the end of a trading day is assumed to be an equally likely random event. What is the probability that a stock will show an increase in its closing price on five consecutive days?

5.24 A recent article in *Quality Progress* (Dennis R. Owens, "The Probability of Reoccurrence: P(r)," April 2007, 40, p. 88) discusses a manufacturing company assessing the chance that its product will fail. The article identifies six independent events that can cause a failure. The probability of each of these events failing is quite low, 0.05, but for a product to ultimately be a success, it must not experience a failure in any of the six events.

a. Use the binomial probability distribution to calculate the probability that a product will ultimately be successful (i.e., that if will not fail).

b. If the probabilities of the six events are not all equal, how could you calculate the probability in (a)?

5.25 A student is taking a multiple-choice exam in which each question has four choices. Assuming that she has no knowledge of the correct answers to any of the questions, she has decided on a strategy in which she will place four balls (marked *A*, *B*, *C*, and *D*) into a box. She randomly selects one ball for each question and replaces the ball in the box. The marking on the ball will determine her answer to the question. There are five multiple-choice questions on the exam. What is the probability that she will get

a. five questions correct?

b. at least four questions correct?

c. no questions correct?

d. no more than two questions correct?

 5.26 In Example 5.4 on page 195, you and two friends decided to go to McDonald's. Instead, suppose that you went to KFC, which last month filled 87.8% of the orders correctly. What is the probability that

a. all three orders will be filled correctly?

b. none of the three will be filled correctly?

c. at least two of the three will be filled correctly?

d. What are the mean and standard deviation of the binomial distribution used in (a) through (c)? Interpret these values.

5.27 In February 2007, The Gallup Poll surveyed adults living in the United States. When asked about the current state of the job market, 45% indicated that now is a good time to be looking for a quality job. The remainder answered no opinion or that now is a bad time to be looking for a quality job. The results were more positive than survey results taken in 2003, but down from the boom years of the late 1990s (Gallup Poll News Service, "Consumer Views of the Economy," **www.galluppoll.com**, April 30, 2007). Suppose that you select a random sample of 10 adults and survey them concerning the current state of the job market. Assume that 45% of the adults in the United States still think that now is a "good time" to be looking for a quality job, and further assume that the number of the 10 adults thinking that now is a "good time" is distributed as a binomial random variable.

a. What are the mean and standard deviation of this distribution?

b. What is the probability that exactly three think that now is a "good time"?

c. What is the probability that three or less think that now is a "good time"?

d. If three adults in your survey indicate that now is a "good time," do you think that 45% of the adults in the United States still think that now is a good time to look for a quality job?

5.28 An article reported that 29% of the home mortgage loans made by Washington Mutual Inc. in 2006 were

high-cost loans, mainly subprime loans made to those with weak credit histories or high debt in relation to income (J. R. Hagerty and A. Carrns, "WaMu Leads in Risky Type of Lending," *The Wall Street Journal*, April 17, 2007, p. A8). If you were to examine five home mortgage loans made by Washington Mutual Inc. in 2006, what is the probability that

a. none are high-cost loans?

b. all five are high-cost loans?

c. at least two are high-cost loans?

d. The article also reported that 15% of the home mortgage loans made by Washington Mutual Inc. in 2006 were granted to second-home owners or investors. Do a similar analysis for this type of loans you did for high-cost loans in (a) through (c)—find the probability that none, all five, and at least two loans were granted to second-home owners or investors. Compare the results for these loans to those of the high-cost loans you computed in (a) through (c).

5.29 When a customer places an order with Rudy's On-Line Office Supplies, a computerized accounting information system (AIS) automatically checks to see if the customer has exceeded his or her credit limit. Past records indicate that the probability of customers exceeding their credit limit is 0.05. Suppose that, on a given day, 20 customers place orders. Assume that the number of customers that the AIS detects as having exceeded their credit limit is distributed as a binomial random variable.

a. What are the mean and standard deviation of the number of customers exceeding their credit limits?

b. What is the probability that 0 customers will exceed their limits?

c. What is the probability that 1 customer will exceed his or her limit?

d. What is the probability that 2 or more customers will exceed their limits?

5.30 In a survey conducted by the Society for Human Resource Management, 68% of workers said that employers have the right to monitor their telephone use ("Snapshots," **usatoday.com**, April 18, 2006). Suppose that a random sample of 20 workers is selected, and they are asked if employers have the right to monitor telephone use. What is the probability that

a. 5 or less of the workers agree?

b. 10 or less of the workers agree?

c. 15 or less of the workers agree?

5.31 Referring to Problem 5.30, when the same workers were asked if employers have the right to monitor their cellphone use, the percentage dropped to 52%. Suppose that the 20 workers are asked if employers have the right to monitor cellphone use. What is the probability that

a. 5 or less of the workers agree?

b. 10 or less of the workers agree?

c. 15 or less of the workers agree?

d. Compare the results of (a) through (c) to those for Problem 5.30.

5.4 POISSON DISTRIBUTION

Many studies are based on counts of the times a particular event occurs in a given *area of opportunity*. An **area of opportunity** is a continuous unit or interval of time, volume, or any physical area in which there can be more than one occurrence of an event. Examples are the surface defects on a new refrigerator, the number of network failures in a day, the number of people arriving at a bank, and the number of fleas on the body of a dog. You can use the **Poisson distribution** to calculate probabilities in situations such as these if the following properties hold:

- You are interested in counting the number of times a particular event occurs in a given area of opportunity. The area of opportunity is defined by time, length, surface area, and so forth.
- The probability that an event occurs in a given area of opportunity is the same for all the areas of opportunity.
- The number of events that occur in one area of opportunity is independent of the number of events that occur in any other area of opportunity.
- The probability that two or more events will occur in an area of opportunity approaches zero as the area of opportunity becomes smaller.

Consider the number of customers arriving during the lunch hour at a bank located in the central business district in a large city. You are interested in the number of customers that arrive each minute. Does this situation match the four properties of the Poisson distribution given above? First, the *event* of interest is a customer arriving, and the *given area of opportunity* is defined as a 1-minute interval. Will zero customers arrive, one customer arrive, two customers arrive, and so on? Second, it is reasonable to assume that the probability that a customer arrives during a 1-minute interval is the same as the probability for all the other 1-minute intervals. Third, the arrival of one customer in any 1-minute interval has no effect on (i.e., is independent of) the arrival of any other customer in any other 1-minute interval. Finally, the probability that two or more customers will arrive in a given time period approaches zero as the time interval becomes small. For example, the probability is virtually zero that two customers will arrive in a time interval of 0.01 second. Thus, you can use the Poisson distribution to determine probabilities involving the number of customers arriving at the bank in a 1-minute time interval during the lunch hour.

The Poisson distribution has one parameter, called λ (the Greek lowercase letter *lambda*), which is the mean or expected number of events per unit. The variance of a Poisson distribution is also equal to λ, and the standard deviation is equal to $\sqrt{\lambda}$. The number of events, X, of the Poisson random variable ranges from 0 to infinity (∞).

Equation (5.14) presents the mathematical expression for the Poisson distribution for computing the probability of X events, given that λ events are expected.

Poisson Distribution

$$P(X) = \frac{e^{-\lambda}\lambda^X}{X!} \tag{5.14}$$

where

$P(X)$ = the probability of X events in an area of opportunity

λ = expected number of events

e = mathematical constant approximated by 2.71828

X = number of events ($X = 0, 1, 2, \ldots, \infty$)

To demonstrate the Poisson distribution, suppose that the mean number of customers who arrive per minute at the bank during the noon-to-1 p.m. hour is equal to 3.0. What is the probability that in a given minute, exactly two customers will arrive? And what is the probability that more than two customers will arrive in a given minute?

Using Equation (5.14) and $\lambda = 3$, the probability that in a given minute exactly two customers will arrive is

$$P(X = 2) = \frac{e^{-3.0}(3.0)^2}{2!} = \frac{9}{(2.71828)^3(2)} = 0.2240$$

To determine the probability that in any given minute more than two customers will arrive,

$$P(X > 2) = P(X = 3) + P(X = 4) + \cdots + P(X = \infty)$$

Because in a probability distribution, all the probabilities must sum to 1, the terms on the right side of the equation $P(X > 2)$ also represent the complement of the probability that X is less than or equal to 2 [i.e., $1 - P(X \le 2)$]. Thus,

$$P(X > 2) = 1 - P(X \le 2) = 1 - [P(X = 0) + P(X = 1) + P(X = 2)]$$

Now, using Equation (5.14),

$$P(X > 2) = 1 - \left[\frac{e^{-3.0}(3.0)^0}{0!} + \frac{e^{-3.0}(3.0)^1}{1!} + \frac{e^{-3.0}(3.0)^2}{2!} \right]$$

$$= 1 - [0.0498 + 0.1494 + 0.2240]$$

$$= 1 - 0.4232 = 0.5768$$

Thus, there is a 57.68% chance that more than two customers will arrive in the same minute.

To avoid drudgery involved in these computations, you can find Poisson probabilities directly from Table E.7 (in Appendix E), a portion of which is reproduced in Table 5.6. Table E.7 provides the probabilities that the Poisson random variable takes on values of $X = 0, 1, 2, \ldots$, for selected values of the parameter λ. To find the probability that exactly two customers will arrive in a given minute when the mean number of customers arriving is 3.0 per minute, you can read the probability corresponding to the row $X = 2$ and column $\lambda = 3.0$ from the table. The result is 0.2240, as demonstrated in Table 5.6.

You can also compute the Poisson probabilities given in Table E.7 by using Microsoft Excel or Minitab, as illustrated in Figures 5.5 and 5.6.

TABLE 5.6

Finding a Poisson Probability for $\lambda = 3$

X	2.1	2.2	....	3.0
0	.1225	.1108	....	.0498
1	.2572	.2438	....	.1494
2	.2700	.2681	....	.2240
3	.1890	.1966	....	.2240
4	.0992	.1082	....	.1680
5	.0417	.0476	....	.1008
6	.0146	.0174	....	.0504
7	.0044	.0055	....	.0216
8	.0011	.0015	....	.0081
9	.0003	.0004	....	.0027
10	.0001	.0001	....	.0008
11	.0000	.0000	....	.0002
12	.0000	.0000	....	.0001

Source: *Table E.7.*

FIGURE 5.5

Microsoft Excel
worksheet for
computing Poisson
probabilities with λ = 3

*See Section E5.4 or P5.3 to
create this.*

	A	B	C	D	E
1	Customer Arrivals Analysis				
2					
3		Data			
4	Mean/Expected number of events of interest:				3
5					
6	Poisson Probabilities Table				
7	X	P(X)			
8	0	0.049787	=POISSON(A8, E4, FALSE)		
9	1	0.149361	=POISSON(A9, E4, FALSE)		
10	2	0.224042	=POISSON(A10, E4, FALSE)		
11	3	0.224042	=POISSON(A11, E4, FALSE)		
12	4	0.168031	=POISSON(A12, E4, FALSE)		
13	5	0.100819	=POISSON(A13, E4, FALSE)		
14	6	0.050409	=POISSON(A14, E4, FALSE)		
15	7	0.021604	=POISSON(A15, E4, FALSE)		
16	8	0.008102	=POISSON(A16, E4, FALSE)		
17	9	0.002701	=POISSON(A17, E4, FALSE)		
18	10	0.000810	=POISSON(A18, E4, FALSE)		
19	11	0.000221	=POISSON(A19, E4, FALSE)		
20	12	0.000055	=POISSON(A20, E4, FALSE)		
21	13	0.000013	=POISSON(A21, E4, FALSE)		
22	14	0.000003	=POISSON(A22, E4, FALSE)		
23	15	0.000001	=POISSON(A23, E4, FALSE)		
24	16	0.000000	=POISSON(A24, E4, FALSE)		
25	17	0.000000	=POISSON(A25, E4, FALSE)		
26	18	0.000000	=POISSON(A26, E4, FALSE)		
27	19	0.000000	=POISSON(A27, E4, FALSE)		
28	20	0.000000	=POISSON(A28, E4, FALSE)		

FIGURE 5.6

Minitab results for
computing Poisson
probabilities with λ = 3

*See Section M5.2 to
create this.*

```
            Poisson with mean = 3

        x   P( X = x )
        0    0.049787
        1    0.149361
        2    0.224042
        3    0.224042
        4    0.168031
        5    0.100819
        6    0.050409
        7    0.021604
        8    0.008102
        9    0.002701
       10    0.000810
       11    0.000221
       12    0.000055
       13    0.000013
       14    0.000003
       15    0.000001
```

EXAMPLE 5.5

COMPUTING POISSON PROBABILITIES

The number of work-related injuries per month in a manufacturing plant is known to follow a
Poisson distribution with a mean of 2.5 work-related injuries a month. What is the probability that
in a given month no work-related injuries occur? That at least one work-related injury occurs?

SOLUTION Using Equation (5.14) on page 198 with $\lambda = 2.5$ (or using Table E.7 or Microsoft Excel or Minitab), the probability that in a given month no work-related injuries occur is

$$P(X = 0) = \frac{e^{-2.5}(2.5)^0}{0!} = \frac{1}{(2.71828)^{2.5}(1)} = 0.0821$$

The probability that there will be no work-related injuries in a given month is 0.0821 or 8.21%. Thus,

$$P(X \geq 1) = 1 - P(X = 0)$$
$$= 1 - 0.0821$$
$$= 0.9179$$

The probability that there will be at least one work-related injury is 0.9179 or 91.79%.

PROBLEMS FOR SECTION 5.4

Learning the Basics

5.32 Assume a Poisson distribution.
a. If $\lambda = 2.5$, find $P(X = 2)$.
b. If $\lambda = 8.0$, find $P(X = 8)$.
c. If $\lambda = 0.5$, find $P(X = 1)$.
d. If $\lambda = 3.7$, find $P(X = 0)$.

5.33 Assume a Poisson distribution.
a. If $\lambda = 2.0$, find $P(X \geq 2)$.
b. If $\lambda = 8.0$, find $P(X \geq 3)$.
c. If $\lambda = 0.5$, find $P(X \leq 1)$.
d. If $\lambda = 4.0$, find $P(X \geq 1)$.
e. If $\lambda = 5.0$, find $P(X \leq 3)$.

5.34 Assume a Poisson distribution with $\lambda = 5.0$. What is the probability that
a. $X = 1$?
b. $X < 1$?
c. $X > 1$?
d. $X \leq 1$?

Applying the Concepts

5.35 Assume that the number of network errors experienced in a day on a local area network (LAN) is distributed as a Poisson random variable. The mean number of network errors experienced in a day is 2.4. What is the probability that in any given day
a. zero network errors will occur?
b. exactly one network error will occur?
c. two or more network errors will occur?
d. less than three network errors will occur?

SELF Test **5.36** The quality control manager of Marilyn's Cookies is inspecting a batch of chocolate-chip cookies that has just been baked. If the production process is in control, the mean number of chip parts per cookie is 6.0. What is the probability that in any particular cookie being inspected
a. less than five chip parts will be found?
b. exactly five chip parts will be found?
c. five or more chip parts will be found?
d. either four or five chip parts will be found?

5.37 Refer to Problem 5.36. How many cookies in a batch of 100 should the manager expect to discard if company policy requires that all chocolate-chip cookies sold have at least four chocolate-chip parts?

5.38 The U.S. Department of Transportation maintains statistics for mishandled bags per 1,000 airline passengers. In 2005, Jet Blue had 4.06 mishandled bags per 1,000 passengers (extracted from M. Mullins, "Out of Place," *USA Today*, March 24, 2006, p. 10A). What is the probability that in the next 1,000 passengers, Jet Blue will have
a. no mishandled bags?
b. at least one mishandled bag?
c. at least two mishandled bags?
d. Compare the results in (a) through (c) to those of Delta in Problem 5.39(a) through (c).

5.39 The U.S. Department of Transportation maintains statistics for mishandled bags per 1,000 airline passengers. In 2005, Delta had 7.09 mishandled bags per 1,000 passengers (extracted from M. Mullins, "Out of Place," *USA*

Today, March 24, 2006, p. 10A). What is the probability that in the next 1,000 passengers, Delta will have
a. no mishandled bags?
b. at least one mishandled bag?
c. at least two mishandled bags?
d. Compare the results in (a) through (c) to those of Jet Blue in Problem 5.38(a) through (c).

5.40 Based on past experience, it is assumed that the number of flaws per foot in rolls of grade 2 paper follows a Poisson distribution with a mean of 1 flaw per 5 feet of paper (0.2 flaw per foot). What is the probability that in a
a. 1-foot roll, there will be at least 2 flaws?
b. 12-foot roll, there will be at least 1 flaw?
c. 50-foot roll, there will be greater than or equal to 5 flaws and less than or equal to 15 flaws?

5.41 J.D. Power and Associates calculates and publishes various statistics concerning car quality. The initial quality score measures the number of problems per new car sold. For 2007 model cars, Ford had 1.27 problems per car. Dodge had 1.32 problems per car (S. Carty, "Ford Moves Up in Quality Survey," *USA Today*, June 7, 2007, p. 3B). Let the random variable X be equal to the number of problems with a newly purchased 2007 Ford.
a. What assumptions must be made in order for X to be distributed as a Poisson random variable? Are these assumptions reasonable?
Making the assumptions as in (a), if you purchased a 2007 Ford, what is the probability that the new car will have
b. zero problems?
c. two or less problems?
d. Give an operational definition for *problem*. Why is the operational definition important in interpreting the initial quality score?

5.42 Refer to Problem 5.41. If you purchased a 2007 Dodge, what is the probability that the new car will have

a. zero problems?
b. two or less problems?
c. Compare your answers in (a) and (b) to those for the Ford in Problem 5.41(b) and (c).

5.43 Refer to Problem 5.41. The same article reported that in 2006, Ford had 1.20 problems per car, and Dodge had 1.56 problems per car. If you purchased a 2006 Ford, what is the probability that the new car will have
a. zero problems?
b. two or less problems?
c. Compare your answers in (a) and (b) to those for the 2007 Ford in Problem 5.41(b) and (c).

5.44 Refer to Problem 5.43. If you purchased a 2006 Dodge, what is the probability that the new car will have
a. zero problems?
b. two or less problems?
c. Compare your answers in (a) and (b) to those for the 2007 Dodge in Problem 5.42(a) and (b).

5.45 A toll-free phone number is available from 9 a.m. to 9 p.m. for your customers to register complaints about a product purchased from your company. Past history indicates that an average of 0.4 calls are received per minute.
a. What properties must be true about the situation described here in order to use the Poisson distribution to calculate probabilities concerning the number of phone calls received in a 1-minute period?
Assuming that this situation matches the properties discussed in (a), what is the probability that during a 1-minute period
b. zero phone calls will be received?
c. three or more phone calls will be received?
d. What is the maximum number of phone calls that will be received in a 1-minute period 99.99% of the time?

5.5   HYPERGEOMETRIC DISTRIBUTION

Both the binomial distribution and the **hypergeometric distribution** are concerned with the number of events of interest in a sample containing n observations. One of the differences in these two probability distributions is in the way that the samples are selected. For the binomial distribution, the sample data are selected *with* replacement from a *finite* population or *without* replacement from an *infinite* population. Thus, the probability of an event of interest, π, is constant over all observations, and the outcome of any particular observation is independent of any other. For the hypergeometric distribution, the sample data are selected *without* replacement from a *finite* population. Thus, the outcome of one observation is dependent on the outcomes of the previous observations.

Consider a population of size N. Let A represent the total number of events of interest in the population. The hypergeometric distribution is then used to find the probability of X events of interest in a sample of size n, selected without replacement. Equation (5.15) presents the mathematical expression of the hypergeometric distribution for finding the probability of X events of interest, given a knowledge of n, N, and A.

Hypergeometric Distribution

$$P(X) = \frac{\binom{A}{X}\binom{N-A}{n-X}}{\binom{N}{n}} \tag{5.15}$$

where

$P(X)$ = the probability of X events of interest, given knowledge of n, N, and A

n = sample size

N = population size

A = number of events of interest in the population

$N - A$ = number of events that are not of interest in the population

X = number of events of interest in the sample

$\binom{A}{X} = {}_AC_X$ [see Equation (5.10) on p. 190]

The number of events of interest in the sample, represented by X, cannot be greater than the number of events of interest in the population, A, or the sample size, n. Thus, the range of the hypergeometric random variable is limited to the sample size or to the number of events of interest in the population, whichever is smaller.

Equation (5.16) defines the mean of the hypergeometric distribution, and Equation (5.17) defines the standard deviation.

Mean of the Hypergeometric Distribution

$$\mu = E(X) = \frac{nA}{N} \tag{5.16}$$

Standard Deviation of the Hypergeometric Distribution

$$\sigma = \sqrt{\frac{nA(N-A)}{N^2}}\sqrt{\frac{N-n}{N-1}} \tag{5.17}$$

In Equation (5.17), the expression $\sqrt{\frac{N-n}{N-1}}$ is a **finite population correction factor** that results from sampling without replacement from a finite population.

To illustrate the hypergeometric distribution, suppose that you are forming a team of 8 managers from different departments within your company. Your company has a total of 30 managers, and 10 of these people are from the finance department. If members of the team are to be selected at random, what is the probability that the team will contain 2 managers from the finance department? Here, the population of $N = 30$ managers within the company is finite. In addition, $A = 10$ are from the finance department. A team of $n = 8$ members is to be selected.

Using Equation (5.15),

$$P(X = 2) = \frac{\dbinom{10}{2}\dbinom{20}{6}}{\dbinom{30}{8}}$$

$$= \frac{\dfrac{10!}{2!(8)!}\dfrac{(20)!}{(6)!(14)!}}{\dfrac{30!}{8!(22)!}}$$

$$= 0.298$$

Thus, the probability that the team will contain two members from the finance department is 0.298, or 29.8%.

Such computations can become tedious, especially as N gets large. However, you can compute hypergeometric probabilities by using Microsoft Excel or Minitab. Figures 5.7 and 5.8 present Microsoft Excel and Minitab results for the team-formation example, where the number of managers from the finance department (i.e., the number of events of interest in the sample) can be equal to 0, 1, 2, . . . , 8. (Note that Minitab uses the letter M instead of A to represent the number of events of interest in the population.)

FIGURE 5.7

Microsoft Excel worksheet for the team member example

See Section E5.5 or P5.4 to create this.

	A	B	
1	**Team Formation Analysis**		
2			
3	**Data**		
4	Sample size	8	
5	No. of events of interest in population	10	
6	Population size	30	
7			
8	**Hypergeometric Probabilities Table**		
9	X	P(X)	
10	0	0.0215	=HYPGEOMDIST(A10, B4, B5, B6)
11	1	0.1324	=HYPGEOMDIST(A11, B4, B5, B6)
12	2	0.2980	=HYPGEOMDIST(A12, B4, B5, B6)
13	3	0.3179	=HYPGEOMDIST(A13, B4, B5, B6)
14	4	0.1738	=HYPGEOMDIST(A14, B4, B5, B6)
15	5	0.0491	=HYPGEOMDIST(A15, B4, B5, B6)
16	6	0.0068	=HYPGEOMDIST(A16, B4, B5, B6)
17	7	0.0004	=HYPGEOMDIST(A17, B4, B5, B6)
18	8	0.0000	=HYPGEOMDIST(A18, B4, B5, B6)

FIGURE 5.8

Minitab results for the team member example

See Section M5.3 to create this.

```
Hypergeometric with N = 30, M = 10, and n = 8

x    P( X = x )
0      0.021523
1      0.132447
2      0.298005
3      0.317872
4      0.173836
5      0.049083
6      0.006817
7      0.000410
8      0.000008
```

PROBLEMS FOR SECTION 5.5

Learning the Basics

5.46 Determine the following:
a. If $n = 4$, $N = 10$, and $A = 5$, find $P(X = 3)$.
b. If $n = 4$, $N = 6$, and $A = 3$, find $P(X = 1)$.
c. If $n = 5$, $N = 12$, and $A = 3$, find $P(X = 0)$.
d. If $n = 3$, $N = 10$, and $A = 3$, find $P(X = 3)$.

5.47 Referring to Problem 5.46, compute the mean and standard deviation for the hypergeometric distributions described in (a) through (d).

Applying the Concepts

 **5.48** An auditor for the Internal Revenue Service is selecting a sample of 6 tax returns for an audit. If 2 or more of these returns are "improper," the entire population of 100 tax returns will be audited. What is the probability that the entire population will be audited if the actual number of improper returns in the population is
a. 25?
b. 30?
c. 5?
d. 10?
e. Discuss the differences in your results, depending on the actual number of improper returns in the population.

5.49 The dean of a business school wishes to form an executive committee of 5 from among the 40 tenured faculty members at the school. The selection is to be random, and at the school there are 8 tenured faculty members in accounting. What is the probability that the committee will contain

a. none of them?
b. at least 1 of them?
c. not more than 1 of them?
d. What is your answer to (a) if the committee consists of 7 members?

5.50 From a shipment of 30 cars being sent to a local automobile dealer, 4 are SUVs. What is the probability that if 4 cars arrive at a particular dealership,
a. all 4 are SUVs?
b. none are SUVs?
c. at least 1 is an SUV?
d. What are your answers to (a) through (c) if 6 cars being shipped are SUVs?

5.51 A state lottery is conducted in which 6 winning numbers are selected from a total of 54 numbers. What is the probability that if 6 numbers are randomly selected,
a. all 6 numbers will be winning numbers?
b. 5 numbers will be winning numbers?
c. none of the numbers will be winning numbers?
d. What are your answers to (a) through (c) if the 6 winning numbers are selected from a total of 40 numbers?

5.52 In a shipment of 15 sets of golf clubs, 3 are left-handed. If 4 sets of golf clubs are selected, what is the probability that
a. exactly 1 is left-handed?
b. at least 1 is left-handed?
c. no more than 2 are left-handed?
d. What is the mean number of left-handed sets of golf clubs that you would expect to find in the sample of 4 sets of golf clubs?

5.6 ✺ (CD-ROM TOPIC) USING THE POISSON DISTRIBUTION TO APPROXIMATE THE BINOMIAL DISTRIBUTION

Under certain circumstances, the Poisson distribution can be used to approximate the binomial distribution. To study this topic, go to the section5.6.pdf file located on the Student CD-ROM that accompanies this book.

SUMMARY

In this chapter, you have studied mathematical expectation, the covariance, and the binomial, Poisson, and hypergeometric distributions. In the Using Statistics scenario, you

learned how to calculate probabilities from the binomial distribution concerning the observation of tagged invoices in the accounting information system used by the Saxon

Home Improvement Company. In the following chapter, you will study several important continuous distributions including the normal distribution.

To help decide what probability distribution to use for a particular situation, you need to ask the following questions:

• Is there a fixed number of observations, n, each of which is classified as an event of interest or not an event of interest? Or is there an area of opportunity? If there is a fixed number of observations, n, each of which is classified as an event of interest or not an event of interest, you use the binomial or hypergeometric distribution. If there is an area of opportunity, you use the Poisson distribution.

• In deciding whether to use the binomial or hypergeometric distribution, is the probability of an event of interest constant over all trials? If yes, you can use the binomial distribution. If no, you can use the hypergeometric distribution.

Probability Distributions—More Likely Than You Think

From the Authors' Desktop

At first glance, probability distributions seem so abstract as to be not applicable in your daily life. Although the theory behind these distributions is perhaps the single most challenging topic in this book, the applications of probability distributions are a lot more accessible than you might first realize.

Taking the topics in the order in which they appeared in the chapter, the covariance and portfolio risk represents the foundation for what you need to know in order to develop portfolios in finance. Of course, to keep things simple, the example in the chapter examined only two alternatives. In developing an actual portfolio, many different alternative investments would be considered.

The binomial distribution, originally developed back in the eighteenth century for games of chance, finds applications today in the securities marketplace (to some, the ultimate game of chance!). Some examples include the relationship between the S & P index during the first five days of the year and the entire year (see Problem 5.70 on page 210), the likelihood

of equaling the record of 14 consecutive daily increases in the Dow Jones Industrial Average set in 1897 (E. S. Browning, "Dow Ends Run at History," *The Wall Street Journal*, April 12, 2007, p. C1), and the possible relationship between the winner of the National Football League Super Bowl and the performance of the Dow Jones Industrial Average (see Problem 5.71 on page 210).

Even though the Poisson distribution might sound a bit fishy (*poisson* is the French word for fish), you may have crossed paths with this distribution waiting in line at a bank, a toll plaza, and yes, waiting to buy a Filet-O-Fish sandwich or other item at a local McDonald's. If you ever wondered why there is only one line (or why there is a separate line for each server) and how the bank, toll authority, or restaurant determined how many servers should be available at a certain time, you have discovered applications of waiting line or queuing theory. Queuing theory depends on the Poisson distribution for the distribution of the arrivals and depends on the exponential distribution (to be covered in Section 6.5) for

the distribution of how long it takes to be served.

Don't like to wait in lines? How about the chance that you will have a certain number of problems with your new car or that an airline will lose a piece of luggage that you checked, or that you will lose more than a certain number of balls in an 18-hole round of golf? Answers to these types of questions also depend on the Poisson distribution.

Finally, you might one day "take a chance" on the hypergeometric distribution, if you play *Powerball* or other lottery-type games. If you really want to know more than "your chance of winning may vary," you can use the hypergeometric distribution to compute the probability of winning a prize in the lottery (see Problem 5.74 on page 210 for one example) or the probability that the lottery ticket you purchased won't be worth anything.

So keep your eyes and ears open, and something related to probability distributions is bound to enter your work life or everyday life.

KEY EQUATIONS

Expected Value, μ, of a Discrete Random Variable

$$\mu = E(X) = \sum_{i=1}^{N} X_i P(X_i) \qquad (5.1)$$

Variance of a Discrete Random Variable

$$\sigma^2 = \sum_{i=1}^{N} [X_i - E(X)]^2 P(X_i) \qquad (5.2)$$

Standard Deviation of a Discrete Random Variable

$$\sigma = \sqrt{\sigma^2} = \sqrt{\sum_{i=1}^{N} [X_i - E(X)]^2 P(X_i)} \qquad (5.3)$$

Covariance

$$\sigma_{XY} = \sum_{i=1}^{N} [X_i - E(X)][Y_i - E(Y)]P(X_iY_i) \qquad (5.4)$$

Expected Value of the Sum of Two Random Variables

$$E(X + Y) = E(X) + E(Y) \qquad (5.5)$$

Variance of the Sum of Two Random Variables

$$Var(X + Y) = \sigma_{X+Y}^2 = \sigma_X^2 + \sigma_Y^2 + 2\sigma_{XY} \qquad (5.6)$$

Standard Deviation of the Sum of Two Random Variables

$$\sigma_{X+Y} = \sqrt{\sigma_{X+Y}^2} \qquad (5.7)$$

Portfolio Expected Return

$$E(P) = wE(X) + (1 - w)E(Y) \qquad (5.8)$$

Portfolio Risk

$$\sigma_p = \sqrt{w^2\sigma_X^2 + (1-w)^2\sigma_Y^2 + 2w(1-w)\sigma_{XY}} \qquad (5.9)$$

Combinations

$$_nC_X = \frac{n!}{X!(n-X)!} \qquad (5.10)$$

Binomial Distribution

$$P(X) = \frac{n!}{X!(n-X)!}\pi^X(1-\pi)^{n-X} \qquad (5.11)$$

Mean of the Binomial Distribution

$$\mu = E(X) = n\pi \qquad (5.12)$$

Standard Deviation of the Binomial Distribution

$$\sigma = \sqrt{\sigma^2} = \sqrt{Var(X)} = \sqrt{n\pi(1-\pi)} \qquad (5.13)$$

Poisson Distribution

$$P(X) = \frac{e^{-\lambda}\lambda^X}{X!} \qquad (5.14)$$

Hypergeometric Distribution

$$P(X) = \frac{\binom{A}{X}\binom{N-A}{n-X}}{\binom{N}{n}} \qquad (5.15)$$

Mean of the Hypergeometric Distribution

$$\mu = E(X) = \frac{nA}{N} \qquad (5.16)$$

Standard Deviation of the Hypergeometric Distribution

$$\sigma = \sqrt{\frac{nA(N-A)}{N^2}}\sqrt{\frac{N-n}{N-1}} \qquad (5.17)$$

KEY TERMS

area of opportunity   198
binomial distribution   189
covariance, σ_{XY} 185
expected value of the sum of two
   random variables   186
expected value, μ, of a discrete random
   variable   181
finite population correction
   factor   203

hypergeometric distribution   202
mathematical model   189
Poisson distribution   198
portfolio   187
portfolio expected return   187
portfolio risk   187
probability distribution for a discrete
   random variable   180
rule of combinations   190

standard deviation of a discrete
   random variable   182
standard deviation of the sum of two
   random variables   186
variance of a discrete random
   variable   182
variance of the sum of two random
   variables   186

CHAPTER REVIEW PROBLEMS

Checking Your Understanding

5.53 What is the meaning of the expected value of a probability distribution?

5.54 What are the four properties that must be present in order to use the binomial distribution?

5.55 What are the four properties that must be present in order to use the Poisson distribution?

5.56 When do you use the hypergeometric distribution instead of the binomial distribution?

Applying the Concepts

5.57 Event insurance allows promoters of sporting and entertainment events to protect themselves from financial losses due to uncontrollable circumstances such as rainouts. For example, each spring, Cincinnati's Downtown Council puts on the Taste of Cincinnati. This is a rainy time of year in Cincinnati, and the chance of receiving an inch or more of rain during a spring weekend is about one out of four. An article in the *Cincinnati Enquirer*, by Jim Knippenberg ("Chicken Pox Means 3 Dog Night Remedy," *Cincinnati Enquirer*, May 28, 1997, p. E1), gave the details for an insurance policy purchased by the Downtown Council. The policy would pay $100,000 if it rained more than an inch during the weekend festival. The cost of the policy was reported to be $6,500.
a. Determine whether you believe that these dollar amounts are correct. (*Hint:* Calculate the expected value of the profit to be made by the insurance company.)
b. Assume that the dollar amounts are correct. Is this policy a good deal for Cincinnati's Downtown Council?

5.58 Between 1872 and 2000, stock prices rose in 74% of the years (M. Hulbert, "The Stock Market Must Rise in 2002? Think Again," *The New York Times*, December 6, 2001, Business, p. 6). Based on this information, and assuming a binomial distribution, what do you think the probability is that the stock market will rise
a. next year?
b. the year after next?
c. in four of the next five years?
d. in none of the next five years?
e. For this situation, what assumption of the binomial distribution might not be valid?

5.59 The mean cost of a phone call handled by an automated customer-service system is $0.45. The mean cost of a phone call passed on to a "live" operator is $5.50. However, as more and more companies have implemented automated systems, customer annoyance with such systems has grown. Many customers are quick to leave the automated system when given an option such as "Press zero to talk to a customer-service representative." According to the Center for Client Retention, 40% of all callers to automated customer-service systems automatically opt to go to a live operator when given the chance (J. Spencer, "In Search of the Operator," *The Wall Street Journal*, May 8, 2002, p. D1).

If 10 independent callers contact an automated customer-service system, what is the probability that
a. 0 will automatically opt to talk to a live operator?
b. exactly 1 will automatically opt to talk to a live operator?
c. 2 or less will automatically opt to talk to a live operator?
d. all 10 will automatically opt to talk to a live operator?
e. If all 10 automatically opt to talk to a live operator, do you think that the 40% figure given in the article applies to this particular system? Explain.

5.60 One theory concerning the Dow Jones Industrial Average is that it is likely to increase during U.S. presidential election years. From 1964 through 2004, the Dow Jones Industrial Average increased in 9 of the 11 U.S. presidential election years. Assuming that this indicator is a random event with no predictive value, you would expect that the indicator would be correct 50% of the time.
a. What is the probability of the Dow Jones Industrial Average increasing in 9 or more of the 11 U.S. presidential election years if the true probability of an increase in the Dow Jones Industrial Average is 0.50?
b. Read Problem 5.58 and note that the Dow Jones Industrial Average increased in 74% of the years studied. What is the probability of the Dow Jones Industrial Average increasing in 9 or more of the 11 U.S. presidential election years if the probability of an increase in the Dow Jones Industrial Average is 0.74?

5.61 Priority Mail is the U.S. Postal Service's alternative to commercial express mail companies such as FedEx. An article in *The Wall Street Journal* presented some interesting conclusions comparing Priority Mail shipments with the much less expensive first-class shipments (R. Brooks, "New Data Reveal 'Priority Mail' Is Slower Than a Stamp," *The Wall Street Journal*, May 29, 2002, p. D1). When comparing shipments intended for delivery in three days, first-class deliveries failed to deliver on time 19% of the time, whereas Priority Mail failed 33% of the time. Note that at the time of the article, first-class deliveries started as low as $0.34, and Priority Mail started at $3.50.

If 10 items are to be shipped first-class to 10 different destinations claimed to be in a three-day delivery location, what is the probability that
a. 0 items will take more than three days?
b. exactly 1 item will take more than three days?

c. 2 or more will take more than three days?

d. What are the mean and the standard deviation of the probability distribution?

5.62 Refer to Problem 5.61. If the shipments are made using Priority Mail, what is the probability that

a. 0 items will take more than three days?

b. exactly 1 will take more than three days?

c. 2 or more will take more than three days?

d. What are the mean and the standard deviation of the probability distribution?

e. Compare the results of (a) through (c) to those of Problem 5.61(a) through (c).

5.63 Cinema advertising is increasing. Normally 60 to 90 seconds long, these advertisements are longer and more extravagant, and they tend to have more captive audiences than television advertisements. Thus, it is not surprising that the recall rates for viewers of cinema advertisements are higher than those for television advertisements. According to survey research conducted by the ComQUEST division of BBM Bureau of Measurement in Toronto, the probability a viewer will remember a cinema advertisement is 0.74, whereas the probability a viewer will remember a 30-second television advertisement is 0.37 (N. Hendley, "Cinema Advertising Comes of Age," *Marketing Magazine*, May 6, 2002, p. 16).

a. Is the 0.74 probability reported by the BBM Bureau of Measurement best classified as *a priori* probability, empirical probability, or subjective probability?

b. Suppose that 10 viewers of a cinema advertisement are randomly sampled. Consider the random variable defined by the number of viewers who recall the advertisement. What assumptions must be made in order to assume that this random variable is distributed as a binomial random variable?

c. Assuming that the number of viewers who recall the cinema advertisement is a binomial random variable, what are the mean and standard deviation of this distribution?

d. Based on your answer to (c), if none of the viewers can recall the ad, what can be inferred about the 0.74 probability given in the article?

5.64 Refer to Problem 5.63. Compute the probability that of the 10 viewers of the cinema advertisement,

a. exactly 0 can recall the advertisement.

b. all 10 can recall the advertisement.

c. more than half can recall the advertisement.

d. 8 or more can recall the advertisement.

5.65 Refer to Problem 5.63. For television advertisements, using the given probability of recall, 0.37, compute the probability that of the 10 viewers,

a. exactly 0 can recall the advertisement.

b. all 10 can recall the advertisement.

c. more than half can recall the advertisement.

d. 8 or more can recall the advertisement.

e. Compare the results of (a) through (d) to those of Problem 5.64(a) through (d).

5.66 A survey conducted by Neilsen/Net Ratings (J. Angwin and K. Delaney, "My Space's Pact with Google Hits a Snag," *The Wall Street Journal*, February 7, 2007, p. B3) it indicated that 51% of the searches conducted in the United States used Google as the search engine. Suppose that you are to randomly call 10 Internet users in the United States and ask them to name the search engine they used. Using the results of the Neilsen/Net Ratings study, what is the probability that

a. all 10 will have used Google as the search engine?

b. exactly 5 will have used Google as the search engine?

c. at least 5 will have used Google as the search engine?

d. less than 5 will have used Google as the search engine?

e. What is the expected number of people who have used Google as the search engine? Explain the practical meaning of this number.

5.67 A study by the Center for Financial Services Innovation showed that in 2004 only 64% of U.S. income earners aged 15 and older had a bank account (A. Carrns, "Banks Court a New Client," *The Wall Street Journal*, March 16, 2007, p. D1).

If a random sample of 20 U.S. income earners aged 15 and older is selected, what is the probability that

a. all 20 have a bank account?

b. no more than 15 have a bank account?

c. more than 10 have a bank account?

d. What assumptions did you have to make to answer (a) through (c)?

5.68 One of the retail industry's biggest frustrations is customers who abuse the return and exchange policies (S. Kang, "New Return Policy: Retailers Say 'No' to Serial Exchangers," *The Wall Street Journal*, November 29, 2004, pp. B1, B3). In a recent year, returns were 13% of sales in department stores. Consider a sample of 20 customers who make a purchase at a department store. Use the binomial model to answer the following questions:

a. What is the expected value, or mean, of the binomial distribution?

b. What is the standard deviation of the binomial distribution?

c. What is the probability that none of the 20 customers will make a return?

d. What is the probability that no more than 2 of the customers will make a return?

e. What is the probability that 3 or more of the customers will make a return?

5.69 Refer to Problem 5.68. In the same year, returns were 1% of sales in grocery stores.

a. What is the expected value, or mean, of the binomial distribution?

b. What is the standard deviation of the binomial distribution?

c. What is the probability that none of the 20 customers will make a return?

d. What is the probability that no more than 2 of the customers will make a return?

e. What is the probability that 3 or more of the customers will make a return?

f. Compare the results of (a) through (e) to those of Problem 5.68(a) through (e).

5.70 One theory concerning the S&P 500 index is that if it increases during the first five trading days of the year, it is likely to increase during the entire year. From 1950 through 2006, the S&P 500 index had these early gains in 37 years. In 31 of these 37 years, the S&P 500 index increased. Assuming that this indicator is a random event with no predictive value, you would expect that the indicator would be correct 50% of the time. What is the probability of the S&P 500 index increasing in 31 or more years if the true probability of an increase in the S&P 500 index is

a. 0.50?

b. 0.70?

c. 0.90?

d. Based on the results of (a) through (c), what do you think is the probability that the S&P 500 index will increase if there is an early gain in the first five trading days of the year? Explain.

5.71 *Spurious correlation* refers to the apparent relationship between variables that either have no true relationship or are related to other variables that have not been measured. One widely publicized stock market indicator in the United States that is an example of spurious correlation is the relationship between the winner of the National Football League Super Bowl and the performance of the Dow Jones Industrial Average in that year. The indicator states that when a team representing the National Football Conference wins the Super Bowl, the Dow Jones Industrial Average will increase in that year. When a team representing the American Football Conference wins the Super Bowl, the Dow Jones Industrial Average will decline in that year. Since the first Super Bowl was held in 1967 through 2006, the indicator has been correct 32 out of 40 times. Assuming that this indicator is a random event with no predictive value, you would expect that the indicator would be correct 50% of the time.

a. What is the probability that the indicator would be correct 32 or more times in 40 years?

b. What does this tell you about the usefulness of this indicator?

5.72 Worldwide golf ball sales total more than $1 billion annually. One reason for such a large number of golf ball purchases is that golfers lose them at a rate of 4.5 per 18-hole round ("Snapshots," **www.usatoday.com**, January 29,

2004). Assume that the number of golf balls lost in an 18-hole round is distributed as a Poisson random variable.

a. What assumptions need to be made so that the number of golf balls lost in an 18-hole round is distributed as a Poisson random variable?

Making the assumptions given in (a), what is the probability that

b. 0 balls will be lost in an 18-hole round?

c. 5 or less balls will be lost in an 18-hole round?

d. 6 or more balls will be lost in an 18-hole round?

5.73 According to a Virginia Tech survey, college students make an average of 11 calls per day on their cellphone. Moreover, 80% of the students surveyed indicated that their parents pay their cellphone expenses (Jean Elliot, "Professor Researches Cell Phone Usage among Students," **www.physorg.com**, February 26, 2007).

a. What distribution can you use to model the number of calls a student makes in a day?

b. If you select a student at random, what is the probability that he or she makes more than 10 calls in a day? More than 15? More than 20?

c. If you select a random sample of 10 students, what distribution can you use to model the proportion of students who have parents that pay their cellphone expenses?

d. Using the distribution selected in (c), what is the probability that all 10 have parents that pay their cellphone expenses? At least 9? At least 8?

5.74 Mega Millions is one of the most popular lottery games in the United States. Participating states in Mega Millions are Georgia, Illinois, Maryland, Massachusetts, Michigan, New Jersey, New York, Ohio, and Virginia. Rules for playing and the list of prizes are given below ("Win Megamoney Playing Ohio's Biggest Jackpot Game," Ohio Lottery Headquarters, 2002):

Rules:

- Select five numbers from a pool of numbers from 1 to 52 and one Mega Ball number from a second pool of numbers from 1 to 52.
- Each wager costs $1.

Prizes:

- Match all five numbers + Mega Ball—win jackpot (minimum of $10,000,000)
- Match all five numbers—win $175,000
- Match four numbers + Mega Ball—win $5,000
- Match four numbers—win $150
- Match three numbers + Mega Ball—win $150
- Match two numbers + Mega Ball—win $10
- Match three numbers—win $7
- Match one number + Mega Ball—win $3
- Match Mega Ball—win $2

Find the probability of winning
a. the jackpot.
b. the $175,000 prize. (Note that this requires matching all five numbers but not matching the Mega Ball.)
c. $5,000.
d. $150.
e. $10.
f. $7.
g. $3.
h. $2.
i. nothing.
j. All stores selling Mega Millions tickets are required to have a brochure that gives complete game rules and probabilities of winning each prize (the probability of having a losing ticket is not given). The slogan for all lottery games in the state of Ohio is "Play Responsibly. Odds Are, You'll Have Fun." Do you think Ohio's slogan and the requirement of making available complete game rules and probabilities of winning is an ethical approach to running the lottery system?

MANAGING THE *SPRINGVILLE HERALD*

The *Herald* marketing department is seeking to increase home-delivery sales through an aggressive direct-marketing campaign that includes mailings, discount coupons, and telephone solicitations. Feedback from these efforts indicates that getting their newspapers delivered early in the morning is a very important factor for both prospective as well as existing subscribers. After several brainstorming sessions, a team consisting of members from the marketing and circulation departments decided that guaranteeing newspaper delivery by a specific time could be an important selling point in retaining and getting new subscribers. The team concluded that the *Herald* should offer a guarantee that customers will receive their newspapers by a certain time or else that day's issue is free.

To assist the team in setting a guaranteed delivery time, Al Leslie, the research director, determined that the circulation department had data that showed the percentage of newspapers yet undelivered every quarter hour from 6 a.m. to 8 a.m. Jan Shapiro remembered that customers were asked on their subscription forms at what time they would be looking for their copy of the *Herald* to be delivered. These data were subsequently combined and posted on an internal *Herald* Web page. (See `Circulation_Data.htm` in the Herald Case folder on the Student CD-ROM or go to **www.prenhall.com/HeraldCase/Circulation_Data.htm**).

EXERCISES

Review the internal data and propose a reasonable time (to the nearest quarter hour) to guarantee delivery. To help explore the effects of your choice, calculate the following probabilities:

SH5.1 If a sample of 50 customers is selected on a given day, what is the probability, given your selected delivery time, that
 a. less than 3 customers will receive a free newspaper?
 b. 2, 3, or 4 customers will receive a free newspaper?
 c. more than 5 customers will receive a free newspaper?

SH5.2 Consider the effects of improving the newspaper delivery process so that the percentage of newspapers that go undelivered by your guaranteed delivery time decreases by 2%. If a sample of 50 customers is selected on a given day, what is the probability, given your selected delivery time (and the delivery improvement), that
 a. less than 3 customers will receive a free newspaper?
 b. 2, 3, or 4 customers will receive a free newspaper?
 c. more than 5 customers will receive a free newspaper?

WEB CASE

Apply your knowledge about expected value and the covariance in this continuing Web Case from Chapters 3 and 4.

Visit the EndRun Bulls and Bears Web page, at **www.prenhall.com/Springville/ER_BullsandBears.htm** (or open the Web page file from the Student CD-ROM Web Case folder), read the claims, and examine the supporting data. Then answer the following:

1. Are there any "catches" about the claims the Web site makes for the rate of return of Happy Bull and Worried Bear Funds?

2. What subjective data influence the rate-of-return analyses of these funds? Could EndRun be accused of making false and misleading statements? Why or why not?

3. The expected-return analysis seems to show that the Worried Bear Fund has a greater expected return than the Happy Bull Fund. Should a rational investor never invest in the Happy Bull Fund? Why or why not?

REFERENCES

1. Bernstein, P. L., *Against the Gods: The Remarkable Story of Risk* (New York: Wiley, 1996).
2. Emery, D. R., J. D. Finnerty, and J. D. Stowe, *Corporate Financial Management*, 3rd ed. (Upper Saddle River, NJ: Prentice Hall, 2007).
3. Kirk, R. L., ed., *Statistical Issues: A Reader for the Behavioral Sciences* (Belmont, CA: Wadsworth, 1972).
4. Levine, D. M., P. Ramsey, and R. Smidt, *Applied Statistics for Engineers and Scientists Using Microsoft Excel and Minitab* (Upper Saddle River, NJ: Prentice Hall, 2001).
5. *Microsoft Excel 2007* (Redmond, WA: Microsoft Corp., 2007).
6. *Minitab Version 15* (State College, PA: Minitab, Inc., 2006).
7. Moscove, S. A., M. G. Simkin, and A. Bagranoff, *Core Concepts of Accounting Information Systems*, 10th ed. (New York: Wiley, 2007).

Appendix E5
Using Microsoft Excel for Discrete Probability Distributions

E5.1 Computing the Expected Value of a Discrete Random Variable

You compute the expected value of a discrete random variable by making entries in the **Discrete** worksheet of the **Expected Value.xls** workbook. This worksheet uses the SUM and SQRT (square root) functions to calculate its statistics.

Figure E5.1 shows a completed worksheet using the mortgage probability distribution of Table 5.1 on page 181. To adapt this worksheet to other problems that have more or less than seven outcomes, first select the cell range **A5:E5**. To add table rows, right-click and click **Insert**. (If a box of options appears, click **Shift cells down** and then click **OK**.) Then, copy the formulas in cell range C4:E4 down through the new table rows and enter the new X and $P(X)$ values in columns A and B.

To delete table rows, right-click and click **Delete**. (If a box of options appears, click **Shift cells up** and then click **OK**.) Enter a corrected list of X values starting with **1** in cell A5 in column A and enter the new $P(X)$ values in column B.

E5.2 Computing Portfolio Expected Return and Portfolio Risk

You compute the portfolio expected return and the portfolio risk of two investments by opening to the **Portfolio** worksheet of the **Portfolio.xls** workbook (see Figure E5.2). This worksheet already contains the entries for the estimated returns for the investment data of Table 5.4 on page 185. To adapt this worksheet to other problems, change the probabilities and outcomes table data and the **Weight Assigned to X** value. If your problem does not have three

	A	B	C	D	E	F	G	H	
1	Discrete Random Variable Probability Distribution								
2							Statistics		
3	X	P(X)	X*P(X)	[X-E(X)]^2	[X-E(X)]^2*P(X)		Expected value	2.8	=SUM(C:C)
4	0	0.10	0	7.84	0.784		Variance	2.46	=SUM(E:E)
5	1	0.10	0.1	3.24	0.324		Standard deviation	1.57	=SQRT(H4)
6	2	0.20	0.4	0.64	0.128				
7	3	0.30	0.9	0.04	0.012		X*P(X)	[X - E(X)]^2	[X - E(X)]^2*P(X)
8	4	0.15	0.6	1.44	0.216		=A4 * B4	=(A4 - H3)^2	=D4 * B4
9	5	0.10	0.5	4.84	0.484		=A5 * B5	=(A5 - H3)^2	=D5 * B5
10	6	0.05	0.3	10.24	0.512		=A6 * B6	=(A6 - H3)^2	=D6 * B6
							=A7 * B7	=(A7 - H3)^2	=D7 * B7
							=A8 * B8	=(A8 - H3)^2	=D8 * B8
							=A9 * B9	=(A9 - H3)^2	=D9 * B9

FIGURE E5.1
Discrete worksheet

	A	B	C	D
1	Portfolio Expected Return and Risk			
2				
3	Probabilities & Outcomes:	P	X	Y
4		0.2	-100	200
5		0.5	100	50
6		0.3	250	-100
7				
8	Weight Assigned to X	0.5		
9				
10	Statistics			
11	E(X)	105	=SUMPRODUCT(B4:B6, C4:C6)	
12	E(Y)	35	=SUMPRODUCT(B4:B6, D4:D6)	
13	Variance(X)	14725	=SUMPRODUCT(B4:B6, H4:H6)	
14	Standard Deviation(X)	121.3466	=SQRT(B13)	
15	Variance(Y)	11025	=SUMPRODUCT(B4:B6, I4:I6)	
16	Standard Deviation(Y)	105	=SQRT(B15)	
17	Covariance(XY)	-12675	=SUMPRODUCT(B4:B6, J4:J6)	
18	Variance(X+Y)	400	=B13 + B15 + 2 * B17	
19	Standard Deviation(X+Y)	20	=SQRT(B18)	
20				
21	Portfolio Management			
22	Weight Assigned to X	0.5	=B8	
23	Weight Assigned to Y	0.5	=1 - B22	
24	Portfolio Expected Return	70	=B22 * B11 + B23 * B12	
25	Portfolio Risk	10	=SQRT(B22^2 * B13 + B23^2 * B15 + 2 * B22 * B23 * B17)	

FIGURE E5.2
Portfolio worksheet

outcomes, first select **row 5** and then add or delete rows one at a time by right-clicking row 5 and clicking either **Insert** or **Delete**. (If you inserted rows, you will also have to copy formulas down to those new rows.)

The worksheet features the **SUMPRODUCT(*cell range 1, cell range 2*)** function, which computes the sum of the products of corresponding elements of two cell ranges (or arrays, in mathematical terms). In this worksheet, the first array/cell range is always the set of $P(X_iY_i)$ probabilities. To compute the variance, standard deviation, and covariance, the worksheet uses a calculation area in rows F through J (not shown in Figure E5.2).

E5.3 Computing Binomial Probabilities

You compute binomial probabilities by making entries in the **Binomial** worksheet of the `Binomial.xls` workbook. This worksheet (shown in Figure 5.2 on page 194) already contains the entries for the tagged orders example of Section 5.3. To adapt this worksheet to other problems, change the **Sample size** and **Probability of an event of interest** values in cells B4 and B5. If your problem has a sample size other than 4, first select **row 15** and then add or delete rows one at a time by right-clicking row 15 and clicking either **Insert** or **Delete** and adjusting the X values in column A. (If you inserted rows, you will also have to copy formulas down to those new rows.)

The worksheet features the **BINOMDIST(*X, n, π, cumulative*)** function in which X is the number of events of interest, n is the sample size, π is the probability of an event

of interest, and *cumulative* is a True or False value. When *cumulative* is **True**, the function computes the probability of X or fewer events of interest; when *cumulative* is **False**, the function computes the probability of exactly X events of interest.

E5.4 Computing Poisson Probabilities

You compute Poisson probabilities by making entries in the **Poisson** worksheet of the `Poisson.xls` workbook. This worksheet (shown in Figure 5.5 on page 200) already contains the entries for the bank customer arrivals problem of Section 5.4. To adapt this worksheet to other problems, change the **Mean/Expected number of events of interest value** in cell **E4**.

The worksheet features the **POISSON(*X, lambda, cumulative*)** function in which X is the number of events of interest, *lambda* is the average or expected number of events of interest, and *cumulative* is a True or False value. When *cumulative* is **True**, the function computes the probability of X or fewer events of interest; when *cumulative* is **False**, the function computes the probability of exactly X events of interest.

E5.5 Computing Hypergeometric Probabilities

You compute Hypergeometric probabilities by making entries in the **Hypergeometric** worksheet of the `Hypergeometric.xls` workbook. This worksheet (shown in Figure 5.7 on page 204) already contains the entries for the team formation problem of Section 5.5. To adapt this worksheet to other problems, change the **Sample size**, **No. of events of interest in population**, and **Population size** in the cell range **B4:B6**. If your problem has a sample size other than 8, first select **row 11**, then right-click and click either **Insert** (or **Delete**) to add (or delete) rows one at a time. Finish by adjusting the X values in column A. (If you inserted rows, you will also have to copy formulas down to those new rows.)

The worksheet features the **HYPERGEOMDIST(X, n, A, N)** function in which X is the number of events of interest, n is the sample size, A is the number of events of interest in the population, and N is the population size. When *cumulative* is **False**, the function computes the probability of exactly X events of interest.

Appendix P5
Using PHStat2 for Discrete Probability Distributions

P5.1 Computing Portfolio Expected Return & Portfolio Risk

To compute the portfolio expected return and the portfolio risk of two investments, use **PHStat → Decision-Making → Covariance and Portfolio Analysis**. This procedure creates a covariance (and portfolio analysis) worksheet into which you add the probabilities and outcomes. Click **Portfolio Management Analysis** to include the portfolio analysis section on the worksheet and create a worksheet similar to Figure E5.2 on page 213.

194 using the sample size, probability of an event of interest, and an outcomes range that you specify. If you click **Cumulative Probabilities**, the binomial table will include additional columns for $P(\leq X)$, $P(<X)$, $P(>X)$, and $P(\geq X)$. If you click **Histogram**, the procedure uses Excel charting features to create a histogram on a separate sheet.

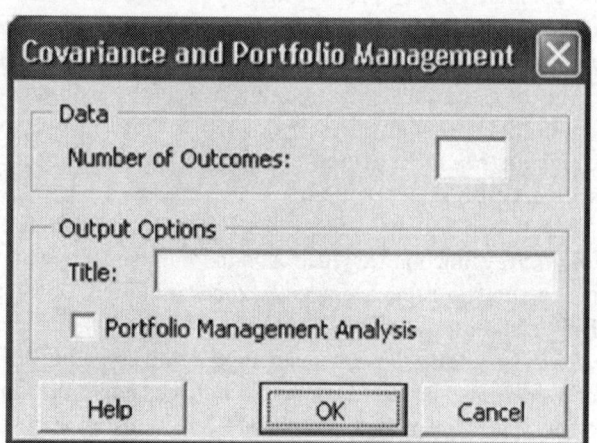

P5.2 Computing Binomial Probabilities

To compute binomial probabilities, use **PHStat → Probability & Prob. Distributions → Binomial**. This procedure creates a worksheet similar to Figure 5.2 on page

P5.3 Computing Poisson Probabilities

To compute Poisson probabilities, use **PHStat → Probability & Prob. Distributions → Poisson**. This procedure creates a worksheet similar to Figure 5.5 on page 200 using the mean or expected number of events of interest that you specify. If you select the **Cumulative Probabilities** check box, the Poisson table will include additional columns for $P(\leq X)$, $P(<X)$, $P(>X)$, and $P(\geq X)$. If you click **Histogram**, the procedure uses Excel charting features to create a histogram on a separate sheet.

page 204 using the sample size, number of events of interest in the population, and population size that you specify. If you click **Histogram**, the procedure uses Excel charting features to create a histogram on a separate sheet.

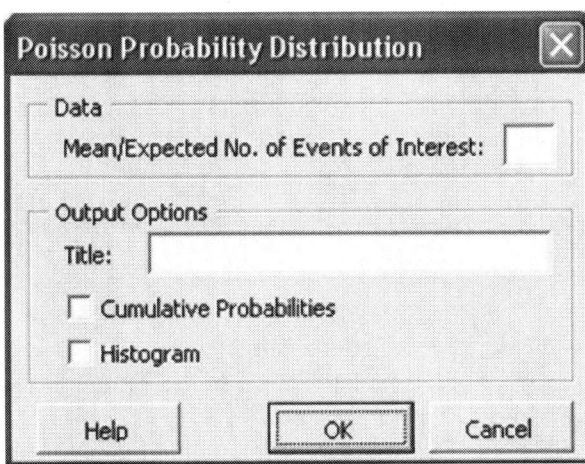

P5.4 Computing Hypergeometric Probabilities

To compute hypergeometric probabilities, use **PHStat → Probability & Prob. Distributions → Hypergeometric**. This procedure creates a worksheet similar to Figure 5.7 on

Appendix M5
Using Minitab for Discrete Probability Distributions

M5.1 Computing Binomial Probabilities

To compute binomial probabilities for the Section 5.3 accounting information system example, shown in Figure 5.3 on page 194:

1. Open to a new, blank worksheet.
2. Enter the values **0, 1, 2, 3**, and **4** in rows 1 to 5 of column C1, leaving the unnumbered variable label cell at the top of the column empty.
3. Select **Calc → Probability Distributions → Binomial**.

In the Binomial Distribution dialog box (see Figure M5.1 on page 216):

4. Click **Probability** (to compute the probabilities of exactly X events of interest for all values of X).

5. Enter **4** (the sample size) in the **Number of trials** box.
6. Enter **.1** in the **Event probability** box.
7. Click **Input column** and enter **C1** in its box.
8. Click **OK**.

M5.2 Computing Poisson Probabilities

To compute Poisson probabilities for the Section 5.4 bank customer arrival example, shown in Figure 5.6 on page 200:

1. Open to a new, blank worksheet.
2. Enter the values **0** through **15** in rows 1 to 16 of column C1, leaving the unnumbered variable label cell at the top of the column empty.
3. Select **Calc → Probability Distributions → Poisson**.

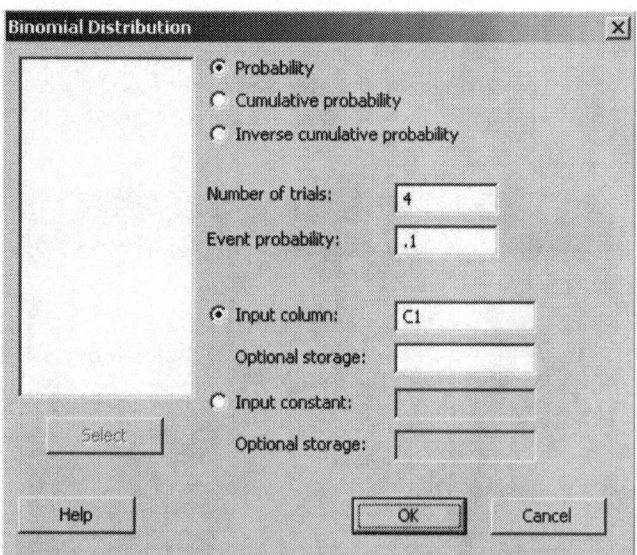

FIGURE M5.1

Minitab Binomial Distribution dialog box

In the Poisson Distribution dialog box (see Figure M5.2 below):

4. Click **Probability** (to compute the probabilities of exactly X events for all values of X).
5. Enter **3** (the λ value) in the **Mean** box.
6. Click **Input column** and enter **C1** in its box.
7. Click **OK**.

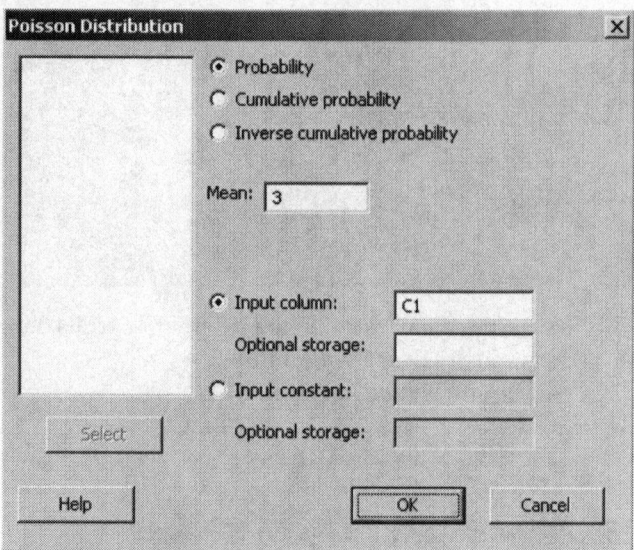

FIGURE M5.2

Minitab Poisson Distribution dialog box

M5.3 Computing Hypergeometric Probabilities

To compute hypergeometric probabilities for the Section 5.5 team formation example, shown in Figure 5.8 on page 204:

1. Open to a new, blank worksheet.
2. Enter the values **0, 1, 2, 3, 4, 5, 6, 7,** and **8** in rows 1 to 9 of column C1, leaving the unnumbered variable label cell at the top of the column empty.
3. Select **Calc → Probability Distributions → Hypergeometric**.

In the Hypergeometric Distribution dialog box (see Figure M5.3):

4. Click **Probability** (to compute the probability of exactly X events for all values of X).
5. Enter **30** (the population size) in the **Population size (N)** box.
6. Enter **10** in the **Event count in population (M)** box.
7. Enter **8** (the sample size) in the **Sample size (n)** box.
8. Click **Input column** and enter **C1** in its box.
9. Click **OK**.

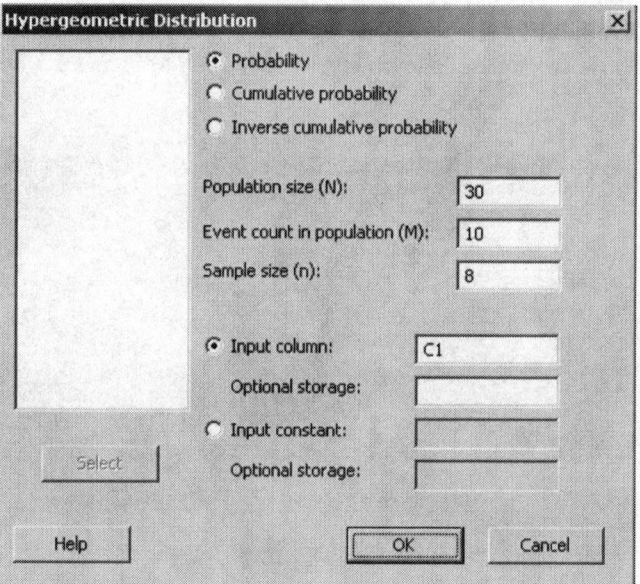

FIGURE M5.3

Minitab Hypergeometric Distribution dialog box

CHAPTER
SIX

THE NORMAL DISTRIBUTION AND OTHER CONTINUOUS DISTRIBUTIONS

LEARNING OBJECTIVES

In this chapter, you learn:

- To compute probabilities from the normal distribution
- To use the normal probability plot to determine whether a set of data is approximately normally distributed
- To compute probabilities from the uniform distribution
- To compute probabilities from the exponential distribution
- To approximate binomial probabilities using the normal distribution

USING STATISTICS @ OurCampus!

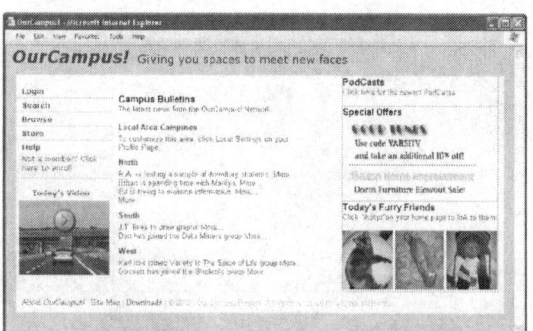

You are a designer for the OurCampus! Web site, which targets college students. To attract and retain customers, you need to make sure that the home page downloads quickly. Both the design of the home page and the load on the company's Web servers affect the download time. To check how fast the home page loads, you open a Web browser on a PC at the corporate offices of OurCampus! and measure the download time—the amount of time in seconds that pass from first linking to the Web site until the home page is fully displayed.

Past data indicate that the mean download time is 7 seconds and that the standard deviation is 2 seconds. Approximately two-thirds of the download times are between 5 and 9 seconds, and about 95% of the download times are between 3 and 11 seconds. In other words, the download times are distributed as a bell-shaped curve, with a clustering around the mean of 7 seconds. How could you use this information to answer questions about the download times of the current home page?

In Chapter 5, Saxon Home Improvement Company managers wanted to be able to solve problems about the number of tagged items in a given sample size. As an OurCampus! Web designer, you face a different task, one that involves a continuous measurement because a download time could be any value and not just a whole number. How can you answer questions about this *continuous numerical variable*, such as:

- What proportion of the home page downloads take more than 10 seconds?
- How many seconds elapse before 10% of the downloads are complete?
- How many seconds elapse before 99% of the downloads are complete?
- How would redesigning the home page to download faster affect the answers to these questions?

As in Chapter 5, you can use a probability distribution as a model. Reading this chapter will help you learn about characteristics of continuous probability distributions and how to use the normal, uniform, and exponential distributions to solve business problems.

6.1 CONTINUOUS PROBABILITY DISTRIBUTIONS

A **continuous probability density function** is the mathematical expression that defines the distribution of the values for a continuous random variable. Figure 6.1 graphically displays the three continuous probability density functions discussed in this chapter.

FIGURE 6.1

Three continuous distributions

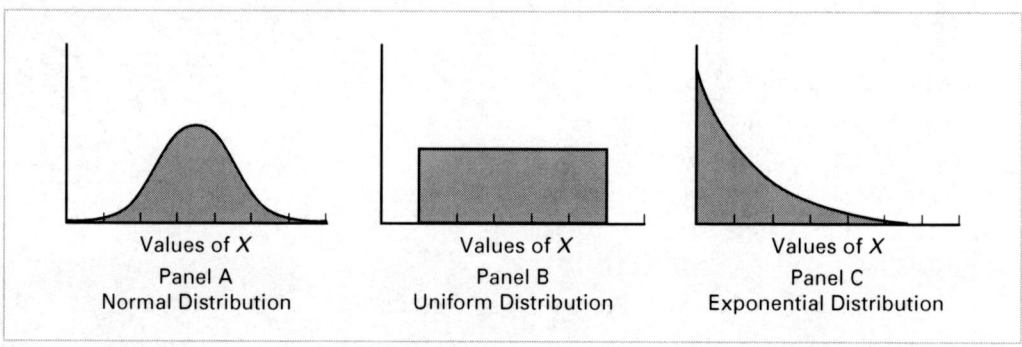

Values of X	Values of X	Values of X
Panel A	Panel B	Panel C
Normal Distribution	Uniform Distribution	Exponential Distribution

Panel A depicts a normal distribution. The normal distribution is symmetrical and bell shaped, implying that most values tend to cluster around the mean, which, due to the distribution's symmetrical shape, is equal to the median. Although the values in a normal distribution can range from negative infinity to positive infinity, the shape of the distribution makes it very unlikely that extremely large or extremely small values will occur.

Panel B depicts a uniform distribution where each value has an equal probability of occurrence anywhere in the range between the smallest value, *a*, and the largest value, *b*. Sometimes referred to as the rectangular distribution, the uniform distribution is symmetrical and therefore the mean equals the median.

Panel C illustrates an exponential distribution. This distribution is skewed to the right, making the mean larger than the median. The range for an exponential distribution is zero to positive infinity, but the distribution's shape makes the occurrence of extremely large values unlikely.

6.2 THE NORMAL DISTRIBUTION

The **normal distribution** (sometimes referred to as the *Gaussian distribution*) is the most common continuous distribution used in statistics. The normal distribution is vitally important in statistics for three main reasons:

- Numerous continuous variables common in business have distributions that closely resemble the normal distribution.
- The normal distribution can be used to approximate various discrete probability distributions.
- The normal distribution provides the basis for *classical statistical inference* because of its relationship to the *Central Limit Theorem* (which is discussed in Section 7.4).

The normal distribution is represented by the classic bell shape shown in Panel A of Figure 6.1. In the normal distribution, you can calculate the probability that various values occur within certain ranges or intervals. However, the *exact* probability of a *particular value* from a continuous distribution such as the normal distribution is zero. This property distinguishes continuous variables, which are measured, from discrete variables, which are counted. As an example, time (in seconds) is measured and not counted. Therefore, you can determine the probability that the download time for a home page on a Web browser is between 7 and 10 seconds, or the probability that the download time is between 8 and 9 seconds, or the probability that the download time is between 7.99 and 8.01 seconds. However, the probability that the download time is *exactly* 8 seconds is zero.

The normal distribution has several important theoretical properties:

- It is symmetrical and thus its mean and median are equal.
- It is bell shaped in its appearance.
- Its interquartile range is equal to 1.33 standard deviations. Thus, the middle 50% of the values are contained within an interval of two-thirds of a standard deviation below the mean and two-thirds of a standard deviation above the mean.
- It has an infinite range ($-\infty < X < \infty$).

In practice, many variables have distributions that closely resemble the theoretical properties of the normal distribution. The data in Table 6.1 on page 220 represent the thickness (in inches) of 10,000 brass washers manufactured by a large company. The continuous variable of interest, thickness, can be approximated by the normal distribution. The measurements of the thickness of the 10,000 brass washers cluster in the interval 0.0190 to 0.0192 inch and distribute symmetrically around that grouping, forming a bell-shaped pattern.

Figure 6.2 shows the relative frequency histogram and polygon for the distribution of the thickness of 10,000 brass washers. For these data, the first three theoretical properties of the normal distribution are approximately satisfied. However, the fourth one, having an infinite range, does not hold. The thickness of the washer cannot possibly be zero or below, nor can a washer be so thick that it becomes unusable. From Table 6.1, you see that only 48 out of every

TABLE 6.1

Thickness of 10,000
Brass Washers

Thickness (inches)	Relative Frequency
< 0.0180	48/10,000 = 0.0048
0.0180 < 0.0182	122/10,000 = 0.0122
0.0182 < 0.0184	325/10,000 = 0.0325
0.0184 < 0.0186	695/10,000 = 0.0695
0.0186 < 0.0188	1,198/10,000 = 0.1198
0.0188 < 0.0190	1,664/10,000 = 0.1664
0.0190 < 0.0192	1,896/10,000 = 0.1896
0.0192 < 0.0194	1,664/10,000 = 0.1664
0.0194 < 0.0196	1,198/10,000 = 0.1198
0.0196 < 0.0198	695/10,000 = 0.0695
0.0198 < 0.0200	325/10,000 = 0.0325
0.0200 < 0.0202	122/10,000 = 0.0122
0.0202 or above	48/10,000 = 0.0048
Total	1.0000

FIGURE 6.2

Relative frequency
histogram and polygon
of the thickness of
10,000 brass washers

*Source: Data are taken from
Table 6.1.*

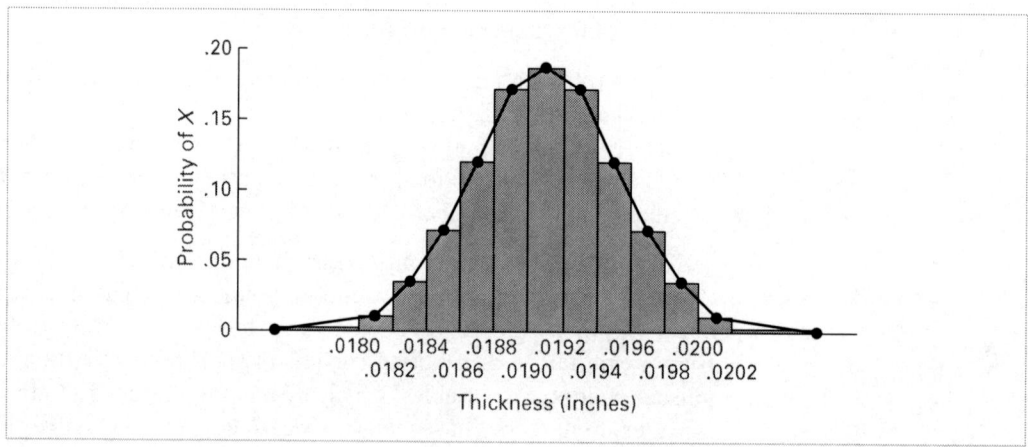

10,000 brass washers manufactured are expected to have a thickness of 0.0202 inch or more, whereas an equal number are expected to have a thickness under 0.0180 inch. Thus, the chance of randomly getting a washer so thin or so thick is 0.0048 + 0.0048 = 0.0096, less than 1 in 100.

The mathematical expression representing a continuous probability density function is denoted by the symbol $f(X)$. For the normal distribution, the **normal probability density function** is given in Equation (6.1).

Normal Probability Density Function

$$f(X) = \frac{1}{\sqrt{2\pi}\sigma} e^{-(1/2)[(X-\mu)/\sigma]^2}$$ (6.1)

where

e = the mathematical constant approximated by 2.71828

π = the mathematical constant approximated by 3.14159

μ = the mean

σ = the standard deviation

X = any value of the continuous variable, where $-\infty < X < \infty$

Because e and π are mathematical constants, the probabilities of the random variable X are dependent only on the two parameters of the normal distribution—the mean, μ, and the standard deviation, σ. Every time you specify a *particular combination* of μ and σ, a *different* normal probability distribution is generated. Figure 6.3 illustrates three different normal distributions.

FIGURE 6.3

Three normal distributions

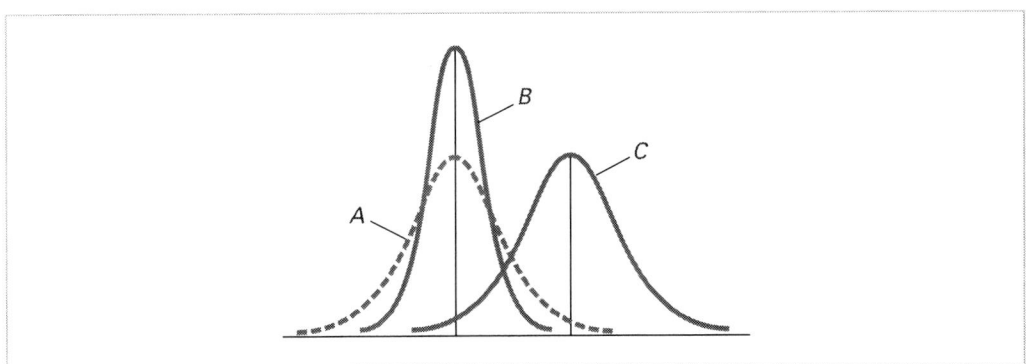

Distributions A and B have the same mean (μ) but have different standard deviations. Distributions A and C have the same standard deviation (σ) but have different means. Distributions B and C differ with respect to both μ and σ.

The mathematical expression in Equation (6.1) is computationally tedious and requires integral calculus. Fortunately, normal probability tables are available, and you *never* need to use Equation (6.1) to make computations of normal distribution probabilities. The first step in finding normal probabilities is to use the **transformation formula**, given in Equation (6.2), to convert any normal random variable, X, to a **standardized normal random variable**, Z.

Transformation Formula

The Z value is equal to the difference between X and the mean, μ, divided by the standard deviation, σ.

$$Z = \frac{X - \mu}{\sigma} \qquad\qquad (6.2)$$

Although the original data for the random variable X had mean μ and standard deviation σ, the standardized random variable, Z, will always have mean $\mu = 0$ and standard deviation $\sigma = 1$.

Any set of normally distributed values can be converted to its standardized form. Then you can determine the desired probabilities by using Table E.2, the **cumulative standardized normal distribution**. To see how the transformation formula is applied and the results are used to find probabilities from Table E.2, recall from the Using Statistics scenario on page 218 that past data indicate that the time to download the Web page is normally distributed, with a mean, $\mu = 7$ seconds and a standard deviation, $\sigma = 2$ seconds. From Figure 6.4 on page 222, you see that every measurement, X, has a corresponding standardized measurement, Z, computed from the transformation formula [Equation (6.2)]. Therefore, a download time of 9 seconds is equivalent to 1 standardized unit (i.e., 1 standard deviation above the mean) because

$$Z = \frac{9 - 7}{2} = +1$$

A download time of 1 second is equivalent to 3 standardized units (3 standard deviations) below the mean because

$$Z = \frac{1-7}{2} = -3$$

Thus, the standard deviation is the unit of measurement. In other words, a time of 9 seconds is 2 seconds (i.e., 1 standard deviation) higher, or *slower*, than the mean time of 7 seconds. Similarly, a time of 1 second is 6 seconds (i.e., 3 standard deviations) lower, or *faster*, than the mean time.

FIGURE 6.4

Transformation of scales

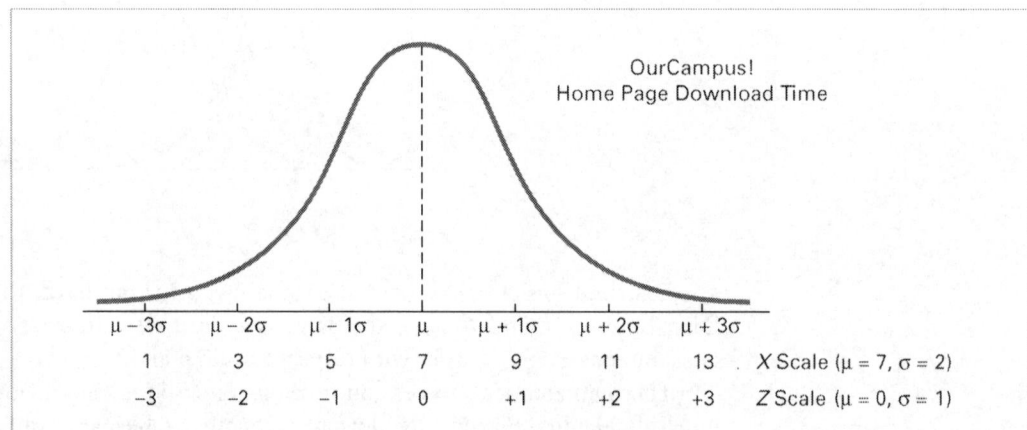

To further illustrate the transformation formula, suppose that the home page of another Web site has a download time that is normally distributed, with a mean, $\mu = 4$ seconds, and a standard deviation, $\sigma = 1$ second. This distribution is illustrated in Figure 6.5.

FIGURE 6.5

A different transformation of scales

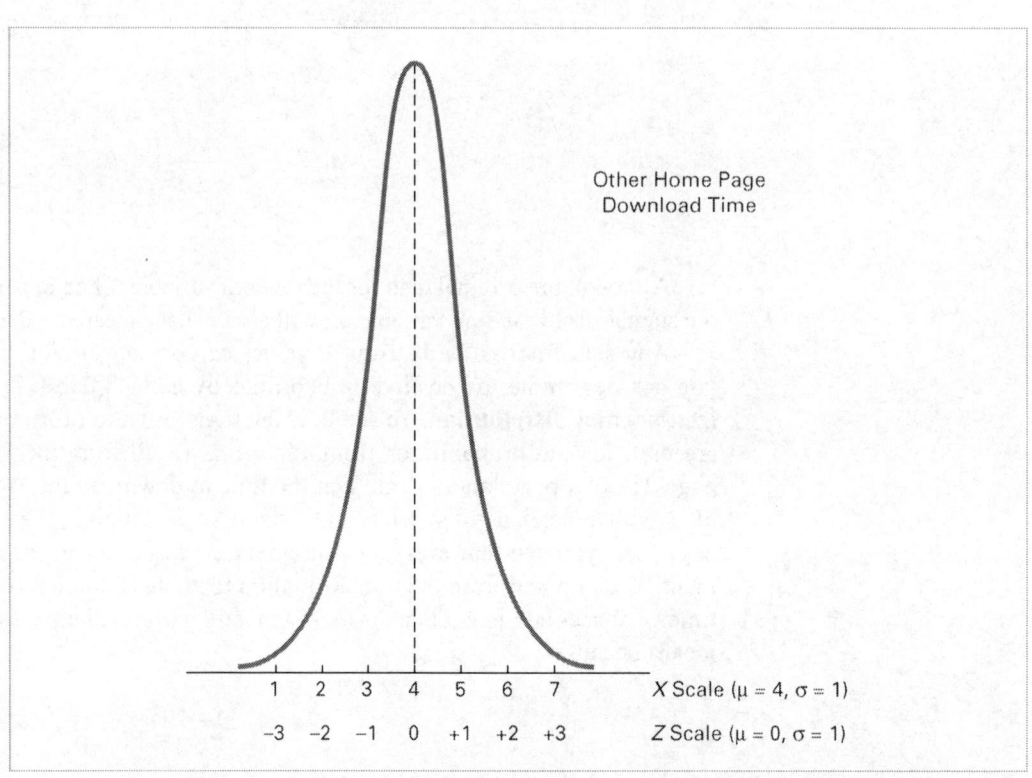

Comparing these results with those of the OurCampus! Web site, you see that a download time of 5 seconds is 1 standard deviation above the mean download time because

$$Z = \frac{5-4}{1} = +1$$

A time of 1 second is 3 standard deviations below the mean download time because

$$Z = \frac{1-4}{1} = -3$$

Suppose you wanted to find the probability that the download time for the OurCampus! site is less than 9 seconds. First, you use Equation (6.2) on page 221 to transform $X = 9$ to standardized Z units. Because $X = 9$ is one standard deviation above the mean, $Z = +1.00$. Next, you use Table E.2 to find the cumulative area under the normal curve less than (i.e., to the left of) $Z = +1.00$. To read the probability or area under the curve less than $Z = +1.00$, you scan down the Z column from Table E.2 until you locate the Z value of interest (in 10ths) in the Z row for 1.0. Next, you read across this row until you intersect the column that contains the 100ths place of the Z value. Therefore, in the body of the table, the tabulated probability for $Z = 1.00$ corresponds to the intersection of the row $Z = 1.0$ with the column $Z = .00$, as shown in Table 6.2, which is extracted from Table E.2. This probability is 0.8413. As illustrated in Figure 6.6, there is an 84.13% chance that the download time will be less than 9 seconds.

TABLE 6.2

Finding a Cumulative Area Under the Normal Curve

Cumulative Probabilities										
Z	.00	.01	.02	.03	.04	.05	.06	.07	.08	.09
0.0	.5000	.5040	.5080	.5120	.5160	.5199	.5239	.5279	.5319	.5359
0.1	.5398	.5438	.5478	.5517	.5557	.5596	.5636	.5675	.5714	.5753
0.2	.5793	.5832	.5871	.5910	.5948	.5987	.6026	.6064	.6103	.6141
0.3	.6179	.6217	.6255	.6293	.6331	.6368	.6406	.6443	.6480	.6517
0.4	.6554	.6591	.6628	.6664	.6700	.6736	.6772	.6808	.6844	.6879
0.5	.6915	.6950	.6985	.7019	.7054	.7088	.7123	.7157	.7190	.7224
0.6	.7257	.7291	.7324	.7357	.7389	.7422	.7454	.7486	.7518	.7549
0.7	.7580	.7612	.7642	.7673	.7704	.7734	.7764	.7794	.7823	.7852
0.8	.7881	.7910	.7939	.7967	.7995	.8023	.8051	.8078	.8106	.8133
0.9	.8159	.8186	.8212	.8238	.8264	.8289	.8315	.8340	.8365	.8389
1.0	.8413	.8438	.8461	.8485	.8508	.8531	.8554	.8577	.8599	.8621

Source: *Extracted from Table E.2.*

FIGURE 6.6

Determining the area less than Z from a cumulative standardized normal distribution

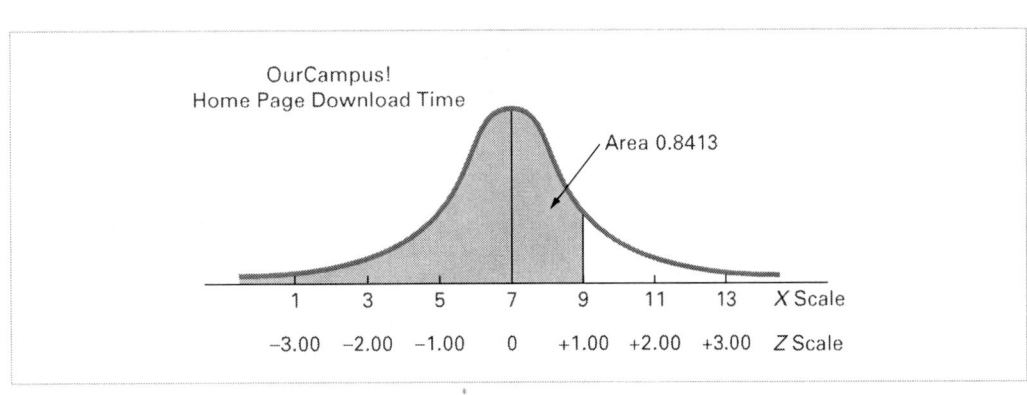

However, for the other home page, you see that a time of 5 seconds is 1 standardized unit above the mean time of 4 seconds. Thus, the probability that the download time will be less than 5 seconds is also 0.8413. Figure 6.7 shows that regardless of the value of the mean, μ, and standard deviation, σ, of a normally distributed variable, Equation (6.2) can transform the problem to Z values.

FIGURE 6.7

Demonstrating a transformation of scales for corresponding cumulative portions under two normal curves

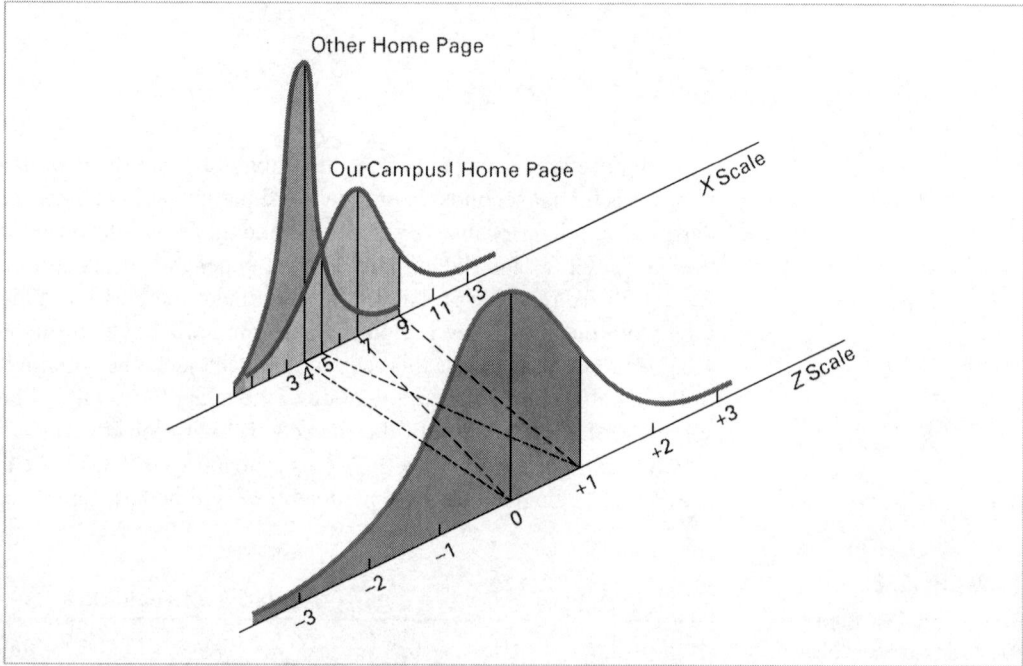

Now that you have learned to use Table E.2 with Equation (6.2), you can answer many questions related to the OurCampus! home page, using the normal distribution.

EXAMPLE 6.1

FINDING $P(X > 9)$

What is the probability that the download time will be more than 9 seconds?

SOLUTION The probability that the download time will be less than 9 seconds is 0.8413 (see Figure 6.6 on page 223). Thus, the probability that the download time will be more than 9 seconds is the *complement* of less than 9 seconds, $1 - 0.8413 = 0.1587$. Figure 6.8 illustrates this result.

FIGURE 6.8

Finding $P(X > 9)$

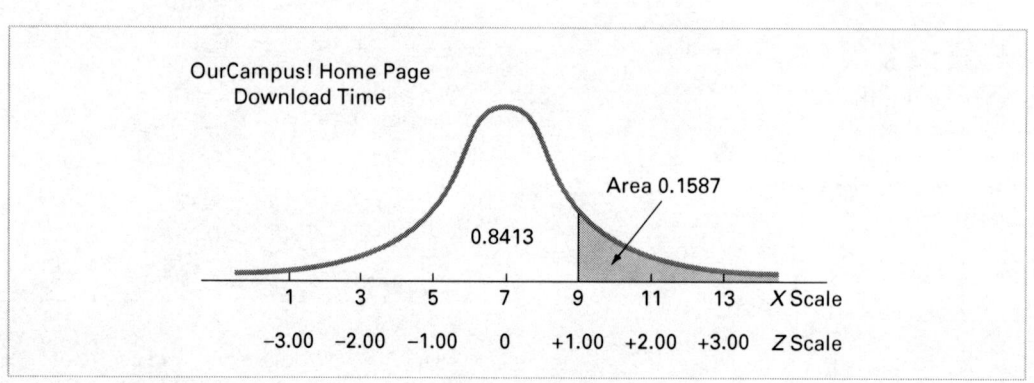

EXAMPLE 6.2

FINDING $P(7 < X < 9)$

What is the probability that the download time will be between 7 and 9 seconds?

SOLUTION From Figure 6.6 on page 223, you can see that the probability that a download time is less than 9 seconds is 0.8413. Now you must determine the probability that the download time will be under 7 seconds and subtract this from the probability that the download time is under 9 seconds. Figure 6.9 illustrates this result.

FIGURE 6.9

Finding $P(7 < X < 9)$

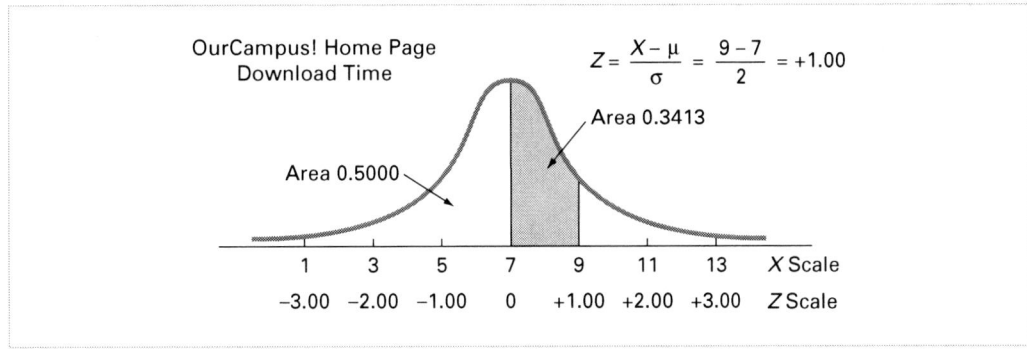

Using Equation (6.2) on page 221,

$$Z = \frac{7-7}{2} = 0.00$$

Using Table E.2 or Table 6.2, the area under the normal curve less than the mean of $Z = 0.00$ is 0.5000. (Because the mean and the median are the same for normally distributed data, 50% of the download times are less than 7 seconds.) Hence, the area under the curve between $Z = 0.00$ and $Z = 1.00$ is $0.8413 - 0.5000 = 0.3413$.

EXAMPLE 6.3

FINDING $P(X < 7$ OR $X > 9)$

What is the probability that the download time will be under 7 seconds or over 9 seconds?

SOLUTION From Figure 6.9, the probability that the download time is between 7 and 9 seconds is 0.3413. The probability that the download time is under 7 seconds or over 9 seconds is its complement, $1 - 0.3413 = 0.6587$.

Another way to view this problem, is to separately calculate the probability of a download time of less than 7 seconds and the probability of a download time of greater than 9 seconds and then add these two probabilities together. Figure 6.10 illustrates this result. Because the mean is seven seconds, 50% of download times are under 7 seconds. From Example 6.1, the probability that the download time is greater than 9 seconds is 0.1587. Hence, the probability that a download time is under 7 or over 9 seconds, $P(X < 7$ or $X > 9)$, is $0.5000 + 0.1587 = 0.6587$.

FIGURE 6.10

Finding $P(X < 7$ or $X > 9)$

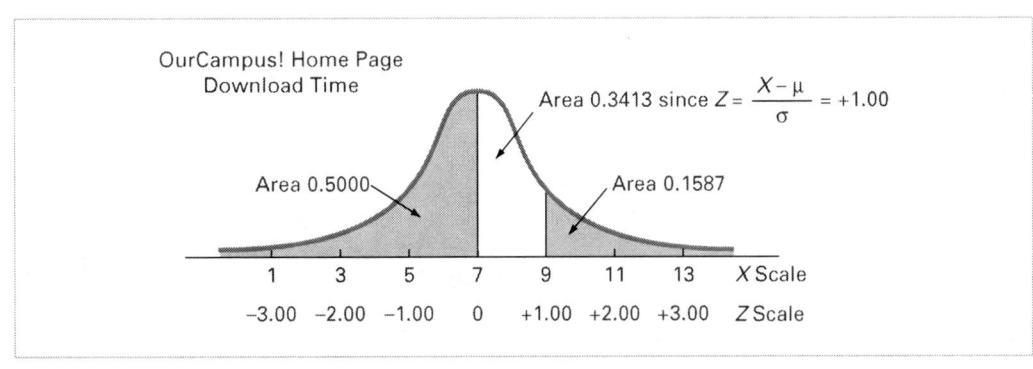

EXAMPLE 6.4   FINDING $P(5 < X < 9)$

What is the probability that the download time will be between 5 and 9 seconds—that is, $P(5 < X < 9)$?

SOLUTION In Figure 6.11, you can see that the area of interest is located between two values, 5 and 9.

FIGURE 6.11

Finding $P(5 < X < 9)$

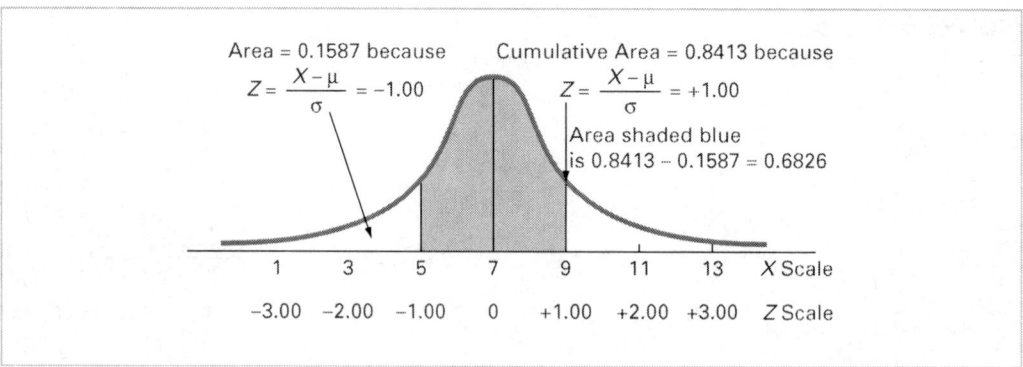

In Example 6.1 on page 224, you already found that the area under the normal curve less than 9 seconds is 0.8413. To find the area under the normal curve less than 5 seconds,

$$Z = \frac{5 - 7}{2} = -1.00$$

Using Table E.2, you look up $Z = -1.00$ and find 0.1587. Thus, the probability that the download time will be between 5 and 9 seconds is $0.8413 - 0.1587 = 0.6826$, as displayed in Figure 6.11.

The result of Example 6.4 enables you to state that for any normal distribution, 68.26% of the values will fall within ± 1 standard deviation of the mean. From Figure 6.12, 95.44% of the values will fall within ± 2 standard deviations of the mean. Thus, 95.44% of the download times are between 3 and 11 seconds. From Figure 6.13, 99.73% of the values are within ± 3 standard deviations above or below the mean. Thus, 99.73% of the download times are between 1 and 13 seconds. Therefore, it is unlikely (0.0027, or only 27 in 10,000) that a download time will be so fast or so slow that it will take under 1 second or more than 13 seconds. In general, you can use 6σ (that is, 3 standard deviations below the mean to 3 standard deviations above the mean) as a practical approximation of the range for normally distributed data.

FIGURE 6.12

Finding $P(3 < X < 11)$

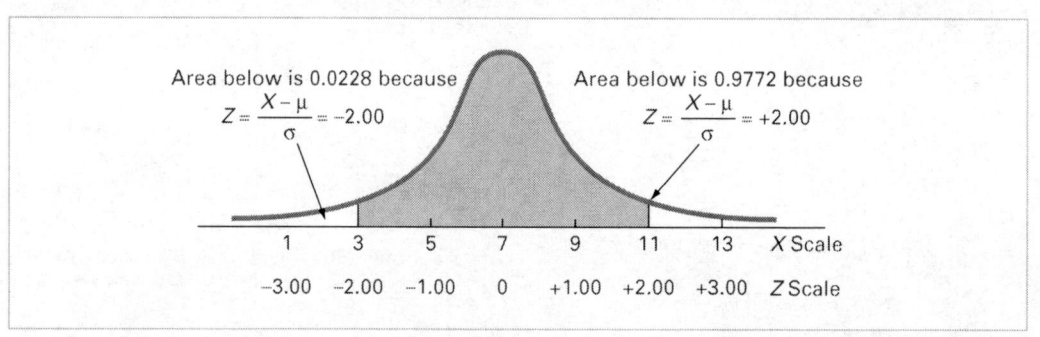

FIGURE 6.13

Finding $P(1 < X < 13)$

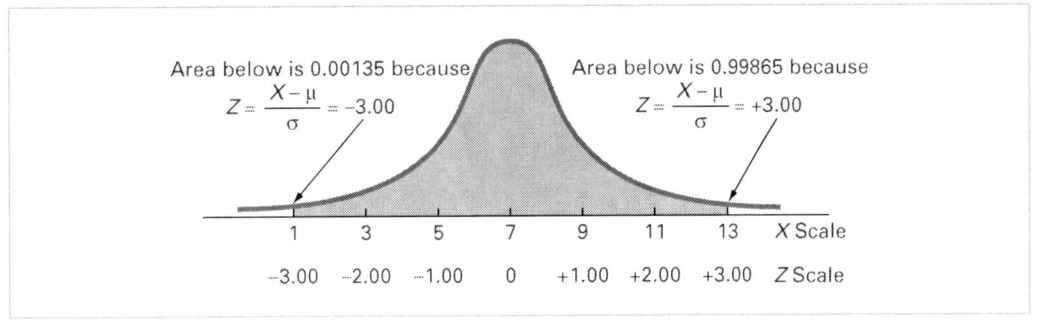

Figures 6.11, 6.12, and 6.13 illustrate how the values of a normal distribution cluster near the mean. For any normal distribution:

*   Approximately 68.26% of the values fall within ±1 standard deviation of the mean.
*   Approximately 95.44% of the values fall within ±2 standard deviations of the mean.
*   Approximately 99.73% of the values fall within ±3 standard deviations of the mean.

This result is the justification for the empirical rule presented on page 112. The accuracy of the empirical rule improves as a data set follows the normal distribution more closely.

EXAMPLE 6.5

FINDING $P(X < 3.5)$

What is the probability that a download time will be under 3.5 seconds?

SOLUTION To calculate the probability that a download time will be under 3.5 seconds, you need to examine the shaded lower-left tail region of Figure 6.14.

FIGURE 6.14

Finding $P(X < 3.5)$

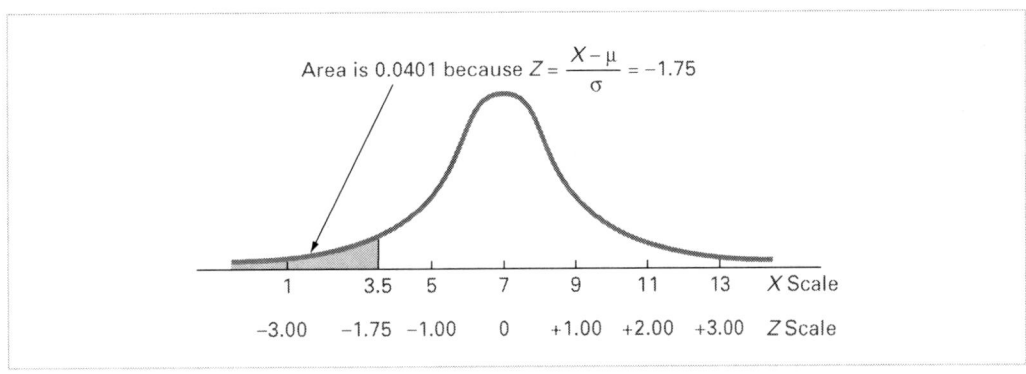

To determine the area under the curve below 3.5 seconds, you first calculate

$$Z = \frac{X - \mu}{\sigma} = \frac{3.5 - 7}{2} = -1.75$$

You then look up the Z value of -1.75 by matching the appropriate Z row (-1.7) with the appropriate Z column (.05), as shown in Table 6.3 on page 228 (which is extracted from Table E.2). The resulting probability or area under the curve less than -1.75 standard deviations below the mean is 0.0401.

TABLE 6.3

Finding a Cumulative Area Under the Normal Curve

					Cumulative Probabilities					
Z	.00	.01	.02	.03	.04	.05	.06	.07	.08	.09
·	·	·	·	·	·		·	·	·	·
·	·	·	·	·	·		·	·	·	·
·	·	·	·	·	·		·	·	·	·
−1.7	.0446	.0436	.0427	.0418	.0409	.0401	.0392	.0384	.0375	.0367
−1.6	.0548	.0537	.0526	.0516	.0505	.0495	.0485	.0475	.0465	.0455

Source: *Extracted from Table E.2.*

Examples 6.1 through 6.5 require you to use the normal table to find an area under the normal curve that corresponds to a specific X value. There are many circumstances in which you want to find the X value that corresponds to a specific area. Examples 6.6 and 6.7 illustrate such situations.

EXAMPLE 6.6

FINDING THE X VALUE FOR A CUMULATIVE PROBABILITY OF 0.10

How much time (in seconds) will elapse before 10% of the downloads are complete?

SOLUTION Because 10% of the home pages are expected to download in under X seconds, the area under the normal curve less than this value is 0.1000. Using the body of Table E.2, you search for the area or probability of 0.1000. The closest result is 0.1003, as shown in Table 6.4 (which is extracted from Table E.2).

TABLE 6.4

Finding a Z Value Corresponding to a Particular Cumulative Area (0.10) Under the Normal Curve

					Cumulative Probabilities					
Z	.00	.01	.02	.03	.04	.05	.06	.07	.08	.09
·	·	·	·	·	·	·	·	·		·
·	·	·	·	·	·	·	·	·		·
·	·	·	·	·	·	·	·	·		·
−1.5	.0668	.0655	.0643	.0630	.0618	.0606	.0594	.0582	.0571	.0559
−1.4	.0808	.0793	.0778	.0764	.0749	.0735	.0721	.0708	.0694	.0681
−1.3	.0968	.0951	.0934	.0918	.0901	.0885	.0869	.0853	.0838	.0823
−1.2	.1151	.1131	.1112	.1093	.1075	.1056	.1038	.1020	.1003	.0985

Source: *Extracted from Table E.2.*

Working from this area to the margins of the table, the Z value corresponding to the particular Z row (−1.2) and Z column (.08) is −1.28 (see Figure 6.15).

FIGURE 6.15

Finding Z to determine X

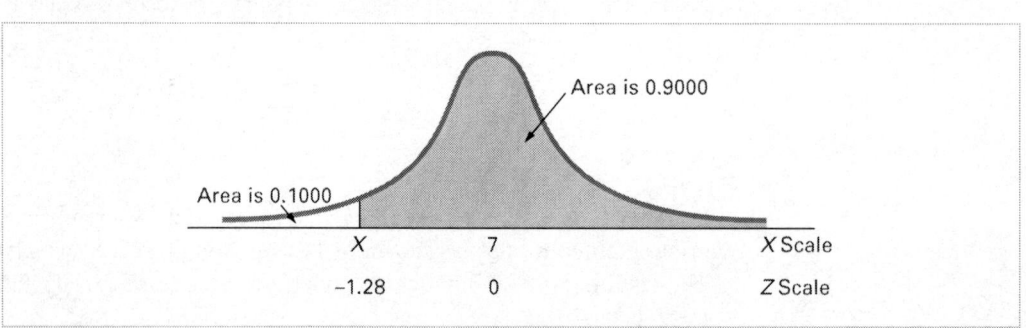

Area is 0.9000

Area is 0.1000

X	7	X Scale
−1.28	0	Z Scale

Once you find Z, you use the transformation formula Equation (6.2) on page 221 to determine the X value, as follows. Let

$$Z = \frac{X - \mu}{\sigma}$$

then

$$X = \mu + Z\sigma$$

Substituting $\mu = 7$, $\sigma = 2$, and $Z = -1.28$,

$$X = 7 + (-1.28)(2) = 4.44 \text{ seconds}$$

Thus, 10% of the download times are 4.44 seconds or less.

In general, you use Equation (6.3) for finding an X value.

Finding An X Value Associated with Known Probability

The X value is equal to the mean μ plus the product of the Z value and the standard deviation σ.

$$X = \mu + Z\sigma \tag{6.3}$$

To find a *particular* value associated with a known probability, follow these steps:

1. Sketch the normal curve and then place the values for the mean and X on the X and Z scales.
2. Find the cumulative area less than X.
3. Shade the area of interest.
4. Using Table E.2, determine the Z value corresponding to the area under the normal curve less than X.
5. Using Equation (6.3), solve for X:

$$X = \mu + Z\sigma$$

EXAMPLE 6.7

FINDING THE X VALUES THAT INCLUDE 95% OF THE DOWNLOAD TIMES

What are the lower and upper values of X, symmetrically distributed around the mean, that include 95% of the download times?

SOLUTION First, you need to find the lower value of X (called X_L). Then you find the upper value of X (called X_U). Because 95% of the values are between X_L and X_U, and because X_L and X_U are equally distant from the mean, 2.5% of the values are below X_L (see Figure 6.16).

FIGURE 6.16

Finding Z to determine X_L

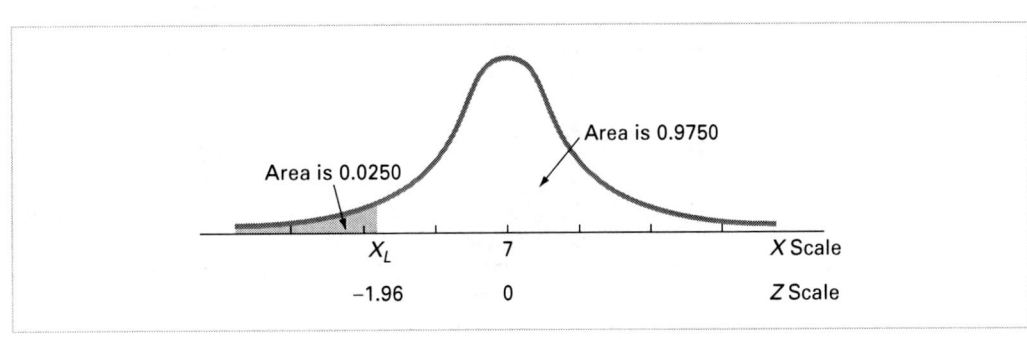

Although X_L is not known, you can find the corresponding Z value because the area under the normal curve less than this Z is 0.0250. Using the body of Table 6.5, you search for the probability 0.0250.

TABLE 6.5

Finding a Z Value Corresponding to a Cumulative Area of 0.025 Under the Normal Curve

					Cumulative Area					
Z	.00	.01	.02	.03	.04	.05	.06	.07	.08	.09
.	.	.	.	.	.	.		.	.	.
.	.	.	.	.	.	.		.	.	.
.	.	.	.	.	.	.		.	.	.
-2.0	.0228	.0222	.0217	.0212	.0207	.0202	.0197	.0192	.0188	.0183
-1.9	.0287	.0281	.0274	.0268	.0262	.0256	.0250	.0244	.0239	.0233
-1.8	.0359	.0351	.0344	.0336	.0329	.0232	.0314	.0307	.0301	.0294

Source: *Extracted from Table E.2.*

Working from the body of the table to the margins of the table, you see that the Z value corresponding to the particular Z row (−1.9) and Z column (.06) is −1.96.

Once you find Z, the final step is to use Equation (6.3) on page 229 as follows:

$$X = \mu + Z\sigma$$
$$= 7 + (-1.96)(2)$$
$$= 7 - 3.92$$
$$= 3.08 \text{ seconds}$$

You use a similar process to find X_U. Because only 2.5% of the home page downloads take longer than X_U seconds, 97.5% of the home page downloads take less than X_U seconds. From the symmetry of the normal distribution, the desired Z value, as shown in Figure 6.17, is +1.96 (because Z lies to the right of the standardized mean of 0). You can also extract this Z value from Table 6.6. You can see that 0.975 is the area under the normal curve less than the Z value of +1.96.

FIGURE 6.17

Finding Z to determine X_U

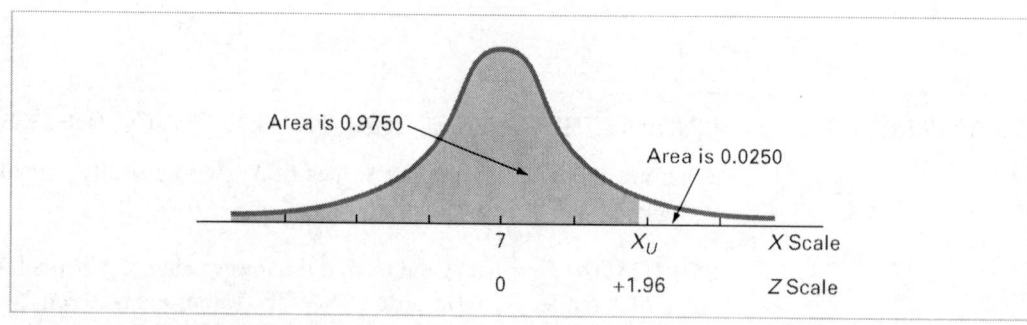

TABLE 6.6

Finding a Z Value Corresponding to a Cumulative Area of 0.975 Under the Normal Curve

					Cumulative Area					
Z	.00	.01	.02	.03	.04	.05	.06	.07	.08	.09
.	.	.	.	.	.	.		.	.	.
.	.	.	.	.	.	.		.	.	.
.	.	.	.	.	.	.		.	.	.
+1.8	.9641	.9649	.9656	.9664	.9671	.9678	.9686	.9693	.9699	.9706
+1.9	.9713	.9719	.9726	.9732	.9738	.9744	.9750	.9756	.9761	.9767
+2.0	.9772	.9778	.9783	.9788	.9793	.9798	.9803	.9808	.9812	.9817

Source: *Extracted from Table E.2.*

Using Equation (6.3) on page 229,

$$X = \mu + Z\sigma$$
$$= 7 + (+1.96)(2)$$
$$= 7 + 3.92$$
$$= 10.92 \text{ seconds}$$

Therefore, 95% of the download times are between 3.08 and 10.92 seconds.

VISUAL EXPLORATIONS: Exploring the Normal Distribution

You can use the Visual Explorations Normal Distribution procedure to see the effects of changes in the mean and standard deviation on the area under a normal distribution curve.

Open the **Visual Explorations.xla** add-in workbook and select **VisualExplorations → Normal Distribution** (Excel 97–2003) or **Add-Ins → VisualExplorations → Normal Distribution** (Excel 2007). You will see a normal curve for the Using Statistics home page download example and a floating control panel that allows you to adjust the shape of the curve and the shaded area under the curve (see illustration below). Use the control panel spinner but-

tons to change the values for the mean, standard deviation, and X value, while noting their effects on the probability of $X <=$ value and the corresponding shaded area under the curve (see illustration below). If you prefer, you can select the **Z Values** option button to see the normal curve labeled with Z values.

Click the **Reset** button to reset the control panel values or click **Help** for additional information about the problem. Click **Finish** when you are done exploring. (Review Section E1.8 on page 20 for more information on using add-ins, if necessary.)

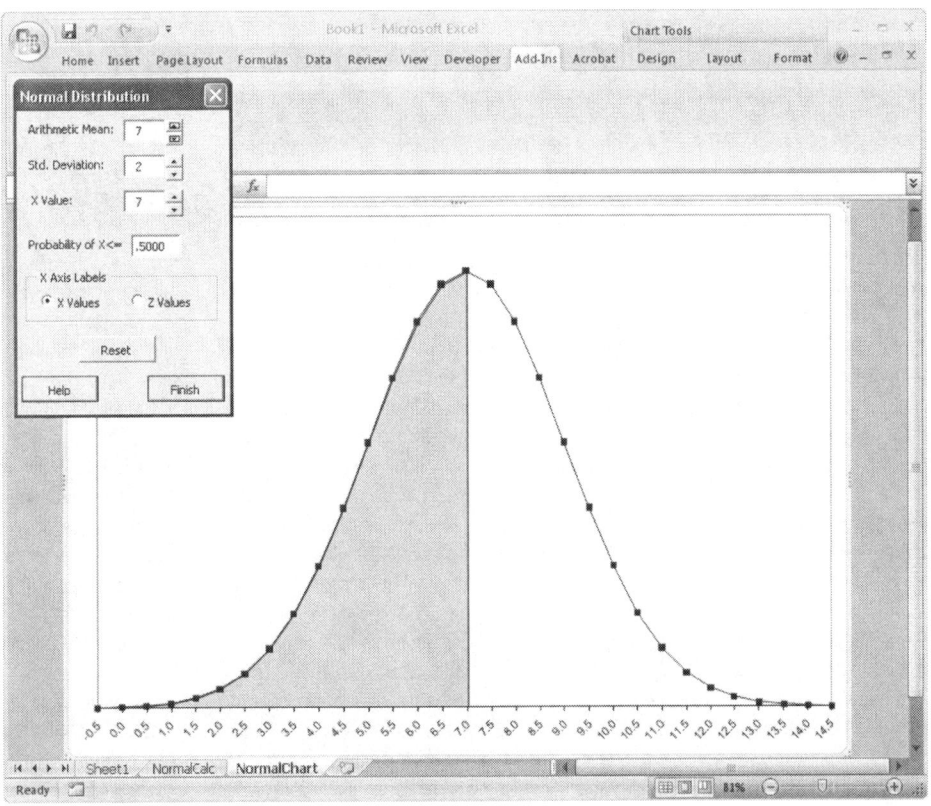

You can also use Microsoft Excel or Minitab to compute normal probabilities. Figure 6.18 illustrates a Microsoft Excel worksheet for Examples 6.5 and 6.6 and Figure 6.19 illustrates Minitab results for Examples 6.1 and 6.6.

FIGURE 6.18

Microsoft Excel worksheet for computing normal probabilities

See Section E6.1 or P6.1 to create this.

	A	B	
1	**Normal Probabilities**		
2			
3	**Common Data**		
4	**Mean**	7	
5	**Standard Deviation**	2	
6			
7	**Probability for X <=**		
8	**X Value**	3.5	
9	**Z Value**	-1.75	=STANDARDIZE(B8, B4, B5)
10	**P(X<=3.5)**	0.0401	=NORMDIST(B8, B4, B5, TRUE)
11			
12	**Find X and Z Given Cum. Pctage.**		
13	**Cumulative Percentage**	10.00%	
14	**Z Value**	-1.2816	=NORMSINV(B13)
15	**X Value**	4.4369	=NORMINV(B13, B4, B5)

FIGURE 6.19

Minitab results for normal probabilities

See Section M6.1 to create this.

Cumulative Distribution Function

Normal with mean = 7 and standard deviation = 2

```
x   P( X <= x )
9     0.841345
```

Inverse Cumulative Distribution Function

Normal with mean = 7 and standard deviation = 2

```
P( X <= x )        x
       0.1    4.43690
```

(The Not-So-Normal Story of) How the Normal Distribution Got Its Name

From the Authors' Desktop

You've already read that the normal distribution is a very important one in statistics. The name "normal" might suggest that other probability distributions are somehow abnormal. This is not the case. In fact, if anything is abnormal, it is the story of how the normal distribution got its name.

The story starts with Abraham de Moivre who, in the early eighteenth century, was computing binomial probabilities for various games of chance and writing such papers as *The Doctrine of Chances*. (A problem in this paper is what led Thomas Bayes to write *An Essay Towards Solving a Problem in the Doctrine of Chances* discussed in the *From the Authors' Desktop* on page 165.) With no computers around at the time, de Moivre had to laboriously hand calculate those probabilities

using the equivalent of Equation 5.11 on page 191 for each solution. As he worked out his solutions for all cases for a certain type of problem, he began to notice that a histogram of his binomial results suggested the trace of a bell-shaped curve. (The normal approximation to the binomial distribution is covered in Section 6.6.)

For this discovery, you might expect that de Moivre would have the distribution named for him. (After all, in Chapter 5 you already have read about a distribution named after its discoverer, Siméon-Denis Poisson.) But no! If anything, the distribution is sometimes called the Gaussian distribution, after the German Carl Frederick Gauss, who, about a century later than de Moivre, used the normal distribution to describe the distribution of errors in measurements made by astronomers. Because

of this application, the normal distribution became known as the Error Curve.

Over time, other researchers discovered that when they measured other things, the same pattern of errors occurred. By the late nineteenth century, some began to conclude that the Error Curve was a fundamental universal law that governed *all* measurements of *any* natural phenomena.

Today we know that not all things conform to the normal distribution, although many do, and that nonnormal distributions are not any less natural than normal ones. For this understanding, we probably have to thank Karl Pearson.

Pearson was a mathematician interested in questions of biological inheritance and evolution. Pearson believed that individuals in populations could show true variability, independent of the variability caused by errors in measurement that astronomers and Gauss had recognized. Although Pearson's concept of individual variability underlies most of the concepts taught in this book, his point of view was radical to some of his contemporaries who saw the world so standardized and "normal." Pearson changed minds by showing that some populations are naturally skewed (coining that word in passing) and he helped put to rest the notion that the normal distribution underlies all phenomena.

Ironically, it was Pearson who did the most to popularize the name "normal" for the distribution discussed in this chapter. Starting with an 1894 paper, Pearson standardized the use of the term *normal* even as he was collecting and describing data that showed how

measurements of phenomena do not naturally or "normally" conform to the "Error Curve."

Today, more than a century after Pearson first published his thoughts, people still make the type of mistakes that Pearson refuted. One of us recalls the story about a upper-level college seminar class of three in which the professor announced one student would get an A, one would get a B, and one would get a C "because grades need to be normally distributed." (That the professor was describing a uniform distribution was a double irony.)

As a student you have probably heard many discussions about grade inflation (undoubtedly a phenomena at many schools). But, have you ever realized that an argument offered as "proof" of this inflation—that there are "too few" low grades because

grades are *skewed* towards A's and B's—wrongly implies that grades should be "normally" distributed. (By the time you finish reading this book, you may realize that because college students represent small non-random samples, there are plenty of reasons to suspect that the distribution of grades would be nonnormal.)

Other misapplications of the normal distribution involve overlooking or not verifying the assumptions the normal distribution makes about the data. Such misuses not only have confounded businesses, but have played a role in important U.S. public policy debates during the past 50 years or so. In the end, remember that just because statisticians call it "normal" doesn't make it so for all cases.

PROBLEMS FOR SECTION 6.2

Learning the Basics

6.1 Given a standardized normal distribution (with a mean of 0 and a standard deviation of 1, as in Table E.2), what is the probability that
a. Z is less than 1.57?
b. Z is greater than 1.84?
c. Z is between 1.57 and 1.84?
d. Z is less than 1.57 or greater than 1.84?

6.2 Given a standardized normal distribution (with a mean of 0 and a standard deviation of 1, as in Table E.2), what is the probability that
a. Z is between −1.57 and 1.84?
b. Z is less than −1.57 or greater than 1.84?
c. What is the value of Z if only 2.5% of all possible Z values are larger?
d. Between what two values of Z (symmetrically distributed around the mean) will 68.26% of all possible Z values be contained?

6.3 Given a standardized normal distribution (with a mean of 0 and a standard deviation of 1, as in Table E.2), what is the probability that
a. Z is less than 1.08?
b. Z is greater than −0.21?
c. Z is less than −0.21 or greater than the mean?
d. Z is less than −0.21 or greater than 1.08?

6.4 Given a standardized normal distribution (with a mean of 0 and a standard deviation of 1, as in Table E.2), determine the following probabilities:

a. $P(Z > 1.08)$
b. $P(Z < -0.21)$
c. $P(-1.96 < Z < -0.21)$
d. What is the value of Z if only 15.87% of all possible Z values are larger?

6.5 Given a normal distribution with $\mu = 100$ and $\sigma = 10$, what is the probability that
a. $X > 75$?
b. $X < 70$?
c. $X < 80$ or $X > 110$?
d. 80% of the values are between what two X values (symmetrically distributed around the mean)?

6.6 Given a normal distribution with $\mu = 50$ and $\sigma = 4$, what is the probability that
a. $X > 43$?
b. $X < 42$?
c. 5% of the values are less than what X value?
d. 60% of the values are between what two X values (symmetrically distributed around the mean)?

Applying the Concepts

6.7 In a recent year, about two-thirds of U.S. households purchased ground coffee. Consider the annual ground coffee expenditures for households purchasing ground coffee, assuming that these expenditures are approximately distributed as a normal random variable with a mean of $45.16 and a standard deviation of $10.00.
a. Find the probability that a household spent less than $25.00.

b. Find the probability that a household spent more than $50.00.
c. What proportion of the households spent between $30.00 and $40.00?
d. 99% of the households spent less than what amount?

✓ SELF Test **6.8** Toby's Trucking Company determined that the distance traveled per truck per year is normally distributed, with a mean of 50.0 thousand miles and a standard deviation of 12.0 thousand miles.
a. What proportion of trucks can be expected to travel between 34.0 and 50.0 thousand miles in the year?
b. What percentage of trucks can be expected to travel either below 30.0 or above 60.0 thousand miles in the year?
c. How many miles will be traveled by at least 80% of the trucks?
d. What are your answers to (a) through (c) if the standard deviation is 10.0 thousand miles?

6.9 The breaking strength of plastic bags used for packaging produce is normally distributed, with a mean of 5 pounds per square inch and a standard deviation of 1.5 pounds per square inch. What proportion of the bags have a breaking strength of
a. less than 3.17 pounds per square inch?
b. at least 3.6 pounds per square inch?
c. between 5 and 5.5 pounds per square inch?
d. 95% of the breaking strengths will be contained between what two values symmetrically distributed around the mean?

6.10 A set of final examination grades in an introductory statistics course is normally distributed, with a mean of 73 and a standard deviation of 8.
a. What is the probability of getting a grade below 91 on this exam?
b. What is the probability that a student scored between 65 and 89?
c. The probability is 5% that a student taking the test scores higher than what grade?
d. If the professor grades on a curve (i.e., gives A's to the top 10% of the class, regardless of the score), are you better off with a grade of 81 on this exam or a grade of 68 on a different exam, where the mean is 62 and the standard deviation is 3? Show your answer statistically and explain.

6.11 A statistical analysis of 1,000 long-distance telephone calls made from the headquarters of the Bricks and Clicks Computer Corporation indicates that the length of these calls is normally distributed, with $\mu = 240$ seconds and $\sigma = 40$ seconds.
a. What is the probability that a call lasted less than 180 seconds?
b. What is the probability that a call lasted between 180 and 300 seconds?
c. What is the probability that a call lasted between 110 and 180 seconds?
d. What is the length of a call if only 1% of all calls are shorter?

6.12 The number of shares traded daily on the New York Stock Exchange (NYSE) is referred to as the *volume* of trading. During the first three months of 2006, daily volume ranged from 1.424 billion to 2.170 billion (NYSE Group, **www.nyse.com**, April 28, 2006). Assume that the number of shares traded on the NYSE is a normally distributed random variable, with a mean of 1.8 billion and a standard deviation of 0.15 billion. For a randomly selected day, what is the probability that the volume is
a. below 1.5 billion?
b. below 1.7 billion?
c. above 2.0 billion?
d. above 2.3 billion?

6.13 Many manufacturing problems involve the matching of machine parts, such as shafts that fit into a valve hole. A particular design requires a shaft with a diameter of 22.000 mm, but shafts with diameters between 21.900 mm and 22.010 mm are acceptable. Suppose that the manufacturing process yields shafts with diameters normally distributed, with a mean of 22.002 mm and a standard deviation of 0.005 mm. For this process, what is
a. the proportion of shafts with a diameter between 21.90 mm and 22.00 mm?
b. the probability that a shaft is acceptable?
c. the diameter that will be exceeded by only 2% of the shafts?
d. What would be your answers in (a) through (c) if the standard deviation of the shaft diameters was 0.004 mm?

6.3 EVALUATING NORMALITY

As discussed in Section 6.2, many continuous variables used in business closely follow a normal distribution. This section presents two approaches for determining whether a set of data can be approximated by the normal distribution:

1. Compare the characteristics of the data with the theoretical properties of the normal distribution.
2. Construct a normal probability plot.

Comparing Data Characteristics to Theoretical Properties

The normal distribution has several important theoretical properties:

- It is symmetrical; thus, the mean and median are equal.
- It is bell shaped; thus, the empirical rule applies.
- The interquartile range equals 1.33 standard deviations.
- The range is approximately equal to 6 standard deviations.

In actual practice, a continuous variable may have characteristics that approximate these theoretical properties. However, many continuous variables are neither normally distributed nor approximately normally distributed. For such variables, the descriptive characteristics of the data do not match well with the properties of a normal distribution. One approach to determining whether a data set follows a normal distribution is to compare the characteristics of the data with the corresponding properties from an underlying normal distribution, as follows:

- Construct charts and observe their appearance. For small- or moderate-sized data sets, construct a stem-and-leaf display or a boxplot. For large data sets, plot a histogram or polygon.
- Compute descriptive numerical measures and compare the characteristics of the data with the theoretical properties of the normal distribution. Compare the mean and median. Is the interquartile range approximately 1.33 times the standard deviation? Is the range approximately 6 times the standard deviation?
- Evaluate how the values in the data are distributed. Determine whether approximately two-thirds of the values lie between the mean and ±1 standard deviation. Determine whether approximately four-fifths of the values lie between the mean and ±1.28 standard deviations. Determine whether approximately 19 out of every 20 values lie between the mean and ±2 standard deviations.

Do the three-year returns discussed in Chapters 2 and 3 (see the Mutual Funds file) have the properties of the normal distribution? Figure 6.20 displays descriptive statistics for these data, and Figure 6.21 presents a boxplot.

FIGURE 6.20

Microsoft Excel descriptive statistics for the 2006 returns

See Section E3.1 to create this. (Use Section M3.1 to create the Minitab equivalent.)

	A	B
1	Return 2006	
2		
3	Mean	12.5142
4	Standard Error	0.2136
5	Median	13.1000
6	Mode	16.6000
7	Standard Deviation	6.2916
8	Sample Variance	39.5840
9	Kurtosis	0.0200
10	Skewness	-0.2982
11	Range	44.0000
12	Minimum	-9.0000
13	Maximum	35.0000
14	Sum	10862.3000
15	Count	868.0000
16	Largest(1)	35.0000
17	Smallest(1)	-9.0000

FIGURE 6.21

Minitab boxplot for the 2006 returns

See Section M3.2 to create this. (Use Section P3.1 to create the PHStat2 equivalent.)

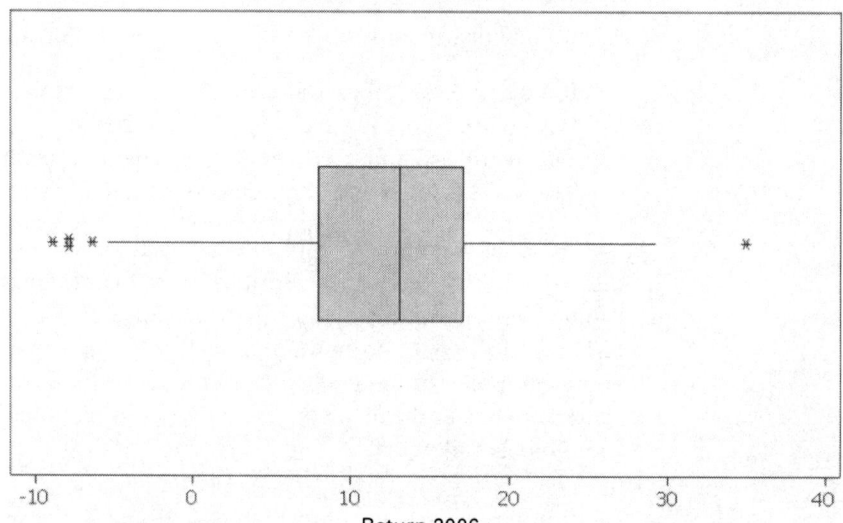

From Figures 6.20 and 6.21 and from an ordered array of the 2006 returns (not shown here), you can make the following statements:

1. The mean of 12.5142 is slightly lower than the median of 13.1. (In a normal distribution, the mean and median are equal.)
2. The boxplot appears symmetrical, with four lower outliers at −9.0, −8.0, −8.0, and −6.5 and one upper outlier at 35.0. (The normal distribution is symmetrical.)
3. The interquartile range of 9.2 is approximately 1.46 standard deviations. (In a normal distribution, the interquartile range is 1.33 standard deviations.)
4. The range of 44 is equal to 6.99 standard deviations. (In a normal distribution, the range is approximately six standard deviations.)
5. 72.2% of the returns are within ±1 standard deviation of the mean. (In a normal distribution, 68.26% of the values lie between the mean ±1 standard deviation.)
6. 87.0% of the returns are within ±1.28 standard deviations of the mean. (In a normal distribution, 80% of the values lie between the mean ±1.28 standard deviations.)

Based on these statements and the criteria given on page 235, the 2006 returns are slightly left-skewed and contain more values closer to the mean than expected. The range is higher than would be expected in a normal distribution, but this is mostly due to the single outlier at 35.0. You can conclude that the data characteristics of the 2006 returns do not greatly differ from the theoretical properties of a normal distribution.

Constructing the Normal Probability Plot

A **normal probability plot** is a graphical approach for evaluating whether data are normally distributed. One common approach is called the **quantile-quantile plot**. In this method, you first transform each ordered value to a Z value. For example, if you have a sample of $n = 19$, the

Z value for the smallest value corresponds to a cumulative area of $\dfrac{1}{n+1} = \dfrac{1}{19+1} = \dfrac{1}{20} = 0.05$.

The Z value for a cumulative area of 0.05 (from Table E.2) is −1.65. Table 6.7 illustrates the entire set of Z values for a sample of $n = 19$.

To construct the quantile-quantile plot, the Z values are plotted on the X axis, and the corresponding values of the variable are plotted on the Y axis. If the data are normally distributed, the values will plot along an approximately straight line. (Minitab uses a slightly different approach that plots the original values on the X axis and a theoretical percentage score based on

TABLE 6.7

Ordered Values and Corresponding Z Values for a Sample of n = 19

Ordered Value	Z Value	Ordered Value	Z Value
1	−1.65	11	0.13
2	−1.28	12	0.25
3	−1.04	13	0.39
4	−0.84	14	0.52
5	−0.67	15	0.67
6	−0.52	16	0.84
7	−0.39	17	1.04
8	−0.25	18	1.28
9	−0.13	19	1.65
10	0.00		

the normal distribution on the Y axis. Once again, if the data are normally distributed, the values will plot along an approximately straight line.)

Figure 6.22 illustrates the typical shape of normal probability plots for a left-skewed distribution (Panel A), a normal distribution (Panel B), and a right-skewed distribution (Panel C). If the data are left-skewed, the curve will rise more rapidly at first and then level off. If the data are normally distributed, the points will plot along an approximately straight line. If the data are right-skewed, the data will rise more slowly at first and then rise at a faster rate for higher values of the variable being plotted.

FIGURE 6.22

Normal probability plots for a left-skewed distribution, a normal distribution, and a right-skewed distribution

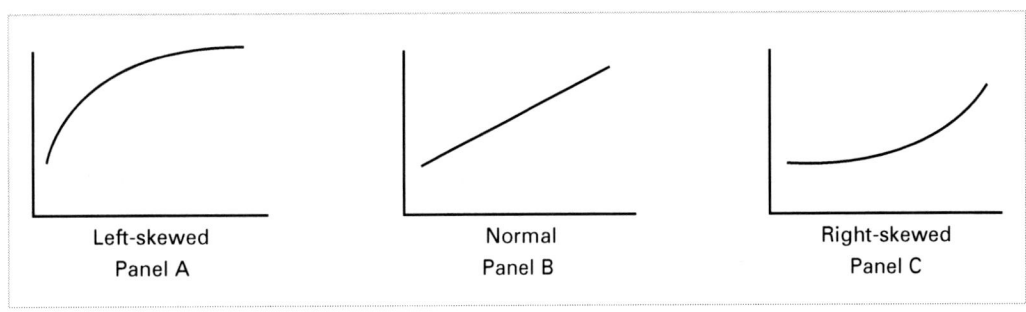

| Left-skewed | Normal | Right-skewed |
| Panel A | Panel B | Panel C |

Figure 6.23 shows a Microsoft Excel quantile-quantile normal probability plot and Figure 6.24 displays a Minitab normal probability plot for the 2006 returns.

FIGURE 6.23

Microsoft Excel normal probability plot for 2006 returns

See Section P6.2 to create this.

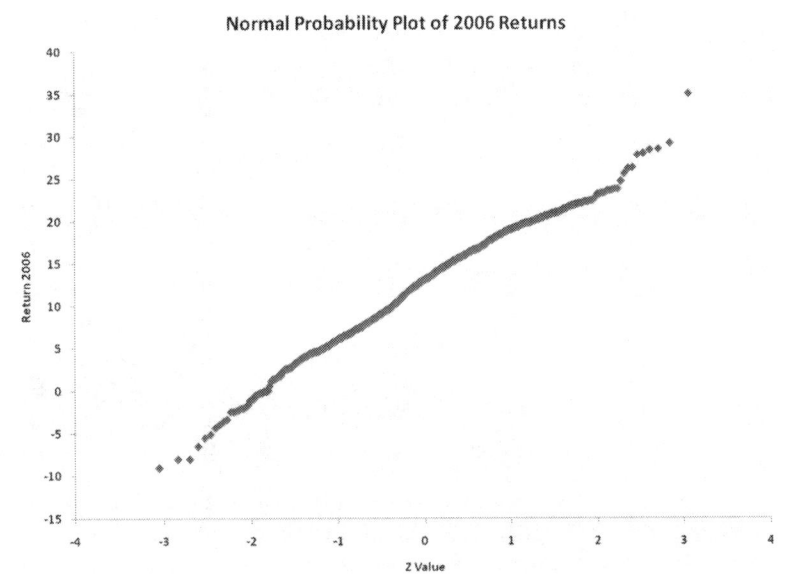

Normal Probability Plot of 2006 Returns

FIGURE 6.24

Minitab normal
probability plot
for 2006 returns

*See Section M6.2 to
create this.*

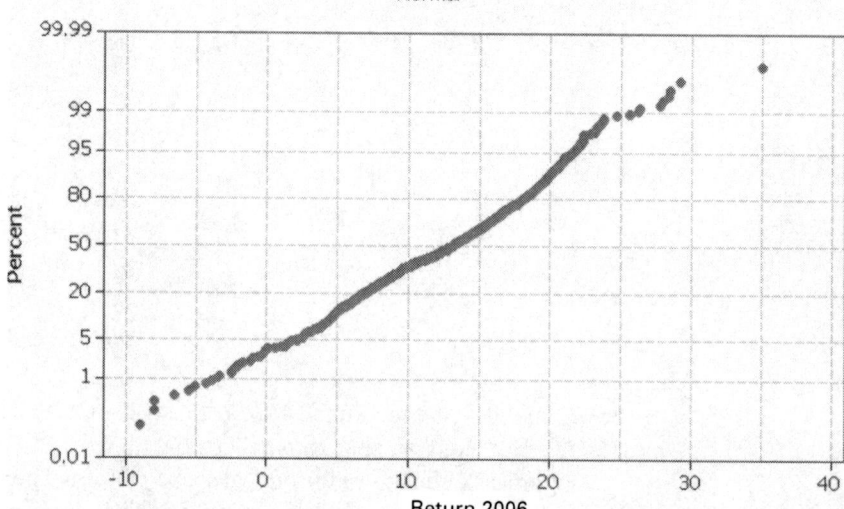

Figures 6.23 and 6.24 shows that the 2006 returns approximate a straight line with the exception of a few outliers at the lower and upper ends of the distribution. Thus, it is reasonable for you to conclude that the 2006 returns do not depart greatly from a normal distribution.

PROBLEMS FOR SECTION 6.3

Learning the Basics

6.14 Show that for a sample of $n = 39$, the smallest and largest Z values are -1.96 and $+1.96$, and the middle (i.e., 20th) Z value is 0.00.

6.15 For a sample of $n = 6$, list the six Z values.

Applying the Concepts

✓SELF **6.16** The data in the file **Chicken** contains the
Test total fat, in grams per serving, for a sample of 20 chicken sandwiches from fast-food chains. The data are as follows:

7 8 4 5 16 20 20 24 19 30 23 30 25 19 29 29 30 30 40 56

Source: *Extracted from "Fast Food: Adding Health to the Menu,"* Consumer Reports, *September 2004, pp. 28–31.*

Decide whether the data appear to be approximately normally distributed by
a. comparing data characteristics to theoretical properties.
b. constructing a normal probability plot.

6.17 As player salaries have increased, the cost of attending games has increased dramatically. The data in the file **BB2006** (extracted from K. Belson, "Oh Yeah, There's a

Ballgame Too," *The New York Times*, October 22, 2006, Business, pp. 1, 7–8) represent the cost of four tickets, two beers, four soft drinks, four hot dogs, two game programs, two baseball caps, and the parking fee for one car for each of the 30 major league teams. Decide whether the data appear to be approximately normally distributed by
a. comparing data characteristics to theoretical properties.
b. constructing a normal probability plot.

6.18 The data in the file **Property Taxes** contain the property taxes per capita for the fifty states and the District of Columbia. Decide whether the data appear to be approximately normally distributed by
a. comparing data characteristics to theoretical properties.
b. constructing a normal probability plot.

6.19 The data in the file **Spending** represent the per-capita spending, in thousands of dollars, for each state in 2004. Decide whether the data appear to be approximately normally distributed by
a. comparing data characteristics to theoretical properties.
b. constructing a normal probability plot.

6.20 One operation of a mill is to cut pieces of steel into parts that will later be used as the frame for front seats in an automotive plant. The steel is cut with a diamond saw and

requires the resulting parts to be within ±0.005 inch of the length specified by the automobile company. The data come from a sample of 100 steel parts and are stored in the file **Steel**. The measurement reported is the difference, in inches, between the actual length of the steel part, as measured by a laser measurement device, and the specified length of the steel part. Decide whether the data appear to be approximately normally distributed by
a. comparing data characteristics to theoretical properties.
b. constructing a normal probability plot.

6.21 The data in the file **Savings** are the yields for a money market account, a one-year certificate of deposit (CD), and a five-year CD for 37 banks in south Florida, as of March 9, 2007 (extracted from **Bankrate.com**, March 9, 2007). For each of the three types of investments, decide whether the data appear to be approximately normally distributed by

a. comparing data characteristics to theoretical properties.
b. constructing a normal probability plot.

6.22 The following data, stored in the file **Utility**, represent the electricity costs in dollars during July 2007 for a random sample of 50 two-bedroom apartments in a large city:

96	171	202	178	147	102	153	197	127	82
157	185	90	116	172	111	148	213	130	165
141	149	206	175	123	128	144	168	109	167
95	163	150	154	130	143	187	166	139	149
108	119	183	151	114	135	191	137	129	158

Decide whether the data appear to be approximately normally distributed by
a. comparing data characteristics to theoretical properties.
b. constructing a normal probability plot.

6.4   THE UNIFORM DISTRIBUTION

In the **uniform distribution**, a value has the same probability of occurrence anywhere in the range between the smallest value, a, and the largest value, b. Because of its shape, the uniform distribution is sometimes called the **rectangular distribution** (see Panel B of Figure 6.1 on page 218). Equation (6.4) defines the continuous probability density function for the uniform distribution.

Uniform Distribution

$$f(X) = \frac{1}{b-a} \text{ if } a \le X \le b \text{ and } 0 \text{ elsewhere} \qquad \textbf{(6.4)}$$

where

$$a = \text{the minimum value of } X$$

$$b = \text{the maximum value of } X$$

Equation (6.5) defines the mean of the uniform distribution.

Mean of the Uniform Distribution

$$\mu = \frac{a+b}{2} \qquad \textbf{(6.5)}$$

Equation (6.6) defines the variance and standard deviation of the uniform distribution.

Variance and Standard Deviation of the Uniform Distribution

$$\sigma^2 = \frac{(b-a)^2}{12} \tag{6.6a}$$

$$\sigma = \sqrt{\frac{(b-a)^2}{12}} \tag{6.6b}$$

One of the most common uses of the uniform distribution is in the selection of random numbers. When you use simple random sampling (see Section 7.1), you assume that each random number comes from a uniform distribution that has a minimum value of 0 and a maximum value of 1.

Figure 6.25 illustrates the uniform distribution with $a = 0$ and $b = 1$. The total area inside the rectangle is equal to the base (1.0) times the height (1.0). Thus, the resulting area of 1.0 satisfies the requirement that the area under any probability density function equals 1.0.

FIGURE 6.25

Probability density function for a uniform distribution with $a = 0$ and $b = 1$

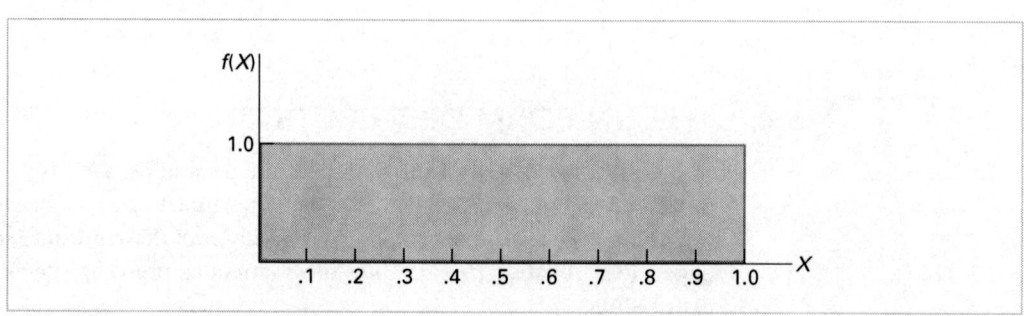

In such a distribution, what is the probability of getting a random number between 0.10 and 0.30? The area between 0.10 and 0.30, depicted in Figure 6.26, is equal to the base (which is $0.30 - 0.10 = 0.20$) times the height (1.0). Therefore,

$$P(0.10 < X < 0.30) = (\text{Base})(\text{Height}) = (0.20)(1.0) = 0.20$$

FIGURE 6.26

Finding $P(0.10 < X < 0.30)$ for a uniform distribution with $a = 0$ and $b = 1$

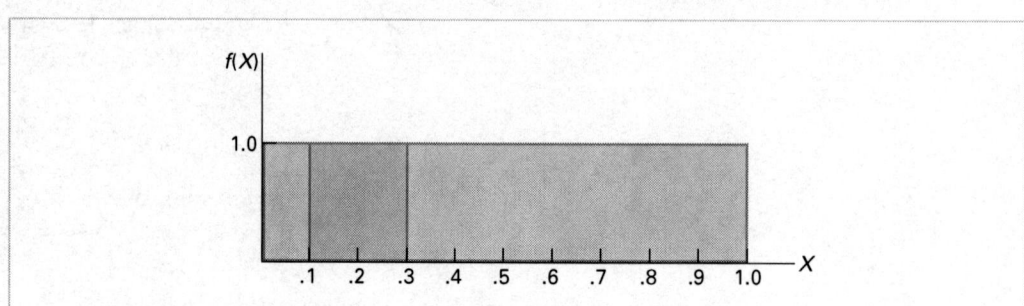

From Equations (6.5) and (6.6), the mean and standard deviation of the uniform distribution for $a = 0$ and $b = 1$ are computed as follows:

$$\mu = \frac{a+b}{2}$$

$$= \frac{0+1}{2} = 0.5$$

and

$$\sigma^2 = \frac{(b-a)^2}{12}$$

$$= \frac{(1-0)^2}{12}$$

$$= \frac{1}{12} = 0.0833$$

$$\sigma = \sqrt{0.0833} = 0.2887$$

Thus, the mean is 0.5 and the standard deviation is 0.2887.

PROBLEMS FOR SECTION 6.4

Learning the Basics

6.23 Suppose you sample one value from a uniform distribution with $a = 0$ and $b = 10$. What is the probability that the value will be
a. between 5 and 7?
b. between 2 and 3?
c. What is the mean?
d. What is the standard deviation?

Applying the Concepts

SELF Test **6.24** The time between arrivals of customers at a bank during the noon-to-1 p.m. hour has a uniform distribution between 0 to 120 seconds. What is the probability that the time between the arrival of two customers will be
a. less than 20 seconds?
b. between 10 and 30 seconds?
c. more than 35 seconds?
d. What are the mean and standard deviation of the time between arrivals?

6.25 A study of the time spent shopping in a supermarket for a market basket of 20 specific items showed an approximately uniform distribution between 20 minutes and 40 minutes. What is the probability that the shopping time will be
a. between 25 and 30 minutes?
b. less than 35 minutes?

c. What are the mean and standard deviation of the shopping time?

6.26 How long does it take you to download a game for your iPod? According to Apple's technical support site, **www.apple.com/support/itunes**, downloading an iPod game using a broadband connection should take 3 to 6 minutes. Assume that the download times are uniformly distributed between 3 and 6 minutes. If you download a game, what is the probability that the download time will be
a. less than 3.3 minutes?
b. less than 4 minutes?
c. between 4 and 5 minutes?
d. What are the mean and standard deviation of the download times?

6.27 The scheduled commuting time on the Long Island Rail Road from Glen Cove to New York City is 65 minutes. Suppose that the actual commuting time is uniformly distributed between 64 and 74 minutes. What is the probability that the commuting time will be
a. less than 70 minutes?
b. between 65 and 70 minutes?
c. greater than 65 minutes?
d. What are the mean and standard deviation of the commuting time?

6.5 THE EXPONENTIAL DISTRIBUTION

The **exponential distribution** is a continuous distribution that is right-skewed and ranges from zero to positive infinity (see Panel C of Figure 6.1 on page 218). The exponential distribution is widely used in waiting-line (i.e., queuing) theory to model the length of time between arrivals in processes such as customers at a bank's ATM, patients entering a hospital emergency room, and hits on a Web site.

The exponential distribution is defined by a single parameter, its mean, λ, the mean number of arrivals per unit of time. The value $1/\lambda$ is equal to the mean time between arrivals. For example, if the mean number of arrivals in a minute is $\lambda = 4$, then the mean time between arrivals is $1/\lambda = 0.25$ minutes, or 15 seconds. Equation (6.7) defines the probability that the length of time before the next arrival is less than X.

Exponential Distribution

$$P(\text{Arrival time} < X) = 1 - e^{-\lambda X} \qquad \textbf{(6.7)}$$

where

e = the mathematical constant approximated by 2.71828

λ = the mean number of arrivals per unit

X = any value of the continuous variable where $0 < X < \infty$

To illustrate the exponential distribution, suppose that customers arrive at a bank's ATM at a rate of 20 per hour. If a customer has just arrived, what is the probability that the next customer will arrive within 6 minutes (i.e., 0.1 hour)? For this example, $\lambda = 20$ and $X = 0.1$. Using Equation (6.7),

$$P(\text{Arrival time} < 0.1) = 1 - e^{-20(0.1)}$$
$$= 1 - e^{-2}$$
$$= 1 - 0.1353 = 0.8647$$

Thus, the probability that a customer will arrive within 6 minutes is 0.8647, or 86.47%. You can also use Microsoft Excel or Minitab to compute this probability (see Figures 6.27 or 6.28). Note that Minitab uses the mean time between arrivals $(1/\lambda)$ as the mean in Figure 6.28.

FIGURE 6.27

Microsoft Excel worksheet for finding exponential probabilities (mean = λ)

See Section E6.3 or P6.3 to create this.

	A	B
1	**Exponential Probability**	
2		
3	**Data**	
4	Mean	20
5	X Value	0.1
6		
7	**Results**	
8	P(<=X)	0.8647 =EXPONDIST(B5, B4, TRUE)

FIGURE 6.28

Minitab results for finding exponential probabilities (mean = $1/\lambda$)

See Section M6.3 to create this.

```
Exponential with mean = 0.05

   x   P( X <= x )
   0.1     0.864665
```

EXAMPLE 6.8   COMPUTING EXPONENTIAL PROBABILITIES

In the ATM example, what is the probability that the next customer will arrive within 3 minutes (i.e., 0.05 hour)?

SOLUTION For this example, $\lambda = 20$ and $X = 0.05$. Using Equation (6.7),

$$P(\text{Arrival time} < 0.05) = 1 - e^{-20(0.05)}$$

$$= 1 - e^{-1}$$

$$= 1 - 0.3679 = 0.6321$$

Thus, the probability that a customer will arrive within 3 minutes is 0.6321, or 63.21%.

PROBLEMS FOR SECTION 6.5

Learning the Basics

6.28 Given an exponential distribution with $\lambda = 10$, what is the probability that the arrival time is
a. less than $X = 0.1$?
b. greater than $X = 0.1$?
c. between $X = 0.1$ and $X = 0.2$?
d. less than $X = 0.1$ or greater than $X = 0.2$?

6.29 Given an exponential distribution with $\lambda = 30$, what is the probability that the arrival time is
a. less than $X = 0.1$?
b. greater than $X = 0.1$?
c. between $X = 0.1$ and $X = 0.2$?
d. less than $X = 0.1$ or greater than $X = 0.2$?

6.30 Given an exponential distribution with $\lambda = 5$, what is the probability that the arrival time is
a. less than $X = 0.3$?
b. greater than $X = 0.3$?
c. between $X = 0.3$ and $X = 0.5$?
d. less than $X = 0.3$ or greater than $X = 0.5$?

Applying the Concepts

6.31 Autos arrive at a toll plaza located at the entrance to a bridge at the rate of 50 per minute during the 5:00–6:00 p.m. hour. If an auto has just arrived,
a. what is the probability that the next auto will arrive within 3 seconds (0.05 minute)?
b. what is the probability that the next auto will arrive within 1 second (0.0167 minute)?
c. What are your answers to (a) and (b) if the rate of arrival of autos is 60 per minute?
d. What are your answers to (a) and (b) if the rate of arrival of autos is 30 per minute?

SELF Test 6.32 Customers arrive at the drive-up window of a fast-food restaurant at a rate of 2 per minute during the lunch hour.
a. What is the probability that the next customer will arrive within 1 minute?
b. What is the probability that the next customer will arrive within 5 minutes?
c. During the dinner time period, the arrival rate is 1 per minute. What are your answers to (a) and (b) for this period?

6.33 Telephone calls arrive at the information desk of a large computer software company at a rate of 15 per hour.
a. What is the probability that the next call will arrive within 3 minutes (0.05 hour)?
b. What is the probability that the next call will arrive within 15 minutes (0.25 hour)?
c. Suppose the company has just introduced an updated version of one of its software programs, and telephone calls are now arriving at a rate of 25 per hour. Given this information, redo (a) and (b).

6.34 An on-the-job injury occurs once every 10 days on average at an automobile plant. What is the probability that the next on-the-job injury will occur within
a. 10 days?
b. 5 days?
c. 1 day?

6.35 The time between unplanned shutdowns of a power plant has an exponential distribution with a mean of 20 days. Find the probability that the time between two unplanned shutdowns is
a. less than 14 days.
b. more than 21 days.
c. less than 7 days.

6.36 Golfers arrive at the starter's booth of a public golf course at a rate of 8 per hour during the Monday-to-Friday midweek period. If a golfer has just arrived,
a. what is the probability that the next golfer will arrive within 15 minutes (0.25 hour)?
b. what is the probability that the next golfer will arrive within 3 minutes (0.05 hour)?
c. The actual arrival rate on Fridays is 15 per hour. What are your answers to (a) and (b) for Fridays?

6.37 TrafficWeb.org claims that it can deliver 10,000 hits to a Web site in the next 60 days for only $21.50 (**www.trafficweb.org**, July 16, 2007). If this amount of Web site traffic is experienced, then the time between hits has a mean of 8.64 minutes (or 0.116 per minute). Assume that your Web site does get 10,000 hits in the next 60 days and that the time between hits has an exponential distribution. What is the probability that the time between two hits is
a. less than 5 minutes?
b. less than 10 minutes?
c. more than 15 minutes?
d. Do you think it is reasonable to assume that the time between hits has an exponential distribution?

6.6 THE NORMAL APPROXIMATION TO THE BINOMIAL DISTRIBUTION

In Sections 6.2 and 6.3 you learned about the normal probability distribution. In this section, you will learn how to use the normal distribution to approximate the binomial distribution (see Section 5.3). Recall that the binomial distribution is a discrete distribution where the random variable X is the number of events of interest occurring in a sample of n trials. Calculating exact probabilities of X using Equation (5.11) on page 191 becomes very tedious when n is large, and thus, it is often useful to approximate the probability using the normal approximation introduced in this section.

Need for a Correction for Continuity Adjustment

When using the normal distribution to approximate the binomial distribution, you can get more accurate approximations of the probabilities if you use a correction for continuity adjustment. There are two major reasons for using the correction. First, discrete random variables that follow the binomial distribution can take on only integer values, whereas a continuous random variable such as the normal can take on any values within a continuum or interval. Second, with a continuous distribution such as the normal, the probability of getting a specific value of a random variable is zero. However, when the normal distribution is used to approximate a discrete distribution, you can use a correction for continuity adjustment to get the approximate probability of a specific value of the binomial distribution.

Consider an experiment in which you toss a fair coin 10 times. Suppose you want to compute the probability of getting *exactly* 4 heads. Whereas a discrete random variable can have only an integer value (such as 4), a continuous random variable used to approximate it could take on any values within an interval around that specified value, as demonstrated on the accompanying scale:

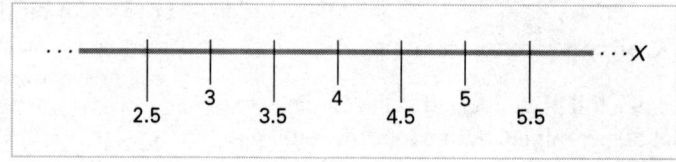

The correction for continuity adjustment requires adding or subtracting 0.5 from the value or values of the discrete random variable X as needed. To use the normal distribution to approximate the probability of getting *exactly* 4 heads (i.e., $X = 4$), you need to find the area under the normal curve from $X = 3.5$ to $X = 4.5$, the lower and upper boundaries of 4. To determine the approximate probability of getting *at least* 4 heads, you find the area under the normal curve greater than or equal to $X = 3.5$, since 3.5 is the lower boundary of 4. Similarly, to determine the approximate probability of getting *at most* 4 heads, you find the area under the normal curve equal to or less than $X = 4.5$, because 4.5 is the upper boundary of 4.

When using the normal distribution to approximate discrete probability distributions, wording is particularly important. To determine the approximate probability of getting *fewer* than 4 heads, you find the area under the normal curve less than or equal to $X = 3.5$. To determine the approximate probability of getting *more than* 4 heads, you find the area under the normal curve greater than or equal to $X = 4.5$. To determine the approximate probability of getting 4 *through* 7 heads, you find the area under the normal curve from $X = 3.5$ to $X = 7.5$.

Approximating the Binomial Distribution

In Section 5.3 you learned that the binomial distribution is symmetrical (like the normal distribution) whenever $\pi = 0.5$. When $\pi \neq 0.5$, the binomial distribution is not symmetrical. However, the closer π is to 0.5 and the larger the sample size n, the more symmetric the distribution becomes. On the other hand, the larger the sample size, the more tedious it is to compute the exact probabilities of a specific number of items of interest by using Equation (5.11) on page 191. Fortunately, whenever the sample size is large, you can use the normal distribution to approximate the exact probabilities of a specific number of items of interest.

As a general rule, you can use the normal distribution to approximate the binomial distribution whenever both $n\pi$ and $n(1 - \pi)$ are at least 5. From Section 5.3, you know that the mean of the binomial distribution is

$$\mu = n\pi$$

and the standard deviation of the binomial distribution is

$$\sigma = \sqrt{n\pi(1 - \pi)}$$

Substituting these results into the transformation formula [Equation (6.2) on page 221],

$$Z = \frac{X - \mu}{\sigma}$$

$$= \frac{X - n\pi}{\sqrt{n\pi(1 - \pi)}}$$

so that, for large enough n, the random variable Z is approximately normally distributed. Hence, you find approximate probabilities corresponding to the values of the discrete random variable X, by using Equation (6.8).

Normal Approximation to the Binomial Distribution

$$Z = \frac{X_a - n\pi}{\sqrt{n\pi(1 - \pi)}} \tag{6.8}$$

where

$\mu = n\pi$, mean of the binomial distribution

$\sigma = \sqrt{n\pi(1 - \pi)}$, standard deviation of the binomial distribution

X_a = adjusted number of items of interest for the discrete random variable X, such that $X_a = X - 0.5$ or $X_a = X + 0.5$ as appropriate

EXAMPLE 6.9

USING THE NORMAL DISTRIBUTION TO APPROXIMATE THE BINOMIAL DISTRIBUTION

You select a random sample of $n = 1,600$ tires from an ongoing production process in which 8% of all such tires produced are defective. What is the probability that 150 or fewer tires will be defective?

SOLUTION Because both $n\pi = 1,600(0.08) = 128$ and $n(1 - \pi) = 1,600(0.92) = 1,472$ are greater than 5, you can use the normal distribution to approximate the binomial. Here X_a, the adjusted number of defective tires, is 150.5.

$$Z = \frac{X_a - n\pi}{\sqrt{n\pi(1 - \pi)}} = \frac{150.5 - 128}{\sqrt{(1,600)(0.08)(0.92)}} = \frac{22.5}{10.85} = +2.07$$

Using Table E.2, the area under the curve to the left of $Z = +2.07$ is 0.9808 (see Figure 6.29).

FIGURE 6.29

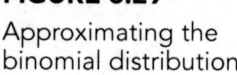

Approximating the binomial distribution

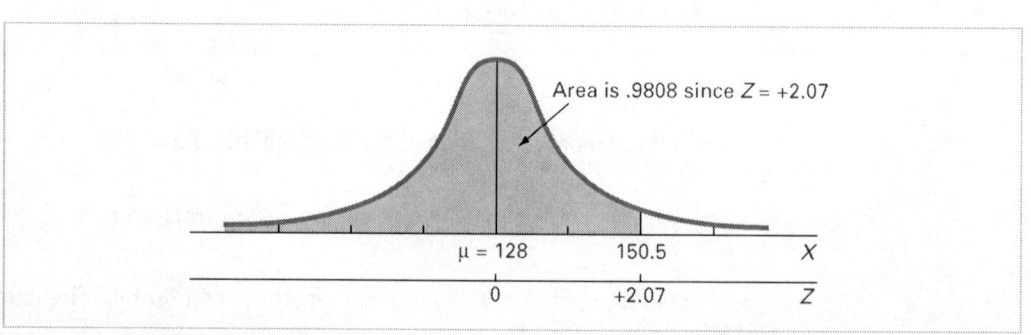

Suppose that you want to approximate the probability of getting *exactly* 150 defective tires. The correction for continuity defines the integer value of interest to range from one-half unit below it to one-half unit above it. Therefore, you define the probability of getting 150 defective tires as the area (under the normal curve) between 149.5 and 150.5. Using Equation (6.8), you approximate the probability as follows:

$$Z = \frac{150.5 - 128}{\sqrt{(1,600)(0.08)(0.92)}} = \frac{22.5}{10.85} = +2.07$$

and

$$Z = \frac{149.5 - 128}{\sqrt{(1,600)(0.08)(0.92)}} = \frac{21.5}{10.85} = +1.98$$

From Table E.2, the area under the normal curve less than $X = 150.5$ ($Z = +2.07$) is 0.9808 and the area under the curve less than $X = 149.5$ ($Z = +1.98$) is 0.9761. Thus, the approximate probability of getting 150 defective tires is the difference in the two areas, 0.0047.

PROBLEMS FOR SECTION 6.6

Learning the Basics

6.38 For $n = 100$ and $\pi = 0.20$, use the normal distribution to approximate the probability that
a. $X = 25$.
b. $X > 25$.
c. $X \leq 25$.
d. $X < 25$.

6.39 For $n = 100$ and $\pi = 0.40$, use the normal distribution to approximate the probability that
a. $X = 40$.
b. $X > 40$.
c. $X \leq 40$.
d. $X < 40$.

Applying the Concepts

6.40 Consider an experiment in which you toss a fair coin 10 times and count the number of heads. Use Equation (5.11) on page 191, Table E.6, or Microsoft Excel, or Minitab to determine the probability of getting:
a. 4 heads.
b. at least 4 heads.
c. 4 through 7 heads.
d. Use the normal approximation to the binomial distribution to approximate the probabilities in (a) through (c).

6.41 For short domestic flights, an airline has three different choices on its snack menu—pretzels, potato chips, and cookies. Based on past experience, the airline feels that each snack is equally likely to be chosen. If there are 150 passengers on a particular flight, what is the *approximate* probability that:
a. at least 60 will choose cookies for a snack?
b. exactly 60 will choose cookies for a snack?
c. less than 60 will choose cookies for a snack?
d. If the airline has 70 of each type of snack available on the flight, what is the likelihood that a passenger will not be able to get the snack that he or she desires?

6.42 Stock options are usually awarded at the price of a company's shares on the date of the grant. A recent study (E. Awata, "Backdated Options May Snare Some Directors," *USA Today*, March 29, 2007, pp. 1B, 2B) found evidence that many outside directors received grants at the lowest price in a given month. Of 17,512 grants before the Sarbanes-Oxley Act tightened Security and Exchange Commission disclosure rules, 1,726 were at the lowest price in a given month. Assume that there is an average of 21 days in a month on which grants can be made. How likely do you think it is that these results or more extreme results could have occurred if the grant is equally likely to be given on any day of the month?

SUMMARY

In this chapter, you used the normal distribution in the Using Statistics scenario to study the time to download a Web page. In addition, you studied the uniform distribution, the exponential distribution, the normal probability plot, and the normal approximation to the binomial distribution. In Chapter 7, the normal distribution is used in developing the subject of statistical inference.

KEY EQUATIONS

Normal Probability Density Function

$$f(X) = \frac{1}{\sqrt{2\pi}\sigma} e^{-(1/2)[(X-\mu)/\sigma]^2} \quad (6.1)$$

Transformation Formula

$$Z = \frac{X - \mu}{\sigma} \quad (6.2)$$

Finding an X Value Associated with Known Probability

$$X = \mu + Z\sigma \quad (6.3)$$

Uniform Distribution

$$f(X) = \frac{1}{b-a} \quad (6.4)$$

Mean of the Uniform Distribution

$$\mu = \frac{a+b}{2} \qquad \text{(6.5)}$$

Variance and Standard Deviation of the Uniform Distribution

$$\sigma^2 = \frac{(b-a)^2}{12} \qquad \text{(6.6a)}$$

$$\sigma = \sqrt{\frac{(b-a)^2}{12}} \qquad \text{(6.6b)}$$

Exponential Distribution

$$P(\text{Arrival time} < X) = 1 - e^{-\lambda X} \qquad \text{(6.7)}$$

Normal Approximation to the Binomial Distribution

$$Z = \frac{X_a - n\pi}{\sqrt{n\pi(1-\pi)}} \qquad \text{(6.8)}$$

KEY TERMS

continuous probability density
   function 218
cumulative standardized normal
   distribution 221
exponential distribution 241

normal distribution 219
normal probability density
   function 220
normal probability plot 236
quantile-quantile plot 236

rectangular distribution 239
standardized normal random
   variable 221
transformation formula 221
uniform distribution 239

CHAPTER REVIEW PROBLEMS

Checking Your Understanding

6.43 Why is it that only one normal distribution table such as Table E.2 is needed to find any probability under the normal curve?

6.44 How do you find the area between two values under the normal curve?

6.45 How do you find the X value that corresponds to a given percentile of the normal distribution?

6.46 What are some of the distinguishing properties of a normal distribution?

6.47 How does the shape of the normal distribution differ from those of the uniform and exponential distributions?

6.48 How can you use the normal probability plot to evaluate whether a set of data is normally distributed?

6.49 Under what circumstances can you use the exponential distribution?

6.50 When can you use the normal distribution to approximate the binomial distribution?

Applying the Concepts

6.51 An industrial sewing machine uses ball bearings that are targeted to have a diameter of 0.75 inch. The lower and upper specification limits under which the ball bearings can operate are 0.74 inch and 0.76 inch, respectively. Past experience has indicated that the actual diameter of the ball bearings is approximately normally distributed, with a mean of 0.753 inch and a standard deviation of 0.004 inch. What is the probability that a ball bearing is
a. between the target and the actual mean?
b. between the lower specification limit and the target?
c. above the upper specification limit?
d. below the lower specification limit?
e. 93% of the diameters are greater than what value?

6.52 The fill amount of soft drink bottles is normally distributed, with a mean of 2.0 liters and a standard deviation of 0.05 liter. If bottles contain less than 95% of the listed net content (1.90 liters, in this case), the manufacturer may be subject to penalty by the state office of consumer affairs. Bottles that have a net content above 2.10 liters may cause excess spillage upon opening. What proportion of the bottles will contain

a. between 1.90 and 2.0 liters?
b. between 1.90 and 2.10 liters?
c. below 1.90 liters or above 2.10 liters?
d. 99% of the bottles contain at least how much soft drink?
e. 99% of the bottles contain an amount that is between which two values (symmetrically distributed) around the mean?

6.53 In an effort to reduce the number of bottles that contain less than 1.90 liters, the bottler in Problem 6.52 sets the filling machine so that the mean is 2.02 liters. Under these circumstances, what are your answers in (a) through (e)?

6.54 An orange juice producer buys all his oranges from a large orange grove. The amount of juice squeezed from each of these oranges is approximately normally distributed, with a mean of 4.70 ounces and a standard deviation of 0.40 ounce.

a. What is the probability that a randomly selected orange will contain between 4.70 and 5.00 ounces of juice?
b. What is the probability that a randomly selected orange will contain between 5.00 and 5.50 ounces of juice?
c. 77% of the oranges will contain at least how many ounces of juice?
d. 80% of the oranges contain between what two values (in ounces of juice), symmetrically distributed around the population mean?

6.55 Data concerning 71 of the best-selling domestic beers in the United States are located in the file **Domesticbeer**. The values for three variables are included: percentage alcohol, number of calories per 12 ounces, and number of carbohydrates (in grams) per 12 ounces. For each of the three variables, decide whether the data appear to be approximately normally distributed. Support your decision through the use of appropriate statistics and graphs.
Source: *Extracted from* **www.Beer100.com**, *May 4, 2007.*

6.56 The evening manager of a restaurant was very concerned about the length of time some customers were waiting in line to be seated. She also had some concern about the seating times—that is, the length of time between when a customer is seated and the time he or she leaves the restaurant. Over the course of one week, 100 customers (no more than 1 per party) were randomly selected, and their waiting and seating times (in minutes) were recorded in the file **Wait**.
a. Think about your favorite restaurant. Do you think waiting times more closely resemble a uniform, exponential, or normal distribution?

b. Again, think about your favorite restaurant. Do you think seating times more closely resemble a uniform, exponential, or normal distribution?
c. Construct a histogram and a normal probability plot of the waiting times. Do you think these waiting times more closely resemble a uniform, exponential, or normal distribution?
d. Construct a histogram and a normal probability plot of the seating times. Do you think these seating times more closely resemble a uniform, exponential, or normal distribution?

6.57 At the end of 2006, all the major stock market indexes had posted strong gains in the previous 12 months. The mean one-year return for stocks in the S&P 500, a group of 500 very large companies, was 13.62%. The mean one-year return for companies in the Russell 2000, a group of 2000 small companies, was 17%. Historically, the one-year returns are approximately normal, the standard deviation in the S&P 500 is approximately 20%, and the standard deviation in the Russell 2000 is approximately 35%.
a. What is the probability that a stock in the S&P 500 gained 25% or more in the last year? gained 50% or more?
b. What is the probability that a stock in the S&P 500 lost money in the last year? lost 25% or more? lost 50% or more?
c. Repeat (a) and (b) for a stock in the Russell 2000.
d. Write a short summary on your findings. Be sure to include a discussion of the risks associated with a large standard deviation.

6.58 *The New York Times* reported (L. J. Flynn, "Tax Surfing," March 25, 2002, p. C10) that the mean time to download the home page for the Internal Revenue Service, **www.irs.gov**, is 0.8 second. Suppose that the download time is normally distributed with a standard deviation of 0.2 second. What is the probability that a download time is
a. less than 1 second?
b. between 0.5 and 1.5 seconds?
c. above 0.5 second?
d. 99% of the download times are above how many seconds?
e. 95% of the download times are between what two values, symmetrically distributed around the mean?

6.59 The same article mentioned in Problem 6.58 also reported that the mean download time for the H&R Block Web site, **www.hrblock.com**, is 2.5 seconds. Suppose that the download time is normally distributed with a standard deviation of 0.5 second. What is the probability that a download time is
a. less than 1 second?
b. between 0.5 and 1.5 seconds?

c. above 0.5 second?

d. 99% of the download times are above how many seconds?

e. Compare the results for the IRS site computed in Problem 6.58 to those of the H&R Block site.

6.60 When obtaining a mortgage, the borrower will pay closing costs to the lender. These costs vary from bank to bank, and from state to state. Bankrate.com conducted a survey in all fifty states to identify average closing costs on a $200,000 loan, assuming a 20-percent down payment and good credit. The file Closing includes the average rate for all fifty states and the District of Columbia for 2006, along with the state rank.

Source: *Extracted from "Closing Cost Survey,"* **www.bankrate.com**, *May 15, 2007.*

a. Is the distribution of state closing costs approximately distributed as a normal random variable?

b. The variable "RANK 2006" includes 51 numbers, 1, 2, 3, . . . , 51. What type of distribution does this column of numbers resemble? Construct a graphical display that supports your answer.

6.61 (Class Project) According to Burton G. Malkiel, the daily changes in the closing price of stock follow a *random walk*—that is, these daily events are independent of each other and move upward or downward in a random manner—and can be approximated by a normal distribution. To test this theory, use either a newspaper or the Internet to select one company traded on the NYSE, one company traded on the American Stock Exchange, and one company traded on the NASDAQ and then do the following:

  1. Record the daily closing stock price of each of these companies for six consecutive weeks (so that you have 30 values per company).

  2. Record the daily changes in the closing stock price of each of these companies for six consecutive weeks (so that you have 30 values per company).

For each of your six data sets, decide whether the data are approximately normally distributed by

a. examining the stem-and-leaf display, histogram or polygon, and boxplot.

b. comparing data characteristics to theoretical properties.

c. constructing a normal probability plot.

d. Discuss the results of (a) through (c). What can you say about your three stocks with respect to daily closing prices and daily changes in closing prices? Which, if any, of the data sets are approximately normally distributed?

Note: The random-walk theory pertains to the daily changes in the closing stock price, not the daily closing stock price.

Team Projects

The data file Mutual Funds contains information regarding nine variables from a sample of 868 mutual funds. The variables are:

  Category—Type of stocks comprising the mutual fund (small cap, mid cap, large cap)

  Objective—Objective of stocks comprising the mutual fund (growth or value)

  Assets—In millions of dollars

  Fees—Sales charges (no or yes)

  Expense ratio—Ratio of expenses to net assets, in percentage

  Risk—Risk-of-loss factor of the mutual fund (low, average, high)

  2006 return—Twelve-month return in 2006

  Three-year return—Annualized return, 2004–2006

  Five-year return—Annualized return, 2002–2006

6.62 For the expense ratio, three-year return, and five-year return, decide whether the data are approximately normally distributed by

a. comparing data characteristics to theoretical properties.

b. constructing a normal probability plot.

Student Survey Data Base

6.63 Problem 1.27 on page 14 describes a survey of 50 undergraduate students (see the file Undergradsurvey). For these data, for each numerical variable, decide whether the data are approximately normally distributed by

a. comparing data characteristics to theoretical properties.

b. constructing a normal probability plot.

6.64 Problem 1.27 on page 14 describes a survey of 50 undergraduate students (see the file Undergradsurvey).

a. Select a sample of 50 undergraduate students and conduct a similar survey for those students.

b. For the data collected in (a), repeat (a) and (b) of Problem 6.63.

c. Compare the results of (b) to those of Problem 6.63.

6.65 Problem 1.28 on page 14 describes a survey of 40 MBA students (see the file Gradsurvey). For these data, for each numerical variable, decide whether the data are approximately normally distributed by

a. comparing data characteristics to theoretical properties.

b. constructing a normal probability plot.

6.66 Problem 1.28 on page 14 describes a survey of 40 MBA students (see the file Gradsurvey).

a. Select a sample of 40 graduate students and conduct a similar survey for those students.

b. For the data collected in (a), repeat (a) and (b) of Problem 6.65.

c. Compare the results of (b) to those of Problem 6.65.

MANAGING THE *SPRINGVILLE HERALD*

The production department of the newspaper has embarked on a quality improvement effort. Its first project relates to the blackness of the newspaper print. Each day, a determination needs to be made concerning how black the newspaper is printed. Blackness is measured on a standard scale in which the target value is 1.0. Data collected over the past year indicate that the blackness is normally distributed, with a mean of 1.005 and a standard deviation of 0.10. Each day, one spot on the first newspaper printed is chosen, and the blackness of the spot is measured. The blackness of the newspaper is considered acceptable if the blackness of a spot is between 0.95 and 1.05.

EXERCISES

SH6.1 Assuming that the distribution has not changed from what it was in the past year, what is the probability that the blackness of the spot is

  a. less than 1.0?
  b. between 0.95 and 1.0?
  c. between 1.0 and 1.05?
  d. less than 0.95 or greater than 1.05?

SH6.2 The objective of the production team is to reduce the probability that the blackness is below 0.95 or above 1.05. Should the team focus on process improvement that lowers the mean to the target value of 1.0 or on process improvement that reduces the standard deviation to 0.075? Explain.

WEB CASE

Apply your knowledge about the normal distribution in this Web Case, which extends the Using Statistics scenario from this chapter.

To satisfy concerns of potential advertisers, the management of OurCampus! has undertaken a research project to learn the amount of time it takes users to download a complex video features page. The marketing department has collected data and has made some claims based on the assertion that the data follow a normal distribution. These data and conclusions can be found in a report located on the internal Web page **www.prenhall.com/Springville/**

Our_DownloadResearch.htm (or in the file with the same name in the Student CD-ROM Web Case folder).

Read this marketing report and then answer the following:

1. Can the collected data be approximated by the normal distribution?

2. Review and evaluate the conclusions made by the OurCampus! marketing department. Which conclusions are correct? Which ones are incorrect?

3. If OurCampus! could improve the mean time by five minutes, how would the probabilities change?

REFERENCES

1. Gunter, B., "Q-Q Plots," *Quality Progress* (February 1994), 81–86.
2. Levine, D. M., P. Ramsey, and R. Smidt, *Applied Statistics for Engineers and Scientists Using Microsoft Excel and Minitab* (Upper Saddle River, NJ: Prentice Hall, 2001).
3. *Microsoft Excel 2007* (Redmond, WA: Microsoft Corp., 2007).
4. Miller, J., "Earliest Known Uses of Some of the Words of Mathematics," **http://members.aol.com/jeff570/n.html**
5. *Minitab for Windows Version 15* (State College, PA: Minitab, Inc., 2006).
6. Pearl, R., "Karl Pearson, 1857–1936," *Journal of the American Statistical Association*, 31 (1936), 653–664.
7. Pearson, E. S., "Some Incidents in the Early History of Biometry and Statistics, 1890–94," *Biometrika*, 52 (1965), 3–18.
8. Walker, H., "The Contributions of Karl Pearson," *Journal of the American Statistical Association*, 53 (1958), 11–22.

Appendix E6
Using Microsoft Excel to Compute Probabilities from the Normal Distribution and Other Continuous Distributions

E6.1 Computing Normal Probabilities

You compute normal probabilities by using either the **Normal** or **Normal Expanded** worksheets of the `Normal.xls` workbook. The **Normal** worksheet, shown in Figure 6.18 on page 232, contains the entries to solve the Example 6.5 and 6.6 problems on pages 227–228. Change the **Mean, Standard Deviation, X Value**, and/or **Cumulative Percentage** to solve similar problems. Use the **Normal Expanded** worksheet (part of which is shown in Figure E6.1) to compute all types of normal probabilities. In these worksheets, the STANDARDIZE function returns the Z value for a specific X value, mean, and standard deviation; the NORMDIST function returns the area or probability of less than a given X value for a specific mean and standard deviation; the NORMSINV function returns the Z value for a given probability of less than a given X, and the

NORMINV function returns the X value for a given probability, mean, and standard deviation.

E6.2 Creating Normal Probability Plots

There are no Microsoft Excel features that directly create normal probability plots. Use PHStat2 (see Section P6.2) to create a normal probability plot in Excel.

E6.3 Computing Exponential Probabilities

You compute exponential probabilities by making entries in the **Exponential** worksheet of the `Exponential.xls` workbook. This worksheet (see Figure 6.27 on page 242) uses the **EXPONDIST(X *value, mean*, True)** function to compute the exponential probability for the bank ATM problem of Section 6.5. To adapt this worksheet for other problems, change the **Mean** and **X Value** values in cells B4 and B5.

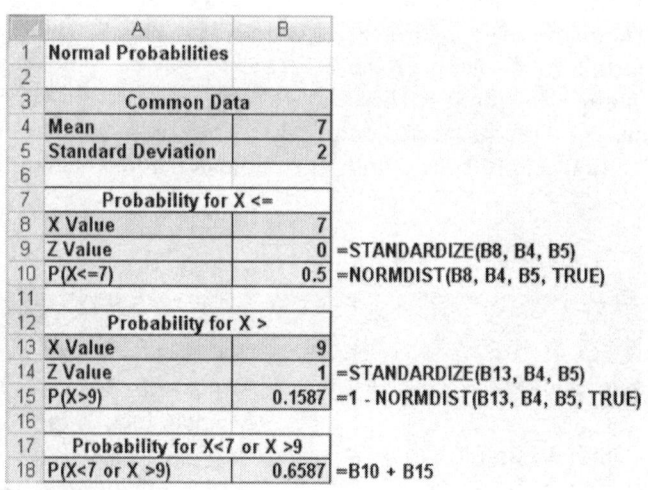

FIGURE E6.1

Normal Expanded worksheet (columns A and B)

Appendix P6
Using PHStat2 to Compute Probabilities from the Normal Distribution and Other Continuous Distributions

P6.1 Computing Normal Probabilities

To compute normal probabilities, use **PHStat → Probability & Prob. Distributions → Normal**. The procedure creates a normal probabilities worksheet, similar to Figure 6.18 on page 232, that solves one or more types of normal probability problems based on the Input Options you select.

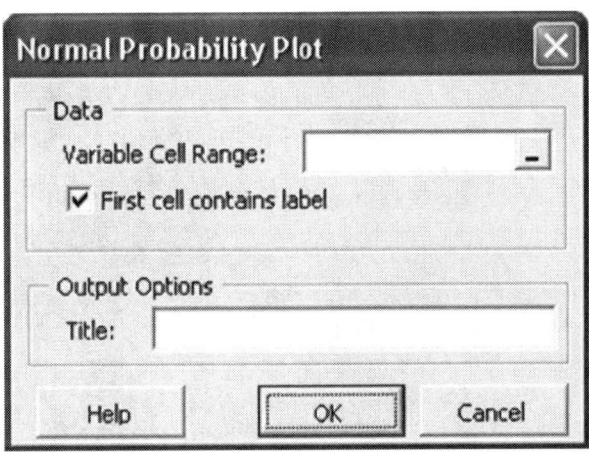

P6.2 Creating Normal Probability Plots

To create a normal probability plot, use **PHStat2 → Probability & Prob. Distributions → Normal Probability Plot**. This procedure uses Excel charting features to create a normal probability plot from data from a custom worksheet that the procedure also creates.

The procedure creates a **Plot** worksheet on which the *Z* values to be plotted are calculated using the NORMSINV function. The procedure then uses Excel charting features

to create a normal probability plot from the calculated *Z* values and the data in the **Variable Cell Range**.

P6.3 Computing Exponential Probabilities

To compute exponential probabilities, use **PHStat → Probability & Prob. Distributions → Exponential**. This procedure creates a worksheet similar to Figure 6.27 on page 242 using the mean per unit (*lambda*) and *X* value that you specify.

Appendix M6
Using Minitab to Compute Probabilities from the Normal Distribution and Other Continuous Distributions

M6.1 Computing Normal Probabilities

To illustrate computing normal probabilities, to find the probability that a download time is less than 9 seconds with $\mu = 7$ and $\sigma = 2$:

1. Open to a new, blank worksheet.
2. Enter **9** in the row 1 cell of column C1, leaving the unnumbered variable label cell at the top of the column empty.
3. Select **Calc → Probability Distributions → Normal**.

In the Normal Distribution dialog box (see Figure M6.1):

4. Click **Cumulative probability**.
5. Enter **7** in the **Mean** box.
6. Enter **2** in the **Standard deviation** box.
7. Click **Input column** and enter **C1** in its box.
8. Click **OK** (to create the results shown in the top portion of Figure 6.19 on page 232).

To find the Z value corresponding to a cumulative area of 0.10:

1. Continue with the same worksheet and enter **.10** in the row 1 cell of column C2.
2. Select **Calc → Probability Distributions → Normal**.

In the Normal Distribution dialog box (see Figure M6.1):

3. Click **Inverse cumulative probability**.
4. Enter **7** in the **Mean** box
5. Enter **2** in the **Standard deviation** box.
6. Click **Input Column** and enter **C2** in its box.
7. Click **OK** (to create the results displayed in the bottom portion of Figure 6.19 on page 232).

M6.2 Creating Normal Probability Plots

To create a normal probability plot for the 2006 returns of mutual funds:

1. Open the **Mutual Funds.mtw** worksheet.
2. Select **Graph → Probability Plot**.
3. In the Probability Plots dialog box gallery, click **Single** and then click **OK**.

In the Probability Plot - Single dialog box (see Figure M6.2):

4. Enter **'Return 2006'** in the **Graph variables** box.
5. Click **Distribution**.

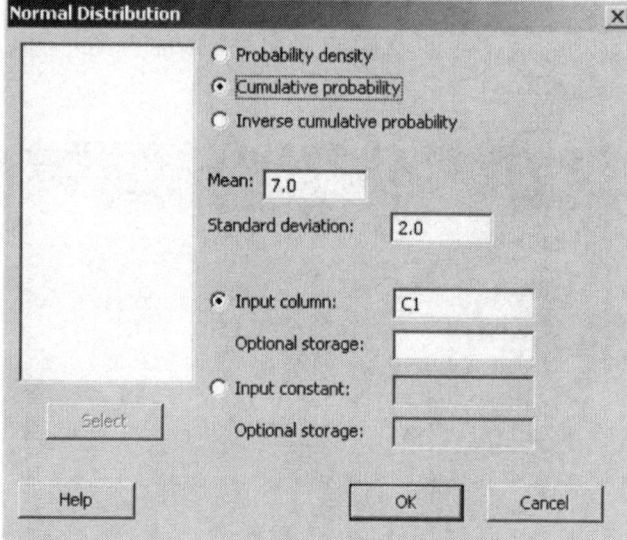

FIGURE M6.1
Minitab Normal Distribution dialog box

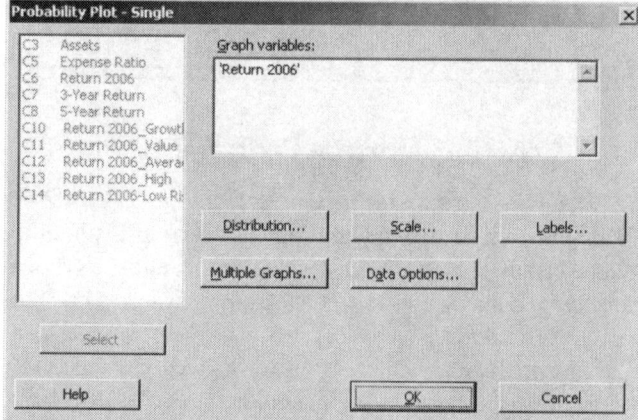

FIGURE M6.2
Minitab Probability Plot - Single dialog box

6. In the Probability Plot - Distribution dialog box (see Figure M6.3), select **Normal** from the **Distribution** drop-down list and then click **OK** to return to the Probability Plot - Single dialog box.
7. Back in the Probability Plot - Single dialog box, click **OK** (to create the plot).

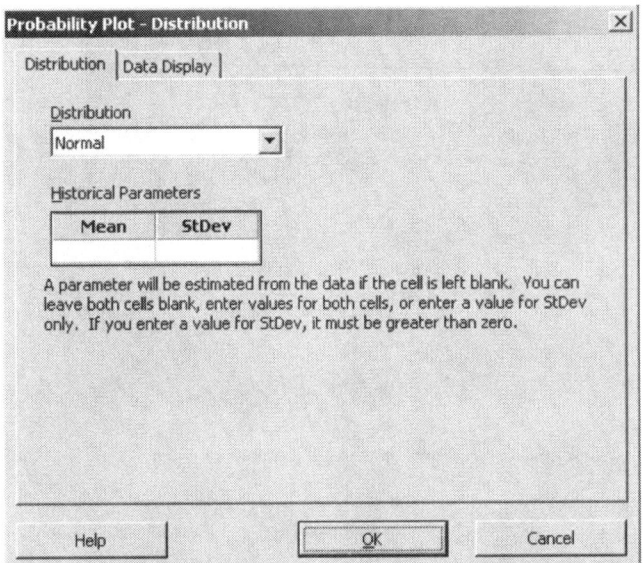

FIGURE M6.3
Minitab Probability Plot - Distribution

M6.3 Computing Exponential Probabilities

To compute exponential probabilities for the Section 6.5 ATM customer-arrival example on page 242:

1. Open to a new, blank worksheet.
2. Enter **.1** in the row 1 cell of column C1, leaving the unnumbered variable label cell at the top of the column empty.
3. Select **Calc → Probability Distributions → Exponential**.

In the Exponential Distribution dialog box (see Figure M6.4):

4. Click **Cumulative probability**.
5. Enter **.05** in the **Scale** box. (Minitab defines Scale as the mean time *between* arrivals, $1/\lambda = 1/20 = 0.05$, not the mean number of arrivals, $\lambda = 20$.)
6. Click **Input column** and enter **C1** in its box.
7. Click **OK** (to compute the probability).

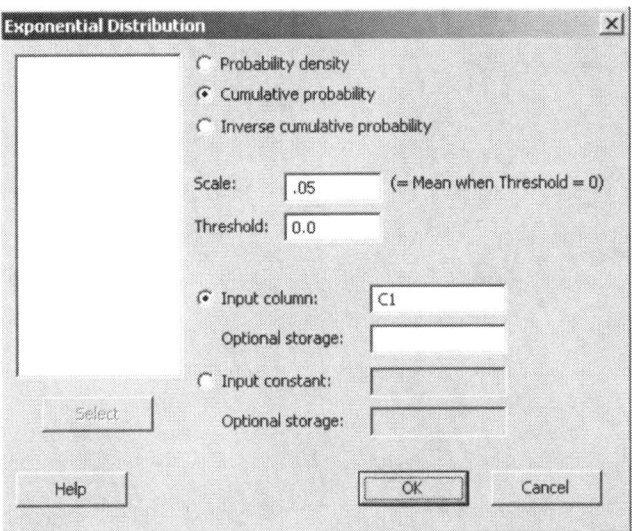

FIGURE M6.4
Minitab Exponential Distribution dialog box

CHAPTER SEVEN

SAMPLING AND SAMPLING DISTRIBUTIONS

LEARNING OBJECTIVES

In this chapter, you learn:

- To distinguish between different sampling methods
- The concept of the sampling distribution
- To compute probabilities related to the sample mean and the sample proportion
- The importance of the Central Limit Theorem

USING STATISTICS @ Oxford Cereals

Oxford Cereals fills thousands of boxes of cereal during an eight-hour shift. As the plant operations manager, you are responsible for monitoring the amount of cereal placed in each box. To be consistent with package labeling, boxes should contain a mean of 368 grams of cereal. Because of the speed of the process, the cereal weight varies from box to box, causing some boxes to be underfilled and others overfilled. If the process is not working properly, the mean weight in the boxes could vary too much from the label weight of 368 grams to be acceptable.

Because weighing every single box is too time-consuming, costly, and inefficient, you must take a sample of boxes. For each sample you select, you plan to weigh the individual boxes and calculate a sample mean. You need to determine the probability that such a sample mean could have been randomly selected from a population whose mean is 368 grams. Based on your analysis, you will have to decide whether to maintain, alter, or shut down the cereal-filling process.

In Chapter 6, you used the normal distribution to study the distribution of download times for the OurCampus! Web site. In this chapter, you need to make a decision about the cereal-filling process, based on the weights of a sample of cereal boxes packaged at Oxford Cereals. You will learn different methods of sampling and about sampling distributions and how to use them to solve business problems.

7.1 TYPES OF SAMPLING METHODS

In Section 1.3, a sample was defined as the portion of a population that has been selected for analysis. Rather than selecting every item in the population, statistical sampling procedures focus on collecting a small representative group of the larger population. The results of the sample are then used to estimate characteristics of the entire population. There are three main reasons for selecting a sample:

- Selecting a sample is less time-consuming than selecting every item in the population.
- Selecting a sample is less costly than selecting every item in the population.
- An analysis of a sample is less cumbersome and more practical than an analysis of the entire population.

The sampling process begins by defining the **frame**. The frame is a listing of items that make up the population. Frames are data sources such as population lists, directories, or maps. Samples are drawn from frames. Inaccurate or biased results can result if a frame excludes certain portions of the population. Using different frames to generate data can lead to dissimilar conclusions.

After you select a frame, you draw a sample from the frame. As illustrated in Figure 7.1, there are two kinds of samples: nonprobability samples and probability samples.

In a **nonprobability sample**, you select the items or individuals without knowing their probabilities of selection. Thus, the theory that has been developed for probability sampling cannot be applied to nonprobability samples. A common type of nonprobability sampling is **convenience sampling**. In convenience sampling, items selected are easy, inexpensive, or convenient to sample. For example, if you were sampling tires stacked in a warehouse, it would be much more convenient to sample tires that were at the top of a stack than tires that were at the bottom of a stack. In many cases, participants in the sample select themselves. For example, many

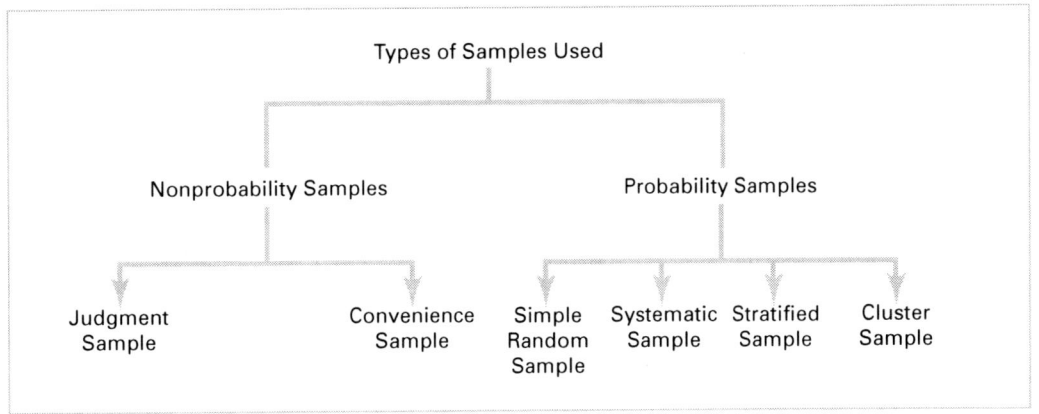

companies conduct surveys by giving visitors to their Web site the opportunity to complete survey forms and submit them electronically. The responses to these surveys can provide large amounts of data quickly and inexpensively, but the sample consists of self-selected Web users. For many studies, only a nonprobability sample such as a judgment sample is available. In a **judgment sample**, you get the opinions of preselected experts in the subject matter. Although the experts may be well informed, you cannot generalize their results to the general public.

Nonprobability samples can have certain advantages, such as convenience, speed, and low cost. However, their lack of accuracy due to selection bias and the fact that the results cannot be used for statistical inference more than offset these advantages.

In a **probability sample**, you select the items based on known probabilities. Whenever possible, you should use probability sampling methods. Probability samples allow you to make unbiased inferences about the population of interest. The four types of probability samples most commonly used are simple random, systematic, stratified, and cluster samples. These sampling methods vary in their cost, accuracy, and complexity.

Simple Random Samples

In a **simple random sample**, every item from a frame has the same chance of selection as every other item. In addition, every sample of a fixed size has the same chance of selection as every other sample of that size. Simple random sampling is the most elementary random sampling technique. It forms the basis for the other random sampling techniques.

With simple random sampling, you use n to represent the sample size and N to represent the frame size. You number every item in the frame from 1 to N. The chance that you will select any particular member of the frame on the first selection is $1/N$.

You select samples with replacement or without replacement. **Sampling with replacement** means that after you select an item, you return it to the frame, where it has the same probability of being selected again. Imagine that you have a fishbowl containing N business cards. On the first selection, you select the card for Judy Craven. You record pertinent information and replace the business card in the bowl. You then mix up the cards in the bowl and select the second card. On the second selection, Judy Craven has the same probability of being selected again, $1/N$. You repeat this process until you have selected the desired sample size, n. However, usually you do not want the same item to be selected again.

Sampling without replacement means that once you select an item, you cannot select it again. The chance that you will select any particular item in the frame—for example, the business card for Judy Craven—on the first draw is $1/N$. The chance that you will select any card not previously selected on the second draw is now 1 out of $N - 1$. This process continues until you have selected the desired sample of size n.

See Sections P7.1 or M7.1 to create a random sample without replacement.

Regardless of whether you have sampled with or without replacement, "fishbowl" methods of sample selection have a major drawback—the ability to thoroughly mix the cards and randomly select the sample. As a result, fishbowl methods are not very useful. You need to use less cumbersome and more scientific methods of selection.

One such method uses a **table of random numbers** (see Table E.1 in Appendix E) for selecting the sample. A table of random numbers consists of a series of digits listed in a randomly generated sequence (see reference 7). Because the numeric system uses 10 digits (0, 1, 2, . . . , 9), the chance that you will randomly generate any particular digit is equal to the probability of generating any other digit. This probability is 1 out of 10. Hence, if you generate a sequence of 800 digits, you would expect about 80 to be the digit 0, 80 to be the digit 1, and so on. Because every digit or sequence of digits in the table is random, the table can be read either horizontally or vertically. The margins of the table designate row numbers and column numbers. The digits themselves are grouped into sequences of five in order to make reading the table easier.

To use Table E.1 instead of a fishbowl for selecting the sample, you first need to assign code numbers to the individual items of the frame. Then you generate the random sample by reading the table of random numbers and selecting those individuals from the frame whose assigned code numbers match the digits found in the table. You can better understand the process of sample selection by examining Example 7.1.

EXAMPLE 7.1

SELECTING A SIMPLE RANDOM SAMPLE BY USING A TABLE OF RANDOM NUMBERS

A company wants to select a sample of 32 full-time workers from a population of 800 full-time employees in order to collect information on expenditures concerning a company-sponsored dental plan. How do you select a simple random sample?

SOLUTION The company decides to conduct an e-mail survey. Assuming that not everyone will respond to the survey, you need to send more than 32 surveys to get the necessary 32 responses. Assuming that 8 out of 10 full-time workers will respond to such a survey (i.e., a response rate of 80%), you decide to send 40 surveys. Because you want to send the 40 surveys to 40 different individuals, you should sample without replacement.

The frame consists of a listing of the names and e-mail addresses of all $N = 800$ full-time employees taken from the company personnel files. Thus, the frame is a complete listing of the population. To select the random sample of 40 employees from this frame, you use a table of random numbers. Because the frame size (800) is a three-digit number, each assigned code number must also be three digits so that every full-time worker has an equal chance of selection. You assign a code of 001 to the first full-time employee in the population listing, a code of 002 to the second full-time employee in the population listing, and so on, until a code of 800 is assigned to the Nth full-time worker in the listing. Because $N = 800$ is the largest possible coded value, you discard all three-digit code sequences greater than 800 (i.e., 801 through 999 and 000).

To select the simple random sample, you choose an arbitrary starting point from the table of random numbers. One method you can use is to close your eyes and strike the table of random numbers with a pencil. Suppose you used this procedure and you selected row 06, column 05, of Table 7.1 (which is extracted from Table E.1) as the starting point. Although you can go in any direction, in this example you read the table from left to right, in sequences of three digits, without skipping.

The individual with code number 003 is the first full-time employee in the sample (row 06 and columns 05–07), the second individual has code number 364 (row 06 and columns 08–10), and the third individual has code number 884. Because the highest code for any employee is 800, you discard the number 884. Individuals with code numbers 720, 433, 463, 363, 109, 592, 470, and 705 are selected third through tenth, respectively.

You continue the selection process until you get the required sample size of 40 full-time employees. If any three-digit sequence repeats during the selection process, you discard the repeating sequence because you are sampling without replacement.

TABLE 7.1

Using a Table of Random Numbers

	Row	00000 12345	00001 67890	11111 12345	11112 67890	22222 12345	22223 67890	33333 12345	33334 67890
					Column				
	01	49280	88924	35779	00283	81163	07275	89863	02348
	02	61870	41657	07468	08612	98083	97349	20775	45091
	03	43898	65923	25078	86129	78496	97653	91550	08078
	04	62993	93912	30454	84598	56095	20664	12872	64647
	05	33850	58555	51438	85507	71865	79488	76783	31708
Begin	06	97340	03364	88472	04334	63919	36394	11095	92470
selection	07	70543	29776	10087	10072	55980	64688	68239	20461
(row 06,	08	89382	93809	00796	95945	34101	81277	66090	88872
column 5)	09	37818	72142	67140	50785	22380	16703	53362	44940
	10	60430	22834	14130	96593	23298	56203	92671	15925
	11	82975	66158	84731	19436	55790	69229	28661	13675
	12	39087	71938	40355	54324	08401	26299	49420	59208
	13	55700	24586	93247	32596	11865	63397	44251	43189
	14	14756	23997	78643	75912	83832	32768	18928	57070
	15	32166	53251	70654	92827	63491	04233	33825	69662
	16	23236	73751	31888	81718	06546	83246	47651	04877
	17	45794	26926	15130	82455	78305	55058	52551	47182
	18	09893	20505	14225	68514	46427	56788	96297	78822
	19	54382	74598	91499	14523	68479	27686	46162	83554
	20	94750	89923	37089	20048	80336	94598	26940	36858
	21	70297	34135	53140	33340	42050	82341	44104	82949
	22	85157	47954	32979	26575	57600	40881	12250	73742
	23	11100	02340	12860	74697	96644	89439	28707	25815
	24	36871	50775	30592	57143	17381	68856	25853	35041
	25	23913	48357	63308	16090	51690	54607	72407	55538

Source: *Extracted from The Rand Corporation,* A Million Random Digits with 100,000 Normal Deviates *(Glencoe, IL: The Free Press, 1955) and displayed in Table E.1 in Appendix E.*

Systematic Samples

In a **systematic sample**, you partition the N items in the frame into n groups of k items, where

$$k = \frac{N}{n}$$

You round k to the nearest integer. To select a systematic sample, you choose the first item to be selected at random from the first k items in the frame. Then, you select the remaining $n-1$ items by taking every kth item thereafter from the entire frame.

If the frame consists of a listing of prenumbered checks, sales receipts, or invoices, a systematic sample is faster and easier to take than a simple random sample. A systematic sample is also a convenient mechanism for collecting data from telephone books, class rosters, and consecutive items coming off an assembly line.

To take a systematic sample of $n = 40$ from the population of $N = 800$ full-time employees, you partition the frame of 800 into 40 groups, each of which contains 20 employees. You then select a random number from the first 20 individuals and include every twentieth individual after the first selection in the sample. For example, if the first random number you select is 008, your subsequent selections are 028, 048, 068, 088, 108, . . . , 768, and 788.

Although they are simpler to use, simple random sampling and systematic sampling are generally less efficient than other, more sophisticated, probability sampling methods. Even greater possibilities for selection bias and lack of representation of the population characteristics occur when using systematic samples than with simple random samples. If there is a pattern in the frame, you could have severe selection biases. To overcome the potential problem of disproportionate representation of specific groups in a sample, you can use either stratified sampling methods or cluster sampling methods.

Stratified Samples

In a **stratified sample**, you first subdivide the N items in the frame into separate subpopulations, or **strata**. A stratum is defined by some common characteristic, such as gender or year in school. You select a simple random sample within each of the strata and combine the results from the separate simple random samples. Stratified sampling is more efficient than either simple random sampling or systematic sampling because you are ensured of the representation of items across the entire population. The homogeneity of items within each stratum provides greater precision in the estimates of underlying population parameters.

EXAMPLE 7.2   SELECTING A STRATIFIED SAMPLE

A company wants to select a sample of 32 full-time workers from a population of 800 full-time employees in order to estimate expenditures from a company-sponsored dental plan. Of the full-time employees, 25% are managers and 75% are nonmanagerial workers. How do you select the stratified sample in order for the sample to represent the correct percentage of managers and nonmanagerial workers?

SOLUTION If you assume an 80% response rate, you need to send 40 surveys to get the necessary 32 responses. The frame consists of a listing of the names and e-mail addresses of all $N = 800$ full-time employees included in the company personnel files. Because 25% of the full-time employees are managers, you first separate the frame into two strata: a subpopulation listing of all 200 managerial-level personnel and a separate subpopulation listing of all 600 full-time nonmanagerial workers. Because the first stratum consists of a listing of 200 managers, you assign three-digit code numbers from 001 to 200. Because the second stratum contains a listing of 600 nonmanagerial workers, you assign three-digit code numbers from 001 to 600.

To collect a stratified sample proportional to the sizes of the strata, you select 25% of the overall sample from the first stratum and 75% of the overall sample from the second stratum. You take two separate simple random samples, each of which is based on a distinct random starting point from a table of random numbers (Table E.1). In the first sample, you select 10 managers from the listing of 200 in the first stratum, and in the second sample, you select 30 nonmanagerial workers from the listing of 600 in the second stratum. You then combine the results to reflect the composition of the entire company.

Cluster Samples

In a **cluster sample**, you divide the N items in the frame into several clusters so that each cluster is representative of the entire population. **Clusters** are naturally occurring designations, such as counties, election districts, city blocks, households, or sales territories. You then take a random sample of one or more clusters and study all items in each selected cluster. If clusters are large, a probability-based sample taken from a single cluster is all that is needed.

Cluster sampling is often more cost-effective than simple random sampling, particularly if the population is spread over a wide geographic region. However, cluster sampling often requires a larger sample size to produce results as precise as those from simple random sampling or stratified sampling. A detailed discussion of systematic sampling, stratified sampling, and cluster sampling procedures can be found in reference 1.

PROBLEMS FOR SECTION 7.1

Learning the Basics

7.1 For a population containing $N = 902$ individuals, what code number would you assign for
a. the first person on the list?
b. the fortieth person on the list?
c. the last person on the list?

7.2 For a population of $N = 902$, verify that by starting in row 05, column 1 of the table of random numbers (Table E.1), you need only six rows to select a sample of $n = 60$ *without* replacement.

7.3 Given a population of $N = 93$, starting in row 29 of the table of random numbers (Table E.1), and reading across the row, select a sample of $n = 15$
a. *without* replacement.
b. *with* replacement.

Applying the Concepts

7.4 For a study that consists of personal interviews with participants (rather than mail or phone surveys), explain why simple random sampling might be less practical than some other sampling methods.

7.5 You want to select a random sample of $n = 1$ from a population of three items (which are called A, B, and C). The rule for selecting the sample is: Flip a coin; if it is heads, pick item A; if it is tails, flip the coin again; this time, if it is heads, choose B; if it is tails, choose C. Explain why this is a probability sample but not a simple random sample.

7.6 A population has four members (called A, B, C, and D). You would like to select a random sample of $n = 2$, which you decide to do in the following way: Flip a coin; if it is heads, the sample will be items A and B; if it is tails, the sample will be items C and D. Although this is a random sample, it is not a simple random sample. Explain why. (If you did Problem 7.5, compare the procedure described there with the procedure described in this problem.)

7.7 The registrar of a college with a population of $N = 4,000$ full-time students is asked by the president to conduct a survey to measure satisfaction with the quality of life on campus. The following table contains a breakdown of the 4,000 registered full-time students, by gender and class designation:

Class Designation

Gender	Fr.	So.	Jr.	Sr.	Total
Female	700	520	500	480	2,200
Male	560	460	400	380	1,800
Total	1,260	980	900	860	4,000

The registrar intends to take a probability sample of $n = 200$ students and project the results from the sample to the entire population of full-time students.
a. If the frame available from the registrar's files is an alphabetical listing of the names of all $N = 4,000$ registered full-time students, what type of sample could you take? Discuss.
b. What is the advantage of selecting a simple random sample in (a)?
c. What is the advantage of selecting a systematic sample in (a)?
d. If the frame available from the registrar's files is a listing of the names of all $N = 4,000$ registered full-time students compiled from eight separate alphabetical lists, based on the gender and class designation breakdowns shown in the class designation table, what type of sample should you take? Discuss.
e. Suppose that each of the $N = 4,000$ registered full-time students lived in one of the 10 campus dormitories. Each dormitory accommodates 400 students. It is college policy to fully integrate students by gender and class designation in each dormitory. If the registrar is able to compile a listing of all students by dormitory, explain how you could take a cluster sample.

7.8 Prenumbered sales invoices are kept in a sales journal. The invoices are numbered from 0001 to 5000.
a. Beginning in row 16, column 1, and proceeding horizontally in Table E.1, select a simple random sample of 50 invoice numbers.
b. Select a systematic sample of 50 invoice numbers. Use the random numbers in row 20, columns 5–7, as the starting point for your selection.
c. Are the invoices selected in (a) the same as those selected in (b)? Why or why not?

7.9 Suppose that 5,000 sales invoices are separated into four strata. Stratum 1 contains 50 invoices, stratum 2 contains 500 invoices, stratum 3 contains 1,000 invoices, and stratum 4 contains 3,450 invoices. A sample of 500 sales invoices is needed.
a. What type of sampling should you do? Why?
b. Explain how you would carry out the sampling according to the method stated in (a).
c. Why is the sampling in (a) not simple random sampling?

7.2 EVALUATING SURVEY WORTHINESS

Surveys are used to collect data. Nearly every day, you read or hear about survey or opinion poll results in newspapers, on the Internet, or on radio or television. To identify surveys that lack objectivity or credibility, you must critically evaluate what you read and hear by examining the worthiness of the survey. First, you must evaluate the purpose of the survey, why it was conducted, and for whom it was conducted. A survey conducted to satisfy curiosity is mainly for entertainment. Its result is an end in itself rather than a means to an end.

The second step in evaluating the worthiness of a survey is to determine whether it was based on a probability or nonprobability sample (as discussed in Section 7.1). You need to remember that the only way to make valid statistical inferences from a sample to a population is through the use of a probability sample. Surveys that use nonprobability sampling methods are subject to serious, perhaps unintentional, biases that may make the results meaningless.

Survey Error

Even when surveys use random probability sampling methods, they are subject to potential errors. There are four types of survey errors:

- Coverage error
- Nonresponse error
- Sampling error
- Measurement error

Well-designed surveys reduce or minimize these four types of errors, often at considerable cost.

Coverage Error The key to proper sample selection is an adequate frame. Remember, a frame is an up-to-date list of all the items from which you will select the sample. **Coverage error** occurs if certain groups of items are excluded from this frame so that they have no chance of being selected in the sample. Coverage error results in a **selection bias**. If the frame is inadequate because certain groups of items in the population were not properly included, any random probability sample selected will provide an estimate of the characteristics of the frame, not the *actual* population.

Nonresponse Error Not everyone is willing to respond to a survey. In fact, research has shown that individuals in the upper and lower economic classes tend to respond less frequently to surveys than do people in the middle class. **Nonresponse error** arises from the failure to collect data on all items in the sample and results in a **nonresponse bias**. Because you cannot always assume that persons who do not respond to surveys are similar to those who do, you need to follow up on the nonresponses after a specified period of time. You should make several attempts to convince such individuals to complete the survey. The follow-up responses are then compared to the initial responses in order to make valid inferences from the survey (reference 1). The mode of response you use affects the rate of response. The personal interview and the telephone interview usually produce a higher response rate than does the mail survey—but at a higher cost.

Sampling Error A sample is selected because it is simpler, less costly, and more efficient. However, chance dictates which individuals or items will or will not be included in the sample. **Sampling error** reflects the variation, or "chance differences," from sample to sample, based on the probability of particular individuals or items being selected in the particular samples.

When you read about the results of surveys or polls in newspapers or magazines, there is often a statement regarding a margin of error, such as "the results of this poll are expected to be within ±4 percentage points of the actual value." This **margin of error** is the sampling error. You can reduce sampling error by taking larger sample sizes, although this also increases the cost of conducting the survey.

Measurement Error   In the practice of good survey research, you design a questionnaire with the intention of gathering meaningful information. But you have a dilemma here: Getting meaningful measurements is often easier said than done. Consider the following proverb:

A person with one watch always knows what time it is;
A person with two watches always searches to identify the correct one;
A person with ten watches is always reminded of the difficulty in measuring time.

Unfortunately, the process of measurement is often governed by what is convenient, not what is needed. The measurements you get are often only a proxy for the ones you really desire. Much attention has been given to measurement error that occurs because of a weakness in question wording (reference 2). A question should be clear, not ambiguous. Furthermore, in order to avoid *leading questions*, you need to present them in a neutral manner.

Three sources of **measurement error** are ambiguous wording of questions, the Hawthorne effect, and respondent error. As an example of ambiguous wording, in November 1993, the U.S. Department of Labor reported that the unemployment rate in the United States had been underestimated for more than a decade because of poor questionnaire wording in the Current Population Survey. In particular, the wording had led to a significant undercount of women in the labor force. Because unemployment rates are tied to benefit programs such as state unemployment compensation, survey researchers had to rectify the situation by adjusting the questionnaire wording.

The "Hawthorne effect" occurs when the respondent feels obligated to please the interviewer. Proper interviewer training can minimize the Hawthorne effect.

Respondent error occurs as a result of an overzealous or underzealous effort by the respondent. You can minimize this error in two ways: (1) by carefully scrutinizing the data and then recontacting those individuals whose responses seem unusual and (2) by establishing a program of recontacting a small number of randomly chosen individuals in order to determine the reliability of the responses.

Ethical Issues

Ethical considerations arise with respect to the four types of potential errors that can occur when designing surveys: coverage error, nonresponse error, sampling error, and measurement error. Coverage error can result in selection bias and becomes an ethical issue if particular groups or individuals are *purposely* excluded from the frame so that the survey results are more favorable to the survey's sponsor. Nonresponse error can lead to nonresponse bias and becomes an ethical issue if the sponsor knowingly designs the survey so that particular groups or individuals are less likely than others to respond. Sampling error becomes an ethical issue if the findings are purposely presented without reference to sample size and margin of error so that the sponsor can promote a viewpoint that might otherwise be truly insignificant. Measurement error becomes an ethical issue in one of three ways: (1) a survey sponsor chooses leading questions that guide the responses in a particular direction; (2) an interviewer, through mannerisms and tone, purposely creates a Hawthorne effect or otherwise guides the responses in a particular direction; or (3) a respondent willfully provides false information.

Ethical issues also arise when the results of nonprobability samples are used to form conclusions about the entire population. When you use a nonprobability sampling method, you need to explain the sampling procedures and state that the results cannot be generalized beyond the sample.

Probability Sampling vs. Web-Based Surveys

From the Authors' Desktop

In Sections 7.1 and 7.2, you learned that statistical inferences about populations can only be made by analyzing data collected from probability samples. This type of sampling has been the "gold standard" in survey research for more than fifty years. Companies using surveys based on probability sampling typically make a great effort (and spend large sums) to deal with coverage error, nonresponse error, sampling error, and measurement error.

A recent article (T. Crampton, "About Online Surveys, Traditional Pollsters Are Somewhat Disappointed," **www.nytimes.com/2007/05/31/business media**), reported that some survey companies are offering an Internet alternative to traditional surveys based on random sampling. YouGov, a British company, is planning to introduce Internet-based polling in the United States for the 2008 presidential election.

YouGov uses a large panel of respondents who answer questions online. These panelists

supposedly come from a diverse group with special efforts made to include people who are less likely to use the Internet. In addition, panelists are paid to participate. This method of sampling (and the fact that respondents are paid and are not volunteers) makes Web-based sampling scientifically unacceptable to traditional pollsters.

Despite these concerns, YouGov has partnered with Polimetrix, an online company based in Palo Alto, California, to conduct surveys in the United States. The founder of Polimetrix, Professor Douglas Rivers of Stanford University, claims that the margin of error of Polimetrix polls is similar to telephone polls. YouGov's chief executive, Nadhim Zahawi, points out that modern technology, such as cell phones, has made old-fashioned polls more unreliable due to the increased difficulty of contacting people at home. In fact, a recent article (M. Thee, "Cellphones Challenge Poll Sampling," *The New York Times*, December 7, 2007, p. A27)

indicated that cellphone-only households make up 16% of the households in the United States.

However, Leendert de Voogd, managing director of TSN Opinion in Brussels, believes that "Internet polling is like the Wild West, with no rules, no sheriff, and no reference points." He believes that only polling with probability sampling will deliver valid results. On the other hand, Professor Anthony King of the University of Essex does not believe that Internet polling fails to reflect a nation's population. According to Professor King, "There is no evidence to suggest that people who use the Internet are fundamentally different from those without it. One mad, awful lady living in a poor neighborhood without Internet does not differ much from her mad, awful friend next door who goes online."

Perhaps only time will tell who is right and perhaps we will know more after the 2008 U.S. presidential election.

PROBLEMS FOR SECTION 7.2

Applying the Concepts

7.10 "A survey indicates that the vast majority of college students own their own personal computers." What information would you want to know before you accepted the results of this survey?

7.11 A simple random sample of $n = 300$ full-time employees is selected from a company list containing the names of all $N = 5,000$ full-time employees in order to evaluate job satisfaction.
a. Give an example of possible coverage error.
b. Give an example of possible nonresponse error.
c. Give an example of possible sampling error.
d. Give an example of possible measurement error.

7.12 Business professor Thomas Callarman traveled to China more than a dozen times from 2000 to 2005. He warns people about believing everything they read about surveys conducted in China and gives two specific reasons. Callarman stated, "First, things are changing so rapidly that what you hear today may not be true tomorrow. Second, the people who answer the surveys may tell you what they think you want to hear, rather than what they really believe" (T. E. Callarman, "Some Thoughts on China," *Decision Line*, March, 2006, pp. 1, 43–44).

a. List the four types (or categories) of survey error discussed in this section.
b. Which categories best describe the types of survey error discussed by Professor Callarman?

7.13 The gourmet foods industry is expected to exceed $62 billion in sales by the year 2009. A survey conducted by Packaged Facts indicates that one-fifth of American adults consider themselves "gourmet consumers" ("Galloping Gourmet," *The Progressive Grocer*, January 1, 2006, pp. 80–81). What additional information would you want to know before you accepted the results of the survey?

7.14 Only 10% of Americans rated their financial situation as "excellent," according to a Gallup Poll taken April 10–13, 2006. However, 41% rated their financial situation as "good," 37% said "only fair," and 12% "poor" (J. M. Jones, "Americans More Worried About Meeting Basic Financial Needs," *The Gallup Poll*, **galluppoll.com**, April 25, 2006). What additional information would you want to know before you accepted the results of the survey?

7.15 In May of 2007, one of the nation's most respected cardiologists, Dr. Steven Nissen, reported his troubling analysis of the heavily prescribed diabetes drug Avandia. His analysis showed a 43% higher risk of heart attacks among patients taking Avandia, compared to other drugs used for the same condition. Furthermore, patients taking Avandia exhibited a 64% higher risk of cardiovascular death (S. Rubenstein, "What Diabetes Patients Need to Know," *The Wall Street Journal*, May 22, 2007, p. D2). What additional information would you want to know in order to make better-informed decisions regarding Avandia?

7.16 A study investigating the effects of CEO succession on the stock performance of large publicly held corporations also investigated the demographics of the newly announced CEOs. The mean and standard deviation of the new CEO's age were 53.3 and 5.97, respectively. The mean and standard deviation of the number of years the new CEO had been with the firm were 20.1 and 12.6, respectively. 93.6% of the new CEOs held college degrees, 30.4% held MBAs, and 3.2% held doctorates (J. C. Rhim, J. V. Peluchette, and I. Song, "Stock Market Reactions and Firm Performance Surrounding CEO Succession: Antecedents of Succession and Successor Origin," *Mid-American Journal of Business*, Spring 2006, pp. 21–30). What additional information would you want to know before you accepted the results of this study?

7.3 SAMPLING DISTRIBUTIONS

In many applications, you want to make inferences that are based on statistics calculated from samples to estimate the values of population parameters. In the next two sections, you will learn about how the sample mean (a statistic) is used to estimate the population mean (a parameter) and how the sample proportion (a statistic) is used to estimate the population proportion (a parameter). Your main concern when making a statistical inference is drawing conclusions about a population, *not* about a sample. For example, a political pollster is interested in the sample results only as a way of estimating the actual proportion of the votes that each candidate will receive from the population of voters. Likewise, as plant operations manager for Oxford Cereals, you are only interested in using the sample mean weight calculated from a sample of cereal boxes for estimating the mean weight contained in a population of boxes.

In practice, you select a single random sample of a predetermined size from the population. Hypothetically, to use the sample statistic to estimate the population parameter, you could examine *every* possible sample of a given size that could occur. A **sampling distribution** is the distribution of the results if you actually selected all possible samples. The single result you obtain in practice is just one of the results in the sampling distribution.

7.4 SAMPLING DISTRIBUTION OF THE MEAN

In Chapter 3, several measures of central tendency, including the mean, median, and mode, were discussed. Undoubtedly, the mean is the most widely used measure of central tendency. The sample mean is often used to estimate the population mean. The **sampling distribution of the mean** is the distribution of all possible sample means if you select all possible samples of a given size.

The Unbiased Property of the Sample Mean

The sample mean is **unbiased** because the mean of all the possible sample means (of a given sample size, n) is equal to the population mean, μ. A simple example concerning a population of four administrative assistants demonstrates this property. Each assistant is asked to type the same page of a manuscript. Table 7.2 presents the number of errors. This population distribution is shown in Figure 7.2.

TABLE 7.2

Number of Errors Made by Each of Four Administrative Assistants

Administrative Assistant	Number of Errors
Ann	$X_1 = 3$
Bob	$X_2 = 2$
Carla	$X_3 = 1$
Dave	$X_4 = 4$

FIGURE 7.2

Number of errors made
by a population of four
administrative assistants

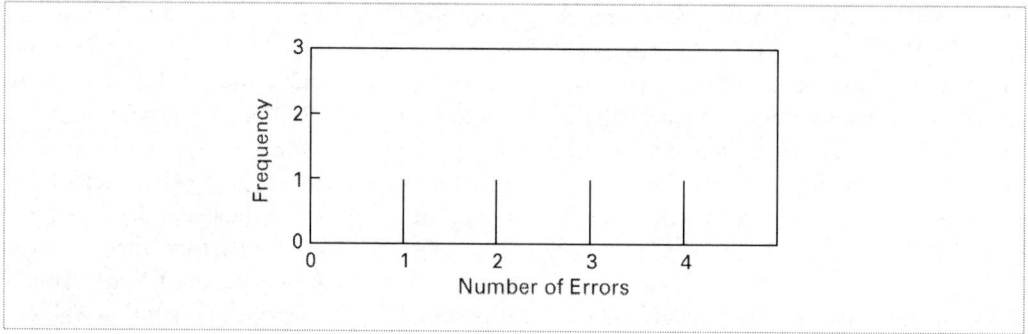

When you have the data from a population, you compute the mean by using Equation (7.1).

Population Mean

The population mean is the sum of the values in the population divided by the population size, N.

$$\mu = \frac{\sum_{i=1}^{N} X_i}{N} \tag{7.1}$$

You compute the population standard deviation, σ, using Equation (7.2):

Population Standard Deviation

$$\sigma = \sqrt{\frac{\sum_{i=1}^{N} (X_i - \mu)^2}{N}} \tag{7.2}$$

Thus, for the data of Table 7.1,

$$\mu = \frac{3 + 2 + 1 + 4}{4} = 2.5 \text{ errors}$$

and

$$\sigma = \sqrt{\frac{(3 - 2.5)^2 + (2 - 2.5)^2 + (1 - 2.5)^2 + (4 - 2.5)^2}{4}} = 1.12 \text{ errors}$$

If you select samples of two administrative assistants *with* replacement from this population, there are 16 possible samples ($N^n = 4^2 = 16$). Table 7.3 lists the 16 possible sample outcomes. If you average all 16 of these sample means, the mean of these values, $\mu_{\bar{X}}$, is equal to 2.5, which is also the mean of the population μ.

Because the mean of the 16 sample means is equal to the population mean, the sample mean is an unbiased estimator of the population mean. Therefore, although you do not know how close the sample mean of any particular sample selected comes to the population mean,

TABLE 7.3

All 16 Samples of n = 2 Administrative Assistants from a Population of N = 4 Administrative Assistants When Sampling with Replacement

Sample	Administrative Assistants	Sample Outcomes	Sample Means
1	Ann, Ann	3, 3	$\bar{X}_1 = 3$
2	Ann, Bob	3, 2	$\bar{X}_2 = 2.5$
3	Ann, Carla	3, 1	$\bar{X}_3 = 2$
4	Ann, Dave	3, 4	$\bar{X}_4 = 3.5$
5	Bob, Ann	2, 3	$\bar{X}_5 = 2.5$
6	Bob, Bob	2, 2	$\bar{X}_6 = 2$
7	Bob, Carla	2, 1	$\bar{X}_7 = 1.5$
8	Bob, Dave	2, 4	$\bar{X}_8 = 3$
9	Carla, Ann	1, 3	$\bar{X}_9 = 2$
10	Carla, Bob	1, 2	$\bar{X}_{10} = 1.5$
11	Carla, Carla	1, 1	$\bar{X}_{11} = 1$
12	Carla, Dave	1, 4	$\bar{X}_{12} = 2.5$
13	Dave, Ann	4, 3	$\bar{X}_{13} = 3.5$
14	Dave, Bob	4, 2	$\bar{X}_{14} = 3$
15	Dave, Carla	4, 1	$\bar{X}_{15} = 2.5$
16	Dave, Dave	4, 4	$\bar{X}_{16} = 4$
			$\mu_{\bar{X}} = 2.5$

you are at least assured that the mean of all the possible sample means that could have been selected is equal to the population mean.

Standard Error of the Mean

Figure 7.3 illustrates the variation in the sample means when selecting all 16 possible samples. In this small example, although the sample means vary from sample to sample, depending on which two administrative assistants are selected, the sample means do not vary as much as the individual values in the population. That the sample means are less variable than the individual values in the population follows directly from the fact that each sample mean averages together all the values in the sample. A population consists of individual outcomes that can take on a wide range of values, from extremely small to extremely large. However, if a sample contains an extreme value, although this value will have an effect on the sample mean, the effect is reduced because the value is averaged with all the other values in the sample. As the sample size increases, the effect of a single extreme value becomes smaller because it is averaged with more values.

FIGURE 7.3

Sampling distribution of the mean, based on all possible samples containing two administrative assistants

Source: Data are from Table 7.3

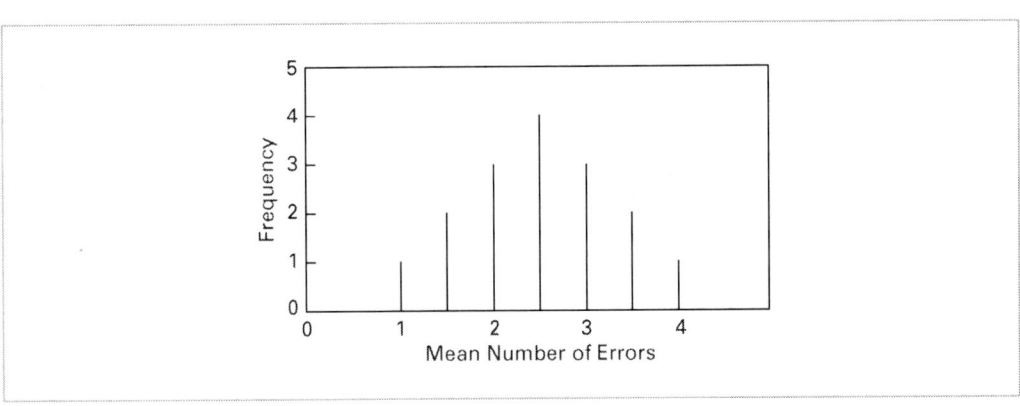

The value of the standard deviation of all possible sample means, called the **standard error of the mean**, expresses how the sample means vary from sample to sample. Equation (7.3) defines the standard error of the mean when sampling *with* replacement or *without* replacement from large or infinite populations.

Standard Error of the Mean

The standard error of the mean, $\sigma_{\bar{X}}$, is equal to the standard deviation in the population, σ, divided by the square root of the sample size, n.

$$\sigma_{\bar{X}} = \frac{\sigma}{\sqrt{n}} \tag{7.3}$$

Therefore, as the sample size increases, the standard error of the mean decreases by a factor equal to the square root of the sample size.

You can also use Equation (7.3) as an approximation of the standard error of the mean when the sample is selected without replacement if the sample contains less than 5% of the entire population. Example 7.3 computes the standard error of the mean for such a situation. (See the section 7.6.pdf file on the Student CD-ROM that accompanies this book for the case in which more than 5% of the population is contained in a sample selected without replacement.)

EXAMPLE 7.3

COMPUTING THE STANDARD ERROR OF THE MEAN

Returning to the cereal-filling process described in the Using Statistics scenario on page 258, if you randomly select a sample of 25 boxes without replacement from the thousands of boxes filled during a shift, the sample contains far less than 5% of the population. Given that the standard deviation of the cereal-filling process is 15 grams, compute the standard error of the mean.

SOLUTION Using Equation (7.3) with $n = 25$ and $\sigma = 15$, the standard error of the mean is

$$\sigma_{\bar{X}} = \frac{\sigma}{\sqrt{n}} = \frac{15}{\sqrt{25}} = \frac{15}{5} = 3$$

The variation in the sample means for samples of $n = 25$ is much less than the variation in the individual boxes of cereal (i.e., $\sigma_{\bar{X}} = 3$ while $\sigma = 15$).

Sampling from Normally Distributed Populations

Now that the concept of a sampling distribution has been introduced and the standard error of the mean has been defined, what distribution will the sample mean, $\bar{X}$, follow? If you are sampling from a population that is normally distributed with mean, μ, and standard deviation, σ, then regardless of the sample size, n, the sampling distribution of the mean is normally distributed, with mean, $\mu_{\bar{X}} = \mu$, and standard error of the mean, $\sigma_{\bar{X}} = \sigma/\sqrt{n}$.

In the simplest case, if you take samples of size $n = 1$, each possible sample mean is a single value from the population because

$$\bar{X} = \frac{\sum_{i=1}^{n} X_i}{n} = \frac{X_1}{1} = X_1$$

Therefore, if the population is normally distributed, with mean, μ, and standard deviation, σ, the sampling distribution of $\bar{X}$ for samples of $n = 1$ must also follow the normal distribution, with mean $\mu_{\bar{X}} = \mu$ and standard error of the mean $\sigma_{\bar{X}} = \sigma/\sqrt{1} = \sigma$. In addition, as the sample size increases, the sampling distribution of the mean still follows a normal distribution, with $\mu_{\bar{X}} = \mu$, but the standard error of the mean decreases, so that a larger proportion of sample means are closer to the population mean. Figure 7.4 below illustrates this reduction in variability. Note that 500 samples of 1, 2, 4, 8, 16, and 32 were randomly selected from a normally distributed population. From the polygons in Figure 7.4, you can see that, although the sampling distribution of the mean is approximately[1] normal for each sample size, the sample means are distributed more tightly around the population mean as the sample size increases.

FIGURE 7.4

Sampling distributions of the mean from 500 samples of sizes $n = 1$, 2, 4, 8, 16, and 32 selected from a normal population

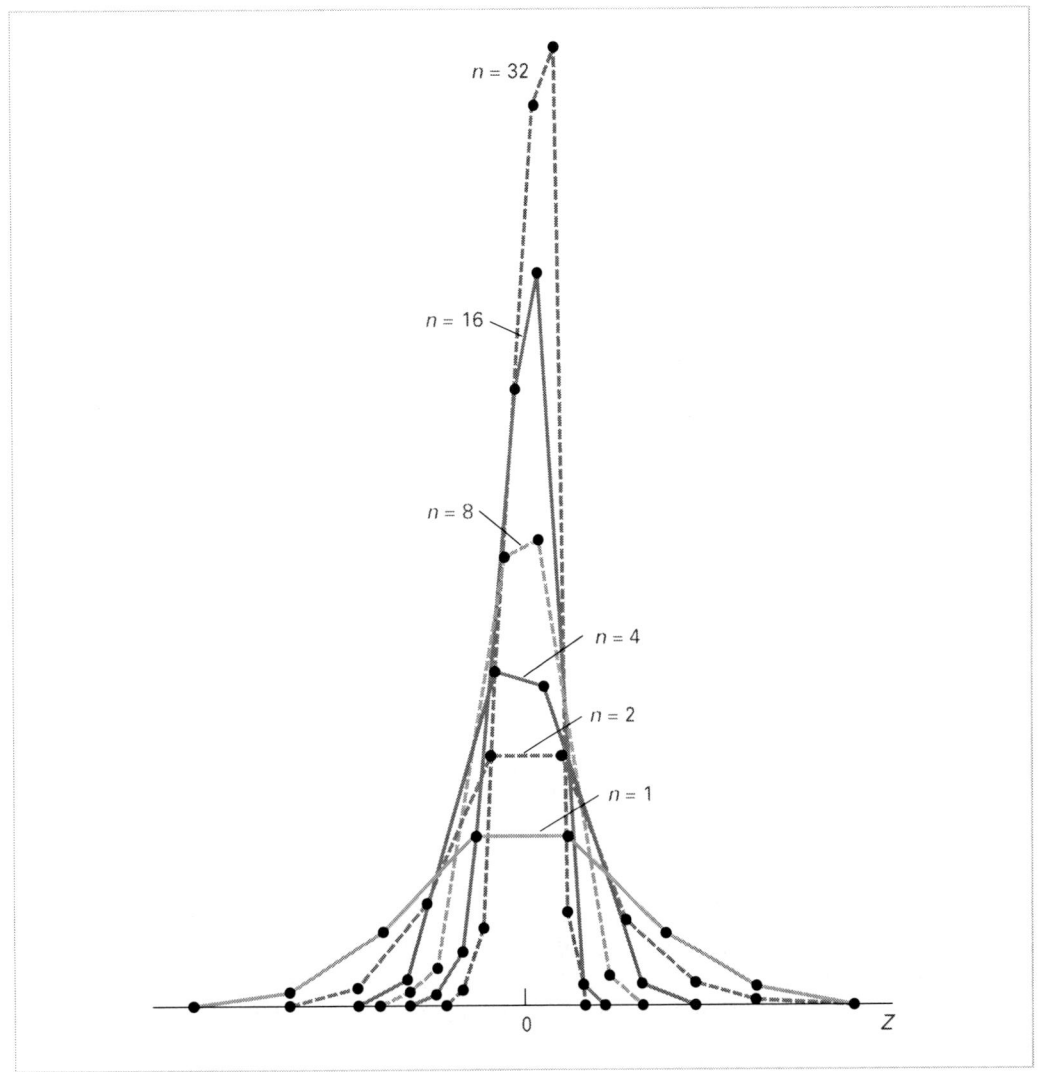

To further examine the concept of the sampling distribution of the mean, consider the Using Statistics scenario described on page 258. The packaging equipment that is filling 368-gram boxes of cereal is set so that the amount of cereal in a box is normally distributed, with a mean of 368 grams. From past experience, you know the population standard deviation for this filling process is 15 grams.

If you randomly select a sample of 25 boxes from the many thousands that are filled in a day and the mean weight is computed for this sample, what type of result could you expect? For example, do you think that the sample mean could be 368 grams? 200 grams? 365 grams?

The sample acts as a miniature representation of the population, so if the values in the population are normally distributed, the values in the sample should be approximately normally distributed. Thus, if the population mean is 368 grams, the sample mean has a good chance of being close to 368 grams.

How can you determine the probability that the sample of 25 boxes will have a mean below 365 grams? From the normal distribution (Section 6.2), you know that you can find the area below any value X by converting to standardized Z values:

$$Z = \frac{X - \mu}{\sigma}$$

In the examples in Section 6.2, you studied how any single value, X, differs from the population mean. Now, in this example, you want to study how a sample mean, $\bar{X}$ differs from the population mean. Substituting $\bar{X}$ for X, $\mu_{\bar{X}}$ for μ, and $\sigma_{\bar{X}}$ for σ in the equation above results in Equation (7.4).

Finding Z for the Sampling Distribution of the Mean

The Z value is equal to the difference between the sample mean, $\bar{X}$, and the population mean, μ, divided by the standard error of the mean, $\sigma_{\bar{X}}$.

$$Z = \frac{\bar{X} - \mu_{\bar{X}}}{\sigma_{\bar{X}}} = \frac{\bar{X} - \mu}{\frac{\sigma}{\sqrt{n}}} \qquad (7.4)$$

To find the area below 365 grams, from Equation (7.4),

$$Z = \frac{\bar{X} - \mu_{\bar{X}}}{\sigma_{\bar{X}}} = \frac{365 - 368}{\frac{15}{\sqrt{25}}} = \frac{-3}{3} = -1.00$$

The area corresponding to $Z = -1.00$ in Table E.2 is 0.1587. Therefore, 15.87% of all the possible samples of 25 boxes have a sample mean below 365 grams.

The preceding statement is not the same as saying that a certain percentage of *individual* boxes will have less than 365 grams of cereal. You compute that percentage as follows:

$$Z = \frac{X - \mu}{\sigma} = \frac{365 - 368}{15} = \frac{-3}{15} = -0.20$$

The area corresponding to $Z = -0.20$ in Table E.2 is 0.4207. Therefore, 42.07% of the *individual* boxes are expected to contain less than 365 grams. Comparing these results, you see that many more *individual boxes* than *sample means* are below 365 grams. This result is explained by the fact that each sample consists of 25 different values, some small and some large. The averaging process dilutes the importance of any individual value, particularly when the sample size is large. Thus, the chance that the sample mean of 25 boxes is far away from the population mean is less than the chance that a *single* box is far away.

Examples 7.4 and 7.5 show how these results are affected by using different sample sizes.

EXAMPLE 7.4

THE EFFECT OF SAMPLE SIZE n ON THE COMPUTATION OF $\sigma_{\bar{X}}$

How is the standard error of the mean affected by increasing the sample size from 25 to 100 boxes?

SOLUTION If $n = 100$ boxes, then using Equation (7.3) on page 270:

$$\sigma_{\bar{X}} = \frac{\sigma}{\sqrt{n}} = \frac{15}{\sqrt{100}} = \frac{15}{10} = 1.5$$

The fourfold increase in the sample size from 25 to 100 reduces the standard error of the mean by half—from 3 grams to 1.5 grams. This demonstrates that taking a larger sample results in less variability in the sample means from sample to sample.

EXAMPLE 7.5

THE EFFECT OF SAMPLE SIZE n ON THE CLUSTERING OF MEANS IN THE SAMPLING DISTRIBUTION

If you select a sample of 100 boxes, what is the probability that the sample mean is below 365 grams?

SOLUTION Using Equation (7.4) on page 272,

$$Z = \frac{\bar{X} - \mu_{\bar{X}}}{\sigma_{\bar{X}}} = \frac{365 - 368}{\frac{15}{\sqrt{100}}} = \frac{-3}{1.5} = -2.00$$

From Table E.2, the area less than $Z = -2.00$ is 0.0228. Therefore, 2.28% of the samples of 100 boxes have means below 365 grams, as compared with 15.87% for samples of 25 boxes.

Sometimes you need to find the interval that contains a fixed proportion of the sample means. You need to determine a distance below and above the population mean containing a specific area of the normal curve. From Equation (7.4) on page 272,

$$Z = \frac{\bar{X} - \mu}{\frac{\sigma}{\sqrt{n}}}$$

Solving for $\bar{X}$ results in Equation (7.5).

> **Finding $\bar{X}$ for the Sampling Distribution of the Mean**
>
> $$\bar{X} = \mu + Z\frac{\sigma}{\sqrt{n}}$$ (7.5)

Example 7.6 illustrates the use of Equation (7.5).

EXAMPLE 7.6

DETERMINING THE INTERVAL THAT INCLUDES A FIXED PROPORTION OF THE SAMPLE MEANS

In the cereal-fill example, find an interval symmetrically distributed around the population mean that will include 95% of the sample means based on samples of 25 boxes.

SOLUTION If 95% of the sample means are in the interval, then 5% are outside the interval. Divide the 5% into two equal parts of 2.5%. The value of Z in Table E.2 corresponding to an area of 0.0250 in the lower tail of the normal curve is −1.96, and the value of Z corresponding to a cumulative area of 0.975 (i.e., 0.025 in the upper tail of the normal curve) is +1.96. The lower value of $\bar{X}$ (called $\bar{X}_L$) and the upper value of $\bar{X}$ (called $\bar{X}_U$) are found by using Equation (7.5):

$$\bar{X}_L = 368 + (-1.96)\frac{15}{\sqrt{25}} = 368 - 5.88 = 362.12$$

$$\bar{X}_U = 368 + (1.96)\frac{15}{\sqrt{25}} = 368 + 5.88 = 373.88$$

Therefore, 95% of all sample means based on samples of 25 boxes are between 362.12 and 373.88 grams.

Sampling from Non-Normally Distributed Populations— The Central Limit Theorem

Thus far in this section, only the sampling distribution of the mean for a normally distributed population has been considered. However, in many instances, either you know that the population is not normally distributed or it is unrealistic to assume that the population is normally distributed. An important theorem in statistics, the Central Limit Theorem, deals with this situation.

> **THE CENTRAL LIMIT THEOREM**
>
> The **Central Limit Theorem** states that as the sample size (i.e., the number of values in each sample) gets *large enough*, the sampling distribution of the mean is approximately normally distributed. This is true regardless of the shape of the distribution of the individual values in the population.

What sample size is large enough? A great deal of statistical research has gone into this issue. As a general rule, statisticians have found that for many population distributions, when the sample size is at least 30, the sampling distribution of the mean is approximately normal. However, you can apply the Central Limit Theorem for even smaller sample sizes if the population distribution is approximately bell shaped. In the uncommon case in which the distribution is extremely skewed or has more than one mode, you may need sample sizes larger than 30 to ensure normality.

Figure 7.5 illustrates the application of the Central Limit Theorem to different populations. The sampling distributions from three different continuous distributions (normal, uniform, and exponential) for varying sample sizes ($n = 2, 5, 30$) are displayed.

FIGURE 7.5

Sampling distribution of the mean for different populations for samples of $n = 2, 5,$ and 30

See Section E7.2, P7.2, or M7.2 to create a simulated sampling distribution.

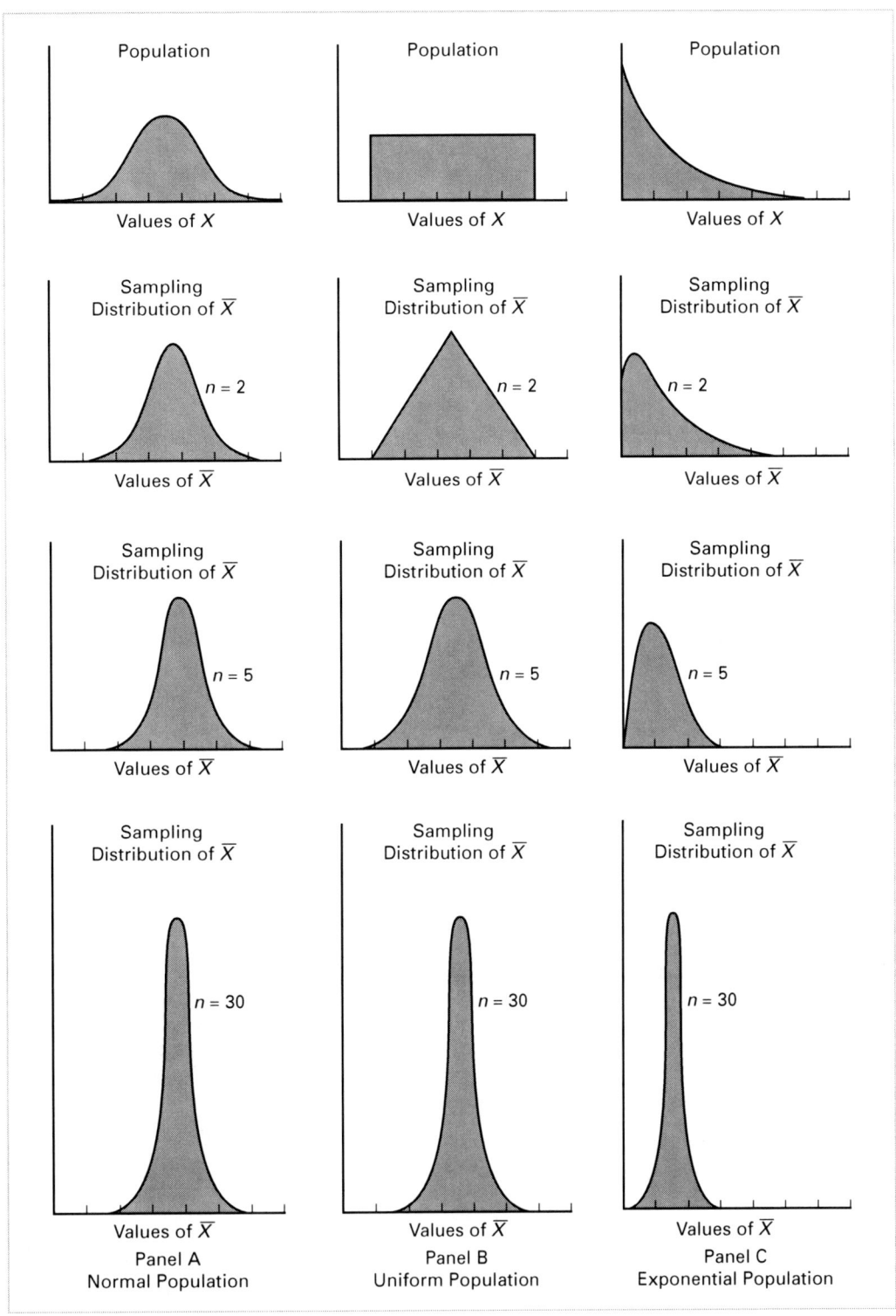

Panel A
Normal Population

Panel B
Uniform Population

Panel C
Exponential Population

In each of the panels, because the sample mean has the property of being unbiased, the mean of any sampling distribution is always equal to the mean of the population.

Panel A of Figure 7.5 shows the sampling distribution of the mean selected from a normal population. As mentioned earlier in this section, when the population is normally distributed, the sampling distribution of the mean is normally distributed for any sample size. [You can measure the variability by using the standard error of the mean, Equation (7.3), on page 270.]

Panel B of Figure 7.5 depicts the sampling distribution from a population with a uniform (or rectangular) distribution (see Section 6.4). When samples of size $n = 2$ are selected, there is a peaking, or *central limiting*, effect already working. For $n = 5$, the sampling distribution is bell shaped and approximately normal. When $n = 30$, the sampling distribution looks very similar to a normal distribution. In general, the larger the sample size, the more closely the sampling distribution will follow a normal distribution. As with all cases, the mean of each sampling distribution is equal to the mean of the population, and the variability decreases as the sample size increases.

Panel C of Figure 7.5 presents an exponential distribution (see Section 6.5). This population is extremely right-skewed. When $n = 2$, the sampling distribution is still highly right-skewed but less so than the distribution of the population. For $n = 5$, the sampling distribution is slightly right-skewed. When $n = 30$, the sampling distribution looks approximately normal. Again, the mean of each sampling distribution is equal to the mean of the population, and the variability decreases as the sample size increases.

VISUAL EXPLORATIONS: Exploring Sampling Distributions

Use the Visual Explorations **Two Dice Probability** procedure to observe the effects of simulated throws on the frequency distribution of the sum of the two dice. Open the `Visual Explorations.xla` add-in workbook and select **VisualExplorations → Two Dice Probability** (Excel 97-2003) or **Add-Ins → VisualExplorations → Two Dice Probability** (Excel 2007). The procedure produces a worksheet that contains an empty frequency distribution table and histogram and a floating control panel (see below).

Click the **Tally** button to tally a set of throws in the frequency distribution table and histogram. Optionally, use the spinner buttons to adjust the number of throws per tally (round). Click the **Help** button for more information about this simulation. Click **Finish** when you are done with this exploration.

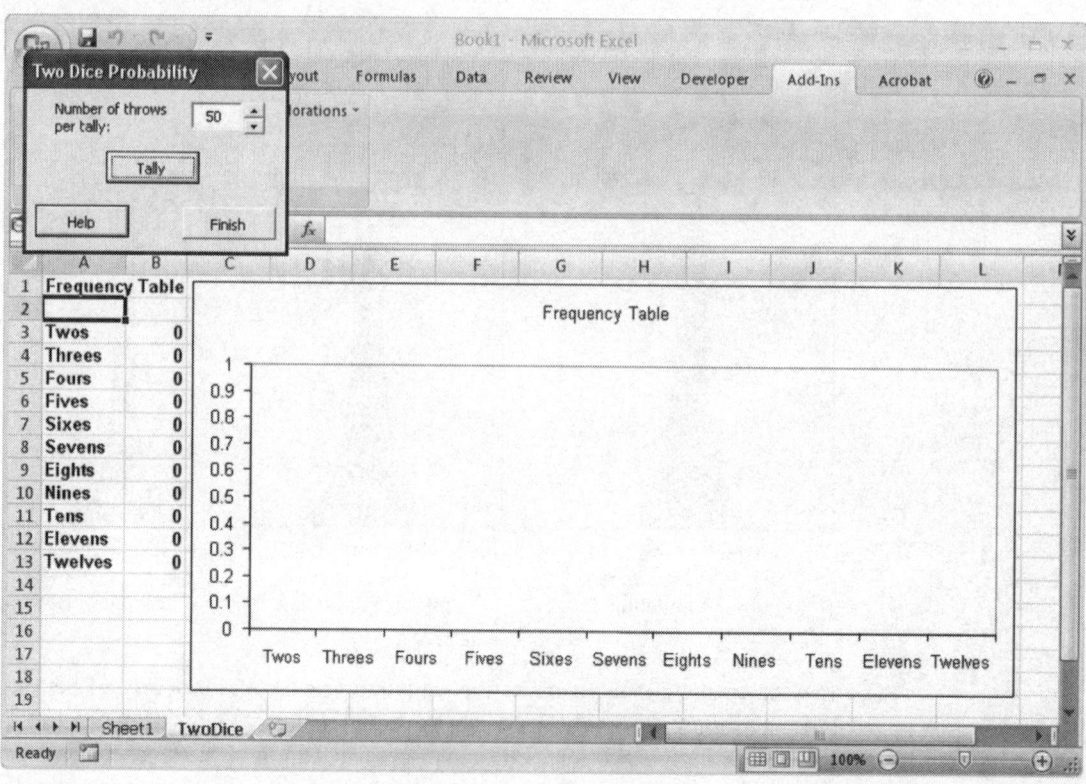

Using the results from the normal, uniform, and exponential distributions, you can reach the following conclusions regarding the Central Limit Theorem:

- For most population distributions, regardless of shape, the sampling distribution of the mean is approximately normally distributed if samples of at least size 30 are selected.
- If the population distribution is fairly symmetric, the sampling distribution of the mean is approximately normal for samples as small as size 5.
- If the population is normally distributed, the sampling distribution of the mean is normally distributed, regardless of the sample size.

The Central Limit Theorem is of crucial importance in using statistical inference to draw conclusions about a population. It allows you to make inferences about the population mean without having to know the specific shape of the population distribution.

PROBLEMS FOR SECTION 7.4

Learning the Basics

7.17 Given a normal distribution with $\mu = 100$ and $\sigma = 10$, if you select a sample of $n = 25$, what is the probability that $\bar{X}$ is
a. less than 95?
b. between 95 and 97.5?
c. above 102.2?
d. There is a 65% chance that $\bar{X}$ is above what value?

7.18 Given a normal distribution with $\mu = 50$ and $\sigma = 5$, if you select a sample of $n = 100$, what is the probability that $\bar{X}$ is
a. less than 47?
b. between 47 and 49.5?
c. above 51.1?
d. There is a 35% chance that $\bar{X}$ is above what value?

Applying the Concepts

7.19 For each of the following three populations, indicate what the sampling distribution for samples of 25 would consist of:
a. Travel expense vouchers for a university in an academic year
b. Absentee records (days absent per year) in 2007 for employees of a large manufacturing company
c. Yearly sales (in gallons) of unleaded gasoline at service stations located in a particular state

7.20 The following data represent the number of days absent per year in a population of six employees of a small company:

1   3   6   7   9   10

a. Assuming that you sample without replacement, select all possible samples of $n = 2$ and construct the sampling distribution of the mean. Compute the mean of all the sample means and also compute the population mean. Are they equal? What is this property called?
b. Repeat (a) for all possible samples of $n = 3$.
c. Compare the shape of the sampling distribution of the mean in (a) and (b). Which sampling distribution has less variability? Why?
d. Assuming that you sample with replacement, repeat (a) through (c) and compare the results. Which sampling distributions have the least variability—those in (a) or (b)? Why?

7.21 The diameter of a brand of Ping-Pong balls is approximately normally distributed, with a mean of 1.30 inches and a standard deviation of 0.04 inch. If you select a random sample of 16 Ping-Pong balls,
a. what is the sampling distribution of the mean?
b. what is the probability that the sample mean is less than 1.28 inches?
c. what is the probability that the sample mean is between 1.31 and 1.33 inches?
d. The probability is 60% that the sample mean will be between what two values, symmetrically distributed around the population mean?

7.22 The U.S. Census Bureau announced that the median sales price of new houses sold in April 2007 was $229,100, whereas the mean sales price was $299,100 (**www.census. gov/newhomesales**, June 21, 2007). Assume that the standard deviation of the prices is $90,000.
a. If you select samples of $n = 2$, describe the shape of the sampling distribution of $\bar{X}$.
b. If you select samples of $n = 100$, describe the shape of the sampling distribution of $\bar{X}$.
c. If you select a random sample of $n = 100$, what is the probability that the sample mean will be less than $300,000?
d. If you select a random sample of $n = 100$, what is the probability that the sample mean will be between $275,000 and $290,000?

7.23 Time spent using e-mail per session is normally distributed, with $\mu = 8$ minutes and $\sigma = 2$ minutes. If you select a random sample of 25 sessions,

a. what is the probability that the sample mean is between 7.8 and 8.2 minutes?

b. what is the probability that the sample mean is between 7.5 and 8 minutes?

c. If you select a random sample of 100 sessions, what is the probability that the sample mean is between 7.8 and 8.2 minutes?

d. Explain the difference in the results of (a) and (c).

 7.24 The amount of time a bank teller spends with each customer has a population mean, μ, of 3.10 minutes and standard deviation, σ, of 0.40 minute. If you select a random sample of 16 customers,

a. what is the probability that the mean time spent per customer is at least 3 minutes?

b. there is an 85% chance that the sample mean is less than how many minutes?

c. What assumption must you make in order to solve (a) and (b)?

d. If you select a random sample of 64 customers, there is an 85% chance that the sample mean is less than how many minutes?

7.25 *The New York Times* reported (L. J. Flynn, "Tax Surfing," *The New York Times*, March 25, 2002, p. C10) that the mean time to download the home page for the Internal Revenue Service (IRS), **www.irs.gov**, was 0.8 second. Suppose that the download time was normally distributed, with a standard deviation of 0.2 second. If you select a random sample of 30 download times,

a. what is the probability that the sample mean is less than 0.75 second?

b. what is the probability that the sample mean is between 0.70 and 0.90 second?

c. the probability is 80% that the sample mean is between what two values, symmetrically distributed around the population mean?

d. the probability is 90% that the sample mean is less than what value?

7.26 The article discussed in Problem 7.25 also reported that the mean download time for the H&R Block Web site, **www.hrblock.com**, was 2.5 seconds. Suppose that the download time for the H&R Block Web site was normally distributed, with a standard deviation of 0.5 second. If you select a random sample of 30 download times,

a. what is the probability that the sample mean is less than 2.75 seconds?

b. what is the probability that the sample mean is between 2.70 and 2.90 seconds?

c. the probability is 80% that the sample mean is between what two values symmetrically distributed around the population mean?

d. the probability is 90% that the sample mean is less than what value?

7.5   SAMPLING DISTRIBUTION OF THE PROPORTION

Consider a categorical variable that has only two categories, such as the customer prefers your brand or the customer prefers the competitor's brand. Of interest is the proportion of items belonging to one of the categories—for example, the proportion of customers that prefers your brand. The population proportion, represented by π, is the proportion of items in the entire population with the characteristic of interest. The sample proportion, represented by p, is the proportion of items in the sample with the characteristic of interest. The sample proportion, a statistic, is used to estimate the population proportion, a parameter. To calculate the sample proportion, you assign the two possible outcomes scores of 1 or 0 to represent the presence or absence of the characteristic. You then sum all the 1 and 0 scores and divide by n, the sample size. For example, if, in a sample of five customers, three preferred your brand and two did not, you have three 1s and two 0s. Summing the three 1s and two 0s and dividing by the sample size of 5 gives you a sample proportion of 0.60.

Sample Proportion

$$p = \frac{X}{n} = \frac{\text{Number of items having the characteristic of interest}}{\text{Sample size}} \quad (7.6)$$

The sample proportion, p, takes on values between 0 and 1. If all items have the characteristic, you assign each a score of 1, and p is equal to 1. If half the items have the characteristic, you assign half a score of 1 and assign the other half a score of 0, and p is equal to 0.5. If none of the items have the characteristic, you assign each a score of 0, and p is equal to 0.

In Section 7.4, you learned that the sample mean, $\bar{X}$, is an unbiased estimator of the population mean, μ. Similarly, the statistic p is an unbiased estimator of the population proportion,

π. By analogy to the sampling distribution of the mean whose standard error is $\sigma_{\bar{X}} = \dfrac{\sigma}{\sqrt{n}}$, the **standard error of the proportion**, σ_p, is given in Equation (7.7).

Standard Error of the Proportion

$$\sigma_p = \sqrt{\frac{\pi(1-\pi)}{n}} \qquad\qquad \textbf{(7.7)}$$

The **sampling distribution of the proportion** follows the binomial distribution, as discussed in Section 5.3. However, you can use the normal distribution to approximate the binomial distribution when $n\pi$ and $n(1-\pi)$ are each at least 5 (see Section 6.6). In most cases in which inferences are made about the proportion, the sample size is substantial enough to meet the conditions for using the normal approximation (see reference 1). Therefore, in many instances, you can use the normal distribution to estimate the sampling distribution of the proportion.

Substituting p for $\bar{X}$, π for μ, and $\sqrt{\dfrac{\pi(1-\pi)}{n}}$ for $\dfrac{\sigma}{\sqrt{n}}$ in Equation (7.4) on page 272 results in Equation (7.8).

Finding Z for the Sampling Distribution of the Proportion

$$Z = \frac{p - \pi}{\sqrt{\dfrac{\pi(1-\pi)}{n}}} \qquad\qquad \textbf{(7.8)}$$

To illustrate the sampling distribution of the proportion, suppose that the manager of the local branch of a savings bank determines that 40% of all depositors have multiple accounts at the bank. If you select a random sample of 200 depositors, the probability that the sample proportion of depositors with multiple accounts is less than 0.30 is calculated as follows: Because $n\pi = 200(0.40) = 80 \geq 5$ and $n(1-\pi) = 200(0.60) = 120 \geq 5$, the sample size is large enough to assume that the sampling distribution of the proportion is approximately normally distributed. Using Equation (7.8),

$$Z = \frac{p - \pi}{\sqrt{\dfrac{\pi(1-\pi)}{n}}}$$

$$= \frac{0.30 - 0.40}{\sqrt{\dfrac{(0.40)(0.60)}{200}}} = \frac{-0.10}{\sqrt{\dfrac{0.24}{200}}} = \frac{-0.10}{0.0346}$$

$$= -2.89$$

Using Table E.2, the area under the normal curve less than -2.89 is 0.0019. Therefore, if the true proportion of items of interest in the population is 0.40, then only 0.19% of the samples of $n = 200$ would be expected to have sample proportions less than 0.30.

PROBLEMS FOR SECTION 7.5

Learning the Basics

7.27 In a random sample of 64 people, 48 are classified as "successful."
a. Determine the sample proportion, p, of "successful" people.
b. If the population proportion is 0.70, determine the standard error of the proportion.

7.28 A random sample of 50 households was selected for a telephone survey. The key question asked was, "Do you or any member of your household own a cellular telephone with a built-in camera?" Of the 50 respondents, 15 said yes and 35 said no.
a. Determine the sample proportion, p, of households with cellular telephones with built-in cameras.
b. If the population proportion is 0.40, determine the standard error of the proportion.

7.29 The following data represent the responses (Y for yes and N for no) from a sample of 40 college students to the question "Do you currently own shares in any stocks?"

N N Y N N Y N Y N Y N N Y N Y Y N N N Y
N Y N N N N Y N N Y Y N N N Y N N Y N N

a. Determine the sample proportion, p, of college students who own shares of stock.
b. If the population proportion is 0.30, determine the standard error of the proportion.

Applying the Concepts

✓SELF Test **7.30** A political pollster is conducting an analysis of sample results in order to make predictions on election night. Assuming a two-candidate election, if a specific candidate receives at least 55% of the vote in the sample, then that candidate will be forecast as the winner of the election. If you select a random sample of 100 voters, what is the probability that a candidate will be forecast as the winner when
a. the true percentage of her vote is 50.1%?
b. the true percentage of her vote is 60%?
c. the true percentage of her vote is 49% (and she will actually lose the election)?
d. If the sample size is increased to 400, what are your answers to (a) through (c)? Discuss.

7.31 You plan to conduct a marketing experiment in which students are to taste one of two different brands of soft drink. Their task is to correctly identify the brand tasted. You select a random sample of 200 students and assume that the students have no ability to distinguish between the two brands. (Hint: If an individual has no ability to distinguish between the two soft drinks, then each brand is equally likely to be selected.)
a. What is the probability that the sample will have between 50% and 60% of the identifications correct?
b. The probability is 90% that the sample percentage is contained within what symmetrical limits of the population percentage?
c. What is the probability that the sample percentage of correct identifications is greater than 65%?
d. Which is more likely to occur—more than 60% correct identifications in the sample of 200 or more than 55% correct identifications in a sample of 1,000? Explain.

7.32 An online quiz available at **www.pewinternet. org/quiz** divides up people according to their usage of the computer. In a survey of 4,001 respondents, 8% were classified as productivity enhancers who are comfortable with technology and use the Internet for its practical value (M. Himowitz, "How to Tell What Kind of Tech User You Are," *Newsday*, May 27, 2007, p. F6). Suppose you select a sample of 400 students at your school, and the population proportion of productivity enhancers is 0.08.
a. What is the probability that in the sample, less than 10% of the students will be productivity enhancers?
b. What is the probability that in the sample, between 6% and 10% of the students will be productivity enhancers?
c. What is the probability that in the sample, more than 5% of the students will be productivity enhancers?
d. If a sample of 100 is taken, how does this change your answers to (a) through (c)?

7.33 Companies often make flextime scheduling available to help recruit and keep women employees who have children at home. Other workers sometimes view these flextime schedules as unfair. An article in *USA Today* indicates that 25% of male employees state that they have to pick up the slack for moms working flextime schedules (D. Jones, "Poll Finds Resentment of Flextime," **usatoday.com**, May 11, 2007). Suppose you select a random sample of 100 male employees working for companies offering flextime.
a. What is the probability that 25% or fewer male employees will indicate that they have to pick up the slack for moms working flextime?

b. What is the probability that 20% or fewer will indicate that they have to pick up the slack for moms working flextime?

c. If a random sample of 500 is taken, how does this change your answers to (a) and (b)?

7.34 According to Gallup's annual poll on personal finances, even though most U.S. workers reported living comfortably now, many expected a downturn in their lifestyle when they stop working. Approximately half said they have enough money to live comfortably now and expected to do so in the future (J. M. Jones, "Only Half of Non-Retirees Expect to be Comfortable in Retirement," *The Gallup Poll*, **galluppoll.com**, May 2, 2006). If you select a random sample of 200 U.S. workers,

a. what is the probability that the sample will have between 45% and 55% who say they have enough money to live comfortably now and expect to do so in the future?

b. the probability is 90% that the sample percentage will be contained within what symmetrical limits of the population percentage?

c. the probability is 95% that the sample percentage will be contained within what symmetrical limits of the population percentage?

7.35 New research shows (J. O'Donnell, "Gen Y Sits on Top of Consumer Food Chain," *USA Today*, October 11, 2006, p. 3B) that members of generation Y (people born from 1982 to 2000) have a great say in household purchases. Specifically, 68% of Gen Y people have a say in computer purchases. Suppose you select a sample of 100 Gen Y respondents.

a. What is the probability that the sample percentage will be contained between 65% and 75%?

b. The probability is 90% that the sample percentage will be contained within what symmetrical limits of the population percentage?

c. The probability is 95% that the sample percentage will be contained within what symmetrical limits of the population percentage?

d. Suppose you selected a sample of 400 respondents. How does this change your answers in (a) through (c)?

7.36 Yahoo HotJobs reported that 56% of full-time office workers believe that dressing-down can affect jobs, salaries, or promotions (J. Yang and K. Carter, "Dress Can Affect Size of Paycheck," **usatoday.com**, May 9, 2007).

a. Suppose that you take a sample of 100 full-time workers. If the true population proportion of workers who believe that dressing-down can affect jobs, salaries, or promotions is 0.56, what is the probability that less than half in your sample hold that same belief?

b. Suppose that you take a sample of 500 full-time workers. If the true population proportion of workers who believe that dressing-down can affect jobs, salaries, or promotions is 0.56, what is the probability that less than half in your sample hold that same belief?

c. Discuss the effect of sample size on the sampling distribution of the proportion in general, and the effect on the probabilities in (a) and (b).

7.37 The IRS discontinued random audits in 1988. Instead, the IRS conducts audits on returns deemed questionable by its Discriminant Function System (DFS), a complicated and highly secretive computerized analysis system. In an attempt to reduce the proportion of "no-change" audits (i.e., audits that uncover that no additional taxes are due), the IRS only audits returns that the DFS scores as highly questionable. The proportion of no-change audits has risen over the years and is currently approximately 0.25 (T. Herman, "Unhappy Returns: IRS Moves to Bring Back Random Audits," *The Wall Street Journal*, June 20, 2002, p. A1). Suppose that you select a random sample of 100 audits. What is the probability that the sample has

a. between 24% and 26% no-change audits?

b. between 20% and 30% no-change audits?

c. more than 30% no-change audits?

7.38 Referring to Problem 7.37, the IRS announced that it planned to resume totally random audits in 2002. Suppose that you select a random sample of 200 totally random audits and that 90% of all the returns filed would result in no-change audits. What is the probability that the sample has

a. between 89% and 91% no-change audits?

b. between 85% and 95% no-change audits?

c. more than 95% no-change audits?

7.6 🌐 (CD-ROM TOPIC) SAMPLING FROM FINITE POPULATIONS

In this section, sampling without replacement from finite populations is considered. For further discussion, see `section 7.6.pdf` on the Student CD-ROM that accompanies this book.

SUMMARY

In this chapter, you studied four common probability sampling methods—simple random, systematic, stratified, and cluster. You also studied the sampling distribution of the sample mean, the Central Limit Theorem, and the sampling distribution of the sample proportion. You learned that the sample mean is an unbiased estimator of the population mean, and the sample proportion is an unbiased estimator of the population proportion. By observing the mean weight in a sample of cereal boxes filled by Oxford Cereals, you were able to reach conclusions concerning the mean weight in the population of cereal boxes. In the next five chapters, the techniques of confidence intervals and tests of hypotheses commonly used for statistical inference are discussed.

KEY EQUATIONS

Population Mean

$$\mu = \frac{\sum_{i=1}^{N} X_i}{N} \tag{7.1}$$

Population Standard Deviation

$$\sigma = \sqrt{\frac{\sum_{i=1}^{N} (X_i - \mu)^2}{N}} \tag{7.2}$$

Standard Error of the Mean

$$\sigma_{\bar{X}} = \frac{\sigma}{\sqrt{n}} \tag{7.3}$$

Finding Z for the Sampling Distribution of the Mean

$$Z = \frac{\bar{X} - \mu_{\bar{X}}}{\sigma_{\bar{X}}} = \frac{\bar{X} - \mu}{\dfrac{\sigma}{\sqrt{n}}} \tag{7.4}$$

Finding $\bar{X}$ for the Sampling Distribution of the Mean

$$\bar{X} = \mu + Z\frac{\sigma}{\sqrt{n}} \tag{7.5}$$

Sample Proportion

$$p = \frac{X}{n} \tag{7.6}$$

Standard Error of the Proportion

$$\sigma_p = \sqrt{\frac{\pi(1 - \pi)}{n}} \tag{7.7}$$

Finding Z for the Sampling Distribution of the Proportion

$$Z = \frac{p - \pi}{\sqrt{\dfrac{\pi(1 - \pi)}{n}}} \tag{7.8}$$

KEY TERMS

Central Limit Theorem   274
cluster   262
cluster sample   262
convenience sampling   258
coverage error   264
frame   258
judgment sample   259
margin of error   265
measurement error   265
nonprobability sample   258

nonresponse bias   264
nonresponse error   264
probability sample   259
sampling distribution   267
sampling distribution of the mean   267
sampling distribution of the proportion   279
sampling error   264
sampling with replacement   259

sampling without replacement   259
selection bias   264
simple random sample   259
standard error of the mean   270
standard error of the proportion   279
strata   262
stratified sample   262
systematic sample   261
table of random numbers   260
unbiased   267

CHAPTER REVIEW PROBLEMS

Checking Your Understanding

7.39 Why is the sample mean an unbiased estimator of the population mean?

7.40 Why does the standard error of the mean decrease as the sample size, n, increases?

7.41 Why does the sampling distribution of the mean follow a normal distribution for a large enough sample size, even though the population may not be normally distributed?

7.42 What is the difference between a population and a sampling distribution?

7.43 Under what circumstances does the sampling distribution of the proportion approximately follow the normal distribution?

7.44 What is the difference between probability and non-probability sampling?

7.45 What are some potential problems with using "fishbowl" methods to select a simple random sample?

7.46 What is the difference between sampling *with* replacement versus *without* replacement?

7.47 What is the difference between a simple random sample and a systematic sample?

7.48 What is the difference between a simple random sample and a stratified sample?

7.49 What is the difference between a stratified sample and a cluster sample?

Applying the Concepts

7.50 An industrial sewing machine uses ball bearings that are targeted to have a diameter of 0.75 inch. The lower and upper specification limits under which the ball bearing can operate are 0.74 inch (lower) and 0.76 inch (upper). Past experience has indicated that the actual diameter of the ball bearings is approximately normally distributed, with a mean of 0.753 inch and a standard deviation of 0.004 inch. If you select a random sample of 25 ball bearings, what is the probability that the sample mean is
a. between the target and the population mean of 0.753?
b. between the lower specification limit and the target?
c. greater than the upper specification limit?
d. less than the lower specification limit?
e. The probability is 93% that the sample mean diameter will be greater than what value?

7.51 The fill amount of bottles of a soft drink is normally distributed, with a mean of 2.0 liters and a standard deviation of 0.05 liter. If you select a random sample of 25 bottles, what is the probability that the sample mean will be
a. between 1.99 and 2.0 liters?
b. below 1.98 liters?
c. greater than 2.01 liters?
d. The probability is 99% that the sample mean amount of soft drink will be at least how much?
e. The probability is 99% that the sample mean amount of soft drink will be between which two values (symmetrically distributed around the mean)?

7.52 An orange juice producer buys all his oranges from a large orange grove that has one variety of orange. The amount of juice squeezed from these oranges is approximately normally distributed, with a mean of 4.70 ounces and a standard deviation of 0.40 ounce. Suppose that you select a sample of 25 oranges.
a. What is the probability that the sample mean amount of juice will be at least 4.60 ounces?
b. The probability is 70% that the sample mean amount of juice will be contained between what two values symmetrically distributed around the population mean?
c. The probability is 77% that the sample mean amount of juice will be greater than what value?

7.53 In his management information systems textbook, Professor David Kroenke raises an interesting point: "If 98% of our market has Internet access, do we have a responsibility to provide non-Internet materials to that other 2%?" (D. M. Kroenke, *Using MIS*, Upper Saddle River, NJ: Prentice Hall, 2007, p. 29a). Suppose that 98% of the customers in your market have Internet access and you select a random sample of 500 customers. What is the probability that the sample has
a. greater than 99% with Internet access?
b. between 97% and 99% with Internet access?
c. less than 97% with Internet access?

7.54 Mutual funds reported strong earnings in the fourth quarter of 2006. Especially strong growth occurred in mutual funds consisting of companies focusing on Latin America. This population of mutual funds earned a mean return of 22.5% in the fourth quarter (I. Salisbury, "Trying to Put 3.28 Billion to Work," *The Wall Street Journal*, January 4, 2007). Assume that the returns for the Latin America mutual funds were distributed as a normal random variable, with a mean of 22.5 and a standard deviation of 20. If you selected a random sample of 10 funds from this population, what is the probability that the sample would have a mean return
a. less than 0—that is, a loss?
b. between 0 and 20?
c. greater than 10?

7.55 The same article as in Problem 7.54 reported that mutual funds focusing on Europe had a mean return of 12.2% during this time. Assume that the returns for the Europe mutual funds were distributed as a normal random variable, with a mean of 12.2 and a standard deviation of 12. If you select an individual fund from this population, what is the probability that it would have a return
a. less than 0—that is, a loss?
b. between 0 and 20?
c. greater than 10?
If you selected a random sample of 10 funds from this population, what is the probability that the sample would have a mean return
d. less than 0—that is, a loss?
e. between 0 and 20?
f. greater than 10?
g. Compare your results in parts (d) through (f) to (a) through (c).
h. Compare your results in parts (d) through (f) to Problem 7.54 (a) through (c).

7.56 Telephone interviews have traditionally been the number one tool in political polling. Recently, many have argued that Internet polling is faster and less expensive and produces a higher response rate. Dr. Doug Usher, a leading authority on political polling, agrees that the telephone poll is still the gold standard in political polls due to its superior statistical reliability even though it is getting harder to reach people via the telephone with the growing use of caller ID and the fact that many younger people no longer have landlines (D. Usher, "The Internet's Unfulfilled Promise for Political Polling," www.mysterypollster.com, June 30, 2005). What concerns, if any, do you have on Internet polling?

7.57 A survey sponsored by The American Dietetic Association and the agribusiness giant ConAgra found that 53% of office workers take 30 minutes or less for lunch each day. Approximately 37% take 30 to 60 minutes, and 10% take more than an hour ("Snapshots," usatoday.com, April 26, 2006).
a. What additional information would you want to know before you accepted the results of the survey?
b. Discuss the four types of survey errors in the context of this survey.
c. One of the types of survey errors discussed in part (b) should have been measurement error. Explain how the root cause of measurement error in this survey could be the Hawthorne effect.

7.58 In a survey conducted by AOL and the Associated Press, less than 25% of adults use instant messaging (IM), and almost 75% of adults who use IM use e-mail more often than IM. The survey also showed that almost 50% of teens use IM, and almost 75% of teens who use IM use IM more often than e-mail (M. Levitt, "Bridging the Collaboration Age Gap with Unified Communications and Web 2.0," *KM World*, June 2007, p. 10).
a. What other information would you want to know before you used the results of this survey?
b. Suppose you work for AOL and wanted to investigate IM and e-mail usage by AOL users. Define the population, frame, and sampling method you would use.

7.59 Connecticut shoppers spend more on women's clothing than do shoppers in any other state, according to a survey conducted by MapInfo. The mean spending per household in Connecticut was $975 annually ("Snapshots," usatoday.com, April 17, 2006).
a. What other information would you want to know before you accepted the results of this survey?
b. Suppose that you wished to conduct a similar survey for the geographic region you live in. Describe the population for your survey.
c. Explain how you could minimize the chance of coverage error in this type of survey.
d. Explain how you could minimize the chance of nonresponse error in this type of survey.
e. Explain how you could minimize the chance of sampling error in this type of survey.
f. Explain how you could minimize the chance of measurement error in this type of survey.

7.60 Technology enables the rise of extreme workers who work more than 60 hours per week (S. Armour, "Hi, I'm Joan, and I'm a Workaholic," *USA Today*, May 23, 2007, pp. 1B, 2B). 90% of male extreme workers said that they work long hours because their jobs are stimulating or challenging or provide an adrenaline rush. However, 46% of male extreme workers said that working long hours undermined their relationship with their spouse or partner.
a. What other information would you want to know before you accepted the results of this study?
b. If you were to perform a similar study in the geographic area where you live, define a population, frame, and sampling method you could use.

7.61 (Class Project) The table of random numbers is an example of a uniform distribution because each digit is equally likely to occur. Starting in the row corresponding to the day of the month in which you were born, use the table of random numbers (Table E.1) to take one digit at a time.

Select five different samples each of $n = 2$, $n = 5$, and $n = 10$. Compute the sample mean of each sample. Develop a frequency distribution of the sample means for the results of the entire class, based on samples of sizes $n = 2$, $n = 5$, and $n = 10$.

What can be said about the shape of the sampling distribution for each of these sample sizes?

7.62 (Class Project) Toss a coin 10 times and record the number of heads. If each student performs this experiment five times, a frequency distribution of the number of heads can be developed from the results of the entire class. Does this distribution seem to approximate the normal distribution?

7.63 (Class Project) The number of cars waiting in line at a car wash is distributed as follows:

Number of Cars	Probability
0	0.25
1	0.40
2	0.20
3	0.10
4	0.04
5	0.01

You can use the table of random numbers (Table E.1) to select samples from this distribution by assigning numbers as follows:

1. Start in the row corresponding to the day of the month in which you were born.
2. Select a two-digit random number.
3. If you select a random number from 00 to 24, record a length of 0; if from 25 to 64, record a length of 1; if from 65 to 84, record a length of 2; if from 85 to 94, record a length of 3; if from 95 to 98, record a length of 4; if 99, record a length of 5.

Select samples of $n = 2$, $n = 5$, and $n = 10$. Compute the mean for each sample. For example, if a sample of size 2

results in the random numbers 18 and 46, these would correspond to lengths of 0 and 1, respectively, producing a sample mean of 0.5. If each student selects five different samples for each sample size, a frequency distribution of the sample means (for each sample size) can be developed from the results of the entire class. What conclusions can you reach concerning the sampling distribution of the mean as the sample size is increased?

7.64 (Class Project) Using Table E.1, simulate the selection of different-colored balls from a bowl as follows:

1. Start in the row corresponding to the day of the month in which you were born.
2. Select one-digit numbers.
3. If a random digit between 0 and 6 is selected, consider the ball white; if a random digit is a 7, 8, or 9, consider the ball red.

Select samples of $n = 10$, $n = 25$, and $n = 50$ digits. In each sample, count the number of white balls and compute the proportion of white balls in the sample. If each student in the class selects five different samples for each sample size, a frequency distribution of the proportion of white balls (for each sample size) can be developed from the results of the entire class. What conclusions can you reach about the sampling distribution of the proportion as the sample size is increased?

7.65 (Class Project) Suppose that step 3 of Problem 7.64 uses the following rule: "If a random digit between 0 and 8 is selected, consider the ball to be white; if a random digit of 9 is selected, consider the ball to be red." Compare and contrast the results in this problem and those in Problem 7.64.

MANAGING THE *SPRINGVILLE HERALD*

Continuing its quality improvement effort first described in the Chapter 6 "Managing the *Springville Herald*" case, the production department of the newspaper has been monitoring the blackness of the newspaper print. As before, blackness is measured on a standard scale in which the target value is 1.0. Data collected over the past year indicate that the blackness is normally distributed, with a mean of 1.005 and a standard deviation of 0.10.

EXERCISE

SH7.1 Each day, 25 spots on the first newspaper printed are chosen, and the blackness of the spots is measured.

Assuming that the distribution has not changed from what it was in the past year, what is the probability that the mean blackness of the spots is
  a. less than 1.0?
  b. between 0.95 and 1.0?
  c. between 1.0 and 1.05?
  d. less than 0.95 or greater than 1.05?
  e. Suppose that the mean blackness of today's sample of 25 spots is 0.952. What conclusion can you make about the blackness of today's newspaper based on this result? Explain.

WEB CASE

Apply your knowledge about sampling distributions in this Web Case, which reconsiders the Oxford Cereals Using Statistics scenario.

The advocacy group Consumers Concerned About Cereal Cheaters (CCACC) suspects that cereal companies, including Oxford Cereals, are cheating consumers by packaging cereals at less than labeled weights. Visit the organization's home page at **www.prenhall.com/ Springville/ConsumersConcerned.htm** (or open the `ConsumersConcerned.htm` file in the Student CD-ROM Web Case folder), examine their claims and supporting data, and then answer the following:

1. Are the data collection procedures that the CCACC uses to form its conclusions flawed? What procedures could the group follow to make their analysis more rigorous?

2. Assume that the two samples of five cereal boxes (one sample for each of two cereal varieties) listed on the CCACC Web site were collected randomly by organization members. For each sample, do the following:

a. Calculate the sample mean.

b. Assume that the standard deviation of the process is 15 grams and a population mean is 368 grams. Calculate the percentage of all samples for each process that have a sample mean less than the value you calculated in (a).

c. Again, assuming that the standard deviation is 15 grams, calculate the percentage of individual boxes of cereal that have a weight less than the value you calculated in (a).

3. What, if any, conclusions can you form by using your calculations about the filling processes of the two different cereals?

4. A representative from Oxford Cereals has asked that the CCACC take down its page discussing shortages in Oxford Cereals boxes. Is that request reasonable? Why or why not?

5. Can the techniques discussed in this chapter be used to prove cheating in the manner alleged by the CCACC? Why or why not?

REFERENCES

1. Cochran, W. G., *Sampling Techniques*, 3rd ed. (New York: Wiley, 1977).

2. Gallup, G. H., *The Sophisticated Poll-Watcher's Guide* (Princeton, NJ: Princeton Opinion Press, 1972).

3. Goleman, D., "Pollsters Enlist Psychologists in Quest for Unbiased Results," *The New York Times*, September 7, 1993, pp. C1, C11.

4. Hahn, G., and W. Meeker, *Statistical Intervals, A Guide for Practioners* (New York: John Wiley and Sons, Inc., 1991).

5. *Microsoft Excel 2007* (Redmond, WA: Microsoft Corp., 2007).

6. *Minitab for Windows Version 15* (State College, PA: Minitab, Inc., 2006).

7. Rand Corporation, *A Million Random Digits with 100,000 Normal Deviates* (New York: The Free Press, 1955).

Appendix E7
Using Microsoft Excel for Sampling and Sampling Distributions

E7.1 Creating Simple Random Samples Without Replacement

No Microsoft Excel features directly create simple random samples. Use PHStat2 Section P7.1 to create such samples.

E7.2 Creating Simulated Sampling Distributions

You create simulated sampling distributions by first using the ToolPak Random Number Generation procedure to create a worksheet of multiple random samples and then adding formulas to that worksheet to compute the sample means and other appropriate measures.

To start, select **Tools → Data Analysis** and in the Data Analysis dialog box, click **Random Number Generation** and then click **OK**. In the Random Number Generation dialog box (shown at right), enter the number of samples as the **Number of Variables** and enter the sample size of each sample as the **Number of Random Numbers.** Select the type of distribution from the **Distribution** drop-down list and make entries in the Parameters area, the contents of which vary according to the distribution selected. (If you select the **Discrete** option, you will need to be opened to a

worksheet that contains a table of X and $P(X)$ values and enter the range of the table as the **Value and Probability Input Range**.). To finish, click **New Worksheet Ply** and then **OK**.

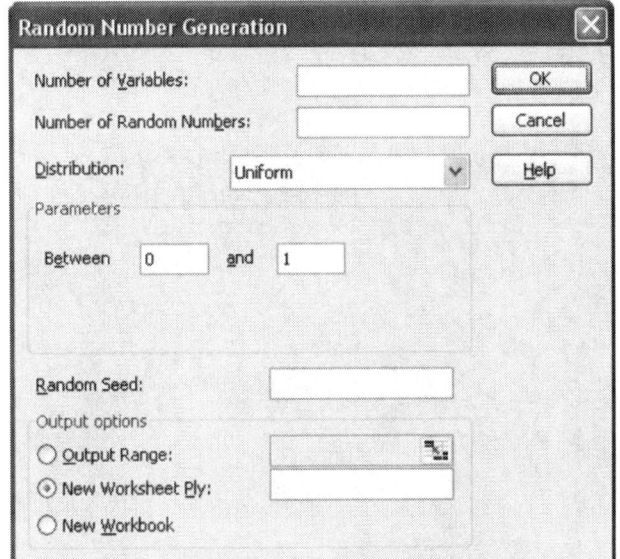

Appendix P7
Using PHStat2 for Sampling and Sampling Distributions

P7.1 Creating Simple Random Samples Without Replacement

To create a random sample without replacement use **PHStat → Sampling → Random Sample Generation**. In the Random Sample Generation dialog box (shown below), click **Select values from range** to have the procedure create the random sample for the values in the **Values Cell Range**. The created random sample appears on a new worksheet.

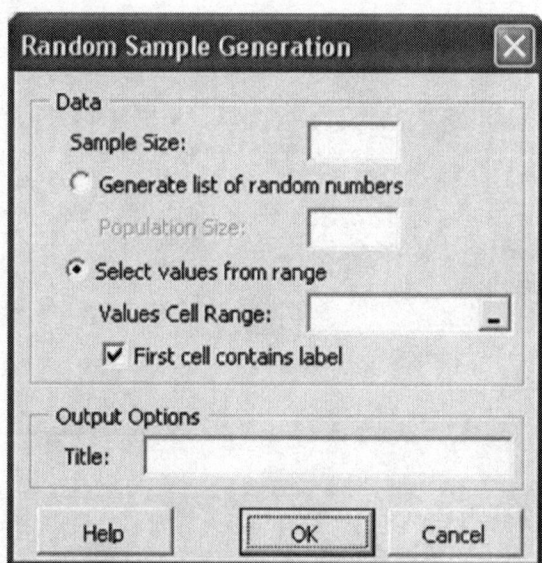

P7.2 Creating Simulated Sampling Distributions

To create a simulated sampling distribution, use **PHStat → Sampling → Sampling Distributions Simulation**. This procedure creates a worksheet using the ToolPak Random Number Generation procedure and the number of samples, sample size, and a type of distribution that you specify.

The procedure adds the sample means, the overall mean, and the standard error of the mean to the worksheet created by the ToolPak procedure. If you click **Histogram**, the procedure uses the ToolPak Histogram procedure to create a histogram of the simulation. (The histogram will contain a number of minor errors as discussed in Section E2.9.)

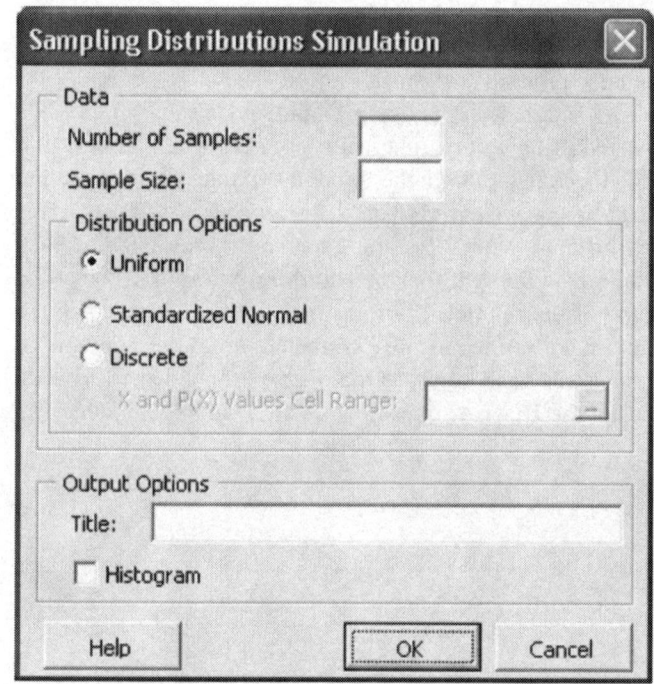

Appendix M7
Using Minitab for Sampling and Sampling Distributions

M7.1 Creating Simple Random Samples Without Replacement

To create a random sample of size 40 from a frame of size 800 as in Example 7.1 on page 260,

1. Select **Calc → Make Patterned Data → Simple Set of Numbers**.

In the Simple Set of Numbers dialog box (see Figure M7.1):

2. Enter **C1** in the **Store patterned data in** box.
3. Enter **1** in the **From first value** box.
4. Enter **800** in the **To last value** box.
5. Click **OK**.

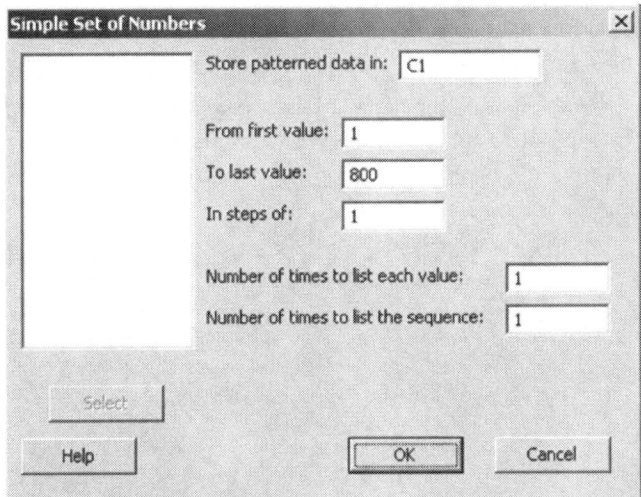

FIGURE M7.1

Minitab Simple Set of Numbers dialog box

With the worksheet containing the numbers in column C1:

6. Select **Calc → Random Data → Sample From Columns**.

In the Sample From Columns dialog box (see Figure M7.2):

7. Enter **40** in the **Number of rows to sample** box.
8. Enter **C1** in the **From columns** box.
9. Enter **C2** in the **Store samples in** box.
10. Click **OK**.

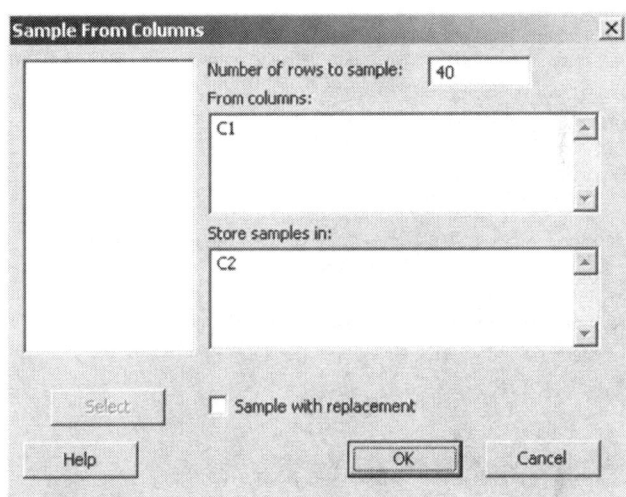

FIGURE M7.2

Minitab Sample From Columns dialog box

M7.2 Creating Simulated Sampling Distributions

To develop a simulation of the sampling distribution of the mean from a uniformly distributed population with 100 samples of $n = 30$:

1. Select **Calc → Random Data → Uniform**.

In the Uniform Distribution dialog box (see Figure M7.3):

2. Enter **100** in the **Number of rows of data to generate** box.
3. Enter **C1–C30** in the **Store in column(s)** box.
4. Enter **0.0** in the **Lower endpoint** box
5. Enter **1.0** in the **Upper endpoint** box.
6. Click **OK**.

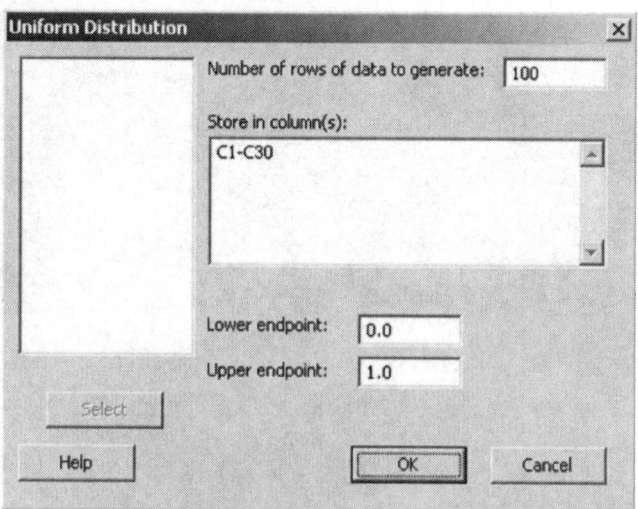

FIGURE M7.3

Minitab Uniform Distribution dialog box

One hundred rows of values are now entered in columns C1–C30. To calculate row statistics for each of the 100 samples:

1. Select **Calc → Row Statistics**.

In the Row Statistics dialog box (see Figure M7.4):

2. Click **Mean**.
3. Enter **C1–C30** in the **Input variables** box.
4. Enter **C31** in the **Store result in** box.
5. Click **OK**.

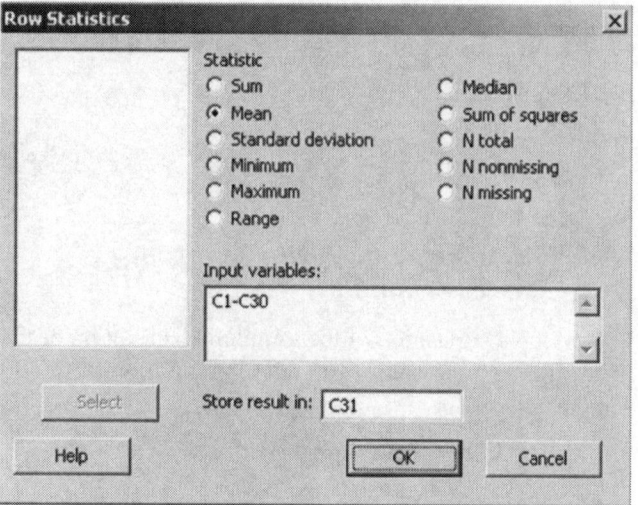

FIGURE M7.4

Minitab Row Statistics dialog box

The mean for each of the 100 samples is stored in column C31. To compute statistics for the set of 100 sample means:

1. Select **Stat → Basic Statistics → Display Descriptive Statistics**.
2. In the Display Descriptive Statistics dialog box, enter **C31** in the **Variables** box and then click **OK**.

To generate a histogram of the 100 sample means:

1. Select **Graph → Histogram** and do the following:

In the Histograms dialog box:

2. Select **Simple**.
3. Click **OK**.

In the Histogram - Simple dialog box:

4. Enter **C31** in the **Graph variables** box.
5. Click **OK**.

To create a simulation of the sampling distribution of the mean for a normal population:

1. Select **Calc → Random Data → Normal**.

In the Normal Distribution dialog box:

2. Enter **100** in the **Number of rows of data to generate** box.
3. Enter **C1–C30** in the **Store in column(s)** box.
4. Enter a value for μ in the **Mean** box.
5. Enter a value for σ in the **Standard deviation** box.
6. Click **OK**.

You can calculate row statistics (descriptive statistics for the set of 100 samples) and create a histogram by adapting the instructions given for a uniformly distributed population.

CHAPTER
EIGHT

CONFIDENCE INTERVAL ESTIMATION

LEARNING OBJECTIVES

In this chapter, you learn:

- To construct and interpret confidence interval estimates for the mean and the proportion
- How to determine the sample size necessary to develop a confidence interval for the mean or proportion
  How to use confidence interval estimates in auditing

USING STATISTICS @ Saxon Home Improvement

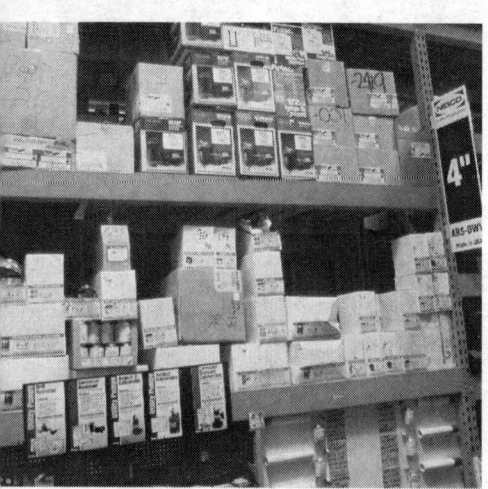

Saxon Home Improvement distributes home improvement supplies in the northeastern United States. As a company accountant, you are responsible for the accuracy of the integrated inventory management and sales information system. You could review the contents of each and every record to check the accuracy of this system, but such a detailed review would be time-consuming and costly. A better approach is to use statistical inference techniques to draw conclusions about the population of all records from a relatively small sample collected during an audit. At the end of each month, you could select a sample of the sales invoices to estimate the following:

- The mean dollar amount listed on the sales invoices for the month.
- The frequency of occurrence of errors that violate the internal control policy of the warehouse. Such errors include making a shipment when there is no authorized warehouse removal slip, failure to include the correct account number, and shipping the incorrect home improvement item.
- The total dollar amount listed on the sales invoices for the month.
- Any differences between the dollar amounts on the sales invoices and the amounts entered into the sales information system.

How accurate are the results from the samples and how do you use this information? Are the sample sizes large enough to give you the information you need?

In Section 7.4, you used the Central Limit Theorem and knowledge of the population distribution to determine the percentage of sample means that are within certain distances of the population mean. For instance, in the cereal-fill example used throughout Chapter 7 (see Example 7.6 on page 274), you can conclude that 95% of all sample means are between 362.12 and 373.88 grams. This is an example of *deductive* reasoning because the conclusion is based on taking something that is true in general (for the population) and applying it to something specific (the sample means).

To get the results that Saxon Home Improvement needs requires *inductive* reasoning. Inductive reasoning lets you use some specifics to make broader generalizations. You cannot guarantee that the broader generalizations are absolutely correct, but with a careful choosing of the specifics and a rigorous methodology, you can get useful conclusions. As a Saxon accountant, you need to use inferential statistics, the process of using sample results (the "some specifics") to *estimate* ("the making of the broader generalization") unknown population parameters such as a population mean or a population proportion. Note that statisticians use the word *estimate* in the same sense of the everyday usage, something you are reasonably certain about, but cannot flatly say is absolutely correct.

You estimate population parameters using either point estimates or interval estimates. A **point estimate** is the value of a single sample statistic. A **confidence interval estimate** is a range of numbers, called an interval, constructed around the point estimate. The confidence interval is constructed such that the probability that the population parameter is located somewhere within the interval is known.

Suppose you want to estimate the mean GPA of all the students at your university. The mean GPA for all the students is an unknown population mean, denoted by μ. You select a sample of students and find that the sample mean is 2.80. The sample mean, $\bar{X} = 2.80$, is a point estimate of the population mean, μ. How accurate is 2.80? To answer this question, you must construct a confidence interval estimate.

Recall that the sample mean, $\bar{X}$, is a point estimate of the population mean, μ. However, the sample mean varies from sample to sample because it depends on the items selected in the sample. By taking into account the known variability from sample to sample (see Section 7.4 on the sampling distribution of the mean), you can develop the interval estimate for the population mean. The interval constructed should have a specified confidence of correctly estimating the value of the population parameter, μ. In other words, there is a specified confidence that μ is somewhere in the range of numbers defined by the interval.

Suppose that after studying this chapter, you find that a 95% confidence interval for the mean GPA at your university is $(2.75 \leq \mu \leq 2.85)$. You can interpret this interval estimate by stating that you are 95% confident that the mean GPA at your university is between 2.75 and 2.85. There is a 5% chance that the mean GPA is below 2.75 or above 2.85.

After learning about the confidence interval for the mean, you will learn how to develop an interval estimate for the population proportion. Then you will learn how large a sample to select when constructing confidence intervals and how to perform several important estimation procedures accountants use when performing audits.

8.1 CONFIDENCE INTERVAL ESTIMATION FOR THE MEAN (σ KNOWN)

In Section 7.4, you used the Central Limit Theorem and knowledge of the population distribution to determine the percentage of sample means that are within certain distances of the population mean. Suppose that in the cereal-fill example, you wished to estimate the population mean, using the information from a single sample. Thus, rather than taking $\mu \pm (1.96)(\sigma/\sqrt{n})$ to find the upper and lower limits around μ, as in Section 7.4, you substitute the sample mean, $\bar{X}$, for the unknown μ and use $\bar{X} \pm (1.96)(\sigma/\sqrt{n})$ as an interval to estimate the unknown μ. Although in practice you select a single sample of n values and compute the mean, $\bar{X}$, in order to understand the full meaning of the interval estimate, you need to examine a hypothetical set of all possible samples of n values.

Suppose that a sample of $n = 25$ boxes has a mean of 362.3 grams. The interval developed to estimate μ is $362.3 \pm (1.96)(15)/(\sqrt{25})$ or 362.3 ± 5.88. The estimate of μ is

$$356.42 \leq \mu \leq 368.18$$

Because the population mean, μ (equal to 368), is included within the interval, this sample results in a correct statement about μ (see Figure 8.1).

FIGURE 8.1

Confidence interval estimates for five different samples of $n = 25$ taken from a population where $\mu = 368$ and $\sigma = 15$

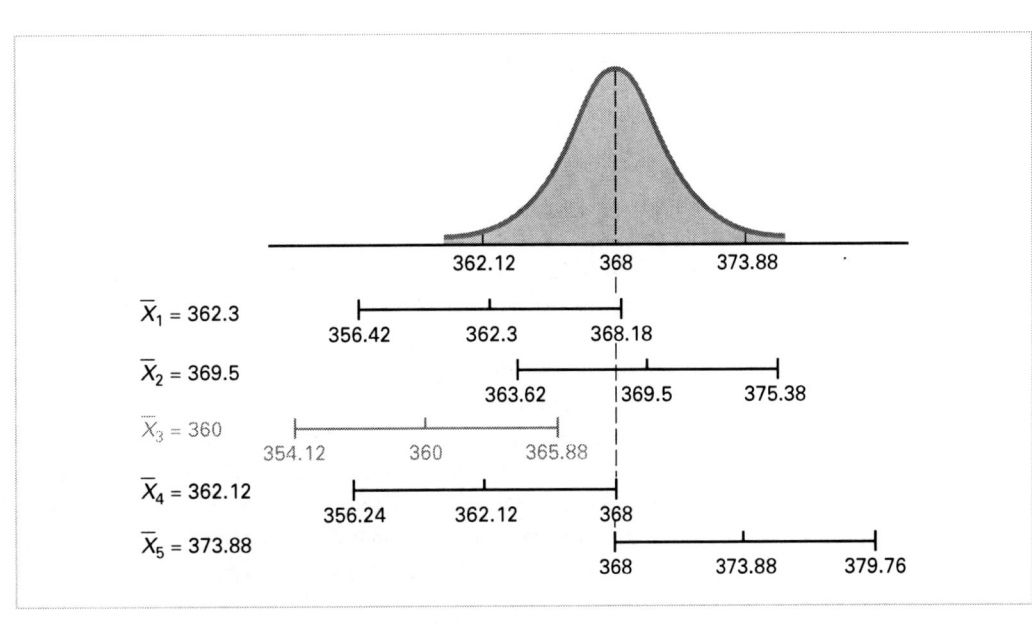

To continue this hypothetical example, suppose that for a different sample of $n = 25$ boxes, the mean is 369.5. The interval developed from this sample is

$$369.5 \pm (1.96)(15)/(\sqrt{25})$$

or 360 ± 5.88. The estimate is

$$363.62 \leq \mu \leq 375.38$$

Because the population mean, μ (equal to 368), is also included within this interval, this statement about μ is correct.

Now, before you begin to think that correct statements about μ are always made by developing a confidence interval estimate, suppose a third hypothetical sample of $n = 25$ boxes is selected and the sample mean is equal to 360 grams. The interval developed here is $360 \pm (1.96)(15)/(\sqrt{25})$, or 360 ± 5.88. In this case, the estimate of μ is

$$354.12 \leq \mu \leq 365.88$$

This estimate is *not* a correct statement because the population mean, μ, is not included in the interval developed from this sample (see Figure 8.1). Thus, for some samples, the interval estimate of μ is correct, but for others it is incorrect. In practice, only one sample is selected, and because the population mean is unknown, you cannot determine whether the interval estimate is correct. To resolve this dilemma of sometimes having an interval that provides a correct estimate and sometimes having an interval that provides an incorrect estimate, you need to determine the proportion of samples producing intervals that result in correct statements about the population mean, μ. To do this, consider two other hypothetical samples: the case in which $\bar{X} = 362.12$ grams and the case in which $\bar{X} = 373.88$ grams. If $\bar{X} = 362.12$, the interval is $362.12 \pm (1.96)(15)/(\sqrt{25})$, or 362.12 ± 5.88. This leads to the following interval:

$$356.24 \leq \mu \leq 368.00$$

Because the population mean of 368 is at the upper limit of the interval, the statement is a correct one (see Figure 8.1).

When $\bar{X} = 373.88$, the interval is $373.88 \pm (1.96)(15)/(\sqrt{25})$, or 373.88 ± 5.88. The interval estimate for the mean is

$$368.00 \leq \mu \leq 379.76$$

In this case, because the population mean of 368 is included at the lower limit of the interval, the statement is correct.

In Figure 8.1, you see that when the sample mean falls anywhere between 362.12 and 373.88 grams, the population mean is included *somewhere* within the interval. In Example 7.6 on page 274, you found that 95% of the sample means fall between 362.12 and 373.88 grams. Therefore, 95% of all samples of $n = 25$ boxes have sample means that include the population mean within the interval developed.

Because, in practice, you select only one sample of size n, and μ is unknown, you never know for sure whether your specific interval includes the population mean. However, if you take all possible samples of n and compute their sample means, 95% of the intervals will include the population mean, and only 5% of them will not. In other words, you have 95% confidence that the population mean is somewhere in your interval.

Consider once again the first sample discussed in this section. A sample of $n = 25$ boxes had a sample mean of 362.3 grams. The interval constructed to estimate μ is:

$$362.3 \pm (1.96)(15) / (\sqrt{25})$$
$$362.3 \pm 5.88$$
$$356.42 \leq \mu \leq 368.18$$

The interval from 356.42 to 368.18 is referred to as a 95% confidence interval. The following box contains an interpretation of the interval that most business professionals will understand. (For a technical discussion of different ways to interpret confidence intervals, see Reference 3.)

> "I am 95% confident that the mean amount of cereal in the population of boxes is somewhere between 356.42 and 368.18 grams."

To assist in your understanding of the meaning of the confidence interval, the following example concerns the order-filling process at a Web site. Filling orders consists of several steps including receiving an order, picking the parts of the order, checking the order, packing, and shipping the order. The data in the file **Order** consists of the time in minutes to fill orders for a population of 200 on a recent day. Although in practice, the population characteristics are rarely known, for this population of orders, the mean μ is known to be equal to 69.637 minutes and the standard deviation σ is known to be equal to 10.411 minutes. To illustrate how the sample mean and sample standard deviation can vary from one sample to another, 20 different samples of $n = 10$ were selected from the population of 200 orders and the sample mean and sample standard deviation (and other statistics) were calculated for each sample using Minitab. Figure 8.2 shows these results.

FIGURE 8.2

Minitab sample statistics and 95% confidence intervals for 20 samples of $n = 10$ selected from the population of 200 orders

Variable	Count	Mean	StDev	Minimum	Median	Maximum	Range	95% CI
Sample 1	10	74.15	13.39	56.10	76.85	97.70	41.60	(67.6973, 80.6027)
Sample 2	10	61.10	10.60	46.80	61.35	79.50	32.70	(54.6473, 67.5527)
Sample 3	10	74.36	6.50	62.50	74.50	84.00	21.50	(67.9073, 80.8127)
Sample 4	10	70.40	12.80	47.20	70.95	84.00	36.80	(63.9473, 76.8527)
Sample 5	10	62.18	10.85	47.10	59.70	84.00	36.90	(55.7273, 68.6327)
Sample 6	10	67.03	9.68	51.10	69.60	83.30	32.20	(60.5773, 73.4827)
Sample 7	10	69.03	8.81	56.60	68.85	83.70	27.10	(62.5773, 75.4827)
Sample 8	10	72.30	11.52	54.20	71.35	87.00	32.80	(65.8473, 78.7527)
Sample 9	10	68.18	14.10	50.10	69.95	86.20	36.10	(61.7273, 74.6327)
Sample 10	10	66.67	9.08	57.10	64.65	86.10	29.00	(60.2173, 73.1227)
Sample 11	10	72.42	9.76	59.60	74.65	86.10	26.50	(65.9673, 78.8727)
Sample 12	10	76.26	11.69	50.10	80.60	87.00	36.90	(69.8073, 82.7127)
Sample 13	10	65.74	12.11	47.10	62.15	86.10	39.00	(59.2873, 72.1927)
Sample 14	10	69.99	10.97	51.00	73.40	84.60	33.60	(63.5373, 76.4427)
Sample 15	10	75.76	8.60	61.10	75.05	87.80	26.70	(69.3073, 82.2127)
Sample 16	10	67.94	9.19	56.70	67.70	87.80	31.10	(61.4873, 74.3927)
Sample 17	10	71.05	10.48	50.10	71.15	86.20	36.10	(64.5973, 77.5027)
Sample 18	10	71.68	7.96	55.60	72.35	82.60	27.00	(65.2273, 78.1327)
Sample 19	10	70.97	9.83	54.40	70.05	84.60	30.20	(64.5173, 77.4227)
Sample 20	10	74.48	8.80	62.00	76.25	85.70	23.70	(68.0273, 80.9327)

From Figure 8.2, you can see the following:

1. The sample statistics differ from sample to sample. The sample means vary from 61.10 to 76.26 minutes, the sample standard deviations vary from 6.50 to 14.10 minutes, the sample medians vary from 59.70 to 76.85 minutes, and the sample ranges vary from 21.50 to 41.60 minutes.

2. Some of the sample means are greater than the population mean of 69.637 minutes, and some of the sample means are less than the population mean.
3. Some of the sample standard deviations are greater than the population standard deviation of 10.411 minutes, and some of the sample standard deviations are less than the population standard deviation.
4. The variation in the sample range from sample to sample is much more than the variation in the sample standard deviation.

The fact that sample statistics vary from sample to sample is called sampling error. Sampling error is the variation that occurs due to selecting a single sample from the population. The size of the sampling error is primarily based on the amount of variation in the population and on the sample size. Larger samples have less sampling error than small samples, but will cost more.

The last column of Figure 8.2 contains twenty 95% confidence interval estimates of the population mean order-filling time based on the results of those 20 samples of $n = 10$. Begin by examining the first sample selected. The sample mean is 74.15 minutes, and the interval estimate for the population mean is $67.6973 - 80.6027$ minutes. In a typical study, you would not know for sure whether this interval estimate is correct because you rarely know the value of the population mean. However, for this example *concerning the order-filling times*, the population mean is known to be 69.637 minutes. If you examine the interval $67.6973 - 80.6027$ minutes, you see that the population mean of 69.637 minutes is located *between* these lower and upper limits. Thus, the first sample provides a correct estimate of the population mean in the form of an interval estimate. Looking over the other 19 samples, you see that similar results occur for all the other samples *except* for samples 2, 5, and 12. For each of the intervals generated (other than samples 2, 5, and 12), the population mean of 69.637 minutes is located *somewhere* within the interval.

For sample 2, the sample mean is 61.10 minutes, and the interval is 54.6473 to 67.5527 minutes; for sample 5, the sample mean is 62.18, and the interval is between 55.7273 and 68.6327; whereas for sample 12, the sample mean is 76.26, and the interval is between 69.8073 and 82.7127 minutes. The population mean of 69.637 minutes is *not* located within any of these intervals, and any estimate of the population mean made using these intervals is incorrect.

In some situations, you might want a higher degree of confidence (such as 99%) of including the population mean within the interval. In other cases, you might accept less confidence (such as 90%) of correctly estimating the population mean. In general, the **level of confidence** is symbolized by $(1 - \alpha) \times 100\%$, where α is the proportion in the tails of the distribution that is outside the confidence interval. The proportion in the upper tail of the distribution is $\alpha/2$, and the proportion in the lower tail of the distribution is $\alpha/2$. You use Equation (8.1) to construct a $(1 - \alpha) \times 100\%$ confidence interval estimate of the mean with σ known.

Confidence Interval for the Mean (σ Known)

$$\bar{X} \pm Z_{\alpha/2} \frac{\sigma}{\sqrt{n}}$$

or

$$\bar{X} - Z_{\alpha/2} \frac{\sigma}{\sqrt{n}} \leq \mu \leq \bar{X} + Z_{\alpha/2} \frac{\sigma}{\sqrt{n}} \tag{8.1}$$

where $Z_{\alpha/2}$ is the value corresponding to an upper-tail probability of $\alpha/2$ from the standardized normal distribution (i.e., a cumulative area of $1 - \alpha/2$).

The value of $Z_{\alpha/2}$ needed for constructing a confidence interval is called the **critical value** for the distribution. 95% confidence corresponds to an α value of 0.05. The critical Z value corresponding to a cumulative area of 0.975 is 1.96 because there is 0.025 in the upper tail of the distribution and the cumulative area less than $Z = 1.96$ is 0.975.

There is a different critical value for each level of confidence, $1 - \alpha$. A level of confidence of 95% leads to a Z value of 1.96 (see Figure 8.3). 99% confidence corresponds to an α value of 0.01. The Z value is approximately 2.58 because the upper-tail area is 0.005 and the cumulative area less than $Z = 2.58$ is 0.995 (see Figure 8.4).

FIGURE 8.3

Normal curve for determining the Z value needed for 95% confidence

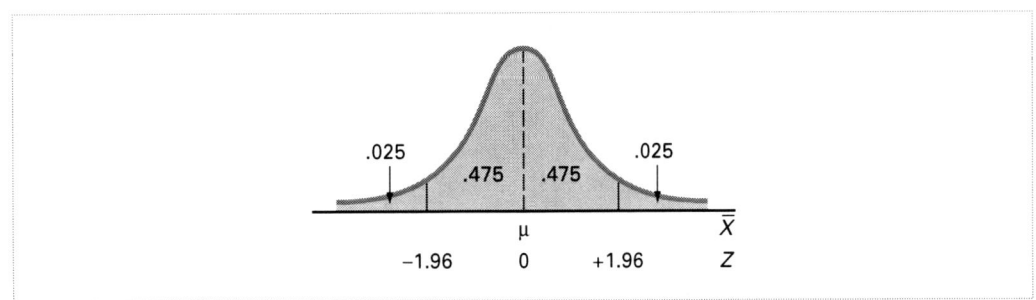

FIGURE 8.4

Normal curve for determining the Z value needed for 99% confidence

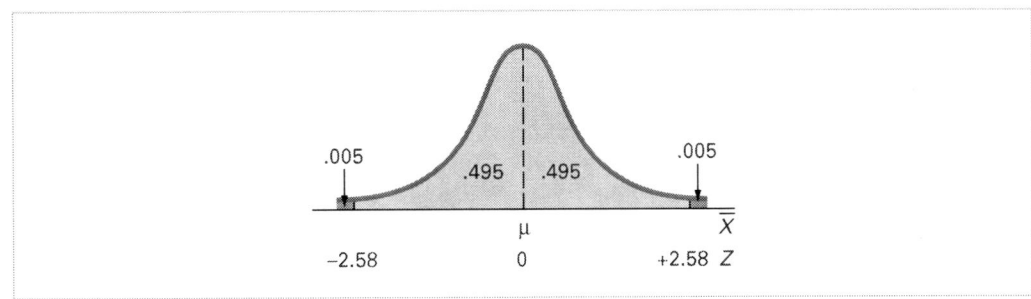

Now that various levels of confidence have been considered, why not make the confidence level as close to 100% as possible? Before doing so, you need to realize that any increase in the level of confidence is achieved only by widening (and making less precise) the confidence interval. There is no "free lunch" here. You would have more confidence that the population mean is within a broader range of values; however, this might make the interpretation of the confidence interval less useful. The trade-off between the width of the confidence interval and the level of confidence is discussed in greater depth in the context of determining the sample size in Section 8.4. Example 8.1 illustrates the application of the confidence interval estimate.

EXAMPLE 8.1

ESTIMATING THE MEAN PAPER LENGTH WITH 95% CONFIDENCE

A paper manufacturer has a production process that operates continuously throughout an entire production shift. The paper is expected to have a mean length of 11 inches, and the standard deviation of the length is 0.02 inch. At periodic intervals, a sample is selected to determine whether the mean paper length is still equal to 11 inches or whether something has gone wrong in the production process to change the length of the paper produced. You select a random sample of 100 sheets, and the mean paper length is 10.998 inches. Construct a 95% confidence interval estimate for the population mean paper length.

SOLUTION Using Equation (8.1) on page 296, with $Z_{\alpha/2} = 1.96$ for 95% confidence,

$$\bar{X} \pm Z_{\alpha/2}\frac{\sigma}{\sqrt{n}} = 10.998 \pm (1.96)\frac{0.02}{\sqrt{100}}$$

$$= 10.998 \pm 0.00392$$

$$10.99408 \le \mu \le 11.00192$$

Thus, with 95% confidence, you conclude that the population mean is between 10.99408 and 11.00192 inches. Because the interval includes 11, the value indicating that the production process is working properly, you have no reason to believe that anything is wrong with the production process.

To see the effect of using a 99% confidence interval, examine Example 8.2.

EXAMPLE 8.2   ESTIMATING THE MEAN PAPER LENGTH WITH 99% CONFIDENCE

Construct a 99% confidence interval estimate for the population mean paper length.

SOLUTION Using Equation (8.1) on page 296, with $Z_{\alpha/2} = 2.58$ for 99% confidence,

$$\bar{X} \pm Z_{\alpha/2}\frac{\sigma}{\sqrt{n}} = 10.998 \pm (2.58)\frac{0.02}{\sqrt{100}}$$

$$= 10.998 \pm 0.00516$$

$$10.99284 \le \mu \le 11.00316$$

Once again, because 11 is included within this wider interval, you have no reason to believe that anything is wrong with the production process.

As discussed in Section 7.4, the sampling distribution of the sample mean $\bar{X}$ is normally distributed if the population for your characteristic of interest X is a normal distribution. And, if the population of X is not a normal distribution, the Central Limit Theorem almost always ensures that $\bar{X}$ is normally distributed when n is large. However, when dealing with a small sample size and a population of X that is not a normal distribution, the sampling distribution of $\bar{X}$ is not normally distributed and therefore the confidence interval discussed in this section is inappropriate. In practice, however, as long as the sample size is large enough and the population is not very skewed, you can use the confidence interval defined in Equation (8.1) to estimate the population mean when σ is known. To assess the assumption of normality, you can evaluate the shape of the sample data by using a histogram, stem-and-leaf display, boxplot, or normal probability plot.

Can You Ever *Really* Know Sigma?

From the Authors' Desktop

Section 8.1 discusses the concept of the confidence interval estimate, how to develop it, and how to interpret it. The discussion limited itself to the case where the population standard deviation, sigma, is known. But, can you ever *really* know sigma? Probably not, but it is much easier to explain the confidence interval estimate using an example where the population standard deviation, sigma, is known. If sigma is known, then you can use the normal distribution, with which you are already famil-

iar from Chapters 6 and 7. In Section 8.2, you will learn how to construct confidence interval estimates when sigma is not known, and you will use the *t* distribution instead of the normal distribution.

In virtually all real-world business applications, you do not know the standard deviation of the population. If, for a particular case, you knew the population standard deviation, you would also already know (or could compute) the population mean. Why is that so? You could only know the population standard

deviation if you have access to all of the population data. And if you knew all of the population data, you could compute the population mean. There would be no need to employ the *inductive* reasoning of inferential statistics to estimate the population mean.

So why study the confidence interval estimate of the mean when sigma is known? Because it is a good way to understand the confidence interval concept—a very important concept to know when studying the rest of this book.

PROBLEMS FOR SECTION 8.1

Learning the Basics

8.1 If $\bar{X} = 85$, $\sigma = 8$, and $n = 64$, construct a 95% confidence interval estimate of the population mean, μ.

8.2 If $\bar{X} = 125$, $\sigma = 24$, and $n = 36$, construct a 99% confidence interval estimate of the population mean, μ.

8.3 A market researcher collects a simple random sample of $n = 100$ customers from its population of two million customers. After analyzing the sample, she states that she has 95% confidence that the mean annual income of its two million customers is between $70,000 and $85,000. Explain the meaning of this statement.

8.4 If you were to collect a set of data, either from an entire population or from a random sample taken from that population:
a. Which statistical measure would you compute first: the mean or the standard deviation? Explain.

b. What does your answer to (a) tell you about the "practicality" of using the confidence interval estimate formula given in Equation (8.1)?

8.5 Consider the confidence interval estimate discussed in Problem 8.3. Suppose that the population mean annual income is $71,000. Is the confidence interval estimate stated in Problem 8.3 correct? Explain.

8.6 You are working as an assistant to the dean of institutional research at your university. She wants to survey members of the alumni association who obtained their baccalaureate degrees 5 years ago to learn what their starting salaries were in their first full-time job after receiving their degrees. A sample of 100 alumni is to be randomly selected from the list of 2,500 graduates in that class. If her goal is to construct a 95% confidence interval estimate of the population mean starting salary, why is it unlikely that you will be able to use Equation (8.1) on page 296 for this purpose? Explain.

8.2 CONFIDENCE INTERVAL ESTIMATION FOR THE MEAN (σ UNKNOWN)

Just as the mean of the population, μ, is usually unknown, you virtually never know the standard deviation of the population, σ. Therefore, you need to construct a confidence interval estimate of μ, using the sample statistic S as an estimate of the population parameter σ.

Student's *t* Distribution

At the beginning of the twentieth century, William S. Gosset, a statistician for Guinness Breweries in Ireland (see reference 4), wanted to make inferences about the mean when σ was unknown. Because Guinness employees were not permitted to publish research work under their own names, Gosset adopted the pseudonym "Student." The distribution that he developed is known as **Student's *t* distribution** and is commonly referred to as the *t* distribution.

If the random variable *X* is normally distributed, then the following statistic has a *t* distribution with *n* − 1 **degrees of freedom**:

$$t = \frac{\bar{X} - \mu}{\dfrac{S}{\sqrt{n}}}$$

This expression has the same form as the *Z* statistic in Equation (7.4) on page 272, except that *S* is used to estimate the unknown σ.

Properties of the *t* Distribution

The *t* distribution looks very similar to the standardized normal distribution. Both distributions are symmetrical and bell shaped with means and medians equal to zero. However, the *t* distribution has more area in the tails and less in the center than does the standardized normal distribution (see Figure 8.5). Because *S* is used to estimate the unknown σ, the values of *t* are more variable than those for *Z*.

FIGURE 8.5

Standardized normal distribution and *t* distribution for 5 degrees of freedom

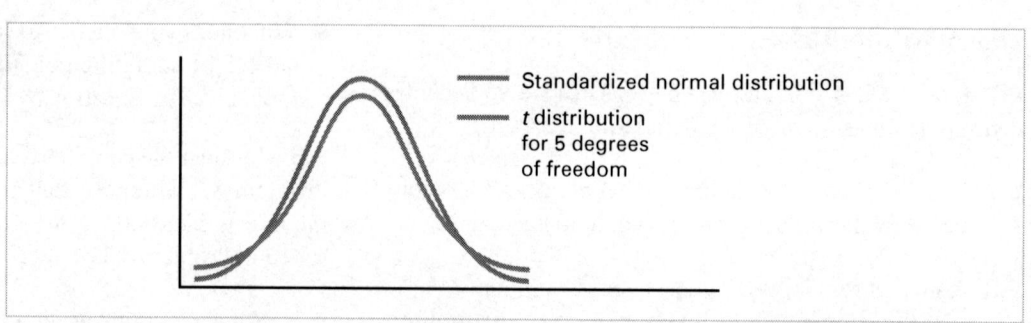

Standardized normal distribution

t distribution for 5 degrees of freedom

The degrees of freedom, *n* − 1, are directly related to the sample size, *n*. The concept of *degrees of freedom* is discussed further on pages 301 through 302. As the sample size and degrees of freedom increase, *S* becomes a better estimate of σ, and the *t* distribution gradually approaches the standardized normal distribution, until the two are virtually identical. With a sample size of about 120 or more, *S* estimates σ precisely enough so that there is little difference between the *t* and *Z* distributions.

As stated earlier, the *t* distribution assumes that the random variable *X* is normally distributed. In practice, however, when the sample size is large enough and the population is not very skewed, in most cases you can use the *t* distribution to estimate the population mean when σ is unknown. When dealing with a small sample size and a skewed population distribution, the confidence interval estimate may not provide a valid estimate of the population mean. To assess the assumption of normality, you can evaluate the shape of the sample data by using a histogram, stem-and-leaf display, boxplot, or normal probability plot. However, the usefulness of any of these graphs to evaluate normality is limited when you have a small sample size.

You find the critical values of *t* for the appropriate degrees of freedom from the table of the *t* distribution (see Table E.3). The columns of the table present the most commonly needed cumulative probabilities and corresponding upper-tail areas. The rows of the table represent the degrees of freedom. The critical *t* values are found in the cells of the table. For example, with 99 degrees of freedom, if you want 95% confidence, you find the appropriate value of *t*, as shown in Table 8.1. The 95% confidence level means that 2.5% of the values (an area of 0.025) are in each tail of the distribution. Looking in the column for a cumulative probability of 0.975 and an upper-tail area of 0.025 in the row corresponding to 99 degrees of freedom gives you a critical value for *t* of 1.9842 (see Figure 8.6). Because *t* is a symmetrical distribution with a mean of 0, if the upper-tail value is +1.9842, the value for the lower-tail area (lower 0.025) is −1.9842. A *t* value of −1.9842 means that the probability that *t* is less than −1.9842 is 0.025, or 2.5%.

 Note that for a 95% confidence interval, you will always use a cumulative probability of 0.975 and an upper-tail area of 0.025. Similarly, for a 99% confidence interval, use 0.995 and 0.005, and for a 90% confidence interval use 0.95 and 0.05.

TABLE 8.1

Determining the Critical Value from the *t* Table for an Area of 0.025 in Each Tail with 99 Degrees of Freedom

	Cumulative Probabilities					
	.75	.90	.95	.975	.99	.995
	Upper Tail Areas					
Degrees of Freedom	.25	.10	.05	.025	.01	.005
1	1.0000	3.0777	6.3138	12.7062	31.8207	63.6574
2	0.8165	1.8856	2.9200	4.3027	6.9646	9.9248
3	0.7649	1.6377	2.3534	3.1824	4.5407	5.8409
4	0.7407	1.5332	2.1318	2.7764	3.7469	4.6041
5	0.7267	1.4759	2.0150	2.5706	3.3649	4.0322
.	.	.	.	.	.	.
.	.	.	.	.	.	.
.	.	.	.	.	.	.
96	0.6771	1.2904	1.6609	1.9850	2.3658	2.6280
97	0.6770	1.2903	1.6607	1.9847	2.3654	2.6275
98	0.6770	1.2902	1.6606	1.9845	2.3650	2.6269
99	0.6770	1.2902	1.6604	1.9842	2.3646	2.6264
100	0.6770	1.2901	1.6602	1.9840	2.3642	2.6259

Source: *Extracted from Table E.3.*

FIGURE 8.6

t distribution with 99 degrees of freedom

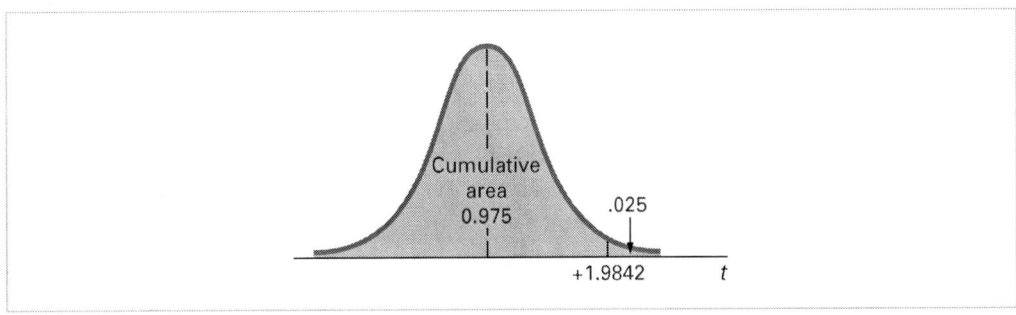

The Concept of Degrees of Freedom

In Chapter 3, you learned that the numerator of the sample variance, S^2 [see Equation (3.6) on page 98], requires the computation of

$$\sum_{i=1}^{n}(X_i - \bar{X})^2$$

In order to compute S^2, you first need to know $\bar{X}$. Therefore, only $n-1$ of the sample values are free to vary. This means that you have $n-1$ degrees of freedom. For example, suppose a sample of five values has a mean of 20. How many values do you need to know before you can determine the remainder of the values? The fact that $n=5$ and $\bar{X}=20$ also tells you that

$$\sum_{i=1}^{n} X_i = 100$$

because

$$\frac{\sum_{i=1}^{n} X_i}{n} = \bar{X}$$

Thus, when you know four of the values, the fifth one is *not* free to vary because the sum must add to 100. For example, if four of the values are 18, 24, 19, and 16, the fifth value must be 23 so that the sum equals 100.

The Confidence Interval Statement

Equation (8.2) defines the $(1-\alpha) \times 100\%$ confidence interval estimate for the mean with σ unknown.

Confidence Interval for the Mean (σ Unknown)

$$\bar{X} \pm t_{\alpha/2} \frac{S}{\sqrt{n}}$$

or

$$\bar{X} - t_{\alpha/2} \frac{S}{\sqrt{n}} \leq \mu \leq \bar{X} + t_{\alpha/2} \frac{S}{\sqrt{n}} \qquad (8.2)$$

where $t_{\alpha/2}$ is the critical value corresponding to an upper-tail probability of $\alpha/2$ from the t distribution with $n-1$ degrees of freedom (i.e., a cumulative area of $1-\alpha/2$).

To illustrate the application of the confidence interval estimate for the mean when the standard deviation, σ, is unknown, recall the Saxon Home Improvement Company Using Statistics scenario presented on page 292. You wanted to estimate the mean dollar amount listed on the sales invoices for the month. You select a sample of 100 sales invoices from the population of sales invoices during the month, and the sample mean of the 100 sales invoices is $110.27, with a sample standard deviation of $28.95. For 95% confidence, the critical value from the t distribution (as shown in Table 8.1) is 1.9842. Using Equation (8.2),

$$\bar{X} \pm t_{\alpha/2} \frac{S}{\sqrt{n}}$$

$$= 110.27 \pm (1.9842) \frac{28.95}{\sqrt{100}}$$

$$= 110.27 \pm 5.74$$

$$\$104.53 \leq \mu \leq \$116.01$$

A Microsoft Excel worksheet for these data is presented in Figure 8.7.

FIGURE 8.7

Microsoft Excel worksheet to compute a confidence interval estimate for the mean sales invoice amount for the Saxon Home Improvement Company

See Section E8.2 or P8.2 to create this. (Minitab users, see Section M8.2 to create the equivalent results.)

	A	B	
1	Estimate for the Mean Sales Invoice Amount		
2			
3	Data		
4	Sample Standard Deviation	28.95	
5	Sample Mean	110.27	
6	Sample Size	100	
7	Confidence Level	95%	
8			
9	Intermediate Calculations		
10	Standard Error of the Mean	2.8950	=B4/SQRT(B6)
11	Degrees of Freedom	99	=B6 - 1
12	t Value	1.9842	=TINV(1 - B7, B11)
13	Interval Half Width	5.7443	=B12 * B10
14			
15	Confidence Interval		
16	Interval Lower Limit	104.53	=B5 - B13
17	Interval Upper Limit	116.01	=B5 + B13

Thus, with 95% confidence, you conclude that the mean amount of all the sales invoices is between $104.53 and $116.01. The 95% confidence level indicates that if you selected all possible samples of 100 (something that is never done in practice), 95% of the intervals developed would include the population mean somewhere within the interval. The validity of this confidence interval estimate depends on the assumption of normality for the distribution of the amount of the sales invoices. With a sample of 100, the normality assumption is not overly restrictive (see the Central Limit Theorem on page 274), and the use of the t distribution is likely appropriate. Example 8.3 further illustrates how you construct the confidence interval for a mean when the population standard deviation is unknown.

EXAMPLE 8.3

ESTIMATING THE MEAN FORCE REQUIRED TO BREAK ELECTRIC INSULATORS

A manufacturing company produces electric insulators. If the insulators break when in use, a short circuit is likely. To test the strength of the insulators, you carry out destructive testing to determine how much *force* is required to break the insulators. You measure force by observing how many pounds are applied to the insulator before it breaks. Table 8.2 lists 30 values from this experiment, which are located in the file **Force**. Construct a 95% confidence interval estimate for the population mean force required to break the insulator.

TABLE 8.2

Force (in Pounds) Required to Break the Insulator

1,870	1,728	1,656	1,610	1,634	1,784	1,522	1,696	1,592	1,662
1,866	1,764	1,734	1,662	1,734	1,774	1,550	1,756	1,762	1,866
1,820	1,744	1,788	1,688	1,810	1,752	1,680	1,810	1,652	1,736

SOLUTION Figure 8.8 shows that the sample mean is $\bar{X}$ = 1,723.4 pounds and the sample standard deviation is S = 89.55 pounds. Using Equation (8.2) on page 302 to construct the confidence interval, you need to determine the critical value from the t table using the row for 29 degrees of freedom. For 95% confidence, you use the column corresponding to an upper-tail area of 0.025 and a cumulative probability of 0.975. From Table E.3, you see that $t_{\alpha/2} = 2.0452$. Thus, using $\bar{X} = 1{,}723$, $S = 89.55$, $n = 30$, and $t_{\alpha/2} = 2.0452$,

$$\bar{X} \pm t_{\alpha/2} \frac{S}{\sqrt{n}}$$

$$= 1{,}723.4 \pm (2.0452) \frac{89.55}{\sqrt{30}}$$

$$= 1{,}723.4 \pm 33.44$$

$$1{,}689.96 \leq \mu \leq 1{,}756.84$$

FIGURE 8.8

Minitab confidence interval estimate for the mean amount of force required to break electric insulators

See Section M8.2 to create this. (Use Section E8.2 or P8.2 to create the Excel equivalent.)

One-Sample T: Force

Variable	N	Mean	StDev	SE Mean	95% CI
Force	30	1723.4	89.6	16.3	(1690.0, 1756.8)

You conclude with 95% confidence that the mean breaking force required for the population of insulators is between 1,689.96 and 1,756.84 pounds. The validity of this confidence interval estimate depends on the assumption that the force required is normally distributed. Remember, however, that you can slightly relax this assumption for large sample sizes. Thus, with a sample of 30, you can use the *t* distribution even if the amount of force required is only slightly left-skewed. From the normal probability plot displayed in Figure 8.9 or the boxplot displayed in Figure 8.10, the amount of force required appears only slightly left-skewed. Thus, the *t* distribution is appropriate for these data.

FIGURE 8.9

Minitab normal probability plot for the amount of force required to break electric insulators

See Section M6.2 to create this. (PHStat2 users, see Section P6.2 to create an equivalent chart.)

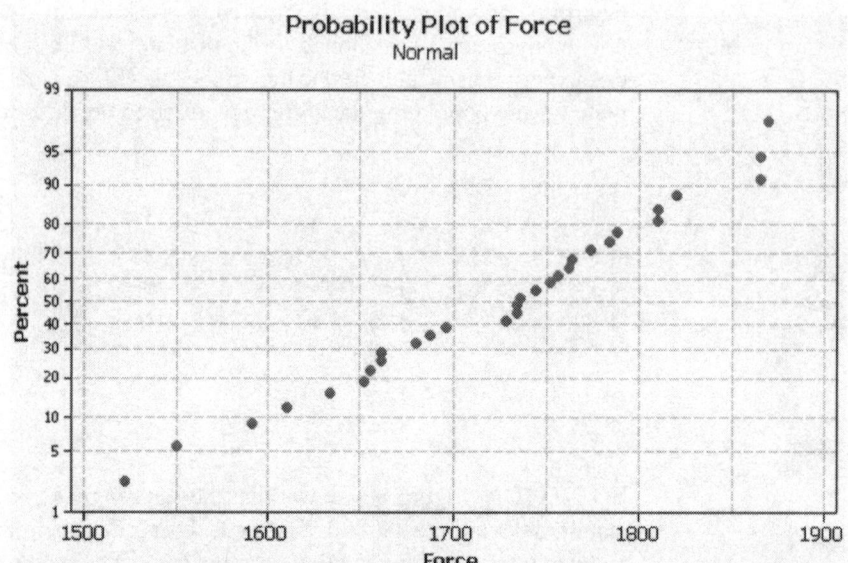

Probability Plot of Force
Normal

FIGURE 8.10

Minitab boxplot for the amount of force required to break electric insulators

See Section M3.4 to create this. (Microsoft Excel users, see Section E3.3 or P3.1 to create an equivalent chart.)

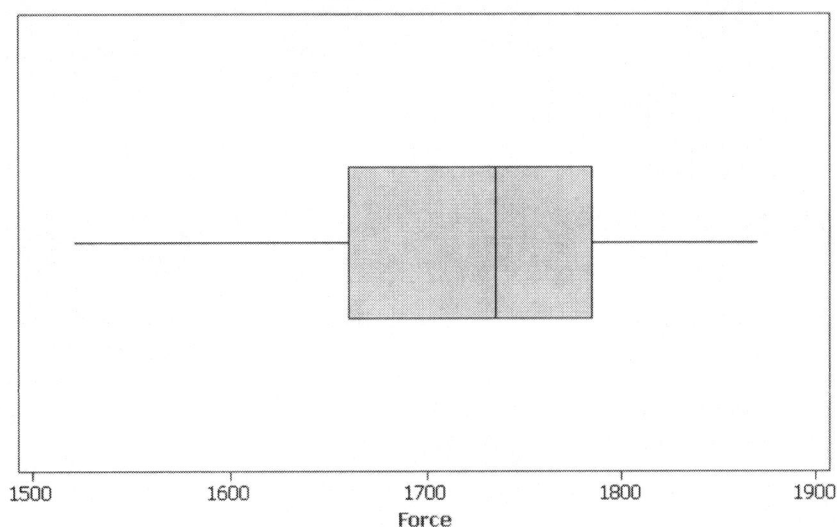

The interpretation of the confidence interval when σ is unknown is the same as when σ is known. To illustrate the fact that the confidence interval for the mean varies more when σ is unknown, return to the example concerning the order-filling times discussed in Section 8.1 on page 295. Suppose that, in this case, you do not know the population standard deviation. Figure 8.11 shows the results for each of 20 samples of n = 10 orders.

FIGURE 8.11

Minitab confidence interval estimates of the mean for 20 samples of n = 10 selected from the population of 200 orders with σ unknown

See Section M8.2 to create this. (Microsoft Excel users, see Section E8.2 or P8.2 to create equivalent results.)

Variable	N	Mean	StDev	SE Mean	95% CI
Sample 1	10	71.64	7.58	2.40	(66.22, 77.06)
Sample 2	10	67.22	10.95	3.46	(59.39, 75.05)
Sample 3	10	67.97	14.83	4.69	(57.36, 78.58)
Sample 4	10	73.90	10.59	3.35	(66.33, 81.47)
Sample 5	10	67.11	11.12	3.52	(59.15, 75.07)
Sample 6	10	68.12	10.83	3.43	(60.37, 75.87)
Sample 7	10	65.80	10.85	3.43	(58.03, 73.57)
Sample 8	10	77.58	11.04	3.49	(69.68, 85.48)
Sample 9	10	66.69	11.45	3.62	(58.50, 74.88)
Sample 10	10	62.55	8.58	2.71	(56.41, 68.69)
Sample 11	10	71.12	12.82	4.05	(61.95, 80.29)
Sample 12	10	70.55	10.52	3.33	(63.02, 78.08)
Sample 13	10	65.51	8.16	2.58	(59.67, 71.35)
Sample 14	10	64.90	7.55	2.39	(59.50, 70.30)
Sample 15	10	66.22	11.21	3.54	(58.20, 74.24)
Sample 16	10	70.43	10.21	3.23	(63.12, 77.74)
Sample 17	10	72.04	6.25	1.98	(67.57, 76.51)
Sample 18	10	73.91	11.29	3.57	(65.83, 81.99)
Sample 19	10	71.49	9.76	3.09	(64.51, 78.47)
Sample 20	10	70.15	10.84	3.43	(62.39, 77.91)

From Figure 8.11, observe that the standard deviation of the samples varies from 6.25 (sample 17) to 14.83 (sample 3). Thus, the width of the confidence interval developed varies from 8.94 in sample 17 to 21.22 in sample 3. Because you know that the population mean order time $\mu = 69.637$ minutes, you can see that the interval for sample 8 (69.68 – 85.48) and the interval for sample 10 (56.41 – 68.69) do not correctly estimate the population mean. All the other intervals correctly estimate the population mean. Once again, remember that in practice you select only one sample of a given size and you have no way of knowing for sure whether this one sample provides a confidence interval that includes the population mean.

PROBLEMS FOR SECTION 8.2

Learning the Basics

8.7 If $\bar{X} = 75$, $S = 24$, and $n = 36$, and assuming that the population is normally distributed, construct a 95% confidence interval estimate of the population mean, μ.

8.8 Determine the critical value of t in each of the following circumstances:
a. $1 - \alpha = 0.95$, $n = 10$
b. $1 - \alpha = 0.99$, $n = 10$
c. $1 - \alpha = 0.95$, $n = 32$
d. $1 - \alpha = 0.95$, $n = 65$
e. $1 - \alpha = 0.90$, $n = 16$

8.9 Assuming that the population is normally distributed, construct a 95% confidence interval estimate for the population mean for each of the following samples:

Sample A: 1, 1, 1, 1, 8, 8, 8, 8
Sample B: 1, 2, 3, 4, 5, 6, 7, 8

Explain why these two samples produce different confidence intervals even though they have the same mean and range.

8.10 Assuming that the population is normally distributed, construct a 95% confidence interval for the population mean, based on the following sample of size $n = 7$: 1, 2, 3, 4, 5, 6, and 20. Change the number 20 to 7 and recalculate the confidence interval. Using these results, describe the effect of an outlier (i.e., an extreme value) on the confidence interval.

Applying the Concepts

8.11 A stationery store wants to estimate the mean retail value of greeting cards that it has in its inventory. A random sample of 100 greeting cards indicates a mean value of $2.55 and a standard deviation of $0.44.
a. Assuming a normal distribution, construct a 95% confidence interval estimate of the mean value of all greeting cards in the store's inventory.
b. Suppose there were 2,500 greeting cards in the store's inventory. How are the results in (a) useful in assisting the store owner to estimate the total value of her inventory?

SELF Test **8.12** Southside Hospital in Bay Shore, New York, commonly conducts stress tests to study the heart muscle after a person has a heart attack. Members of the diagnostic imaging department conducted a quality improvement project to try to reduce the turnaround time for stress tests. Turnaround time is defined as the time from when the test is ordered to when the radiologist signs off on the test results. Initially, the mean turnaround time for a stress test was 68 hours. After incorporating changes into the stress-test process, the quality improvement team collected a sample of 50 turnaround times. In this sample, the mean turnaround time was 32 hours, with a standard deviation of 9 hours (extracted from E. Godin, D. Raven, C. Sweetapple, and F. R. Del Guidice, "Faster Test Results," *Quality Progress*, January 2004, 37(1), pp. 33–39).
a. Construct a 95% confidence interval estimate for the population mean turnaround time.
b. Interpret the interval constructed in (a).
c. Do you think the quality improvement project was a success?

8.13 The U.S. Department of Transportation requires tire manufacturers to provide tire performance information on the sidewall of the tire to better inform prospective customers when making purchasing decisions. One very important measure of tire performance is the tread wear index, which indicates the tire's resistance to tread wear compared with a tire graded with a base of 100. This means that a tire with a grade of 200 should last twice as long, on average, as a tire graded with a base of 100. A consumer organization wants to estimate the actual tread wear index of a brand name of tires that claims "graded 200" on the sidewall of the tire. A random sample of $n = 18$ indicates a sample mean tread wear index of 195.3 and a sample standard deviation of 21.4.
a. Assuming that the population of tread wear indexes is normally distributed, construct a 95% confidence interval estimate of the population mean tread wear index for tires produced by this manufacturer under this brand name.
b. Do you think that the consumer organization should accuse the manufacturer of producing tires that do not meet the performance information provided on the sidewall of the tire? Explain.
c. Explain why an observed tread wear index of 210 for a particular tire is not unusual, even though it is outside the confidence interval developed in (a).

8.14 The data in the file **Movieprices** contain the price for two tickets with online service charges, large popcorn, and two medium soft drinks at a sample of six theater chains:

$36.15 $31.00 $35.05 $40.25 $33.75 $43.00

Source: *Extracted from K. Kelly, "The Multiplex Under Siege," The Wall Street Journal, December 24–25, 2005, pp. P1, P5.*

a. Construct a 95% confidence interval estimate for the population mean price for two tickets with online service charges, large popcorn, and two medium soft drinks, assuming a normal distribution.

b. Interpret the interval constructed in (a).

8.15 The data in the file **Sedans** represents the overall miles per gallon (MPG) of 2007 family sedans (4 cylinder).

Model	MPG	Model	MPG
Volkswagen Passat	24	Mazda	23
Nissan Altima	25	Ford Fusion	23
Toyota Camry Hybrid	34	Mercury Milan	23
Honda Accord	24	Toyota Prius	44
Kia Optima	23	Chevrolet Malibu	24
Toyota Camry LE	24	Mitsubishi Galant	23
Subaru Legacy	18	Pontiac G6	22
Hyundai Sonata	23	Chrysler Sebring	23

Source: *Extracted from "Vehicle Ratings," Consumer Reports, April 2007, pp. 36–37.*

a. Construct a 95% confidence interval estimate for the population mean miles per gallon of 2007 family sedans (4 cylinder) assuming a normal distribution.

b. Interpret the interval constructed in (a).

c. Compare the results in (a) to those in Problem 8.16(a).

8.16 The data in the file **SUV** represents the overall miles per gallon (MPG) of 2007 small SUVs.

Model	MPG	Model	MPG
Toyota RAV4 6-cyl	22	Mazda Tribute	18
Hyundai Santa Fe	18	Mercury	18
Toyota RAV4 4-cyl	23	Mariner Luxury	
Subaru Forester	20	Nissan Xterra	17
Sports 2.5 XT		Honda Element	21
Honda CR-V	21	Suzuki Grand Vitara	18
Subaru Forester	22	Chevrolet Equinox	18
Sports 2.5 X		Pontiac Torrent	18
Mitsubishi Outlander	19	Jeep Compass	22
Hyundai Tucson	18	Saturn Vue	19
Kia Sportage	18	Saturn Vue Hybrid	24
Ford Escape Hybrid	26	Kia Sorento	15
Mercury	26	Jeep Liberty	15
Mariner Hybrid		Toyota FJ Cruiser	17
Suzuki XL-7	17	Dodge Nitro	16
Ford Escape	18	Jeep Wrangler	15

Source: *Extracted from "Vehicle Ratings," Consumer Reports, April 2007, pp. 42–43.*

a. Construct a 95% confidence interval estimate for the population mean miles per gallon of 2007 small SUVs assuming a normal distribution.

b. Interpret the interval constructed in (a).

c. Compare the results in (a) to those in Problem 8.15(a).

8.17 The data in the file **Chicken** represent the total fat, in grams per serving, for a sample of 20 chicken sandwiches from fast-food chains. The data are as follows:

7	8	4	5	16	20	20	24	19	30
23	30	25	19	29	29	30	30	40	56

Source: *Extracted from "Fast Food: Adding Health to the Menu," Consumer Reports, September 2004, pp. 28–31.*

a. Construct a 95% confidence interval for the population mean total fat, in grams per serving.

b. Interpret the interval constructed in (a).

c. What assumption must you make about the population distribution in order to construct the confidence interval estimate in (a)?

d. Do you think that the assumption needed in order to construct the confidence interval estimate in (a) is valid? Explain.

8.18 One of the major measures of the quality of service provided by any organization is the speed with which it responds to customer complaints. A large family-held department store selling furniture and flooring, including carpet, had undergone a major expansion in the past several years. In particular, the flooring department had expanded from 2 installation crews to an installation supervisor, a measurer, and 15 installation crews. Last year, there were 50 complaints concerning carpet installation. The following data, also in the file **Furniture**, represent the number of days between the receipt of a complaint and the resolution of the complaint:

54	5	35	137	31	27	152	2	123	81	74	27
11	19	126	110	110	29	61	35	94	31	26	5
12	4	165	32	29	28	29	26	25	1	14	13
13	10	5	27	4	52	30	22	36	26	20	23
33	68										

a. Construct a 95% confidence interval estimate of the population mean number of days between the receipt of a complaint and the resolution of the complaint.

b. What assumption must you make about the population distribution in order to construct the confidence interval estimate in (a)?

c. Do you think that the assumption needed in order to construct the confidence interval estimate in (a) is valid? Explain.

d. What effect might your conclusion in (c) have on the validity of the results in (a)?

8.19 In New York State, savings banks are permitted to sell a form of life insurance called savings bank life insurance

(SBLI). The approval process consists of underwriting, which includes a review of the application, a medical information bureau check, possible requests for additional medical information and medical exams, and a policy compilation stage in which the policy pages are generated and sent to the bank for delivery. The ability to deliver approved policies to customers in a timely manner is critical to the profitability of this service to the bank. During a period of one month, a random sample of 27 approved policies was selected, and the total processing time, in days, was as shown below and stored in the file **Insurance**:

73 19 16 64 28 28 31 90 60 56 31 56 22 18
45 48 17 17 17 91 92 63 50 51 69 16 17

a. Construct a 95% confidence interval estimate of the population mean processing time.
b. What assumption must you make about the population distribution in order to construct the confidence interval estimate in (a)?
c. Do you think that the assumption needed in order to construct the confidence interval estimate in (a) is valid? Explain.

8.20 The data in the file **BatteryLife** represent the battery life (in shots) for a sample of twelve three-pixel digital cameras:

300 180 85 170 380 460 260 35 380 120 110 240

Source: *Extracted from "Cameras: More Features in the Mix,"* Consumer Reports, *July 2005, pp. 14–18.*

a. Construct a 95% confidence interval estimate for the population mean battery life (in shots).
b. What assumption do you need to make about the population of interest to construct the interval in (a)?
c. Given the data presented, do you think the assumption needed in (a) is valid? Explain.

8.21 One operation of a mill is to cut pieces of steel into parts that are used later in the frame for front seats in an automobile. The steel is cut with a diamond saw and requires the resulting parts to be within ±0.005 inch of the length specified by the automobile company. The measurement reported from a sample of 100 steel parts (and stored in the file **Steel**) is the difference, in inches, between the actual length of the steel part, as measured by a laser measurement device, and the specified length of the steel part. For example, the first observation, −0.002, represents a steel part that is 0.002 inch shorter than the specified length.

a. Construct a 95% confidence interval estimate of the population mean difference between the actual length of the steel part and the specified length of the steel part.
b. What assumption must you make about the population distribution in order to construct the confidence interval estimate in (a)?
c. Do you think that the assumption needed in order to construct the confidence interval estimate in (a) is valid? Explain.
d. Compare the conclusions reached in (a) with those of Problem 2.25 on page 47.

8.3   CONFIDENCE INTERVAL ESTIMATION FOR THE PROPORTION

This section extends the concept of the confidence interval to categorical data. Here you are concerned with estimating the proportion of items in a population having a certain characteristic of interest. The unknown population proportion is represented by the Greek letter π. The point estimate for π is the sample proportion, $p = X/n$, where n is the sample size and X is the number of items in the sample having the characteristic of interest. Equation (8.3) defines the confidence interval estimate for the population proportion.

Confidence Interval Estimate for the Proportion

$$p \pm Z_{\alpha/2}\sqrt{\frac{p(1-p)}{n}}$$

or

$$p - Z_{\alpha/2}\sqrt{\frac{p(1-p)}{n}} \le \pi \le p + Z_{\alpha/2}\sqrt{\frac{p(1-p)}{n}} \tag{8.3}$$

where

$$p = \text{sample proportion} = \frac{X}{n} = \frac{\text{Number of items having the characteristic}}{\text{Sample size}}$$

$\pi = \text{population proportion}$

$Z_{\alpha/2} = \text{critical value from the standardized normal distribution}$

$n = \text{sample size}$

Note: To use this interval, the sample size n must be large enough to ensure that both X and $n - X$ are greater than 5.

You can use the confidence interval estimate of the proportion defined in Equation (8.3) to estimate the proportion of sales invoices that contain errors (see the Using Statistics scenario on page 292). Suppose that in a sample of 100 sales invoices, 10 contain errors. Thus, for these data, $p = X/n = 10/100 = 0.10$. Using Equation (8.3) and $Z_{\alpha/2} = 1.96$ for 95% confidence,

$$p \pm Z_{\alpha/2}\sqrt{\frac{p(1-p)}{n}}$$

$$= 0.10 \pm (1.96)\sqrt{\frac{(0.10)(0.90)}{100}}$$

$$= 0.10 \pm (1.96)(0.03)$$

$$= 0.10 \pm 0.0588$$

$$0.0412 \le \pi \le 0.1588$$

Therefore, you have 95% confidence that between 4.12% and 15.88% of all the sales invoices contain errors. Figure 8.12 shows a Microsoft Excel worksheet for these data and Figure 8.13 shows Minitab results.

FIGURE 8.12

Microsoft Excel worksheet to construct a confidence interval estimate for the proportion of sales invoices that contain errors

See Section E8.3 or P8.3 to create this.

	A	B	
1	Proportion of In-Error Sales Invoices		
2			
3	Data		
4	Sample Size	100	
5	Number of Successes	10	
6	Confidence Level	95%	
7			
8	Intermediate Calculations		
9	Sample Proportion	0.1	=B5/B4
10	Z Value	-1.9600	=NORMSINV((1 - B6)/2)
11	Standard Error of the Proportion	0.03	=SQRT(B9 * (1 - B9)/B4)
12	Interval Half Width	0.0588	=ABS(B10 * B11)
13			
14	Confidence Interval		
15	Interval Lower Limit	0.0412	=B9 - B12
16	Interval Upper Limit	0.1588	=B9 + B12

FIGURE 8.13

Minitab confidence interval estimate for the proportion of sales invoices that contain errors

See Section M8.3 to create this.

```
Sample   X    N   Sample p        95% CI
1       10   100  0.100000   (0.041201, 0.158799)

Using the normal approximation.
```

Example 8.4 illustrates another application of a confidence interval estimate for the proportion.

EXAMPLE 8.4

ESTIMATING THE PROPORTION OF NONCONFORMING NEWSPAPERS PRINTED

The operations manager at a large newspaper wants to estimate the proportion of newspapers printed that have a nonconforming attribute, such as excessive ruboff, improper page setup, missing pages, or duplicate pages. A random sample of $n = 200$ newspapers is selected from all the newspapers printed during a single day. In this sample, 35 contain some type of nonconformance. Construct and interpret a 90% confidence interval for the proportion of newspapers printed during the day that have a nonconforming attribute.

SOLUTION Using Equation (8.3),

$$p = \frac{X}{n} = \frac{35}{200} = 0.175, \text{ and with a 90\% level of confidence } Z_{\alpha/2} = 1.645$$

$$p \pm Z_{\alpha/2}\sqrt{\frac{p(1-p)}{n}}$$

$$= 0.175 \pm (1.645)\sqrt{\frac{(0.175)(0.825)}{200}}$$

$$= 0.175 \pm (1.645)(0.0269)$$

$$= 0.175 \pm 0.0442$$

$$0.1308 \leq \pi \leq 0.2192$$

You conclude with 90% confidence that between 13.08% and 21.92% of the newspapers printed on that day have some type of nonconformance.

Equation (8.3) contains a Z statistic because you can use the normal distribution to approximate the binomial distribution when the sample size is sufficiently large. In Example 8.4, the confidence interval using Z provides an excellent approximation for the population proportion because both X and $n - X$ are greater than 5. However, if you do not have a sufficiently large sample size, you should use the binomial distribution rather than Equation (8.3) (see references 1, 2, and 7). The exact confidence intervals for various sample sizes and proportions of successes have been tabulated by Fisher and Yates (reference 2) and can be computed using Minitab.

PROBLEMS FOR SECTION 8.3

Learning the Basics

8.22 If $n = 200$ and $X = 50$, construct a 95% confidence interval estimate of the population proportion.

8.23 If $n = 400$ and $X = 25$, construct a 99% confidence interval estimate of the population proportion.

Applying the Concepts

SELF Test **8.24** The telephone company wants to estimate the proportion of households that would purchase an additional telephone line if it were made available at a substantially reduced installation cost. A random sample of

500 households is selected. The results indicate that 135 of the households would purchase the additional telephone line at a reduced installation cost.

a. Construct a 99% confidence interval estimate of the population proportion of households that would purchase the additional telephone line.

b. How would the manager in charge of promotional programs concerning residential customers use the results in (a)?

8.25 CareerBuilder.com surveyed 1,124 moms who were currently employed full-time. Of the women surveyed, 281 said that they were dissatisfied with their work-life balance, and 495 said that they would take a pay cut to spend more time with their kids (extracted from D. Jones, "Poll Finds Resentment of Flextime," **usatoday.com**, May 11, 2007).

a. Construct a 95% confidence interval estimate for the population proportion of moms employed full-time who are dissatisfied with their work-life balance.

b. Construct a 95% confidence interval estimate for the population proportion of moms employed full-time who would take a pay cut to spend more time with their kids.

c. Write a short summary of the information derived from (a) and (b).

8.26 In a survey conducted for American Express, 27% of small business owners indicated that they never check in with the office when on vacation (extracted from "Snapshots," **usatoday.com**, April 18, 2006). The article did not disclose the sample size used in the study.

a. Suppose that the survey was based on 500 small business owners. Construct a 95% confidence interval estimate for the population proportion of small business owners who never check in with the office when on vacation.

b. Suppose that the survey was based on 1,000 small business owners. Construct a 95% confidence interval estimate for the population proportion of small business owners who never check in with the office when on vacation.

c. Discuss the effect of sample size on the confidence interval estimate.

8.27 The start of the twenty-first century saw many corporate scandals and many individuals lost faith in business. In a 2007 poll conducted by the New York City-based Edelman Public Relations firm, 57% of respondents say they trust business to "do what is right." This percentage was the highest in the annual survey since 2001 (extracted from G. Colvin, "Business is Back!" *Fortune*, May 14, 2007, pp. 40–48).

a. Construct a 95% confidence interval estimate of the population proportion of individuals who trust business to "do what is right" assuming that the poll surveyed:
  1. 100 individuals.
  2. 200 individuals.
  3. 300 individuals.

b. Discuss the effect that sample size has on the width of confidence intervals.

c. Interpret the interval in (a).

8.28 A survey of 705 workers (extracted from "Snapshots," *USA Today*, March 21, 2006, p. 1B) were asked how much they used the Internet at work. 423 said they used it within limits, and 183 said that they did not use the Internet at work.

a. Construct a 95% confidence interval estimate for the proportion of all workers who use the Internet within limits.

b. Construct a 95% confidence interval estimate for the proportion of all workers who did not use the Internet at work.

8.29 When do Americans decide what to make for dinner? An online survey (extracted from N. Hellmich, "Americans Go for the Quick Fix for Dinner," *USA Today*, February 14, 2005, p. 1B) indicated that 74% of Americans decided either at the last minute or that day. Suppose that the survey was based on 500 respondents.

a. Construct a 95% confidence interval estimate for the proportion of Americans who decided what to make for dinner either at the last minute or that day.

b. Construct a 99% confidence interval for the proportion of Americans who decided what to make for dinner either at the last minute or that day.

c. Which interval is wider? Explain why this is true.

8.30 In a survey of 894 respondents with salaries below $100,000 per year, 367 indicated that the primary reason for staying on their job was interesting job responsibilities (extracted from "Snapshots: What Is the Primary Reason for Staying on Your Job?" *USA Today*, October 5, 2005, p. 1B).

a. Construct a 95% confidence interval estimate for the proportion of all workers whose primary reason for staying on their job was interesting job responsibilities.

b. Interpret the interval constructed in (a).

8.31 The utility of mobile devices raises new questions about the intrusion of work into personal life. In a recent survey by **CareerJournal.com** (extracted from P. Kitchen, "Can't Turn It Off," *Newsday*, October 20, 2006, pp. F4–F5), 158 of 473 employees responded that they typically took work with them on vacation and 85 responded that there are unwritten and unspoken expectations that they stay connected.

a. Construct a 95% confidence interval estimate for the population proportion of employees who typically take work with them on vacation.

b. Construct a 95% confidence interval estimate for the population proportion of employees who said that there are unwritten and unspoken expectations that they stay connected.

c. Interpret the intervals in (a) and (b).

d. Explain the difference in the results in (a) and (b).

8.4   DETERMINING SAMPLE SIZE

In each confidence interval developed so far in this chapter, the sample size was reported along with the results with little discussion of the width of the resulting confidence interval. In the business world, sample sizes are determined prior to data collection to ensure that the confidence interval is narrow enough to be useful in making decisions. Determining the proper sample size is a complicated procedure, subject to the constraints of budget, time, and the amount of acceptable sampling error. In the Saxon Home Improvement example, if you want to estimate the mean dollar amount of the sales invoices, you must determine in advance how large a sampling error to allow in estimating the population mean. You must also determine, in advance, the level of confidence (i.e., 90%, 95%, or 99%) to use in estimating the population parameter.

Sample Size Determination for the Mean

To develop an equation for determining the appropriate sample size needed when constructing a confidence interval estimate of the mean, recall Equation (8.1) on page 296:

$$\bar{X} \pm Z_{\alpha/2} \frac{\sigma}{\sqrt{n}}$$

The amount added to or subtracted from $\bar{X}$ is equal to half the width of the interval. This quantity represents the amount of imprecision in the estimate that results from sampling error. The **sampling error**[1], e, is defined as

[1]*In this context, some statisticians refer to e as the* **"margin of error."**

$$e = Z_{\alpha/2} \frac{\sigma}{\sqrt{n}}$$

Solving for n gives the sample size needed to construct the appropriate confidence interval estimate for the mean. "Appropriate" means that the resulting interval will have an acceptable amount of sampling error.

Sample Size Determination for the Mean

The sample size, n, is equal to the product of the $Z_{\alpha/2}$ value squared and the standard deviation, σ, squared, divided by the square of the sampling error, e,

$$n = \frac{Z_{\alpha/2}^2 \sigma^2}{e^2} \tag{8.4}$$

---

[2]*You use Z instead of t because, to determine the critical value of t, you need to know the sample size, but you do not know it yet. For most studies, the sample size needed is large enough that the standardized normal distribution is a good approximation of the t distribution.*

To determine the sample size, you must know three factors:

1. The desired confidence level, which determines the value of $Z_{\alpha/2}$, the critical value from the standardized normal distribution[2]
2. The acceptable sampling error, e
3. The standard deviation, σ

In some business-to-business relationships that require estimation of important parameters, legal contracts specify acceptable levels of sampling error and the confidence level required. For companies in the food or drug sectors, government regulations often specify sampling errors and confidence levels. In general, however, it is usually not easy to specify the two factors needed to determine the sample size. How can you determine the level of confidence and sampling error? Typically, these questions are answered only by the subject matter expert (i.e., the individual most familiar with the variables under study). Although 95% is the most common confidence level used, if more confidence is desired, then 99% might be more appropriate; if less confidence is deemed acceptable, then 90% might be used. For the sampling error, you should think not of how much sampling error you would like to have (you really do not want any error) but of how much you can tolerate when reaching conclusions from the confidence interval.

In addition to specifying the confidence level and the sampling error, you need an estimate of the standard deviation. Unfortunately, you rarely know the population standard deviation, σ. In some instances, you can estimate the standard deviation from past data. In other situations, you can make an educated guess by taking into account the range and distribution of the variable. For example, if you assume a normal distribution, the range is approximately equal to 6σ (i.e., $\pm 3\sigma$ around the mean) so that you estimate σ as the range divided by 6. If you cannot estimate σ in this way, you can conduct a small-scale study and estimate the standard deviation from the resulting data.

To explore how to determine the sample size needed for estimating the population mean, consider again the audit at Saxon Home Improvement. In Section 8.2, you selected a sample of 100 sales invoices and constructed a 95% confidence interval estimate of the population mean sales invoice amount. How was this sample size determined? Should you have selected a different sample size?

Suppose that, after consultation with company officials, you determine that a sampling error of no more than $\pm\$5$ is desired, along with 95% confidence. Past data indicate that the standard deviation of the sales amount is approximately \$25. Thus, $e = \$5$, $\sigma = \$25$, and $Z_{\alpha/2} = 1.96$ (for 95% confidence). Using Equation (8.4),

$$n = \frac{Z_{\alpha/2}^2 \sigma^2}{e^2} = \frac{(1.96)^2(25)^2}{(5)^2}$$

$$= 96.04$$

Because the general rule is to slightly oversatisfy the criteria by rounding the sample size up to the next whole integer, you should select a sample of size 97. Thus, the sample of size $n = 100$ used on page 302 is close to what is necessary to satisfy the needs of the company, based on the estimated standard deviation, desired confidence level, and sampling error. Because the calculated sample standard deviation is slightly higher than expected, \$28.95 compared to \$25.00, the confidence interval is slightly wider than desired. Figure 8.14 shows a Microsoft Excel worksheet to determine the sample size.

FIGURE 8.14

Microsoft Excel worksheet for determining sample size for estimating the mean sales invoice amount for the Saxon Home Improvement Company

See Section E8.4 or P8.4 to create this.

	A	B	
1	For Mean Sales Invoice Amount		
2			
3	Data		
4	Population Standard Deviation	25	
5	Sampling Error	5	
6	Confidence Level	95%	
7			
8	Intermediate Calculations		
9	Z Value	-1.9600	=NORMSINV((1 - B6)/2)
10	Calculated Sample Size	96.0365	=((B9 * B4)/B5)^2
11			
12	Result		
13	Sample Size Needed	97	=ROUNDUP(B10, 0)

Example 8.5 illustrates another application of determining the sample size needed to develop a confidence interval estimate for the mean.

EXAMPLE 8.5

DETERMINING THE SAMPLE SIZE FOR THE MEAN

Returning to Example 8.3 on page 303, suppose you want to estimate the population mean force required to break the insulator to within ±25 pounds with 95% confidence. On the basis of a study taken the previous year, you believe that the standard deviation is 100 pounds. Find the sample size needed.

SOLUTION Using Equation (8.4) on page 312 and $e = 25$, $\sigma = 100$, and $Z_{\alpha/2} = 1.96$ for 95% confidence,

$$n = \frac{Z_{\alpha/2}^2 \sigma^2}{e^2} = \frac{(1.96)^2 (100)^2}{(25)^2}$$

$$= 61.47$$

Therefore, you should select a sample size of 62 insulators because the general rule for determining sample size is to always round up to the next integer value in order to slightly oversatisfy the criteria desired. An actual sampling error slightly larger than 25 will result if the sample standard deviation calculated in this sample of 62 is greater than 100 and slightly smaller if the sample standard deviation is less than 100.

Sample Size Determination for the Proportion

So far in this section, you have learned how to determine the sample size needed for estimating the population mean. Now suppose that you want to determine the sample size necessary for estimating a population proportion.

To determine the sample size needed to estimate a population proportion, π, you use a method similar to the method for a population mean. Recall that in developing the sample size for a confidence interval for the mean, the sampling error is defined by

$$e = Z_{\alpha/2} \frac{\sigma}{\sqrt{n}}$$

When estimating a proportion, you replace σ with $\sqrt{\pi(1-\pi)}$. Thus, the sampling error is

$$e = Z_{\alpha/2} \sqrt{\frac{\pi(1-\pi)}{n}}$$

Solving for n, you have the sample size necessary to develop a confidence interval estimate for a proportion.

Sample Size Determination for the Proportion

The sample size n is equal to the product of $Z_{\alpha/2}$ squared, the population proportion, π, and 1 minus the population proportion, π, divided by the square of the sampling error, e,

$$n = \frac{Z_{\alpha/2}^2 \pi(1-\pi)}{e^2} \tag{8.5}$$

To determine the sample size, you must know three factors:

1. The desired confidence level, which determines the value of $Z_{\alpha/2}$, the critical value from the standardized normal distribution
2. The acceptable sampling error (or margin of error), e
3. The population proportion, π

In practice, selecting these quantities requires some planning. Once you determine the desired level of confidence, you can find the appropriate $Z_{\alpha/2}$ value from the standardized normal distribution. The sampling error, e, indicates the amount of error that you are willing to tolerate in estimating the population proportion. The third quantity, π, is actually the population parameter that you want to estimate! Thus, how do you state a value for what you are taking a sample in order to determine?

Here you have two alternatives. In many situations, you may have past information or relevant experience that provide an educated estimate of π. Or, if you do not have past information or relevant experience, you can try to provide a value for π that would never *underestimate* the sample size needed. Referring to Equation (8.5), you can see that the quantity $\pi(1 - \pi)$ appears in the numerator. Thus, you need to determine the value of π that will make the quantity $\pi(1 - \pi)$ as large as possible. When $\pi = 0.5$, the product $\pi(1 - \pi)$ achieves its maximum value. To show this result, consider the following values of π, along with the accompanying products of $\pi (1 - \pi)$:

When $\pi = 0.9$, then $\pi(1 - \pi) = (0.9)(0.1) = 0.09$
When $\pi = 0.7$, then $\pi(1 - \pi) = (0.7)(0.3) = 0.21$
When $\pi = 0.5$, then $\pi(1 - \pi) = (0.5)(0.5) = 0.25$
When $\pi = 0.3$, then $\pi(1 - \pi) = (0.3)(0.7) = 0.21$
When $\pi = 0.1$, then $\pi(1 - \pi) = (0.1)(0.9) = 0.09$

Therefore, when you have no prior knowledge or estimate of the population proportion, π, you should use $\pi = 0.5$ for determining the sample size. Using $\pi = 0.5$ produces the largest possible sample size and results in the narrowest and most precise confidence interval. This increased precision comes at the cost of spending more time and money for an increased sample size. Also, note that if you use $\pi = 0.5$ instead of the actual sample proportion in developing the confidence interval, you will overestimate the sample size needed, because you will get a confidence interval narrower than originally intended.

Returning to the Saxon Home Improvement Using Statistics scenario, suppose that the auditing procedures require you to have 95% confidence in estimating the population proportion of sales invoices with errors to within ±0.07. The results from past months indicate that the largest proportion has been no more than 0.15. Thus, using Equation (8.5) on page 314 and $e = 0.07$, $\pi = 0.15$, and $Z_{\alpha/2} = 1.96$ for 95% confidence,

$$n = \frac{Z_{\alpha/2}^2 \pi(1-\pi)}{e^2}$$
$$= \frac{(1.96)^2(0.15)(0.85)}{(0.07)^2}$$
$$= 99.96$$

Because the general rule is to round the sample size up to the next whole integer to slightly oversatisfy the criteria, a sample size of 100 is needed. Thus, the sample size needed to satisfy the requirements of the company, based on the estimated proportion, desired confidence level, and sampling error, is equal to the sample size taken on page 309. The actual confidence interval is narrower than required because the sample proportion is 0.10, whereas 0.15 was used for π in Equation (8.5). Figure 8.15 shows a Microsoft Excel worksheet for determining sample size.

FIGURE 8.15

Microsoft Excel
worksheet for
determining sample
size for estimating the
proportion of sales
invoices with errors for
the Saxon Home
Improvement Company

*See Section E8.5 or P8.5 to
create this.*

	A	B	
1	For Proportion of In-Error Sales Invoices		
2			
3	Data		
4	Estimate of True Proportion	0.15	
5	Sampling Error	0.07	
6	Confidence Level	95%	
7			
8	Intermediate Calculations		
9	Z Value	-1.9600	=NORMSINV((1 - B6)/2)
10	Calculated Sample Size	99.9563	=(B9^2 * B4 * (1 - B4))/B5^2
11			
12	Result		
13	Sample Size Needed	100	=ROUNDUP(B10, 0)

Example 8.6 provides another application of determining the sample size for estimating the population proportion.

EXAMPLE 8.6

DETERMINING THE SAMPLE SIZE FOR THE POPULATION PROPORTION

You want to have 90% confidence of estimating the proportion of office workers who respond to e-mail within an hour to within ±0.05. Because you have not previously undertaken such a study, there is no information available from past data. Determine the sample size needed.

SOLUTION Because no information is available from past data, assume that $\pi = 0.50$. Using Equation (8.5) on page 314 and $e = 0.05$, $\pi = 0.50$, and $Z_{\alpha/2} = 1.645$ for 90% confidence,

$$n = \frac{Z_{\alpha/2}^2 \pi (1 - \pi)}{e^2}$$

$$= \frac{(1.645)^2 (0.50)(0.50)}{(0.05)^2}$$

$$= 270.6$$

Therefore, you need a sample of 271 office workers to estimate the population proportion to within ±0.05 with 90% confidence.

PROBLEMS FOR SECTION 8.4

Learning the Basics

8.32 If you want to be 95% confident of estimating the population mean to within a sampling error of ±5 and the standard deviation is assumed to be 15, what sample size is required?

8.33 If you want to be 99% confident of estimating the population mean to within a sampling error of ±20 and the standard deviation is assumed to be 100, what sample size is required?

8.34 If you want to be 99% confident of estimating the population proportion to within a sampling error of ±0.04, what sample size is needed?

8.35 If you want to be 95% confident of estimating the population proportion to within a sampling error of ±0.02 and there is historical evidence that the population proportion is approximately 0.40, what sample size is needed?

Applying the Concepts

√ SELF Test **8.36** A survey is planned to determine the mean annual family medical expenses of employees of a large company. The management of the company wishes to be 95% confident that the sample mean is correct to within ±$50 of the population mean annual family medical

expenses. A previous study indicates that the standard deviation is approximately $400.
a. How large a sample size is necessary?
b. If management wants to be correct to within ±$25, how many employees need to be selected?

8.37 If the manager of a paint supply store wants to estimate the mean amount of paint in a 1-gallon can to within ±0.004 gallon with 95% confidence and also assumes that the standard deviation is 0.02 gallon, what sample size is needed?

8.38 If a quality control manager wants to estimate the mean life of lightbulbs to within ±20 hours with 95% confidence and also assumes that the population standard deviation is 100 hours, how many lightbulbs need to be selected?

8.39 If the inspection division of a county weights and measures department wants to estimate the mean amount of soft-drink fill in 2-liter bottles to within ±0.01 liter with 95% confidence and also assumes that the standard deviation is 0.05 liter, what sample size is needed?

8.40 A consumer group wants to estimate the mean electric bill for the month of July for single-family homes in a large city. Based on studies conducted in other cities, the standard deviation is assumed to be $25. The group wants to estimate the mean bill for July to within ±$5 with 99% confidence.
a. What sample size is needed?
b. If 95% confidence is desired, how many homes need to be selected?

8.41 An advertising agency that serves a major radio station wants to estimate the mean amount of time that the station's audience spends listening to the radio daily. From past studies, the standard deviation is estimated as 45 minutes.
a. What sample size is needed if the agency wants to be 90% confident of being correct to within ±5 minutes?
b. If 99% confidence is desired, how many listeners need to be selected?

8.42 A growing niche in the restaurant business is gourmet-casual breakfast, lunch, and brunch. Chains in this group include Le Peep, Good Egg, Eggs & I, First Watch, and Eggs Up Grill. The mean per-person check for First Watch is approximately $7, and the mean per-person check for Eggs Up Grill is $6.50 (extracted from J. Hayes, "Competition Heats Up as Breakfast Concepts Eye Growth," *Nation's Restaurant News*, April 24, 2006, pp. 8, 66).
a. Assuming a standard deviation of $2.00, what sample size is needed to estimate the mean per-person check for Good Egg to within ±$0.25 with 95% confidence?
b. Assuming a standard deviation of $2.50, what sample size is needed to estimate the mean per-person check for Good Egg to within ±$0.25 with 95% confidence?
c. Assuming a standard deviation of $3.00, what sample size is needed to estimate the mean per-person check for Good Egg to within ±$0.25 with 95% confidence?
d. Discuss the effect of variation on selecting the sample size needed.

8.43 The U.S. Department of Transportation defines an airline flight as being "on time" if it lands less than 15 minutes after the scheduled time shown in the carrier's computerized reservation system. Cancelled and diverted flights are counted as late. A study of the 10 largest U.S. domestic airlines found Southwest Airlines to have the lowest proportion of late arrivals, at 0.1577 (extracted from N. Tsikriktsis and J. Heineke, "The Impact of Process Variation on Customer Dissatisfaction: Evidence from the U.S. Domestic Airline Industry," *Decision Sciences*, Winter 2004, 35(1), pp. 129–142). Suppose you were asked to perform a follow-up study for Southwest Airlines in order to update the estimated proportion of late arrivals. How many airline flights do you need to sample in order to estimate the population proportion to within an error of
a. ±0.06 with 95% confidence?
b. ±0.04 with 95% confidence?
c. ±0.02 with 95% confidence?

8.44 In 2005, 34% of workers reported that their jobs were more difficult, with more stress, and 37% reported that they worry about retiring comfortably (extracted from S. Armour, "Money Worries Hinder Job Performance," *USA Today*, October 5, 2005, p. D1). Consider a follow-up study to be conducted in the near future.
a. What sample size is needed to estimate the population proportion of workers who reported that their jobs were more difficult, with more stress, to within ±0.02 with 95% confidence?
b. How many workers need to be sampled in order to estimate the population proportion of workers who worried about retiring comfortably to within ±0.02 with 95% confidence?
c. Compare the results of (a) and (b). Explain why these results differ.
d. If you were to design the follow-up study, would you use one sample and ask the respondents both questions, or would you select two separate samples? Explain the rationale behind your decision.

8.45 What proportion of people hit snags with online transactions? According to a poll conducted by Harris Interactive, 89% hit snags with online transactions (extracted from "Snapshots: Top Online Transaction Trouble," *USA Today*, April 4, 2006, p. 1D).
a. To conduct a follow-up study that would provide 95% confidence that the point estimate is correct to within ±0.04 of the population proportion, how large a sample size is required?

b. To conduct a follow-up study that would provide 99% confidence that the point estimate is correct to within ±0.04 of the population proportion, how many people need to be sampled?

c. To conduct a follow-up study that would provide 95% confidence that the point estimate is correct to within ±0.02 of the population proportion, how large a sample size is required?

d. To conduct a follow-up study that would provide 99% confidence that the point estimate is correct to within ±0.02 of the population proportion, how many people need to be sampled?

e. Discuss the effects of changing the desired confidence level and the acceptable sampling error on sample size requirements.

8.46 A poll of 1,286 young adult cellphone users was conducted in March 2006. These cellphone users, aged 18 to 29, were actively engaged in multiple uses of their cellphones. The data suggest that 707 took still pictures with their phones, 604 played games, and 360 used the Internet (extracted from "Poll: Cellphones Are Annoying but Invaluable," **usatoday.com**, April 3, 2006). Construct a 95% confidence interval estimate of the population proportion of young adults that used their cellphone to

a. take still pictures.

b. play games.

c. use the Internet.

d. You have been asked to update the results of this study. Determine the sample size necessary to estimate the population proportions in (a) through (c) to within ±0.02 with 95% confidence.

8.47 A study of 658 CEOs conducted by the Conference Board reported that 250 stated that their company's greatest concern was sustained and steady top-line growth (extracted from "Snapshots: CEOs' Greatest Concerns," *USA Today*, May 8, 2006, p. 1D).

a. Construct a 95% confidence interval for the proportion of CEOs whose greatest concern was sustained and steady top-line growth.

b. Interpret the interval constructed in (a).

c. To conduct a follow-up study to estimate the population proportion of CEOs whose greatest concern was sustained and steady top-line growth to within ±0.01 with 95% confidence, how many CEOs would you survey?

8.48 In 2007, oil companies posted huge profits and consumers paid record high prices at the gas pump. The president of Shell Oil stated that "we know for a fact that the favorability rating of oil companies today ranges from 10–15%" (extracted from D. J. Lynch, "Shell Oil Tries Different Path to Engage Public Opinion," **usatoday.com**, May 14, 2007).

a. If you conduct a follow-up study to estimate the population proportion of individuals who view oil companies favorably, would you use a π of 0.10, 0.15, or 0.50 in the sample size formula? Discuss.

b. Using your answer to (a), find the sample size necessary to estimate the population proportion to within ±0.03 with 95% certainty.

8.49 The Department of Commerce announced that the national rental vacancy rate during the first quarter of 2007 was 10.1%. The report noted that the proportion of rentals vacant was 0.101 with a 95% confidence interval and margin of error of 0.004 (extracted from R. R. Callis and L. B. Cavanaugh, "Census Bureau Reports on Residential Vacancies and Homeownership," *United States Department of Commerce News*, April 27, 2007, p.1).

a. Construct a 95% confidence interval estimate for the national rental vacancy rate.

b. Interpret the interval found in (a).

c. If the estimate reported was constructed using the methods in this section, what sample size was required?

8.5   APPLICATIONS OF CONFIDENCE INTERVAL ESTIMATION IN AUDITING

This chapter has focused on estimating either the population mean or the population proportion. In previous chapters, you have studied applications to different business scenarios. Auditing is one of the areas in business that makes widespread use of probability sampling methods in order to construct confidence interval estimates.

AUDITING

Auditing is the collection and evaluation of evidence about information relating to an economic entity, such as a sole business proprietor, a partnership, a corporation, or a government agency, in order to determine and report on how well the information corresponds to established criteria.

Auditors rarely examine a complete population of information. Instead, they rely on estimation techniques based on the probability sampling methods you have studied in this text. The following list contains some of the reasons sampling is advantageous compared to examining the entire population.

- Sampling is less time-consuming.
- Sampling is less costly.
- Sampling provides an objective way of estimating the sample size in advance.
- Sampling provides results that are objective and defensible. Because the sample size is based on demonstrable statistical principles, the audit is defensible before one's superiors and in a court of law.
- Sampling provides an estimate of the sampling error and therefore allows auditors to generalize their findings to the population with a known sampling error.
- Sampling is often more accurate for drawing conclusions about large populations than other methods. Examining every item in large populations is time-consuming and therefore often subject to more nonsampling error than statistical sampling.
- Sampling allows auditors to combine, and then evaluate collectively, samples collected by different individuals.

Estimating the Population Total Amount

In auditing applications, you are often more interested in developing estimates of the population **total amount** than the population mean. Equation (8.6) shows how to estimate a population total amount.

Estimating the Population Total Amount

The point estimate for the population total is equal to the population size, N, times the sample mean.

$$\text{Total} = N\bar{X} \qquad (8.6)$$

Equation (8.7) defines the confidence interval estimate for the population total.

Confidence Interval Estimate for the Total Amount

$$N\bar{X} \pm N(t_{\alpha/2})\frac{S}{\sqrt{n}}\sqrt{\frac{N-n}{N-1}} \qquad (8.7)$$

where $t_{\alpha/2}$ is the critical value corresponding to an upper-tail probability of $\alpha/2$ from the t distribution with $n-1$ degrees of freedom (i.e., a cumulative area of $1-\alpha/2$).

To demonstrate the application of the confidence interval estimate for the population total amount, return to the Saxon Home Improvement Using Statistics scenario on page 292. One of the auditing tasks is to estimate the total dollar amount of all sales invoices for the month. If there are 5,000 invoices for that month and $\bar{X} = \$110.27$, then using Equation (8.6),

$$N\bar{X} = (5,000)(\$110.27) = \$551,350$$

If $n = 100$ and $S = \$28.95$, then using Equation (8.7) with $t_{\alpha/2} = 1.9842$ for 95% confidence and 99 degrees of freedom,

$$N\bar{X} \pm N(t_{\alpha/2})\frac{S}{\sqrt{n}}\sqrt{\frac{N-n}{N-1}} = 551{,}350 \pm (5{,}000)(1.9842)\frac{28.95}{\sqrt{100}}\sqrt{\frac{5{,}000-100}{5{,}000-1}}$$

$$= 551{,}350 \pm 28{,}721.295(0.99005)$$

$$= 551{,}350 \pm 28{,}436$$

$$\$522{,}914 \le \text{Population total} \le \$579{,}786$$

Therefore, with 95% confidence, you estimate that the total amount of sales invoices is between \$522,914 and \$579,786. Figure 8.16 shows a Microsoft Excel worksheet for these data.

FIGURE 8.16

Microsoft Excel worksheet for the confidence interval estimate of the total amount of all invoices for the Saxon Home Improvement Company

See Section E8.6 or P8.6 to create this.

	A	B	
1	**Total Amount of All Sales Invoices**		
2			
3	**Data**		
4	Population Size	5000	
5	Sample Mean	110.27	
6	Sample Size	100	
7	Sample Standard Deviation	28.95	
8	Confidence Level	95%	
9			
10	**Intermediate Calculations**		
11	Population Total	551350.00	=B4 * B5
12	FPC Factor	0.9900	=SQRT((B4 - B6)/(B4 - 1))
13	Standard Error of the Total	14330.9521	=(B4 * B7 * B12)/SQRT(B6)
14	Degrees of Freedom	99	=B6 - 1
15	t Value	1.9842	=TINV(1 - B8, B14)
16	Interval Half Width	28435.72	=B15 * B13
17			
18	**Confidence Interval**		
19	Interval Lower Limit	522914.28	=B11 - B16
20	Interval Upper Limit	579785.72	=B11 + B16

Example 8.7 further illustrates the population total.

EXAMPLE 8.7   DEVELOPING A CONFIDENCE INTERVAL ESTIMATE FOR THE POPULATION TOTAL

An auditor is faced with a population of 1,000 vouchers and wants to estimate the total value of the population of vouchers. A sample of 50 vouchers is selected, with the following results:

$$\text{Mean voucher amount } (\bar{X}) = \$1{,}076.39$$

$$\text{Standard deviation } (S) = \$273.62$$

Construct a 95% confidence interval estimate of the total amount for the population of vouchers.

SOLUTION Using Equation (8.6) on page 319, the point estimate of the population total is

$$N\bar{X} = (1{,}000)(1{,}076.39) = \$1{,}076{,}390$$

From Equation (8.7) on page 319, a 95% confidence interval estimate of the population total amount is

$$(1,000)(1,076.39) \pm (1,000)(2.0096)\frac{273.62}{\sqrt{50}}\sqrt{\frac{1,000-50}{1,000-1}}$$

$$= 1,076,390 \pm 77,762.878(0.97517)$$

$$= 1,076,390 \pm 75,832$$

$$\$1,000,558 \le \text{Population total} \le \$1,152,222$$

Therefore, with 95% confidence, you estimate that the total amount of the vouchers is between $1,000,558 and $1,152,222.

Difference Estimation

An auditor uses **difference estimation** when he or she believes that errors exist in a set of items and he or she wants to estimate the magnitude of the errors based only on a sample. The following steps are used in difference estimation:

1. Determine the sample size required.
2. Calculate the differences between the values reached during the audit and the original values recorded. The difference in value i, denoted D_i, is equal to 0 if the auditor finds that the original value is correct, is a positive value when the audited value is larger than the original value, and is negative when the audited value is smaller than the original value.
3. Compute the mean difference in the sample, $\bar{D}$, by dividing the total difference by the sample size, as shown in Equation (8.8).

Mean Difference

$$\bar{D} = \frac{\sum_{i=1}^{n} D_i}{n} \tag{8.8}$$

where D_i = Audited value − Original value

4. Compute the standard deviation of the differences, S_D, as shown in Equation (8.9). *Remember that any item that is not in error has a difference value of 0.*

Standard Deviation of the Difference

$$S_D = \sqrt{\frac{\sum_{i=1}^{n}(D_i - \bar{D})^2}{n-1}} \tag{8.9}$$

5. Use Equation (8.10) to construct a confidence interval estimate of the total difference in the population.

Confidence Interval Estimate for the Total Difference

$$N\bar{D} \pm N(t_{\alpha/2})\frac{S_D}{\sqrt{n}}\sqrt{\frac{N-n}{N-1}} \tag{8.10}$$

where $t_{\alpha/2}$ is the critical value corresponding to an upper-tail probability of $\alpha/2$ from the t distribution with $n-1$ degrees of freedom (i.e., a cumulative area of $1-\alpha/2$).

The auditing procedures for Saxon Home Improvement require a 95% confidence interval estimate of the difference between the audited dollar amounts on the sales invoices and the amounts originally entered into the integrated inventory and sales information system. Suppose that in a sample of 100 sales invoices, you have 12 invoices in which the audited dollar amount on the sales invoice and the amount originally entered into the integrated inventory management and sales information system is different. These 12 differences (stored in the file **Plumbinv**) are

$9.03 $7.47 $17.32 $8.30 $5.21 $10.80 $6.22 $5.63 $4.97 $7.43 $2.99 $4.63

The other 88 invoices are not in error. Their *differences* are each 0. Thus,

$$\bar{D} = \frac{\sum_{i=1}^{n} D_i}{n} = \frac{90}{100} = 0.90$$

[3]In the numerator below, there are 100 differences. Each of the last 88 are equal to $(0-0.9)^2$.

and[3]

$$S_D = \sqrt{\frac{\sum_{i=1}^{n}(D_i - \bar{D})^2}{n-1}}$$

$$= \sqrt{\frac{(9.03-0.9)^2 + (7.47-0.9)^2 + \cdots + (0-0.9)^2}{100-1}}$$

$$S_D = 2.752$$

Using Equation (8.10), construct the 95% confidence interval estimate for the total difference in the population of 5,000 sales invoices as follows:

$$(5,000)(0.90) \pm (5,000)(1.9842)\frac{2.752}{\sqrt{100}}\sqrt{\frac{5,000-100}{5,000-1}}$$

$$= 4,500 \pm 2,702.91$$

$$\$1,797.09 \le \text{Total difference} \le \$7,202.91$$

Thus, the auditor estimates with 95% confidence that the total difference between the sales invoices as determined during the audit and the amount originally entered into the accounting system is between $1,797.09 and $7,202.91. Figure 8.17 shows an Excel worksheet for these data.

FIGURE 8.17

Microsoft Excel worksheet for the total difference between the invoice amounts found during the audit and the amounts originally entered into the accounting system for the Saxon Home Improvement Company

See Section E8.7 or P8.7 to create this.

	A	B	
1	**Total Difference In Actual and Entered**		
2			
3	**Data**		
4	**Population Size**	**5000**	
5	**Sample Size**	**100**	
6	**Confidence Level**	**95%**	
7			
8	Intermediate Calculations		
9	Sum of Differences	90.0000	=SUM(DifferencesData!A:A)
10	Average Difference in Sample	0.9	=B9/B5
11	Total Difference	4500	=B4 * B10
12	Standard Deviation of Differences	2.7518	=SQRT(E16)
13	FPC Factor	0.9900	=SQRT((B4 - B5)/(B4 - 1))
14	Standard Error of the Total Diff.	1362.2064	=(B4 * B12 * B13)/SQRT(B5)
15	Degrees of Freedom	99	=B5 - 1
16	*t* Value	1.9842	=TINV(1 - B6, B15)
17	Interval Half Width	2702.9129	=B16 * B14
18			
19	Confidence Interval		
20	**Interval Lower Limit**	**1797.09**	=B11 - B17
21	**Interval Upper Limit**	**7202.91**	=B11 + B17

In the previous example, all 12 differences are positive because the audited amount on the sales invoice is more than the amount originally entered into the accounting system. In some circumstances, you could have negative errors. Example 8.8 illustrates such a situation.

EXAMPLE 8.8   DIFFERENCE ESTIMATION

Returning to Example 8.7 on page 320, suppose that 14 vouchers in the sample of 50 vouchers contain errors. The values of the 14 errors are listed below and stored in the file `Difftest`. Observe that two differences are negative:

$75.41 $38.97 $108.54   −$37.18 $62.75 $118.32   −$88.84

$127.74 $55.42 $39.03 $29.41 $47.99 $28.73 $84.05

Construct a 95% confidence interval estimate of the total difference in the population of 1,000 vouchers.

SOLUTION For these data,

$$\bar{D} = \frac{\sum\limits_{i=1}^{n} D_i}{n} = \frac{690.34}{50} = 13.8068$$

and

$$S_D = \sqrt{\frac{\sum\limits_{i=1}^{n} (D_i - \bar{D})^2}{n-1}}$$

$$= \sqrt{\frac{(75.41 - 13.8068)^2 + (38.97 - 13.8068)^2 + \cdots + (0 - 13.8068)^2}{50 - 1}}$$

$$= 37.427$$

Using Equation (8.10) on page 322, construct the confidence interval estimate for the total difference in the population as follows:

$$(1,000)(13.8068) \pm (1,000)(2.0096)\frac{37.427}{\sqrt{50}}\sqrt{\frac{1,000-50}{1,000-1}}$$

$$= 13,806.8 \pm 10,372.4$$

$$\$3,434.40 \leq \text{Total difference} \leq \$24,179.20$$

Therefore, with 95% confidence, you estimate that the total difference in the population of vouchers is between \$3,434.40 and \$24,179.20.

One-Sided Confidence Interval Estimation of the Rate of Noncompliance with Internal Controls

Organizations use internal control mechanisms to ensure that individuals act in accordance with company guidelines. For example, Saxon Home Improvement requires that an authorized warehouse-removal slip be completed before goods are removed from the warehouse. During the monthly audit of the company, the auditing team is charged with the task of estimating the proportion of times goods were removed without proper authorization. This is referred to as the *rate of noncompliance with the internal control*. To estimate the rate of noncompliance, auditors take a random sample of sales invoices and determine how often merchandise was shipped without an authorized warehouse-removal slip. The auditors then compare their results with a previously established tolerable exception rate, which is the maximum allowable proportion of items in the population not in compliance. When estimating the rate of noncompliance, it is commonplace to use a **one-sided confidence interval**. That is, the auditors estimate an upper bound on the rate of noncompliance. Equation (8.11) defines a one-sided confidence interval for a proportion.

One-Sided Confidence Interval for a Proportion

$$\text{Upper bound} = p + Z_\alpha\sqrt{\frac{p(1-p)}{n}}\sqrt{\frac{N-n}{N-1}} \qquad (8.11)$$

where Z_α = the value corresponding to a cumulative area of $(1 - \alpha)$ from the standardized normal distribution (i.e., a right-hand tail probability of α).

If the tolerable exception rate is higher than the upper bound, the auditor concludes that the company is in compliance with the internal control. If the upper bound is higher than the tolerable exception rate, the auditor has failed to prove that the company is in compliance. The auditor may then request a larger sample.

Suppose that in the monthly audit, you select 400 sales invoices from a population of 10,000 invoices. In the sample of 400 sales invoices, 20 are in violation of the internal control. If the tolerable exception rate for this internal control is 6%, what should you conclude? Use a 95% level of confidence.

The one-sided confidence interval is computed using $p = 20/400 = 0.05$ and $Z_\alpha = 1.645$. Using Equation (8.11),

$$\text{Upper bound} = p + Z_\alpha\sqrt{\frac{p(1-p)}{n}}\sqrt{\frac{N-n}{N-1}} = 0.05 + 1.645\sqrt{\frac{0.05(1-0.05)}{400}}\sqrt{\frac{10,000-400}{10,000-1}}$$

$$= 0.05 + 1.645(0.0109)(0.98) = 0.05 + 0.0176 = 0.0676$$

Thus, you have 95% confidence that the rate of noncompliance is less than 6.76%. Because the tolerable exception rate is 6%, the rate of noncompliance may be too high for this internal control. In other words, it is possible that the noncompliance rate for the population is higher than the rate deemed tolerable. Therefore, you should request a larger sample.

In many cases, the auditor is able to conclude that the rate of noncompliance with the company's internal controls is acceptable. Example 8.9 illustrates such an occurrence.

EXAMPLE 8.9   ESTIMATING THE RATE OF NONCOMPLIANCE

A large electronics firm writes 1 million checks a year. An internal control policy for the company is that the authorization to sign each check is granted only after an invoice has been initialed by an accounts payable supervisor. The company's tolerable exception rate for this control is 4%. If control deviations are found in 8 of the 400 invoices sampled, what should the auditor do? To solve this, use a 95% level of confidence.

SOLUTION The auditor constructs a 95% one-sided confidence interval for the proportion of invoices in noncompliance and compares this to the tolerable exception rate. Using Equation (8.11) on page 324, $p = 8/400 = 0.02$, and $Z_\alpha = 1.645$ for 95% confidence,

$$\text{Upper bound} = p + Z_\alpha \sqrt{\frac{p(1-p)}{n}} \sqrt{\frac{N-n}{N-1}} = 0.02 + 1.645 \sqrt{\frac{0.02(1-0.02)}{400}} \sqrt{\frac{1{,}000{,}000 - 400}{1{,}000{,}000 - 1}}$$

$$= 0.02 + 1.645(0.007)(0.9998) = 0.02 + 0.0115 = 0.0315$$

The auditor concludes with 95% confidence that the rate of noncompliance is less than 3.15%. Because this is less than the tolerable exception rate, the auditor concludes that the internal control compliance is adequate. In other words, the auditor is more than 95% confident that the rate of noncompliance is less than 4%.

PROBLEMS FOR SECTION 8.5

Learning the Basics

8.50 A sample of 25 is selected from a population of 500 items. The sample mean is 25.7, and the sample standard deviation is 7.8. Construct a 99% confidence interval estimate of the population total.

8.51 Suppose that a sample of 200 (see the file **Itemerr**) is selected from a population of 10,000 items. Of these, 10 items are found to have errors of the following amounts:

13.76	42.87	34.65	11.09	14.54
22.87	25.52	9.81	10.03	15.49

Construct a 95% confidence interval estimate of the total difference in the population.

8.52 If $p = 0.04$, $n = 300$, and $N = 5,000$, calculate the upper bound for a one-sided confidence interval estimate of the population proportion, π, using the following levels of confidence:

a. 90%
b. 95%
c. 99%

Applying the Concepts

8.53 A stationery store wants to estimate the total retail value of the 1,000 greeting cards it has in its inventory. Construct a 95% confidence interval estimate of the population total value of all greeting cards that are in inventory if a random sample of 100 greeting cards indicates a mean value of $2.55 and a standard deviation of $0.44.

SELF Test **8.54** The personnel department of a large corporation employing 3,000 workers wants to estimate the family dental expenses of its employees to determine the feasibility of providing a dental insurance plan. A random sample of 10 employees reveals the following family dental expenses (in dollars) (see the **Dental** file):

110   362   246   85   510   208   173   425   316   179

Construct a 90% confidence interval estimate of the total family dental expenses for all employees in the preceding year.

8.55 A branch of a chain of large electronics stores is conducting an end-of-month inventory of the merchandise in stock. There were 1,546 items in inventory at that time. A sample of 50 items was randomly selected, and an audit was conducted, with the following results:

Value of Merchandise

$$\bar{X} = \$252.28 \qquad S = \$93.67$$

Construct a 95% confidence interval estimate of the total value of the merchandise in inventory at the end of the month.

8.56 A customer in the wholesale garment trade is often entitled to a discount for a cash payment for goods. The amount of discount varies by vendor. A sample of 150 items selected from a population of 4,000 invoices at the end of a period of time (see the Discount file) revealed that in 13 cases, the customer failed to take the discount to which he or she was entitled. The amounts (in dollars) of the 13 discounts that were not taken were as follows:

6.45 15.32   97.36 230.63 104.18 84.92 132.76
66.12 26.55 129.43   88.32   47.81 89.01

Construct a 99% confidence interval estimate of the population total amount of discounts not taken.

8.57 Econe Dresses is a small company that manufactures women's dresses for sale to specialty stores. It has 1,200 inventory items, and the historical cost is recorded on a first in, first out (FIFO) basis. In the past, approximately 15% of the inventory items were incorrectly priced. However, any misstatements were usually not significant. A sample of 120 items was selected (see the Fifo file), and the historical cost of each item was compared with the

audited value. The results indicated that 15 items differed in their historical costs and audited values. These values were as follows:

Sample Number	Historical Cost ($)	Audited Value ($)	Sample Number	Historical Cost ($)	Audited Value ($)
5	261	240	60	21	210
9	87	105	73	140	152
17	201	276	86	129	112
18	121	110	95	340	216
28	315	298	96	341	402
35	411	356	107	135	97
43	249	211	119	228	220
51	216	305			

Construct a 95% confidence interval estimate of the total population difference in the historical cost and audited value.

8.58 Tom and Brent's Alpine Outfitters conduct an annual audit of its financial records. An internal control policy for the company is that a check can be issued only after the accounts payable manager initials the invoice. The tolerable exception rate for this internal control is 0.04. During an audit, a sample of 300 invoices is examined from a population of 10,000 invoices, and 11 invoices are found to violate the internal control.
a. Calculate the upper bound for a 95% one-sided confidence interval estimate for the rate of noncompliance.
b. Based on (a), what should the auditor conclude?

8.59 An internal control policy for Rhonda's Online Fashion Accessories requires a quality assurance check before a shipment is made. The tolerable exception rate for this internal control is 0.05. During an audit, 500 shipping records were sampled from a population of 5,000 shipping records, and 12 were found that violated the internal control.
a. Calculate the upper bound for a 95% one-sided confidence interval estimate for the rate of noncompliance.
b. Based on (a), what should the auditor conclude?

8.6 CONFIDENCE INTERVAL ESTIMATION AND ETHICAL ISSUES

Ethical issues relating to the selection of samples and the inferences that accompany them can occur in several ways. The major ethical issue relates to whether confidence interval estimates are provided along with the sample statistics. To provide a sample statistic without also including the confidence interval limits (typically set at 95%), the sample size used, and an interpretation of the meaning of the confidence interval in terms that a person untrained in statistics can understand raises ethical issues. Failure to include a confidence interval estimate might mislead the user of the results into thinking that the point estimate is all that is needed to predict the population characteristic with certainty. Thus, it is important that you indicate the interval estimate in a prominent place in any written communication, along with a simple explanation of the meaning of the confidence interval. In addition, you should highlight the sample size and sampling error.

One of the most common areas where ethical issues concerning confidence intervals occurs is in the publication of the results of political polls. Often, the results of the polls are highlighted on the front page of the newspaper, and the sampling error involved along with the methodology used is printed on the page where the article is continued, often in the middle of the newspaper. To ensure an ethical presentation of statistical results, the confidence levels, sample size, sampling error, and confidence limits should be made available for all surveys and other statistical studies.

8.7 ⊙ (CD-ROM TOPIC) ESTIMATION AND SAMPLE SIZE DETERMINATION FOR FINITE POPULATIONS

In this section, confidence intervals are developed and the sample size is determined for situations in which sampling is done without replacement from a finite population. For further discussion, see section 8.7.pdf on the Student CD-ROM that accompanies this book.

SUMMARY

This chapter discusses confidence intervals for estimating the characteristics of a population, along with how you can determine the necessary sample size. You learned how an accountant at Saxon Home Improvement can use the sample data from an audit to estimate important population parameters such as the total dollar amount on invoices and the proportion of shipments made without the proper authorization. Table 8.3 provides a list of topics covered in this chapter.

TABLE 8.3

Summary of Topics in Chapter 8

Type of Analysis	Type of Data	
	Numerical	**Categorical**
Confidence interval for a population parameter	Confidence interval estimate for the mean (Sections 8.1 and 8.2)	Confidence interval estimate for the proportion (Section 8.3)
	Confidence interval estimate for the total and the mean difference (Section 8.5)	One-sided confidence interval estimate for the proportion (Section 8.5)

To determine what equation to use for a particular situation, you need to answer two questions:

- Are you developing a confidence interval or are you determining sample size?

- Do you have a numerical variable or do you have a categorical variable?

The next four chapters develop a hypothesis-testing approach to making decisions about population parameters.

KEY EQUATIONS

Confidence Interval for the Mean (σ Known)

$$\bar{X} \pm Z_{\alpha/2} \frac{\sigma}{\sqrt{n}}$$

or

$$\bar{X} - Z_{\alpha/2} \frac{\sigma}{\sqrt{n}} \leq \mu \leq \bar{X} + Z_{\alpha/2} \frac{\sigma}{\sqrt{n}} \qquad (8.1)$$

Confidence Interval for the Mean (σ Unknown)

$$\bar{X} \pm t_{\alpha/2} \frac{S}{\sqrt{n}}$$

or

$$\bar{X} - t_{\alpha/2} \frac{S}{\sqrt{n}} \leq \mu \leq \bar{X} + t_{\alpha/2} \frac{S}{\sqrt{n}} \qquad (8.2)$$

Confidence Interval Estimate for the Proportion

$$p \pm Z_{\alpha/2}\sqrt{\frac{p(1-p)}{n}}$$

or

$$p - Z_{\alpha/2}\sqrt{\frac{p(1-p)}{n}} \le \pi \le p + Z_{\alpha/2}\sqrt{\frac{p(1-p)}{n}} \quad (8.3)$$

Sample Size Determination for the Mean

$$n = \frac{Z_{\alpha/2}^2 \sigma^2}{e^2} \quad (8.4)$$

Sample Size Determination for the Proportion

$$n = \frac{Z_{\alpha/2}^2 \pi(1-\pi)}{e^2} \quad (8.5)$$

Estimating the Population Total Amount

$$\text{Total} = N\bar{X} \quad (8.6)$$

Confidence Interval Estimate for the Total Amount

$$N\bar{X} \pm N(t_{\alpha/2})\frac{S}{\sqrt{n}}\sqrt{\frac{N-n}{N-1}} \quad (8.7)$$

Mean Difference

$$\bar{D} = \frac{\sum_{i=1}^{n} D_i}{n} \quad (8.8)$$

Standard Deviation of the Difference

$$S_D = \sqrt{\frac{\sum_{i=1}^{n}(D_i - \bar{D})^2}{n-1}} \quad (8.9)$$

Confidence Interval Estimate for the Total Difference

$$N\bar{D} \pm N(t_{\alpha/2})\frac{S_D}{\sqrt{n}}\sqrt{\frac{N-n}{N-1}} \quad (8.10)$$

One-Sided Confidence Interval for a Proportion

$$\text{Upper bound} = p + Z_{\alpha}\sqrt{\frac{p(1-p)}{n}}\sqrt{\frac{N-n}{N-1}} \quad (8.11)$$

KEY TERMS

auditing 318
confidence interval estimate 292
critical value 297
degrees of freedom 300
difference estimation 321
level of confidence 296
margin of error 312
one-sided confidence interval 324
point estimate 292
sampling error 312
Student's t distribution 300
total amount 319

CHAPTER REVIEW PROBLEMS

Checking Your Understanding

8.60 Why can you never really have 100% confidence of correctly estimating the population characteristic of interest?

8.61 When are you able to use the t distribution to develop the confidence interval estimate for the mean?

8.62 Why is it true that for a given sample size, n, an increase in confidence is achieved by widening (and making less precise) the confidence interval?

8.63 Under what circumstances do you use a one-sided confidence interval instead of a two-sided confidence interval?

8.64 When would you want to estimate the population total instead of the population mean?

8.65 How does difference estimation differ from estimation of the mean?

Applying the Concepts

8.66 You work in the corporate office for a nationwide convenience store franchise that operates nearly 10,000 stores. The per-store daily customer count has been steady at 900 for some time (i.e., the mean number of customers in a store in one day is 900). To increase the customer count, the franchise is considering cutting coffee prices by approximately half. The 12-ounce size will now be $.59 instead of $.99, and the 16-ounce size will be $.69 instead of $1.19. Even with this reduction in price, the franchise will have a 40% gross margin on coffee. To test the new initiative, the franchise has reduced coffee prices in a sample of 34 stores, where customer counts have been running almost exactly at the national average of 900. After four weeks, the sample stores stabilize at a mean customer count of 974 and a standard deviation of 96. This increase seems like a substantial amount to you, but it also seems like a pretty small sample. Is there some way to get a feel for what the mean per-store count in all the stores will be if you cut coffee prices nationwide? Do you think reducing coffee prices is a good strategy for increasing the mean customer count?

8.67 Companies are spending more time screening applicants than in the past. A study of 102 recruiters conducted by ExecuNet found that 77 did Internet research on candidates (extracted from P. Kitchen, "Don't Let Any 'Digital Dirt' Bury Your Job Prospects," *Newsday*, August 21, 2005, p. A59).
a. Construct a 95% confidence interval estimate of the population proportion of recruiters who do Internet research on candidates.
b. Based on (a), is it correct to conclude that more than 70% of recruiters do Internet research on candidates?
c. Suppose that the study uses a sample size of 400 recruiters and 302 did Internet research on candidates. Construct a 95% confidence interval estimate of the population proportion of recruiters who do Internet research on candidates.
d. Based on (c), is it correct to conclude that more than 70% of recruiters do Internet research on candidates?
e. Discuss the effect of sample size on your answers to (a) through (d).

8.68 High-fructose corn syrup (HFCS) was created in the 1970s and is used today in a wide variety of foods and beverages. HFCS is cheaper than sugar and is about 75% sweeter than sucrose. Some researchers think that HFCS is linked to the growing obesity problem in the United States (extracted from P. Lempert, "War of the Sugars," *Progressive Grocer*, April 15, 2006, p. 20). The following consumer views are from a nationwide survey of 1,114 responses:

Views on HFCS	Yes	No
Are you concerned about consuming HFCS?	80%	20%
Do you think HFCS should be banned in food sold to schools?	88%	12%
Do you think HFCS should be banned in all foods?	56%	44%

Construct a 95% confidence interval estimate of the population proportion of people who
a. are concerned about consuming HFCS.
b. think HFCS should be banned in food sold to schools.
c. think HFCS should be banned in all foods.
d. You are in charge of a follow-up survey. Determine the sample size necessary to estimate the proportions in (a) through (c) to within ±0.02 with 95% confidence.

8.69 Often, after a period of time, items that were considered luxuries become necessities. A survey by the Pew Research Center of 2,000 U.S. adults 18 and over (extracted from S. Jayson, "Luxuries of the Past Become Necessities," *USA Today*, December 15, 2006, p. 6A) found the following percentages that considered each of the following items as necessities
• Car—91%
• Home air conditioner—70%
• TV set—64%
• Car air-conditioning—59%
• Home computer—51%
• Cellphone—49%
• Cable or satellite TV—33%
• High-speed Internet—29%
• Flat-screen TV—5%
• IPod—3%

Construct a 95% confidence interval estimate for each of these questions. Based on these results, what conclusions can you reach about the items that Americans consider necessities?

8.70 A market researcher for a consumer electronics company wants to study the television viewing habits of residents of a particular area. A random sample of 40 respondents is selected, and each respondent is instructed to keep a detailed record of all television viewing in a particular week. The results are as follows:
• Viewing time per week: $\bar{X} = 15.3$ hours, $S = 3.8$ hours.
• 27 respondents watch the evening news on at least 3 weeknights.
a. Construct a 95% confidence interval estimate for the mean amount of television watched per week in this city.
b. Construct a 95% confidence interval estimate for the population proportion who watch the evening news on at least 3 weeknights per week.
Suppose that the market researcher wants to take another survey in a different city. Answer these questions:
c. What sample size is required to be 95% confident of estimating the population mean to within ±2 hours and assumes that the population standard deviation is equal to 5 hours?
d. How many respondents need to be selected to be 95% confident of being within ±0.035 of the population pro-

portion who watch the evening news on at least 3 week-nights if no previous estimate is available?

e. Based on (c) and (d), how many respondents should the market researcher select if a single survey is being conducted?

8.71 The real estate assessor for a county government wants to study various characteristics of single-family houses in the county. A random sample of 70 houses reveals the following:

- Heated area of the houses (in square feet): $\bar{X} = 1,759$, $S = 380$.
- 42 houses have central air-conditioning.

a. Construct a 99% confidence interval estimate of the population mean heated area of the houses.

b. Construct a 95% confidence interval estimate of the population proportion of houses that have central air-conditioning.

8.72 The personnel director of a large corporation wishes to study absenteeism among clerical workers at the corporation's central office during the year. A random sample of 25 clerical workers reveals the following:

- Absenteeism: $\bar{X} = 9.7$ days, $S = 4.0$ days.
- 12 clerical workers were absent more than 10 days.

a. Construct a 95% confidence interval estimate of the mean number of absences for clerical workers during the year.

b. Construct a 95% confidence interval estimate of the population proportion of clerical workers absent more than 10 days during the year.

Suppose that the personnel director also wishes to take a survey in a branch office. Answer these questions:

c. What sample size is needed to have 95% confidence in estimating the population mean absenteeism to within ±1.5 days if the population standard deviation is estimated to be 4.5 days?

d. How many clerical workers need to be selected to have 90% confidence in estimating the population proportion to within ±0.075 if no previous estimate is available?

e. Based on (c) and (d), what sample size is needed if a single survey is being conducted?

8.73 The market research director for Dotty's Department Store wants to study women's spending on cosmetics. A survey of the store's credit card holders is designed in order to estimate the proportion of women who purchase their cosmetics primarily from Dotty's Department Store and the mean yearly amount that women spend on cosmetics. A previous survey found that the standard deviation of the amount women spend on cosmetics in a year is approximately $18.

a. What sample size is needed to have 99% confidence of estimating the population mean to within ±$5?

b. How many of the store's credit card holders need to be selected to have 90% confidence of estimating the population proportion to within ±0.045?

c. Based on the results in (a) and (b), how many of the store's credit card holders should be sampled? Explain.

8.74 The branch manager of a nationwide bookstore chain wants to study characteristics of her store's customers. She decides to focus on two variables: the amount of money spent by customers and whether the customers would consider purchasing educational DVDs relating to graduate preparation exams, such as the GMAT, GRE, or LSAT. The results from a sample of 70 customers are as follows:

- Amount spent: $\bar{X} = \$28.52$, $S = \$11.39$.
- 28 customers stated that they would consider purchasing the educational DVDs.

a. Construct a 95% confidence interval estimate of the population mean amount spent in the bookstore.

b. Construct a 90% confidence interval estimate of the population proportion of customers who would consider purchasing educational DVDs.

Assume that the branch manager of another store in the chain wants to conduct a similar survey in his store. Answer the following questions:

c. What sample size is needed to have 95% confidence of estimating the population mean amount spent in his store to within ±$2 if the standard deviation is assumed to be $10?

d. How many customers need to be selected to have 90% confidence of estimating the population proportion who would consider purchasing the educational DVDs to within ±0.04?

e. Based on your answers to (c) and (d), how large a sample should the manager take?

8.75 The branch manager of an outlet (Store 1) of a nationwide chain of pet supply stores wants to study characteristics of her customers. In particular, she decides to focus on two variables: the amount of money spent by customers and whether the customers own only one dog, only one cat, or more than one dog and/or cat. The results from a sample of 70 customers are as follows:

- Amount of money spent: $\bar{X} = \$21.34$, $S = \$9.22$.
- 37 customers own only a dog.
- 26 customers own only a cat.
- 7 customers own more than one dog and/or cat.

a. Construct a 95% confidence interval estimate of the population mean amount spent in the pet supply store.

b. Construct a 90% confidence interval estimate of the population proportion of customers who own only a cat.

The branch manager of another outlet (Store 2) wishes to conduct a similar survey in his store. The manager does not have access to the information generated by the manager of Store 1. Answer the following questions:

c. What sample size is needed to have 95% confidence of estimating the population mean amount spent in his store to within ±$1.50 if the standard deviation is estimated to be $10?

d. How many customers need to be selected to have 90% confidence of estimating the population proportion of customers who own only a cat to within ± 0.045?

e. Based on your answers to (c) and (d), how large a sample should the manager take?

8.76 The owner of a restaurant that serves continental food wants to study characteristics of his customers. He decides to focus on two variables: the amount of money spent by customers and whether customers order dessert. The results from a sample of 60 customers are as follows:

- Amount spent: $\bar{X} = \$38.54$, $S = \$7.26$.
- 18 customers purchased dessert.

a. Construct a 95% confidence interval estimate of the population mean amount spent per customer in the restaurant.

b. Construct a 90% confidence interval estimate of the population proportion of customers who purchase dessert.

The owner of a competing restaurant wants to conduct a similar survey in her restaurant. This owner does not have access to the information of the owner of the first restaurant. Answer the following questions:

c. What sample size is needed to have 95% confidence of estimating the population mean amount spent in her restaurant to within $\pm\$1.50$, assuming that the standard deviation is estimated to be \$8?

d. How many customers need to be selected to have 90% confidence of estimating the population proportion of customers who purchase dessert to within ± 0.04?

e. Based on your answers to (c) and (d), how large a sample should the owner take?

8.77 The manufacturer of "Ice Melt" claims its product will melt snow and ice at temperatures as low as $0°$ Fahrenheit. A representative for a large chain of hardware stores is interested in testing this claim. The chain purchases a large shipment of 5-pound bags for distribution. The representative wants to know with 95% confidence, within ± 0.05, what proportion of bags of Ice Melt perform the job as claimed by the manufacturer.

a. How many bags does the representative need to test? What assumption should be made concerning the population proportion? (This is called *destructive testing*; that is, the product being tested is destroyed by the test and is then unavailable to be sold.)

b. The representative tests 50 bags, and 42 of them do the job as claimed. Construct a 95% confidence interval estimate for the population proportion that will do the job as claimed.

c. How can the representative use the results of (b) to determine whether to sell the Ice Melt product?

8.78 An auditor needs to estimate the percentage of times a company fails to follow an internal control procedure. A sample of 50 from a population of 1,000 items is selected, and in 7 instances, the internal control procedure was not followed.

a. Construct a 90% one-sided confidence interval estimate of the population proportion of items in which the internal control procedure was not followed.

b. If the tolerable exception rate is 0.15, what should the auditor conclude?

8.79 An auditor for a government agency needs to evaluate payments for doctors' office visits paid by Medicare in a particular zip code during the month of June. A total of 25,056 visits occurred during June in this area. The auditor wants to estimate the total amount paid by Medicare to within $\pm\$5$ with 95% confidence. On the basis of past experience, she believes that the standard deviation is approximately \$30.

a. What sample size should she select?

Using the sample size selected in (a), an audit is conducted with the following results.

Amount of Reimbursement

$\bar{X} = \$93.70$ $S = \$34.55$

In 12 of the office visits, an incorrect amount of reimbursement was provided. For the 12 office visits in which there was an incorrect reimbursement, the differences between the amount reimbursed and the amount that the auditor determined should have been reimbursed were as follows (and are stored in the file Medicare):

$17 $25 $14   –$10 $20 $40 $35 $30 $28 $22 $15 $5

b. Construct a 90% confidence interval estimate of the population proportion of reimbursements that contain errors.

c. Construct a 95% confidence interval estimate of the population mean reimbursement per office visit.

d. Construct a 95% confidence interval estimate of the population total amount of reimbursements for this geographic area in June.

e. Construct a 95% confidence interval estimate of the total difference between the amount reimbursed and the amount that the auditor determined should have been reimbursed.

8.80 A home furnishings store that sells bedroom furniture is conducting an end-of-month inventory of the beds (mattress, bed spring, and frame) in stock. An auditor for the store wants to estimate the mean value of the beds in stock at that time. She wants to have 99% confidence that her estimate of the mean value is correct to within $\pm\$100$. On the basis of past experience, she estimates that the standard deviation of the value of a bed is \$200.

a. How many beds should she select?

b. Using the sample size selected in (a), an audit was conducted, with the following results:

$\bar{X} = \$1,654.27$ $S = \$184.62$

Construct a 99% confidence interval estimate of the total value of the beds in stock at the end of the month if there were 258 beds in stock.

8.81 A quality characteristic of interest for a tea-bag-filling process is the weight of the tea in the individual bags. In this example, the label weight on the package indicates that the mean amount is 5.5 grams of tea in a bag. If the bags are underfilled, two problems arise. First, customers may not be able to brew the tea to be as strong as they wish. Second, the company may be in violation of the truth-in-labeling laws. On the other hand, if the mean amount of tea in a bag exceeds the label weight, the company is giving away product. Getting an exact amount of tea in a bag is problematic because of variation in the temperature and humidity inside the factory, differences in the density of the tea, and the extremely fast filling operation of the machine (approximately 170 bags per minute). The following data (stored in the file Teabags) are the weights, in grams, of a sample of 50 tea bags produced in one hour by a single machine:

5.65 5.44 5.42 5.40 5.53 5.34 5.54 5.45 5.52 5.41
5.57 5.40 5.53 5.54 5.55 5.62 5.56 5.46 5.44 5.51
5.47 5.40 5.47 5.61 5.53 5.32 5.67 5.29 5.49 5.55
5.77 5.57 5.42 5.58 5.58 5.50 5.32 5.50 5.53 5.58
5.61 5.45 5.44 5.25 5.56 5.63 5.50 5.57 5.67 5.36

a. Construct a 99% confidence interval estimate of the population mean weight of the tea bags.
b. Is the company meeting the requirement set forth on the label that the mean amount of tea in a bag is 5.5 grams?

8.82 A manufacturing company produces steel housings for electrical equipment. The main component part of the housing is a steel trough that is made out of a 14-gauge steel coil. It is produced using a 250-ton progressive punch press with a wipe-down operation that puts two 90-degree forms in the flat steel to make the trough. The distance from one side of the form to the other is critical because of weatherproofing in outdoor applications. The widths (in inches) and stored in the file Trough from a sample of 49 troughs follows:

8.312 8.343 8.317 8.383 8.348 8.410 8.351 8.373 8.481 8.422
8.476 8.382 8.484 8.403 8.414 8.419 8.385 8.465 8.498 8.447
8.436 8.413 8.489 8.414 8.481 8.415 8.479 8.429 8.458 8.462
8.460 8.444 8.429 8.460 8.412 8.420 8.410 8.405 8.323 8.420
8.396 8.447 8.405 8.439 8.411 8.427 8.420 8.498 8.409

a. Construct a 95% confidence interval estimate of the mean width of the troughs.
b. Interpret the interval developed in (a).

8.83 The manufacturer of Boston and Vermont asphalt shingles knows that product weight is a major factor in the customer's perception of quality. The last stage of the

assembly line packages the shingles before they are placed on wooden pallets. Once a pallet is full (a pallet for most brands holds 16 squares of shingles), it is weighed, and the measurement is recorded. The file Pallet contains the weight (in pounds) from a sample of 368 pallets of Boston shingles and 330 pallets of Vermont shingles.
a. For the Boston shingles, construct a 95% confidence interval estimate of the mean weight.
b. For the Vermont shingles, construct a 95% confidence interval estimate of the mean weight.
c. Evaluate whether the assumption needed for (a) and (b) has been seriously violated.
d. Based on the results of (a) and (b), what conclusions can you reach concerning the mean weight of the Boston and Vermont shingles?

8.84 The manufacturer of Boston and Vermont asphalt shingles provides its customers with a 20-year warranty on most of its products. To determine whether a shingle will last as long as the warranty period, accelerated-life testing is conducted at the manufacturing plant. Accelerated-life testing exposes the shingle to the stresses it would be subject to in a lifetime of normal use via a laboratory experiment that takes only a few minutes to conduct. In this test, a shingle is repeatedly scraped with a brush for a short period of time, and the shingle granules removed by the brushing are weighed (in grams). Shingles that experience low amounts of granule loss are expected to last longer in normal use than shingles that experience high amounts of granule loss. In this situation, a shingle should experience no more than 0.8 grams of granule loss if it is expected to last the length of the warranty period. The file Granule contains a sample of 170 measurements made on the company's Boston shingles and 140 measurements made on Vermont shingles.
a. For the Boston shingles, construct a 95% confidence interval estimate of the mean granule loss.
b. For the Vermont shingles, construct a 95% confidence interval estimate of the mean granule loss.
c. Evaluate whether the assumption needed for (a) and (b) has been seriously violated.
d. Based on the results of (a) and (b), what conclusions can you reach concerning the mean granule loss of the Boston and Vermont shingles?

Report Writing Exercises
8.85 Referring to the results in Problem 8.82 concerning the width of a steel trough, write a report that summarizes your conclusions.

Team Project
8.86 Refer to the team project on page 67. Construct all appropriate confidence interval estimates of the population characteristics of low-risk, average-risk, and high-risk

mutual funds. Include these estimates in a report to the vice president for research at the financial investment service (The data are stored in the Mutual Funds file).

Student Survey Database

8.87 Problem 1.27 on page 14 describes a survey of 50 undergraduate students (see the file Undergradsurvey).
a. For these data, for each variable, construct a 95% confidence interval estimate of the population characteristic.
b. Write a report that summarizes your conclusions.

8.88 Problem 1.27 on page 14 describes a survey of 50 undergraduate students (see the file Undergradsurvey).
a. Select a sample of 50 undergraduate students at your school and conduct a similar survey for those students.

b. For the data collected in (a), repeat (a) and (b) of Problem 8.87.
c. Compare the results of (b) to those of Problem 8.87.

8.89 Problem 1.28 on page 14 describes a survey of 40 MBA students (see the file Gradsurvey).
a. For these data, for each variable, construct a 95% confidence interval estimate of the population characteristic.
b. Write a report that summarizes your conclusions.

8.90 Problem 1.28 on page 14 describes a survey of 40 MBA students (see the file Gradsurvey).
a. Select a sample of 40 graduate students in your MBA program and conduct a similar survey for those students.
b. For the data collected in (a), repeat (a) and (b) of Problem 8.89.
c. Compare the results of (b) to those of Problem 8.89.

MANAGING THE *SPRINGVILLE HERALD*

The marketing department has been considering ways to increase the number of new subscriptions and increase the rate of retention among customers who agreed to a trial subscription. Following the suggestion of Assistant Manager Lauren Adler, the department staff designed a survey to help determine various characteristics of readers of the newspaper who were not home-delivery subscribers. The survey consists of the following 10 questions:

1. Do you or a member of your household ever purchase the *Springville Herald*?
   (1) Yes   (2) No
   [If the respondent answers no, the interview is terminated.]
2. Do you receive the *Springville Herald* via home delivery?
   (1) Yes   (2) No
   [If no, skip to question 4.]
3. Do you receive the *Springville Herald*:
   (1) Monday–Saturday (2) Sunday only (3) Every day
   [If every day, skip to question 9.]
4. How often during the Monday–Saturday period do you purchase the *Springville Herald*?
   (1) Every day
   (2) Most days
   (3) Occasionally or never
5. How often do you purchase the *Springville Herald* on Sundays?
   (1) Every Sunday
   (2) 2–3 Sundays per month
   (3) No more than once a month

6. Where are you most likely to purchase the *Springville Herald*?
   (1) Convenience store
   (2) Newsstand/candy store
   (3) Vending machine
   (4) Supermarket
   (5) Other
7. Would you consider subscribing to the *Springville Herald* for a trial period if a discount were offered?
   (1) Yes   (2) No
   [If no, skip to question 9.]
8. The *Springville Herald* currently costs $0.50 Monday–Saturday and $1.50 on Sunday, for a total of $4.50 per week. How much would you be willing to pay per week to get home delivery for a 90-day trial period?
9. Do you read a daily newspaper other than the *Springville Herald*?
   (1) Yes   (2) No
10. As an incentive for long-term subscribers, the newspaper is considering the possibility of offering a card that would provide discounts at certain restaurants in the Springville area to all subscribers who pay in advance for six months of home delivery. Would you want to get such a card under the terms of this offer?
    (1) Yes   (2) No

The group agreed to use a random-digit dialing method to poll 500 local households by telephone. Using this approach, the last four digits of a telephone number are randomly selected to go with an area code and exchange (the first 6 digits of a 10-digit telephone number). Only those pairs of area codes and exchanges that were for the Springville city area were used for this survey.

Of the 500 households selected, 94 households either refused to participate, could not be contacted after repeated attempts, or represented telephone numbers that were not in service. The summary results are as follows:

Households That Purchase the *Springville Herald*

	Frequency
Yes	352
No	54

Households with Home Delivery

	Frequency
Yes	136
No	216

Type of Home Delivery Subscription

	Frequency
Monday–Saturday	18
Sunday only	25
7 days a week	93

Purchase Behavior of Nonsubscribers for Monday–Saturday Editions

	Frequency
Every day	78
Most days	95
Occasionally or never	43

Purchase Behavior of Nonsubscribers for Sunday Editions

	Frequency
Every Sunday	138
2–3 Sundays a month	54
No more than once a month	24

Nonsubscribers' Purchase Location

	Frequency
Convenience store	74
Newsstand/candy store	95
Vending machine	21
Supermarket	13
Other locations	13

Would Consider Trial Subscription If Offered a Discount

	Frequency
Yes	46
No	170

Rate ($) Willing to Pay per Week (data file SH8) for a 90-Day Home-Delivery Trial Subscription

4.15 3.60 4.10 3.60 3.60 3.60 4.40 3.15 4.00 3.75 4.00
3.25 3.75 3.30 3.75 3.65 4.00 4.10 3.90 3.50 3.75 3.00
3.40 4.00 3.80 3.50 4.10 4.25 3.50 3.90 3.95 4.30 4.20
3.50 3.75 3.30 3.85 3.20 4.40 3.80 3.40 3.50 2.85 3.75
3.80 3.90

Read a Daily Newspaper Other Than the *Springville Herald*

	Frequency
Yes	138
No	214

Would Prepay Six Months to Receive a Restaurant Discount Card

	Frequency
Yes	66
No	286

EXERCISES

SH8.1 Some members of the marketing department are concerned about the random-digit dialing method used to collect survey responses. Prepare a memorandum that examines the following issues:
- The advantages and disadvantages of using the random-digit dialing method.
- Possible alternative approaches for conducting the survey and their advantages and disadvantages.

SH8.2 Analyze the results of the survey of Springville households. Write a report that discusses the marketing implications of the survey results for the *Springville Herald*.

WEB CASE

Apply your knowledge about confidence interval estimation in this Web Case, which extends the OurCampus! Web Case from Chapter 6.

Among its other features, the OurCampus! Web site allows customers to purchase OurCampus! LifeStyles merchandise online. To handle payment processing, the management of OurCampus! has contracted with the following firms:
- PayAFriend (PAF): an online payment system with which customers and businesses such as OurCampus!

register in order to exchange payments in a secure and convenient manner without the need for a credit card.
- Continental Banking Company (Conbanco): a processing services provider that allows OurCampus! customers to pay for merchandise using nationally recognized credit cards issued by a financial institution.

To reduce costs, the management is considering eliminating one of these two payment systems. However, Virginia Duffy of the sales department suspects that customers use the two forms of payment in unequal numbers and that customers display different buying behaviors when using the two forms of payment. Therefore, she would like to first determine:

a. the proportion of customers using PAF and the proportion of customers using a credit card to pay for their purchases.
b. the mean purchase amount when using PAF and the mean purchase amount when using a credit card.

Assist Ms. Duffy by preparing an appropriate analysis based on a random sample of 50 transactions that she has prepared and placed in an internal file on the OurCampus! Web site, **www.prenhall.com/Springville/OurCampus_ PymtSample.htm** or open **OurCampus_PymtSample. htm** from the Student CD-ROM Web Case folder. Summarize your findings and determine whether Ms. Duffy's conjectures about OurCampus! customer purchasing behaviors are correct. If you want the sampling error to be no more than $3 when estimating the mean purchase amount, is Ms. Duffy's sample large enough to perform a valid analysis?

REFERENCES

1. Cochran, W. G., *Sampling Techniques*, 3rd ed. (New York: Wiley, 1977).
2. Fisher, R. A., and F. Yates, *Statistical Tables for Biological, Agricultural and Medical Research*, 5th ed. (Edinburgh: Oliver & Boyd, 1957).
3. Hahn, G., and W. Meeker, *Statistical Intervals, A Guide for Practioners*, (New York: John Wiley and Sons, Inc., 1991).
4. Kirk, R. E., ed., *Statistical Issues: A Reader for the Behavioral Sciences* (Belmont, CA: Wadsworth, 1972).
5. Larsen, R. L., and M. L. Marx, *An Introduction to Mathematical Statistics and Its Applications*, 4th ed. (Upper Saddle River, NJ: Prentice Hall, 2006).
6. *Microsoft Excel 2007* (Redmond, WA: Microsoft Corp., 2007).
7. *Minitab for Windows Version 15* (State College, PA: Minitab, Inc., 2006).
8. Snedecor, G. W., and W. G. Cochran, *Statistical Methods*, 7th ed. (Ames, IA: Iowa State University Press, 1980).

Appendix E8
Using Microsoft Excel for Confidence Interval Estimation

E8.1 Computing the Confidence Interval Estimate for the Mean (σ Known)

You compute the confidence interval estimate for the mean (σ known) by making entries in the **CIE_SK** worksheet of the `CIE sigma known.xls` workbook. This worksheet uses the **NORMSINV($P < X$)** and **CONFIDENCE(1-*confidence level, population standard deviation, sample size*)** functions to compute the Z value and interval half width for the Example 8.1 mean paper length problem on page 297. To adapt this worksheet to other problems, change the population standard deviation, sample mean, sample size, and confidence level values in the tinted cells B4 through B7, and enter a new title in cell A1.

E8.2 Computing the Confidence Interval Estimate for the Mean (σ Unknown)

You compute the confidence interval estimate for the mean (σ unknown) by making entries in the **CIE_SU** worksheet of the `CIE sigma unknown.xls` workbook. The worksheet (see Figure 8.7 on page 303) uses the **TINV(1-*confidence level, degrees of freedom*)** function to determine the critical value from the t distribution and compute the interval half width for the Section 8.2 Saxon Home Improvement Company example. To adapt this worksheet to other problems, change the sample statistics and confidence level values in the tinted cells B4 through B7, and enter a new title in cell A1.

E8.3 Computing the Confidence Interval Estimate for the Proportion

You compute the confidence interval estimate for the proportion by making entries in the **CIE_P** worksheet of the `CIE Proportion.xls` workbook. The worksheet (see Figure 8.12 on page 309) uses the **NORMSINV(*P < X*)** function to determine the *Z* value and uses the square root function to compute the standard error of the proportion for the Section 8.3 Saxon Home Improvement Company example. To adapt this worksheet to other problems, change the sample size, number of successes, and confidence level values in the tinted cells B4, B5, and B6, and enter a new title in cell A1.

E8.4 Computing the Sample Size Needed for Estimating the Mean

You compute the sample size needed for estimating the mean by making entries in the **SampleSize_M** worksheet of the `Sample Size Mean.xls` workbook. The worksheet (see Figure 8.14 on page 313) uses the **NORMSINV(*P < X*)** function to compute the *Z* value and uses the **ROUNDUP(*value*)** function to round up the sample size needed to the next higher integer for the Section 8.4 Saxon Home Improvement Company example. To adapt this worksheet to other problems, change the population standard deviation, sampling error, and confidence level values in the tinted cells B4, B5, and B6, and enter a new title in cell A1.

E8.5 Computing the Sample Size Needed for Estimating the Proportion

You compute the sample size needed for estimating the proportion by making entries in the **SampleSize_P** worksheet of the `Sample Size Proportion.xls` workbook. The worksheet (see Figure 8.15 on page 316) uses the **ROUNDUP(*value*)** function to round up the sample size needed to the next higher integer for the Section 8.4 Saxon Home Improvement Company example. To adapt this worksheet to other problems, change the estimate of true proportion, sampling error, and confidence level values in the tinted cells B4 through B6, and enter a new title in cell A1.

E8.6 Computing the Confidence Interval Estimate for the Population Total

You compute the confidence interval estimate for the population total by making entries in the **CIE_T** worksheet of the `CIE Total.xls` workbook. This worksheet (see Figure

8.16 on page 320) uses the **TINV(1-*confidence level, degrees of freedom*)** function to determine the critical value from the *t* distribution and the interval half width for the Section 8.5 Saxon Home Improvement Company population total example. To adapt this worksheet to other problems, change the population size, sample mean, sample size, sample standard deviation, and confidence level values in the tinted cells B4 through B8, and enter a new title in cell A1.

E8.7 Computing the Confidence Interval Estimate for the Total Difference

You compute the confidence interval estimate for the total difference by making entries in the **CIE_TD** worksheet of the `CIE Total Difference.xls` workbook. This worksheet (see Figure 8.17 on page 323) uses the **TINV(1-*confidence level, degrees of freedom*)** function to determine the critical value from the *t* distribution and the interval half width for the Section 8.5 Saxon Home Improvement Company total difference example. The worksheet also contains a calculation area in cell range D9:E16 that counts and sums the differences computed in column B of a **DifferencesData** worksheet. (Neither cell range is shown in Figure 8.17. See the **CIE_TD Formulas** and the **DifferencesData Formulas** worksheets for more information about these ranges and the formulas they contain.)

To adapt this worksheet to other problems, change both the CIE_TD and DifferencesData worksheet. In the CIE_TD sheet, change the population size, sample mean, sample size, sample standard deviation, and confidence level values in the tinted cells B4 through B6, and enter a new title in cell A1. In the DiffererencesData worksheet, enter the differences in column A. Then adjust column B by either copying down the formula in cell B13 to all rows with difference data if you have more than 12 differences, or by deleting unnecessary column B formulas if you have less than 12 differences.

E8.8 Computing Finite Correction Factors

The workbooks for confidence interval estimates of the mean and proportion and for computing the sample size needed for estimating the mean or proportion include **FPC** worksheets that calculate the finite population correction factor. Use these FPC worksheets if the sampling was done without replacement from a finite population (see Section 8.7).

Appendix P8
Using PHStat2 for Confidence Interval Estimation

P8.1 Computing the Confidence Interval Estimate for the Mean (σ Known)

To compute the confidence interval estimate for the mean (σ known), use **PHStat → Confidence Intervals → Estimate for the Mean, sigma known**. This procedure creates a worksheet (similar to the **CIE_SK** worksheet of the **CIE sigma known.xls** workbook) using the population standard deviation, sample mean, sample size, and confidence level values that you specify. If you have unsummarized data, click **Sample Statistics Unknown** and the procedure will calculate the sample statistics for you.

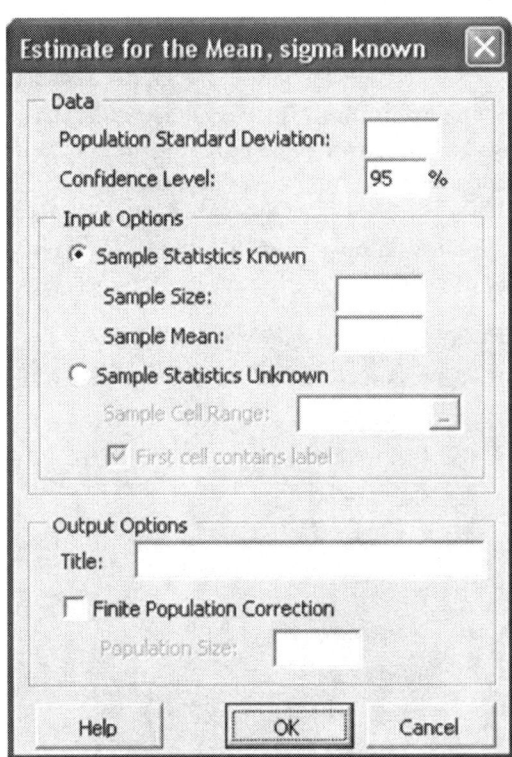

P8.2 Computing the Confidence Interval Estimate for the Mean (σ Unknown)

To compute the confidence interval estimate for the mean (σ unknown), use **PHStat → Confidence Intervals → Estimate for the Mean, sigma unknown**. This procedure

creates a worksheet similar to Figure 8.7 on page 303 using the sample statistics and a confidence level value that you specify. If you have unsummarized data, click **Sample Statistics Unknown** and the procedure will calculate the sample statistics for you.

P8.3 Computing the Confidence Interval Estimate for the Proportion

To compute the confidence interval estimate for the proportion, use **PHStat → Confidence Intervals → Estimate for the Proportion**. This procedure creates a worksheet similar to Figure 8.12 on page 309 using the sample size, number of successes, and confidence level values that you specify. Click **Finite Population Correction** if the sampling is done without replacement from a finite population (see Section 8.7).

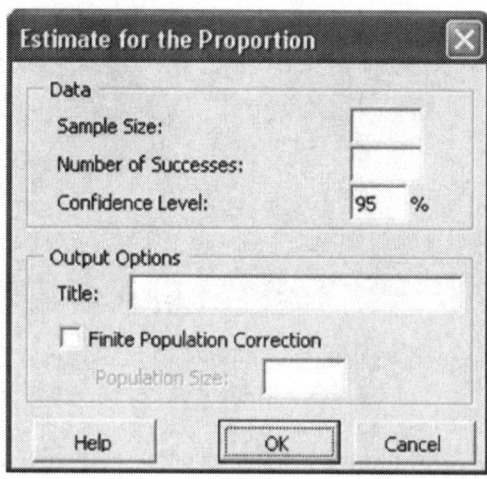

sampling is done without replacement from a finite population (see Section 8.7).

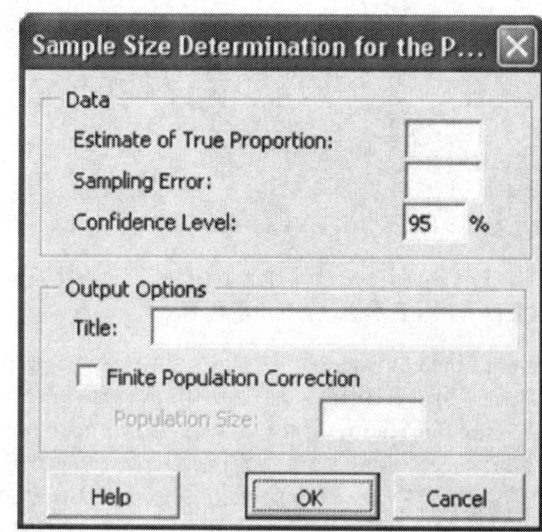

P8.4 Computing the Sample Size Needed for Estimating the Mean

To compute the sample size needed for estimating the mean, use **PHStat → Sample Size → Determination for the Mean**. This procedure creates a worksheet similar to Figure 8.14 on page 313 using the population standard deviation, sampling error, and confidence level values that you specify. Click **Finite Population Correction** if the sampling is done without replacement from a finite population (see Section 8.7).

P8.6 Computing the Confidence Interval Estimate for the Population Total Amount

To compute the confidence interval estimate for the population total, use **PHStat → Confidence Intervals → Estimate for the Population Total**. The procedure creates a worksheet similar to Figure 8.16 on page 320 using the population size, confidence level, sample mean, sample size, and sample standard deviation that you specify. If you have unsummarized data, click **Sample Statistics Unknown** and the procedure will calculate the sample statistics for you.

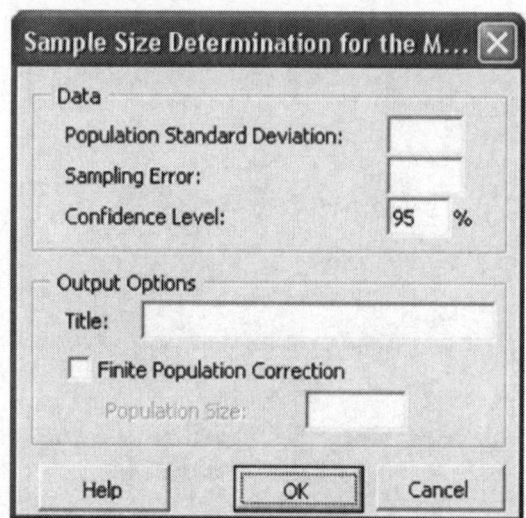

P8.5 Computing the Sample Size Needed for Estimating the Proportion

To compute the sample size needed for estimating the proportion, use **PHStat → Sample Size → Determination for the Proportion**. This procedure creates a worksheet similar to Figure 8.15 on page 316 using the estimate of true proportion, sampling error, and confidence level values that you specify. Click **Finite Population Correction** if the

P8.7 Computing the Confidence Interval Estimate for the Total Difference

To compute the confidence interval estimate for the total difference, use **PHStat → Confidence Intervals → Estimate for the Total Difference**. This procedure creates a worksheet similar to Figure 8.17 on page 323 using the sample size, population size, and confidence level values that you specify.

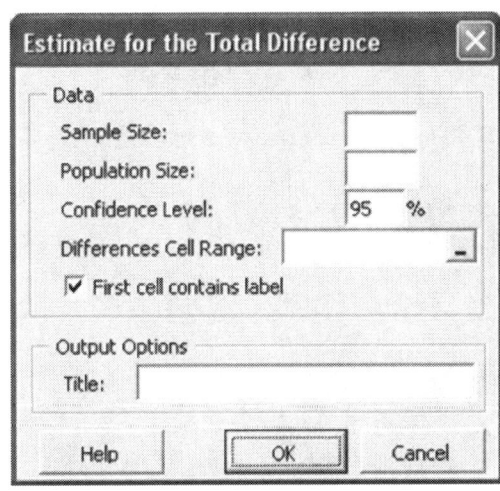

Appendix M8
Using Minitab for Confidence Interval Estimation

M8.1 Computing the Confidence Interval Estimation for the Mean (σ Known)

To compute a confidence interval estimate for the mean when σ is known

1. Select **Stat → Basic Statistics → 1-Sample Z**.

In the 1-Sample Z (Test and Confidence Interval) dialog box

2. Click **Samples in columns**.
3. Enter the variable name in the **Samples in columns** box.
4. Enter the value for σ in the **Standard deviation** box.
5. Click **Options.**

In the 1-Sample Z - Options dialog box:

6. Enter the level of confidence in the **Confidence level** box.
7. Click **OK** (to return to the previous dialog box).
8. Back in the first dialog box, click **OK** (to compute the confidence interval estimate).

M8.2 Computing the Confidence Interval Estimation for the Mean (σ Unknown)

To compute the confidence interval estimate for the population mean force required to break the insulators presented in Figure 8.8 on page 304:

1. Open the Force.mtw worksheet.
2. Select **Stat → Basic Statistics → 1-Sample t**.

In the 1-Sample t (Test and Confidence Interval) dialog box (see Figure M8.1):

3. Click **Samples in columns** and enter **Force** in its box. (For summarized data, click **Summarized data** and enter the sample size, sample mean, and sample standard deviation in their respective boxes.)
4. Click **Options**.

FIGURE M8.1

Minitab 1-Sample t (Test and Confidence Interval) dialog box

In the 1-Sample t - Options dialog box (see Figure M8.2):

5. Enter **95.0** in the **Confidence level** box.
6. Click **OK**.
7. Back in the first dialog box, click **OK**.

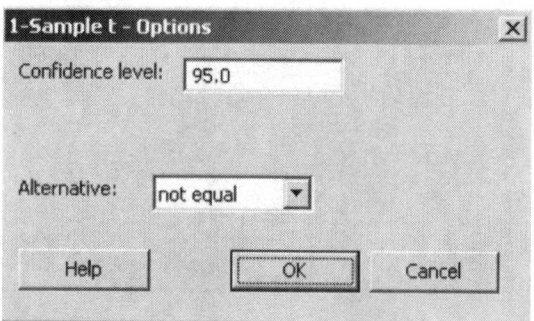

FIGURE M8.2

Minitab 1-Sample t - Options dialog box

M8.3 Computing the Confidence Interval Estimation for the Proportion

To compute the confidence interval estimate for the population proportion for the Saxon Home Improvement Company problem of Section 8.3 on page 309:

1. Select **Stat → Basic Statistics → 1 Proportion**.

In the 1 Proportion (Test and Confidence Interval) dialog box (see Figure M8.3):

2. Click **Summarized data**.
3. Enter **10** in the **Number of events** box.
4. Enter **100** in the **Number of trials** box.
5. Click **Options**.

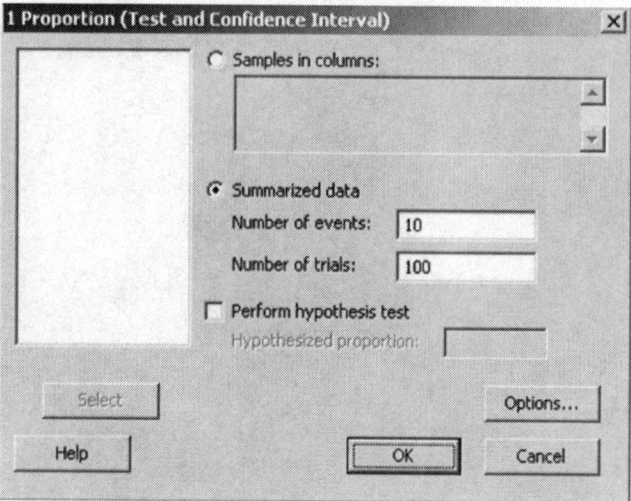

FIGURE M8.3

Minitab 1 Proportion (Test and Confidence Interval) dialog box

In the 1 Proportion-Options dialog box (see Figure M8.4):

6. Enter **95** in the **Confidence level** box.
7. Select **not equal** from the **Alternative** drop-down list.
8. Click **Use test and interval based on normal distribution**.
9. Click **OK**.
10. Back in the first dialog box, click **OK**.

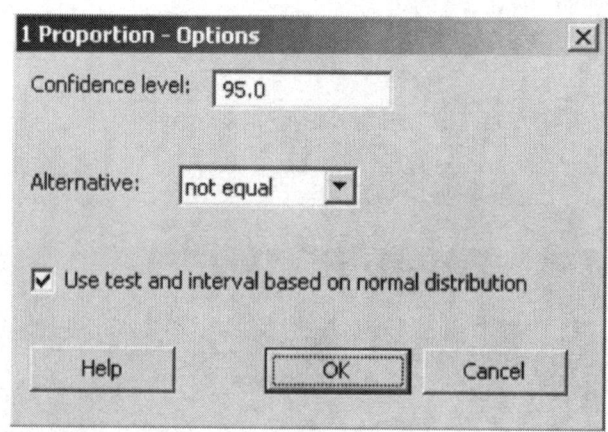

FIGURE M8.4

Minitab 1 Proportion - Options dialog box

CHAPTER
NINE

USING STATISTICS @ Oxford Cereals, Part II

LEARNING OBJECTIVES

In this chapter, you learn:

- The basic principles of hypothesis testing
- How to use hypothesis testing to test a mean or proportion
- The assumptions of each hypothesis-testing procedure, how to evaluate them, and the consequences if they are seriously violated
- How to avoid the pitfalls involved in hypothesis testing
- Ethical issues involved in hypothesis testing

USING STATISTICS @ Oxford Cereals, Part II

As in Chapter 7, you again find yourself as plant operations manager for Oxford Cereals. You are responsible for monitoring the amount in each cereal box filled. Company specifications require a mean weight of 368 grams per box. It is your responsibility to adjust the process when the mean fill weight in the population of boxes deviates from 368 grams. How can you rationally make the decision whether or not to adjust the process when it is impossible to weigh every single box as it is being filled? You begin by selecting and weighing a random sample of 25 cereal boxes. After computing a sample mean, how do you proceed?

In Chapter 7, you learned methods to determine whether a sample mean is consistent with a known population mean. In this Oxford Cereals scenario, you seek to use a sample mean to validate a claim about the population mean, a somewhat different problem. For this type of problem, you use an inferential method called **hypothesis testing**. Hypothesis testing requires that you state a claim unambiguously. In this scenario, the claim is that the population mean is 368 grams. You examine a sample statistic to see if it better supports the stated claim, called the *null hypothesis*, or the mutually exclusive alternative (for this scenario, that the population mean is not 368 grams).

In this chapter, you will learn several applications of hypothesis testing. You will learn how to make inferences about a population parameter by *analyzing differences* between the results observed, the sample statistic, and the results you would expect to get if an underlying hypothesis were actually true. For the Oxford Cereals scenario, hypothesis testing would allow you to infer one of the following:

- The mean weight of the cereal boxes in the sample is a value consistent with what you would expect if the mean of the entire population of cereal boxes is 368 grams.
- The population mean is not equal to 368 grams because the sample mean is significantly different from 368 grams.

9.1   FUNDAMENTALS OF HYPOTHESIS-TESTING METHODOLOGY

Hypothesis testing typically begins with some theory, claim, or assertion about a particular parameter of a population. For example, your initial hypothesis about the cereal example is that the process is working properly, so the mean fill is 368 grams, and no corrective action is needed.

The Null and Alternative Hypotheses

The hypothesis that the population parameter is equal to the company specification is referred to as the null hypothesis. A **null hypothesis** is always one of status quo and is identified by the symbol H_0. Here the null hypothesis is that the filling process is working properly, and therefore the mean fill is the 368-gram specification provided by Oxford Cereals. This is stated as

$$H_0: \mu = 368$$

Even though information is available only from the sample, the null hypothesis is written in terms of the population. Remember, your focus is on the population of all cereal boxes. The sample statistic is used to make inferences about the entire filling process. One inference may be that the results observed from the sample data indicate that the null hypothesis is false. If the null hypothesis is considered false, something else must be true.

Whenever a null hypothesis is specified, an alternative hypothesis is also specified, and it must be true if the null hypothesis is false. The **alternative hypothesis**, H_1, is the opposite of the null hypothesis, H_0. This is stated in the cereal example as

$$H_1: \mu \neq 368$$

The alternative hypothesis represents the conclusion reached by rejecting the null hypothesis. The null hypothesis is rejected when there is sufficient evidence from the sample information that the null hypothesis is false. In the cereal example, if the weights of the sampled boxes are sufficiently above or below the expected 368-gram mean specified by Oxford Cereals, you reject the null hypothesis in favor of the alternative hypothesis that the mean fill is different from 368 grams. You stop production and take whatever action is necessary to correct the problem. If the null hypothesis is not rejected, you should continue to believe in the status quo, that the process is working correctly and therefore no corrective action is necessary. In this second circumstance, you have not proven that the process is working correctly. Rather, you have failed to prove that it is working incorrectly, and therefore you continue your belief (although unproven) in the null hypothesis.

In hypothesis testing, you reject the null hypothesis when the sample evidence suggests that it is far more likely that the alternative hypothesis is true. However, failure to reject the null hypothesis is not proof that it is true. You can never prove that the null hypothesis is correct because the decision is based only on the sample information, not on the entire population. Therefore, if you fail to reject the null hypothesis, you can only conclude that there is insufficient evidence to warrant its rejection. The following key points summarize the null and alternative hypotheses:

- The null hypothesis, H_0, represents the status quo or the current belief in a situation.
- The alternative hypothesis, H_1, is the opposite of the null hypothesis and represents a research claim or specific inference you would like to prove.
- If you reject the null hypothesis, you have statistical proof that the alternative hypothesis is correct.
- If you do not reject the null hypothesis, you have failed to prove the alternative hypothesis. The failure to prove the alternative hypothesis, however, does not mean that you have proven the null hypothesis.
- The null hypothesis, H_0, always refers to a specified value of the population parameter (such as μ), not a sample statistic (such as $\bar{X}$).
- The statement of the null hypothesis always contains an equal sign regarding the specified value of the population parameter (e.g., $H_0: \mu = 368$ grams).
- The statement of the alternative hypothesis never contains an equal sign regarding the specified value of the population parameter (e.g., $H_1: \mu \neq 368$ grams).

EXAMPLE 9.1

THE NULL AND ALTERNATIVE HYPOTHESES

You are the manager of a fast-food restaurant. You want to determine whether the waiting time to place an order has changed in the past month from its previous population mean value of 4.5 minutes. State the null and alternative hypotheses.

SOLUTION The null hypothesis is that the population mean has not changed from its previous value of 4.5 minutes. This is stated as

$$H_0: \mu = 4.5$$

The alternative hypothesis is the opposite of the null hypothesis. Because the null hypothesis is that the population mean is 4.5 minutes, the alternative hypothesis is that the population mean is not 4.5 minutes. This is stated as

$$H_1: \mu \neq 4.5$$

The Critical Value of the Test Statistic

The logic of hypothesis testing involves determining how likely the null hypothesis is to be true by considering the information gathered in a sample. In the Oxford Cereal Company scenario, the null hypothesis is that the mean amount of cereal per box in the entire filling process is 368 grams (the population parameter specified by the company). You select a sample of boxes from the filling process, weigh each box, and compute the sample mean. This statistic is an estimate of the corresponding parameter (the population mean, μ). Even if the null hypothesis is true, the statistic (the sample mean, $\bar{X}$) is likely to differ from the value of the parameter (the population mean, μ) because of variation due to sampling. However, you expect the sample statistic to be close to the population parameter if the null hypothesis is true. If the sample statistic is close to the population parameter, you have insufficient evidence to reject the null hypothesis. For example, if the sample mean is 367.9, you conclude that the population mean has not changed (i.e., $\mu = 368$) because a sample mean of 367.9 is very close to the hypothesized value of 368. Intuitively, you think that it is likely that you could get a sample mean of 367.9 from a population whose mean is 368.

However, if there is a large difference between the value of the statistic and the hypothesized value of the population parameter, you conclude that the null hypothesis is false. For example, if the sample mean is 320, you conclude that the population mean is not 368 (i.e., $\mu \neq 368$), because the sample mean is very far from the hypothesized value of 368. In such a case, you conclude that it is very unlikely to get a sample mean of 320 if the population mean is really 368. Therefore, it is more logical to conclude that the population mean is not equal to 368. Here you reject the null hypothesis.

Unfortunately, the decision-making process is not always so clear-cut. Determining what is "very close" and what is "very different" is arbitrary without clear definitions. Hypothesis-testing methodology provides clear definitions for evaluating differences. Furthermore, it enables you to quantify the decision-making process by computing the probability of getting a given sample result if the null hypothesis is true. You calculate this probability by determining the sampling distribution for the sample statistic of interest (e.g., the sample mean) and then computing the particular **test statistic** based on the given sample result. Because the sampling distribution for the test statistic often follows a well-known statistical distribution, such as the standardized normal distribution or t distribution, you can use these distributions to help determine whether the null hypothesis is true.

Regions of Rejection and Nonrejection

The sampling distribution of the test statistic is divided into two regions, a **region of rejection** (sometimes called the critical region) and a **region of nonrejection** (see Figure 9.1). If the test statistic falls into the region of nonrejection, you do not reject the null hypothesis. In the Oxford Cereals scenario, you conclude that there is insufficient evidence that the population mean fill is different from 368 grams. If the test statistic falls into the rejection region, you reject the null hypothesis. In this case, you conclude that the population mean is not 368 grams.

The region of rejection consists of the values of the test statistic that are unlikely to occur if the null hypothesis is true. These values are much more likely to occur if the null hypothesis is false. Therefore, if a value of the test statistic falls into this *rejection region*, you reject the null hypothesis because that value is unlikely if the null hypothesis is true.

To make a decision concerning the null hypothesis, you first determine the **critical value** of the test statistic. The critical value divides the nonrejection region from the rejection region.

FIGURE 9.1

Regions of rejection
and nonrejection in
hypothesis testing

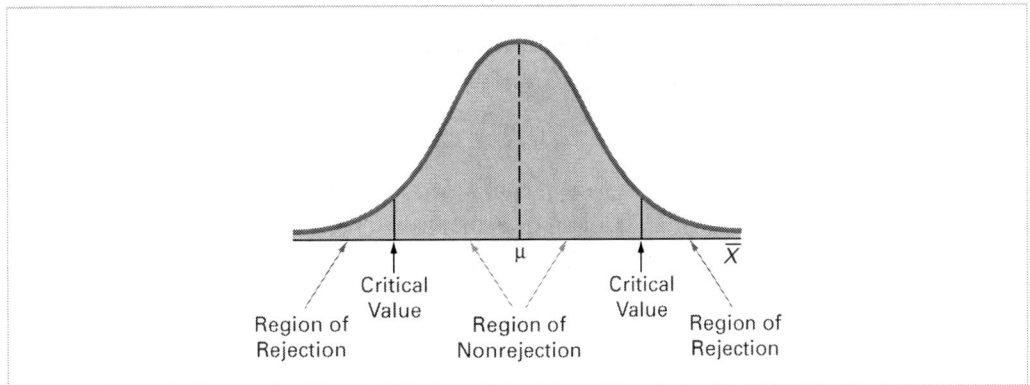

Determining this critical value depends on the size of the rejection region. The size of the rejection region is directly related to the risks involved in using only sample evidence to make decisions about a population parameter.

Risks in Decision Making Using Hypothesis Testing

When using a sample statistic to make decisions about a population parameter, there is a risk that you will reach an incorrect conclusion. You can make two different types of errors when applying hypothesis testing, Type I and Type II errors.

> A **Type I error** occurs if you reject the null hypothesis, H_0, when it is true and should not be rejected. The probability of a Type I error occurring is α.
>
> A **Type II error** occurs if you do not reject the null hypothesis, H_0, when it is false and should be rejected. The probability of a Type II error occurring is β.

In the Oxford Cereals scenario, you make a Type I error if you conclude that the population mean fill is *not* 368 when it *is* 368. This error causes you to adjust the filling process even though the process is working properly. Thus, a Type I error is a "false alarm". You make a Type II error if you conclude that the population mean fill *is* 368 when it is *not* 368. Here, you would allow the process to continue without adjustment even though adjustments are needed. Thus, a Type II error represents a "missed opportunity".

The Level of Significance (α)   The probability of committing a Type I error, denoted by α (the lowercase Greek letter *alpha*), is referred to as the **level of significance** of the statistical test. Traditionally, you control the Type I error by deciding the risk level, α, that you are willing to have of rejecting the null hypothesis when it is true. Because you specify the level of significance before the hypothesis test is performed, the risk of committing a Type I error, α, is directly under your control. Traditionally, you select levels of 0.01, 0.05, or 0.10. The choice of a particular risk level for making a Type I error depends on the cost of making a Type I error. After you specify the value for α, you can then determine the critical values that divide the rejection and nonrejection regions. You know the size of the rejection region because α is the probability of rejection when the null hypothesis is true. From this, you can then determine the critical value or values that divide the rejection and nonrejection regions.

The Confidence Coefficient   The complement of the probability of a Type I error, $(1 - \alpha)$, is called the confidence coefficient. When multiplied by 100%, the confidence coefficient yields the confidence level that was studied when constructing confidence intervals (see Section 8.1).

The **confidence coefficient**, $(1 - \alpha)$, is the probability that you will not reject the null hypothesis, H_0, when it is true and should not be rejected. The **confidence level** of a hypothesis test is $(1 - \alpha) \times 100\%$.

In terms of hypothesis testing, the confidence coefficient represents the probability of concluding that the value of the parameter as specified in the null hypothesis is plausible when it is true. In the Oxford Cereals scenario, the confidence coefficient measures the probability of concluding that the population mean fill is 368 grams when it is actually 368 grams.

The β Risk   The probability of committing a Type II error is denoted by β (the lowercase Greek letter *beta*). Unlike a Type I error, which you control by the selection of α, the probability of making a Type II error depends on the difference between the hypothesized and actual values of the population parameter. Because large differences are easier to find than small ones, if the difference between the hypothesized and actual values of the population parameter is large, β is small. For example, if the population mean is 330 grams, there is a small chance (β) that you will conclude that the mean has not changed from 368. However, if the difference between the hypothesized and actual values of the parameter is small, β is large. For example, if the population mean is actually 367 grams, there is a large chance (β) that you will conclude that the mean is still 368 grams.

The Power of a Test   The complement of the probability of a Type II error, $(1 - \beta)$, is called the power of a statistical test.

The **power of a statistical test**, $(1 - \beta)$, is the probability that you will reject the null hypothesis when it is false and should be rejected.

In the Oxford Cereals scenario, the power of the test is the probability that you will correctly conclude that the mean fill amount is not 368 grams when it actually is not 368 grams. For a detailed discussion of the power of the test, see Section 9.5.

Risks in Decision Making: A Delicate Balance   Table 9.1 illustrates the results of the two possible decisions (do not reject H_0 or reject H_0) that you can make in any hypothesis test. You can make a correct decision or make one of two types of errors.

TABLE 9.1

Hypothesis Testing and Decision Making

Statistical Decision	Actual Situation	
	H_0 True	H_0 False
Do not reject H_0	Correct decision Confidence $= (1 - \alpha)$	Type II error P (Type II error) $= \beta$
Reject H_0	Type I error P (Type I error) $= \alpha$	Correct decision Power $= (1 - \beta)$

One way to reduce the probability of making a Type II error is by increasing the sample size. Large samples generally permit you to detect even very small differences between the hypothesized values and the actual population parameters. For a given level of α, increasing the sample size decreases β and therefore increases the power of the test to detect that the null hypothesis, H_0, is false. However, there is always a limit to your resources, and this affects the decision as to how large a sample you can take. Thus, for a given sample size, you must consider the trade-offs between the two possible types of errors. Because you can directly control the risk of Type I error, you can reduce this risk by selecting a smaller value for α. For example, if the negative consequences associated with making a Type I error are substantial, you could select $\alpha = 0.01$ instead of 0.05. However, when you decrease α, you increase β, so reducing the risk of a Type I error results in an increased risk of a Type II error. However, if you wish to reduce β, you could select a larger value for α. Therefore, if it is important to try to avoid a Type II error, you can select α of 0.05 or 0.10 instead of 0.01.

In the Oxford Cereals scenario, the risk of a Type I error involves concluding that the mean fill amount has changed from the hypothesized 368 grams when it actually has not changed. The risk of a Type II error involves concluding that the mean fill amount has not changed from the hypothesized 368 grams when it actually has changed. The choice of reasonable values for α and β depends on the costs inherent in each type of error. For example, if it is very costly to change the cereal-fill process, you would want to be very confident that a change is needed before making any changes. In this case, the risk of a Type I error is more important, and you would choose a small α. However, if you want to be very certain of detecting changes from a mean of 368 grams, the risk of a Type II error is more important, and you would choose a higher level of α.

Now that you have been introduced to hypothesis testing, recall that in the Using Statistics scenario on page 342, Oxford Cereals wants to determine whether the cereal-fill process is working properly (i.e., whether the mean fill throughout the entire packaging process remains at the specified 368 grams, and no corrective action is needed). To evaluate the 368-gram requirement, you take a random sample of 25 boxes, weigh each box, and then evaluate the difference between the sample statistic and the hypothesized population parameter by comparing the mean weight (in grams) from the sample to the expected mean of 368 grams specified by the company. The null and alternative hypotheses are

$$H_0: \mu = 368$$
$$H_1: \mu \neq 368$$

When the standard deviation, σ, is known (which rarely occurs), you use the **Z test for the mean** if the population is normally distributed. If the population is not normally distributed, you can still use the Z test if the sample size is large enough for the Central Limit Theorem to take effect (see Section 7.4). Equation (9.1) defines the Z-test statistic Z_{STAT} for determining the difference between the sample mean, $\bar{X}$, and the population mean, μ, when the standard deviation, σ, is known.

Z Test for the Mean (σ Known)

$$Z_{STAT} = \frac{\bar{X} - \mu}{\frac{\sigma}{\sqrt{n}}} \tag{9.1}$$

In Equation (9.1), the numerator measures the difference between the observed sample mean, $\bar{X}$, and the hypothesized mean, μ. The denominator is the standard error of the mean, so Z_{STAT} represents the difference between $\bar{X}$ and μ in standard error units.

The Critical Value Approach to Hypothesis Testing

In the critical value approach to hypothesis testing, the observed value of the Z_{STAT} test statistic, Equation (9.1), is compared to critical values. The critical values are expressed as standardized Z values (i.e., in standard error units). For example, if you use a level of significance of 0.05, the size of the rejection region is 0.05. Because the rejection region is divided into the two tails of the distribution (this is called a **two-tail test**), you divide the 0.05 into two equal parts of 0.025 each. A rejection region of 0.025 in each tail of the normal distribution results in a cumulative area of 0.025 below the lower critical value and a cumulative area of 0.975 below the upper critical value (i.e., an area of 0.025 in the upper tail). According to the cumulative standardized normal distribution table (Table E.2), the critical values that divide the rejection and nonrejection regions are −1.96 and +1.96. Figure 9.2 illustrates that if the mean is actually 368 grams, as H_0 claims, the values of the Z_{STAT} test statistic have a standardized normal distribution centered at $Z = 0$ (which corresponds to an $\bar{X}$ value of 368 grams). Values of Z_{STAT} greater than +1.96 or less than −1.96 indicate that $\bar{X}$ is sufficiently different from the hypothesized $\mu = 368$ that it is unlikely that such an $\bar{X}$ value would occur if H_0 were true.

FIGURE 9.2

Testing a hypothesis about the mean (σ known) at the 0.05 level of significance

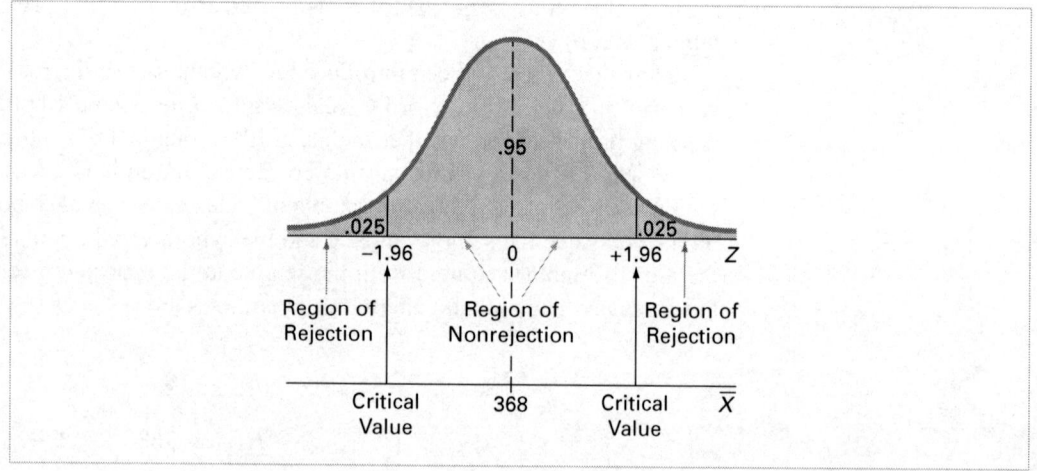

Therefore, the decision rule is

$$\text{Reject } H_0 \text{ if } Z_{STAT} > +1.96$$

$$\text{or if } Z_{STAT} < -1.96;$$

$$\text{otherwise, do not reject } H_0.$$

Suppose that the sample of 25 cereal boxes indicates a sample mean, $\bar{X}$, of 372.5 grams, and the population standard deviation, σ, is 15 grams. Using Equation (9.1) on page 347,

$$Z_{STAT} = \frac{\bar{X} - \mu}{\dfrac{\sigma}{\sqrt{n}}} - \frac{372.5 - 368}{\dfrac{15}{\sqrt{25}}} = +1.50$$

Because $Z_{STAT} = +1.50$ is between −1.96 and +1.96, you do not reject H_0 (see Figure 9.3). You continue to believe that the mean fill amount is 368 grams. To take into account the possibility of a Type II error, you state the conclusion as "there is insufficient evidence that the mean fill is different from 368 grams."

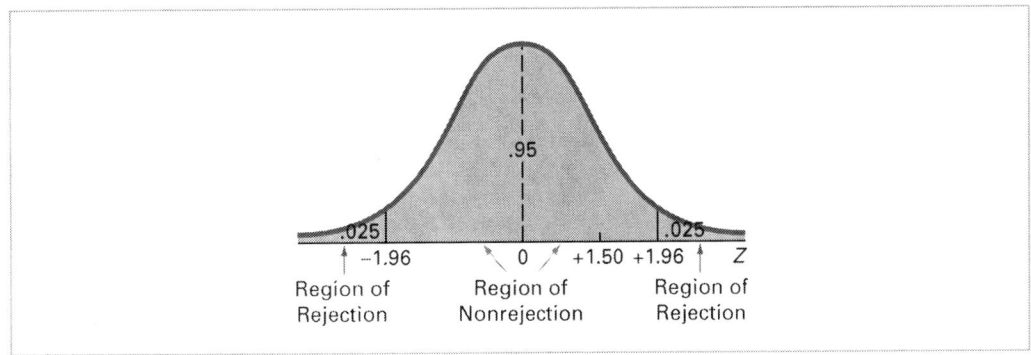

Exhibit 9.1 provides a summary of the critical value approach to hypothesis testing.

EXHIBIT 9.1 THE SIX-STEP METHOD OF HYPOTHESIS TESTING

1. State the null hypothesis, H_0, and the alternative hypothesis, H_1.
2. Choose the level of significance, α, and the sample size, n. The level of significance is based on the relative importance of the risks of committing Type I and Type II errors in the problem.
3. Determine the appropriate test statistic and sampling distribution.
4. Determine the critical values that divide the rejection and nonrejection regions.
5. Collect the sample data and compute the value of the test statistic.
6. Make the statistical decision and state the managerial conclusion. If the test statistic falls into the nonrejection region, you do not reject the null hypothesis. If the test statistic falls into the rejection region, you reject the null hypothesis. The managerial conclusion is written in the context of the real-world problem.

EXAMPLE 9.2

APPLYING THE SIX-STEP METHOD OF HYPOTHESIS TESTING
AT OXFORD CEREALS

State the six-step method of hypothesis testing at Oxford Cereals.

SOLUTION

Step 1 State the null and alternative hypotheses. The null hypothesis, H_0, is always stated as a mathematical expression using population parameters. In testing whether the mean fill is 368 grams, the null hypothesis states that μ equals 368. The alternative hypothesis, H_1, is also stated as a mathematical expression using population parameters. Therefore, the alternative hypothesis states that μ is not equal to 368 grams.

Step 2 Choose the level of significance and the sample size. You choose the level of significance, α, according to the relative importance of the risks of committing Type I and Type II errors in the problem. The smaller the value of α, the less risk there is of making a Type I error. In this example, making a Type I error means that you conclude that the population mean is not 368 grams when it is 368 grams. Thus, you will take corrective action on the filling process even though the process is working properly. Here, $\alpha = 0.05$ is selected. The sample size, n, is 25.

Step 3 Select the appropriate test statistic. Because σ is known from information about the filling process, you use the normal distribution and the Z_{STAT} test statistic.

Step 4 Determine the rejection region. Critical values for the appropriate test statistic are selected so that the rejection region contains a total area of α when H_0 is true and the nonrejection region contains a total area of $1 - \alpha$ when H_0 is true. Because $\alpha = 0.05$ in the cereal example, the critical values of the Z_{STAT} test statistic are -1.96 and $+1.96$. The rejection region is therefore $Z_{STAT} < -1.96$ or $Z_{STAT} > +1.96$. The nonrejection region is $-1.96 < Z_{STAT} < +1.96$.

Step 5 Collect the sample data and compute the value of the test statistic. In the cereal example, $\bar{X} = 372.5$, and the value of the test statistic is $Z_{STAT} = +1.50$.

Step 6 State the statistical decision and the managerial conclusion. First, determine whether the test statistic has fallen into the rejection region or the nonrejection region. For the cereal example, $Z_{STAT} = +1.50$ is in the region of nonrejection because $-1.96 < Z_{STAT} = +1.50 < +1.96$. Because the test statistic falls into the nonrejection region, the statistical decision is to not reject the null hypothesis, H_0. The managerial conclusion is that insufficient evidence exists to prove that the mean fill is different from 368 grams. No corrective action on the filling process is needed.

EXAMPLE 9.3

TESTING AND REJECTING A NULL HYPOTHESIS

You are the manager of a fast-food restaurant. You want to determine whether the population mean waiting time to place an order has changed in the past month from its previous population mean value of 4.5 minutes. From past experience, you can assume that the population is normally distributed with a population standard deviation of 1.2 minutes. You select a sample of 25 orders during a one-hour period. The sample mean is 5.1 minutes. Use the six-step approach listed in Exhibit 9.1 on page 399 to determine whether there is evidence at the 0.05 level of significance that the population mean waiting time to place an order has changed in the past month from its previous population mean value of 4.5 minutes.

SOLUTION

Step 1 The null hypothesis is that the population mean has not changed from its previous value of 4.5 minutes:

$$H_0: \mu = 4.5$$

The alternative hypothesis is the opposite of the null hypothesis. Because the null hypothesis is that the population mean is 4.5 minutes, the alternative hypothesis is that the population mean is not 4.5 minutes:

$$H_1: \mu \neq 4.5$$

Step 2 You have selected a sample of $n = 25$. The level of significance is 0.05 (i.e., $\alpha = 0.05$).

Step 3 Because σ is assumed known, you use the normal distribution and the Z_{STAT} test statistic.

Step 4 Because $\alpha = 0.05$, the critical values of the Z_{STAT} test statistic are -1.96 and $+1.96$. The rejection region is $Z_{STAT} < -1.96$ or $Z_{STAT} > +1.96$. The nonrejection region is $-1.96 < Z_{STAT} < +1.96$.

Step 5 You collect the sample data and compute $\bar{X} = 5.1$. Using Equation (9.1) on page 347, you compute the test statistic:

$$Z_{STAT} = \frac{\bar{X} - \mu}{\dfrac{\sigma}{\sqrt{n}}} = \frac{5.1 - 4.5}{\dfrac{1.2}{\sqrt{25}}} = 2.50$$

Step 6 Because $Z_{STAT} = 2.50 > 1.96$, you reject the null hypothesis. You conclude that there is evidence that the population mean waiting time to place an order has changed from its previous value of 4.5 minutes. The mean waiting time for customers is longer now than it was last month.

The *p*-Value Approach to Hypothesis Testing

Most software packages, including Microsoft Excel and Minitab, compute the *p*-value when performing a test of hypothesis.

> The ***p*-value** is the probability of getting a test statistic equal to or more extreme than the sample result, given that the null hypothesis, H_0, is true. The *p*-value is often referred to as the *observed level of significance*.

The decision rules for rejecting H_0 in the *p*-value approach are

- If the *p*-value is greater than or equal to α, do not reject the null hypothesis.
- If the *p*-value is less than α, reject the null hypothesis.

Many people confuse these rules, mistakenly believing that a high *p*-value is grounds for rejection. You can avoid this confusion by remembering the following mantra:

> If the *p*-value is low, then H_0 must go.

To understand the *p*-value approach, consider the Oxford Cereals scenario. You tested whether the mean fill was equal to 368 grams. The test statistic resulted in a Z_{STAT} value of +1.50, and you did not reject the null hypothesis because +1.50 was less than the upper critical value of +1.96 and more than the lower critical value of −1.96.

To use the *p*-value approach for the *two-tail test*, you find the probability of getting a test statistic Z_{STAT} that is equal to or *more extreme than* 1.50 standard error units from the center of a standardized normal distribution. In other words, you need to compute the probability of a Z_{STAT} value greater than +1.50, along with the probability of a Z_{STAT} value less than −1.50. Table E.2 shows that the probability of a Z_{STAT} value below −1.50 is 0.0668. The probability of a value below +1.50 is 0.9332, and the probability of a value above +1.50 is 1 − 0.9332 = 0.0668. Therefore, the *p*-value for this two-tail test is 0.0668 + 0.0668 = 0.1336 (see Figure 9.4). Thus, the probability of a test statistic equal to or more extreme than the sample result is 0.1336. Because 0.1336 is greater than $\alpha = 0.05$, you do not reject the null hypothesis.

FIGURE 9.4

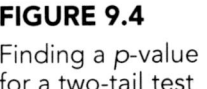

Finding a *p*-value for a two-tail test

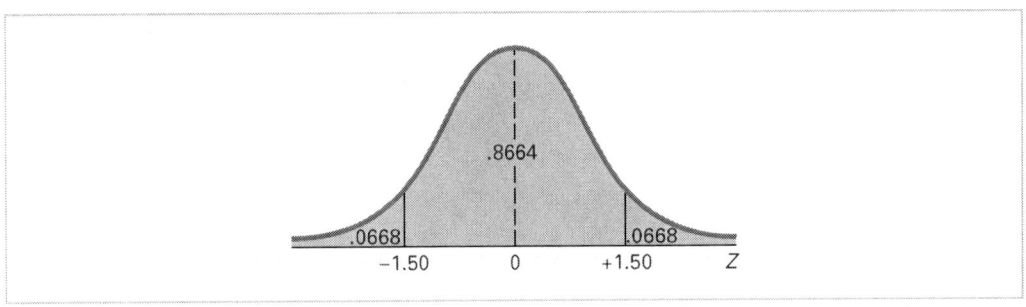

In this example, the observed sample mean is 372.5 grams, 4.5 grams above the hypothesized value, and the *p*-value is 0.1336. Thus, if the population mean is 368 grams, there is a 13.36% chance that the sample mean differs from 368 grams by more than 4.5 grams (i.e., is ≥ 372.5 grams or ≤ 363.5 grams). Therefore, even though 372.5 is above the hypothesized value of 368, a result as extreme as or more extreme than 372.5 is not highly unlikely when the population mean is 368.

Unless you are dealing with a test statistic that follows the normal distribution, you will only be able to approximate the *p*-value from the tables of the distribution. However, Microsoft Excel and Minitab routinely compute the *p*-values in each hypothesis-testing procedure. Once you understand the *p*-value approach, and assuming that you are using software such as Microsoft Excel or Minitab, you can just use the *p*-value approach instead of the critical value approach.

Figure 9.5 shows a Microsoft Excel worksheet for the cereal-filling example discussed in this section.

FIGURE 9.5

Microsoft Excel *Z*-test results for the cereal-fill example

See Section E9.1 or P9.1 to create this. (Minitab users, see Section M9.1 to create the equivalent results.)

	A	B	
1	Cereal-Filling Process Hypothesis Test		
2			
3	**Data**		
4	Null Hypothesis μ=	368	
5	Level of Significance	0.05	
6	Population Standard Deviation	15	
7	Sample Size	25	
8	Sample Mean	372.5	
9			
10	Intermediate Calculations		
11	Standard Error of the Mean	3	=B6/SQRT(B7)
12	Z Test Statistic	1.5	=(B8 - B4)/B11
13			
14	**Two-Tail Test**		
15	Lower Critical Value	-1.9600	=NORMSINV(B5/2)
16	Upper Critical Value	1.9600	=NORMSINV(1 - B5/2)
17	*p*-Value	0.1336	=2 * (1 - NORMSDIST(ABS(B12)))
18	Do not reject the null hypothesis		=IF(B17 < B5, "Reject the null hypothesis", "Do not reject the null hypothesis")

Exhibit 9.2 provides a summary of the *p*-value approach for hypothesis testing.

EXHIBIT 9.2 THE FIVE-STEP *p*-VALUE APPROACH TO HYPOTHESIS TESTING

1. State the null hypothesis, H_0, and the alternative hypothesis, H_1.
2. Choose the level of significance, α, and the sample size, n. The level of significance is based on the relative importance of the risks of committing Type I and Type II errors in the problem.
3. Determine the appropriate test statistic and the sampling distribution.
4. Collect the sample data, compute the value of the test statistic, and compute the *p*-value.
5. Make the statistical decision and state the managerial conclusion. If the *p*-value is greater than or equal to α, you do not reject the null hypothesis. If the *p*-value is less than α, you reject the null hypothesis. Remember the mantra: If the *p*-value is low, then H_0 must go. The managerial conclusion is written in the context of the real-world problem.

EXAMPLE 9.4

TESTING AND REJECTING A NULL HYPOTHESIS, USING THE *p*-VALUE APPROACH

You are the manager of a fast-food restaurant. You want to determine whether the population mean waiting time to place an order has changed in the past month from its previous value of 4.5 minutes. From past experience, you can assume that the population standard deviation is 1.2 minutes. You select a sample of 25 orders during a one-hour period. The sample mean is 5.1 minutes. Use the five-step *p*-value approach of Exhibit 9.2 to determine whether there is evidence that the population mean waiting time to place an order has changed in the past month from its previous population mean value of 4.5 minutes.

SOLUTION

Step 1   The null hypothesis is that the population mean has not changed from its previous value of 4.5 minutes:

$$H_0: \mu = 4.5$$

The alternative hypothesis is the opposite of the null hypothesis. Because the null hypothesis is that the population mean is 4.5 minutes, the alternative hypothesis is that the population mean is not 4.5 minutes:

$$H_1: \mu \neq 4.5$$

Step 2 You have selected a sample of $n = 25$. You choose a 0.05 level of significance (i.e., $\alpha = 0.05$).

Step 3 Select the appropriate test statistic. Because σ is assumed known, you use the normal distribution and the Z_{STAT} test statistic.

Step 4 You collect the data and compute $\bar{X} = 5.1$. Using Equation (9.1) on page 347, you compute the test statistic as follows:

$$Z_{STAT} = \frac{\bar{X} - \mu}{\dfrac{\sigma}{\sqrt{n}}} = \frac{5.1 - 4.5}{\dfrac{1.2}{\sqrt{25}}} = 2.50$$

To find the probability of getting a Z_{STAT} test statistic that is equal to or more extreme than 2.50 standard error units from the center of a standardized normal distribution, you compute the probability of a Z_{STAT} value greater than 2.50 along with the probability of a Z_{STAT} value less than -2.50. From Table E.2, the probability of a Z_{STAT} value below -2.50 is 0.0062. The probability of a value below $+2.50$ is 0.9938. Therefore, the probability of a value above $+2.50$ is $1 - 0.9938 = 0.0062$. Thus, the p-value for this two-tail test is $0.0062 + 0.0062 = 0.0124$.

Step 5 Because the p-value $= 0.0124 < \alpha = 0.05$, you reject the null hypothesis. You conclude that there is evidence that the population mean waiting time to place an order has changed from its previous population mean value of 4.5 minutes. The mean waiting time for customers is longer now than it was last month.

A Connection Between Confidence Interval Estimation and Hypothesis Testing

This chapter and Chapter 8 discuss the two major components of statistical inference: confidence interval estimation and hypothesis testing. Although they are based on the same set of concepts, they are used for different purposes. In Chapter 8, confidence intervals were used to estimate parameters. In this chapter, hypothesis testing is used for making decisions about specified values of population parameters. Hypothesis tests are used when trying to prove that a parameter is less than, more than, or not equal to a specified value. Proper interpretation of a confidence interval, however, can also indicate whether a parameter is less than, more than, or not equal to a specified value. For example, in this section, you tested whether the population mean fill amount was different from 368 grams by using Equation (9.1) on page 347:

$$Z_{STAT} = \frac{\bar{X} - \mu}{\dfrac{\sigma}{\sqrt{n}}}$$

Instead of testing the null hypothesis that $\mu = 368$ grams, you can reach the same conclusion by constructing a confidence interval estimate of μ. If the hypothesized value of $\mu = 368$ is contained within the interval, you do not reject the null hypothesis because 368 would not be considered an unusual value. However, if the hypothesized value does not fall into the interval, you reject the null hypothesis because "$\mu = 368$ grams" is then considered an unusual value. Using Equation (8.1) on page 296 and the following data:

$$n = 25, \bar{X} = 372.5 \text{ grams}, \sigma = 15 \text{ grams}$$

for a confidence level of 95% (i.e., $\alpha = 0.05$),

$$\bar{X} \pm Z_{\alpha/2} \frac{\sigma}{\sqrt{n}}$$

$$372.5 \pm (1.96)\frac{15}{\sqrt{25}}$$

$$372.5 \pm 5.88$$

so that

$$366.62 \le \mu \le 378.38$$

Because the interval includes the hypothesized value of 368 grams, you do not reject the null hypothesis. There is insufficient evidence that the mean fill amount over the entire filling process is not 368 grams. You reached the same decision by using two-tail hypothesis testing.

Can You Ever *Really* Know Sigma Part II?

From the Authors' Desktop

Section 9.1 discusses the fundamentals of hypothesis testing. Just as in Chapter 8 when confidence intervals were developed, using an example in which the population standard deviation σ is known makes it much easier to explain the fundamentals of hypothesis testing. With a known population standard deviation, you can use the normal distribution and compute p-values from the tables of the normal distribution.

In virtually all situations, you do not know the standard deviation of the population. If you did, you would also know the population mean and therefore would not need to test a hypothesis about it. So, use this section to understand the fundamentals of hypothesis testing, but don't think that, in practice, you will ever know the population standard deviation σ.

PROBLEMS FOR SECTION 9.1

Learning the Basics

9.1 For H_0: $\mu = 100$, H_1: $\mu \ne 100$, and for a sample of size n, why is β larger if the actual value of μ is 90 than if the actual value of μ is 75?

9.2 If you use a 0.05 level of significance in a (two-tail) hypothesis test, what will you decide if $Z_{STAT} = +2.21$?

9.3 If you use a 0.10 level of significance in a (two-tail) hypothesis test, what is your decision rule for rejecting a null hypothesis that the population mean is 500 if you use the Z test?

9.4 If you use a 0.01 level of significance in a (two-tail) hypothesis test, what is your decision rule for rejecting H_0: $\mu = 12.5$ if you use the Z test?

9.5 What is your decision in Problem 9.4 if $Z_{STAT} = -2.61$?

9.6 What is the *p*-value if, in a two-tail hypothesis test, $Z_{STAT} = +2.00$?

9.7 In Problem 9.6, what is your statistical decision if you test the null hypothesis at the 0.10 level of significance?

9.8 What is the *p*-value if, in a two-tail hypothesis test, $Z_{STAT} = -1.38$?

Applying the Concepts

9.9 In the U.S. legal system, a defendant is presumed innocent until proven guilty. Consider a null hypothesis, H_0, that the defendant is innocent, and an alternative hypothesis, H_1, that the defendant is guilty. A jury has two possible decisions: Convict the defendant (i.e., reject the null hypothesis) or do not convict the defendant (i.e., do not reject the null hypothesis). Explain the meaning of the risks of committing either a Type I or Type II error in this example.

9.10 Suppose the defendant in Problem 9.9 is presumed guilty until proven innocent, as in some other judicial systems. How do the null and alternative hypotheses differ from those in Problem 9.9? What are the meanings of the risks of committing either a Type I or Type II error here?

9.11 The U.S. Food and Drug Administration (FDA) is responsible for approving new drugs. Many consumer groups feel that the approval process is too easy and, therefore, too many drugs are approved that are later found to be unsafe. On the other hand, a number of industry lobbyists are pushing for a more lenient approval process so that pharmaceutical companies can get new drugs approved more easily and quickly (extracted from R. Sharpe, "FDA Tries to Find Right Balance on Drug Approvals," *The Wall Street Journal*, April 20, 1999, p. A24). Consider a null hypothesis that a new, unapproved drug is unsafe and an alternative hypothesis that a new, unapproved drug is safe.

a. Explain the risks of committing a Type I or Type II error.
b. Which type of error are the consumer groups trying to avoid? Explain.
c. Which type of error are the industry lobbyists trying to avoid? Explain.
d. How would it be possible to lower the chances of both Type I and Type II errors?

SELF Test **9.12** As a result of complaints from both students and faculty about lateness, the registrar at a large university wants to adjust the scheduled class times to allow for adequate travel time between classes and is ready to undertake a study. Until now, the registrar has believed that there should be 20 minutes between scheduled classes. State the null hypothesis, H_0, and the alternative hypothesis, H_1.

9.13 Do students at your school study more, less, or about the same as at other business schools? *Business Week* reported that at the top 50 business schools, students studied an average of 14.6 hours (extracted from "Cracking the Books," SPECIAL REPORT/Online Extra, **www.businessweek.com**, March 19, 2007). Set up a hypothesis test to try to prove that the mean number of hours studied at your school is different from the 14.6 hour benchmark reported by *Business Week*.
a. State the null and alternative hypotheses.
b. What is a Type I error for your test?
c. What is a Type II error for your test?

9.14 The manager of a paint supply store wants to determine whether the amount of paint contained in 1-gallon cans purchased from a nationally known manufacturer actually averages 1 gallon. State the null and alternative hypotheses.

9.15 The quality control manager at a lightbulb factory needs to determine whether the mean life of a large shipment of lightbulbs is equal to the specified value of 375 hours. State the null and alternative hypotheses.

9.2 *t* TEST OF HYPOTHESIS FOR THE MEAN (σ UNKNOWN)

In virtually all hypothesis-testing situations concerning the population mean, μ, you do not know the population standard deviation, σ. Instead, you use the sample standard deviation, *S*. If you assume that the population is normally distributed, then the sampling distribution of the mean follows a *t* distribution with $n - 1$ degrees of freedom and you use the ***t* test for the mean**. If the population is not normally distributed, you can still use the *t* test if the sample size is large enough for the Central Limit Theorem to take effect (see Section 7.4). Equation (9.2) defines the test statistic for determining the difference between the sample mean, $\bar{X}$, and the population mean, μ, when using the sample standard deviation, *S*.

t Test of Hypothesis for the Mean (σ Unknown)

$$t_{STAT} = \frac{\bar{X} - \mu}{\frac{S}{\sqrt{n}}} \qquad (9.2)$$

where the t_{STAT} test statistic follows a *t* distribution having $n - 1$ degrees of freedom.

To illustrate the use of this *t* test, return to the Using Statistics scenario concerning the Saxon Home Improvement Company on page 292. Over the past five years, the mean amount per sales invoice is $120. As an accountant for the company, you need to inform the finance department if this amount changes. In other words, the hypothesis test is used to try to prove that the mean amount per sales invoice is increasing or decreasing.

The Critical Value Approach

To perform this two-tail hypothesis test, you use the six-step method listed in Exhibit 9.1 on page 349.

Step 1 H_0: $\mu = \$120$
H_1: $\mu \neq \$120$

The alternative hypothesis contains the statement you are trying to prove. If the null hypothesis is rejected, then there is statistical proof that the population mean amount per sales invoice is no longer $120. If the statistical conclusion is "do not reject H_0," then you will conclude that there is insufficient evidence to prove that the mean amount differs from the long-term mean of $120.

Step 2 You have selected a sample of $n = 12$. You decide to use $\alpha = 0.05$.

Step 3 Because σ is unknown, you use the *t* distribution and the t_{STAT} test statistic. You must assume that the population of sales invoices is normally distributed. This assumption is discussed on pages 358–360.

Step 4 For a given sample size, *n*, the test statistic t_{STAT} follows a *t* distribution with $n - 1$ degrees of freedom. The critical values of the *t* distribution with $12 - 1 = 11$ degrees of freedom are found in Table E.3, as illustrated in Table 9.2 and Figure 9.6. The alternative hypothesis, H_1, $\mu \neq \$120$ is two-tail. Thus, the area in the rejection region of the *t* distribution's left (lower) tail is 0.025, and the area in the rejection region of the *t* distribution's right (upper) tail is also 0.025.

From the *t* table as given in Table E.3, a portion of which is shown in Table 9.2, the critical values are ±2.2010. The decision rule is

Reject H_0 if $t_{STAT} < -t_{\alpha/2} = -2.2010$

or if $t_{STAT} > t_{\alpha/2} = +2.2010$;

otherwise, do not reject H_0.

Step 5 A random sample of 12 sales invoices is selected. The dollar amounts for the 12 invoices are given below (and in the file **Invoices**):

108.98	152.22	111.45	110.59	127.46	107.26
93.32	91.97	111.56	75.71	128.58	135.11

TABLE 9.2

Determining the Critical Value from the *t* Table for an Area of 0.025 in Each Tail with 11 Degrees of Freedom

	Cumulative Probabilities					
	.75	.90	.95	.975	.99	.995
	Upper-Tail Areas					
Degrees of Freedom	.25	.10	.05	.025	.01	.005
1	1.0000	3.0777	6.3138	12.7062	31.8207	63.6574
2	0.8165	1.8856	2.9200	4.3027	6.9646	9.9248
3	0.7649	1.6377	2.3534	3.1824	4.5407	5.8409
4	0.7407	1.5332	2.1318	2.7764	3.7469	4.6041
5	0.7267	1.4759	2.0150	2.5706	3.3649	4.0322
6	0.7176	1.4398	1.9432	2.4469	3.1427	3.7074
7	0.7111	1.4149	1.8946	2.3646	2.9980	3.4995
8	0.7064	1.3968	1.8595	2.3060	2.8965	3.3554
9	0.7027	1.3830	1.8331	2.2622	2.8214	3.2498
10	0.6998	1.3722	1.8125	2.2281	2.7638	3.1693
11	0.6974	1.3634	1.7959	2.2010	2.7181	3.1058

Source: *Extracted from Table E.3.*

FIGURE 9.6

Testing a hypothesis about the mean (σ unknown) at the 0.05 level of significance with 11 degrees of freedom

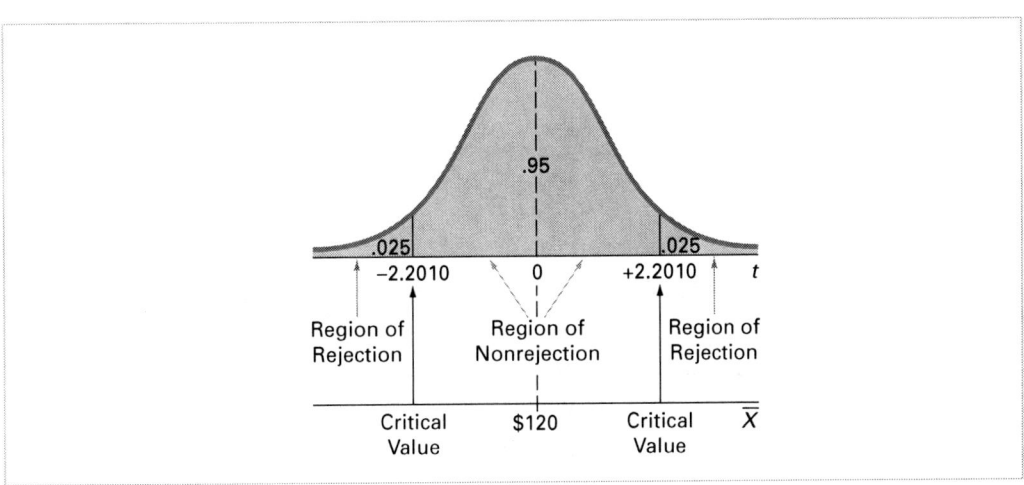

Using Equations (3.1) and (3.7) on pages 91 and 98, or Microsoft Excel or Minitab as shown in Figures 9.7 and 9.8,

$$\bar{X} = \frac{\sum_{i=1}^{n} X_i}{n} = \$112.85 \quad \text{and} \quad S = \sqrt{\frac{\sum_{i=1}^{n}(X_i - \bar{X}_i)^2}{n-1}} = \$20.80$$

From Equation (9.2) on page 356,

$$t_{STAT} = \frac{\bar{X} - \mu}{\frac{S}{\sqrt{n}}} = \frac{112.85 - 120}{\frac{20.80}{\sqrt{12}}} = -1.1908$$

Step 6 Because $-2.2010 < t_{STAT} = -1.1908 < 2.2010$, you do not reject H_0. You have insufficient evidence to conclude that the mean amount per sales invoice differs from \$120. You should inform the finance department that the audit suggests that the mean amount per invoice has not changed.

FIGURE 9.7

Microsoft Excel results for the *t* test of sales invoices

See Section E9.2 or P9.2 to create this.

	A	B	
1	t Test for the Hypothesis of the Mean		
2			
3	Data		
4	Null Hypothesis $\mu=$	120	
5	Level of Significance	0.05	
6	Sample Size	12	
7	Sample Mean	112.85	
8	Sample Standard Deviation	20.8	
9			
10	Intermediate Calculations		
11	Standard Error of the Mean	6.0044	=B8/SQRT(B6)
12	Degrees of Freedom	11	=B6 - 1
13	t Test Statistic	-1.1908	=(B7 - B4)/B11
14			
15	Two-Tail Test		
16	Lower Critical Value	-2.2010	=-(TINV(B5, B12))
17	Upper Critical Value	2.2010	=TINV(B5, B12)
18	p-Value	0.2588	=TDIST(ABS(B13), B12, 2)
19	Do not reject the null hypothesis		=IF(B18 < B5, "Reject the null hypothesis", "Do not reject the null hypothesis")

FIGURE 9.8

Minitab results for the *t* test of sales invoices

See Section M9.2 to create this.

```
Test of mu = 120 vs not = 120


Variable   N     Mean   StDev   SE Mean      95% CI        T      P
Amount    12   112.85   20.80     6.00   (99.64, 126.07)  -1.19  0.259
```

The *p*-Value Approach

Steps 1–3 These steps are the same as in the critical value approach on page 356.

Step 4 From the Microsoft Excel worksheet of Figure 9.7 or from the Minitab results of Figure 9.8, $t_{STAT} = -1.19$ and the *p*-value = 0.259.

Step 5 The Microsoft Excel results in Figure 9.7 and the Minitab results in Figure 9.8 give the *p*-value for this two-tail test as 0.259. Because the *p*-value of 0.259 is greater than $\alpha = 0.05$, you do not reject H_0. The data provide insufficient evidence to conclude that the mean amount per sales invoice differs from $120. You should inform the finance department that the audit suggests that the mean amount per invoice has not changed. The *p*-value indicates that if the null hypothesis is true, the probability that a sample of 12 invoices could have a sample mean that differs by $7.15 or more from the stated $120 is 0.259. In other words, if the mean amount per sales invoice is truly $120, then there is a 25.9% chance of observing a sample mean below $112.85 or above $127.15.

In the preceding example, it is incorrect to state that there is a 25.9% chance that the null hypothesis is true. This misinterpretation of the *p*-value is sometimes used by those not properly trained in statistics. Remember that the *p*-value is a conditional probability, calculated by *assuming* that the null hypothesis is true. In general, it is proper to state the following:

If the null hypothesis is true, there is a (*p*-value)*100% chance of observing a test statistic at least as contradictory to the null hypothesis as the sample result.

Checking Assumptions

You use the *t* test when the population standard deviation, σ, is not known and is estimated using the sample standard deviation, *S*. To use the *t* test, you assume that the data represent a random sample from a population that is normally distributed. In practice, as long as the sample size is not very small and the population is not very skewed, the t distribution provides a good approximation to the sampling distribution of the mean when σ is unknown.

There are several ways to evaluate the normality assumption necessary for using the t test. You can observe how closely the sample statistics match the normal distribution's theoretical properties. You can also use a histogram, stem-and-leaf display, boxplot, or normal probability plot. For details on evaluating normality, see Section 6.3 on page 234.

Figure 9.9 presents descriptive statistics generated by Microsoft Excel. Figure 9.10 is a Microsoft Excel boxplot. Figure 9.11 on page 360 is a Microsoft Excel normal probability plot.

FIGURE 9.9

Microsoft Excel descriptive statistics for the sales invoice data

See Section E3.1 to create this. (Minitab users, see Section M3.1 to create the equivalent results.)

	A	B
1	**Invoice Amount**	
2		
3	Mean	112.8508
4	Standard Error	6.003863
5	Median	111.02
6	Mode	#N/A
7	Standard Deviation	20.79799
8	Sample Variance	432.5565
9	Kurtosis	0.172708
10	Skewness	0.133638
11	Range	76.51
12	Minimum	75.71
13	Maximum	152.22
14	Sum	1354.21
15	Count	12
16	Largest(1)	152.22
17	Smallest(1)	75.71

FIGURE 9.10

Microsoft Excel boxplot for the sales invoice data

See Section E3.3 or P3.1 to create this. (Minitab users, see Section M3.2 to create the equivalent chart.)

Boxplot of Invoice Amount

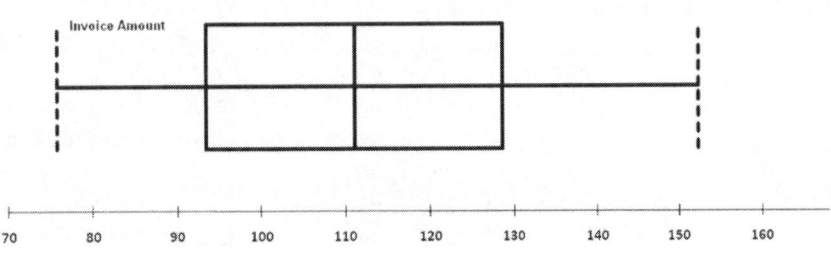

The mean is very close to the median and the points on the normal probability plot appear to be increasing approximately in a straight line. The boxplot appears approximately symmetrical. Thus, you can assume that the population of sales invoices is approximately normally distributed. The normality assumption is valid, and therefore the auditor's results are valid.

The t test is a **robust** test. It does not lose power if the shape of the population departs somewhat from a normal distribution, particularly when the sample size is large enough to enable the test statistic t to be influenced by the Central Limit Theorem (see Section 7.4).

FIGURE 9.11

Microsoft Excel normal probability plot for the sales invoice data

See Section P6.2 to create this. (Minitab users, see Section M6.2 to create the equivalent chart.)

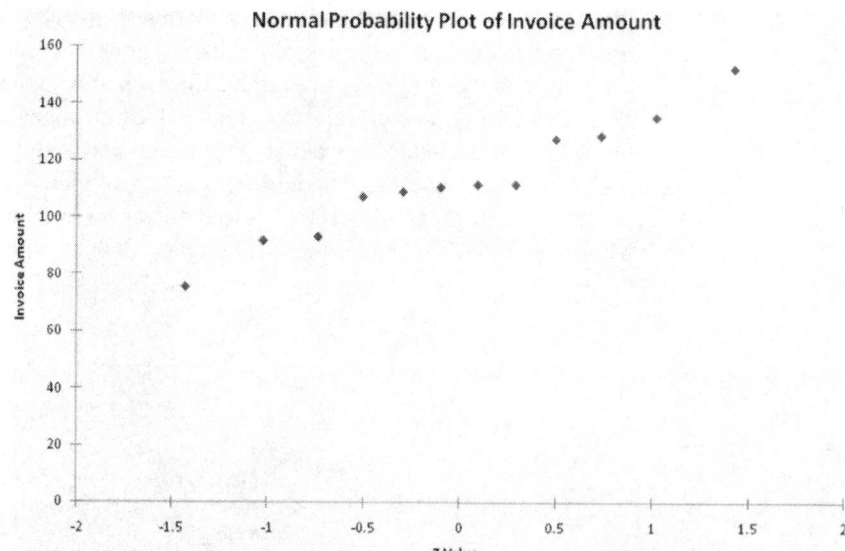

Normal Probability Plot of Invoice Amount

However, you can reach erroneous conclusions and can lose statistical power if you use the *t* test incorrectly. If the sample size, *n*, is small (i.e., less than 30) and you cannot easily make the assumption that the underlying population is at least approximately normally distributed, then *nonparametric* testing procedures are more appropriate (see references 1 and 2).

PROBLEMS FOR SECTION 9.2

Learning the Basics

9.16 If, in a sample of $n = 16$ selected from a normal population, $\bar{X} = 56$ and $S = 12$, what is the value of t_{STAT} if you are testing the null hypothesis H_0: $\mu = 50$?

9.17 In Problem 9.16, how many degrees of freedom are there in the *t* test?

9.18 In Problems 9.16 and 9.17, what are the critical values of *t* if the level of significance, α, is 0.05 and the alternative hypothesis, H_1, is $\mu \neq 50$?

9.19 In Problems 9.16, 9.17, and 9.18, what is your statistical decision if the alternative hypothesis, H_1, is $\mu \neq 50$?

9.20 If, in a sample of $n = 16$ selected from a left-skewed population, $\bar{X} = 65$ and $S = 21$, would you use the *t* test to test the null hypothesis H_0: $\mu = 60$? Discuss.

9.21 If, in a sample of $n = 160$ selected from a left-skewed population, $\bar{X} = 65$ and $S = 21$, would you use the *t* test to test the null hypothesis H_0: $\mu = 60$? Discuss.

Applying the Concepts

9.22 Late payment of medical claims can add to the cost of health care. An article (M. Freudenheim, "The Check Is Not in the Mail," *The New York Times*, May 25, 2006, pp. C1, C6) reported that the mean time from the date of service to the date of payment for one insurance company was 41.4 days during a recent period. Suppose that a sample of 100 medical claims is selected during the latest time period. The sample mean time from the date of service to the date of payment was 39.6 days, and the sample standard deviation was 7.4 days.
a. Using the 0.05 level of significance, is there evidence that the population mean has changed from 41.4 days?
b. What is your answer in (a) if you use the 0.01 level of significance?
c. What is your answer in (a) if the sample mean is 38.2 days and the sample standard deviation is 10.7 days?
d. Because the sample size is 100, do you need to be concerned about the shape of the population distribution when conducting the *t*-test in (a)? Explain.

9.23 An article (N. Hellmich, "'Supermarket Guru' Has a Simple Mantra," *USA Today*, June 19, 2002, p. 70)

claimed that the typical supermarket trip takes a mean of 22 minutes. Suppose that in an effort to test this claim, you select a sample of 50 shoppers at a local supermarket. The mean shopping time for the sample of 50 shoppers is 25.36 minutes, with a standard deviation of 7.24 minutes. Using the 0.10 level of significance, is there evidence that the mean shopping time at the local supermarket is different from the claimed value of 22 minutes?

✓ SELF Test **9.24** You are the manager of a restaurant for a fast-food franchise. Last month, the mean waiting time at the drive-through window for branches in your geographical region, as measured from the time a customer places an order until the time the customer receives the order, was 3.7 minutes. You select a random sample of 64 orders. The sample mean waiting time is 3.57 minutes, with a sample standard deviation of 0.8 minute.
a. At the 0.05 level of significance, is there evidence that the population mean waiting time is different from 3.7 minutes?
b. Because the sample size is 64, do you need to be concerned about the shape of the population distribution when conducting the *t*-test in (a)? Explain.

9.25 A manufacturer of chocolate candies uses machines to package candies as they move along a filling line. Although the packages are labeled as 8 ounces, the company wants the packages to contain a mean of 8.17 ounces so that virtually none of the packages contain less than 8 ounces. A sample of 50 packages is selected periodically, and the packaging process is stopped if there is evidence that the mean amount packaged is different from 8.17 ounces. Suppose that in a particular sample of 50 packages, the mean amount dispensed is 8.159 ounces, with a sample standard deviation of 0.051 ounce.
a. Is there evidence that the population mean amount is different from 8.17 ounces? (Use a 0.05 level of significance.)
b. Determine the *p*-value and interpret its meaning.

9.26 The data in the file **MoviePrices** contain prices (in dollars) for two tickets, with online service charges, large popcorn, and two medium soft drinks at a sample of six theater chains:

36.15   31.00   35.05   40.25   33.75   43.00

Source: *Extracted from K. Kelly, "The Multiplex Under Siege," The Wall Street Journal, December 24–25, 2005, pp. P1, P5.*

a. At the 0.05 level of significance, is there evidence that the mean price for two tickets, with online service charges, large popcorn, and two medium soft drinks, is different from $35?
b. Determine the *p*-value in (a) and interpret its meaning.
c. What assumption must you make about the population distribution in order to conduct the *t* test in (a) and (b)?

d. Because the sample size is 6, do you need to be concerned about the shape of the population distribution when conducting the *t* test in (a)? Explain.

9.27 In New York State, savings banks are permitted to sell a form of life insurance called savings bank life insurance (SBLI). The approval process consists of underwriting, which includes a review of the application, a medical information bureau check, possible requests for additional medical information and medical exams, and a policy compilation stage in which the policy pages are generated and sent to the bank for delivery. The ability to deliver approved policies to customers in a timely manner is critical to the profitability of this service. During a period of one month, a random sample of 27 approved policies is selected, and the total processing time, in days, is recorded (as stored in the **Insurance** file):

73   19   16   64   28   28   31   90   60   56   31   56   22   18
45   48   17   17   17   91   92   63   50   51   69   16   17

a. In the past, the mean processing time was 45 days. At the 0.05 level of significance, is there evidence that the mean processing time has changed from 45 days?
b. What assumption about the population distribution is needed in order to conduct the *t* test in (a)?
c. Use a boxplot or a normal probability plot to evaluate the assumption made in (b).
d. Do you think that the assumption needed in order to conduct the *t* test in (a) is valid? Explain.

9.28 The following data (see the **Drink** file) represent the amount of soft-drink filled in a sample of 50 consecutive 2-liter bottles. The results, listed horizontally in the order of being filled, were:

2.109 2.086 2.066 2.075 2.065 2.057 2.052 2.044 2.036 2.038

2.031 2.029 2.025 2.029 2.023 2.020 2.015 2.014 2.013 2.014

2.012 2.012 2.012 2.010 2.005 2.003 1.999 1.996 1.997 1.992

1.994 1.986 1.984 1.981 1.973 1.975 1.971 1.969 1.966 1.967

1.963 1.957 1.951 1.951 1.947 1.941 1.941 1.938 1.908 1.894

a. At the 0.05 level of significance, is there evidence that the mean amount of soft drink filled is different from 2.0 liters?
b. Determine the *p*-value in (a) and interpret its meaning.
c. In (a), you assumed that the distribution of the amount of soft drink filled was normally distributed. Evaluate this assumption using a boxplot or a normal probability plot.
d. Do you think that the assumption needed in order to conduct the *t* test in (a) is valid? Explain.
e. Examine the values of the 50 bottles in their sequential order, as given in the problem. Is there a pattern to the results? If so, what impact might this pattern have on the validity of the results in (a)?

9.29 One of the major measures of the quality of service provided by any organization is the speed with which it responds to customer complaints. A large family-held department store selling furniture and flooring, including carpet, had undergone a major expansion in the past several years. In particular, the flooring department had expanded from 2 installation crews to an installation supervisor, a measurer, and 15 installation crews. Last year there were 50 complaints concerning carpet installation. The following data (stored in the Furniture file) represent the number of days between the receipt of a complaint and the resolution of the complaint:

54	5	35	137	31	27	152	2	123	81	74	27
11	19	126	110	110	29	61	35	94	31	26	5
12	4	165	32	29	28	29	26	25	1	14	13
13	10	5	27	4	52	30	22	36	26	20	23
33	68										

a. The installation supervisor claims that the mean number of days between the receipt of a complaint and the resolution of the complaint is 20 days. At the 0.05 level of significance, is there evidence that the claim is not true (i.e., that the mean number of days is different from 20)?
b. What assumption about the population distribution is needed in order to conduct the t test in (a)?
c. Use a boxplot or a normal probability plot to evaluate the assumption made in (b).
d. Do you think that the assumption needed in order to conduct the t test in (a) is valid? Explain.

9.30 A manufacturing company produces steel housings for electrical equipment. The main component part of the housing is a steel trough that is made out of a 14-gauge steel coil. It is produced using a 250-ton progressive punch press with a wipe-down operation that puts two 90-degree forms in the flat steel to make the trough. The distance from one side of the form to the other is critical because of weatherproofing in outdoor applications. The company requires that the width of the trough be between 8.31 inches and 8.61 inches. The file Trough contains the widths of the troughs, in inches, for a sample of $n = 49$.

8.312 8.343 8.317 8.383 8.348 8.410 8.351 8.373 8.481 8.422
8.476 8.382 8.484 8.403 8.414 8.419 8.385 8.465 8.498 8.447
8.436 8.413 8.489 8.414 8.481 8.415 8.479 8.429 8.458 8.462
8.460 8.444 8.429 8.460 8.412 8.420 8.410 8.405 8.323 8.420
8.396 8.447 8.405 8.439 8.411 8.427 8.420 8.498 8.409

a. At the 0.05 level of significance, is there evidence that the mean width of the troughs is different from 8.46 inches?
b. What assumption about the population distribution is needed in order to conduct the t test in (a)?
c. Evaluate the assumption made in (b).
d. Do you think that the assumption needed in order to conduct the t test in (a) is valid? Explain.

9.31 One operation of a steel mill is to cut pieces of steel into parts that are used in the frame for front seats in an automobile. The steel is cut with a diamond saw and requires the resulting parts to be within ±0.005 inch of the length specified by the automobile company. The data in the file Steel come from a sample of 100 steel parts. The measurement reported is the difference, in inches, between the actual length of the steel part, as measured by a laser measurement device, and the specified length of the steel part. For example, a value of –0.002 represents a steel part that is 0.002 inch shorter than the specified length.
a. At the 0.05 level of significance, is there evidence that the mean difference is not equal to 0.0 inches?
b. Construct a 95% confidence interval estimate of the population mean. Interpret this interval.
c. Compare the conclusions reached in (a) and (b).
d. Because $n = 100$, do you have to worry about the normality assumption needed for the t test and t interval?

9.32 In Problem 3.67 on page 135, you were introduced to a tea-bag-filling operation. An important quality characteristic of interest for this process is the weight of the tea in the individual bags. The data in the file Teabags are provided in an ordered array of the weight, in grams, of a sample of 50 tea bags produced during an eight-hour shift.
a. Is there evidence that the mean amount of tea per bag is different from 5.5 grams (use $\alpha = 0.01$)?
b. Construct a 99% confidence interval estimate of the population mean amount of tea per bag. Interpret this interval.
c. Compare the conclusions reached in (a) and (b).

9.33 Although many people think they can put a meal on the table in a short period of time, a recent article reported that they end up spending about 40 minutes doing so (extracted from N. Hellmich, "Americans Go for the Quick Fix for Dinner," *USA Today*, February 14, 2006). Suppose another study is conducted to test the validity of this statement. A sample of 25 people is selected, and the length of time to prepare and cook dinner (in minutes) is recorded, with the following results (stored in the file Dinner).

44.0 51.9 49.7 40.0 55.5 33.0 43.4 41.3 45.2 40.7 41.1 49.1 30.9
45.2 55.3 52.1 55.1 38.8 43.1 39.2 58.6 49.8 43.2 47.9 46.6

a. Is there evidence that the population mean time to prepare and cook dinner is different from 40 minutes? Use the p-value approach and a level of significance of 0.05.
b. What assumption about the population distribution is needed in order to conduct the t test in (a)?
c. Make a list of the various ways you could evaluate the assumption noted in (b).
d. Evaluate the assumption noted in (b) and determine whether the t test in (a) is valid.

9.3   ONE-TAIL TESTS

In Section 9.1, hypothesis testing was used to examine the question of whether the population mean amount of cereal filled is 368 grams. The alternative hypothesis (H_1: $\mu \ne 368$) contains two possibilities: Either the mean is less than 368 grams, or the mean is more than 368 grams. For this reason, the rejection region is divided into the two tails of the sampling distribution of the mean. In Section 9.2, once again a two-tail test was used to determine whether the mean amount per invoice had changed from $120.

In contrast to these two examples, many situations require an alternative hypothesis that focuses on a *particular direction*. For example, the population mean is *less than* a specified value. One such situation involves the service time at the drive-through window of a fast-food restaurant. The speed with which customers are served is of critical importance to the success of the service (see **www.qsrmagazine.com/reports/drive-thru_time_study**). In a recent study, McDonald's had a mean service time of 163.9 seconds, which was the fourth best in the industry. Suppose that McDonald's has embarked on a quality improvement effort to reduce the service time and has developed improvements to the service process at the drive-through. The new process will be tested in a sample of 25 stores. Because McDonald's would only want to institute the new process in all of its stores if it resulted in *decreased* drive-through time, the entire rejection region is located in the lower tail of the distribution.

The Critical Value Approach

You wish to determine whether the new drive-through process has a mean that is less than 163.9 seconds. To perform this one-tail hypothesis test, you use the six-step method listed in Exhibit 9.1 on page 349.

Step 1

$$H_0: \mu \ge 163.9$$

$$H_1: \mu < 163.9$$

The alternative hypothesis contains the statement you are trying to prove. If the conclusion of the test is "reject H_0," there is statistical proof that the mean drive-through time is less than the drive-through time in the old process. This would be reason to change the drive-through process for the entire population of stores. If the conclusion of the test is "do not reject H_0," then there is insufficient evidence to prove that the mean drive-through time in the new process is significantly less than the drive-through time in the old process. If this occurs, there would be insufficient reason to institute the new drive-through process in the population of stores.

Step 2   You have selected a sample size of $n = 25$ stores. You decide to use $\alpha = 0.05$.

Step 3   Because σ is unknown, you use the t distribution and the t_{STAT} test statistic. You must assume that the service time is normally distributed.

Step 4   The rejection region is entirely contained in the lower tail of the sampling distribution of the mean because you want to reject H_0 only when the sample mean is significantly less than 163.9 seconds. When the entire rejection region is contained in one tail of the sampling distribution of the test statistic, the test is called a **one-tail** or **directional test**. If the alternative hypothesis includes the *less than* sign, the critical value of t is negative. As shown in Table 9.3 and Figure 9.12, because the entire rejection region is in the lower tail of the t distribution and contains an area of 0.05, the critical value of the t test statistic with $25 - 1 = 24$ degrees of freedom is -1.7109.

The decision rule is

$$\text{Reject } H_0 \text{ if } t_{STAT} < -1.7109;$$

$$\text{otherwise, do not reject } H_0.$$

TABLE 9.3

Determining the Critical Value from the *t* Table for an Area of 0.05 in the Lower Tail with 24 Degrees of Freedom

	Cumulative Probabilities					
	.75	.90	.95	.975	.99	.995
	Upper-Tail Areas					
Degrees of Freedom	.25	.10	.05	.025	.01	.005
1	1.0000	3.0777	6.3138	12.7062	31.8207	63.6574
2	0.8165	1.8856	2.9200	4.3027	6.9646	9.9248
3	0.7649	1.6377	2.3534	3.1824	4.5407	5.8409
.	.	.	.	.	.	.
.	.	.	.	.	.	.
.	.	.	.	.	.	.
23	0.6853	1.3195	1.7139	2.0687	2.4999	2.8073
24	0.6848	1.3178	1.7109	2.0639	2.4922	2.7969
25	0.6844	1.3163	1.7081	2.0595	2.4851	2.7874

Source: *Extracted from Table E.3.*

FIGURE 9.12

One-tail test of hypothesis for a mean (σ known) at the 0.05 level of significance

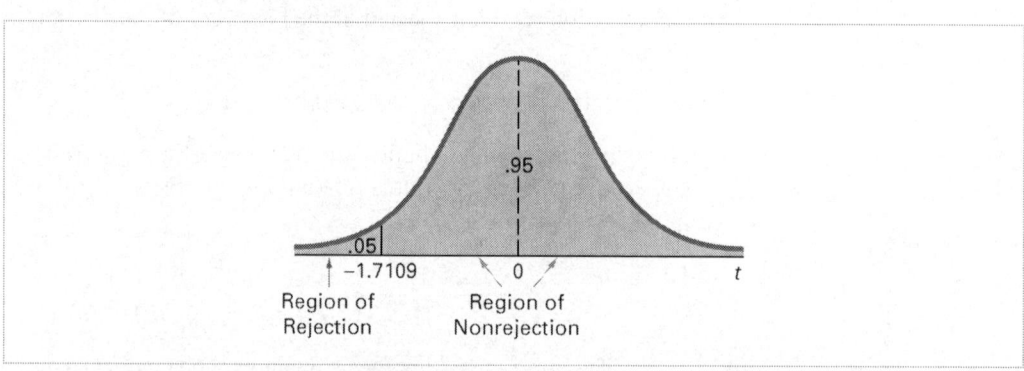

Step 5   You select a sample of 25 stores and find that the sample mean service time at the drive-through equals 152.7 seconds and the sample standard deviation equals 20 seconds. Using $n = 25$, $\bar{X} = 152.7$, $S = 20$, and Equation (9.2) on page 356,

$$t_{STAT} = \frac{\bar{X} - \mu}{\dfrac{S}{\sqrt{n}}} = \frac{152.7 - 163.9}{\dfrac{20}{\sqrt{25}}} = -2.80$$

Step 6   Because $t_{STAT} = -2.80 < -1.7109$, you reject the null hypothesis (see Figure 9.12). You conclude that the mean service time at the drive-through is below 163.9 seconds. There is sufficient evidence to change the drive-through process for the entire population of stores.

The *p*-Value Approach

Use the five steps listed in Exhibit 9.2 on page 352 to illustrate the *t* test for the drive-through time study using the *p*-value approach.

Steps 1–3   These steps are the same as in the critical value approach on page 363.

Step 4 $t_{STAT} = -2.80$ (see step 5 of the critical value approach). Because the alternative hypothesis indicates a rejection region entirely in the *lower* tail of the sampling distribution, to compute the *p*-value you need to find the probability that the *t*-value will be *less than* the t_{STAT} test statistic of -2.80. From Figure 9.13, the *p*-value is 0.0050.

FIGURE 9.13

Microsoft Excel *t* test results for the drive-through time study

See Section E9.1 or P9.1 to create this. (Minitab users, see Section M9.1 to create the equivalent results.)

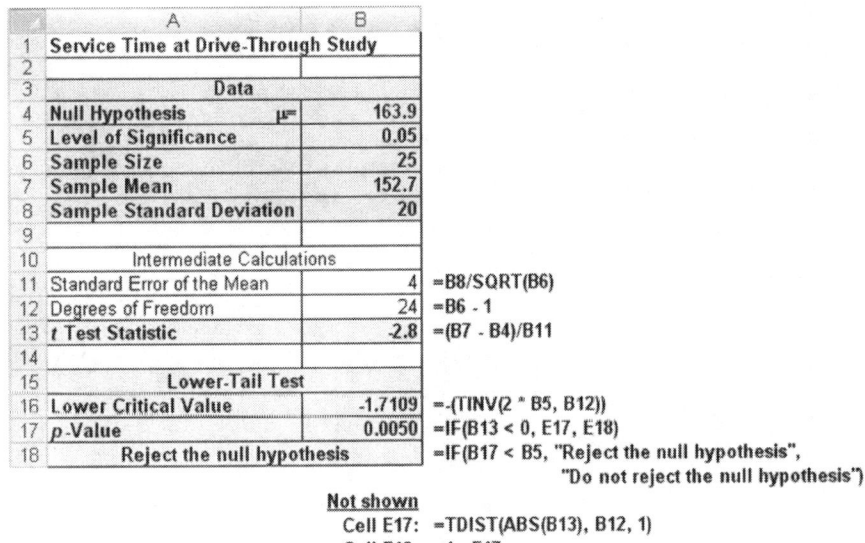

Step 5   The *p*-value of 0.0050 is less than $\alpha = 0.05$ (see Figure 9.14). You reject H_0, and conclude that the mean service time at the drive-through is less than 163.9 seconds. There is sufficient evidence to change the drive-through process for the entire population of stores.

FIGURE 9.14

Determining the *p*-value for a one-tail test

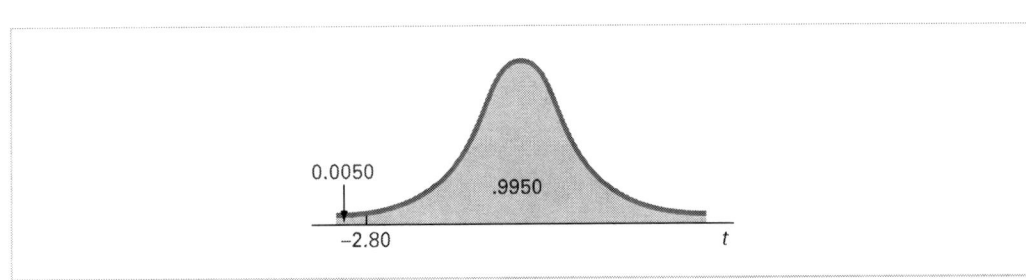

EXAMPLE 9.5   A ONE-TAIL TEST FOR THE MEAN

A company that manufactures chocolate bars is particularly concerned that the mean weight of a chocolate bar is not greater than 6.03 ounces. A sample of 50 chocolate bars is selected, and the sample mean is 6.034 ounces and the sample standard deviation is 0.02 ounces. Using the $\alpha = 0.01$ level of significance, is there evidence that the population mean weight of the chocolate bars is greater than 6.03 ounces?

SOLUTION   Using the critical value approach,

Step 1
$$H_0: \mu \le 6.03$$
$$H_1: \mu > 6.03$$

Step 2   You have selected a sample size of $n = 50$. You decide to use $\alpha = 0.01$.

Step 3   Because σ is unknown, you use the *t* distribution and the t_{STAT} test statistic.

Step 4   The rejection region is entirely contained in the upper tail of the sampling distribution of the mean because you want to reject H_0 only when the sample mean is significantly greater than 6.03 ounces. Because the entire rejection region is in the upper tail of the *t* distribution and contains an area of 0.01, the critical value of the *t* with $50 - 1 = 49$ degrees of freedom is 2.4049 (see Table E.3).

The decision rule is

$$\text{Reject } H_0 \text{ if } t_{STAT} > 2.4049;$$

$$\text{otherwise, do not reject } H_0.$$

Step 5 You select a sample of 50 chocolate bars, and the sample mean weight is 6.034 ounces. Using $n = 50$, $\bar{X} = 6.034$, $S = 0.02$, and Equation (9.2) on page 356,

$$t_{STAT} = \frac{\bar{X} - \mu}{\dfrac{S}{\sqrt{n}}} = \frac{6.034 - 6.03}{\dfrac{0.02}{\sqrt{50}}} = 1.414$$

Step 6 Because $t_{STAT} = 1.414 < 2.4049$, or using Microsoft Excel or Minitab, the p-value is $0.0818 > 0.01$, you do not reject the null hypothesis. There is insufficient evidence to conclude that the population mean weight is greater than 6.03 ounces.

To perform one-tail tests of hypotheses, you must properly formulate H_0 and H_1. A summary of the null and alternative hypotheses for one-tail tests is as follows:

- The null hypothesis, H_0, represents the status quo or the current belief in a situation.
- The alternative hypothesis, H_1, is the opposite of the null hypothesis and represents a research claim or specific inference you would like to prove.
- If you reject the null hypothesis, you have statistical proof that the alternative hypothesis is correct.
- If you do not reject the null hypothesis, then you have failed to prove the alternative hypothesis. The failure to prove the alternative hypothesis, however, does not mean that you have proven the null hypothesis.
- The null hypothesis always refers to a specified value of the *population parameter* (such as μ), not to a *sample statistic* (such as $\bar{X}$).
- The statement of the null hypothesis *always* contains an equal sign regarding the specified value of the parameter (e.g., $H_0: \mu \geq 163.9$).
- The statement of the alternative hypothesis *never* contains an equal sign regarding the specified value of the parameter (e.g., $H_1: \mu < 163.9$).

PROBLEMS FOR SECTION 9.3

Learning the Basics

9.34 In a one-tail hypothesis test where you reject H_0 only in the *upper* tail, what is the p-value if $Z_{STAT} = +2.00$?

9.35 In Problem 9.34, what is your statistical decision if you test the null hypothesis at the 0.05 level of significance?

9.36 In a one-tail hypothesis test where you reject H_0 only in the *lower* tail, what is the p-value if $Z_{STAT} = -1.38$?

9.37 In Problem 9.36, what is your statistical decision if you test the null hypothesis at the 0.01 level of significance?

9.38 In a one-tail hypothesis test where you reject H_0 only in the *lower* tail, what is the p-value if $Z_{STAT} = +1.38$?

9.39 In Problem 9.38, what is the statistical decision if you test the null hypothesis at the 0.01 level of significance?

9.40 In a one-tail hypothesis test where you reject H_0 only in the *upper* tail, what is the critical value of the t-test statistic with 10 degrees of freedom at the 0.01 level of significance?

9.41 In Problem 9.40, what is your statistical decision if $t_{STAT} = +2.39$?

9.42 In a one-tail hypothesis test where you reject H_0 only in the *lower* tail, what is the critical value of the t_{STAT} test statistic with 20 degrees of freedom at the 0.01 level of significance?

9.43 In Problem 9.42, what is your statistical decision if $t_{STAT} = -1.15$?

Applying the Concepts

SELF Test **9.44** The Glen Valley Steel Company manufactures steel bars. If the production process is working properly, it turns out steel bars that are normally distributed with mean length of *at least* 2.8 feet. Longer steel bars can be used or altered, but shorter bars must be scrapped. You select a sample of 25 bars, and the mean length is 2.73 feet and the sample standard deviation is 0.20 foot. Do you need to adjust the production equipment?
a. If you test the null hypothesis at the 0.05 level of significance, what decision do you make using the critical value approach to hypothesis testing?
b. If you test the null hypothesis at the 0.05 level of significance, what decision do you make using the *p*-value approach to hypothesis testing?
c. Interpret the meaning of the *p*-value in this problem.
d. Compare your conclusions in (a) and (b).

9.45 You are the manager of a restaurant that delivers pizza to college dormitory rooms. You have just changed your delivery process in an effort to reduce the mean time between the order and completion of delivery from the current 25 minutes. A sample of 36 orders using the new delivery process yields a sample mean of 22.4 minutes and a sample standard deviation of 6 minutes.
a. Using the six-step critical value approach, at the 0.05 level of significance, is there evidence that the population mean delivery time has been reduced below the previous population mean value of 25 minutes?
b. At the 0.05 level of significance, use the five-step *p*-value approach.
c. Interpret the meaning of the *p*-value in (b).
d. Compare your conclusions in (a) and (b).

9.46 Children in the United States account directly for $36 billion in sales annually. When their indirect influence over product decisions from stereos to vacations is considered, the total economic spending affected by children in the United States is $290 billion. It is estimated that by age 10, a child makes an average of more than five trips a week to a store (extracted from M. E. Goldberg, G. J. Gorn, L. A. Peracchio, and G. Bamossy, "Understanding Materialism Among Youth," *Journal of Consumer Psychology*, 2003, 13(3), pp. 278–288). Suppose that you want to prove that children in your city average more than five trips a week to a store. Let µ represent the population mean number of times children in your city make trips to a store.
a. State the null and alternative hypotheses.
b. Explain the meaning of the Type I and Type II errors in the context of this scenario.
c. Suppose that you carry out a similar study in the city in which you live. You take a sample of 100 children and find that the mean number of trips to the store is 5.47 and the sample standard deviation of the number of trips to the store is 1.6. At the 0.01 level of significance, is there evidence that the population mean number of trips to the store is greater than 5 per week?
d. Interpret the meaning of the *p*-value in (c).

9.47 The waiting time to check out of a supermarket has had a population mean of 10.73 minutes. Recently, in an effort to reduce the waiting time, the supermarket has experimented with a system in which there is a single waiting line with multiple checkout servers. A sample of 100 customers was selected, and their mean waiting time to check out was 9.52 minutes with a sample standard deviation of 5.8 minutes.
a. At the 0.05 level of significance, using the critical value approach to hypothesis testing, is there evidence that the population mean waiting time to check out is less than 10.73 minutes?
b. At the 0.05 level of significance, using the *p*-value approach to hypothesis testing, is there evidence that the population mean waiting time to check out is less than 10.73 minutes?
c. Interpret the meaning of the *p*-value in this problem.
d. Compare your conclusions in (a) and (b).

9.4 Z TEST OF HYPOTHESIS FOR THE PROPORTION

In some situations, you want to test a hypothesis about the proportion of events of interest in the population, π, rather than testing the population mean. To begin, you select a random sample and compute the **sample proportion**, $p = X/n$. You then compare the value of this statistic to the hypothesized value of the parameter, π, in order to decide whether to reject the null hypothesis. If the number of events of interest (X) and the number of events that are not of interest ($n - X$) are each at least five, the sampling distribution of a proportion approximately follows a normal distribution. You use the **Z test for the proportion** given in Equation (9.3) to perform the hypothesis test for the difference between the sample proportion, p, and the hypothesized population proportion, π.

Z Test for the Proportion

$$Z_{STAT} = \frac{p - \pi}{\sqrt{\dfrac{\pi(1 - \pi)}{n}}}$$

(9.3)

where

$$p = \text{sample proportion} = \frac{X}{n} = \frac{\text{Number of events of interest in the sample}}{\text{Sample size}}$$

π = hypothesized proportion of events of interest in the population

The Z_{STAT} test statistic approximately follows a standardized normal distribution when X and $(n - X)$ are each at least 5.

To illustrate the Z test for a proportion, consider a survey that sought to determine whether customer service is better or worse at e-commerce sites than it is at physical stores (extracted from "Consumers Happier With E-Commerce," *USA Today Snapshots*, March 13, 2007, p. 1B). Of 1,100 respondents, 561 stated that customer service was better at e-commerce sites than at physical stores. For this survey, the null and alternative hypotheses are stated as follows:

H_0: $\pi = 0.50$ (i.e., half of all consumers believe that customer service is better at e-commerce sites than at physical stores)

H_1: $\pi \neq 0.50$ (i.e., either less than half or more than half of all consumers believe that customer service is better at e-commerce sites than at physical stores)

Alternatively, by multiplying the numerator and denominator by n, you can write the Z_{STAT} test statistic in terms of the number of events of interest, X, as shown in Equation (9.4).

Z Test for the Proportion in Terms of the Number of Events of Interest

$$Z_{STAT} = \frac{X - n\pi}{\sqrt{n\pi(1 - \pi)}}$$

(9.4)

The Critical Value Approach

Because you are interested in determining whether the population proportion of consumers who believe that customer service is better at e-commerce sites than at physical stores is 0.50, you use a two-tail test. If you select the $\alpha = 0.05$ level of significance, the rejection and nonrejection regions are set up as in Figure 9.15, and the decision rule is

Reject H_0 if $Z_{STAT} < -1.96$ or if $Z_{STAT} > +1.96$;

otherwise, do not reject H_0.

FIGURE 9.15

Two-tail test of hypothesis for the proportion at the 0.05 level of significance

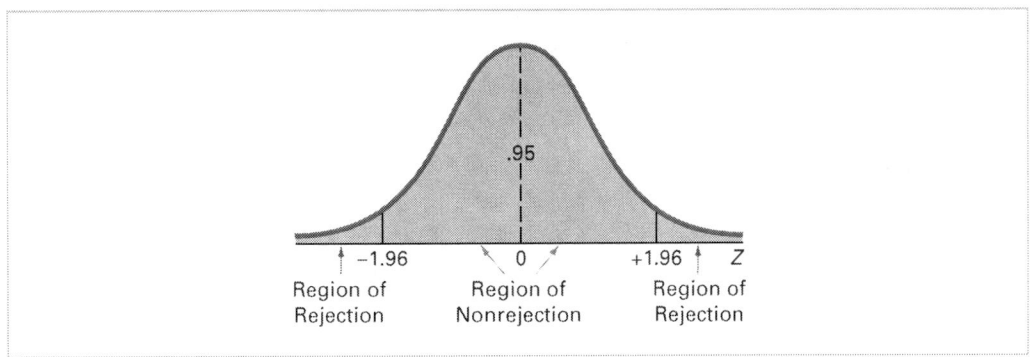

Because 561 of the 1,100 respondents stated that customer service was better at e-commerce sites than at physical stores,

$$p = \frac{561}{1,100} = 0.51$$

Using Equation (9.3),

$$Z_{STAT} = \frac{p - \pi}{\sqrt{\frac{\pi(1-\pi)}{n}}} = \frac{0.51 - 0.50}{\sqrt{\frac{0.50(1-0.50)}{1,100}}} = \frac{0.01}{0.0151} = 0.6633$$

or, using Equation (9.4),

$$Z_{STAT} = \frac{X - n\pi}{\sqrt{n\pi(1-\pi)}} = \frac{561 - (1,100)(0.50)}{\sqrt{1,100(0.50)(0.50)}} = \frac{11}{16.5831} = 0.6633$$

Because $-1.96 < Z_{STAT} = 0.6633 < 1.96$, you do not reject H_0. There is insufficient evidence that the population proportion of all consumers who believe that customer service is better at e-commerce sites than at physical stores is not 0.50. Figure 9.16 presents a Microsoft Excel worksheet and Figure 9.17 presents Minitab results for these data.

FIGURE 9.16

Microsoft Excel results for the survey of whether customer service is better or worse at e-commerce sites than it is at physical stores

See Section E9.3 or P9.3 to create this.

	A	B	
1	Z Test of Hypothesis for the Proportion		
2			
3	Data		
4	Null Hypothesis p=	0.5	
5	Level of Significance	0.05	
6	Number of Items of Interest	561	
7	Sample Size	1100	
8			
9	Intermediate Calculations		
10	Sample Proportion	0.5100	=B6/B7
11	Standard Error	0.0151	=SQRT(B4*(1 - B4)/B7)
12	Z Test Statistic	0.6633	=(B10 - B4)/B11
13			
14	Two-Tail Test		
15	Lower Critical Value	-1.9600	=NORMSINV(B5/2)
16	Upper Critical Value	1.9600	=NORMSINV(1 - B5/2)
17	p-Value	0.5071	=2 * (1 - NORMSDIST(ABS(B12)))
18	Do not reject the null hypothesis		=IF(B17 < B5, "Reject the null hypothesis", "Do not reject the null hypothesis")

See Section M9.3 to create this.

FIGURE 9.17

Minitab results for the survey of whether customer service is better or worse at e-commerce sites than it is at physical stores

```
Sample    X     N   Sample p        95% CI          Z-Value  P-Value
1        561  1100  0.510000  (0.480458, 0.539542)    0.66    0.507

Using the normal approximation.
```

The p-Value Approach

As an alternative to the critical value approach, you can compute the p-value. For this two-tail test in which the rejection region is located in the lower tail and the upper tail, you need to find the area below a Z value of -0.66 and above a Z value of $+0.66$. Figures 9.16 and 9.17 report a p-value of 0.507. Because this value is greater than the selected level of significance $(\alpha = 0.05)$, you do not reject the null hypothesis.

EXAMPLE 9.6

TESTING A HYPOTHESIS FOR A PROPORTION

A fast-food chain has developed a new process to ensure that orders at the drive-through are filled correctly. The previous process filled orders correctly 85% of the time. Based on a sample of 100 orders using the new process, 94 were filled correctly. At the 0.01 level of significance, can you conclude that the new process has increased the proportion of orders filled correctly?

SOLUTION The null and alternative hypotheses are

H_0: $\pi \leq 0.85$ (i.e., the population proportion of orders filled correctly using the new process is less than or equal to 0.85)

H_1: $\pi > 0.85$ (i.e., the population proportion of orders filled correctly using the new process is greater than 0.85)

Using Equation (9.3) on page 368,

$$p = \frac{X}{n} = \frac{94}{100} = 0.94$$

$$Z_{STAT} = \frac{p - \pi}{\sqrt{\dfrac{\pi(1-\pi)}{n}}} = \frac{0.94 - 0.85}{\sqrt{\dfrac{0.85(1-0.85)}{100}}} = \frac{0.09}{0.0357} = 2.52$$

The p-value for $Z_{STAT} > 2.52$ is 0.0059.

Using the critical value approach, you reject H_0 if $Z_{STAT} > 2.33$. Using the p-value approach, you reject H_0 if the p-value < 0.01. Because $Z_{STAT} = 2.52 > 2.33$ or the p-value $= 0.0059 < 0.01$, you reject H_0. You have evidence that the new process has increased the proportion of correct orders above 0.85.

PROBLEMS FOR SECTION 9.4

Learning the Basics

9.48 If, in a random sample of 400 items, 88 are defective, what is the sample proportion of defective items?

9.49 In Problem 9.48, if the null hypothesis is that 20% of the items in the population are defective, what is the value of Z_{STAT}?

9.50 In Problems 9.48 and 9.49, suppose you are testing the null hypothesis H_0: $\pi = 0.20$ against the two-tail alternative hypothesis H_1: $\pi \neq 0.20$ and you choose the level of significance $\alpha = 0.05$. What is your statistical decision?

Applying the Concepts

9.51 Late payment of medical claims can add to the cost of health care. An article (M. Freudenheim, "The Check Is Not in the Mail," *The New York Times*, May 25, 2006, pp. C1, C6) reported that for one insurance company, 85.1% of the claims were paid in full when first submitted. Suppose that the insurance company developed a new payment system in an effort to increase this percentage. A sample of 200 claims processed under this system revealed that 180 of the claims were paid in full when first submitted.

a. At the 0.05 level of significance, is there evidence that the population proportion of claims processed under this new system is higher than the article reported for the previous system?

b. Compute the *p*-value and interpret its meaning.

9.52 On Memorial Day weekend in 2007, gas prices in the United States reached an all-time high. An Ohio newspaper conducted a survey to see how its readers were reacting to the high prices. Of the 720 readers surveyed, 377 indicated that they planned to cut back on driving (extracted from "Gasoline Usage Poll," *The Oxford Press*, **www.oxfordpress.com**, May 24, 2007). Using a 0.05 level of significance and the 5-step *p*-value approach, can you prove that more than half of *The Oxford Press* readers planned to cut back on driving?

9.53 A *Wall Street Journal* article suggested that age bias was a growing problem in the corporate world (extracted from C. Hymowitz, "Top Executives Chase Youthful Appearance, but Miss Real Issue," *The Wall Street Journal*, February 17, 2004, p. B1). In 2001, an estimated 78% of executives believed that age bias was a serious problem. In a 2004 study by ExecuNet, 82% of the executives surveyed considered age bias a serious problem. The sample size for the 2004 study was not disclosed. Suppose 50 executives were surveyed.

a. At the 0.05 level of significance, use the six-step critical value approach to hypothesis testing to try to prove that the 2004 proportion of executives who believed that age bias was a serious problem has increased.

b. Use the five-step *p*-value approach. Interpret the meaning of the *p*-value.

c. Suppose that the sample size used was 1,000. Redo (a) and (b).

d. Discuss the effect that sample size had on the outcome of this analysis and, in general, the effect that sample size plays in hypothesis testing.

 9.54 A *Wall Street Journal* poll ("What's News Online," *The Wall Street Journal*, March 30, 2004, p. D7) asked respondents if they trusted energy-efficiency ratings on cars and appliances; 552 responded yes, and 531 responded no.

a. At the 0.05 level of significance, use the six-step critical value approach to hypothesis testing to try to prove that the percentage of people who trust energy-efficiency ratings differs from 50%.

b. Use the five-step *p*-value approach. Interpret the meaning of the *p*-value.

9.55 One of the biggest issues facing e-retailers is the ability to reduce the proportion of customers who cancel their transactions after they have selected their products. It has been estimated that about half of prospective customers cancel their transactions after they have selected their products (extracted from B. Tedeschi, "E-Commerce, a Cure for Abandoned Shopping Carts: A Web Checkout System That Eliminates the Need for Multiple Screens," *The New York Times*, February 14, 2005, p. C3). Suppose that a company changed its Web site so that customers could use a single-page checkout process rather than multiple pages. A sample of 500 customers who had selected their products were provided with the new checkout system. Of these 500 customers, 210 cancelled their transactions after they had selected their products.

a. At the 0.01 level of significance, is there evidence that the population proportion of customers who select products and then cancel their transaction is less than 0.50 with the new system?

b. Suppose that a sample of $n = 100$ customers (instead of $n = 500$ customers) were provided with the new checkout system and that 42 of those customers cancelled their transactions after they had selected their products. At the 0.01 level of significance, is there evidence that the population proportion of customers who select products and then cancel their transaction is less than 0.50 with the new system?

c. Compare the results of (a) and (b) and discuss the effect that sample size has on the outcome, and, in general, in hypothesis testing.

9.56 A recent study by the Pew Internet and American Life Project (**pewinternet.org**) found that Americans had a complex and ambivalent attitude toward technology (extracted from M. Himowitz, "How to Tell What Kind of Tech User You Are," *Newsday*, May 27, 2007, p. F6). The study reported that 8% of the respondents were "Omnivores" who are gadget lovers, text messengers, and online gamers who often had their own blogs, Web pages, video makers, and YouTube posters. You believe that the percentage of students at your school who are Omnivores is greater than 8% and you plan to carry out a study to prove that this is so.

a. State the null and alternative hypothesis.

You select a sample of 200 students at your school and find that 30 students can be classified as Omnivores.

b. Use either the six-step critical value hypothesis-testing approach or the five-step *p*-value approach to determine at the 0.05 level of significance whether there is evidence that the percentage of Omnivores at your school is greater than 8%.

9.5 THE POWER OF A TEST

Section 9.1 defined Type I and Type II errors and their associated risks. Recall that α represents the probability that you reject the null hypothesis when it is true and should not be rejected, and β represents the probability that you do not reject the null hypothesis when it is false and should be rejected. The power of the test, $1 - \beta$, is the probability that you correctly reject a false null hypothesis. This probability depends on how different the actual population parameter is from the value being hypothesized (under H_0), the value of α used, and the sample size. If there is a large difference between the population parameter and the hypothesized value, the power of the test will be much greater than if the difference between the population parameter and the hypothesized value is small. Selecting a larger value of α makes it easier to reject H_0 and therefore increases the power of a test. Increasing the sample size increases the precision in the estimates and therefore increases the ability to detect differences in the parameters and increases the power of a test.

In this section, the power of a statistical test is illustrated using the Oxford Cereals scenario. The filling process is subject to periodic inspection from a representative of the consumer affairs office. The representative's job is to detect the possible "short weighting" of boxes (i.e., cereal boxes are being sold that, on average have less than the specified 368 grams). Thus, the representative is interested in determining whether there is evidence that the cereal boxes have a mean weight that is less than 368 grams. The null and alternative hypotheses are as follows:

$$H_0: \mu \geq 368 \text{ (filling process is working properly)}$$

$$H_1: \mu < 368 \text{ (filling process is not working properly)}$$

The representative is willing to accept the company's claim that the standard deviation σ equals 15 grams. Therefore, you can use the Z test. Using Equation (9.1) on page 347, with $\bar{X}_L$ (the lower critical $\bar{X}$ value) substituted for $\bar{X}$, you can find the value of $\bar{X}$ that enables you to reject the null hypothesis:

$$Z_\alpha = \frac{\bar{X}_L - \mu}{\dfrac{\sigma}{\sqrt{n}}}$$

$$Z_\alpha \frac{\sigma}{\sqrt{n}} = \bar{X}_L - \mu$$

$$\bar{X}_L = \mu + Z_\alpha \frac{\sigma}{\sqrt{n}}$$

Because you have a one-tail test with a level of significance of 0.05, the value of Z_α is equal to –1.645 (see Figure 9.18). The sample size $n = 25$. Therefore,

$$\bar{X}_L = 368 + (-1.645)\frac{(15)}{\sqrt{25}} = 368 - 4.935 = 363.065$$

The decision rule for this one-tail test is

$$\text{Reject } H_0 \text{ if } \bar{X} < 363.065;$$

$$\text{otherwise do not reject } H_0.$$

FIGURE 9.18

Determining the lower critical value for a one-tail Z test for a population mean at the 0.05 level of significance

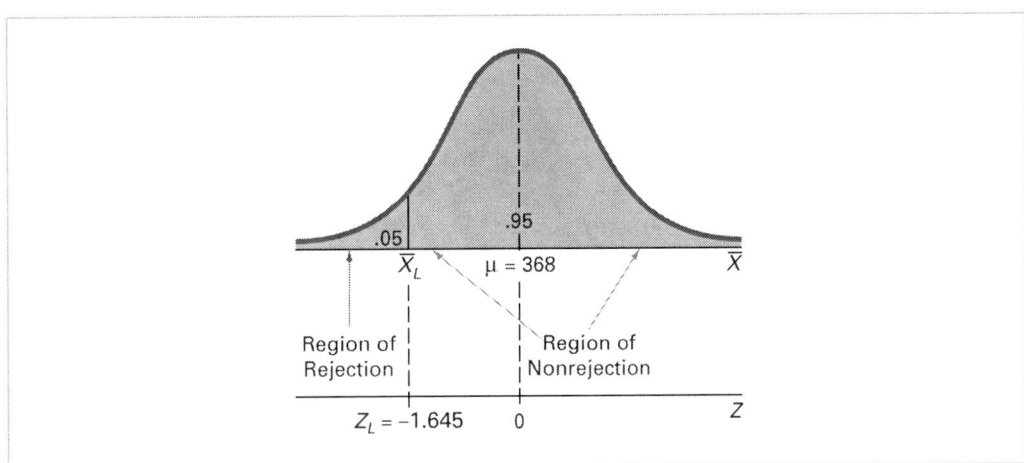

The decision rule states that if, in a random sample of 25 boxes, the sample mean is less than 363.065 grams, you reject the null hypothesis, and the representative concludes that the process is not working properly.

The power of the test measures the probability of concluding that the process is not working properly for differing values of the true population mean. What is the power of the test if the actual population mean is 360 grams? To determine the chance of rejecting the null hypothesis when the population mean is 360 grams, you need to determine the area under the normal curve below $\bar{X}_L = 363.065$ grams. Using Equation (9.1), with the population mean $\mu = 360$,

$$Z_{STAT} = \frac{\bar{X} - \mu}{\dfrac{\sigma}{\sqrt{n}}}$$

$$= \frac{363.065 - 360}{\dfrac{15}{\sqrt{25}}} = 1.02$$

From Table E.2, there is an 84.61% chance that the Z value is less than +1.02. This is the power of the test when the population mean is 360 grams (see Figure 9.19 on page 374). The probability (β) that you will not reject the null hypothesis ($\mu = 368$) is $1 - 0.8461 = 0.1539$. Thus, the probability of committing a Type II error is 15.39%.

FIGURE 9.19

Determining the power of the test and the probability of a Type II error when $\mu = 360$ grams

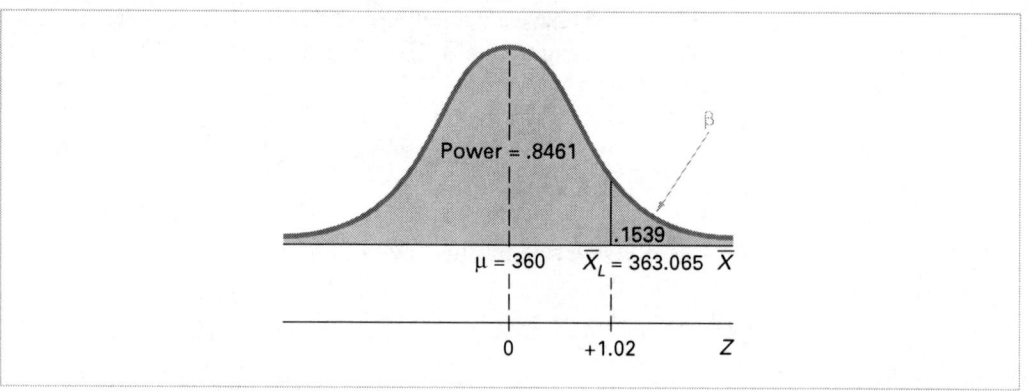

Now that you have determined the power of the test if the population mean were equal to 360, you can calculate the power for any other value of μ. For example, what is the power of the test if the population mean is 352 grams? Assuming the same standard deviation, sample size, and level of significance, the decision rule is

$$\text{Reject } H_0 \text{ if } \overline{X} < 363.065;$$

$$\text{otherwise do not reject } H_0.$$

Once again, because you are testing a hypothesis for a mean, from Equation (9.1)

$$Z_{STAT} = \frac{\overline{X} - \mu}{\dfrac{\sigma}{\sqrt{n}}}$$

If the population mean shifts down to 352 grams (see Figure 9.20), then

$$Z_{STAT} = \frac{363.065 - 352}{\dfrac{15}{\sqrt{25}}} = 3.69$$

FIGURE 9.20

Determining the power of the test and the probability of a Type II error when $\mu = 352$ grams

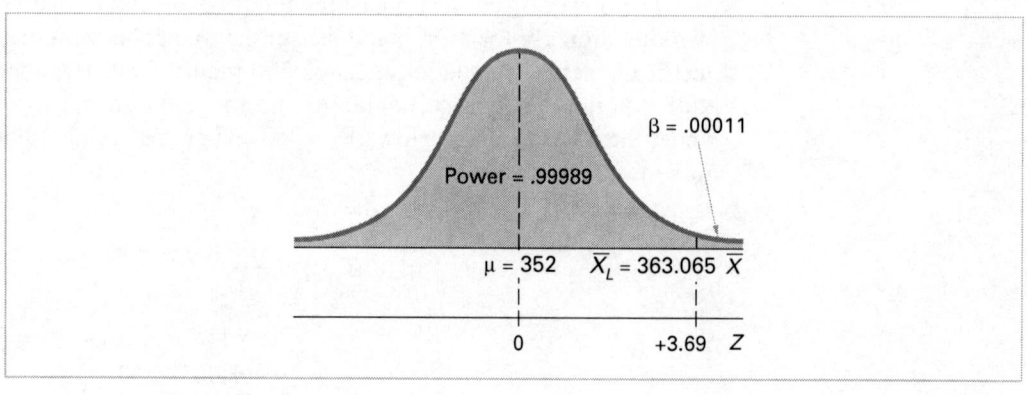

From Table E.2, there is a 99.989% chance that the Z value is less than +3.69. This is the power of the test when the population mean is 352. The probability (β) that you will not reject the null hypothesis ($\mu = 368$) is $1 - 0.99989 = 0.00011$. Thus, the probability of committing a Type II error is only 0.011%.

In the preceding two examples the power of the test is high, and the chance of committing a Type II error is low. In the next example, you compute the power of the test when the population mean is equal to 367 grams—a value that is very close to the hypothesized mean of 368 grams.

Once again, from Equation (9.1),

$$Z_{STAT} = \frac{\bar{X} - \mu}{\dfrac{\sigma}{\sqrt{n}}}$$

If the population mean is equal to 367 grams (see Figure 9.21), then

$$Z_{STAT} = \frac{363.065 - 367}{\dfrac{15}{\sqrt{25}}} = -1.31$$

FIGURE 9.21

Determining the power of the test and the probability of a Type II error when $\mu = 367$ grams

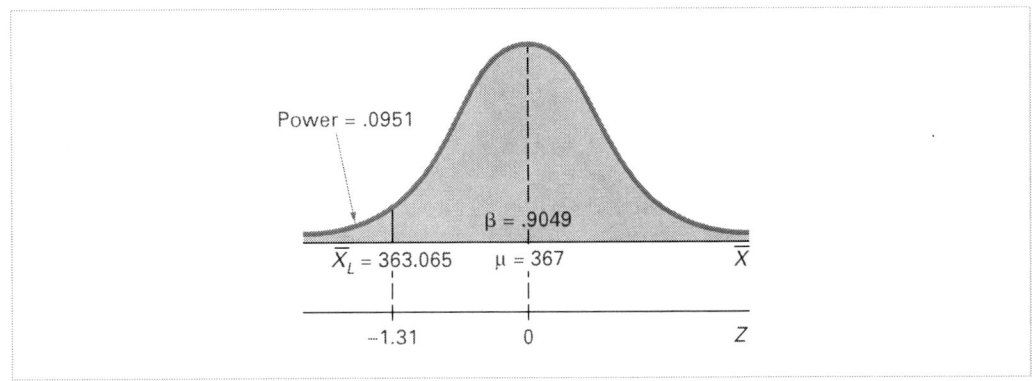

From Table E.2, the probability less than $Z = -1.31$ is 0.0951 (or 9.51%). Because the rejection region is in the lower tail of the distribution, the power of the test is 9.51% and the chance of making a Type II error is 90.49%.

Figure 9.22 illustrates the power of the test for various values of μ (including the three values examined). This graph is called a **power curve**.

FIGURE 9.22

Power curve of the cereal-box-filling process for H_1: $\mu < 368$ grams

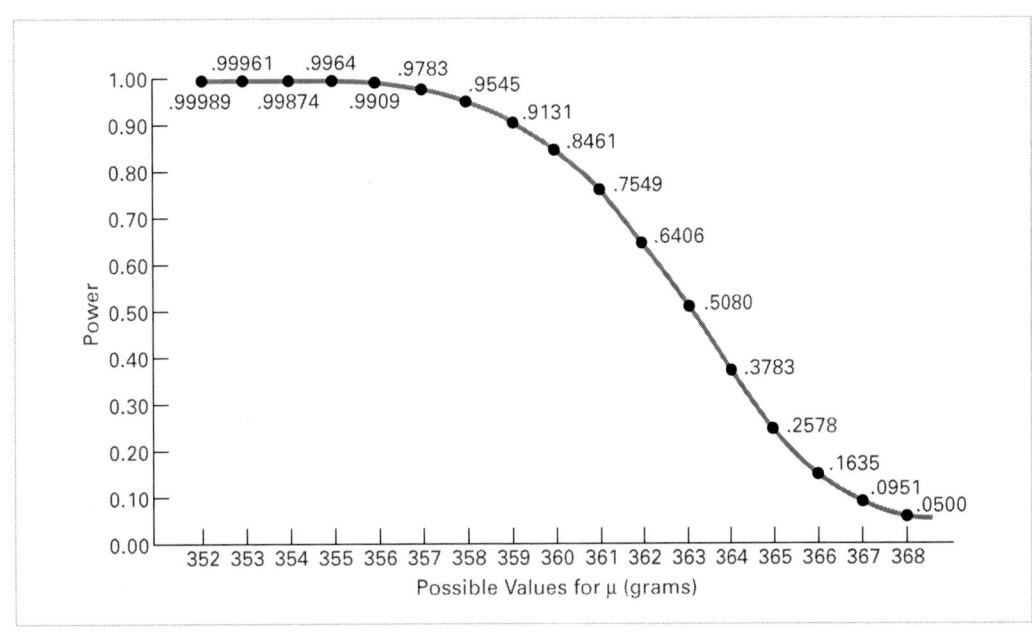

[1]For situations involving one-tail tests in which the actual mean is greater than the hypothesized mean, the converse would be true. The larger the actual mean compared with the hypothesized mean, the greater is the power. For two-tail tests, the greater the distance between the actual mean and the hypothesized mean, the greater the power of the test.

From Figure 9.22, you can see that the power of this one-tail test increases sharply (and approaches 100%) as the population mean takes on values farther below the hypothesized mean of 368 grams. Clearly, for this one-tail test, the smaller the actual mean μ the greater the power to detect this difference.[1] For values of μ close to 368 grams, the power is small because the test cannot effectively detect small differences between the actual population mean and the hypothesized value of 368 grams. When the population mean approaches 368 grams, the power of the test approaches α, the level of significance (which is 0.05 in this example). Figure 9.23 summarizes the computations for the three cases combined.

FIGURE 9.23

Determining the power of the test for varying values of the population mean

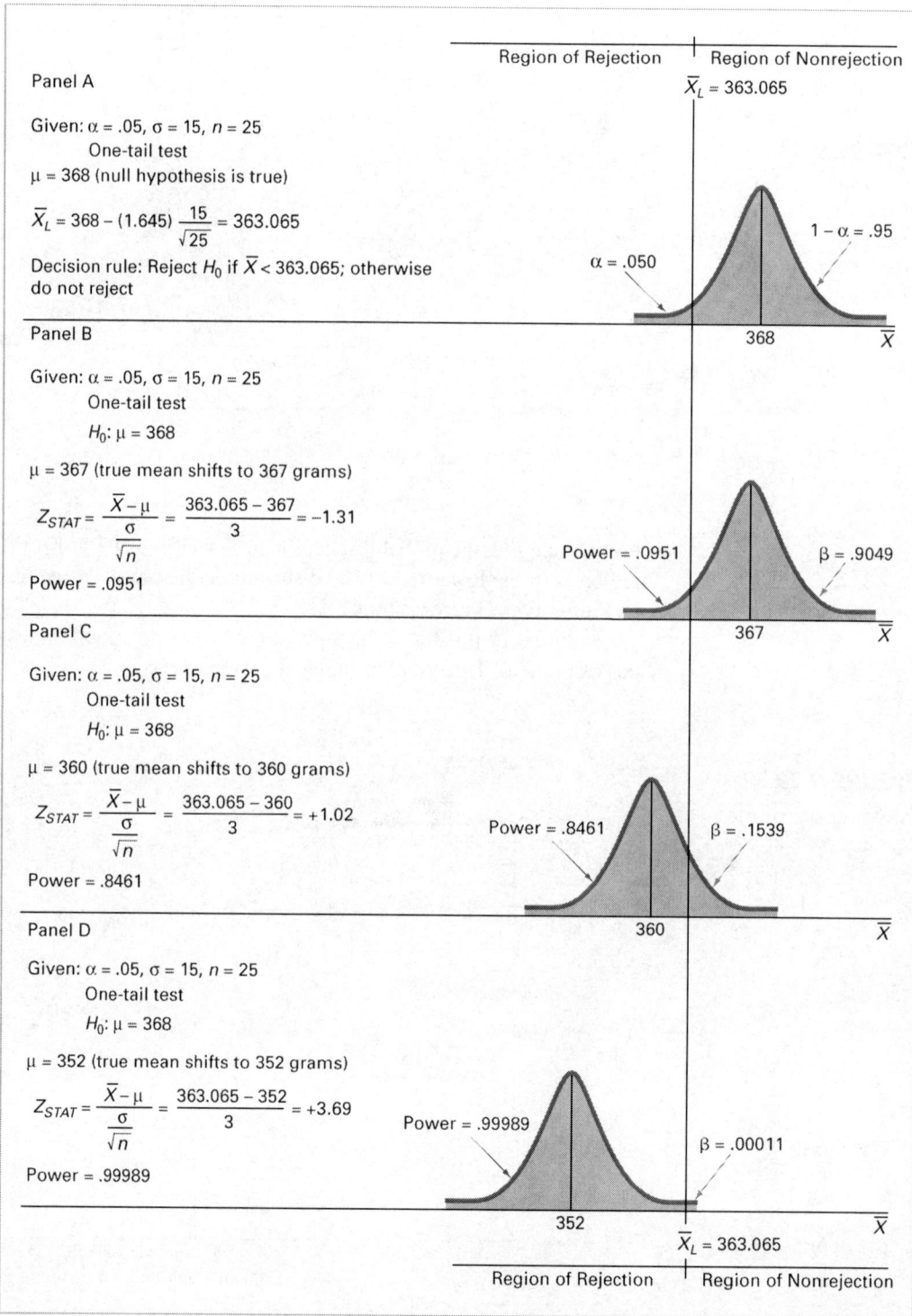

Panel A

Given: $\alpha = .05$, $\sigma = 15$, $n = 25$
    One-tail test
$\mu = 368$ (null hypothesis is true)

$\bar{X}_L = 368 - (1.645)\dfrac{15}{\sqrt{25}} = 363.065$

Decision rule: Reject H_0 if $\bar{X} < 363.065$; otherwise do not reject

Panel B

Given: $\alpha = .05$, $\sigma = 15$, $n = 25$
    One-tail test
    H_0: $\mu = 368$

$\mu = 367$ (true mean shifts to 367 grams)

$Z_{STAT} = \dfrac{\bar{X} - \mu}{\dfrac{\sigma}{\sqrt{n}}} = \dfrac{363.065 - 367}{3} = -1.31$

Power $= .0951$

Panel C

Given: $\alpha = .05$, $\sigma = 15$, $n = 25$
    One-tail test
    H_0: $\mu = 368$

$\mu = 360$ (true mean shifts to 360 grams)

$Z_{STAT} = \dfrac{\bar{X} - \mu}{\dfrac{\sigma}{\sqrt{n}}} = \dfrac{363.065 - 360}{3} = +1.02$

Power $= .8461$

Panel D

Given: $\alpha = .05$, $\sigma = 15$, $n = 25$
    One-tail test
    H_0: $\mu = 368$

$\mu = 352$ (true mean shifts to 352 grams)

$Z_{STAT} = \dfrac{\bar{X} - \mu}{\dfrac{\sigma}{\sqrt{n}}} = \dfrac{363.065 - 352}{3} = +3.69$

Power $= .99989$

You can see the drastic changes in the power of the test for differing values of the actual population means by reviewing the different panels of Figure 9.23. From panels *A* and *B* you can see that when the population mean does not greatly differ from 368 grams, the chance of rejecting the null hypothesis is not large. However, once the population mean shifts substantially below the hypothesized 368 grams, the power of the test greatly increases, approaching its maximum value of 1 (or 100%).

In the above discussion, a one-tail test with $\alpha = 0.05$ and $n = 25$ was used. The type of statistical test (one-tail versus two-tail), the level of significance, and the sample size all affect the power. Three basic conclusions regarding the power of the test are summarized below:

1. A one-tail test is more powerful than a two-tail test.
2. An increase in the level of significance (α) results in an increase in power. A decrease in α results in a decrease in power.
3. An increase in the sample size n results in an increase in power. A decrease in the sample size n results in a decrease in power.

PROBLEMS FOR SECTION 9.5

Applying the Concepts

9.57 A coin-operated soft-drink machine is designed to discharge on average, at least 7 ounces of beverage per cup with a standard deviation of 0.2 ounce. The amount of beverage per cup is normally distributed. If you select a random sample of 16 cups and you are willing to have an $\alpha = 0.05$ risk of committing a Type I error, compute the power of the test and the probability of a Type II error (β) if the population mean amount dispensed is actually
a. 6.9 ounces per cup.
b. 6.8 ounces per cup.

9.58 Refer to Problem 9.57. If you are willing to only have an $\alpha = 0.01$ risk of committing a Type I error, compute the power of the test and the probability of a Type II error (β) if the population mean amount dispensed is actually
a. 6.9 ounces per cup.
b. 6.8 ounces per cup.
c. Compare the results in (a) and (b) of this problem and in Problem 9.57. What conclusion can you reach?

9.59 Refer to Problem 9.57. If you select a random sample of 25 cups and are willing to have an $\alpha = 0.05$ risk of committing a Type I error, compute the power of the test and the probability of a Type II error (β) if the population mean amount dispensed is actually
a. 6.9 ounces per cup.
b. 6.8 ounces per cup.
c. Compare the results in (a) and (b) of this problem and in Problem 9.57. What conclusion can you reach?

9.60 A tire manufacturer produces tires that have a mean life of at least 25,000 miles when the production process is working properly. Based on past experience, the standard deviation of the tires is 3,500 miles and the tire life is normally distributed. The operations manager stops the production process if there is evidence that the population mean tire life is below 25,000 miles. If you select a random sample of 100 tires and you are willing to have an $\alpha = 0.05$ risk of committing a Type I error, compute the power of the test and the probability of a Type II error (β) if the population mean life is actually
a. 24,000 miles.
b. 24,900 miles.

9.61 Refer to Problem 9.60. If you are willing to only have an $\alpha = 0.01$ risk of committing a Type I error, compute the power of the test and the probability of a Type II error (β) if the population mean life is actually
a. 24,000 miles.
b. 24,900 miles.
c. Compare the results in (a) and (b) of this problem and (a) and (b) in Problem 9.60. What conclusion can you reach?

9.62 Refer to Problem 9.60. If you select a random sample of 25 tires and are willing to have an $\alpha = 0.05$ risk of committing a Type I error, compute the power of the test and the probability of a Type II error (β) if the population mean life is actually
a. 24,000 miles.
b. 24,900 miles.

c. Compare the results in (a) and (b) of this problem and (a) and (b) in Problem 9.60. What conclusion can you reach?

9.63 Refer to Problem 9.60. If the operations manager stops the process when there is evidence that the population mean life is different from 25,000 miles (either less than or greater than) and a random sample of 100 tires is selected along with a level of significance of $\alpha = 0.05$, compute the power of the test and the probability of a Type II error (β) if the population mean life is actually

a. 24,000 miles.

b. 24,900 miles.

c. Compare the results in (a) and (b) of this problem and (a) and (b) in Problem 9.60. What conclusion can you reach?

9.6 POTENTIAL HYPOTHESIS-TESTING PITFALLS AND ETHICAL ISSUES

To this point, you have studied the fundamental concepts of hypothesis testing. You have used hypothesis testing to analyze differences between sample statistics and hypothesized population parameters in order to make business decisions concerning the underlying population characteristics. You have also learned how to evaluate the risks involved in making these decisions.

When planning to carry out a hypothesis test based on a survey, research study, or designed experiment, you must ask several questions to ensure that you use proper methodology. You need to raise and answer questions such as the following in the planning stage:

1. What is the goal of the survey, study, or experiment? How can you translate the goal into a null hypothesis and an alternative hypothesis?
2. Is the hypothesis test a two-tail test or one-tail test?
3. Can you select a random sample from the underlying population of interest?
4. What kinds of data will you collect in the sample? Are the variables numerical or categorical?
5. At what level of significance should you conduct the hypothesis test?
6. Is the intended sample size large enough to achieve the desired power of the test for the level of significance chosen?
7. What statistical test procedure should you use and why?
8. What conclusions and interpretations can you reach from the results of the hypothesis test?

Failing to consider these questions early in the planning process can lead to biased or incomplete results. Proper planning can help ensure that the statistical study will provide objective information needed to make good business decisions.

Statistical Significance versus Practical Significance You need to make the distinction between the existence of a statistically significant result and its practical significance in the context within a field of application. Sometimes, due to a very large sample size, you may get a result that is statistically significant but has little practical significance. For example, suppose that prior to a national marketing campaign focusing on a series of expensive television commercials, you believe that the proportion of people who recognize your brand is 0.30. At the completion of the campaign, a survey of 20,000 people indicates that 6,168 recognized your brand. A one-tail test trying to prove that the proportion is now greater than 0.30 results in a p-value of 0.0047 and the correct statistical conclusion is that the proportion of consumers recognizing your brand name has now increased. Was the campaign successful? The result of the hypothesis test indicates a statistically significant increase in brand awareness, but is this increase practically important? The population proportion is now estimated at 6,168/20,000 = 0.3084, or 30.84%. This increase is less than 1% more than the hypothesized value of 30%. Did the large expenses associated with the marketing campaign produce a result with a meaningful increase in brand awareness? Because of the minimal real-world impact an increase of less than 1% has on the overall marketing strategy and the huge expenses associated with the marketing campaign, you should conclude that the campaign was not successful. On the other hand, if the campaign increased brand awareness by 20%, you could conclude that the campaign was successful.

Ethical Issues   You also need to distinguish between poor research methodology and unethical behavior. Ethical considerations arise when the hypothesis-testing process is manipulated. Some of the areas where ethical issues can arise include the use of human subjects in experiments, data collection method, the type of test (one-tail or two-tail test), the choice of the level of significance, data snooping, the cleansing and discarding of data, and the failure to report pertinent findings.

Informed Consent from Human Respondents Being "Treated"   Ethical considerations require that any individual who is to be subjected to some "treatment" in an experiment be made aware of the research endeavor and any potential behavioral or physical side effects. The person should also provide informed consent before participating.

Data Collection Method—Randomization   To eliminate the possibility of potential biases in the results, you must use proper data collection methods. To draw meaningful conclusions, the data must be the outcome of a random sample from a population or from an experiment in which a **randomization** process was used in which respondents are randomly assigned to groups. Potential respondents should not be permitted to self-select for a study, nor should they be purposely selected. Aside from the potential ethical issues that may arise, such a lack of randomization can result in serious coverage errors or selection biases that destroy the integrity of the study.

Type of Test—Two-Tail or One-Tail Test   If prior information is available that leads you to test the null hypothesis against a specifically directed alternative, then a one-tail test is more powerful than a two-tail test. However, if you are interested only in *differences* from the null hypothesis, not in the *direction* of the difference, the two-tail test is the appropriate procedure to use. For example, if previous research and statistical testing have already established the difference in a particular direction, or if an established scientific theory states that it is possible for results to occur in only one direction, then a one-tail test is appropriate. You should never change the direction of a test after the data are collected.

Choice of Level of Significance, α   In a well-designed study, you select the level of significance, α, before data collection occurs. You cannot alter the level of significance after the fact to achieve a specific result. You should always report the *p*-value, not just the conclusions of the hypothesis test.

Data Snooping   **Data snooping** involves performing a hypothesis test on a set of data, looking at the results, and only then specifying the level of significance or deciding whether to use a one-tail or two-tail test. This unethical approach is never permissible. You must make these decisions before the data are collected in order to achieve valid conclusions. In addition, you cannot arbitrarily change or discard extreme or unusual values in order to alter the results of the hypothesis tests.

Cleansing and Discarding of Data   In the data preparation stage of editing, coding, and transcribing, you have an opportunity to review the data for any extreme or unusual values. After reviewing the data, you should construct a stem-and-leaf display and/or a boxplot to determine whether there are possible outliers to double-check against the original data.

The process of data cleansing raises a major ethical question. Should you ever remove a value from a study? The answer is a qualified yes. If you can determine that a measurement is incomplete or grossly in error because of some equipment problem or unusual behavioral occurrence unrelated to the study, you can discard the value. Sometimes you have no choice—an individual may decide to quit a particular study he or she has been participating in before a final measurement can be made. In a well-designed experiment or study, you should decide, in advance, on all rules regarding the possible discarding of data.

Reporting of Findings   In conducting research, you should document both good and bad results. You should not just report the results of hypothesis tests that show statistical significance but omit those for which there is insufficient evidence in the findings. In instances in which there is insufficient evidence to reject H_0, you must make it clear that this does not prove that the null hypothesis is true. What the result does indicate is that with the sample size used, there is not enough information to *disprove* the null hypothesis.

Summary   To summarize, in discussing ethical issues concerning hypothesis testing, the key is *intent*. You must distinguish between poor data analysis and unethical practice. Unethical practice occurs when researchers *intentionally* create a selection bias in data collection, manipulate the treatment of human subjects without informed consent, use data snooping to select the type of test (two-tail or one-tail) and/or level of significance, discard values that do not support a stated hypothesis, or fail to report pertinent findings.

SUMMARY

This chapter presented the foundation of hypothesis testing. You learned how to perform tests on the population mean and on the population proportion. You also learned how an operations manager of a production facility can use hypothesis testing to monitor and improve a cereal-fill process.

In deciding which test to use, you should ask the following question:

Does the test involve a numerical variable or a categorical variable? If the test involves a categorical variable, use the Z test for the proportion. If the test involves a numerical variable, use the t test for the mean.

Table 9.4 provides a list of topics covered in this chapter.

TABLE 9.4

Summary of Topics in Chapter 9

Type of Analysis	Type of Data	
	Numerical	**Categorical**
Hypothesis test concerning a single parameter	t test of hypothesis for the mean (Section 9.2)	Z test of hypothesis for the proportion (Section 9.4)

KEY EQUATIONS

Z **Test for the Mean (σ Known)**

$$Z_{STAT} = \frac{\bar{X} - \mu}{\dfrac{\sigma}{\sqrt{n}}} \qquad (9.1)$$

t **Test for the Mean (σ Unknown)**

$$t_{STAT} = \frac{\bar{X} - \mu}{\dfrac{S}{\sqrt{n}}} \qquad (9.2)$$

Z Test for the Proportion

$$Z_{STAT} = \frac{p - \pi}{\sqrt{\dfrac{\pi(1-\pi)}{n}}} \qquad (9.3)$$

Z Test for the Proportion in Terms of the Number of Events of Interest

$$Z_{STAT} = \frac{X - n\pi}{\sqrt{n\pi(1-\pi)}} \qquad (9.4)$$

KEY TERMS

α (level of significance)   345
alternative hypothesis (H_1) 343
β risk   346
confidence coefficient   346
confidence level   346
critical value   344
data snooping   379
directional test   363
hypothesis testing   342

level of significance (α) 345
null hypothesis (H_0) 342
one-tail test   363
p-value   351
power curve   375
power of a statistical test   346
randomization   379
region of nonrejection   344
region of rejection   344

robust   359
sample proportion   367
t test for the mean   355
test statistic   344
two-tail test   348
Type I error   345
Type II error   345
Z test for the mean   347
Z test for the proportion   367

CHAPTER REVIEW PROBLEMS

Checking Your Understanding

9.64 What is the difference between a null hypothesis, H_0, and an alternative hypothesis, H_1?

9.65 What is the difference between a Type I error and a Type II error?

9.66 What is meant by the power of a test?

9.67 What is the difference between a one-tail test and a two-tail test?

9.68 What is meant by a p-value?

9.69 How can a confidence interval estimate for the population mean provide conclusions to the corresponding two tail hypothesis test for the population mean?

9.70 What is the six-step critical value approach to two-tail hypothesis testing?

9.71 What is the five-step p-value approach to hypothesis testing?

9.72 What are some of the ethical issues involved with performing a hypothesis test?

Applying the Concepts

9.73 An article in *Marketing News* (T. T. Semon, "Consider a Statistical Insignificance Test," *Marketing News*, February 1, 1999) argued that the level of significance used when comparing two products is often too low—that is, sometimes you should be using an α value greater than 0.05. Specifically, the article recounted testing the proportion of potential customers with a preference for product 1 over product 2. The null hypothesis was that the population proportion of potential customers preferring product 1 was 0.50, and the alternative hypothesis was that it was not equal to 0.50. The p-value for the test was 0.22. The article suggested that, in some cases, this should be enough evidence to reject the null hypothesis.

a. State the null and alternative hypotheses for this example in statistical terms.
b. Explain the risks associated with Type I and Type II errors in this case.
c. What would be the consequences if you rejected the null hypothesis for a p-value of 0.22?
d. Why do you think the article suggested raising the value of α?
e. What would you do in this situation?
f. What is your answer in (e) if the p-value equals 0.12? What if it equals 0.06?

9.74 La Quinta Motor Inns developed a computer model to help predict the profitability of sites that are being considered as locations for new hotels. If the computer model predicts large profits, La Quinta buys the proposed site and builds a new hotel. If the computer model predicts small or moderate profits, La Quinta chooses not to proceed with that site (extracted from S. E. Kimes and J. A. Fitzsimmons, "Selecting Profitable Hotel Sites at La Quinta Motor Inns," *Interfaces*, Vol. 20, March–April 1990, pp. 12–20). This decision-making procedure can be expressed in the hypothesis-testing framework. The null hypothesis is that the site is not a profitable location. The alternative hypothesis is that the site is a profitable location.

a. Explain the risks associated with committing a Type I error in this case.

b. Explain the risks associated with committing a Type II error in this case.

c. Which type of error do you think the executives at La Quinta Motor Inns are trying hard to avoid? Explain.

d. How do changes in the rejection criterion affect the probabilities of committing Type I and Type II errors?

9.75 In 2006, Visa wanted to move away from its long-running television advertising theme of "Visa, it's everywhere you want to be." During the Winter Olympics, Visa featured Olympians in commercials with a broader message, including security, check cards, and payment technologies such as contactless processing. One of the first commercials featured snowboarder Lindsey Jacobellis being coached to calm down before a big race by imagining that her Visa Check Card got stolen. A key metric for the success of television advertisements is the proportion of viewers who "like the ads a lot." Harris Ad Research Service conducted a study of 903 adults who viewed the new Visa advertisement and reported that 54 indicated that they "like the ad a lot." According to Harris, the proportion of a typical television advertisement receiving the "like the ad a lot" score is 0.21 (extracted from T. Howard, "Visa to Change Strategies in Upcoming Ads," **usatoday.com**, January 23, 2006).

a. Use the six-step critical value approach to hypothesis testing and a 0.05 level of significance to try to prove that the new Visa ad is less successful than a typical television advertisement.

b. Use the five-step p-value approach to hypothesis testing and a 0.05 level of significance to try to prove that the new Visa ad is less successful than a typical television advertisement.

c. Compare the results of (a) and (b).

9.76 The owner of a gasoline station wants to study gasoline purchasing habits by motorists at his station. He selects a random sample of 60 motorists during a certain week, with the following results:

- The amount purchased was $\bar{X} = 11.3$ gallons, $S = 3.1$ gallons.
- 11 motorists purchased premium-grade gasoline.

a. At the 0.05 level of significance, is there evidence that the population mean purchase was different from 10 gallons?

b. Determine the p-value in (a).

c. At the 0.05 level of significance, is there evidence that fewer than 20% of all the motorists at the station purchased premium-grade gasoline?

d. What is your answer to (a) if the sample mean equals 10.3 gallons?

e. What is your answer to (c) if 7 motorists purchased premium-grade gasoline?

9.77 An auditor for a government agency is assigned the task of evaluating reimbursement for office visits to physicians paid by Medicare. The audit was conducted on a sample of 75 of the reimbursements, with the following results:
In 12 of the office visits, an incorrect amount of reimbursement was provided.
The amount of reimbursement was $\bar{X} = \$93.70$, $S = \$34.55$.

a. At the 0.05 level of significance, is there evidence that the population mean reimbursement was less than $100?

b. At the 0.05 level of significance, is there evidence that the proportion of incorrect reimbursements in the population was greater than 0.10?

c. Discuss the underlying assumptions of the test used in (a).

d. What is your answer to (a) if the sample mean equals $90?

e. What is your answer to (b) if 15 office visits had incorrect reimbursements?

9.78 A bank branch located in a commercial district of a city has developed an improved process for serving customers during the noon-to-1:00 p.m. lunch period. The waiting time (defined as the time the customer enters the line until he or she reaches the teller window) of all customers during this hour is recorded over a period of 1 week. A random sample of 15 customers (see the data file **Bank1**) is selected, and the results are as follows:

4.21	5.55	3.02	5.13	4.77	2.34	3.54	3.20
4.50	6.10	0.38	5.12	6.46	6.19	3.79	

a. At the 0.05 level of significance, is there evidence that the population mean waiting time is less than 5 minutes?

b. What assumption about the population distribution is needed in order to conduct the t test in (a)?

c. Use a boxplot or a normal probability plot to evaluate the assumption made in (b).

d. Do you think that the assumption needed in order to conduct the t test in (a) is valid? Explain.

e. As a customer walks into the branch office during the lunch hour, she asks the branch manager how long she can expect to wait. The branch manager replies, "Almost certainly not longer than 5 minutes." On the basis of the results of (a), evaluate this statement.

9.79 A manufacturing company produces electrical insulators. If the insulators break when in use, a short circuit is likely to occur. To test the strength of the insulators, destructive testing is carried out to determine how much *force* is required to break the insulators. Force is measured by observing the number of pounds of force applied to the insulator before it breaks. The following data (stored in the `Force` file) are from 30 insulators subject to this testing:

1,870 1,728 1,656 1,610 1,634 1,784 1,522 1,696 1,592 1,662

1,866 1,764 1,734 1,662 1,734 1,774 1,550 1,756 1,762 1,866

1,820 1,744 1,788 1,688 1,810 1,752 1,680 1,810 1,652 1,736

a. At the 0.05 level of significance, is there evidence that the population mean force is greater than 1,500 pounds?
b. What assumption about the population distribution is needed in order to conduct the *t* test in (a)?
c. Use a histogram, boxplot, or a normal probability plot to evaluate the assumption made in (b).
d. Do you think that the assumption needed in order to conduct the *t* test in (a) is valid? Explain.

9.80 An important quality characteristic used by the manufacturer of Boston and Vermont asphalt shingles is the amount of moisture the shingles contain when they are packaged. Customers may feel that they have purchased a product lacking in quality if they find moisture and wet shingles inside the packaging. In some cases, excessive moisture can cause the granules attached to the shingle for texture and coloring purposes to fall off the shingle, resulting in appearance problems. To monitor the amount of moisture present, the company conducts moisture tests. A shingle is weighed and then dried. The shingle is then reweighed, and, based on the amount of moisture taken out of the product, the pounds of moisture per 100 square feet are calculated. The company would like to show that the mean moisture content is less than 0.35 pound per 100 square feet. The data file `Moisture` includes 36 measurements (in pounds per 100 square feet) for Boston shingles and 31 for Vermont shingles.
a. For the Boston shingles, is there evidence at the 0.05 level of significance that the population mean moisture content is less than 0.35 pound per 100 square feet?
b. Interpret the meaning of the *p*-value in (a).
c. For the Vermont shingles, is there evidence at the 0.05 level of significance that the population mean moisture content is less than 0.35 pound per 100 square feet?
d. Interpret the meaning of the *p*-value in (c).
e. What assumption about the population distribution is needed in order to conduct the *t* tests in (a) and (c)?
f. Use a histogram, boxplot, or a normal probability plot to evaluate the assumption made in (a) and (c).
g. Do you think that the assumption needed in order to conduct the *t* tests in (a) and (c) is valid? Explain.

9.81 Studies conducted by the manufacturer of Boston and Vermont asphalt shingles have shown product weight

to be a major factor in the customer's perception of quality. Moreover, the weight represents the amount of raw materials being used and is therefore very important to the company from a cost standpoint. The last stage of the assembly line packages the shingles before the packages are placed on wooden pallets. Once a pallet is full (a pallet for most brands holds 16 squares of shingles), it is weighed, and the measurement is recorded. The data file `Pallet` contains the weight (in pounds) from a sample of 368 pallets of Boston shingles and 330 pallets of Vermont shingles.
a. For the Boston shingles, is there evidence that the population mean weight is different from 3,150 pounds?
b. Interpret the meaning of the *p*-value in (a).
c. For the Vermont shingles, is there evidence that the population mean weight is different from 3,700 pounds?
d. Interpret the meaning of the *p*-value in (c).
e. In (a) through (d), do you have to worry about the normality assumption? Explain.

9.82 The manufacturer of Boston and Vermont asphalt shingles provides its customers with a 20-year warranty on most of its products. To determine whether a shingle will last as long as the warranty period, accelerated-life testing is conducted at the manufacturing plant. Accelerated-life testing exposes the shingle to the stresses it would be subject to in a lifetime of normal use in a laboratory setting via an experiment that takes only a few minutes to conduct. In this test, a shingle is repeatedly scraped with a brush for a short period of time, and the shingle granules removed by the brushing are weighed (in grams). Shingles that experience low amounts of granule loss are expected to last longer in normal use than shingles that experience high amounts of granule loss. The data file `Granule` contains a sample of 170 measurements made on the company's Boston shingles and 140 measurements made on Vermont shingles.
a. For the Boston shingles, is there evidence that the population mean granule loss is different from 0.50 gram?
b. Interpret the meaning of the *p*-value in (a).
c. For the Vermont shingles, is there evidence that the population mean granule loss is different from 0.50 gram?
d. Interpret the meaning of the *p*-value in (c).
e. In (a) through (d), do you have to worry about the normality assumption? Explain.

Report Writing Exercises

9.83 Referring to the results of Problems 9.80 through 9.82 concerning Boston and Vermont shingles, write a report that evaluates the moisture level, weight, and granule loss of the two types of shingles.

MANAGING THE *SPRINGVILLE HERALD*

Continuing its monitoring of the blackness of the newspaper print, first described in the Chapter 6 Managing the *Springville Herald* case, the production department of the newspaper wants to ensure that the mean blackness of the print for all newspapers is at least 0.97 on a standard scale in which the target value is 1.0. A random sample of 50 newspapers was selected, and the blackness of one spot on each of the 50 newspapers measured (and stored in the **SH9** file).

0.854	1.023	1.005	1.030	1.219	0.977	1.044	0.778	1.122	1.114
1.091	1.086	1.141	0.931	0.723	0.934	1.060	1.047	0.800	0.889
1.012	0.695	0.869	0.734	1.131	0.993	0.762	0.814	1.108	0.805
1.223	1.024	0.884	0.799	0.870	0.898	0.621	0.818	1.113	1.286
1.052	0.678	1.162	0.808	1.012	0.859	0.951	1.112	1.003	0.972

Calculate the sample statistics and determine whether there is evidence that the population mean blackness is less than 0.97. Write a memo to management that summarizes your conclusions.

WEB CASE

Apply your knowledge about hypothesis testing in this Web Case, which continues the cereal-fill-packaging dispute Web Case from Chapter 7.

In response to the negative statements made by the Consumers Concerned About Cereal Cheaters (CCACC) in the Chapter 7 Web Case, Oxford Cereals recently conducted an experiment concerning cereal packaging. The company claims that the results of the experiment refute the CCACC allegations that Oxford Cereals has been cheating consumers by packaging cereals at less than labeled weights. Review the Oxford Cereals' press release and supporting documents that describe the experiment at the company's Web site, **www.prenhall.com/Springville/**

OC_FullUp.htm, or open OC_FullUp.htm from the Student CD-ROM Web Case folder, and then answer the following:

1. Are the results of the experiment valid? Why or why not? If you were conducting the experiment, is there anything you would change?

2. Do the results support the claim that Oxford Cereals is not cheating its customers?

3. Is the claim of the Oxford Cereals CEO that many cereal boxes contain *more* than 368 grams surprising? Is it true?

4. Could there ever be a circumstance in which the results of the Oxford Cereals experiment *and* the CCACC's results are both correct? Explain.

REFERENCES

1. Bradley, J. V., *Distribution-Free Statistical Tests* (Upper Saddle River, NJ: Prentice Hall, 1968).
2. Daniel, W., *Applied Nonparametric Statistics*, 2nd ed. (Boston: Houghton Mifflin, 1990).
3. *Microsoft Excel 2007* (Redmond, WA: Microsoft Corp., 2007).
4. *Minitab for Windows Version 15* (State College, PA: Minitab, Inc., 2006).

Appendix E9
Using Microsoft Excel for One-Sample Tests

E9.1 Using the Z Test for the Mean (σ Known)

You perform the Z test for the mean (σ known) by making entries in either the **ZMean_TT** (see Figure 9.5 on page 352) or **ZMean_All** worksheets of the **Z Mean.xls** workbook. These worksheets use the **NORMSINV($P < X$)** function to determine the lower and upper critical values and use the **NORMSDIST(Z *value*)** function to compute the p-values from the Z value calculated in cell B12. The worksheets also use the **IF(*comparison, what to do if comparison holds, what to do if comparison fails*)** function to determine whether or not you should reject the null hypothesis. (Although shown as two lines in Figure 9.5, the function is entered as a single, continuous line.)

The **ZMean_TT** worksheet applies the two-tail Z test to the Example 9.2 cereal-filling process on page 349. The similar **ZMean_All** worksheet includes the two-tail test, the upper one-tail test, and the lower one-tail test on one worksheet. To adapt these worksheets to other problems, change the null hypothesis, level of significance, population standard deviation, sample size, and sample mean values, in the tinted cells B4 through B8, as is necessary.

E9.2 Using the t Test for the Mean (σ Unknown)

You perform the t test for the mean (σ unknown) by making entries in either the **TMean_TT** (see Figure 9.7 on page 358) or **TMean_All** worksheets of the **T Mean.xls** workbook. These worksheets use the **TINV(1-*confidence level, degrees of freedom*)** function to determine the lower and upper critical values and use the **TDIST(ABS(*t*), *degrees of freedom, tails*)** function in which **ABS(*t*)** is the absolute value of the t_{STAT} test statistic, and ***tails*** is either 1, for a one-tail test, or 2, for a two-tail test, to compute the p-values. The worksheets also use the IF function to determine whether or not you should reject the null hypothesis (see related material in Section P9.1).

The **TMean_TT** worksheet applies the two-tail t test to the Section 9.2 sales invoices example on page 356. The similar **TMean_All** worksheet includes the two-tail test, the upper one-tail test, and the lower one-tail test on one worksheet. To adapt these worksheets to other problems, change the null hypothesis, level of significance, sample size, sample mean, and sample standard deviation values, in the tinted cells B4 through B8, as is necessary.

E9.3 Using the Z Test for the Proportion

You perform the Z test for the proportion by making entries in either the **ZProp_TT** (see Figure 9.16 on page 369) or **ZProp_All** worksheets of the **Z Proportion.xls** workbook. These worksheets use the **NORMSINV($P < X$)** function to determine the lower and upper critical values and use the **NORMSDIST(Z *value*)** function to compute the p-values. The worksheets also use the IF function to determine whether or not you should reject the null hypothesis (see related material in Section P9.1).

The **ZProp_TT** worksheet applies the two-tail Z test to the Section 9.4 example concerning customer satisfaction on pages 368–369. The **ZProp_All** worksheet includes the two-tail test, the upper one-tail test, and the lower one-tail test on one worksheet. To adapt these worksheets to other problems, enter the appropriate null hypothesis, level of significance, sample size, sample mean, and sample standard deviation values, in the tinted cells B4 through B8, as is necessary.

Appendix P9
Using PHStat2 for One-Sample Tests

P9.1 Using the Z Test for the Mean (σ Known)

To perform the Z test for the mean (σ known), use **PHStat → One-Sample Tests → Z Test for the Mean, sigma known**. This procedure creates a worksheet similar to Figure 9.5 on page 352 using the test option you click and the null hypothesis, significance, population standard deviation, sample size, and sample mean values that you specify. If you have unsummarized data, click **Sample Statistics Unknown** and the procedure will calculate the sample statistics for you.

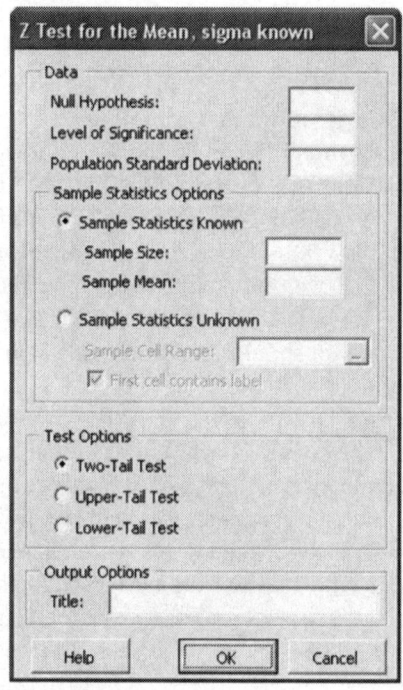

P9.2 Using the t Test for the Mean (σ Unknown)

To perform the *t* test for the mean (σ unknown), use **PHStat → One-Sample Tests → t Test for the Mean, sigma unknown**. The procedure creates a worksheet similar to Figure 9.7 on page 358 using the test option you click and the null hypothesis, level of significance, sample size, sample mean, and sample standard deviation values you specify. If you have unsummarized data, click **Sample Statistics Unknown** and the procedure will calculate the sample statistics for you.

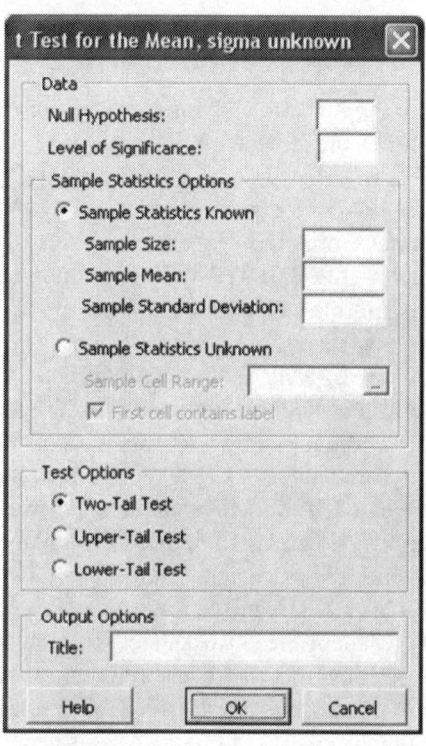

P9.3 Using the Z Test for the Proportion

To perform the *Z* test for the proportion use **PHStat → One-Sample Tests → Z Test for the Proportion**. The procedure creates a worksheet similar to Figure 9.16 on page 369 using the test option you click and the null hypothesis, level of significance, number of events of interest, and sample size values that you specify.

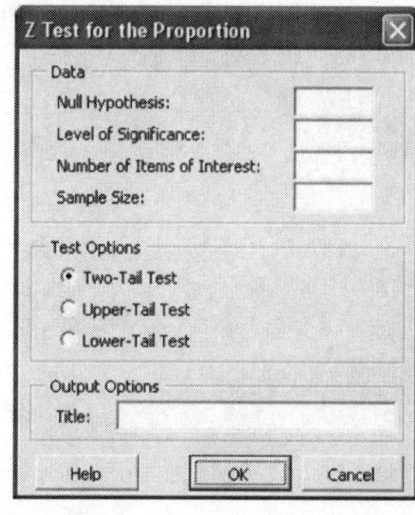

Appendix M9
Using Minitab for One-Sample Tests

M9.1 Using the Z Test of Hypothesis for the Mean (σ Known)

To perform a test for the mean, return to the Oxford Cereals example discussed in Example 9.2 on pages 349–350.

1. Open a blank worksheet.
2. Select **Stat → Basic Statistics → 1-Sample Z**.

In the 1-Sample Z (Test and Confidence Interval) dialog box (see Figure M9.1):

3. Click **Summarized data**.
4. Enter **25** in the **Sample size** box.
5. Enter **372.5** in the **Mean** box.
6. Enter **15** in the **Standard deviation** box.
7. Click **Perform hypothesis test**.
8. Enter **368** in the **Hypothesized mean** box.
9. Click **Options**.

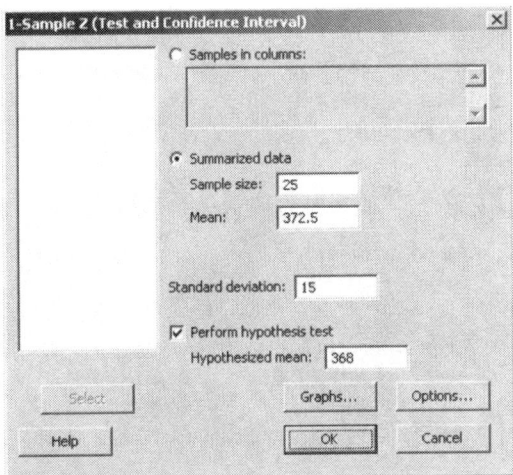

FIGURE M9.1

Minitab 1-Sample Z (Test and Confidence Interval) dialog box

In the 1-Sample Z - Options dialog box (see Figure M9.2):

10. Make sure that **95.0** is in the **Confidence level** box.
11. Select **not equal** from the **Alternative** drop-down list. (This selection performs a two-tail test. Select **less than** or **greater than** to perform a one-tail test.)
12. Click **OK** [to return to the 1-Sample Z (Test and Confidence Interval) dialog box].
13. Click **OK** (to perform the test).

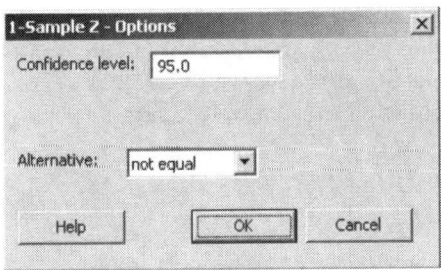

FIGURE M9.2

Minitab 1-Sample Z - Options dialog box

M9.2 Using the t Test of Hypothesis for the Mean (σ Unknown)

To illustrate the test of hypothesis for the mean when σ is unknown, return to the Saxon Home Improvement Company invoice example discussed in Section 9.2 on pages 356–358.

1. Open the **Invoices.mtw** worksheet.
2. Select **Stat → Basic Statistics → 1-Sample t**.

In the 1-Sample t (Test and Confidence Interval) dialog box (see Figure M9.3):

3. Click **Sample in columns**.
4. Enter **Amount** in the **Sample in columns** box.
5. Click **Perform hypothesis test**.
6. Enter **120** in the **Hypothesized mean** box.
7. Click **Options**.

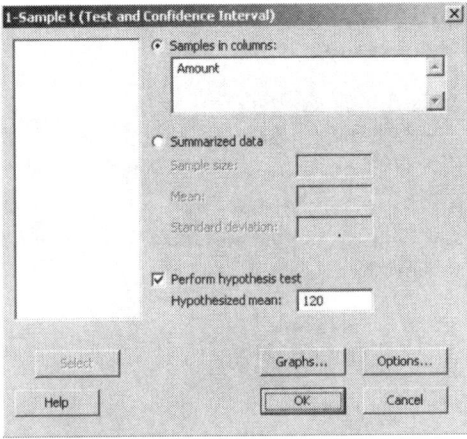

FIGURE M9.3

Minitab 1-Sample t (Test and Confidence Interval) dialog box

In the 1-Sample t - Options dialog box (see Figure M9.4)

8. Make sure that **95.0** is entered in the **Confidence level** box.
9. Select **not equal** from the **Alternative** drop-down list. (This selection performs a two-tail test. Select **less than** or **greater than** to perform a one-tail test.)
10. Click **OK** [to return to the 1-Sample t (Test and Confidence Interval) dialog box].
11. *Optional.* To create a boxplot, click **Graphs**. In the Minitab 1-Sample t - Graphs dialog box, click **Boxplot of data** and then click **OK** to return to the 1-Sample t dialog box.
12. Click **OK** (to perform the test).

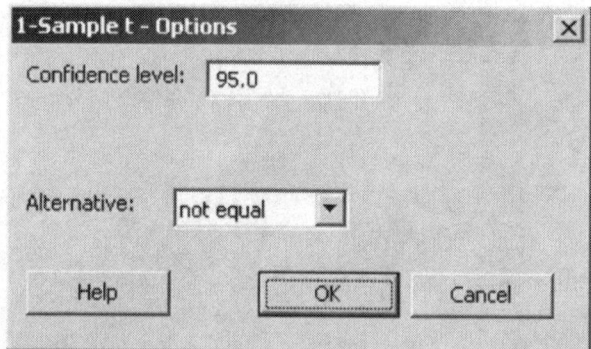

FIGURE M9.4

Minitab 1-Sample t - Options dialog box

M9.3 Using the Z Test for the Proportion

To illustrate the Z test for the proportion, return to the Section 9.4 example examining whether customer service was better at e-commerce sites than at physical stores.

1. Select **Stat → Basic Statistics → 1 Proportion**.

In the 1 Proportion (Test and Confidence Interval) dialog box (see Figure M9.5):

2. Click **Summarized data**.
3. Enter **561** in the **Number of events** box.
4. Enter **1100** in the **Number of trials** box.
5. Click **Perform hypothesis test**.
6. Enter **0.50** in the **Hypothesized proportion** box.
7. Click **Options**.

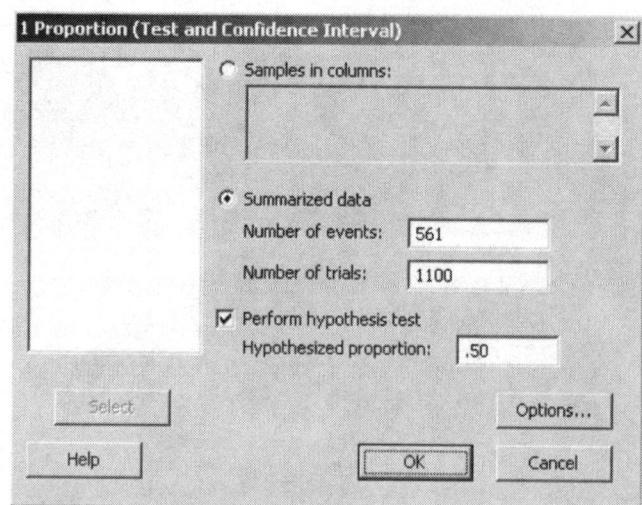

FIGURE M9.5

Minitab 1-Proportion (Test and Confidence Interval) dialog box

In the 1 Proportion - Options dialog box (see Figure M9.6):

8. Make sure that **95.0** is entered in the **Confidence level** box.
9. Select **not equal** from the **Alternative** drop-down list. (This selection performs a two-tail test. Select **less than** or **greater than** to perform a one-tail test.)
10. Click **Use test and interval based on normal distribution**.
11. Click **OK** [to return to the 1 Proportion (Test and Confidence Interval) dialog box].
12. Click **OK** (to perform the test).

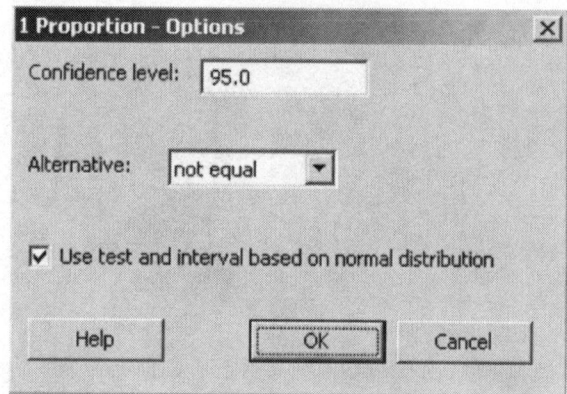

FIGURE M9.6

1 Proportion - Options dialog box

CHAPTER
TEN

TWO-SAMPLE TESTS

LEARNING OBJECTIVES

In this chapter, you learn how to use hypothesis testing for comparing the difference between:

- The means of two independent populations
- The means of two related populations
- Two proportions
- The variances of two independent populations

USING STATISTICS @ BLK Foods

Does the type of display used in a supermarket affect the sales of products? As the regional sales manager for BLK Foods, you want to compare the sales volume of the BLK Cola when the product is placed in the normal shelf location to the sales volume when the product is featured in a special end-aisle display. To test the effectiveness of the end-aisle displays, you select 20 stores from the BLK supermarket chain that all experience similar storewide sales volumes. You then randomly assign 10 of the 20 stores to sample 1 and 10 to sample 2. The managers of the 10 stores in sample 1 place the BLK Cola in the normal shelf location alongside the other cola products. The 10 stores in sample 2 use the special end-aisle promotional display. At the end of one week, the sales of BLK Cola are recorded. How can you determine whether sales of BLK Cola using the end-aisle displays are the same as those when the cola is placed in the normal shelf location? How can you decide if the variability in BLK cola sales from store to store is the same for the two types of displays? How could you use the answers to these questions to improve sales of BLK Colas?

Hypothesis testing provides a *confirmatory* approach to data analysis. In Chapter 9, you learned a variety of commonly used hypothesis-testing procedures that relate to a single sample of data selected from a single population. In this chapter, you learn how to extend hypothesis testing to procedures that compare statistics from two samples of data selected from two populations. One such extension would be asking the question, "Are the mean weekly sales of BLK Cola when using the normal shelf location equal to the mean weekly sales of BLK Cola when placed in an end-aisle display?"

10.1   COMPARING THE MEANS OF TWO INDEPENDENT POPULATIONS

Pooled-Variance *t* Test for the Difference Between Two Means

Suppose that you take a random sample of n_1 from the first population and a random sample of n_2 from the second population. The data collected in each sample are from a numerical variable. In the first population, the mean is represented by the symbol μ_1 and the standard deviation is represented by the symbol σ_1. In the second population, the mean is represented by the symbol μ_2 and the standard deviation is represented by the symbol σ_2.

In almost all cases, the variances of the two populations are not known. The only information you usually have are the sample means and the sample variances. If you assume that the samples are randomly and independently selected from populations that are normally distributed and that the population variances are equal (i.e., $\sigma_1^2 = \sigma_2^2$), you can use a **pooled-variance *t* test** to determine whether there is a significant difference between the means of the two populations. If the populations are not normally distributed, the pooled-variance *t* test is still appropriate if the sample sizes are large enough (typically n_1 and $n_2 \geq 30$; see the Central Limit Theorem in Section 7.4 on page 274).

To test the null hypothesis of no difference in the means of two independent populations:

$$H_0: \mu_1 = \mu_2 \text{ or } \mu_1 - \mu_2 = 0$$

against the alternative that the means are not the same

$$H_1: \mu_1 \neq \mu_2 \text{ or } \mu_1 - \mu_2 \neq 0$$

you use the pooled-variance t-test statistic t_{STAT} shown in Equation (10.1). The pooled-variance t test gets its name from the fact that the test statistic pools or combines the two sample variances S_1^2 and S_2^2 to compute S_p^2, the best estimate of the variance common to both populations under the assumption that the two population variances are equal.[1]

[1]When the two sample sizes are equal (i.e., $n_1 = n_2$), the equation for the pooled variance can be simplified to

$$S_p^2 = \frac{S_1^2 + S_2^2}{2}$$

Pooled-Variance t Test for the Difference Between Two Means

$$t_{STAT} = \frac{(\bar{X}_1 - \bar{X}_2) - (\mu_1 - \mu_2)}{\sqrt{S_p^2\left(\dfrac{1}{n_1} + \dfrac{1}{n_2}\right)}} \tag{10.1}$$

where

$$S_p^2 = \frac{(n_1 - 1)S_1^2 + (n_2 - 1)S_2^2}{(n_1 - 1) + (n_2 - 1)}$$

and

S_p^2 = pooled variance

$\bar{X}_1$ = mean of the sample taken from population 1

S_1^2 = variance of the sample taken from population 1

n_1 = size of the sample taken from population 1

$\bar{X}_2$ = mean of the sample taken from population 2

S_2^2 = variance of the sample taken from population 2

n_2 = size of the sample taken from population 2

The t_{STAT} test statistic follows a t distribution with $n_1 + n_2 - 2$ degrees of freedom.

For a given level of significance α, in a two-tail test, you reject the null hypothesis if the computed t_{STAT} test statistic is greater than the upper-tail critical value from the t distribution or if the computed t_{STAT} test statistic is less than the lower-tail critical value from the t distribution. Figure 10.1 displays the regions of rejection.

In a one-tail test in which the rejection region is in the lower tail, you reject the null hypothesis if the computed t_{STAT} test statistic is less than the lower-tail critical value from the t distribution. In a one-tail test in which the rejection region is in the upper tail, you reject the null hypothesis if the computed t_{STAT} test statistic is greater than the upper-tail critical value from the t distribution.

FIGURE 10.1

Regions of rejection and nonrejection for the pooled-variance t test for the difference between the means (two-tail test)

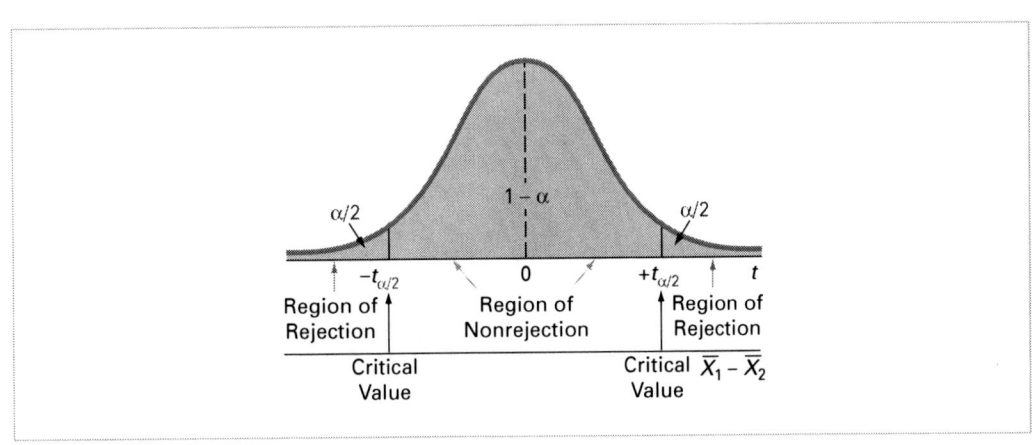

To demonstrate the use of the pooled-variance t test, return to the Using Statistics scenario on page 390. You want to determine whether the mean weekly sales of BLK Cola are the same when using a normal shelf location and when using an end-aisle display. There are two populations of interest. The first population is the set of all possible weekly sales of BLK Cola *if* all the BLK supermarkets used the normal shelf location. The second population is the set of all possible weekly sales of BLK Cola *if* all the BLK supermarkets used the end-aisle displays. The first sample contains the weekly sales of BLK Cola from the 10 stores selected to use the normal shelf location, and the second sample contains the weekly sales of BLK Cola from the 10 stores selected to use the end-aisle display. Table 10.1 contains the cola sales (in number of cases) for the two samples (see the **Cola** file).

TABLE 10.1

Comparing BLK Cola Weekly Sales from Two Different Display Locations (in Number of Cases)

Display Location									
Normal					**End-Aisle**				
22	34	52	62	30	52	71	76	54	67
40	64	84	56	59	83	66	90	77	84

The null and alternative hypotheses are

$$H_0: \mu_1 = \mu_2 \text{ or } \mu_1 - \mu_2 = 0$$

$$H_1: \mu_1 \neq \mu_2 \text{ or } \mu_1 - \mu_2 \neq 0$$

Assuming that the samples are from normal populations having equal variances, you can use the pooled-variance t test. The t_{STAT} test statistic follows a t distribution with $10 + 10 - 2 = 18$ degrees of freedom. Using $\alpha = 0.05$ level of significance, you divide the rejection region into the two tails for this two-tail test (i.e., two equal parts of 0.025 each). Table E.3 shows that the critical values for this two-tail test are +2.1009 and −2.1009. As shown in Figure 10.2, the decision rule is:

$$\text{Reject } H_0 \text{ if } t_{STAT} > +2.1009$$

$$\text{or if } t_{STAT} < -2.1009;$$

$$\text{otherwise do not reject } H_0.$$

FIGURE 10.2

Two-tail test of hypothesis for the difference between the means at the 0.05 level of significance with 18 degrees of freedom

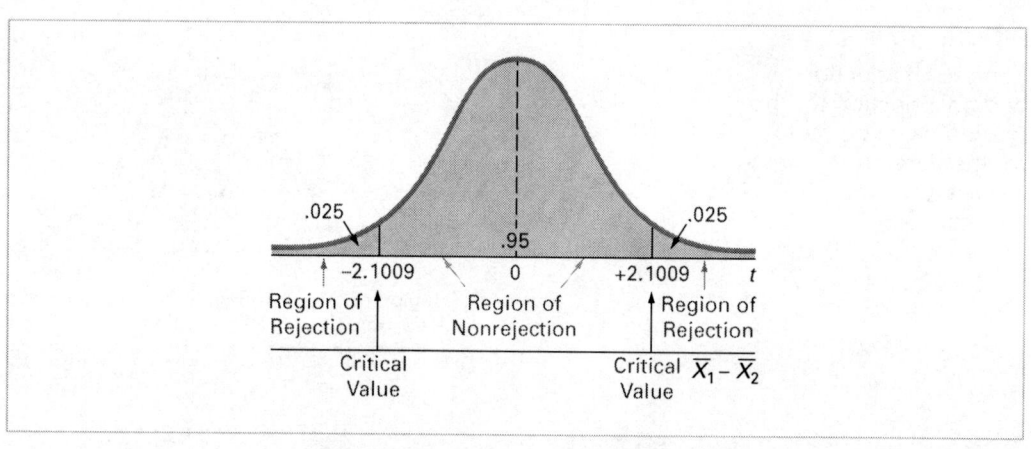

From Figures 10.3 or 10.4, the computed t_{STAT} test statistic for this test is -3.0446 and the p-value is 0.0070.

FIGURE 10.3

Microsoft Excel t-test results for the two display locations

See Section E10.2 to create this.

	A	B	C
1	t-Test: Two-Sample Assuming Equal Variances		
2			
3		*Normal*	*End-Aisle*
4	Mean	50.3	72
5	Variance	350.6778	157.3333
6	Observations	10	10
7	Pooled Variance	254.0056	
8	Hypothesized Mean Difference	0	
9	df	18	
10	t Stat	-3.0446	
11	P(T<=t) one-tail	0.0035	
12	t Critical one-tail	1.7341	
13	P(T<=t) two-tail	0.0070	
14	t Critical two-tail	2.1009	

FIGURE 10.4

Minitab t-test results for the two display locations

See Section M10.2 to create this.

```
Two-sample T for Sales_Normal vs Sales_EndAisle

                N   Mean   StDev   SE Mean
Sales_Normal    10  50.3   18.7     5.9
Sales_EndAisle  10  72.0   12.5     4.0


Difference = mu (Sales_Normal) - mu (Sales_EndAisle)
Estimate for difference:  -21.70
95% CI for difference:  (-36.67, -6.73)

T-Test of difference = 0 (vs not =): T-Value = -3.04  P-Value = 0.007  DF = 18
Both use Pooled StDev = 15.9376
```

Using Equation (10.1) on page 391 and the descriptive statistics provided in Figures 10.3 and 10.4,

$$t_{STAT} = \frac{(\bar{X}_1 - \bar{X}_2) - (\mu_1 - \mu_2)}{\sqrt{S_p^2 \left(\frac{1}{n_1} + \frac{1}{n_2} \right)}}$$

where

$$S_p^2 = \frac{(n_1 - 1)S_1^2 + (n_2 - 1)S_2^2}{(n_1 - 1) + (n_2 - 1)}$$

$$= \frac{9(350.6778) + 9(157.3333)}{9 + 9} = 254.0056$$

Therefore,

$$t_{STAT} = \frac{(50.3 - 72.0) - 0.0}{\sqrt{254.0056 \left(\frac{1}{10} + \frac{1}{10} \right)}} = \frac{-21.7}{\sqrt{50.801}} = -3.0446$$

You reject the null hypothesis because $t_{STAT} = -3.0446 < -2.1009$. The p-value (as computed from Microsoft Excel or Minitab) is 0.0070. In other words, the probability that $t_{STAT} > 3.0446$ or $t_{STAT} < -3.0446$ is equal to 0.0070. This p-value indicates that if the population means are equal, the probability of observing a difference this large or larger in the two sample means is only 0.0070. Because the p-value is less than $\alpha = 0.05$, there is sufficient evidence to reject the null hypothesis. You can conclude that the mean sales are different for the normal shelf location and the end-aisle location. Based on these results, the sales are lower for the normal location (i.e., higher for the end-aisle location). Example 10.1 provides another application of the pooled-variance t test.

EXAMPLE 10.1

TESTING FOR THE DIFFERENCE IN THE MEAN DELIVERY TIMES

A local pizza restaurant and a local branch of a national chain are located across the street from a college campus. The local pizza restaurant advertises that they deliver to the dormitories faster than the national chain. In order to determine whether this advertisement is valid, you and some friends have decided to order 10 pizzas from the local pizza restaurant and 10 pizzas from the national chain, all at different times. The delivery times in minutes (see the Pizzatime file) are shown in Table 10.2:

TABLE 10.2

Delivery Times (in minutes) for Local Pizza Restaurant and National Pizza Chain

Local	Chain	Local	Chain
16.8	22.0	18.1	19.5
11.7	15.2	14.1	17.0
15.6	18.7	21.8	19.5
16.7	15.6	13.9	16.5
17.5	20.8	20.8	24.0

At the 0.05 level of significance, is there evidence that the mean delivery time for the local pizza restaurant is less than the mean delivery time for the national pizza chain?

SOLUTION Because you want to know whether the mean is *lower* for the local pizza restaurant than for the national pizza chain, you have a one-tail test with the following null and alternative hypotheses:

$H_0: \mu_1 \geq \mu_2$ (The mean delivery time for the local pizza restaurant is equal to or greater than the mean delivery time for the national pizza chain.)
$H_1: \mu_1 < \mu_2$ (The mean delivery time for the local pizza restaurant is less than the mean delivery time for the national pizza chain.)

Figure 10.5 displays Microsoft Excel results of the pooled t test for these data.

FIGURE 10.5

Microsoft Excel results of the pooled t test for the pizza delivery time data

See Section E10.2 to create this. (Minitab users, see Section M10.2 to create equivalent results.)

	A	B	C
1	t-Test: Two-Sample Assuming Equal Variances		
2			
3		Local	Chain
4	Mean	16.7	18.88
5	Variance	9.5822	8.2151
6	Observations	10	10
7	Pooled Variance	8.8987	
8	Hypothesized Mean Difference	0	
9	df	18	
10	t Stat	-1.6341	
11	P(T<=t) one-tail	0.0598	
12	t Critical one-tail	1.7341	
13	P(T<=t) two-tail	0.1196	
14	t Critical two-tail	2.1009	

Using Equation (10.1) on page 391,

$$t_{STAT} = \frac{(\bar{X}_1 - \bar{X}_2) - (\mu_1 - \mu_2)}{\sqrt{S_p^2 \left(\frac{1}{n_1} + \frac{1}{n_2} \right)}}$$

where

$$S_p^2 = \frac{(n_1 - 1)S_1^2 + (n_2 - 1)S_2^2}{(n_1 - 1) + (n_2 - 1)}$$

$$= \frac{9(9.5822) + 9(8.2151)}{9 + 9} = 8.8987$$

Therefore,

$$t_{STAT} = \frac{(16.7 - 18.88) - 0.0}{\sqrt{8.8987 \left(\frac{1}{10} + \frac{1}{10} \right)}} = \frac{-2.18}{\sqrt{1.7797}} = -1.6341$$

You do not reject the null hypothesis because tSTAT = -1.6341 > -1.7341. The p-value (as computed from Microsoft Excel) is 0.0598. This *p*-value indicates that the probability that $t_{STAT} < $ -1.6341 is equal to 0.0598. In other words, if the population means are equal, the probability that the sample mean delivery time for the local pizza restaurant is at least 2.18 minutes faster than the national chain is 0.0598. Because the p-value is greater than a = 0.05, there is insufficient evidence to reject the null hypothesis. Based on these results, there is insufficient evidence for the local pizza restaurant to make the advertising claim that they have a faster delivery time.

In testing for the difference between the means, you assume that the populations are normally distributed with equal variances. For situations in which the two populations have equal variances, the pooled-variance *t* test is **robust** (or not sensitive) to moderate departures from the assumption of normality, provided that the sample sizes are large. In such situations, you can use the pooled-variance *t* test without serious effects on its power. However, if you cannot assume that both populations are normally distributed, you have two choices. You can use a nonparametric procedure, such as the Wilcoxon rank sum test (covered in Section 12.6), that does not depend on the assumption of normality for the two populations, or you can use a normalizing transformation (see reference 6) on each of the outcomes and then use the pooled-variance *t* test.

To check the assumption of normality in each of the two populations, observe the boxplot of the sales for the two display locations in Figure 10.6 on page 396. For these two small samples, there appears to be only moderate departure from normality, so the assumption of normality needed for the *t* test is not seriously violated.

Confidence Interval Estimate for the Difference Between Two Means

Instead of, or in addition to, testing for the difference in the means of two independent populations, you can use Equation (10.2) to develop a confidence interval estimate of the difference in the means.

FIGURE 10.6

Minitab boxplot for the sales for two display locations

See Section M3.2 to create this. (PHStat2 users, see Section P3.4 to create an equivalent chart.)

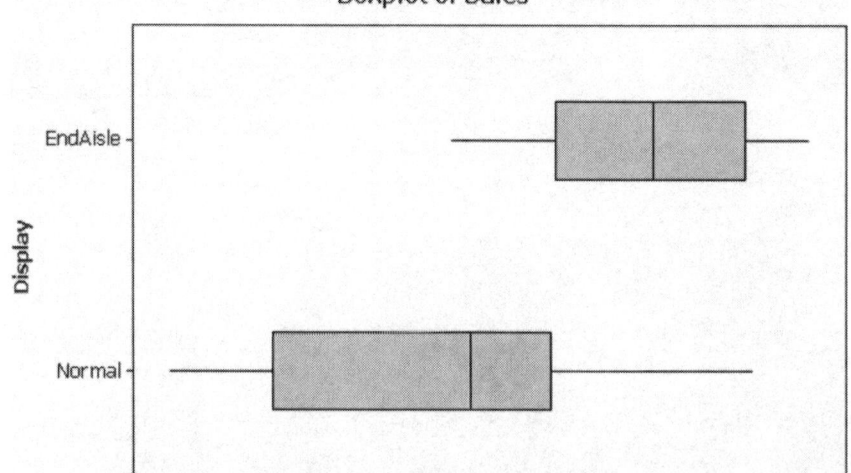

Confidence Interval Estimate of the Difference in the Means of Two Independent Populations

$$(\bar{X}_1 - \bar{X}_2) \pm t_{\alpha/2}\sqrt{S_p^2\left(\frac{1}{n_1} + \frac{1}{n_2}\right)} \qquad (10.2)$$

or

$$(\bar{X}_1 - \bar{X}_2) - t_{\alpha/2}\sqrt{S_p^2\left(\frac{1}{n_1} + \frac{1}{n_2}\right)} \le \mu_1 - \mu_2 \le (\bar{X}_1 - \bar{X}_2) + t_{\alpha/2}\sqrt{S_p^2\left(\frac{1}{n_1} + \frac{1}{n_2}\right)}$$

where $t_{\alpha/2}$ is the critical value of the t distribution with $n_1 + n_2 - 2$ degrees of freedom for an area of $\alpha/2$ in the upper tail.

For the sample statistics pertaining to the two aisle locations reported in Figures 10.3 or 10.4 on page 393, using 95% confidence, and Equation (10.2),

$$\bar{X}_1 = 50.3, \; n_1 = 10, \; \bar{X}_2 = 72, \; n_2 = 10, \; S_p^2 = 254.0056, \text{ and with } 10 + 10 - 2$$

$$= 18 \text{ degrees of freedom, } t_{0.025} = 2.1009$$

$$(50.3 - 72) \pm (2.1009)\sqrt{254.0056\left(\frac{1}{10} + \frac{1}{10}\right)}$$

$$-21.7 \pm (2.1009)(7.1275)$$

$$-21.7 \pm 14.97$$

$$-36.67 \le \mu_1 - \mu_2 \le -6.73$$

Therefore, you are 95% confident that the difference in mean sales between the normal aisle location and the end-aisle location is between −36.67 cases of cola and −6.73 cases of cola. In other words, the end-aisle location sells, on average, 6.73 to 36.67 cases more than the normal aisle location. From a hypothesis-testing perspective, because the interval does not include zero, you reject the null hypothesis of no difference between the means of the two populations.

Separate-Variance t Test for the Difference Between Two Means

In testing for the difference between the means of two independent populations when the population variances are assumed to be equal, the sample variances are pooled together into a common estimate S_p^2. However, if you cannot make this assumption, then the pooled-variance t test is inappropriate. In this case, you should use the **separate-variance t test** developed by Satterthwaite (see reference 5). This test procedure includes the two separate sample variances in the computation of the t-test statistic. Equation (10.3) defines the test statistic for the separate-variance t test.

Separate-Variance t Test for the Difference in Two Means

$$t_{STAT} = \frac{(\bar{X}_1 - \bar{X}_2) - (\mu_1 - \mu_2)}{\sqrt{\dfrac{S_1^2}{n_1} + \dfrac{S_2^2}{n_2}}} \tag{10.3}$$

where

$\bar{X}_1$ = mean of the sample taken from population 1

S_1^2 = variance of the sample taken from population 1

n_1 = size of the sample taken from population 1

$\bar{X}_2$ = mean of the sample taken from population 2

S_2^2 = variance of the sample taken from population 2

n_2 = size of the sample taken from population 2

The separate-variance t_{STAT} test statistic approximately follows a t distribution with degrees of freedom V equal to the integer portion of the following computation.

Computing Degrees of Freedom in the Separate-Variance t Test

$$V = \frac{\left(\dfrac{S_1^2}{n_1} + \dfrac{S_2^2}{n_2}\right)^2}{\dfrac{\left(\dfrac{S_1^2}{n_1}\right)^2}{n_1 - 1} + \dfrac{\left(\dfrac{S_2^2}{n_2}\right)^2}{n_2 - 1}} \tag{10.4}$$

For a given level of significance α, in a two-tail test you reject the null hypothesis if the computed t_{STAT} test statistic is greater than the upper-tail critical value $t_{\alpha/2}$ from the t distribution with V degrees of freedom or if the computed t_{STAT} test statistic is less than the lower-tail critical value $-t_{\alpha/2}$ from the t distribution with V degrees of freedom. Thus, the decision rule is

Reject H_0 if $t_{STAT} > t_{\alpha/2}$

or if $t_{STAT} < -t_{\alpha/2}$;

otherwise, do not reject H_0.

Return to the Using Statistics scenario on page 390 concerning the display location of BLK Cola. Using Equation (10.4), the separate-variance t_{STAT} test statistic is approximated by a t distribution with $V = 15$ degrees of freedom, the integer portion of the following computation.

$$V = \frac{\left(\dfrac{S_1^2}{n_1} + \dfrac{S_2^2}{n_2}\right)^2}{\dfrac{\left(\dfrac{S_1^2}{n_1}\right)^2}{n_1 - 1} + \dfrac{\left(\dfrac{S_2^2}{n_2}\right)^2}{n_2 - 1}}$$

$$= \frac{\left(\dfrac{350.6778}{10} + \dfrac{157.3333}{10}\right)^2}{\dfrac{\left(\dfrac{350.6778}{10}\right)^2}{9} + \dfrac{\left(\dfrac{157.3333}{10}\right)^2}{9}} = 15.72$$

Using $\alpha = 0.05$, the upper and lower critical values for this two-tail test found in Table E.3 are $+2.1315$ and -2.1315. As depicted in Figure 10.7, the decision rule is

$$\text{Reject } H_0 \text{ if } t_{STAT} > +2.1315$$

$$\text{or if } t_{STAT} < -2.1315;$$

$$\text{otherwise do not reject } H_0.$$

FIGURE 10.7

Two-tailed test of hypothesis for the difference between the means at the 0.05 level of significance with 15 degrees of freedom

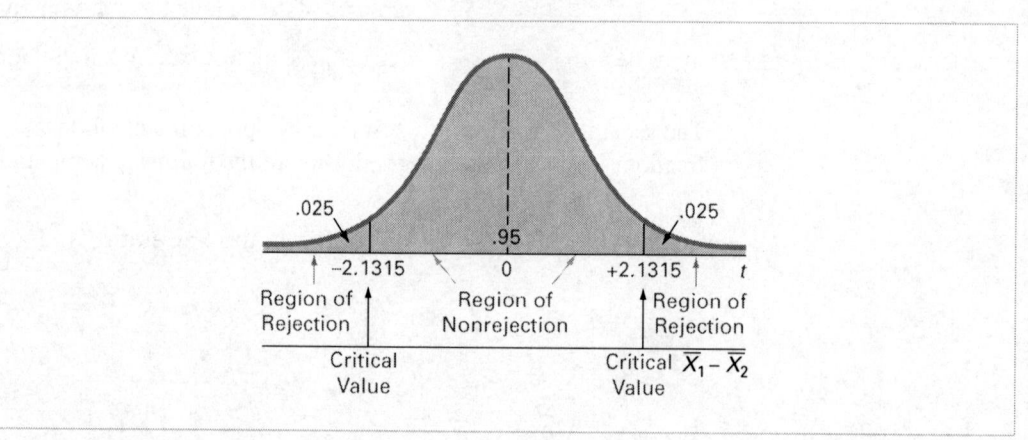

Using Equation (10.3) on page 397 and the descriptive statistics provided in Figures 10.3 and 10.4 on page 393,

$$t_{STAT} = \frac{(\bar{X}_1 - \bar{X}_2) - (\mu_1 - \mu_2)}{\sqrt{\dfrac{S_1^2}{n_1} + \dfrac{S_2^2}{n_2}}}$$

$$= \frac{50.3 - 72}{\sqrt{\left(\dfrac{350.6778}{10} + \dfrac{157.3333}{10}\right)}} = \frac{-21.7}{\sqrt{50.801}} = -3.04$$

Using a 0.05 level of significance, you reject the null hypothesis because $t_{STAT} = -3.04446 < -2.1315$.

Figure 10.8 illustrates Microsoft Excel results for this separate-variance t test, and Figure 10.9 illustrates Minitab output. Note that Excel rounds the degrees of freedom while Minitab uses the integer portion.

FIGURE 10.8

Microsoft Excel results of the separate-variance t test for the display location data

See Section E10.4 to create this.

	A	B	C
1	t-Test: Two-Sample Assuming Unequal Variances		
2			
3		*Normal*	*End-Aisle*
4	Mean	50.3	72
5	Variance	350.6778	157.3333
6	Observations	10	10
7	Hypothesized Mean Difference	0	
8	df	16	
9	t Stat	-3.0446	
10	P(T<=t) one-tail	0.0039	
11	t Critical one-tail	1.7459	
12	P(T<=t) two-tail	0.0077	
13	t Critical two-tail	2.1199	

FIGURE 10.9

Minitab results of the separate-variance t test for the display location data

See Section M10.2 to create this.

```
Two-sample T for Sales_Normal vs Sales_EndAisle

              N   Mean   StDev   SE Mean
Sales_Normal  10  50.3   18.7    5.9
Sales_EndAisle 10  72.0   12.5    4.0


Difference = mu (Sales_Normal) - mu (Sales_EndAisle)
Estimate for difference: -21.70
95% CI for difference: (-36.89, -6.51)
T-Test of difference = 0 (vs not =): T-Value = -3.04  P-Value = 0.008  DF = 15
```

"This Call May Be Monitored . . . ."

From the Authors' Desktop

If you have ever used a telephone to seek customer service, you've probably heard at least once a message that begins "this call may be monitored . . . " Most of the time the message explains the monitoring is for "quality assurance purposes," but do companies really monitor your calls to improve quality?

From one of our previous students, we've learned that a certain large financial corporation really does monitor calls for quality purposes. This student was asked to develop an improved training program for a call center that was hiring people to answer phone calls customers make about outstanding loans. For feedback and evaluation, she planned to randomly select phone calls received by each new employee and rate the employee on ten aspects of the call including did the employee maintain a pleasant tone with the customer?

Who You Gonna Call?

She presented her plan to her boss for approval, but her boss, remembering the words of a famous statistician, said, "In God we trust, all others must bring data." That is, her boss wanted proof that her new training program would improve customer service. Faced with such a request, who would you call? She called one of us. "Hey professor, you'll never believe why I called. I work for a large company and in the project I am currently working on, I have to put some of the statistics you taught us to work! Can you help?" The answer was "Yes" and together they formulated this test:

- Randomly assign the 60 most recent hires into two training programs. Half would go through the preexisting training program, and half would be trained using the new program.
- At the end of the first month, compare the mean score for the 30 employees in the

new training program against the mean score for the 30 employees in the preexisting training program.

She listened as her professor explained, "What you are trying to prove is that the mean score from the new training program is higher than the mean score from the current program. You can make the null hypothesis that the means are equal, and see if you can reject it in favor of the alternative that the mean score from the new program is higher."

"Or, as you used to say, 'if the p-value is low, H_0 must go!'—yes, I do remember!" she replied. Her professor chuckled and said, "Yes, that's correct. And if you can reject H_0, you will have the proof to present to your boss." She thanked him for his help and got back to work with the newfound confidence that she would be able to successfully apply the t test that compares the means of two independent populations.

In Figures 10.8 and 10.9 the test statistic $t_{STAT} = -3.0446$ and the p-value is $0.008 < 0.05$. Thus, the results for the separate-variance t test are almost exactly the same as those of the pooled-variance t test. The assumption of equality of population variances had no real effect on the results. Sometimes, however, the results from the pooled-variance and separate-variance t tests conflict because the assumption of equal variances is violated. Therefore, it is important that you evaluate the assumptions and use those results as a guide in appropriately selecting a test procedure. In Section 10.4, the F test is used to determine whether there is evidence of a difference in the two population variances. The results of that test can help you determine which of the t tests—pooled-variance or separate-variance—is more appropriate.

PROBLEMS FOR SECTION 10.1

Learning the Basics

10.1 If you have samples of $n_1 = 12$ and $n_2 = 15$, in performing the pooled-variance t test, how many degrees of freedom do you have?

10.2 Assume that you have a sample of $n_1 = 8$, with the sample mean $\bar{X}_1 = 42$, and a sample standard deviation of $S_1 = 4$, and you have an independent sample of $n_2 = 15$ from another population with a sample mean of $\bar{X}_2 = 34$ and the sample standard deviation $S_2 = 5$.
a. What is the value of the pooled-variance t_{STAT} test statistic for testing $H_0 : \mu_1 = \mu_2$?
b. In finding the critical value $t_{\alpha/2}$, how many degrees of freedom are there?
c. Using the level of significance $\alpha = 0.01$, what is the critical value for a one-tail test of the hypothesis $H_0 : \mu_1 \leq \mu_2$ against the alternative $H_1 : \mu_1 > \mu_2$?
d. What is your statistical decision?

10.3 What assumptions about the two populations are necessary in Problem 10.2?

10.4 Referring to Problem 10.2, construct a 95% confidence interval estimate of the population mean difference between μ_1 and μ_2.

10.5 Referring to Problem 10.2, using the separate-variance t test, how many degrees of freedom do you have?

10.6 Referring to Problem 10.2, using the separate-variance t test, at the 0.01 level of significance, is there evidence of a difference in the means of the two populations?

Applying the Concepts

10.7 The operations manager at a lightbulb factory wants to determine whether there is any difference in the mean life expectancy of bulbs manufactured on two different types of machines. A random sample of 25 lightbulbs from machine I indicates a sample mean of 375 hours and a sample standard deviation of 100 hours, and a similar sample of 25 from machine II indicates a sample mean of 362 hours and a sample standard deviation of 125 hours.
a. Using the 0.05 level of significance, and assuming that the population variances are equal, is there any evidence of a difference in the mean life of bulbs produced by the two types of machines?
b. Using the 0.05 level of significance, and assuming that the population variances are not equal, is there any evidence of a difference in the mean life of bulbs produced by the two types of machines?

10.8 The purchasing director for an industrial parts factory is investigating the possibility of purchasing a new type of milling machine. She determines that the new machine will be purchased if there is evidence that the parts produced have a higher mean breaking strength than those from the old machine. A sample of 100 parts taken from the old machine indicates a sample mean of 65 kilograms and a sample standard deviation of 10 kilograms, and a similar sample of 100 from the new machine indicates a sample mean of 72 kilograms and a sample standard deviation of 9 kilograms.
a. Using the 0.01 level of significance, and assuming that the population variances are equal, is there evidence that the purchasing director should buy the new machine?
b. Using the 0.01 level of significance, and assuming that the population variances are not equal, is there evidence of a difference in the mean breaking strength of the two machines?

10.9 Millions of dollars are spent each year on diet foods. Trends such as the low-fat diet or the low-carb Atkins diet have led to a host of new products. A study by Dr. Linda Stern of the Philadelphia Veterans Administration Hospital compared weight loss between obese patients on a low-fat diet and obese patients on a low-carb diet (extracted from R. Bazell, "Study Casts Doubt on Advantages of Atkins Diet," **msnbc.com**, May 17, 2004). Let μ_1 represent the mean number of pounds obese patients on a low-fat diet lose in six months and μ_2 represent the mean number of pounds obese patients on a low-carb diet lose in six months.

a. State the null and alternative hypotheses if you want to test whether the mean weight loss between the two diets is equal.

b. In the context of this study, what is the meaning of a Type I error?

c. In the context of this study, what is the meaning of a Type II error?

d. Suppose that a sample of 100 obese patients on a low-fat diet lost a mean of 7.6 pounds in six months, with a sample standard deviation of 3.2 pounds, whereas a sample of 100 obese patients on a low-carb diet lost a mean of 6.7 pounds in six months, with a sample standard deviation of 3.9 pounds. Assuming that the population variances are equal and using a 0.05 level of significance, is there evidence of a difference in the mean weight loss of obese patients between the low-fat and low-carb diets?

10.10 When do children in the United States develop preferences for brand-name products? In a study reported in the *Journal of Consumer Psychology* (extracted from G. W. Achenreiner and D. R. John, "The Meaning of Brand Names to Children: A Developmental Investigation," *Journal of Consumer Psychology*, 2003, 13(3), pp. 205–219), marketers showed children identical pictures of athletic shoes. One picture was labeled Nike, and one was labeled K-Mart. The children were asked to evaluate the shoes based on their appearance, quality, price, prestige, favorableness, and preference for owning. A score from 2 (highest product evaluation possible) to −2 (lowest product evaluation possible) was recorded for each child. The following table reports the results of the study:

Age by Brand	Sample Size	Sample Mean	Sample Standard Deviation
Age 8			
Nike	27	0.89	0.98
K-Mart	22	0.86	1.07
Age 12			
Nike	39	0.88	1.01
K-Mart	41	0.09	1.08
Age 16			
Nike	35	0.41	0.81
K-Mart	33	−0.29	0.92

a. Conduct a pooled-variance t test for the difference between the two means for each of the three age groups. Use a level of significance of 0.05.

b. What assumptions are needed to conduct the tests in (a)?

c. Write a brief summary of your findings.

10.11 Digital cameras have taken over the majority of the point-and-shoot camera market. One of the important

features of a camera is the battery life as measured by the number of shots taken until the battery needs to be recharged. The data in the file **Digitalcameras** contain the battery life of 31 subcompact cameras and 15 compact cameras (extracted from "Cameras," *Consumer Reports*, November 2006, pp. 20–21).

a. Assuming that the population variances from both types of digital cameras are equal, is there evidence of a difference in the mean battery life between the two types of digital cameras?

b. Determine the p-value in (a) and interpret its meaning.

c. Assuming that the population variances from both types of digital cameras are equal, construct and interpret a 95% confidence interval estimate of the difference between the population mean battery life of the two types of digital cameras.

✓ SELF Test **10.12** The Computer Anxiety Rating Scale (CARS) measures an individual's level of computer anxiety, on a scale from 20 (no anxiety) to 100 (highest level of anxiety). Researchers at Miami University administered CARS to 172 business students. One of the objectives of the study was to determine whether there is a difference in the level of computer anxiety experienced by female and male business students. They found the following:

	Males	Females
$\bar{X}$	40.26	36.85
S	13.35	9.42
n	100	72

Source: *Extracted from T. Broome and D. Havelka, "Determinants of Computer Anxiety in Business Students,"* The Review of Business Information Systems, *Spring 2002, 6(2), pp. 9–16.*

a. At the 0.05 level of significance, is there evidence of a difference in the mean computer anxiety experienced by female and male business students?

b. Determine the p-value and interpret its meaning.

c. What assumptions do you have to make about the two populations in order to justify the use of the t test?

10.13 A company making plastic optical components for bar code scanners was studying inconsistencies in an optical measurement called tilt. The company knew that scanners work best when the tilt measurement is small. Two different types of locking mechanisms used in the mold produced the following results:

	Taper Locks	Locking Pins
$\bar{X}$	1.262	0.561
S	0.297	0.307
n	20	20

Source: *Extracted from J. Duncan, "Ghosts in Your Process? Who Ya Gonna Call?"* Quality Progress, *May 2005, pp. 52–57.*

a. Assuming that the population variances are equal and the populations are normally distributed, at the 0.05 level of significance, is there evidence of a difference in the means between taper locks and locking pins?

b. Repeat (a), assuming that the population variances are not equal.

c. Compare the results of (a) and (b).

10.14 A bank with a branch located in a commercial district of a city has developed an improved process for serving customers during the noon-to-1 p.m. lunch period. The waiting time (operationally defined as the time elapsed from when the customer enters the line until he or she reaches the teller window) needs to be shortened to increase customer satisfaction. A random sample of 15 customers is selected (and stored in the file **Bank1**), and the results (in minutes) are as follows:

4.21   5.55   3.02   5.13   4.77   2.34   3.54   3.20

4.50   6.10   0.38   5.12   6.46   6.19   3.79

Suppose that another branch, located in a residential area, is also concerned with the noon-to-1 p.m. lunch period. A random sample of 15 customers is selected (and stored in the file **Bank2**), and the results are as follows:

9.66   5.90   8.02   5.79   8.73   3.82   8.01   8.35

10.49   6.68   5.64   4.08   6.17   9.91   5.47

a. Assuming that the population variances from both banks are equal, is there evidence of a difference in the mean waiting time between the two branches? (Use $\alpha = 0.05$.)

b. Determine the p-value in (a) and interpret its meaning.

c. In addition to equal variances, what other assumption is necessary in (a)?

d. Construct and interpret a 95% confidence interval estimate of the difference between the population means in the two branches.

10.15 Repeat Problem 10.14(a), assuming that the population variances in the two branches are not equal. Compare the results with those of Problem 10.14(a).

10.16 In intaglio printing, a design or figure is carved beneath the surface of hard metal or stone. Suppose that an experiment is designed to compare differences in mean surface hardness of steel plates used in intaglio printing (measured in indentation numbers), based on two different surface conditions—untreated and treated by lightly polishing with emery paper. In the experiment, 40 steel plates are randomly assigned—20 that are untreated, and 20 that are treated. The data are shown here and stored in the file **Intaglio**:

Untreated		Treated	
164.368	177.135	158.239	150.226
159.018	163.903	138.216	155.620
153.871	167.802	168.006	151.233
165.096	160.818	149.654	158.653
157.184	167.433	145.456	151.204
154.496	163.538	168.178	150.869
160.920	164.525	154.321	161.657
164.917	171.230	162.763	157.016
169.091	174.964	161.020	156.670
175.276	166.311	167.706	147.920

a. Assuming that the population variances from both conditions are equal, is there evidence of a difference in the mean surface hardness between untreated and treated steel plates? (Use $\alpha = 0.05$.)

b. Determine the p-value in (a) and interpret its meaning.

c. In addition to equal variances, what other assumption is necessary in (a)?

d. Construct and interpret a 95% confidence interval estimate of the difference between the population means from treated and untreated steel plates.

10.17 Repeat Problem 10.16(a), assuming that the population variances from untreated and treated steel plates are not equal. Compare the results with those of Problem 10.16(a).

10.18 The director of training for an electronic equipment manufacturer is interested in determining whether different training methods have an effect on the productivity of assembly-line employees. She randomly assigns 42 recently hired employees into two groups of 21. The first group receives a computer-assisted, individual-based training program, and the other receives a team-based training program. Upon completion of the training, the employees are evaluated on the time (in seconds) it takes to assemble a part. The results are in the data file **Training**.

a. Assuming that the variances in the populations of training methods are equal, is there evidence of a difference between the mean assembly times (in seconds) of employees trained in a computer-assisted, individual-based program and those trained in a team-based program? (Use a 0.05 level of significance.)

b. In addition to equal variances, what other assumption is necessary in (a)?

c. Repeat (a), assuming that the population variances are not equal.

d. Compare the results of (a) and (c).

e. Assuming normality and equal variances, construct and interpret a 95% confidence interval estimate of the difference between the population means of the two training methods.

10.19 Nondestructive evaluation is a method that is used to describe the properties of components or materials without causing any permanent physical change to the units. It includes the determination of properties of materials and the classification of flaws by size, shape, type, and location. This method is most effective for detecting surface flaws and characterizing surface properties of electrically conductive materials. Recently, data were collected that classified each component as having a flaw or not based on manual inspection and operator judgment and also reported the size of the crack in the material. Do the components classified as unflawed have a smaller mean crack size than components classified as flawed? The results in terms of crack size

(in inches) are in the data file **Crack** (extracted from B. D. Olin and W. Q. Meeker, "Applications of Statistical Methods to Nondestructive Evaluation," *Technometrics*, 38, 1996, p. 101).

a. Assuming that the population variances are equal, is there evidence that the mean crack size is smaller for the unflawed specimens than for the flawed specimens? (Use $\alpha = 0.05$.)

b. Repeat (a), assuming that the population variances are not equal.

c. Compare the results of (a) and (b).

10.2 COMPARING THE MEANS OF TWO RELATED POPULATIONS

The hypothesis-testing procedures examined in Section 10.1 enable you to make comparisons and examine differences in the means of two *independent* populations. In this section, you will learn about a procedure for analyzing the difference between the means of two populations when you collect sample data from populations that are related—that is, when results of the first population are *not* independent of the results of the second population.

There are two situations that involve related data between populations. Either you take repeated measurements from the same set of items or individuals or you match items or individuals according to some characteristic. In either situation, you are interested in the *difference between the two related values* rather than the *individual values* themselves.

When you take **repeated measurements** on the same items or individuals, you assume that the same items or individuals will behave alike if treated alike. Your objective is to show that any differences between two measurements of the same items or individuals are due to different treatment conditions. For example, when performing a taste-testing experiment comparing two beverages, you can use each person in the sample as his or her own control so that you can have *repeated measurements* on the same individual.

The second situation that involves related data between populations is when you have **matched samples**. Here items or individuals are paired together according to some characteristic of interest. For example, in test marketing a product under two different advertising campaigns, a sample of test markets can be *matched* on the basis of the test market population size and/or demographic variables. By accounting for the differences in test market population size and/or demographic variables, you are better able to measure the effects of the two different advertising campaigns.

Regardless of whether you have matched samples or repeated measurements, the objective is to study the difference between two measurements by reducing the effect of the variability that is due to the items or individuals themselves. Table 10.3 on page 404 shows the differences in the individual values for two related populations. To read this table, let $X_{11}, X_{12}, \ldots, X_{1n}$ represent the n values from a sample. And let $X_{21}, X_{22}, \ldots, X_{2n}$ represent either the corresponding n matched values from a second sample or the corresponding n repeated measurements from the initial sample. Then, $D_1, D_2, \ldots, D_n$ will represent the corresponding set of n difference *scores* such that

$$D_1 = X_{11} - X_{21}, D_2 = X_{12} - X_{22}, \ldots, \text{and } D_n = X_{1n} - X_{2n}.$$

To test for the mean difference between two related populations, you treat the difference scores, each D_i, as values from a single sample.

TABLE 10.3

Determining the
Difference Between
Two Related Samples

	Sample		
Value	**1**	**2**	**Difference**
1	X_{11}	X_{21}	$D_1 = X_{11} - X_{21}$
2	X_{12}	X_{22}	$D_2 = X_{12} - X_{22}$
.	.	.	.
.	.	.	.
.	.	.	.
i	X_{1i}	X_{2i}	$D_i = X_{1i} - X_{2i}$
.	.	.	.
.	.	.	.
.	.	.	.
n	X_{1n}	X_{2n}	$D_n = X_{1n} - X_{2n}$

Paired t Test

If you assume that the difference scores are randomly and independently selected from a population that is normally distributed, you can use the **paired t test for the mean difference** in related populations to determine whether there is a significant population mean difference. Like the one-sample t test developed in Section 9.2 [see Equation (9.2) on page 356], the t-test statistic developed here follows the t distribution, with $n - 1$ degrees of freedom. Although you must assume that the population is normally distributed, as long as the sample size is not very small and the population is not highly skewed, you can use the paired t test.

To test the null hypothesis that there is no difference in the means of two related populations:

$$H_0: \mu_D = 0 \text{ (where } \mu_D = \mu_1 - \mu_2)$$

against the alternative that the means are not the same:

$$H_1: \mu_D \neq 0$$

you compute the t_{STAT} test statistic using Equation (10.5).

Paired t Test for the Mean Difference

$$t_{STAT} = \frac{\bar{D} - \mu_D}{\dfrac{S_D}{\sqrt{n}}} \tag{10.5}$$

where

$$\mu_D = \text{hypothesized mean difference}$$

$$\bar{D} = \frac{\displaystyle\sum_{i=1}^{n} D_i}{n}$$

$$S_D = \sqrt{\frac{\displaystyle\sum_{i=1}^{n} (D_i - \bar{D})^2}{n-1}}$$

The t_{STAT} test statistic follows a t distribution with $n - 1$ degrees of freedom.

For a two-tail test with a given level of significance, α, you reject the null hypothesis if the computed t_{STAT} test statistic is greater than the upper-tail critical value $t_{\alpha/2}$ from the t distribution, or if the computed t_{STAT} test statistic is less than the lower-tail critical value $-t_{\alpha/2}$ from the t distribution. The decision rule is

$$\text{Reject } H_0 \text{ if } t_{STAT} > t_{\alpha/2}$$

$$\text{or if } t_{STAT} < -t_{\alpha/2};$$

$$\text{otherwise, do not reject } H_0.$$

The following example illustrates the use of the t test for the mean difference. The Automobile Association of America (AAA) conducted a mileage test to compare the gasoline mileage from real-life driving done by AAA members and results of driving done according to government standards (extracted from J. Healey, "Fuel Economy Calculations to Be Altered," *USA Today*, January 11, 2006, p. 1B).

What is the best way to design an experiment to compare the gasoline mileage from real-life driving done by AAA members and results of driving done according to government standards? One approach is to take two independent samples and then use the hypothesis tests discussed in Section 10.1. In this approach, you would use one set of automobiles to test the real-life driving done by AAA members. Then you would use a second set of different automobiles to test the results of driving done according to government standards.

However, because the first set of automobiles to test the real-life driving done by AAA members may get lower or higher gasoline mileage than the second set of automobiles, this is not a good approach. A better approach is to use a repeated-measurements experiment. In this experiment, you use one set of automobiles. For each automobile, you conduct a test of real-life driving done by an AAA member and a test of driving done according to government standards. Measuring the two gasoline mileages for the same automobiles serves to reduce the variability in the gasoline mileages compared with what would occur if you used two independent sets of automobiles. This approach focuses on the differences between the real-life driving done by an AAA member and the driving done according to government standards.

Table 10.4 displays results (stored in the file AAAMileage) from a sample of $n = 9$ automobiles from such an experiment.

TABLE 10.4

Repeated Measurements of Gasoline Mileage for Real-Life Driving by AAA Members and Driving Done According to Government Standards

Model	Members	Government	Difference (D_i)
2005 Ford F-150	14.3	16.8	−2.5
2005 Chevrolet Silverado	15.0	17.8	−2.8
2002 Honda Accord LX	27.8	26.2	+1.6
2002 Honda Civic	27.9	33.2	−5.3
2004 Honda Civic Hybrid	48.8	47.6	+1.2
2002 Ford Explorer	16.8	18.3	−1.5
2005 Toyota Camry	23.7	28.5	−4.8
2003 Toyota Corolla	32.8	33.1	−0.3
2005 Toyota Prius	37.3	44.0	−6.7

You want to determine whether there is any difference in the mean gasoline mileage between the real-life driving done by an AAA member and the driving done according to government standards. In other words, is there evidence that the mean gasoline mileage is different between the two types of driving? Thus, the null and alternative hypotheses are

H_0: $\mu_D = 0$ (There is no difference in mean gasoline mileage between the real-life driving done by an AAA member and the driving done according to government standards.)
H_1: $\mu_D \neq 0$ (There is a difference in mean gasoline mileage between the real-life driving done by an AAA member and the driving done according to government standards.)

Choosing the level of significance of $\alpha = 0.05$ and assuming that the differences are normally distributed, you use the paired t test [Equation (10.5)]. For a sample of $n = 9$ automobiles, there are $n - 1 = 8$ degrees of freedom. Using Table E.3, the decision rule is

$$\text{Reject } H_0 \text{ if } t_{STAT} > t_{0.025} = 2.3060;$$

$$\text{or if } t_{STAT} < -t_{0.025} = -2.3060;$$

$$\text{otherwise, do not reject } H_0.$$

For the $n = 9$ differences (see Table 10.4), the sample mean difference is

$$\bar{D} = \frac{\sum_{i=1}^{n} D_i}{n} = \frac{-21.1}{9} = -2.3444$$

and

$$S_D = \sqrt{\frac{\sum_{i=1}^{n}(D_i - \bar{D})^2}{n-1}} = 2.893575$$

From Equation (10.5) on page 404,

$$t_{STAT} = \frac{\bar{D} - \mu_D}{\dfrac{S_D}{\sqrt{n}}} = \frac{-2.3444 - 0}{\dfrac{2.893575}{\sqrt{9}}} = -2.4307$$

Because $t_{STAT} = -2.4307$ is less than -2.3060, you reject the null hypothesis, H_0 (see Figure 10.10). There is evidence of a difference in mean gasoline mileage between the real-life driving done by an AAA member and the driving done according to government standards. Real-life driving results in a lower mean gasoline mileage.

FIGURE 10.10

Two-tail paired t test at the 0.05 level of significance with 8 degrees of freedom

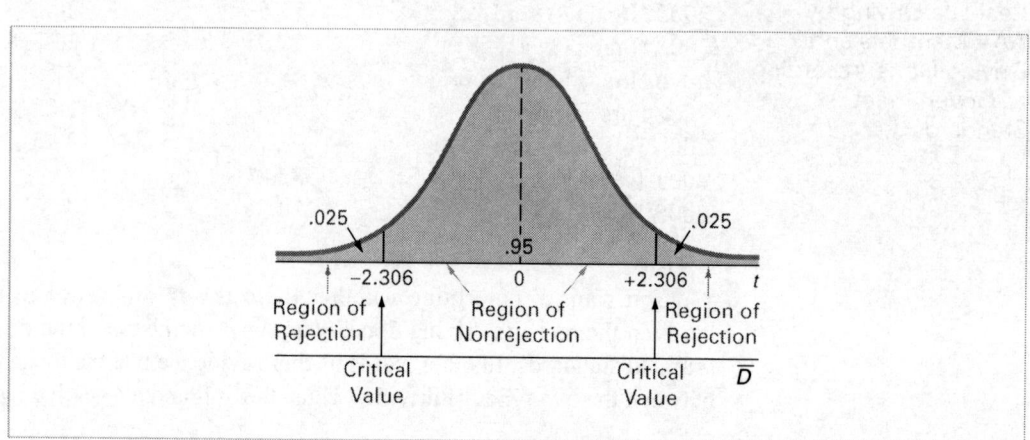

You can compute this test statistic along with the p-value by using Microsoft Excel or Minitab (see Figures 10.11 and 10.12). Because the p-value $= 0.0412 < \alpha = 0.05$, you reject H_0. The p-value indicates that if the two types of driving have the same population mean gasoline

FIGURE 10.11

Microsoft Excel results of paired *t* test for the car mileage data

See Section E10.6 to create this worksheet.

	A	B	C
1	t-Test: Paired Two Sample for Means		
2			
3		*Members*	*Government*
4	Mean	27.1556	29.5
5	Variance	129.5528	125.0025
6	Observations	9	9
7	Pearson Correlation	0.9673	
8	Hypothesized Mean Difference	0	
9	df	8	
10	t Stat	-2.4307	
11	P(T<=t) one-tail	0.0206	
12	t Critical one-tail	1.8595	
13	P(T<=t) two-tail	0.0412	
14	t Critical two-tail	2.3060	

FIGURE 10.12

Minitab results of paired *t* test for the car mileage data

See Section M10.3 to create this.

```
Paired T-Test and CI: Owner, Government

Paired T for Owner - Government

                N    Mean   StDev   SE Mean
Owner           9   27.16   11.38     3.79
Government      9   29.50   11.18     3.73
Difference      9   -2.344  2.894     0.965


95% CI for mean difference: (-4.569, -0.120)
T-Test of mean difference = 0 (vs not = 0): T-Value = -2.43  P-Value = 0.041
```

mileage, the probability that one type of driving would have a sample mean that was 2.3444 miles per gallon less than the other type is 0.0412. Because this probability is less than $\alpha = 0.05$, you conclude that the alternative hypothesis is true.

From Figure 10.13, observe that the boxplot shows approximate symmetry. Thus, the data do not greatly contradict the underlying assumption of normality. If a boxplot, histogram, or normal probability plot reveals that the assumption of underlying normality in the population is severely violated, then the *t* test is inappropriate. If this occurs, you can use either a *nonparametric* procedure that does not make the assumption of underlying normality (see Section 12.7) or make a data transformation (see reference 6), and then recheck the assumptions to determine whether you should use the *t* test.

FIGURE 10.13

Minitab results of boxplot for the car mileage data

See Section M3.2 to create this. (PHStat2 users, see Section P3.1 to create an equivalent chart.)

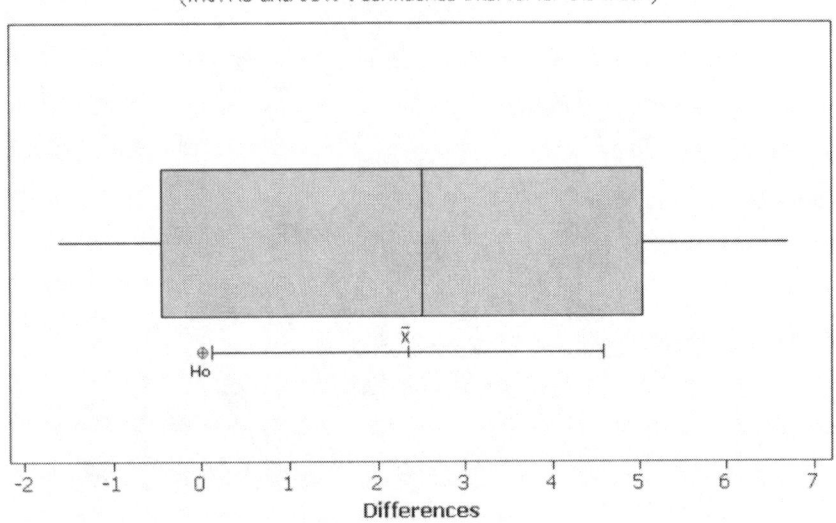

EXAMPLE 10.2

PAIRED *t* TEST OF PIZZA DELIVERY TIMES

Recall from Example 10.1 on page 394 that a local pizza restaurant situated across the street from a college campus advertises that it delivers to the dormitories faster than the local branch of a national pizza chain. In order to determine whether this advertisement is valid, you and some friends have decided to order 10 pizzas from the local pizza restaurant and 10 pizzas from the national chain. In fact, each time you ordered a pizza from the local pizza restaurant, your friends ordered a pizza from the national pizza chain. Thus, you have matched samples. For each of the ten times pizzas were ordered, you have one measurement from the local pizza restaurant and one from the national chain. At the 0.05 level of significance, is the mean delivery time for the local pizza restaurant less than the mean delivery time for the national pizza chain?

SOLUTION Use the paired *t* test to analyze the data in Table 10.5 (see the file Pizzatime). Figure 10.14 illustrates Microsoft Excel paired *t*-test results for the pizza delivery data and Figure 10.15 shows Minitab results.

TABLE 10.5

Delivery Times for Local Pizza Restaurant and National Pizza Chain

Time	Local	Chain	Difference
1	16.8	22.0	−5.2
2	11.7	15.2	−3.5
3	15.6	18.7	−3.1
4	16.7	15.6	1.1
5	17.5	20.8	−3.3
6	18.1	19.5	−1.4
7	14.1	17.0	−2.9
8	21.8	19.5	2.3
9	13.9	16.5	−2.6
10	20.8	24.0	−3.2
			−21.8

FIGURE 10.14

Microsoft Excel paired *t*-test results for the pizza delivery data

See Section E10.6 to create this.

	A	B	C
1	t-Test: Paired Two Sample for Means		
2			
3		Local	Chain
4	Mean	16.7	18.88
5	Variance	9.5822	8.2151
6	Observations	10	10
7	Pearson Correlation	0.7141	
8	Hypothesized Mean Difference	0	
9	df	9	
10	t Stat	-3.0448	
11	P(T<=t) one-tail	0.0070	
12	t Critical one-tail	1.8331	
13	P(T<=t) two-tail	0.0139	
14	t Critical two-tail	2.2622	

FIGURE 10.15

Minitab paired *t*-test results for the pizza delivery data

See Section M10.3 to create this.

```
Paired T-Test and CI: Local, Chain

Paired T for Local - Chain

                 N    Mean   StDev   SE Mean
Local           10  16.700   3.096    0.979
Chain           10  18.880   2.866    0.906
Difference      10  -2.180   2.264    0.716


95% upper bound for mean difference: -0.868
T-Test of mean difference = 0 (vs < 0): T-Value = -3.04  P-Value = 0.007
```

The null and alternative hypotheses are

H_0: $\mu_D \geq 0$ (Mean delivery time for the local pizza restaurant is greater than or equal to the mean delivery time for the national pizza chain.)
H_1: $\mu_D < 0$ (Mean delivery time for the local pizza restaurant is less than the mean delivery time for the national pizza chain.)

Choosing the level of significance $\alpha = 0.05$ and assuming that the differences are normally distributed, you use the paired t test [Equation (10.5) on page 404]. For a sample of $n = 10$ delivery times, there are $n - 1 = 9$ degrees of freedom. Using Table E.3, the decision rule is

$$\text{Reject } H_0 \text{ if } t_{STAT} < -t_{0.05} = -1.8331;$$

$$\text{otherwise, do not reject } H_0.$$

For $n = 10$ differences (see Table 10.5), the sample mean difference is

$$\bar{D} = \frac{\sum_{i=1}^{n} D_i}{n} = \frac{-21.8}{10} = -2.18$$

and the sample standard deviation of the difference is

$$S_D = \sqrt{\frac{\sum_{i=1}^{n}(D_i - \bar{D})^2}{n-1}} = 2.2641$$

From Equation (10.5) on page 404,

$$t_{STAT} = \frac{\bar{D} - \mu_D}{\frac{S_D}{\sqrt{n}}} = \frac{-2.18 - 0}{\frac{2.2641}{\sqrt{10}}} = -3.0448$$

Because $t_{STAT} = -3.0448$ is less than -1.8331, you reject the null hypothesis H_0 (the p-value is $0.0070 < 0.05$). There is evidence that the mean delivery time is lower for the local pizza restaurant than for the national pizza chain.

This conclusion is different from the one you reached in Example 10.1 on page 394 when you used the pooled-variance t test for these data. By pairing the delivery times, you are able to focus on the differences between the two pizza delivery services and not the variability created by ordering pizzas at different times of day. The paired t test is a more powerful statistical procedure that is better able to detect the difference between the two pizza delivery services.

Confidence Interval Estimate for the Mean Difference

Instead of, or in addition to, testing for the difference between the means of two related populations, you can use Equation (10.6) to construct a confidence interval estimate of the mean difference.

Confidence Interval Estimate for the Mean Difference

$$\bar{D} \pm t_{\alpha/2} \frac{S_D}{\sqrt{n}} \tag{10.6}$$

or

$$\bar{D} - t_{\alpha/2} \frac{S_D}{\sqrt{n}} \le \mu_D \le \bar{D} + t_{\alpha/2} \frac{S_D}{\sqrt{n}}$$

where $t_{\alpha/2}$ is the critical value of the t distribution with $n-1$ degrees of freedom for an area of $\alpha/2$ in the upper tail.

Return to the example comparing gasoline mileage generated by real-life driving and by government standards. Using Equation (10.6), $\bar{D} = -2.3444$, $S_D = 2.8936$, $n = 9$, and $t_{\alpha/2} = 2.306$ (for 95% confidence and $n - 1 = 8$ degrees of freedom),

$$-2.3444 \pm (2.306) \frac{2.8936}{\sqrt{9}}$$

$$-2.3444 \pm 2.2242$$

$$-4.5686 \le \mu_D \le -0.1202$$

Thus, with 95% confidence, the mean difference in gasoline mileage between the real-life driving done by an AAA member and the driving done according to government standards is between −4.5686 and −0.1202 miles per gallon. Because the interval estimate contains only values less than zero, you can conclude that there is a difference in the population means. The mean miles per gallon for the real-life driving done by an AAA member is less than the mean miles per gallon for the driving done according to government standards.

PROBLEMS FOR SECTION 10.2

Learning the Basics

10.20 An experimental design for a paired t test has 20 pairs of identical twins. How many degrees of freedom are there in this t test?

10.21 An experiment requires a measurement before and after the presentation of a stimulus to each of 15 subjects. In the analysis of the data collected from this experiment, how many degrees of freedom are there in the test?

Applying the Concepts

SELF Test **10.22** Nine experts rated two brands of Colombian coffee in a taste-testing experiment. A rating on a 7-point scale (1 = extremely unpleasing, 7 = extremely pleasing) is given for each of four character-

istics: taste, aroma, richness, and acidity. The following data (stored in the file **Coffee**) displays the summated ratings—accumulated over all four characteristics.

EXPERT	BRAND	
	A	B
C.C.	24	26
S.E.	27	27
E.G.	19	22
B.L.	24	27
C.M.	22	25
C.N.	26	27
G.N.	27	26
R.M.	25	27
P.V.	22	23

a. At the 0.05 level of significance, is there evidence of a difference in the mean summated ratings between the two brands?

b. What assumption is necessary about the population distribution in order to perform this test?

c. Determine the *p*-value in (a) and interpret its meaning.

d. Construct and interpret a 95% confidence interval estimate of the difference in the mean summated ratings between the two brands.

10.23 In industrial settings, alternative methods often exist for measuring variables of interest. The data in the file **Measurement** (coded to maintain confidentiality) represent measurements in-line that were collected from an analyzer during the production process and from an analytical lab (extracted from M. Leitnaker, "Comparing Measurement Processes: In-line Versus Analytical Measurements," *Quality Engineering*, 13, 2000–2001, pp. 293–298).

a. At the 0.05 level of significance, is there evidence of a difference in the mean measurements in-line and from an analytical lab?

b. What assumption is necessary about the population distribution in order to perform this test?

c. Use a graphical method to evaluate the validity of the assumption in (a).

d. Construct and interpret a 95% confidence interval estimate of the difference in the mean measurements in-line and from an analytical lab.

10.24 Can students save money by comparison shopping for textbooks at Amazon.com? To investigate this possibility, a random sample of 15 textbooks used during the Spring 2007 semester at Miami University was selected. The prices for these textbooks at both a local bookstore and through Amazon.com were recorded. The prices for the textbooks are given below (and are stored in the file **Textbook**):

Book Name	Book Store	Amazon
Principles of Microeconomics	120.00	101.22
Calculus: Early Transcendentals	137.50	115.33
Exploring Wine	65.00	37.05
Manual de Gramatica	82.75	71.36
Deviant Behavior	90.00	83.00
Modern Architecture Since 1900	39.95	26.37
Rise of Christianity	40.00	26.40
Commercial Banking	120.00	108.99
A Romance of a Republic	25.00	14.99
Chemistry in Context	133.75	102.30
Universal Principles of Design	40.00	26.40
In Mixed Company	79.50	68.76
International Marketing	154.75	126.15
Russia & Western Civilization	30.95	31.95
Enterprise Information Systems	155.75	126.97

a. At the 0.01 level of significance, is there evidence of a difference between the mean price of textbooks at the local bookstore and Amazon.com?

b. What assumption is necessary about the population distribution in order to perform this test?

c. Construct a 99% confidence interval estimate of the mean difference in price. Interpret the interval.

d. Compare the results of (a) and (c).

10.25 A newspaper article discussed the opening of a Whole Foods Market in the Time-Warner building in New York City. The following data (stored in the file **Wholefoods1**) compared the prices of some kitchen staples at the new Whole Foods Market and at the Fairway supermarket located about 15 blocks from the Time-Warner building:

Item	Whole Foods	Fairway
Half-gallon milk	2.19	1.35
Dozen eggs	2.39	1.69
Tropicana orange juice (64 oz.)	2.00	2.49
Head of Boston lettuce	1.98	1.29
Ground round, 1 lb.	4.99	3.69
Bumble Bee tuna, 6 oz. can	1.79	1.33
Granny Smith apples (1 lb.)	1.69	1.49
Box DeCecco linguini	1.99	1.59
Salmon steak, 1 lb.	7.99	5.99
Whole chicken, per pound	2.19	1.49

Source: *Extracted from W. Grimes, "A Pleasure Palace Without the Guilt,"* The New York Times, *February 18, 2004, pp. F1, F5.*

a. At the 0.01 level of significance, is there evidence that the mean price is higher at Whole Foods Market than at the Fairway supermarket?

b. Interpret the meaning of the *p*-value in (a).

c. What assumption is necessary about the population distribution in order to perform the test in (a)?

10.26 Multiple myeloma, or blood plasma cancer, is characterized by increased blood vessel formulation (angiogenesis) in the bone marrow that is a predictive factor in survival. One treatment approach used for multiple myeloma is stem cell transplantation with the patient's own stem cells. The following data (stored in the file **Myeloma**) represent the bone marrow microvessel density for patients who had a complete response to the stem cell transplant (as measured by blood and urine tests). The measurements were taken immediately prior to the stem cell transplant and at the time the complete response was determined:

Patient	Before	After
1	158	284
2	189	214
3	202	101
4	353	227
5	416	290
6	426	176
7	441	290

Source: *Extracted from S. V. Rajkumar, R. Fonseca, T. E. Witzig, M. A. Gertz, and P. R. Greipp, "Bone Marrow Angiogenesis in Patients Achieving Complete Response After Stem Cell Transplantation for Multiple Myeloma," Leukemia, 1999, 13, pp. 469–472.*

a. At the 0.05 level of significance, is there evidence that the mean bone marrow microvessel density is higher before the stem cell transplant than after the stem cell transplant?

b. Interpret the meaning of the *p*-value in (a).

c. Construct and interpret a 95% confidence interval estimate of the mean difference in bone marrow microvessel density before and after the stem cell transplant.

d. What assumption is necessary about the population distribution in order to perform the test in (a)?

10.27 Over the past year, the vice president for human resources at a large medical center has run a series of three-month workshops aimed at increasing worker motivation and performance. To check the effectiveness of the workshops, she selected a random sample of 35 employees from the personnel files and recorded their most recent annual performance ratings, along with their ratings prior to attending the workshops. The data are stored in the file `Perform`. The Microsoft Excel results shown at right provide both descriptive and inferential information. State your findings and conclusions in a report to the vice president for human resources.

	A	B
1	**Difference**	
2		
3	Mean	-5.2571
4	Standard Error	1.9478
5	Median	-5
6	Mode	-10
7	Standard Deviation	11.5232
8	Sample Variance	132.7849
9	Kurtosis	1.1038
10	Skewness	0.1103
11	Range	61
12	Minimum	-34
13	Maximum	27
14	Sum	-184
15	Count	35
16	Largest(1)	27
17	Smallest(1)	-34

	A	B	C
1	t-Test: Paired Two Sample for Means		
2			
3		*Before*	*After*
4	Mean	74.5429	79.8
5	Variance	80.9025	37.1647
6	Observations	35	35
7	Pearson Correlation	-0.1342	
8	Hypothesized Mean Difference	0	
9	df	34	
10	t Stat	-2.6990	
11	P(T<=t) one-tail	0.0054	
12	t Critical one-tail	1.6909	
13	P(T<=t) two-tail	0.0108	
14	t Critical two-tail	2.0322	

10.28 The data in the file `Concrete1` represent the compressive strength, in thousands of pounds per square inch (psi), of 40 samples of concrete taken two and seven days after pouring.

Source: *Extracted from O. Carrillo-Gamboa and R. F. Gunst, "Measurement-Error-Model Collinearities," Technometrics, 34, 1992, pp. 454–464.*

a. At the 0.01 level of significance, is there evidence that the mean strength is lower at two days than at seven days?

b. What assumption is necessary about the population distribution in order to perform this test?

c. Find the *p*-value in (a) and interpret its meaning.

10.3 COMPARING TWO POPULATION PROPORTIONS

Often, you need to make comparisons and analyze differences between two population proportions. You can perform a test for the difference between two proportions selected from independent populations by using two different methods. This section presents a procedure whose test statistic, Z_{STAT}, is approximated by a standardized normal distribution. In Section 12.1, a procedure is developed whose test statistic, χ^2_{STAT}, is approximated by a chi-square distribution. As you will see, the results from these two tests are equivalent.

Z Test for the Difference Between Two Proportions

In evaluating differences between two population proportions, you can use a **Z test for the difference between two proportions**. The Z_{STAT} test statistic is based on the difference between two sample proportions ($p_1 - p_2$). This test statistic, given in Equation (10.7), approximately follows a standardized normal distribution for large enough sample sizes.

Z Test for the Difference Between Two Proportions

$$Z_{STAT} = \frac{(p_1 - p_2) - (\pi_1 - \pi_2)}{\sqrt{\bar{p}(1-\bar{p})\left(\frac{1}{n_1} + \frac{1}{n_2}\right)}} \tag{10.7}$$

with

$$\bar{p} = \frac{X_1 + X_2}{n_1 + n_2} \qquad p_1 = \frac{X_1}{n_1} \qquad p_2 = \frac{X_2}{n_2}$$

where

p_1 = proportion of items of interest in sample 1

X_1 = number of items of interest in sample 1

n_1 = sample size of sample 1

π_1 = proportion of items of interest in population 1

p_2 = proportion of items of interest in sample 2

X_2 = number of items of interest in sample 2

n_2 = sample size of sample 2

π_2 = proportion of items of interest in population 2

$\bar{p}$ = pooled estimate of the population proportion of items of interest

The Z_{STAT} test statistic approximately follows a standardized normal distribution.

Under the null hypothesis, you assume that the two population proportions are equal ($\pi_1 = \pi_2$). Because the pooled estimate for the population proportion is based on the null hypothesis, you combine, or pool, the two sample proportions to compute an overall estimate of the common population proportion. This estimate is equal to the number of items of interest in the two samples combined ($X_1 + X_2$) divided by the total sample size from the two samples combined ($n_1 + n_2$).

As shown in the following table, you can use this Z test for the difference between population proportions to determine whether there is a difference in the proportion of items of interest in the two populations (two-tail test) or whether one population has a higher proportion of items of interest than the other population (one-tail test):

Two-Tail Test	One-Tail Test	One-Tail Test
$H_0: \pi_1 = \pi_2$	$H_0: \pi_1 \geq \pi_2$	$H_0: \pi_1 \leq \pi_2$
$H_1: \pi_1 \neq \pi_2$	$H_1: \pi_1 < \pi_2$	$H_1: \pi_1 > \pi_2$

where

π_1 = proportion of items of interest in population 1

π_2 = proportion of items of interest in population 2

To test the null hypothesis that there is no difference between the proportions of two independent populations:

$$H_0: \pi_1 = \pi_2$$

against the alternative that the two population proportions are not the same:

$$H_1: \pi_1 \neq \pi_2$$

use the Z_{STAT} test statistic, given by Equation (10.7). For a given level of significance α, reject the null hypothesis if the computed Z_{STAT} test statistic is greater than the upper-tail critical value from the standardized normal distribution, or if the computed Z_{STAT} test statistic is less than the lower-tail critical value from the standardized normal distribution.

To illustrate the use of the Z test for the equality of two proportions, suppose that you are the manager of T.C. Resort Properties, a collection of five upscale resort hotels located on two tropical islands. On one of the islands, T.C. Resort Properties has two hotels, the Beachcomber and the Windsurfer. In tabulating the responses to the single question, "Are you likely to choose this hotel again?" 163 of 227 guests at the Beachcomber responded yes, and 154 of 262 guests at the Windsurfer responded yes. At the 0.05 level of significance, is there evidence of a significant difference in guest satisfaction (as measured by the likelihood to return to the hotel) between the two hotels?

The null and alternative hypotheses are

$$H_0: \pi_1 = \pi_2 \quad \text{or} \quad \pi_1 - \pi_2 = 0$$
$$H_1: \pi_1 \neq \pi_2 \quad \text{or} \quad \pi_1 - \pi_2 \neq 0$$

Using the 0.05 level of significance, the critical values are −1.96 and +1.96 (see Figure 10.16), and the decision rule is

Reject H_0 if $Z_{STAT} < -1.96$

or if $Z_{STAT} > +1.96$;

otherwise, do not reject H_0.

FIGURE 10.16

Regions of rejection and nonrejection when testing a hypothesis for the difference between two proportions at the 0.05 level of significance

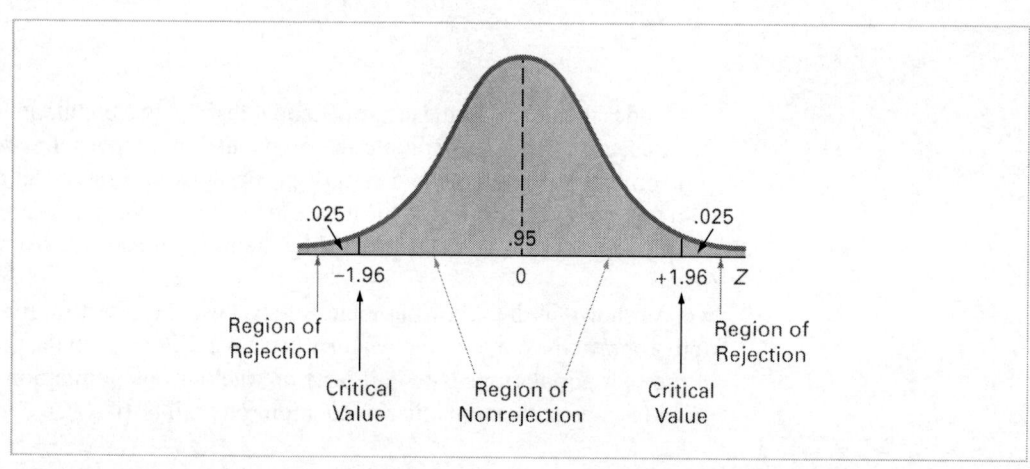

Using Equation (10.7) on page 413,

$$Z_{STAT} = \frac{(p_1 - p_2) - (\pi_1 - \pi_2)}{\sqrt{\bar{p}(1-\bar{p})\left(\dfrac{1}{n_1} + \dfrac{1}{n_2}\right)}}$$

where

$$p_1 = \frac{X_1}{n_1} = \frac{163}{227} = 0.7181 \quad p_2 = \frac{X_2}{n_2} = \frac{154}{262} = 0.5878$$

and

$$\bar{p} = \frac{X_1 + X_2}{n_1 + n_2} = \frac{163 + 154}{227 + 262} = \frac{317}{489} = 0.6483$$

so that

$$
\begin{aligned}
Z_{STAT} &= \frac{(0.7181 - 0.5878) - (0)}{\sqrt{0.6483(1 - 0.6483)\left(\dfrac{1}{227} + \dfrac{1}{262}\right)}} \\[2mm]
&= \frac{0.1303}{\sqrt{(0.228)(0.0082)}} \\[2mm]
&= \frac{0.1303}{\sqrt{0.00187}} \\[2mm]
&= \frac{0.1303}{0.0432} = +3.0088
\end{aligned}
$$

Using the 0.05 level of significance, reject the null hypothesis because Z_{STAT} = +3.0088 > +1.96. The p-value is 0.0026 (calculated from Table E.2 or from the Microsoft Excel results of Figure 10.17 or the Minitab results of Figure 10.18 on page 416), and indicates that if the null hypothesis is true, the probability that a Z_{STAT} test statistic is less than −3.0088 is 0.0013, and, similarly, the probability that a Z_{STAT} test statistic is greater than +3.0088 is 0.0013. Thus, for this two-tail test, the p-value is 0.0013 + 0.0013 = 0.0026. Because 0.0026 < α = 0.05, you reject the null hypothesis. There is evidence to conclude that the two hotels are significantly different with respect to guest satisfaction; a greater proportion of guests are willing to return to the Beachcomber than to the Windsurfer.

EXAMPLE 10.3

TESTING FOR THE DIFFERENCE IN TWO PROPORTIONS

Technology has led to the rise of extreme workers who are on the job 60 hours a week or more. One of the reasons cited by employees about why they worked long hours was that they loved their job because it is stimulating/challenging/provides an adrenaline rush (extracted from S. Armour, "Hi, I'm Joan and I'm a Workaholic," *USA Today*, May 23, 2007, pp. 1B, 2B). Suppose that the survey of 1,564 workaholics included 786 men and 778 women, and that 707 men and 638 women loved their job because it is stimulating/challenging/provides an

See Section E10.7 or P10.4 to create this.

FIGURE 10.17

Microsoft Excel results for the Z test for the difference between two proportions for the hotel guest satisfaction problem

	A	B
1	Z Test for Differences in Two Proportions	
2		
3	Data	
4	Hypothesized Difference	0
5	Level of Significance	0.05
6	Group 1	
7	Number of Items of Interest	163
8	Sample Size	227
9	Group 2	
10	Number of Items of Interest	154
11	Sample Size	262
12		
13	Intermediate Calculations	
14	Group 1 Proportion	0.7181
15	Group 2 Proportion	0.5878
16	Difference in Two Proportions	0.1303
17	Average Proportion	0.6483
18	Z Test Statistic	3.0088
19		
20	Two-Tail Test	
21	Lower Critical Value	-1.9600
22	Upper Critical Value	1.9600
23	p-Value	0.0026
24	Reject the null hypothesis	

Formulas (column C):
- Row 14: =B7/B8
- Row 15: =B10/B11
- Row 16: =B14 - B15
- Row 17: =(B7 + B10)/(B8 + B11)
- Row 18: =(B16 - B4)/SQRT(B17 * (1 - B17) * (1/B8 + 1/B11))
- Row 21: =NORMSINV(B5/2)
- Row 22: =NORMSINV(1 - B5/2)
- Row 23: =2 * (1 - NORMSDIST(ABS(B18)))
- Row 24: =IF(B23 < B5, "Reject the null hypothesis", "Do not reject the null hypothesis")

FIGURE 10.18

Minitab results for the Z test for the difference between two proportions for the hotel guest satisfaction problem

See Section M10.4 to create this.

```
Test and CI for Two Proportions

Sample   X     N   Sample p
1       163   227  0.718062
2       154   262  0.587786


Difference = p (1) - p (2)
Estimate for difference:  0.130275
95% CI for difference:  (0.0467379, 0.213813)
Test for difference = 0 (vs not = 0):  Z = 3.01  P-Value = 0.003
```

adrenaline rush. At the 0.05 level of significance, you would like to determine whether the proportion of workaholic men who love their job because it is stimulating/challenging/provides an adrenaline rush is greater than the proportion of women.

SOLUTION Because you want to know whether there is evidence that the proportion of workaholic men who love their job because it is stimulating/challenging/provides an adrenaline rush is *greater* than the proportion of women, you have a one-tail test. The null and alternative hypotheses are

H_0: $\pi_1 \leq \pi_2$ (Proportion of workaholic men who love their job because it is stimulating /challenging/provides an adrenaline rush is less than or equal to the proportion of women.)
H_1: $\pi_1 > \pi_2$ (Proportion of workaholic men who love their job because it is stimulating /challenging/provides an adrenaline rush is greater than the proportion of women.)

Using the 0.05 level of significance, for the one-tail test in the upper tail, the critical value is +1.645. The decision rule is

$$\text{Reject } H_0 \text{ if } Z_{STAT} > +1.645;$$

$$\text{otherwise, do not reject } H_0.$$

Using Equation (10.7) on page 413,

$$Z_{STAT} = \frac{(p_1 - p_2) - (\pi_1 - \pi_2)}{\sqrt{\bar{p}(1-\bar{p})\left(\frac{1}{n_1} + \frac{1}{n_2}\right)}}$$

where

$$p_1 = \frac{X_1}{n_1} = \frac{707}{786} = 0.8995 \quad p_2 = \frac{X_2}{n_2} = \frac{638}{778} = 0.8201$$

and

$$\bar{p} = \frac{X_1 + X_2}{n_1 + n_2} = \frac{707 + 638}{786 + 778} = \frac{1,345}{1,564} = 0.8600$$

so that

$$Z_{STAT} = \frac{(0.8995 - 0.8201) - (0)}{\sqrt{0.86(1-0.86)\left(\frac{1}{786} + \frac{1}{778}\right)}}$$

$$= \frac{0.0794}{\sqrt{(0.1204)(0.0025575)}}$$

$$= \frac{0.0794}{\sqrt{0.0003079}}$$

$$= \frac{0.0794}{0.017547} = +4.5266$$

Using the 0.05 level of significance, you reject the null hypothesis because $Z_{STAT} = +4.5266 > +1.645$. The p-value is approximately 0.0000. Therefore, if the null hypothesis is true, the probability that a Z_{STAT} test statistic is greater than +4.526 is approximately 0.0000 (which is less than $\alpha = 0.05$). You conclude that there is evidence that the proportion of workaholic men who love their job because it is stimulating/challenging/provides an adrenaline rush is greater than the proportion of women.

Confidence Interval Estimate for the Difference Between Two Proportions

Instead of, or in addition to, testing for the difference between the proportions of two independent populations, you can construct a confidence interval estimate of the difference between the two proportions using Equation (10.8).

Confidence Interval Estimate for the Difference Between Two Proportions

$$(p_1 - p_2) \pm Z_{\alpha/2} \sqrt{\frac{p_1(1-p_1)}{n_1} + \frac{p_2(1-p_2)}{n_2}} \qquad (10.8)$$

or

$$(p_1 - p_2) - Z_{\alpha/2} \sqrt{\frac{p_1(1-p_1)}{n_1} + \frac{p_2(1-p_2)}{n_2}} \leq (\pi_1 - \pi_2)$$

$$\leq (p_1 - p_2) + Z_{\alpha/2} \sqrt{\frac{p_1(1-p_1)}{n_1} + \frac{p_2(1-p_2)}{n_2}}$$

To construct a 95% confidence interval estimate of the population difference between the proportion of guests who would return to the Beachcomber and who would return to the Windsurfer, you use the results on page 415 or from Figures 10.17 or 10.18 on page 416:

$$p_1 = \frac{X_1}{n_1} = \frac{163}{227} = 0.7181 \qquad p_2 = \frac{X_2}{n_2} = \frac{154}{262} = 0.5878$$

Using Equation (10.8),

$$(0.7181 - 0.5878) \pm (1.96) \sqrt{\frac{0.7181(1-0.7181)}{227} + \frac{0.5878(1-0.5878)}{262}}$$

$$0.1303 \pm (1.96)(0.0426)$$

$$0.1303 \pm 0.0835$$

$$0.0468 \leq (\pi_1 - \pi_2) \leq 0.2138$$

Thus, you have 95% confidence that the difference between the population proportion of guests who would return again to the Beachcomber and the Windsurfer is between 0.0468 and 0.2138. In percentages, the difference is between 4.68% and 21.38%. Guest satisfaction is higher at the Beachcomber than at the Windsurfer.

PROBLEMS FOR SECTION 10.3

Learning the Basics

10.29 Let $n_1 = 100$, $X_1 = 50$, $n_2 = 100$, and $X_2 = 30$.
a. At the 0.05 level of significance, is there evidence of a significant difference between the two population proportions?
b. Construct a 95% confidence interval estimate of the difference between the two population proportions.

10.30 Let $n_1 = 100$, $X_1 = 45$, $n_2 = 50$, and $X_2 = 25$.
a. At the 0.01 level of significance, is there evidence of a significant difference between the two population proportions?

b. Construct a 99% confidence interval estimate of the difference between the two population proportions.

Applying the Concepts

10.31 A sample of 500 shoppers was selected in a large metropolitan area to determine various information concerning consumer behavior. Among the questions asked was, "Do you enjoy shopping for clothing?" Of 240 males, 136 answered yes. Of 260 females, 224 answered yes.
a. Is there evidence of a significant difference between males and females in the proportion that enjoy shopping for clothing at the 0.01 level of significance?

b. Find the *p*-value in (a) and interpret its meaning.

c. Construct and interpret a 99% confidence interval estimate of the difference between the proportion of males and females who enjoy shopping for clothing.

d. What are your answers to (a) through (c) if 206 males enjoyed shopping for clothing?

10.32 An article referencing a survey conducted by AP-LOL Learning Services claims that parents are more confident than teachers that their schools will meet the standards set by the No Child Left Behind Act. The survey asked parents (and teachers), "How confident are you that your child's school (the school where you work) will meet the standards by the deadline?" The responses to that question are given in the following table:

	Parents	**Teachers**
Very confident	401	162
Not very confident	684	648
Totals	1,085	810

Source: *Extracted from B. Feller, "Teachers More Likely Skeptics of No Child," The Cincinnati Enquirer, April 20, 2006, p. A4.*

a. Set up the null and alternative hypotheses needed to try to prove that the population proportion of parents that are very confident that their child's school will meet the standards by the deadline is greater than the population proportion of teachers that are very confident that the school where they work will meet standards by the deadline.

b. Conduct the hypothesis test defined in (a), using a 0.05 level of significance.

c. Does the result of your test in (b) make it appropriate for the article to claim that parents are more confident than teachers?

10.33 The results of a study conducted as part of a yield-improvement effort at a semiconductor manufacturing facility provided defect data for a sample of 450 wafers. The following contingency table presents a summary of the responses to two questions: "Was a particle found on the die that produced the wafer?" and "Is the wafer good or bad?"

QUALITY OF WAFER

PARTICLES	**Good**	**Bad**	**Totals**
Yes	14	36	50
No	320	80	400
Totals	334	116	450

Source: *Extracted from S.W. Hall, "Analysis of Defectivity of Semiconductor Wafers by Contingency Table," Proceedings Institute of Environmental Sciences, Vol. 1, 1994, pp. 177–183.*

a. At the 0.05 level of significance, is there evidence of a significant difference between the proportion of good and bad wafers that have particles?

b. Determine the *p*-value in (a) and interpret its meaning.

c. Construct and interpret a 95% confidence interval estimate of the difference between the population proportion of good and bad wafers that contain particles.

d. What conclusions can you reach from this analysis?

✓ SELF Test **10.34** According to an Ipsos poll, the perception of unfairness in the U.S. tax code is spread fairly evenly across income groups, age groups, and education levels. In an April 2006 survey of 1,005 adults, Ipsos reported that almost 60% of all people said the code is unfair, whereas slightly more that 60% of those making more than $50,000 viewed the code as unfair (extracted from "People Cry Unfairness," *The Cincinnati Enquirer*, April 16, 2006, p. A8). Suppose that the following contingency table represents the specific breakdown of responses:

	INCOME LEVEL		
U.S. TAX CODE	**Less Than $50,000**	**More Than $50,000**	**Total**
Fair	225	180	405
Unfair	280	320	600
Total	505	500	1,005

a. At the 0.05 level of significance, is there evidence of a difference in the proportion of adults who think the U.S. tax code is unfair between the two income groups?

b. Find the *p*-value in (a) and interpret its meaning.

10.35 Are women more risk averse in the stock market? A sample of men and women were asked the following question: "If both the stock market and a stock you owned dropped 25% in three months, would you buy more shares while the price is low?" (extracted from "Snapshots: Women Are More Risk Adverse in the Stock Market," *USA Today*, September 25, 2006, p. 1C). Of 965 women, 338 said yes. Of 1,066 men, 554 said yes.

a. At the 0.05 level of significance, is there evidence that the proportion of women who would buy more shares while the price is low is less than the proportion of men?

b. Find the *p*-value in (a) and interpret its meaning.

10.36 An experiment was conducted to study the choices made in mutual fund selection. Undergraduate and MBA students were presented with different S&P 500 index funds that were identical except for fees. Suppose 100 undergraduate students and 100 MBA students were selected. Partial results are shown in the following table:

	STUDENT GROUP	
FUND	**Undergraduate**	**MBA**
Highest-cost fund	27	18
Not-highest-cost fund	73	82

Source: *Extracted from J. Choi, D. Laibson, and B. Madrian, "Why Does the Law of One Practice Fail? An Experiment on Mutual Funds,"* **www.som.yale.edu/faculty/jjc83/fees.pdf.**

a. At the 0.05 level of significance, is there evidence of a difference between undergraduate and MBA students in the proportion who selected the highest-cost fund?
b. Find the p-value in (a) and interpret its meaning.

10.37 Where people turn for news is different for various age groups (extracted from P. Johnson, "Young People Turn to the Web for News," *USA Today*, March 23, 2006, p. 9D). Suppose that a study conducted on this issue was based on 200 respondents who were between the ages of 36 and 50, and 200 respondents who were above age 50. Of the 200 respondents who were between the ages of 36 and 50, 82 got their news primarily from newspapers. Of the 200 respondents who were above age 50, 104 got their news primarily from newspapers.

a. Is there evidence of a significant difference in the proportion that get their news primarily from newspapers between those respondents 36 to 50 years old and those above 50 years old? (Use $\alpha = 0.05$.)
b. Determine the p-value in (a) and interpret its meaning.
c. Construct and interpret a 95% confidence interval estimate of the difference between the population proportion of respondents who get their news primarily from newspapers between those respondents 36 to 50 years old and those above 50 years old.

10.4   F TEST FOR THE DIFFERENCE BETWEEN TWO VARIANCES

Often you need to determine whether two independent populations have the same amount of variability. By testing variances, you can detect differences in the amount of variability. One important reason to test for the difference between the variances of two populations is to determine whether to use the pooled-variance t test (which assumes equal variances) or the separate-variance t test (which does not assume equal variances) while comparing two means.

The test for the difference between the variances of two independent populations is based on the ratio of the two sample variances. If you assume that each population is normally distributed, then the ratio S_1^2/S_2^2 follows the F distribution (see Table E.5). The critical values of the **F distribution** in Table E.5 depend on the degrees of freedom in the two samples. The degrees of freedom in the numerator of the ratio are for the first sample, and the degrees of freedom in the denominator are for the second sample. The first sample taken from the first population is defined as the sample that has the *larger* sample variance. The second sample taken from the second population is the sample with the *smaller* sample variance. Equation (10.9) defines the **F-test for the equality of two variances**.

F-Test Statistic for Testing the Equality of Two Variances

The F_{STAT} test statistic is equal to the variance of sample 1 (the larger sample variance) divided by the variance of sample 2 (the smaller sample variance).

$$F_{STAT} = \frac{S_1^2}{S_2^2} \tag{10.9}$$

where

S_1^2 = variance of sample 1 (the larger sample variance)

S_2^2 = variance of sample 2 (the smaller sample variance)

n_1 = size of sample 1

n_2 = size of sample 2

$n_1 - 1$ = degrees of freedom from sample 1 (i.e., the numerator degrees of freedom)

$n_2 - 1$ = degrees of freedom from sample 2 (i.e., the denominator degrees of freedom)

The F_{STAT} test statistic follows an F distribution with $n_1 - 1$ and $n_2 - 1$ degrees of freedom.

For a given level of significance, α, to test the null hypothesis of equality of population variances:

$$H_0: \sigma_1^2 = \sigma_2^2$$

against the alternative hypothesis that the two population variances are not equal:

$$H_1: \sigma_1^2 \neq \sigma_2^2$$

because the F_{STAT} test statistic is defined as the larger sample variance divided by the smaller sample variance, you reject the null hypothesis if the computed F_{STAT} test statistic is greater than the upper-tail critical value, $F_{\alpha/2}$, from the F distribution with $n_1 - 1$ degrees of freedom in the numerator and $n_2 - 1$ degrees of freedom in the denominator. Thus, the decision rule is

$$\text{Reject } H_0 \text{ if } F_{STAT} > F_{\alpha/2};$$
$$\text{otherwise, do not reject } H_0.$$

To illustrate how to use the F test to determine whether the two variances are equal, return to the Using Statistics scenario on page 390 concerning the sales of BLK Cola in two different aisle locations. To determine whether to use the pooled-variance t test or the separate-variance t test in Section 10.1, you can test the equality of the two population variances. The null and alternative hypotheses are

$$H_0: \sigma_1^2 = \sigma_2^2$$
$$H_1: \sigma_1^2 \neq \sigma_2^2$$

Because you are defining sample 1 as having the larger sample variance, the rejection region in the upper tail of the F distribution contains $\alpha/2$. Using the level of significance $\alpha = 0.05$, the rejection region in the upper tail contains 0.025 of the distribution.

Because there are samples of 10 stores for each of the two display locations, there are $10 - 1 = 9$ degrees of freedom in the numerator (the sample with the larger variance) and also in the denominator (the sample with the smaller variance). $F_{\alpha/2}$, the upper-tail critical value of the F distribution, is found directly from Table E.5, a portion of which is presented in Table 10.6 on page 422. Because there are 9 degrees of freedom in the numerator and 9 degrees of freedom in the denominator, you find the upper-tail critical value, $F_{\alpha/2}$, by looking in the column labeled 9 and the row labeled 9. Thus, the upper-tail critical value of this F distribution is 4.03. Therefore the decision rule is

$$\text{Reject } H_0 \text{ if } F_{STAT} > F_{0.025} = 4.03;$$
$$\text{otherwise, do not reject } H_0.$$

Using Equation (10.9) on page 420 and the cola sales data (see Table 10.1 on page 392),

$$F_{STAT} = \frac{S_1^2}{S_2^2}$$

$$= \frac{350.6778}{157.3333} = 2.2289$$

TABLE 10.6

Finding the Upper-Tail Critical Value of F with 9 and 9 Degrees of Freedom for Upper-Tail Area of 0.025

Denominator df_2	Cumulative Probabilities = 0.975 Upper-Tail Area = 0.025 Numerator df_1						
	1	2	3	...	7	8	9
1	647.80	799.50	864.20	...	948.20	956.70	963.30
2	38.51	39.00	39.17	...	39.36	39.37	39.39
3	17.44	16.04	15.44	...	14.62	14.54	14.47
.			.	.			
.			.	.			
.			.	.			
7	8.07	6.54	5.89	...	4.99	4.90	4.82
8	7.57	6.06	5.42	...	4.53	4.43	4.36
9	7.21	5.71	5.08	...	4.20	4.10	4.03

Source: *Extracted from Table E.5.*

Because $F_{STAT} = 2.2289 < 4.03$, you do not reject H_0. The p-value is 0.2482 for a two-tail test as shown in Figure 10.20 (twice the p-value for the one-tail test shown in the Microsoft Excel results in Figure 10.19). Because $0.2482 > 0.05$, you conclude that there is no significant difference in the variability of the sales of cola for the two display locations. Notice that in Figure 10.20, Minitab reports the F statistic as 0.45, the reciprocal of 2.2289. This occurs because Minitab assigns samples in alphabetical order, so EndAisle is assigned to the numerator (sample 1) and Normal is assigned to the denominator (sample 2).

FIGURE 10.19

Microsoft Excel F test results for the BLK Cola sales data

See Section E10.9 or P10.5 to create this.

	A	B	C
1	F-Test Two-Sample for Variances		
2			
3		Normal	End-Aisle
4	Mean	50.3	72
5	Variance	350.6778	157.3333
6	Observations	10	10
7	df	9	9
8	F	2.2289	
9	P(F<=f) one-tail	0.1241	
10	F Critical one-tail	3.1789	

FIGURE 10.20

Minitab F test results for the BLK Cola sales data

See Section M10.5 to create this.

```
Display    N    Lower    StDev    Upper
EndAisle   10   8.2048   12.5433  25.2578
Normal     10   12.2494  18.7264  37.7085


F-Test (Normal Distribution)
Test statistic = 0.45, p-value = 0.248
```

In testing for a difference between two variances using the F test described in this section, you assume that each of the two populations is normally distributed. The F test is very sensitive to the normality assumption. If boxplots or normal probability plots suggest even a mild departure from normality for either of the two populations, you should not use the F test. If this happens, you should use the Levene test (see Section 11.1) or a nonparametric approach (see references 1 and 2).

In testing for the equality of variances as part of assessing the validity of the pooled-variance t test procedure, the F test is a two-tail test with $\alpha/2$ in the upper tail. However, when you are interested in examining the variability in situations other than the pooled-variance t test, the F test is often a one-tail test. Example 10.4 illustrates a one-tail test.

EXAMPLE 10.4   A ONE-TAIL TEST FOR THE DIFFERENCE BETWEEN TWO VARIANCES

Shipments of meat, meat by-products, and other ingredients are mixed together in several filling lines at a pet food canning factory. Operations managers suspect that, although the mean amount filled per can of pet food is usually the same, the variability of the cans filled in line A is greater than that of line B. The following data from a sample of eight-ounce cans is as follows:

	Line A	Line B
$\bar{X}$	8.005	7.997
S	0.012	0.005
n	11	16

At the 0.05 level of significance, is there evidence that the variance in line A is greater than the variance in line B? Assume that the population amounts filled are normally distributed.

SOLUTION The null and alternative hypotheses are

$$H_0: \sigma_A^2 \leq \sigma_B^2$$

$$H_1: \sigma_A^2 > \sigma_B^2$$

The F_{STAT} test statistic is given by Equation (10.9) on page 420:

$$F_{STAT} = \frac{S_1^2}{S_2^2}$$

You use Table E.5 to find the upper critical value of the F distribution. With $n_1 - 1 = 11 - 1 = 10$ degrees of freedom in the numerator, $n_2 - 1 = 16 - 1 = 15$ degrees of freedom in the denominator, and $\alpha = 0.05$, the upper critical value, $F_{0.05}$, is 2.54.

The decision rule is

Reject H_0 if $F_{STAT} > 2.54$;

otherwise, do not reject H_0.

From Equation (10.9) on page 420,

$$F_{STAT} = \frac{S_1^2}{S_2^2}$$

$$= \frac{(0.012)^2}{(0.005)^2} = 5.76$$

Because $F_{STAT} = 5.76 > 2.54$, you reject H_0. Using a 0.05 level of significance, you conclude that there is evidence that the variance of line A is greater than the variance of line B. In other words, the amount of pet food in the cans filled by line A is more variable than the amount of pet food in cans filled by line B.

PROBLEMS FOR SECTION 10.4

Learning the Basics

10.38 Determine the upper-tail critical values of F, in each of the following two-tail tests:
a. $\alpha = 0.10$, $n_1 = 16$, $n_2 = 21$
b. $\alpha = 0.05$, $n_1 = 16$, $n_2 = 21$
c. $\alpha = 0.01$, $n_1 = 16$, $n_2 = 21$

10.39 Determine the upper-tail critical value of F in each of the following one-tail tests:
a. $\alpha = 0.05$, $n_1 = 16$, $n_2 = 21$
b. $\alpha = 0.01$, $n_1 = 16$, $n_2 = 21$

10.40 The following information is available for two samples drawn from independent normally distributed populations:

$$\text{Population A:} \quad n = 25 \quad S^2 = 16$$
$$\text{Population B:} \quad n = 25 \quad S^2 = 25$$

a. Which sample variance do you place in the numerator of F_{STAT}?
b. What is the value of F_{STAT}?

10.41 The following information is available for two samples drawn from independent normally distributed populations:

$$\text{Population A:} \quad n = 25 \quad S^2 = 161.9$$
$$\text{Population B:} \quad n = 25 \quad S^2 = 133.7$$

What is the value of F_{STAT} if you are testing the null hypothesis $H_0: \sigma_1^2 = \sigma_2^2$?

10.42 In Problem 10.41, how many degrees of freedom are there in the numerator and denominator of the F test?

10.43 In Problems 10.41 and 10.42, what is the upper critical value for F if the level of significance, α, is 0.05 and the alternative hypothesis is $H_1: \sigma_1^2 \neq \sigma_2^2$?

10.44 In Problems 10.41 through 10.43, what is your statistical decision?

10.45 The following information is available for two samples selected from independent but very right-skewed populations:

$$\text{Population A:} \quad n = 16 \quad S^2 = 47.3$$
$$\text{Population B:} \quad n = 13 \quad S^2 = 36.4$$

Should you use the F test to test the null hypothesis of equality of variances? Discuss.

10.46 In Problem 10.45, assume that two samples are selected from independent normally distributed populations.
a. At the 0.05 level of significance, is there evidence of a difference between σ_1^2 and σ_2^2?

b. Suppose that you want to perform a one-tail test. At the 0.05 level of significance, what is the upper-tail critical value of F to determine whether there is evidence that $\sigma_1^2 > \sigma_2^2$? What is your statistical decision?

Applying the Concepts

10.47 A professor in the accounting department of a business school claims that there is much more variability in the final exam scores of students taking the introductory accounting course who are not majoring in accounting than for students taking the course who are majoring in accounting. Random samples of 13 non-accounting majors and 10 accounting majors are taken from the professor's class roster in his large lecture, and the following results are computed based on the final exam scores:

$$\text{Non-Accounting:} \quad n = 13 \quad S^2 = 210.2$$
$$\text{Accounting:} \quad n = 10 \quad S^2 = 36.5$$

a. At the 0.05 level of significance, is there evidence to support the professor's claim?
b. Interpret the p-value.
c. What assumption do you need to make in (a) about the two populations in order to justify your use of the F test?

SELF Test **10.48** The Computer Anxiety Rating Scale (CARS) measures an individual's level of computer anxiety, on a scale from 20 (no anxiety) to 100 (highest level of anxiety). Researchers at Miami University administered CARS to 172 business students. One of the objectives of the study was to determine whether there is a difference between the level of computer anxiety experienced by female students and male students. They found the following:

	Males	Females
$\bar{X}$	40.26	36.85
S	13.35	9.42
n	100	72

Source: *Extracted from T. Broome and D. Havelka, "Determinants of Computer Anxiety in Business Students,"* The Review of Business Information Systems, *Spring 2002, 6(2), pp. 9–16.*

a. At the 0.05 level of significance, is there evidence of a difference in the variability of the computer anxiety experienced by males and females?
b. Interpret the p-value.
c. What assumption do you need to make about the two populations in order to justify the use of the F test?
d. Based on (a) and (b), which t test defined in Section 10.1 should you use to test whether there is a significant difference in mean computer anxiety for female and male students?

10.49 A bank with a branch located in a commercial district of a city has developed an improved process for serving customers during the noon-to-1 p.m. lunch period. The waiting time (defined as the time elapsed from when the customer enters the line until he or she reaches the teller window) needs to be shortened to increase customer satisfaction. A random sample of 15 customers is selected (and stored in the file Bank1), and the results (in minutes) are as follows:

4.21 5.55 3.02 5.13 4.77 2.34 3.54 3.20
4.50 6.10 0.38 5.12 6.46 6.19 3.79

Suppose that another branch, located in a residential area, is also concerned with the noon-to-1 p.m. lunch period. A random sample of 15 customers is selected (and stored in the file Bank2), and the results (in minutes) are as follows:

9.66 5.90 8.02 5.79 8.73 3.82 8.01 8.35
10.49 6.68 5.64 4.08 6.17 9.91 5.47

a. Is there evidence of a difference in the variability of the waiting time between the two branches? (Use $\alpha = 0.05$.)
b. Determine the p-value in (a) and interpret its meaning.
c. What assumption about the population distribution of the two banks is necessary in (a)? Is the assumption valid for these data?
d. Based on the results of (a), is it appropriate to use the pooled-variance t test to compare the means of the two branches?

10.50 Digital cameras have taken over the majority of the point-and-shoot camera market. One of the important features of a camera is the battery life as measured by the number of shots taken until the battery needs to be recharged. The data in the file Digitalcameras contains the battery life of 31 subcompact cameras and 15 compact cameras (extracted from "Cameras," *Consumer Reports*, November 2006, pp. 20–21)
a. Is there evidence of a difference in the variability of the battery life between the two types of digital cameras? (Use $\alpha = 0.05$.)

b. Determine the p-value in (a) and interpret its meaning.
c. What assumption about the population distribution of the two types of cameras is necessary in (a)? Is the assumption valid for these data?
d. Based on the results of (a), which t test defined in Section 10.1 should you use to compare the mean battery life of the two types of cameras?

10.51 The director of training for a company that manufactures electronic equipment is interested in determining whether different training methods have an effect on the productivity of assembly-line employees. She randomly assigns 21 of the 42 recently hired employees to a computer-assisted, individual-based training program. The other 21 are assigned to a team-based training program. Upon completion of the training, the employees are evaluated on the time (in seconds) it takes to assemble a part. The results are in the data file Training.
a. Using a 0.05 level of significance, is there evidence of a difference between the variances in assembly times (in seconds) of employees trained in a computer-assisted, individual-based program and those trained in a team-based program?
b. On the basis of the results in (a), which t test defined in Section 10.1 should you use to compare the means of the two training programs? Discuss.

10.52 Is there a difference in the variation of the yield of different types of investment between banks? The following data, from the file Bankyield, represent the nationwide highest yields for money market accounts and five-year CDs as of March 12, 2007:

Money Market Accounts	Five-Year CD
5.35 5.31 5.30 5.30 5.25	5.95 5.89 5.83 5.83 5.79

Source: *Extracted from Bankrate.com, March 12, 2007.*

At the 0.05 level of significance, is there evidence of a difference in the variance of the yield between money market accounts and five-year CDs? Assume that the population yields are normally distributed.

SUMMARY

In this chapter, you were introduced to a variety of two-sample tests. For situations in which the samples are independent, you learned statistical test procedures for analyzing possible differences between means, variances, and proportions. In addition, you learned a test procedure that is frequently used when analyzing differences between the means of two related samples. Remember that you need to select the test that is most appropriate for a given set of conditions and to critically investigate the validity of the assumptions underlying each of the hypothesis-testing procedures.

The roadmap in Figure 10.21 illustrates the steps needed in determining which two-sample test of hypothesis to use. The following are the questions you need to consider.

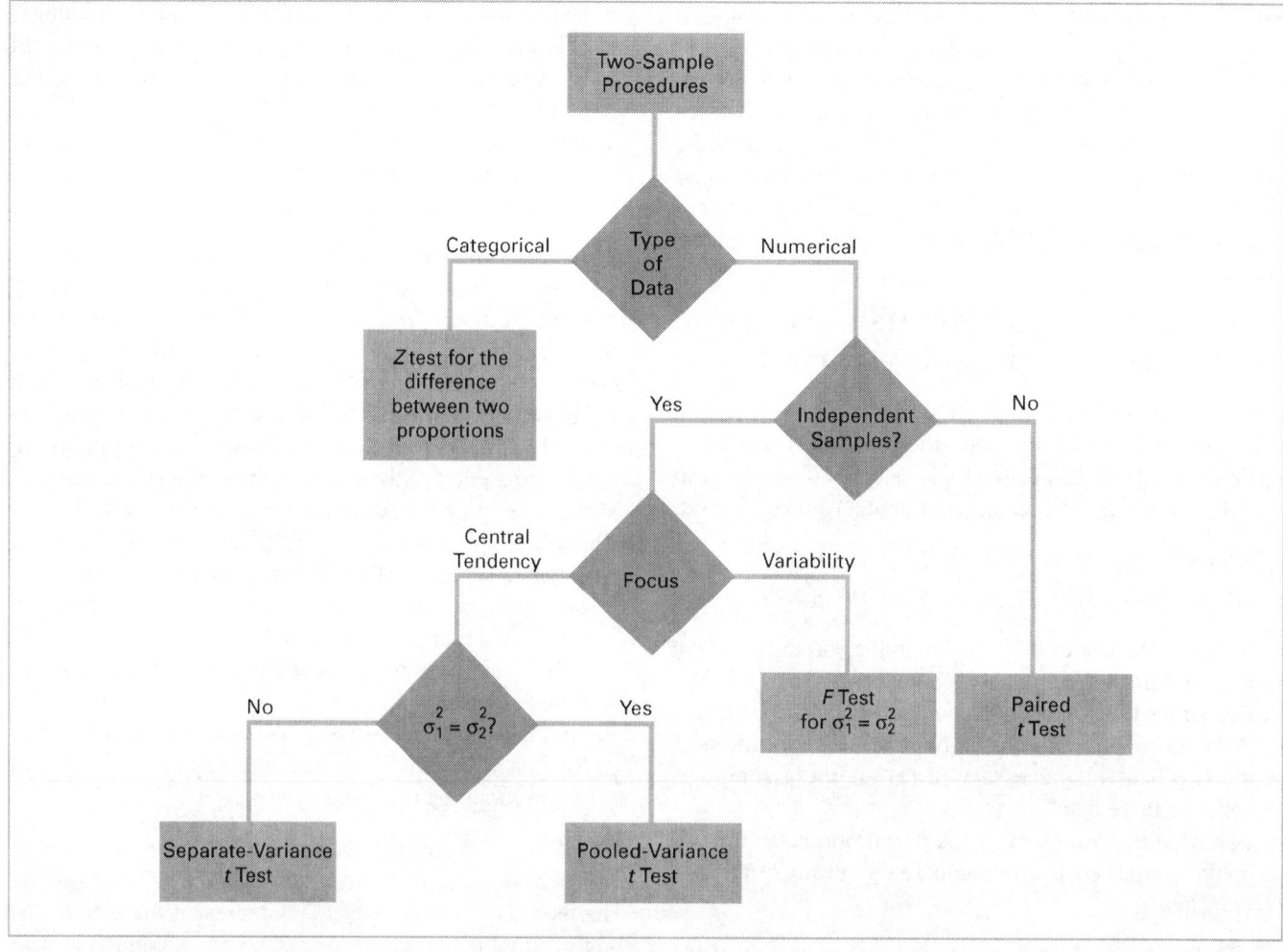

FIGURE 10.21   Roadmap for selecting a two-sample test of hypothesis

1. What type of data do you have? If you are dealing with categorical variables, use the Z test for the difference between two proportions. (This test assumes independent samples.)

2. If you have a numerical variable, determine whether you have independent samples or related samples. If you have related samples, use the paired t test.

3. If you have independent samples, is your focus on variability or central tendency? If the focus is variability, use the F test.

4. If your focus is central tendency, determine whether you can assume that the variances of the two populations are equal. (This assumption can be tested using the F test.)

5. If you can assume that the two populations have equal variances, use the pooled-variance t test. If you cannot assume that the two populations have equal variances, use the separate-variance t test.

Table 10.7 provides a list of topics covered in this chapter.

TABLE 10.7

Summary of Topics in Chapter 10

| Type of Analysis | Types of Data | |
	Numerical	Categorical
Comparing two populations	t tests for the difference in the means of two independent populations (Section 10.1)	Z test for the difference between two proportions (Section 10.3)
	Paired t test (Section 10.2)	
	F test for the difference between two variances (Section 10.4)	

KEY EQUATIONS

Pooled-Variance t Test for the Difference Between Two Means

$$t_{STAT} = \frac{(\bar{X}_1 - \bar{X}_2) - (\mu_1 - \mu_2)}{\sqrt{S_p^2\left(\dfrac{1}{n_1} + \dfrac{1}{n_2}\right)}} \qquad (10.1)$$

Confidence Interval Estimate of the Difference in the Means of Two Independent Populations

$$(\bar{X}_1 - \bar{X}_2) \pm t_{\alpha/2}\sqrt{S_p^2\left(\dfrac{1}{n_1} + \dfrac{1}{n_2}\right)} \qquad (10.2)$$

or

$$(\bar{X}_1 - \bar{X}_2) - t_{\alpha/2}\sqrt{S_p^2\left(\dfrac{1}{n_1} + \dfrac{1}{n_2}\right)} \le \mu_1 - \mu_2$$

$$\le (\bar{X}_1 - \bar{X}_2) + t_{\alpha/2}\sqrt{S_p^2\left(\dfrac{1}{n_1} + \dfrac{1}{n_2}\right)}$$

Separate-Variance t Test for the Difference in Two Means

$$t_{STAT} = \frac{(\bar{X}_1 - \bar{X}_2) - (\mu_1 - \mu_2)}{\sqrt{\dfrac{S_1^2}{n_1} + \dfrac{S_2^2}{n_2}}} \qquad (10.3)$$

Computing Degrees of Freedom in the Separate-Variance t Test

$$V = \frac{\left(\dfrac{S_1^2}{n_1} + \dfrac{S_2^2}{n_2}\right)^2}{\dfrac{\left(\dfrac{S_1^2}{n_1}\right)^2}{n_1 - 1} + \dfrac{\left(\dfrac{S_2^2}{n_2}\right)^2}{n_2 - 1}} \qquad (10.4)$$

Paired t Test for the Mean Difference

$$t_{STAT} = \frac{\bar{D} - \mu_D}{\dfrac{S_D}{\sqrt{n}}} \qquad (10.5)$$

Confidence Interval Estimate for the Mean Difference

$$\bar{D} \pm t_{\alpha/2}\frac{S_D}{\sqrt{n}} \qquad (10.6)$$

or

$$\bar{D} - t_{\alpha/2}\frac{S_D}{\sqrt{n}} \le \mu_D \le \bar{D} + t_{\alpha/2}\frac{S_D}{\sqrt{n}}$$

Z Test for the Difference Between Two Proportions

$$Z_{STAT} = \frac{(p_1 - p_2) - (\pi_1 - \pi_2)}{\sqrt{\bar{p}(1 - \bar{p})\left(\dfrac{1}{n_1} + \dfrac{1}{n_2}\right)}} \qquad (10.7)$$

Confidence Interval Estimate for the Difference Between Two Proportions

$$(p_1 - p_2) \pm Z_{\alpha/2}\sqrt{\left(\frac{p_1(1 - p_1)}{n_1} + \frac{p_2(1 - p_2)}{n_2}\right)} \qquad (10.8)$$

or

$$(p_1 - p_2) - Z_{\alpha/2}\sqrt{\frac{p_1(1 - p_1)}{n_1} + \frac{p_2(1 - p_2)}{n_2}} \le (\pi_1 - \pi_2)$$

$$\le (p_1 - p_2) + Z_{\alpha/2}\sqrt{\frac{p_1(1 - p_1)}{n_1} + \frac{p_2(1 - p_2)}{n_2}}$$

F Test for the Equality of Two Variances

$$F_{STAT} = \frac{S_1^2}{S_2^2} \qquad (10.9)$$

KEY TERMS

CHAPTER REVIEW PROBLEMS

Checking Your Understanding

10.53 What are some of the criteria used in the selection of a particular hypothesis-testing procedure?

10.54 Under what conditions should you use the pooled-variance *t* test to examine possible differences in the means of two independent populations?

10.55 Under what conditions should you use the *F* test to examine possible differences in the variances of two independent populations?

10.56 What is the distinction between two independent populations and two related populations?

10.57 What is the distinction between repeated measurements and matched items?

10.58 Under what conditions should you use the paired *t* test for the mean difference?

10.59 When you have two independent populations, explain the similarities and differences between the test of hypothesis for the difference between the means and the confidence interval estimate of the difference between the means.

Applying the Concepts

10.60 A study compared music compact disc prices for Internet-based retailers and traditional brick-and-mortar retailers [extracted from L. Zoonky and S. Gosain, "A Longitudinal Price Comparison for Music CDs in Electronic and Brick-and-Mortar Markets: Pricing Strategies in Emergent Electronic Commerce," *Journal of Business Strategies*, Spring 2002, 19(1), pp. 55–72]. Before collecting the data, the researchers carefully defined several research hypotheses, including:

1. The price dispersion on the Internet is lower than the price dispersion in the brick-and-mortar market.
2. Prices in electronic markets are lower than prices in physical markets.

a. Consider research hypothesis 1. Write the null and alternative hypotheses in terms of population parameters. Carefully define the population parameters used.

b. Define a Type I and Type II error for the hypotheses in (a).
c. What type of statistical test should you use?
d. What assumptions are needed to perform the test you selected?
e. Repeat (a) through (d) for research hypothesis 2.

10.61 The pet-drug market is growing very rapidly. Before new pet drugs can be introduced into the marketplace, they must be approved by the U.S. Food and Drug Administration (FDA). In 1999, the Novartis company was trying to get Anafranil, a drug to reduce dog anxiety, approved. According to an article (E. Tanouye, "The Ow in Bowwow: With Growing Market in Pet Drugs, Makers Revamp Clinical Trials," *The Wall Street Journal*, April 13, 1999), Novartis had to find a way to translate a dog's anxiety symptoms into numbers that could be used to prove to the FDA that the drug had a statistically significant effect on the condition.

a. What is meant by the phrase *statistically significant effect*?
b. Consider an experiment in which dogs suffering from anxiety are divided into two groups. One group will be given Anafranil, and the other will be given a placebo (i.e., a drug without active ingredients). How can you translate a dog's anxiety symptoms into numbers? In other words, define a continuous variable, X_1, that measures the effectiveness of the drug Anafranil, and X_2, that measures the effectiveness of the placebo.
c. Building on your answer to part (b), define the null and alternative hypotheses for this study.

10.62 In response to lawsuits filed against the tobacco industry, many companies, such as Philip Morris, are running television advertisements that are supposed to educate teenagers about the dangers of smoking. Are these tobacco industry antismoking campaigns successful? Are state-sponsored antismoking commercials more effective? An article (G. Fairclough, "Philip Morris's Antismoking Campaign Draws Fire," *The Wall Street Journal*, April 6, 1999, p. B1) discussed a study in California that compared commercials made by the state of California and commercials produced by

Philip Morris. Researchers showed the state ads and the Philip Morris ads to a group of California teenagers and measured the effectiveness of both. The researchers concluded that the state ads were more effective in relaying the dangers of smoking than the Philip Morris ads. The article suggests, however, that the study is not *statistically reliable* because the sample size was too small and because the study specifically selected participants who are considered more likely to start smoking than others.

a. How do you think the researchers measured effectiveness?

b. Define the null and alternative hypotheses for this study.

c. Explain the risks associated with Type I and Type II errors in this study.

d. What type of test is most appropriate in this situation?

e. What do you think is meant by the phrase *statistically reliable*?

10.63 Do male and female students study the same amount per week? In 2007, 58 sophomore business students were surveyed at a large university, which has over 1000 sophomore business students each year. The file **Studytime** contains the gender and the number of hours spent studying in a typical week for the sampled students.

a. At the 0.05 level of significance, is there a difference in the variance of the study time for male students and female students?

b. Using the results of (a), which *t* test is appropriate to compare the mean study time for male and female students?

c. At the 0.05 level of significance, conduct the test selected in (b).

d. Write a short summary of your findings.

10.64 Two professors wanted to study how students from their two universities compared in their capabilities of using Excel spreadsheets in undergraduate information systems courses (extracted from H. Howe and M. G. Simkin, "Factors Affecting the Ability to Detect Spreadsheet Errors," *Decision Sciences Journal of Innovative Education*, January 2006, pp. 101–122). A comparison of the student demographics was also performed. One school is a state university in the Western United States, and the other school is a state university in the Eastern United States. The following table contains information regarding the ages of the students:

School	Sample Size	Mean Age	Standard Deviation
Western	93	23.28	6.29
Eastern	135	21.16	1.32

a. Using a 0.01 level of significance, is there evidence of a difference between the variances in age of students at the Western school and at the Eastern school?

b. Discuss the practical implications of the test performed in (a). Address, specifically, the impact equal (or unequal) variances in age has on teaching an undergraduate information systems course.

c. To test for a difference in the mean age of students, is it most appropriate to use the pooled-variance *t* test or the separate-variance *t* test?

The following table contains information regarding the years of spreadsheet usage of the students:

School	Sample Size	Mean Years	Standard Deviation
Western	93	2.6	2.4
Eastern	135	4.0	2.1

d. Using a 0.01 level of significance, is there evidence of a difference between the variances in years of spreadsheet usage of students at the Western school and at the Eastern school?

e. Based on the results of (d), use the most appropriate test to determine, at the 0.01 level of significance, whether there is evidence of a difference in the mean years of spreadsheet usage of students at the Western school and at the Eastern school.

10.65 The data file **Restaurants** contains the ratings for food, decor, service, and the price per person for a sample of 50 restaurants located in an urban area and 50 restaurants located in a suburban area. Completely analyze the differences between urban and suburban restaurants for the variables food rating, decor rating, service rating, and price per person, using $\alpha = 0.05$.

Source: *Extracted from* Zagat Survey 2006: New York City Restaurants *and* Zagat Survey 2005–2006: Long Island Restaurants.

10.66 A computer information systems professor is interested in studying the amount of time it takes students enrolled in the introduction to computers course to write and run a program in Visual Basic. The professor hires you to analyze the following results (in minutes) from a random sample of nine students (the data are stored in the **VB** file):

10   13   9   15   12   13   11   13   12

a. At the 0.05 level of significance, is there evidence that the population mean amount is greater than 10 minutes? What will you tell the professor?

b. Suppose the computer professor, when checking her results, realizes that the fourth student needed 51 minutes rather than the recorded 15 minutes to write and run the Visual Basic program. At the 0.05 level of significance, reanalyze the question posed in (a), using the revised data. What will you tell the professor now?

c. The professor is perplexed by these paradoxical results and requests an explanation from you regarding the justification for the difference in your findings in (a) and (b). Discuss.

d. A few days later, the professor calls to tell you that the dilemma is completely resolved. The original number 15 (the fourth data value) was correct, and therefore your findings in (a) are being used in the article she is writing for a computer journal. Now she wants to hire you to compare the results from that group of introduction to computers students against those from a sample of 11 computer majors in order to determine whether there is evidence that computer majors can write a Visual Basic program in less time than introductory students. For the computer majors, the sample mean is 8.5 minutes, and the sample standard deviation is 2.0 minutes. At the 0.05 level of significance, completely analyze these data. What will you tell the professor?

e. A few days later, the professor calls again to tell you that a reviewer of her article wants her to include the *p*-value for the "correct" result in (a). In addition, the professor inquires about an unequal-variances problem, which the reviewer wants her to discuss in her article. In your own words, discuss the concept of *p*-value and also describe the unequal-variances problem. Then, determine the *p*-value in (a) and discuss whether the unequal-variances problem had any meaning in the professor's study.

10.67 An article in *The New York Times* (A. Jennings, "What's Good for a Business Can be Hard on Friends," *The New York Times*, August 4, 2007, pp. C1–C2) reported that according to a poll, the mean number of cellphone calls per month was 290 for 18- to 24-year-olds and 194 for 45- to 54-year-olds, whereas the mean number of text messages per month was 290 for 18- to 24-year-olds and 57 for 45- to 54-year-olds. Suppose that the poll was based on a sample of 100 18- to 24-year-olds and 100 45- to 54-year-olds, and that the standard deviation of the number of cellphone calls per month was 100 for 18- to 24-year-olds and 90 for 45- to 54-year-olds, whereas the standard deviation of the number of text messages per month was 90 for 18- to 24-year-olds and 77 for 45- to 54-year-olds.

Use a level of significance of 0.05.

a. Is there evidence of a difference in the variances of the number of cellphone calls per month for 18- to 24-year-olds and 45- to 54-year-olds?

b. Is there evidence of a difference in the mean number of cellphone calls per month for 18- to 24-year-olds and 45- to 54-year-olds?

c. Construct and interpret a 95% confidence interval estimate of the difference in the mean number of cellphone calls per month for 18- to 24-year-olds and 45- to 54-year-olds.

d. Is there evidence of a difference in the variances of the number of text messages per month for 18- to 24-year-olds and 45- to 54-year-olds?

e. Is there evidence of a difference in the mean number of text messages per month for 18- to 24-year-olds and 45- to 54-year-olds?

f. Construct and interpret a 95% confidence interval estimate of the difference in the mean number of text messages per month for 18- to 24-year-olds and 45- to 54-year-olds.

g. Based on the results of (a) through (f), what conclusions can you make concerning cellphone and text message usage between 18- to 24-year-olds and 45- to 54-year-olds?

10.68 The lengths of life (in hours) of a sample of 40 100-watt lightbulbs produced by manufacturer A and a sample of 40 100-watt lightbulbs produced by manufacturer B are in the file Bulbs. Completely analyze the differences between the lengths of life of the bulbs produced by the two manufacturers (use α = 0.05).

10.69 A hotel manager is concerned with increasing the return rate for hotel guests. One aspect of first impressions by guests relates to the time it takes to deliver the guest's luggage to the room after check-in to the hotel. A random sample of 20 deliveries on a particular day were selected in Wing A of the hotel, and a random sample of 20 deliveries were selected in Wing B. The results are stored in the file Luggage. Analyze the data and determine whether there is a difference in the mean delivery time in the two wings of the hotel. (Use α = 0.05.)

10.70 A survey of 500 men and 500 women designed to study financial tensions between couples asked how likely they were to hide purchases, cash, or investments from their partners. The results were as follows:

	LIKELY TO HIDE	
TYPE	**Men**	**Women**
Auto-related	66	36
Cash	126	133
Clothes	62	116
Electronics	79	56
Entertainment	96	76
Food	74	94
Investments	76	52
Travel	53	39

Source: *Extracted from L. Wei, "Your Money Manager as Financial Therapist,"* The Wall Street Journal, *November 5–6, 2005, p. B4.*

For *each type of purchase*, determine whether there is a difference between men and women at the 0.05 level of significance.

10.71 As more Americans use cellphones, they question where it is okay to talk on cellphones. The following is a table of results, in percentages, for 2000 and 2006 (extracted from W. Koch, "Businesses Put a Lid on Chatter-boxes," *USA Today*, February 7, 2006, p. 3A). Suppose the survey was based on 100 respondents in 2000 and 100 respondents in 2006.

OKAY TO TALK ON A CELL PHONE IN A	YEAR	
	2000	**2006**
Bathroom	39	38
Movie/theater	11	2
Car	76	63
Supermarket	60	66
Public transit	52	45
Restaurant	31	21

For *each type of location*, determine whether there is a difference between 2000 and 2006 in the proportion who think it is okay to talk on a cellphone. (Use the 0.05 level of significance.)

10.72 Many companies are finding that customers are using various types of online content before purchasing products (extracted from K. Spors, "How Are We Doing?" *The Wall Street Journal*, November 13, 2006, p. R9). The following results are the percentages of adults and youths who use various sources of online content. Suppose the survey was based on 100 adults and 100 youths.

TYPE OF ONLINE CONTENT	USE ONLINE CONTENT	
	Adult	**Youth**
Customer product ratings/reviews	71	81
For sale listings with seller ratings	69	77
For sale listings without seller ratings	58	65
Online classified ads	57	66
Message-board posts	57	71
Web blogs	55	67
Dating site profiles/personals	49	59
Peer-generated and peer-reference information	49	68
Peer-posted event listings	46	71

For *each type of online content*, determine whether there is a difference between adults and youths in the proportion who use the type of online content at the 0.05 level of significance.

10.73 The manufacturer of Boston and Vermont asphalt shingles knows that product weight is a major factor in the customer's perception of quality. Moreover, the weight represents the amount of raw materials being used and is therefore very important to the company from a cost standpoint. The last stage of the assembly line packages the shingles before they are placed on wooden pallets. Once a pallet is full (a pallet for most brands holds 16 squares of shingles), it is weighed, and the measurement is recorded. The data file **Pallet** contains the weight (in pounds) from a sample of 368 pallets of Boston shingles and 330 pallets of Vermont shingles. Completely analyze the differences in the weights of the Boston and Vermont shingles, using $\alpha = 0.05$.

10.74 The manufacturer of Boston and Vermont asphalt shingles provides its customers with a 20-year warranty on most of its products. To determine whether a shingle will last as long as the warranty period, accelerated-life testing is conducted at the manufacturing plant. Accelerated-life testing exposes the shingle to the stresses it would be subject to in a lifetime of normal use in a laboratory setting via an experiment that takes only a few minutes to conduct. In this test, a shingle is repeatedly scraped with a brush for a short period of time, and the shingle granules removed by the brushing are weighed (in grams). Shingles that experience low amounts of granule loss are expected to last longer in normal use than shingles that experience high amounts of granule loss. In this situation, a shingle should experience no more than 0.8 grams of granule loss if it is expected to last the length of the warranty period. The data file **Granule** contains a sample of 170 measurements made on the company's Boston shingles and 140 measurements made on Vermont shingles. Completely analyze the differences in the granule loss of the Boston and Vermont shingles, using $\alpha = 0.05$.

Report Writing Exercise

10.75 Referring to the results of Problems 10.73 and 10.74 concerning the weight and granule loss of Boston and Vermont shingles, write a report that summarizes your conclusions.

Team Project

The data file **Mutual Funds** contains information regarding nine variables from a sample of 868 mutual funds. The variables are

Category—Type of stocks comprising the mutual fund (small cap, mid cap, or large cap)

Objective—Objective of stocks comprising the mutual fund (growth or value)

Assets—In millions of dollars

Fees—Sales charges (no or yes)

Expense ratio—Ratio of expenses to net assets, in percentage

2006 return—Twelve-month return in 2006

Three-year return—Annualized return, 2004–2006

Five-year return—Annualized return, 2002–2006
Risk—Risk-of-loss factor of the mutual fund (low, average, or high)

10.76 Completely analyze the difference between mutual funds without fees and mutual funds with fees in terms of 2006 return, three-year return, five-year return, and expense ratio. Write a report summarizing your findings.

10.77 Completely analyze the difference between mutual funds that have a growth objective and mutual funds that have a value objective in terms of 2006 return, three-year return, five-year return, and expense ratio. Write a report summarizing your findings.

Student Survey Data Base

10.78 Problem 1.27 on page 14 describes a survey of 50 undergraduate students (see the file Undergradsurvey). For these data,
a. at the 0.05 level of significance, is there evidence of a difference between males and females in grade point average, expected starting salary, salary expected in five years, age, and spending on textbooks and supplies?
b. at the 0.05 level of significance, is there evidence of a difference between those students who plan to go to graduate school and those who do not plan to go to grad-

uate school in grade point average, expected starting salary, salary expected in five years, age, and spending on textbooks and supplies?

10.79 Problem 1.27 on page 14 describes a survey of 50 undergraduate students (see the file Undergradsurvey).
a. Select a sample of 50 undergraduate students at your school and conduct a similar survey for them.
b. For the data collected in (a), repeat (a) and (b) of Problem 10.78.
c. Compare the results of (b) to those of Problem 10.78.

10.80 Problem 1.28 on page 14 describes a survey of 40 MBA students (see the file Gradsurvey). For these data, at the 0.05 level of significance, is there evidence of a difference between males and females in age, undergraduate grade point average, graduate grade point average, GMAT score, expected salary upon graduation, salary expected in five years, and spending on textbooks and supplies?

10.81 Problem 1.28 on page 14 describes a survey of 40 MBA students (see the file Gradsurvey).
a. Select a sample of 40 graduate students in your MBA program and conduct a similar survey for those students.
b. For the data collected in (a), repeat Problem 10.80.
c. Compare the results of (b) to those of Problem 10.80.

MANAGING THE *SPRINGVILLE HERALD*

A marketing department team is charged with improving the telemarketing process in order to increase the number of home-delivery subscriptions sold. After several brainstorming sessions, it was clear that the longer a caller speaks to a respondent, the greater the chance that the caller will sell a home-delivery subscription. Therefore, the team decided to find ways to increase the length of the phone calls.

Initially, the team investigated the impact that the time of a call might have on the length of the call. Under current arrangements, calls were made in the evening hours, between 5:00 p.m. and 9:00 p.m., Monday through Friday. The team wanted to compare the length of calls made early in the evening (before 7:00 p.m.) with those made later in the evening (after 7:00 p.m.) to determine whether one of these time periods is more conducive to lengthier calls and, correspondingly, to increased subscription sales. The team selected a sample of 30 female callers who staff the telephone bank on Wednesday evenings and randomly assigned 15 of them to the "early" time period and 15 to the "later" time period. The callers knew that the team was observing their efforts that evening but didn't know which calls were monitored. The callers had been trained to make their telephone presentations in a structured manner. They were to read from a script, and

their greeting was personal but informal ("Hi, this is Leigh Richardson from the *Springville Herald*. May I speak to Stuart Knoll?").

Measurements were taken on the length of the call (defined as the difference, in seconds, between the time the person answered the phone and the time he or she hung up). The results (stored in the file SH10) are presented in Table SH10.1.

TABLE SH10.1

Length of Calls, in Seconds, Based on Time of Call—Early Versus Late in the Evening

Time of Call		Time of Call	
Early	Late	Early	Late
41.3	37.1	40.6	40.7
37.5	38.9	33.3	38.0
39.3	42.2	39.6	43.6
37.4	45.7	35.7	43.8
33.6	42.4	31.3	34.9
38.5	39.0	36.8	35.7
32.6	40.9	36.3	47.4
37.3	40.5		

EXERCISES

SH10.1 Analyze the data in Table SH10.1 and write a report to the marketing department team that indicates your findings. Include an attached appendix in which you discuss the reason you selected a particular statistical test to compare the two independent groups of callers.

SH10.2 Suppose that instead of the research design described here, there were only 15 callers sampled, and each caller was to be monitored twice in the evening— once in the early time period and once in the later time period. Thus, in Table SH10.1, each pair of values represents a particular caller's two measurements. Reanalyze these data and write a report for presentation to the team that indicates your findings.

SH10.3 What other variables should be investigated next? Why?

WEB CASE

Apply your knowledge about hypothesis testing in this Web Case, which continues the cereal-fill packaging dispute Web Case from Chapters 7 and 9.

Even after the recent public experiment about cereal box weights, the Consumers Concerned About Cereal Cheaters (CCACC) remains convinced that Oxford Cereals has misled the public. The group has created and posted a document in which it claims that cereal boxes produced at Plant Number 2 in Springville weigh less than the claimed mean of 368 grams. Visit the CCACC More Cheating page

at **www.prenhall.com/Springville/MoreCheating.htm** (or open this Web page file from the Student CD-ROM Web Case folder) and then answer the following:

1. Do the CCACC's results prove that there is a statistical difference in the mean weights of cereal boxes produced at Plant Numbers 1 and 2?

2. Perform the appropriate analysis to test the CCACC's hypothesis. What conclusions can you reach based on the data?

REFERENCES

1. Conover, W. J., *Practical Nonparametric Statistics*, 3rd ed. (New York: Wiley, 2000).
2. Daniel, W., *Applied Nonparametric Statistics*, 2nd ed. (Boston: Houghton Mifflin, 1990).
3. *Microsoft Excel 2007* (Redmond, WA: Microsoft Corp., 2007).
4. *Minitab for Windows Version 15* (State College, PA: Minitab, Inc., 2006).
5. Satterthwaite, F. E., "An Approximate Distribution of Estimates of Variance Components," *Biometrics Bulletin*, 2(1946): 110–114.
6. Snedecor, G. W., and W. G. Cochran, *Statistical Methods*, 8th ed. (Ames, IA: Iowa State University Press, 1989).
7. Winer, B. J., D. R. Brown, and K. M. Michels, *Statistical Principles in Experimental Design*, 3rd ed. (New York: McGraw-Hill, 1989).

Appendix E10
Using Microsoft Excel for Two-Sample Tests

E10.1 Stacking and Unstacking Data

Unsummarized data for two (or more) samples can be entered as **stacked** or **unstacked** worksheet data. In a stacked arrangement, all the variable values appear in a single column next to a column that identifies the sample to which individual values belong. In an unstacked arrangement, the values for each sample appear in separate columns.

Specific ToolPak procedures or Excel worksheets for analyses involving two or more samples will require that your data be arranged either as stacked or unstacked data. If you need to change stacked data into its unstacked equivalent, you can sort your data by sample and then cut and paste the data of the second sample (now in contiguous rows) to a new column. (Use row 1 in that column to identify the second sample.) Likewise, to stack unstacked data, you can copy the data of the second sample to below the first sample and then add a column that identifies the sample. The `StackedAndUnstacked.xls` workbook illustrates both the stacked and unstacked arrangement of the BLK Cola weekly sales data of Table 10.1 on page 392.

E10.2 Using the Pooled-Variance *t* test (unsummarized data)

For unsummarized data, you perform the pooled-variance *t* test by using the ToolPak t-Test: Two-Sample Assuming Equal Variances procedure.

Open to the worksheet containing the unsummarized data for the two samples. Select **Tools → Data Analysis** (Excel 97–2003) or **Data → Data Analysis** (Excel 2007). Then select **t-Test: Two-Sample Assuming Equal Variances** from the **Analysis Tools** list and then click **OK**. In the procedure's dialog box (shown below), enter the cell range of one sample as the **Variable 1 Range** and the cell range of the other sample as the **Variable 2 Range.** Enter the **Hypothesized Mean Difference**, click **Labels**, and click **OK**. Results appear on a new worksheet. Figure 10.3 on page 393 shows the results for the Table 10.1 BLK Cola sales data.

E10.3 Using the Pooled-Variance *t* test (summarized data)

For summarized data, you perform the pooled-variance *t* test by making entries in the **PVt** worksheet of the `Pooled-Variance T.xls` workbook. This worksheet (see Figure E10.1 and E10.2) uses the **TINV(1-*confidence level,***

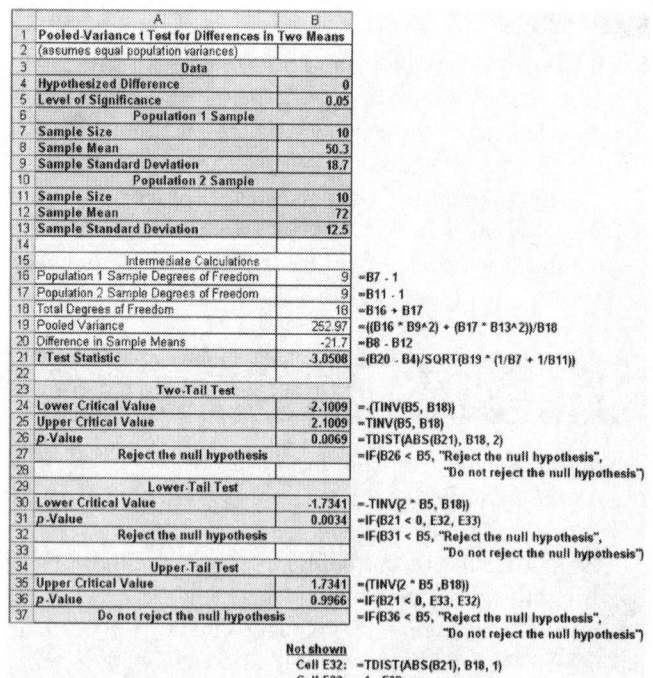

FIGURE E10.1 PVt worksheet

	D	E	
1			
2			
3	**Confidence Interval Estimate**		
4	**of the Difference Between Two Means**		
5			
6	**Data**		
7	**Confidence Level**	95%	
8			
9	Intermediate Calculations		
10	Degrees of Freedom	18	=B16 + B17
11	*t* Value	2.1009	=TINV(1 - E7, E10)
12	Interval Half Width	14.9437	=(E11 * SQRT(B19 * (1/B7 + 1/B11)))
13			
14	**Confidence Interval**		
15	**Interval Lower Limit**	-36.6437	=B20 - E12
16	**Interval Upper Limit**	-6.7563	=B20 + E12

FIGURE E10.2
Confidence interval estimate area of PVt worksheet

degrees of freedom) function to determine the lower and upper critical values. The worksheet also uses the **TDIST(ABS(*t*), *degrees of freedom, tails*)** function, in which **ABS(*t*)** is the absolute value of the *t*-test statistic, and *tails* is either 1, for a one-tail test, or 2, for a two-tail test, to help compute the *p*-values. IF functions in cells B31 and B36 select which one of two values computed in a calculations area (not shown in Figure E10.3) to use. IF functions in cells A27, A32, and A37 determine which one of two phrases will be displayed in those cells.

The worksheet contains entries based on the Table 10.1 BLK Cola weekly sales data. To adapt this worksheet to other problems, change, as is necessary, the hypothesized difference, level of significance, and the sample statistics of the two samples in cells B4, B5, B7:B9, and B11:B13. If you do not want to include a confidence interval estimate in your worksheet (see Figure E10.2), select and delete the cell range D3:E16.

E10.4 Using the Separate-Variance *t* test (unsummarized data)

For unsummarized data, you perform the separate-variance *t* test by using the ToolPak t-Test: Two-Sample Assuming Unequal Variances procedure. (There is no equivalent procedure for summarized data in Microsoft Excel.)

Open to the worksheet containing the unsummarized data for the two samples. Select **Tools → Data Analysis** (Excel 97–2003) or **Data → Data Analysis** (Excel 2007). Then select **t-Test: Two-Sample Assuming Unequal Variances** from the **Data Analysis** list and click **OK**. In the procedure's dialog box (shown below), enter the cell range of one sample as the **Variable 1 Range** and the cell range of the other sample as the **Variable 2 Range**. Enter the **Hypothesized Mean Difference**, click **Labels**, and click **OK**. Figure 10.8 on page 399 shows the results of applying this procedure to the Table 10.1 BLK Cola weekly sales data.

E10.5 Using the Separate-Variance *t* test (summarized data)

For summarized data, you perform the separate-variance *t* test by making entries in the SVt worksheet of the **Separate-Variance T.xls** workbook. This worksheet (see Figure E10.3) uses the TINV and TDIST functions in ways similar to their use in the pooled-variance worksheet (see Section E10.3). IF functions in cells B32 and B37 select which one of two values computed in a calculations area (not shown in Figure E10.3) to use. IF functions in cells

A28, A33, and A38 determine which one of two phrases will be displayed in those cells.

The worksheet contains entries based on the Table 10.1 BLK Cola weekly sales data. To adapt this worksheet to other problems, change, as is necessary, the hypothesized difference, level of significance, and the sample statistics of the two samples in cells B4, B5, B7:B9, and B11:B13.

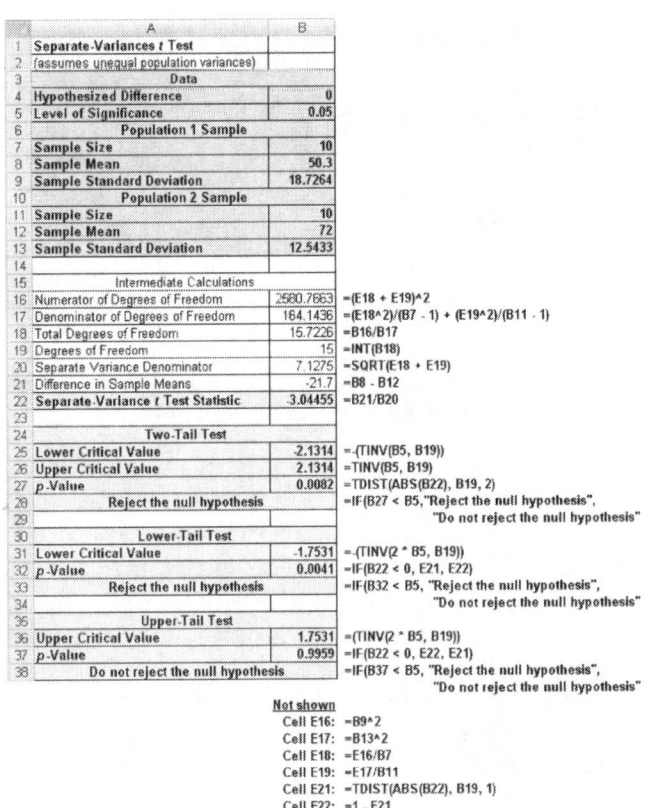

FIGURE E10.3

Separate-variance (SVt) worksheet

E10.6 Using the Paired *t* Test (unsummarized data)

For unsummarized data, you perform the paired *t* test by using the ToolPak t-Test: Paired Two Sample for Mean procedure. (There is no equivalent procedure for summarized data in Microsoft Excel.)

Open to the worksheet containing the unsummarized data for the two samples. Select **Tools → Data Analysis** (Excel 97–2003) or **Data → Data Analysis** (Excel 2007). Then select **t-Test: Paired Two Sample for Means** from the **Data Analysis** list and click **OK**. In the procedure's dialog box (shown at the top of page 436), enter the cell range of one sample as the **Variable 1 Range** and the cell range of the other sample as the **Variable 2 Range**. Enter the

Hypothesized Mean Difference, click **Labels**, and click **OK**. Figure 10.11 on page 407 shows the results for the Table 10.4 car mileage data.

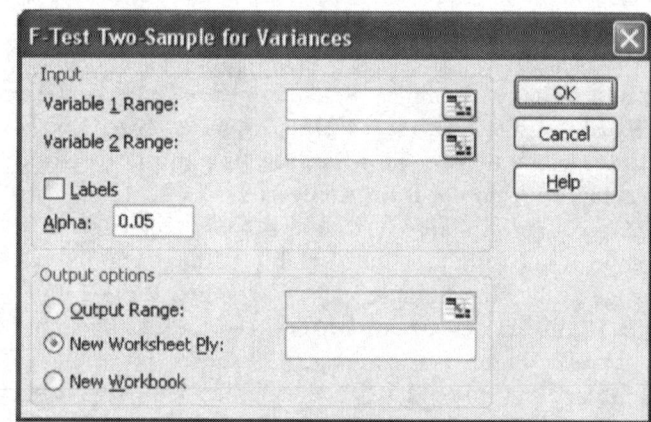

E10.7 Using the *Z* Test for the Difference Between Two Proportions

For summarized data, you perform the *Z* test for the difference between two proportions by making entries in either the **ZTP_TT** or **ZTP_All** worksheets of the `Z Two Proportions.xls` workbook. These worksheets use the **NORMSINV**(*P<X*) function to determine the lower and upper critical values and use the **NORMSDIST**(*Z value*) function to compute the *p*-values from the *Z* value calculated in cell B12. IF functions in cell A24 and in A29 and A34 determine which one of two phrases will be displayed in those cells.

The **ZTP_TT** worksheet (see Figure 10.17 on page 416) applies the two-tail *Z* test to the Section 10.3 guest satisfaction example. The **ZTP_All** worksheet includes the two-tail test, the upper one-tail test, and the lower one-tail test on one worksheet and contains a confidence interval estimate of the difference between the two proportions. To adapt these worksheets to other problems, enter the hypothesized difference, level of significance, and the number of items of interest and sample size for each sample in cells B4, B5, B7, B8, B10, and B11, as is necessary.

E10.8 Using the *F* Test for the Difference Between Two Variances (unsummarized data)

For unsummarized data, you use the *F* test for the difference between two variances by using the ToolPak F Test Two-Sample for Variances procedure.

Open to the worksheet containing the unsummarized data for the two samples. Select **Tools** → **Data Analysis** (Excel 97–2003) or **Data** → **Data Analysis** (Excel 2007). Then select **F Test Two-Sample for Variances** from the **Data Analysis** list and click **OK**. In the procedure's dialog box (shown below), enter the cell range of one sample as the **Variable 1 Range** and the cell range of the other sample as the **Variable 2 Range**. Click **Labels** and click **OK**. Results appear on a new worksheet. Figure 10.19 on page 422 shows results for the Table 10.1 BLK Cola weekly sales data.

E10.9 Using the *F* Test for the Difference Between Two Variances (summarized data)

For summarized data, you perform the *F* test for the difference between two variances by making entries in the **F Two Variances** worksheet of the `F Two Variances.xls` workbook.

	A	B	
1	F Test for Differences in Two Variances		
2			
3	**Data**		
4	Level of Significance	0.05	
5	**Larger-Variance Sample**		
6	Sample Size	10	
7	Sample Standard Deviation	18.7264	
8	**Smaller-Variance Sample**		
9	Sample Size	10	
10	Sample Standard Deviation	12.543	
11			
12	**Intermediate Calculations**		
13	F Test Statistic	2.2290	=B7^2/B10^2
14	Population 1 Sample Degrees of Freedom	9	=B6 - 1
15	Population 2 Sample Degrees of Freedom	9	=B9 - 1
16			
17	**Two-Tail Test**		
18	Upper Critical Value	4.0260	=FINV(B4/2, B14, B15)
19	*p*-Value	0.2482	=2 * E17
20	Do not reject the null hypothesis		=IF(B20 < B4, "Reject the null hypothesis", "Do not reject the null hypothesis")
21			
22	**Upper-Tail Test**		
23	Upper Critical Value	3.1789	=FINV(B4, B14, B15)
24	*p*-Value	0.1241	=E17
25	Do not reject the null hypothesis		=IF(B24 < B4, "Reject the null hypothesis", "Do not reject the null hypothesis")

Not shown
Cell E17: =FDIST(B13, B14, B15)

FIGURE E10.4
F Two Variances worksheet

The worksheet uses the **FINV(*upper-tailed* p-*value*, *numerator degrees of freedom, denominator degrees of freedom*)** function, in which ***upper-tailed* p-*value*** is the probability that F will be greater than the value, to compute the upper and lower critical values and **FDIST(F-*test statistic, numerator degrees of freedom, denominator degrees of freedom*)** function to compute the *p*-values.

The worksheet (shown in Figure E10.4) applies the F test to the Section 10.4 BLK Cola weekly sales example. Because sample 1 has been defined as the sample with the

larger variance, a lower-tail test section is unnecessary in this worksheet.

To adapt this worksheet to other problems, change the level of significance and the sample statistics for the two population samples in the tinted cells B4, B6, B7, B9, and B10. Should you inadvertently enter the data of the sample with the largest standard deviation as the "smaller-variance sample," IF functions in cells A28 and A29 (not shown in Figure E10.4) will display messages asking you to review your entries.

Appendix P10
Using PHStat2 for Two-Sample Tests

P10.1 Stacking and Unstacking Data

Specific PHStat2 or ToolPak procedures or Excel worksheets for analyses involving two or more samples will require that your data be arranged either as stacked or unstacked data.

To stack data, use **PHStat → Data Preparation → Stack Data.** This procedure places the data of the **Unstacked Data Cell Range** into a new worksheet containing two columns, one for the sample labels, the other for the data. The **Unstacked Data Cell Range** must be a contiguous multiple-column cell range in which each column contains the data of a sample.

of the samples. The **Grouping Variable Cell Range** must be a single-column cell range containing the sample labels and the **Stacked Data Cell Range** must be a single-column cell range containing the data.

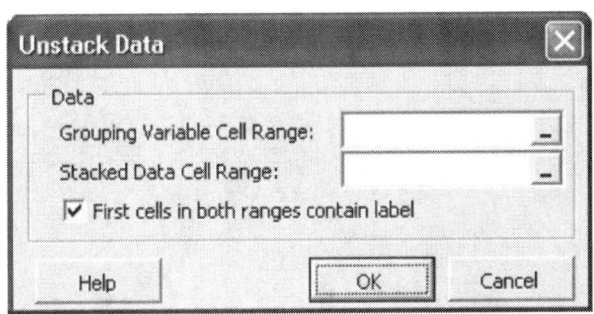

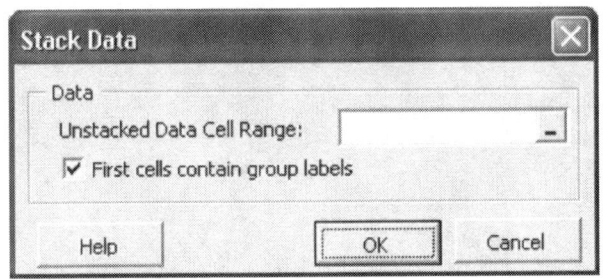

To unstack data, use **PHStat → Data Preparation → Unstack Data.** This procedure places data into a new worksheet in which each column contains the data for one

P10.2 Using the Pooled-Variance t Test

To perform the pooled-variance *t* test, use **PHStat → Two-Sample Tests → Pooled-Variance t Test.** This procedure creates a worksheet similar to Figure E10.1 on page 434, based on the test option and the hypothesized difference, level of significance, and the sample statistics values that you specify. If you click **Confidence Interval Estimate**, the worksheet will also include a confidence interval estimate in columns D and E (shown in Figure E10.2 on page 434).

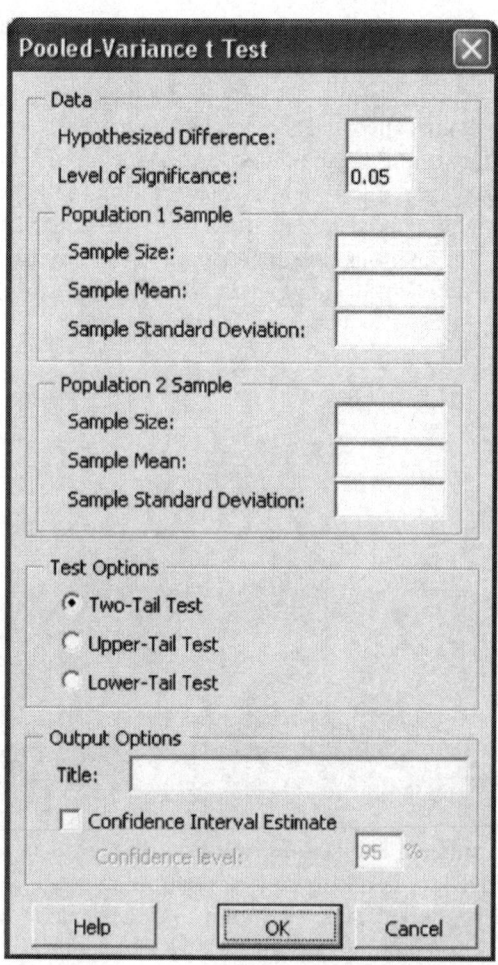

P10.3 Using the Separate-Variance *t* Test

To perform the separate-variance *t* test, use **PHStat →
Two-Sample Tests → Separate-Variance t Test**. This procedure creates a worksheet similar to Figure E10.3 on page
435, based on the test option and the hypothesized difference, level of significance, and the sample statistics values
that you specify.

P10.4 Using the *Z* Test for the Difference Between Two Proportions

To perform the *Z* test for the differences in two proportions, use **PHStat → Two-Sample Tests → Z Test for the Differences in Two Proportions**. This procedure creates a worksheet similar to Figure 10.17 on page 416, based on the test option and the null hypothesis, level of significance, number of items of interest, and sample size values that you specify.

P10.5 Using the *F* Test for the Difference Between Two Variances

To perform the *F* test for the difference between two variances, use **PHStat → Two-Sample Tests → F Test for the Differences in Two Variances**. This procedure creates a worksheet similar to Figure E10.3 on page 435, based on the level of significance, sample statistics values, and the test option that you specify.

Appendix M10
Using Minitab for Two-Sample Tests

M10.1 Stacking and Unstacking Data

Unsummarized data for two (or more) samples can be entered as **stacked** or **unstacked** worksheet data. As first mentioned in Section M2.1 on page 81, in a stacked arrangement, all the values for a variable appear in a single column next to a column that identifies the sample to which individual values belong. In an unstacked arrangement, the values for each sample appear in separate columns.

Although most Minitab procedures accept either stacked or unstacked data, you may discover situations when you need to change your data arrangement. To change stacked data into its unstacked equivalent, select **Data → Unstack Columns**. In the Unstack Columns dialog box enter the column that identifies the sample in the **Using subscripts in** box. Likewise, to stack unstacked data, select **Data → Stack → Columns** and enter the columns to be stacked in the **Stack the following columns** box. The `Cola.mtw` worksheet illustrates both the stacked and unstacked arrangement of the BLK Cola weekly sales data of Table 10.1 on page 392.

M10.2 Using the *t* Test for the Difference Between Two Means

To illustrate the *t* test of the difference in two means:

1. Open the `Cola.mtw` worksheet.
2. Select **Stat → Basic Statistics → 2-Sample t**.

In the 2-Sample t (Test and Confidence Interval) dialog box (see Figure M10.1):

3. Click **Samples in one column** and enter **Sales** in the **Samples** box and **Display** in the **Subscripts** box. (If you had unstacked data, you would click **Samples in different columns** and enter the column names in the **First** and **Second** boxes.)
4. Click **Assume equal variances** to perform the pooled-variance *t* test. (To perform the separate-variance *t* test, leave this unchecked.)
5. Click **Options**.

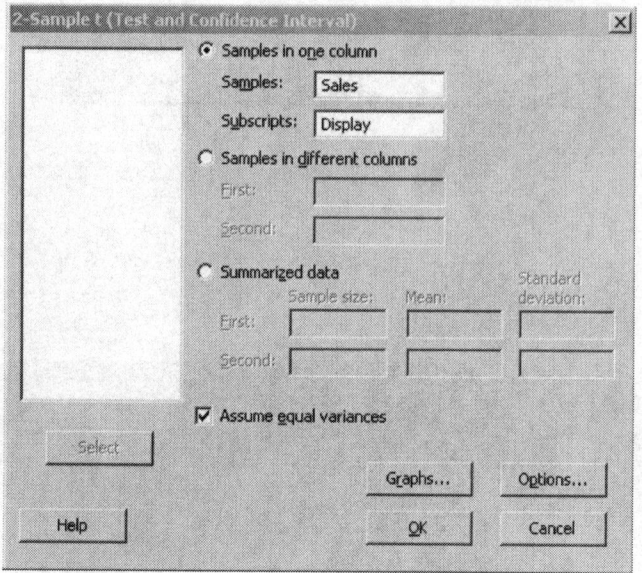

FIGURE M10.1
2-Sample t (Test and Confidence Interval) dialog box

In the 2-Sample t - Options dialog box (see Figure M10.2):

6. Leave the **Confidence level** and **Test difference** values unchanged.

7. Select **not equal** from the **Alternative** drop-down list to perform the two-tail test. (To perform a one-tail test, select **less than** or **greater than**.)
8. Click **OK**.

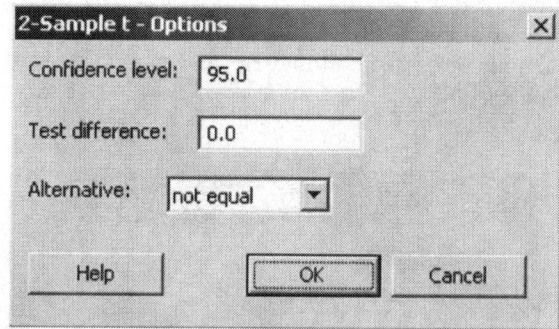

FIGURE M10.2
2-Sample t - Options dialog box

9. Back in the 2-Sample t (Test and Confidence Interval) dialog box, click **Graphs**.
10. In the 2-Sample t - Graphs dialog box (not shown), click **Boxplots of data** and then click **OK**.
11. Back in the 2-Sample t (Test and Confidence Interval) dialog box, click **OK**.

To get the results in Figure 10.4 on page 393, you need to unstack the data.

1. Select **Data → Unstack Columns**.
2. Enter **Sales** in the **Unstack the data in** box.
3. Enter **Display** in the **Using subscripts in** box.
4. Click **After last column in use**.
5. Click **OK**.
6. Rename the **Sales_Normal** column as **Normal** and rename the **Sales_End_Aisle** column as **EndAisle**. (This will simplify entering their names.)

Then repeat the 11-step instructions, changing step 3 as follows: Click **Samples in different columns**. Enter **Normal** in the **First** box and enter **EndAisle** in the **Second** box.

M10.3 Using the Paired *t* Test

To illustrate the paired *t* test,

1. Open the `AAAMileage.mtw` worksheet.
2. Select **Stat → Basic Statistics → Paired t**.

In the Paired *t* (Test and Confidence Interval) dialog box (see Figure M10.3):

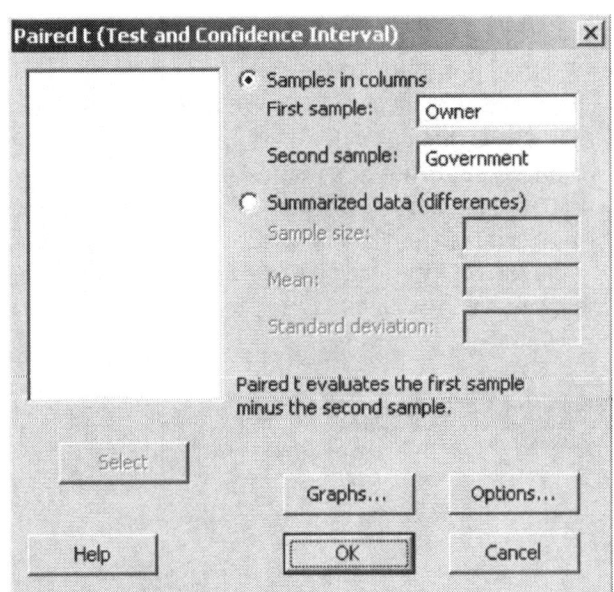

FIGURE M10.3

Paired t (Test and Confidence Interval) dialog box

3. Click **Samples in columns**.
4. Enter **Owner** in the **First sample** box.
5. Enter **Government** in the **Second sample** box.
6. Click **Options**.

In the Paired t - Options dialog box (see Figure M10.4),

7. Leave the **Confidence level** and **Test mean** values unchanged.
8. Select **not equal** from the **Alternative** drop-down list to perform the two-tail test shown on page 407.
9. Click **OK**.
10. Back in the Paired t (Test and Confidence Interval) dialog box, click **Graphs**.

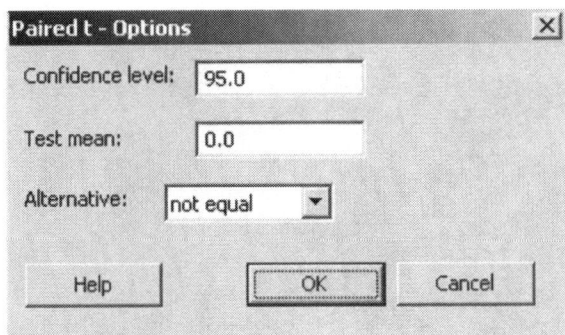

FIGURE M10.4

Paired t - Options dialog box

In the Paired t - Graphs dialog box (see Figure M10.5),

11. Click **Boxplot of differences**.
12. Click **OK**.
13. Back in the Paired t (Test and Confidence Interval) dialog box, click **OK**.

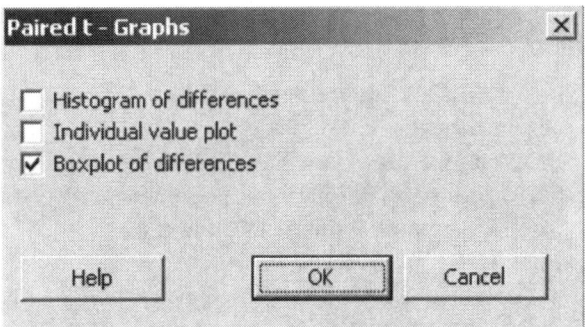

FIGURE M10.5

Paired t - Graphs dialog box

M10.4 Using the *Z* Test for the Difference between Two Proportions

To illustrate the test for the difference between two proportions, using the example shown in Figure 10.18 on page 416,

1. Select **Stat → Basic Statistics → 2 Proportions**.

In the 2 Proportions (Test and Confidence Interval) dialog box (see Figure M10.6),

2. Click **Summarized data**.
3. In the **First** row, enter **163** in the **Events** box and **227** in the **Trials** box.
4. In the **Second** row, enter **154** in the **Events** box and **262** in the **Trials** box.
5. Click **Options**.

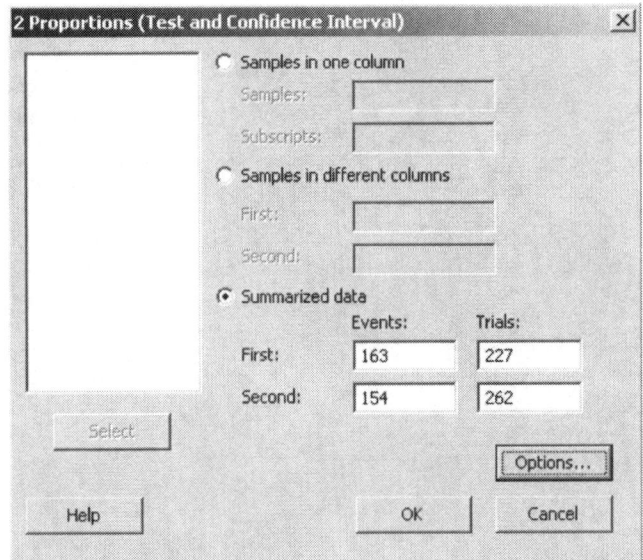

FIGURE M10.6

2 Proportions (Test and Confidence Interval) dialog box

In the 2 Proportions - Options dialog box (see Figure M10.7),

6. Leave the **Confidence level** and **Test difference** values unchanged.
7. Select **not equal** from the **Alternative** drop-down list to perform the two-tail test presented on page 415.
8. Click **Use pooled estimate of p for test**.
9. Click **OK**.
10. Back in the 2-Proportions (Test and Confidence Interval) dialog box click **OK**.

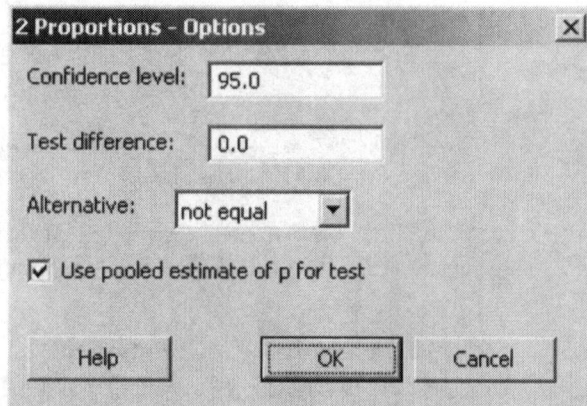

FIGURE M10.7
2 Proportions - Options dialog box

M10.5 Using the *F* Test for the Difference Between Two Variances

To illustrate the *F* test of the difference in two variances as shown in Figure 10.20 on page 422,

1. Open the `Cola.mtw` worksheet.
2. Select **Stat → Basic Statistics → 2 Variances**.

In the 2 Variances dialog box (see Figure M10.8),

3. Click **Samples in one column**.
4. Enter **Sales** in the **Samples** box, and enter **Display** in the **Subscripts** box. (If you have unstacked data, click **Samples in different columns** and enter the names of the two columns in the **First** and **Second** boxes. If you have summarized data instead of the actual data, click **Summarized data** and enter the sample size and variance for each sample.)
5. Click **OK**.

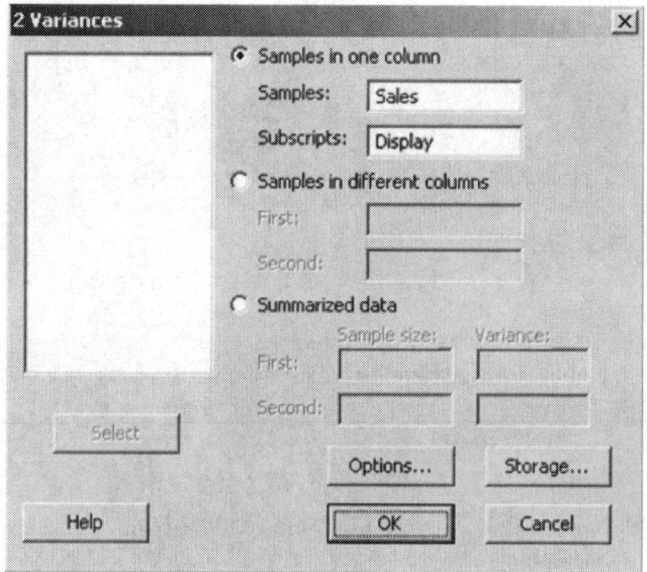

FIGURE M10.8
2 Variances dialog box

APPENDICES

A. REVIEW OF ARITHMETIC, ALGEBRA, AND LOGARITHMS

A.1   RULES FOR ARITHMETIC OPERATIONS

RULE	EXAMPLE
1. $a + b = c$ and $b + a = c$	$2 + 1 = 3$ and $1 + 2 = 3$
2. $a + (b + c) = (a + b) + c$	$5 + (7 + 4) = (5 + 7) + 4 = 16$
3. $a - b = c$ but $b - a \neq c$	$9 - 7 = 2$ but $7 - 9 \neq 2$
4. $(a)(b) = (b)(a)$	$(7)(6) = (6)(7) = 42$
5. $(a)(b + c) = ab + ac$	$(2)(3 + 5) = (2)(3) + (2)(5) = 16$
6. $a \div b \neq b \div a$	$12 \div 3 \neq 3 \div 12$
7. $\dfrac{a+b}{c} = \dfrac{a}{c} + \dfrac{b}{c}$	$\dfrac{7+3}{2} = \dfrac{7}{2} + \dfrac{3}{2} = 5$
8. $\dfrac{a}{b+c} \neq \dfrac{a}{b} + \dfrac{a}{c}$	$\dfrac{3}{4+5} \neq \dfrac{3}{4} + \dfrac{3}{5}$
9. $\dfrac{1}{a} + \dfrac{1}{b} = \dfrac{b+a}{ab}$	$\dfrac{1}{3} + \dfrac{1}{5} = \dfrac{5+3}{(3)(5)} = \dfrac{8}{15}$
10. $\left(\dfrac{a}{b}\right)\left(\dfrac{c}{d}\right) = \left(\dfrac{ac}{bd}\right)$	$\left(\dfrac{2}{3}\right)\left(\dfrac{6}{7}\right) = \left(\dfrac{(2)(6)}{(3)(7)}\right) = \dfrac{12}{21}$
11. $\dfrac{a}{b} \div \dfrac{c}{d} = \dfrac{ad}{bc}$	$\dfrac{5}{8} \div \dfrac{3}{7} = \left(\dfrac{(5)(7)}{(8)(3)}\right) = \dfrac{35}{24}$

A.2   RULES FOR ALGEBRA: EXPONENTS AND SQUARE ROOTS

RULE	EXAMPLE
1. $(X^a)(X^b) = X^{a+b}$	$(4^2)(4^3) = 4^5$
2. $(X^a)^b = X^{ab}$	$(2^2)^3 = 2^6$
3. $(X^a/X^b) = X^{a-b}$	$\dfrac{3^5}{3^3} = 3^2$
4. $\dfrac{X^a}{X^a} = X^0 = 1$	$\dfrac{3^4}{3^4} = 3^0 = 1$
5. $\sqrt{XY} = \sqrt{X}\sqrt{Y}$	$\sqrt{(25)(4)} = \sqrt{25}\sqrt{4} = 10$
6. $\sqrt{\dfrac{X}{Y}} = \dfrac{\sqrt{X}}{\sqrt{Y}}$	$\sqrt{\dfrac{16}{100}} = \dfrac{\sqrt{16}}{\sqrt{100}} = 0.40$

A.3   RULES FOR LOGARITHMS

Base 10

Log is the symbol used for base-10 logarithms:

RULE	EXAMPLE
1. $\log(10^a) = a$	$\log(100) = \log(10^2) = 2$
2. If $\log(a) = b$, then $a = 10^b$	If $\log(a) = 2$, then $a = 10^2 = 100$
3. $\log(ab) = \log(a) + \log(b)$	$\log(100) = \log[(10)(10)] = \log(10) + \log(10) = 1 + 1 = 2$
4. $\log(a^b) = (b)\log(a)$	$\log(1{,}000) = \log(10^3) = (3)\log(10) = (3)(1) = 3$
5. $\log(a/b) = \log(a) - \log(b)$	$\log(100) = \log(1{,}000/10)$
	$= \log(1{,}000) - \log(10) = 3 - 1 = 2$

EXAMPLE

Take the base-10 logarithm of each side of the following equation:

$$Y = \beta_0 \beta_1^X \varepsilon$$

SOLUTION: Apply rules 3 and 4:

$$\log(Y) = \log(\beta_0 \beta_1^X \varepsilon)$$

$$= \log(\beta_0) + \log(\beta_1^X) + \log(\varepsilon)$$

$$= \log(\beta_0) + (X)\log(\beta_1) + \log(\varepsilon)$$

Base e

ln is the symbol used for base e logarithms, commonly referred to as natural logarithms. e is Euler's number, and $e \cong 2.718282$:

RULE	EXAMPLE
1. $\ln(e^a) = a$	$\ln(7.389056) = \ln(e^2) = 2$
2. If $\ln(a) = b$, then $a = e^b$	If $\ln(a) = 2$, then $a = e^2 = 7.389056$
3. $\ln(ab) = \ln(a) + \ln(b)$	$\ln(100) = \ln[(10)(10)]$
	$\ln(10) + \ln(10) = 2.302585 + 2.302585 = 4.605170$
4. $\ln(a^b) = (b)\ln(a)$	$\ln(1{,}000) = \ln(10^3) = 3\ln(10) = 3(2.302585) = 6.907755$
5. $\ln(a/b) = \ln(a) - \ln(b)$	$\ln(100) = \ln(1{,}000/10) = \ln(1{,}000) - \ln(10)$
	$= 6.907755 - 2.302585 = 4.605170$

EXAMPLE

Take the base e logarithm of each side of the following equation:

$$Y = \beta_0 \beta_1^X \varepsilon$$

SOLUTION: Apply rules 3 and 4:

$$\ln(Y) = \ln(\beta_0 \beta_1^X \varepsilon)$$

$$= \ln(\beta_0) + \ln(\beta_1^X) + \ln(\varepsilon)$$

$$= \ln(\beta_0) + (X)\ln(\beta_1) + \ln(\varepsilon)$$

B.   SUMMATION NOTATION, STATISTICAL SYMBOLS, AND GREEK ALPHABET

B.1   SUMMATION NOTATION

The symbol Σ, the Greek capital letter sigma, is used to denote "taking the sum of." Consider a set of n values for variable X. The expression $\sum_{i=1}^{n} X_i$ means that these n values are to be added together. Thus:

$$\sum_{i=1}^{n} X_i = X_1 + X_2 + X_3 + \cdots + X_n$$

The following problem illustrates the use of summation notation. Consider five values of a variable X: $X_1 = 2$, $X_2 = 0$, $X_3 = -1$, $X_4 = 5$, and $X_5 = 7$. Thus:

$$\sum_{i=1}^{5} X_i = X_1 + X_2 + X_3 + X_4 + X_5 = 2 + 0 + (-1) + 5 + 7 = 13$$

In statistics, the squared values of a variable are often summed. Thus:

$$\sum_{i=1}^{n} X_i^2 = X_1^2 + X_2^2 + X_3^2 + \cdots + X_n^2$$

and, in the example above:

$$\sum_{i=1}^{5} X_i^2 = X_1^2 + X_2^2 + X_3^2 + X_4^2 + X_5^2$$

$$= 2^2 + 0^2 + (-1)^2 + 5^2 + 7^2$$

$$= 4 + 0 + 1 + 25 + 49$$

$$= 79$$

$\sum_{i=1}^{n} X_i^2$, the summation of the squares, is *not* the same as $\left(\sum_{i=1}^{n} X_i \right)^2$, the square of the sum:

$$\sum_{i=1}^{n} X_i^2 \neq \left(\sum_{i=1}^{n} X_i \right)^2$$

In the example given earlier, the summation of squares is equal to 79. This is not equal to the square of the sum, which is $13^2 = 169$.

Another frequently used operation involves the summation of the product. Consider two variables, X and Y, each having n values. Then:

$$\sum_{i=1}^{n} X_i Y_i = X_1 Y_1 + X_2 Y_2 + X_3 Y_3 + \cdots + X_n Y_n$$

Continuing with the previous example, suppose there is a second variable, Y, whose five values are $Y_1 = 1$, $Y_2 = 3$, $Y_3 = -2$, $Y_4 = 4$, and $Y_5 = 3$. Then,

$$\sum_{i=1}^{n} X_i Y_i = X_1 Y_1 + X_2 Y_2 + X_3 Y_3 + X_4 Y_4 + X_5 Y_5$$

$$= (2)(1) + (0)(3) + (-1)(-2) + (5)(4) + (7)(3)$$

$$= 2 + 0 + 2 + 20 + 21$$

$$= 45$$

In computing $\sum_{i=1}^{n} X_i Y_i$, realize that the first value of X is multiplied by the first value of Y, the second value of X is multiplied by the second value of Y, and so on. These products are then summed in order to compute the desired result. However, the summation of products is *not* equal to the product of the individual sums:

$$\sum_{i=1}^{n} X_i Y_i \neq \left(\sum_{i=1}^{n} X_i \right) \left(\sum_{i=1}^{n} Y_i \right)$$

In this example,

$$\sum_{i=1}^{5} X_i = 13$$

and

$$\sum_{i=1}^{5} Y_i = 1 + 3 + (-2) + 4 + 3 = 9$$

so that

$$\left(\sum_{i=1}^{5} X_i \right) \left(\sum_{i=1}^{5} Y_i \right) = (13)(9) = 117$$

However,

$$\sum_{i=1}^{5} X_i Y_i = 45$$

The following table summarizes these results:

VALUE	X_i	Y_i	$X_i Y_i$
1	2	1	2
2	0	3	0
3	−1	−2	2
4	5	4	20
5	7	3	21
	$\sum_{i=1}^{5} X_i = 13$	$\sum_{i=1}^{5} Y_i = 9$	$\sum_{i=1}^{5} X_i Y_i = 45$

RULE 1 The summation of the values of two variables is equal to the sum of the values of each summed variable:

$$\sum_{i=1}^{n}(X_i + Y_i) = \sum_{i=1}^{n}X_i + \sum_{i=1}^{n}Y_i$$

Thus,

$$\sum_{i=1}^{5}(X_i + Y_i) = (2+1) + (0+3) + (-1+(-2)) + (5+4) + (7+3)$$

$$= 3 + 3 + (-3) + 9 + 10$$

$$= 22$$

$$\sum_{i=1}^{5}X_i + \sum_{i=1}^{5}Y_i = 13 + 9 = 22$$

RULE 2 The summation of a difference between the values of two variables is equal to the difference between the summed values of the variables:

$$\sum_{i=1}^{n}(X_i - Y_i) = \sum_{i=1}^{n}X_i - \sum_{i=1}^{n}Y_i$$

Thus,

$$\sum_{i=1}^{5}(X_i - Y_i) = (2-1) + (0-3) + (-1-(-2)) + (5-4) + (7-3)$$

$$= 1 + (-3) + 1 + 1 + 4$$

$$= 4$$

$$\sum_{i=1}^{5}X_i - \sum_{i=1}^{5}Y_i = 13 - 9 = 4$$

RULE 3 The sum of a constant times a variable is equal to that constant times the sum of the values of the variable:

$$\sum_{i=1}^{n}cX_i = c\sum_{i=1}^{n}X_i$$

where c is a constant. Thus, if $c = 2$,

$$\sum_{i=1}^{5}cX_i = \sum_{i=1}^{5}2X_i = (2)(2) + (2)(0) + (2)(-1) + (2)(5) + (2)(7)$$

$$= 4 + 0 + (-2) + 10 + 14$$

$$= 26$$

$$c\sum_{i=1}^{5}X_i = 2\sum_{i=1}^{5}X_i = (2)(13) = 26$$

RULE 4 A constant summed n times will be equal to n times the value of the constant.

$$\sum_{i=1}^{n} c = nc$$

where c is a constant. Thus, if the constant $c = 2$ is summed 5 times,

$$\sum_{i=1}^{5} c = 2 + 2 + 2 + 2 + 2 = 10$$

$$nc = (5)(2) = 10$$

EXAMPLE

Suppose there are six values for the variables X and Y, such that $X_1 = 2$, $X_2 = 1$, $X_3 = 5$, $X_4 = -3$, $X_5 = 1$, $X_6 = -2$, and $Y_1 = 4$, $Y_2 = 0$, $Y_3 = -1$, $Y_4 = 2$, $Y_5 = 7$, and $Y_6 = -3$. Compute each of the following:

(a) $\sum_{i=1}^{6} X_i$

(f) $\sum_{i=1}^{6} (X_i + Y_i)$

(b) $\sum_{i=1}^{6} Y_i$

(g) $\sum_{i=1}^{6} (X_i - Y_i)$

(c) $\sum_{i=1}^{6} X_i^2$

(h) $\sum_{i=1}^{6} (X_i - 3Y_i + 2X_i^2)$

(d) $\sum_{i=1}^{6} Y_i^2$

(i) $\sum_{i=1}^{6} (cX_i)$, where $c = -1$

(e) $\sum_{i=1}^{6} X_i Y_i$

(j) $\sum_{i=1}^{6} (X_i - 3Y_i + c)$, where $c = +3$

ANSWERS
(a) 4 (b) 9 (c) 44 (d) 79 (e) 10 (f) 13 (g) −5 (h) 65 (i) −4 (j) −5

References

1. Bashaw, W. L., *Mathematics for Statistics* (New York: Wiley, 1969).
2. Lanzer, P., *Basic Math: Fractions, Decimals, Percents* (Hicksville, NY: Video Aided Instruction, 2006).
3. Levine, D., *The MBA Primer: Business Statistics* (Cincinnati, OH: Southwestern Publishing, 2000).
4. Levine, D., *Statistics* (Hicksville, NY: Video Aided Instruction, 2006).
5. Shane, H., *Algebra 1* (Hicksville, NY: Video Aided Instruction, 2006).

B.2   STATISTICAL SYMBOLS

+ add   × multiply

− subtract   ÷ divide

= equal to   ≠ not equal to

≅ approximately equal to

> greater than   < less than

≥ greater than or equal to   ≤ less than or equal to

B.3   GREEK ALPHABET

GREEK LETTER		LETTER NAME	ENGLISH EQUIVALENT	GREEK LETTER		LETTER NAME	ENGLISH EQUIVALENT
A	α	Alpha	a	N	ν	Nu	n
B	β	Beta	b	Ξ	ξ	Xi	x
Γ	γ	Gamma	g	O	o	Omicron	ŏ
Δ	δ	Delta	d	Π	π	Pi	p
E	ε	Epsilon	ē	P	ρ	Rho	r
Z	ζ	Zeta	z	Σ	σ	Sigma	s
H	η	Eta	ē	T	τ	Tau	t
Θ	θ	Theta	th	Y	υ	Upsilon	u
I	ι	Iota	i	Φ	φ	Phi	ph
K	κ	Kappa	k	X	χ	Chi	ch
Λ	λ	Lambda	l	Ψ	ψ	Psi	ps
M	μ	Mu	m	Ω	ω	Omega	ō

C.   BASIC COMPUTING SKILLS

C.1   INTRODUCTION

Using Microsoft Excel or Minitab with this book requires certain basic computing skills. If you have ever sent an instant message, surfed the Web, played music or games through a computer, or written word-processed assignments, you probably have already mastered these skills required to use the end-of-chapter appendices. If you already have the basic computing skills that this book requires, this appendix will introduce you to the vocabulary and conventions used in this book to present computer-related operations.

C.2   MOUSING OPERATIONS

You make extensive use of your mouse (or equivalent pointing device) to move an onscreen mouse pointer as you operate Excel or Minitab. Microsoft Windows expects your mouse to have one mouse button designated as the primary button (this is typically the left button) and another button designated as the secondary button (typically the right button). Throughout the appendices, you will need to distinguish among the following seven mousing verbs that involve moving the mouse and one of these two buttons:

Click, Select, and **Clear**   These verbs tell you to move the mouse pointer over the object of the instruction and press the primary button. Click suggests that an action is completed when you press the primary button, as in "click the **OK** button." Select suggests that you will be choosing or highlighting a choice from an onscreen list *or* opening a new onscreen list or submenu. Selecting something is typically followed by clicking something else, as in "select the file name and then click **OK**." Clear is the click operation that clears the checkmark in an onscreen check box (see Figure C.2 on page 900).

Double-click This verb tells you to move the **mouse pointer** over an object and click the primary button twice in rapid succession. You double-click program icons on the Windows Desktop to open programs, and you double-click onscreen objects such as parts of a chart to further edit or format them.

Right-click This verb tells you to move the mouse pointer over an object and click the secondary button. You right-click onscreen objects to display a **shortcut menu** of commands from which you click or select an action.

Drag and **Drag-and-drop** These verbs represent a two-step process. In the first step, you move the mouse pointer over an object and press and hold down the primary button while you move the mouse pointer somewhere else. In the second step, you move the mouse pointer somewhere else and release the primary button. Drag suggests that you are selecting part of a whole; drag-and-drop suggests that you are moving an entire whole. You drag the mouse to select contiguous parts of a worksheet or to move or resize the borders of onscreen windows, but you drag-and-drop a Windows Desktop icon to move it from one part of the screen to another.

C.3   WINDOW ELEMENTS

The "windows" in Microsoft Windows are onscreen rectangular frames that divide the screen. When you open a program, Microsoft Windows displays a program window, the typical elements of which are shown in Figures C.1 and C.2 and explained in Table C.1. As you use a program, the program will display **dialog boxes**, specialized windows that contain messages or ask you to make entries and selections. Figure C.3 shows two examples of dialog boxes and the elements commonly found in all dialog boxes and explained in Table C.2.

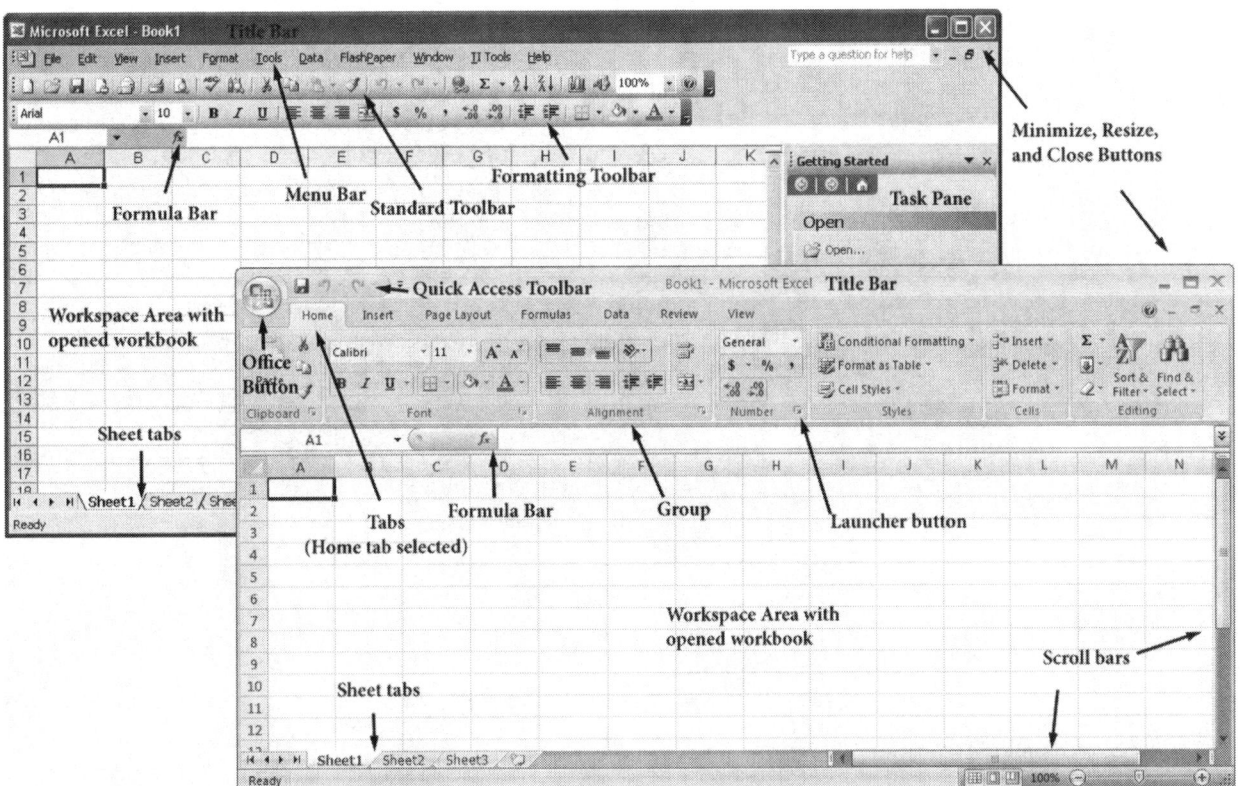

FIGURE C.1 Microsoft Excel 2003 and Microsoft Excel 2007 Program Windows

TABLE C.1

Program Window
Elements

Element	Function
Title bar	Displays the name of the program and contains the Minimize, Resize, and Close buttons for the program window. You drag and drop the title bar to reposition a program window on your screen.
Minimize, Resize, and Close buttons	Change the display of the program window. **Minimize** hides the window without closing the program, **Resize** permits you to change the size of the window, and **Close** removes the window from the screen and closes the program. A second set of these buttons that appear in Microsoft Excel perform the three actions for the currently active worksheet. (Similar buttons, obscured in Figure C.2, perform the same functions for the Minitab Session and Worksheet area.)
Menu Bar	The horizontal list of words at the top of the window that represent sets of commands. You select a menu bar word and typically reveal another list of command choices that either lead to some direct action, the display of a dialog box, or the display of another list of choices.
Toolbars	An array of clickable buttons that serve as shortcuts to program commands.
Task Pane	A closable window that lists clickable links that represent shortcuts to menu and toolbar operations (seen only in Excel 2002 and 2003).
Ribbon	Distinctive of Excel 2007, the Ribbon with its **Tabs** and **Tab Groups** performs the combined functions of a menu bar, task pane, and toolbars. Some tab groups contain **Launcher Buttons** that display dialog boxes, task panes, or **galleries**, illustrated sets of choices.
Office Button and Quick Access Toolbar	Other distinctive features of Excel 2007. The **Office Button** displays a menu of commonly issued commands similar to the File menu in other programs and gives you access to many Excel options settings. The **Quick Access Toolbar** (to the immediate right of the Office Button) displays shortcuts to commonly used commands.
Worksheet area	Displays the currently opened workbooks (Excel) or worksheets (Minitab). In Excel, this area also contains **Sheet tabs** on which you can double-click to go a specific sheet in a workbook. (Although you can open more than one Excel workbook or more than one Minitab worksheet at one time in a worksheet area, no instructions in this book will ever ask you to do so.)
Scroll bars	Allow you to travel horizontally or vertically through a worksheet to reveal parts that cannot otherwise be seen, for example, row 100.

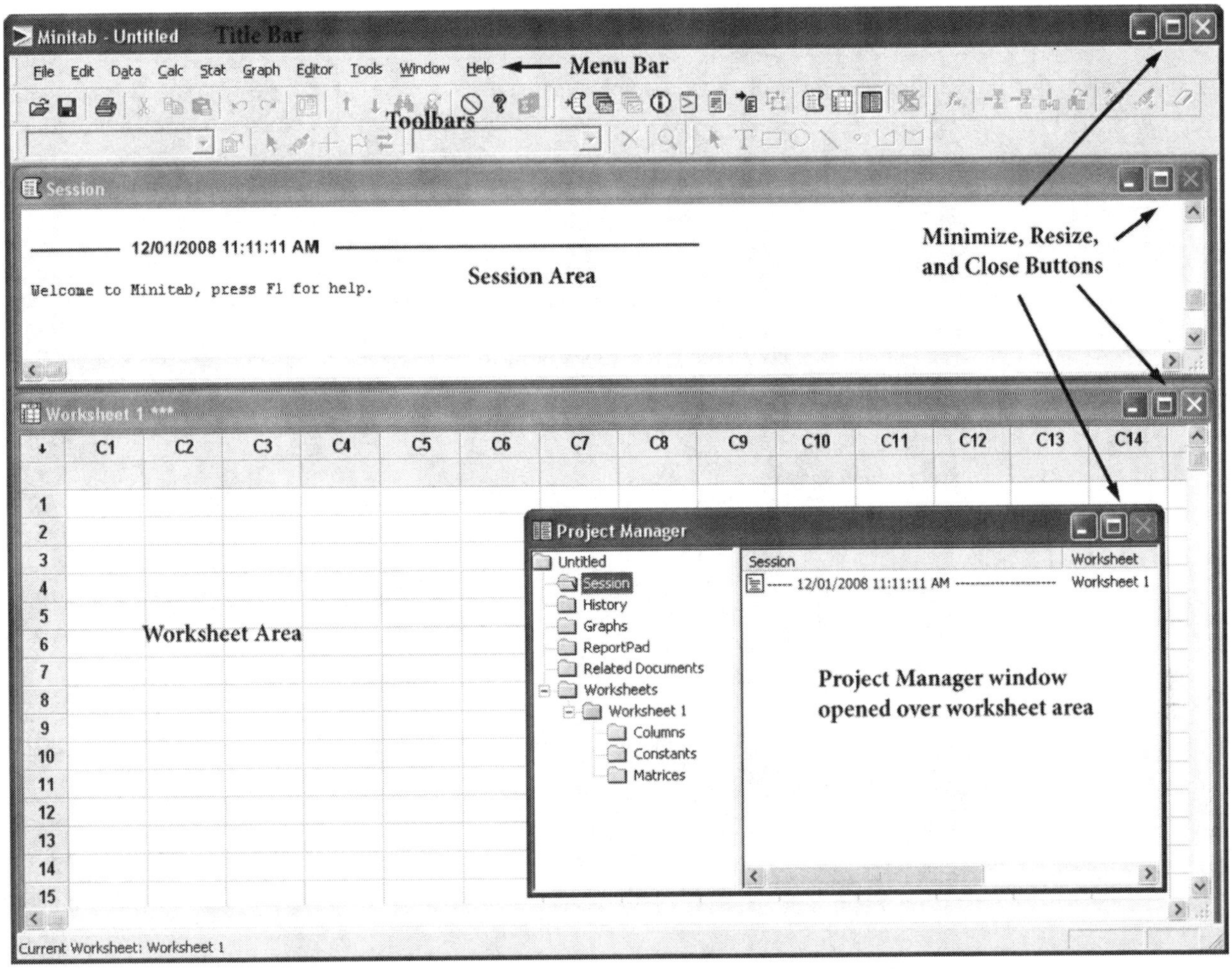

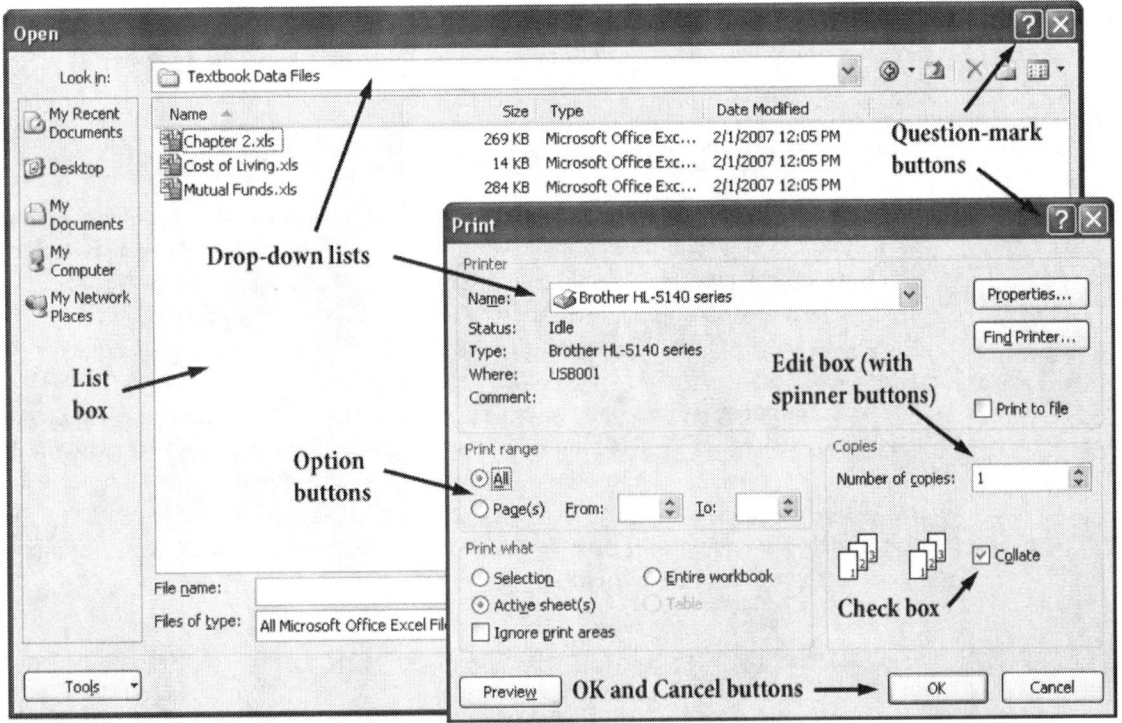

FIGURE C.2 Minitab 15 Program Windows

FIGURE C.3 Dialog box elements

TABLE C.2

Dialog Box Elements

Element	Function
Command buttons	Clickable areas that cause a program to take some action. Many dialog boxes contain an **OK button** that causes a program to take an action using the current entries and selections in the dialog box as well as a **Cancel button** that closes a dialog box and cancels the pending operation associated with the dialog box.
List boxes	Display lists of choices available to you. Should a list exceed the dimensions of a list box, you will see **scroll buttons** or **sliders** (not shown in Figure C.3) that you can click to reveal choices not currently displayed. In Minitab, you will frequently select an item from a list box and then press a command button to perform some action.
Drop-down lists	Display lists of choices when you click over them.
Edit boxes	Areas into which you type entries. Some edit boxes contain drop-down lists or **spinner buttons** that you can use to complete the entry. Excel edit boxes for cell ranges typically contain a button that allows you to drag the mouse over a cell range as an alternative to typing the cell range.
Option buttons	Present you with a set of mutually exclusive choices. When you click one option button, all the other option buttons in the set are cleared.
Check boxes	Present you with optional actions that are not mutually exclusive choices. Unlike with option buttons, clicking a check box does not affect the status of other check boxes, and more than one check box can be checked at a time. Clicking a check box that contains a checkmark **clears** the check box as discussed in Section C.2.
Question-mark buttons	Display help messages related to a dialog box. Dialog boxes that do not contain a question-mark button typically contain a command button labeled **Help** that performs this function. (Minitab dialog boxes contain only Help command buttons.)

C.4 USEFUL KEYS AND KEYSTROKE COMBINATIONS

In Microsoft Excel and Minitab, certain keystrokes and keystroke combinations (one or more keys held down as you press another key) represent useful shortcuts. For data entry, pressing the **Backspace** key when typing an entry erases typed characters to the left of the current position, one character at a time. Pressing the **Delete** key erases characters to the right of the cursor, one character at a time. Pressing either the **Enter** or **Tab** keys finalizes an entry typed into a worksheet cell.

For program functions, the **Esc** key cancels a dialog box or action and is often equivalent to clicking a dialog box's Cancel button. Pressing the combination **Ctrl+C** (while holding down the **Ctrl** key, press the **C** key) copies a worksheet entry and pressing **Crtl+V** can paste that copy into a second worksheet cell. Pressing the combinations **Ctrl+P** and **Ctrl+S** are shortcuts to printing and saving things, respectively. When all else fails, pressing **F1** (function key #1) usually displays the help system for the program you are using.

C.5 CONVENTIONS USED IN THIS BOOK

In its instructions for Microsoft Excel and Minitab, this book uses several typographic conventions. In the previous section, you have already been introduced to the convention used for a keystroke combination (e.g., **Ctrl+C**). Throughout this book, the targets of mousing operations are boldfaced, as in "Click **Labels** " or "Click **OK**." For dialog boxes that are divided into sub-titled areas or tabs, the book identifies the area or tab as in "click **All** in the **Page range** section" or "in the **Context** tab of the Help dialog box, click the first entry." When object names or labels can vary due to context, the book uses italics as a placeholder for a specific object, as in "Select *variable column*."

To describe a sequence of menu bar or ribbon selections, the book uses an arrow symbol to link selections. For example, when the book says, "**File → New**", first select File and then from the list of choices that appears, select New. ("**File → New**" would be a valid sequence in Excel 97–2003 and in Minitab; the equivalent Excel 2007 sequence would be "**Office Button → New**".) In the PHStat2 appendices, selection sequences are given relative to the PHStat menu, for example, as **PHStat → Descriptive Statistics → Boxplot**. If you use Excel 2007, you will need to click the **Add-Ins** ribbon tab first in order to use these selection sequences.

D. STUDENT CD-ROM CONTENTS

D.1 STUDENT CD-ROM OVERVIEW

The Student CD-ROM packaged with this book contains various resources to support your learning of statistics. You can use the small Windows "start" program included on the CD-ROM to copy and install the contents of the CD-ROM to your computer system or manually explore the CD-ROM contents.

The following CD-ROM folders contain learning resources used in this book.

Excel Data Files

Located in the **Browse** folder, the **Excel Data Files** folder contains the Microsoft Excel workbook files (with the extension .xls) used in the examples and problems in this text. A detailed list of the files appears in Section D.2.

Minitab Data Files

Located in the **Browse** folder, the **Minitab Data Files** folder contains the Minitab worksheet files (with the extension .mtw) used in the examples and problems in this text. A detailed list of the files appears in Section D.2.

Herald Case

Located in the **Browse** folder, the **Herald Case** folder contains the files for the "Managing the *Springville Herald*" case. (These files are also available online at the URLs listed in the case.)

Web Case

Located in the **Browse** folder, the **Web Case** folder contains the files for all the Web Cases that appear at the end of chapters. (These files are also available online at the URLs listed in each case.)

PHStat2

Located in the **Install** folder, the **PHStat2** folder contains the PHStat2 version 2.8 setup program. Run this program to install PHStat2 on a Windows PC. (For more information, see Appendix F and the **PHStat2 readme file** in the CD_ROM PHStat2 folder.)

Excel Workbooks

Located in the **Browse** folder, the Microsoft Excel workbooks folder contains the workbooks described and used in the Excel appendices sections. Copies of these files also appear in the Excel Data Files folder.

Visual Explorations in Statistics

Located in the **Browse** folder, Visual Explorations contains the files necessary to use the Visual Explorations in Statistics add-in workbook (`Visual Explorations.xla`). Before using this workbook, you should review the "Macro Security Issues" part of Section E1.8 on pages 20–21 and you may also want to consult the Appendix F FAQs. You can open and use the `Visual Explorations.xla` file directly from the CD in Microsoft Excel. If you prefer to use Visual Explorations without the CD present, copy the files `Visual Explorations.xla` and `Veshelp.chm` to the folder of your choice. (The `Veshelp.chm` file contains the orientation and help files for this add-in.)

Student CD-ROM Topics

Located in the **Browse** folder, the Student CD-ROM Topics folder contains supplemental textbook sections as electronic Adobe Reader files with the extension .pdf. You will need the Adobe Acrobat reader program installed on your system in order to read these sections. (In the Install folder is a version of the Adobe Reader that you can install on your system, if necessary.)

D.2 DATA FILE DESCRIPTIONS

The following presents in alphabetical order, a listing of the data files that can be found in both the **Excel Data Files** and **Minitab Data Files** folder. Elsewhere in this book, these file names appear in a special typeface, for example as Mutual Funds.

AAAMILEAGE Gasoline mileage from AAA members and combined city-highway driving gasoline mileage according to current government standards (Chapters 10, 12)

ACCESS Coded access read times (in msec), file size, programmer group, and buffer size (Chapter 11)

ACT ACT scores for type of course (rows) and length of course (columns) (Chapter 11)

ACT-ONEWAY ACT scores by groups (Chapter 11)

ADVERTISE Sales (in thousands of dollars), radio ads (in thousands of dollars), and newspaper ads (in thousands of dollars) for 22 cities (Chapters 14, 15)

ADVERTISING Sales (in millions of dollars) and newspaper ads (in thousands of dollars) (Chapter 15)

AMPHRS Capacity of batteries (Chapter 12)

ANGLE Subgroup number and angle (Chapter 18)

ANSCOMBE Data sets A, B, C, and D—each with 11 pairs of X and Y values (Chapter 13)

AUTO Miles per gallon, horsepower, and weight for a sample of 50 car models (Chapters 14, 15)

BANK1 Waiting time (in minutes) spent by a sample of 15 customers at a bank located in a commercial district (Chapters 3, 9, 10, 12)

BANK2 Waiting time (in minutes) spent by a sample of 15 customers at a bank located in a residential area (Chapters 3, 10, 12)

BANKING Banking preference and percentage (Chapter 2)

BANKTIME Waiting times of bank customers (Chapter 18)

BANKYIELD Yield for money market account and yield for five-year CD (Chapters 3, 10)

BASEBALL Team, attendance, high temperature on game day, winning percentage of home team, opponent's winning percentage, game played on Friday, Saturday, or Sunday (0 = no, 1 = yes), promotion held (0 = no, 1 = yes) (Chapter 19)

BASKET Year, price of bread, beef, eggs, and lettuce (Chapter 16)

BATTERYLIFE Life of a camera battery, in number of shots (Chapters 2, 3, 8)

BB2001 Team; league (0 = American, 1 = National); wins; earned run average; runs scored; hits allowed; walks allowed; saves; errors; average ticket prices; fan cost index; regular season gate receipts; local television, radio, and cable revenues; other local operating revenues; player compensation and benefits; national and other local expenses; and income from baseball operations (Chapter 19)

BB2006 Team, league (0 = American, 1 = National), wins, earned run average, runs scored, hits allowed, walks allowed, saves, errors, and cost of attending a game (Chapters 2, 6, 13, 14, 15)

BBREVENUE Team, value, and revenue (Chapter 13)

BEDBATH Year, coded year, and number of stores opened (Chapter 16)

BESTREST State, city, restaurant, hotel, cost (estimated price of dinner, including one drink and tip), and rating (1 to 100, with 1 the top-rated restaurant) (Chapter 3)

BREAKFAST Menu choice and delivery time difference for early and late (Chapter 11)

BREAKFAST2 Menu choice and delivery time difference for early and late (Chapter 11)

BREAKSTW Breaking strength for operators (rows) and machines (columns) (Chapter 11)

BULBS Length of life of 40 lightbulbs from manufacturer A (=1) and 40 lightbulbs from manufacturer B (=2) (Chapters 2, 10)

CABERNET California and Washington ratings (Chapter 12)

CABOT Year and revenue for Cabot Corporation (Chapter 16)

CANISTER Day and number of nonconforming film canisters (Chapter 18)

CDYIELD Yield of money market account, 6-month CD, 1-year CD, 2.5-year CD, and 5-year CD (Chapters 11, 12)

CEO Company and total compensation of CEOs (Chapters 2, 3)

CHICKEN Sandwich, calories, fat (in grams), saturated fat (in grams), carbohydrates (in grams), and sodium (in milligrams) (Chapters 2, 3, 6, 8)

CIRCUITS Thickness of semiconductor wafers, by batch and position (Chapters 11, 12)

CIRCULATION Magazine, reported newsstand sales, and audited newsstand sales (Chapter 13)

CLOSING Rank, state, and closing costs (Chapter 6)

COCACOLA Year, coded year, and operating revenues (in billions of dollars) at Coca-Cola Company (Chapter 16)

COFFEE Rating of coffees, by expert and brand (Chapters 10, 11, 12)

COFFEEDRINK Product, calories, and fat in coffee drinks (Chapters 3, 13)

COFFEEPRICE Year and price per pound of coffee in the United States (Chapter 16)

COLA Sales for normal and end-aisle locations (Chapters 10, 12)

COLASPC Day, total number of cans filled, and number of unacceptable cans (over a 22-day period) (Chapter 18)

COLLEGES-BASKETBALL School, coach's salary for 2005–2006, expenses for 2004–2005, revenues for 2004–2005 (in millions of dollars), and winning percentage in 2005–2006 (Chapters 2, 3, 13)

COLLEGETUITION State, tuition, and change in tuition (Chapter 3)

COMPLAINTS Day and number of complaints (Chapter 18)

COMPUTERS Download time of three brands of computers (Chapter 11)

COMPUTERS2 Download time, brand, and browser (Chapter 11)

CONCRETE1 Compressive strength after two days and seven days (Chapters 10, 12)

CONCRETE2 Compressive strength after 2 days, 7 days, and 28 days (Chapters 11, 12)

CONTEST2001 Returns for experts, readers, and dart throwers (Chapters 11, 12)

COST OF LIVING City, overall cost rating, apartment rent, and costs of a cup of coffee, a hamburger, dry cleaning a men's suit, toothpaste, and movie tickets (Chapters 2, 3)

CPI-U Year, coded year, and value of CPI-U, the consumer price index (Chapter 16)

CRACK Type of crack and crack size (Chapters 10, 12)

CREDIT Month, coded month, credit charges (Chapter 16)

CURRENCY Year, coded year, and mean annual exchange rates (against the U.S. dollar) for the Canadian dollar, Japanese yen, and English pound (Chapter 16)

CUSTSALE Week number, number of customers, and sales (in thousands of dollars) over a period of 15 consecutive weeks (Chapter 13)

DAILYNASDAQ Date and NASDAQ value (Chapter 16)

DATING Year and number of subscribers (Chapter 2)

DEALS Year and number of mergers and acquisitions from January 1 to January 11 (Chapters 2, 16)

DELIVERY Customer number, number of cases, and delivery time (Chapter 13)

DENTAL Annual family dental expenses for 10 employees (Chapter 8)

DIFFTEST Differences in the sales invoices and actual amounts from a sample of 50 vouchers (Chapter 8)

DIGITALCAMERAS Battery life, camera type, life for subcompact cameras, life for compact cameras (Chapters 10, 12)

DINNER Time to prepare and cook dinner (Chapter 9)

DISCOUNT The amount of discount taken from 150 invoices (Chapter 8)

DISPRAZ Price, price squared, and sales of disposable razors in 15 stores (Chapter 15)

DJIA Year, coded year, and Dow Jones Industrial Average at the end of the year (Chapter 16)

DOMESTICBEER Brand, alcohol percentage, calories, and carbohydrates in U.S. domestic beers (Chapters 2, 3, 6, 15)

DOWMARKETCAP Company, ticker symbol, and market capitalization, in billions of dollars (Chapter 3)

DRILL Time to drill additional 5 feet, depth, and type of hole (Chapter 14)

DRINK Amount of soft drink filled in a subgroup of 50 consecutive 2-liter bottles (Chapters 2, 9)

DRYCLEAN Day, number of items returned (Chapter 18)

ELECTRICITY Year and cost of electricity (Chapter 16)

ELECUSE Electricity consumption (in kilowatts) and mean temperature (in degrees Fahrenheit) over a consecutive 24-month period (Chapter 13)

ENERGY State and per-capita kilowatt hour use (Chapter 3)

ENERGY2 Year, price of electricity, natural gas, and fuel oil (Chapter 16)

ERRORSPC Number of nonconforming items and number of accounts processed over 39 days (Chapter 18)

ERWAITING Emergency room waiting time (in minutes) at the main facility and at satellite 1, satellite 2, and satellite 3 (Chapters 11, 12)

ESPRESSO Tamp (the distance in inches between the espresso grounds and the top of the portafilter) and time (the number of seconds the heart, body, and crema are separated) (Chapter 13)

FEDRECEIPT Year, coded year, and federal receipts (in billions of current dollars) (Chapter 16)

FFCHAIN Raters and restaurant ratings (Chapters 11, 12)

FIFO Historical cost (in dollars) and audited value (in dollars) for a sample of 120 inventory items (Chapter 8)

FIRERUNS Week and number of fire runs (Chapter 18)

FLYASH Fly ash percentage, fly ash percentage squared, and strength (Chapter 15)

FORCE Force required to break an insulator (Chapters 2, 3, 8, 9)

FORD Quarter, coded quarter, revenue, and three dummy variables for quarters (Chapter 16)

FOULSPC Number of foul shots made and number taken over 40 days (Chapter 18)

FREEPORT Address, appraised value, property size (acres), house size, age, number of rooms, number of bathrooms, and number of cars that can be parked in the garage located in Freeport, New York (Chapter 15)

FRUIT Fruit and year, price, and quantity (Chapter 16)

FUNDTRAN Day, number of new investigations, and number of investigations closed over a 30-day period (Chapter 18)

FURNITURE Days between receipt and resolution of a sample of 50 complaints regarding purchased furniture (Chapters 2, 3, 8, 9)

GAS Week and price per gallon, in cents (Chapter 2)

GASOLINE Year, gasoline price, 1980 price index, and 1995 price index (Chapter 16)

GCFREEROSLYN Address, appraised value, location, property size (acres), house size, age, number of rooms, number of bathrooms, and number of cars that can be parked in the garage in Glen Cove, Freeport, and Roslyn, New York (Chapter 15)

GCROSLYN Address, appraised value, location, property size (acres), house size, age, number of rooms, number of bathrooms, and number of cars that can be parked in the garage in Glen Cove and Roslyn, New York (Chapter 15)

GDP Year and real gross domestic product (Chapter 16)

GE Year, coded year, and stock price (Chapter 16)

GEAR Tooth size, part positioning, and gear distortion (Chapter 11)

GLENCOVE Address, appraised value, property size (acres), house size, age, number of rooms, number of bathrooms, and number of cars that can be parked in the garage in Glen Cove, New York (Chapters 14, 15)

GOLFBALL Distance for designs 1, 2, 3, and 4 (Chapters 11, 12)

GPIGMAT GMAT scores and GPI for 20 students (Chapter 13)

GRADSURVEY Gender, age (as of last birthday), height (in inches), major, current cumulative grade point average, undergraduate area of specialization, undergraduate cumulative grade point average, GMAT score, current employment status, number of different full-time jobs held in the past 10 years, expected salary upon completion of MBA (in thousands of dollars), anticipated salary after 5 years of experience after MBA (in thousands of dollars), satisfaction with student advisement services on campus, and amount spent for books and supplies this semester (Chapters 1, 2, 3, 4, 6, 8, 10, 11, 12)

GRANULE Granule loss in Boston and Vermont shingles (Chapters 3, 8, 9, 10)

HARNSWELL Day and diameter of cam rollers (in inches) for samples of five parts produced in each of 30 batches (Chapter 18)

HEMLOCKFARMS Asking price, hot tub, rooms, lake view, bathrooms, bedrooms, loft/den, finished basement, and number of acres (Chapter 15)

HOMES Price, location, condition, bedrooms, bathrooms, and other rooms (Chapter 19)

HOSPADM Day, number of admissions, mean processing time (in hours), range of processing times, and proportion of laboratory rework (over a 30-day period) (Chapter 18)

HOTEL1 Day, number of rooms, number of nonconforming rooms per day over a 28-day period, and proportion of nonconforming items (Chapter 18)

HOTEL2 Day and delivery time for subgroups of five luggage deliveries per day over a 28-day period (Chapter 18)

HOUSE1 Selling price (in thousands of dollars), assessed value (in thousands of dollars), type (new = 0, old = 1), and time period of sale for 30 houses (Chapters 13, 14, 15)

HOUSE2 Assessed value (in thousands of dollars), size (in thousands of square feet), and age (in years) for 15 houses (Chapters 13, 14)

HOUSE3 Assessed value (in thousands of dollars), size (in thousands of square feet), and presence of a fireplace for 15 houses (Chapter 14)

HOUSING Quarter and units (Chapter 16)

HTNGOIL Monthly consumption of heating oil (in gallons), temperature (in degrees Fahrenheit), attic insulation (in inches), and style (0 = not ranch, 1 = ranch) (Chapters 14, 15)

ICECREAM Daily temperature (in degrees Fahrenheit) and sales (in thousands of dollars) for 21 days (Chapter 13)

INDICES Year and total rate of return (in percentage) for the Dow Jones Industrial Average (DJIA), the Standard & Poor's 500 (S&P 500), and the technology-heavy NASDAQ Composite (NASDAQ) (Chapter 3)

INSURANCE Processing time for insurance policies (Chapters 3, 8, 9)

INTAGLIO Surface hardness of untreated and treated steel plates (Chapters 10, 12)

INVOICE Number of invoices processed and amount of time (in hours) for 30 days (Chapter 13)

INVOICES Amount recorded (in dollars) from a sample of 12 sales invoices (Chapter 9)

ITEMERR Amount of error (in dollars) from a sample of 200 items (Chapter 8)

KEYBOARD DEFECTS Defect and frequency (Chapter 2)

LARGEST BONDS Five-year return of bond funds (Chapter 3)

LAUNDRY Dirt (in pounds) removed for detergent brands (rows) and cycle times (columns) (Chapter 11)

LOGPURCH Annual spending ($000) purchase (0 = no, 1 = yes), additional credit cards (0 = no, 1 = yes) (Chapter 14)

LOCATE Sales volume (in thousands of dollars) for front, middle, and rear locations (Chapters 11, 12)

LUGGAGE Delivery time, in minutes, for luggage in Wing A and Wing B of a hotel (Chapters 10, 12)

MANAGERS Sales (ratio of yearly sales divided by the target sales value for that region), score from the Wonderlic Personnel Test, score on the Strong-Campbell Interest Inventory Test, number of years of selling experience prior to becoming a sales manager, and whether the sales manager has a degree in electrical engineering (0 = no, 1 = yes) (Chapter 15)

MBA Success (0 = no, 1 = yes), GPA score, GMAT score (Chapter 14)

MCDONALDS Year, coded year, and annual total revenues (in billions of dollars) at McDonald's Corporation (Chapter 16)

MEASUREMENT Sample, in-line measurement, and analytical lab measurement (Chapters 10, 12)

MEDICARE Difference in amount reimbursed and amount that should have been reimbursed for office visits (Chapter 8)

MEDREC Day, number of discharged patients, and number of records not processed for a 30-day period (Chapter 18)

METALS Year and the total rate of return (in percentage) for platinum, gold, and silver (Chapter 3)

MILEAGE Mileage of autos calculated by owner, currently reported by the government, and forecasted according to government plans (Chapters 2, 3, 13)

MOISTURE Moisture content of Boston shingles and Vermont shingles (Chapter 9)

MOVIE Box office gross (in millions) and DVD sales (in thousands) (Chapter 13)

MOVIEPRICES Movie chain and prices (Chapters 2, 3, 8, 9)

MOVIES Year and movie attendance (Chapters 2, 16)

MOVING Labor hours, cubic feet, number of large pieces of furniture, and availability of an elevator (Chapters 13, 14)

MUSICONLINE Album/artist and prices at iTunes, Wal-Mart, MusicNow, Musicmatch, and Napster (Chapters 11, 12)

MUTUALFUNDS Category, objective, assets, fees, expense ratio, 2006 return, three-year return, five-year return, and risk (Chapters 2, 3, 4, 6, 8, 10, 11, 12, 15)

MYELOMA Patient, measurement before transplant, and measurement after transplant (Chapter 10)

NATURALGAS Coded quarter, price, and three dummy variables for quarters (Chapter 16)

NBA2007 Team, number of wins, points per game (for team, opponent, and the difference between team and opponent), field goal (shots made) percentage (for team, opponent, and the difference between team and opponent), turnovers (losing the ball before a shot is taken) per game (for team, opponent, and the difference between team and opponent), offensive rebound percentage, and defensive rebound percentage (Chapters 14, 15)

NEIGHBOR Selling price (in thousands of dollars), number of rooms, and neighborhood location (east = 0, west = 1) for 20 houses (Chapter 14)

OMNIPOWER Bars sold, price (in cents), and promotion expenses (in dollars) (Chapter 14)

ORDER Time in a restaurant (Chapter 8)

O-RING Flight number, temperature, and O-ring damage index (Chapter 13)

OYSTERS Year, coded year, and number of bushels harvested (Chapter 16)

PAIN-RELIEF Temperature, brand of pain relief tablet, and time to dissolve (Chapter 11)

PALLET Weight of Boston and weight of Vermont shingles (Chapters 2, 8, 9, 10)

PARACHUTE Tensile strength of parachutes from suppliers 1, 2, 3, and 4 (Chapters 11, 12)

PARACHUTE2 Tensile strength for looms and suppliers (Chapter 11)

PASTA Weight for type of pasta (rows) and cooking time (columns) (Chapter 11)

PEN Gender, ad, and product rating (Chapters 11, 12)

PERFORM Performance rating before and after motivational training (Chapters 10, 12)

PETFOOD Shelf space (in feet), weekly sales (in dollars), and aisle location (back = 0, front = 1) (Chapters 13, 14)

PHONE Time (in minutes) to clear telephone line problems and location (I and II) for samples of 20 customer problems reported to each of the two office locations (Chapter 19)

PHOTO Density for developer strength (rows) and development time (columns) (Chapter 11)

PIZZAHUT Gender (0 = female, 1 = male), price, and purchase behavior (0 = no, 1 = yes) (Chapter 14)

PIZZATIME Time period, delivery time for local restaurant, delivery time for national chain (Chapter 10)

PLUMBINV Difference in dollars between actual amounts recorded on sales invoices and the amounts entered into the accounting system (Chapter 8)

POLIO Year and incidence rates per 100,000 persons of reported poliomyelitis (Chapter 16)

POTATO Percentage of solids content in filter cake, acidity (in pH), lower pressure, upper pressure, cake thickness, varidrive speed, and drum speed setting for 54 measurements (Chapter 15)

PROPERTYTAXES State and property taxes per capita (Chapters 2, 6)

PROTEIN Calories (in grams), protein, percentage of calories from fat, percentage of calories from saturated fat, and cholesterol (in mg) for 25 popular protein foods (Chapter 2)

PTFALLS Month and patient falls (Chapter 18)

PUMPKIN Circumference and weight of pumpkins (Chapter 13)

RADON Solar radiation, soil temperature, vapor pressure, wind speed, relative humidity, dew point, ambient temperature, and radon concentration (Chapter 15)

RAISINS Weight of packages of raisins (Chapter 12)

REDWOOD Height, diameter, and bark thickness (Chapter 14)

RENT Monthly rental cost (in dollars) and apartment size (in square footage) for a sample of 25 apartments (Chapter 13)

RESTAURANTS Location, food rating, decor rating, service rating, summated rating, coded location (0 = urban, 1 = suburban), and price of restaurants (Chapters 2, 10, 13, 14)

RESTAURANTS2 Location, food rating, decor rating, service rating, summated rating, coded location (0 = urban, 1 = suburban), and price of restaurants (Chapter 19)

ROSLYN Address, appraised value, property size (acres), house size, age, number of rooms, number of bathrooms, and number of cars that can be parked in the garage in Roslyn, New York (Chapter 15)

RUDYBIRD Day, total cases sold, and cases of Rudybird sold (Chapter 18)

RXDRUGS Name of drug, price at two U.S. online drug stores and at Aptecha (Chapter 11)

S&PINDEX Coded quarters, end-of-quarter values of the quarterly Standard & Poor's Composite Stock Price Index, and three quarterly dummy variables (Chapter 16)

SAFETY Tour, number of unsafe acts (Chapter 18)

SATISFACTION Satisfaction (0 = no, 1 = yes), delivery time difference, previous stay at hotel (0 = no, 1 = yes) (Chapter 14)

SAVINGS Bank, money market rate, one-year CD rate, and five-year CD rate (Chapters 2, 3, 6)

SCRUBBER Airflow, water flow, recirculating water flow, orifice diameter, and NTU (Chapter 15)

SEALANT Sample number, sealant strength for Boston shingles, and sealant strength for Vermont shingles (Chapter 18)

SEDANS Model and miles per gallon (Chapters 3, 8)

SH2 Day and number of calls received at the help desk (Chapters 2, 3)

SH8 Rate ($) willing to pay for the newspaper (Chapter 8)

SH9 Blackness of newsprint (Chapter 9)

SH10 Length of early calls (in seconds), length of late calls (in seconds), and difference (in seconds) (Chapter 10)

SH11-1 Call, presentation plan (structured = 1, semistructured = 2, unstructured = 3), and length of call (in seconds) (Chapter 11)

SH11-2 Gender of caller, type of greeting, and length of call (Chapter 11)

SH13 Hours per month spent telemarketing and number of new subscriptions per month over a 24-month period (Chapter 13)

SH14 Hours per week spent telemarketing, number of new subscriptions, and type of presentation (Chapter 14)

SH16 Month and number of home-delivery subscriptions over the most recent 24-month period (Chapter 16)

SH18-1 Day, number of ads with errors, number of ads, and number of errors over a 25-day period (Chapter 18)

SH18-2 Day and newsprint blackness measures for each of five spots made over 25 consecutive weekdays (Chapter 18)

SITE Store number, square footage (in thousands of square feet), and sales (in millions of dollars) in 14 Sunflowers Apparel stores (Chapter 13)

SPENDING State and per-capita federal spending ($000) in 2004 (Chapters 2, 3, 6)

SPONGE Day, number of sponges produced, number of nonconforming sponges, proportion of nonconforming sponges (Chapter 18)

SPORTING Sales, age, annual population growth, income, percentage with high school diploma, and percentage with college diploma (Chapters 13, 15)

SPWATER Sample number and amount of magnesium (Chapter 18)

STANDBY Standby hours, staff, remote hours, Dubner hours, and labor hours for 26 weeks (Chapters 14, 15)

STATES State, commuting time, percentage of homes with more than eight rooms, median income, and percentage of housing that costs more than 30% of family income (Chapter 2)

STEEL Error in actual length and specified length (Chapters 2, 6, 8, 9)

STOCKS & BONDS Date, closing price of the Dow Jones Industrial Average, and closing price of Vanguard Long-Term Bond Index Fund (Chapter 13)

STOCKS2006 Week and closing weekly stock price for S&P, Target, Sara Lee, and GE (Chapters 2, 13)

STRATEGIC Year and billions of barrels in U.S. strategic oil reserve (Chapter 16)

STUDYTIME Gender and study time (Chapter 10)

SUPERMARKET Day, number of customers, and check-out time (Chapter 13)

SUV Model, miles per gallon (Chapters 3, 8)

TAX Quarterly sales tax receipts (in thousands of dollars) for 50 business establishments (Chapter 3)

TAXES County taxes (in dollars) and age of house (in years) for 19 single-family houses (Chapter 15)

TEA3 Sample number and weight of tea bags (Chapter 18)

TEABAGS Weight of tea bags (Chapters 3, 8, 9)

TELESPC Number of orders and number of corrections over 30 days (Chapter 18)

TELLER Number of errors by tellers (Chapter 18)

TENSILE Sample number and strength (Chapter 18)

TESTRANK Rank scores for 10 people trained using a "traditional" method (Method = 0) and 10 people trained using an "experimental" method (Method = 1) (Chapter 12)

TEXTBOOK Textbook, book store price, and Amazon price (Chapters 10, 12)

THEMEPARKS Name of location and admission price for one-day tickets (Chapter 3)

TIMES Times to get ready (Chapter 3)

TOMATO Fertilizer and yield (Chapter 15)

TOMATOES Year and price per pound in the United States (Chapter 16)

TOYSRUS Quarter, coded quarter, revenue, and three dummy variables for quarters (Chapter 16)

TRADE Day, number of undesirable trades, and number of total trades made over a 30-day period (Chapter 18)

TRADES Day, number of incoming calls, and number of trade executions per day over a 35-day period (Chapter 13)

TRAINING Assembly time and training program (team-based = 0, individual-based = 1) (Chapters 10, 12)

TRANSMIT Day and number of errors in transmission (Chapter 18)

TRANSPORT Days and patient transport times (in minutes) for samples of four patients per day over a 30-day period (Chapter 18)

TRASHBAGS Weight required to break four brands of trash bags (Chapters 11, 12)

TREASURY Year and interest rate (Chapter 16)

TROUGH Width of trough (Chapters 2, 3, 8, 9)

TRSNYC Year, unit value of variable A, and unit value of variable B (Chapter 16)

TSMODEL1 Years, coded years, and three time series (I, II, III) (Chapter 16)

TSMODEL2 Years, coded years, and two time series (I, II) (Chapter 16)

TUITION2006 School, in-state tuition and fees, and out-of-state tuition and fees (Chapter 3)

TVCHANNELS Year and the number of TV channels received (Chapter 2)

UNDERGRADSURVEY Gender, age (*as of last birthday*), height (*in inches*), class designation, major, graduate school intention, cumulative grade point average, expected starting salary (in thousands of dollars), anticipated salary after five years of experience (in thousands of dollars), current employment status, number of campus club/group/organization/team affiliations, satisfaction with student advisement services on campus, and amount spent on books and supplies this semester (Chapters 1, 2, 3, 4, 6, 8, 10, 11, 12)

UNDERWRITING Score on proficiency exam, score on end of training exam, and training method (Chapter 14)

UNEMPLOY Year, month, and monthly unemployment rates (Chapters 2, 16)

UNLEADED Year, month, and price (Chapter 16)

UTILITY Utilities charges for 50 one-bedroom apartments (Chapters 2, 6)

VB Time (in minutes) for nine students to write and run a Visual Basic program (Chapter 10)

WAIT Waiting times and seating times, in minutes (Chapter 6)

WALMART Quarter and quarterly revenues (Chapter 16)

WARECOST Distribution cost (in thousands of dollars), sales (in thousands of dollars), and number of orders for 24 months (Chapters 13, 14, 15)

WAREHSE Number of units handled per day and employee number (Chapter 18)

WHITNEY1 Type (1 = kidney, 2 = shrimp), shift, and weight in ounces (Chapter 19)

WHITNEY2 Type (1 = kidney, 2 = shrimp), shift, time, nonconformances, and volume (Chapter 19)

WHITNEY3 Type (1 = kidney, 2 = shrimp), shift, time, and weight in ounces (Chapter 19)

WHITNEY4 Type (1 = fine, 2 = chunky) and weight in ounces (Chapter 19)

WHITNEY5 Type (1 = kidney, 2 = shrimp, 3 = chicken liver, 4 = salmon, 5 = beef) and ounces eaten (Chapter 19)

WHITNEY6 Piece size (F = fine, C = chunky), fill height (L = low, C = current), and coded weight in ounces (Chapter 19)

WHOLEFOODS1 Item, price at Whole Foods, and price at Fairway (Chapters 10, 12)

WHOLEFOODS2 Item, price at Whole Foods, price at Gristede's, price at Fairway, and price at Stop & Shop (Chapters 11, 12)

WINE Summated ratings of different wines by experts (Chapter 11)

WIP Processing times at each of two plants (A = 1, B = 2) (Chapter 19)

WONDERLIC School, average Wonderlic score of football players trying out for the NFL, and graduation rate (Chapters 2, 3, 13)

WORKFORCE Year, population, and size of the workforce (Chapter 16)

WRIGLEY Year, coded year, actual revenue, consumer price index, and real revenue (Chapter 16)

YARN Breaking strength, pressure, yarn sample, and side-by-side aspect (nozzle = 1, opposite = 2) (Chapter 11)

YIELD Cleansing step, etching step, and yield (Chapter 11)

E. TABLES

E. TABLES

TABLE E.1

Table of Random Numbers

Row	Column							
	00000 12345	00001 67890	11111 12345	11112 67890	22222 12345	22223 67890	33333 12345	33334 67890
01	49280	88924	35779	00283	81163	07275	89863	02348
02	61870	41657	07468	08612	98083	97349	20775	45091
03	43898	65923	25078	86129	78496	97653	91550	08078
04	62993	93912	30454	84598	56095	20664	12872	64647
05	33850	58555	51438	85507	71865	79488	76783	31708
06	97340	03364	88472	04334	63919	36394	11095	92470
07	70543	29776	10087	10072	55980	64688	68239	20461
08	89382	93809	00796	95945	34101	81277	66090	88872
09	37818	72142	67140	50785	22380	16703	53362	44940
10	60430	22834	14130	96593	23298	56203	92671	15925
11	82975	66158	84731	19436	55790	69229	28661	13675
12	30987	71938	40355	54324	08401	26299	49420	59208
13	55700	24586	93247	32596	11865	63397	44251	43189
14	14756	23997	78643	75912	83832	32768	18928	57070
15	32166	53251	70654	92827	63491	04233	33825	69662
16	23236	73751	31888	81718	06546	83246	47651	04877
17	45794	26926	15130	82455	78305	55058	52551	47182
18	09893	20505	14225	68514	47427	56788	96297	78822
19	54382	74598	91499	14523	68479	27686	46162	83554
20	94750	89923	37089	20048	80336	94598	26940	36858
21	70297	34135	53140	33340	42050	82341	44104	82949
22	85157	47954	32979	26575	57600	40881	12250	73742
23	11100	02340	12860	74697	96644	89439	28707	25815
24	36871	50775	30592	57143	17381	68856	25853	35041
25	23913	48357	63308	16090	51690	54607	72407	55538
26	79348	36085	27973	65157	07456	22255	25626	57054
27	92074	54641	53673	54421	18130	60103	69593	49464
28	06873	21440	75593	41373	49502	17972	82578	16364
29	12478	37622	99659	31065	83613	69889	58869	29571
30	57175	55564	65411	42547	70457	03426	72937	83792
31	91616	11075	80103	07831	59309	13276	26710	73000
32	78025	73539	14621	39044	47450	03197	12787	47709
33	27587	67228	80145	10175	12822	86687	65530	49325
34	16690	20427	04251	64477	73709	73945	92396	68263
35	70183	58065	65489	31833	82093	16747	10386	59293
36	90730	35385	15679	99742	50866	78028	75573	67257
37	10934	93242	13431	24590	02770	48582	00906	58595
38	82462	30166	79613	47416	13389	80268	05085	96666
39	27463	10433	07606	16285	93699	60912	94532	95632
40	02979	52997	09079	92709	90110	47506	53693	49892
41	46888	69929	75233	52507	32097	37594	10067	67327
42	53638	83161	08289	12639	08141	12640	28437	09268
43	82433	61427	17239	89160	19666	08814	37841	12847
44	35766	31672	50082	22795	66948	65581	84393	15890
45	10853	42581	08792	13257	61973	24450	52351	16602
46	20341	27398	72906	63955	17276	10646	74692	48438
47	54458	90542	77563	51839	52901	53355	83281	19177
48	26337	66530	16687	35179	46560	00123	44546	79896
49	34314	23729	85264	05575	96855	23820	11091	79821
50	28603	10708	68933	34189	92166	15181	66628	58599

continued

TABLE E.1

Table of Random Numbers (*Continued*)

Row	00000 12345	00001 67890	11111 12345	11112 67890	22222 12345	22223 67890	33333 12345	33334 67890
51	66194	28926	99547	16625	45515	67953	12108	57846
52	78240	43195	24837	32511	70880	22070	52622	61881
53	00833	88000	67299	68215	11274	55624	32991	17436
54	12111	86683	61270	58036	64192	90611	15145	01748
55	47189	99951	05755	03834	43782	90599	40282	51417
56	76396	72486	62423	27618	84184	78922	73561	52818
57	46409	17469	32483	09083	76175	19985	26309	91536
58	74626	22111	87286	46772	42243	68046	44250	42439
59	34450	81974	93723	49023	58432	67083	36876	93391
60	36327	72135	33005	28701	34710	49359	50693	89311
61	74185	77536	84825	09934	99103	09325	67389	45869
62	12296	41623	62873	37943	25584	09609	63360	47270
63	90822	60280	88925	99610	42772	60561	76873	04117
64	72121	79152	96591	90305	10189	79778	68016	13747
65	95268	41377	25684	08151	61816	58555	54305	86189
66	92603	09091	75884	93424	72586	88903	30061	14457
67	18813	90291	05275	01223	79607	95426	34900	09778
68	38840	26903	28624	67157	51986	42865	14508	49315
69	05959	33836	53758	16562	41081	38012	41230	20528
70	85141	21155	99212	32685	51403	31926	69813	58781
71	75047	59643	31074	38172	03718	32119	69506	67143
72	30752	95260	68032	62871	58781	34143	68790	69766
73	22986	82575	42187	62295	84295	30634	66562	31442
74	99439	86692	90348	66036	48399	73451	26698	39437
75	20389	93029	11881	71685	65452	89047	63669	02656
76	39249	05173	68256	36359	20250	68686	05947	09335
77	96777	33605	29481	20063	09398	01843	35139	61344
78	04860	32918	10798	50492	52655	33359	94713	28393
79	41613	42375	00403	03656	77580	87772	86877	57085
80	17930	00794	53836	53692	67135	98102	61912	11246
81	24649	31845	25736	75231	83808	98917	93829	99430
82	79899	34061	54308	59358	56462	58166	97302	86828
83	76801	49594	81002	30397	52728	15101	72070	33706
84	36239	63636	38140	65731	39788	06872	38971	53363
85	07392	64449	17886	63632	53995	17574	22247	62607
86	67133	04181	33874	98835	67453	59734	76381	63455
87	77759	31504	32832	70861	15152	29733	75371	39174
88	85992	72268	42920	20810	29361	51423	90306	73574
89	79553	75952	54116	65553	47139	60579	09165	85490
90	41101	17336	48951	53674	17880	45260	08575	49321
91	36191	17095	32123	91576	84221	78902	82010	30847
92	62329	63898	23268	74283	26091	68409	69704	82267
93	14751	13151	93115	01437	56945	89661	67680	79790
94	48462	59278	44185	29616	76537	19589	83139	28454
95	29435	88105	59651	44391	74588	55114	80834	85686
96	28340	29285	12965	14821	80425	16602	44653	70467
97	02167	58940	27149	80242	10587	79786	34959	75339
98	17864	00991	39557	54981	23588	81914	37609	13128
99	79675	80605	60059	35862	00254	36546	21545	78179
00	72335	82037	92003	34100	29879	46613	89720	13274

Source: *Partially extracted from the Rand Corporation,* A Million Random Digits with 100,000 Normal Deviates *(Glencoe, IL, The Free Press, 1955).*

TABLE E.2

The Cumulative Standardized Normal Distribution

Entry represents area under the cumulative standardized normal distribution from $-\infty$ to Z

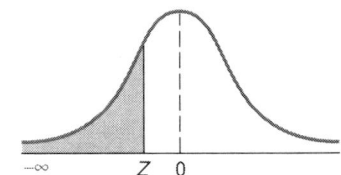

	Cumulative Probabilities									
Z	**0.00**	**0.01**	**0.02**	**0.03**	**0.04**	**0.05**	**0.06**	**0.07**	**0.08**	**0.09**
−6.0	0.000000001									
−5.5	0.000000019									
−5.0	0.000000287									
−4.5	0.000003398									
−4.0	0.000031671									
−3.9	0.00005	0.00005	0.00004	0.00004	0.00004	0.00004	0.00004	0.00004	0.00003	0.00003
−3.8	0.00007	0.00007	0.00007	0.00006	0.00006	0.00006	0.00006	0.00005	0.00005	0.00005
−3.7	0.00011	0.00010	0.00010	0.00010	0.00009	0.00009	0.00008	0.00008	0.00008	0.00008
−3.6	0.00016	0.00015	0.00015	0.00014	0.00014	0.00013	0.00013	0.00012	0.00012	0.00011
−3.5	0.00023	0.00022	0.00022	0.00021	0.00020	0.00019	0.00019	0.00018	0.00017	0.00017
−3.4	0.00034	0.00032	0.00031	0.00030	0.00029	0.00028	0.00027	0.00026	0.00025	0.00024
−3.3	0.00048	0.00047	0.00045	0.00043	0.00042	0.00040	0.00039	0.00038	0.00036	0.00035
−3.2	0.00069	0.00066	0.00064	0.00062	0.00060	0.00058	0.00056	0.00054	0.00052	0.00050
−3.1	0.00097	0.00094	0.00090	0.00087	0.00084	0.00082	0.00079	0.00076	0.00074	0.00071
−3.0	0.00135	0.00131	0.00126	0.00122	0.00118	0.00114	0.00111	0.00107	0.00103	0.00100
−2.9	0.0019	0.0018	0.0018	0.0017	0.0016	0.0016	0.0015	0.0015	0.0014	0.0014
−2.8	0.0026	0.0025	0.0024	0.0023	0.0023	0.0022	0.0021	0.0021	0.0020	0.0019
−2.7	0.0035	0.0034	0.0033	0.0032	0.0031	0.0030	0.0029	0.0028	0.0027	0.0026
−2.6	0.0047	0.0045	0.0044	0.0043	0.0041	0.0040	0.0039	0.0038	0.0037	0.0036
−2.5	0.0062	0.0060	0.0059	0.0057	0.0055	0.0054	0.0052	0.0051	0.0049	0.0048
−2.4	0.0082	0.0080	0.0078	0.0075	0.0073	0.0071	0.0069	0.0068	0.0066	0.0064
−2.3	0.0107	0.0104	0.0102	0.0099	0.0096	0.0094	0.0091	0.0089	0.0087	0.0084
−2.2	0.0139	0.0136	0.0132	0.0129	0.0125	0.0122	0.0119	0.0116	0.0113	0.0110
−2.1	0.0179	0.0174	0.0170	0.0166	0.0162	0.0158	0.0154	0.0150	0.0146	0.0143
−2.0	0.0228	0.0222	0.0217	0.0212	0.0207	0.0202	0.0197	0.0192	0.0188	0.0183
−1.9	0.0287	0.0281	0.0274	0.0268	0.0262	0.0256	0.0250	0.0244	0.0239	0.0233
−1.8	0.0359	0.0351	0.0344	0.0336	0.0329	0.0322	0.0314	0.0307	0.0301	0.0294
−1.7	0.0446	0.0436	0.0427	0.0418	0.0409	0.0401	0.0392	0.0384	0.0375	0.0367
−1.6	0.0548	0.0537	0.0526	0.0516	0.0505	0.0495	0.0485	0.0475	0.0465	0.0455
−1.5	0.0668	0.0655	0.0643	0.0630	0.0618	0.0606	0.0594	0.0582	0.0571	0.0559
−1.4	0.0808	0.0793	0.0778	0.0764	0.0749	0.0735	0.0721	0.0708	0.0694	0.0681
−1.3	0.0968	0.0951	0.0934	0.0918	0.0901	0.0885	0.0869	0.0853	0.0838	0.0823
−1.2	0.1151	0.1131	0.1112	0.1093	0.1075	0.1056	0.1038	0.1020	0.1003	0.0985
−1.1	0.1357	0.1335	0.1314	0.1292	0.1271	0.1251	0.1230	0.1210	0.1190	0.1170
−1.0	0.1587	0.1562	0.1539	0.1515	0.1492	0.1469	0.1446	0.1423	0.1401	0.1379
−0.9	0.1841	0.1814	0.1788	0.1762	0.1736	0.1711	0.1685	0.1660	0.1635	0.1611
−0.8	0.2119	0.2090	0.2061	0.2033	0.2005	0.1977	0.1949	0.1922	0.1894	0.1867
−0.7	0.2420	0.2388	0.2358	0.2327	0.2296	0.2266	0.2236	0.2206	0.2177	0.2148
−0.6	0.2743	0.2709	0.2676	0.2643	0.2611	0.2578	0.2546	0.2514	0.2482	0.2451
−0.5	0.3085	0.3050	0.3015	0.2981	0.2946	0.2912	0.2877	0.2843	0.2810	0.2776
−0.4	0.3446	0.3409	0.3372	0.3336	0.3300	0.3264	0.3228	0.3192	0.3156	0.3121
−0.3	0.3821	0.3783	0.3745	0.3707	0.3669	0.3632	0.3594	0.3557	0.3520	0.3483
−0.2	0.4207	0.4168	0.4129	0.4090	0.4052	0.4013	0.3974	0.3936	0.3897	0.3859
−0.1	0.4602	0.4562	0.4522	0.4483	0.4443	0.4404	0.4364	0.4325	0.4286	0.4247
−0.0	0.5000	0.4960	0.4920	0.4880	0.4840	0.4801	0.4761	0.4721	0.4681	0.4641

continued

TABLE E.2

The Cumulative Standardized Normal Distribution (*Continued*)

Entry represents area under the cumulative standardized normal distribution from $-\infty$ to Z

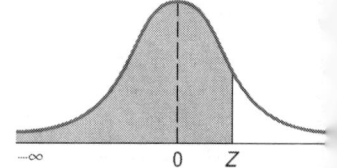

| Z | \multicolumn{10}{c}{Cumulative Probabilities} |
	0.00	0.01	0.02	0.03	0.04	0.05	0.06	0.07	0.08	0.09
0.0	0.5000	0.5040	0.5080	0.5120	0.5160	0.5199	0.5239	0.5279	0.5319	0.5359
0.1	0.5398	0.5438	0.5478	0.5517	0.5557	0.5596	0.5636	0.5675	0.5714	0.5753
0.2	0.5793	0.5832	0.5871	0.5910	0.5948	0.5987	0.6026	0.6064	0.6103	0.6141
0.3	0.6179	0.6217	0.6255	0.6293	0.6331	0.6368	0.6406	0.6443	0.6480	0.6517
0.4	0.6554	0.6591	0.6628	0.6664	0.6700	0.6736	0.6772	0.6808	0.6844	0.6879
0.5	0.6915	0.6950	0.6985	0.7019	0.7054	0.7088	0.7123	0.7157	0.7190	0.7224
0.6	0.7257	0.7291	0.7324	0.7357	0.7389	0.7422	0.7454	0.7486	0.7518	0.7549
0.7	0.7580	0.7612	0.7642	0.7673	0.7704	0.7734	0.7764	0.7794	0.7823	0.7852
0.8	0.7881	0.7910	0.7939	0.7967	0.7995	0.8023	0.8051	0.8078	0.8106	0.8133
0.9	0.8159	0.8186	0.8212	0.8238	0.8264	0.8289	0.8315	0.8340	0.8365	0.8389
1.0	0.8413	0.8438	0.8461	0.8485	0.8508	0.8531	0.8554	0.8577	0.8599	0.8621
1.1	0.8643	0.8665	0.8686	0.8708	0.8729	0.8749	0.8770	0.8790	0.8810	0.8830
1.2	0.8849	0.8869	0.8888	0.8907	0.8925	0.8944	0.8962	0.8980	0.8997	0.9015
1.3	0.9032	0.9049	0.9066	0.9082	0.9099	0.9115	0.9131	0.9147	0.9162	0.9177
1.4	0.9192	0.9207	0.9222	0.9236	0.9251	0.9265	0.9279	0.9292	0.9306	0.9319
1.5	0.9332	0.9345	0.9357	0.9370	0.9382	0.9394	0.9406	0.9418	0.9429	0.9441
1.6	0.9452	0.9463	0.9474	0.9484	0.9495	0.9505	0.9515	0.9525	0.9535	0.9545
1.7	0.9554	0.9564	0.9573	0.9582	0.9591	0.9599	0.9608	0.9616	0.9625	0.9633
1.8	0.9641	0.9649	0.9656	0.9664	0.9671	0.9678	0.9686	0.9693	0.9699	0.9706
1.9	0.9713	0.9719	0.9726	0.9732	0.9738	0.9744	0.9750	0.9756	0.9761	0.9767
2.0	0.9772	0.9778	0.9783	0.9788	0.9793	0.9798	0.9803	0.9808	0.9812	0.9817
2.1	0.9821	0.9826	0.9830	0.9834	0.9838	0.9842	0.9846	0.9850	0.9854	0.9857
2.2	0.9861	0.9864	0.9868	0.9871	0.9875	0.9878	0.9881	0.9884	0.9887	0.9890
2.3	0.9893	0.9896	0.9898	0.9901	0.9904	0.9906	0.9909	0.9911	0.9913	0.9916
2.4	0.9918	0.9920	0.9922	0.9925	0.9927	0.9929	0.9931	0.9932	0.9934	0.9936
2.5	0.9938	0.9940	0.9941	0.9943	0.9945	0.9946	0.9948	0.9949	0.9951	0.9952
2.6	0.9953	0.9955	0.9956	0.9957	0.9959	0.9960	0.9961	0.9962	0.9963	0.9964
2.7	0.9965	0.9966	0.9967	0.9968	0.9969	0.9970	0.9971	0.9972	0.9973	0.9974
2.8	0.9974	0.9975	0.9976	0.9977	0.9977	0.9978	0.9979	0.9979	0.9980	0.9981
2.9	0.9981	0.9982	0.9982	0.9983	0.9984	0.9984	0.9985	0.9985	0.9986	0.9986
3.0	0.99865	0.99869	0.99874	0.99878	0.99882	0.99886	0.99889	0.99893	0.99897	0.99900
3.1	0.99903	0.99906	0.99910	0.99913	0.99916	0.99918	0.99921	0.99924	0.99926	0.99929
3.2	0.99931	0.99934	0.99936	0.99938	0.99940	0.99942	0.99944	0.99946	0.99948	0.99950
3.3	0.99952	0.99953	0.99955	0.99957	0.99958	0.99960	0.99961	0.99962	0.99964	0.99965
3.4	0.99966	0.99968	0.99969	0.99970	0.99971	0.99972	0.99973	0.99974	0.99975	0.99976
3.5	0.99977	0.99978	0.99978	0.99979	0.99980	0.99981	0.99981	0.99982	0.99983	0.99983
3.6	0.99984	0.99985	0.99985	0.99986	0.99986	0.99987	0.99987	0.99988	0.99988	0.99989
3.7	0.99989	0.99990	0.99990	0.99990	0.99991	0.99991	0.99992	0.99992	0.99992	0.99992
3.8	0.99993	0.99993	0.99993	0.99994	0.99994	0.99994	0.99994	0.99995	0.99995	0.99995
3.9	0.99995	0.99995	0.99996	0.99996	0.99996	0.99996	0.99996	0.99996	0.99997	0.99997
4.0	0.999968329									
4.5	0.999996602									
5.0	0.999999713									
5.5	0.999999981									
6.0	0.999999999									

TABLE E.3

Critical Values of t

For a particular number of degrees of freedom, entry represents the critical value of t corresponding to a specified upper-tail area (α).

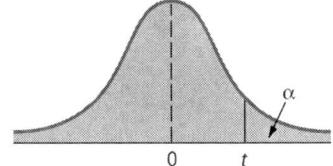

Degrees of Freedom	Cumulative Probabilities					
	0.75	0.90	0.95	0.975	0.99	0.995
	Upper-Tail Areas					
	0.25	0.10	0.05	0.025	0.01	0.005
1	1.0000	3.0777	6.3138	12.7062	31.8207	63.6574
2	0.8165	1.8856	2.9200	4.3027	6.9646	9.9248
3	0.7649	1.6377	2.3534	3.1824	4.5407	5.8409
4	0.7407	1.5332	2.1318	2.7764	3.7469	4.6041
5	0.7267	1.4759	2.0150	2.5706	3.3649	4.0322
6	0.7176	1.4398	1.9432	2.4469	3.1427	3.7074
7	0.7111	1.4149	1.8946	2.3646	2.9980	3.4995
8	0.7064	1.3968	1.8595	2.3060	2.8965	3.3554
9	0.7027	1.3830	1.8331	2.2622	2.8214	3.2498
10	0.6998	1.3722	1.8125	2.2281	2.7638	3.1693
11	0.6974	1.3634	1.7959	2.2010	2.7181	3.1058
12	0.6955	1.3562	1.7823	2.1788	2.6810	3.0545
13	0.6938	1.3502	1.7709	2.1604	2.6503	3.0123
14	0.6924	1.3450	1.7613	2.1448	2.6245	2.9768
15	0.6912	1.3406	1.7531	2.1315	2.6025	2.9467
16	0.6901	1.3368	1.7459	2.1199	2.5835	2.9208
17	0.6892	1.3334	1.7396	2.1098	2.5669	2.8982
18	0.6884	1.3304	1.7341	2.1009	2.5524	2.8784
19	0.6876	1.3277	1.7291	2.0930	2.5395	2.8609
20	0.6870	1.3253	1.7247	2.0860	2.5280	2.8453
21	0.6864	1.3232	1.7207	2.0796	2.5177	2.8314
22	0.6858	1.3212	1.7171	2.0739	2.5083	2.8188
23	0.6853	1.3195	1.7139	2.0687	2.4999	2.8073
24	0.6848	1.3178	1.7109	2.0639	2.4922	2.7969
25	0.6844	1.3163	1.7081	2.0595	2.4851	2.7874
26	0.6840	1.3150	1.7056	2.0555	2.4786	2.7787
27	0.6837	1.3137	1.7033	2.0518	2.4727	2.7707
28	0.6834	1.3125	1.7011	2.0484	2.4671	2.7633
29	0.6830	1.3114	1.6991	2.0452	2.4620	2.7564
30	0.6828	1.3104	1.6973	2.0423	2.4573	2.7500
31	0.6825	1.3095	1.6955	2.0395	2.4528	2.7440
32	0.6822	1.3086	1.6939	2.0369	2.4487	2.7385
33	0.6820	1.3077	1.6924	2.0345	2.4448	2.7333
34	0.6818	1.3070	1.6909	2.0322	2.4411	2.7284
35	0.6816	1.3062	1.6896	2.0301	2.4377	2.7238
36	0.6814	1.3055	1.6883	2.0281	2.4345	2.7195
37	0.6812	1.3049	1.6871	2.0262	2.4314	2.7154
38	0.6810	1.3042	1.6860	2.0244	2.4286	2.7116
39	0.6808	1.3036	1.6849	2.0227	2.4258	2.7079
40	0.6807	1.3031	1.6839	2.0211	2.4233	2.7045
41	0.6805	1.3025	1.6829	2.0195	2.4208	2.7012
42	0.6804	1.3020	1.6820	2.0181	2.4185	2.6981
43	0.6802	1.3016	1.6811	2.0167	2.4163	2.6951
44	0.6801	1.3011	1.6802	2.0154	2.4141	2.6923
45	0.6800	1.3006	1.6794	2.0141	2.4121	2.6896
46	0.6799	1.3002	1.6787	2.0129	2.4102	2.6870
47	0.6797	1.2998	1.6779	2.0117	2.4083	2.6846
48	0.6796	1.2994	1.6772	2.0106	2.4066	2.6822

continued

TABLE E.3

Critical Values of *t*
(*Continued*)

	Cumulative Probabilities					
	0.75	0.90	0.95	0.975	0.99	0.995
	Upper-Tail Areas					
Degrees of Freedom	0.25	0.10	0.05	0.025	0.01	0.005
49	0.6795	1.2991	1.6766	2.0096	2.4049	2.6800
50	0.6794	1.2987	1.6759	2.0086	2.4033	2.6778
51	0.6793	1.2984	1.6753	2.0076	2.4017	2.6757
52	0.6792	1.2980	1.6747	2.0066	2.4002	2.6737
53	0.6791	1.2977	1.6741	2.0057	2.3988	2.6718
54	0.6791	1.2974	1.6736	2.0049	2.3974	2.6700
55	0.6790	1.2971	1.6730	2.0040	2.3961	2.6682
56	0.6789	1.2969	1.6725	2.0032	2.3948	2.6665
57	0.6788	1.2966	1.6720	2.0025	2.3936	2.6649
58	0.6787	1.2963	1.6716	2.0017	2.3924	2.6633
59	0.6787	1.2961	1.6711	2.0010	2.3912	2.6618
60	0.6786	1.2958	1.6706	2.0003	2.3901	2.6603
61	0.6785	1.2956	1.6702	1.9996	2.3890	2.6589
62	0.6785	1.2954	1.6698	1.9990	2.3880	2.6575
63	0.6784	1.2951	1.6694	1.9983	2.3870	2.6561
64	0.6783	1.2949	1.6690	1.9977	2.3860	2.6549
65	0.6783	1.2947	1.6686	1.9971	2.3851	2.6536
66	0.6782	1.2945	1.6683	1.9966	2.3842	2.6524
67	0.6782	1.2943	1.6679	1.9960	2.3833	2.6512
68	0.6781	1.2941	1.6676	1.9955	2.3824	2.6501
69	0.6781	1.2939	1.6672	1.9949	2.3816	2.6490
70	0.6780	1.2938	1.6669	1.9944	2.3808	2.6479
71	0.6780	1.2936	1.6666	1.9939	2.3800	2.6469
72	0.6779	1.2934	1.6663	1.9935	2.3793	2.6459
73	0.6779	1.2933	1.6660	1.9930	2.3785	2.6449
74	0.6778	1.2931	1.6657	1.9925	2.3778	2.6439
75	0.6778	1.2929	1.6654	1.9921	2.3771	2.6430
76	0.6777	1.2928	1.6652	1.9917	2.3764	2.6421
77	0.6777	1.2926	1.6649	1.9913	2.3758	2.6412
78	0.6776	1.2925	1.6646	1.9908	2.3751	2.6403
79	0.6776	1.2924	1.6644	1.9905	2.3745	2.6395
80	0.6776	1.2922	1.6641	1.9901	2.3739	2.6387
81	0.6775	1.2921	1.6639	1.9897	2.3733	2.6379
82	0.6775	1.2920	1.6636	1.9893	2.3727	2.6371
83	0.6775	1.2918	1.6634	1.9890	2.3721	2.6364
84	0.6774	1.2917	1.6632	1.9886	2.3716	2.6356
85	0.6774	1.2916	1.6630	1.9883	2.3710	2.6349
86	0.6774	1.2915	1.6628	1.9879	2.3705	2.6342
87	0.6773	1.2914	1.6626	1.9876	2.3700	2.6335
88	0.6773	1.2912	1.6624	1.9873	2.3695	2.6329
89	0.6773	1.2911	1.6622	1.9870	2.3690	2.6322
90	0.6772	1.2910	1.6620	1.9867	2.3685	2.6316
91	0.6772	1.2909	1.6618	1.9864	2.3680	2.6309
92	0.6772	1.2908	1.6616	1.9861	2.3676	2.6303
93	0.6771	1.2907	1.6614	1.9858	2.3671	2.6297
94	0.6771	1.2906	1.6612	1.9855	2.3667	2.6291
95	0.6771	1.2905	1.6611	1.9853	2.3662	2.6286
96	0.6771	1.2904	1.6609	1.9850	2.3658	2.6280
97	0.6770	1.2903	1.6607	1.9847	2.3654	2.6275
98	0.6770	1.2902	1.6606	1.9845	2.3650	2.6269
99	0.6770	1.2902	1.6604	1.9842	2.3646	2.6264
100	0.6770	1.2901	1.6602	1.9840	2.3642	2.6259
110	0.6767	1.2893	1.6588	1.9818	2.3607	2.6213
120	0.6765	1.2886	1.6577	1.9799	2.3578	2.6174
∞	0.6745	1.2816	1.6449	1.9600	2.3263	2.5758

TABLE E.4

Critical Values of χ^2

For a particular number of degrees of freedom, entry represents the critical value of χ^2 corresponding to a specified upper-tail area (α).

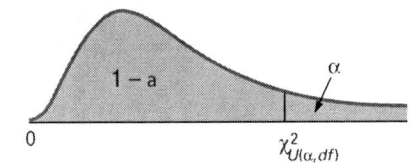

Degrees of Freedom	Cumulative Probabilities											
	0.005	0.01	0.025	0.05	0.10	0.25	0.75	0.90	0.95	0.975	0.99	0.995
	Upper Tail Areas (α)											
	0.995	0.99	0.975	0.95	0.90	0.75	0.25	0.10	0.05	0.025	0.01	0.005
1			0.001	0.004	0.016	0.102	1.323	2.706	3.841	5.024	6.635	7.879
2	0.010	0.020	0.051	0.103	0.211	0.575	2.773	4.605	5.991	7.378	9.210	10.597
3	0.072	0.115	0.216	0.352	0.584	1.213	4.108	6.251	7.815	9.348	11.345	12.838
4	0.207	0.297	0.484	0.711	1.064	1.923	5.385	7.779	9.488	11.143	13.277	14.860
5	0.412	0.554	0.831	1.145	1.610	2.675	6.626	9.236	11.071	12.833	15.086	16.750
6	0.676	0.872	1.237	1.635	2.204	3.455	7.841	10.645	12.592	14.449	16.812	18.458
7	0.989	1.239	1.690	2.167	2.833	4.255	9.037	12.017	14.067	16.013	18.475	20.278
8	1.344	1.646	2.180	2.733	3.490	5.071	10.219	13.362	15.507	17.535	20.090	21.955
9	1.735	2.088	2.700	3.325	4.168	5.899	11.389	14.684	16.919	19.023	21.666	23.589
10	2.156	2.558	3.247	3.940	4.865	6.737	12.549	15.987	18.307	20.483	23.209	25.188
11	2.603	3.053	3.816	4.575	5.578	7.584	13.701	17.275	19.675	21.920	24.725	26.757
12	3.074	3.571	4.404	5.226	6.304	8.438	14.845	18.549	21.026	23.337	26.217	28.299
13	3.565	4.107	5.009	5.892	7.042	9.299	15.984	19.812	22.362	24.736	27.688	29.819
14	4.075	4.660	5.629	6.571	7.790	10.165	17.117	21.064	23.685	26.119	29.141	31.319
15	4.601	5.229	6.262	7.261	8.547	11.037	18.245	22.307	24.996	27.488	30.578	32.801
16	5.142	5.812	6.908	7.962	9.312	11.912	19.369	23.542	26.296	28.845	32.000	34.267
17	5.697	6.408	7.564	8.672	10.085	12.792	20.489	24.769	27.587	30.191	33.409	35.718
18	6.265	7.015	8.231	9.390	10.865	13.675	21.605	25.989	28.869	31.526	34.805	37.156
19	6.844	7.633	8.907	10.117	11.651	14.562	22.718	27.204	30.144	32.852	36.191	38.582
20	7.434	8.260	9.591	10.851	12.443	15.452	23.828	28.412	31.410	34.170	37.566	39.997
21	8.034	8.897	10.283	11.591	13.240	16.344	24.935	29.615	32.671	35.479	38.932	41.401
22	8.643	9.542	10.982	12.338	14.042	17.240	26.039	30.813	33.924	36.781	40.289	42.796
23	9.260	10.196	11.689	13.091	14.848	18.137	27.141	32.007	35.172	38.076	41.638	44.181
24	9.886	10.856	12.401	13.848	15.659	19.037	28.241	33.196	36.415	39.364	42.980	45.559
25	10.520	11.524	13.120	14.611	16.473	19.939	29.339	34.382	37.652	40.646	44.314	46.928
26	11.160	12.198	13.844	15.379	17.292	20.843	30.435	35.563	38.885	41.923	45.642	48.290
27	11.808	12.879	14.573	16.151	18.114	21.749	31.528	36.741	40.113	43.194	46.963	49.645
28	12.461	13.565	15.308	16.928	18.939	22.657	32.620	37.916	41.337	44.461	48.278	50.993
29	13.121	14.257	16.047	17.708	19.768	23.567	33.711	39.087	42.557	45.722	49.588	52.336
30	13.787	14.954	16.791	18.493	20.599	24.478	34.800	40.256	43.773	46.979	50.892	53.672

For larger values of degrees of freedom (df) the expression $Z = \sqrt{2\chi^2} - \sqrt{2(df)-1}$ may be used and the resulting upper-tail area can be found from the cumulative standardized normal distribution (Table E.2).

TABLE E.5

Critical Values of F

For a particular combination of numerator and denominator degrees of freedom, entry represents the critical values of F corresponding to the cumulative probability $(1 - \alpha)$ and a specified upper-tail area (α).

$\alpha = 0.05$

Cumulative Probabilities = 0.95

Upper Tail Areas = 0.05

Denominator, df_2	Numerator, df_1																		
	1	2	3	4	5	6	7	8	9	10	12	15	20	24	30	40	60	120	∞
1	161.40	199.50	215.70	224.60	230.20	234.00	236.80	238.90	240.50	241.90	243.90	245.90	248.00	249.10	250.10	251.10	252.20	253.30	254.30
2	18.51	19.00	19.16	19.25	19.30	19.33	19.35	19.37	19.38	19.40	19.41	19.43	19.45	19.45	19.46	19.47	19.48	19.49	19.50
3	10.13	9.55	9.28	9.12	9.01	8.94	8.89	8.85	8.81	8.79	8.74	8.70	8.66	8.64	8.62	8.59	8.57	8.55	8.53
4	7.71	6.94	6.59	6.39	6.26	6.16	6.09	6.04	6.00	5.96	5.91	5.86	5.80	5.77	5.75	5.72	5.69	5.66	5.63
5	6.61	5.79	5.41	5.19	5.05	4.95	4.88	4.82	4.77	4.74	4.68	4.62	4.56	4.53	4.50	4.46	4.43	4.40	4.36
6	5.99	5.14	4.76	4.53	4.39	4.28	4.21	4.15	4.10	4.06	4.00	3.94	3.87	3.84	3.81	3.77	3.74	3.70	3.67
7	5.59	4.74	4.35	4.12	3.97	3.87	3.79	3.73	3.68	3.64	3.57	3.51	3.44	3.41	3.38	3.34	3.30	3.27	3.23
8	5.32	4.46	4.07	3.84	3.69	3.58	3.50	3.44	3.39	3.35	3.28	3.22	3.15	3.12	3.08	3.04	3.01	2.97	2.93
9	5.12	4.26	3.86	3.63	3.48	3.37	3.29	3.23	3.18	3.14	3.07	3.01	2.94	2.90	2.86	2.83	2.79	2.75	2.71
10	4.96	4.10	3.71	3.48	3.33	3.22	3.14	3.07	3.02	2.98	2.91	2.85	2.77	2.74	2.70	2.66	2.62	2.58	2.54
11	4.84	3.98	3.59	3.36	3.20	3.09	3.01	2.95	2.90	2.85	2.79	2.72	2.65	2.61	2.57	2.53	2.49	2.45	2.40
12	4.75	3.89	3.49	3.26	3.11	3.00	2.91	2.85	2.80	2.75	2.69	2.62	2.54	2.51	2.47	2.43	2.38	2.34	2.30
13	4.67	3.81	3.41	3.18	3.03	2.92	2.83	2.77	2.71	2.67	2.60	2.53	2.46	2.42	2.38	2.34	2.30	2.25	2.21
14	4.60	3.74	3.34	3.11	2.96	2.85	2.76	2.70	2.65	2.60	2.53	2.46	2.39	2.35	2.31	2.27	2.22	2.18	2.13
15	4.54	3.68	3.29	3.06	2.90	2.79	2.71	2.64	2.59	2.54	2.48	2.40	2.33	2.29	2.25	2.20	2.16	2.11	2.07
16	4.49	3.63	3.24	3.01	2.85	2.74	2.66	2.59	2.54	2.49	2.42	2.35	2.28	2.24	2.19	2.15	2.11	2.06	2.01
17	4.45	3.59	3.20	2.96	2.81	2.70	2.61	2.55	2.49	2.45	2.38	2.31	2.23	2.19	2.15	2.10	2.06	2.01	1.96
18	4.41	3.55	3.16	2.93	2.77	2.66	2.58	2.51	2.46	2.41	2.34	2.27	2.19	2.15	2.11	2.06	2.02	1.97	1.92
19	4.38	3.52	3.13	2.90	2.74	2.63	2.54	2.48	2.42	2.38	2.31	2.23	2.16	2.11	2.07	2.03	1.98	1.93	1.88
20	4.35	3.49	3.10	2.87	2.71	2.60	2.51	2.45	2.39	2.35	2.28	2.20	2.12	2.08	2.04	1.99	1.95	1.90	1.84
21	4.32	3.47	3.07	2.84	2.68	2.57	2.49	2.42	2.37	2.32	2.25	2.18	2.10	2.05	2.01	1.96	1.92	1.87	1.81
22	4.30	3.44	3.05	2.82	2.66	2.55	2.46	2.40	2.34	2.30	2.23	2.15	2.07	2.03	1.98	1.94	1.89	1.84	1.78
23	4.28	3.42	3.03	2.80	2.64	2.53	2.44	2.37	2.32	2.27	2.20	2.13	2.05	2.01	1.96	1.91	1.86	1.81	1.76
24	4.26	3.40	3.01	2.78	2.62	2.51	2.42	2.36	2.30	2.25	2.18	2.11	2.03	1.98	1.94	1.89	1.84	1.79	1.73
25	4.24	3.39	2.99	2.76	2.60	2.49	2.40	2.34	2.28	2.24	2.16	2.09	2.01	1.96	1.92	1.87	1.82	1.77	1.71
26	4.23	3.37	2.98	2.74	2.59	2.47	2.39	2.32	2.27	2.22	2.15	2.07	1.99	1.95	1.90	1.85	1.80	1.75	1.69
27	4.21	3.35	2.96	2.73	2.57	2.46	2.37	2.31	2.25	2.20	2.13	2.06	1.97	1.93	1.88	1.84	1.79	1.73	1.67
28	4.20	3.34	2.95	2.71	2.56	2.45	2.36	2.29	2.24	2.19	2.12	2.04	1.96	1.91	1.87	1.82	1.77	1.71	1.65
29	4.18	3.33	2.93	2.70	2.55	2.43	2.35	2.28	2.22	2.18	2.10	2.03	1.94	1.90	1.85	1.81	1.75	1.70	1.64
30	4.17	3.32	2.92	2.69	2.53	2.42	2.33	2.27	2.21	2.16	2.09	2.01	1.93	1.89	1.84	1.79	1.74	1.68	1.62
40	4.08	3.23	2.84	2.61	2.45	2.34	2.25	2.18	2.12	2.08	2.00	1.92	1.84	1.79	1.74	1.69	1.64	1.58	1.51
60	4.00	3.15	2.76	2.53	2.37	2.25	2.17	2.10	2.04	1.99	1.92	1.84	1.75	1.70	1.65	1.59	1.53	1.47	1.39
120	3.92	3.07	2.68	2.45	2.29	2.17	2.09	2.02	1.96	1.91	1.83	1.75	1.66	1.61	1.55	1.50	1.43	1.35	1.25
∞	3.84	3.00	2.60	2.37	2.21	2.10	2.01	1.94	1.88	1.83	1.75	1.67	1.57	1.52	1.46	1.39	1.32	1.22	1.00

continued

TABLE E.5
Critical Values of F (Continued)

α = 0.025

Cumulative Probabilities = 0.975

Upper Tail Areas = 0.025

Numerator, df_1

Denominator, df_2	1	2	3	4	5	6	7	8	9	10	12	15	20	24	30	40	60	120	∞
1	647.80	799.50	864.20	899.60	921.80	937.10	948.20	956.70	963.30	968.60	976.70	984.90	993.10	997.20	1,001.00	1,006.00	1,010.00	1,014.00	1,018.00
2	38.51	39.00	39.17	39.25	39.30	39.33	39.36	39.39	39.39	39.40	39.41	39.43	39.45	39.46	39.46	39.47	39.48	39.49	39.50
3	17.44	16.04	15.44	15.10	14.88	14.73	14.62	14.54	14.47	14.42	14.34	14.25	14.17	14.12	14.08	14.04	13.99	13.95	13.90
4	12.22	10.65	9.98	9.60	9.36	9.20	9.07	8.98	8.90	8.84	8.75	8.66	8.56	8.51	8.46	8.41	8.36	8.31	8.26
5	10.01	8.43	7.76	7.39	7.15	6.98	6.85	6.76	6.68	6.62	6.52	6.43	6.33	6.28	6.23	6.18	6.12	6.07	6.02
6	8.81	7.26	6.60	6.23	5.99	5.82	5.70	5.60	5.52	5.46	5.37	5.27	5.17	5.12	5.07	5.01	4.96	4.90	4.85
7	8.07	6.54	5.89	5.52	5.29	5.12	4.99	4.90	4.82	4.76	4.67	4.57	4.47	4.42	4.36	4.31	4.25	4.20	4.14
8	7.57	6.06	5.42	5.05	4.82	4.65	4.53	4.43	4.36	4.30	4.20	4.10	4.00	3.95	3.89	3.84	3.78	3.73	3.67
9	7.21	5.71	5.08	4.72	4.48	4.32	4.20	4.10	4.03	3.96	3.87	3.77	3.67	3.61	3.56	3.51	3.45	3.39	3.33
10	6.94	5.46	4.83	4.47	4.24	4.07	3.95	3.85	3.78	3.72	3.62	3.52	3.42	3.37	3.31	3.26	3.20	3.14	3.08
11	6.72	5.26	4.63	4.28	4.04	3.88	3.76	3.66	3.59	3.53	3.43	3.33	3.23	3.17	3.12	3.06	3.00	2.94	2.88
12	6.55	5.10	4.47	4.12	3.89	3.73	3.61	3.51	3.44	3.37	3.28	3.18	3.07	3.02	2.96	2.91	2.85	2.79	2.72
13	6.41	4.97	4.35	4.00	3.77	3.60	3.48	3.39	3.31	3.25	3.15	3.05	2.95	2.89	2.84	2.78	2.72	2.66	2.60
14	6.30	4.86	4.24	3.89	3.66	3.50	3.38	3.29	3.21	3.15	3.05	2.95	2.84	2.79	2.73	2.67	2.61	2.55	2.49
15	6.20	4.77	4.15	3.80	3.58	3.41	3.29	3.20	3.12	3.06	2.96	2.86	2.76	2.70	2.64	2.59	2.52	2.46	2.40
16	6.12	4.69	4.08	3.73	3.50	3.34	3.22	3.12	3.05	2.99	2.89	2.79	2.68	2.63	2.57	2.51	2.45	2.38	2.32
17	6.04	4.62	4.01	3.66	3.44	3.28	3.16	3.06	2.98	2.92	2.82	2.72	2.62	2.56	2.50	2.44	2.38	2.32	2.25
18	5.98	4.56	3.95	3.61	3.38	3.22	3.10	3.01	2.93	2.87	2.77	2.67	2.56	2.50	2.44	2.38	2.32	2.26	2.19
19	5.92	4.51	3.90	3.56	3.33	3.17	3.05	2.96	2.88	2.82	2.72	2.62	2.51	2.45	2.39	2.33	2.27	2.20	2.13
20	5.87	4.46	3.86	3.51	3.29	3.13	3.01	2.91	2.84	2.77	2.68	2.57	2.46	2.41	2.35	2.29	2.22	2.16	2.09
21	5.83	4.42	3.82	3.48	3.25	3.09	2.97	2.87	2.80	2.73	2.64	2.53	2.42	2.37	2.31	2.25	2.18	2.11	2.04
22	5.79	4.38	3.78	3.44	3.22	3.05	2.93	2.84	2.76	2.70	2.60	2.50	2.39	2.33	2.27	2.21	2.14	2.08	2.00
23	5.75	4.35	3.75	3.41	3.18	3.02	2.90	2.81	2.73	2.67	2.57	2.47	2.36	2.30	2.24	2.18	2.11	2.04	1.97
24	5.72	4.32	3.72	3.38	3.15	2.99	2.87	2.78	2.70	2.64	2.54	2.44	2.33	2.27	2.21	2.15	2.08	2.01	1.94
25	5.69	4.29	3.69	3.35	3.13	2.97	2.85	2.75	2.68	2.61	2.51	2.41	2.30	2.24	2.18	2.12	2.05	1.98	1.91
26	5.66	4.27	3.67	3.33	3.10	2.94	2.82	2.73	2.65	2.59	2.49	2.39	2.28	2.22	2.16	2.09	2.03	1.95	1.88
27	5.63	4.24	3.65	3.31	3.08	2.92	2.80	2.71	2.63	2.57	2.47	2.36	2.25	2.19	2.13	2.07	2.00	1.93	1.85
28	5.61	4.22	3.63	3.29	3.06	2.90	2.78	2.69	2.61	2.55	2.45	2.34	2.23	2.17	2.11	2.05	1.98	1.91	1.83
29	5.59	4.20	3.61	3.27	3.04	2.88	2.76	2.67	2.59	2.53	2.43	2.32	2.21	2.15	2.09	2.03	1.96	1.89	1.81
30	5.57	4.18	3.59	3.25	3.03	2.87	2.75	2.65	2.57	2.51	2.41	2.31	2.20	2.14	2.07	2.01	1.94	1.87	1.79
40	5.42	4.05	3.46	3.13	2.90	2.74	2.62	2.53	2.45	2.39	2.29	2.18	2.07	2.01	1.94	1.88	1.80	1.72	1.64
60	5.29	3.93	3.34	3.01	2.79	2.63	2.51	2.41	2.33	2.27	2.17	2.06	1.94	1.88	1.82	1.74	1.67	1.58	1.48
120	5.15	3.80	3.23	2.89	2.67	2.52	2.39	2.30	2.22	2.16	2.05	1.94	1.82	1.76	1.69	1.61	1.53	1.43	1.31
∞	5.02	3.69	3.12	2.79	2.57	2.41	2.29	2.19	2.11	2.05	1.94	1.83	1.71	1.64	1.57	1.48	1.39	1.27	1.00

continued

TABLE E.5

Critical Values of F (Continued)

α = 0.01

Cumulative Probabilities = 0.99

Upper Tail Areas = 0.01

Denominator, df_2	Numerator, df_1																		
	1	2	3	4	5	6	7	8	9	10	12	15	20	24	30	40	60	120	∞
1	4,052.00	4,999.50	5,403.00	5,625.00	5,764.00	5,859.00	5,928.00	5,982.00	6,022.00	6,056.00	6,106.00	6,157.00	6,209.00	6,235.00	6,261.00	6,287.00	6,313.00	6,339.00	6,366.00
2	98.50	99.00	99.17	99.25	99.30	99.33	99.36	99.37	99.39	99.40	99.42	99.43	44.45	99.46	99.47	99.47	99.48	99.49	99.50
3	34.12	30.82	29.46	28.71	28.24	27.91	27.67	27.49	27.35	27.23	27.05	26.87	26.69	26.60	26.50	26.41	26.32	26.22	26.13
4	21.20	18.00	16.69	15.98	15.52	15.21	14.98	14.80	14.66	14.55	14.37	14.20	14.02	13.93	13.84	13.75	13.65	13.56	13.46
5	16.26	13.27	12.06	11.39	10.97	10.67	10.46	10.29	10.16	10.05	9.89	9.72	9.55	9.47	9.38	9.29	9.20	9.11	9.02
6	13.75	10.92	9.78	9.15	8.75	8.47	8.26	8.10	7.98	7.87	7.72	7.56	7.40	7.31	7.23	7.14	7.06	6.97	6.88
7	12.25	9.55	8.45	7.85	7.46	7.19	6.99	6.84	6.72	6.62	6.47	6.31	6.16	6.07	5.99	5.91	5.82	5.74	5.65
8	11.26	8.65	7.59	7.01	6.63	6.37	6.18	6.03	5.91	5.81	5.67	5.52	5.36	5.28	5.20	5.12	5.03	4.95	4.86
9	10.56	8.02	6.99	6.42	6.06	5.80	5.61	5.47	5.35	5.26	5.11	4.96	4.81	4.73	4.65	4.57	4.48	4.40	4.31
10	10.04	7.56	6.55	5.99	5.64	5.39	5.20	5.06	4.94	4.85	4.71	4.56	4.41	4.33	4.25	4.17	4.08	4.00	3.91
11	9.65	7.21	6.22	5.67	5.32	5.07	4.89	4.74	4.63	4.54	4.40	4.25	4.10	4.02	3.94	3.86	3.78	3.69	3.60
12	9.33	6.93	5.95	5.41	5.06	4.82	4.64	4.50	4.39	4.30	4.16	4.01	3.86	3.78	3.70	3.62	3.54	3.45	3.36
13	9.07	6.70	5.74	5.21	4.86	4.62	4.44	4.30	4.19	4.10	3.96	3.82	3.66	3.59	3.51	3.43	3.34	3.25	3.17
14	8.86	6.51	5.56	5.04	4.69	4.46	4.28	4.14	4.03	3.94	3.80	3.66	3.51	3.43	3.35	3.27	3.18	3.09	3.00
15	8.68	6.36	5.42	4.89	4.56	4.32	4.14	4.00	3.89	3.80	3.67	3.52	3.37	3.29	3.21	3.13	3.05	2.96	2.87
16	8.53	6.23	5.29	4.77	4.44	4.20	4.03	3.89	3.78	3.69	3.55	3.41	3.26	3.18	3.10	3.02	2.93	2.81	2.75
17	8.40	6.11	5.18	4.67	4.34	4.10	3.93	3.79	3.68	3.59	3.46	3.31	3.16	3.08	3.00	2.92	2.83	2.75	2.65
18	8.29	6.01	5.09	4.58	4.25	4.01	3.84	3.71	3.60	3.51	3.37	3.23	3.08	3.00	2.92	2.84	2.75	2.66	2.57
19	8.18	5.93	5.01	4.50	4.17	3.94	3.77	3.63	3.52	3.43	3.30	3.15	3.00	2.92	2.84	2.76	2.67	2.58	2.49
20	8.10	5.85	4.94	4.43	4.10	3.87	3.70	3.56	3.46	3.37	3.23	3.09	2.94	2.86	2.78	2.69	2.61	2.52	2.42
21	8.02	5.78	4.87	4.37	4.04	3.81	3.64	3.51	3.40	3.31	3.17	3.03	2.88	2.80	2.72	2.64	2.55	2.46	2.36
22	7.95	5.72	4.82	4.31	3.99	3.76	3.59	3.45	3.35	3.26	3.12	2.98	2.83	2.75	2.67	2.58	2.50	2.40	2.31
23	7.88	5.66	4.76	4.26	3.94	3.71	3.54	3.41	3.30	3.21	3.07	2.93	2.78	2.70	2.62	2.54	2.45	2.35	2.26
24	7.82	5.61	4.72	4.22	3.90	3.67	3.50	3.36	3.26	3.17	3.03	2.89	2.74	2.66	2.58	2.49	2.40	2.31	2.21
25	7.77	5.57	4.68	4.18	3.85	3.63	3.46	3.32	3.22	3.13	2.99	2.85	2.70	2.62	2.54	2.45	2.36	2.27	2.17
26	7.72	5.53	4.64	4.14	3.82	3.59	3.42	3.29	3.18	3.09	2.96	2.81	2.66	2.58	2.50	2.42	2.33	2.23	2.13
27	7.68	5.49	4.60	4.11	3.78	3.56	3.39	3.26	3.15	3.06	2.93	2.78	2.63	2.55	2.47	2.38	2.29	2.20	2.10
28	7.64	5.45	4.57	4.07	3.75	3.53	3.36	3.23	3.12	3.03	2.90	2.75	2.60	2.52	2.44	2.35	2.26	2.17	2.06
29	7.60	5.42	4.54	4.04	3.73	3.50	3.33	3.20	3.09	3.00	2.87	2.73	2.57	2.49	2.41	2.33	2.23	2.14	2.03
30	7.56	5.39	4.51	4.02	3.70	3.47	3.30	3.17	3.07	2.98	2.84	2.70	2.55	2.47	2.39	2.30	2.21	2.11	2.01
40	7.31	5.18	4.31	3.83	3.51	3.29	3.12	2.99	2.89	2.80	2.66	2.52	2.37	2.29	2.20	2.11	2.02	1.92	1.80
60	7.08	4.98	4.13	3.65	3.34	3.12	2.95	2.82	2.72	2.63	2.50	2.35	2.20	2.12	2.03	1.94	1.84	1.73	1.60
120	6.85	4.79	3.95	3.48	3.17	2.96	2.79	2.66	2.56	2.47	2.34	2.19	2.03	1.95	1.86	1.76	1.66	1.53	1.38
∞	6.63	4.61	3.78	3.32	3.02	2.80	2.64	2.51	2.41	2.32	2.18	2.04	1.88	1.79	1.70	1.59	1.47	1.32	1.00

continued

TABLE E.5
Critical Values of F (Continued)

α = 0.005

Cumulative Probabilities = 0.995

Upper Tail Areas = 0.005

Numerator, df_1

Denominator, df_2	1	2	3	4	5	6	7	8	9	10	12	15	20	24	30	40	60	120	∞
1	16,211.00	20,000.00	21,615.00	22,500.00	23,056.00	23,437.00	23,715.00	23,925.00	24,091.00	24,224.00	24,426.00	24,630.00	24,836.00	24,910.00	25,044.00	25,148.00	25,253.00	25,359.00	25,465.00
2	198.50	199.00	199.20	199.20	199.30	199.30	199.40	199.40	199.40	199.40	199.40	199.40	199.40	199.50	199.50	199.50	199.50	199.50	199.50
3	55.55	49.80	47.47	46.19	45.39	44.84	44.43	44.13	43.88	43.69	43.39	43.08	42.78	42.62	42.47	42.31	42.15	41.99	41.83
4	31.33	26.28	24.26	23.15	22.46	21.97	21.62	21.35	21.14	20.97	20.70	20.44	20.17	20.03	19.89	19.75	19.61	19.47	19.32
5	22.78	18.31	16.53	15.56	14.94	14.51	14.20	13.96	13.77	13.62	13.38	13.15	12.90	12.78	12.66	12.53	12.40	12.27	12.11
6	18.63	14.54	12.92	12.03	11.46	11.07	10.79	10.57	10.39	10.25	10.03	9.81	9.59	9.47	9.36	9.24	9.12	9.00	8.88
7	16.24	12.40	10.88	10.05	9.52	9.16	8.89	8.68	8.51	8.38	8.18	7.97	7.75	7.65	7.53	7.42	7.31	7.19	7.08
8	14.69	11.04	9.60	8.81	8.30	7.95	7.69	7.50	7.34	7.21	7.01	6.81	6.61	6.50	6.40	6.29	6.18	6.06	5.95
9	13.61	10.11	8.72	7.96	7.47	7.13	6.88	6.69	6.54	6.42	6.23	6.03	5.83	5.73	5.62	5.52	5.41	5.30	5.19
10	12.83	9.43	8.08	7.34	6.87	6.54	6.30	6.12	5.97	5.85	5.66	5.47	5.27	5.17	5.07	4.97	4.86	4.75	4.61
11	12.23	8.91	7.60	6.88	6.42	6.10	5.86	5.68	5.54	5.42	5.24	5.05	4.86	4.75	4.65	4.55	4.44	4.34	4.23
12	11.75	8.51	7.23	6.52	6.07	5.76	5.52	5.35	5.20	5.09	4.91	4.72	4.53	4.43	4.33	4.23	4.12	4.01	3.90
13	11.37	8.19	6.93	6.23	5.79	5.48	5.25	5.08	4.94	4.82	4.64	4.46	4.27	4.17	4.07	3.97	3.87	3.76	3.65
14	11.06	7.92	6.68	6.00	5.56	5.26	5.03	4.86	4.72	4.60	4.43	4.25	4.06	3.96	3.86	3.76	3.66	3.55	3.41
15	10.80	7.70	6.48	5.80	5.37	5.07	4.85	4.67	4.54	4.42	4.25	4.07	3.88	3.79	3.69	3.58	3.48	3.37	3.26
16	10.58	7.51	6.30	5.64	5.21	4.91	4.69	4.52	4.38	4.27	4.10	3.92	3.73	3.64	3.54	3.44	3.33	3.22	3.11
17	10.38	7.35	6.16	5.50	5.07	4.78	4.56	4.39	4.25	4.14	3.97	3.79	3.61	3.51	3.41	3.31	3.21	3.10	2.98
18	10.22	7.21	6.03	5.37	4.96	4.66	4.44	4.28	4.14	4.03	3.86	3.68	3.50	3.40	3.30	3.20	3.10	2.99	2.87
19	10.07	7.09	5.92	5.27	4.85	4.56	4.34	4.18	4.04	3.93	3.76	3.59	3.40	3.31	3.21	3.11	3.00	2.89	2.78
20	9.94	6.99	5.82	5.17	4.76	4.47	4.26	4.09	3.96	3.85	3.68	3.50	3.32	3.22	3.12	3.02	2.92	2.81	2.69
21	9.83	6.89	5.73	5.09	4.68	4.39	4.18	4.02	3.88	3.77	3.60	3.43	3.24	3.15	3.05	2.95	2.84	2.73	2.61
22	9.73	6.81	5.65	5.02	4.61	4.32	4.11	3.94	3.81	3.70	3.54	3.36	3.18	3.08	2.98	2.88	2.77	2.66	2.55
23	9.63	6.73	5.58	4.95	4.54	4.26	4.05	3.88	3.75	3.64	3.47	3.30	3.12	3.02	2.92	2.82	2.71	2.60	2.48
24	9.55	6.66	5.52	4.89	4.49	4.20	3.99	3.83	3.69	3.59	3.42	3.25	3.06	2.97	2.87	2.77	2.66	2.55	2.43
25	9.48	6.60	5.46	4.84	4.43	4.15	3.94	3.78	3.64	3.54	3.37	3.20	3.01	2.92	2.82	2.72	2.61	2.50	2.38
26	9.41	6.54	5.41	4.79	4.38	4.10	3.89	3.73	3.60	3.49	3.33	3.15	2.97	2.87	2.77	2.67	2.56	2.45	2.33
27	9.34	6.49	5.36	4.74	4.34	4.06	3.85	3.69	3.56	3.45	3.28	3.11	2.93	2.83	2.73	2.63	2.52	2.41	2.29
28	9.28	6.44	5.32	4.70	4.30	4.02	3.81	3.65	3.52	3.41	3.25	3.07	2.89	2.79	2.69	2.59	2.48	2.37	2.25
29	9.23	6.40	5.28	4.66	4.26	3.98	3.77	3.61	3.48	3.38	3.21	3.04	2.86	2.76	2.66	2.56	2.45	2.33	2.21
30	9.18	6.35	5.24	4.62	4.23	3.95	3.74	3.58	3.45	3.34	3.18	3.01	2.82	2.73	2.63	2.52	2.42	2.30	2.18
40	8.83	6.07	4.98	4.37	3.99	3.71	3.51	3.35	3.22	3.12	2.95	2.78	2.60	2.50	2.40	2.30	2.18	2.06	1.93
60	8.49	5.79	4.73	4.14	3.76	3.49	3.29	3.13	3.01	2.90	2.74	2.57	2.39	2.29	2.19	2.08	1.96	1.83	1.69
120	8.18	5.54	4.50	3.92	3.55	3.28	3.09	2.93	2.81	2.71	2.54	2.37	2.19	2.09	1.98	1.87	1.75	1.61	1.43
∞	7.88	5.30	4.28	3.72	3.35	3.09	2.90	2.74	2.62	2.52	2.36	2.19	2.00	1.90	1.79	1.67	1.53	1.36	1.00

Source: Reprinted from E. S. Pearson and H. O. Hartley, eds., Biometrika Tables for Statisticians, 3rd ed., 1966, by permission of the Biometrika Trustees.

TABLE E.6

TABLE OF BINOMIAL PROBABILITIES (BEGINS ON THE FOLLOWING PAGE)

TABLE E.6
Table of Binomial Probabilities

For a given combination of n and p, entry indicates the probability of obtaining a specified value of X. To locate entry, **when $p \le .50$**, read p across the top heading and both n and X down the left margin; **when $p \ge .50$**, read p across the bottom heading and both n and X up the right margin.

											p										
n	X	0.01	0.02	0.03	0.04	0.05	0.06	0.07	0.08	0.09	0.10	0.15	0.20	0.25	0.30	0.35	0.40	0.45	0.50	X	n
2	0	0.9801	0.9604	0.9409	0.9216	0.9025	0.8836	0.8649	0.8464	0.8281	0.8100	0.7225	0.6400	0.5625	0.4900	0.4225	0.3600	0.3025	0.2500	2	
	1	0.0198	0.0392	0.0582	0.0768	0.0950	0.1128	0.1302	0.1472	0.1638	0.1800	0.2550	0.3200	0.3750	0.4200	0.4550	0.4800	0.4950	0.5000	1	
	2	0.0001	0.0004	0.0009	0.0016	0.0025	0.0036	0.0049	0.0064	0.0081	0.0100	0.0225	0.0400	0.0625	0.0900	0.1225	0.1600	0.2025	0.2500	0	2
3	0	0.9703	0.9412	0.9127	0.8847	0.8574	0.8306	0.8044	0.7787	0.7536	0.7290	0.6141	0.5120	0.4219	0.3430	0.2746	0.2160	0.1664	0.1250	3	
	1	0.0294	0.0576	0.0847	0.1106	0.1354	0.1590	0.1816	0.2031	0.2236	0.2430	0.3251	0.3840	0.4219	0.4410	0.4436	0.4320	0.4084	0.3750	2	
	2	0.0003	0.0012	0.0026	0.0046	0.0071	0.0102	0.0137	0.0177	0.0221	0.0270	0.0574	0.0960	0.1406	0.1890	0.2389	0.2880	0.3341	0.3750	1	
	3	0.0000	0.0000	0.0000	0.0001	0.0001	0.0002	0.0003	0.0005	0.0007	0.0010	0.0034	0.0080	0.0156	0.0270	0.0429	0.0640	0.0911	0.1250	0	3
4	0	0.9606	0.9224	0.8853	0.8493	0.8145	0.7807	0.7481	0.7164	0.6857	0.6561	0.5220	0.4096	0.3164	0.2401	0.1785	0.1296	0.0915	0.0625	4	
	1	0.0388	0.0753	0.1095	0.1416	0.1715	0.1993	0.2252	0.2492	0.2713	0.2916	0.3685	0.4096	0.4219	0.4116	0.3845	0.3456	0.2995	0.2500	3	
	2	0.0006	0.0023	0.0051	0.0088	0.0135	0.0191	0.0254	0.0325	0.0402	0.0486	0.0975	0.1536	0.2109	0.2646	0.3105	0.3456	0.3675	0.3750	2	
	3	0.0000	0.0000	0.0001	0.0002	0.0005	0.0008	0.0013	0.0019	0.0027	0.0036	0.0115	0.0256	0.0469	0.0756	0.1115	0.1536	0.2005	0.2500	1	
	4	0.0000	—	0.0000	0.0000	0.0000	0.0000	0.0000	0.0000	0.0001	0.0001	0.0005	0.0016	0.0039	0.0081	0.0150	0.0256	0.0410	0.0625	0	4
5	0	0.9510	0.9039	0.8587	0.8154	0.7738	0.7339	0.6957	0.6591	0.6240	0.5905	0.4437	0.3277	0.2373	0.1681	0.1160	0.0778	0.0503	0.0312	5	
	1	0.0480	0.0922	0.1328	0.1699	0.2036	0.2342	0.2618	0.2866	0.3086	0.3280	0.3915	0.4096	0.3955	0.3601	0.3124	0.2592	0.2059	0.1562	4	
	2	0.0010	0.0038	0.0082	0.0142	0.0214	0.0299	0.0394	0.0498	0.0610	0.0729	0.1382	0.2048	0.2637	0.3087	0.3364	0.3456	0.3369	0.3125	3	
	3	0.0000	0.0001	0.0003	0.0006	0.0011	0.0019	0.0030	0.0043	0.0060	0.0081	0.0244	0.0512	0.0879	0.1323	0.1811	0.2304	0.2757	0.3125	2	
	4	0.0000	0.0000	0.0000	0.0000	0.0000	0.0001	0.0001	0.0002	0.0003	0.0004	0.0022	0.0064	0.0146	0.0283	0.0488	0.0768	0.1128	0.1562	1	
	5	—	0.0000	0.0000	0.0000	0.0000	0.0000	0.0000	0.0000	0.0000	0.0000	0.0001	0.0003	0.0010	0.0024	0.0053	0.0102	0.0185	0.0312	0	5
6	0	0.9415	0.8858	0.8330	0.7828	0.7351	0.6899	0.6470	0.6064	0.5679	0.5314	0.3771	0.2621	0.1780	0.1176	0.0754	0.0467	0.0277	0.0156	6	
	1	0.0571	0.1085	0.1546	0.1957	0.2321	0.2642	0.2922	0.3164	0.3370	0.3543	0.3993	0.3932	0.3560	0.3025	0.2437	0.1866	0.1359	0.0937	5	
	2	0.0014	0.0055	0.0120	0.0204	0.0305	0.0422	0.0550	0.0688	0.0833	0.0984	0.1762	0.2458	0.2966	0.3241	0.3280	0.3110	0.2780	0.2344	4	
	3	0.0000	0.0002	0.0005	0.0011	0.0021	0.0036	0.0055	0.0080	0.0110	0.0146	0.0415	0.0819	0.1318	0.1852	0.2355	0.2765	0.3032	0.3125	3	
	4	—	0.0000	0.0000	0.0000	0.0001	0.0002	0.0003	0.0005	0.0008	0.0012	0.0055	0.0154	0.0330	0.0595	0.0951	0.1372	0.1861	0.2344	2	
	5	—	0.0000	0.0000	0.0000	0.0000	0.0000	0.0000	0.0000	0.0000	0.0001	0.0004	0.0015	0.0044	0.0102	0.0205	0.0369	0.0609	0.0937	1	
	6	—	—	—	0.0000	0.0000	0.0000	0.0000	0.0000	0.0000	0.0000	0.0000	0.0001	0.0002	0.0007	0.0018	0.0041	0.0083	0.0156	0	6

n	X	0.50	0.55	0.60	0.65	0.70	0.75	0.80	0.85	0.90	0.91	0.92	0.93	0.94	0.95	0.96	0.97	0.98	0.99
7	7	0.0078	0.0152	0.0280	0.0490	0.0824	0.1335	0.2097	0.3206	0.4783	0.5168	0.5578	0.6017	0.6485	0.6983	0.7514	0.8080	0.8681	0.9321
	6	0.0547	0.0872	0.1306	0.1848	0.2471	0.3115	0.3670	0.3960	0.3720	0.3578	0.3396	0.3170	0.2897	0.2573	0.2192	0.1749	0.1240	0.0659
	5	0.1641	0.2140	0.2613	0.2985	0.3177	0.3115	0.2753	0.2097	0.1240	0.1061	0.0886	0.0716	0.0555	0.0406	0.0274	0.0162	0.0076	0.0020
	4	0.2734	0.2918	0.2903	0.2679	0.2269	0.1730	0.1147	0.0617	0.0230	0.0175	0.0128	0.0090	0.0059	0.0036	0.0019	0.0008	0.0003	0.0000
	3	0.2734	0.2388	0.1935	0.1442	0.0972	0.0577	0.0287	0.0109	0.0026	0.0017	0.0011	0.0007	0.0004	0.0002	0.0001	0.0001	0.0000	0.0000
	2	0.1641	0.1172	0.0774	0.0466	0.0250	0.0115	0.0043	0.0012	0.0002	0.0001	0.0001	0.0000	0.0000	0.0000	0.0000	0.0000	0.0000	—
	1	0.0547	0.0320	0.0172	0.0084	0.0036	0.0013	0.0004	0.0001	0.0000	0.0000	0.0000	0.0000	0.0000	0.0000	0.0000	0.0000	—	—
	0	0.0078	0.0037	0.0016	0.0006	0.0002	0.0001	0.0000	0.0000	—	—	—	—	—	—	—	—	—	—
8	8	0.0039	0.0084	0.0168	0.0319	0.0576	0.1001	0.1678	0.2725	0.4305	0.4703	0.5132	0.5596	0.6096	0.6634	0.7214	0.7837	0.8508	0.9227
	7	0.0312	0.0548	0.0896	0.1373	0.1977	0.2670	0.3355	0.3847	0.3826	0.3721	0.3570	0.3370	0.3113	0.2793	0.2405	0.1939	0.1389	0.0746
	6	0.1094	0.1569	0.2090	0.2587	0.2965	0.3115	0.2936	0.2376	0.1488	0.1288	0.1087	0.0888	0.0695	0.0515	0.0351	0.0210	0.0099	0.0026
	5	0.2187	0.2568	0.2787	0.2786	0.2541	0.2076	0.1468	0.0839	0.0331	0.0255	0.0189	0.0134	0.0089	0.0054	0.0029	0.0013	0.0004	0.0001
	4	0.2734	0.2627	0.2322	0.1875	0.1361	0.0865	0.0459	0.0185	0.0046	0.0031	0.0021	0.0013	0.0007	0.0004	0.0002	0.0001	0.0000	0.0000
	3	0.2187	0.1719	0.1239	0.0808	0.0467	0.0231	0.0092	0.0026	0.0004	0.0002	0.0001	0.0001	0.0000	0.0000	0.0000	0.0000	—	—
	2	0.1094	0.0703	0.0413	0.0217	0.0100	0.0038	0.0011	0.0002	0.0000	0.0000	0.0000	0.0000	0.0000	0.0000	—	—	—	—
	1	0.0312	0.0164	0.0079	0.0033	0.0012	0.0004	0.0001	0.0000	0.0000	0.0000	0.0000	0.0000	—	—	—	—	—	—
	0	0.0039	0.0037	0.0016	0.0002	0.0001	0.0000	0.0000	0.0000	—	—	—	—	—	—	—	—	—	—
9	9	0.0020	0.0046	0.0101	0.0207	0.0404	0.0751	0.1342	0.2316	0.3874	0.4279	0.4722	0.5204	0.5730	0.6302	0.6925	0.7602	0.8337	0.9135
	8	0.0176	0.0339	0.0605	0.1004	0.1556	0.2253	0.3020	0.3679	0.3874	0.3809	0.3695	0.3525	0.3292	0.2985	0.2597	0.2116	0.1531	0.0830
	7	0.0703	0.1110	0.1612	0.2162	0.2668	0.3003	0.3020	0.2597	0.1722	0.1507	0.1285	0.1061	0.0840	0.0629	0.0433	0.0262	0.0125	0.0034
	6	0.1641	0.2119	0.2508	0.2716	0.2668	0.2336	0.1762	0.1069	0.0446	0.0348	0.0261	0.0186	0.0125	0.0077	0.0042	0.0019	0.0006	0.0001
	5	0.2461	0.2600	0.2508	0.2194	0.1715	0.1168	0.0661	0.0283	0.0074	0.0052	0.0034	0.0021	0.0012	0.0006	0.0003	0.0001	0.0000	0.0000
	4	0.2461	0.2128	0.1672	0.1181	0.0735	0.0390	0.0165	0.0050	0.0008	0.0005	0.0003	0.0002	0.0001	0.0000	0.0000	0.0000	—	—
	3	0.1641	0.1160	0.0743	0.0424	0.0210	0.0087	0.0028	0.0006	0.0001	0.0000	0.0000	0.0000	0.0000	0.0000	—	—	—	—
	2	0.0703	0.0407	0.0212	0.0098	0.0039	0.0012	0.0003	0.0001	0.0000	0.0000	0.0000	—	—	—	—	—	—	—
	1	0.0176	0.0083	0.0035	0.0013	0.0004	0.0001	0.0000	0.0000	0.0000	—	—	—	—	—	—	—	—	—
	0	0.0020	0.0017	0.0007	0.0002	0.0001	0.0000	0.0000	0.0000	—	—	—	—	—	—	—	—	—	—
10	10	0.0010	0.0025	0.0060	0.0135	0.0282	0.0563	0.1074	0.1969	0.3487	0.3894	0.4344	0.4840	0.5386	0.5987	0.6648	0.7374	0.8171	0.9044
	9	0.0098	0.0207	0.0403	0.0725	0.1211	0.1877	0.2684	0.3474	0.3874	0.3851	0.3777	0.3643	0.3438	0.3151	0.2770	0.2281	0.1667	0.0914
	8	0.0439	0.0763	0.1209	0.1757	0.2335	0.2816	0.3020	0.2759	0.1937	0.1714	0.1478	0.1234	0.0988	0.0746	0.0519	0.0317	0.0153	0.0042
	7	0.1172	0.1665	0.2150	0.2522	0.2668	0.2503	0.2013	0.1298	0.0574	0.0452	0.0343	0.0248	0.0168	0.0105	0.0058	0.0026	0.0008	0.0001
	6	0.2051	0.2384	0.2508	0.2377	0.2001	0.1460	0.0881	0.0401	0.0112	0.0078	0.0052	0.0033	0.0019	0.0010	0.0004	0.0001	0.0000	0.0000
	5	0.2461	0.2340	0.2007	0.1536	0.1029	0.0584	0.0264	0.0085	0.0015	0.0009	0.0005	0.0003	0.0001	0.0001	0.0000	0.0000	—	—
	4	0.2051	0.1596	0.1115	0.0689	0.0368	0.0162	0.0055	0.0012	0.0001	0.0001	0.0000	0.0000	0.0000	0.0000	—	—	—	—
	3	0.1172	0.0746	0.0425	0.0212	0.0090	0.0031	0.0008	0.0001	0.0000	0.0000	0.0000	—	—	—	—	—	—	—
	2	0.0439	0.0229	0.0106	0.0043	0.0014	0.0004	0.0001	0.0000	0.0000	—	—	—	—	—	—	—	—	—
	1	0.0098	0.0042	0.0016	0.0005	0.0001	0.0000	0.0000	0.0000	—	—	—	—	—	—	—	—	—	—
	0	0.0010	0.0003	0.0001	0.0000	0.0000	0.0000	0.0000	0.0000	—	—	—	—	—	—	—	—	—	—

continued

TABLE E.6
Table of Binomial Probabilities (Continued)

n = 20

X	0.01	0.02	0.03	0.04	0.05	0.06	0.07	0.08	0.09	0.10	0.15	0.20	0.25	0.30	0.35	0.40	0.45	0.50	X
0	0.8179	0.6676	0.5438	0.4420	0.3585	0.2901	0.2342	0.1887	0.1516	0.1216	0.0388	0.0115	0.0032	0.0008	0.0002	0.0000	0.0000	—	20
1	0.1652	0.2725	0.3364	0.3683	0.3774	0.3703	0.3526	0.3282	0.3000	0.2702	0.1368	0.0576	0.0211	0.0068	0.0020	0.0005	0.0001	0.0000	19
2	0.0159	0.0528	0.0988	0.1458	0.1887	0.2246	0.2521	0.2711	0.2818	0.2852	0.2293	0.1369	0.0699	0.0278	0.0100	0.0031	0.0008	0.0002	18
3	0.0010	0.0065	0.0183	0.0364	0.0596	0.0860	0.1139	0.1414	0.1672	0.1901	0.2428	0.2054	0.1339	0.0716	0.0323	0.0123	0.0040	0.0011	17
4	0.0000	0.0006	0.0024	0.0065	0.0133	0.0233	0.0364	0.0523	0.0703	0.0898	0.1821	0.2182	0.1897	0.1304	0.0738	0.0350	0.0139	0.0046	16
5	—	0.0000	0.0002	0.0009	0.0022	0.0048	0.0088	0.0145	0.0222	0.0319	0.1028	0.1746	0.2023	0.1789	0.1272	0.0746	0.0365	0.0148	15
6	—	0.0000	0.0000	0.0001	0.0003	0.0008	0.0017	0.0032	0.0055	0.0089	0.0454	0.1091	0.1686	0.1916	0.1712	0.1244	0.0746	0.0370	14
7	—	—	0.0000	0.0000	0.0000	0.0001	0.0002	0.0005	0.0011	0.0020	0.0160	0.0545	0.1124	0.1643	0.1844	0.1659	0.1221	0.0739	13
8	—	—	0.0000	0.0000	0.0000	0.0000	0.0000	0.0001	0.0002	0.0004	0.0046	0.0222	0.0609	0.1144	0.1614	0.1797	0.1623	0.1201	12
9	—	—	—	—	—	—	—	0.0000	0.0000	0.0001	0.0011	0.0074	0.0271	0.0654	0.1158	0.1597	0.1771	0.1602	11
10	—	—	—	—	—	—	—	—	—	0.0000	0.0002	0.0020	0.0099	0.0308	0.0686	0.1171	0.1593	0.1762	10
11	—	—	—	—	—	—	—	—	—	—	0.0000	0.0005	0.0030	0.0120	0.0336	0.0710	0.1185	0.1602	9
12	—	—	—	—	—	—	—	—	—	—	0.0000	0.0001	0.0008	0.0039	0.0136	0.0355	0.0727	0.1201	8
13	—	—	—	—	—	—	—	—	—	—	—	0.0000	0.0002	0.0010	0.0045	0.0146	0.0366	0.0739	7
14	—	—	—	—	—	—	—	—	—	—	—	0.0000	0.0000	0.0002	0.0012	0.0049	0.0150	0.0370	6
15	—	—	—	—	—	—	—	—	—	—	—	—	0.0000	0.0000	0.0003	0.0013	0.0049	0.0148	5
16	—	—	—	—	—	—	—	—	—	—	—	—	—	—	0.0000	0.0003	0.0013	0.0046	4
17	—	—	—	—	—	—	—	—	—	—	—	—	—	—	—	0.0000	0.0002	0.0011	3
18	—	—	—	—	—	—	—	—	—	—	—	—	—	—	—	—	0.0000	0.0002	2
19	—	—	—	—	—	—	—	—	—	—	—	—	—	—	—	—	—	0.0000	1
20	—	—	—	—	—	—	—	—	—	—	—	—	—	—	—	—	—	—	0
X	0.99	0.98	0.97	0.96	0.95	0.94	0.93	0.92	0.91	0.90	0.85	0.80	0.75	0.70	0.65	0.60	0.55	0.50	X

n = 20

TABLE E.7

Table of Poisson Probabilities

For a given value of λ, entry indicates the probability of a specified value of X.

λ

X	0.1	0.2	0.3	0.4	0.5	0.6	0.7	0.8	0.9	1.0
0	0.9048	0.8187	0.7408	0.6703	0.6065	0.5488	0.4966	0.4493	0.4066	0.3679
1	0.0905	0.1637	0.2222	0.2681	0.3033	0.3293	0.3476	0.3595	0.3659	0.3679
2	0.0045	0.0164	0.0333	0.0536	0.0758	0.0988	0.1217	0.1438	0.1647	0.1839
3	0.0002	0.0011	0.0033	0.0072	0.0126	0.0198	0.0284	0.0383	0.0494	0.0613
4	0.0000	0.0001	0.0003	0.0007	0.0016	0.0030	0.0050	0.0077	0.0111	0.0153
5	0.0000	0.0000	0.0000	0.0001	0.0002	0.0004	0.0007	0.0012	0.0020	0.0031
6	0.0000	0.0000	0.0000	0.0000	0.0000	0.0000	0.0001	0.0002	0.0003	0.0005
7	0.0000	0.0000	0.0000	0.0000	0.0000	0.0000	0.0000	0.0000	0.0000	0.0001

λ

X	1.1	1.2	1.3	1.4	1.5	1.6	1.7	1.8	1.9	2.0
0	0.3329	0.3012	0.2725	0.2466	0.2231	0.2019	0.1827	0.1653	0.1496	0.1353
1	0.3662	0.3614	0.3543	0.3452	0.3347	0.3230	0.3106	0.2975	0.2842	0.2707
2	0.2014	0.2169	0.2303	0.2417	0.2510	0.2584	0.2640	0.2678	0.2700	0.2707
3	0.0738	0.0867	0.0998	0.1128	0.1255	0.1378	0.1496	0.1607	0.1710	0.1804
4	0.0203	0.0260	0.0324	0.0395	0.0471	0.0551	0.0636	0.0723	0.0812	0.0902
5	0.0045	0.0062	0.0084	0.0111	0.0141	0.0176	0.0216	0.0260	0.0309	0.0361
6	0.0008	0.0012	0.0018	0.0026	0.0035	0.0047	0.0061	0.0078	0.0098	0.0120
7	0.0001	0.0002	0.0003	0.0005	0.0008	0.0011	0.0015	0.0020	0.0027	0.0034
8	0.0000	0.0000	0.0001	0.0001	0.0001	0.0002	0.0003	0.0005	0.0006	0.0009
9	0.0000	0.0000	0.0000	0.0000	0.0000	0.0000	0.0001	0.0001	0.0001	0.0002

λ

X	2.1	2.2	2.3	2.4	2.5	2.6	2.7	2.8	2.9	3.0
0	0.1225	0.1108	0.1003	0.0907	0.0821	0.0743	0.0672	0.0608	0.0550	0.0498
1	0.2572	0.2438	0.2306	0.2177	0.2052	0.1931	0.1815	0.1703	0.1596	0.1494
2	0.2700	0.2681	0.2652	0.2613	0.2565	0.2510	0.2450	0.2384	0.2314	0.2240
3	0.1890	0.1966	0.2033	0.2090	0.2138	0.2176	0.2205	0.2225	0.2237	0.2240
4	0.0992	0.1082	0.1169	0.1254	0.1336	0.1414	0.1488	0.1557	0.1622	0.1680
5	0.0417	0.0476	0.0538	0.0602	0.0668	0.0735	0.0804	0.0872	0.0940	0.1008
6	0.0146	0.0174	0.0206	0.0241	0.0278	0.0319	0.0362	0.0407	0.0455	0.0504
7	0.0044	0.0055	0.0068	0.0083	0.0099	0.0118	0.0139	0.0163	0.0188	0.0216
8	0.0011	0.0015	0.0019	0.0025	0.0031	0.0038	0.0047	0.0057	0.0068	0.0081
9	0.0003	0.0004	0.0005	0.0007	0.0009	0.0011	0.0014	0.0018	0.0022	0.0027
10	0.0001	0.0001	0.0001	0.0002	0.0002	0.0003	0.0004	0.0005	0.0006	0.0008
11	0.0000	0.0000	0.0000	0.0000	0.0000	0.0001	0.0001	0.0001	0.0002	0.0002
12	0.0000	0.0000	0.0000	0.0000	0.0000	0.0000	0.0000	0.0000	0.0000	0.0001

λ

X	3.1	3.2	3.3	3.4	3.5	3.6	3.7	3.8	3.9	4.0
0	0.0450	0.0408	0.0369	0.0334	0.0302	0.0273	0.0247	0.0224	0.0202	0.0183
1	0.1397	0.1340	0.1217	0.1135	0.1057	0.0984	0.0915	0.0850	0.0789	0.0733
2	0.2165	0.2087	0.2008	0.1929	0.1850	0.1771	0.1692	0.1615	0.1539	0.1465
3	0.2237	0.2226	0.2209	0.2186	0.2158	0.2125	0.2087	0.2046	0.2001	0.1954
4	0.1734	0.1781	0.1823	0.1858	0.1888	0.1912	0.1931	0.1944	0.1951	0.1954
5	0.1075	0.1140	0.1203	0.1264	0.1322	0.1377	0.1429	0.1477	0.1522	0.1563
6	0.0555	0.0608	0.0662	0.0716	0.0771	0.0826	0.0881	0.0936	0.0989	0.1042
7	0.0246	0.0278	0.0312	0.0348	0.0385	0.0425	0.0466	0.0508	0.0551	0.0595
8	0.0095	0.0111	0.0129	0.0148	0.0169	0.0191	0.0215	0.0241	0.0269	0.0298
9	0.0033	0.0040	0.0047	0.0056	0.0066	0.0076	0.0089	0.0102	0.0116	0.0132
10	0.0010	0.0013	0.0016	0.0019	0.0023	0.0028	0.0033	0.0039	0.0045	0.0053
11	0.0003	0.0004	0.0005	0.0006	0.0007	0.0009	0.0011	0.0013	0.0016	0.0019
12	0.0001	0.0001	0.0001	0.0002	0.0002	0.0003	0.0003	0.0004	0.0005	0.0006
13	0.0000	0.0000	0.0000	0.0000	0.0001	0.0001	0.0001	0.0001	0.0002	0.0002
14	0.0000	0.0000	0.0000	0.0000	0.0000	0.0000	0.0000	0.0000	0.0000	0.0001

continued

ABLE E.7

able of Poisson
robabilities
Continued)

					λ					
X	4.1	4.2	4.3	4.4	4.5	4.6	4.7	4.8	4.9	5.0
0	0.0166	0.0150	0.0136	0.0123	0.0111	0.0101	0.0091	0.0082	0.0074	0.0067
1	0.0679	0.0630	0.0583	0.0540	0.0500	0.0462	0.0427	0.0395	0.0365	0.0337
2	0.1393	0.1323	0.1254	0.1188	0.1125	0.1063	0.1005	0.0948	0.0894	0.0842
3	0.1904	0.1852	0.1798	0.1743	0.1687	0.1631	0.1574	0.1517	0.1460	0.1404
4	0.1951	0.1944	0.1933	0.1917	0.1898	0.1875	0.1849	0.1820	0.1789	0.1755
5	0.1600	0.1633	0.1662	0.1687	0.1708	0.1725	0.1738	0.1747	0.1753	0.1755
6	0.1093	0.1143	0.1191	0.1237	0.1281	0.1323	0.1362	0.1398	0.1432	0.1462
7	0.0640	0.0686	0.0732	0.0778	0.0824	0.0869	0.0914	0.0959	0.1002	0.1044
8	0.0328	0.0360	0.0393	0.0428	0.0463	0.0500	0.0537	0.0575	0.0614	0.0653
9	0.0150	0.0168	0.0188	0.0209	0.0232	0.0255	0.0280	0.0307	0.0334	0.0363
10	0.0061	0.0071	0.0081	0.0092	0.0104	0.0118	0.0132	0.0147	0.0164	0.0181
11	0.0023	0.0027	0.0032	0.0037	0.0043	0.0049	0.0056	0.0064	0.0073	0.0082
12	0.0008	0.0009	0.0011	0.0014	0.0016	0.0019	0.0022	0.0026	0.0030	0.0034
13	0.0002	0.0003	0.0004	0.0005	0.0006	0.0007	0.0008	0.0009	0.0011	0.0013
14	0.0001	0.0001	0.0001	0.0001	0.0002	0.0002	0.0003	0.0003	0.0004	0.0005
15	0.0000	0.0000	0.0000	0.0000	0.0001	0.0001	0.0001	0.0001	0.0001	0.0002

					λ					
X	5.1	5.2	5.3	5.4	5.5	5.6	5.7	5.8	5.9	6.0
0	0.0061	0.0055	0.0050	0.0045	0.0041	0.0037	0.0033	0.0030	0.0027	0.0025
1	0.0311	0.0287	0.0265	0.0244	0.0225	0.0207	0.0191	0.0176	0.0162	0.0149
2	0.0793	0.0746	0.0701	0.0659	0.0618	0.0580	0.0544	0.0509	0.0477	0.0446
3	0.1348	0.1293	0.1239	0.1185	0.1133	0.1082	0.1033	0.0985	0.0938	0.0892
4	0.1719	0.1681	0.1641	0.1600	0.1558	0.1515	0.1472	0.1428	0.1383	0.1339
5	0.1753	0.1748	0.1740	0.1728	0.1714	0.1697	0.1678	0.1656	0.1632	0.1606
6	0.1490	0.1515	0.1537	0.1555	0.1571	0.1584	0.1594	0.1601	0.1605	0.1606
7	0.1086	0.1125	0.1163	0.1200	0.1234	0.1267	0.1298	0.1326	0.1353	0.1377
8	0.0692	0.0731	0.0771	0.0810	0.0849	0.0887	0.0925	0.0962	0.0998	0.1033
9	0.0392	0.0423	0.0454	0.0486	0.0519	0.0552	0.0586	0.0620	0.0654	0.0688
10	0.0200	0.0220	0.0241	0.0262	0.0285	0.0309	0.0334	0.0359	0.0386	0.0413
11	0.0093	0.0104	0.0116	0.0129	0.0143	0.0157	0.0173	0.0190	0.0207	0.0225
12	0.0039	0.0045	0.0051	0.0058	0.0065	0.0073	0.0082	0.0092	0.0102	0.0113
13	0.0015	0.0018	0.0021	0.0024	0.0028	0.0032	0.0036	0.0041	0.0046	0.0052
14	0.0006	0.0007	0.0008	0.0009	0.0011	0.0013	0.0015	0.0017	0.0019	0.0022
15	0.0002	0.0002	0.0003	0.0003	0.0004	0.0005	0.0006	0.0007	0.0008	0.0009
16	0.0001	0.0001	0.0001	0.0001	0.0001	0.0002	0.0002	0.0002	0.0003	0.0003
17	0.0000	0.0000	0.0000	0.0000	0.0000	0.0000	0.0001	0.0001	0.0001	0.0001

					λ					
X	6.1	6.2	6.3	6.4	6.5	6.6	6.7	6.8	6.9	7.0
0	0.0022	0.0020	0.0018	0.0017	0.0015	0.0014	0.0012	0.0011	0.0010	0.0009
1	0.0137	0.0126	0.0116	0.0106	0.0098	0.0090	0.0082	0.0076	0.0070	0.0064
2	0.0417	0.0390	0.0364	0.0340	0.0318	0.0296	0.0276	0.0258	0.0240	0.0223
3	0.0848	0.0806	0.0765	0.0726	0.0688	0.0652	0.0617	0.0584	0.0552	0.0521
4	0.1294	0.1249	0.1205	0.1162	0.1118	0.1076	0.1034	0.0992	0.0952	0.0912
5	0.1579	0.1549	0.1519	0.1487	0.1454	0.1420	0.1385	0.1349	0.1314	0.1277
6	0.1605	0.1601	0.1595	0.1586	0.1575	0.1562	0.1546	0.1529	0.1511	0.1490
7	0.1399	0.1418	0.1435	0.1450	0.1462	0.1472	0.1480	0.1486	0.1489	0.1490
8	0.1066	0.1099	0.1130	0.1160	0.1188	0.1215	0.1240	0.1263	0.1284	0.1304
9	0.0723	0.0757	0.0791	0.0825	0.0858	0.0891	0.0923	0.0954	0.0985	0.1014
10	0.0441	0.0469	0.0498	0.0528	0.0558	0.0588	0.0618	0.0649	0.0679	0.0710
11	0.0245	0.0265	0.0285	0.0307	0.0330	0.0353	0.0377	0.0401	0.0426	0.0452
12	0.0124	0.0137	0.0150	0.0164	0.0179	0.0194	0.0210	0.0277	0.0245	0.0264
13	0.0058	0.0065	0.0073	0.0081	0.0089	0.0098	0.0108	0.0119	0.0130	0.0142
14	0.0025	0.0029	0.0033	0.0037	0.0041	0.0046	0.0052	0.0058	0.0064	0.0071

continued

TABLE E.7

Table of Poisson
Probabilities
(*Continued*)

					λ					
X	6.1	6.2	6.3	6.4	6.5	6.6	6.7	6.8	6.9	7.0
15	0.0010	0.0012	0.0014	0.0016	0.0018	0.0020	0.0023	0.0026	0.0029	0.0033
16	0.0004	0.0005	0.0005	0.0006	0.0007	0.0008	0.0010	0.0011	0.0013	0.0014
17	0.0001	0.0002	0.0002	0.0002	0.0003	0.0003	0.0004	0.0004	0.0005	0.0006
18	0.0000	0.0001	0.0001	0.0001	0.0001	0.0001	0.0001	0.0002	0.0002	0.0002
19	0.0000	0.0000	0.0000	0.0000	0.0000	0.0000	0.0000	0.0001	0.0001	0.0001

					λ					
X	7.1	7.2	7.3	7.4	7.5	7.6	7.7	7.8	7.9	8.0
0	0.0008	0.0007	0.0007	0.0006	0.0006	0.0005	0.0005	0.0004	0.0004	0.0003
1	0.0059	0.0054	0.0049	0.0045	0.0041	0.0038	0.0035	0.0032	0.0029	0.0027
2	0.0208	0.0194	0.0180	0.0167	0.0156	0.0145	0.0134	0.0125	0.0116	0.0107
3	0.0492	0.0464	0.0438	0.0413	0.0389	0.0366	0.0345	0.0324	0.0305	0.0286
4	0.0874	0.0836	0.0799	0.0764	0.0729	0.0696	0.0663	0.0632	0.0602	0.0573
5	0.1241	0.1204	0.1167	0.1130	0.1094	0.1057	0.1021	0.0986	0.0951	0.0916
6	0.1468	0.1445	0.1420	0.1394	0.1367	0.1339	0.1311	0.1282	0.1252	0.1221
7	0.1489	0.1486	0.1481	0.1474	0.1465	0.1454	0.1442	0.1428	0.1413	0.1396
8	0.1321	0.1337	0.1351	0.1363	0.1373	0.1382	0.1388	0.1392	0.1395	0.1396
9	0.1042	0.1070	0.1096	0.1121	0.1144	0.1167	0.1187	0.1207	0.1224	0.1241
10	0.0740	0.0770	0.0800	0.0829	0.0858	0.0887	0.0914	0.0941	0.0967	0.0993
11	0.0478	0.0504	0.0531	0.0558	0.0585	0.0613	0.0640	0.0667	0.0695	0.0722
12	0.0283	0.0303	0.0323	0.0344	0.0366	0.0388	0.0411	0.0434	0.0457	0.0481
13	0.0154	0.0168	0.0181	0.0196	0.0211	0.0227	0.0243	0.0260	0.0278	0.0296
14	0.0078	0.0086	0.0095	0.0104	0.0113	0.0123	0.0134	0.0145	0.0157	0.0169
15	0.0037	0.0041	0.0046	0.0051	0.0057	0.0062	0.0069	0.0075	0.0083	0.0090
16	0.0016	0.0019	0.0021	0.0024	0.0026	0.0030	0.0033	0.0037	0.0041	0.0045
17	0.0007	0.0008	0.0009	0.0010	0.0012	0.0013	0.0015	0.0017	0.0019	0.0021
18	0.0003	0.0003	0.0004	0.0004	0.0005	0.0006	0.0006	0.0007	0.0008	0.0009
19	0.0001	0.0001	0.0001	0.0002	0.0002	0.0002	0.0003	0.0003	0.0003	0.0004
20	0.0000	0.0000	0.0001	0.0001	0.0001	0.0001	0.0001	0.0001	0.0001	0.0002
21	0.0000	0.0000	0.0000	0.0000	0.0000	0.0000	0.0000	0.0000	0.0001	0.0001

					λ					
X	8.1	8.2	8.3	8.4	8.5	8.6	8.7	8.8	8.9	9.0
0	0.0003	0.0003	0.0002	0.0002	0.0002	0.0002	0.0002	0.0002	0.0001	0.0001
1	0.0025	0.0023	0.0021	0.0019	0.0017	0.0016	0.0014	0.0013	0.0012	0.0011
2	0.0100	0.0092	0.0086	0.0079	0.0074	0.0068	0.0063	0.0058	0.0054	0.0050
3	0.0269	0.0252	0.0237	0.0222	0.0208	0.0195	0.0183	0.0171	0.0160	0.0150
4	0.0544	0.0517	0.0491	0.0466	0.0443	0.0420	0.0398	0.0377	0.0357	0.0337
5	0.0882	0.0849	0.0816	0.0784	0.0752	0.0722	0.0692	0.0663	0.0635	0.0607
6	0.1191	0.1160	0.1128	0.1097	0.1066	0.1034	0.1003	0.0972	0.0941	0.0911
7	0.1378	0.1358	0.1338	0.1317	0.1294	0.1271	0.1247	0.1222	0.1197	0.1171
8	0.1395	0.1392	0.1388	0.1382	0.1375	0.1366	0.1356	0.1344	0.1332	0.1318
9	0.1256	0.1269	0.1280	0.1290	0.1299	0.1306	0.1311	0.1315	0.1317	0.1318
10	0.1017	0.1040	0.1063	0.1084	0.1104	0.1123	0.1140	0.1157	0.1172	0.1186
11	0.0749	0.0776	0.0802	0.0828	0.0853	0.0878	0.0902	0.0925	0.0948	0.0970
12	0.0505	0.0530	0.0555	0.0579	0.0604	0.0629	0.0654	0.0679	0.0703	0.0728
13	0.0315	0.0334	0.0354	0.0374	0.0395	0.0416	0.0438	0.0459	0.0481	0.0504
14	0.0182	0.0196	0.0210	0.0225	0.0240	0.0256	0.0272	0.0289	0.0306	0.0324
15	0.0098	0.0107	0.0116	0.0126	0.0136	0.0147	0.0158	0.0169	0.0182	0.0194
16	0.0050	0.0055	0.0060	0.0066	0.0072	0.0079	0.0086	0.0093	0.0101	0.0109
17	0.0024	0.0026	0.0029	0.0033	0.0036	0.0040	0.0044	0.0048	0.0053	0.0058
18	0.0011	0.0012	0.0014	0.0015	0.0017	0.0019	0.0021	0.0024	0.0026	0.0029
19	0.0005	0.0005	0.0006	0.0007	0.0008	0.0009	0.0010	0.0011	0.0012	0.0014
20	0.0002	0.0002	0.0002	0.0003	0.0003	0.0004	0.0004	0.0005	0.0005	0.0006
21	0.0001	0.0001	0.0001	0.0001	0.0001	0.0002	0.0002	0.0002	0.0002	0.0003
22	0.0000	0.0000	0.0000	0.0000	0.0001	0.0001	0.0001	0.0001	0.0001	0.0001

continued

ABLE E.7

able of Poisson
robabilities
Continued)

					λ					
X	9.1	9.2	9.3	9.4	9.5	9.6	9.7	9.8	9.9	10
0	0.0001	0.0001	0.0001	0.0001	0.0001	0.0001	0.0001	0.0001	0.0001	0.0000
1	0.0010	0.0009	0.0009	0.0008	0.0007	0.0007	0.0006	0.0005	0.0005	0.0005
2	0.0046	0.0043	0.0040	0.0037	0.0034	0.0031	0.0029	0.0027	0.0025	0.0023
3	0.0140	0.0131	0.0123	0.0115	0.0107	0.0100	0.0093	0.0087	0.0081	0.0076
4	0.0319	0.0302	0.0285	0.0269	0.0254	0.0240	0.0226	0.0213	0.0201	0.0189
5	0.0581	0.0555	0.0530	0.0506	0.0483	0.0460	0.0439	0.0418	0.0398	0.0378
6	0.0881	0.0851	0.0822	0.0793	0.0764	0.0736	0.0709	0.0682	0.0656	0.0631
7	0.1145	0.1118	0.1091	0.1064	0.1037	0.1010	0.0982	0.0955	0.0928	0.0901
8	0.1302	0.1286	0.1269	0.1251	0.1232	0.1212	0.1191	0.1170	0.1148	0.1126
9	0.1317	0.1315	0.1311	0.1306	0.1300	0.1293	0.1284	0.1274	0.1263	0.1251
10	0.1198	0.1210	0.1219	0.1228	0.1235	0.1241	0.1245	0.1249	0.1250	0.1251
11	0.0991	0.1012	0.1031	0.1049	0.1067	0.1083	0.1098	0.1112	0.1125	0.1137
12	0.0752	0.0776	0.0799	0.0822	0.0844	0.0866	0.0888	0.0908	0.0928	0.0948
13	0.0526	0.0549	0.0572	0.0594	0.0617	0.0640	0.0662	0.0685	0.0707	0.0729
14	0.0342	0.0361	0.0380	0.0399	0.0419	0.0439	0.0459	0.0479	0.0500	0.0521
15	0.0208	0.0221	0.0235	0.0250	0.0265	0.0281	0.0297	0.0313	0.0330	0.0347
16	0.0118	0.0127	0.0137	0.0147	0.0157	0.0168	0.0180	0.0192	0.0204	0.0217
17	0.0063	0.0069	0.0075	0.0081	0.0088	0.0095	0.0103	0.0111	0.0119	0.0128
18	0.0032	0.0035	0.0039	0.0042	0.0046	0.0051	0.0055	0.0060	0.0065	0.0071
19	0.0015	0.0017	0.0019	0.0021	0.0023	0.0026	0.0028	0.0031	0.0034	0.0037
20	0.0007	0.0008	0.0009	0.0010	0.0011	0.0012	0.0014	0.0015	0.0017	0.0019
21	0.0003	0.0003	0.0004	0.0004	0.0005	0.0006	0.0006	0.0007	0.0008	0.0009
22	0.0001	0.0001	0.0002	0.0002	0.0002	0.0002	0.0003	0.0003	0.0004	0.0004
23	0.0000	0.0001	0.0001	0.0001	0.0001	0.0001	0.0001	0.0001	0.0002	0.0002
24	0.0000	0.0000	0.0000	0.0000	0.0000	0.0000	0.0000	0.0001	0.0001	0.0001

X	λ = 20	X	λ = 20	X	λ = 20	X	λ = 20
0	0.0000	10	0.0058	20	0.0888	30	0.0083
1	0.0000	11	0.0106	21	0.0846	31	0.0054
2	0.0000	12	0.0176	22	0.0769	32	0.0034
3	0.0000	13	0.0271	23	0.0669	33	0.0020
4	0.0000	14	0.0387	24	0.0557	34	0.0012
5	0.0001	15	0.0516	25	0.0446	35	0.0007
6	0.0002	16	0.0646	26	0.0343	36	0.0004
7	0.0005	17	0.0760	27	0.0254	37	0.0002
8	0.0013	18	0.0844	28	0.0181	38	0.0001
9	0.0029	19	0.0888	29	0.0125	39	0.0001

F.   STUDENT CD-ROM AND SOFTWARE FAQs

Use this appendix to find answers to the most frequently asked questions about using the resources on the Student CD-ROM and using Microsoft Excel and PHStat2.

F.1   ABOUT THE STUDENT CD-ROM

What does the Student CD-ROM contain?
The Student CD-ROM contains six categories of files that support this book:

1. **Data files.** These files contain the data used in chapter examples or named in problems. They exist as both Excel workbook files (in the **.xls** format, compatible with all Excel versions) and Minitab worksheet (**.mtw**) files. See Appendix D.2 for a complete listing of data files included on the Student CD-ROM.
2. **Case files.** These files, a mix of data and document files as well as facsimiles of Web page files, support both the *Managing the Springville Herald* running case and the various Web Cases.
3. **Student CD-ROM topic files.** These files are bonus chapter sections included as Adobe Reader (**.pdf** format) files.
4. **Excel appendix workbooks.** These files are Microsoft Excel workbooks that contain model solutions for applying Microsoft Excel to various statistical analyses. Most are designed as fill-in-the-data templates that can be reused indefinitely.
5. **Visual Explorations files.** These files support Visual Explorations, the interactive Excel add-in that illustrates selected statistical concepts.
6. **Windows applications.** These files are specific to Microsoft Windows XP or Vista (any version) and include the PHStat2 setup program, the Adobe Reader setup program, and the Student CD-ROM's own "start" program that simplifies access to the contents of the Student CD-ROM.

Can I use the Student CD-ROM with an Apple Mac running the Mac OS?
Although the Student CD-ROM is marked "For Windows," most Mac users will be able to retrieve and use the first five categories of files listed in the previous answer.

Does the Student CD-ROM contain Microsoft Excel or Minitab?
No, these programs must be acquired separately. Specially priced student-oriented versions of Microsoft Office (containing Excel) are available at many retailers and select retailers, including **mypearsonstore.com**, sell the student version of Minitab.

Can I copy the Excel workbook files to my local hard disk or other storage device?
Yes, you can, and you are encouraged to do so. Windows users can use the CD-ROM's own "start" program to facilitate this task. Some files that you copy may be reported as being a "read-only" file. If you make changes to such files, you will need to save the file under a different name.

Can I buy a replacement Student CD-ROM disk?
No, Student CD-ROM disks are not sold separately. However, a PHStat2 version either identical or similar to the one included on the Student CD-ROM is available for separate purchase.

F.2   ABOUT MICROSOFT EXCEL

Will I need access to my original Microsoft Office/Excel CDs or DVD?
Yes, if you are using PHStat2 you may need to use the original program disks if the Analysis ToolPak and Analysis ToolPak–VBA (referred to as the "ToolPak" in this book) has not been installed on your system.

What Microsoft Office security settings should I use? How do I change Office security settings?
See Section E1.8, "Using Add-ins" on page 20 for specific answers to these questions. If you plan to use the Prentice Hall PHStat2 Excel add-in, also read the PHStat2 readme file on the Student CD-ROM.

How can I check to see if the ToolPak has been installed in Excel 97–2003?
Open Excel and select **Tools → Add-Ins** and in the Add-Ins dialog box that appears, verify that **Analysis ToolPak** (and **Analysis ToolPak–VBA**, if using PHStat2) is checked in the **Add-Ins available** list. If **Analysis ToolPak** does not appear, you will need to install it separately.

How can I check to see if the ToolPak has been installed in Excel 2007?
Open Excel and click the **Office Button**. In the Office Button pane, click **Excel Options**. In the Excel options dialog box that appears, click **Add-Ins** in the left pane and look for **Analysis ToolPak** (and **Analysis ToolPak–VBA**, if using PHStat2) under **Active Application Add-ins**. If they do not appear, click **Go** and continue with the instructions for using the Add-Ins dialog box presented in the answer for Excel 97–2003.

How can I install the ToolPak?
Close Microsoft Excel and rerun the Microsoft Office or Microsoft Excel setup program. When the setup program runs, choose the option that allows you to add components. This option is variously described as the **modify**, **add**, or **custom** option. Then, select install **Analysis ToolPak** (and **Analysis ToolPak–VBA**, if using PHStat2). You may need access to the original Microsoft Office/Excel setup CD-ROMs or DVDs to complete this task.

Do I need to run a setup program to use the Visual Explorations add-in workbook (Visual Explorations.xla)?
No, you can copy the files and install the files from the Visual Explorations folder on the Student CD-ROM and use this add-in file as you would use any of the workbook data files. You will need to properly adjust your Microsoft Office security settings (see Section E1.8 on page 20) in order to use this add-in.

In Excel 97–2003, how can I specify the custom settings that you recommend?
First, select **Tools → Customize**. In the Customize dialog box, clear (uncheck) the **Menus show recently used commands first** check box if it is checked and click the **Close** button. Then select **Tools → Options**. In the Options dialog box, click the **Calculation** tab and verify that the **Automatic** option button of the Calculation group has been selected. Click the **Edit** tab and verify that all check boxes except the **Fixed decimal, Provide feedback with Animation,** and **Enable automatic percent entry** have been selected. (Excel 97 does not contain an Automatic percent entry check box.) Click the **General** tab and verify that the **R1C1 reference style** check box is cleared, and, if using Excel 97, check the **Macro virus protection** check box. Enter **3** as the number of **Sheets in new workbook**, select **Arial** from the **Standard font** list, and select **10** from the **Size** drop-down list. Then click **OK** to finish the customization.

In Excel 2007, how can I specify the custom settings that you recommend?
First, click the **Office Button** and then click **Excel Options**. In the Excel Options dialog box, click **Formulas** in the left panel. In the **Formulas** right pane, click **Automatic** under Workbook Calculation and verify that all check boxes are checked except **Enable iterative calculation, R1C1 reference style,** and **Formulas referring to empty cells**. For greater customization, click **Advanced** in the left panel and scroll through the **Advanced options for working with Excel** that appears in the right panel. Click **OK** when finished.

F.3 ABOUT PHSTAT2

What is PHStat2?
PHStat2 is software that makes operating Microsoft Excel as distraction free as possible. As a student studying statistics,

you can focus mainly on learning statistics and not worry about having to fully master Excel first. When PHStat2 is combined with the ToolPak add-in supplied with Microsoft Excel, just about all statistical methods taught in an introductory statistics course can be illustrated using Microsoft Excel.

I do not want to use an add-in that will not be available in my business environment. Any comments?
Chapter 1 talks about these issues in detail. To summarize those pages, PHStat2 helps you learn Microsoft Excel, and using PHStat2 will not leave you any less equipped to work with Microsoft Excel in a setting where it is not available.

What do I need to do in order to begin using PHStat2?
You run the PHStat2 setup program (setup.exe) that is included on the Student CD-ROM. To use this program successfully, you must have logged in to Windows using an account that has administrator or software-installing privileges. (Student and faculty accounts to log in to networked computers in academic settings typically do not have this privilege. If you have such an account, ask your network or lab technician for assistance.) If you are using Windows Vista or certain firewall or security-suite programs, you may see messages asking you to permit or allow certain system operations as the PHStat2 setup runs. (If you decline permission, PHStat2 will not be successfully set up.)

What are the technical requirements for setting up and adding PHStat2 to my system?
If your system can run Microsoft Excel, it can also run PHStat2. You need approximately up to 10 MB hard disk free space during the setup process and up to 3 MB hard disk space after PHStat2 is installed. You must also ensure that the Microsoft Excel Analysis ToolPak and Analysis ToolPak–VBA add-ins have been installed. (See related question in Section F.2.)

Are updates to PHStat2 available?
Yes, free minor updates to resolve issues may be available for download from the PHStat2 Web site (**www.prenhall.com/phstat**). When you visit that Web site, note that the Student CD-ROM contains version 2.8 of PHStat2.

How can I identify which version of PHStat2 I have?
Open Microsoft Excel with PHStat2 and select **Help for PHStat** from the PHStat menu. A dialog box will display your current XLA and DLL version numbers. The XLA version number identifies the version of PHStat2 you have. Both of these numbers will initially be 2.8.0 after you set up PHStat2 from the Student CD-ROM.

Where can I get help setting up PHStat2?
First, carefully review the Student CD-ROM PHStat2 readme file. If your problem is unresolved, visit the PHStat2 Web site (**www. prenhall.com/phstat**) for further information. If your problem is still unresolved, contact Pearson Education technical support at **247pearsoned.custhelp.com**.

Where can I find tips for using PHStat2?

While your classmates and instructor can be the best source of tips, you can also visit the online PHStat2 community at **phstatcommunity.org**.

F.4   ABOUT MINITAB

Which versions of Minitab can I use with this book?

You should use Minitab 14 or Minitab 15 when following the instructions in the Minitab appendices. There is a student version of Minitab that can be bundled with the book.

F.5   ADDITIONAL INFORMATION FOR NEW MICROSOFT EXCEL 2007 USERS

I do not see the menu for an add-in workbook that I opened. Where is it?

Unlike earlier versions of Excel that allowed add-ins to add menus to the menu bar, Excel 2007 places all add-in menus under the Add-ins tab. If you click Add-ins, you find the menus of all properly loaded add-ins.

What does "Compatibility Mode" mean?

When you see "Compatibility Mode" in the title bar, Excel 2007 is telling you that you are using a workbook compatible with earlier Excel versions. When you save such a workbook, Excel 2007 will automatically use the .xls file format of earlier versions.

How can I update an older (.xls) workbook to the Excel 2007 .xlsx workbook format?

The simplest way is to open the workbook file and select **Office Button → Convert**. Then save your file (select **Office Button → Save**). You can also open the workbook file and select **Office Button → Save As** and in the Save As dialog box, select **Excel Workbook (*.xlsx)** from the **Save as type** list.

Self-Test Solutions and Answers to Selected Even-Numbered Problems

The following represent worked-out solutions to Self-Test Problems and brief answers to most of the even-numbered problems in the text. For more detailed solutions, including explanations, interpretations, and Excel and Minitab output, see the *Student Solutions Manual*.

CHAPTER 1

1.2 Small, medium, and large sizes imply order but do not specify how much more soft drink is added at increasing levels.

1.4 (a) The number of telephones is a numerical variable that is discrete because the outcome is a count. It is ratio scaled because it has a true zero point. **(b)** The length of the longest long-distance call is a numerical variable that is continuous because any value within a range of values can occur. It is ratio scaled because it has a true zero point. **(c)** Whether there is a cell phone in the household is a categorical variable because the answer can be only yes or no. This also makes it a nominal-scaled variable. **(d)** Same answer as in (c).

1.6 (a) Categorical, nominal scale. **(b)** Numerical, continuous, ratio scale. **(c)** Numerical, discrete, ratio scale. **(d)** Numerical, discrete, ratio scale.

1.8 (a) Numerical, continuous, ratio scale. **(b)** Numerical, discrete, ratio scale. **(c)** Numerical, continuous, ratio scale. **(d)** Categorical, nominal scale.

1.10 The underlying variable, ability of the students, may be continuous, but the measuring device, the test, does not have enough precision to distinguish between the two students.

1.24 (a) A primary data source collected through a survey was used in this study. **(b)** Deciding what to make for dinner at home at the last minute. **(c)** The amount of time to prepare dinner.

1.26 (a) Cat owner households in the United States. **(b)** 1. Categorical. 2. Categorical. 3. Numerical, discrete. 4. Categorical.

CHAPTER 2

2.4 (b) The Pareto chart is best for portraying these data because it not only sorts the frequencies in descending order, it also provides the cumulative polygon on the same scale. **(c)** You can conclude that friends/family account for the largest percentage of 45%. When other, news media, and online user reviews are added to friends/family, this accounts for 83%.

2.6 (b) 88%. **(d)** The Pareto chart allows you to see which sources account for most of the electricity.

2.8 (b) The bar chart is more suitable if the purpose is to compare the categories. The pie chart is more suitable if the main objective is to investigate the portion of the whole that is in a particular category.

2.10 (b) Rooms dirty, rooms not stocked, and rooms needing maintenance have the largest number of complaints, so focusing on these categories can reduce the number of complaints the most.

2.12 Stem-and-leaf display of finance scores:

5	34
6	9
7	4
8	0
9	38

$n = 7$

2.14 50 74 74 76 81 89 92.

2.16 (a) Ordered array: Cost($) 120, 130, 132, 134, 134, 139, 141, 146, 148, 149, 154, 157, 158, 159, 163, 170, 170, 175, 180, 183, 186, 191, 192, 194, 202, 207, 209, 209, 219, 288
(b) Stem-and-leaf display:

Stem unit: 10

12	0
13	0 2 4 4 9
14	1 6 8 9
15	4 7 8 9
16	3
17	0 0 5
18	0 3 6
19	1 2 4
20	2 7 9 9
21	9
22	
23	
24	
25	
26	
27	
28	8

(c) The stem-and-leaf display provides more information because it not only orders values from the smallest to the largest into stems and leaves, it also conveys information on how the values distribute and cluster over the range of the data.
(d) The costs of attending a baseball game do not appear to be concentrating around any particular value. In fact, the costs appear to spread evenly between $130 and $210 with the exception of an outlier at $288 for Boston.

2.18 (a) Ordered array:

4 5 7 8 16 19 19 20 20 23 24 25 29 29 30 30 30 30 40 56

(b) Stem-and-leaf display for fat; stem, 10 unit:

0	4 5 7 8
1	6 9 9
2	0 0 3 4 5 9 9
3	0 0 0 0
4	0
5	6

(c) The stem-and-leaf display conveys more information than the ordered array. You can also obtain a sense of the distribution of the data from the stem-and-leaf display. **(d)** They are concentrated around 29 and 30.

2.20 (a) 10 but less than 20, 20 but less than 30, 30 but less than 40, 40 but less than 50, 50 but less than 60, 60 but less than 70, 70 but less than 80, 80 but less than 90, 90 but less than 100. **(b)** 10. **(c)** 15, 25, 35, 45, 55, 65, 75, 85, 95.

2.22 (a)

Electricity Costs	Frequency	Percentage
$80 up to $99	4	8%
$100 up to $119	7	14
$120 up to $139	9	18
$140 up to $159	13	26
$160 up to $179	9	18
$180 up to $199	5	10
$200 up to $219	3	6

(c)

Electricity Costs	Frequency	Percentage	Cumulative %
$99	4	8.00%	8.00%
$119	7	14.00	22.00
$139	9	18.00	40.00
$159	13	26.00	66.00
$179	9	18.00	84.00
$199	5	10.00	94.00
$219	3	6.00	100.00

(d) The majority of utility charges are clustered between $120 and $180.

2.24 The property taxes per capita appear to be right-skewed with approximately 90% falling between $399 and $1,700, and the remaining 10% falling between $1,700 and $2,100. The center is at about $1,000.

2.26 (a)

Width	Frequency	Percentage
8.310–8.329	3	6.12%
8.330–8.349	2	4.08
8.350–8.369	1	2.04
8.370–8.389	4	8.16
8.390–8.409	5	10.20
8.410–8.429	16	31.65
8.430–8.449	5	10.20
8.450–8.469	5	10.20
8.470–8.489	6	12.24
8.490–8.509	2	4.08

(d) All the troughs will meet the company's requirements of between 8.31 and 8.61 inches wide.

2.28 (a)

Bulb Life (hrs)	% Less Than	Percentage, Mfgr A	Percentage, Mfgr B
650–749	750	7.5%	0.0%
750–849	850	12.5	5.0
850–949	950	50.0	20.0
950–1,049	1,050	22.5	40.0
1,050–1,149	1,150	7.5	22.5
1,150–1,249	1,250	0.0	12.5

(c)

Bulb Life (hrs)	Percentage Less Than, Mfgr A	Percentage Less Than, Mfgr B
650–749	7.5%	0.0%
750–849	20.0	5.0
850–949	70.0	25.0
950–1049	92.5	65.0
1050–1149	100.0	87.5
1150–1249	100.0	100.0

(d) Manufacturer B produces bulbs with longer lives than Manufacturer A. The cumulative percentage for Manufacturer B shows 65% of its bulbs lasted less than 1,050 hours, contrasted with 70% of Manufacturer A's bulbs, which lasted less than 950 hours. None of Manufacturer A's bulbs lasted more than 1,149 hours, but 12.5% of Manufacturer B's bulbs lasted between 1,150 and 1,249 hours. At the same time, 7.5% of Manufacturer A's bulbs lasted less than 750 hours, whereas all of Manufacturer B's bulbs lasted at least 750 hours.

2.30 (a) Table of frequencies for all student responses:

STUDENT MAJOR CATEGORIES

GENDER	A	C	M	Totals
Male	14	9	2	25
Female	6	6	3	15
Totals	20	15	5	40

(b) Table of percentages based on overall student responses:

STUDENT MAJOR CATEGORIES

GENDER	A	C	M	Totals
Male	35.0%	22.5%	5.0%	62.5%
Female	15.0	15.0	7.5	37.5
Totals	50.0	37.5	12.5	100.0

(c) Table based on row percentages:

STUDENT MAJOR CATEGORIES

GENDER	A	C	M	Totals
Male	56.0%	36.0%	8.0%	100.0%
Female	40.0	40.0	20.0	100.0
Totals	50.0	37.5	12.5	100.0

(d) Table based on column percentages:

STUDENT MAJOR CATEGORIES

GENDER	A	C	M	Totals
Male	70.0%	60.0%	40.0%	62.5%
Female	30.0	40.0	60.0	37.5
Totals	100.0	100.0	100.0	100.0

2.32 (a) Contingency table:

	CONDITION OF DIE		
QUALITY	**No Particles**	**Particles**	**Totals**
Good	320	14	334
Bad	80	36	116
Totals	400	50	450

Table of total percentages:

	CONDITION OF DIE		
QUALITY	**No Particles**	**Particles**	**Totals**
Good	71%	3%	74%
Bad	18	8	26
Totals	89	11	100

Table of row percentages:

	CONDITION OF DIE		
QUALITY	**No Particles**	**Particles**	**Totals**
Good	96%	4%	100%
Bad	69	31	100
Totals	89	11	100

Table of column percentages:

	CONDITION OF DIE		
QUALITY	**No Particles**	**Particles**	**Totals**
Good	80%	28%	74%
Bad	20	72	26
Totals	100	100	100

(c) The data suggest that there is some association between condition of the die and the quality of wafer because more good wafers are produced when no particles are found in the die, and more bad wafers are produced when there are particles found in the die.

2.34 (a) Table of row percentages:

ENJOY SHOPPING FOR CLOTHING	GENDER		
	Male	**Female**	**Total**
Yes	38%	62%	100%
No	74	26	100
Total	48	52	100

Table of column percentages:

ENJOY SHOPPING FOR CLOTHING	GENDER		
	Male	**Female**	**Total**
Yes	57%	86%	72%
No	43	14	28
Total	100	100	100

Table of total percentages:

ENJOY SHOPPING FOR CLOTHING	GENDER		
	Male	**Female**	**Total**
Yes	27%	45%	72%
No	21	7	28
Total	48	52	100

(c) A higher percentage of females enjoy shopping for clothing.

2.36 (b) The number of MBA and undergraduate students who choose the lowest-cost fund and the second-lowest-cost fund is about the same. More MBA students chose the third-lowest cost fund whereas more undergraduate students chose the highest cost fund.

2.38 (b) Yes, there is a strong positive relationship between X and Y. As X increases, so does Y.

2.40 (b) There is a positive relationship between owner mileage and current government standard mileage.

2.42 (b) There appears to be a positive relationship between the coachs' salary and revenue. **(c)** Yes, this is borne out by the data.

2.44 (b) The unemployment rate was stable at around 4% from January 2000 to around January 2001. Then it trended upward and leveled off at around 6% by December 2001. Around October 2003, it started to trend downward and reached about 4.5% by December 2006.

2.46 (b) There is an obvious upward trend in the average number of TV channels that the U.S. home received from 1985 to 2005. **(c)** With extrapolation, you would predict the average number of TV channels that the U.S. home will receive in 2010 to be around 140.

2.64 (c) The publisher gets the largest portion (64.8%) of the revenue. About half (32.2%) of the revenue received by the publisher covers manufacturing costs. The publisher's marketing and promotion account for the next largest share of the revenue, at 15.4%. Author, bookstore employee salaries and benefits, and publisher administrative costs and taxes each account for around 10% of the revenue, whereas the publisher after-tax profit, bookstore operations, bookstore pretax profit, and freight constitute the "trivial few" allocations of the revenue. Yes, the bookstore gets twice the revenue of the authors.

2.66 (b) In 2005, the United States relied on petroleum heavily, followed by coal and natural gas as major sources of energy, whereas renewable fuels accounted for less than 4% of the total consumption. Wood accounted for more than half of the renewable energy consumption.

2.68 (b) The Pareto plot is most appropriate because it not only sorts the frequencies in descending order, it also provides the cumulative polygon on the same scale. **(d)** The Pareto plot is most appropriate because it not only sorts the frequencies in descending order, it also provides the cumulative polygon on the same scale. **(e)** "Paid search" constitutes the largest category on U.S. online ad spending at 43%. Excluding the generic keyword "sneakers," searches using the keywords "sneaker pimps" and "Jordan sneaker" make up the majority of the searches for sneakers on specific brands.

2.70 (a)

DESSERT	GENDER		
ORDERED	Male	Female	Total
Yes	71%	29%	100%
No	48	52	100
Total	53	47	100

DESSERT	GENDER		
ORDERED	Male	Female	Total
Yes	30%	14%	23%
No	70	86	77
Total	100	100	100

DESSERT	BEEF ENTRÉE		
ORDERED	Yes	No	Total
Yes	52%	48%	100%
No	25	75	100
Total	31	69	100

DESSERT	BEEF ENTRÉE		
ORDERED	Yes	No	Total
Yes	38%	16%	23%
No	62	84	77
Total	100	100	100

DESSERT	BEEF ENTRÉE		
ORDERED	Yes	No	Total
Yes	12%	11%	23%
No	19	58	77
Total	31	69	100

(b) If the owner is interested in finding out the percentage of males and females who order dessert or the percentage of those who order a beef entrée and a dessert among all patrons, the table of total percentages is most informative. If the owner is interested in the effect of gender on ordering of dessert or the effect of ordering a beef entrée on the ordering of dessert, the table of column percentages will be most informative. Because dessert is usually ordered after the main entrée, and the owner has no direct control over the gender of patrons, the table of row percentages is not very useful here. **(c)** 30% of the men ordered desserts, compared to 14% of the women; men are more than twice as likely to order desserts as women. Almost 38% of the patrons ordering a beef entrée ordered dessert, compared to 16% of patrons ordering all other entrees. Patrons ordering beef are more than 2.3 times as likely to order dessert as patrons ordering any other entrée.

2.72 (a) 23575R15 accounts for over 80% of the warranty claims. **(b)** 91.82% of the warranty claims are from the ATX model. **(c)** Tread separation accounts for 73.23% of the warranty claims among the ATX model. **(d)** The number of claims is evenly distributed among the three incidents; other/unknown incidents account for almost 40% of the claims, tread separation accounts for about 35% of the claims, and blowout accounts for about 25% of the claims.

2.74 (c) Majority (about 71%) of the beers have percentage alcohol between 4.1% and 5.1% with one beer (O'Doul's) containing only 0.4% alcohol. There are two clusters in the distribution of calories. About 60% of the beers have between 135 and 175 calories and another cluster of 25% has between 95 and 115 calories. The distribution of carbohydrates is slightly right-skewed with carbohydrates for Sam Adams Cream Stout having a value equal to 23.9. There appears to be a positive relationship between percentage alcohol in a beer and its calories content. There is also an obvious positive relationship between calories content and carbohydrates content. Percentage alcohol content and calories content do not appear to be related.

2.76 (c) The distribution of the yields of the money market accounts is right-skewed with almost 80% of them having a return of less than 1.2% whereas only about 16% of them have yields higher than 2.0%. The distribution of the yields of one-year CDs is uniform between 3.4% and 5.4% with only about 16% of them having a yield of less than 3.4%. About 65% of the five-year CDs have yields that fall between 3.4% and 4.6%. Only 5% of them have yields that are lower than 3.4% and about 19% of them have yields higher than 5.0%. There appear to be positive relationships between all pairs of yields with one-year CDs and five-year CDs demonstrating the strongest positive relationship.

2.78 (a)

Frequencies (Boston)		
Weight (Boston)	Frequency	Percentage
3,015 but less than 3,050	2	0.54%
3,050 but less than 3,085	44	11.96
3,085 but less than 3,120	122	33.15
3,120 but less than 3,155	131	35.60
3,155 but less than 3,190	58	15.76
3,190 but less than 3,225	7	1.90
3,225 but less than 3,260	3	0.82
3,260 but less than 3,295	1	0.27

(b)

Frequencies (Vermont)		
Weight (Vermont)	Frequency	Percentage
3,550 but less than 3,600	4	1.21%
3,600 but less than 3,650	31	9.39
3,650 but less than 3,700	115	34.85
3,700 but less than 3,750	131	39.70
3,750 but less than 3,800	36	10.91
3,800 but less than 3,850	12	3.64
3,850 but less than 3,900	1	0.30

(d) 0.54% of the Boston shingles pallets are underweight, whereas 0.27% are overweight. 1.21% of the Vermont shingles pallets are underweight, whereas 3.94% are overweight.

2.80 (a), (c)

Calories	Frequency	Percentage	Limit	Percentage Less Than
50 but less than 100	3	12%	100	12%
100 but less than 150	3	12	150	24
150 but less than 200	9	36	200	60
200 but less than 250	6	24	250	84
250 but less than 300	3	12	300	96
300 but less than 350	0	0	350	96
350 but less than 400	1	4	400	100

Protein	Frequency	Percentage	Limit	Percentage Less Than
16 but less than 20	1	4%	20	4%
20 but less than 24	5	20	24	24
24 but less than 28	8	32	28	56
28 but less than 32	9	36	32	92
32 but less than 36	2	8	36	100

Calories from Fat	Frequency	Percentage	Limit	Percentage Less Than
0% but less than 10%	3	12%	10	12%
10% but less than 20%	4	16	20	28
20% but less than 30%	2	8	30	36
30% but less than 40%	5	20	40	56
40% but less than 50%	3	12	50	68
50% but less than 60%	5	20	60	88
60% but less than 70%	2	8	70	96
70% but less than 80%	1	4	80	100

Calories from Saturated Fat	Frequency	Percentage	Limit	Percentage Less Than
0% but less than 5%	6	24%	5	24%
5% but less than 10%	2	8	10	32
10% but less than 15%	5	20	15	52
15% but less than 20%	5	20	20	72
20% but less than 25%	5	20	25	92
25% but less than 30%	2	8	30	100

Cholesterol	Frequency	Percentage	Limit	Percentage Less Than
0 but less than 50	2	8%	50	8%
50 but less than 100	17	68	100	76
100 but less than 150	4	16	150	92
150 but less than 200	1	4	200	96
200 but less than 250	0	0	250	96
250 but less than 300	0	0	300	96
300 but less than 350	0	0	350	96
350 but less than 400	0	0	400	96
400 but less than 450	0	0	450	96
450 but less than 500	1	4	500	100

(d) The sampled fresh red meats, poultry, and fish vary from 98 to 397 calories per serving, with the highest concentration between 150 to 200 calories. One protein source, spareribs, with 397 calories, is more than 100 calories above the next highest caloric food. The protein content of the sampled foods varies from 16 to 33 grams, with 68% of the data values falling between 24 and 32 grams. Spareribs and fried liver are both very different from other foods sampled—the former on calories and the latter on cholesterol content.

2.82 (c) Total fat seems to be most closely related to calories because the points in the scatter plot are closer to the imaginary line that passes through the data points.

2.84 (b) There is a downward trend in the amount filled. **(c)** The amount filled in the next bottle will most likely be below 1.894 liter. **(d)** The scatter plot of the amount of soft drink filled against time reveals the trend of the data, whereas a histogram only provides information on the distribution of the data.

CHAPTER 3

3.2 (a) Mean = 7, median = 7, mode = 7. **(b)** Range = 9, interquartile range = 5, S^2 = 10.8, S = 3.286, CV = 46.948%. **(c)** Z scores: 0, −0.913, 0.609, 0, −1.217, 1.522. None of the Z scores are larger than 3.0 or smaller than −3.0. There is no outlier. **(d)** Symmetric because mean = median.

3.4 (a) Mean = 2, median = 7, mode = 7. **(b)** Range = 17, interquartile range = 14.5, S^2 = 62, S = 7.874, CV = 393.7%. **(d)** Left-skewed because mean < median.

3.6 (a)

	Grade X	Grade Y
Mean	575	575.4
Median	575	575
Standard deviation	6.40	2.07

(b) If quality is measured by central tendency, Grade X tires provide slightly better quality because X's mean and median are both equal to the expected value, 575 mm. If, however, quality is measured by consistency, Grade Y provides better quality because, even though Y's mean is only slightly larger than the mean for Grade X, Y's standard deviation is much smaller. The range in values for Grade Y is 5 mm compared to the range in values for Grade X, which is 16 mm.

(c)

	Grade X	Grade Y, Altered
Mean	575	577.4
Median	575	575
Standard deviation	6.40	6.11

When the fifth Y tire measures 588 mm rather than 578 mm, Y's mean inner diameter becomes 577.4 mm, which is larger than X's mean inner diameter, and Y's standard deviation increases from 2.07 mm to 6.11 mm. In this case, X's tires are providing better quality in terms of the mean inner diameter, with only slightly more variation among the tires than Y's.

3.8 (a) Mean = 36.53, median = 35.6. **(b)** Variance = 19.27, standard deviation = 4.39, range = 12, coefficient of variation = 12.02%. **(c)** The mean is only slightly larger than the median, so the data is only slightly right-skewed. **(d)** The mean cost is $36.53 and the median cost is $35.60. The average scatter of cost around the mean is $4.39. The difference between the highest and the lowest cost is $12.

3.10 (a) Mean = 19.25, median = 18, mode = 18. **(b)** Variance = 9.3056, standard deviation = 3.0505, range = 11, coefficient of variation = 15.85%. **(c)** Because the mean is larger than the median, the data are right-skewed. **(d)** The distributions of MPG of both 4 cylinder family sedans and small SUVs are skewed to the right. The mean MPG of 4 cylinder sedans is 5.75 higher than that of small SUVs. The average scatter of the MPG of 4 cylinder sedans is higher than that for small SUVs. The difference between the highest and the lowest MPG of sedans is also higher than that of SUVs. There is an obvious outlier in the MPG in Toyota Prius among the 4 cylinder family sedans whereas there is not an obvious outlier in the MPG among the small SUVs.

3.12 (a) Mean = 226.67, median = 210, first quartile = 110, third quartile = 380. **(b)** Variance = 17,756.06, standard deviation = 133.25, range = 425, interquartile range = 270, CV = 58.79%. There is no outlier because none of the Z scores has an absolute value that is greater than 3.0. **(c)** The data appear to be skewed to the right because the mean is greater than the median.

3.14 (a) Mean = 46.8, median = 42.5. **(b)** Range = 34, variance = 123.29, standard deviation = 11.10. **(c)** The admission price for one-day tickets is slightly skewed to the right because the mean is slightly greater than the median. **(d)(a)** Mean = 50.8, median = 42.5, first quartile = 40, third quartile = 62. **(b)** Range = 69, variance = 382.84, standard deviation = 19.57. **(c)** The admission price for one-day tickets is skewed to the right because the mean is much greater than the median due to the much higher price of the first observation, at $98.

3.16 (a) Mean = 7.11, median = 6.68. **(b)** Variance = 4.336, standard deviation = 2.082, range = 6.67, interquartile range = 3.09, CV = 29.27%. **(c)** Because the mean is greater than the median, the distribution is right-skewed. **(d)** The mean and median are both greater than 5 minutes. The distribution is right-skewed, meaning that there are some unusually high values. Further, 13 of the 15 bank customers sampled (or 86.7%) had waiting times greater than 5 minutes. So the customer is likely to experience a waiting time in excess of 5 minutes. The manager overstated the bank's service record in responding that the customer would "almost certainly" not wait longer than 5 minutes for service.

3.18 (a) $\bar{R}_G = [(1+3.614)(1-0.78)]^{\frac{1}{2}} - 1 = 0.7512\%$. **(b)** If you purchased $1,000 of TASER stock at the start of 2004, its value at the end of 2005 was $1,007.51. **(c)** If you purchased $1,000 of TASER stock at the start of 2004, its value at the end of 2005 was $82.95 lower than that of GE stock. **(d)** $\bar{R}_G = [(1+3.614)(1-0.78)(1+0.093)]^{\frac{1}{3}} - 1 = 3.5234\%$.

3.20 (a) Platinum = 18.45%, Gold = 17.98%, Silver = 23.32%. **(b)** All three metals achieved positive rates of return over the five-year period with silver yielding the highest rate of return at 23.32%, followed by platinum at 18.45% and gold at 17.98%. **(c)** In general, investments in the metal market achieved a higher rate of return than investments in the stock market from 2002 to 2006.

3.22 (a) Population mean, μ = 6. **(b)** Population standard deviation, σ = 1.673, population variance, σ^2 = 2.8.

3.24 (a) 68%. **(b)** 95%. **(c)** Not calculable, 75%, 88.89%. **(d)** $\mu - 4\sigma$ to $\mu + 4\sigma$ or −2.8 to 19.2.

3.26 (a) Mean = 12,999.2158, variance = 14,959,700.52, standard deviation = 3,867.7772. **(b)** 64.71%, 98.04%, and 100% of these states have mean per-capita energy consumption within 1, 2, and 3 standard deviations of the mean, respectively. **(c)** This is consistent with 68%, 95%, and 99.7%, according to the empirical rule. **(d)(a)** Mean = 12,857.7402, variance = 14,238,110.67, standard deviation = 3,773.3421. **(b)** 66%, 98%, and 100% of these states have a mean per-capita energy consumption within 1, 2, and 3 standard deviations of the mean, respectively. **(c)** This is consistent with 68%, 95%, and 99.7% according to the empirical rule.

3.28 (a) 25. **(b)** 11.010.

3.30 (a) March mean = $4,720, April mean = $4,400. **(b)** March S = $2,250.08, April S = $2,657.30. **(c)** No, the means are close relative to the size of the standard deviations. The standard deviations are about $400 apart.

3.32 (a) A: mean = 40.435, B: mean = 36.831. **(b)** A: S = 11.097, B: S = 8.334. **(c)** Yes, division B appears to have younger employees who are less variable in age than in division A.

3.34 (a) 4, 9, 5. **(b)** 3, 4, 7, 9, 12. **(c)** The distances between the median and the extremes are close, 4 and 5, but the differences in the tails are

different (1 on the left and 3 on the right), so this distribution is slightly right-skewed. **(d)** In 3.2 (d), because mean = median, the distribution was said to be symmetric. The box part of the graph is symmetric, but the tails show right-skewness.

3.36 (a) −6.5, 8, 14.5. **(b)** −8, −6.5, 7, 8, 9. **(c)** The shape is left-skewed. **(d)** This is consistent with the answer in 3.4 (d).

3.38 (a), (b) Five-number summary: 35 110 210 380 460. **(c)** The distribution is slightly skewed to the right.

3.40 (a) First Quartile = 17, Third Quartile = 22, Interquartile Range = 5. **(b)** Five-number summary: 15 17 18 22 26. **(c)** The MPG of small SUVs is right-skewed.

3.42 (a) Commercial district five-number summary: 0.38 3.2 4.5 5.55 6.46. Residential area five-number summary: 3.82 5.64 6.68 8.73 10.49. **(b)** Commercial district: The distribution is skewed to the left. Residential area: The distribution is skewed slightly to the right. **(c)** The central tendency of the waiting times for the bank branch located in the commercial district of a city is lower than that of the branch located in the residential area. There are a few longer than normal waiting times for the branch located in the residential area, whereas there are a few exceptionally short waiting times for the branch located in the commercial area.

3.44 U.S. stocks are highly correlated with the German stock market, somewhat correlated with the Brazilian stock market, and not very correlated with the Japanese stock market.

3.46 (a) cov(X, Y) = 591.667. **(b)** r = 0.7196. **(c)** The correlation coefficient is more valuable for expressing the relationship between calories and fat because it does not depend on the units used to measure calories and fat. **(d)** There is a strong positive linear relationship between calories and fat.

3.48 (a) cov(X, Y) = 1.2132. **(b)** $S_X^2 = 0.1944, S_Y^2 = 20.4054$

$$r = \frac{\text{cov}(X,Y)}{S_X S_Y} = \frac{1.2132}{(0.4409)(4.5172)} = 0.6092$$

(c) There is a moderate positive linear relationship between the coachs' salary and revenue.

3.62 (a) Mean = 43.89, median = 45, 1st quartile = 18, 3rd quartile = 63. **(b)** Range = 76, interquartile range = 45, variance = 639.2564, standard deviation = 25.28, CV = 57.61%. **(c)** The distribution is skewed to the right because there are a few policies that require an exceptionally long period to be approved. **(d)** The mean approval process takes 43.89 days, with 50% of the policies being approved in less than 45 days. 50% of the applications are approved between 18 and 63 days. About 67% of the applications are approved between 18.6 and 69.2 days.

3.64 (a) Mean = 8.421, median = 8.42, range = 0.186, S = 0.0461. The mean and median width are both 8.42 inches. The range of the widths is 0.186 inch, and the average scatter around the mean is 0.0461 inch. **(b)** 8.312, 8.404, 8.42, 8.459, 8.498. **(c)** Even though mean = median, the left tail is slightly longer so the distribution is slightly left-skewed. **(d)** All the troughs in this sample meet the specifications.

3.66 (a), (b)
Excel output:

	In-State Tuition/Fees	Out-of-State Tuition/Fees
Mean	6841.8155	17167.71
Median	6340	16340
Mode	7062	14901
Standard Deviation	2212.2215	4274.009
Sample Variance	4893924.034	18267150
Kurtosis	4.29574	−0.33509
Skewness	1.3504	0.5244
Range	14466	20007
Minimum	3094	8965
Maximum	17560	28972
Sum	704707	1768274
Count	103	103
First Quartile	5378	13928
Third Quartile	8143	20134
Interquartile Range	2765	6206
Coefficient of Variation	32.33%	24.90%

(c) Both in-state and out-of-state tuition and fees are right-skewed.

(d) $r = \dfrac{\text{cov}(X,Y)}{S_X S_Y} = 0.4911$.

(e) Both in-state and out-of-state tuition and fees are right-skewed due to the outliers in the right tails. There is a moderate positive linear relationship between in-state and out-of-state tuition and fees. Those schools with high in-state tuition and fees tend to also have high out-of-state tuition and fees.

3.68 (a) Boston: 0.04, 0.17, 0.23, 0.32, 0.98; Vermont: 0.02, 0.13, 0.20, 0.28, 0.83. **(b)** Both distributions are right-skewed. **(c)** Both sets of shingles did quite well in achieving a granule loss of 0.8 gram or less. The Boston shingles had only two data points greater than 0.8 gram. The next highest to these was 0.6 gram. These two data points can be considered outliers. Only 1.176% of the shingles failed the specification. In the Vermont shingles, only one data point was greater than 0.8 gram. The next highest was 0.58 gram. Thus, only 0.714% of the shingles failed to meet the specification.

3.70 (a) 0.80. **(b)** 0.53. **(c)** 0.92. **(d)** Total fat seems to be most closely related to calories because it has the highest correlation coefficient with calories.

3.72 (a) Mean = 7.5273, median = 7.263, first quartile = 6.353, third quartile = 8.248. **(b)** Range = 7.416, interquartile range = 1.895, variance = 2.6609, standard deviation = 1.6312, CV = 21.67%. **(c)** The data are skewed to the right. **(d)** The per-capita spending by the 50 states is right-skewed because a few states spend a lot more than the rest.

CHAPTER 4

4.2 (a) Simple events include selecting a red ball. **(b)** Selecting a white ball.

4.4 (a) 60/100 = 3/5 = 0.6. **(b)** 10/100 = 1/10 = 0.1. **(c)** 35/100 = 7/20 = 0.35. **(d)** 9/10 = 0.9.

4.6 (a) Mutually exclusive, not collectively exhaustive. **(b)** Not mutually exclusive, not collectively exhaustive. **(c)** Mutually exclusive, not collectively exhaustive. **(d)** Mutually exclusive, collectively exhaustive.

4.8 (a) "Makes less than \$50,000." **(b)** "Makes less than \$50,000 and tax code is unfair." **(c)** The complement of "tax code is fair" is "tax code is

unfair." **(d)** "Tax code is fair and makes less than \$50,000" is a joint event because it consists of two characteristics or attributes.

4.10 (a) "A wafer is good." **(b)** "A wafer is good and no particle was found on the die." **(c)** "Bad wafer." **(d)** A wafer that is a "good wafer" and was produced by a die "with particles" is a joint event because it consists of two characteristics.

4.12 (a) P(Selected the highest-cost fund) = (27+18)/200 = 0.225. **(b)** P(Selected the highest-cost fund and is an undergraduate) = 27/200 = 0.135. **(c)** P(Selected the highest-cost fund or is an undergraduate) = (45+100−27)/200 = 0.59. **(d)** The probability of "selected the highest-cost fund or is an undergraduate" includes the probability of "selected the highest-cost fund," plus the probability of "undergraduate minus the joint probability of highest-cost fund and undergraduate."

4.14 (a) 360/500 = 18/25 = 0.72. **(b)** 224/500 = 56/125 = 0.448. **(c)** 396/500 = 99/125 = 0.792. **(d)** 500/500 = 1.00.

4.16 (a) 10/30 = 1/3 = 0.33. **(b)** 20/60 = 1/3 = 0.33. **(c)** 40/60 = 2/3 = 0.67. **(d)** Because $P(A \mid B) = P(A) = 1/3$, events A and B are independent.

4.18 $\frac{1}{2}$ = 0.5.

4.20 Because $P(A \text{ and } B) = 0.20$ and $P(A) P(B) = 0.12$, events A and B are not independent.

4.22 (a) 36/116 = 0.3103. **(b)** 14/334 = 0.0419. **(c)** 320/334 = 0.9581 P(No particles) = 400/450 = 0.8889. Because P(No particles | Good) ≠ P(No particles), "a good wafer" and "a die with no particle" are not independent.

4.24 (a) P(Selected the highest-cost fund | Is an undergraduate) = 27/100 = 0.27. **(b)** P(Is an undergraduate | Selected the highest-cost fund) = 27/(27+18) = 0.6. **(c)** The conditional events are reversed. **(d)** Because P(Selected the highest-cost fund | Is an undergraduate) = 0.27 is not equal to P(Selected the highest-cost fund) = 0.225, the two events "student group" and "fund selected" are not independent.

4.26 (a) 0.025/0.6 = 0.0417. **(b)** 0.015/0.4 = 0.0375. **(c)** Because P(Needs warranty repair | Manufacturer based in U.S.) = 0.0417 and P(Needs warranty repair) = 0.04, the two events are not independent.

4.28 (a) 0.0045. **(b)** 0.012. **(c)** 0.0059. **(d)** 0.0483.

4.30 0.095.

4.32 (a) 0.736. **(b)** 0.997.

4.34 (a) $P(B' \mid O) = \dfrac{(0.5)(0.3)}{(0.5)(0.3)+(0.25)(0.7)} = 0.4615$. **(b)** $P(O) = 0.175 + 0.15 = 0.325$.

4.36 (a) P(Huge success | Favorable review) = 0.099/0.459 = 0.2157; P(Moderate success | Favorable review) = 0.14/0.459 = 0.3050; P(Break even | Favorable review) = 0.16/0.459 = 0.3486; P(Loser | Favorable review) = 0.06/0.459 = 0.1307. **(b)** P(Favorable review) = 0.459.

4.38 3^{10} = 59,049.

4.40 (a) 2^7 = 128. **(b)** 6^7 = 279,936. **(c)** There are two mutually exclusive and collectively exhaustive outcomes in (a) and six in (b).

4.42 (8)(4)(3)(3) = 288.

4.44 5! = (5)(4)(3)(2)(1) = 120. Not all these orders are equally likely because the teams have a different probability of finishing first through fifth.

4.46 $n!$ = 6! = 720.

4.48 $\dfrac{8!}{2!6!} = 28.$

4.50 4,950.

4.62 (a) $P(\text{all three are Republican}) = (0.3)^3 = 0.027.$ **(b)** $P(\text{all three are Democrats}) = 0.34^3 = 0.0393.$ **(c)** $P(\text{all three are Independents}) = 0.36^3 = 0.0467.$ **(d)** $P(\text{one Republican, one Democrat, and one Independent}) = (0.3)(0.34)(0.36) = 0.0367.$ **(e)** The approach you used in (a) through (d) is an example of empirical probability because the probability of each type of voters was obtained using the relative frequency of that type of voters.

4.64 (a)

		Age		
		18–25	26–40	Total
Goals	Getting Rich	405	310	715
	Other	95	190	285
	Total	500	500	1000

(b) Simple event: "Has a goal of getting rich." Joint event: "Has a goal of getting rich and is between 18–25 years old." **(c)** $P(\text{Has a goal of getting rich}) = 715/1000 = 0.715.$ **(d)** $P(\text{Has a goal of getting rich and is in the 26–40-year-old group}) = 310/1000 = 0.31.$

4.66 (a) 0.0225. **(b)** $3,937.5 \cong 3,938$ can be expected to read the advertisement and place an order. **(c)** 0.03. **(d)** 5,250 can be expected to read the advertisement and place an order.

4.68 (a) 0.4712. **(b)** Because the probability that a fatality involved a rollover, given that the fatality involved an SUV, a van, or a pickup is 0.4712, which is almost twice the probability that a fatality involved a rollover with any vehicle type, at 0.24, SUVs, vans, and pickups are generally more prone to rollover accidents.

CHAPTER 5

5.2 (a) C: $\mu = 2$, D: $\mu = 2$. **(b)** C: $\sigma = 1.414$, D: $\sigma = 1.095$. **(c)** Distribution C is uniform and symmetric; Distribution D is symmetric and has a single mode.

5.4 (a) $\mu = 0(0.10) + 1(0.20) + 2(0.45) + 3(0.15) + 4(0.05) + 5(0.05) = 2.0.$

(b) $\sigma = \sqrt{\begin{array}{l}(0-2)^2(0.10)+(1-2)^2(0.20)+(2-2)^2(0.45)+(3-2)^2(0.15) \\ +(4-2)^2(0.05)+(5-2)^2(0.05)\end{array}}$

$= 1.183.$

5.6 (a)

X	P(X)
$\$-1$	21/36
$\$+1$	15/36

(b)

X	P(X)
$\$-1$	21/36
$\$+1$	15/36

(c)

X	P(X)
$\$-1$	30/36
$\$+4$	6/36

(d) $\$-0.167$ for each method of play.

5.8 (a) 2.105769. **(b)** 1.467063.

5.10 (a) 90; 30. **(b)** 126.10, 10.95. **(c)** $-1,300.$ **(d)** 120.

5.12 (a) 9.5 minutes. **(b)** 1.9209 minutes.

5.14

$X*P(X)$	$Y*P(Y)$	$(X-\mu_X)^2*P(X)$	$(Y-\mu_Y)^2*P(Y)$	$(X-\mu_X)(Y-\mu_Y)*P(XY)$
−10	5	2,528.1	129.6	−572.4
0	45	1,044.3	5,548.8	−2,407.2
24	−6	132.3	346.8	−214.2
45	−30	2,484.3	3,898.8	−3,112.2

(a) $E(X) = \mu_X = \sum_{i=1}^{N} X_i P(X_i) = 59$, $E(Y) = \mu_Y = \sum_{i=1}^{N} Y_i P(Y_i) = 14$

$\sigma_X = \sqrt{\sum_{i=1}^{N}[X_i - E(X)]^2\, P(X_i)} = 78.6702$

(b)

$\sigma_Y = \sqrt{\sum_{i=1}^{N}[Y_i - E(Y)]^2\, P(Y_i)} = 99.62$

(c) $\sigma_{XY} = \sum_{i=1}^{N}[X_i - E(X)][Y_i - E(Y)]P(X_iY_i) = -6,306$

(d) Stock X gives the investor a lower standard deviation while yielding a higher expected return, so the investor should select stock X.

5.16 (a) \$71; \$97. **(b)** 61.88; 84.27. **(c)** 5,113. **(d)** Risk-averse investors would invest in stock X, whereas risk takers would invest in stock Y.

5.18 (a) $E(X) = \$77$; $E(Y) = \$97$. **(b)** $\sigma_X = 39.76$; $\sigma_Y = 108.95$. **(c)** $\sigma_{XY} = 4161$. **(d)** The common stock fund gives the investor a higher expected return than the corporate bond fund, but also has a standard deviation more than 2.5 times higher than that for the corporate bond fund. An investor should carefully weigh the increased risk.

5.20 (a) 0.5997. **(b)** 0.0016. **(c)** 0.0439. **(d)** 0.4018.

5.22

	Mean	Standard Deviation
(a)	0.40	0.600
(b)	1.60	0.980
(c)	4.00	0.894
(d)	1.50	0.866

5.24 (a) $P(X = 0) = 0.7351.$ **(b)** If the probabilities of the six events are not all equal, then you would calculate the probability in (a) by multiplying together the probability of no failure in each of the six events.

5.26 Given $\pi = 0.878$ and $n = 3$,

(a) $P(X = 3) = \dfrac{n!}{X!(n-x)!}\pi^X(1-\pi)^{n-X} = \dfrac{3!}{3!0!}(0.878)^3(0.122)^0 = 0.6768.$

(b) $P(X = 0) = \dfrac{n!}{X!(n-x)!}\pi^X(1-\pi)^{n-X} = \dfrac{3!}{0!3!}(0.878)^0(0.122)^3 = 0.0018.$

(c) $P(X \geq 2) = P(X = 2) + P(X = 3)$

$= \dfrac{3!}{2!1!}(0.878)^2(0.122)^1 + \dfrac{3!}{3!0!}(0.878)^3(0.122)^0 = 0.9590.$

(d) $E(X) = n\pi = 3(0.878) = 2.634$ $\sigma_X = \sqrt{n\pi(1-\pi)}$

$= \sqrt{3(0.878)(0.122)} = 0.5669.$

5.28 (a) 0.1804. **(b)** 0.00205. **(c)** 0.4511. **(d)** 0.4437, 0.00000, 0.1648. The probability of loans to second home owners or investors is lower, so the chance of no loans to these individuals is higher.

5.30 (a) $P(X \leq 5) = .00009919$. **(b)** $P(X \leq 10) = 0.0719$. **(c)** $P(X \leq 15) = 0.8173$.

5.32 (a) 0.2565. **(b)** 0.1396. **(c)** 0.3033. **(d)** 0.0247.

5.34 (a) 0.0337. **(b)** 0.0067. **(c)** 0.9596. **(d)** 0.0404.

5.36 (a)
$$P(X < 5) = P(X = 0) + P(X = 1) + P(X = 2) + P(X = 3) + P(X = 4)$$
$$= \frac{e^{-6}(6)^0}{0!} + \frac{e^{-6}(6)^1}{1!} + \frac{e^{-6}(6)^2}{2!} + \frac{e^{-6}(6)^3}{3!} + \frac{e^{-6}(6)^4}{4!}$$
$$= 0.002479 + 0.014873 + 0.044618 + 0.089235 + 0.133853$$
$$= 0.2851.$$

(b) $P(X = 5) = \dfrac{e^{-6}(6)^5}{5!} = 0.1606$.

(c) $P(X \geq 5) = 1 - P(X < 5) = 1 - 0.2851 = 0.7149$.

(d) $P(X = 4 \text{ or } X = 5) = P(X = 4) + P(X = 5) = \dfrac{e^{-6}(6)^4}{4!} + \dfrac{e^{-6}(6)^5}{5!}$
$$= 0.2945.$$

5.38 $\lambda = 4.06$. **(a)** $P(X = 0) = 0.0172$. **(b)** $P(X \geq 1) = 0.9828$. **(c)** $P(X \geq 2) = 0.9127$.

5.40 (a) 0.0176. **(b)** 0.9093. **(c)** 0.9220.

5.42 (a) 0.2671. **(b)** 0.8525. **(c)** Because Ford had a lower mean rate of problems per car in 2007 compared to Dodge, the probability of a randomly selected Ford having zero problems and the probability of no more than 2 problems are both higher than their values for Dodge.

5.44 (a) 0.2101. **(b)** 0.7936. **(c)** Because Dodge had a lower mean rate of problems per car in 2007 compared to 2006, the probability of a randomly selected Dodge having zero problems and the probability of no more than 2 problems are both higher in 2007 than their values in 2006.

5.46 (a) 0.238. **(b)** 0.2. **(c)** 0.1591. **(d)** 0.0083.

5.48 (a) If $n = 6$, $A = 25$, and $N = 100$,
$$P(X \geq 2) = 1 - [P(X = 0) + P(X = 1)]$$
$$= 1 - \left[\frac{\binom{25}{0}\binom{100-25}{6-0}}{\binom{100}{6}} + \frac{\binom{25}{1}\binom{100-25}{6-1}}{\binom{100}{6}} \right]$$
$$= 1 - [0.1689 + 0.3620] = 0.4691.$$

(b) If $n = 6$, $A = 30$, and $N = 100$,
$$P(X \geq 2) = 1 - [P(X = 0) + P(X = 1)]$$
$$= 1 - \left[\frac{\binom{30}{0}\binom{100-30}{6-0}}{\binom{100}{6}} + \frac{\binom{30}{1}\binom{100-30}{6-1}}{\binom{100}{6}} \right]$$
$$= 1 - [0.1100 + 0.3046] = 0.5854.$$

(c) If $n = 6$, $A = 5$, and $N = 100$,
$$P(X \geq 2) = 1 - [P(X = 0) + P(X = 1)]$$
$$= 1 - \left[\frac{\binom{5}{0}\binom{100-5}{6-0}}{\binom{100}{6}} + \frac{\binom{5}{1}\binom{100-5}{6-1}}{\binom{100}{6}} \right]$$
$$= 1 - [0.7291 + 0.2430] = 0.0279.$$

(d) If $n = 6$, $A = 10$, and $N = 100$,
$$P(X \geq 2) = 1 - [P(X = 0) + P(X = 1)]$$
$$= 1 - \left[\frac{\binom{10}{0}\binom{100-10}{6-0}}{\binom{100}{6}} + \frac{\binom{10}{1}\binom{100-10}{6-1}}{\binom{100}{6}} \right]$$
$$= 1 - [0.5223 + 0.3687] = 0.1090.$$

(e) The probability that the entire group will be audited is very sensitive to the true number of improper returns in the population. If the true number is very low ($A = 5$), the probability is very low (0.0279). When the true number is increased by a factor of 6 ($A = 30$), the probability the group will be audited increases by a factor of almost 21 (0.5854).

5.50 (a) $P(X = 4) = 0.00003649$. **(b)** $P(X = 0) = 0.5455$. **(c)** $P(X \geq 1) = 0.4545$. **(d)** $X = 6$. **(a)** $P(X = 4) = 0.0005$. **(b)** $P(X = 0) = 0.3877$. **(c)** $P(X \geq 1) = 0.6123$.

5.52 (a) $P(X = 1) = 0.4835$. **(b)** $P(X \geq 1) = 0.6374$. **(c)** $P(X \leq 2) = 0.9912$. **(d)** $\mu = n \times (A/N) = 0.8$.

5.58 (a) 0.74. **(b)** 0.74. **(c)** 0.3898. **(d)** 0.0012. **(e)** The assumption of independence may not be true.

5.60 (a) If $\pi = 0.50$ and $n = 11$, $P(X \geq 9) = 0.0327$. **(b)** If $\pi = 0.74$ and $n = 11$, $P(X \geq 9) = 0.4247$.

5.62 (a) 0.018228. **(b)** 0.089782. **(c)** 0.89199. **(d)** Mean = 3.3, standard deviation = 1.486943.

5.64 (a) 0.0000. **(b)** 0.04924. **(c)** 0.909646. **(d)** 0.49578.

5.66 (a) 0.0012. **(b)** 0.2456. **(c)** 0.6474. **(d)** 0.3526. **(e)** $E(X) = n\pi = 5.1$. Google can expect that slightly more than half of the people use its search engine.

5.68 (a) $\mu = n\pi = 2.6$. **(b)** $\sigma = \sqrt{n\pi(1-\pi)} = 1.5040$. **(c)** $P(X = 0) = 0.0617$. **(d)** $P(X \leq 2) = 0.5080$. **(e)** $P(X \geq 3) = 0.4920$.

5.70 (a) If $\pi = 0.50$ and $n = 37$, $P(X \geq 31) = 0.0000$. **(b)** If $\pi = 0.70$ and $n = 37$, $P(X \geq 31) = 0.0216$. **(c)** If $\pi = 0.90$ and $n = 36$, $P(X \geq 37) = 0.8564$. **(d)** Based on the results in (a)–(c), the probability that the Standard & Poor's 500 index will increase if there is an early gain in the first five trading days of the year is very likely to be close to 0.90 because that yields a probability of 85.64% that at least 31 of the 37 years the Standard & Poor's 500 index will increase the entire year.

5.72 (a) The assumptions needed are (i) the probability that a golfer loses a golf ball in a given interval is constant, (ii) the probability that a golfer loses more than one golf ball approaches 0 as the interval gets smaller, and (iii) the probability that a golfer loses a golf ball is independent from interval to interval. **(b)** 0.0111. **(c)** 0.70293. **(d)** 0.29707.

5.74 (a) Virtually zero. **(b)** 0.00000037737. **(c)** 0.00000173886. **(d)** 0.000168669. **(e)** 0.0011998. **(f)** 0.00407937. **(g)** 0.006598978. **(h)** 0.0113502. **(i)** 0.976601.

CHAPTER 6

6.2 (a) 0.9089. **(b)** 0.0911. **(c)** +1.96. **(d)** −1.00 and +1.00.

6.4 (a) 0.1401. **(b)** 0.4168. **(c)** 0.3918. **(d)** +1.00.

6.6 (a) 0.9599. **(b)** 0.0228. **(c)** 43.42. **(d)** 46.64 and 53.36.

6.8 (a) $P(34 < X < 50) = P(-1.33 < Z < 0) = 0.4082$. **(b)** $P(X < 30) + P(X > 60) = P(Z < -1.67) + P(Z > 0.83) = 0.0475 + (1.0 - 0.7967) = 0.2508$. **(c)** $P(Z < -0.84) \cong 0.20$, $Z = -0.84 = \dfrac{X - 50}{12}$. $X = 50 - 0.84(12) = 39.92$ thousand miles, or 39,920 miles. **(d)** The smaller standard deviation makes the Z values larger.

(a) $P(34 < X < 50) = P(-1.60 < Z < 0) = 0.4452$.
(b) $P(X < 30) + P(X > 60) = P(Z < -2.00) + P(Z > 1.00) = 0.0228 + (1.0 - 0.8413) = 0.1815$.
(c) $X = 50 - 0.84(10) = 41.6$ thousand miles, or 41,600 miles.

6.10 (a) 0.9878. **(b)** 0.8185. **(c)** 86.16%. **(d)** Option 1: Because your score of 81% on this exam represents a Z score of 1.00, which is below the minimum Z score of 1.28, you will not earn an A grade on the exam under this grading option. Option 2: Because your score of 68% on this exam represents a Z score of 2.00, which is well above the minimum Z score of 1.28, you will earn an A grade on the exam under this grading option. You should prefer Option 2.

6.12 (a) 0.0228. **(b)** 0.2525. **(c)** 0.0912. **(d)** 0.0004.

6.14 With 39 values, the smallest of the standard normal quantile values covers an area under the normal curve of 0.025. The corresponding Z value is −1.96. The middle (20th) value has a cumulative area of 0.50 and a corresponding Z value of 0.0. The largest of the standard normal quantile values covers an area under the normal curve of 0.975, and its corresponding Z value is +1.96.

6.16 (a) Mean = 23.2, median = 23.5, range = 52, standard deviation = 12.3868, $6(S_X) = 6(12.3868) = 74.3205$, interquartile range = 14, $1.33(S_X) = 1.33(12.3868) = 16.4744$. The mean is almost equal to the median; the range is smaller than 6 times the standard deviation, and the interquartile range is slightly smaller than 1.33 times the standard deviation. The data appear to be approximately normally distributed but slightly skewed to the right. **(b)** The normal probability plot suggests that the data are skewed to the right.

6.18 (a) Mean = 1040.863, median = 981, range = 1732, $6(S_X) = 2571.2310$, interquartile range = 593, $1.33(S_X) = 569.9562$. There are 62.75%, 78.43%, and 94.12% of the observations that fall within 1, 1.28, and 2 standard deviations of the mean, respectively, as compared to the approximate theoretical 66.67%, 80%, and 95%. Because the mean is slightly larger than the median, the interquartile range is slightly larger than 1.33 times the standard deviation, and the range is much smaller than 6 times the standard deviation, the data appear to deviate slightly from the normal distribution. **(b)** The normal probability plot suggests that the data appear to be slightly right-skewed.

6.20 (a) Interquartile range = 0.0025, $S_X = 0.0017$, range = 0.008, $1.33(S_X) = 0.0023$, $6(S_X) = 0.0102$. Because the interquartile range is close to $1.33(S_X)$ and the range is also close to $6(S_X)$, the data appear to be approximately normally distributed. **(b)** The normal probability plot suggests that the data appear to be approximately normally distributed.

6.22 (a) Five-number summary: 82 127 148.5 168 213; mean = 147.06, mode = 130, range = 131, interquartile range = 41, standard deviation = 31.69. The mean is very close to the median. The five-number summary suggests that the distribution is approximately symmetrical around the median. The interquartile range is very close to 1.33 times the standard deviation. The range is about $50 below 6 times the standard deviation. In general, the distribution of the data appears to closely resemble a normal distribution. **(b)** The normal probability plot confirms that the data appear to be approximately normally distributed.

6.24 (a) $(20 - 0)/120 = 0.1667$. **(b)** $(30 - 10)/120 = 0.1667$. **(c)** $(120 - 35)/120 = 0.7083$. **(d)** Mean = 60, standard deviation = 34.641.

6.26 (a) 0.1. **(b)** 0.3333. **(c)** 0.3333. **(d)** Mean = 4.5, standard deviation = 0.8660.

6.28 (a) 0.6321. **(b)** 0.3679. **(c)** 0.2326. **(d)** 0.7674.

6.30 (a) 0.7769. **(b)** 0.2231. **(c)** 0.1410. **(d)** 0.8590.

6.32 (a) For $\lambda = 2$, $P(X \le 1) = 0.864665$. **(b)** For $\lambda = 2$, $P(X \le 5) = 0.99996$. **(c)** For $\lambda = 1$, $P(X \le 1) = 0.6321$, for $\lambda = 1$, $P(X \le 1) = 0.9933$.

6.34 (a) 0.6321. **(b)** 0.3935. **(c)** 0.0952.

6.36 (a) 0.8647. **(b)** 0.3297. **(c)(a)** 0.9765. **(b)** 0.5276.

6.38 (a) 0.0457. **(b)** 0.0846. **(c)** 0.9154. **(d)** 0.8697.

6.40 (a) 0.2051. **(b)** 0.8281. **(c)** 0.7734. **(d)(a)** 0.2045. **(b)** 0.8286. **(c)** 0.7717.

6.42 If the grant is equally likely to be given on any day of the month, the probability of seeing the results or more extreme results is virtually 0.

6.52 (a) 0.4772. **(b)** 0.9544. **(c)** 0.0456. **(d)** 1.8835. **(e)** 1.8710 and 2.1290.

6.54 (a) 0.2734. **(b)** 0.2038. **(c)** 4.404 ounces. **(d)** 4.188 ounces and 5.212 ounces.

6.56 (a) Waiting time will more closely resemble an exponential distribution. **(b)** Seating time will more closely resemble a normal distribution. **(c)** Both the histogram and normal probability plot suggest that waiting time more closely resembles an exponential distribution. **(d)** Both the histogram and normal probability plot suggest that seating time more closely resembles a normal distribution.

6.58 (a) 0.8413. **(b)** 0.9330. **(c)** 0.9332. **(d)** 0.3347. **(e)** 0.4080 and 1.1920.

6.60 (a) Mean = 3,019.7255, median = 2,972, range = 1174, $6(S_X) = 1,393.4693$, interquartile range = 284, $1.33(S_X) = 308.8857$. There are 70.59%, 86.27%, and 96.08% of the observations that fall within 1, 1.28, and 2 standard deviations of the mean, respectively, as compared to the approximate theoretical 66.67%, 80%, and 95%. Because the mean is slightly larger than the median, the interquartile range is slightly smaller than 1.33 times the standard deviation, and the range is much smaller than 6 times the standard deviation, the data appear to deviate slightly from the normal distribution. The normal probability plot suggests that the data appear to be slightly right-skewed. **(b)** The variable RANK 2006 has a uniform distribution between 1 and 52.

CHAPTER 7

7.2 Sample without replacement: Read from left to right in three-digit sequences and continue unfinished sequences from the end of the row to the beginning of the next row:

Row 05: 338 505 855 551 438 855 077 186 579 488 767 833 170
Rows 05–06: 897
Row 06: 340 033 648 847 204 334 639 193 639 411 095 924
Rows 06–07: 707
Row 07: 054 329 776 100 871 007 255 980 646 886 823 920 461
Row 08: 893 829 380 900 796 959 453 410 181 277 660 908 887
Rows 08–09: 237
Row 09: 818 721 426 714 050 785 223 801 670 353 362 449
Rows 09–10: 406

Note: All sequences above 902 and duplicates are discarded.

7.4 A simple random sample would be less practical for personal interviews because of travel costs (unless interviewees are paid to go to a central interviewing location).

7.6 Here all members of the population are equally likely to be selected, and the sample selection mechanism is based on chance. But selection of two elements is not independent; for example, if A is in the sample, we know that B is also and that C and D are not.

7.8 (a)

Row 16: 2323 6737 5131 8888 1718 0654 6832 4647 6510 4877
Row 17: 4579 4269 2615 1308 2455 7830 5550 5852 5514 7182
Row 18: 0989 3205 0514 2256 8514 4642 7567 8896 2977 8822
Row 19: 5438 2745 9891 4991 4523 6847 9276 8646 1628 3554
Row 20: 9475 0899 2337 0892 0048 8033 6945 9826 9403 6858
Row 21: 7029 7341 3553 1403 3340 4205 0823 4144 1048 2949
Row 22: 8515 7479 5432 9792 6575 5760 0408 8112 2507 3742
Row 23: 1110 0023 4012 8607 4697 9664 4894 3928 7072 5815
Row 24: 3687 1507 7530 5925 7143 1738 1688 5625 8533 5041
Row 25: 2391 3483 5763 3081 6090 5169 0546

Note: All sequences above 5,000 are discarded. There were no repeating sequences.

(b) 089 189 289 389 489 589 689 789 889 989
1089 1189 1289 1389 1489 1589 1689 1789 1889 1989
2089 2189 2289 2389 2489 2589 2689 2789 2889 2989
3089 3189 3289 3389 3489 3589 3689 3789 3889 3989
4089 4189 4289 4389 4489 4589 4689 4789 4889 4989

(c) With the single exception of invoice #0989, the invoices selected in the simple random sample are not the same as those selected in the systematic sample. It would be highly unlikely that a simple random sample would select the same units as a systematic sample.

7.10 Before accepting the results of a survey of college students, you might want to know, for example:

Who funded the survey? Why was it conducted? What was the population from which the sample was selected? What sampling design was used? What mode of response was used: a personal interview, a telephone interview, or a mail survey? Were interviewers trained? Were survey questions field-tested? What questions were asked? Were they clear, accurate, unbiased, and valid? What operational definition of "vast majority" was used? What was the response rate? What was the sample size?

7.12 (a) The four types of survey errors are: coverage error, nonresponse error, sampling error, and measurement error. **(b)** When people who answer the survey tell you what they think you want to hear, rather than what they really believe, it introduces the halo effect, which is a source of measurement error. Also, every survey will have sampling error that reflects the chance differences from sample to sample, based on the probability of particular individuals being selected in the particular sample.

7.14 Before accepting the results of the survey, you might want to know, for example:

Who funded the study? Why was it conducted? What was the population from which the sample was selected? What sampling design was used? What mode of response was used: a personal interview, a telephone interview, or a mail survey? Were interviewers trained? Were survey questions field-tested? What other questions were asked? Were they clear, accurate, unbiased, and valid? What was the response rate? What was the margin of error? What was the sample size? What was the frame being used?

7.16 Before accepting the results of the survey, you might want to know, for example:

Who funded the study? Why was it conducted? What was the population from which the sample was selected? What was the frame being used? What sampling design was used? What mode of response was used: a personal interview, a telephone interview, or a mail survey? Were interviewers trained? Were survey questions field-tested? What other questions were asked? Were they clear, accurate, unbiased, and valid? What was the response rate? What was the margin of error? What was the sample size?

7.18 (a) Virtually zero. **(b)** 0.1587. **(c)** 0.0139. **(d)** 50.195.

7.20 (a) Both means are equal to 6. This property is called unbiasedness. **(c)** The distribution for $n = 3$ has less variability. The larger sample size has resulted in sample means being closer to μ.

7.22 (a) When $n = 2$, the shape of the sampling distribution of $\bar{X}$ should closely resemble the shape of the distribution of the population from which the sample is selected. Because the mean is larger than the median, the distribution of the sales price of new houses is skewed to the right, and so is the sampling distribution of $\bar{X}$. **(b)** If you select samples of $n = 100$, the shape of the sampling distribution of the sample mean will be very close to a normal distribution with a mean of \$299,100 and a standard deviation of \$9,000. **(c)** 0.5398. **(d)** 0.1523.

7.24 (a) $P(\bar{X} > 3) = P(Z > -1.00) = 1.0 - 0.1587 = 0.8413$.
(b) $P(Z < 1.04) = 0.85$; $\bar{X} = 3.10 + 1.04(0.1) = 3.204$.

(c) To be able to use the standardized normal distribution as an approximation for the area under the curve, you must assume that the population is approximately symmetrical. **(d)** $P(Z < 1.04) = 0.85$; $\bar{X} = 3.10 + 1.04(0.05) = 3.152$.

7.26 (a) 0.9969. **(b)** 0.0142. **(c)** 2.3830 and 2.6170. **(d)** 2.6170.
Note: These answers are computed using Microsoft Excel. They may be slightly different when Table E.2 is used.

7.28 (a) 0.30. **(b)** 0.0693.

7.30 (a) $\pi = 0.501$, $\sigma_P = \sqrt{\frac{\pi(1-\pi)}{n}} = \sqrt{\frac{0.501(1-0.501)}{100}} = 0.05$
$P(p > 0.55) = P(Z > 0.98) = 1.0 - 0.8365 = 0.1635$.

(b) $\pi = 0.60$, $\sigma_P = \sqrt{\frac{\pi(1-\pi)}{n}} = \sqrt{\frac{0.6(1-0.6)}{100}} = 0.04899$
$P(p > 0.55) = P(Z > -1.021) = 1.0 - 0.1539 = 0.8461$.

(c) $\pi = 0.49$, $\sigma_P = \sqrt{\frac{\pi(1-\pi)}{n}} = \sqrt{\frac{0.49(1-0.49)}{100}} = 0.05$
$P(p > 0.55) = P(Z > 1.20) = 1.0 - 0.8849 = 0.1151$.

(d) Increasing the sample size by a factor of 4 decreases the standard error by a factor of 2.
(a) $P(p > 0.55) = P(Z > 1.96) = 1.0 - 0.9750 = 0.0250$.
(b) $P(p > 0.55) = P(Z > -2.04) = 1.0 - 0.0207 = 0.9793$.
(c) $P(p > 0.55) = P(Z > 2.40) = 1.0 - 0.9918 = 0.0082$.

7.32 (a) 0.9298. **(b)** 0.8596. **(c)** 0.9865. **(d)(a)** 0.7695. **(b)** 0.5390. **(c)** 0.8656.

7.34 (a) Because $n = 200$, which is quite large, you use the sample proportion to approximate the population proportion and, hence, $\pi = 0.50$.

$$\mu_P = \pi = 0.5, \sigma_P = \sqrt{\frac{\pi(1-\pi)}{n}} = \sqrt{\frac{0.5(0.5)}{200}} = 0.0354$$

$P(0.45 < \pi < 0.55) = P(-1.4142 < Z < 1.4142) = 0.8427$.
(b) $P(A < \pi < B) = P(-1.6449 < Z < 1.6449) = 0.90$. $A = 0.50 - 1.6449(0.0354) = 0.4418$. $B = 0.50 + 1.6449(0.0354) = 0.5582$. The probability is 90% that the sample percentage will be contained within 5.8% symmetrically around the population percentage.
(c) $P(A < \pi < B) = P(-1.96 < Z < +1.96) = 0.95$. $A = 0.50 - 1.96(0.0354) = 0.4306$. $B = 0.50 + 1.96(0.0354) = 0.5694$. The probability is 95% that the sample percentage will be contained within 6.94% symmetrically around the population percentage.

7.36 (a) 0.1134. **(b)** 0.0034. **(c)** Increasing the sample size by a factor of 5 decreases the standard error by a factor of $\sqrt{5}$. The sampling distribution of the proportion becomes more concentrated around the true proportion of 0.56 and, hence, the probability in (b) becomes smaller than that in (a).

7.38 (a) 0.3626. **(b)** 0.9816. **(c)** 0.0092.

Note: These answers are computed using Microsoft Excel. They may be slightly different when Table E.2 is used.

7.50 (a) 0.4999. **(b)** 0.00009. **(c)** 0. **(d)** 0. **(e)** 0.7518.

7.52 (a) 0.8944. **(b)** 4.617; 4.783. **(c)** 4.641.

7.54 (a) 0.0002. **(b)** 0.3461. **(c)** 0.9759.

7.56 Even though Internet polling is less expensive and faster and offers higher response rates than telephone surveys, it is a self-selection response method. Because respondents who choose to participate in the survey may not represent the view of the public, the data collected may not be appropriate for making inferences about the general population.

7.58 (a) Before accepting the results of this survey, you would like to know (i) how big is the sample size, (ii) what is the purpose of the survey, (iii) what sampling method is being used, (iv) what is the frame being used, (v) what is the response rate, and (vi) how the questions are being phrased. **(b)** The population will be all the AOL users. The frame can be compiled from the list of the AOL subscribers. Because there are two natural strata in the population, adults and teens, a stratified sampling method should be used to better represent the population.

7.60 (a) Before accepting the results of this survey, you would like to know (i) how big is the sample size, (ii) what is the purpose of the survey, (iii) what sampling method is being used, (iv) what is the frame being used, (v) what is the response rate, and (vi) how the questions are being phrased. **(b)** The population will be all the working males in the geographic region. The frame can be compiled from the list of men who file income tax returns in the region. Because not all extreme workers have a spouse or partner, you might be interested in knowing whether there is any connection between being an extreme worker and maintaining a relationship. So a stratified sample could be used to ensure that those who have a spouse or partner and those who do not are equally represented. These two strata can be identified through their income tax filing status.

CHAPTER 8

8.2 $114.68 \leq \mu \leq 135.32$.

8.4 (a) You would compute the mean first because you need the mean to compute the standard deviation. If you had a sample, you would compute the sample mean. If you had the population mean, you would compute the population standard deviation. **(b)** If you have a sample, you are computing the sample standard deviation, not the population standard deviation needed in Equation (8.1). If you have a population and have computed the population mean and population standard deviation, you don't need a confidence interval estimate of the population mean because you already know the mean.

8.6 Equation (8.1) assumes that you know the population standard deviation. Because you are selecting a sample of 100 from the population, you are computing a sample standard deviation, not the population standard deviation.

8.8 (a) 2.2622. **(b)** 3.2498. **(c)** 2.0395. **(d)** 1.9977. **(e)** 1.7531.

8.10 $-0.12 \leq \mu \leq 11.84$, $2.00 \leq \mu \leq 6.00$. The presence of the outlier increases the sample mean and greatly inflates the sample standard deviation.

8.12 (a) $32 \pm (2.0096)(9)/\sqrt{50}$; $29.44 \leq \mu \leq 34.56$. **(b)** The quality improvement team can be 95% confident that the population mean turnaround time is between 29.44 hours and 34.56 hours. **(c)** The project was a success because the initial turnaround time of 68 hours does not fall into the interval.

8.14 (a) $31.9267 \leq \mu \leq 41.1399$. **(b)** You can be 95% confident that the population mean price for two tickets with online service charges, large popcorn, and two medium soft drinks is somewhere between \$31.93 and \$41.14.

8.16 (a) $18.0671 \leq \mu \leq 20.4329$. **(b)** You can be 95% confident that the population mean miles per gallon of 2007 small SUVs is somewhere between 18.0671 and 20.4329. **(c)** Because the 95% confidence interval for population mean miles per gallon of 2007 small SUVs does not overlap with that for the population mean miles per gallon of 2007 family sedans, you are 95% confident that the population mean miles per gallon of 2007 small SUVs is lower than that of 2007 family sedans.

8.18 (a) $31.12 \leq \mu \leq 54.96$. **(b)** The number of days is approximately normally distributed. **(c)** No, the outliers skew the data. **(d)** Because the sample size is fairly large, at $n = 50$, the use of the t distribution is appropriate.

8.20 (a) $142.00 \leq \mu \leq 311.33$. **(b)** The population distribution needs to be normally distributed. **(c)** Both the normal probability plot and the boxplot show that the distribution for battery life is approximately normally distributed.

8.22 $0.19 \leq \pi \leq 0.31$.

8.24 (a) $p = \dfrac{X}{n} = \dfrac{135}{500} = 0.27$

$$p \pm Z\sqrt{\frac{p(1-p)}{n}} = 0.27 \pm 2.58\sqrt{\frac{0.27(0.73)}{500}} \qquad 0.2189 \leq \pi \leq 0.3211.$$

(b) The manager in charge of promotional programs concerning residential customers can infer that the proportion of households that would purchase an additional telephone line if it were made available at a substantially reduced installation cost is somewhere between 0.22 and 0.32, with 99% confidence.

8.26 (a) $0.2311 \leq \pi \leq 0.3089$. **(b)** $0.2425 \leq \pi \leq 0.2975$. **(c)** The larger the sample size, the narrower is the confidence interval, holding everything else constant.

8.28 (a) $0.5638 \leq \pi \leq 0.6362$. **(b)** $0.2272 \leq \pi \leq 0.2920$.

8.30 (a) $0.3783 \leq \pi \leq 0.4427$. **(b)** You can be 95% confident that the population proportion of all workers whose primary reason for staying on their job is interesting job responsibilities is somewhere between 0.3783 and 0.4427.

8.32 $n = 35$.

8.34 $n = 1,041$.

8.36 (a) $n = \dfrac{Z^2\sigma^2}{e^2} = \dfrac{(1.96)^2(400)^2}{50^2} = 245.86$

Use $n = 246$.

(b) $n = \dfrac{Z^2\sigma^2}{e^2} = \dfrac{(1.96)^2(400)^2}{25^2} = 983.41$

Use $n = 984$.

8.38 $n = 97$.

8.40 (a) $n = 167$. **(b)** $n = 97$.

8.42 (a) $n = 246$. **(b)** $n = 385$. **(c)** $n = 554$. **(d)** When there is more variability in the population, a larger sample is needed to accurately estimate the mean.

8.44 (a) $n = 2,156$. **(b)** $n = 2,239$. **(c)** The sample size is larger in (b) than in (a) because the estimate of the true proportion is closer to 0.5 in (b) than in (a). **(d)** If you were to design the follow-up study, you would use one sample and ask the respondents both questions rather than selecting two separate samples because it costs more to select two samples than one.

8.46 (a) $p = 0.5498$; $0.5226 \leq \pi \leq 0.5770$. **(b)** $p = 0.4697$; $0.4424 \leq \pi \leq 0.4970$. **(c)** $p = 0.2799$; $0.2554 \leq \pi \leq 0.3045$. **(d) (a)** $n = 2,378$. **(b)** $= 2,393$. **(c)** $= 1,936$.

8.48 (a) If you conduct a follow-up study to estimate the population proportion of individuals who view oil companies favorably, you would use a π of 0.15 in the sample size formula because it provides the most conservative value based on past information on the proportion. **(b)** $n = 545$.

8.50 $\$10,721.53 \leq \text{Total} \leq \$14,978.47$.

8.52 (a) 0.054. **(b)** 0.0586. **(c)** 0.066.

8.54 $(3,000)(\$261.40) \pm (3,000)(1.8331)\dfrac{(138.8046)}{\sqrt{10}}\left(\sqrt{\dfrac{3,000-10}{3,000-1}}\right)$

$\$543,176.96 \leq \text{Total} \leq \$1,025,224.04$.

8.56 $\$5,443 \leq \text{Total difference} \leq \$54,229$.

8.58 (a) 0.0542. **(b)** Because the upper bound is higher than the tolerable exception rate of 0.04, the auditor should request a larger sample.

8.66 $940.50 \leq \mu \leq 1007.50$. Based on the evidence gathered from the sample of 34 stores, the 95% confidence interval for the mean per-store count in all of the franchise's stores is from 940.50 to 1,007.50. With a 95% level of confidence, the franchise can conclude that the mean per-store count in all its stores is somewhere between 940.50 and 1,007.50, which is larger than the original average of 900 mean per-store count before the price reduction. Hence, reducing coffee prices is a good strategy to increase the mean customer count.

8.68 (a) $p = 0.80$, $0.7765 \leq \pi \leq 0.8235$. **(b)** $p = 0.88$, $0.8609 \leq \pi \leq 0.8991$. **(c)** $p = 0.56$, $0.5309 \leq \pi \leq 0.5891$. **(d) (a)** $n = 1,537$. **(b)** $n = 1,015$. **(c)** $n = 2,367$.

8.70 (a) $14.085 \leq \mu \leq 16.515$. **(b)** $0.530 \leq \pi \leq 0.820$. **(c)** $n = 25$. **(d)** $n = 784$. **(e)** If a single sample were to be selected for both purposes, the larger of the two sample sizes ($n = 784$) should be used.

8.72 (a) $8.049 \leq \mu \leq 11.351$. **(b)** $0.284 \leq \pi \leq 0.676$. **(c)** $n = 35$. **(d)** $n = 121$. **(e)** If a single sample were to be selected for both purposes, the larger of the two sample sizes ($n = 121$) should be used.

8.74 (a) $\$25.80 \leq \mu \leq \$31.24$. **(b)** $0.3037 \leq \pi \leq 0.4963$. **(c)** $n = 97$. **(d)** $n = 423$. **(e)** If a single sample were to be selected for both purposes, the larger of the two sample sizes ($n = 423$) should be used.

8.76 (a) $\$36.66 \leq \mu \leq \$40.42$. **(b)** $0.2027 \leq \pi \leq 0.3973$. **(c)** $n = 110$. **(d)** $n = 423$. **(e)** If a single sample were to be selected for both purposes, the larger of the two sample sizes ($n = 423$) should be used.

8.78 (a) $\pi \leq 0.2013$. **(b)** Because the upper bound is higher than the tolerable exception rate of 0.15, the auditor should request a larger sample.

8.80 (a) $n = 27$. **(b)** $\$402,652.53 \leq \text{Population total} \leq \$450,950.79$.

8.82 (a) $8.41 \leq \mu \leq 8.43$. **(b)** With 95% confidence, the population mean width of troughs is somewhere between 8.41 and 8.43 inches.

8.84 (a) $0.2425 \leq \mu \leq 0.2856$. **(b)** $0.1975 \leq \mu \leq 0.2385$. **(c)** The amounts of granule loss for both brands are skewed to the right, but the sample sizes are large enough. **(d)** Because the two confidence intervals do not overlap, you can conclude that the mean granule loss of Boston shingles is higher than that of Vermont shingles.

CHAPTER 9

9.2 Because $Z_{STAT} = +2.21 > 1.96$, reject H_0.

9.4 Reject H_0 if $Z_{STAT} < -2.58$ or if $Z_{STAT} > 2.58$.

9.6 p-value $= 0.0456$.

9.8 p-value $= 0.1676$.

9.10 H_0: Defendant is guilty; H_1: Defendant is innocent. A Type I error would be not convicting a guilty person. A Type II error would be convicting an innocent person.

9.12 H_0: $\mu = 20$ minutes. 20 minutes is adequate travel time between classes. H_1: $\mu \neq 20$ minutes. 20 minutes is not adequate travel time between classes.

9.14 H_0: $\mu = 1.00$. The mean amount of paint per one-gallon can is one gallon. H_1: $\mu \neq 1.00$. The mean amount of paint per one-gallon can differs from one gallon.

9.16 $t_{STAT} = 2.00$

9.18 (a) ± 2.1315.

9.20 No, you should not use a t test because the original population is left-skewed and the sample size is not large enough for the t test to be valid.

9.22 (a) Because $t_{STAT} = -2.4324 < -1.9842$, reject H_0. There is enough evidence to conclude that the population mean has changed from 41.4 days. **(b)** Because $t_{STAT} = -2.4324 > -2.6264$, do not reject H_0. There is not enough evidence to conclude that the population mean has changed from 41.4 days. **(c)** Because $t_{STAT} = -2.9907 < -1.9842$, reject H_0. There is enough evidence to conclude that the population mean has changed from 41.4 days. **(d)** No, the large sample size ensures that the use of the t test is appropriate.

9.24 (a) $t_{STAT} = (3.57 - 3.70)/\sqrt{64} = -1.30$; Because $-1.9983 < t_{STAT} = -1.30 < 1.9983$ and the p-value of $0.1984 > 0.05$ There is no evidence that the population mean waiting time is different from 3.7 minutes. **(b)** Since $n = 64$, the central limit theorem should ensure that the sampling distribution of the mean is approximately normal. In general, the t-test is appropriate for this sample size except for the case where the population is extremely skewed or bimodal.

9.26 (a) Because $-2.5706 < t_{STAT} = 0.8556 < 2.5706$, do not reject H_0. There is not enough evidence to conclude that the mean price for two tickets, with online service charges, large popcorn, and two medium soft drinks, is different from \$35. **(b)** The p-value is 0.4313. If the population mean is \$35, the probability of observing a sample of six theater chains that will result in a sample mean farther away from the hypothesized value than this sample is 0.4313. **(c)** That the distribution of prices is normally distributed. **(d)** With a small sample size, it is difficult to evaluate the assumption of normality. However, the distribution may be symmetric because the mean and the median are close in value.

9.28 (a) Because $-2.0096 < t_{STAT} = 0.114 < 2.0096$, do not reject H_0. There is no evidence that the mean amount is different from two liters. **(b)** p-value = 0.9095. **(c)** and **(d)** Yes, the data appear to have met the normality assumption. **(e)** The amount of fill is decreasing over time. Therefore, the t test is invalid.

9.30 (a) Because $t_{STAT} = -5.9355 < -2.0106$, reject H_0. There is enough evidence to conclude that mean widths of the troughs is different from 8.46 inches. **(b)** That the population distribution is normal. **(c)** Although the distribution of the widths is left-skewed, the large sample size means that the validity of the t test is not seriously affected.

9.32 (a) Because $-2.68 < t_{STAT} = 0.094 < 2.68$, do not reject H_0. **(b)** $5.462 \le \mu \le 5.542$. **(c)** The conclusions are the same.

9.34 p-value = 0.0228.

9.36 p-value = 0.0838.

9.38 p-value = 0.9162.

9.40 $t_{STAT} = 2.7638$.

9.42 $t_{STAT} = -2.5280$.

9.44 (a) $t_{STAT} = (2.73 - 2.80)/0.2/\sqrt{25} = -1.75$; Because $t_{STAT} = -1.75 < -1.7109$, reject H_0. **(b)** p-value = $0.0464 < 0.05$, reject H_0. **(c)** The probability of getting a sample mean of 2.73 feet or less if the population mean is 2.8 feet is 0.0464. **(d)** They are the same.

9.46 (a) H_0: $\mu \le 5$; H_1: $\mu > 5$. **(b)** A Type I error occurs when you conclude that children take a mean of more than five trips a week to the store when in fact they take a mean of no more than five trips a week to the store. A Type II error occurs when you conclude that children take a mean of no more than five trips a week to the store when in fact they take a mean of more than five trips a week to the store. **(c)** Because $t_{STAT} = 2.9375 > 2.3263$ or the p-value of 0.0021 is less than 0.01, reject H_0. There is enough evidence to conclude the population mean number of trips to the store is greater than five per week. **(d)** The probability that the sample mean is 5.47 trips or more when the null hypothesis is true is 0.0021.

9.48 $p = 0.22$.

9.50 Do not reject H_0.

9.52 $Z_{STAT} = 1.2671$, p-value = 0.1026. Because $0.1026 > 0.05$, do not reject H_0. There is not enough evidence to show that more than half of *The Oxford Press* readers planned to cut back on driving.

9.54 (a) H_0: $\pi = 0.5$; H_1: $\pi \ne 0.5$. Decision rule: If $Z_{STAT} > 1.96$ or $Z_{STAT} < -1.96$, reject H_0.

$$p = \frac{552}{1,083} = 0.5097$$

Test statistic:

$$Z_{STAT} = \frac{p - \pi}{\sqrt{\dfrac{\pi(1-\pi)}{n}}} = \frac{0.5097 - 0.5}{\sqrt{\dfrac{0.5(1-0.5)}{1,083}}} = 0.6381$$

Because $-1.96 < Z_{STAT} = 0.6381 < 1.96$, do not reject H_0 and conclude that there is not enough evidence to show that the percentage of people who trust energy-efficiency ratings differs from 50%. **(b)** p-value = 0.5234. Because the p-value of $0.5234 > 0.05$, do not reject H_0.

9.56 (a) H_0: $\pi \le 0.08$. No more than 8% of students at your school are Omnivores. H_1: $\pi > 0.08$. More than 8% of students at your school are Omnivores. **(b)** $Z_{STAT} = 3.6490$, p-value = 0.0001316. Because $Z_{STAT} = 3.6490 > 1.96$ or p-value = $0.0001316 < 0.05$, reject H_0. There is enough evidence to show that the percentage of Omnivores at your school is greater than 8%.

9.58 (a) power = 0.3721β = 0.6279. **(b)** power = 0.9529β = 0.0471. **(c)** Holding everything else constant, the greater the distance from the true mean to the hypothesized mean, the higher is the power of the test and the lower is the probability of committing a Type II error. Holding everything else constant, the smaller the level of significance, the lower is the power of the test and the higher is the probability of committing a Type II error.

9.60 (a) power = 0.8873β = 0.1127. **(b)** power = 0.0871β = 0.9129.

9.62 (a) power = 0.4144β = 0.5856. **(b)** power = 0.0665β = 0.9335. **(c)** Holding everything else constant, the larger the sample size, the higher is the power of the test and the lower is the probability of committing a Type II error.

9.74 (a) Buying a site that is not profitable. **(b)** Not buying a profitable site. **(c)** Type I. **(d)** If the executives adopt a less stringent rejection criterion by buying sites for which the computer model predicts moderate or large profit, the probability of committing a Type I error will increase. Many more of the sites the computer model predicts that will generate moderate profit may end up not being profitable at all. On the other hand, the less stringent rejection criterion will lower the probability of committing a Type II error since more potentially profitable sites will be purchased.

9.76 (a) Because $t_{STAT} = 3.248 > 2.0010$, reject H_0. **(b)** p-value = 0.0019. **(c)** Because $Z_{STAT} = -0.32 > -1.645$, do not reject H_0. **(d)** Because $-2.0010 < t_{STAT} = 0.75 < 2.0010$, do not reject H_0. **(e)** Because $t_{STAT} = -1.61 > -1.645$, do not reject H_0.

9.78 (a) Because $t_{STAT} = -1.69 > -1.7613$, do not reject H_0. **(b)** The data are from a population that is normally distributed. **(c)** and **(d)** With the exception of one extreme point, the data are approximately normally distributed. **(e)** There is insufficient evidence to state that the waiting time is less than five minutes.

9.80 (a) Because $t_{STAT} = -1.47 > -1.6896$, do not reject H_0. **(b)** p-value = 0.0748. If the null hypothesis is true, the probability of obtaining a t_{STAT} of -1.47 or more extreme is 0.0748. **(c)** Because $t_{STAT} = -3.10 < -1.6973$, reject H_0. **(d)** p-value = 0.0021. If the null hypothesis is true, the probability of obtaining a t_{STAT} of -3.10 or more extreme is 0.0021. **(e)** The data in the population are assumed to be normally distributed.

(f) Both boxplots suggest that the data are skewed slightly to the right, more so for the Boston shingles. However, the very large sample sizes mean that the results of the t-test are relatively insensitive to the departure from normality.

9.82 (a) $t_{STAT} = -21.61$, reject H_0. **(b)** p-value = 0.0000. **(c)** $t_{STAT} = -27.19$, reject H_0. **(d)** p-value = 0.0000. **(e)** Because of the large sample sizes, you do not need to be concerned with the normality assumption.

CHAPTER 10

10.2 (a) $t = 3.8959$. **(b)** $df = 21$. **(c)** 2.5177. **(d)** Because $t_{STAT} = 3.8959 > 2.5177$, reject H_0.

10.4 $3.73 \le \mu_1 - \mu_2 \le 12.27$.

10.6 Because $t_{STAT} = 4.1779 > 2.8982$ or p-value = 0.0006 < 0.05, reject H_0. There is evidence of a difference in the means of the two populations.

10.8 (a) Because $t_{STAT} = 5.2031 > 2.33$ or p-value = 0.0000 < 0.01, reject H_0. There is enough evidence to conclude that the mean breaking strength of parts produced by the new machine is greater than the mean breaking strength of parts produced by the old machine. **(b)** Because $t_{STAT} = 5.2031 > 2.33$ or p-value = 0.0000 < 0.01, reject H_0. There is enough evidence to conclude that the mean breaking strength of parts produced by the new machine is greater than the mean breaking strength of parts produced by the old machine. (The answers to (a) and (b) are the same because of the large sample size and the minimal difference between the variances.)

10.10 (a) Because $-2.0117 < t_{STAT} = 0.1023 < 2.0117$, do not reject H_0. There is no evidence of a difference in the two means for the age 8 group. Because $t_{STAT} = 3.375 > 1.9908$, reject H_0. There is evidence of a difference in the two means for the age 12 group. Because $t_{STAT} = 3.3349 > 1.9966$, reject H_0. There is evidence of a difference in the two means for the age 16 group. **(b)** The test results show that children in the United States begin to develop preferences for brand-name products as early as age 12.

10.12 (a) $H_0: \mu_1 = \mu_2$, where Populations: 1 = Males, 2 = Females.
$H_1: \mu_1 \neq \mu_2$
Decision rule: $df = 170$. If $t_{STAT} < -1.974$ or $t_{STAT} > 1.974$, reject H_0.
Test statistic:

$$S_p^2 = \frac{(n_1-1)(S_1^2)+(n_2-1)(S_2^2)}{(n_1-1)+(n_2-1)}$$

$$= \frac{(99)(13.35^2)+(71)(9.42^2)}{99+71} = 140.8489$$

$$t_{STAT} = \frac{(\bar{X}_1-\bar{X}_2)-(\mu_1-\mu_2)}{\sqrt{S_p^2\left(\frac{1}{n_1}+\frac{1}{n_2}\right)}}$$

$$= \frac{(40.26-36.85)-0}{\sqrt{140.8489\left(\frac{1}{100}+\frac{1}{72}\right)}} = 1.859$$

Decision: Because $-1.974 < t_{STAT} = 1.859 < 1.974$, do not reject H_0. There is not enough evidence to conclude that the mean computer anxiety experienced by males and females is different. **(b)** p-value = 0.0648. **(c)** In order to use the pooled-variance t test, you need to assume that the populations are normally distributed with equal variances.

10.14 (a) Because $t_{STAT} = -4.1343 < -2.0484$, reject H_0. **(b)** p-value = 0.0003. **(c)** The original populations of waiting times are approximately normally distributed. **(d)** $-4.2292 \le \mu_1 - \mu_2 \le -1.4268$.

10.16 (a) Because $t_{STAT} = 4.10 > 2.024$, reject H_0. There is evidence of a difference in the mean surface hardness between untreated and treated steel plates. **(b)** p-value = 0.0002. The probability that two samples have a mean difference of 9.3634 or more is 0.02% if there is no difference in the mean surface hardness between untreated and treated steel plates. **(c)** You need to assume that the population distribution of hardness of both untreated and treated steel plates is normally distributed. **(d)** $4.7447 \le \mu_1 - \mu_2 \le 13.9821$.

10.18 (a) Because $t_{STAT} = -2.1522 < -2.0211$, reject H_0. There is enough evidence to conclude that the mean assembly times, in seconds, are different between employees trained in a computer-assisted, individual-based program and those trained in a team-based program. **(b)** You must assume that each of the two independent populations is normally distributed. **(c)** Because $t_{STAT} = -2.152 < -2.052$ or p-value = 0.041 < 0.05, reject H_0. **(d)** The results in (a) and (c) are the same. **(e)** $-4.52 \le \mu_1 - \mu_2 \le -0.14$. You are 95% confident that the difference between the population means of the two training methods is between -4.52 and -0.14.

10.20 $df = 19$.

10.22 (a) $t_{STAT} = (-1.5566)/(1.424)/\sqrt{9} = -3.2772$; Because $t_{STAT} = -3.2772 < -2.306$ or p-value = 0.0112 < 0.05, reject H_0. There is enough evidence of a difference in the mean summated ratings between the two brands. **(b)** You must assume that the distribution of the differences between the two ratings is approximately normal. **(c)** p-value is 0.0112. The probability of obtaining a mean difference in ratings that gives rise to a test statistic that deviates from 0 by 3.2772 or more in either direction is 0.0112 if there is no difference in the mean summated ratings between the two brands. **(d)** $-2.6501 \le \mu_D \le -0.4610$. You are 95% confident that the mean difference in summated ratings between brand A and brand B is somewhere between -2.6501 and -0.4610.

10.24 (a) Because $t_{STAT} = 6.7876 > 2.9768$ or p-value = 0.0000 < 0.01, reject H_0. There is evidence to conclude that there is a difference between the mean price of textbooks at the local bookstore and Amazon.com. **(b)** You must assume that the distribution of the differences between the measurements is approximately normal. **(c)** $\$9.27 \le \mu_D \le \$23.25$. You are 99% confident that the mean difference between the price of textbooks at the local bookstore and Amazon.com is somewhere between $9.27 and $23.25. **(d)** The results in (a) and (c) are the same. The hypothesized value of 0 for the difference in the price of textbooks between the local bookstore and Amazon.com is outside the 99% confidence interval.

10.26 (a) Because $t_{STAT} = 1.8425 < 1.943$, do not reject H_0. There is not enough evidence to conclude that the mean bone marrow microvessel density is higher before the stem cell transplant than after the stem cell transplant. **(b)** p-value = 0.0575. The probability that the t statistic for the mean difference in density is 1.8425 or more is 5.75% if the mean density is not higher before the stem cell transplant than after the stem cell transplant. **(c)** $-28.26 \le \mu_D \le 200.55$. You are 95% confident that the mean difference in bone marrow microvessel density before and after the stem cell transplant is somewhere between -28.26 and 200.55.

10.28 (a) Because $t_{STAT} = -9.3721 < -2.4258$, reject H_0. **(b)** The population of differences in strength is approximately normally distributed. **(c)** $p = 0.000$.

10.30 (a) Because $-2.58 \le Z_{STAT} = -0.58 \le 2.58$, do not reject H_0. **(b)** $-0.273 \le \pi_1 - \pi_2 \le 0.173$.

10.32 (a) $H_0: \pi_1 \le \pi_2$. $H_1: \pi_1 > \pi_2$. Populations: 1 = parents, 2 = teachers.

(b) Because $Z_{STAT} = 7.9918 > 1.6449$, reject H_0. There is sufficient evidence to conclude that the population proportion of parents that are very confident that their child's school will meet the standards by the deadline is greater than the population proportion of teachers that are very confident that the school where they work will meet standards by the deadline. **(c)** Yes, the result in (b) makes it appropriate for the article to claim that parents are more confident.

10.34 (a) H_0: $\pi_1 = \pi_2$. H_1: $\pi_1 \neq \pi_2$. Decision rule: If $|Z_{STAT}| > 1.96$, reject H_0.
Test statistic:

$$\bar{p} = \frac{X_1 + X_2}{n_1 + n_2} = \frac{280 + 320}{505 + 500} = 0.5970$$

$$Z_{STAT} = \frac{(p_1 - p_2) - (\pi_2 - \pi_2)}{\sqrt{\bar{p}(1 - \bar{p})\left(\frac{1}{n_1} + \frac{1}{n_2}\right)}} = \frac{(0.5545 - 0.64) - 0}{\sqrt{0.5970(1 - 0.5970)\left(\frac{1}{505} + \frac{1}{500}\right)}}$$

$$= -2.7644.$$

Decision: Because $Z_{STAT} = -2.7644 < -1.96$, reject H_0. There is sufficient evidence to conclude that there is a difference in the proportion of adults who think the U.S. tax code is unfair between the two income groups. **(b)** p-value = 0.0057. The probability of obtaining a difference in proportions that gives rise to a test statistic that deviates from 0 by 2.7644 or more in either direction is 0.0057 if there is no difference in the proportion of adults who think the U.S. tax code is unfair between the two income groups.

10.36 (a) Because $-1.96 < Z_{STAT} = 1.5240 < 1.96$, do not reject H_0. There is insufficient evidence of a difference between undergraduate and MBA students in the proportion who selected the highest-cost fund. **(b)** p-value = 0.1275. The probability of obtaining a difference in proportions that gives rise to a test statistic that deviates from 0 by 1.5240 or more in either direction is 0.1275 if there is no difference between undergraduate and MBA students in the proportion who selected the highest-cost fund.

10.38 (a) 2.20. **(b)** 2.57. **(c)** 3.50.

10.40 (a) Population B. $S^2 = 25$. **(b)** 1.5625.

10.42 $df_{numerator} = 24$, $df_{denominator} = 24$.

10.44 Because $F_{STAT} = 1.2109 < 2.27$, do not reject H_0.

10.46 (a) Because $F_{STAT} = 1.2995 < 3.18$, do not reject H_0. **(b)** Because $F_{STAT} = 1.2995 < 2.62$, do not reject H_0.

10.48 (a) $H_0 : \sigma_1^2 = \sigma_2^2$. $H_1 : \sigma_1^2 \neq \sigma_2^2$.
Decision rule: If $F_{STAT} > 1.556$, reject H_0.

Test statistic: $F_{STAT} = \frac{S_1^2}{S_2^2} = \frac{(13.35)^2}{(9.42)^2} = 2.008$.

Decision: Because $F_{STAT} = 2.008 > 1.556$, reject H_0. There is enough evidence to conclude that the two population variances are different. **(b)** p-value = 0.0022. **(c)** The test assumes that each of the two populations is normally distributed. **(d)** Based on (a) and (b), a separate-variance t test should be used.

10.50 (a) Because $F_{STAT} = 1.0389 < 2.7324$ or p-value = 0.9789 > 0.05, do not reject H_0. There is not enough evidence of a difference in the variability of the battery life between the two types of digital cameras.

(b) p-value = 0.9789. The probability of obtaining a sample that yields a test statistic more extreme than 1.0389 is 0.9789 if there is no difference in the two population variances. **(c)** The test assumes that the two populations are both normally distributed. **(d)** Based on (a) and (b), a pooled-variance t test should be used.

10.52 Because $F_{STAT} = 3.0866 < 6.3852$, do not reject H_0. There is not enough evidence of a difference in the variance of the yield between money market accounts and five-year CDs.

10.60 (a) $H_0 : \sigma_1^2 \geq \sigma_2^2$ and $H_0 : \sigma_1^2 < \sigma_2^2$. **(b)** Type I error: Rejecting the null hypothesis that the price variance on the Internet is no lower than the price variance in the brick-and-mortar market when the price variance on the Internet is no lower than the price variance in the brick-and-mortar market. Type II error: Failing to reject the null hypothesis that price variance on the Internet is no lower than the price variance in the brick-and-mortar market when the price variance on the Internet is lower than the price variance in the brick-and-mortar market. **(c)** An F test for differences in two variances can be used. **(d)** You need to assume that each of the two populations is normally distributed.
(e) (a) H_0: $\mu_1 \geq \mu_2$ and H_1: $\mu_1 < \mu_2$. **(b)** Type I error: Rejecting the null hypothesis that the mean price in the electronic market is no lower than the mean price in the physical market when the mean price in the electronic market is no lower than the mean price in the physical market. Type II error: Failing to reject the null hypothesis that the mean price in the electronic market is no lower than the mean price in the physical market when the mean price in the electronic market is lower than the mean price in the physical market. **(c)** A pooled t test or a separate-variance t test for the difference in the means can be used. **(d)** You must assume that the distribution of the prices in the electronic market and in the physical market are approximately normally distributed.

10.62 (a) The researchers can ask the teenagers, after viewing each ad, to rate the dangers of smoking, using a scale from 0 to 10, with 10 representing the most dangerous. **(b)** H_0: $\mu_T \geq \mu_S$ and H_1: $\mu_T < \mu_S$. **(c)** Type I error is the error made by concluding that ads produced by the state are more effective than those produced by Philip Morris even though it is not true. The risk of Type I error here is that teenagers can miss the opportunity from the better ads produced by Philip Morris to recognize the true dangers of smoking and the additional expenses the state will have to incur to produce and run the ads. Type II error is the error made by concluding that ads produced by Philip Morris are no less effective than those produced by the state even though ads produced by the state are more effective. The risk of Type II error here is that more teenagers will miss the opportunity to recognize the true dangers of smoking from the ads produced by the state. **(d)** Because both ads are shown to the same group of teenagers, a paired t test for the mean difference is most appropriate. **(e)** Statistically reliable here means the conclusions drawn from the test are reliable because all the assumptions needed for the test to be valid are fulfilled.

10.64 (a) Because $F_{STAT} = 22.7067 > F_\alpha = 1.6275$, reject H_0. There is enough evidence to conclude that there is a difference between the variances in age of students at the Western school and at the Eastern school. **(b)** Because there is a difference between the variances in the age of students at the Western school and at the Eastern school, schools should take that into account when designing their curriculum to accommodate the larger variance in age of students in the state university in the Western United States. **(c)** It is more appropriate to use a separate-variance t test. **(d)** Because $F_{STAT} = 1.3061 < 1.6275$, do not reject H_0. There is not enough evidence to conclude that there is a difference between the variances in years of spreadsheet usage of students at the Western school and at the Eastern school. **(e)** Using the pooled-variance t test, because

$t_{STAT} = -4.6650 < -2.5978$, reject H_0. There is enough evidence of a difference in the mean years of spreadsheet usage of students at the Western school and at the Eastern school.

10.66 (a) Because $t_{STAT} = 3.3282 > 1.8595$, reject H_0. There is enough evidence to conclude that the introductory computer students required more than a mean of 10 minutes to write and run a program in Visual Basic. **(b)** Because $t_{STAT} = 1.3636 < 1.8595$, do not reject H_0. There is not enough evidence to conclude that the introductory computer students required more than a mean of 10 minutes to write and run a program in Visual Basic. **(c)** Although the mean time necessary to complete the assignment increased from 12 to 16 minutes as a result of the increase in one data value, the standard deviation went from 1.8 to 13.2, which reduced the t value. **(d)** Because $F_{STAT} = 1.2308 < 3.8549$, do not reject H_0. There is not enough evidence to conclude that the population variances are different for the Introduction to Computers students and computer majors. Hence, the pooled-variance t test is a valid test to determine whether computer majors can write a Visual Basic program in less time than introductory students, assuming that the distributions of the time needed to write a Visual Basic program for both the Introduction to Computers students and the computer majors are approximately normally distributed. Because $t_{STAT} = 4.0666 > 1.7341$, reject H_0. There is enough evidence that the mean time is higher for Introduction to Computers students than for computer majors. **(e)** p-value $= 0.000362$. If the true population mean amount of time needed for Introduction to Computer students to write a Visual Basic program is no more than 10 minutes, the probability of observing a sample mean greater than the 12 minutes in the current sample is 0.0362%. Hence, at a 5% level of significance, you can conclude that the population mean amount of time needed for Introduction to Computer students to write a Visual Basic program is more than 10 minutes. As illustrated in part (d), in which there is not enough evidence to conclude that the population variances are different for the Introduction to Computers students and computer majors, the pooled-variance t test performed is a valid test to determine whether computer majors can write a Visual Basic program in less time than introductory students, assuming that the distribution of the time needed to write a Visual Basic program for both the Introduction to Computers students and the computer majors are approximately normally distributed.

10.68 From the boxplot and the summary statistics, both distributions are approximately normally distributed. $F_{STAT} = 1.056 < 1.89$. There is insufficient evidence to conclude that the two population variances are significantly different at the 5% level of significance. $t_{STAT} = -5.084 < -1.99$. At the 5% level of significance, there is sufficient evidence to reject the null hypothesis of no difference in the mean life of the bulbs between the two manufacturers. You can conclude that there is a significant difference in the mean life of the bulbs between the two manufacturers.

10.70 Population 1 is men and population 2 is women. Auto-related: Because $Z_{STAT} = 3.1346 > 1.96$, reject H_0. There is sufficient evidence to conclude that there is a difference between men and women. Cash: Because $-1.96 < Z_{STAT} = -0.5053 < 1.96$, do not reject H_0. There is insufficient evidence to conclude that there is a difference between men and women. Clothes: Because $Z_{STAT} = -4.4642 < -1.96$, reject H_0. There is sufficient evidence to conclude that there is a difference between men and women. Electronics: Because $Z_{STAT} = 2.1284 > 1.96$, reject H_0. There is sufficient evidence to conclude that there is a difference between men and women. Entertainment: Because $-1.96 < Z_{STAT} = 1.6759 < 1.96$, do not reject H_0. There is insufficient evidence to conclude that there is a difference between men and women. Food: Because $-1.96 < Z_{STAT} = -1.6917 < 1.96$, do not reject H_0. There is insufficient evidence to conclude that there is a difference between men and women. Investments: Because

$Z_{STAT} = 2.2717 > 1.96$, reject H_0. There is sufficient evidence to conclude that there is a difference between men and women. Travel: Because $-1.96 < Z_{STAT} = 1.5318 < 1.96$, do not reject H_0. There is insufficient evidence to conclude that there is a difference between men and women.

10.72 Customer Product Rating Reviews: $-1.96 < Z_{STAT} = -1.6557 < 1.96$ and p-value $= 0.0978 > 0.05$, do not reject H_0. There is not enough evidence that there is a difference between adults and youths in the proportion who use customer product ratings/reviews. For sale listings with seller ratings: $-1.96 < Z_{STAT} = -1.2742 < 1.96$ and p-value $= 0.2026 > 0.05$, do not reject H_0. There is not enough evidence that there is a difference between adults and youths in the proportion who use for sale listings with seller ratings. For sale listings without seller ratings: $-1.96 < Z_{STAT} = -1.0172 < 1.96$ and p-value $= 0.3090 > 0.05$, do not reject H_0. There is not enough evidence that there is a difference between adults and youths in the proportion who use for sale listings without seller ratings. Online classified ads: $-1.96 < Z_{STAT} = -1.3079 < 1.96$ and p-value $= 0.1909 > 0.05$, do not reject H_0. There is not enough evidence that there is a difference between adults and youths in the proportion who use online classified ads. Message-board posts: $Z_{STAT} = -2.0624 < -1.96$ and p-value $= 0.0392 < 0.05$, reject H_0. There is enough evidence that there is a difference between adults and youths in the proportion who use message-board posts. Web blogs: $-1.96 < Z_{STAT} = -1.7397 < 1.96$ and p-value $= 0.0819 > 0.05$, do not reject H_0. There is not enough evidence that there is a difference between adults and youths in the proportion who use Web blogs. Dating site profile/personals: $= -1.96 < Z_{STAT} = -1.4188 < 1.96$ and p-value $= 0.1560 > 0.05$, do not reject H_0. There is not enough evidence that there is a difference between adults and youths in the proportion who use dating site profiles/personals. Peer-generated and peer-referenced information: $Z_{STAT} = -2.7267 < -1.96$ and p-value $= 0.0064 < 0.05$, reject H_0. There is enough evidence that there is a difference between adults and youths in the proportion who use peer-generated and peer-referenced information. Peer-posted event listings: $Z_{STAT} = -3.5878 < -1.96$ and p-value $= 0.0003 < 0.05$, reject H_0. There is enough evidence that there is a difference between adults and youths in the proportion who use peer-posted event listings.

10.74 The normal probability plots suggest that the two populations are not normally distributed. An F test is inappropriate for testing the difference in two variances. The sample variances for Boston and Vermont shingles are 0.0203 and 0.015, respectively. Because $t_{STAT} = 3.015 > 1.967$ or the p-value $= 0.0028 < \alpha = 0.05$, reject H_0. There is sufficient evidence to conclude that there is a difference in the mean granule loss of Boston and Vermont shingles.

Index